The Way

The Way

RELIGIOUS THINKERS
OF THE RUSSIAN EMIGRATION IN
PARIS AND THEIR JOURNAL,
1925–1940

ANTOINE ARJAKOVSKY

Translated by Jerry Ryan
Edited by John A. Jillions and Michael Plekon
Foreword by Rowan Williams

UNIVERSITY OF NOTRE DAME PRESS
NOTRE DAME, INDIANA

English Language Edition Copyright © 2013 University of Notre Dame
Notre Dame, Indiana 46556
All Rights Reserved
www.undpress.nd.edu
Manufactured in the United States of America

Translated by Jerry Ryan from *La Génération des penseurs religieux de l'émigration russe: La revue* La Voie *(Put'), 1925–1940* by Antoine Arjakovsky, published by L'Esprit et la Lettre, Kiev-Paris, 2002. © L'Esprit et la Lettre, 2002

Licensed by Antoine Arjakovsky, Paris, France

Library of Congress Cataloging-in-Publication Data

Arzhakovskii, Antuan, 1966–
 [Génération des penseurs religieux de l'émigration russe. English]
 The way : religious thinkers of the Russian emigration in Paris and their journal, 1925/1940 / Antoine Arjakovsky ; translated by Jerry Ryan ; edited by John A. Jillions and Michael Plekon ; foreword by Rowan Williams. — English language edition.
     pages cm
 "Translated by Jerry Ryan from La génération des penseurs religieux de l'émigration russe : la revue La Voie (Put'), 1925/1940 by Antoine Arjakovsky, published by L'Esprit et la Lettre, Kiev-Paris, 2002"—T.p. verso.
 Includes bibliographical references and index.
 ISBN-13: 978-0-268-02040-8 (paperback : alkaline paper)
 ISBN-10: 0-268-02040-X (paperback : alkaline paper)
 1. Russians—France—Paris—Religion—History—20th century. 2. Put' (Paris, France) 3. Russians—France—Paris—Biography. 4. Immigrants—France—Paris—Biography. 5. Intellectuals—France—Paris—Biography. 6. Theologians—France—Paris—Biography. 7. Russian periodicals—France—Paris—History—20th century
 8. Paris (France)—Intellectual life—20th century. 9. Paris (France)—Religious life and customs. 10. Paris (France)—Ethnic relations—History—20th century
 I. Jillions, John A. II. Plekon, Michael, 1948– III. Title.
   DC718.R8A78 2013
   944'.004917100922—dc23
                      2013022544

∞ *The paper in this book meets the guidelines for permanence and durability of the Committee on Production Guidelines for Book Longevity of the Council on Library Resources.*

CONTENTS

Foreword   vii
   Rowan Williams

Acknowledgments   xi
   Michael Plekon

Note on Transliteration and Other Conventions   xiii

Introduction   1
   The Project and Its Background   1
   A Brief Description of the Journal   17
   The Epistemological Stance of Russian Religious Thought   21

PART ONE
A Modernist Journal (1925–1929)   33
   A Generation of Modernist Intellectuals   36
   The Modernist Constellation   87
   The Ecumenical Commitment: The Affirmation of the East   138
      in Relation to the West

PART TWO
A Nonconformist Journal (1930–1935)   189
   Introduction: New Outlooks   189
   The Ecclesial Frontiers of a Generation   207
   The Paris School   275
   An Ecclesial Commitment off the Beaten Path   323

PART THREE
A Spiritual Journal (1935–1940) — 375

    The Paradigm of the Spirit — 375
    The *Raskol* of a Generation of Intellectuals — 381
    Two Conflicting Spiritualities — 428
    The Common Horizon of the War and the New Jerusalem — 470

Conclusion: The Two "Bodies" of the Review — 519

    The End of the Review's History (1940–1948) — 519
    The Recollections of a Generation in Russia — 530
    The Development of Memory in France — 551

Afterword to the English Translation — 571

Notes — 584

References: Articles Published in *The Way* — 670

Index — 717

FOREWORD

The intellectual creativity of the Russian emigration in Paris is a fairly well-known phenomenon, chronicled very ably by Marc Raeff, with its immediate historical background narrated more recently, with great vividness, by Lesley Chamberlain. But there has been a lack of more detailed studies of the sheer variety of convictions and visions to be found among the émigrés, and of the complicated interweaving of secular and religious politics in Russian Paris.

The main source for following this tangled story is the periodical *Put'*, "The Way," which from 1925 to 1940 was one of the major vehicles for philosophical and religious discussion among the émigrés. It represented unashamedly the legacy of pre-Revolutionary debates, in which aesthetics, politics, and theology mingled freely in a philosophical climate very alien to many Western observers, yet undeniably lively and critical. The presiding genius in this world, and the creator of *Put'*, was Nikolai Berdyaev, still probably the best-known Russian émigré philosopher in Western intellectual circles: a man of strong and idiosyncratic personal conviction (it is a great mistake, though a frequent one, to regard him as somehow *typical* of Eastern Orthodox religious thinking), but quite content to allow the periodical he edited to carry dramatically diverse and opposed argumentation about virtually every area of its interests.

It is salutary for a Western reader to see how integrally theological and political or philosophical questions are bound together in these pages. Neither Berdyaev nor all of his contributors were conventional orthodox (or Orthodox) believers, but they shared the view that fundamental issues of value, judgment, and virtue could not be intelligently pursued without reference to theology. They rightly saw the direct relevance of theology to all of the most basic issues around the definition of the human, and, whatever their personal commitment to the Church, they were prepared to involve theology in these discussions and to take it with complete critical seriousness.

Antoine Arjakovsky, in this magisterial survey of the history of *Put'*, has at last given the wider scholarly world the chance of absorbing and reflecting on this remarkable history. He traces numerous arguments through their various stages, with clarity and patience—the debates over what we might call "Russian exceptionalism" (what did it mean to believe that Russian identity was somehow spiritually distinct from that of other nations, more clearly marked by Providence?), over the possibilities of a Christian and Orthodox version of socialist politics, over the degree to which the Church could allow its agenda to be shaped by both local and global political realities, and much else. We can follow here the debates around the "Eurasian" movement, which attracted several significant figures for a time with its conviction that Russia could not simply look westwards for its cultural and spiritual future, before dissolving into irreparable conflicts. Very importantly, we can trace the fierce controversies about the distinctively Russian theology of Divine Wisdom, *Sophia*, with its roots partly in nineteenth-century Russian speculation and literature and partly in a wider world of Kabbalistic and hermetic imagery. The great Sergius Bulgakov had developed this theology in its most sophisticated form as a way of holding together insights about economics, art, politics, and doctrine, and Arjakovsky does full justice to the range of Bulgakov's genius. But it suited some both in Moscow and elsewhere in the emigration to label this as heresy; and the ensuing controversy proved to be one of the most divisive and bitter in the history of the Paris community. We see also how the long shadow of fascism and the outbreak of war in 1939 affected the émigrés, and how, ultimately, the periodical came to an end in the face of the pressures of the German invasion: several of those who had been actively involved in *Put'* were to offer the final and most effective kind of theological witness in the form of martyrdom at the hands of the Third Reich.

But in addition to a full and sympathetic account of all this, Arjakovsky adds an invaluable afterword about the retrieval of this heritage in the Russia of more recent times. From a very cautious admission that émigré thinking was not entirely a morass of counter-revolutionary mythology, Russian commentators came to see the world of *Put'* more and more as a kind of ideal for intellectual renewal in the homeland. Sometimes this involved ignoring the contradictions and ambivalence of much of the

Parisian material; and there were plenty of voices to point out that there was still disagreement over the theological probity of some of the religious speculations to be found there. But there is no denying that the legacy of *Put'* was of great significance for countless younger thinkers and artists in Russia around the time of *perestroika* and in the 1990s; nor is it dead today. The first flush of enthusiastic reprinting of work by the Paris intellectuals passed quite quickly, but sustained scholarly engagement continues. And the reputation of some of the central figures involved in the periodical is growing rapidly among non-Russian thinkers and scholars: Bulgakov, to take only the most obvious example, has received more attention in the last ten to fifteen years than in the preceding half century.

Arjakovsky's conclusion is that this particular style of weaving together the theological, the political, and the creative is more than ever necessary across the globe, not merely in a Russia that is once again struggling with whether it can manage democracy and transparency in governance. The sense of a vacuum in political and economic thinking throughout Europe and the North Atlantic world is recognized by believers and many secularists alike, and there is a widespread agreement that we must find the language for a renewed "humanistic" politics (in the sense of a politics attuned to the real capacities of the human spirit rather than to managerial, consumerist, and functionalist nostrums). In this welcome and deeply stimulating book (expertly translated and freshly updated), Professor Arjakovsky has offered a treasury of material for such fresh thinking, as well as telling a story of extraordinary intellectual adventure in the most challenging of circumstances.

Rowan Williams
Archbishop of Canterbury

Lambeth Palace, February 2011

ACKNOWLEDGMENTS

First of all, Antoine Arjakovsky is to be thanked for the enormous contribution that this study makes. It illumines a significant part of the history of the Russian emigration and its literature. More specifically, it holds up for us a diverse, often contentious group of scholars, teachers, and writers who struggled, almost a century ago, to bring the Christian tradition as experienced in the Eastern Church into conversation with Christians of the West. Today, we still find ourselves challenged to bring together the Church and the world, Christianity and culture. The creativity and openness of these thinkers remain very valuable to us. If I could sum up what they hold out, despite their profound disagreements, it is the idea that Christianity is a "living tradition," not a finished, closed system. The Spirit, as one of the liturgical prayers puts it, "is everywhere, filling all things."

This is a comprehensive, thorough, and demanding study that connects with many other issues, some of which the author touches upon, especially in the conclusion and in his afterword—the relationship of Russia to the rest of Europe and the world, the state of ecumenical work and relationships among the churches, and the quest for unity not only within the Orthodox churches but across the churches that confess Christ as Lord.

Jerry Ryan is to be thanked for a daunting task of translation. Natalia Ermolaev contributed mightily by correcting transliterations and translations. John Jillions provided a thorough reading and editing. At the University of Notre Dame Press, Rebecca DeBoer assumed the challenge of copyediting, and former press director Barbara Hanrahan was supportive from the first proposal of this project of translation. To these and others who assisted, many thanks.

Michael Plekon

NOTE ON TRANSLITERATION AND OTHER CONVENTIONS

The transliteration from Russian used here follows the Library of Congress system (without diacritical marks). Slight modifications have been made in the case of proper names for the sake of readability: the soft sign -ь- is omitted from proper names; the vowel modifier -й- is transcribed as -i- in first names ending in -ai or -ei (such as Nikolai, Sergei); -ий appears as -ii in first names (Dimitrii, Georgii; with the exception of "Evlogy"), but -y in last names (Troitsky, Mochulsky). Certain personal names with a standard English version deviate from this pattern, for example, Berdyaev (rather than Berdiaev), Sergius (rather than Sergei or Sergii) Bulgakov, George (rather than Georgii) Fedotov, Paul (rather than Pavel) Evdokimov, Georges (rather than Georgii) Florovsky, and Nicolas (rather than Nikolai) Zernov. Ecclesiastical names are generally rendered in their Greek or English, rather than Russian, variants: Sergius (not Sergii), Paisius (not Paisii), Theophanes (not Feofan), and Anthony (not Antonii). An important exception is Evlogy (rather than Eulogius).

All Cyrillic quotations are given in the new (post-1917) orthography.

———

Articles published in the Russian-language journal *Put'* (*The Way*) are cited in the notes and occasionally in main text using the abbreviation system detailed in the References section at the back of the book, which contains a comprehensive listing, by author, of the articles published in *The Way*. Apart from minor alterations necessitated by the change from French to English transliterations of Russian authors' names, the References list preserves the order and citation system of the original French edition. For example, the four articles published in *The Way* by Nikolai N. Afanasiev are identified in chronological order as A1, A2, A3, and A4, respectively; the article by A. A. Alexandrov is A5; the article by R. (Raymond) de Becker is B1; and so forth. A final letter "R," as in "A2R," indicates that the article in *The Way* is a review of another work.

The original French edition often translated original Russian titles into French for ease of reading. Similarly, many Russian titles have been translated here into English rather than preserving or restoring their original titles.

In addition, many of the texts cited and quoted here are English translations of French texts that originally appeared in Russian. While some effort was made to compare the English translation to the original Russian, this was not done exhaustively.

Introduction

This study has a threefold aim: to facilitate access to the prestigious journal *Put'*, or *The Way*,[1] which is still little known; to explain the resurgence of interest in it in Russia and France in the last decade; and, finally, to test my methodology, which attempts to elaborate a synthesis between the historical truth and the accuracy of memory. Before presenting a brief overview of *The Way*, I shall describe this three-pronged project in detail, using a primary definition of Russian religious thought as a means of delimiting my field of investigation.

THE PROJECT AND ITS BACKGROUND

The State of Research on *The Way*

The Way: A Journal of Russian Religious Thought, a journal in the Russian language, was published quarterly in Paris from 1925 to 1940 by the Academy of Religious Philosophy, directed by Nikolai Alexandrovich Berdyaev. Scholars ranging from the French Slavist Pierre Pascal, who described the sixty-one issues of *The Way* as "uncommonly substantial,"[2] to the American-based historian of the Russian emigration, Marc Raeff, who stressed its "high level of erudition," have agreed that the journal is one of the most brilliant in all Russian intellectual history.[3] The French theologian Olivier Clément remarked that, thanks to Berdyaev's *The Way*, Orthodox thought untiringly increased its awareness of French thought on similar subjects and, testing itself, grew more profound.[4] Though the journal was held in high esteem by several eminent specialists in Russian philosophy, it remained little known in France and the USSR for different reasons until the early 1990s.

As for its obscurity in France, this can be explained by the fact that only six articles (out of 606), written by Berdyaev and Lev Shestov, were translated into French in the interwar period.[5] Moreover, when they were published in French there was no reference to *The Way*, as their publishers wanted to present them as "new" texts. Thus, Berdyaev's "The Truth and Lies of Communism" appeared in the first issue of Emmanuel Mounier's journal *Esprit* (October 1932) and helped set its nonconformist tone, with no mention of its prior publication in *The Way*. After World War II, another twenty articles from *The Way*, by Berdyaev, Shestov, Sergius Bulgakov, Mother Maria Skobtsova, and Georges Florovsky, appeared in French, but that was all.[6] If the Francophone public had no opportunity to hear of the journal, the Russian reading public in France likewise had very limited access to it. In fact, except for three research libraries—the Bibliothèque Nationale, the library of the St. Sergius Institute, and the Turgenev Library—one cannot find a complete run of *The Way* in France.[7]

At present, there is not a single monograph on *The Way*. There does exist a general index of the publications of the YMCA Press between 1941 and 1956, compiled by Fedor Pianov, which includes a chronological index of the issues of *The Way*. The latter was published in France by the Russian-American YMCA publishing house. In 1986, the Russian Academic Group, which held its meetings in the 1930s at the editorial office of *The Way* and later took refuge in the United States, commissioned A. P. Obolensky to prepare a subject index to *The Way*. It was published in New York that same year, prefaced by a three-page introduction.[8]

In 1990, Marc Raeff, himself a son of Russian émigrés in Paris in the interwar period, devoted six pages to *The Way* in his *Russia Abroad: A Cultural History of the Russian Emigration (1919–1939)*. This is the first brief but comprehensive presentation of the journal. Raeff's working hypothesis is that the Russian émigrés, who were knit together by their shared emotional experience of the Russian Revolution, formed a homogeneous society. This justifies a sociopolitical analysis of its origins, character, and cultural dynamics. Despite the many rifts within it, in Raeff's view, the Russian émigrés of the interwar period were politically, culturally, and psychologically united. He recalls that two main questions hammered at the émigré consciousness, from New York to Vladivostok: "What brought on the Revolution? What is the future of the Communist system?" Clearly more interested in the sociopolitical aspects of the emigration than the intellectual ones,[9] Raeff calls *The Way* "the most significant religious journal of the Russian emigration ... representing the best that émigré life had to offer."[10]

In the USSR, only the few individuals who were called upon to combat the emigration ideologically had access to *The Way*. It was kept in the special collections of the Communist Party, such as the Literary Archives of the Lenin Library in Moscow. Several issues of the journal turned up in Moscow during the "Thaw" and circulated secretly, primarily through ecclesiastical channels.[11] The first real discovery of *The Way* took place in 1992, when the journal *Moskva*, through the Inform Progress Publishers, issued a reprint of the first six issues (September 1925 to January 1927) in 50,000 copies. In the hyperinflation of 1992–93 the publishing house, which had collected subscriptions to publish further issues of *The Way*, went bankrupt. Thus, republication of *The Way* in Russia was interrupted. The complete run of the journal was finally made available in 1993, when Militsa Zernov, widow of Nicolas Zernov, a principal contributor, bequeathed her husband's library to the Moscow Library of Foreign Literature, directed by Ekaterina Geneva. Until 1988, the Center for Religious Literature of the Russian Emigration, along with the Museum of the Russian Emigration (founded by Alexander Solzhenitsyn and Nikita Struve), was the principal place where the public could have access to *The Way*. Thanks to the journal's significance, to the desire of many researchers from the former USSR to gain access to it, and finally, to the initiative of Professor F. Poliakov (a Russian émigré living in Munich), who collaborated with the Moscow Patriarchate to resume the republication begun in 1992, the entire journal was published (in Russian) on a CD-ROM in 1998. The CD-ROM included a twenty-one page introduction, "Grains of a Unique Bread: An Index of the Articles and Publications of *The Way*," by the priest Boris Danilenko, director of the Library of the Holy Synod in Moscow. The Synodal Library received the blessing of the Patriarch of Moscow, Alexii II, whose personal endorsement graces the cover of the CD-ROM: "I deem it indispensable for theological schools to have copies of *The Way* as it fills the gaps in our theological thought caused by the Revolution."[12]

Produced with the cooperation of the publisher Martis and the American Business Forms Company, this reprint of *The Way* was envisioned as the first in a series of Russian reprints on CD-ROMs, intended to include (using English translations of their titles) "The Encyclopedia of Orthodox Theology (1901–1911)," "Russian Theologians and Church Historians of the Emigration," "The Journals of Theological Academies in Russia," and "The Greek and Slavic Archives of the Library of the Holy Synod." Since there are no copyright restrictions on *The Way*, one can imagine that in just a few years the journal will be widely accessible to scholars from Moscow to Kiev to Paris. A case in point already is Yakov Krotov's website, www.krotov.info.[13]

Thus, although it enjoyed great intellectual prestige, *The Way* was largely unknown in the West and the East for many years. I want to present, for the first time, a synthesis of the articles it contained, while also providing a historical context to facilitate access not only for specialists but also for the wider public, who will now be able to consult this brilliant journal.

The Way: A Locus of Memory

Shortly after the creation of *The Way* in 1925, but, more importantly, from its final issue in 1940 up to Russian independence in 1991, it became a "locus of memory." Pierre Nora defines this phrase as follows:

> Above all, a locus of memory presupposes the straddling of two orders of reality: 1) a tangible, palpable reality, at times material, at others, less so, that is inscribed in space, time, language, and tradition; and 2) a purely symbolic reality, bearing history.... Thus a locus of memory is any meaningful unity of the material or ideal order which is transformed—through human intention and thanks to the effects of time—into the memorial patrimony of a certain community.[14]

Although *The Way* is inscribed into the place and time of the Paris emigration of the interwar period, it is also very much a symbolic reality for the descendants of this emigration in the West, as it is for intellectuals, clergy, and politicians of the new Russia after 1991. I will analyze the evolution of memory in the journal at the end of this study, but my interest here is to explain the journal's symbolic dimension and its relevance to the present day. As "an organ of Russian religious thought" in the collective memory, *The Way* has become a reference point for a generation of intellectuals sharing a particular history. The myth of the émigré religious intelligentsia—it is fitting to speak of myth when narratives vary as a function of different memory communities—is more or less the following.[15] (This narrative story of mine, which I present in italics, is in the genre of a memoir. I have carefully kept inaccuracies and imprecisions characteristic of mythic discourse.)

In the beginning, meaning at the end of the nineteenth century, several Russian intellectuals (today some claim that they were of Ukrainian or Baltic origin), concerned with finding authenticity and truth [pravda-istina] (without making a distinction between the two), looked to the West, broke with their ancestral ancient faith, and became Marxists. After a turbulent period marked by arrests, incarceration, and scholarly work, these intellectuals—under the influence of Friedrich Nietzsche, Arthur Rimbaud, and Immanuel Kant—experienced a profound crisis and became idealists. Then—under the influence of Vladimir Solovyov, the church fathers, and Fyodor Dostoevsky—they returned like prodigal sons to the bosom of the Church and became true patriots. In their collection "Landmarks" [Vekhi], they criticized their erstwhile revolutionary confreres for separating speculative truth [umozritel'naia istina] from practical truth [prakticheskaia pravda]. But their warning went unheeded. A series of catastrophes was unleashed upon Russia: war, revolution, civil war. Lenin, striving to get rid of his old enemies, spared them at the last minute and sent them into exile. In 1922, as their ship left the Baltic port, the intellectuals looked out onto the horizon and watched the storm clouds gathering over Russia. So began their long "way of the cross," marked by poverty, division, homesickness, and Western intellectuals' failure to understand the uniqueness of Russian philosophy. But the Russian intellectuals did not sit idly by; they took advantage of the freedoms offered by their adoptive countries. After the 1923 Congress of Psherov, where they experienced "a veritable descent of the Holy Spirit," the older generation of intellectuals was reborn as they united with the younger émigrés. And then together they created a truly prophetic movement, which had no analogue since the establishment of the Byzantine "symphony" of power in the fourth century, and which aimed for the liberation of the Church from state authority, the churching of one's entire life [votserkovlenie vsei zhizni], and, finally, "bringing the meaning of the icon to the West." Opposing military counter-revolutionary activity on religious grounds, these intellectuals were fully resolved—like the Jews in Babylonian exile—to prepare Russia's future through a spiritual and cultural renaissance. Gathering around institutions of higher learning, initiating a youth movement, publishing house, and a journal, they opened up a brilliant page in Russian intellectual history by publishing numerous philosophical treatises, theological works, and even novels. But the "Paris School," as this movement later came to be known, was too audacious. This audacity—and particularly the sophiological teachings—was severely reprimanded when some Russian bishops condemned sophiological doctrine as heresy. When World War II broke out, these Russian intellectuals fought heroically against the occupiers, always sustaining prayers for Russia under German invasion. The story ends tragically. At the end of their lives, some fell victim to the "devastating illness of Soviet patriotism." Having devoted so many years to spiritual struggle, they all died, like Moses, without entering the Promised Land.

This myth or "little memoir," as Alain Brossat has called it, which is not about institutions, suddenly became the center of attention in the 1980s.[16] Georges Nivat, citing V. Bolshakov's 1990 work on the emigration, underscores the mythical conception of this emigration, like the myths of "the thirteenth tribe of Israel."[17] He writes: "The Russian emigration is not the only wave of displaced persons in the twentieth century, nor the only one to lead a miserable existence. But it is the only one to conceive of itself as a 'New Israel,' or a 'New Mayflower,' having taking away from its morally tainted homeland the elements of a moral renewal, just as the Puritans did when they fled Europe in the seventeenth century."[18] Memory, Nora states, is "the most vulnerable to all manner of manipulation," and is marked by "long periods of quiescence and sudden moments of revitalization."[19] In general, one can say that if, in Russia, the end of the Soviet Union engendered an immense desire to find once more the thread of the pre-revolutionary national history that the emigration symbolized, in France the end of the political emigration—brought about by a liberated Russia—provoked in the descendants of these intellectuals a profound desire to communicate the universal dimension of the intellectual, social, and ecclesiastical heritage of the writers of *The Way*.

As the witnesses to the noncommunist past disappeared, the memory of the emigration in the USSR and in Russia in 1989–91 passed from a negative connotation to a positive image. Vyacheslav Kostikov, a former diplomat who had worked in the French Embassy in Paris and who became Yeltsin's spokesperson in 1991–93, published a book entitled *Let Us Not Curse the Exiles* (*Ne budem proklinat' izgnanie*) in a sizeable edition—100,000 copies. In it, the political and cultural life of the emigration was presented in the USSR in a relatively positive light for the first time. In the first chapter, "Memory Awakened," the author recalls the episode of the "philosopher's steamship" in typical *nomenklatura* style. Citing Fedor Stepun, one of the exiled thinkers and a contributor to *The Way*, Kostikov justifies his changed attitude towards the emigration by dividing it into two camps. He mentions those who were the last survivors of the old monarchist guard, who had learned nothing from the revolution or from emigration, the group Stepun pejoratively called *emigrantshchina*. "They rejected the future in the name of the past, but they were not numerous, those infected by the '*emigrantshchina*' virus. It was not they who had determined the spiritual and cultural life of the emigration."[20]

Although this might be expressed differently, for a great many Russian intellectuals the rediscovery of the "spiritual and cultural life of the emigration" offered the hope of reestablishing a bond with the past and finding themselves in it. In the two-page preface to the republication of the first six issues of *The Way* in 1992, Aleksander Abramov, professor of philosophy at the Russian State Humanities University, stresses the "burning relevance" of its publication to the present moment in Russian life and announces that "this republication of *The Way* may well become a significant event in our spiritual life."[21] That same year, a new journal called *The Way* was inaugurated in Moscow. Its goals were "to reveal and continue the intellectual tradition of the interwar generation and thus to foster the formation of a united intellectual space embracing the East and the West."[22] The journal's editor-in-chief was Anatolii Yakovlev (son of Aleksander Yakovlev, ideological adviser to the *Politburo* in 1988–91). The younger Yakovlev, in his capacity as editor of *Problems of Philosophy* (*Voprosy filosofii*) in 1989–92, had encouraged the broad dissemination of articles and books on religious philosophy by émigré authors during the *perestroika* years. In his editorial in the first issue of the new journal, *The Way*, he writes:

> The fact that we are living in a time of great social change is but subjective. Obviously, the house in which three generations of Russians have lived has collapsed before our eyes. But we have survived. And the only thing we still have is our inner spiritual life.... Now that the conversation about our circumstances or the interior movements of the spirit has begun, it has become possible to philosophize.... A very rich tradition exists, from the pre- and post-revolutionary years, which may remain inaccessible.... We must rediscover this tradition, and then hope for the miracle of its eventual transformation into an original living philosophy.[23]

Finally, from the clergy, Fr. Danilenko's introduction to the republication of *The Way* on the CD-ROM is most insightful. Later on I will analyze the "deformations of memory" in this introduction in some detail, as well as the precious insights these distortions give us into the present state of religious consciousness in Russia. Here, I merely repeat Fr. Danilenko's conclusion, from April 5, 1998, which addresses the power and feeling of indebtedness towards the past that certain clerics feel as they rejoin the profound movement of the whole of contemporary Russian society:

> Ste. Geneviève-des-Bois, Tegel, Olchany... those cemeteries abroad and still others became the final refuge for the contributors to *The Way*. Why did such a long and sorrowful voyage have to end in burial far from the homeland? "Truly, truly I say to you, if a seed of grain falls into the earth and dies not, it remains alone; if it dies, it bears much fruit" (John 12:24).

In the memory of the emigration, *The Way* is looked upon similarly, as a conduit from the past to the future, both on the intellectual level and on the political and religious ones. Raeff points out that the need to forge a unity with the old Russia is evident in the very name of the journal, a name taken over from an illustrious pre-revolutionary publishing house. The cultural unity of the emigration crystallized for Raeff in that name. "In these different expressions," he wrote, "the word 'way' was the guarantor of

Russian cultural identity and the most important element in the intelligentsia's consciousness. In émigré literature it became even more important for the collective identity as language was the most obvious sign of membership in a specific group."[24] Thus, the use of the pre-revolutionary orthography in the journal was profoundly symbolic. Nikita Struve, the French academic and son of the Russian emigration, and director of the YMCA Press (the main publisher of Berdyaev's journal), published a work entitled *Seventy Years of the Russian Emigration (1919–1989)* in 1996, in which he follows up on the reflections of his American colleague. Struve writes that *The Way* played the same role as a rallying point and unifying force that *Contemporary Annals* (*Sovremennye zapiski*) played in the literary sphere.[25] Looking back (with the benefit of hindsight), Struve takes note of the end of the emigration and foists a new task on its heirs. In his opinion, the emigration, "despite snares and dangers, fulfilled its mission by building a 'Russia abroad' which now forms one body with the Russia that is rising from the ruins, to help it cement itself to the Russia of tomorrow."[26]

Keeping the journal in memory is important not only for the Russian emigration. For Olivier Clément, a French intellectual who converted to Orthodoxy after reading the religious thought of members of the emigration, the legacy of *The Way* lay in the advent of an original philosophy that sought a synthesis between logic and "mytho-logic."[27] Unwieldy at times, these attempts at synthesis, if one carefully discerns them, are rich in potential for the future. In a chapter entitled "For a Future in Common," from his 1997 book *Rome autrement*, Clément imagines a rapprochement between Bulgakov's theology and ecology.

> It is incumbent upon man, the priest of the world, to offer the spiritual essences of things to God in the Christian sacrifice of reintegration. We must give this transfiguring vision all its cultural and social import and enrich ecology with it. The great Russian sophiological thinkers attempted to do this early in the century. Their conceptualizations were, no doubt, clumsy, but we should reconsider their meditations on Wisdom—the mystery which is found above all in the eighth chapter of Proverbs in which God and the Creation appear mutually interpenetrating. Through Wisdom the old myths of the consecrated Earth can be integrated into Christianity as a kind of poetics of communion. And without doubt there is a mystical bond between Wisdom and the Mother of God in which earth at last finds a face.[28]

According to Hélène d'Encausse, a French professor of Georgian origin, the rapprochement between Russian religious thought and modernity was of great political import. She describes the politicians and intellectuals grouped around Dimitrii Likhachev thus:

> For this group the intellectual and philosophical heritage of the early twentieth century is so rich as to serve as a reference point for the Russia they were seeking. Berdyaev, Bulgakov, and Simeon Frank were philosophers who found an alternative to Marxism in Christian values. Though they had been unknown in the USSR, they could enrich a reemerging Russian thought. In this Christianity, the key thing for political culture was that there was no room, according to Likhachev, for intolerance and the exclusion of "others."[29]

Finally, for Michel Evdokimov, emeritus professor of literature in France, an Orthodox priest, and the son of the celebrated émigré intellectual Paul Evdokimov, the Orthodox heirs of the spiritual message of *The Way* must now turn resolutely towards the future as "messengers" or liaisons, making it their mission to Russia and the new democracies of the former USSR and the Orthodox countries in general, to help them integrate "what is best in modernity." In a chapter entitled, characteristically, "Orthodoxy Faces the Future," he writes:

> In countries such as Russia, modernity is viewed negatively. Yet one wants to preserve its positive aspects. The same view is held in countries with a majority Orthodox population, such as Greece, countries situated just this side of the Iron Curtain. We have before us the enormous challenge to calm spirits, to avoid condemnations at sword point if not by the axe, of all that modernity bears with it, that is to say, the good and the bad.[30]

Thus, what is at stake is a threefold process of discovery, precipitated by Russian religious thought. First, we must measure the political aspect of the present-day grafting of émigré ideas in the Soviet body politic. Even though it is not the main subject of this book, we must point out that it depends on the changes in the political regime in Russia; on the relations of the Orthodox Church with the state and the society; and finally, on the evolution of the strategy of the Orthodox Church in Europe and the wider world.

The second matter at stake is of an intellectual order. Certain problems have remained suspended at the heart of Russian thought, and certain themes have reemerged regularly in publications without ever being integrated into the general culture, and they must be taken up again in the present. These are personalism, sophiology, and, more generally, the epistemological status of religious thought, to which I shall return in this introduction. On the other hand, what about the interest in Russia manifested by French professors and intellectuals? Is it simply a matter of fashion, or is it indicative of a genuine desire to do away with the intellectual partitioning of Europe into two camps? Is the thought of the Russian emigration a synthesis of German idealism and Byzantine patristic thought, condemned to remain "at the margins" of "religious philosophy"?[31] Or do the current attempts of Ricoeur, Breton, or Yannaras permit us to envisage a single Europe from the Atlantic to Siberia? I do not claim to answer these questions definitively here, but I end with a discussion of the present integration of Russian philosophy in universities and other institutions of higher learning in the new Russia.

Finally, the third matter at stake concerns the church itself. As Constantine Andronikov has written, the emergence of a body of modern Orthodox thought for the first time since St. Gregory Palamas (14th c.) has major consequences for the level of ecumenism as well as the practical life of the world's 200 million Orthodox Christians.[32] Whether it be the issue of the contemporary reform of the World Council of Churches, founded in part by some of the writers of *The Way*, or the matter of the reform of the liturgical language for tens of millions of believers who can no longer pray in Slavonic, or the secularization of the majority of Orthodox countries of Europe—all these issues are not without consequence. Yet, here again, the contribution to these debates in this volume will be to highlight as succinctly and faithfully as possible those "time bombs" that the contributors to *The Way* left in their wake.

An Adapted Methodology

It is fair to say that the tragic tale of the Russian intellectual generation put forward above is a "poeticization," which bears little relation to the historical reality of the journal and its collaborators. If Bulgakov, son of a line of six generations of priests, could lose his faith upon reading *Das Kapital*, his Parisian colleague at the St. Sergius Institute, Lev Zander, was always faithful to his childhood religion, which he maintained from St. Petersburg to the Côte d'Azur. Simeon Frank was also expelled from Russia in the philosophers' boat, but Shestov simply took the Geneva-Paris train in 1923. Not all religious thinkers left Russia, as the examples of Alexei Losev and Pavel Florensky attest. Of the collaborators in the renowned *Landmarks* collection, only three went on to write in *The Way*.

The "state of grace" achieved at the Congress of Psherov lasted only three years. In 1926, the Serbian Brotherhood abandoned the "movement." Without the aid of Protestant organizations such as the YMCA, the World Student Christian Federation, or the Anglican Church, the emigration would have been a flash in the pan. The lack of mutual comprehension between Russian and French intellectuals was a further factor. Nevertheless, Berdyaev's oeuvre was translated into more than fifteen languages in the period in question. The "Paris School" thought it had a common center, embracing many mutually opposing currents.[33] Certain contributors, such as Mother Maria Skobtsova, did in fact give their lives in the name of freedom during the War, but others simply departed for the United States, or for Germany, to collaborate during the Russian Campaign of 1941 with the Wehrmacht's propaganda machine. It is true that the great historian of Russian religiosity, George Fedotov, is buried in New York State, but Lev Karsavin died somewhere in the Gulag and is buried in Siberia.

One could cite many other half-truths evoked by memory. Of course, such minor details seem insignificant against the background of the great adventure called "the ways of Russian theology," as in the title of Florovsky's 1936 work, or "the Russian idea," as in Berdyaev's title in 1946, or even "the Russian religious renaissance of the twentieth century," as in the title of Zernov's book of 1963. All three wrote in *The Way*, but one could add the essays of others as well—Vasilii Zenkovsky, Nikolai Lossky, Fedotov, or Mother Maria Skobtsova—these authors resumed on their own the legend of a great tradition of interrupted national thought, of which they were the last blooms. Attempting to raise memory to the level of the sacred, they were unable to free it of many very prosaic details.

Given this situation, the question of scholarly method arises and, more generally, that of "truth in history." Convinced that truth in history is always a rewriting, Ricoeur points out in his 1998 article "The Mark of the Past" that the question of truth raises more the issue of "veracity-reliability" than that of "truth-proof."[34] This does not mean that the historian is consigned to the shadows of provisional truths. For Antoine Prost, history has a method, that is to say, a definite complex of intellectual procedures such that anyone who respects those procedures and poses the same questions to his source materials will necessarily reach the same conclusions.[35] He puts the historical methods in two groups, investigation and systematization, each of which is supported by its own type of proof, factual proof or systematic proof, respectively. In the first case, the historian proceeds like a judge confronting different kinds of evidence, weighing them against each other, and neglecting no detail. In the second case, the historian enunciates truths that have validity for a certain assemblage of facts, based on a certain number of examples or, better yet, on the construction of quantifiable indicators.

This study is based on a combination of these two methods in the attempt to position ourselves as close as possible to the journal, or "to make ourselves contemporary to the (historical) actor," to use Raymond Aron's expression from his 1937 *Introduction to the Philosophy of History*.[36] Certainly, factual investigation and examples are limited approaches, a fact of which I remain aware. As Jacques Revel, one of the most prominent proponents of microhistory in France, humorously wrote, "the investigation of microscopic detail can at times give the impression that the historian held a microphone up to ants."[37] One would wish to inscribe these chronological investigations into the framework of a more global problem. I will have occasion to return to this.

According to historian Christophe Charle, only a complete history that contrasts intellectuals by periods and countries can help us understand them in their complexity and evolution.[38] Using Pierre Bourdieu's minimal definition of an intellectual as "a professional handler of symbolic goods," Charle rejects the motion of a single definition for intellectual phenomena. On the other hand, he recommends balancing the comparative sociology of intellectuals with a comparative morphology and analysis of the symbolic and political representations that give meaning to social specifiers.[39]

Nevertheless, the procedures of a historian rely on quotations and eyewitness reports. If applied anarchically, outside a strict common frame of reference, they can result in the researcher making his informants say what he wants to hear, by his choosing to stress those opinions closest to his own.[40] To avoid this pitfall, Bernard Lepetit suggests that one must construct one's subjects like a cartographer, keeping an adequate scale in mind.[41] This is why I have elected to limit my investigation to a defined corpus of texts, the sixty-one issues of *The Way*. Inasmuch as the historian endeavors to be impartial, to "laicize" or "secularize" memory, and to apply a rigorous critical method, does he not risk leaving out some important element of truth, by reproducing the epistemological deletions of the positivist school that Michel Foucault decries in *The Order of Things* (*Les mots et les choses*)? By clearly distinguishing between memory and history, does he not sidestep what memory tries, however awkwardly, to tell us is really the deeper meaning of an event that a group wishes to transmit at all costs, in an obstinate and blind fashion? This is because no political regime or regime of philosophical truth is in a position to comprehend it. Certainly, one must question the perennial ideological use and widespread acceptance of the sacrosanct myth of this intellectual generation that the Russian intellectuals elaborated themselves in their lifetime and later filled in with émigré or Soviet testimony over a fifty-year period. But if the notion of "memory of the clan" is shocking, historian Jeffrey Andrew Barash has questioned anew the Hegelian concept of a universal memory based on the myth of absolute certainty, in the illusion that the trace is adequate to the event.[42] According to Ricoeur, one approximates truth much better "by putting memory back into the movement of change with the expectation of the future and the 'presence' of the past." History is nothing if it is not ordered memory, and oblivion is not its antonym but rather a form of memory. In chasing constantly after a past that is always in question, inasmuch as one imagines it as "lost," must not one at a certain point ask: "What are we making of our memory for today and tomorrow?"[43] The fact is that the possibility of a plural memory bursts forth. Just as the authors collected by Pierre Nora show, his resplendent memory lets us weld together a collective memory that tends less to legitimize identity and more to manifest wounds, something full of potential and of faulty sources of misinformation, of repressions that touch the heart of our present pluralistic existence.[44] In his 1988 *History and Memory*, Jacques Le Goff calls on the historian to lighten the heavy burden of the past. Ricoeur invites today's historian to take another step and see to it that the debt to the past is not only a burden, but that "the legacy of the past is also a resource."[45]

From this perspective, the intellectual is not merely a social actor, a professional manipulating symbolic goods; he is also a locus of memory himself. According to Nora, the intellectual is the result of a long cycle of his/her own developing self-consciousness as an intellectual. Le Goff revealed that the medieval cleric is the ancestor of our present-day intellectual.[46] Paul Bénichou has shown the monk's development into an intellectual—via the humanists, the Republic of Letters, the Enlightenment thinkers, and the symbolist poets—and that this amounts to the progressive formation throughout Europe of a spiritual laity.[47] Russian medieval historian Dimitrii Likhachev, for his part, insisted in the same way on the religious roots of the Russian intelligentsia.[48] He maintains that the first Russian intellectual appeared at the end of the fifteenth century—well before Pyotr Boborykin, one of the first to use the term "intelligentsia" in Russia in 1860. This was an Orthodox monk of Italian origin, Maxim the Greek.[49] The main trait of a representative of the intelligentsia, according to Likhachev, is his rejection of despotism, on the one hand, and his fully national and universal character, on the other. "Russia," he writes, "undoubtedly belongs to Europe by dint of its religion and culture. Even if it is not the only milieu linking Russia to Europe, the intelligentsia is the main one."[50] The mutual acknowledgment by French and Russian intellectuals in France in the 1920s that they belonged to the same intellectual group is evidence of the European dimension of the Russian intelligentsia, which fact gives us a basis for viewing the intellectual as a "locus of memory."

According to Nora, intellectual generations themselves are loci of memory, crucibles of all the complexes, but also a central resource for memory. For an intellectual generation is both the product of memory or an effort to retrieve memory and, at the same time, a violent affirmation of a horizontal identity, usually political or cultural, which takes precedence over all other forms of vertical solidarity.[51] In other words, the memory of a generation of intellectuals is the triangular relation among the state, the society, and the individual, where the vital choices of a united community are formed, at times unconsciously. In this sense, the generation itself is the forger of the bond of memory. These latter constitute for Nora "the tissue of the generation's temporary identity and the reference points of their own memory."[52] Moreover, the "exploration of a generation's memory begins with an inventory of those loci."[53] Jean-François Sirenelli studied the generation of Jean-Paul Sartre and Raymond Aron, concentrating on the *khâgne* [*classes préparatoires aux grandes écoles (CPGE)*] preparatory courses for the superior schools, the equivalent of our top prep schools, one of the loci of memory for the intellectuals of the interwar period.[54] Focusing on the *Landmarks* anthology, Jutta Scherrer has described the milieu of the religious-philosophical societies of Moscow, St. Petersburg, and Kiev, which marked the consciousness of identity among Russian intellectuals of the early twentieth century.[55] Scherrer demonstrated that the generation led by Sergius Bulgakov and Nikolai Berdyaev, two leading contributors to the review, defined itself against the intellectual tradition that extends from Vissarion Belinsky to Georgii Plekhanov and Vladimir Lenin. Oriented from 1900 towards metaphysical and religious problems, and desiring dialogue with official Orthodoxy, "the generation of God-seekers" continued their critique of the Communist intelligentsia after the revolution in the collection *De Profundis*.

Continuing this approach, I will situate *The Way* within a political, social, and ecclesiastical context constituted by four entities: the YMCA Publishing House, the St. Sergius Theological Institute, the Academy of Religious Philosophy, and the Russian Student Christian Movement.[56] I will further observe that the emigration of Berdyaev's and Bulgakov's generation, but also that of George Fedotov and Mother Maria (Skobtsova), while remaining aloof from the Communist intelligentsia, powerfully vindicates its intellectual identity by markedly affirming its connection in memory to the tradition of Alexei Khomiakov and Vladimir Solovyov and by correcting the ideological interpretation of the Kingdom of God on earth.[57] In the history of Russian thought, it symbolized the reconciliation of a stream of formerly alienated intelligensia with the Orthodox Church.

Thus, one can posit the problem inherent in the present research: to blend the microcosmic method with that of symbolic history, to write the minute chronological narrative of the discordant actions of the journal's contributors, while seeing to it that we constantly question these intellectuals' sense of self through their engagement in the *polis*, the public arena, the organization of a space for discussion and orientation towards others. By this dual approach we shall bring to light a part of the special individual creativity of each contributor; their personal conflicts and ruptures in behavior from one period to the next and from day to day; the slowly growing consciousness of self for several intellectuals through their involvement in the journal and with different groups; and the growth of their modernist identity (1925–29), then their nonconformist identity (1930–35),[58] and finally, their spiritual identity (1935–40). Thus, by revealing the context in which *The Way* was produced, we shall avoid reducing the memory of an intellectual generation to small isolated events, but we shall also be invited to participate in a dialogue that, though invisible, is still ongoing in the present. Between a vision of the past which is but the participation in the past that is always with us, between passing a damaged memory through a sieve and remaining faithful to the secret truth of myth, our research will consist in tracing definitively the sad contours of wounded memories. To do so is to allow this broken memory perhaps to be transfigured, as Ricoeur recommends, from repetitious memory to creative memory, to fully forgetting the past and turning towards the future, having once and for all obtained grace.

A BRIEF DESCRIPTION OF THE JOURNAL

The history of European intellectuals of the interwar period is necessarily based, as Michel Trébitsch and Nicole Racine have shown, on the words of journals and weekly publications, the veritable laboratories of a society's debates.[59] A journal, by confronting the intellectual and his age, but also the intellectual and the group to which he belongs, is the best means for feeling the pulse of a generation. Jacques Julliard has written:

> The true journal is a family. The value of each member in it is not measured as in the outside world by quality or abundance of productions, but by his place in the family's structure. Literally and figuratively, the family-journal is a meeting place; it is a natural place to work, discuss, or simply warm one's soul. The disappearance of such a journal when it occurs is a collective trauma.... The echo of a journal is not proportional to its circulation.[60]

For its part, the Russian intelligentsia after the early nineteenth century had always had the habit of organizing its debates in "thick journals" (*tolstye zhurnaly*). Franco Venturi, in his voluminous study of Russian populism, emphasized the importance of the Moscow journal *The Moscow Observer* (*Moskovskii nabliudatel'*) and the St. Petersburg-based *Fatherland*

Notes (*Otechestvennye zapiski*). Belinsky's famous "Letter to Gogol," a political, philosophical, and artistic testament penned in 1848, is one of the best examples of "publicistics"(*publitsistika*), a new literary genre that vacillates between a lay sermon and a spiritual pamphlet, and which appeared in Russian journals at this time. In the Russian mentality up to the present day, journals symbolize their eras. This is the case for *The World of Art* (*Mir iskusstva*) of Diaghilev for the Silver Age and for Aleksandr Tvardovsky's *New World* (*Novy mir*) for the period of "The Thaw."[61]

This is certainly the case with *The Way* for the emigration after 1917. We are justified in considering *The Way* as a locus of memory, that is, as a locus, circumscribed in time and space, in whose bosom the consciousness of an intellectual generation united by the shock of revolution and exile and by the memory of the Russian past was gradually and progressively taking shape.

The Way was intended to be the direct heir of the Put' publishing house, founded in Moscow in 1909 by Berdyaev and other writers with the financial support of Margarita Morozova, which continued until 1919. Thus, *The Way* set itself the task of carrying forward the intellectual and spiritual renewal of the Silver Age.[62]

The entire journal consists of sixty-one issues and nine supplements, containing 400 articles and 206 book reviews. The rhythm of publication was irregular, essentially for financial reasons.[63] Between 1925 and 1940, four issues came out annually on the average, with variations—ranging from three issues (in 1939) to seven (in 1931). The size of the issues averaged ninety pages, but no. 4 for 1928 consisted of 195 pages, more than six times the size of the final issue of 1940 (thirty-one pages). Circulation was around one thousand copies.[64]

The journal had 127 named contributors, to which we must add six anonymous articles and three signed by a single letter or the initials of the author. Seventy-seven authors contributed a single article, thirty-four contributed from 1 to 5 articles, nine from 6 to 10, and twelve from 11 to 40. The last group of twelve must be considered the nucleus of the journal, since they furnished half of the journal's intellectual content: 343 articles and reviews out of the total 606. These were the editor Nikolai Berdyaev (48 articles, 51 reviews), followed by Georges Florovsky (12, 26), Vasilii Zenkovsky (10, 24), Boris Vysheslavtsev (14, 15), Simeon Frank (16, 11), Vladimir Ilyin (11, 14), Sergius Bulgakov (21, 2), George Fedotov (15, 5),

Nikolai Lossky (8, 5), Nicolas Zernov (10, 3), Nikolai Arseniev (10, 1), and finally, Sergei (later Father and then Bishop Cassian) Bezobrazov (5, 6).

The oldest contributor was Nikolai Glubokovsky, born in 1863, and the youngest Raymond de Becker, born in 1912. Two "generations" or age groups collaborated from the beginning to the end: that of the "fathers," born between 1860 and 1890, who had completed their education before the October Revolution, and that of the "sons," born after 1890 and profoundly influenced by World War I, the Bolshevik Revolution, the civil war, and exile. From 1930 onward the "sons" became dominant in the journal, even though the older group, with a few exceptions, remained faithful until the journal's demise. The last living contributor was Valentina Zander, who died in 1989.

The majority of the authors were Russian Orthodox. Nevertheless, the journal opened its columns broadly—to Catholics, such as Cardinal Andrieu, Paul Archambault, Elisabeth Belenson-Elson, Raymond de Becker, Jacques Maritain, Julia Sazonova, Fr. G. Bennigsen, Stanislas Fumet, Lev Kozlovsky, Augustin Jakubiziak, Pope Pius XI, and an anonymous Catholic contributor; to Protestants, such as Pastor Christoph Blumhardt, Hans Erenburg, Gustav Kuhlmann, Samuel Kavert, Fritz Lieb, and Paul Tillich; and to the Anglicans Paul F. Anderson, S. L. Ollard, a contributor identified as K. A., Frank Gavin, and Kenneth Kirk.

The Way was primarily a European journal in its contributors and readership, with correspondents in Asia and the United States. The nucleus of the journal's contributors resided in Paris (Berdyaev, Florovsky, Zenkovsky, Boris Vysheslavtsev, Vladimir Ilyin, Bulgakov), but close to half of the contributors lived in the French provinces, such as Alexander Elchaninov (Nice) and Nikolai Alexeev (Strasbourg), or lived abroad, such as Frank, Nikolai Bubnov, Dmitrii Chizhevsky, Fedor Stepun, Paul Tillich, Igor Smolitsch, and Vasilii Sezeman (Germany); Piotr Bitsilli, Sergei Chetverikov, Vyacheslav Lebedev, Maria Litviak, Nikolai Lossky, Pavel Novgorodtsev, Piotr Savitsky, Nikolai Trubetskoy, and Evgenii Spektorsky (Czechoslovakia); Fr. Alexei B., the two authors identified as a Russian monk and a priest of Petrograd, and Fr. Nalimov (USSR); N. Zernov, G. Bennigsen, and S. L. Ollard (England); Piotr Lopukhin, Rostislav Pletnev, and Sergei Troitsky (Yugoslavia); Anastasia Polotebneva and Pope Pius XI (Italy); Nikolai Arseniev and Lev Kozlovsky (Poland); Fritz Lieb and Mikhail Volkonsky (Switzerland); Georgii Tsebrikov and Victor Ekkersdorf

(Belgium); Frank Gavin and Samuel Kavert (United States); Nikolai Glubokovsky (Bulgaria); T. S. Ku (China); Alexander Vanovsky (Japan); and Valentina Zander (Latvia).

The journal aimed to bring together and make known various currents of Russian religious thought. In the majority of cases, the contributors dealt with problems arising in the tradition of the Eastern Church. On the cover of each issue appeared the Christological sign "chi-rho XP," framed by *alpha* and *omega*. However, from its inception, *The Way* was open to all spiritual horizons. In its pages we find discussion of Japanese mythology (V2) and Italian Protestantism (P9), Taoism in China and the Catholic youth movement in Germany (Z17R), Rudolph Steiner's anthroposophy (T17), Jewish mysticism (B6), Anglican theology (A40), and Buddhism (K29). One can estimate the number of articles dealing directly with Orthodoxy's relations with other confessions at 10 percent.

The originality of *The Way* lay in its treatment of secular problems from a religious perspective. This is why it has a more generalist than specialist character. It does, of course, treat of philosophy, theology, psychology, science, history, politics, art and literature, and so forth. The diversity of subject matter is accompanied by a similar diversity of genres. We find the more popular *publitsistika* side by side with metaphysical treatises, travel narratives, reviews of French and other non-Russian books, chronicles, extracts from intimate journals, historiographical studies, monographs on writers, the publication of nineteenth-century correspondence from readers, and exegesis of Holy Scripture.

Although the scarcity of archival materials makes it difficult to provide precise data, there is enough information to determine the public towards which the journal was targeted.[65] The nucleus of readers was comprised of Russian émigré intellectuals in the Paris region. An essential part of these still practiced an intellectual profession (creative writers such as Remizov or Shmelev), or were journalists, such as Ilya Fondaminsky or S. Gessen, but they also included readers such as Piotr Ivanov and Nikolai Reimers, a porter and taxi driver, respectively. Ivan Shmelev, celebrated for his 1923 story of the cruelties of the revolution, "The Sun of the Dead," wrote to Berdyaev on the occasion of the journal's debut: "How grateful to you I am for *The Way*. It is a remarkable journal and so necessary. For me it is my daily bread, the water of life."[66] Not all of the intellectuals lived in Paris. Historian Mikhail Karpovich was teaching in New York. The theologian Troitsky resided in Belgrade and Lebedev in Prague. There was also an equal proportion of well-known clerics among the audience: bishops, such as Metropolitan Evlogy of the Russian community of Europe, but also Bishop Theophilus (Pashkovsky) of Chicago and later Metropolitan of the North American Diocese of the Russian Orthodox Church; and priests, such as Lev Zander's father-in-law Fr. Kalashnikov of Paris, Fr. Iswolsky of Brussels, and finally, Fr. Lev Liperovsky, Secretary-General of the Russian Student Christian Movement.

Russian émigré students comprised the third group of readers, among them regular participants in courses at the St. Sergius Institute in Paris, such as Dimitrii Klepinin or Alexander Schmemann, and those in the Academy of Religious Philosophy, such as its two secretaries Georgii Kazachkin and Paul Evdokimov. Others were in contact through the Russian Student Christian Movement, such as Tamara Baimakova in Riga and Stefan Chertkov in Sofia. Finally, the journal benefited from the distribution system of the YMCA Press, which gave it a circle of readers who were enthusiasts of Russian culture or Christians of an ecumenical stripe. Notable among the former were the German writer Hermann Keyserling, French professors Edouard Petit, Paul Boyer, and Ferdinand Lot, and Italian professor Ettore Lo Gatto. Among the latter were the Catholics Monsignor Michel D'Herbigny, Fr. Lev Gillet of the Benedictine Monastery of Amay-sur-Meuse, the Greek Catholic Metropolitan of Ukraine Andrei Sheptytsky, the missionaries John Mott and Donald Lowrie of the World Student Christian Association and the YMCA, the theologians Rudolph Otto and Paul Tillich, and Anglicans such as Canon J. A. Douglas and Bishop Walter Frere of Truro. And the journal also reached to Harbin, China, where there was a branch of the American YMCA Press publishing in Russian, as well as to a number of leading American universities. *The Way* could boast an audience that bridged all divisions of generation, religious faith, or nationality.

THE EPISTEMOLOGICAL STANCE OF RUSSIAN RELIGIOUS THOUGHT

A historical work such as this, which examines a journal and an intellectual generation of philosophers and theologians, must span several disciplines and ask itself, first, What was the nature of the Russian thought of which *The Way* was the mouthpiece? The unresolved question of the epistemological stance of Russian thought is particularly important in the works of Berdyaev, Bulgakov, Nikolai Lossky, and Shestov and must be broached here, even if briefly.

What Is "Russian Religious Thought"?

From Vysheslavtsev's inquiry into the "eternal" in Russian philosophy to Zenkovsky's *Russian Thinkers and Europe*, one gnawing problem afflicted the contributors to the journal: "Who are we? What is our identity? Why does the West not understand us?" In parallel fashion, we find Berdyaev meditating on the "mysterious" France of Joris-Karl Huysmans and Léon Bloy and the rapprochement of Pierre Suvchinsky's works with those of Igor Stravinsky, Claude Debussy, Henri Bergson, and Marcel Proust, all in a desire to find the common ground of Russian culture and that of the West.[67] These parallel attitudes appear so often that we must take seriously the Russians' reproach to their French and German counterparts that they failed to understand them. Even more so than in the case of Pyotr Chaadaev's *The Vindication of a Madman* in the present renaissance in Russia of religious philosophy defined as specifically "Russian," this phenomenon exceeds the framework of the journal and embraces several centuries of Russian cultural history. Furthermore, eminent European intellectuals—from Carl Jung, Mounier, and Edmund Husserl, who were in contact with Vysheslavtsev, Berdyaev, and Shestov, to Jacques Derrida, Hans-Georg Gadamer, and Albert Camus, who had read some of the authors of *The Way*—found Russian thought sufficiently original to attract their interest.

A conference on Russian religious thought in Aix-en-Provence in 1968 brought these thinkers together under the rubric of "idealist philosophy."[68] In a doctoral thesis on the religious renaissance of the Russian fin-de-siècle, Michel Grabar has challenged this definition. In his view, before the Russian Revolution these thinkers had stated the impossibility of the subject's positing himself as an aesthetic, natural, or ethical subject in the framework of what was then called "idealism." Therefore they elaborated a critique of idealism under the influence of Nietzsche, Dostoevsky, and Solovyov, or they arrived at, thanks to a protean formulation and Platonic formulation, a "realistic symbolism."[69] In the framework of the present study of *The Way*, we will not return to this study's conclusions. Rather, the historical approach here is to examine how Russian thought conceived of itself and what it became, beginning with precise examples crystallized on the pages of the journal. Moreover, after consideration of the definitions that Russian intellectuals applied to their own thought, we shall give broad outlines of the genealogical contours they used for their spiritual identities. Thus, we shall proceed to disengage this thought from the nationalist entrapment in which it remains in Russia today, due to pride and resentment. Finally, we will expose the equally necessary philosophical assessment based on the Christian revelation of "the Humanity of God" (*Bogochelovechestvo*) inscribed in the very heart of modernity.

An Evolving Self-Definition

For the above reasons, we shall confine ourselves to three basic statements. First, the intellectuals of *The Way* consciously grouped themselves around the standard of "Russian religious thought," which they used internally. Second, they sought to find common ground with their European counterparts and defined their thought as sophiology (Bulgakov), personalism (Berdyaev), or existentialism (Shestov). Nevertheless, they were conscious of belonging to the same generation. And third, these thinkers became increasingly aware of the "mytho-logical" dimension of their thought, which was not contradicted by other contributors to the journal in the late 1930s. It went largely uncomprehended by the European intellectuals of the interwar period.

The first statement above allows us to delimit the intellectual profile of the generation of *The Way*. Having rejected Kant's prohibition against penetration into the depths of the thing-in-itself, these readers of Nietzsche went ahead and flushed out the myths, symbols, and dogmas appealing to very specific forms of religiosity that lay behind apparently objective, authoritative concepts. Giving primacy to the Christian myth over the Nietzschean, Marxist, and Freudian myths—even while writing about these three thinkers—they cut themselves off from intellectuals who rejected the authority of religion or the appeal to religion in their argumentation. That is why one finds little trace in the journal of nonreligious authors from the Russian Empire who were exiled in France, such as Emmanuel Lévinas, Alexandre Koyré, and Georges Gurvitch.

On the other hand, the Orthodox profile of most contributors did not prevent the journal from publishing a Jewish thinker such as Shestov, the Catholic Maritain, or the Protestant theologian Tillich. The second statement above indicates a certain diversity of thought. Some, calling themselves professional theologians, such as Bulgakov and Florovsky, insisted on Christian dogma as the basis of their thought. Others, like Berdyaev, whose visiting card read "Man of Letters, Professor of Philosophy," but also Frank and N. Lossky, tried to show that the person is more a mythical notion than a concept. Lastly, there were others, such as Shestov and Adolf Lazarev, who wanted their thought to rest wholly on that form of certitude which we call religious faith. The milieu for the reception of the work of this generation of contributors could vary from Anglican seminaries to Paul Desjardins' gatherings of writers, including Gide and Bergson among others (the group known as the Décades de Pontigny), and from the Protestant journal *Le Semeur* to the important and scholarly *Revue de philosophie et des religions*.

The third statement requires more precision. There are two principal definitions of the word "mythology": first, Mircea Eliade's notion of mythology as the systematic study of mythical narratives recounting events of the fabulous age of beginnings—*illud tempus* ("in that time");[70] and second, mythology as understood by Berdyaev, Shestov, or Bulgakov, which is not a theoretical discipline of knowledge. The thinkers writing in *The Way* understood mythology in a totally different sense from Eliade, one derived ultimately from Schelling but interpreted phenomenologically, namely, as a type of symbolic formation of being and of human thought.[71] Therefore, to avoid confusion, and without going into the many symbolist, structuralist, and functionalist interpretations of it in the West, I translate these Russian thinkers' sense of *mifologiia* as "mytho-logy" and, in the adjectival form, "mytho-logic."

The Genealogy of Mytho-logic Thought

Genealogy is one of the traditional forms of self-definition for these Russian thinkers. Berdyaev cites as his intellectual predecessors Jacob Boehme, Kant, and Dostoevsky, and Shestov points to Job, Blaise Pascal, and Søren Kierkegaard. Florovsky situates himself in the tradition from St. Simeon the New Theologian to St. Philaret (Drozdov) of Moscow, via St. Gregory Palamas. It does not make sense to attempt to construct a narrative of "the sources and the meaning" or a sense of "a growing consciousness of self," which is protean and eminently personal. Nevertheless, the constant, passionate references to the past in the journal articles show that Byzantine patristic literature, and the violence of the debates on Russian spiritual history that pitted Florovsky, Fedotov, and Bulgakov against each other, force us into the dialogue among both the French and the Russian intellectuals on their understanding of mythos and logos. Only thus will we avoid misunderstandings. This justifies a brief presentation, not of the mythic origins of national thought, but of some elements of the general culture of this group, born out of the Silver Age and reassembled in *The Way*. Here, three important elements in their inherited self-consciousness can be distinguished: patristic mytho-logy, idealist mytho-logy, and symbolist mytho-logy.

Patristic Mytho-logy

The Greek philosopher Christos Yannaras has given fresh consideration to the Russian thinkers' discourse on Being,[72] most notably that of Sergei Trubetskoy's essay "The Doctrine of Logos" (1900).[73] Yannaras explains the difference between mystical experience and logical experience as follows. The logos signifies and reveals the fact of the relation of the spirit with the mode of manifestation of beings and cosmic harmony, the fact that human logos conforms and corresponds to logical modes which constitute Being. In effect, in myth, which is always a narration, reason never functions simply to describe sense experience or an intelligible approach to reality. It aims to communicate consciousness in the mode in which life is realized. In this case, reason functions as judgment and imagination. Yannaras's definition of myth is the following:

> Myth is the history of something produced by imagination. It reproduces actions and the relations which are relevant to the sensual domain but in the way in which the mind imagines them while judging them. That is to say, it separates what is essential for the realization of life from that which is only ancillary to it.[74]

These existential actions reproduced in myth and expressed in language via symbols are the relations of persons.

In the same way, in logical consciousness, the essence is not something completed, but rather a participation in becoming, in life's development as a social and cosmic fact. Logical thought is a semantics of essences. In it, the concept of definition determines the singularity of the essence as a discourse of differences. Declarative discourse, the action of demonstrating, reveals not only the singularity of being as a universal, but also the model of this singularity. Yet one must always keep in mind that it is within the framework of the *polis*, not individually and not autonomously, that common reason is achieved with the logos of communion of the citizens of the polity.

The difference between mythical and logical experience is one of participation in communal reason. That is why thought has such difficulty synthesizing them into one expression. But the history of thought shows that their increasing separation has curbed their realization in life. In effect, a personified image that uses myth has the tendency to identify itself with what it signifies, so that it cannot distinguish the alterity of each intelligible reality. In the same way, abstract and impersonal notions lose their semantic character easily and are subject to the arbitrary interpretation of a single individual, and can no longer be taken as the last word on Being.

It is from this separation of myth and logos, between image and life, and between image and word, that one must make a detour towards the problem of Being, in order to give the patristic definition of mytho-logic thinking for a second time. Ontology is discourse on Being. We can distinguish briefly, in the history of thought, three discourses on Being: the ontic conception, the rational conception, and finally, the personal one. The ontic conception of Being treats it as if it were something that really exists. The rationalist conception, because it is still inscribed in the substantialist vision of the ontic conception, is displaced from the question of mythos to that of logos. Thought, doubling back on itself, poses the problem of discourse on Being and adopts the criterion of conformity of the human logos (which becomes reason) with the logos of beings-in-themselves or beings-with-relation-to-us. This approach presupposes the same conception of the knowing subject and the known object, as autonomous ontic individualities. Finally, the personal conception is based, as S. Trubetskoy writes, on "the religious ideal of Judaism." It shares with the rational approach the distinction between human beings and the cosmos, more clearly than within the ontic conception. But it refuses the rational reduction of truth to the adequacy of the concept to the thing conceived.

The personal understanding of Being returns to the ontic conception of truth as a universal, dynamic, and social matter of life.[75] Using the apophatic method, that is, the logic of negation (*affranchissement*) of all the determinant notions of consciousness, the personal conception of Being consists in a new return of thought to the problem of the mythical nature of Being.

For the Cappadocian Fathers, what lies at the origin of the personal vision of Being is first a revelation of spirit: The ontical vision of God imprisoned in its essence and of man overwhelmed by cosmic time became impossible. This spiritual turn gave life back to Being and integrated history as the space-time of the personal relationship between man and the Creator. For Gregory of Nyssa and John of Damascus, "to be" and "to be in relation" became identical. Whoever or whatever is at issue, two things are necessary at once: to be oneself (*hypostasis*) and being in relation (*prosopon*). Only in the relationship does identity appear to have ontological meaning. This discourse derives from the new representation of God's unique nature, not in an abstract substance (*ousia*), but in the Father, as *prosopon* and *hypostasis*.[76] Far from separating the discourse on God and the love of wisdom, Gregory of Nyssa, Maximus the Confessor, and Nicholas Cabasilas took up anew the initial intuition of Greek philosophy of Being as a given living reality that can only be spoken of in mythic terms, which makes it more intelligible in discourse. The Christian Church calls these men its "Fathers" precisely because of their ability to communicate their revelation of God the Trinity logically.

The Cappadocian philosophers, by taking Aristotle's distinction between primary essence (the individual attributes of the subject), which is for them its *hypostasis* in the sense of self-consciousness, and secondary essence (modes of common participation in Being), *ousia*, introduce in addition to those two terms a third notion, energy (*energoumenon*), as the realization of unique relations by each subject, or of similar relations by numerous subjects.

> We call the energies of the essence of man those capacities for the common participation of persons in Being (knowing, desiring, creating, loving), while at the same time it is a leaving, an existential ex-stasis in regard to this common mode, that is to say, the existential alterity/otherness of each concrete person, but also the knowing-participation in the alterity of other essences and other individuals.[77]

Facing the problem of Being, and moving thus from the problem of the *what* to the question of the *how*, this movement of thought saw Being not as a substance but as a person. Besides the great types of the Same and the Other, a third generic type, that of the Self which founds its own hypostasis, was emerging in consciousness.

One can date the advent of Christian mytho-logic discourse from the personalist ontology of the Cappodocians. Here, mytho-logic thought is the discourse oriented towards the universal harmony of the logical faculties of man with Being, considered as a person in view of the living out of life.

Idealist Mytho-logy

Modernity transferred the discovery of the personal dimension of divine Being to the level of the human *Cogito*. But according to Paul Ricoeur, after the exaltation of the *Cogito* by René Descartes, an alternative was posed to European philosophical consciousness by a representation of the Perfect that was more Hellenistic than patristic. "Either the *Cogito* is a foundation, but it is a sterile truth to which one can add nothing without rupture in the order of causes, or it is the idea of the Perfect that underlies it in the condition of finite being, and the primary truth loses its aura of being the primary foundation."[78] In the first case, for Malebranche and then Spinoza, "the *Cogito* becomes an abstract truth." In the second case, for the idealist current running through Kant, Johann Fichte, and Husserl, "the certitude of God's existence is ruptured by the same seal of subjectivity as the certitude of my own existence."[79] In both cases the representation of the divine logos as static and immutable and the way of individual reasoning founded on hyperbolic doubt leads in the twentieth century to a new turn of thought towards myth. This results, with the "I doubt better than Descartes doubts" of Nietzsche, in the bankruptcy of the self-proclaimed subject and the collapse of a certain type of certainty.[80]

Thus, the rehabilitation of myth in philosophy is the accomplishment of German idealism in its effort to find once more the meaning of the Absolute. It starts from Kant but is in total opposition to him. Friedrich Schelling's (1775–1854) reflections on myth and revelation were pivotal for the history of Russian thought. Schelling states unequivocally that myth is not allegorical but "tautegoric." He writes: "For it [the mythology], the gods are beings who really exist, who are nothing else but what they signify they are."[81] For him, however, myth does not belong, like a sign, to the order of thought, but rather belongs to the order of emotional affect and will. It is always the individual who, in Fichte's thought, projects himself and objectifies his aspirations in society, art, and religion. The novelty of this discovery lies in the fact that the individual thus reveals the presence of symbols in himself, symbols which have the same universality as concepts. But in this way Schelling was proposing an Absolute beyond thought, even while giving it the contingency of a historical revelation. For Hegel (1770–1831), an absolute that renounces thought is not an absolute.[82] The absolute thus must force the experience of alterity and schism in order to posit itself as an Absolute.

Nineteenth-century Russian thinkers, from Ivan Kireevsky to Vladimir Solovyov, were profoundly influenced by Schelling's realist concept of myth and by Hegelian ontologism. But as the heirs of a renewal of Orthodox spirituality, they could not admit the "erroneous" (according to Solovyov) notion that "what is known in the self is outside of us and does not act upon us except in an exterior manner."[83] The evolution of German thought on Russian soil definitely produced, as much for Belinsky as for his opposite, Dostoevsky, a denial of personhood. As Koyré wrote, all Slavophile thought from Kireevsky to Khomiakov rejects the abstract character of Hegelian thought.[84] Russian religious thought agrees that there is no rational bridge between the transcendental and the immanent, but holds that this is not sufficient to separate man from the profundity of being.

Mytho-logy of Russian Religious Thought

Here, once more, it is not a question of defining a uniform system of thought, whose diversity and evolution will then be studied. We must simply posit the special character of a current of thought that appears at the beginning of the twentieth century in Russia and its roots in the wider development of European philosophy described above. We shall not retrace the Greek, French, or German sources of Russian thought, or the dimensions of Russian Symbolism—more meandering than linear—as it appeared in figures as diverse as S. Trubetskoy, Andrei Bely, and Vyacheslav Ivanov. We shall concentrate on the integrality of the movement produced in *The Way* in the 1920s and 1930s.

In 1927 Berdyaev wrote in the journal, "mytho-logic thought has much more contact with being than logical thought."[85] Mythology was not for him a reference to "narratives of societies where the State was established,"

> Dogma has a philosophical meaning and dogmatic philosophy devotes all its efforts to the unveiling of this meaning and makes of it a kind of general metaphysics. Since philosophy does not have access except to that which it is questioning or why it is "surprised," the content of a philosophy and its measure are determined by its problematics. This is why philosophy's ability to include the dogmatic meaning of the Trinity is determined by the degree to which the inner problem of the Trinity emerges within it, at least as a postulate.[96]

For the Russian theologian, knowledge of the truth was not an elaboration of rational notions, but rather involved a full value judgment, a creative participation of the human spirit created in the image of God, of the divine Logos.

Likewise, for Florovsky, dogma, more surely than myth—understood in its Hegelian interpretation—allowed him to reflect on the reality of the world, on its created dimension. If the mainstream of the neo-patristic tradition—represented by two contributors to the journal, Georges Florovsky and Vladimir Lossky, themselves disciples of Bulgakov and Lev Karsavin—undertook a radical critique of ideas still carrying the taint of abstract idealism, still, as far as they and their elders were concerned, they did not question the movement of that thought which turned from biblical revelation to *realiora* in an antinomian and eschatological way. In a 1930 article entitled "The Dispute concerning German Idealism," Florovsky, even though he was a strong critic of German idealist mythology, rejected the dualism of "Christianity or metaphysics," introduced after the Protestant Reformation. The Greek patristic path, for Florovsky, responded exactly to the problem of undertaking "attempts at 'the churching of Hellenism,' to create an authentic 'Christian metaphysics.'"[97]

The mytho-logy of Russian thought, then, is a personal and generational immersion in the space that stretches between poetic or religious myth, and thought. Mytho-logy is the living relationship of myth and thought, that is, an event, or in Russian, *so-bytie*—"a being-with," an encounter.

PART ONE

A Modernist Journal

(1925–1929)

The formation of the consciousness of a generation is the fruit of complex processes and can be understood as a mythological phenomenon.[1] Raoul Girardet has shown that in periods of historical upheaval, a society's collective consciousness loses its traditional points of reference. That gives rise to a mythical effervescence within minority groups, which are the most threatened.[2] Myth, despite its objectively refutable interpretation of reality, offers certain keys to explain the chaos of facts and events and the mobilization of these groups' energies.[3] According to W. Otto, the original mythic process is such that it imperiously demands to be imitated, or, more exactly, to be re-accomplished. Man seeks through his corporal nature, through cult, and through his actions and words to incarnate his representation of the divine.[4]

At the end of the First World War, the French public wanted its government officials to erase the traces and aftermath of the war and lead the country back to the happy prewar epoch. S. Berstein maintains that the aspiration to return to a golden age included several myths, such as nostalgia for a stable currency and vague references to the "good life" of the *Belle Époque*, which the French sought anew through intoxication with jazz and the new enjoyment of consumption.[5] However, the blow of the occupation of the Ruhr in October 1923 and the inability of the National Bloc between 1919 and 1924 to solve the crisis in public finances forced the French to understand, despite much confusion, that the war, rather than being a parenthesis, had brought forth a new world and a new way of living. In this sense, France in 1925 was living out the last days of the postwar period. The awareness that things were different due to the structural effects of the war was first formulated by intellectuals such as Alain and Paul Valéry and was communicated gradually to society in general after Poincaré returned to power in July 1926. The devaluation of the franc in 1928, the rise of German nationalism from the summer of 1929, and finally, the Wall Street crash on October 24, 1929, destroyed the myth of a golden age. In 1929, four years after the great exposition of decorative arts at the Trocadéro, a new generation of French, born after 1900, reached the age of political and intellectual responsibility in a state of unrest but also with demands for a new realism compared to the idealist, progressive, and pacifist generation born before 1880.[6]

At the same time, the majority of émigrés from Russia understood that the consolidation of Stalin's power in Russia had devastated their plans to return to their native land, and there was a palpable increase in demands for French naturalization.[7] Until this point, they had lived in a nostalgic frame of mind, hoping to encounter the good old days of Imperial Russia once more.[8] Such a context vindicated the modernist identity of the authors of *The Way*. Specifically, the common will towards a new interpretation of religious doctrine within the bosom of Orthodoxy takes on its full meaning. In effect, Berdyaev's and Karsavin's generation, born of the Silver Age and welded together by common emotional experience and exile, was animated by a search that was itself mytho-logic (as explained in the introduction to this volume), but with a completely new understanding of the Kingdom of God on earth.

In an article about A. Gornostaev's book on Dostoevsky and N. Fedorov, Berdyaev based himself on the "fathers" of *The Way* generation to define the "fundamental, unique, and central" problematic of Russian religious thought as "the Kingdom of God on earth," and to avoid the millenarianism of the formula "the search for the truth on earth."[9] In like manner, Bulgakov, in his lecture "Concerning the Kingdom of God" at St. Albans in 1927, insisted on the Christological, antinomian, and eschatological dimensions of this symbolic figure. It indicates the possibility of encountering the spiritual world from this world, from the terrestrial world, thanks to the unity perfected in Christ (the God-man) of the two natures, human and divine. Inspired by Fedorov's myth of the common task, Bulgakov's philosophy of history is profoundly dynamic.[10] "The advent of the Kingdom of God on earth," Bulgakov writes, "is an event [*sobytie*], not only metaphysical but historical; also it is not accomplished in the inner world of man via repentance only, it is a change in the relation of God to the world, a *Parousia*."[11] This eschatological search for the Kingdom, based on the deification of man and the transfiguration of the cosmos, is radically opposed to the nostalgic hope, dominated by the primary notion of the Fall, of finding a new golden age in Russian history.[12]

Dominated by the same demand for realism as the younger generation of French intellectuals, who were born to urban life after the hostilities ended, the generation of Russian intellectuals expelled by Communism incarnated their mythic ideal between 1925 and 1929 in an involvement that was resolutely *modernist*. The modernism of these Orthodox intellectuals is seen in the editorial of the first issue of *The Way* as a call to "spiritual creativity" within the framework of the Orthodox Church and a call to struggle against "the reactionary trend" that was constantly being reaffirmed in the 1930s. It should be distinguished from a comparable trend in the thought of Lucien Laberthonnière, Adolf von Harnack, Henri Bergson, and Alfred Loisy, which was broken by papal condemnation between 1907 and 1914, because it pertains to a radically different context and did not take on the form of a dispute. However, the above writers were visited by Russian intellectuals and had in turn their own infatuation with Claudel, Desjardins, or Léon Bloy for the work of Melchior de Vogüe on the Russian novel. They had in common a certain will to combat the "cultural underdevelopment" of religious research (the expression of H. I. Marrou) and to confront church authorities. This allows us to speak of a certain proximity of the Orthodox intellectuals to the modernist current of the prewar period. Above all, the term "modernism" was used pejoratively by those criticizing the contributors to *The Way* both in Orthodox and ecumenical circles. We hear Bishop d'Herbigny, prelate-in-charge of the Papal Institute, uttering his chronic polemic on the Russian emigration in 1931.

> The Karlovtsy synod decried the "modernism" of the directors of the Theological School of Paris and the [Russian Student Christian]

Movement. The lecture of Professor S. Bezobrazov at the Congress of Bierville (1926) confirms this. Without any protest from his audience, Bezobrazov allowed only one source for divine revelation—Holy Scripture: the subsequent tradition is nothing but illustration and commentary by men in which each believer arrives individually at a grasp of the true meaning of the Bible. According to him, the Ecumenical Council itself cannot speak infallibly [a reference to article B97 in *The Way*].[13]

Below, we shall study the basic aspects and evolution of this group's modernist engagement, from its intellectual reflection (in the next main section, "A Generation of Modernist Intellectuals"), to its ecclesiastical, social, and political positions (in the section "The Modernist Constellation"), and finally, the integration into the European intelligentsia of the contributors to the journal (in the section "The Ecumenical Commitment: The Affirmation of the East in Relation to the West").

A GENERATION OF MODERNIST INTELLECTUALS

In the editorial in the first issue of *The Way*, the editors declare that they consider themselves Orthodox and place themselves within "the traditions of Russian creative religious thought."[14] That is why they appeal to "the names of Khomiakov, Dostoevsky, Solovyov, Bukharev, Fedorov, and Nesmelov, all of whom are close and dear to the editors of this journal."[15] Taken together, these six names represent for the authors of *The Way* a new current in Russian religious thought quite distinct from that of Tolstoy, Leontiev, and Rozanov.[16] In 1935, Berdyaev, in hindsight, called it "modernist"—this "path," this original representation of the Kingdom and the locus of their new Russian identity, which the group wished to preserve in the emigration.[17] The 1925 editorial read as follows:

> There may be within Orthodoxy new currents of creativity, renewal, and rebirth [*obnovliayushchee*] necessary to confront new challenges. The status of the Orthodox Church in the world has sharply and catastrophically changed, and before it stand new tasks. A new type of Orthodox soul is taking shape, one that is more active and respon-

sible, more creative, more virile and daring. Russian religious thought contains creative ideas that can contribute to a general Christian renaissance.[18]

The "modernism" of the six individuals mentioned above consisted, for the editors, in their need to be independent from all forms of power. Their vision of the world, inspired by the church's dogmatic symbolism and ecclesiastical involvement, was directed towards the unity of Christian churches. We are speaking here of a memorial reconstruction, inasmuch as the Caesaropapist ideology of Solovyov, the critique of rationalism in Dostoevsky, and Khomiakov's rejection of "Protestant heresy" are well known. Nevertheless, these six names—from Solovyov's speech against capital punishment to Nesmelov's anthropology, and from Khomiakov's encyclopedism to Fedorov's thirst for a new renaissance—indicate a movement of thought towards intellectual, political, and ecclesiastical modernity.

The renewal of Orthodox tradition that this generation demanded thus differed from the Western version of Modernism, which was centered on problems of science versus faith. But it shares with the *Sillon* of Marc Sangnier the same thirst for social justice. And it shares with Fr. Loisy a desire for renewed interpretations of the scriptures, and finally, with Charles Péguy, that thirst for universality that does not contradict love for one's native land.

In the first editorial (March 6, 1925), which Berdyaev intended to serve as a guide for the editorial group, he made his position explicit. He wrote that the support which the Christian churches extended to the schism of the "Living Church" in Russia after the Revolution showed a different understanding of church reform in the Eastern and Western churches. That difference is what lay behind the following words and the modernist thrust of the journal.

> The current Christian renaissance and its creativity is neither a rupture from nor a struggle with the Orthodox Church. Rather, it is renewal [*obnovlenie*] and development within the Church, and is linked and united with all that is eternal in it. Russian Christianity is unthinkable outside the framework of the Orthodox Church, thus any attempt at renewal must be made from within it. The "Living Church"

of their banishment from Russia and went abroad to do doctoral work. Vysheslavtsev traveled to Rome in 1908–9, to Paris, and most important, to Berlin and Marburg, where he met the neo-Kantians Paul Natorp and Nicolai Hartmann and wrote his doctoral thesis, "The Ethics of Fichte." Frank went to Berlin in 1899 to take Georg Simmel's course on economics. After a period in Berlin, where Nikolai Lossky studied with M. Wundt, and then in Leipzig with Wilhelm Windelband, Lossky decided to translate Kant's *The Critique of Pure Reason* into Russian. Italy also attracted Russian intellectuals. Berdyaev marveled at Rome and Florence, while Karsavin spent two years in Tuscany writing his doctoral dissertation, "The Foundations of Medieval Religiosity."

The collaborators of *The Way* were likewise of diverse social backgrounds. Among the professions of their fathers, one finds doctors (S. Frank, L. Zander), a judge (E. Spektorsky), a school principal (V. Ilyin), a choreographer (L. Karsavin), a priest (S. Bulgakov), a military officer (A. Elchaninov), and merchants (P. Novgorodtsev, A. Remizov). Some were from aristocratic families, mostly landowners or government functionaries more or less recently raised to the nobility, or from military families (Archimandrite Ioann Shahovskoy, Berdyaev, G. Fedotov, N. Lossky, E. Skobtsova, Grigorii Trubetskoy, N. Trubetskoy). Their level of affluence also varied, and while no one was of proletarian origin, some, like Remizov, had financially difficult childhoods. A. Kartashev was the only one hailing from the peasantry. This variety of social backgrounds is equaled by the diversity of their native towns, which included Moscow (B. Vysheslavtsev, N. Alekseev, Ioann Shahovskoy, S. Frank, Remizov, N. Trubetskoy), Kiev (Berdyaev), St. Petersburg (S. Bezobrazov, L. Karsavin, L. and V. Zander), Vyborg (V. Sezeman), Riga (E. Skobtsova), Saratov (Fedotov), Odessa (Florovsky), Tula (Archimandrite Cyprian Kern), Ekaterinburg (D. Klepinin), small provincial towns (Bulgakov, Lossky, Elchaninov, Ilyin, Kartashev, M. Kurdiumov, P. Novgorodtsev, Spektorsky, Zenkovsky), and cities abroad (Arseniev in Stockholm). However, certain regional groupings among them had formed after they completed their higher education and before they met in Paris. Thus, one can distinguish a Muscovite group centered around Professor Novgorodtsev (Vysheslavtsev, Frank, later Bulgakov and Florovsky), a Kievan group around Professor G. Chelpanov (Berdyaev, Ilyin, and Zenkovsky), to which one could also add I. Lagovsky and Spektorsky, and a Petersburg group surrounding the professor of medieval history I. Grevs (Karsavin, Kartashev, and Fedotov).

A Similar Intellectual Trajectory
Tempted early on, under the influence of Lavrov and Mikhailovsky, by populism and positivism, Berdyaev, N. Lossky, and later Zenkovsky, Ilyin, and Florovsky chose to major in natural sciences at the university level. Deeply affected by their reading of *Das Kapital* and by political changes, they reoriented their studies, taking up law (Alekseev, Berdyaev, Bulgakov, Novgorodtsev, Frank, Speransky, Vysheslavtsev), political science (Bulgakov, Frank, P. Savitsky, N. Timashev), or history (N. Arseniev, A. Elchaninov, Karsavin, N. Lossky, Fedotov, Florovsky). Finally, from roughly 1908 up to the Revolution, their reading of Nietzsche, Kant, and above all, Solovyov led a part of the Russian intellectual elite to turn to philosophy (Berdyaev, Ilyin, Lossky, Vysheslavtsev, Novgorodtsev, V. Sezeman, Zander, Zenkovsky) or theology (Bezobrazov, S. Chetverikov, N. Glubokovsky, Kartashev, S. Troitsky, Skobtsova). Elizabeth Skobtsova was the first woman in Russia to complete study at a theological seminary. Some of the contributors rose to the upper levels of university education, becoming associate professors (Arseniev, D. Chizhevsky, Elchaninov, Florovsky, Ilyin, Fedotov, Troitsky, Zander, Zenkovsky) and then full professors (Bulgakov, Kartashev, Vysheslavtsev, Karsavin, Novgorodtsev, N. Trubetskoy).

The similarity of their intellectual trajectory shows the philosophical evolution of this generation, first from positivism and Marxism and then, from 1900 on, neo-Kantianism and a return to metaphysics.[23] This evolution created new bonds and fostered new groupings, such as the religious-philosophical meetings in St. Petersburg from 1901 to 1903, the Religious-Philosophical Society in Moscow, St. Petersburg, and Kiev from 1906, and circles such as Vyacheslav Ivanov's "Tower," as well as journals such as *Russian Thought* (*Russkaia mysl'*) from 1880, *Questions of Philosophy and Psychology* (*Voprosy filosofii i psikhologii*) from 1889, *The New Way* (*Novyi put'*) (1903–4), and *Problems of Life* (*Voprosy zhizni*) (1905), the newspapers *Liberation* (*Osvobozhdenie*) (1902–5), *Moscow Weekly* (*Moskovskii ezhenedel'nik*) (edited by E. N. and G. N. Trubetskoy) (1906–10), and *The Stock Exchange News* (*Birzhevye vedomosti*) during the war years, and the anthologies *Questions of Idealism* (*Voprosy idealizma*) (1902), *Landmarks* (*Vekhi*) (1909), *About V. Solovyov* (*O V. Solovyove*) (1911), *De Profundis* (*Iz glubiny*) (1918), and *O. Spengler and the Decline of Europe* (*O. Shpengler i zakat Evropy*) (1922). These were the "meeting points" that brought together the following writers between 1900 and 1917: Berdyaev, Alekseev, Arseniev, Belenson, Bezobrazov, Bulgakov, Elchaninov, Fedotov, Frank, Glubokovsky,

Ilyin, Karsavin, Klepinin, Lossky, O. Nalimov, Novgorodtsev, Remizov, V. Sezeman, Skobtsova, Speransky, Troitsky, G. Trubetskoy, Vysheslavtsev, and Zenkovsky.

Several books written after 1909 by people who would become collaborators of *The Way* are characteristic of their final period of rupture with neo-Kantian idealism and their attempt to find Being in its totality once more. Berdyaev's book *The Philosophy of Freedom* (*Filosofiia svobody*) (1911) affirmed the primacy of ontology over the theory of knowledge and thus completed a movement of thought that had been launched in Russia in the 1830s. Referring explicitly to Khomiakov and I. Kireevsky, he writes: "The truest way to reach knowledge cannot and should not be through the channel of rationalism and intellectualism. Rather, it must be solely through the complete and total life of the spirit."[24] The following year, Bulgakov, in his second doctoral dissertation, *The Philosophy of Economy* (*Filosofiia khoziaistva*), rejected all materialism and phenomenology and appealed to the Solovyovan intuition of the divine Sophia for an understanding of the world as the field where economic activity takes place. He interpreted Sophia biblically, as the organizing activity of man in the cosmos in accordance with the divine model called the Wisdom of God. For him, it is not man who creates myth, but myth which expresses itself through man. From such a perspective, the mytho-logic approach of the ancients, in the myth of Gaia and the Great Mother giving birth to the children of earth, is, for Bulgakov, much more satisfactory from the scientific point of view than the materialist myth which holds that absolute chance fashioned life through evolution from dead matter, from a "little sack of jumping atoms."[25] Bulgakov preferred to base himself on the ontological, anthropological, and cosmological tradition of St. Athanasius of Alexandria and St. Gregory of Nyssa, which saw economics not only as the rational administration of the city, but also as the transformation by humanization of inert and mechanical nature into a living organism.[26] Finally, in the same Solovyovan tradition, S. Frank's *Knowledge and Being* from 1915 (Petrograd) argued that the object of all cognition is the Unknown, the "Other" of metaphysics, which is not the correlative of the "Same," but which transcends the opposition between logical identity and alterity. Thus, what the senses and conceptual cognition see are things and ideas; only "living knowledge," that is, the spirit, sees what is primary. He concluded his work as follows: "The originality of this 'living knowledge' lies precisely in that it destroys the opposition between the object and knowledge of the object; thus to know something in this sense is precisely to be what one knows, or to live its own life."[27]

A Neo-Slavophile Political Involvement
This philosophical evolution was accomplished largely by a change in political involvement. Here, again, there were striking common traits: involvement in the Socialist or Socialist-Revolutionary parties in their university years (Bulgakov, Berdyaev, Frank, Lossky, Skobtsova, Fedotov, Alekseev, Aleksey Remizov); expulsion from the university, arrest, or exile (Berdyaev, Fedotov, Alekseev, Remizov, Frank, Lossky); after 1900, illegal militant activity in the Constitutional Democrat Party (Berdyaev, Bulgakov, Frank, Pavel Novgorodtsev, Vysheslavtsev, N. Lossky); and finally, rejection after 1905 of leftist parties, liberal criticism of the autocracy, and progressive activity in the church (Bulgakov, Berdyaev—through the involvement of Father Alexei Mechev—G. Trubetskoy, Anton Kartashev, Lev Zander, Zenkovsky, Fedotov, Alexander Elchaninov, Lev Karsavin, S. V. Troitsky, Vysheslavtsev).[28] They became active in the neo-Slavophile movement on the eve of the First World War, seeking once again a synthesis of spirituality and patriotism. There were, of course, exceptions. Florovsky was neither arrested nor exiled. Skobtsova was elected People's Commissar (Social Revolutionary) for Public Health and Education in 1918 by the Revolutionary Committee of Anapa and remained faithful to her earlier involvements for a long period. Frank continued to write in the Cadet Party organ, *Russian Thought* (*Russkaia mysl'*), until 1923. Nevertheless, the editorial posture of *De Profundis* (Moscow, 1918) summed up, over and above different analyses of the revolution itself, the spirit of the signatories of the collection's editorial board (Berdyaev, Bulgakov, Novgorodtsev, Frank) and that of the whole generation. All the writers shared, with the same ardor, the conviction that positive principles in social life have their roots in the depths of religious consciousness. Breaking the connection with religious consciousness was, for all of them, a misfortune and a crime.[29]

The Ecclesiastical Criticism of Symbolism

The identity of the collaborators of *The Way*, as constituted by their social origins and changing intellectual and political affiliations, was essentially based on their common religious seeking and their ecclesial involvement. By 1925 a common point of reference for this generation as a whole was membership in or affiliation with the Orthodox Church.

The Loyal Sons
Two groups can be distinguished among them: those who were always faithful to the Christianity of their childhood, and those who followed the path of the Prodigal Son. The loyal sons include Florovsky, Bezobrazov, Troitsky, Arseniev, Zander, Kartashev, and Glubokovsky. Lev Zander encountered the faith of other Christians at a young age. As an adolescent, during the long periods his family spent in the south of France before the Revolution, he discovered Roman Catholicism, which was for him both familiar and alien. After 1922 the World Student Christian Federation elected to hold its general meeting in Beijing, and Zander was chosen along with Lev Liperovsky and A. Nikitin to represent the Russian Student Christian Movement. Similarly, Arseniev's childhood was open to Western faiths. His pious mother made him acquaint himself with the literature of the Rhineland mystics of the thirteenth century and the *Fioretti* of St. Francis of Assisi. He learned German, French, Spanish, and Italian and could read Goethe and Racine in the original. Later, under the influence of the great Russian Hellenist, Vyacheslav Ivanov, he discovered the spirituality of antiquity and became an expert in the Mt. Athos tradition of the Jesus Prayer and the prayer of the heart.

The Prodigal Sons
The majority of contributors to the journal, however, experienced some sort of conversion. Most, like Zenkovsky, Bulgakov, Berdyaev, Skobtsova, and Fedotov, had been baptized in the Orthodox Church but had distanced themselves from it, only to return to it at a mature age. Zenkovsky was the grandson of a priest. His father, the choir director in the village of Proskurov, had him singing in the choir as a young boy, but at the age of seventeen, he read in Dmitri Pisarev that "words and illusions will pass, but not deeds," and became an atheist.[30] Later he returned to the church, thanks to the help of a dear friend, to Kant and Solovyov, and to Victor Hugo's *Les Misérables*, which he had read in his teens. In 1919 he became a member of the Church Council of Ukraine.

Sergius Bulgakov hailed from a family of seven generations of priests, going back to the reign of Ivan the Terrible. He was placed in a seminary by his parents at an early age. But between the age of sixteen, when he left the seminary, and twenty-four, when he spent a day in the Dresden Art Gallery and was moved by the smile of Raphael's Sistine Madonna, he rejected all forms of transcendence. Finally, in 1901, when he was around thirty years old, and after a long intellectual evolution, the contemplation of a sunset in the Caucasus, and a meeting with an aged hermit who was filled with compassion for the world, Bulgakov abandoned his atheism. He arrived at the understanding that it was the very experience of transcendence that gave him knowledge of it, and that, just as in philosophy or science, religion is based on an a priori synthetic judgment, on a "Thou art." Several years later, in 1905, he was ready to take communion. At that time he discovered the Fathers of the Church and the tradition of religious philosophy that extends from Khomiakov through Solovyov. Under the influence of his friend Fr. Pavel Florensky, he was ordained on June 24, 1918, the day of the Holy Spirit, with the blessing of Patriarch Tikhon (Belavin).[31]

The life of Pavel Florensky and his book *The Pillar and Ground of the Truth* exerted considerable influence on Nikolai Lossky. The latter had been expelled from St. Petersburg University in 1894 for political views, and later, by the irony of fate, lost his professional position because of his religious beliefs.

Like Bulgakov, many intellectuals of the Silver Age passed from a religiously inspired socialism to a Christianity marked by a concern for social problems. Elizabeth Skobtsova began her career as a poet in the Symbolist milieu of St. Petersburg. Her first collection of poems, *The Scythian Shards*, which came out in 1912, had an Acmeist tone. Four years later, while doing social work in the worst neighborhoods of St. Petersburg, she published her second collection, *Ruth*, which was clearly inspired by the Bible.

At the same time, during the Revolution, George Fedotov ceased his revolutionary activity within the Social Democrat Party. Along with his friend A. Meyer, he founded a brotherhood called "Christ and Freedom."[32] Its aim was to be open to ecumenism and not attached to any particular church. Orthodox believers, some Protestants, and many Jews open to Christianity participated. No credo was imposed. Only the solemn promise "Christ and Freedom" was obligatory. As a sign of their belonging to the universal church, they all recited the "Our Father" in Latin, German, and Slavonic. In the first issue of the journal of the brotherhood, *Free Voices* (*Svobodnye golosa*), the editorial staff writes: "We are seeking a new way [*novyi put'*] ... to save the truth of socialism through the truth of the spirit, and save the world through the truth of socialism."[33]

Berdyaev experienced the universal church from his infancy. His mother, who had received a French education and who was "afraid to address God with the familiarity customary in the Eastern Church," passed on to him her love for Catholic piety. His father, who admired Rousseau and Tolstoy, liked to read the Bible but rejected the way the church had compromised itself in the course of history. Through his grandmother—who was secretly religious—and his nanny he had his first contacts with the Russian folk (*narod*) and discovered the Orthodox tradition. This education, which was completed by his studies in the corps of the cadets and by his readings, awakened his spiritual curiosity. Later, he frequented St. Petersburg occultist circles, Zosima's hermitage, and meetings that took place in the tavern near the Church of Florus and Laurus on Miasnitskii street in Moscow, where one could find Baptists, Evangelicals, and members of the "Bessmertnik" sect—that is, members of the ordinary *narod*. It is in this context that Berdyaev, when he was about twenty-seven years old, had a decisive spiritual experience. He refers to it briefly in his memoirs:

> One particular moment from this summer in the country comes to mind, as I was walking in the garden, in early evening, and my heart was heavy. . . . Clouds hung overhead. Darkness was setting, but a light was suddenly ignited in my soul. I do not call this an abrupt "conversion" because I was neither a skeptic nor a materialist nor an atheist nor an agnostic before this moment, and my internal contradictions did not cease after it.[34]

From this moment Berdyaev intensified his public condemnation of the intolerance of the Orthodox Church while, at the same time, drawing nearer to it. He was particularly sensitive on the subject of personal freedom, and he continually battled against obscurantism and fanaticism. In 1913, the Holy Synod, exasperated by the philosopher's defense of the onomatodox monks (*imiaslavtsy*, "worshippers of the Name"),[35] finally initiated a process of excommunication for blasphemy. This process was interrupted by the war. Later, in the middle of the revolution, his wife, Lydia Judifevna, decided to convert to Catholicism. Thus Berdyaev rediscovered the creative tension between Orthodoxy and Catholicism within his very household.

Finally, Simeon Frank had the distinction of coming from a Jewish family immersed in German culture. He lost his father when he was very young, and his childhood was principally marked by the gentle and scholarly presence of his maternal grandfather, a practicing Jew. When his grandfather was near death, he summoned the child and made him swear upon his deathbed to always remain faithful to the Jewish religion. His discovery of the thought of Solovyov, his marriage in 1908 to a Russian Orthodox woman, and his own spiritual journey finally led Frank to convert. In 1912 he became Orthodox and yet retained the profound conviction that he had not contradicted the promise made to his grandfather.

Points in Common
Whatever might have been their spiritual trajectories, the generation of Berdyaev and Kartashev shared a growing awareness that the interpretation—as modernist as it might be—of the realities signified by myths, symbols, and dogma[36] only made sense if it was situated within the tradition of the church.[37] Unlike Ivanov, Shestov, or Dmitrii Merezhkovsky, Berdyaev and Kartashev believed that dogma points towards authentic reality, for it symbolizes the spiritual experience and deep life of the whole church. This "realistic symbolism" rejects—to use Bulgakov's words—"fossilized ecclesiasticism," "willful mysticism,"[38] or "fainthearted a-dogmatism"[39] because it is rooted in the living tradition of the church. All three, the myth, the symbol, and the dogma, are born of a religious experience, pass inevitably into thought, and tend to find expression in words. In 1916 Bulgakov wrote:

> Dogma is a means for signaling through concepts that which is not a concept, and which finds itself above logical thought through its abstract aspect. It is, however, a conceptual enunciation, a logical transcription of what is contained in the religious experience. . . . On the one hand, it is a judgment expressed in concepts and, consequently, an immanent reasoning process, auto-generated and continual; on the other hand it transcends thought and introduces a discontinuity.[40]

In 1920–21, while in Crimea, Bulgakov completed two books, *The Philosophy of the Word* (*Filosofiia slova*) and *The Tragedy of Philosophy* (*Tragediia filosofii*), which are essential for understanding the evolution of the mytho-logical discourse from Byzantine thought to Russian thought.

These two books were not well known in the émigré community since the first was not published until after Bulgakov's death, and the second was published in German at Darmstadt in 1927. This explains why the "linguistic turn"—the discovery that there is no thought without expression, nor is there word without thought—which the Russian philosopher elaborated in these works was misunderstood during his lifetime. These two books are of considerable interest, however, for the measure in which they mark a rupture in the history of Russian religious thought between the period of so-called "realistic symbolism"[41] and the period in which the mytho-logical discourse becomes aware of itself.

In 1921, Bulgakov acknowledged that language, nature, and myth are a given, and assigned reason the task of seizing their meaning. Thus, he made the transition from formal logic to hermeneutics, the logic of comprehension. Since a thought is expressed in language by means of language, as Bulgakov writes in *The Tragedy of Philosophy*:

> We can say that at the basis of self-awareness, as with every thought-act which seals this awareness, lies a trinitarity of moments [*troistvennost' momentov*], a tri-unity expressed by the simple judgment: *I am A*. If we restate this in grammatical and logical terms—subject [*podlezhashchee*], predicate [*skazuemoe*], copula [or, linking verb: *sviazka*]—we could say that the foundation of self-awareness is the sentence [*predlozhenie*].... The self-contained I ... finds within itself the image of being [*obraz bytiia*], and expressing itself through the "predicate," recognizes this image as its own fruit, as a self-revelation that is the copula.... The essence and image of being is embedded in the sentence; the sentence carries its mystery within itself, for in it is hidden the figure of the trinitarity.[42]

Within the structure of linguistic expression, Bulgakov identifies the "Self" (*samost'*) (the hypostasis) from the nature of the "Self" (thought, spirit), which reveals itself within the "I" (*ia*) and within the framework of the "I," and, finally, the self-affirmation of the "Self" in the "I" (existence [*bytie*]).

Using this as a starting point, Bulgakov qualifies the entire history of modern thought as monistic because it dissolves the three terms into a single one in the name of the correspondence of rationality with substance. Bulgakov distinguishes among the different systems of monistic thought. The first kind, which stems from the subject (the abstract hypostasis), results in idealistic systems (Kant). The second kind stems from the predicate and, in identifying hypostasis and substance, leads to panlogistic systems (Hegel, Fichte). And finally, the third kind stems from the copula between subject and predicate. By rejecting impersonal being (the hypostasis, which is secondary in regard to substance), it results in the mystical, empirical, and materialistic variants of realist systems (Leibniz, Spinoza, Schelling). For Bulgakov, this monism has its dogmatic counterpart in the heresy of monarchianism.[43] He adds, "the 'substance' exists not only 'in itself' (as the subject), it exists simultaneously 'for itself' (as the predicate), and also 'in itself and for itself' (in the copula), as being [*kak bytie*]."[44]

Having arrived at this stage of his reflection, Bulgakov takes the decisive step for his demonstration by elaborating a "philosophy of trinitarity [*troichnosti*]." The hermeneutic of judgment leads to a "metaphysics" of the Trinitarian God, who created man in his image. Bulgakov writes: "The tri-unique nature of the human spirit is the living witness of the Holy Trinity; likewise its revelation, the ecclesial dogma, is the only satisfactory premise which enables our thought to conceptualize the human spirit."[45]

By this discovery of the richness of the symbolic, mythological, and dogmatic tradition of the church, the generation of Berdyaev and Bulgakov prepared the way for the important return of some of the intelligentsia to the church during the somber years of exile. This return was preceded by a resounding polemic. In the 1909 collection *Landmarks*, Berdyaev, Bulgakov, and Frank denounced the radical ignorance, sectarian intolerance, and atheistic positivism of Russian intellectuals.[46] The reactions to the collection reveal the novelty of this perspective.[47] The Social Democrat Party, the Revolutionary Socialists, and the Constitutional Democrats were unanimous in rejecting what they called this "Salvation Army literature."[48] The feeling that the intellectuals were betraying their common mission of opposing the state led Lenin to call *Landmarks* an "encyclopedia of abjuration" and to exclude those authors qualified as renegades.[49] For his part, Anthony Khrapovitsky, bishop of Volhynia and representative of the official church, publicly expressed his gratitude for the collection but only retained the call to repentance, which meant, in his mind, the submission of the intelligentsia to the ecclesiastical hierarchy.[50] In the end, the symbolist intellectuals fell out among themselves. Dimitrii Merezhkovsky condemned the "reactionary" bent of the authors of *Landmarks*. Andrei Bely lamented the reactions against the collection expressed in the press, which he compared to "a summary execution pronounced by a military court martial."[51]

This unanimity against the authors of *Landmarks* does not recognize the two different roads taken by Russian intelligentsia who contributed to *The Way*. The fact that Kartashev, Troitsky, G. Trubetskoy, and Bulgakov— who was elected representative of the establishments of higher education of Moscow—all participated in the 1917–18 Council of the Russian Church is a testimony to their common awareness of the necessity of church reform. This reform took place through the restoration of the patriarchate and the participation of both clergy and lay people in the work of the council. In September 1917, the assembly adopted a revised constitution, which affirmed the principle of conciliarity. The supreme authority of the church would be the council, which would assemble, in principle, every three years and be accepted by the whole of the church. At each level of hierarchy, an elected council would designate and assist the priest or prelate in charge.[52] By reintroducing the principle of authority and personal responsibility in the church, while retaining the principle that truth can only be found in conciliarity, the generation of Bulgakov and Kartashev testified to the Christological deepening of the Russian ecclesial consciousness, rooted in the patristic renewal and the philosophy of the Silver Age. These decisions in fact consecrated the recognition by the "clerics" of the priestly dignity of all those baptized in the church and the recognition by the participating "intellectuals" of the Christological foundations of the apostolic succession. Unlike the Slavophile generation of Khomiakov, which insisted on the spiritual underpinnings and invisible dimension of the church, this generation dared to reaffirm that Christianity also professes that the visible church should anticipate the Kingdom of God on earth. Although he was wary of church authorities, Berdyaev still appreciated the political consequences of the reform. For the reform of the Russian Church meant the end of the "symphony" between the Tsar, the anointed one of God, and the patriarch. It culminated in the separation of church and state on January 23, 1918. Kartashev, who had become minister of religious affairs under the provisional government, definitively eliminated the function of Ober-Procurator of the Holy Synod.

The Common Experience of Exile

In addition to the fact that they all belonged to the Silver Age, to an epoch of ecclesial commitment, the authors of *The Way* also shared the experience of revolution and exile. The Parisian review was the place where people of the emigration came together, yet their conditions of exile, their political opinions, and their age differences were markedly distinct. Among them were those who, like Alekseev, Arseniev, Elisabeth Belenson, Chetverikov, Florovsky, Ilyin, Kartashev, Klepinin, Lopukhin, Piotr Savitsky, Igor Smolitsch, Eugene Spektorsky, Suvchinsky, N. Trubetskoy, and Zenkovsky, had left Russia promptly during the civil war and wartime Communism. Others took advantage of the NEP (New Economic Policy) to deliberately go abroad (Bezobrazov, Elchaninov, Fedotov, Novgorodtsev, Remizov, V. Sezeman, and L. Zander). A third group was expelled in 1922.[53] On August 31, 1922, the Central Committee of the Russian Communist Party announced in *Pravda* its decision to order the secret police (the GPU, ancestor of the KGB) to expel to the provinces and foreign countries the most active counter-revolutionaries among the "milieus of the intelligentsia who sympathized with the cadets and the SR" (Socialist Revolutionaries). We now know that this expulsion was decided by Lenin himself and publicly approved by Trotsky the day before.[54] Among "the 160 most active bourgeois ideologues" were Bulgakov, Karsavin, Berdyaev, Frank, N. Lossky, Fyodor Stepun, and Vysheslavtsev. A first "philosophers' boat" left Russia in the month of September, through the Baltic Sea, for Germany; as for Bulgakov, he was expelled in the second boat, on December 30, 1922, via the Black Sea.

A Spiritual Criticism of the Revolution
For these intellectuals, exile strengthened the sentiment of belonging to the tradition of modernist thought as embodied in Khomiakov, Dostoevsky, and Solovyov. As has been noted, this is characterized by political, social, and ecclesiastical independence. It will suffice to recall some of the best-known examples: the interdiction by censorship and the prohibition of publication of his works outside Russia that was imposed on Khomiakov due to his virulent criticism of the "decadent scholasticism" of the *Dogmatic Theology* of Metropolitan Makarii (Bulgakov); the exclusion of Solovyov from the university because of his position against the death

penalty; the condemnation to death of Dostoevsky for his participation in the Petrashevsky Circle; and the problems of Aleksandr Bukharev with the official authorities of the Holy Synod, which led him to his voluntary departure from the priesthood and monastic life in order to preserve his freedom. On the occasion of the tenth anniversary of the journal, in 1935, Berdyaev wrote:

> The principal religious and philosophical forces were concentrated around the publishing house The Way. The journal *The Way* continues these same traditions. It is indisputable that Russian religious thought at the beginning of the twentieth century was a modernism reposing on Orthodox soil, in the sense that one could already call the thought of Khomiakov, of Solovyov, of Dostoevsky, and of Bukharev modernistic. This represents a progress outside of the categories of traditional and official Orthodoxy.[55]

In the context of exile, this intellectual modernism manifested itself in a common spiritual interpretation of historical events by those who wrote for the journal. On November 26, 1922, in Berlin, Berdyaev presided over the opening session of the Academy of Religious Philosophy in the presence of the principal personalities of the Russian emigration. To the surprise of all, the Russian philosopher, in the course of his presentation, condemned all forms of political and military counter-revolutionary activity and challenged the émigrés to give proof of a creative attitude. For Berdyaev, the causes of the ruptures that were tearing apart the world were only an expression of an interior spiritual rupture. He concluded by inviting émigrés to rediscover the religious meaning of life in order to bring about the political and social rebirth of the motherland. This position was reaffirmed three years later in an editorial of *The Way* by a group of expelled philosophers:

> The Russian emigration is not made up of innocents in opposition to the guilty who live in Russia. It is made up of guilty people, and its positive spiritual mission can only be accomplished if it recognizes its culpability. Those of the "right wing" must recognize this as much as those of the "left wing." The cultured element of Russian society, horrified today by the anti-Christian visage of the Revolution, had strayed a thousand times from the Christian commandments and had given

little thought to realizing the truth of Christianity. The path of opposition to the Christian commandments and of denial of Christian truth will now continue to its final destination with the Bolsheviks. But it was not the Bolsheviks who started out on this path. All of us, those on the right as well as those on the left, have opened this path and made use of it for a longer or shorter time.... The task of the cultured segment of the emigration is to become spiritually aware of this truth: there is only one possible movement against the kingdom of the Antichrist ... that which realizes the truth of Christ and takes its inspiration from that truth.[56]

This spiritual vision, shared by the contributors to *The Way*, does not exclude a more philosophical criticism of the foundations of socialism. In an article entitled "The Paradoxes of Communism" published in March 1926, Vysheslavtsev criticized the Marxist theory that capitalism fatally leads to the concentration of capital, a phenomenon that would weaken the development of entrepreneurial shareholders and trade unionism.[57] In "The Two Paths of Social Development," published four months later, Vysheslavtsev fine-tuned his criticism by pointing out that the fundamental contradiction of socialism lies in its failure to understand the nature of law. Marx's hostility towards the state, based on that of Henri de Saint-Simon, was, in reality, a hostility towards the law, which imposes a limit on the all-powerful nature of socialist norms.[58]

More profoundly, the contributors to *The Way*, whether they were monarchists (Arseniev, Bulgakov, Andrei Karpov, Zenkovsky, Sergei Bezobrazov, Kartashev, G. Trubetskoy) or republicans (Alekseev, Berdyaev, Skobtsova, N. Lossky, Novgorodtsev, Fedotov) fundamentally agreed, at least until 1927, on the recognition of the religious sources of the revolution and, hence, the need to vanquish Bolshevism by deepening the spirituality of the Russian religious conscience. This position was especially original among the Christian intelligentsia. Already, in 1923, it had provoked a rupture in Berlin among the authors of the collection *De Profundis*, with Berdyaev and Frank supporting it and Piotr Struve favoring the continuation of the civil war.

A Criticism of Western Spirituality
Corresponding to the spiritual criticism of the Revolution was the criticism of Western spirituality as a whole. In an editorial of *The Way*, the

editors write: "The capitalist society is no less anti-Christian than the Communist society.... A Christian society must be constructed over the ruins of the bourgeois society. We must take advantage of this favorable situation and not reconstruct the decayed anti-Christian society of the past."[59] The great majority of the authors of *The Way*, as noted above, belonged to the neo-Slavophile current of the immigration. Inspired by Khomiakov, Solovyov, and Dostoevsky, the generation of Berdyaev and Bulgakov gathered, prior to the revolution, around the publishing house with the same name as the journal would have—The Way (Put'). This publishing house had condemned the secularization of Western civilization in the wake of the Renaissance. Their writings, and above all their articles between 1917 and 1926, unanimously recognized the decline of Europe[60] and radically criticized "rationalistic" Western metaphysics and its exaggerated faith in man. In their view, these factors had led to the burgeoning of evolutionary ideologies, liberalism, and socialism.[61] In 1926, in the third issue of the journal, Berdyaev, in an article written three years earlier and entitled "The Bourgeois Spirit," presents the ontological and spiritual foundations of the bourgeoisie, which he characterizes as extreme attachment and servitude to this world. According to the Russian philosopher, the mechanical, industrial, and capitalist civilization of Europe and America has dethroned the figures of the knight, philosopher, and poet to put in their place the new figure of the "bourgeois," athirst for universal domination, often pious, and a conqueror and organizer. Only a reduction of needs and appetites, a diminution of that vital appetite that engenders "the anguish, the worry, the increasingly hectic movement, the incapability of living in the present moment," can once again permit the creative flame to aspire to the Heavenly City.[62] For Berdyaev, the first bourgeois was "the architect of the Tower of Babel," the first to have rationalized the future harmony of the earthly paradise.[63] In the same issue of *The Way*, Zenkovsky, for his part, wrote that the emergence of a bourgeois ethic had a more historical source in "blessed Augustine," who was the first to turn away from the theonomic ethic that affirmed that the person is not free except in God. In his view, this fatal option would result, in the eighteenth century, in Kant's justification of autonomous ethics, according to which "the starry sky is above me and the moral law is within me."[64] When, according to Kant, the person is no longer the subject but the object of ethical activity and is submitted to the categorical imperatives, the transcendent force of God becomes useless.

Zenkovsky summed up his argument by stating that this is why "religious immanentism," that is, the diabolical affirmation that religious and creative powers come only from one's self, is the "key for understanding the very essence of the spiritual life of Europe in these modern times."[65] Florovsky continued the debate in the following issue of July 1926. For him, this immanentism, which affirmed social progress in the framework of history, obscured man's hope of freeing himself from creation, of suppressing the distance that separates duty and reality.[66]

For the heirs of Dostoevsky, this "chiliasm" of the nineteenth century was in a process of decay. That is why they considered the development of a certain relativism in matters of political philosophy as a positive phenomenon. In his article entitled "The Religious Foundations of Society," Frank points out that since life in Russia "has become hellish," all the ideals of society, socialism included, have lost the source of their vitality. "No one can really believe, with all his soul, in 'democracy' with its 'liberty' and 'equality' nor in 'progress' or 'enlightenment.'"[67] Berdyaev also, in January 1927, justified relativism in politics.

> The State and society are rooted in the absolute, but that does not give them the right to erect their relative forms and manifestations as absolutes. To make the relative absolute, to refuse to recognize the rights of what is relative, the tendency to see everything either as an immediate theophany or a diabolical manifestation and the anti-Christ himself, is the principal sin of Russian reflection on the State and society. Such a position negates purely human activity, our responsibilities in the affairs of this world and in the construction of human society.[68]

In the end, for the contributors to *The Way*, democracy was not the Kingdom of God upon earth. As Novgorodtsev put it, "Like any other system it can be better or worse according to the spiritual forces people invest in it."[69] These writers were equally aware of the pagan origins of Fascism. As early as 1926, Berdyaev denounced right-wing German nationalists for their "paganism and hatred of Christianity."[70] The common foundation for the political activity of the Russian émigrés who wrote for *The Way* was the desire to Christianize society or—to use the expression most often employed—the "churching of life" (*Votserkovlenie zhizni*).

The Relative Openness to the Eurasian Movement

The neo-Slavophile sympathies of this generation of authors of *The Way* explains the favorable reception given to the ideas of the young Eurasianist movement in journal articles.[71] The Eurasianist movement began in 1920 in Sofia with a generation of intellectuals born in the 1890s. S. N. Trubetskoy, Savitsky, Suvchinsky, and Florovsky published their first manifesto in 1921—a collection of articles entitled *Exodus to the East* (*Iskhod k vostoku*). Later the movement extended to all of Europe and became very active. It organized Eurasianist seminars in all of the large centers of the Russian emigration and published seven collections between 1920 and 1931, a *Eurasianist Chronicle* (*Evraziiskaia khronika*) (1925–37), a journal *Versts* (*Versty*) (1926–28), a weekly (1928–29), *Eurasianist Notebooks* (*Evroziiskie tetradi*) (1934–36), and many brochures.[72] In the Sofia manifesto, the four authors remark that the Old World has collapsed with ancient Russia and affirm that the East, still full of spiritual reserves, will become the new *hegemon* (spiritual leader) of a new Europe.[73] In the second collection, *On the Roads* (*Na putiakh*), published in Berlin in 1922, Suvchinsky specifies that the Russian Revolution was more a geocultural event than a sociopolitical one insofar as it is the affirmation of a geocultural era, that is, Eurasia as a self-contained continent.[74] These considerations were supported by phonology—the new science (of sound patterns in language) invented by N. Trubetskoy. The latter justifies his Christian-based Eurasianism in an article entitled "The Tower of Babel and the Confusion of Tongues," published in *Eurasianist Annals* (*Evraziiskii vremennik*). He writes:

> The appeal of Christ to teach all nations, baptizing them in the name of the Father, of the Son, and of the Holy Spirit, has not been carried out because missionary work was transformed into being an instrument of Europeanization, a means of establishing a homogeneous universal culture. We have tried to show that this culture is hostile to God.[75]

This new science of phonology revealed the existence of a Eurasian group whose common characteristics were the absence of tone in their languages and an organization consonant with this fact. From a historical perspective, the Zoroastrian sources of Russian religious terminology, the choice of the Byzantine religion by Vladimir, and, finally, the fusion of Russia and the Horde during the period of the Tatar domination of Genghis Khan, confirm this presence of "Turanian" (i.e., Central Asian) elements in the Russian culture. This is why, in Florovsky's opinion, the revolution, if it wanted to succeed, should return to its Russian sources and reject the international element of Bolshevism.[76]

Certain Eurasian theses were subject to severe criticism by Berdyaev, beginning with the very first issue of *The Way*. In his review of the fourth issue of the *Eurasianist Chronicle*, the Russian philosopher criticized the movement for its lack of universalism, its approach to Eurasia (which he found too geographical, racial, and national), its ritualistic and folkloric vision of Orthodoxy, its hatred of Catholicism, and its criticism of the intelligentsia. These doctrinal insufficiencies can be explained, in Berdyaev's opinion, by the primacy given by young émigrés to action and emotion, as opposed to reflection. There is also a danger, he warned, that the movement might become a "Russian Fascism."[77]

Although *The Way* never defined itself as Eurasianist, about a third of its Russian contributors participated in the movement at one time or another (Alekseev, Arseniev, Berdyaev, Fedotov, Florovsky, Frank, Ilyin, Karsavin, Kartashev, Klepinin, Remizov, Savitsky, V. Sezeman, Suvchinsky, N. Trubetskoy, Vysheslavtsev). Berdyaev recognized the originality of S. Trubetskoy's "Turano-Tatar" conception of Russian history and qualified the Eurasian movement as being "a unique ideological current of the post-Revolution emigration."[78]

The main point that Berdyaev and S. Trubetskoy shared was their mytho-logical understanding of Russian identity, following the tradition of Dostoevsky and Solovyov. In 1888, Trubetskoy had identified the "Russian idea" with the quest for the Kingdom of God and, more precisely, for the restoration of the divine Trinity on earth, that is, a quest for "the complete realization of the social Trinity where each of the three principal organic unities, the Church, the State, and society, is absolutely free and sovereign not by separating itself from the others or absorbing them or destroying them but by affirming its absolute solidarity with them."[79] In the same spirit, as affirmed in an editorial of *The Way*, the heirs of Solovyov agreed that "the Russian idea has always been a religious idea. It is the concept of Holy Russia and not the imperialist concept Great Russia."[80] Unlike Solovyov, however, the intellectuals of *The Way*, Berdyaev as well as Florovsky, no longer believed in a "theocratic utopia"[81] but rather in a "Christification" (*okhristovlenie*) of life from within,[82] that is, in an ecclesial justification of all the spheres of culture and in a Christian transfiguration of society, economy, and the state.

A Tradition of Mytho-logical Speculation

During the 1920s, in order to be heard, the Russian authors presented themselves to their Western colleagues as representatives of a renewed ontological approach. But the ensuing confrontation with Western intellectuals whose theses had seemed, a priori, very similar to theirs, and the painful lack of understanding encountered by the contributors to *The Way*, reinforced their intention of representing an original form of thought. In the following pages, I analyze this confrontation as it is reflected in the journal during the period 1925–29. I then trace the sources and different interpretations of myth and, finally, present the characteristics of Russian mytho-logical speculation.

The Confrontations with Western Thought as Reflected in the Journal

The authors of *The Way* were basically at odds with the neo-Kantianism and neo-Hegelianism of the European philosophers of the 1920s. On the other hand, phenomenology, which was more concrete, was received more favorably in the pages of the journal. Let us examine their relationship with these three philosophical movements.

The Russian Philosophers and Neo-Kantianism
In 1925, Ernst Cassirer, the most eminent representative of the neo-Kantian Marburg School, published the second volume of *The Philosophy of Symbolic Forms*, which dealt with the philosophy of mythology and of religion. S. L. Frank in "The Neo-Kantian Philosophy of Mythology," which appeared in the issue of July 1926, and then N. Lossky in "Mythical Thought and Contemporary Scientific Thought," in December 1928, both reviewed Cassirer's work in *The Way*, and both noted the great erudition of this disciple of Hermann Cohen. However, both thought that the transcendental method was not satisfactory for the understanding of mythical thought. Lossky criticized Cassirer for seeing mythical thought as a "construction" of the activity of the intellect and not as the faculty of immedi-

ately seizing the living and dynamic reality of things.[83] Frank argued that in Cassirer's system, "there is no faith in an immutable reality which one discovers and relates to; this discovery and consequent relationship can, by themselves (contrary to all types of transcendentalism), justify and thus render consistent and significative (and not just psychologically interesting) the analysis of the religious conscience."[84] The opposition of the categories of mythological and scientific approaches that Cassirer set up, inspired by Schelling, could only clash with the symbolist and realist metaphysics of the two Russians. Lossky and Frank both used the example of number in their reply to the German philosopher. Their conception, inspired by Florensky, is close to the idea of the neo-Pythagoreans, according to which number can only be understood by the Unknown, which it manifests, for there is neither logical nor mathematical determination in it.[85] In a more systematic fashion, Lossky examined, one after the other, the foundations of contemporary scientific thought using recent discoveries in physics and biology. Lossky was himself in favor of a radical empirical method, which takes into account sensory, intellectual, and mystical experience. In his view, only a philosophy of knowledge intuition, Anglo-American realism, or what he calls "organic, concrete ideal-realism," can integrate the scientific and mythical perspectives in a unified whole.[86] Actually, for Lossky, only the concept of a substantive actor permits one to seize causality in a truly dynamic manner and not simply as "the order of the harmonious appearance of events in time."[87]

The Russian Philosophers and Neo-Hegelianism
On the other hand, R. Kroner,[88] Jean Wahl, and Berdyaev agreed in recognizing that Hegel's thought, shaped by Meister Eckhart, Boehme, and Luther, was marked by an awareness of the transcendence of God. In his review of the "brilliant and original" book of J. Wahl,[89] Berdyaev rejoiced that "even objective savants are beginning to understand that the whole history of philosophy is full of theological and mytho-logical elements, depends on a religious source, and belongs to the history of the spiritual life."[90] However, he laments that Wahl did not sense the religious impotency of Hegel's romantic mytho-logy.

> For Hegel the final word is philosophy and not religion. The unhappy consciousness is overcome, and joy and plenitude are attained through

philosophy. What is original about Hegel is that he wants to carry life over to philosophy. . . . Everything is realized in consciousness. For Hegel, even Christ's wounds become identified with the contradictions of reason. . . . Hegel wanted to rationalize the irrational mystery of religious life. This was the grandiose and daring goal of his philosophy. But instead, Hegel irrationalized comprehension, as Kroner rightly points out. In Hegel's system, comprehension lost its mind [*poniatie soshlo s uma*].[91]

The Russian Philosophers and Phenomenology
The fact that Husserl (1859–1938) and his disciples went beyond the psychologism and subjectivism in vogue in the European departments of philosophy at the beginning of the century, and their elaboration of a philosophical method that emphasized the contemplation of essences rather than the causal description of facts, had a very real influence on Russian religious thinking. Alexei Losev (1893–1988) was one of the rare disciples of Husserl who lived in Russia during the 1920s. He was well known by the authors of *The Way* since he had twice presented lectures at conferences of the Free Academy of Spiritual Culture (*Vol'naia akademiia dukhovnoi kul'tury*), founded by Berdyaev. One was entitled "The Ontology of Plato" and the other "The Unity of Plato's Dialogues 'Parmenides' and 'Timaeus.'" According to Frank, Losev was the most "lively" philosopher in the Soviet Union. In 1928, Frank reviewed three of Losev's works published at his own expense in the USSR—*The Philosophy of the Name, The Dialectic of Artistic Forms*, and *The Cosmos of the Ancients and Modern Science*. Frank underscored the fact that, despite Losev's rejection of metaphysics, an apophatic perspective towards being can be found in his philosophy in which the name reveals itself as myth, namely, as the self-revelation of the deepest reality.[92]

All the same, the rejection of "ontological instances" by the German phenomenologists Nicolai Hartmann (1882–1950), a former student of Lossky at St. Petersburg, and Max Scheler (1874–1928) was the principal point of contention between the Russian and German philosophers in *The Way*. Frank reviewed Hartmann's *Ethics*, which appeared in 1926,[93] and wrote the obituary of Max Scheler, whom he considered "the most talented thinker of contemporary Germany,"[94] in the October 1928 issue. In these two articles, Frank argued that the dynamics of this philosophy, based on human freedom, transformed itself into moralism when the divine principle of the person was denied.[95] On the other hand, in his December 1928 review of Heidegger's *Being and Time,* Vasily Sezeman judged the work as "the most remarkable book published in the last ten to fifteen years."[96] Sezeman writes that since the fundamental ontological principle is concrete in Heidegger's thought, the phenomenological analysis becomes truly synthetic and much more convincing than the analytical approach of Husserl's phenomenology. While for Sezeman, the fundamental problem with Heidegger, the *Dasein*—which he translates as "being-consciousness" (*bytie-soznanie*)—is on the level of the philosophy of knowledge, for Gurvitch, who followed the interpretation of O. Becker in a 1930 article entitled *Current Tendencies of German Philosophy,* Heidegger's philosophy represented a synthesis of the principles of phenomenology and post-Kantian idealism. These interpretations would be further developed and completed in the early 1930s, especially by Berdyaev, N. Lossky, and Frank. Heidegger's book, in which being is founded on care, held interest for Russian religious philosophy because it was part of the elaboration of a new metaphysics based on the experience of the mystery of being and not on traditional onto-theology.

The Different Mytho-logical Systems in Russian Thought

The Hesychastic Current in the Journal
The spiritual tradition preserved in the Russian Church was not only the common foundation of Russian mytho-logical speculation but also one of the sources of the diversity of views concerning the myth of being. The modernism of Russian religious thought was marked, above all, by hesychastic spirituality, the summit of the Eastern spiritual tradition. This is why the contributors to the review published several articles on this spirituality between 1925 and 1929. In 1925, Vysheslavtsev wrote an article entitled "The Meaning of the Heart in Religion." Subsequently, between 1925 and 1927, Fr. Chetverikov completed a voluminous study on the life of St. Paisius Velichkovsky. In the January 1926 issue, N. Lossky reviewed the books of Ilyin, on St. Seraphim of Sarov, and of Zaitsev, on St. Sergius of Radonezh. In July 1926, the review published extracts of texts of the saints Basil the Great, Gregory the Theologian, John Chrysostom, Macarius the

Great, Simeon the New Theologian, Mark of Ephesus, and Gregory Palamas. In the May 1929 issue, Florovsky presented the life of St. Simeon the New Theologian. And finally, Smolitsch, in the November 1929 issue, presented the life of the "great *starets* (elder)," Nil of Sora.

The term *hesychasm* comes from the Greek word *hesychia*, which means peace, silence, and the sweetness of union with God when one has arrived at spontaneous prayer. By the invocation of God's name, the uncreated light of the divine energies illuminates one's whole being and leads to a restoration and glorification of human nature.[97] This encounter, writes Vysheslavtsev, begins in the human heart—understood as the "symbol," the meeting place of the transcendent and the immanent.[98] The prayer that springs from the heart, if it is to take flight, must purify the consciousness of all images and concepts so that, in a reconstituted "intelligent heart," the energy of the Spirit might embrace and begin to transform one's whole being.[99] The Russian intelligentsia, from Khomiakov to Dostoevsky, were deeply marked by this spirituality. From a theological point of view, this spirituality rejected all forms of objectification of the transcendent and led to the apophatic method. Thus Bulgakov, in *The Unfading Light*, prefaced the exposition of his sophiological doctrine with an entire chapter dedicated to the phenomenology of the representations of the divine nothingness in the history of thought from Plato to Kant.[100]

The Different Receptions of Hesychastic Spirituality
But hesychastic texts, which were becoming increasingly popular as evidenced by the publication of *The Way of the Pilgrim* (*Otkrovennye rasskazy strannika*) at the end of the nineteenth century, were partially cut by the censor when Theophan the Recluse translated them into Russian. Theophan thus kept only the moral and ascetical aspects of the *Philokalia*, which he translated as *Dobrotoliubie*. Among the authors of *The Way*, there could be found both unconditional partisans of the *Philokalia*, such as Fr. Chetverikov, who insisted in his article in the April 1927 issue on the necessity for the faithful to confide completely in a spiritual director,[101] and detractors, such as Berdyaev, for whom the love of freedom opposed any form of spiritual mediation in the Church.[102] Vysheslavtsev situated himself in the middle between Chetverikov and Berdyaev. In his September 1925 article he tried to show that the prayer of the heart was not a disguised form of irrationality that negated the world and was linked to a

simple ascetic technique. It is true, he wrote, that all of the wisdom of the Hindu tradition is founded upon ideas developed in the Upanishads, according to which my true "I," the self (*samost'*), is in the heart.[103] But this true "I," he continued, was not the love which united that which was distinct and diverse. It confused Atman and Brahman, rejected *eros*, the source of suffering, and denied the reality of the world. The patristic tradition, however, up to St. Seraphim of Sarov, taught that love is the true essence of the person and that the pure of heart shall see God, but on the condition of not separating soul and body, intelligence and heart.[104] On two more occasions, Vysheslavtsev would return to this distinction between Buddhism and Christianity in the pages of *The Way*, and this is indicative of the importance of the question among the younger members of the Russian immigration. In October 1928, Vysheslavtsev reviewed a book on Eastern and Western mysticism by the German phenomenologist Rudolf Otto, and in December he gave an analysis of Theosophic doctrine. In both cases, Vysheslavtsev distinguished the high theistic and antinomic mysticism of the Upanishads, of Sankara and of Krishnamurti, from the Buddhism and syncretism of Annie Besant.[105] All the same, he distanced himself from Otto, his colleague and friend,[106] and observed that the God of Sankara is more static than the God of Meister Eckhart and, on this level, that only Christian mysticism, based on the Incarnation, permits us to grasp the personal dimension of love.[107]

The Various Attempts to Continue Solovyov's Synthesis
Whether the emphasis is on the hypostasis of the Father, of the Son, or of the Holy Spirit, the Russian spiritual tradition is centered on the mystery of the Incarnation, on what it calls the myth of the person. However, within Russian mytho-logical thought, some seek to approach the mystical realities by looking, first of all, at the Divine Persons; some tend towards Divine Wisdom; and, finally, some seek to understand the mystery of the personal unity of the Three Hypostases. A difference in the spiritual approach goes in tandem with a difference of logical interpretation, and it provoked a rift between the authors who remained faithful to the quest for spiritual Being in a continuation of the tradition of the Cappadocians and of Solovyov (Lossky, Frank, Zenkovsky, Karsavin, and others), and those who sought new modes of intelligibility, whether kataphatic or apophatic, for the mystery of the Divine Person, in the tradition of Gregory Palamas

but also in that of German mysticism and Dostoevsky (Bulgakov, Berdyaev, Florovsky, and so on).

As indicated by the articles published in *The Way* in 1925, there was a tension between these two approaches, centered on Solovyov. In an article entitled "Vladimir Solovyov and His Successors in Russian Religious Philosophy," which was published in 1925 and appeared in *The Way* in 1926, Lossky proposed that the originality of Russian religious philosophy resided in its realistic and personal relationship to Being: "Russian philosophy, as expressed by Solovyov and his successors, is particularly attached to the teachings about concrete-ideal living principles (such as the personal, living Logos, Sophia, Adam-Kadmon, each human individual spirit) and the doctrine of their incarnation."[108]

Even if the authors of *The Way* agreed in recognizing Solovyov as one of their spiritual masters, nevertheless, a line of demarcation can be drawn between the continuers of and the detractors from his philosophy of the total-unity or pan-unity (*vseedinstvo*). The concept of pan-unity emphasized the ontological principle of the absolute unity of the multiple forms, according to which all the elements of this multiplicity are, on a transrational level, identical both among themselves and in their relationship with the whole, thus forming a sort of polyphonic order. The division among the intellectuals of the review was in evidence during the conference organized by the Academy of Religious Philosophy on November 1, 1925, which was dedicated to Solovyov on the occasion of the twenty-fifth anniversary of his death.

In the camp of those who followed the *vseedinstvo* doctrine, Vysheslavtsev came forward to highlight the Neoplatonic sources of Solovyov's thought.[109] According to him, Solovyov found the concept in the works of Nicolas of Cusa, who, in turn, followed the inspiration of Dionysius the Areopagite. In Vysheslavtsev's opinion, the tradition attempted to synthesize the philosophy of Plotinus, who situated this pan-unity in the sphere of ideas (*kosmos noetos*), and Christianity, which, with St. Paul, affirmed that such a unity is only possible in the person who is in communion. He concludes that this is why Dionysius the Areopagite had identified the world of ideas with the world of the divine plan prior to creation. Karsavin, in his "Prolegomena for a Study of Personhood,"[110] published in August 1928, also aligned himself with this tradition. He stressed the personal character of this pan-unity, which leads to the unveiling of an infinite hierarchy of "pan-unities," in which each actualizes in itself those that are superior and actualizes itself in those that are inferior. This example is a perfect illustration of the following statement, written by Vysheslavtsev in 1928 on the occasion of Emile Bréhier's new translation of the *Enneads* of Plotinus: "Russian philosophy, insofar as it is original, will always be Neoplatonic."[111]

But this thesis was not shared by all the contributors to the journal. Even before the revolution, Bulgakov and Berdyaev had distanced themselves from this Platonic tradition. During the conference at the Academy of Religious Philosophy, the latter, on several occasions, expressed his dismay that Solovyov had not been more critical of Plato's utopian moralism and rationalism.[112] During this same commemorative session, Bulgakov, although he recognized that Solovyov was "a confessor of the faith,"[113] called attention to the lack of clarity in the philosopher's thought, thus indicating that he had nothing to add to the criticism that he had already formulated in *The Unfading Light* in 1916. Finally, Florovsky, unlike Berdyaev, but in continuity with Bulgakov, denounced the Gnostic tendencies in Solovyov's thought.[114]

Characteristics of Mytho-Logical Thought

An Antinomian Approach
In spite of these diverse interpretations of Solovyov's philosophy, the contributors to *The Way* felt as though they belonged to a common tradition of thought. In a 1935 article, Berdyaev writes: "All of us, and in the same way, see an opposition between religious thought and rationalism which legitimizes an expression of the knowledge of God through rational concepts. This signifies the recognition that antinomianism is best suited for the mysteries of Christian revelation."[115]

The antinomian character of modern Russian thought should be studied closely. The fact is that mythical thought uses a form of logic which can be called—in contrast to the philosophers' logic of non-contradiction— a logic of ambiguity, of obscurity, of polarity. Since the time of Aristotle, logical thought advances the following law: "The same attribute cannot at the same time belong and not belong to the same subject and in the same respect."[116] A thing cannot be, at the same time, itself and its contrary. Modern Russian thought, from the beginning of the century and as expressed in the pages of *The Way* in the years between the two world wars, attempted to go beyond the reciprocal exclusion of *logos* and *mythos* by formulating, in an original manner, the antinomian relation of being and of the world.

Florensky, "the Russian Pascal of the twentieth century," according to Rozanov, wanted to construct a synthesis of the metaphysics of Heraclitus and Kant with the dogmatic tradition of the church, a synthesis that affirmed the hypostatic unity of the two natures, divine and human, without confusion and without separation. In his book *The Pillar and Ground of the Truth*, published in 1914 by The Way of Moscow (republished in Berlin by Rossica in 1929 and immediately announced [A25R] and commented upon in *The Way* by Ilyin [I21R] and Florovsky [F43R]), Florensky wrote that the truth itself was antinomian, for if it were not, reason, always operating on its own level, would not have any support and would be unable to see any nonrational object.[117] Truth is a judgment that contains the limit of all its refutations. In this major work, Florensky gave the logical definition of antinomy: "If the antithesis brings about the thesis and if, at the same time, the thesis causes the antithesis, the ensemble of the thesis and antithesis, if it is not false, is an antinomy."[118] According to Florensky, this antinomian understanding of the truth was only possible in the measure in which it is announced to the creature by God.[119] Truth existed only if a creature existed along with God.[120]

It is especially on this point that the thought of Florensky and Bulgakov differed from Kant. In *The Critique of Pure Reason*, Kant described the state of the creature by proposing that it was equally true to say that the world had a final cause—freedom—and that it could not have such a cause. Kant resolved the contradiction by referring freedom to what is intelligible in itself and causality to the realm of phenomena.[121] For Bulgakov, transcendental philosophy thus took away God's freedom. There could be no logical bridge between the transcendent and absolute God, that is, the divine darkness, and the immanent, revealed God. God created the world ex nihilo.[122] The very first axiom of Russian modernist thought, from Solovyov to Bulgakov, rested on the postulate that the being of the world was created. From this stemmed the antinomy between God and the world, which allowed one to affirm simultaneously that God is perfectly transcendent to the world and that the world is perfectly transparent to God. In his own manner, Berdyaev formulated this mytho-logical representation, which was particular to modernist Russian thought, in the September 1929 issue of *The Way*, in the course of a review of Shestov's book *In Job's Balances*: "It is impossible to know God through concepts; he can only be known through myths. This world, the only world, does not exist because it is submitted to the eternal law of reason enthroned above it, because it is organized à la Aristotle, but because it is the creation of the unique God."[123]

Creation as the Central Myth and the Problem of Evil
This antinomian understanding of truth based on the myth of the creation of the world by God enables us to grasp certain aspects of Russian modernist thought as found in *The Way* and to follow their evolution. In this line of thinking, the mode of causality, which consists in referring things to the original archetype of the myth, is the only way that the work of the Logos in the world can be understood.[124] In a course given at the Academy of Religious Philosophy in 1929 on "The Six Days of Creation," Vladimir Ilyin formulated his approach to knowledge and myth. In his view, this perpetual reference to the origin is based on the postulate that the reality signified by the myth has ontological priority to the myth, because otherwise there would be no correspondence between the cause and the effect.[125] This is why knowledge, be it scientific or religious, proceeds by hypotheses, that is, by the affirmation of an original mysterious fact. This could be the biblical "In the beginning," just as it could be the Kantian "thing in itself."[126]

It is for this reason that the biblical account in Genesis was so often commented upon in *The Way*. Among the theologians, Troitsky, in a series of articles on marriage in *The Way* in 1928–29, commented on the patristic understanding of the original fall as related in Genesis.[127] Likewise, among the philosophers, the principal debate between Berdyaev and Shestov (who was not yet a member of the review) during the 1920s consisted in differing interpretations of the myth of the Fall. For Shestov, original sin began when man wanted to live from the fruits of the tree of the knowledge of good and evil. Because he represents the world as the place where the laws of reason and the ethic of good and evil hold sway, man continues to live separated from the tree of life.[128] Differing with his old friend, Berdyaev believed that original sin took place first in the sphere of being prior to its manifestation in the sphere of knowledge. In the September 1929 issue of *The Way*, he wrote that sin is, above all, "life outside of God."[129] For Shestov, law, what is permitted and what is forbidden, was an integral part of paradise. For Berdyaev, law was absent from the garden of Eden since social relations prior to the fall could only be based on grace.[130]

This constant reference to beginnings in the Russian modernist tradition expresses itself through an inquiry into the origin of evil and a continuous effort to construct a theodicy acceptable to the Christian conscience. In *The Way*, Frank drew the line that distinguished the generation of religious philosophers who returned to the church from the other émigré philosophers. This consisted in an interpretation of evil that was neither rationalist nor irrational. For Frank, the intellectual I. Eihenvald, the translator of the complete works of Schopenhauer into Russian, maintained a rationalist interpretation of the world even though he was tormented by the problem of evil.[131] Inversely, according to Berdyaev, the rationalist interpretation of evil was the source of the irrationalism of Shestov, and it was what prevented him from having an ontological understanding of the world—thus making it difficult to communicate with it.[132] In spite of these divergences between Berdyaev and Shestov, this intellectual process, which was shared by most Russian philosophers and which consists in taking the problem of evil as a starting point for treating the most diverse questions of the philosophy of knowledge, should be considered as a common ground of Russian religious thought. This process is the context in which the different interpretations of the origin of evil are distinct or identical.

Dostoevsky's "The Legend of the Grand Inquisitor" was the most daring attempt of nineteenth-century Russian religious thought to overcome rationalism by the elaboration of a new theodicy. Berdyaev, in *The Spirit of Dostoevsky*, published in Russian in Prague in 1923 and in French in Paris in 1929,[133] argued that "The Legend" was the refutation of the evolutionist theory of evil, which considered evil as a moment in the evolution of good. In an article published in April 1927, entitled "Some Reflections on Theodicy," he pointed out the intention of the novelist to show the absurdity of a naturalist theodicy that resolved the problem of evil by the theory of satisfaction offered to an immovable God through the sacrifice of Golgotha.[134] For Berdyaev, as for Dostoevsky, Christ, who incarnates the meeting of the divine and human principles in freedom, was the only possible response to the figure of the Grand Inquisitor and to the Euclidean spirit that constructed a world order free of all evil and all responsibility. But in "The Legend," Dostoevsky was content with reminding us, through the silent figure of Christ, that love was deeper and stronger than evil. Berdyaev, for his part, wanted to do more than echo this, and in so doing, pass from a negative theology to a positive theology.

> God created the world not out of his own nature or out of *materia prima* as the ancients believed, but from nothing. This nothing is freedom. That means that God created the world out of freedom. Put differently, God freely created a world which is free. But the freedom which engenders evil comes from the nothingness which is pure possibility. We must admit that this freedom is not the nature created by God for, in such a case, it would be determined. God's nature could only be orientated towards what is good. The freedom which is capable of engendering evil is pure possibility enfolded in nothingness, in the abyss, where the category of being is inapplicable. Outside of God there is no being; outside of God is the nothingness out of which the world was created. This is the freedom which precedes the creation of the world. This mystery can only be approached in an antinomian manner.[135]

The line of tension between ontologism and personalism within the generation of the contributors to the review is again evident here. Lossky, in the steps of Lev Mikhailovich Lopatin, professed an ideal-realism inspired by the monadology of Leibniz and the Platonism of Nicolas of Cusa. In his review of Lossky's book *The Freedom of the Will*, published in 1926, Berdyaev distanced himself from a vision of freedom that he found too substantialist and too static, and which makes any theodicy and any anthropodicy—the justification of God and man given the existence of evil—impossible. "How, in this case, can the fact of the existence of evil be understood?" he asked.[136] Berdyaev believed that the unity of the two natures, the divine and the human, in Christ allows us to understand authentic freedom as the tension in mankind towards God and not as a simple choice between good and evil. In such a perspective, theodicy inaugurates a new anthropodicy. Berdyaev cites the patristic adage that God became man so that man might become God. Only the symbolic language of sacrificial love, which is an expression of the experience of the mystery—and not of concepts or logic—permits the formulation of a theodicy and an anthropodicy.

In his article in the January 1928 issue, entitled "A Tragic Theodicy," Vysheslavtsev also referred to Dostoevsky. For Vysheslavtsev, evil cannot be conceptualized, for that, in itself, would mean accepting it. Taking a stand against Raskolnikov, who calls for the elimination of the "harmful lice" for the good of humanity, Vysheslavtsev believed that man cannot put himself in the place of Providence in his ethical judgments, for that would inevitably lead him to justify suffering. But Providence does not have any common measure with the historical necessity of this world. Vysheslavtsev wrote:

> Man has no right to take Hegel's historico-philosophical viewpoint (that of the "Absolute Spirit") or that of the theodicy of Leibniz. To say that "all is for the best in the best of all possible worlds" is as base and immoral as to say that "history is progress in the awareness of freedom." For that means justifying the crimes of history (for example, the evils of the revolution) as a necessary step in the development of history.[137]

Those who, with Epicurus, Comte, and Marx, believed that it was possible to surmount the tragedy of evil in this world are accused of rationalism of the same kind as that of the Stoics or Thomas Aquinas, who wanted to see the will of God, united to that of man, in each instance of suffering. For Vysheslavtsev, history only made sense if the fundamental antinomy was respected—that God exists everywhere and nowhere, that he is both transcendent and immanent to everything. Here again, only the symbolic image of the relationships of love within the Trinity permits us to realize the personal meaning of the coming together, both tragic and filled with the light of the Kingdom, of the divine and human natures in the here and now.

An Eschatological Mode of Thought
Eschatology, understood as a sphere of knowledge, is the study of the end times and of the end of the world, which, according to a linear concept of time, will consummate history.[138] Taken as a mode of the participation of the intelligence in being, eschatology is the attempt to integrate the end

of history in the representation of the world by thought and by action. Russian modernist thought is characterized by a constant reference to the last things, but according to an antinomian conception of time and not merely according to a cyclic or linear conception.

It is understandable why Frank was especially attentive to the scientific debate on evolution. For him, myth was a story of the beginning and of the end of the world that gave the only answer to the question of the evolution of species. In the January 1929 issue, in reviewing the German paleontologist Edgar Dacque's *Urwelt, Sage und Menschheit*,[139] Frank marveled at the fact that humanity was able to preserve the memory of several million years of evolution in its myths.[140] A year later, in an article entitled "The New German Literature on the Philosophy of Anthropology," dedicated to the works of Dacque, the biologist L. Bolk, and the philosopher Max Scheler,[141] Frank showed that the vital impulse (*élan vital*) of Bergson was much more in harmony with the discoveries of science than the evolutionist theory of Darwin. For Frank, this was why biology was no longer based on the genealogical method but "on a 'symbolic' approach, which consisted in proceeding from empirical organic species, considered as symbols of the creative ideas, to these ideas themselves."[142] The discoveries of science signified that myth, as story, was constituted at the same time as the world, as the meeting place of the transcendent and the immanent, and that it is the expression of its most precious essence. But this essence, for the Russian mytho-logical tradition, was eternal—at the same time as it was perpetually in movement. This is why the myth expressed both the retrospective memory of the beginning and the projective memory of the end. Thus, according to Florensky, memory was meta-rational, a category of the Spirit.[143]

If the development of Russian religious thought is to be considered as a mytho-logical process itself, it is necessary to pinpoint the contours and the evolution of its eschatology, from Solovyov to the generation of the émigré Russian philosophers. In fact, it was through the eschatology of Khomiakov and Dostoevsky that the modernist generation of the authors of *The Way* became aware of the deepest meaning of Russian identity, namely, the quest for the Kingdom of God on earth. This mytho-logical eschatology developed within the journal during the 1920s as a result of the evolution of the memory of the intellectual tradition[144] among the different contributors to *The Way*. Already at the beginning of the century, the generation of Berdyaev had identified itself with the profoundly tragic eschatology of Dostoevsky, which differed from the more optimistic eschatology of Khomiakov.[145] The eschatological memory of the émigrés was turned towards the figures of Dostoevsky and Solovyov during the first years of exile, but from 1927 onward it shifted noticeably towards that of Fedorov.

It is well known that the Judeo-Christian eschatological visions represent a major innovation as compared with that of antiquity. Just as the Judeo-Christian cosmogony was unique, the Christian end of the world will be unique. It will be announced by a period of chaos, the reign of the Antichrist, and will precede the Second Coming of Christ and the Last Judgment. The tension between the joyous memory of the Second Coming, confessed in the liturgy, and the pessimistic and millenniarist representation of the Apocalypse makes the evolution of the eschatology of the Russian modernist thinkers understandable. Solovyov, near the end of his life, had written a book, *The Tale of the Antichrist*, which resolved the tragic sense of history in an eschatological manner. Whereas for Dostoevsky, the face of the one who divides and sows dissension was that of the Roman Grand Inquisitor, for Solovyov, only the unity of the churches would enable them to vanquish the supreme temptation of which the Antichrist is the figure, a sweet-talking propagandist for the rights of humanity in opposition to God.

In the first years of the journal this tale was the object of several commentaries. In the fifth issue of *The Way*, one finds, along with a 1894 letter of Solovyov to Tolstoy on the resurrection of Christ,[146] an article by D. Shakhovskoy entitled "On the Rights of Discussion,"[147] and one by Fedotov entitled "On the Goodness of the Antichrist."[148] While both articles agree in recognizing the prophetic character of the tale, the first disagreed with the humanist character of Solovyov's Antichrist and showed, using quotations from Lenin, that this has been transformed into a "bestialism." Fedotov, on the contrary, following Solovyov, tried to rehabilitate humanism in a Christian perspective—which is different from that of antiquity. That is why the one announces the first trumpets of the Apocalypse, while the other vigorously criticizes fatalism, the scorn for the humanity of God among the intellectuals who recently returned to the church, and their fierce asceticism.[149]

Two years later, after N. Setnitsky, a Soviet disciple of Fedorov, visited France, the attention of the authors of *The Way* was focused more clearly on the thought of this latter figure, which eclipsed, to a certain extent, the eschatology of Solovyov in the pages of the journal.[150] Berdyaev based himself on the theses of Nikolai Fedorov in commenting on Solovyov's tale. To be sure, in an article in April 1927 dedicated to Fedorov's *The Philosophy of the Common Task,* Berdyaev noted the insufficiencies of Fedorov's project, which essentially consisted in a lack of understanding of the mystical significance of death and a naturalization of the sacraments.[151] The following year, however, on the occasion of Fedorov's birthday, Berdyaev presented his work in a more positive light.[152] The vast superiority of Fedorov in comparison with Solovyov, writes Berdyaev, is his active and creative concept of eschatology. For Fedorov, the resurrection is not just a work of the grace of God. It is also the result of human activity.

Modernist Aspects of the Intellectual Debate

The fact that Russian religious thought has roots in the mytho-logical tradition of the nineteenth century enables us to understand the uniformity of the intellectual generation that contributed to *The Way* from 1925 to 1929. It can be said that the myth of the *Parousia,* Christ's Second Coming, was the a priori synthetic judgment of the anthropologic, cosmologic, and ecclesiological thought of this modernist generation. It is precisely the fluid and dynamic character of this thought that also explains the internal contradiction within the journal.

Anthropocentric Reflection

The anthropological reflection among the contributors to the journal was modernist in virtue of the originality of its conclusions in the realm of political philosophy and cultural creativity. But the authors differed on the final causes of creativity.

The Relativity of the State
Berdyaev's first article in *The* Way had a significant title—"The Kingdom of God and the Kingdom of Caesar." The originality of his approach lay in his understanding of the relationship between the spiritual world and the terrestrial world—a relationship both ontological and antinomic, pneumatological and Christological. Berdyaev reminded the reader that, according

to St. Macarius, each person is called to become a king, priest, and prophet. This is why the Second Coming of Christ on the earth will be preceded by the following signs: the use of force to bring in the Kingdom will be renounced, Caesar will no longer be deified by Christians, East and West will draw closer, and social justice will be accomplished in all truth and not merely symbolically.[153] In "The Religious Foundations of Society," Frank wrote that the state has religious significance because of the barrier it erects against chaos, but, as Solovyov claims, "the function of the State is not to create paradise but to avoid hell."[154] The relationship with an ideal form of the state was the object of lively discussions in the review. Yet the generation of Berdyaev and Fedotov differed from that of Khomiakov, Dostoevsky, and Solovyov in the sense that the idealized concept of the rural commune was absent from their preoccupations.[155] On the other hand, they shared with their elders the convictions that every tear would be wiped away and that, in the Kingdom of God, philosophical truth could not be disassociated from social truth. Fedorov believed that salvation is not just individual but also social and cosmic. For Berdyaev, that is "a Russian truth," for the Russian people are always characterized by their compassion for the misery of the masses, by their sense of the importance of the resurrection of Christ, and by their expectation of the eternal resurrection for all.[156]

The Justification of Culture
This anthropological understanding of the Kingdom is the basis of the task that Russian religious thought has given itself since the time of Bukharev, namely, to justify culture. In his article entitled "The Culture of Technology and the Christian Ideal," N. Lossky drew up a table of contemporary scientific progress—from the jet engine to antibiotics. He did not propose rejecting technical progress (traditionally considered diabolic) but rather advocated delving deeper into its spiritual foundations to the point where "God will be all in all."[157] It is thus that humanity will be able to detach itself from its possessive attitude towards the world, founded on the forces of separation, and will be able to arrive at the Kingdom, characterized by the free and desired reunion of all essences in a single organic body.

In *The Meaning of the Creative Act*, published in Moscow by the publishing house Put' in 1914, Berdyaev laid down the theurgic foundations of culture, that is, the divine sources of human creation.[158] In an article dedicated to Solovyov and published in *The Way* in the January 1926 issue, Berdyaev argued that in Russia, a nominalist theology often suspected culture of leading man away from the path of salvation. But God does not ask the justification of man. He asks his love and the transformation of the world. To realize God's plan for the world, to transfigure the cosmos, it is necessary to legitimate science, society, art, and even philosophy— notwithstanding the Buddhist and philocalistic tendencies of the Russian spirit. "St. Athanasius the Great," exclaimed Berdyaev, "invented the concept of *homoousios*, 'of the same essence,' in a state of creativity, not of humility."[159]

This relationship to culture and to the world explains the diversity of the themes touched on in *The Way*, from Freudian psychoanalysis[160] to the poetry of Rilke,[161] and from the role of Action Française[162] to the cult of the superman in Europe during the period between the two wars.[163] Characteristic of this generation, as compared to that of Khomiakov or Ivanov, a refugee in Italy, was a thirst for realism, an eschatological relationship to creation and not simply a nostalgic one, and a desire to transport one's self into the tangible future of the Kingdom to come and not into an aesthetic delight in the static beauty of the world. In 1917, Berdyaev wrote concerning V. Ivanov: "When he speaks of theurgy and appeals to theurgy, he is thinking about it in the context of art, of culture, as the enchantment of forms descending into this world. But if a theurgy is possible, it will come forth from the limits of culture and art and supposes a catastrophic surpassing of the limits of this world."[164] This explains why literature found so little place in *The Way*. Until 1927 the review published news of a religious character by Remizov, Ekkersdorf, and Tsebrikov,[165] but it then quickly passed on to the more realistic genre of *publitsistika*.

The Two Approaches to Creativity
Two types of approaches to creativity can be discerned among the generation of the contributors to the journal. The first position, represented by Bulgakov and Ilyin, saw creativity as a fact which above all was divine and sacramental, while the second, represented by Berdyaev and Elizabeth (later Mother Maria) Skobtsova, saw it as the prophetic response of man to God. Thus Ilyin, in several of his reviews, insisted on the fact that the liturgy is an anticipation of the Kingdom. In his October 1928 review of the works of the German Benedictine monk Chrysostom Panfoeder on the liturgy,

Ilyin renders homage to the author and takes up his idea of the church as a liturgical community (*liturgische Gemeinschaft*). In this sense, the eternal and luminous archetype of the liturgical life is the Holy Trinity.[166]

Elizabeth Skobtsova, a poet prior to the Russian Revolution, interested herself in the 1920s in the philosophy of Khomiakov, Solovyov, and Dostoevsky, but she only published articles of the *publitsistika* genre in *The Way*, that is, essays connecting philosophical and theological themes to issues of everyday life. In "The Holy Land" and in "The Search for Synthesis," she reflected on the possibility of encounter between the principles of maternity and childhood, of birth and creation, of divinity and humanity. In the second article, written in May 1929, the emphasis was more prophetic. Faithful to the tradition of Solovyov, she concluded by asking herself what would be "the correct path" towards the *Parousia*.

> Battles should not be waged to prove the divine, or human essence, nor for the depopulated Church, nor for humanism—right now we must fight for Divine Humanity. Yes, we must completely and to the fullest degree raise the cupola of the Church over our heads. We must completely and to the fullest degree accept the mystery of Revelation. And at the same time, we must completely and to the fullest degree affirm and bless not only the right, but also the obligation of humanity to do its human work. All branches of human creativity—science, art, society, government, creation, the quests for new winged utopias, perceiving the sole truth and thousands of truths, the struggle for the emancipation of the worker, affirming the right to work, the attempts to create a new international collective life, populism—everywhere that there is a spark of individual or collective creativity, where human freedom is individually or collectively affirmed, and where a person is obligated to be free—all of this is sanctified and blessed.[167]

Cosmological Reflection

In the tradition of Russian religious philosophy, the transfiguration of the cosmos is one of the characteristic principles of the *Parousia*. This properly cosmological dimension of modernist thought was particularly salient in sophiological thinking. In the work of Bulgakov, the Kingdom, the Glory, and the Reign of God are simply biblical figures for the Wisdom of God. This approach was inaugurated in the seventeenth century by the Lutheran cobbler and mystic, Jakob Boehme (1575–1624), and continued in Russia during the eighteenth century by Hryhorii Skovoroda (1722–94) and Nikolai Novikov (1744–1818). In the nineteenth and twentieth centuries it was taken up by Bukharev, Solovyov, Fedorov, Florensky, Bulgakov, Berdyaev, Zenkovsky, and Ilyin, among others. Sophiology in Russia was a constantly renewed effort to trace out a modernist vision of the world as a counterpart to traditional philosophy and theology, using, on the one hand, the traditional Christian concept of theanthropy, and, on the other hand, the Boehmian intuition of God's interior life, of the abyss as the foundation of Being. Berdyaev, Dmitry Chizhevsky, Frank, Ilyin, Karsavin, and Reinhold von Walter all made several references to the work of the German theosophist. Although each has his own interpretation of the work of Boehme, they all interpret his thought in a mytho-logical sense. Berdyaev, in writing about Boehme, described him primarily as "a creator of myths," who thought "on a mytho-logical register and not by concepts."[168] In contrast to this mytho-logical approach is the 1929 study of the émigré Russian philosopher Alexander Koyré.[169] In his review of this book, Berdyaev recognized the author's merits but took exception to his skepticism and historical relativism, which, he claimed, led Koyré to judge Boehme's doctrine on Sophia as naïve as well as furnishing an excuse for the credit given by Boehme to astrology and alchemy. By trying to rationally systematize Boehme's work—Berdyaev wrote—Koyré neglected the symbolic character of his vision of the world.

As early as 1926, Berdyaev had presented Boehme as "one of the greatest geniuses of humanity," as a visionary penetrated by the Bible, Paracelsus, and the Kabbalah, whose fundamental originality with respect to the wisdom of the ancients and scholasticism was to have understood Being in an antinomian manner.[170] At the beginning of Being, even before the birth of the divine Trinity, there is, in Berdyaev's reading of Boehme, unfathomable freedom, the passionate desire of nothingness to become something: God surges from the depths of the Divinity, from inexpressible nothingness. When Boehme sees the darkness at the foundation of Being, he names this undetermined source *Ungrund*.[171] However, when he sees the light in the depths of God, he calls it Sophia or Wisdom of God. For Boehme, the theogonic, cosmogonic, and anthropogonic dynamic has its source in the irrational life of Being. That is why his anthropology, which supposes man's irrational freedom and his creative capacity, is more

Christological than that of Luther, for whom freedom is swallowed up by grace. In this sense, Boehme was, for Berdyaev, the founder of an original metaphysical voluntarism that determined the history of modern German philosophy.

The Patristic Interpretation of the Myth of Sophia
In *The Way* there were three interpretations of sophiology—patristic, dogmatic, and metaphysical. Among those who favored the patristic interpretation were Karsavin, Florovsky, and Ilyin. In the January 1926 issue, Karsavin, in the name of some of the Eurasians, criticized the Russian intelligentsia of the nineteenth century and "its aesthetic-religious decadence, its Latinism, and its sophianism."[172] The following year he became more explicit by criticizing the Manichaeism of Boehme, who gives Lucifer, the personification of evil, an exaggerated importance.[173] According to Florovsky's criticism of Sergei Lukianov on the sophiological sources of Solovyov's thought, and of E. de Faye on Origen,[174] and according to Ilyin's review of Bulgakov's book on the angels,[175] it appeared that the reaction of these Orthodox theologians against the doctrine of the Wisdom of God had to do, essentially, with its Gnostic character and the fact that it is "imported from the West." No one, however, denied its place in the church. Its scriptural, patristic, and liturgical origins are unquestionable. In the book of Proverbs, Wisdom says of herself: "Yahweh created me as the first fruits of his work, before the most ancient of his works. I was established from eternity, from the beginning, before the earth came into being."[176] St. Gregory Palamas taught that Wisdom was the energy of the energies of God and that these alone are accessible to the creature, while the Essence of God remains outside of the creature's grasp. And, finally, the architectural and iconographical presence of Wisdom, particularly in Russian history, testified that there was, historically, an uninterrupted cult of the Wisdom of God. This aspect was especially developed by Fedorov—excerpts from certain of his unpublished manuscripts on this theme were posthumously published in *The Way* in 1929[177]—and by Florensky in *The Pillar and Ground of the Truth.*

The Dogmatic Interpretation of the Myth of Sophia
When all was said and done, the patristic criticism of sophiology was in line with what Bulgakov had already written in 1916 in *The Unfading*

Light about the excessive "rationalism"[178] in Solovyov's understanding of the figure of Sophia and the absence of a logical rupture between Nothingness and God in the visions of Boehme.[179] This did not deter Bulgakov from believing that the emergence of the sophiological problematic in the conscience of humanity was an important event. In 1926 he wrote that this problematic had its place in the symbolic history of "the dogmatic development of the Church," according to Solovyov. In fact, in Bulgakov's mind, the sophiological perspective defines a particular interpretation of the ensemble of dogmas and doctrines—from those that concern the Trinity and the Incarnation to those that have not yet been dogmatically defined in Orthodoxy, such as the role of the Mother of God, of social service, and, above all, of the church. Between 1925 and 1929, Bulgakov published a number of works on these issues: *The Saints Peter and John* (1926), *The Tragedy of Philosophy* (1927), *The Friend of the Bridegroom* (1927), *The Burning Bush* (1928), the "Chapters on Trinitarity" (1928), and *Jacob's Ladder* (1929). In these, Bulgakov analogically identified the Wisdom of God with the Mother of God, the church, and the world. Similarly, in *The Way*, nine of the ten articles published by Bulgakov during this period were devoted to the formulation of a Christian doctrine of the church which is not separated from the doctrine concerning the Mother of God or that concerning the cosmos. His theology employed a method that was both iconographic and phenomenological. His first trilogy, which he dedicated to the Virgin (*The Burning Bush*), to St. John the Baptist (*The Friend of the Bridegroom*), and to the angels (*Jacob's Ladder*), followed the pattern of the icon of the *Deisis* or "Intercession," which represents the Wisdom of God in creation. In a lecture given on July 7, 1926, at the St. Sergius Institute, entitled "Saint Sergius's Blessed Precepts for the Russian Theological Tradition," Bulgakov pointed out the intentionality of Russian spirituality through the study of the religious representations of the most venerated saint in Russian history. He wrote: "In the life of St. Sergius we know, we intuitively sense, this love for the divine cosmos which sparkles in this fallen world: this forest in which he lived in the middle of nature, this bear who was his friend."[180] But the Russian saint also had a vision of the Holy Virgin. The cosmological dimension of the Spirit-Bearing Mother of God is also quite traditional. Specific to the Russian liturgical commemoration of Sophia, however, is its linkage with the Marian feasts of the liturgical calendar. This is in contrast to Byzantine spirituality, which connected the cult of Sophia to the feasts of Christ.[181] Last, Bulgakov writes, the Mother of God or the Divine Wisdom appeared to St. Sergius accompanied by the apostles Peter and John, and this signifies that she also represents the church in the Russian religious conscience.

The Metaphysical Interpretation of the Myth of Sophia
Berdyaev's metaphysical interpretation of sophiology was distinct from those of Karsavin and Bulgakov. Berdyaev replied vigorously to those émigrés who used the theses of Karsavin to condemn sophiology. In an October 1928 article entitled "Obscurantism," Berdyaev accuses Pobedonostsev, Stalin, Miliukov, and the bishops of the Russian Orthodox Church Outside Russia (ROCOR) of being obscurantists—but he also includes "the contemporary young people of the emigration who are obsessed by the heresy of 'gnoseomachy' or struggle against or resistance to any philosophical or theological knowledge."[182] The metaphysical source of Christian obscurantism and the persecution that victimized religious philosophy from Khomiakov to Nesmelov, according to Berdyaev, came from the church's refusal to rethink its traditional explanation of evil and the fall. While venturing to affirm that certain questions have not been resolved by the tradition of the church, Berdyaev also distanced himself from Boehme and Solovyov's understanding of the former, such as the latter expressed it in his 1876 treatise on Sophia.[183] In 1929 Berdyaev wrote:

> The *Ungrund* is the original freedom, irrational, somber, still undetermined. Freedom is not evil but it makes evil possible, within it are potentialities of evil as well as good. Potentiality, in Boehme's view, consists in this—that it introduces the *Ungrund* into the very divinity and thus authorizes the existence of a dark principle in God. It would be more just to say that the *Ungrund*, i.e., the original liberty, lies outside of God, outside of being and precedes every already determined being.[184]

In 1916 Bulgakov had reproached Berdyaev for relying on Boehme. In a review of Bulgakov's book on angels in the May 1929 issue, Berdyaev gave his response. Berdyaev admitted that the Thomistic opposition between the natural and the supernatural, Luther's rejection of the divinity of the cosmos and of the cult of the Mother of God, and, last, the moralist and noncosmic asceticism of traditional Orthodoxy had created the need for the formulation of a new, specifically Christian cosmology in which all of the life of the world is seen as the symbol of the divinity. But Berdyaev feared that Bulgakov's cosmology took precedence over his anthropology. His incapacity to resolve the problem of the fall of the angels witnessed to the lesser importance he gave to the question of evil and man's freedom.[185] In Berdyaev's view, the potential freedom of which Bulgakov wrote was sophianic—it has its source in God and not in nothingness. For Berdyaev, this would explain the entanglement of Bulgakov's images and the lack of eschatological vigor in his thought.

At the end of the 1920s, Elizabeth Skobtsova tried to synthesize these two positions. As she saw it, while for Bulgakov the cosmos could only come forth from the depths of the Divinity by way of birth, for Berdyaev the world comes forth through freedom by means of a creative act. The awareness of this antinomy between the works of Berdyaev and Bulgakov among the contributors to the review in 1930 is fundamental, since it determines, in great part, the convergence in the 1930s of the two currents—the anthropologic-dualist-prophetic, and the cosmological-monist-sacramental—of the religious thought of the Russian emigration and their distancing of themselves from the neo-patristic current.

Ecclesiological Reflection

A Spirit-Centered Ecclesiology
For Khomiakov, the quest for the Kingdom of God on earth would be decisive for both his theory of knowledge and his ecclesiology. His doctrine of conciliarity or catholicity (*sobornost'*) was the affirmation of a philosophy of knowledge of universal communion which anticipated the moment when God would be all in all. According to this perspective, love is the foundation of knowledge—but love is a gift of God assuring knowledge of the truth for all mankind. This is why the frontiers of knowledge corresponded to the limits of the church. Among the works of Khomiakov can be found this passage, which is very important for understanding the ecclesiology of the religious thought of the emigration:

> The Truth, inaccessible to the isolated intellect, is only accessible to the collectivity of intellects united by love. This trait distinguishes

Orthodox thought from all others; from the Latins who hold to an exterior authority and from the Protestants who release people to the point of leaving them in freedom in the deserts of abstract reasoning.[186]

This link between philosophy of knowledge and ecclesiology in the understanding of catholicity in Russian religious thought appears often in contributions to *The Way*. In the March 1927 issue, Zenkovsky, in "Freedom and *Sobornost*'," used the doctrine of *sobornost*' to show the insufficiencies of the Protestant conception of freedom and its historical implications. Protestant catholicity, for him, was merely psychological. Because it came into being as a reaction to Catholic authoritarianism, the Protestant church has rejected any incarnation in history and has continued to nourish itself from the eschatology of the Christians of the first centuries.[187] But Zenkovsky admits that "the doctrine of the *sobornost*' of the Church has yet to be fully formulated."[188]

Actually there were several problems. If, as Zenkovsky affirmed,[189] ecclesiology should reflect the intertrinitarian relations, how should the relationship between the Son and the Holy Spirit be understood? If the church is the Body of Christ according to the apostolic definition, how should we envisage the connection between human freedom and divine freedom in the second hypostasis of the Trinity? And finally, and above all, if the foundation of the Trinity is love, how should we understand the principle of authority in the visible and invisible church? Khomiakov denied any form of authority in the church, whether of the bishop or that of God Himself, because "no visible sign"[190] other than mutual love can serve to guarantee the truth. This spiritual understanding of truth tended to deny the human source of the freedom of Christ and, with it, the Christological foundations of the visible church and apostolic authority. By not recognizing any head of the church other than Christ, who, since the Ascension, is seated at the right hand of the Father, Khomiakov was justifying the autocratic power of the sovereign upon earth as "head of the people in ecclesiastical affairs and in this sense head of the local Church."[191]

The Eurasian theologians of the emigration continued this approach and delved deeper into its implications. In an article written in August 1926 and entitled "On Heavenly and Earthly *Sobornost*'," Ilyin used Khomiakov's book *On the Church*[192] to show the link between the Roman dogma of the *Filioque*—which affirmed that the Spirit proceeds not only from the Father but also from the Son—and Caesaropapism—which disrupted the harmony of catholicity. Ilyin also linked the *Filioque* with the dogma of papal infallibility, which sets the bishop of Rome over the councils. For him, "the only true power is divine power,"[193] which enables humanity, in its pluralism, to become the Body of Christ, "and this in no way concerns the techniques of government whose forms do not in any way determine its content."[194] Karsavin, in his "Prolegomena for a Study of Personhood [*lichnost'*]," justified this non-incarnation of divine power by the fact that the hypostasis of Christ, which in the Trinity represents the unity of the many, is of divine nature and not of human nature. The same can be said of the hypostatic dimension of the individual. "As a creature," he writes, "man is not a person but rather a sort of substratum without a face." It is, therefore, God's transcendence which assures the individual of his ability to join with others, or humanity's symphonic character.[195] In this same way, the state gives the nation its collective identity. Thus the church, as an organic divine-human body which embraces within itself the state and the nation, cannot separate the one from the other. Karsavin uses this reasoning to denounce (on several occasions) the absence of the Roman Church's consideration of the national sources of the Eastern Church.

A Christocentric Ecclesiology
Florovsky likewise used Khomiakov's doctrine of *sobornost'* to justify his ecclesiology. However, certainly because of his origins in the clerical world, Florovsky was struck by the reforms of the Council of 1917 more than were his contemporaries. His understanding of catholicity was, in fact, more Christ-centered than that of Khomiakov. In April 1927, when he was breaking with the Eurasianist movement, he wrote, with regard to an article about a book by Johann Moehler on the church which had been republished in Germany, that the foundations of the doctrine of the German theologian concerning catholicity are not sufficiently Christ-centered—and this could lead to erroneously identifying the Body of Christ with the Holy Spirit.[196] In "The House of the Father," published in the same issue, Florovsky argued that Christ is indeed the sole head of the church. For him, the doctrine of the double nature of the church, visible and invisible, is an extension of the Chalcedonian dogma of the two distinct but not divided natures of Christ. Florovsky understood this

mysterious unity in a manner that is essentially sacramental,[197] for in the Eucharist the pilgrim church can enter into communion with its Spouse through the intermediary of the Holy Spirit transmitted by Christ to his apostles before his Ascension.[198]

This more eschatological approach made it possible to justify the principle of episcopal authority in the church as the guarantee of the apostolic tradition. Florovsky cited the 1848 encyclical of the Eastern patriarchs, which declared that "the bishop is as necessary for the Church as breath is for man and the sun for the world."[199] He toned down his approach in 1927 by invoking "the adequate expression of Khomiakov," according to which it is the Holy Spirit and not a human being who preserves tradition in the church.[200] But two years later, in his article entitled "The Eucharist and *Sobornost*'," published in the November 1929 issue, Florovsky reaffirmed that "the real and ontological unity" of Christians which is accomplished in the liturgy[201] is only possible through the mediation of the priest or bishop who represents Christ. Therefore, for Florovsky, the Eucharist is the foundation stone of ecclesiology because "each 'little Church' is not just a part but a concentrated figure [*stiazhennyi obraz*] of the whole Church without being separated from its unity and plenitude. It is for this that, during each liturgy, the whole Church is present and participates in a mysterious but real way."[202]

While admitting that Christ is the source of episcopal authority, Berdyaev, who was closer to Khomiakov and company, in the November 1926 issue, refused to consider the hierarchical principle as the sole source of grace in the church insofar as the union of man with God through the Holy Spirit goes beyond the frontiers of the Eucharist alone and can be of a prophetic nature. For Berdyaev, the Spirit of God also acts through man's freedom. Taking a stand against any monophysite interpretation of the dogma of Chalcedon, he cited Bukharev on "the kenosis of Christ on earth" and reaffirmed the human and creative nature of Christ.

> The bishop directs the hierarchical order of the Church, affirms ecclesial unity, protects the Orthodox tradition. But he has no power over all the creative activity of the individual and of the people; their knowledge, their social work, their creative initiatives in the spiritual life do not belong to the bishop. Even Catholicism recognizes that the ministry belongs to all Christians and that all Christians are priests.

That which does not have official, juridical, and formal recognition can and should be recognized as being potentially ecclesiastical. The churching of life is an invisible process. . . . The Kingdom of God arrives imperceptibly in the depths of human hearts.[203]

A Wisdom-Centered Ecclesiology
From the very first issue of *The Way*, Bulgakov tried to resolve this antinomy between authority and freedom by inaugurating a series of five voluminous articles entitled "Notes on the Doctrine of the Church." For Bulgakov, the church has Christ as its foundation but also the Holy Spirit. It is founded by Christ and realized through Pentecost. This twofold origin of the church can only be interpreted in a sophiological and eschatological manner. In November 1926, Bulgakov wrote that "the Wisdom of God is the Church."[204] According to the Fathers, God created the world with the church in view. Since the essence of the church is the divine life, which manifests itself in creation, it will not be accomplished until "God becomes all, in all."[205] In this perspective, the relationship between the second and third hypostases should be formulated, Bulgakov insisted, not in terms of procession following the categories of Neoplatonic philosophy, but by symbols which refer to their personal love. Basing himself on Scripture,[206] Bulgakov speaks of the "repose" (*pochivanie*) of the Holy Spirit on Christ.

> Just as, in the pre-eternal life of the Holy Trinity, the Holy Spirit reposes on the Son, revealing the Father, the Incarnation of Christ in the world would have remained incomplete if it had not brought with it the descent of the Holy Spirit, who is essentially and inseparably linked to Christ. This is why the deification of humanity is accomplished by the Incarnation of Christ with the power of the Holy Spirit, knowing that the Son and the Spirit are sent by the Father and reveal him.[207]

Bulgakov's Christology makes it possible to consider the church as the life of grace in the Spirit (and, consequently, in Christ) and as the Holy Spirit who lives in humanity. There can be no doubt that authority in the visible church is of divine-human character. But the modernism of Bulgakov's theses consists in his not projecting the use of this supreme authority upon an individual person. In his second "Notes on the Doctrine of the Church," published in January 1926, Bulgakov claimed that there cannot be an exterior organism of infallibility and domination in the church—be it the pope or councils—since Christ is the sole head of the church. On the other hand, there is a real visible authority in the church expressed by the union of the apostles, presbyters, and laity in the Holy Spirit during the Council of Jerusalem and formulated thus: "It has seemed good to the Holy Spirit and to us."[208]

Thus, by formulating the modalities of the union between the second and third persons of the Trinity in a more hypostatic context, Bulgakov laid the theological foundations for the rediscovery of the royal, priestly, and prophetic dignity of all the baptized in the Orthodox Church. Yet he did not resolve the difficult question of the limits or boundaries of the church—a problem that would focus the attention of the Russian intellectuals during the 1930s.

They were united by their common origins, by the experience of exile, and by their shared desire to recover the living tradition of the church in a context of creative freedom. However, the authors of *The Way* only gradually became aware, between 1925 and 1929, of how they differed among themselves in their interpretations of what the modernity of Orthodox discourse represented. On the level of spiritual experience, two currents became clearly distinct by 1929: the neo-patristic tendency represented by Florovsky or Chetverikov, and the one influenced more heavily by German philosophy and represented by Berdyaev or Frank. On the level of mytho-logical discourse there were also two different orientations: that situated in continuity with the Neoplatonism inherited from Solovyov (Vysheslavtsev), and that which would resolutely develop a sophiological discourse (Bulgakov) or a personalist discourse (Berdyaev). But the reciprocal mistrusts, which were legacies of the past, between the cosmocentric and anthropocentric currents prevented Bulgakov and Berdyaev from noticing the similarities of their discourse. On the other hand, the authors of the journal, in their desire to prevent divisions in the church of the emigration, showed a particular prudence in putting their perspectives forward. Moreover, since they wanted to transmit an authentically Eastern Orthodox message and were faced with a Western culture apparently very alien to their vision of the world, their affirmation of a common Byzantine spiritual identity contributed, throughout this period, to mask the differences of spiritual experience. It was only at the end of this period, after the schism of 1926 had revealed that the modernist and conservative currents would persist for the long term, and after their myth of the West progressively fell apart, that the authors of the review passed to a new phase of their evolution—that of the affirmation of self in its alterity. Before studying this new nonconformist period (1930–35), however, it seems better to continue the story of the modernist period of the review by discussing, on the one hand, the social, political, and ecclesial engagement of this generation of the Russian immigrants, and, on the other hand, the commitment of French intellectuals to seek contacts between the East and the West.

THE MODERNIST CONSTELLATION

The unchanging characteristics of mythical narrative make possible the discernment of what Raoul Girardet calls "mythical constellations," that is, "structural ensembles which have a real homogeneity and a consistent specificity."[209] The Russian emigration organized itself and evolved according to structural ensembles of myths belonging to a common theme. The eschatological quest for the Kingdom of God on earth, founded on the theme of mankind's deification and transformation, was radically opposed to the hope, nostalgic and "dominated by the primal notion of a fall,"[210] of recovering the golden age of Russian history, which meant for them the "Holy Rus" before the 1905–1917 revolutions.

The vast majority of the émigrés sought, fundamentally, stability, a return to the pre-revolution situation, and the warmth of the protective intimacy of a closed community. This aspiration of the émigrés was represented by a good part of the monarchist enclaves in their midst and of the bishops of the Russian Orthodox Church Outside Russia (ROCOR). As will be shown below, the generation of Berdyaev, on the contrary, established itself between 1925 and 1929 in a modernist constellation, namely, in a social, religious, and cultural ensemble characterized by the common conviction that a movement, a reform, is possible in the church and, consequently, in history. Moreover, notwithstanding their intellectual and political oppositions, the modernist identity of this generation was reinforced by a phenomenon of reaction against the legendary tales propagated about them in émigré circles. Very quickly, in fact, the liberal and reform-minded intellectuals of *The Way* were connected by the most reactionary groups to the traditional figures of the Antichrist: the Jews and Freemasons. At the center of this mythology of a global conspiracy, the American-based Young Men's Christian Association (YMCA) provided (as will also be seen) the ideal support, as a sort of octopus with tentacles reaching to the far corners of the world. This virulent opposition finally culminated, in 1927, in a schism within the Russian émigré church.

But strangely enough, as Girardet writes, "there is no rupture, no irreducible confrontation between the powers of nostalgia and those of hope but rather a continuity, an indispensable complementarity."[211] When, after the schism, the exterior ascendancy lost its sway over the modernist intellectuals, tension sprang up within the review itself between two attitudes— the sacralization of the past and the prophetic annunciation of its renaissance. This would have grave consequences.

The Schism in Formation (September 1925–June 1926)

In the editorial of the September 1925 issue of *The Way*, the authors recognized the historical fact of the Russian Revolution and argued that the future of Russia was linked to "the spiritual condition of the people."[212] But between 1925 and 1929, *The Way* was caught up in polemical issues that were raging in the émigré community. As in all emigrations of a political nature, the point of departure for these polemics was most often linked to the relationship the one or other group had with the mother country. It will be useful to briefly recall the main events that took place within the Russian Church between 1917 and 1925, before studying the positions of the authors of the review in the face of the first schism, which tore that church apart in 1921–22.

The Question of Jurisdiction

The Background
In 1919, when confronted with the first persecutions of the church by the Russian government,[213] Tikhon Belavin (1865–1925), the former archbishop of Yaroslavl, then of Vilnius, and, finally, patriarch of Moscow, adopted a position of political neutrality towards the government. This

position was questioned by the Russian Church of the emigration. The synod of the Russian Church, which emigrated after the revolution to Sremski Karlovtsy, a small city northwest of Belgrade, held a council from November 21 to December 3, 1921, presided over by Metropolitan Anthony Khrapovitsky (1863–1936), the president of the administration of the Russian Orthodox Church Outside Russia,[214] in the presence of around 150 clergy and lay people (among them General Pyotr Wrangel, commanding general of the White Army), in view of setting itself up as an autonomous church in submission to the patriarch of Moscow. But on November 30, pressured by Count George Grabbe, Metropolitan Anthony published a letter entitled "To the Children of the Russian Church Dispersed and in Exile," in which he proposed the restoration of the Romanov dynasty in Russia. This was done against the advice of both Metropolitan Evlogy (1858–1946),[215] the temporary administrator of the Russian Churches of Western Europe, and the theologian Sergei Troitsky.[216]

As a sign of his disapproval of this act, which was in fact political, the patriarch, in January 1922, confirmed Metropolitan Evlogy as the head of the new diocese of Western Europe. However, following decrees of the Soviet government on February 10 and 13 ordering the seizure of church property—including liturgical objects—in order to alleviate a famine, the patriarch, on February 28, made a public protest. On May 5, perhaps under coercion, he decided to dissolve the synod of the ROCOR, but the following week he was imprisoned and prevented from exercising his functions. On May 18, 1922, a group of clerics and lay people—composed of Bishop Anthony, Bishop Leonid (Verninsky), the priests A. Vvedensky and V. Krasnitsky, and Professor Titlinov, who represented the presbyterial left wing that was overruled in the council of 1917—decided, with the complicity of the Soviet government, to assume the succession of the patriarch and create a renewed church, "The Living Church" (*Zhivaia Tserkov'*). On the political level, this church accepted Soviet authority—and shut its eyes to the persecution of recalcitrant Christians—and in the religious domain, it favored a second marriage for widowed priests, the marriage of bishops, the introduction of the Gregorian calendar, and changing the liturgy from Slavonic to Russian.

The bishops of Karlovtsy reacted by condemning this external and internal fracturing of the Russian Church by those in power and, on June 2, addressed a letter of protest to the Soviet government. The reply was violent.

Benjamin Kazansky, the metropolitan of Petrograd, was executed on August 13, and sixty-six bishops and about eight thousand members of the clergy were deported.[217] These persecutions led to the creation of the Temporary Synod of ROCOR by metropolitans Anthony and Evlogy on September 2, 1922. This synod held a council from May 31 to June 8, 1923, and confirmed Metropolitan Evlogy as the head of the diocese of Western Europe. This decision "contradicted the principle of catholicity" as it had been defined at the council of 1917–18 since the erection of dioceses was reserved to the patriarchal jurisdiction.[218]

The Support for the Patriarch
In the first issue of *The Way*, P. Ivanov and G. Trubetskoy vigorously condemned the Living Church schism.[219] Ivanov, a recent émigré from the Soviet Union, described the events he lived through to his compatriots in the issue of September 1925. In July 1922, Ivanov wrote, the High Commission of the Living Church split into three rival groups and resolved to organize a council (*sobor*). Ivanov participated in the diocesan congress of Moscow on April 23, 1923, which was to elect the Muscovite delegates to the council. The participants in the congress, according to Ivanov, were subjected to pressures and threatened by Krasnitsky with detention by the political police, the GPU, if they did not elect the delegates proposed by the Living Church.[220] These delegates were finally elected, and on May 2, 1923, the council began its work. The High Commission of the Living Church, which was favorable to the revolution and hostile to anything that opposed it, rejected the decisions of the General Council of 1917–18 and, always in the name of the principle of catholicity, decided to transfer the supreme power in the church from the council to the synod and to depose Patriarch Tikhon.[221] But on June 26 the patriarch was released by the government and immediately issued a pastoral letter opposing this decision. In this letter he reaffirmed his loyalty to the regime and repeated his condemnation of the machinations of the council of Karlovtsy. The liberation of Patriarch Tikhon weakened the position of the Living Church considerably, and many reformist bishops—among them the metropolitan of Vladimir and Nizhnii-Novgorod, Sergius (Stragorodsky)—rejoined the ranks of the patriarchal church. After the death of the patriarch on April 8, 1925, Metropolitan Sergius, designated by the interplay of successions as "the replacement of the guardian of the patriarchal throne," suc-

ceeded, in May 1926, in imposing himself over the metropolitans Grigorii of Ekaterinburg and Iosif of Leningrad as the head of a new Patriarchal Holy Synod of the Russian Church. G. Trubetskoy published an article in the September 1925 issue of *The Way*, an article enriched with personal recollections of this period, in which he justifies the loyalty of the patriarch and compares it to that of St. Alexei, who, "during the adolescence of Dimitrii Donskoy, was not afraid to submit himself to the Mongol Horde."[222]

Echoes of Russia
Four months later the review published an anonymous article written in Russia describing the state of the Russian Church. According to the historian Michel Heller, "the years 1923–1926 were, for the citizens of the Soviet Republic, years of hope and waiting, one of the most tranquil epochs of Soviet history."[223] This general optimism also appeared in the article in *The Way*. Its author condemned the "anti-Christian power"[224] and described a few instances of persecution. Yet the article tended to relativize these cases by situating them in the overall context of Russia, which the author considered "transitory."[225] He stressed the anti-religious propaganda but did not mention any executions.[226] "Today priests are not killed and worship is seldom interfered with; . . . the deported bishops and priests are returning to their dioceses and parishes after having completed their sentences. . . . Communist power prefers killing the spirit and not the flesh."[227] On the other hand, the author insisted on the need for a renewal of the Russian Church, which would include the collapse of the "Living Church," the return of the intelligentsia to the church, liturgical renewal, and the development of monastic life.[228] Such a renaissance of Holy Russia was again confirmed by V. Speransky in the November 1926 issue of *The Way*.[229]

The New Structures Surrounding the Review

The review's support of the pro-Tikhon tendency of the church, the memories of those intellectuals who were still in Russia in 1921, the devastating effect of the council of Karlovtsy, and, finally, the optimistic testimonies concerning the evolution of the regime go a long way towards explaining the intentions of the generation of Berdyaev, Bulgakov, and Zenkovsky. They wanted to create, in the emigration, as early as 1922, educational and publishing institutions that were still nonexistent in Russia, in order to perpetuate the Russian Orthodox renewal inaugurated by the council of 1917. In their eyes, the spiritual liberation of the Russian Church loomed on the horizon, and new minds had to be formed for catechizing the people in order to prevent a return to the traditional synodal church. It is in this context that many institutions came into being: the YMCA created a publishing house, the YMCA Press (1923), to which were affiliated an institute for the formation of the laity, the Academy of Religious Philosophy (APR) (1922), and the review *The Way* (1925). It also supported the creation of a youth movement, the Russian Student Christian Movement (1923),[230] and a theological seminary, the St. Sergius Orthodox Theological Institute (1925). Before examining the ecclesial options of the authors of *The Way* during the 1925–29 period, we should recall the stages in the formation of the modernist milieu of the emigration.

The Patronage of the YMCA: The YMCA Press, the Academy, The Way
The support given to the Russian émigrés by John Mott, at that time General Secretary of the World Student Christian Federation and president of the YMCA, was decisive. The goal of the YMCA was "to forge a Christian personality and promote a Christian society."[231] Following his stay in Russia in 1899 and another in 1909 with Ruth Rouse, the movement Lighthouse (*Maiak*),[232] a Russian branch of the YMCA, was founded in 1905 in St. Petersburg. The circles of Christian students who gathered around Baron Paul Nikolai, a Lutheran of Finnish origin, became in 1913 the Russian Student Christian Movement, headed by V. F. Marcinkovsky,[233] belonging to the World Student Christian Federation. During the war, the Russian branch of the YMCA was given the task of organizing material aid to prisoners of war, and Paul Anderson, a Presbyterian from Iowa, was sent to Moscow by the American office of the YMCA to coordinate operations. Under pressure from Soviet ambassador Maxim Litvinov, the YMCA left Russia on July 15, 1920, and set up shop in Berlin. Paul Anderson then dedicated himself to developing programs of social action among Russian émigré students. In this he was supported by the leaders of the YMCA in Europe, E. MacNaughten, D. Lowrie, G. Kuhlmann, and D. Davis. The YMCA financed a technical school in Sofia and Narva and a Russian polytechnic school by correspondence in Berlin and created several student hostels in Germany. Beginning in 1920, in Geneva, the World Alliance of

the YMCA published Russian works for prisoners of war under the direction of an American Methodist of Russian descent, Julius F. Hecker. Ethan Colton, the director of the YMCA in New York, decided to entrust the project of editing the works of the exiled Russian émigrés to Paul Anderson. In 1922 Anderson bought a printing press in Prague, making possible the creation of a genuine printing shop, the YMCA Press.[234] As director of the YMCA Press, Anderson named Berdyaev as responsible for everything it published.

Soon after the revolution, circles of Christian students were established across Europe, notably in Belgrade in collaboration with the Academy of Theology and N. Zernov, N. Klepinin, N. Afanasiev, and P. Lodyzhensky. After the general conference of the World Student Christian Federation at Tianjin, China, in April 1922, at which three former members of Lighthouse, Liperovsky, Nikitin, and Zander participated, John Mott decided to help the different groups of exiled Russian students in Europe join together in a federation.[235] On July 31, 1922, Paul Anderson organized a conference of students near Berlin with the participation of A. Bely, P. Novgorodtsev, and Zenkovsky.

Through Fiodor Pianov,[236] another former member of Lighthouse, Anderson met Vysheslavtsev and Berdyaev, who had just been expelled from Russia, and agreed to finance the Academy of Religious Philosophy. This was the descendant of the Free Academy of Spiritual Culture, which Berdyaev had founded at Moscow in 1919 with the permission of Lev Kamenev, the Commissar of the People.[237] The Academy of Religious Philosophy was founded by philosophers who were expelled when the Society of Russian Philosophy (the SPR) was repressed at the end of the summer of 1922.[238] The Academy was inaugurated on November 26, 1922, at the French lyceum of Berlin[239] by a lecture by Berdyaev in the presence of Metropolitan Evlogy. The success of the Academy encouraged the YMCA to publish the books of contemporary Orthodox religious thinkers and to entrust the editorial direction of the YMCA Press to Berdyaev and Vysheslavtsev. The guiding principle of the YMCA was "the preservation and development of Russian Christian culture."[240] The first work, published in Berlin in 1924, was a collection of articles of an entire generation—Vysheslavtsev, Berdyaev, Karsavin, Zenkovsky, Frank, N. Lossky, and Arseniev—entitled *Problems of the Russian Religious Conscience*.[241] According to Pianov's account of the activities of the Academy during the years 1924–25, "the

Academy is the sole living spiritual center in Berlin." Very soon it established links with the German intellectual world—notably with H. Keyserling and Max Scheler, who, in 1924, came to give a conference on "The Meaning of Suffering."[242] But from this point resources began to decline. Of the five hundred and twenty-seven Russian émigré students in Berlin, thirty-seven[243] were regular students in the courses given by Frank, Karsavin, Ivan Ilyin, and Vladimir Ilyin.[244]

As of 1924, for economic, political, and cultural reasons,[245] Paris became the center of the Russian emigration. The émigrés, increasingly overwhelmed by galloping inflation in Germany, turned towards France, which, after the war, was in need of workers. An estimated 31,347 Russians were living in France in 1921. Five years later there were 67,218. In 1931 their number was 71,928. Since the Congress of Vienna, Paris had also become the political capital of choice for the Russian emigration. It was there that, in 1921, the National Committee of Monarchists, presided over by Kartashev, was founded, as well as the Democratic Union, directed by Miliukov. Paris also attracted the cultural activities of the Russian intelligentsia. The first important daily newspapers of the emigration—from both the left wing (*The Latest News* [*Poslednie novosti*]) and the right wing (*Renaissance* [*Vozrozhdenie*])—were founded in the 1920–25 period. The group of philosophers who belonged to the SPR of Prague, founded in February 1924, turned towards Paris as of 1925. One after the other, Bulgakov, Georges Gurvitch, Sergei Gessen, Zenkovsky, Florovsky, Spektorsky, and Nikolai Alekseev emigrated to France, leaving only N. Lossky, D. Chizhevsky (the secretary), I. Lapshin, P. Savitsky, and B.V. Yakovenko in Prague.

Berdyaev then decided—in agreement with Paul Anderson in Berlin and Vysheslavtsev and Shestov in Paris—to move the seat of the Russian-American publishing house and that of the Academy to the French capital. The Academy remained, nonetheless, in contact with the Russian philosophers of the SPR of Berlin and Prague through the review *The Way*.[246] On November 9, 1924, in the hall of the School of Advanced Social Studies of the Sorbonne, 16 rue de la Sorbonne, Berdyaev, accompanied by Vysheslavtsev, Kartashev, and G. Trubetskoy, resumed the activities of the Academy with a lecture, "The Religious Significance of the Contemporary Crisis." A week later the Academy began its regular classes at 11 rue de Jean de Beauvais, at the center of the publishing house Le Semeur—a sign of its proximity to the Catholic modernist current.[247] For fifty francs a year, students could follow the courses of Arseniev on "Orthodoxy, Catholicism and Protestantism," of Kartashev on "The History of Primitive Christianity," of Berdyaev on "The History of Russian Spiritual Movements," and of Vysheslavtsev on "Good and Evil in Christian Doctrine," with occasional conferences of professors still living in Prague or Berlin, such as Bulgakov, Zenkovsky, or Frank.[248]

There were five steps in the creation of the review *The Way*. It began with a conversation between Berdyaev, Vysheslavtsev, Anderson, and Kuhlmann on a sunny afternoon in July 1924, at a café in the Place des Ternes in Paris.[249] The project took shape during three meetings of the four men on October 6, November 14, and December 4, 1924. John Mott, the president of the YMCA and World Student Christian Federation, gave his consent for the creation of a journal in Russian and of a high level of erudition, whose goal would be to assure the meeting between the Christian West and the Christian East. The first meeting took place at Saint-Cloud.[250] Berdyaev gave the journal its two principal orientations: the deepening of the philosophical and religious conscience of Russian Christians, without falling into dry abstractions, and an openness to every religious, ecumenical, or intellectual manifestation. Berdyaev specified that the review should assure a "spiritual leadership" vis-à-vis the Russian Student Christian Movement and the "Russian intelligentsia" and avoid attempts to return to the religiosity of the old regime.[251] In Berdyaev's mind, this should be undertaken by a group of intellectuals who were part of the St. Sophia Brotherhood (Bulgakov, Frank, Zenkovsky, Kartashev). The editorial committee was composed of Berdyaev as editor-in-chief, Vysheslavtsev as assistant editor and the person responsible for the review's technical preparation, and Kuhlmann as second assistant editor. Thus, from the very beginning, the only review in the world of intellectuals that defined itself as Orthodox was ecumenical, since Kuhlmann was himself a Protestant.

In the second meeting, held at St. Cloud on November 14,[252] the four participants shelved the project of an administrative committee made up of two Russians, two representatives of the YMCA, and some American, German, and French members, who would represent universities. After a heated discussion, the four men decided that the publishing house responsible for the publication of the review would not be the YMCA Press but rather the Academy of Religious Philosophy (APR), which was itself financed by the YMCA. On the other hand, however, "from a legal and administrative point of view, the YMCA could be considered as having responsibility for the review by putting its publication and diffusion material, as well as its personnel, at the disposition of the review."[253] Here can be found a trait that would be decisive in the history of the review—for by thus posing their conditions, the two Russian intellectuals were assuring full freedom of creativity and opinion. In fact, even if Anderson were opposed to the editorial policy of Berdyaev in his capacity as editor-in-chief of the YMCA, he left the editor-in-chief of the review completely free insofar as the review depended exclusively on the APR. The third meeting was held at Berdyaev's residence in Clamart.[254] A permanent editorial staff was chosen, consisting of Bulgakov, Zenkovsky, Frank, Karsavin, Kartashev, G. Trubetskoy, N. Lossky, and Arseniev, so that "the different tendencies of Russian religious thought might have the possibility to express themselves" and also so that "a whole group—and not just the editor—with the same spiritual approaches might share the responsibility of the review."[255]

In the course of the evening, the four men discussed different names for the review without arriving at a decision. Among those proposed were "Faith and Life," "Time and Eternity," "Patmos," "Sophia," "Sobor," and "Charis." All agreed, however, on the theme of the first issue: "The Spiritual Crisis of the Present Times." It was not until December 12, at the YMCA headquarters at 11 rue de Jean de Beauvais, that the four—along with Bulgakov and Zenkovsky—decided, it seems, to call the journal *The Way*.[256] Although it cannot be proved, Berdyaev and Bulgakov were probably the ones who came up with this name. Indeed, both of them had participated in Merezhkovsky's review, *The New Way* (*Novyi put'*), which was published in St. Petersburg between 1903 and 1904. Both had also participated in the publishing house The Way (Put'), which, between 1909 and 1916, and thanks to the financial support of the wealthy philanthropist M. K. Morozova, published original articles including ones by Florensky and Frank. Moreover, both authors always sought to clarify the evolution of their thought as well as that of their generation by the works they coauthored, such as *Problems of Idealism* in 1902, which announced their shift from Marxism to Idealism, *Landmarks* in 1909, which marked their rejection of a certain tendency of a radical and intolerant intelligentsia, *De Profundis* in 1918, in which they vigorously denounced the revolution, and *Problems of the Russian Religious Conscience* in 1924, which confirmed their return to the religious preoccupations of the émigrés of the Russian intelligentsia. Consequently, the title of the review symbolized the affirmation of the continuity of the intellectual tradition of Russian religious thought.

The final step in the creation of the review was the meeting of the four with John Mott, E. MacNaughten, and E. T. Colton of the administration of the YMCA on May 2, 1925, at Annemasse, near Geneva.[257] Berdyaev reiterated to Mott that it was the common desire of the authors to contribute to "a creative reform within the Orthodox Church as opposed to a reactionary form of Orthodoxy."[258] Mott, for his part, reaffirmed the editorial autonomy of the review. In the end, it was agreed that a structure of administrative direction would be created that would include Mott (or Colton), Kuhlmann, Berdyaev, Vysheslavtsev, and a third Russian to be named and that an editorial committee would be set up with the participation of two Russians, an American (Paul Micou), an Englishman, and a Swiss (Kuhlmann)—all under the authority of Berdyaev. The editor-in-chief would have the responsibility of soliciting articles from Russian writers representative of all different tendencies (such as the new names Zaitsev, Florovsky, Bezobrazov, Ilyin, Chetverikov).[259] Finally, they decided to put out a brochure announcing the review as follows:

> *The Way* is the organ of Russian Orthodox thought. It seeks to continue the tradition linked to the names of Khomiakov, Dostoevsky, and Solovyov and believes in the possibility of a creative development within Orthodoxy. The catastrophe which has occurred in Russia and the worldwide crisis changes the situation of the Christian Churches and confers new responsibilities on Orthodoxy. The review *The Way* will have to respond to this new creative questioning. At the same time it will make the spiritual currents in Europe and the life and thought of the other Christian confessions known to the Russians.[260]

The Theological Institute
At the Tianjin congress, John Mott had also promised the Russian delegates that he would support the project of creating a school of theology—an idea that came from the émigrés and had at its center Kartashev, Novgorodtsev, and P. Struve. All seminaries and theological academies in Russia had been closed in 1918, and there was no place in Europe that could perpetuate the great Russian theological tradition and apply the

ecclesiastical reforms from the council of 1917–18. In the spring of 1920, Patriarch Tikhon had given his blessing to Metropolitan Benjamin of Petrograd and the priest Nicolas Chukov for the creation of an Orthodox institute of theology. This institute was both traditional and modernist, in that women were admitted to take courses and the faculty was recruited from former academic professors such as Kartashev and university professors such as N. Lossky, Bezobrazov, and Karsavin. After Lenin expelled the group of non-Bolshevist intellectuals in 1922, the institute began to have financial problems. It finally closed in the spring of 1923. In May 1924, Mott, Zenkovsky, and Bulgakov agreed to establish the new institute in Prague. However, in December 1922, Metropolitan Evlogy decided to follow the movement of his faithful to France and to transfer the seat of his metropolis to Paris. In January 1924, he entrusted to Mikhail Ossorgin and Grigorii Trubetskoy the task of finding a new place of worship for the thousands of Russian émigrés of Paris. On July 18, 1924, the day of the feast of St. Sergius in the Orthodox calendar, Ossorgin purchased a property in Paris for the sum of 320,000 francs. It was spacious enough to become the intellectual and spiritual center of the Russian emigration. The property was located at 92 rue de Crimée in the 19th arrondissment.[261] It had been bought in 1857 by the German Lutheran pastor Friedrich von Bodelschwing and subsequently requisitioned by the French government during World War I. Thanks to the contributions of émigrés and the financial support of the YMCA and the World Student Christian Federation (91,400 francs), the Anglican support group for the Russian Church, and the Jewish benefactor M. A. Ginzburg, the purchasing price was covered.

On Sunday, March 1, 1925, Metropolitan Evlogy celebrated the first liturgy and officially inaugurated the St. Sergius Theological Institute. The parish was entrusted to Archimandrite Ioann Leonchukov and Metropolitan Evlogy, who became the rector of the Institute. There was an immediate rush of candidates for both the student body and the faculty. In the course of three months, ninety students from all over Europe applied, but only nineteen were retained to finish the year of preparatory training, which ran from March to October 1925. The professors of the Institute arrived gradually between March and October 1925. Some came from the ranks of the academies of theology, as was the case for Kartashev (Dean, as well as a scholar in History of the Church, Russian, Hebrew), Bishop Benjamin (Old Testament, Liturgics, Moral Theology, Canon Law), and Ossorgin (Rubrics); but principally they came from the academic world of the university, such as Bezobrazov (New Testament studies), Fr. Bulgakov (Old Testament, Dogmatic Theology), Fedotov (Hagiography, History of the Western Church), Florovsky (Patristics), P. Kovalevsky (Latin), V. Ilyin (Liturgics), Vysheslavtsev (Moral Theology), L. Zander (Logic, Comparative Theology), and Zenkovsky (Philosophy, Psychology, Education, Apologetics). In his article on the St. Sergius Institute published in *The Way* in the September 1925 issue, Bezobrazov justified this choice of faculty by situating the Institute in continuity with both the theological schools of the nineteenth century and the line of lay Russian religious thought inaugurated by Khomiakov, whom he considered—in the manner of these new professors of modernist tendencies—a "Doctor of the Church."[262]

The Youth Movement
All students at St. Sergius belonged to the new Russian Student Christian Movement (RSCM), created in 1923. The founding congress took place at Psherov, near Prague, from October 1 to 7. Both Ruth Rouse and Donald Lowrie of the World Student Christian Federation and the YMCA, respectively, were present.[263] The thirty-three delegates—students from the Baltic countries, France, Yugoslavia, Czechoslovakia, Bulgaria, and Germany—distrusted the pre-revolutionary Russian intelligentsia, whom they considered responsible for the revolution. Yet the two generations of intellectuals—one coming from the Silver Age, the other from the revolution—recognized one another as a unique group and decided to form the RSCM. The charisma of Bulgakov, Berdyaev, Kartashev, and Zenkovsky and the daily celebration of the liturgy eased their mutual distrust. A. Nikitin decided to convert to Orthodoxy. The eschatological sentiment of belonging to the end of the Constantinian period of the Orthodox Church marked by the Byzantine "symphony" explains the prophetic character of the new movement's two principal objectives: the "churching" of life and the mission of "presenting the icon to the West."

Frank was quick to realize the historical significance of the RSCM congress. As he explained the following year in a book entitled *The Fall of the Idols*, the meeting between the two generations was made possible both by the progressive reentry into the church of the intelligentsia and by the collapse of the revolutionary ideals.[264] Building on the enthusiasm of the congress, Bulgakov, Berdyaev, Kartashev, and Zenkovsky also decided to establish the Brotherhood of St. Sophia, whose goal was to continue the philosophical and religious initiatives that had existed prior to the revolution and to maintain a link among the Russian intellectuals dispersed across Europe. The foundational meeting of the brotherhood was held in Paris in the same month as the first RSCM congress, October 1923.

The YMCA was the principal sponsor of the Russian Student Christian Movement. Given the exodus of the émigrés to Paris and the dynamism of the Parisian circles animated by Piotr Kovalevsky and Paul Evdokimov, the first secretary of the Academy of Religious Philosophy, the RSCM set up its central headquarters in Paris in 1924. Its general secretary, Lev Liperovsky, immediately coordinated the activity of the catechetical schools for children and the classes for biblical studies and general culture, and, on December 1, 1925, the first issue of the RSCM review *The Messenger* (*Vestnik RSKhD*) appeared under the editorship of Lagovsky and Zernov. In "The Religious Youth Movements in the Russian Emigration," published in the September 1925 issue of *The Way*, Zenkovsky, who had been elected president at the congress, described the goals of the movement as they were formulated at Psherov:

> The renewal [*perestroika*] of one's whole life according to the principles of Orthodoxy, the turning towards an integral (ecclesial) culture—this is the guiding idea of the religious movement among Russian youth.... The creative task [*delo*] (in the sense of *The Philosophy of the Common Task* of Fedorov) which determines the logic of the whole movement is not the elaboration of an integral vision of the world—as some are already dreaming of realizing—but the "churching" of life.[265]

Further on, the author insists on the freedom of the laity and warns the young intellectuals who were returning to the church en masse against all clericalism. "The spirit of Orthodoxy," Zenkovsky wrote, "reconciles freedom and ecclesial belonging, the patriarchal principle and catholicity."[266] The primacy of the church explained why the RSCM was fundamentally apolitical.[267] This formula was ambiguous, however, for, although it accepted as members both monarchists and republicans, it refused to integrate Communists. In spite of its protestations of neutrality, the movement, by the very context of its foundation, was anti-Bolshevik. The failure to acknowledge this would have serious consequences, as we shall see later on. In conclusion, Zenkovsky affirmed the intent of the RSCM to be open to ecumenism and specified—in a bow to the YMCA and the World Student Christian Federation—that the inevitably fruitful coming together with the Christian West could only be brought about, as was formerly the case in Russia, on the basis of a type of inter-confessionalism held dear by the Protestant churches. Such an ecumenical meeting could only take place in the context of a mutual respect for the ecclesiologies of each confession. This decision represented the victory, within the movement, of the Orthodox tendency of the emigration over and against the position of V. Marcinkovsky and other non-Orthodox members.[268]

The Relationship with the Church

The originality of the institutions discussed above, which were closely interrelated, and the context of exile, which favored a new liberty of expression, immediately posed the problem of the place in the church of this new category of Christians engaged in the world and their relationship with the church hierarchy. The logic of the conflict between the modernist and conservative trends in the Russian Church was more symbolic than rational. Indeed, the memory of Russia's past, of Imperial Russia, and of the revolution played a role infinitely more important than the theological, canonical, and political oppositions invoked by both sides.

The Collaboration between the Russian Orthodox Church Outside Russia (ROCOR) and the YMCA
In 1921 the council of Karlovtsy, mindful of ancient fears, had harshly condemned the YMCA and the movement Lighthouse. According to the signatories, "these two organizations are a Masonic plot against Christianity."[269] Thus Anderson, so as not to get on the wrong side of the religious authorities, sought by every possible means to collaborate with Metropolitan Anthony Khrapovitsky. In 1923 the YMCA officially addressed Bishop Benjamin, asking him to recommend a list of writings to be used by the circles of Russian students under their tutelage. Bishop Benjamin replied to Kuhlmann on October 24, 1923, sending a list of the spiritual works of the bishops Ignatius Brianchaninov and Theophan the Recluse. As for theological literature, the bishop recommended *The Orthodox*

Doctrine of Salvation by Metropolitan Sergius (Stragorodsky) and *The Unfading Light* by Bulgakov, although, he made clear, "with the exception of the chapters on Sophia."[270]

But on September 4, 1924, in *New Time* (*Novoe Vremia*), the organ of the Russian monarchists published in Belgrade, Metropolitan Anthony inaugurated a series of articles disapproving of Bulgakov's ideas on sophiology. On the basis of the presentation that Bulgakov made in 1917 in *The Unfading Light*, where the Russian theologian had awkwardly—although in quotation marks—applied the term *hypostasis* to Sophia,[271] Metropolitan Anthony criticized sophiology as "a complete heresy contradicting the fundamental dogma of the Christian faith concerning the three hypostases in the unique Divinity."[272]

This theological dispute was compounded by other, more general considerations. In the course of the second RSCM congress,[273] the participants became aware of the abyss separating them from the representatives of traditional Orthodoxy. The congress took place between July 21 and 28, 1925, at the chateau of the Countess of Montmor at Argeron in Normandy, with the participation of delegates from Paris, Lyon, Marseille, Montpellier, and Strasbourg, as well as Berlin, Prague, London, Brussels, Louvain, Belgrade, Sofia, Spain, and Mexico. Lev Zander, in his report on the congress, mentions the intervention of Bishop Benjamin, who gave precedence to the salvation of the individual Christian over social work. He vigorously opposed the theses of Berdyaev by affirming that the Constantinian period of history was not finished and that it was not the task of the Christian to transform the world, for, in his mind, "the Kingdom of God cannot be realized on earth."[274]

The articles of Metropolitan Anthony in *New Time* encouraged the monarchists—most of whom were hostile to the modernist wing of the Russian Church, to the intelligentsia, and to the West—to condemn the new Parisian institutions. On April 3, 1925, A. Pogodin published an article in *New Time* representing the YMCA as a "rationalist sect," "pro-Semite," and "Masonic," the offshoot of a country whose only identity is the "thirst for gold."

> As is well known, Semitism, which is well organized, is trying to usurp the spiritual life of Christian peoples. The *Protocols of the Elders of Zion* describes how that will be done. In any case, Semitism seeks to con-

trol all organizations that have an influence on the spiritual life of the Christian peoples of Europe. Freemasonry is only a simple toy in the hands of the Jews. It is possible that associations having nothing in common with Semitism fall into their net. Even the YMCA has not resisted such a destiny.... Some young Jews who pretend to be Christians have assumed leadership roles in the YMCA.... Many speak of principles of humanity, of justice, of a religion of humanity, of the destruction of confessional churches to be replaced by a cult of human-divinity.[275]

The generation of intellectuals gathered together in the St. Sergius Institute, the St. Sophia Brotherhood, the Academy, *The Way*, and the RSCM counterattacked immediately. In the *Evening News* (*Vechernoe vremia*), Bulgakov replied to Metropolitan Anthony, affirming that he had never preached a God in four hypostases.[276] On November 13, 1924, the metropolitan published an article reaffirming his previous positions. Moreover, Bulgakov, in his article "Hypostasis and Hypostaticity," published in Prague in 1925 in the collection dedicated to P. Struve, had replied more theologically by repeating that Sophia is not a hypostasis but rather an essence potentially capable of being personified. Finally, on June 7, 1926, on the eve of a new meeting of the synod, Fr. Bulgakov, in an address at the St. Sergius Institute and published by *The Way* in November, explained the Trinitarian doctrine in the Orthodox tradition while carefully avoiding any reference to Sophia.[277]

Moreover, Metropolitan Anthony agreed to participate in the third general conference of the RSCM, held at Hopovo in Serbia on September 11–17, 1925. The congress was dedicated to the question of the movement's structure. As conference participants, N. Klepinin and Bulgakov agreed with Metropolitan Anthony's proposition in favor of a movement of confraternities, or brotherhoods, each with its own statutes.[278] This meant accepting, in the place of a federative and lay organization along the lines of the World Student Christian Federation, a structure that privileged the authority of the local bishop, since confraternities, from their beginnings in the sixteenth century in the Eastern Church, had always been submitted to the episcopal hierarchy. This "territorialization" of the movement was confirmed at the congress of the Orthodox students of the Balkans and Southern Europe held in Ban Kostenec in Bulgaria in May 1926, with the presence of metropolitans Evlogy and Anthony.[279] Definitively reassured of Bulgakov's orthodoxy, Metropolitan Anthony agreed that the YMCA Press could publish his book, *The Dogma of Redemption.* After a stay at the St. Sergius Institute, Metropolitan Anthony himself wrote an article very favorable to the new institute in the April 30, 1926, issue of *Renaissance.*[280]

The Debate between the Monarchists and Republicans in the Review
In spite of reciprocal affinities, the members of the review were divided between monarchists and republicans. Consequently, the political debate was a source of tension between the modernist current of the emigration and the ROCOR. Berdyaev took it upon himself to reply to the monarchist publications of Belgrade with an article entitled "Joseph de Maistre and Freemasonry," which was published in the June 1926 issue of *The Way.* Berdyaev's testimony laid bare the irrationality of conspiracy logic: "The question of Freemasonry is both posed and discussed in an atmosphere of moral barbarism created by panic and fear in the face of the revolution.... The quest of Judeo-Masonry, for protocols of worldwide Masonry, is of the same nature as the Bolshevik quest for agents of the worldwide counter-revolutionary bourgeois conspiracy."[281]

Berdyaev pointed out the Christian and humanist sources of the first English Freemasons and, in spite of his hostility to the atheism of the Grand Orient (the largest of France's Masonic lodges, and one of the oldest in Europe), declared himself in favor of the project of a federation of European states. More fundamentally, Berdyaev responded to the monarchists by refuting the principal thesis of the theorist of autocracy, M. Zyzykin, concerning the "eighth sacrament."[282] In his September 1925 article, "The Kingdom of God and the Kingdom of Caesar," Berdyaev wrote that the anointing of the Tsar, practiced in the Russian Church since the reign of Paul I, was the final result of the theocratic utopia of the Jewish people and of a confusion between the Kingdom of Caesar, "which belongs to time," and the Kingdom of God, which "belongs to eternity." For Berdyaev, Christian theocracy is eschatological and can recognize only Christ as tsar.[283]

A. Petrov, a monarchist from Prague who was closely associated with N. Markov and N. Talberg, leaders in the High Monarchist Council, replied to Berdyaev on October 29, 1925. Using the ecclesiology of Bishop Ignatius Brianchaninov[284] as a starting point, Petrov reaffirmed the religious foundations of the monarchy. But the real criticism of Berdyaev by the philosopher from Prague is found near the end of the article:

The overall tone of the social philosophy [of Berdyaev] is unacceptable for the young generation because it calls for patience in the face of the evil which triumphs in our country, in our homeland, and not for an armed struggle against it. The evil within us can be overcome interiorly; that should be the religious task of every Christian. But this concrete earthly evil which now invades our homeland can only be vanquished by bringing together the religious strengths of all her sons and assembling her warriors under the shadow of the Holy Cross and the banners of the tsar.[285]

This article caused a division among the authors of the review. The article by G. Trubetskoy, "The Debate over the Monarchy," published in the following issue, is indicative of the monarchist sympathies of some of them. More profoundly, this attack by Petrov revealed the symbolic implications of the political debate that agitated the émigré community during the period between the two world wars, for it openly confronted the question of evil and the use of force—a particularly sensitive question in a social context favorable to the propagation of myths.

The Debate on the Use of Force
On June 14, 1925, in Berlin, Ivan Ilyin (1883–1954), one of the conference speakers of the Academy of Religious Philosophy,[286] published a book in Russian entitled *The Resistance to the Forces of Evil.* Here Ilyin, in opposition to the Tolstoy-inspired and pacifist intelligentsia, put forth the doctrine, drawn from the New Testament, of the sword as the foundation of love and thus justified the armed counter-revolution in Russia. The emigration community was split between the two sides. The monarchists behind P. Struve[287] and the daily right-wing paper *Renaissance* were favorable to the position of Ilyin, while the democrats, behind I. Demidov[288] and the left-wing daily *Latest News* (*Poslednie novosti*), were opposed. The polemic went beyond the boundaries of the emigration community. *Pravda*, the journal of the Soviet Communist Party in Moscow, in its June 19, 1925, issue, reacted strongly against Ilyin's "reactionary" book.[289] Among the intellectuals who took part in the polemic were Boris Suvarin and A. Bilimovich, partisans of Ilyin, and, among his detractors, Maxim Gorky, I. Eihenvald, Z. Gippius, and F. Stepun.

This polemic led Berdyaev to decide to leave the Brotherhood of St. Sophia, since P. Struve was one of its members. On September 23, 1925,

Berdyaev wrote to Bulgakov, asking him to tell the other members of his decision (the rest of the letter concerns the editorial work for the first issues of the review).[290] In his response, Bulgakov regretted Berdyaev's decision and recognized that political tensions have found their way even into the brotherhood.[291] The most intense moment of the polemic coincided with an attempt to establish political unity within the Russian emigration in April 1926. P. Struve, editor-in-chief of *Renaissance*, organized a congress of the Russian émigrés at the Majestic Hotel in Paris on April 4, 1926, in the hope of reuniting the political forces of the emigration. He failed due to the refusal of the non-monarchist parties to participate in the congress. Henceforth the emigration community was divided into several camps, and this blocked any hope of success for counter-revolutionary political unity.

Berdyaev participated in the polemic in the April and June issues of 1926. In his response to Petrov, he turned up the heat.[292] In his view, royal power, from the times of the Egyptian pharaohs, is linked more to "totemism" than to Christianity. According to Berdyaev, nothing in the Bible indicates that the Trinity is a monarchy. On the other hand, Berdyaev did not deny, in principle, the possibility of opposing evil by force, but he reaffirmed that the émigré community's struggle against Bolshevism could take place only on a spiritual level. "I don't believe in the sword of the emigration," writes Berdyaev, "that has long since been changed into a cardboard sword."[293] The article by G. Trubetskoy, published in the June 1926 issue, formulated the opinion—which was rather widespread among the émigrés—that it was tactically harmful to criticize the pre-revolutionary period because that would amount to playing the game of the Bolsheviks and the Living Church.[294] For Berdyaev, on the contrary, the overcoming of Bolshevism could only be "post-revolutionary and not pre-revolutionary."[295] The violence of Berdyaev's criticism of Ilyin's book consists in its making it seem, in the face of any rational logic, that Ilyin and Tolstoy understand evil in essentially the same way. He writes:

> The metaphysical and religious roots of all of I. Ilyin's errors can be found in his monism, or, if we want to use the terminology of the heresies of the first centuries of Christianity, in his monophysitism.... Monophysitism is a false understanding of the mystery of Divine-humanity, the central mystery of Christianity, the mystery of the union

of two natures in a unique person without any diminution of the autonomy of these natures.... The pathos of I. Ilyin is that of an abstract good, of an abstract idea, of an abstract spirit in which man's living face, the soul of man, disappears definitively. But Christianity is not an idea, Christianity is a reality.... The unique good is Christ himself, his Person. "I am the way, the truth and the life." The Sabbath is made for man and not man for the Sabbath. Man is greater than the Sabbath.... Herein lies the absolute difference between Christian morality and the morality of Kant, Fichte, L. Tolstoy, I. Ilyin, and all the other moralists of this world.[296]

This comparison between monism and the monophysitism of Ivan Ilyin is fundamental, for it would also explain the movement—incomprehensible at that moment—during the 1930s of certain intellectuals of the review, such as Boris Vysheslavtsev or Vladimir Ilyin, towards National Socialism. Ivan Ilyin himself moved towards National Socialism but left Germany to live in Switzerland during the Second World War. Such an explanation would lead to incriminating Christians as responsible for the totalitarian ideologies that sprang up during the interwar period. In 1926, Berdyaev did not hesitate to make that step.

> Hegel didn't believe in the Church and replaced it by the State. For him, the State took charge of all the functions of the Church. Such was the result of extreme forms of Protestantism. It is not by chance that in today's Germany the currents of the extreme right, the monarchists and nationalists, are linked to Lutheranism, whose religious energy is transformed, in large part, into national and state-related energy. I. Ilyin's idea of the State is, like Hegel's, a pagan reaction, a return to absolutism and to the pagan deification of the State.[297]

But, Berdyaev went on to say, metaphysical monism was not the exclusive domain of right-wingers. For the foremost inquisitors, "from Robespierre to Dzerzhinsky," were characterized, above all, by their negation of the freedom of evil, by their desire to organize the good against man's freedom. However, Berdyaev added, the justification of capital punishment or of tyrannicide is all the more repugnant when it invokes the Gospel. Ilyin, in his book, used the episode of Jesus violently cleansing the Temple to justify combating the Bolsheviks. Berdyaev turned his opponent's argument against him by showing that the real merchants in the Temple are not those who seek to destroy it but those who believe themselves so full of divine fire that they can use the church for their personal ends.[298] "The Cheka in the name of God," wrote Berdyaev, "is much more abominable than the Cheka in the name of the devil."[299]

The Crisis (June 1926–January 1928)

Events in the Soviet Union and the Evolution of the YMCA

At the fourteenth congress of the Russian Communist Party in December 1925, Stalin became the number one man. Four months later, G. Zinoviev was obliged to leave the Politburo. In November 1927, L. Trotsky and Zinoviev were expelled from the party. This reinforcement of Stalin's power went hand in hand with a revival of anti-religious propaganda. In September 1926, Metropolitan Sergius was arrested. After he had agreed to recognize and submit to the authority of the government, he was allowed to resume his functions in March 1927. On May 20 the government legalized the temporary patriarchal synod headed by Metropolitan Sergius. A week later, Sergius wrote to Metropolitan Evlogy asking him to accept this legalization and make his clergy sign a recognition of "loyalty towards Soviet power." Metropolitan Sergius then wrote a declaration dated July 16 and published in the emigration press on August 19, 1927, in which Soviet authority was recognized as coming from God. This brought with it the obligation for the members of the Russian Church to "share its joys and sufferings." According to Nikita Struve, this declaration "made the Church an active ally of the Soviet government."[300]

The fourth congress of the Russian Student Christian Movement in France took place in July 1927, at Clermont en Argonne, with Metropolitan Evlogy and Bishop Sergius of Prague in attendance. For the first time, the general theme of the congress was Russia. According to a report by Lev Zander published in *The Way* in January 1928, the participants were particularly impressed by a presentation by Lagovsky on the persecution of Christians in Russia.[301] On the basis of a number of testimonies and using quotations from the review *The Atheist* (*Bezbozhnik*), Lagovsky revealed the extent of the anti-religious propaganda in 1926–27 to those participating in the congress and made them sense the "hell"[302] of spiritual life in Russia. In spite of the frightening scenario depicted by Lagovsky, however, there was no change in the optimism of the participants as to the possibility of a religious renaissance in Russia and of a proximate return to the country. Berdyaev encouraged the members of the congress to redouble their efforts and to prepare themselves intellectually in order to be able to struggle, in a near future, for the church and against atheism. Elizabeth Skobtsova announced, in a prophetic tone, that the twelfth hour, the moment of the return to Russia, was at hand. "Something is happening in the world; the axle of the spiritual life is beginning to turn again."[303]

An assessment of the YMCA, of the RSCM, and of the St. Sergius Institute for the year 1926–27 shows a dynamic increase of activities. In the month of November 1926, the YMCA moved its general headquarters to Paris. It rented a twenty-five-room building at 10 Boulevard Montparnasse for its publishing house, the Academy, the RSCM, and the technical school conducted by correspondence.[304] In 1927 the RSCM had about sixteen hundred members. The most active centers were Paris (100 members), Prague (87), Brno (35), Belgrade (30), Nice (30), Berlin (25), Dresden (25), and New York, London, Brussels, Zagreb, Harbin, and Sofia (20 each). *The Way* was distributed in all of these circles—a fact that contributed to the renown of some of its authors. Along these lines, Vysheslavtsev, at the invitation of the RSCM circles in southeast Europe and with YMCA support, gave a lecture tour in the spring of 1927 in Bulgaria, Romania, Serbia, and Greece.[305] Starting in 1926, the movement began to expand in the Baltic countries as well. The RSCM delegated Berdyaev to give a lecture tour in the Baltics in March 1927. In Paris, it began its youth activities in November 1926 by organizing a Sunday School for sixty children and a cultural club for teenagers, led by Maria Zernova. In July 1927, summer camps for boys and girls were inaugurated, and new circles for students were organized. In November, Zenkovsky, after spending six months in the United States supported by the YMCA, created an Office of Religious Pedagogy at the St. Sergius Institute for the formation of groups to work with young people. The books published by the YMCA in 1926 and the four issues of the review *The Way* sold well; N. Klepinin, who was hired by the YMCA Press in 1926 because of his experience in business, succeeded in doubling sales ($3,952 in 1926 as compared with $1,910 in 1925).

This evident burst of activity reinforced the fears of the conservative elements of the émigré community. On November 27, 1926, Paul Anderson wrote a short piece entitled "The YMCA and the Russian Orthodox Church," in which he summed up the press campaign being waged against the American organization. According to his account, the principal criticisms were that the YMCA was "highly centralized," "extremely rich," "had obscure ambitions," and held an "esoteric" doctrine influenced by "the Freemasons" and "the Jews." On the other hand, Anderson admitted abuses of proselytism by the YMCA in Siberia in 1918–1920 and the ignorance of its staff concerning what is specific to Orthodoxy.[306] But for Anderson, the main difficulty lay in the difference of emphasis between the Americans and Russians concerning the divine humanity of Christ. The ideology of the YMCA affirmed the creative aspect of mankind, while the Eastern Church emphasized the grace of God as the source of truth.[307] The realization of this difference led the leaders of the YMCA to redefine the meaning of their activities within the Russian émigré community during a meeting in Paris on July 27, 1927. The YMCA decided to grant complete autonomy to the RSCM in its missionary work with students and young people and to continue to support it financially. In exchange, the RSCM committed itself to respect the principles of interconfessional tolerance, of the preservation of Russian culture, of diversity in its activities, and of "organic" official relations—at least on the level of its most important members—with the YMCA, the YWCA, and the World Student Christian Federation.[308]

The Schism of August 26, 1927

The reinforcement of Stalinist power in the USSR, the declaration of loyalty by Metropolitan Sergius, the radicalization of the political life of the emigration community after the failure of the congress of April 4, 1926, the deterioration of the economic situation of the Russian refugees following the financial crisis of the Briand government in July, and, lastly, the general insecurity made worse by the progressive awareness of a religious threat from without—all precipitated the schism of the Russian Church that took place on August 26, 1927. After the death of Patriarch Tikhon in April 1925, the hierarchy of the synod of the ROCOR assembled at Karlovtsy had elected Metropolitan Anthony as *locum tenens* of the Patriarch.

In May 1925, Kartashev published an article in *Renaissance* denouncing this election as against canon law and accusing the synod of preparing a schism against the patriarchate.[309] The rupture became evident during the annual council of the ROCOR. Metropolitan Evlogy asked the synod to modify their agenda in order to give priority to article 2 of the council's program concerning the relationship of the ROCOR with the administrative center at Moscow. The synod refused to do so and, on June 16, after Metropolitan Evlogy had left, elected Metropolitan Anthony to head the entire ROCOR. Metropolitan Anthony, making use of his new powers, immediately withdrew Germany from the jurisdiction of Metropolitan Evlogy and named Bishop Tikhon (Liashenko) in his place. The next day the council condemned the World Student Christian Federation and the YMCA as Masonic organizations. It forbade members of the Orthodox Church to form groups that would be under the direction of these two institutions and, consequently, of the RSCM. After having heard the report of Archbishop Theophan on the "heretical" doctrine of Bulgakov's sophiology, the council went on to reproach Metropolitan Evlogy for having opened the St. Sergius Institute without the approval of the synod. It decided that St. Sergius Institute should be directly subject to the synod's authority and that it should be purged of all remnants of Freemasonry.[310] The chapter on the RSCM was publicly toned down by Metropolitan Anthony on July 22.[311] Metropolitan Evlogy, however, refused to recognize the decisions of the council and suspended Bishop Tikhon.

On the occasion of its third local congress, held at Clermont near the end of July and with Metropolitan Evlogy present, the RSCM declared that its missionary goals and the attitude of the synod prevented it from "recognizing itself as formally subject to the hierarchy."[312] It was in this context of open schism that the RSCM organized its fourth general assembly on September 1–5 at the Château of Bierville, near Paris; this assembly was to treat the question of its structure. This congress was of primary importance since it determined the ecclesiology and the organization of the movement during the interwar period. Among the delegates of Russian circles in France, Germany, Czechoslovakia, England, Bulgaria, Estonia, Latvia, and Poland, there were two opposing camps. The first group, animated by the younger generation led by P. Lopukhin and N. Klepinin, affirmed the orthodox underpinnings of the movement and pronounced itself in favor of a decentralized structure of brotherhoods grouped around the "spiritual authority"[313] of their bishop, yet leaving the movement administratively autonomous. Since the seat of the movement was in Paris, the two leaders accepted that the RSCM would be under Metropolitan Evlogy but with the condition that it "present an overview of its activities to the synod once a year and follow its recommendations."[314] The second group, headed by representatives of the older generation and the former members of Lighthouse, insisted on the interconfessional, missionary, and autonomous dimensions of the movement. In his report on the congress, L. Zander cites the following words of Berdyaev:

> It is indispensable that we distinguish two ways of understanding the Church: the invisible Church, the Mystical Body of Christ which embraces all that is truly alive, and the visible Church, an earthly and ephemeral construction, a canonical organization. The student movement, because it is made up of the laity, is ecclesial in the original and integral sense of the term.[315]

Faithful to the ecclesiology of the Holy Spirit as formulated by Khomiakov, Berdyaev did not want to institutionalize the organization of the movement in a way that would be overly sympathetic to the Russian Orthodox Church Outside Russia. The congress went along with him but accepted certain compromises. The general assembly constituted itself as the supreme organ of the movement and declared itself in favor of a lay-led and interconfessional organization. Consequently, it elected a board or executive committee composed of lay people and clergy representative of the different circles and confraternities of the movement, with Zenkovsky as president. No bishop and, likewise, no member of the YMCA or of the World Student Christian Federation was part of this committee. For regulating the relations between the movement and the larger sectors of the social and ecclesial worlds, a new council was created composed of four members elected by the board—S. Bulgakov, N. Berdyaev, G. Trubetskoy, and N. Klepinin.

This solution was a compromise that could satisfy no one. On January 23, 1927, Lopukhin gave his assessment of the congress of Bierville in the pages of *The Way*. Taking issue with the opinion of Zander, he believed that the congress had not succeeded in overcoming the conflict between the two tendencies of the movement and lamented that, because of this failure, the position of the Serbian confraternity has been subsequently interpreted by the partisans of Metropolitan Evlogy as clericalist and formalist, while the position of the philosophers of religion has been characterized by the partisans of the synod as disguised "Freemasonry."[316] After the congress, in fact, the real question of the modalities of a structure for the youth movement that was both ecclesial and modernist, namely, a structure valid for the entire Orthodox Church, was abandoned, and in its place a progressively radical opposition between laicism and clericalism developed.

Berdyaev invalidated the weak outcome of the compromise of Bierville in a virulent article against the ROCOR and the "rebirth of the clerical psychology," which appeared in the November issue of *The Way*.[317] He was of the opinion that the schism of the ROCOR was inevitable "sooner or later," and he rejoiced in it because, as he writes, "unity in truth is better than a compromise between truth and error."[318] Berdyaev argued, "The mistrust (of the Synod) towards the Russian Student Christian Movement, the most precious element in the emigration community at this moment, should make manifest to our younger people that outside of liberty of the spirit, there cannot be a Christian renaissance."[319] In the same article, he did not hesitate to radicalize the situation. He pronounced himself in favor of freedom of conscience, that is, against "the exterior organizational unity" in the church, and expressed his firm support for Metropolitan Evlogy in his struggles with the ROCOR. According to Berdyaev, the Synod is "monophysite by its spirit" and "Caesaropapist in its flesh." It had denied any chance at a new life through its nostalgia for the past and had surrounded itself with reactionary elements obsessed by the phobia of "Judeo-Masonry."[320] Berdyaev's article caused a scandal; even in China, Archbishop Innokenty of Beijing, in a letter to Metropolitan Anthony, denounced this "anti-Christian and anti-Orthodox blasphemy" and reproached Metropolitan Evlogy for remaining silent when he should have condemned the guilty author.[321]

For its part, the Karlovtsy synod clearly precipitated the rupture; as long as Metropolitan Sergius remained in prison, its stance against the patriarchal church and the diocese of Metropolitan Evlogy would receive the assent of the majority of the Russian emigration. On January 13, 1927, the synod decided to divest Metropolitan Evlogy of his functions and to confide the administration of the Orthodox churches of Western Europe to Bishop Seraphim of Lubny. The synod announced this decision to the émigrés of Western Europe through a circular letter, dated January 22, exhorting the faithful to cease all communion with the interdicted metropolitan.[322] That same day, Metropolitan Evlogy declared that this decision was anticanonical, broke off all relations with the synod, and decided to continue to administrate the eparchy that Patriarch Tikhon had confided to him.

On March 18, 1927, the synod published a pastoral letter, signed by Metropolitan Anthony and six other bishops, condemning the "modernism" prevalent in the St. Sergius Institute. After responding to the words of Kartashev offered in May 1925, according to which the faculty expressed their wish to remain united to the Church of Russia, the bishops vigorously attacked the professors of the Institute. Their attack singled out in particular the article of Kartashev published in Berlin in 1922 in the second collection of the Eurasianists, entitled "The Reform, the Reformation, and the Accomplishment of the Church."[323] Concerning the modernist intellectuals, the bishops wrote:

> They teach that the "ecclesial consciousness" in the Russian Orthodox Church has been stifled up till now, and their first goal was, then, to liberate it from this yoke. In their opinion, the "ecclesial consciousness" once it was liberated would, in its turn, free the "ecclesial forces of Russia" and enable them to transform the Church right down to its very foundations.[324]

The letter was also directed against the "prophetism" of Berdyaev and the sophiology of Bulgakov:

> Up to the present, with the Apostle Paul and the Fathers of the Church we have only known "Christ crucified, a scandal for the Jews, a folly for the pagans ... Christ, the power of God and the wisdom of God" (1 Cor 1:23–24). They, on the contrary, announce a new doctrine of "Wisdom, the feminine principle in God." Sometimes, for them, this feminine principle is an individual substance, a hypostasis which, without being consubstantial to the Holy Trinity, is not a stranger to it. Sometimes this feminine principle only appears to them as "hypostasized," a capability analogous to the hypostasis ... both interpretations of Wisdom are absolutely foreign to the tradition of the apostles and the teachings of the Fathers.[325]

The letter ends with a summons to Metropolitan Evlogy to return to the right path:

> Metropolitan Evlogy has not condemned the innovators; not only is he not taking any measures against the modernism which is infiltrating the Church from without, but he is choosing people who profess this doctrine to be his collaborators and is entrusting them with the task of forming the future pastors of the Church. . . . Once again we exhort Metropolitan Evlogy . . . to spare us the obligation of judging him as the protector of a new impiety.[326]

These accusations were immediately seized upon by the figurehead of the High Monarchist Council, Markov II, in an article entitled "The Reformers of Orthodoxy," which was published in *The Two-Headed Eagle*, an organ of the monarchist party. Fedotov replied in the April issue of *The Way*. For Fedotov, these attacks against "the Paris theological institute, *The Way*, and several theologians played on the fear of modernism and fidelity to tradition."[327] However, he wrote, in this debate it is not a question of opposing tradition and innovation but of defending the right of "freedom in Orthodox thinking, and the possibility of a living and creative theology."[328]

The support of Metropolitan Sergius in May and then, in June, of the Patriarch of Constantinople Basil III, encouraged Metropolitan Evlogy to convoke a general assembly of his diocese at the St. Sergius Institute on June 20–25, 1927. Of the nearly sixty parishes, only three, two at Nice and one at Menton, defected and passed over to the party of Metropolitan Anthony.[329] Metropolitan Evlogy, who was confirmed by the assembly as head of the provisional eparchy of Western Europe, reaffirmed his support for the St. Sergius Institute, the RSCM, and the Brotherhood of St. Sophia. Following Fedotov, the faculty of St. Sergius who were incriminated by the synod rejected the label of modernist reformers that had been applied to them. In defense of Metropolitan Evlogy, Bulgakov wrote a "manuscript note" in which he responded in detail to the accusations of Archbishop Theophan. The Russian theologian cited the scriptural, liturgical, and patristic testimonies to the doctrine of the Wisdom of God. He also denied trying to introduce a feminine principle into the Trinity in the sense in which Solovyov understood it:

Sophia, as the object of God's love, as the Glory of God or his revelation, is necessarily a living and intelligent essence, for God cannot love an unreal and dead abstraction, but only a concrete being, worthy of love, alive, having the force of life received from the all-life-giving Holy Spirit. But since Sophia is the love of the Holy Trinity, its auto-revelation, how can it not love in return? Since Sophia is not a hypostasis but only the revelation of the three hypostases of the Holy Trinity, it has the faculty of hypostasizing itself, of belonging to a hypostasis, of being its manifestation, of giving itself to it. It is a particular hypostatic condition of hypostasizing itself not through its hypostasis, but through another hypostasis, by the gift of self. It is the force of love, but passive, feminine, it is the gift of self in the acceptance of love, but without the possibility of becoming its own active center.[330]

In the end, Bulgakov considered that the synod's attack on his theological opinions itself suffered from a rationalistic approach towards dogma. In the August issue of *The Way*, V. Ilyin makes a reference to Bulgakov's allusion to the rationalism of Metropolitan Anthony. In his review of the Russian bishop's book *The Dogma of Redemption*, published at Sremski Karlovtsy in 1926, Ilyin reproaches the author for understanding the dogmas of the Trinity and of Redemption from a "moral-psychological" point of view and for being, in general, "anti-ontologist, nominalist, and rationalist."[331]

The council of Karlovtsy, in its meeting of August 20–27, 1927, noted the insubordination of Metropolitan Evlogy and, above all, that of the edicts (*ukazi*) of Metropolitan Sergius. On August 26 it decided to proclaim a state of schism, to suspend Metropolitan Evlogy together with his vicars Vladimir and Sergius, and to confide the diocese of Western Europe to Archbishop Seraphim of Finland. Moreover, although breaking relations with Metropolitan Sergius of Moscow after his declaration of allegiance to Soviet authority, the council of Karlovtsy declared that it would remain faithful to his predecessor, Metropolitan Peter of Krutitsky.

In the August 1927 issue of *The Way*, Ivanov reaffirmed the review's support of Metropolitan Evlogy and lamented the attitude of Metropolitan Anthony and of Bishop Benjamin.[332] The latter, in fact, less and less at ease with the modernist intellectuals of the St. Sergius Institute, of the RSCM, and of the Academy, had left his position as inspector of the Institute during the summer to join the ROCOR.

The Political Reactions

In the fall of 1927, the schism of the church and the declaration of loyalty by Metropolitan Sergius of Moscow revived the debate on the monarchy and on nonresistance to the forces of evil of Bolshevism. Each side dug in behind its position. In October 1927, P. Struve, who was considered too soft, left the editorial team of *Renaissance* under pressure from the conservative businessman A. Gukasov. In *The Way*, the authors were divided into two groups: Zenkovsky,[333] N. Lossky,[334] Karpov,[335] and Arseniev,[336] who were more or less favorable towards I. Ilyin, accepted the "White idea" and saw themselves as following the lead of the holy warriors of Orthodoxy but giving priority to love over evil in the struggle with Bolshevism. Karpov, a monarchist student and member of the Academy, criticized the eschatology of Berdyaev in the pages of *The Way* and affirmed that "man cannot know God since God is a pure spirit which is not incarnated in any form," and this justifies political structures.[337] In his response, Berdyaev conceded this point to his young student but drew the conclusion that, by its very nature, "the form is not absolute and cannot express the inner nature of the Divinity."[338] In this sense a democracy is preferable to a monarchy since it is less absolute. But, he added: "We should consciously direct ourselves neither towards a theocracy nor towards a religious monarchy, nor towards a democracy that would be religious and absolute, but towards the Kingdom of God, which cannot be compared with the forms of this world but which can only be attained by a real Christianization of society."[339]

Arseniev, for his part, lamented that Berdyaev did not take into consideration the religious torch of the new chivalry, zealous to serve the motherland, that was emerging among the younger generation of Russians.[340] For Berdyaev, this "romanticism" and its "idealization of the White movement"[341] were the first symptoms of what the psychologist P. Janet calls the loss of "the function of reality."

The debate on the engagement of the young émigrés was not without consequences. On the right, just as on the left, the younger generation felt increasingly suffocated by exile. From 1926 on, above all, some of them sought more expeditious means for putting themselves at the service of the motherland and for redeeming themselves in the eyes of the Russian government. Thus the Eurasians, adopting a policy completely contrary to that of the monarchists, reached out to Bolshevist Russia, seeking to reestablish a contact with the motherland. (The GPU profited from this to infiltrate the ranks of the monarchists through the intermediary of a secret organization, *Trest*.)[342] Combat on "the ideological front" was another form of service by the Eurasians to the motherland. In this context, until 1928 the Eurasians were Berdyaev's best allies against Ilyin and the right-wing nationalists. As of 1926, Paris had become the center of the Eurasian movement. Karsavin, who, since his response to Berdyaev in the January issue of *The Way*, had become the ideologist of the movement, inaugurated his Eurasian seminar on November 1, 1926, first at Paris and then at Clamart. Suvchinsky, along with Mirsky, launched the review *Versts*. In 1926–27, the Eurasians published several works in Paris. In January 1928, V. Ilyin contributed to *The Way* a short review of a book by Karsavin entitled *The Church, the Person, and the State*, which he found "rich and spiritually nourishing."[343] As for the theses of Ivan Ilyin, V. Ilyin, like Karsavin, justified the death penalty but could not accept that it be understood as the will of God.[344] N. Klepinin justified the religious signification of nationalism but rejected any monophysite or pantheistic attitude.[345] Finally, in his article in the January 1927 issue, "The Dangers of an Abstract Christianity and How They Can Be Overcome," Karsavin reminded the reader that the church cannot have a political program.[346]

Although they condemned the idea of an armed counter-revolution and a return to autocracy, the Eurasians were equally opposed to the angelic idealism of the pre-revolutionary generation of Russian intellectuals. Instead they focused on the concrete forms of a future Russian state. Certain contributors to the review had affirmed on more than one occasion that the form of the state was of little importance to Christians. Frank, following in the footsteps of Solovyov, wrote, in 1925 that the state's function is not to create an earthly paradise but to avoid hell.[347] Along the same lines, Berdyaev had declared that Christianity could not have any preference in the political domain: "Everything is decided by the spiritual content, not by the formal signs. We are no longer able to believe in the absolute signification of juridical and political forms."[348]

In three articles published between November 1926 and August 1927, Alekseev attacked this attitude by arguing that the entire Bible, from the Decalogue to the Book of Daniel to the Apocalypse of John, encourages man to revolt against "the Beast" and not to accept a state when it becomes unjust.[349] To support his thesis, the Russian Eurasian historian also invoked

St. Augustine, Luther, and Nil of Sora (Nil Sorsky). For St. Augustine, he claimed, the very idea of a state was impossible without the acknowledgment of the Christian God.[350] Later, the example of the Reformation showed that, from a biblical point of view, democracy was more compatible with Christianity than monarchy.[351] Alekseev then discussed at length the Russian people's philosophy of the state. The article published in the August 1927 issue of *The Way* had been the topic of a Eurasian seminar on January 10, 1927. According to Alekseev, a defining moment in the political history of Russia was the sixteenth-century conflict between Joseph of Volokalamsk, who justified the absolute authority of autocracy on religious grounds, and Nil of Sora, for whom the state, sinful by nature, could not reflect the divine order.[352] The monks of the Trans-Volga, because, in Alekseev's view, they were closer to the New Testament than the Old, had an image of a tsar who would be relatively close to the people and tend not to oppress them. Prince Kurbsky, influenced by these monks, drew out the political consequences of this spirituality. He proposed transforming the Muscovite monarchy into a constitutional state that would leave room for individual freedoms and limit the authority of the tsar by popular councils.[353] Alekseev concluded his vast fresco of the political history of the Russian people by summarizing, in a phrase, the political philosophy of the Eurasians: "The future [of post-Communist Russia] belongs to an Orthodox constitutional state capable of associating a strong power (principle of dictatorship) with the rights of the people (the principle of revolt, *vol'nitsa*) and the service of social truth."[354]

The violence of the attacks of the monarchist circles against the YMCA and modernism explains—in spite of the divergences between Berdyaev and Alekseev—the Eurasian tone of *The Way* up to 1928. Berdyaev congratulated the Eurasian movement for opposing "the reactionary tendencies which want to use the European bourgeoisie to find a solution for Russia . . . they do not link Orthodoxy and the Russian national spirit to a defined type of state."[355]

But once the August schism with the ROCOR had suppressed, at least for the time being, any threat of a right-wing religious nationalism, Berdyaev immediately distanced himself from the left-wing Orthodox nationalism of the Eurasians. In the August 1927 issue he published two articles criticizing the Eurasians. The first, written by Frank, was called "The Church and the World, Grace and the Law." For Frank, the monistic ideas of Karsavin were similar to those of I. Ilyin in not distinguishing sufficiently between the kingdom of the law and the kingdom of grace. This is why Frank insisted on the distinction between the forms of application of the law and its spiritual content.[356] Berdyaev himself went on the offensive in a review of *An Attempt at a Systematic Exposition* published by the Eurasians in 1926.[357] In this book, the Eurasians, in the name of the eschatological concept of the realization of the Kingdom of God on earth, pronounced themselves in favor of federal political structure for the Russian state, for a centralization of the soviets and for their election by their colleagues, and, finally, for the abolition of individual property. This program, typically Bolshevik, was characterized by Berdyaev as a naturalist and optimistic monism.[358] Politically, it would lead to a "utopian stateism." For Berdyaev, an idea which has the state becoming progressively "churched," to the point where it becomes the church, lacked eschatological inspiration and revealed the rupture between the Eurasian generation and the tradition of creative and religious Russian thought.[359]

The Consequences of the Schism (February 1928–November 1929)

On the eve of the great economic "rupture" launched on December 27, 1929—breaking with Lenin's "New Economic Policy," stepping up forced collectivization of farms, and ordering the destruction of kulaks—Stalin tried to get rid of the last forces hostile to him during the period 1928–29 so as to be free to put his projects into practice. In April 1928, he announced to the country the abrogation of "the civil peace."[360] "We have enemies within, we have enemies without, comrades, and we must not forget it." In the course of that summer, fifty-three engineers and technicians of the mining industry of Donbass were publicly accused of sabotage and espionage and subsequently executed. In April 1929, the sixteenth conference of the Bolshevik party approved a second general purge of all those who opposed Stalin, and the Central Committee stripped Bukharin of his posts of editor-in-chief of *Pravda* and president of the Executive Committee of Komintern. A law was promulgated on April 8 concerning the juridical situation of the church. This law intensified the state's control of parishes. On May 22, Article 13 of the Constitution, which assured the liberty of religious cults, was corrected so as to legalize anti-religious propaganda. Henceforth, religious propaganda would be a crime against the state. The clergy and their families were deprived of their civil rights. The church was forbidden to engage in cultural or charitable activities. Hundreds of churches were demolished, and the seven-day week was abolished.[361]

The Development of Opinion

The Malaise of the Younger Generation
The reinforcement of Stalinist power in Russia produced painful vibrations within the emigration community. The arrest, in the month of January, of P. Vaillant-Couturier and J. Doriot, the principal leaders of the French Communist Party, by the government of Raymond Poincaré in retaliation for the provocations of the Communist International within French borders revealed to the émigrés that the "red menace" was drawing near. This deterioration of the political climate especially affected the youth, both Russian and French. At the end of the 1920s, the "generation of Agathon," born just before the Great War, suddenly realized that "everything is always under threat, and one must make the best of the simplest shelter, of the shortest celebration, of as little fire that can be seen, and of the most humble alcohol in one's iron goblet."[362] To be sure, until October 1929, the solidity of Poincaré, the pacifism of French minister Aristide Briand, and the economic prosperity of France reassured public opinion. The Russian emigration community was always relying on some kind of collapse of the Bolshevik regime. All studies show, however, that during the years 1928–29, its members progressively lost hope of returning to their country anytime soon.[363] For some, this led to a decision to integrate themselves definitively into the West; for others, it led to an increase of militancy in the most active organizations within the emigration community. Among the new post-revolution movements formed by the younger generation during the 1920s, there were—alongside the Russian Student Christian Movement and the Eurasian movement—the fascist movement of Young-Russians (*Mladorossy*) of Alexandr Kazem-Bek and the movement of the National-Bolsheviks led by Prince Yuri Shirinsky-Shikhmatov.[364] These movements shared a common voluntarism and strong nationalism, presented a program of social reforms, and claimed to be of Orthodox inspiration.

But the schism of 1927 had left a deep impression on the ecclesial conscience. After the turmoil of the revolution, the church had been an ark of salvation and a place of appeasement, especially for the youth. For many, the realization that the church, too, was threatened by terrestrial contingencies was a terrible disillusionment. The tragic tone of the articles "Progress and Christianity" by Pogodin,[365] "A Sad Paradise" by Zander,[366] and "In the Power of Temptation" by M. Kurdiumov-Kalash[367] manifested that 1928 was a turning point for the youth of the emigration. The last-mentioned article, published in the October 1928 issue of *The Way*, was a biography of Metropolitan Anthony particularly indicative of the psychological trauma among the émigrés following the schism. For the young people born between 1890 and 1910, who lived through the Great War, the revolution, the civil war, famine, exile, solitude, and, as of 1926, poverty, the schism, and eventually unemployment, these years of 1928–29 corresponded to the realization of belonging to an accursed generation or, to use the title of a book written by one of them, a "generation of which nobody took notice."[368]

The Appearance of Two Directions within the Russian Student Christian Movement

The evolution of the RSCM, the St. Sergius Institute, and the Academy of Religious Philosophy reflects this change of perspective. Very few intellectuals understood the depth of the separation that had just taken place between the ancient Constantinian structure of the church and the new one, born of the revolution. All the same, the schism had immediate repercussions. Beginning in 1928–29, two movements, the neo-traditionalists and the neo-modernists, appeared in the ranks of the RSCM. The St. Sergius Institute and the Academy, the two establishments of advanced religious studies, also took different directions. After the schism with the ROCOR, the traditionalists sought to preserve the church from political passions at the price of a certain withdrawal from the world and of a compromise with those who wanted an ecclesial structure for movements involving the laity. In this respect, the creation of a parish on the property of the RSCM in the summer of 1928 and the nomination of Fr. Sergius Chetverikov as chaplain of the RSCM by Metropolitan Evlogy were significant. Fr. Chetverikov was particularly appreciated as a spiritual director by the youth, but his formation at pre-revolutionary academies of theology did not predispose him favorably towards the new fields of research of the Russian religious philosophers. Yet the parish and fraternity founded on September 8, 1929, were able to respond to the accusations of Freemasonry and give the movement, at least formally, the more traditional structure of a confraternity. The members of this fraternity, centered around the parish of The Presentation of the Virgin in the Temple, were spread out all over Europe: Fr. Chetverikov, Liperovsy, Zenkovsky, Zernov, Lagovsky (Paris), V. Rastorguev (London), G. Bobrovsky (Prague), and V. Slepian (Berlin). Among the books recommended for "the good education of the Orthodox Christian" could be found works of Theophan the Recluse and Ignatius Brianchaninov, the *Philokalia*, and the lives of saints—but not a single work of religious philosophy or even any theological work by Bulgakov. The RSCM also published several brochures giving information about its activities during 1928–29. One of them touched on the rapport between the RSCM and the hierarchy.[369] It gave a large place to Metropolitan Anthony, who was treated on the same level as Metropolitan Evlogy, and recalled the blessing he gave to the movement in the autumn of 1926. In *The Way*, this tendency found expression during the 1928–29 period in the articles of priest-monk Ioann (D. A. Shakhovskoy), entitled "Lent" and "Freedom from the World."[370]

After the schism, Metropolitan Evlogy, for his part, tried to restore an image of respectability to the St. Sergius Institute among the émigré community, the majority of whom were monarchists. In the period 1928–29 the applications for admission had fallen off by 50 percent. During the 1928–29 school year, he invited the professors S. Troitsky, a specialist in canon law, and N. Glubokovsky, a New Testament scholar, to teach for a semester at the Institute.[371] These professors had taken positions in favor of the Tikhonian line of Metropolitan Evlogy and had the advantage of being graduates of Russian theological academies. Moreover, in 1928 and 1930, the St. Sergius Institute published the first two issues of its new journal, *Orthodox Thought* (*Pravoslavnaia mysl'*), which presented annually the state of the work being done by the professors of the institute. The second issue was dedicated to the jubilee of Professor Glubokovsky, celebrating his forty years of academic research. On the very first page it pointed out that Glubokovsky was a professor at the Academy of Theology of St. Petersburg, a member in good standing of the Academy of Russian Sciences, and an honorary member of the Academies of Theology of Moscow, Kiev, and Kazan. All the same, the St. Sergius Institute, which depended entirely on the financial help of Protestant and Anglican institutions, had a difficult time in shaking off the Masonic label given to it by the most radically conservative factions. In 1927, Metropolitan Evlogy created a fraternity, named for St. Sergius of Radonezh, whose function was to strengthen the bonds among the students through common prayer, social work, and publication. It published seventeen hundred copies of the Russian-language *Pages from the St. Sergius Institute*. In 1929 it included most of the thirty-eight students at the institute.

The Debate on Morality
The attitudes of the RSCM and the St. Sergius Institute witness to the fact that the rupture between metropolitans Evology and Anthony was, in the eyes of many traditionalists on both sides, of a political nature, which did not necessarily touch the very foundations of their faith. Indeed, Metropolitan Anthony himself used to refer to Khomiakov as one of his masters.[372] On the other hand, many of those in the Evlogian camp were far from being reformers. This theological and spiritual proximity appeared in three articles by S. Troitsky, published in *The Way* between June 1928 and July 1929, on the Orthodox theology of marriage.[373] The question of marriage is particularly symbolic, for if Christ is the head of the church, he is also its Spouse. Relations within the church are of the same nature as those between married couples. Consequently, the theology of marriage as it evolves in dogmatic theology cannot be indifferent to moral theology. The debate on marriage is also symbolic of the role that this topic played in the formation of the modernist Russian conscience. On the occasion of the meetings of religious philosophers held at St. Petersburg between 1901 and 1903, Rozanov had defended the cult of Dionysius and Osiris against the moralism of Russian philosophy and theology. These meetings brought together, for the first time, intellectuals and members of the church under the chairmanship of Metropolitan Sergius (Stragorodsky) and with the participation of Kartashev. Two discussions were dedicated to marriage as a sacrament and a mystery and to the antinomy between spirit and flesh.[374] The moralist school, of which Metropolitan Anthony was one of the founders,[375] believed that concupiscence is reprehensible and needs to be healed by relationships of love. For Rozanov, however, eros was the source of all creation. On April 5, 1903, the Ober-Procurator of the Holy Synod decided to discontinue these gatherings. The excesses of Rozanov, however, remained etched in the memories of the bishops of the synod. For them, theological modernism was synonymous with paganism. On two occasions—June 15, 1926, the eve of the break between Evlogy and

the synod, and August 21, 1927, the eve of the August 26 schism and excommunication—the council of the ROCOR discussed the matrimonial practices of the émigrés, and on both occasions it reaffirmed its condemnation of divorce and reminded the people that the matrimonial bond is indissoluble. Troitsky had also participated in these meetings while a student at the St. Petersburg Academy of Theology and had been shaped by the moralist theology of Metropolitan Anthony and Solovyov's book *The Meaning of Love*. After a period of exile in Siberia, he became professor of canon law at the faculty of theology of the University of Belgrade and, on the strength of this position, was especially appreciated by Metropolitan Anthony. On the very first page of an article published in the June 1928 issue of *The Way*, Troitsky cites Metropolitan Anthony's book *The Moral Significance of the Dogma of the Holy Trinity*.[376] Later, when he treats of the question of marriage after original sin, he gives his definition of concupiscence: "The sinful and unnatural reunion of the practical reason with the sexual life."[377] This definition could not satisfy the Russian intellectuals who, like Vysheslavtsev, had understood the depth of Rozanov's criticism. But the hour had not yet come to measure the profound depth of the schism that had just separated the diocese of the Russian Church in Western Europe from the ROCOR. Vysheslavtsev would not answer Troitsky in the pages of *The Way* until 1933.

The Beginning of a New Era

The Formation of the Neo-Modernist Group
Among the group of modernist authors who published in *The Way*, some—unlike Zenkovsky, Metropolitan Evlogy, and Troitsky—interpreted the schism with the ROCOR as the beginning of a new era, during which there would finally be a place within the church for reflection, for a shift of thought that would concentrate on the problems of the contemporary world and integrate the acquisitions of modernity. Such an interpretation of events had repercussions within the RSCM, in the review, and at the Academy of Religious Philosophy, but it provoked a clear-cut rupture with the monarchist intellectuals and contributed to their distancing themselves from all these institutions.

On November 13, 1927, Skobtsova, V. Ilyin, and Fedotov created a circle of Russian studies at the RSCM, whose purpose was to rediscover the great Russian intellectual tradition of the nineteenth century. The following year, Berdyaev inaugurated an RSCM seminar on Christianity and Marxism. The annual RSCM congress, on September 10–16, 1928, held at the château of Savez near Amiens, was the occasion for the two sides to clarify the movement's projects. It was only at the cost of passionate discussions that the movement resolved to break out of circles limited to biblical exegesis and dedicate itself more fully to social work. The following year, however, the fact that two well-known personalities of the monarchist right, General E. Miller and K. Zaitsev, were invited to the local congress of the RSCM, held at Clermont in Argonne on June 15–30, 1929, was indicative of the conservative orientation that the movement was taking. At the seventh general congress, held at Boissy, near Paris, on September 16–29, 1929, the conservative tendency headed by Zenkovsky won out definitively over that of Berdyaev. Berdyaev, three years after the congress of Bierville, resigned from the council that he had created in order to open the movement to the exterior world.

In spite of Stalin's crackdown, which could have provoked a vehement anti-Soviet reaction, *The Way* maintained its Eurasian and Tikhonian perspective during the years 1928–29. After the schism, Berdyaev adopted a political perspective opposed to that taken by the St. Sergius Institute and the RSCM. He tried to break off once and for all any links the review might have with the monarchists of the synod. In his eyes, the monarchist and conservative threat was even more troubling than the communist menace. The monarchist contributors, such as G. Trubetskoy, either ceased to publish in the journal or, like Zenkovsky, abandoned the political terrain and concentrated on religious issues. N. S. Timashev published two articles in *The Way*, in April 1928 and in July 1929, on the new relationships between church and state in the Soviet Union. In the 1928 article, Timashev had no illusions about respect for the law by a despotic state: "The organisms of the Cheka—now the GPU—can arrest, deport or execute whomever they want."[378] In addition, Timashev criticized the partiality of Soviet law, which did not recognize the church's juridical rights but authorized teaching materialism in schools. Yet his 1929 commentary on the new law was relatively neutral because he thought it was still too early to pass judgment. In spite of the severity of the law, the author pointed out that the struggle which began on December 27, 1921, between the state and the church concerning church properties seemed to have ended in favor of the church.[379] The Evlogian perspective of the *The Way* was not, therefore, questioned directly until 1929. This was evidenced by a series of four articles by I. Stratonov in 1928–29 enumerating the different schisms that had divided the Russian Church between 1917 and 1929 and, in addition, showing all the troubling similarities between the Living Church and the ROCOR.[380]

The Polemic with P. Struve
In the issue of October 1928, Berdyaev began his article entitled "Obscurantism" with these words: "There are reasons to think that we are entering into an era of obscurantism."[381] For the Russian philosopher, obscurantism is not just about Stalin: "It flourishes in the soviet and communist milieus just as it does in milieus of the emigration. In Italy the young Fascists have burned the library of Benedetto Croce, the greatest philosopher in Italy."[382] As for the emigration community, Berdyaev was aiming especially at the partisans of the synod and, more specifically, Count G. P. Grabbe.[383] These individuals, he wrote, are obsessed by Freemasonry—about which they know next to nothing—and hunt down heresies because they are afraid that their group, which they value above all else, will collapse. V. Ilyin, in his article "Christ and Israel," also criticized the conservatives and their journal, *The Two-Headed Eagle*.[384] Citing Martin Buber and invoking chapters 9–11 of the Letter of Paul to the Romans, he condemned all forms of anti-Semitism.[385] Hassidism and Kabbalism are for him "the natural shining forth of the New Testament within the Old."[386] This theme was also taken up by E. Belenson, a Russian émigré of Jewish origin who had converted to Christianity, in an article published in the October issue and entitled "The Hidden Christ of the Jews."[387]

The virulent article of Berdyaev attacking the obscurantist monarchists did not go unanswered. P. Struve, who had withdrawn to Serbia after his political defeat in 1926 and his dismissal from *Renaissance* in 1927, published an article dated February 2, 1929, in his new daily paper *Russia and Slavism* (*Rossiia i slavianstvo*). This article, scathing and unsigned, was entitled "Berdyaev and the Berdyaevists."[388] The author rejected Berdyaev's lumping together of Bolsheviks and monarchists, denounced the intellectual laziness of the editor of *The Way*, and reaffirmed the need to combat the forces of evil.

Berdyaev replied in May 1929. Significantly, this was the last polemical article he wrote in his column "A Philosopher's Journal." Berdyaev aligned himself resolutely against those who envisaged the emigration community as a contra-revolutionary military camp.[389] After 1927, dialogue was no longer possible between the two camps within the émigré community. In this matter, the schism had disastrous repercussions. What could have united Berdyaev and his opponent, namely, the religious foundations of their political engagement, had been cut off at the root. Along with the primacy he gave to fraternity over hierarchy, Berdyaev differed from the Christian monarchist milieus by the eschatological form of his thought, which was opposed to any type of absolutizing of forms or of norms. For Berdyaev, objectivization is the beginning of the fall. Paralyzed by these forms believed to be eternal, the mind tends to separate ends and means and winds up, little by little, justifying the means by the ends.[390] "What counts," Berdyaev stated, "are not the goals or the ideology but the sources and spiritual foundations of one's life through which the 'way' [*put'*] is determined."[391]

Every time that Berdyaev let himself get caught up in polemics and judged his opponent's arguments as unworthy—even sacrilegious—he always appealed to the tradition of Russian religious thought. In general, this tradition functioned as a defense for the generation of the intellectuals of *The Way* against all forms of secular heresies and was a determining factor in their political, social, and religious behavior. Berdyaev wrote: "Those who think that the ancient empire, the capitalistic industry, the Roman concept of propriety, are authentic Orthodox Christian principles of life are also surely among those who have forgotten that we have had Khomiakov and the Slavophiles, Bukharev, Dostoevsky, Solovyov, Fedorov, and many other seekers of God's truth."[392] The ambiguity in Berdyaev's thought up to 1929 consisted in his maintaining that political action can only be the work of the Spirit and not of the Word. That is why he was unable to formulate any political program and why he identified politics with power, the source of corruption. For the Russian philosopher, the state is, by nature, the result of original sin and should be supported only as a necessary evil. It is in this sense that Berdyaev understood the words of Christ: "Render unto Caesar what is Caesar's."[393] This is also why the only road for the salvation of Russia that Berdyaev felt he could authorize for the émigré community was "to vanquish the temptation of power in one's self."[394] Only then could the outpouring of the Spirit begin.

The Academy, St. Sergius Institute, and the Russian Student Christian Movement Drift Apart
Berdyaev had given a series of lectures at the St. Sergius Institute in 1926.[395] After 1927 he could no longer do this. At the Academy of Religious Philosophy, on the other hand, he affirmed his ecumenical connection loudly and clearly and took pleasure in inaugurating, in January 1928, a series of conferences on "non-Christian spiritual movements," such as Buddhism, Tolstoyism, Theosophy, and Freemasonry. Bulgakov, for his part, was obliged to separate his classes into two kinds. At the St. Sergius Institute he avoided any reference to sophiology; in his seminar on dogmatic theology for the Academy, which convened outside St. Sergius,[396] he could continue his research on sophiology. V. Ilyin, who considered himself a disciple of Bulgakov, reviewed his teacher's book on the angels[397] in the February 1929 issue of *The Way* and set it in contrast to "the knowledge-hating obscurantism of the theological babblings of bureaucratic functionaries."[398] Nor was the Academy afraid of committing itself politically. On April 15, 1929, N. Klepinin began a course on the topic "The Social Problems of the Contemporary World and of Christianity," in which he treated, successively, the themes of neo-capitalism, liberalism, the new forms that the workers' movements were taking in the Anglo-Saxon countries, and the social work of Western Christians. Vysheslavtsev, whose Eurasian commitment was well known, gave a course called "Socialism and Christianity" at the Academy.

Finally, Berdyaev, who was sensitive to the increasing distress among the younger members of the émigré community, began a course on "The Meaning of Life," on November 2, 1928, which ran through the 1928–29 school year. He preceded this course by a public lecture on October 28, whose theme was "Illusions and Realities in the Psychology of the Youth of the Emigration." Previously, in August 1928, Fedotov, in his article "Carmen Saeculare," noted that the separation between the generations in Europe during the 1920s, following the Great War, had never been so profound, and was reminiscent of the opposition in Russia between the generation of the idealists of the 1840s and the nihilists of the 1860s. That same year, Zinaida Gippius gave a lecture on "Russian Literature in Exile" to the *Green Lamp* society, the literary and philosophical circle founded at Passy in 1926 by her husband Dimitrii Merezhkovsky, in which she also pointed out the generational change.[399] Berdyaev's lecture, published in

The Way in December 1928, was thus in the larger context of the accession to responsibilities of the generation born just before the war and the revolution. For him, a sentiment of fear, associated with a need for realism, characterized the psychology of a great many of the younger generation of the émigré community.[400] The more conservative young people of the emigration were intoxicated by all sorts of illusions. They yearned to restore the past, such as the sacred monarchy, or a static and perfect Orthodoxy. But the Kingdom of God, Berdyaev stated, should not be sought either in the past or in the future or in the present moment, but only in eternity. "Only the tension towards eternity, the will turned towards the realization of the eternal, frees people from illusions and phantasms and transforms them into authentic realists."[401] The neurosis provoked by the catastrophe of the revolution explained, according to Berdyaev, the quest for authority, the unrealizable desire to forget, the terror when faced with creative action, and the denunciation of heresies. As for the leftists—and here Berdyaev addresses himself to the Eurasians—the young people only considered the social question from a tactical point of view, as an inevitable concession to the new Soviet order.[402] On the right—and here Berdyaev is thinking this time of the RSCM—the youth forgot that the social progress inherited from the nineteenth century, such as women's emancipation, and the loosening of Puritanism (which the RSCM accomplished by the introduction of mixed summer camps of men and women), were the work of Russian revolutionaries. It was true that the puritanical pedagogy elaborated by Zenkovsky, after his return from the United States, within the Office of Religious Pedagogy at St. Sergius, was particularly hostile "to the corrupting influence of contemporary dances,"[403] such as the Charleston and the Upa-Upa. Berdyaev concluded his article with a warning to the RSCM:

> The sentiment of terror in the face of the revolution can hamper the meeting of the emigration's youth with the young Russia born of the revolution.... The correct spiritual attitude consists in vanquishing the fear of the world, the fear of people, the fear of evil, by the fear of God—and this fear was abolished by absolute love. The sentiment of fear prevents creative activity. People talk of a Christian Student Movement. But a movement can only be creative.... A movement which is not creative can only be mortal and inert; it has within itself that

ennui which is not going to accomplish anything by being pious. . . . Within the Church there are enormous creative tasks—theological and gnostic, apologetic, cultural and social. It is not a question of a movement of churches but a movement in the Church. Many think that there cannot be movement in the Church, that there can only be movement towards the Church, and within the Church is an icy and immobile repose. This is a harmful illusion which should be surpassed. The themes of the Church and of the nation should be taught to young souls. In that respect the Russian Student Christian Movement sees more clearly than the preceding generation. But while affirming the absolute primacy of the spiritual life as an eternal principle, it is necessary, from within this spiritual life, to transform history, society, culture, and thought. It is only then that there will be a truly vital movement. . . . In this way the creative spiritual movement will be faithful to the best traditions of the Russian religious thought of the nineteenth century.[404]

This article had the effect of a bomb. The year 1929 was marked by a polemic between Berdyaev[405] and Kartashev,[406] on the one hand, and Zenkovsky[407] on the other, in the columns of the RSCM *Messenger*. Berdyaev's words, however, were still merely a warning. Until 1930, the conflict between the two tendencies, traditionalist and modernist, of the generation of the authors of the review had not yet appeared in the review itself.[408] The fact of belonging to the diocese of Metropolitan Evlogy took precedence over any differences.

Mounting Tensions

All the same, in the imprecations of Berdyaev during October 1928 against the seekers of heresies, one can discern, between the lines, a warning to the young generation of radical Christian intellectuals. These included Vladimir Lossky, who considered sophiology a gnostic heresy, Florovsky, who published an article in *The Way* in 1929 condemning Origenism and the *apokatastasis* doctrine dear to Bulgakov,[409] and Koyré, whose book on the heresies of Boehme was roundly criticized by Berdyaev in September 1929. And, above all, during the 1927–29 period, there appeared within the modernist movement itself a tension between Fedotov and Berdyaev.

Fedotov, a Eurasian historian, unlike his older colleague, did not consider authority to be relative and transitory in form. As of 1927, when the schism with the ROCOR became evident, he timidly raised his voice from within the Evlogian camp to question the "conservative" attitude of loyalty towards the mother church.[410] This debate was at the origin of the division of the Eurasian movement into two rival camps in 1928, and then of the separation of the Evlogian church from that of Moscow in 1931. This debate entered the pages of *The Way* in the form of a reflection by intellectuals on the sources of holiness.

The Debate on the Archetypes of Holiness
In August 1927, Alekseev, the Eurasian jurist, taking a stance against Berdyaev, noted that the form of the state cannot be a matter of indifference to a Christian. Along the same lines, for Fedotov, the opposition to the synod was primarily structural, whereas for Berdyaev, it was a question of fundamentals. In an article published in April 1927 against the monarchists Markov and Talberg, Fedotov had taken a clear position in favor of Metropolitan Evlogy. But he already distinguished the fundamental question of the canonical status of the Russian Church in the emigration from the polemic whirling around monarchism and religious conservatism: "Do we want to preserve a close link with the Russian Patriarchal Church or should we consider ourselves as an autocephalous Church?"[411] The declaration of Metropolitan Sergius and the exigency of loyalty demanded of the clergy and, consequently, of the faithful of the emigration reinforced the uneasiness of the Russian historian. The Eurasian friends of Fedotov, such as G. Trubetskoy,[412] based themselves on the Mongol period of Russian history and the example of Prince Ivan Kalita to prove that true holiness, as St. Paul recommends, involves respecting the throne. N. Klepinin, in his 1926 work *The Holy, Just, and Great Prince Alexander Nevsky*, wrote that the submission of the Russian prince to the Golden Horde was "his greatest and most difficult work, even if it was an occasion of sin for many, for it allowed Russia to arise from its ruins and to return to its authentic historical path."[413] In August 1927, V. Ilyin published a review in which he congratulated his Eurasian colleague for having so well demonstrated that the Tartar yoke was a salutary protection for the Orthodox Church against the enemy from the West.[414]

On the other hand, in March 1927, the young historian Igor Smolitsch, a former student of the Academy of Religious Philosophy in Berlin, reacted by plunging himself into the study of holiness in Russia. He wrote an article on St. Nil of Sora—which was not published in *The Way* until November 1929—in which he insisted upon the contemplative and mystical dimension of the Trans-Volga monks. Fedotov also decided to conduct some research and within a few months came out with a book entitled *Saint Philip, Metropolitan of Moscow*. In the preface to the book, published by YMCA Press in 1928, he wrote: "We want to convince ourselves that the Church has preserved its independence, its integrity of moral judgment in this difficult task which is the service of the State."[415] St. Philip, whose spirituality was very close to that of Nil of Sora, was venerated by the Russian Church for having refused, on March 22, 1565, to give his blessing to the actions of Ivan the Terrible. Fedotov shows that the metropolitan did not reproach the Tsar for having gone astray dogmatically—for the Tsar scrupulously respected dogma—but for having made a mockery of the social dimension of Christianity through his persecutions. According to his hagiographers and the testimony of Prince Kurbsky,[416] the metropolitan died a martyr, suffocated by a legate of the Tsar on December 23, 1568. For Fedotov, this event is of primary importance in Russian history because it is indicative of the ultimate confrontation between two models of holiness—the Old Testament model and the New Testament model—and it announces an evangelical understanding of the state in Russian history. He wrote: "St. Philip became a martyr not in the name of his faith in Christ, for the Tsar Ivan Vasilevich considered himself the defender of this faith, but in the name of the truth of Christ which the Tsar was defaming.... The Orthodox Kingdom without the truth is only a cadaver whose soul has departed." "There where the body is, the eagles gather."[417]

The Division of the Eurasian Movement
By June 1928 there were already two groups among the Eurasians. On the right, among those opposing Metropolitan Sergius of Moscow, were Alekseev, Fedotov, Bitsilli, Savitsky, and Florovsky. Florovsky had published an article favorable to the Eurasian movement in the January 1926 issue of *The Way*. Two years later, however, he wrote an article for *Contemporary Annals* (*Sovremennye zapiski*) entitled "The Eurasian Temptation," in which he distanced himself from the movement.[418] On the left, among the partisans of loyalty to Soviet power, were L. Karsavin, N. Klepinin, S. Efron (1893–1941), D. Mirsky (1890–1939), P. Suvchinsky, and N. Trubetskoy. The latter did not share the views of Karsavin but felt himself closer to

Suvchinsky than to Savitsky. As he wrote to Suvchinsky on March 10, 1928, "I no longer support Eurasianism, but, through weakness, I remain faithful to my friendship with you."[419]

In 1928, Ilyin and Kurdiumov still sought some kind of equilibrium between these two currents. V. Ilyin, in his review of Fedotov's book in the April 1928 issue of *The Way*, showed some hesitation. Although he recognized the historian's talent, he considered that the idea of the primacy of the holy martyr over the Orthodox Tsar is only valid "in a certain context."[420] Two months later, Kurdiumov made these words of Ilyin more explicit in an article entitled "The Holiness of St. Sergius of Radonezh and the Affair of Metropolitan Sergius." Contradicting Fedotov's thesis, she argued that the great historical difference between Ivan the Terrible and Stalin is that the former believed in his dogmas, whereas the latter is ready to betray Marx and Lenin. Moreover, "Metropolitan Philip was able to speak to Ivan the Terrible of his responsibilities before the Tsar of tsars, of life after death, simply because the tsar believed in eternal life and the final judgment."[421] To be sure, the author admitted, St. Sergius of Radonezh blessed Dmitri Donskoy in 1380 in his battles against the Horde. But that was only because the saint sensed "a will to fight and to vanquish" on the part of the people.[422] But, according to Kurdiumov, the time of rebellion had not yet arrived in Russia because its people were still too hostile to the church. The promise of loyalty made by Metropolitan Sergius "in the face of Soviet power" was thus inevitable. Moreover, it was the only way to stop the disguised persecutions of the government, which, until then, had used the counter-revolution argument to justify its illegal persecutions. Kurdiumov concluded by recalling that "the strength of the Orthodox Church in Russia does not consist in a political opposition to the Soviet order, but in a spiritual opposition of Christian ideals and teachings to the primitive and materialist dogmatism of Marxism and Communism."[423]

The Journal Separates Itself from the Eurasians
This dispute about the archetypes of Russian holiness was followed by a debate over the eschatology of Fedorov, which resulted in the final separation of the two currents in the Eurasian party. As of 1927 there was a renewal of interest among the Eurasians in the ideas of Fedorov, due, in large part, to the publication of his works in Harbin. Fedorov's ideas had elements that attracted the "post-revolutionaries" of the review and Soviet intellectuals of religious inspiration. His anthropological dynamism, his

call for a religious organization and regulation of work, and his perpetual quest for the salutary "work" of the resurrection were all particularly welcome to Eurasians, who were hostile to both "abstraction" and individualism. In this sense, Berdyaev, influenced by the ideas of N. A. Setnitsky, recognized "that there is a formal resemblance between Marx and Fedorov. The separation of the theoretical reason from the practical reason is the original sin of [modern] thought."[424] This formal resemblance was the last hope for the Russian intellectuals of the emigration to find a common language with the intellectuals of Moscow. Along the same lines, this reconciliation between Marx and Fedorov was, for the Eurasian intellectuals, the last attempt at a synthesis before the movement splintered.

In August 1928 a certain unity could still be found among the articles of Florovsky, Fedotov, and Karsavin in *The Way*. All three, with Eurasian emphases, insisted on the creative role of the person and rejected Western secularization, the vector of individualism. In his portrait of Metropolitan Philaret of Moscow, Florovsky insisted on the astonishing dynamism of this Russian theologian and on the fact that, without opposing the Byzantine "symphony," he always underlined the "difference in nature" between the state and the church.[425] Karsavin, in his "Prolegomena for a Study of Personhood," rejected that thesis of individualism according to which the only concrete personal being is the individual person. "The Personal unity of the Tri-hypostatic Divinity shows, on the contrary, the symphonic personal reality of being and thus affirms the formation of the individual person itself as pluri-unity."[426] In "Carmen Saeculare," Fedotov studied the development of contemporary culture and discerned a new dynamism of the person united to the collectivity within European societies.[427] For him, this had political consequences. Fedotov announced "the end of the parliamentary system" and the advent of a new "social monarchy." The old perspective of an atomized individual freedom should make room for the formation of "powerful elementary cells" capable of limiting the power of the state. Fedotov wrote:

> The State, as the coming together of associations, as the center of gravity of complex material and spiritual forces, cannot be despotic. Under these conditions, the dictatorship of the party or of the leaders can be a passage not towards autocracy but towards a republic of the "soviet" type or of "guilds" hierarchically organized and directed by an elected bureau of technical specialists and organizers.[428]

While recognizing that Fedorov's theory on the overcoming of death through a creative, collective effort of the human race was "the most audacious in the history of Christianity," Berdyaev had indicated, in June 1928, that Fedorov's refusal to recognize the irrational freedom of evil in the world had led him to a rationalistic and naturalistic optimism. For Berdyaev, Fedorov exaggerated the power of technology and did not understand the mystical signification of death. That was, doubtlessly, another link between Marx and Fedorov. This optimism and naturalism of the Eurasians, which Berdyaev had already pointed out the previous year,[429] became—after contact with Setnitsky and the rediscovery of Fedorov— the basis of the openly Bolshevik engagement of the left-wing Eurasians in the fall of 1928. In November, Karsavin addressed himself to J. L. Piatakov of the Soviet Embassy in Paris to offer his services. On November 24, 1928, along with Efron and Suvchinsky, he launched the pro-Bolshevik weekly *Eurasia* (*Evraziia*) and left France to teach history at the University of Kaunas in Lithuania, while continuing to write articles for *Eurasia* until June 1929. From the first issue, D. Sviatopolk-Mirsky, the theorist of the Eurasian project of ideocracy, referred to the "precious essay" of A. Gornostaev on Fedorov and Tolstoy.[430] In the third issue, the first "Letters from Russia" appear, in which the anonymous author—probably Setnitsky[431]— declared himself in favor of a synthesis between Marx and Fedorov.[432] Even if it was true that Fedorov would have been hostile to the revolution, wrote Setnitsky, he would have been just as hostile to capitalism, and today he probably would have sought to regulate and coordinate the ocean of energies released since 1917. On December 31, N. Trubetskoy wrote an open letter to the weekly, which was published on January 5, 1929, in which he challenged this illegitimate marriage between Marx and Fedorov and broke away from Suvchinsky. In the following issue, the editorial staff replied by expressing its regrets for such a step but maintaining its position. The editors underlined the mytho-logical dimension of their commitment:

> For many of us, "The Philosophy of the Common Task" has been the key which has enabled us to discover the true content of our own philosophy.... To be sure, we are not Fedorovians, but we consider the central idea of Fedorov just, as an inspired progression towards the myth. We do, however, consider him as our master. Of all the Russian thinkers, he is the one closest to us. This is why we are particularly

interested in his ideas, in the same way as we consider Marx as the Western thinker who best suits us, even if such a declaration would have astonished most Eurasianists two or three years ago. What attracts us most in Marx—and this applies equally to Fedorov—is an orientation towards action, towards a philosophy which is active and not limited to the sole sphere of speculation.[433]

The right-wing Eurasians reacted by organizing a conference-debate on February 10, 1929, at the salon of the Guimet Museum in Paris with Berdyaev, Vysheslavtsev, Alekseev, Fedotov, and Shirinski-Shakhmatov. V. Ilyin, probably to atone for having delayed in choosing sides, presented a virulent paper entitled "Karl Marx, Fedorov, and Eurasianism." In it he condemned the weekly's Bolshevik propaganda and, after the conference, published, along with Savitsky and Alekseev, a brochure entitled "Concerning the Journal *Eurasia* (The Journal *Eurasia* Is Not a Eurasian Publication),"[434] which he sent to all the subscribers of the journal. Finally, in May 1929, under his rubric "A Philosopher's Journal," Berdyaev definitively crossed out the Eurasianist movement and its "abstract" and "illusory" project of ideocracy.[435]

Conclusions on the Schism

The schism of 1927 within the Russian Church of the emigration had very important consequences. In particular, among the intellectuals who contributed to *The Way*, it produced a new, collective awareness of their own identity. The modernist unanimity, born of the enthusiastic period of the council of 1917 and based, on the one hand, on the sense of their all belonging to the tradition of Khomiakov, Dostoevsky, and Fedorov, and, on the other hand, their common recognition of the fact of the revolution, gave way, near the end of the 1920s, to a heavy tension among the authors of the review—between the neo-traditionalists and the neo-modernists, between Eurasianists of the left and Eurasianists of the right, and between partisans of the Russian Church and detractors of Metropolitan Sergius.

Apart from the political events in the Soviet Union, it became apparent that the memories of reciprocal wounds inflicted on the Russian intellectuals and the representatives of the official church during the pre-revolutionary period played an important role in the double separation of the Synod of the Russian Church Outside Russia from both Metropolitan Sergius and Metropolitan Evlogy. But these kinds of arguments are not sufficient to explain the dispute between metropolitans Anthony and Evlogy, who, as it was well known, were old friends and shared common monarchic political principles.

As has been seen in the dispute between P. Struve and Berdyaev on the problem of evil, or in the debate among the Eurasians on the archetypes of holiness, the mytho-logical dimension of the schism is central to a correct understanding of events. In fact, in their political, social, and jurisdictional engagements, the Russian intellectuals and hierarchs of the emigration were obeying a common logic centered on the myth of the church, but were differentiating themselves in the function of this myth and diverging in their interpretations of it.

Thus, there is a paradigmatic link between the successive ecclesiological engagements of the intellectuals in the life of the *polis* and the diverging evolution of their thinking, which, as we have seen, is of a mytho-logical nature. This double, parallel evolution can be understood by considering the movements of an awareness of collective identity among the intellectuals of the review as decisive. The similar phenomenon of generational awareness—from modernism to the shattering of the paradigm—in the relationships of the Russian intellectuals with their Western colleagues confirms this analysis. It is fitting, then, to study the history of these relationships. And that brings up another myth central to the evolution of the Russian intellectual conscience—the myth of the West.

THE ECUMENICAL COMMITMENT: THE AFFIRMATION OF THE EAST IN RELATION TO THE WEST

The exile of approximately a million Russians after the revolution, one of the first great waves of emigration in the twentieth century, contributed to upsetting the traditional structural poles of East and West, both for the Europeans and, especially, for the Russians themselves. The resulting changes in traditional representations varied depending on the models of integration of the foreigners in the different host countries. In France, as Tzvetan Todorov wrote, if the universalist logic of the Declaration of the Rights of the Person and the Citizen was capable of reconciling both religious or ethnic affiliation and citizenship, based on the fact of belonging to the same nation, this logic hit a bump when it was a question of foreigners, "because the foreigner is precisely one who is not part of the nation."[436] But, from 1920 to 1930 the number of foreigners in France tripled, reaching about three million by 1930. After the shock of the Great War, this situation produced a surge of xenophobia, especially towards the Russian émigrés, whose status as stateless persons facilitated the propagation of all sorts of myths.[437] Moreover, political events in Russia—"a knife in the back" for some, "a great light in the East" for others—only served to rekindle what Georges Nivat called "the Russian myth." In the period between the two wars, the massive arrival of Russians in France was at the origin—above all in Paris—of a Russian way of life made up of evenings in the "cabarets of the boyars" and fantastic recitals about the "Russian soul," which had already been characterized in France in the 1880s as "nonchalant and mystic."[438] Ralph Schor remarks that of the 243 novels, plays, and short stories about foreigners that appeared in France during the period between the two world wars, 55 were about Russians—twice as many as for Germans, British, and Americans.[439] Most often these were tales full of clichés about the Russian people, Cossacks caught up in the torment of exile, or Russian princes who had become taxi drivers. Zoé Oldenbourg described the bitterness felt by the Russian émigrés in the face of this romantic enthusiasm, which usually went hand in hand with a profound ignorance of Russian civilization.[440]

For some Russian and French intellectuals, however, the meeting between East and West could only be realized in the depths of a Christian universalism. Indeed, for the modernist generation that emerged from the Silver Age, the cultural frontiers of Europe in 1925 were merely the historical realization of the symbolic frontiers of Christianity and, in a larger sense, the horizontal projection of the division of the world into two spiritual hemispheres. This vision of the world was founded on the Christian conception of the church whose Nicene-Constantinopolitan symbol of faith or creed proclaims that it is "one, holy, catholic and apostolic." For Metropolitan Philaret as well as for Khomiakov, the dogmatic frontiers of Christianity could not "rise up to heaven," since the unity of Christians is in the image of the Trinitarian unity, the archetype of the Kingdom of God upon earth. Solovyov, in his *Story of the Antichrist*, draws out, in an eschatological context, the consequence of this vertical and spiritual representation of the Kingdom, by making the unity of the Christian churches possible at the end of history (yet still within it). Berdyaev, in his book on Dostoevsky, shows that the figure of the Grand Inquisitor in *The Brothers Karamazov* was, for the novelist, not a symbol of the bishop of Rome but of the Antichrist.[441]

The desire of the Russian intellectuals who contributed to *The Way* to incarnate the Kingdom of God on earth through a common ecumenical engagement is in continuity with this modernist interpretation. Here, the road narrowed. Very few Russian émigrés had any knowledge—even partial—of Western Christianity. On the other side, during the 1920s, French intellectuals who, like Abel Miroglio in the world of Protestantism and Jacques Maritain among the Catholics, manifested any interest in Russian religious thought were rare.[442] Ecumenical dialogue among the laity was a recent phenomenon. Those who interested themselves in the nineteenth-century movement of the Holy Alliance in favor of the unity of the churches—such as Abbé Vladimir Guettée, Prince Ivan Gagarin, and, above all, Vladimir Solovyov—envisaged this in terms of personal conversion. Finally, and most important, the evolution of ideas in favor of a rereading of traditional ecclesiology was experienced in a very different manner by the authors of *The Way*, compared to the generation that came from the philosophical circles of the Silver Age and the council of 1917–18. The very fact of participating, in 1925, in a review known for its links with the YMCA testified to the ecumenical engagement of the ensemble of modernists at *The Way*. All the same, their engagement led only progressively to a true dialogue between West and East, depending on the flux of events and the personal evolution of each author.

The commitment of Berdyaev, Trubetskoy, or Florovsky evolved differently and was a function of the modifications of their ecclesiological opinions, of the ecclesial context of the Russian emigration, and, finally, of the attitude of the Western churches and intellectuals. Before the schism with the synod of the Russian Church Outside Russia became evident at the beginning of 1927, and when the Eurasian movement was in its glory, the attitude of the contributors to *The Way* was reserved, careful not to antagonize the bishops of Karlovtsy, and "contained" by the ecclesiology of the church fathers. While some saw above all the openness and grandeur of the West and chose, as did Solovyov, to receive the representatives of "Pope Peter II and Doctor Paulus" without reserve, others, more skeptical of this openness and grandeur, preferred to follow the example of Khomiakov and demand that the Western theologians justify their dogmatic innovations. But the schism of 1927, the diverging attitudes of the Western churches, the integration of one or another in varying degrees into French cultural life—all this together with the evolution of the ecclesiological opinions of the authors of *The Way* would modify the internal equilibrium of the review. During the 1930s, the disciples of Solovyov progressively embarked on roads radically different in their search for the unity of West and East, and this would eventually make their participation in the same journal impossible.

Apart from the external causes mentioned above, we must not overlook the internal logic, symbolic in nature, of this diverging movement in the ecumenical commitment of the intellectuals of the review during the years 1925–29. The common identity of modernist Russian thought was constituted in relationship to the religious and cultural realities implanted in their consciousness by Rome, Geneva, and London. During the 1920s, their first contacts with theologians from these cities, symbolic of Catholicism, Protestantism, and Anglicanism, led the intellectuals of the review to think of themselves as the heirs of the second and third Rome: Constantinople and Moscow, archetypes of the East in Russian religious thought. Berdyaev, Trubetskoy, and Florovsky entered into dialogue with Catholic, Protestant, and Anglican theologians, while situating themselves exclusively as representatives of Eastern Christianity. This was what founded the homogeneity of the review during the 1920s. But if different understandings of ecumenical dialogue appeared among the Russian intellectuals, this was due to the progressive erosion of the myths about the West in the course of contact with daily reality and by the growing awareness on the part of some of them of the profound unity between Eastern and Western Christians. In a 1925 editorial of *The Way* one can find this double relationship of the Other and the Same regarding the West—a position made up of messianism and the sentiment of belonging to a common body, but carrying within itself the seeds of future divergence:

> The Russians can remain faithful to their own kind of religion, affirm their faith, not be afraid to openly recognize its universal significance, and, at the same time, proceeding from the depths of what is typical in their spirituality and their faith, be able to go forth to meet Western

Christians, to collaborate with them and establish strong fraternal relations between Christians of all confessions. The East and the West cannot remain closed in upon themselves and isolated. That should not be understood in the sense of an abstract and sterile interconfessionalism, nor of a horizontal universalism, but as the construction of a great spiritual unity descending vertically into the depths of each confession. Western Europe no longer holds the monopoly of culture—it is worn out. But the East and, above all, the Russian East, takes on a greater worldwide significance than ever before.[443]

The Relationship with Rome

Tense Relations

The Politics of the Holy See and the Newfound Desire for Unity
According to the historian Etienne Fouilloux, the basic policy of Catholicism towards a dissident East during the interwar period was that defined by Leo XIII in 1890—"unionism."[444] This policy sought to highlight those thoroughly Eastern communities that had returned to the bosom of the Roman Church. It was revitalized by the upheavals in the international panorama. With the First World War, the Caesaropapism that had protected state Orthodoxy faded away. Benedict XV and then Pius XI saw this as "an unexpected opportunity to penetrate a world which had been off-limits."[445] On October 15, 1917, the document *Motu proprio Orientalis catholici* announced the creation of the Eastern Pontifical Institute, which had the mission of forming highly trained specialists for the mission to the East. But it was also necessary to neutralize or limit the Anglo-Protestant influence, which was proposing a rival model of East-West encounters through the newly formed ecumenical movement. On November 5, 1920, the Holy Office published a "letter to all the Ordinaries of the world," accusing the YMCA of Freemasonry.[446] Five years later, a pro-Russia commission was created within the new curial Congregation Pro Ecclesia Orientali. This commission was under the presidency of the French Jesuit Michel d'Herbigny (1880–1957), who was a specialist in the work of Solovyov. His policy was to vigorously sustain the schism of the Living Church, to install, more or less clandestinely, a hierarchy and a seminary, and to form future native apostles, religious or lay people, émigrés or Latins, who

had passed to the Eastern Rite.[447] The open door policy of the Roman Church towards the Churches of the East did not only incite plans of conquest among Western Christians. After the slaughters of the Great War, there was a particularly ardent desire for reconciliation among the general population. But the attitude of Michel d'Herbigny deeply offended the Orthodox and provoked a polemic in *The Way* in 1925–26.

The Myth of the Latin West in the Review
In 1923, the Eurasians published an anthology entitled *La Russie et le latinisme* in which they compared "Bolshevism and Latinism, The International and the Vatican"[448] in their common hostility towards Russia. If, for Catholics, the separation between the Roman and the Eastern Church was reduced (improperly) to a question of rites and liturgical prescriptions, for the Eurasians—at least during the first years of the emigration—Catholicism was identified with "Latinism."[449] This explains why the fear of a Vatican plot—and, from the opposite direction, admiration (typical of Westernizing Russian intellectuals) of the Vatican—were such active elements in the review.

In the September 1925 issue of *The Way*, G. Trubetskoy responded to the issues through a review of the November 1924 and the February and May 1925 issues of the publication *Orientalia Christiana*, directed by d'Herbigny. While he lamented that d'Herbigny failed to appreciate the heroism of the persecuted Russian Church and sometimes offered charitable help to the Russian refugees "for propaganda reasons,"[450] Trubetskoy defended the French bishop for his disinterested aid to the Russian people during the famine of 1922.[451] He concluded by speaking in favor of a reunion of the churches based on the Pauline principle of love and not on the principle of a systematic criticism or of a necessarily superficial conversion.

The younger generation, which had known the revolution and then the civil war, was not ready to place such confidence in the Vatican or in the West. In the following issue of *The Way*, the Eurasians reacted by publishing a collective letter signed by Suvchinsky, Karsavin, Florovsky, Savitsky, N. Trubetskoy, and V. Ilyin. Its authors reaffirmed that they "maintain the analogy between the Latins and the Bolsheviks."[452] It was significant that G. Trubetskoy, in his reply to the letter, no longer tried to distinguish between Latinism and Catholicism. On the other hand, he firmly condemned "Uniatism" because this doctrine contradicted the very principle of the separation of the church into Eastern and Western, which was historical and cultural rather than dogmatic. Thus he limited himself to simply showing that it is abusive to identify Latinism with Bolshevism.[453] This defense of Catholicism could not lead to a true, in-depth coming together of Catholicism and Orthodoxy because it was incapable of dissipating the fears of the Eurasians and overestimated the openness of the Catholic episcopate. This was made clear by the ecumenical experience attempted in Belgium by Cardinal Désiré Mercier (1851–1926). Cardinal Mercier, by his vigorous and unselfish action on behalf of the Russian émigrés, embodied the surge of generosity on the part of Western Christians towards the persecuted Russian Church. Along with Lazarist Fernand Portal and the Anglo-Catholic Lord Halifax, Cardinal Mercier had also taken the initiative of organizing private but authorized meetings between French-speaking Catholics and High Church Anglicans. After the fifth such meeting, however, Pius XI gave the order to cease all dialogue.[454]

Berdyaev, who had long-standing sympathies with the "secret" France of Barbey d'Aurevilly and Léon Bloy,[455] adopted a stance different from that of his monarchist and Eurasianist friends. In a more antinomic way, he clearly and openly separated himself from Latinism as well as from Roman universalism in order to better accentuate Catholic spirituality. Berdyaev's attitude towards Roman Catholicism was not without prejudices. In April 1926 he wrote: "Orthodoxy, unlike Catholicism, understands universality vertically, not horizontally. Catholic conscience cherishes, above all, the exterior unity of the universal organization of the Church—to the point that it seems to it that the Church is perishing when this exterior unity is shaken."[456]

By excluding the Latin Vatican from Catholicism, Berdyaev retained only a certain vision of Catholicism. The first issue of *The Way* was supposed to present the spiritual nature of Catholic France through a criticism of official Thomist doctrine and a defense of Léon Bloy. Stanislas Fumet, who, like Berdyaev, was influenced by Bloy,[457] was married to a Russian and had been seeking to meet Berdyaev since December 1924. Berdyaev invited him to write an article for *The Way*, which Berdyaev translated from French into Russian. In this article, "The Pilgrim of the Holy Sepulcher," Fumet drew up a list of "secret France," the underground spiritual France, which included Joan of Arc, Mélanie Calvat (the visionary of La Salette), Joseph de Maistre, Jules Barbey d'Aurévilly, Ernest Hello (1828–1885), and Charles Baudelaire. For Fumet, the originality of Bloy within this intellectual tradition was to have formulated the unutterable. In *L'âme de Napoleon,* Bloy wrote, "every person freely accomplishes a necessary act."[458] Such a conception of Providence was far from being shared by the historian H. Delacroix and the French positivists described by Zenkovsky in the January 1926 issue of *The Way*.[459] This is why Zenkovsky, like Berdyaev, preferred St. Thérèse of Lisieux (St. Thérèse of the Child Jesus) (1873–1897), beatified by the Catholic Church in 1923, as the image of French spiritual life.[460]

In this first issue of *The Way*, Berdyaev accompanied the presentation of spiritual life in France with a similar presentation of religious life in Germany by Arseniev, in which the author likewise insisted on the spiritual dimension rather than the "juridical"[461] aspect of Catholicism. Arseniev dedicated a large part of his article to the liturgical renewal undertaken by Romano Guardini and underlined the need for a Christian realism on the part of the Youth Movement (*Jugendbewegung*) led by the German theologian.[462] The almanac *Das Siegel (ein Jahrbuch des Katholischen Lebens)* appeared in 1925 under the editorship of Fr. Thomas Michels of the Benedictine Abby of Maria Laach near Berlin and belonged to the same movement. Arseniev cites approvingly Fr. Michels's words on the significance of this meeting. For the German priest, the West, corrupted by individualism, is in need of the East to help it recover the dynamism of its constructive genius through a return to the sources of contemplation and mysticism.[463]

This criticism of Latinism by Berdyaev, Zenkovsky, and Arseniev corresponded to a static rather than a dynamic representation of the East and the West. In his review of d'Herbigny's account of a trip to Moscow,[464] Berdyaev, irritated by the cultivated Latin's condescending view of a barbaric country, replied icily to the French cleric.

> Fr. d'Herbigny is a typical representative of Latin culture, of a Latin way of thinking, of a certain Latin rationalism. One senses in him a self-satisfied narrowness and the pride of the Latin civilization. This type of spirituality in the Catholic world is at antipodes with the Russian spiritual mode. German Catholics, especially the Benedictines, are closer to the Russians and understand them better.[465]

In July and November 1926, Arseniev published two more long articles in *The Way* concerning the tragic sources—namely, Oriental—of Greek religion.[466] In the same spirit, Berdyaev, in the November 1926 issue, reviewed

Louis Rougier's book *Celse ou le conflit de la civilisation antique et du christianisme primitif.* This book on Celsus had appeared in 1926 in a new collection dedicated to "Masters of Anti-Christian Thought," which had been founded at the publishing house Éditions du Siècle by the columnist of the anti-patriotic and anti-modernist magazine *Mercure de France.* In his review, the Russian philosopher opposed the Oriental and Dionysian vision of mystical Greece to the Latin and Apollinarian vision. "The sentiment which Christianity inspires in Rougier," Berdyaev stated, "is identical to that which Dostoevsky describes in certain Catholics imbued with the Latin spirit." For Berdyaev, there is little difference between intellectual humanists such as Rougier, Valéry, and Charles Maurras, and the intellectual elite of the Catholic right represented in France by Henri Massis, Maritain, and Etienne Gilson, since they all share the same love for "form and measure" and the same fear and panic when confronted with "the chaos and irrationality which can come forth from the East."[467]

The opposition that Berdyaev proposed between Latin-pagan culture and an underground Catholic spirituality suffered from a certain Manichaeism and was contradicted by the fact that Catholics of Russian origin were often hostile to Slavic eschatologism. In a review in the May 1926 issue of *Orientalia Christiana* of Berdyaev's article "The Kingdom of God and the Kingdom of Caesar," Fr. Ivan Kologrivov, a Russian of the Belgian emigration who had entered the Jesuit order, lamented that the symbolism of the Russian philosopher made it difficult for any stability within the intimate life of the church.[468] On the other hand, not all Latins were necessarily hostile to an authentic openness of Catholicism towards the East. Along these lines, in 1925 Dom Lambert Beaudouin, the father of the second liturgical movement, founded a Benedictine priory of the Eastern rite at Amay-sur-Meuse in Belgium.[469] The monks of this community dedicated themselves to the union of the Catholic and Orthodox Churches in the same spirit as the Abbey of Maria Laach and published a high-quality journal whose Greek title, *Irénikon* (from the liturgy's prayer for "peaceful times"), symbolized its spirit of openness.

The Dialogue between Berdyaev and Maritain
In spite of—or because of—the clichés and misunderstandings on both sides of the Roman question, the dialogue between the two great Christian intellectuals, Berdyaev and Jacques Maritain, which began in 1925

and continued until 1948, is especially representative of the meeting of the Latin and the Byzantine-Russian worlds.[470] Maritain was converted to Christianity by Bloy. Quite naturally, he met Berdyaev through Bloy's widow, at the beginning of 1925. Maritain, whose wife was born in Russia, and Berdyaev, who was married to a Catholic, hit it off immediately. In 1926, Maritain offered to publish, in French, Berdyaev's article "The Destiny of Culture"[471] as part of the collection Roseau d'Or, which he directed with Massis, Fumet, and Lefebvre in collaboration with the Plon publishing house. On November 6, 1926, Maritain informed Berdyaev of his interest in publishing a French translation of the Russian philosopher's historical-sophiological *New Middle Age: Reflections on the Destinies of Russia and of Europe*, which had been published in Berlin in 1924. Maritain wrote: "Your book has such a great importance that I would like it to be presented in French in its strongest and most exhilarating form."[472] It was translated by Fumet's wife and appeared in February 1927.[473] The book was an immediate success among intellectuals such as the sociologist Lucien Lévy-Bruhl,[474] the historian Emile Dermenghem,[475] the leader of the group Décades de Pontigny, Paul Desjardins,[476] and the Reformed Church pastor A. Lecerf,[477] among others.

In spite of his affinity with the "religious realism, objectivism, and ontologism" of Thomism, Berdyaev severely criticized the thinking of the French philosopher in the pages of *The Way*, beginning with an article in the September 1925 issue. In 1919, Maritain, with the help of the Dominican priest Reginald Garrigou-Lagrange, had founded his Thomistic Study Circles in reaction to the modernism of the generation of the "fathers" E. Le Roy (1870–1954) and Maurice Blondel (1861–1949). In his review of the books of Maritain[478] and of Fr. Garrigou-Lagrange,[479] Berdyaev depicts the neo-Thomist movement as a renewal of classical Catholicism. He goes on to say that "this classical Catholicism is, in its spirit, mainly Latin."[480] In opposition to classical Latinism, which excludes any meeting of the natural with the supernatural, Berdyaev preferred to continue to defend the irrationalism of modernist Catholics and the Platonism of Russian religious thinkers. In their name he writes:

> Aristotle and Saint Thomas Aquinas are strangers to us. We are Platonists by our tradition and for us there is no such chasm between the natural and the supernatural. We believe that the more the world,

mankind, and every authentic being is rooted in God, the more the divine energies penetrate the natural order and that only sin and evil can be totally outside of the Divinity. Since the coming of Christ, mankind and the world have changed, the Creator and his creation have been reunited.[481]

These criticisms did not, however, exclude a dialogue between the two intellectuals. In January 1926, Berdyaev published an article that Maritain wrote especially for the Russian readers of the review *The Way*, entitled "Metaphysics and Mysticism." Here Maritain explained the Thomistic understanding of being as both knowable and unattainable and his theory of knowledge, founded on a radical distinction between reason and faith. Maritain ended with a profession of faith in the universal church.

Even if people who have been baptized and have not remained faithful to their calling separate themselves from the Church ... I could never be capable of despising the sufferings and expectations of those who feel that all is lost and all is possible. What do they await? This is what it is important to know: the Antichrist or the second coming of Christ? We, for our part, await the resurrection of the dead and the life of the world to come. We know what we await and we know that what we await surpasses all possibility. There is a difference between those who do not know what to hope for and those who know that what they hope for is inaccessible.[482]

Maritain's approach, in spite of his supra-rational faith in the unity of Christians, suffered from a static vision of the limits of the church. In this sense, his perspective is hardly different from that of Berdyaev, who denied all possibility of a real and visible unity of the churches within history. In April 1926, Berdyaev wrote: "I'm not part of those who are hostile to Catholicism, and, deep down, I hope that, even if the Churches cannot reunite—that can only be a deed of the Holy Spirit—there will be more encounters, more mutual discoveries, more friendship between the Christians of East and West."[483]

Berdyaev may have shared with the Thomists their ontological conception of the world and a spiritual vision of ecumenism, but the Russian philosopher felt closer, intellectually and politically, to the modernist

Christians spearheaded by Maurice Blondel and Fr. Lucien Laberthonnière (1860–1932). These two authors, who were hostile to the movement Action Française, were the principal targets of attacks by the Thomist theologians. Blondel, in his book *L'Action*,[484] published in 1893, tried to reconcile reason and faith, immanence and the supernatural, by the "synthesis of volition, knowledge, and being."[485] Laberthonnière was placed on the Catholic index in 1907, then again in 1913 by Pope Pius X, along with the entire collection of *Annales de Philosophie Chrétienne*, which featured contributions by Loisy, Fr. Rousselot, S.J., and Bergson. In 1922, the followers of Blondel counterattacked against "The Manifesto of the Intellect" by Massis and Ghéon with a pamphlet entitled "The Intellect on Trial." Two years later they founded a new review, *Les Cahiers de la Nouvelle Journée*, directed by Paul Archambault. Berdyaev, who had come into contact with the modernist Catholic movement during his stay in France in 1907, asked the movement to present the thought of Blondel and Laberthonnière to the Russian readers of *The Way*. Archambault's article, "The Philosophy of Action," appeared in the July 1926 issue. Here, the French intellectual tried, above all, to overcome misunderstandings concerning the alleged immanence in the thought of Blondel and Laberthonnière by showing that their philosophy of action overcomes the apparent conflict between intellectualism and pragmatism.

The Common Battle

The encounters between Berdyaev and Catholic intellectuals, both Thomists and modernists, were decisive in the ecumenical advances made by Catholics, Protestants, and Orthodox. In spite of its limits, Berdyaev's position was far in advance of those taken by Florovsky or Trubetskoy. By their openness and informal character, these encounters made possible a limited but authentic dialogue between French and Russian religious thinkers during the interwar period.

The First Ecumenical Meetings of the Academy
In particular, Catholic and Protestant theologians in France were able to formally renew a dialogue for the first time since the Edict of Nantes (1685). Because of their unofficial character, little is known of these meetings of interconfessional theological discussions, which, from 1926 to 1928,

brought together the best of the Parisian Christian intelligentsia, thanks to the initiative of the Academy of Religious Philosophy. In November 1925, Berdyaev informed Suzanne de Dietrich (1891–1981) of his project. De Dietrich was from a family of Alsatian Protestant industrialists. After studies at Lausanne, she had been named Secretary of the Protestant Federation of France (FPF), and then, in 1920, a member of the Executive Committee of the World Student Christian Federation. Through Miroglio, she quickly became friends with Paul Evdokimov and then with Berdyaev. For a time she lodged at the Circle of Parisian Russian students at the headquarters of the FPF. She came into contact with Pastor Marc Boegner (1881–1970), the head of the Reformed Church of France, who was himself close to Fr. Lucién Laberthonnière, whom he had met during the Great War.[486] After delicate negotiations, the first meeting took place on January 4, 1926, at the headquarters of the Russian Academy, 10 Boulevard du Montparnasse, with the participation of Maritain, Fr. Louis (Lev) Gillet, Fr. Laberthonnière, Fr. Augustin Jakubiziak, and Stanislas Fumet for the Catholics; Pastor Philippe Boegner, the Calvinist pastor Lecerf, the Lutheran professor A. Yundt, and Professor Monnier for the Protestants; and, for the Orthodox, Vysheslavtsev, Kartashev, and G. Trubetskoy, along with selected students of the Academy, among whom were Paul Evdokimov and Evgraph Kovalevsky. Later, other theologians participated in these discussion meetings—among them Frs. Battifol, Bopin, Simeterre, and Durantel for the Catholics, Wilfred Monod, Pierre Maury, and Suzanne de Dietrich for the Protestants, and Zander, Karsavin, Bulgakov, M. Lot-Borodin, Zenkovsky, and Zernov for the Orthodox.[487] The first meeting opened with a paper by Berdyaev on the topic "The Nature of Faith." Kovalevsky, one of the members of the Brotherhood of St. Photius, noted that starting with the first meeting, Fr. Gillet was in agreement with the Calvinist Lecerf, and the so-called modernist, Fr. Laberthonnière, was in agreement with the Lutheran Yundt.[488] In the following meetings the opening papers were as follows: Father L. Gillet, "Analogy in the Knowledge of God," with a debate on the relationship between faith and reason; Pastor Lecerf, "Religious Knowledge and the Notion of Dogma," Professor Yundt, "Freedom and Grace from a Lutheran Viewpoint," Karsavin, "The Divinity and Humanity of Jesus Christ and the Problem of Freedom," Maritain, "Created Nature and Its Relationships with God," Florovsky, "The Idea of Creation in Christian Philosophy," Professor Monnier, "The Two Ways of

Understanding Sacrifice," Pastor Lecerf, "Calvin's Idea of the Church," Professor Yundt, "Revelation and Salvation," and Monod, "The Contingency of the Laws of Grace in the Christian Church."[489] These meetings, which were mentioned in *The Way*, were an immediate success. In his memoirs, Berdyaev wrote: "From the start, the enthusiasm and interest which these meetings provoked was very intense. They were too crowded and ran the risk of becoming too 'fashionable.' Each confession was discovering a new world, and yet it was the same Christian world."[490]

From the Myth of the Latin Church to the Myth of the Conquering Church
As a sign of the changing times, in January 1927, a split appeared within the Eurasianist movement concerning their relationship to the magisterium of Rome. Karsavin and Ilyin reaffirm their rejection of Caesaropapism[491] and Uniatism.[492] On the other hand, Fedotov preferred to focus on Péguy, "the soldier, the discoverer of Joan of Arc, the socialist," as well as the French Catholic renewal of the end of the nineteenth century—from the *talas* (churchgoers) of L'Ecole Normale Supérieure to the *Cahiers de la Quinzaine*. He wrote a review of Plon's 1926 publication *Notre cher Péguy* by the Tharaud brothers. Fedotov was especially sensitive to the fact that Péguy, a supporter of Dreyfus and an anti-Thomist, maintained his spirit of independence, refused any form of peaceful compromise, and dared not receive the sacraments, which were considered an outward guarantee of grace.[493] He cites Péguy's words: "God loves France because of its love for freedom and it refuses to submit, for grace and liberty are inseparable."[494]

Through the intermediary of Fr. Lev Gillet, who had become one of the editors of *Irénikon*, Fedotov also discovered the Eastern rite Benedictine community of Amay-sur-Meuse. The sincere thirst for Christian unity on the part of the Benedictine monks disturbed the certitudes of the Eurasian historian. In the April 1927 issue of *The Way*, he published a review of the 1925 and 1926 issues of *Irénikon*. He applauded the condemnation of "The Living Church" by the editorial board of *Irénikon* and its kind reviews of the books published by the YMCA, as well as of *The Way*. The openness of the monks of Amay, to which Zernov testified after a stay at the Benedictine monastery in December 1927,[495] led Fedotov to a more realistic understanding of the Eurasian dichotomy between a Christian East and a decadent West. He drew a distinction between the Latin West of the epoch of the undivided church and the Latin West after the schism.

In an article published in the August 1927 issue, "Saint Genevieve and Saint Simeon the Stylite," Fedotov embraced the image of one church, East and West, breathing together with two lungs. The Russian hagiographer, in reading the life of St. Genevieve of Paris (422–499), discovered that this saint had been providentially put into contact with St. Simeon the Stylite (390–459). Genevieve, the protector of Paris, had learned, through traveling merchants, that "there was a man in Syria by the name of Simeon who had been living on the top of a column for forty years, who was posing many questions to the merchants about Genevieve and who wanted her to pray for him."[496] This small detail in the life of the saint, which Merovingian hagiography had retained, was, for Fedotov, a sign of the belief of the saint's contemporaries in the unity of holiness in the church extending beyond the seas and into far-off countries. Fedotov deepened the symbolic significance of this contact between East and West. Forcing things a bit, he opposed the warrior spirituality, active and charitable, of St. Genevieve of Paris to the contemplative spirituality, ascetical and mystical, of St. Simeon the Stylite. But for Fedotov, both types of holiness have their place in the church:

> [Sts. Simeon and Genevieve] can be considered as orthodox icons of the Eastern and Western Churches. To be sure, there is a very profound and complex mysticism in the Catholic Church and, in principle, Mary was always placed higher than Martha. In the same way Simeon, in the harshness of his asceticism, is characteristic only of the distant Christian East, that of Syria and Egypt, and not of Russian Orthodoxy. Nonetheless, compared to the East, Catholicism will always appear, above all, as an ecclesial form of moral activity turned towards the conquest and reconstruction of the world. Likewise, the Russian Church will not disown Saint Simeon but it will temper and humanize his prayerful asceticism.[497]

All the same, Fedotov attributed the better part to the Christian East, by designating St. Simeon as the heir of Mary. According to the Gospel narrative, Christ does, in fact, give priority to the contemplative spirit of Mary over the dynamism of Martha. Fedotov thus remained faithful to his Eurasian convictions. This evolution of the representations of the East and the West, together with the spiritual discovery of Catholicism and

Protestantism, however, had important consequences for Eurasian ideology as well as for the ecumenical dialogue itself. In the conclusion of his article, Fedotov pointed out that, because of their divisions, the East and the West would succumb—the one to the temptations of monophysite Islam and the other to the Arian heresy propagated by the rationalism of the Enlightenment.[498] Thus, the Russian historian put the ecumenical dialogue in a new perspective. It was no longer a question of returning to a golden age of perfect and unshakeable unity, but rather one of showing the openness and imagination necessary to feed the flame of Christian unity, which often flickers but never goes out.[499]

In spite of his ecumenical openness, Fedotov's Eurasianism could not be judged satisfactory by Berdyaev's standards nor by those of his wife, Lydia Judifevna, who was responsible for the final proofs of the articles submitted to the review. Alongside Fedotov's article, the review published pieces by Reinhold von Walter on the Catholic mystic, Angelus Silesius,[500] and by Julia Sazonova on Western contemplative holiness. The latter, a literary critic for *Contemporary Annals*, had converted to Catholicism while an émigré. In opposing the mysticism of St. Marie-Angelique (1893–1919), of St. Thérèse of Lisieux, and of St. Theophane Venard (d. 1861) to a "militant Catholicism based on political doctrines," Sazonova returned to the Khomiakovian vision of Berdyaev, which separates the invisible church, the first fruits of the Kingdom of God, from the visible church, which belongs to the kingdom of Caesar. Such a conception of the church, pushed to its extreme, led her to represent France as torn between its mystical and spiritual past and its technical and decadent modernity. Compared to Constantinople and Moscow, Paris, in Sazonova's eyes, seems divided between its "Sacre Coeur" and its "Eiffel Tower."[501]

The Common Rejection of Action Française
The warning addressed to Action Française on August 27, 1926, by Cardinal Andrieu, archbishop of Bordeaux, and confirmed on September 5 by the authority of Pius XI was, for most of the authors of *The Way*, unexpected support in their opposition to the monarchists. This courageous decision, confirmed on March 8, 1927, by a decree of the Holy Office that barred obstinate members of the league from the sacraments, inaugurated in France—according to the expression of René Rémond—a "new Pentecost" of the Catholic Church.[502]

The condemnation of Action Française by Pius XI did not go unnoticed by the staff of the journal, either. In the January 1927 issue, the journal published the declarations of two Catholic prelates *in extenso*. These texts were followed by a review written by an anonymous Polish Catholic of the latest book of Merezhkovsky, *The Mystery of the Three*. This Russian symbolist writer, who moved to Paris in 1926 after a long stay in Poland, once again entered into the polemic on resistance to the powers of evil by favoring an armed counter-revolution—a position that could only deepen his alienation from the group of *The Way*. These political opinions were intimately linked to his anti-dogmatic and anti-ecclesial symbolism. He considered Russia "the face of the East turned towards the West" and preached a virulent anti-Catholicism. In his latest work, he had condemned Vatican politics in Russia and affirmed that the blood of martyrs elevated the Russian Orthodox Church above all other churches.[503] In his review of Merezhkovsky's work, the Polish author pointed out that the Roman Church, unlike the Russian Church, knew how to maintain its independence from political power. For him, the Russian Church would do well to learn from the Roman organizational genius. Although the editorial staff of *The Way* judged it necessary to note its disagreement with "certain ideas" of the author, the very fact that this article was published was a sign of the increasing estrangement of the two branches of Russian symbolism as a result of their contact with the spiritual reality of the West. The review did not publish a single article of Merezhkovsky.

In the August 1927 issue, Berdyaev reviewed a book by Massis, *Défense de l'Occident*, that had just been published in the collection Roseau d'Or.[504] While the Russian authors of *The Way*, after their split with the monarchist synod of Karlovtsy, were searching to rediscover the Christian foundations of the West, the decision of the Vatican against Action Française similarly provoked a debate in France over the grandeurs and limitations of the Latin West.[505] During the period 1925–29, two major literary debates took place in the religious intellectual circles of Paris—one about the limits of reason, the other about the defense of the West against the charms of the East. As historian Robert Brasillach put it, "Henri Massis had just published his famous book, but we were also reading translations of Tagore and *Bouddha vivant* by Paul Morand, and Shestov, the Russian Jew, presented us with an odd sort of Pascal."[506] It is interesting to note that Russian thinkers played a decisive role in these two debates, which were deeply intertwined. Thus, in the debate concerning the limits of the West, Maritain and Massis both justified their reaction to the condemnation of Action Française by referring to Russian religious thought.[507]

In his book, Massis defended the rationalist Latin West against the mysticism of other peoples of Eastern Europe, especially against "the Russian people who are returning to their Asian origins," and vigorously condemned the pacifism of Romain Rolland. To support his position he cited *The Way*, the St. Sergius Institute, and the Eurasianist Russian émigré authors and wrote that Berdyaev and Bulgakov preferred "Genghis Khan to Saint Vladimir."[508] Berdyaev's reply in *The Way* was stinging. In his article "The Accusation of the West," he defended the people in revolt in Asia and the anti-colonialism of Gandhi and accused Massis of stifling Europe by maintaining the animosity between France and Germany. In the tradition of Dostoevsky's discourse on Pushkin, Berdyaev wrote:

> Dostoevsky would have found the confirmation of his "Legend of the Grand Inquisitor" in Maurras and Massis. I myself feel like defending Catholicism against Massis. Catholicism is larger and more complex than Latin civilization, with its rationalism, its juridicism, its formalism and classical spirit. . . . One also feels like defending European culture against Massis. European culture is not just Latin culture—it is Romano-Germanic, and in France itself there are not just Latin elements. . . . There is also the Anglo-Saxon world. But for Massis, Europe ends at the Rhine. For Massis, Russia is still Asia and it terrifies him, Germany has Asia for itself and this terrifies him as much as do Russia and India. . . . The errors of judgment that Massis commits regarding Orthodoxy are especially serious and harmful. He doesn't have the least idea of what it is—as is also the case for most foreigners.[509]

Berdyaev was not without prejudices himself in this domain. In his opposition to Latin Rome, he held a geographic and static vision of the East and the West. He affirmed that Christianity, like all other religions, is "of Eastern origin."[510] It is in the name of this spiritual primacy of the East that Berdyaev vigorously defends the Dionysian, eschatological, and prophetic spirit of the Greeks, Jews, and Russians against the pathos of the finalized, completed forms of the West. He was thus very close to Karsavin and Fedotov when he wrote:

We Russians are more linked to Greece than the Latins are. Through the Orthodox Church, Greek patristics and the Platonism which is part of our very being, we belong to the Greek tradition.... and Orthodoxy is a form of Christianity much more faithful to the sources of Christian revelation and much less deformed by the rationalism and juridicalism proper to the Roman spirit.[511]

Such distinctions were judged "extremely necessary"[512] by French Catholic Russophiles.

One of the active centers of Catholicism between the two wars was at L'Ecole Normale Supérieure. It was formed around the group known as "*tala*," which had been founded at the beginning of the century by two Lazarist teachers, M. Portal (1855–1926) and M. Pouget (1847–1933), who were impassioned believers in ecumenism and whose thought was nourished by the Greek Fathers. Their young students Marcel Legaut and Robert Garric were instilled by these two with a sense of the necessity of unity between West and East. After the completion of their studies, they continued to be the driving force behind La Revue des Jeunes, which was under the direction of Fr. Sertillanges. In 1919, Garric had founded the first of his "Social Teams" (*Équipes sociales*) urging class reconciliation. In 1927 he published, in La Revue des Jeunes, a long article about Massis in which he cited Berdyaev.[513] For his part, Archambault replied to Massis by publishing, that same year, the results of two symposia. The first had the theme "the Russian Soul," with articles by Berdyaev, Bulgakov, Miroglio, and Zdziechowsky; the other was devoted to the "Great Debate among French Catholics—Testimonies on Action Française," with articles by J. Vialatoux and G. Bidault.

Finally, in July 1927, Maritain published *Primauté du spirituel* and then, in December, at the request of Pius XI, another volume.[514] In the first of these books, Maritain devoted an entire chapter to Russian Orthodoxy. He lamented that the East underestimates the significance of the Logos and that this is especially the case in Russian religious thought, which has mixed together theology, mysticism, and philosophy without distinguishing among them. But Maritain believed that "the best and most urgent way for Orthodox and Catholics to get to know one another is to know and love one another in the holiest representations of their respective spiritualities."[515] Most important, he made Berdyaev's distinction his own. "The spirit of Orthodoxy," he wrote, "is not the same thing as the Russian spirit. The spirit of Catholicism is not the same thing as the Latin spirit."[516] This comparison allowed Maritain to justify his acceptance of the condemnation of Rome. In *Primauté du spirituel*, he distinguished two ancient Christian spiritual traditions in France—that of St. Louis and St. Joan of Arc, and that of Philip le Bel and Louis XIV. Berdyaev was not unaware of these modifications of historical representations. In his review of these two books by Maritain, as well as of the special issue the same year of the journal *Cahiers de la Nouvelle Journée* dedicated to this issue "Un grand débat catholique et français," which treated of Action Française, Berdyaev wrote:

> The conception of history is linked to a mytho-urgy. Bainville understands the history of France through his monarchist and nationalist myth. He does not see the revolution and its significance in the destiny of France. For others, it is the myth of the revolution which dominates and makes the revolution the central event in the destiny of France—and perhaps of the whole world. Spengler has not recognized the place of Christianity in history, whereas for us it is the force that determines all of history.[517]

Together with Laberthonnière, Berdyaev again defended the "social, republican and democratic Catholicism of Marc Sangnier"[518] against the atheistic and anti-Semite positivism of Charles Maurras, but he did not share the "moralist" vision of left-leaning Catholic modernists. Inversely, the Russian philosopher applauded when Maritain accorded primacy to the spiritual but regretted that this gesture was made in the name of order and of submission to the principle of papal infallibility. Elsewhere, he took issue with Maritain by reaffirming the dependence of philosophical and theological knowledge on spiritual experience.

In any case, the disagreement between Berdyaev and the French intellectuals was based on different philosophical and theological conceptions of freedom. In spite of some lingering odors of Slavophilism specific to the symbolistic authors, the East-West opposition, as Berdyaev envisaged it after his polemic with monarchism, took on a dimension more realistic and, consequently, more universal.[519] In 1926, Berdyaev had written a book on the Slavophile intellectual Leontiev. In 1927, he wrote a more philosophical book, *Spirit and Freedom* (*Filosofiia svobodnoga dukha*), in which the eschatological element takes on a new importance when compared with his 1923 essay, *The Meaning of History* (*Smysl' istorii*). If this evolution is compared to that of Fedotov and Bulgakov, it can be surmised that the living encounter between East and West favored a shift in the Russian modernist conscience from the position of Leontiev towards that of Fedotov, that is, from one concept of eschatology to another, more realistic one.

This new realism, coupled with the demonstration of the Roman Church's power over Action Française,[520] encouraged Berdyaev to become more deeply involved in the ecumenical movement. From April 30 to May 6, he participated, along with Zernov, in a congress organized by the World Student Christian Federation, not far from the Benedictine Abbey of Seckau in Austria. For the first time in a congress of the Federation, there were students belonging to three different Christian confessions and representing ten different European countries. The account of this meeting, which Berdyaev published in *The Way* in August 1927, offered a more optimistic vision of ecumenism than his 1926 account:

> There was the feeling that the time to unite had come, that the time of discords in the Christian world was over. The Protestants are ceasing to live on their protesting and tending towards a greater ecclesial plenitude.... And the Catholic world is becoming less closed in on itself, less exclusive and intolerant, even if this isn't always easy for Catholics. The Orthodox world is also coming out of its isolation as regards Western Christianity.... Only the Holy Spirit can reunite the Churches. But people must prepare the terrain. The division has not appeared in the Church but in sinful humanity, and the fault is shared by all the torn-apart components of the Christian world.[521]

Mortalium animos

A new intervention of the Holy See, however, shook up the points of reference for ecumenical engagement among the authors of *The Way*. On January 6, 1928, Pius XI published an encyclical, *Mortalium animos*, in which he condemned the ecumenical movement and prohibited Catholics from participating in any interconfessional encounter. The pontifical condemnation was especially cruel for those in the West who were in quest of universality[522] and provoked the decision of numerous Catholics, among them some Benedictines, to convert to the Church of the East. But the encyclical did not slow down the ecumenical movement. It only reinforced the hostility of Catholic Slavophiles and the majority of the Russian émigrés towards Rome. Within the Russian modernist generation, the effect of the pontifical condemnation was to strengthen the identification of the contributors of *The Way* with Eastern Christianity. All the same, according to whether the archetype of the East was Moscow or Constantinople, the attitude towards the West varied. The heirs of the Third Rome, Berdyaev, Fedotov, and Bulgakov, put the accent on the possibility, here and now, of bypassing the dogmatic divisions through eschatology. On the other hand, the eschatology of Karsavin, Florovsky, and Ilyin, the apologists of the newborn neo-patristic movement, was characterized by a return in time to the Byzantine epoch, to the times of an undivided Christianity.

The Reaction of the Neo-Byzantine Current
Among the latter, Florovsky was the most virulent during the 1928–29 period in his condemnation of Latinism, papalism, and Catholic proselytism.[523] He published three successive book reviews: in June 1928 he reviewed the edition of *The Orthodox Confession* of Petro Moghila by the Jesuit Fathers of the Pontifical Oriental Institute, in August 1928 the *Theologia Dogmatica Christianorum Orientalum Ab Ecclesia Catholica Dissidentium* by the Assumptionist Fr. Martin Jugie, and finally, in May 1929, the publication by the Jesuit Fr. Irenée Hausherr of an unpublished text of St. Simeon the New Theologian (949–1022), accompanied by his biography written by a disciple, Nicetas Stetathos. The Russian theologian reacted against the distinction made in "uniate" seminaries between Orthodox Christians, separated from the church by error or in good faith, and the Oriental church, considered as an "institutio pseudo-ecclesiastica."[524] According to Florovsky, this distinction corresponds to the "Latin" dualism of soul and body.

In a kind of paradox, Florovsky himself was not exempt from a similar historical dualism. Florovsky discovered in the emigration, with some anxiety, that the divisions among Christians were ontological in depth and not simply cultural, and he wanted to purify the memory of the Christian conscience from the impurity of its historical body. For him, the West had not yet become aware of its "interior schism." This is why he located a separation in the history of Catholicism between its "Orthodox past" and its "non-Orthodox" modernity (which is, alas, very ancient).[525] His desire to radically separate Russian Orthodoxy from any Latin influences, which in his eyes were channels of heresy, actually led him to neglect the dynamic dimension of the Orthodox ecclesial conscience. He denied the contemporary authority of *The Orthodox Confession* of Petro Moghila, Metropolitan of Kiev (1633–46), because of his Latin spirit, but he did not explain how this confession could be approved by the Greek patriarchs of the seventeenth century. Like Kitezh, the city taken over by the Old Believers, Byzantium became for Florovsky the only pure foundation of Christian ecclesial consciousness. In his article on St. Simeon the New Theologian, Florovsky used Spengler's concept of pseudomorphosis to characterize the development—or rather the absence of development and decadence— of Orthodox theology. According to him, the simple hesychastic monk was given the title of "new theologian" by the Eastern Church because he knew how to stand up to the might of ecclesial power, because, for him, holiness was superior to the institution. And most important, in Florovsky's opinion, Simeon was canonized because he placed the interior experience of prayer, the source of all knowledge, above all types of discursive thought, of form and of canon. It was this mystical experience that enabled the saint to compose his divine *Hymns*.[526] But, Florovsky continued, such an understanding of theology was transformed by the corrupting influence of the West, after the fall of the Byzantine Empire, into an Eastern scholasticism usually formulated, moreover, in Latin. Therefore the Russian theologian gave himself the mission of helping the West realize that it is schismatic,[527] on the one hand, and on the other, of recovering the memory of the Byzantine tradition, the unshakeable trunk of the undivided church. Thus the last lines of Florovsky's article, written on March 19, 1929, can be considered as the manifesto of the Orthodox neo-patristic movement.

> Even to the present day Catholic theology mistrusts and questions Byzantine piety. And this mistrust concerns the very essence of the spiritual life of the East and, especially, this particular type of oriental piety conserved and symbolized in the *Philokalia*. "Plenum ineptiae cum pari impietate," as Combefise used to say about intelligent prayer [i.e., the noetic prayer, the "prayer of the heart" of the *Philokalia*]. The

West sharply interrogates the East as to the meaning of Byzantine theology. Our historical amnesia renders the task difficult. Only a complete and philosophical history of Byzantine theology—from St. Maximus to St. Gregory Palamas and St. Mark of Ephesus—can answer such a question. In this history one of the preeminent places belongs to St. Simeon. To give such a response is not only an historical or theological duty; it is a spiritual duty.[528]

The Reaction of the Neo-Slavic Current
After their ecumenical encounters of 1925–27 with Western Christians, Berdyaev, Fedotov, and Bulgakov believed in the actual present unity of the church—not just a past or future one. As of 1928–29, they dedicated themselves to manifesting this in their contributions to the review, each in his own way and in spite of the intolerance of Rome. Thus, Berdyaev clearly shifted his criticism of the West from the cultural domain to the more universal terrain of philosophy and theology. He lashed out at the positivism of Jean Izoulet, a professor of social philosophy at the Collège de France and apostle of an abstract monotheism.[529] In August 1928, the Russian philosopher observed that a new atheism, a dualist humanistic gnosis, more nuanced and spiritual than its predecessor, has installed itself in France in place of materialist and positivist atheism. Berdyaev understood it as his mission and duty to formulate a creative response to the problem of evil by drawing upon what is best in the Christian tradition. To reply to the neo-Marcionism laced with Spinozism confessed by H. Delafosse and L. Gabrilovitch, he invoked both the work of the German Protestant exegete A. von Harnack and the doctrine of the Orthodox Church concerning the kenosis of God.[530]

Fedotov, in his article "Carmen Saeculare," which appeared in the August 1928 issue, proposed a different view of the history of the West. He argued that the collapse of Europe in 1914–18 was the swan song of an atheistic civilization. After having lived in the West for three years, Fedotov admitted that Christian Europe had not perished. Through contacts with French and English intellectuals, Fedotov concluded that the Western Christian Church, a "living memory,"[531] guaranteed that the continuity between generations was not broken and that the experience of centuries—and especially what was best in humanism—was not forgotten. For him, this is the reason a living encounter was being prepared among all Christians of good faith through culture, social movements, and ecumenical commitment. Religious renewal among the young people of the West was already promising—in spite of Rome's authoritarianism—an unprecedented cultural renewal. Fedotov waxed enthusiastic: "In ten years' time these young people will take over the university chairs of the old positivists and idealists and the whole organization of culture, all the contact with the masses who are still atheists, will be in the hands of the Church."[532]

Bulgakov had a more dogmatic attitude with respect to Rome. The text he published in the October 1928 issue of *The Way*, "The Lausanne Conference and the Papal Encyclical" (of Pope Pius XI, *Mortalium Animos*), was the only direct response to the Roman condemnation that appeared in the review. It can therefore be considered as the collective position of the journal on this question. Bulgakov set in opposition the pan-Christic "openness" of the Protestant and Orthodox Churches at the first world conference of Faith and Order at Lausanne in August of 1927 to the "pan-papist" interdiction imposed on Catholics who "participate in congresses with non-Catholics."[533] For Bulgakov, "the faith of Peter is the foundation of the Church," but "papal infallibility has placed a veil over the Gospel."[534] If it is true, he writes, that the canons of the church forbid Christians to speak with heretics, it is to "prevent a dogmatic indifference or even a desire to commit heresies."[535] Bulgakov, who at Lausanne sensed with "a new acuity that the Christian world believes and loves the Lord Jesus Christ"[536] and that the ecumenical movement was not seeking to create a superchurch, declared himself in favor of an active and practical *sobornost'*. "The Church is conciliar," he wrote, "not only in the sense of its catholicity which opposes any spiritual provincialism, but also in the sense of the coming together of hearts, in love and in intellectual unity."[537] To support what he said, he invoked the First Ecumenical Council, in which pagan philosophers were invited to speak. He recalled that Cardinal Mercier himself said: "I do not have the right to look the other way when an occasion presents itself to me to do an act of fraternal charity and Christian hospitality."[538] Bulgakov concluded that the coming together of hearts should inaugurate the formation of a more irenic "symbolic" ecumenism to replace the traditional "accusatory theology."[539]

New Forms of Commitment
The joint participation of Florovsky, Karsavin, and Zenkovsky with Berdyaev, Fedotov, and Bulgakov in the ecumenical movement during the

1927–29 period can only be understood in the light of the eschatological exigencies of the Kingdom of God. For in spite of their different understandings of the nature of the church—and thus of its urban archetype—all of them saw the coming together of the Christian confessions as a victory over temporality and a meeting of East and West.

A new member of the journal, Fr. Lev Gillet, served as a bridge between the two groups. Fr. Lev, who had become acquainted with the authors of the review through the journal *Irénikon*, decided to enter the Eastern Church after the condemnation of Pius XI. He was received in May 1928 at Clamart in the presence of Bulgakov, Berdyaev, Florovsky, and Karsavin.[540] Metropolitan Evlogy, who, in his own words, was thinking of "the future of our denationalized Russian children,"[541] named Fr. Lev the rector of the first French language Orthodox parish, founded in 1928 in the headquarters of the RSCM. The manager of *The Way*, the young viscount Sergius Hautman de Villiers, who, through his mother, had contacts with circles of Russian occultists and who was a member of the St. Photius Brotherhood (whose project was "to make the Catholic West Orthodox"), was commissioned to resume the translation of the liturgical texts from Slavonic into French, a project begun by Fr. Vladimir Guettée. Along with two other members of the brotherhood, Evgraph Kovalevsky and Vladimir Lossky, both defenders—as was their ninth-century holy patron—of Orthodoxy against Latin errors, Fr. Lev published the first Orthodox journal in French. It was entitled *La Voie* (*The Way*), thus maintaining a reference to the Russian language review of the Academy.[542] It could be said that one of the principal poles of attraction for Catholic converts to the Orthodox Church was expressed in the February 1929 issue of *La Voie* by this modernist statement, borrowed from an issue of Berdyaev's review: "Our Church does not recognize any exterior juridical authority."[543]

The encyclical and Father Lev's conversion called into question the validity of the interconfessional conferences that Berdyaev organized at Montparnasse. These ceased in December 1928 due to internal and external causes. Maritain, who could not stomach "the presentations of Fr. Laberthonnière,"[544] was the first to leave, in March. The prohibition of Catholic theologians from participating in the meetings of the Academy by Bishop Rafael Chaptal, the diocesan bishop in charge of émigrés, complicated matters for the other Catholic participants. For his part, Berdyaev came to a more realistic understanding of ecumenical dialogue, and, since he felt a greater intellectual affinity with the Thomist thinkers, he decided to change the formula. On December 17, with Maritain but also with Bulgakov, Fedotov, and Florovsky, he organized an initial informal meeting between Catholic and Orthodox thinkers at his house in Clamart. After the debate concerning the West, some new faces appeared, all of them attracted by the East: Charles du Bos (1882–1939), an essayist close to Proust, Claudel, Valéry, and Gide; Olivier Lacombe (1904), a Belgian philologist professor and a specialist on India; Emile Dermenghem (1892), a specialist in Eastern history and ethnography; Étienne Gilson (1884–1978), a Thomist who specialized in medieval history; Louis Massignon (1883–1962), a professor at the Collège de France and a specialist in Islamic mysticism; Emmanuel Mounier (1905–50), a young philosophy professor; Gabriel Marcel (1889–1973), a phenomenologist philosopher who converted to Catholicism in 1929; Jean Wahl (1888–1974), a philosopher specializing in Hegel; Jules Lebreton, a Jesuit and professor of dogma and Christian history at the Catholic Institute; and Fr. Charles Journet (1891–1975), a Swiss theologian and professor at the University of Fribourg. Berdyaev had met most of these intellectuals either through Maritain and the meetings he organized at his house in Meudon or on the occasion of the Décades de Pontigny, to which Paul Desjardins invited him regularly since the gathering of August 1927, dedicated to Romanticism. He met Charles du Bos in 1924 at the home of his friend Leon Shestov. Berdyaev immediately considered him as one of the most subtle and cultivated of contemporary French intellectuals. Du Bos, who had just converted to Catholicism in 1927, also appreciated Eastern mysticism and accepted an invitation to preside over the meetings at Clamart, as he had done at Pontigny. The first themes for discussion were quite varied: "L'action catholique" (the Catholic Action movement), "the place of the laity in the Church," and "The Old Believers," among others. Count Jean de Pange, who participated regularly in the meetings, noted in his journal that on April 16, 1929, Florovsky gave a presentation on Byzantine mysticism. Rather characteristically, the attention of the French intellectual was aroused when, in the course of his presentation, the Russian theologian remarked that "in the East, there is no distinction between mysticism and theology."[545]

In the September 1929 issue of *The Way*, Zenkovsky praised the new cultural dynamism of the Catholic Church and the efficacy, especially notable in Germany, of Actio Catholica (the Catholic Action movement), a creation of Pius XI.[546] His colleagues at the St. Sergius Institute, Fedotov and Kartashev, reacted in the same way to the ecumenical challenge in spite of their opposing political opinions and their age difference. They participated in ecumenical congresses, above all with the Anglicans, and threw themselves into the study of Holy Russia. Kartashev's first article in *The Way*, "The Influence of the Church on Russian Culture," in the January 1928 issue, was a lecture delivered at the Sorbonne—under the presidency of E. Haumanton—on June 9, 1927, at the occasion of the commemoration of the birth of Pushkin. For his part, Fedotov drew close to less academic Russian intellectuals living at Montparnasse, such as Irina de Mantciarli, the editor of *Cahiers de l'Etoile*, and the young poets N. Otsup, V. Varshavsky, V. Yanovsky, B. Poplavsky, and V. de Vogt. The latter, who had close contacts with the editorial staff of *Annales Contemporaines*, met Robert Sebastien, the editor of *France et Monde*, a publication of Les Humanités Contemporaines, when the debate about the limits of the West was going on. Together they decided to organize the first literary gathering between French and Russian intellectuals. This took place on April 30, 1929, in the salon of Humanités Contemporaines under the presidency of Probus Correard and gave birth to the Studio Franco-Russe (SFR). These meetings sought to deepen East-West relations—which had suddenly sprung up on the occasion of the polemic between Massis and Berdyaev— by a mutual discovery of the cultural riches of Russia and France. Once again, Charles Péguy was a link between French and Russian intellectuals. In fact, the publication of the debates was entrusted to the *Cahiers de la Quinzaine*, the review founded by Péguy in 1899 to oppose anti-Semitism and nationalism in the context of the Dreyfus affair. On October 29, 1929, Robert Sebastien and Vsevolod de Vogt gave separate presentations on the topic "Unrest in Literature." The following month, on November 26, two other intellectuals had their turn. Julia Sazonova, a contributor to *The Way* who was close to Fedotov, spoke on "The Influence of French Literature on Russian Writers since 1900," and Jean Maxence (Pierre Godme), a twenty-three-year-old Thomist École Normale student close to Maurras and a member of the review *Les Cahiers*, founded in 1928, spoke on "The Influence of Russian Literature on French Writers." With an audience including Massis, Maritain, Marcel, Sauvage, Bernanos, and Arnoux, as well as Fedotov, M. Tsvetaeva, B. Zaitsev, Poplavsky, Gazdanov, and Gorodetsky, Sazonova insisted on the distinction between Maupassant—for whom "the forms of life are stable and have their meaning"—and Chekhov—in whose works "no one is in his right place."[547] Maxence pointed out that the epic novel of Tolstoy, which became known in France at the beginning of the nineteenth century thanks to Melchior de Vogue, and the tragic persona of Dostoevsky made known through Rivière, Gide, and Mauriac, had dethroned the image of Pushkin in the way that the French represented the East. Maxence did not arrive at a conclusion. However, such a broadening of the limits of the novel and such a tragic evolution of the representations of the East—a mirror of the West both repugnant and fascinating—only manifested the interior evolution of the French intelligentsia from patriotic triumphalism to universality, from serenity to restlessness.[548]

Bulgakov's engagement should not be considered in the same way as that of Berdyaev and Fedotov. Bulgakov, who was tempted in 1918[549] to convert to Catholicism while he was in Crimea, near the Byzantine walls of Chersonese, entered into the dialogue with the Latin West looking at the long term rather than the immediate future. From Bulgakov's perspective, the only effective form of encounter with respect to Christian unity was an official dialogue, based on a "dogmatic maximalism," among theologians mandated by their respective churches. Since such encounters had been forbidden by the Roman Curia, Bulgakov chose to prepare for the future by dedicating himself, as of 1927, to the principal points of divergence between the Catholic Church and the Orthodox Church. From an Orthodox point of view, the main discrepancies in doctrinal matters concerned the questions of the procession of the Holy Spirit and its relationship to the Son (1054), the Immaculate Conception of the Virgin (1854), and, finally, papal infallibility (1870).

Surprisingly, the divergence concerning the *Filioque*, held up for such a long time by both churches as their principal source of disagreement, was considered minor by Bulgakov. The more realistic approach to the relationship between the hypostases—which already could be observed in Bulgakov in 1926[550]—was clearly affirmed for the first time in 1929 in an article in *The Way*. At the end of his article on the dogma of the Vatican, Bulgakov cites the authority of the Russian theologian V.V. Bolotov and affirms that between the Catholic and Orthodox Church, "the question of the Holy Spirit has ceased to be an '*impedimentum dirimens*.'"[551]

In his book on the Mother of God, *The Burning Bush*, published in 1928 by YMCA Press, Bulgakov showed that a sophiological approach made it possible to transcend the opposition between Catholicism and Orthodoxy concerning the dogma of the Immaculate Conception.[552] In the February and May 1929 issues of *The Way*, Bulgakov published two studies devoted to the dogma of the First Vatican Council concerning papal infallibility. Bulgakov prefaced his voluminous study with this clarification:

> The external reason which motivates the publication of this essay has to do with certain aggressive declarations on the part of Catholics.... The internal motivation is the desire to pose the question which divides West and East in view of an until now unexplored theological approach; moreover this approach to the problem does not stem from a sentiment of hostility, but, on the contrary, from a sincere desire for mutual understanding and from a coming together which is based on such an understanding.[553]

Bulgakov took up the argument of the Old Catholics against the pope as *Vicarius Christi*.[554] He reaffirmed the principles of the undivided church: the bishop is not above the church, he is the representative of grace. His authority is, in reality, that given to him by the church, for the *charisma veritatis* belongs to the whole ecclesial body united in Christ. Bulgakov revealed the motivations, more ultramontane and nationalistic than ecclesial, of the bishops during the First Vatican Council and in particular those of Bishop J.-G. Strossmayer, the administrator of Croatia who wanted to convert Solovyov. Bulgakov placed the debate on the primacy of the pope over the council in its historical perspective. This primacy was affirmed for the first time in the West at the Council of Florence in 1439, when the question of authority in the church was already associated with union with the Orthodox Church.[555] The dogma of infallibility, which, from a juridical point of view, was not necessary to Roman legislation, appears, in this perspective, as the culmination of the Catholic Counter-Reformation. Finally, Bulgakov examined the encyclical itself in more detail and revealed all the manipulations of the dogmatic and canonic traditions on the part of the redactors during the sessions of April 24–July 18, 1870. The thesis of the Russian theologian was that "by proclaiming papal sovereignty, the council annulled itself, it committed dogmatic suicide and formulated its own nonexistence."[556]

Thus, for Bulgakov, if the Vatican I dogma of 1870 is the principal dividing point between the East and the West,[557] the very demonstration of this point indicates that it can be easily surmounted, since the dogmatic unity of the church is not really affected.

Relations with Geneva

Certain Swiss Protestants, who were prejudiced against the Roman magisterium and who did not understand the politics of the YMCA as reflected in the correspondence of Paul Anderson throughout 1925–27,[558] took a dim view of the openness of *The Way* towards the Catholic world. Although ecumenism was born in Protestantism, it owes its development to a number of enlightened personalities. The modern ecumenical movement predated the initiatives of the Russian intellectuals to bring together the Christian churches of France. It first appeared in the nineteenth century thanks to the new place taken by laity, especially young people, in the mission activity of the church and in the progressive rapprochement between East and West since the Holy Alliance and up to the chaos of the First World War. It originated primarily in the churches that issued from the Reformation. The term "ecumenism" was employed in its contemporary sense for the first time around 1846 by the new Universal Evangelical Church.[559] The YMCA, which developed rapidly in the second half of the nineteenth century, prepared the groundwork among young people for the rapprochement of all Christians. The student branch of the YMCA became an autonomous movement on August 19, 1895, when the World Student Christian Federation was founded at the chateau of Vadstena in Sweden.[560] The Federation immediately gave birth to a flock of pioneers of ecumenism. The missionary élan also played an important role. The Faith and Order movement was constituted on the basis of the principle, defined at the World Congress of Missions at Edinburgh on July 14–23, 1910, of henceforth reuniting all the Christian communities who confess "Our Lord Jesus Christ as God and Saviour." At the first meeting of the Federation on May 8, 1913, in New York, the Episcopal bishop Charles Brent (1862–1929) gave the new organization the mission of promoting comparative doctrinal studies in view of a greater understanding among the churches. An Orthodox from Russia, D. Hotovitsky, had been invited to New York. The Orthodox had, in fact, rather quickly taken a position in favor of the ecumenical movement. On June 12, 1902, the patriarch of Constantinople, Joachim III, pronounced his support for a greater unity among sister churches.[561] Patriarch Tikhon, who had lived in the United States, was also favorable to the movement. The First World War precipitated events. On January 18, 1920, the archbishop of Canterbury addressed an appeal to "all the Christian peoples." At the same time, the bishop of Thyateira, Germanos (Stronopoulos) (1872–1951), published the encyclical of Patriarch Dorotheos recommending the forging of greater fraternity (*koinonia*) among Christian churches.[562] Germanos, who was a friend of John Mott, agreed to participate in the executive committee of the Faith and Order movement, with its seat in Geneva, after it was agreed that the powerful Protestant and Anglo-Saxon missions would not seek to extend themselves in the zones of influence of Orthodoxy. Metropolitan Evlogy also participated at this conference and noted in his diary that "right from the first session, one could sense the breath of Christian unity."[563]

Stockholm

As exarch of the Ecumenical Patriarchate at London, Metropolitan Germanos also participated in the first conference of the Life and Work movement at Stockholm in August 1925, the sixteenth centenary of the Council of Nicea (325). This second pole of the ecumenical movement was rooted in the current of social Christianity that appeared at the beginning of the twentieth century. The World Alliance for International Friendship, which had also resulted from this current, never became a group involving diverse churches (a precursor of the World Council of Churches, it was founded in 1914 at a conference in Germany to promote peace). In 1919 the Lutheran bishop of Uppsala, Nathan Söderblom (1866–1931), proposed the creation of a new structure called Life and Work. He invited all Christian churches to participate in order to strive towards unity through their common practice of Christianity rather than a doctrinal rapprochement. Although Cardinal Gasparri refused to participate in Life and Work in April 1921, the Orthodox of Greece and of the Russian emigration joined the new organization.

Dialectical Theology
Among the authors of *The Way*, Paul Anderson, Arseniev, and Glubokovsky participated in the first Stockholm conference on August 19–25, 1925. This conference was the first official confrontation between the Russian religious thought issuing from the Silver Age and the new dialectical theology of the disciples of Karl Barth. Rarely in the history of theology has there been such a radical and fruitful change as that initiated by the theology

of "The Word of God" taught by Karl Barth (1886–1968), a Swiss pastor and professor of theology at the University of Göttingen, based on the second edition of his commentary, *Der Römerbrief* (*Epistle to the Romans*) (1922). This text, which denounced the continuity between the human being and the divine reality championed by the liberal theologians of the nineteenth century, preached the "totally Other God" and became the manifesto of the theologians who contributed to the review *Zwischen den Zeiten*—Eduard Thurneysen, Emil Brunner, Friedrich Gogarten, and Rudolf Bultmann. Inspired by Kierkegaard's philosophy of radical despair, Barth inaugurated a theology of divine judgment (*Krisis*) which returned to the very sources of Protestantism by recalling that God bridges, in an eschatological way and through the pure grace of his Word, the infinite distance between Himself and being.[564] In the first issue of *The Way*, Arseniev and Paul Tillich (1886–1965), a German theologian close to Barth and Berdyaev, presented the principal actors and major characteristics of the dialectical method to a Russian readership.[565] Arseniev professed his enthusiasm for the German theological renewal and, above all, its interest in the liturgy, the church, and "Christian realism." This liturgical renewal, confirmed by Arseniev in another article published in April 1927 and entitled "The Present Situation of Christianity," was accompanied by an ecumenical overture on the part of the evangelical movement Hochkirchlich-Oekumenischer Bund and its journal, *Una Sancta*.[566] Dr. V. Martin, the editor of this monthly, founded in January 1925 and published in Berlin, was particularly open to Russian Orthodoxy. But Arseniev believed that the weight of Western individualism still prevented German theology from grasping the cosmic significance of Christianity and its spirit of universality.[567] Paul Tillich, for his part, shared Barth's insistence on justification by faith alone but believed that a negative theology of God cannot be genuinely dialectical unless it admitted a positive theology as well. This implied that the church, history, and culture should rediscover their importance in the perspective of the coming of the Kingdom of God.[568] Thus, beginning with its very first issue, the position of *The Way* was that there was a place in Europe for different representations of the Kingdom of God upon earth.

The Repercussion of the Conference
The affirmation of Orthodox identity at Geneva could only clash with the ecumenical practice of the Protestant world. In January 1926, *The Way* echoed the Stockholm conference through the intermediary of Samuel

Kavert, the secretary of the Council of Protestant Churches of the USA. Like Anderson, Kavert wanted the ecumenical dialogue to get rid of the formal confessional divisions that were the weighty legacy of historical evolution.[569] In this same spirit, the World Student Christian Federation, in its desire for ecumenical overture, would accept in its ranks only organizations that were open to all confessions. But the Orthodox position, as defined by the Russian Student Christian Movement and the editorial of *The Way*, rejected any form of interconfessionalism. In June 1926, a delegation of Russians, led by Zenkovsky, Zernov, and Kuhlmann, attended the general assembly of the World Student Christian Federation at Nyborg Strand in Denmark in order to resolve the problem posed by the RSCM.[570] After a great deal of discussion, the assembly decided to admit the RSCM as a member of the organization in spite of its confessional character and to finance up to 12 percent of its budget.[571] This decision was due, in great part, to the persuasive talents of the young Swiss Barthian secretary of the YMCA and assistant editor of *The Way*, Gustav Kuhlmann. At the RSCM conference at Hopovo in September 1925 and in the presence of Metropolitan Anthony, Kuhlmann gave a lecture that was particularly revealing of his motivations in seeking church unity.[572] It was reprinted on the occasion of the consultation he organized at Ban' Kostenec in Bulgaria and published in the November 1926 issue of *The Way* under the title "Protestantism and Orthodoxy." The young secretary of the YMCA, after four years of working with students of the Russian emigration, believed that the meeting between Protestantism and Orthodoxy was a meeting of West and East.[573] For Kuhlmann, influenced, like many of his contemporaries, by the ideas of Barth, this meeting was that of the Word and the Symbol, the two eternal principles of the church. This vision of the world separated the West, more sensitive to the prophetical, eschatological, and creative dimension represented by the Word, from the East, which conserves the eternity of the mystic realities of the world hidden in symbols. At the end of his lecture, Kuhlmann proclaimed:

> Here I see the miraculous blessedness of our encounter. You need the dynamism of the word and we have such a thirst to enter into the visible Church of Christ, into the liturgy and sacraments and be in silence there! And, by helping you with your student movements, with your lay movements and their social and missionary labors, where there is enthusiasm for the study of the Holy Scriptures and tradition,

where hearts are open to the spirit of prophesy, to the *hic et nunc* of Christ for our times and our country, and where one draws strength for all that from prayer before God, we receive much more than we give; we receive from you a new vision of the totality and plenitude which opens up in Christ and which lives in the liturgy and sacraments of your Church.[574]

The Debate between Erenberg and Bulgakov
Professor Hans Erenberg (1883–1954), a German Protestant pastor who specialized in Eastern Christianity, was one of the connections for Russian religious thought in Germany. A letter he sent to Bulgakov concerning the relationships between Orthodoxy and Protestantism, published in the November 1926 issue of *The Way*, posed the problem of the reunion of the Eastern and Western churches according to the perspective of Barth. For Erenberg, Orthodox ecclesiology is founded more on dogma and hierarchy than on the Bible. In his view, that allowed Orthodoxy to avoid an individualistic and pietistic spirituality but prevented it from embracing all the people of God.[575] Bulgakov, in his response, cited the First Epistle to the Corinthians, the real cornerstone of his ecumenical engagement. According to the apostle, "love forgives all, believes all, hopes all, supports all; it does not rejoice in injustice but puts its joy in the truth."[576] Further, Bulgakov distinguished between universal Orthodoxy, to which Protestantism belongs in virtue of veneration of the Word of God, and historical Orthodoxy, which should be attentive to Protestant "Biblicism."[577] He clarified that this in no way justifies the anti-ecclesial proselytism of the Stundists in Russia. For, although Bulgakov historically justified the protest against the papacy, he declared that "today the Reformation itself should get rid of Protestantism and return to the Church."[578] Finally, Bulgakov gave his reply on the question of the church but without proceeding very far. Prudently, he drew on Khomiakov, who saw the church as the Body of Christ and not "an assembly of slaves." He concluded by claiming that Protestantism could enter into universal Orthodoxy on the condition that it realize that, in the church, the love of the people of God does not contradict respect for the hierarchy.[579]

Lausanne

The discovery of American Protestantism in 1927 within a Russian Orthodox context of schism (*raskol*), whether directly, as in the case of Zenkovsky, who spent seven months in the United States,[580] or indirectly, through Samuel Kavert and his article "The Different Currents of Religious Life in America,"[581] appearing in the April 1927 issue, gave a certain reassurance to the authors and the more skeptical readers of *The Way* that the openness of the YMCA to ecumenism was sincere. The turning point, however, in the relationship between the authors of *The Way* and the Protestant West took place during the conference of Lausanne, not far from Geneva, on August 2–21, 1927, and practically coincided with the definitive proclamation of the schism by the ROCOR on August 26.

Faith and Order
The first world conference of the Faith and Order movement, held at Lausanne, brought together nearly four hundred delegates from fifty-nine countries. For the first time, the Orthodox world, represented by twenty-two theologians from Armenian, Bulgarian, Greek, Georgian, Romanian, Serbian, and Russian churches (the Russian delegation included Metropolitan Evlogy, Bulgakov, Arseniev, Zankov, and Glubokovsky), met, on an official and theological level, the Western world that issued from the Reformation. The principal representatives of the latter were Bishop Brent of New York; Bishop Gore of Oxford; the editor of the British review *Christian East*, Canon Douglas; the head of the YMCA in New York, Donald E. Davis; the Lutheran archbishop Söderblom of Uppsala; the rector of the University of Heidelberg, Professor Martin Dibelius; the convert from Catholicism and professor at the University of Marburg, Friederich Heiler; the editor of the review *Una Sancta*, Professor V. Martin; the disciple of Barth, Friedrich Gogarten; and the Reformed professor Wilfred Monod.

Reactions in The Way
As Arseniev wrote in the April 1928 issue of *The Way*, this conference was, above all, a unique occasion for the Orthodox world to experience its very concrete—and not just its mystical—unity in the face of the West.[582] This encounter with the West was not without its tensions. For Bulgakov, it was essential to bring up ecclesiological questions concerning the hierarchy in the church, ministry, the sacraments of salvation—especially the Eucharist—and the Mother of God.[583] But when the Russian theologian brought up the theme of the Mother of God, during his presentation on the topic "Ministry in the Church," he was interrupted by the president of the session, A. E. Garvie, an English Congregationalist, who asked him to

return to his seat. Bulgakov refused to move and, thanks to the intervention of Bishop Gore, was able to finish his paper.[584]

In spite of this incident, the first assembly of Faith and Order was so important that many of its participants had the feeling that, after twelve centuries of ruptures, an eighth ecumenical council of the Christian church was in the making—in a different way from earlier councils, perhaps, but very concretely. After the conference, the archpriest S. Zankov (1881–1965), a professor at the University of Sofia, became a fervent partisan of ecumenical dialogue. Following a seminar which he led at the University of Berlin in the summer of 1927, he published a book in German on the Eastern Orthodox Church in order to make it known to the German Protestant world.[585] In it, Zankov upheld the thesis that the expansion of the frontiers of the church primarily depended on the expansion of the ways dogma could be represented.

The Experience of Unity
Consequently, we can distinguish between contributors to *The Way* who participated in the conference of Lausanne and those who did not. Arseniev stated that, at Lausanne, the church was present not as a dream but "as the Reality, already given."[586] Bulgakov himself, in October 1928, enigmatically wrote that "something happened [at the conference of Lausanne], and the participants remembering this event now felt responsible for the future of the ecumenical movement."[587] Six years earlier, in the Crimea, Bulgakov had nearly converted to Catholicism following the example of Solovyov. But on August 12, at Lausanne, when the nearly four hundred participants from all over the world rose to confess their faith in Jesus Christ, Bulgakov encountered something that the Russian philosophical symbolist had not yet experienced in such a way—that the nature of the Church is dynamic, alive and not static. He wrote:

> We cannot accept the divided condition of the Christian world. The wound of this division should always be present in our heart. Orthodox encounters where love is present open the hearts of the non-Orthodox, thanks to their authentic and sincere love for God—and that in despite of all that separates them, often because of historical factors rather than contemporary ones. Orthodoxy is not just the status quo, the condition for arriving at fullness, the treasure of the true

faith conserved unchanging until the consummation of the ages; it is also dynamism, at work in the Christian world, its leaven—one might say it is the internal logic of Christianity.[588]

The Divisions

The Critics of Protestantism
The authors who were most critical of the Protestant world during the 1927–29 period, Florovsky and Zenkovsky, did not share the experiences of Zankov, Bulgakov, and Arseniev at Lausanne. In the April 1928 issue, Florovsky reviewed the book of Zankov and criticized his subjectivism. Florovsky argued that, even if it were true that baptism in the Holy Trinity opened the gates of the church to "those who were strangers to it," it is dangerous to rationalize such a mystery.[589] In his view, the Protestant world was still far from understanding the thought of the Eastern Church. According to Florovsky, Karl Holl, the author of a trilogy on the history of the Orthodox Church published at Tübingen in 1928, was unable to grasp its mystical dimension.[590] Inversely, Emil Brunner, a disciple of Karl Barth, so mistrusted reason in his reaction against "liberal Christology" (Jesusism) that he could not enter into the kerygmatic depths of the Byzantine dogmas.[591] In a new critical review dated June 19, 1929, of the work of the German Protestant historian Hans Koch on the Orthodox Church during the time of Peter the Great, Florovsky said that works such as these only reminded him of his own "unaccomplished duty" of being a critical memorialist of Russia's past.[592]

Zenkovsky, who returned from the United States with negative as well as favorable impressions of Protestantism,[593] published a critical review of a book by the Reformed theologian Wilfrid Monod, one of the participants in the conference of Lausanne,[594] in the February 1929 issue of *The Way*. For him, Monod was witnessing to "the profound contemporary dogmatic crisis of Protestantism" when he triumphantly proclaimed the victory of spiritualism over sacramentalism.[595] In November of the same year, Zenkovsky, addressing the young readers of the journal who might be interested in contemporary religious life in Soviet Russia, warned them against the harmful influence of a book by the former president of the Russian Student Christian Movement, V. Marcinkovsky, who had become one of the leaders of the Russian evangelical movement.[596]

This new tension within the *The Way* after the Lausanne conference was a manifestation of the theological opposition between the neo-eschatological current (Bulgakov) and those who held a unilateral pneumocentrism (Zenkovsky) or Christocentrism (Florovsky). But the polemic that these three waged in the pages of *The Way* should not create misunderstanding. Following the papal condemnation of January 1928, all of them understood that the encounter between East and West would pass principally through Geneva. Moreover, the authors of the journal were not that far apart. Florovsky was not insensitive to the eschatology of Barth, for whom the kerygmatic understanding of the event went in hand with a return to the sources of revelation and thus of history.[597] As for Zenkovsky, he was, by way of Khomiakov, close to the spiritual vision of the church proclaimed by liberal German Protestantism.[598] That is why it is not surprising that Florovsky and Zenkovsky continued to participate in *The Way* and in the ecumenical movement. Conversely, Kuhlmann, who was close to the ideas of Barth, decided in 1928 to convert to Orthodoxy and, in 1929, married the sister of Nicolas Zernov, Maria Zernov, who was the head of the youth section of the RSCM. This decision forced him to quit his functions in the YMCA. He also abandoned his post as assistant editor of the journal, due to his departure from Paris for Geneva, where he began to work within the League of Nations in the field of international intellectual cooperation. On the other hand, in spite of the openness of a Bulgakov or an Arseniev, the view held by the Protestant world of the sacramentalism and contemporary hierarchical structure of the Second and Third Rome, namely, Constantinople and Moscow, could only encourage neo-Byzantines and neo-Muscovites to work together in order to reveal to Geneva the profound and continuing reality of the Christian Rome they represented and of which they were the successors. This is why the years 1928–29 were also the moment of a common affirmation of the Eastern identity of the modernist Russian generation.

The Myth of the East
In this respect, the indirect dialogue within the ranks of *The Way* between Fritz Lieb (1892–1970), a Swiss Protestant theologian, an Evangelical, a Slavophile, and a friend of Barth and Berdyaev, and Bezobrazov, who was close both to Bulgakov and Florovsky at the St. Sergius Institute, is rather representative of this movement of identification. In 1929, Lieb, with the participation of the editor of the review and of Paul Schütz of Leipzig,

founded a new journal in German dedicated to the encounter of Orthodoxy and Protestantism, eloquently entitled *Orient und Occident*.[599] Among the authors of *The Way*, Florovsky, Zenkovsky, Berdyaev, Bulgakov, and Vysheslavtsev participated in this new publication.

In his first article in this new journal, "Orthodoxy and Protestantism," which was translated and published in the May 1929 issue of *The Way* on the occasion of the Orthodox Easter, Lieb, citing Zankov, insisted precisely on the fact that "only the Father and Christ, the head of the One Church (*Una Sancta*), and the Holy Spirit invisibly present in the Church, are perfect, transforming the Church into the true Church, and they are the unique and full guaranty of its infallibility."[600] A disciple of Blumhardt, Lieb was involved in the German socioreligious movement. He pointed out the historical and contemporary sins of Russian Protestants and Evangelicals, criticizing their lack of social commitment and their loss of the prophetic spirit over the course of time. In the view of this Evangelical theologian, the manifestation of unity always begins by a common repentance.[601] For Lieb, a true dialogue could not take place unless Orthodox theologians overcame their clichés about the West and recognized the real presence of God in Protestantism[602]—faithful, in this respect, to the living tradition of "Kireevsky, Khomiakov, Florensky, and Bulgakov." But what Lieb—who, according to the memoirs of Berdyaev, wanted to be called Fedor Ivanovich[603]—especially cherished in the Eastern Church was the faith in the Resurrection and the faith of "Dostoevsky, Solovyov, Florensky, Bulgakov, Berdyaev" in the *apocatastasis*, "the universal salvation of the whole unified human race and of the cosmos."[604] The "Geneva" theologian held up the mirror to the "Muscovite" theologians in these words:

> The original characteristic, the particular gift of the Orthodox Church, is its teaching on the Resurrection. Thanks to this teaching, its thirst for the unity of the Churches will be quenched, its quest will be accomplished. Because of its faith in the Risen Lord, which is so strong and so full of radiant joy, the Eastern Church will have primacy of place when the One Church will be risen under the authority of the One who is risen. The union of the Churches is unthinkable without the Orthodox Church. We Evangelical Christians also confess this faith of the *Unae Sanctae* in the Resurrection, joyfully exclaiming with our Russian brethren "Christ is risen! Indeed he is risen."[605]

Bezobrazov was sensitive to such an image of the East. It echoed that which Solovyov had insinuated in his *A Tale of the Antichrist*—a mystical and Johannine East, distinct from both the Petrine and charity-oriented Rome, and from the Pauline and biblical Geneva. In his exegetical study of the resurrection of Lazarus, which, strangely, only the beloved disciple of Christ mentions,[606] Bezobrazov probed more deeply into the meaning of this distinction. He believed that the Gospel of John should be interpreted symbolically, but this interpretation should not contradict the concrete and historical reality of the facts related by the Evangelist.[607] Lazarus was truly recalled to life by Christ, but this event, in Bezobrazov's opinion, should be understood as the eschatological annunciation of the resurrection of Christ. In his article entitled "The Raising of Lazarus and the Resurrection of Christ," published in the same May 1929 issue as the article by Lieb, Bezobrazov gave a precise comparison of the unfolding of the two miracles. For Bezobrazov, "that which is figured [*proobrazuemoe*] is the accomplishment of the prototype [*proobraz*]; the archetypical figure [*proobraz*] is obscured [*merknet*] in the glory of its accomplishment."[608] This parallel, traditional in the Orthodox Church, which celebrates the feast of Lazarus before Palm Sunday, was Bezobrazov's reply to the expectation of Lieb. Indeed, such an interpretation, unlike traditional liberal exegesis, announced the resurrection of all and the sanctification of the cosmos.[609] Concerning this last point, Bezobrazov gave a cosmic interpretation to the fact that Lazarus' resurrection took place in the full light of day. He believed that the words of Christ concerning the Light,[610] as well as the story of the crowing of the cock, should not be understood as symbolic of the Fall, as in the synoptic Gospels, but as a symbol of the Resurrection, the victory of light over darkness.[611]

The Living Dialogue
The mutual encounter of Protestant and Orthodox theologians in which Lieb placed his hopes contributed to Bezobrazov's realization of the unity between the East and the West. On August 9–10, 1929, at Novi Sad in Serbia, he and Glubokovsky participated in what he called "the first meeting between West and East in order to work together on scholarly and theological questions."[612] This meeting took place in the context of the commission "for worldwide mutual cooperation of theology professors," created at Stockholm during the conference of Life and Work. Under the

presidency of Martin Dibelius, British, German, Czechoslovakian, Austrian, and French professors compared their interpretations of the Epistle of Saint Paul to the Philippians with Greek, Russian, and Serbian theologians. Bezobrazov experienced this meeting as a new Pentecost. Moved by the extreme attentiveness of the Protestants to the sufferings of the Russian Church, he wrote: "We, who, coming from different peoples, have been gathered together by the Holy Spirit, have recognized one another as brothers in Christ, members of the same flock led by the sole pastor, Jesus Christ."[613] Significantly, the only debate, in which Professor Dodd of Mansfield College at Oxford and Bezobrazov of the St. Sergius Institute opposed one another, concerned the eschatological interpretation of the words of the apostle on the resurrection.[614] Bezobrazov linked this passage with the Christological doctrine of Paul[615] concerning the deification by *kenosis* and thus as manifesting that the sufferings of the apostle, in the image of the sufferings of Christ, are the foundation of the apostolic power of the Church.[616] The Easterners received a new vision of faith in the human nature of Christ from the West. Bezobrazov wrote that "the awareness of unity in the confession of the faith was a revelation made to the East by the West."[617]

Relations with London

If only for geographical reasons, contacts between authors of *The Way* and the Anglican Church were slow in developing. In spite of a long tradition of friendship between the Russian Church and the Church of England, vital contacts among theologians of the two confessions were practically nonexistent until January 1927. The very memory of this tradition was revived in the review only in November 1926, when the first meetings between the Continental generation of the Russian emigration and Anglican theologians took place through the mediation of the World Student Christian Federation and the ecumenical movement. In his general presentation of Anglicanism, published in the April 1926 issue of *The Way*, the Anglican theologian S. L. Ollard stated that, since the seventeenth century, Anglo-Catholics, more than any other confession, have been seeking to reestablish union with the Orthodox Church.[618] Several months later, in the November 1926 issue, an anonymous author, "K. A.," recalled the history of these relations. They began in 1690 when the party of Nonjurors, clergy and laity opposed to King William III, was formed under the aegis of the Archbishop of Canterbury. In 1716 the Nonjurors addressed themselves to the patriarchs of the Eastern Church in the hope of establishing a protocol of agreement among the churches and thus emancipating themselves from the authority of the English Crown.[619] The patriarchs refused any compromise, especially concerning the veneration of icons and the honoring of the Mother of God, the saints, and the angels. At the beginning of the nineteenth century, the emergence in the Anglican Church of the Oxford Movement, led by John Henry Newman (1801–90), who converted to Catholicism in 1846, sought to extend the catholicity of the Church of England and revived the project of reuniting the two churches. The friendship between William Palmer (1803–85), who also wound up converting to Catholicism, and Khomiakov and their correspondence from 1844 to 1856 are testimonies to this thirst for universality. Khomiakov liked "soccer and the Yule log"[620] and sincerely believed that the destinies of the world would be decided in Moscow and in London.[621] But the mentalities on both sides were not yet ready. The dialogue again came up against dogmatic oppositions, notably concerning the procession of the Holy Spirit. However, it enabled a new generation of bishops who had studied at Oxford—such as Bishop Gore of Oxford—to familiarize themselves with the ecumenical question and the social commitment of the church.

The revolution, the persecution of Christians in Russia, and the exile of several hundred thousand Russians in the West caused a large surge of sympathy in favor of the martyred church. The Archbishop of Canterbury, Cosmo Gordon Lang (1864–1945), played a decisive role. He officially declared himself in favor of the unity of the churches and gave aid to Patriarch Tikhon. He supported the Russian emigration by creating a fundraising committee to help the Russian clergy and church (Appeal for the Russian Clergy and Church Aid Fund), under the presidency of Dr. Russell Wakefield, the bishop of Birmingham. Finally, in 1925, he organized ceremonies in London to commemorate the sixteen hundredth anniversary of the Council of Nicea. Along with Metropolitan Germanos, the Archbishop of Canterbury invited the patriarchs Photius of Alexandria and Damien of Jerusalem as well as metropolitans Evlogy and Anthony.

These ceremonies were an occasion for the two Russian bishops and their delegation, composed notably of Bishop Benjamin, the rector of

St. Sergius Institute, and N. Glubokovsky, to travel throughout England and form an idea of the piety and catholicity of the English people. They found a sincere impulse of sympathy for the Orthodox Church everywhere.[622] The English press shared this enthusiasm. In its June 1925 issue, the Anglican review, *The Christian East*, considered that "the full union with the venerable Church (the Eastern Orthodox Church) seems only to be awaiting the restoration of political stability in Eastern Europe."[623] They met Bishop Walter Frere of Truro (1863–1938), a member of the Anglican monastic Community of the Resurrection at Mirfield and a specialist in liturgy. Bishop Frere, who felt especially close to Russia, having lived there prior to the revolution, was open to the ecumenical movement and had participated in the encounters of Malines with Cardinal Mercier.

It was only a year after the fact, in July 1926, that *The Way* published the paper given by Glubokovsky at King's College London on June 25, 1925. Glubokovsky put forth the principle that should govern any ecumenical undertaking by citing the words of St. Vincent of Lerins: "in necessariis unitas, in dubiis, libertas, in omnibus autem, caritas" ("unity in necessary things; liberty in doubtful things; charity in all things").[624] Basing themselves on this principle, the heads of the Orthodox and Anglican Churches decided to organize a new Anglo-Orthodox conference at Lambeth Palace in 1930. In the meantime, it was up to the theologians to resolve the principal theological disagreements. The discussion focused from the start on the recognition of the validity of apostolic continuity in the Anglican Church by the Orthodox Church and, consequently, the question of sacramental intercommunion between the two churches. The members of the Episcopalian Church, according to whether they were High Church or Low Church, were divided among themselves on the question of the real presence of Christ in the Eucharist. In January 1927, however, the synod of the Church of England demonstrated its desire to come closer to the Orthodox Church by agreeing to modify certain passages of its Book of Common Prayer that were not in conformity with tradition. The Orthodox were also divided among themselves. Metropolitan Anthony was opposed to recognizing the presence of any grace in the Anglican hierarchy. On the other hand, for the first time in the history of the Orthodox Church, two Orthodox patriarchs, Photius of Alexandria and Dimitrii of Serbia, recognized this hierarchy and accepted, in certain cases, intercommunion between Christians of the two confessions.[625]

The First Anglo-Russian Conference

As a result of all this, the committee for the Appeal for the Russian Clergy and Church Aid Fund decided to support the theological work being done and to give priority to subsidizing the St. Sergius Institute. Beginning in 1926, a considerable sum, 125,000 francs, was contributed annually by the committee; this represented 25 percent of the budget of the Institute.[626] The Anglican movement also supported the British Student Christian Movement (BSCM) in its efforts of collaboration with the Russian Student Christian Movement. In July 1923, the BSCM, through the World Student Christian Federation, had invited two Russian students from Serbia, Nikolai Klepinin and Nicolas Zernov, to its annual congress. Three years later, Zernov was reunited with his British friends from BSCM, Canon Tissington Tatlow and Zoe Fairfield, at the conference of Nyborg Strand. They decided to organize a joint conference of Orthodox and Anglican students—a historical first—with the participation of the Appeal committee, the BSCM, and the RSCM. The conference took place at St. Albans, a town twenty miles from London, on January 11–15, 1927. Although it was late in getting started, the encounter of the Russian visitors with the Anglican Church began with certain advantages. Unlike the ecumenical dialogue with Catholic and Protestant churches, the contacts between the Orthodox and Anglican churches had a clear theological, liturgical, and institutional character. On the first day, Bishop Gore presided over the opening liturgy in the presence of the British professors, the Reverends O. Clarke and Robertson, students from the BSCM, and a delegation of twelve Russian émigrés led by Fr. Sergius Bulgakov, along with Bezobrazov, Kalashnikov, N. Klepinin, and Zernov. After two days dedicated to information concerning the situation of the Russian Church, Bulgakov, on January 13, delivered a paper in English entitled "Orthodoxy and Non-Orthodox Religions," which had already appeared (under a different title) in the July 1926 issue of *The Way*. Being careful not to clash with the Russian Church Outside Russia, the Russian theologian, in his presentation, rejected "any type of Eucharistic intercommunion"[627] because "you cannot follow two ways at the same time." Several years later, Bulgakov would change his opinion.

Bulgakov pointed out, however, that, historically, the Orthodox Church has recognized every person baptized in Christ as a Christian even if that person was separated from Orthodoxy. The Orthodox Church has also recognized, in practice, the existence of a potential hierarchy outside of its visible borders.[628] That meant that "the mystical reality of the Church is not limited by its canonical borders," which, moreover, became outdated in certain cases. Thus Bulgakov justified the movement to reunite the different churches by affirming that the Orthodox Church was one but that ecclesial reality was active outside its borders.[629] According to the report on the St. Albans conference that appeared in *The Way*, the presentation was well received by the Anglican attendees.[630] On the other hand, the Anglicans were opposed to any "metahistoric" interpretation of Scripture and especially to that of the Book of Genesis,[631] such as Bulgakov developed during the debate, while the Russian participants were opposed to the naïve and optimistic vision of the Kingdom of God held by the Anglicans.[632] When it came time to evaluate what they had accomplished, O. Clarke admitted that the conference had opened "a new world" for the participants, "in which we felt at home yet all the while being impressed by its newness."[633] In typical Anglican style, Fr. Clarke affirmed that this mutual discovery was providential and also symbolic of the coming together of Russia and England.[634]

The Birth of the Fellowship

The conference of Lausanne, where Bulgakov and Bishop Gore felt themselves particularly close to one another in their common defense of the First Rome and of the Mother of God in the face of the Protestant world — especially German Protestantism — encouraged the British and Russian students to consolidate their unity in a more concrete way. Moreover, the neo-liturgical movement among the younger members of the Russian emigration — reinforced in 1927 following the schism with the Russian Church Outside Russia — awakened the interest of Anglo-Catholics, who were attracted by the profundity of the Eastern liturgy. Unlike the meetings with Catholic intellectuals organized in Paris by Berdyaev, the encounters between the Russian emigration and the Anglicans took on a dimension which was more sacramental and ecclesial than anthropological and secular. That is why Bulgakov and Florovsky played greater roles in it.

The second conference of Anglican and Orthodox young people, held at St. Albans from December 28 to January 8, 1928,[635] terminated this time with the foundation of a confraternity among the students of the BSCM, those of the St. Sergius Institute, and those of the RSCM—named the Fellowship of St. Alban (the first British martyr) and St. Sergius (of Radonezh) (FSASS). The secretary, Xenia Braikevich, a Russian émigré living in London, and Nicolas Zernov, the editor of *Vestnik RSKhD*, the review of the RSCM, were entrusted with the publication of the journal of the fellowship, *The Journal of the Fellowship of St. Alban and St. Sergius.*

About sixty-five people, twenty-five Russians and forty Anglicans, were present at this conference. The conference presenters, Bishops Gore and Frere, Bulgakov, and Bezobrazov, treated themes that had been broached during the first conference—the interpretation of the Kingdom of God and exegesis.

Bezobrazov's paper, "The Principles of Orthodox Study of the Holy Scriptures," was the result of the confrontation of the two exegetical traditions eleven months previously. It was particularly important since it was the first response of a theologian of the Russian Church of the emigration to twentieth-century Western perspectives and the first attempt at a theoretical formulation of the originality (modernist, even if the term is not necessarily used) of Orthodox exegetical symbolism. Bezobrazov claimed that the basis of the metahistorical approach to Scripture does not rule out any rational approach. It relies on the a priori of faith that the scriptural texts are vehicles of revelation and on the testimony of the texts, of the canon, of the editors, and, above all, of Tradition. Taking a point of departure from this principle and these laws, Bezobrazov established a web of symbolic correspondences between the books of the Old and New Testaments. Using this method, he argued that Genesis should be distinguished from the other books of the Pentateuch and, consequently, not be submitted to a narrow historical approach, such as that employed by the Anglican exegetes, but understood in a metahistorical context. The distance that separated the metahistorical from the historical was, according to Bezobrazov, that which also separated a painted portrait from an icon. "Metahistory does not exclude history," wrote Bezobrazov, "but, though it reveals itself in history, it escapes our understanding."[636] Paul Anderson, one of the architects of the Fellowship among the Anglicans, mentioned in his report on the conference, which appeared in the April 1928 issue of *The Way*, the general reaction of the participants to the presentation of the Russian theologian. In Anderson's opinion, with respect to exegetics, unlike the previous year, "unity was arrived at in spite of differences of approach and religious experience."[637]

Unity was advancing with giant steps. The contributors to the review were also attentive to the more left-leaning modernist currents within the Anglican Church. In the November 1929 issue of *The Way*, V. Grinevich published an article on English religious and philosophical thought. The author opposed "the mystical experience and symbolism" of the new British intelligentsia to the traditional dogmatic approach and argued that the interrogations of the former concerning Darwin's theory of evolution are based on a particular interpretation of the origins of evil.[638] All the same, as was the case in France, the modernist authors of *The Way* had more intellectual affinity with right-wing Christians. In the same issue of *The Way*, Fedotov gave a report on the "conference" of the Fellowship held at High Leigh in England on April 3–8, 1929, describing it as "a new form for us to communicate with the Anglo-Saxons."[639] The papers dedicated to the liturgy were given by Bishop Frere and Fedotov to an audience of about a hundred. In spite of the limited short-term significance of such a conference, the pro-ecumenist Russian historian considered it as "a link in this great enterprise . . . on which our generation will perhaps be called upon to pronounce the decisive word."[640] Indeed, the very perspective of the conference, which posed the question of an approach to ecumenical dialogue that was not simply dogmatic but also sacramental, was, in itself, of universal importance. Fedotov, going beyond Bulgakov's declaration of the previous year, thought that everything that it is humanly possible to do to advance the full sacramental coming together of Orthodox and Anglicans—that is, intercommunion—should be done.[641] Fedotov wrote:

> What can reunion with the local Anglican Church give to the Eastern Orthodox Churches? The answer to this question will either stimulate or dry up the energies of the promoters of this movement. It seems to us that the consequences of such an event are incomparable. The Orthodox Church will exercise its universality in a new way by ceasing to consider itself (according to our limited psychology) as the Church of just the East, linked to a sole geographical or political tradition. It will incorporate into itself, not just potentially but really, a whole new cultural world, by sanctifying what is orthodox in the Latin Middle Ages and, at the same time, all that is worthy and precious in the Reformation. More specifically, this brings the promise of the "churching" of all the enormous social energy of the Anglo-Saxon world as well as its theological research. . . . After the enormous cultural collapse of Russia,

the scientific traditions must be restored and in a new way; in this the aid of England will be especially precious.[642]

Conclusion: Snapshot of an Encounter

As we have seen, the modernist period of the review, from 1925 to 1929, was characterized by the emergence of a milieu of émigré Russian intellectuals who came to Western Europe from all sorts of backgrounds and who were united, in spite of a number of internal divergencies, by their concern to anchor the tradition of symbolic thought in Christian revelation and by a common determination to defend Eastern civilization in the face of the West. In an arbitrary yet significant way, this first period of the journal can end with the report of the eighth session of the Franco-Russian meetings held on May 27, 1930, in Paris and dedicated to the theme of the East and the West. In the course of this meeting between Russian and French intellectuals, although it became clear that the old conceptions of the "Byzantine" East and the "Latin" West were vacuous, Berdyaev took pains to prove that the realities of the East and the West are pure symbols. Henri Massis, given his unexpected absence from the conference, was unable to contradict the position of the Russian philosopher, who maintained that the static and fixed concepts of East and West are inadequate for the realities that they should signify.

In the context of the Franco-Russian group, de Vogt had organized an event involving a debate between the famous activist Massis and Berdyaev, the leader of those opposed to the apologist of Action Française. The report of the event was published in the June 5, 1930, issue of *Cahiers de la Quinzaine*, and Berdyaev's contribution appeared in the August issue of *The Way* that same year. Among others who participated in this meeting were J. Maxence, R. Sebastien, M. Péguy, Henri Ghéon, Daniel Halévy, Robert Honnert, Count Jean de Pange, Fumet, O. Lacombe, and Fr. Lev Gillet representing the French intellectuals, and, on the Russian side, Vysheslavtsev, N. Berberova, N. Gorodetskaya, J. Sazonova, N. Teffi, N. Turgeneva, K. Mochulsky, B. Poplavsky, S. Sharshun, and M. Vishniak, as well as the Grand Duchess Irene of Russia and M. Spolaikovitch, the Yugoslavian minister at Paris.

In the absence of Massis, Berdyaev presented his address first. The Russian philosopher, who was particularly at ease in this kind of debate, did not lose the opportunity to provoke the French intellectuals.

Classicism, in Western European culture and especially in its oldest, most perfect, and refined expression—that of France—so seductive by its clarity, stems from Greco-Roman classicism towards which it seeks to be faithful. Mediterranean civilization is, in its eyes, universal and eternal, while the rest of the world wallows in barbarism.[643]

For Berdyaev, "the concepts of East and West are very mobile." The concept of the East for a Westerner, moreover, is nothing more than a disguised form of the myth of the Other. After showing the absurdity of identifying the concept of the West with that of Latin civilization, Berdyaev defended his idea that "East" and "West" are symbols. While the West symbolized humanism and historical dynamism but also cultural formalism, the East, represented in particular by Russian thought, tended, according to Berdyaev, "to see an activity in the very power of life, and does not permit itself to admit that the form can be applied to matter as something exterior to it."[644]

But Berdyaev pushed the symbolism to its limits and concluded that "the East is the land of revelation." Although he had criticized the identification of the West and Latinism, he restored a geographical meaning to the symbol of the East by affirming that "all religions have arisen from the East."[645] It followed that the West was only a symbol of "the setting sun" and of "civilization." Russia, which belonged both to the East and to the West, should realize the synthesis between Athens and Jerusalem, between intelligence and faith. Berdyaev conceded that Christianity, although originating in the East, is a universal revelation which alone can bring about this synthesis.

Following Berdyaev's presentation, de Vogt had to announce to the audience that, at the last minute, Massis was forced to cancel. Maxence elected to reply to Berdyaev in the name of his friend Massis. The nonconformist writer did not hesitate to point out the contradictions in Berdyaev's argumentation. "The fact that Christianity comes to us from Jerusalem does not prove that the West has not been baptized; it doesn't even prove that the West propagated religions by 'the methods of civilization.'"[646] But, above all, Maxence disputed the symbolic identification of the East with revelation and the West with civilization because, in his opinion, "if these two definitions were true, there would be no possibility of a common language." After the reading of three messages from Maritain, Malraux, and R. Lalou, three speakers, namely, Pange, M. Péguy, and Fumet, then offered a classic defense of Western civilization against the attacks of the Russian philosopher. Vysheslavtsev tried to take an intermediary position by defending Christian Platonism against the Eastern Hindu flight from the world. O. Lacombe, in opposition to certain ambiguous theses of Berdyaev, essentially intoned a hymn to the law and to rights which, far from being obstacles to freedom, are the very conditions of true liberty. But the specialist on Indian culture finished his presentation by coming back to the principal idea of Berdyaev: "It is in a deep and ordered harmony of reason and faith, both of which come from God and which He wants to see associated in a common task, that the union of the East and the West can be consummated in these two universalisms."[647] Fr. Lev Gillet concluded the series of presentations by giving a clear preference to the Gospel foundation rather than any attachment to the East or the West.

Berdyaev, visibly embarrassed at having revealed his own a priori assumptions against the West for all to see, attempted to nuance his propositions. He responded to his critics that by "civilization" he did not at all have in mind a pejorative definition of material culture, but rather of "spiritual culture." He then admitted that the symbolic use of "the words East and West" should not mask the fact that "there is a wonderful religious life in the West."[648] Piqued by the criticism of Russian eschatology, Berdyaev judged that from now on it would be impossible to prove that "his people are the greatest in the world" and dryly opined that "this is a question of faith." He concluded, nonetheless, by repeating his "central idea." "God is neither a God of the West nor a God of the East."[649]

Although it is somewhat arbitrary to regard this meeting in the spring of 1930 as a turning point in the history of *The Way*, it is, however, a fact that after this date, debate on the limits of East and West disappeared from the pages of the review. The time had now arrived for the Russian intellectuals to rid themselves of their preconceived ideas about the West and also to reconsider, in a more antinomian manner, the relationship between the symbol, the myth and dogma, and the realities that these terms designated. Through chance meetings, and each one in his own way, the Russian philosophers henceforth directed their research towards a theme that would become central—theanthropy.

PART TWO

A Nonconformist Journal

(1930–1935)

INTRODUCTION: NEW OUTLOOKS

The Nonconformist Spirit of the 1930s

In the 1930s, Europe experienced "pivotal years" between war and peace, as expressed in the title of Henri Daniel-Rops's book *Les années tournantes*, published in 1932. The consequences of America's Great Depression, which little by little spread throughout Europe, would provoke the great civilization crisis of the thirties, which had been pending since the end of the First World War. It was a crisis of civilization because its political, economic, and social aspects were rooted above all in the death of nineteenth-century bourgeois society. An entire intellectual generation that had reached adulthood by the end of the 1920s suddenly experienced the abyss that separated it from the "blue-horizon" generation, which gloried in indescribable slaughter, and, moreover, whose elders were governing France without even realizing that the twentieth century had begun. Within this generation a group of angry young people would be classified as "nonconformist youth."[1] These individuals would recognize one another, as in any other generation, by subtle behaviors invisible to the uninitiated, whether it be their choice of meeting places or the way they presented their positions; by their attempt to create a political "Third Force" between capitalism and communism or between fascism and democracy; and finally, by their common intellectual reference points.

Above all, this generation was characterized by a particular relationship to life, a demand for realism in the face of the growing darkness ahead. Marked by the inevitable sense that the postwar period was ending, this generation was rightly described by Jean Touchard[2] as neo-traditionalist and neoconservative. But, as shown in *Les non-conformistes des années trente* by Jean-Louis Loubet del Bayle and in *Les années souterraines* by Daniel Lindenberg, this generation was also characterized by a genuine spiritual impulse. In these two historians' descriptions of the generation of Georges Bataille, leader of the Collège de Sociologie, of Denis de Rougemont, spokesman of *La Nouvelle Revue Française* ("A prendre ou à tuer," *NRF*, December 1, 1932), and of Robert Aron and Arnaud Dandieu, the co-authors of *La révolution nécessaire* (1933), they insisted on the burning quest for an existential meaning to life by the entire generation. This search was based on a much more demanding and vigorous humanism than that of the prewar pacifists, by the desire to captivate the world once again through literature as well as through politics, by the urge to belong to an authentic community working outside of national institutions (the church, army, university, political party) in a "grassroots" or "bottom-up" way, or, again, by a revolutionary aspiration to restore the history of a country content with its republican conquests.

Michel Winock, in his work for the journal *Esprit*, affirmed that before looking for sociopolitical explanations for the emergence of the journal, it would be better to qualify its authors—Mounier, Izard, Déléage, and Madaule—as defenders of the "primacy of the spiritual." But this did not mean an escape from politics. Rather, they wanted to affirm the importance of spiritual reality within the realm of politics.[3] In the journal *Esprit*, as well as in the journals of Jean-Pierre Maxence (*Les Cahiers, La Revue Française*), of Jean de Fabrègues (*Réaction*), of Philippe Lamour and André Wurmser (*Plans*), and of Robert Aron and Arnaud Dandieu (*L'Ordre nouveau*), we find the same questioning about the great political forces and about the traditional left-wing/right-wing opposition, with a common aspiration to a better sharing of revenue. In short, we find a rejection of the "established chaos." This generation horizontally brought together different sociopolitical traditions. Whether one belonged to the neoliberal current of Bertrand de Jouvenel and Jacques Rueff, for whom the state should merely have the role of a policeman, or to the neosocialist perspective of André Philip and Denis de Rougemont, for whom the society of the community should prevail against liberal individualism, or, again, to the neo-traditionalist current of Georges Roditi and André Voisin, who would rather use planning, corporations, and trade unions in order to make the economy serve humanity; one finds in all of these groups a demand for an increasing role of the executive over the legislative, a predilection for planning, and the desire to reconcile patriotism and revolution. Because they were living on the fringes of society, the main asset of these nonconformist intellectuals was their openness to any kind of new idea and their eagerness to engage in dialogue. Also, from 1935 onward, the polarization of politics, little by little, would shut down this new third force.

According to Jean-Jacques Becker and Serge Berstein, the deferred realization of the structural effects of the First World War was initiated in the 1920s by certain great thinkers, such as Paul Valéry and Oswald Spengler, and constituted the basis for the nonconformist movement. Reflection on the foundations of Western rationality obviously expanded following the popularization of the works of Freud on the unconscious, of Albert Einstein on relativity, and of Henri Bergson on the vital impulse. Anything that had to do with sexuality, the Orient, the fabulous, and the mythical fascinated intellectuals. There was an interest in new worlds, whether esoteric or tropical. Nietzsche, Sorel, and Proudhon were being read. Above all, the demand for realism united intellectual tendencies. Péguy, the voice of a whole generation, was seen as the poet of the Incarnation, the anti-Kant, the critic of "pure reason." Emmanuel Mounier, in a retrospective article, wrote: "We were quite busy getting rid of our mentors of literature and of the university. We had read neither Marx nor Kierkegaard, nor Jaspers. We were looking for a place to stay between Bergson and Péguy, Maritain and Berdyaev."[4]

Was Berdyaev, the Russian who denounced the bourgeois spirit, one of the fathers of the nonconformist movement, as Mounier's quotation asserts? Or, on the contrary, should one consider that personalism, which is the real achievement of Berdyaev's thought, could not have been systematized in the thirties by the Russian philosopher had he not been in contact with French thought? As to whether it is influence or convergence, Olivier Clément, in the chapter of his book on Berdyaev entitled "Berdyaev et la pensée française," leans towards the second conclusion. Certainly, according to a note Mounier wrote on December 8, 1930, it seems that the idea of the journal *Esprit* and the associated movement started precisely that day, after a meeting at Berdyaev's home. Berdyaev was present at the founding meeting on the following day, and his article "Vérité et mensonge du communisme," published in *The Way* a year earlier, set the tone for the first issue of the journal *Esprit*. Similarly, D. Lindenberg talks about "Berdyaev, Shestov, Gurdiev, and Solovyov" as follows:

> These names are so much help for the French intelligentsia of the twenties and thirties. In a way they are the Lenins, the Trotskys, and the Bukharins for those who strongly dislike materialism and the fact that our modern world is ruled by money. . . . The contact with the thought of the Russian exiles (it would be appropriate to mention also Gurvitch and Lévinas) brought back the combination of theology and politics which had been excluded from French universities because of the conflict between the State and the Church. We know what an enrichment this reunion was for the Church, which thus could reestablish contacts with Islam and Judaism. Bataille received one of his first impressions when reading Shestov, and thanks to Berdyaev's meditations, the themes of Dostoyevsky were spreading everywhere.[5]

Conversely, it is easy to show how the Russian intellectuals, living in Montparnasse, the center of Paris, were influenced by the ideas of their time. Berdyaev published in 1933 in *The Way* an article entitled "*Esprit*, les quêtes spirituelles et sociales de la jeunesse française." Shestov was kept updated by Jules de Gaultier and Benjamin Fondane about publications. Fedotov regularly published in his new journal, *New City*, reviews of the main works of Aron and de Jouvenel. I discuss the relations between French and Russian intellectuals in more detail later. Of current interest is the relationship between the nonconformist current and the authors of *The Way*.

The Nonconformist Aspects of *The Way*

It is clear that, on the political plane, the failure of the monarchist and Eurasian movements (characterized by the splintering of Trubetskoy's group and the pro-Soviet evolution of its left wing) and, on the social plane, the emancipation of the intellectuals collaborating with the review from the conservative currents of the immigrant community, created a favorable climate for the emergence of a nonconformist tendency in *The Way*. But it was on the intellectual level that the rupture appeared most clearly. The February 1930 issue, number 20, could symbolically be chosen as the beginning of this period. This issue contained two decisive articles—which must have surprised an unsuspecting public—by Berdyaev and Bulgakov, respectively. The first was on Jacob Boehme's doctrine of the *Ungrund*, the other was on the dogma of the Eucharist, where, for the first time in the pages of the review, Bulgakov clearly put forth the sophiological foundations of his thought.

As was the case for the French intellectuals, the polarization of political life after the French political crisis of February 6, 1934, got the better of the Russian nonconformist movement as a short-term political project for Soviet Russia. All the same, the cohesion of the group would last until the summer of 1935. For reasons explained in Part Three, I have chosen to conclude the specifically nonconformist period of the review with the July 1935, number 48 issue, which contained an article by Vladimir Veidlé [also Weidle, or Veidle]—quite representative of the era—entitled "The Renaissance of the Marvelous." These timeframes should be viewed with extreme prudence. They are simply points of reference in the continual flux of many individual lives. Having the benefit of the clarity of the lights that illumine our present age, their only claim is to illustrate the continual movement of the collective conscience reflecting upon itself.

Thus *The Way* underwent an authentic change between February 1930 and March 1935. What it shared with the nonconformist movement was mainly a period of intense intellectual activity, of creativity in the realms of literature, philosophy, and theology, which can only be compared to the beacon years of the Silver Age (1909–14). During this period, the review increased its publications, putting out six issues annually in 1930–31 and five annually in 1932–33. It returned to its earlier pattern of four annual issues in 1934–35 only because of the constraints of the financial crisis of the YMCA (the individual issue sold for ten francs, a four-issue subscription cost thirty-five francs). Between January 1930 and March 1935, twenty-seven issues were published, while for a similar five-year period, between September 1925 and December 1929, only nineteen issues were published. To all this activity should be added the beginning, in 1932, of a series of nine supplements to the review. The first four supplements, in 1932, were "Christianity and the Challenge of Contemporary Social Reality," a previously unpublished session of the Academy of Religious Philosophy; Kartashev, "Church and State"; Berdyaev, "The General Orientation of Soviet Philosophy and Militant Atheism"; and Vysheslavtsev, "The Tragedy of Those Elevated and Speculation on Their Fall." As of September 1932, these supplements were published separately, as special additions to the review: Lagovsky, "Collectivization and Religion" (Sept. 1932, no. 35); Florovsky, "The Question of Christian Unity" (Feb. 1933, no. 37); Kurdiumov, "The Church and the New Russia" (May 1933, no. 38); Afanasiev, "The Canons and Canonical Conscience" (July 1933, no. 39); and Stratonov, "The Origins of the Present Organization of the Patriarchal Russian Church." An article by Troitsky entitled "The Pre-Synod of 1932 and the Preparation for the Council," which was announced as a supplement on several occasions, never appeared.

Without a doubt, one finds the same fascination among French intellectuals for the idea of myth as one finds among the Russians. This fascination took the form of an emotional attraction towards the esoteric and the discovery of new worlds, of a resurgence of interest in literary and artistic currents inspired by symbolism, and of a greater reawakening of collective memory. In the December 1930 issue of the review (no. 25), Frank published a long study entitled "Psychoanalysis as a Worldview." Saltykov developed a zodiac exegesis of the Gospels, while Berdyaev and Turgeneva, the sister-in-law of André Biely, discussed the doctrine of metempsychosis in the pages of the journal. Among other things, the journal also published an account of the voyage of S. Ilnitsky to Dahomey and his life among the primitive peoples of the region, an essay dedicated to the Japanese mythology of Kodzik (V2), and two remarkable studies by Veidlé ("The Degeneration of Art" (March 1934) and "The Renaissance of the Marvelous" (July 1935).

Above and beyond the quality of Veidlé's analysis, these studies merit closer attention insofar as they manifest the nonconformist accents of the review. Because of his evolution from aesthetic research of the fabulous to adherence to the Christian myth, Veidlé (1895–1979) is the most characteristic representative of the new group of authors whom Berdyaev incorporated into the review around 1930.[6] In his article on the degeneration of art, Veidlé used examples drawn from painting, photography, cinema, music, literature, and architecture, and argued that the West, incapable of casting off Cartesian doubt, is looking at the end of an epoch. Unless the artists, Veidlé wrote, rediscovered as quickly as possible their sense of the mystery of creation—whose ultimate justification is religious—then, as was the case for the Roman Empire, the gladiator will begin to replace the tragic actor while awaiting the arrival of the barbarians.

> The artist tumbles down from one hell into an another, each one yet more terrible, wandering from the moldy reality to the world of disincarnate forms and returning once again towards the symbols and awaiting their transformation. No understanding, no talent, no knowledge will, by itself, be able to save him, will enable him to find the living word he has lost. The transfiguration is not brought about by methodic doubt, it is a miracle, and the Incarnation is a still greater miracle. Their true meaning is not revealed in philosophy nor in science nor even in art but only in the myths and mysteries of religion.[7]

In his second article, Veidlé continued his reflection by revealing the presence of a hunger for "mytho-creation" in contemporary literature. Whether it be the success of children's literature as exemplified by Jules Verne, Alain Fournier, or Lewis Carroll—characterized by the rejection of traditional forms of causality—or regionalist literature as exemplified by Giono, Francois Mauriac, or Marcel Jouhandeau—whose quest for mythical realism has not been snuffed out by technology or by the frantic rhythms of the megalopolis—Russian critics witnessed that authentic creation is nourished by the marvelous. But Veidlé again insisted on the necessity for the artist to anchor the myths he discovers in faith. "For only faith can separate the mythic—in the deepest sense of the word—from fiction; without faith, the artist can only choose between the inner acceptance of the intellectually dissolute character of his art, or lie to himself by constructing his art while pretending to have faith."[8] Russian critics explained the English literary revival (G. K. Chesterton) as well as the French literary renaissance (Charles Du Bos) by their Anglican and Catholic sources, while, inversely, literature of the Protestant tradition suffers in a conflict with myth. Veidlé finished by mentioning the later work of Rouault: "The straightest road, the road most faithful to the renaissance of the marvelous, even though it is not the only road, is found in the reunion of the artistic creation with the Christian myth and the Christian Church."[9]

Thus the coordinates of the debate changed with respect to those of the 1920s. The double dialogue undertaken by the generation of the authors of *The Way*, the first within Russian speculation itself—between the two currents, cosmological and anthropological—and the second with the European intellectuals—concerning the foundations of rationality—finds a new expression by refocusing reflection on the principal myth of Christianity, that of the God-Man. It could be said that the *Ungrund* of Berdyaev, the Sophia of Bulgakov, or the faith of Shestov (1866–1938)—which made its appearance in the review in June 1930 with an article on Rozanov—are no longer the bases for reflection on the spirit, the angels, or Luther, as was the case in the 1920s, but the very objects of this reflection. During this period, Berdyaev would lay the foundations of a new divine-human anthropology in his book *O Naznachenia Cheloveka* (*The Destiny of Man*).[10] Bulgakov would inaugurate a new trilogy centered on theanthropy/divine-humanity with his treatise on Christ, *Agnets Bozhii* (*The Lamb of God*), and Shestov would publish three studies—"The Second Dimension of Thought" (1930), "Parmenides Enchained: The Sources of Metaphysical Truth" (1932), and "Athens and Jerusalem: In Response to Etienne Gilson's *The Spirit of Medieval Philosophy*"—which traced the contours of a "philosophy which proposes not to accept but rather surpass evidence and which introduces a new dimension into our reflection: the faith."[11]

A second change within the review compared to the preceding period is more of a social nature and assimilates it more closely to the nonconformist movement of the 1930s. There was a significant turnover in the contributors to the review, which favored Russian intellectuals born between 1890 and 1910. These authors, who were too young to know Russia before the revolution, no longer benefited from the legitimacy within the immigration community that was necessary in order to make heard the new accents of their language, which was less "pure," mixed with gallicisms and new references. Whether they were writers, historians, theologians, or philosophers, these authors found themselves, without having been consulted, caught in an awkward position between a Silver Age that didn't want to end (in 1933 Bunin received the Nobel Prize in Literature, and Berdyaev the famous French Institute's prize in philosophy) and "this glow arising in the East," as embodied in a new generation of Soviet intellectuals, which aroused a much greater fascination among the French intellectuals than the "painful road of exile" of the Russian immigrants. Increasingly marginalized by the reinforcement of Stalin's regime and the worsening economic and social situation in France, this generation of authors had the same reasons—and more—to be frustrated as did their French contemporaries. Varshavsky, one of these young writers, born in 1906, who was familiar with the Russian groups and reviews of Paris, published a book of reminiscences in New York in 1956 with the relevant title *Nezamechenoe Pokolenie* (*A Generation Which Nobody Noticed*), in which he compared his generation, stuck between two eras, to that of the 1820s described by Alfred de Musset in *Confessions of a Child of the Century*. For Varshavsky, the 1931 suicide of Boris Poplavsky, the most brilliant poet among the young writers of the exile community, was symbolic of the awkwardness felt by this stratum of the Russian intelligentsia, who were ignored before they could even speak. It would seem that Berdyaev was the first to make such an analysis; deeply moved by the death of the young poet, whom he had appreciated, he published, that same year, a short essay on suicide in response to questions certain young Russian intellectuals at Montparnasse were asking themselves. Nor did he spare any efforts to integrate as many young authors as possible into the review and to promote, at least until 1935, when it was still possible, a dialogue between the different generations and among the different groups of the immigration community. It can even be said that Berdyaev brought about a real transfusion of life into the review, for, between January 1930 and March 1935, 60 percent of the authors of the preceding period dropped out of sight, while, among the newcomers, twenty-four were less than forty years old, bringing the number of young authors up to thirty-five, representing 50 percent of the contributors as opposed to 37 percent in the 1920s.

To allow this young generation to become part of the review, Berdyaev ingeniously manipulated three elements: the natural succession of generations, the ecumenical and cultural change in the editorial policy of the review, and the evolution of the political context of the immigration community. During this period the review lost two of its most eminent collaborators; G. N. Trubetskoy died in 1929 at the age of fifty-five and Fr. Alexander Eltchaninov in 1934 at the age of fifty-three. On the other hand, young philosophers and theologians, often formed in the modernist galaxy, began appearing in the review: Afanasiev, Gillet, A. Glazberg, N. A. Reimers, K. Serezhnikov, B. Vrevsky, Zander, and Zernov. Among the older generation, a number of noted figures had their debut in *The Way*: Lazarev, M. Lot-Borodin, Menshikov, Shestov, Spektorsky, and F. A. Stepun.[12] As for the participation of non-Orthodox authors in the journal, as of 1929 with the departure of Kuhlmann to Switzerland, Berdyaev had undertaken a change of editorial policy concerning ecumenism—first, by not replacing Kuhlmann, which had the effect of making the ecumenical commitments of the review more legitimately Orthodox, and, second, by increasing the number of articles treating the problem of the reunion of the churches but privileging the point of view of Orthodox authors on the grounds that they were more accessible and credible to the readership. Berdyaev did not cease inviting non-Orthodox authors—in that respect he was faithful to his principle of the primacy of the spiritual in these questions—but their number decreased significantly. While there were fourteen non-Orthodox authors in the nineteen issues between 1925 and 1930, there were only five for the twenty-seven issues between 1930 and 1935 (two Catholics, Bennigsen and A. Iakubiziak; one Protestant, F. Gavin; one Anglican, K. Kirk; and one Jew, Shestov). Likewise, on the cultural level, the review began shifting its policy as of 1928 by not publishing more prose and by favoring essays of criticism. This tendency was consolidated and enlarged by an openness to young critics from the immigration community (Ilnitsky, Litviak, Mochulsky, Pletnev, Veidlé), as well as to others no longer young (P. Bitsilli, G. Guesen). Finally, as we have seen, the change in the political context during the 1920s, the fading of the Eurasian movement, the loss of the perspective of returning to Russia, the new political-ecclesial situation, and the worsening of the economic and social condition of the immigrants—all these factors led Berdyaev to invite new and young authors to collaborate with the journal: M. M. Artemiev, H. Gofshtetter, D. Ishevsky, A. Polotebneva, V. Rastorguev, D. Rasheev, and N. Sarafanov.

In addition to the ebullient intellectual character of this period and the process of generational succession, at the same time as the establishment of a dialogue among the diverse currents represented in the review, the third characteristic that drew most of the authors of *The Way* towards the nonconformist preoccupations of their era was their desire to commit themselves concretely on a spiritual level and to reformulate the terms of the political debate outside the usual models. For a number of Russian intellectuals, the new decade corresponded to strong existential decisions on their part, which had been put on hold during the waiting period of the 1920s. Zander and Lagovsky decided to live in the Baltic countries, with a view to developing the activities of the Russian Student Christian Movement, while Zernov opted to install himself definitively in England in order to concentrate on ecumenical activities. In 1932, Bezobrazov decided to become a monk, taking the name of Cassian; Skobtsova also chose to take the monastic habit and, under the religious name of St. Mary of Egypt, as Mother Maria, founded a hostel for the homeless, unemployed, and needy. Florovsky became a priest. The following year saw the conversion of Mochulsky and Veidlé's return to the church. In 1934, Vladimir Ilyin, at the age of forty-three, was married to Vera Pundik.

The quest for the Kingdom of God, whether a personal quest or a political and social quest (a phenomenon that we will observe later on with respect to the formation of new movements such as those of the "new city," the *novogradtsy*) is, as we have seen in the 1920s, one of the constants of this generation of intellectuals, and is not, in itself, linked to the nonconformist movement. By his engagements in the early 1930s in favor of "the truth of Communism" and by his softer opposition against any form of nationalism, Berdyaev was merely continuing to commit himself, as he had done in the 1920s, against the monarchists and Eurasians. What had changed from the preceding period was that Berdyaev was no longer isolated. A group of young intellectual modernists, openly proclaiming their membership in the visible church, succeeded in emancipating themselves from the prevailing idea that the sacred principle of "the primacy of the spiritual" meant that one must remain silent in the domain of the political and social life of the world. As a result, the journal, although not entering the sphere of commentary on disputed issues, multiplied the number of its articles dedicated to social questions, political science, economy, ecology,[13] and political and religious changes in the USSR. These articles were characterized by the desire for economic liberation from the old models of liberalism or socialism and the search for political alternatives to democracies that were neither fascist nor communist. In so doing, the review became a kind of nonconformist workshop trying to elaborate a third way.

Moreover, Berdyaev, who wanted *The Way* to maintain its character of spearheading reflections on theology, philosophy, and human sciences, was in favor of the appearance of another journal that would provide a more adequate framework and a team for treating political and economic questions. In 1931, with the encouragement of Berdyaev, Fedotov, along with Fondaminsky and Stepun, decided to found a new Russian language review, *Novy Grad—New City*. In their editorial-manifesto, the editors wrote: "Along with all those who live in this century, we are convinced that our generation finds itself very intimately involved in social problems, not in seeking theoretical analyses but rather practical solutions."[14] This new review could be seen as a younger sister to *The Way*. Edited by the YMCA Press, which Berdyaev directed, and composed of the principal modernist authors of *The Way*, such as Berdyaev, Bulgakov, Skobtsova, and Vysheslavtsev, its goal was to popularize the ideas debated in *The Way* by linking them with the political, social, and cultural evolution of the USSR and Western Europe. Deliberately disrespectful of the symbolist and pre-revolution generation of the intelligentsia, even sometimes entering into conflict with the generation of its fathers and with Berdyaev in particular, *New City* was, above all, a group of authors (including Berdyaev, Bulgakov, and so on) united by the same spiritual exigencies and belonging to the same intellectual tradition as *The Way*. In the same manifesto of 1931, the editors concluded with phrases that echo Berdyaev:

> The freedom of the person and communitarian truth, the principles of nationality and universality—where can these be reconciled outside of Christianity? . . . But we do not ask someone what he believes in but rather of what spirit he is made. With this motto as a standard, we have come together to struggle for the truth in the New City.[15]

The Renewal of an Intellectual Generation

The Way's nonconformist character having been established, the next step here is to investigate the evolution of the intellectual generation and its memory of what preceded it.

First of all, was it the case that the passage of time, which led to the exclusion of 60 percent of the original authors of the journal, modified the principal foundations of those intellectuals descended from the tradition of the fathers of the nineteenth century: spiritual independence with respect to all types of power, dogmatic symbolism inspired by the Orthodox tradition, and openness towards church unity? Why did the final modernist crystallization of this generation not lead to the journal's demise? How could neo-traditionalist intellectuals such as Florovsky, Chetverikov, and Arseniev continue to engage in dialogue for another four years with a group of younger men with arrogant modernist pretensions, led by Fedotov, Zernov, and Veidlé?

Another series of questions emerges concerning the content of the intellectual debate itself. How could Berdyaev open the pages of *The Way* to Shestov, his implacable philosophical enemy? What role did memory play regarding openness to the nonconformist currents of the journal? What was the influence of the debate with European intellectuals on the internal movement of Russian thought?

Finally, questions must be raised about the cohesion of engagements within the context of the journal in spite of the different choices made by the journal's authors between Moscow and Constantinople. Why didn't the convulsions in the relationships between the jurisdiction of Metropolitan Evlogy and that loyal to Moscow cause a schism within the journal? How could the positions espoused in *The Way*, which Berdyaev was pushing more and more to the left, be supported by monarchists such as Kartashev and Zenkovsky? Was there any connection between the different ecclesial, ecumenical, and political engagements of the authors of the journal?

Although it is certain that the journal, in the years 1930–35, went through a considerable renewal of its contributors by integrating a number of young intellectuals, the disintegrating effect of such a phenomenon on the modernist generation was offset by the stability of a core of twenty-eight authors, whose articles represented 70 percent of the contributions during this period. These authors were: Alekseev, Arseniev, Belenson-Elson, Berdyaev, Bezobrazov, Bubnov, Bulgakov, Chetverikov, Chizhevsky, Fedorov, Fedotov, Florovsky, Frank, Ilyin, Ioann (Shakhovskoy), Ivanov, Karpov, Kartashev, Kurdiumov, Lagovsky, N. Lossky, Sazonova, Skobtsova, Smolitsch, Troitsky, Vysheslavtsev, Zander, and Zenkovsky. It is true that the permanence of the participation of these authors does not resolve the problem of the increasing gap between the two generations, pre- and post-revolution, which constitute the review. What was there in common between the dean of the group, Fr. Sergius Chetverikov, whose spirituality had been forged during his seminary years in Russia, at the end of the nineteenth century, by the severe vision of Theophan the Recluse, and the youngest of the authors, Nicolas Zernov, who debuted in the pages of the review in 1932 and whose spiritual formation took place in the context of the immigration, at the Faculty of Theology at Belgrade, then in the Russian Student Christian Movement under Berdyaev and Bulgakov, and, finally, at Oxford, where he received a doctorate in philosophy in 1932? But if the differences of age, existential experience, and intellectual and spiritual formation were determining factors, they were not enough to shape a dissident generation. The effects of time were much more complex. In fact, Chetverikov was the spiritual father of the Russian Student Christian Movement in 1925–30, when Zernov was its general secretary. Both men also belonged to the Fraternity of the Presentation of the Virgin in the Temple. Likewise, there was more affinity between Chetverikov and Florovsky, who was twenty-six years younger and who would become the second priest of the RSCM in 1932, than between Chetverikov and Shestov, born one year apart but who had no spiritual affinities. Afanasiev, who appeared in the review for the first time in December 1930, was twelve years younger than Zenkovsky, who recommended him to Berdyaev. According to his wife, Marianne, Zenkovsky "was like a father to him."[16] Examples could be multiplied. There is no doubt that the biological concept of generation only captures one aspect of generational reality.

But this only shifts the problem. Indeed, if it is accepted that the incorporation of younger authors into the review did not have a disintegrating effect, how was Berdyaev able to reconcile, in the very structure of *The Way*, authors so prolix, and currents in increasing opposition to one another due to the aggravation of the political, social, and ecclesial climate within the immigration community and, on a more general level, in the Europe of the years between the two world wars? That was the real question for Florovsky and Fedotov, who, even though they belonged to the same "generation," had two totally different visions of Russian history. Shestov and Bulgakov had completely divergent readings of the Bible, and Skobtsova and Ilyin held radically opposed political positions. An easy answer would be to maintain that *The Way* did not have an editorial policy and anyone could contribute an article if it was well written. Such an answer, however, would imply a misunderstanding of the review. First of all, *The Way* had acquired a reputation that did not allow it to be open to any opinion whatsoever. Given the personality of its editor-in-chief and the value he attached to his review with respect to the "spiritual and religious tasks of the Russian immigration" and the history of the intelligentsia, it is difficult to imagine him publishing articles that contradicted the spirit of the tradition of "Khomiakov, Dostoevsky, Solovyov, Bukharev, Nesmelov, Fedorov,"[17] as he put it in what he wrote, along with the other authors, in his editorial of 1925, and which he would repeat several times up until 1940. Moreover, *The Way*, ever since its criticism of the monarchism of certain circles of the Russian Orthodox Church Outside Russia, was so politically, intellectually, and religiously marked that any author who published in its pages became, in the eyes of the monarchist majority of the immigration, compromised with the "School of Paris."

Finally, and most important, the archives of the journal[18] reveal the presence of genuine editorial work, both collective and exacting, concerning the content of the articles. To be sure, the notion of "close collaborators" mentioned on page 3 of the first issues of the journal was quickly replaced, in 1927, by a vaguer formula: "The following authors have published in preceding issues: . . ." But up to 1939, the review kept the inscription "under the direction of N. A. Berdyaev with the collaboration of B. P. Vysheslavtsev" above the list of the already-published authors. This was not out of inertia, because when the masthead had to be revised because of the departure of Kuhlmann, Berdyaev's second editorial secretary, the formula was maintained. It is a fact that, beginning in 1937, a certain number of the authors belonging to the Parisian core stopped participating in the meetings of the editorial staff. This is why Berdyaev chose to tighten up the membership of his editorial committee and make a new start with a new formula. In September 1939, he changed the heading on page 3 for the third time to read "Under the Direction of N. A. Berdyaev" (without Vysheslavtsev) and "With the Participation of . . ." (followed by a limited number of authors who composed the new core group of the journal). These successive changes reveal that although the members of the editorial board varied depending on the times, the collective nature of the editorial work was always respected.

Andrew Blane, Florovsky's biographer, writes that "the meetings of the editorial committee of the review usually took place Sunday evenings in Berdyaev's apartment."[19] Once a month, on Sunday afternoon, Berdyaev organized a public meeting of the Academy of Religious Philosophy at his home, in which most of the Parisian members of the review participated—Zenkovsky, Skobtsova, Ilyin, Fedotov, Florovsky, Bulgakov, Vysheslavtsev, Alekseev, Shestov, Zander, and Lagovsky. Pierre Pascal, who occasionally attended these gatherings, relates that at the end of the day, after often violent discussions, the journal's authors exchanged articles and made their commentaries. Those who could not attend the meeting because of some problem or because they lived abroad sent their recommendations by letter to Berdyaev or Vysheslavtsev. A number of letters concerning the journal can be found in the archives of Berdyaev and Vysheslavtsev. In 1931, Nikolai Lossky recommended to Vysheslavtsev, for publication in *The Way*, articles by Pletnev on the topic "The Influence of Holy Scripture and Spiritual Literature on Dostoevsky," and added that this represented "ten years of work." Only a part of this work appeared in the January 1939 issue of the journal, which indicates that, given the quality of the article, submissions for publication were not lacking. Another example is a second letter of Lossky to Vysheslavtsev, dated August 1, 1931, in which he recommends including in *The Way* a list of the books published by the YMCA Press between 1930 and 1934, "or at least a partial list, in view of the 8th International Conference of Philosophy." Nothing came of this proposal.[20]

During these meetings, it would happen that an article was judged interesting without convincing the majority of the members of the editorial board. If the spirit of the article was the problem, it was published with a footnote warning the reader. Most frequently, however, the article would be sent back to its author for modifications. Two different examples can be cited. In the June 1930 issue, the review published the first and only article of Yakov Menshikov (1888–1953), a student at Berdyaev's seminar at the Academy, entitled "The Soul of Things," an article with anthroposophic accents, focusing on the symbolic in empirical creation. It was accompanied by the following footnote: "The editorial staff opens its pages to an interesting and indicative article, even though its spirit is not in line with the principal orientation of *The Way*."[21] Probably it was Florovsky who insisted that this phrase be added. The memory of the dispute caused by this article remained quite vivid for a long time, since Florovsky, in relating his memories to his biographer several decades later, affirmed that he was particularly angered by Berdyaev's wish to publish articles with esoteric overtones.

But the best example of specifically editorial work concerns the article by Ilyin that appeared in the October 1933 issue, entitled "The Profanation of Tragedy: The Confrontation of Utopia, Love, and Death." This article was actually published a year after it was submitted and after several modifications, as testified by the correspondence between Berdyaev and

Ilyin preserved in the Berdyaev archives at Clamart. In this article, very typical of the author in its mytho-logical approach, its provocative style, and its despairing tone, Ilyin develops the thesis that the "Marxist-Communist Utopia" is the result of the rejection of the doctrine of original sin. This explains why the Soviet system chooses love and death, the foundations of human tragedy, as scapegoats and clothes itself in a Puritan moralism. Ilyin at the time was going through some complex romantic affairs, similar to the "love-passion" of Tristan and Isolde, which he mentions in this article.[22] Thus he rejects, passionately and not without humor, any moralism that comes from "Athos" or "the Kremlin."[23] In his eyes, the organizational principle of the "Marxo-Communists," with their five-year plans and other industrial fronts, tries to take the place of "the old Eros,"[24] while the mystery of death is profaned by a massive and antipersonal terror.[25]

In the course of a meeting of the editorial board sometime in October 1932, Berdyaev devoted himself above all to a criticism of the proximity of this article to the "organistic" theses developed by the poet Ivanov in his pre-revolution writings. He asked Ilyin to correct the content of the article and its exclusively symbolic references. We know that, for Berdyaev, the organizing and personal principle was more profound than the organic and cosmic principle. His criticism was, therefore, a case of the well-known debate between the anthropocentric and cosmocentric currents of the journal, between two political approaches to the situation in the USSR, but also between two generations who had not experienced the Silver Age in the same way. In November 1932, Ilyin, irritated by the criticisms of Berdyaev, decided to write an "Open Letter to Professor N. A. Berdyaev" in which he stated, "the differences which have arisen between us are so fundamental that I believe that it is indispensable to make our discussion public for 'those who have ears' and who, alas, are not very numerous nowadays."[26] Ilyin began with a defense of the Silver Age, by comparing it to the 1860s. But, for Ilyin, that was not the real source of the dispute. The question was of a spiritual order rather than an historical one: "If you and I were not Christian believers, I would be ready to stop this discussion at once."[27] Ilyin criticized Berdyaev for not understanding the role of the Holy Spirit in the tragedy of love and death and for thinking that the technical advances in the Soviet Union were necessarily the work of the Spirit. He concluded: "I would like to hear your point of view concerning the attempts by the current economic Hero-titan to raise up the sign of the Son of Man against the Spirit-Comforter."[28] Although he continued to disagree with Ilyin, Berdyaev did not publish this open letter, but since he was undoubtedly convinced of the nonconformist dimension of the article by the professor of the St. Sergius Institute, he decided to publish it in the October 1933 issue—yet only after its author had agreed to erase all the specific references to Ivanov.

So *The Way* did have an editorial policy and a common concern for remaining within a particular intellectual tradition. Therefore the question needs to be reformulated: What were the factors, internal and external to the journal, which, in spite of the different political, intellectual, and religious differences, allowed the authors to come together as an intellectual generation with the same undertakings, discussing the same questions, engaging in the same initiatives, and, finally, sharing a common nonconformist awareness? There are two ways of responding to this question. The first way is to hold that the "cause" was of a spiritual nature and therefore invisible, imperceptible, unverifiable, and metahistoric. It was a historical fact but it did not follow the laws of rational logic. It was precisely this nonconformist spirit of the 1930s that was dominant at the beginning of the decade. As a spirit of openness, of engagement and tolerance, it did not mechanically extend to all the protagonists of those times, but only to certain chosen milieus, to certain personalities without any apparent coherence. The different paths followed during the 1930s by Mounier, Dandieu, and Aron, who were together in the same circles at the beginning of the decade, demonstrated that nonconformism was a spiritual state rather than an intellectual position. In the course of this narrative, this spiritual state is invoked in order to give a certain logic to the unfolding of events. The second way of responding to the question is on a more strictly historical level: a threefold argument can be advanced to explain the antinomic character, both stable and mobile, of the generation of the authors of the journal: their solidarity in the face of adversity, a common problematic in their intellectual research, and, finally, a common eschatological sentiment that all is possible in the realm of civic engagement. Armed with these two kinds of responses, it is then possible to consider more closely, first, these authors' social, juridical, and political positions; second, their rational reflection on the three visions of the Christian myth of the Triune God (Father–Son–Holy Spirit/Unique Person/Divine-Human Wisdom); and third, the universalist engagement of the authors of *The Way* during the first half of the 1930s.

THE ECCLESIAL FRONTIERS OF A GENERATION

As was the case from 1925 to 1929, a mechanism of solidarity came into play among the authors of *The Way* who felt themselves victims of a lack of comprehension by outsiders. This was essentially the case within the Orthodox Church of the Russian immigrants, who either viewed the YMCA Press as an American octopus, with tentacles reaching across the world, or else considered it too conciliatory towards the Soviet regime. After the schism of 1927, when the conflicting parties were revealed and defined, the struggle, in which the bishops' synod of the Russian Orthodox Church Outside Russia (ROCOR) opposed the collection of modernist groups within the jurisdiction of Metropolitan Evlogy and was supported by the American Protestant publishing house, somewhat diminished. In reaction to a condemnation of the YMCA similar to that of the Russian Orthodox Church Outside Russia on the part of the synod of the Bulgarian Church, John Mott had organized a congress in Sophia, in April 1928, with representatives of the Russian Student Christian Movement and several local hierarchs in order to show the sincerity of the actions undertaken by his movement in countries of Orthodox tradition and to pacify critics for a while. In 1930, however, while relations between the jurisdiction of Metropolitan Evlogy and Metropolitan Sergius of Moscow were deteriorating, the Russian Orthodox Church Outside Russia rekindled hostilities with the Parisian modernist currents by again accusing them of Freemasonry. This was done in order to weaken the position of Metropolitan Evlogy's Western Russian jurisdiction and convince it to submit to the control of the ROCOR synod. After a brief summary of this battle, which once again opposed the Russian Church Outside of Russia and the YMCA, I will show the decisive role assumed by the Academy of Religious Philosophy, the St. Sergius Institute, and the Russian Student Christian Movement in diffusing the tensions produced by this confrontation. I then examine the position of *The Way* and the debate among intellectuals concerning the jurisdictional conflict between Metropolitan Evlogy and Metropolitan Sergius. Finally, I show that the political engagement within the immigrant community by the journal's authors during the 1930–35 period is closely linked with the two other modes of expression, the social and jurisdictional, of the collective conscience of the intelligentsia during this period.

Places of Dialogue

At the beginning of 1930, the accusations of Freemasonry against the YMCA flared up again with renewed vigor in France and especially in the Mediterranean countries of southeast Europe. To counter these accusations, John Mott decided to convoke another congress in Athens on February 25–28, modeled on that of Sofia, with the participation of about forty attendees including Metropolitan Evlogy, some Greek, Romanian, and Bulgarian hierarchs, a number of lay Orthodox delegates, and the team of the YMCA consisting of Donald E. Davis, the administrator for Europe, and Edgar MacNaughten and Paul Anderson, the two administrators for projects in Orthodox countries. In an article which appeared in the June 1930 issue of the review, Zenkovsky reported on this "Congress of Athens." This report is interesting insofar as it revealed all the ambiguities and malaise of the author, who was, at that time, the president of the Russian Student Christian Movement. Although he rejected the accusations of Freemasonry, Zenkovsky justified in part the decisions taken by the Russian and Bulgarian synods, admitting that the interconfessional methods of the YMCA and the World Student Christian Federation were not fully Orthodox. Obviously ill at ease, he added that after the 1928 Congress of Mysore, in India, with the World Student Christian Federation and after those at Sofia and Athens with the YMCA, the situation had been clarified, even if "everything has not been accomplished, all the difficulties have not been surmounted."[29] Although he regretted that such inter-Orthodox meetings were due to the initiative of Protestant organizations, Zenkovsky legitimated the participation of the Russian Student Christian Movement in the ecumenical movement and expressed approval for collaboration with the YMCA in working with youth groups. The ambivalent attitude of Zenkovsky enables us to understand why the Congress of Athens failed to convince the Orthodox of the southeastern Mediterranean, in spite of John Mott's denial of anything like proselytism or Freemasonry.

Metropolitan Evlogy chose to sever his jurisdictional links with the synod of Moscow in February 1931 and placed his diocese under the protection of the patriarch of Constantinople, separating himself from Metropolitan Sergius of Moscow but also distancing himself from the Russian Orthodox Church Outside Russia. After this the polemics concerning the YMCA flared up again with vengeance in 1932–33. A series of documents from the archives of the American publishing house confirms the gravity of the tensions. Following attacks repeated in Bulgaria and France[30] against the "non-ecclesiality" of the Russian Student Christian Movement, because this movement did not—on a strictly juridical plan—recognize the authority of Metropolitan Evlogy in its statutes, Chetverikov published an embarrassed explanation in the July 1932 issue of the *Vestnik RSKhD* (*The Messenger of the Russian Student Christian Movement*). He wrote—not without ambiguity—that "although it maintains friendly relations with the representatives of other confessions . . . the movement believes that it is essential to preserve the purity of Orthodox thought and of Christian life from any human modification or addition." In spite of its very measured tone, this article provoked a violent declaration of the Russian Orthodox Church Outside Russia, which appeared in the August 28, 1932, issue of *Tsarsky Vestnik* and was signed by Metropolitan Anthony Khrapovitsky.[31] In this article, after a long historic survey of the nefarious influence of the Masonic lodges in Russia, the synod of Russian bishops in exile publicly renewed its condemnation of "all those currents and organizations which have any affinities with Freemasonry, theosophy, anthroposophy, . . . and the YMCA." The synod obliged its pastors to henceforth ask their faithful, when they went to confession, if they belonged to any Masonic organizations and to excommunicate them if they answered in the positive.[32]

After an awkward presentation given by a delegate of the Russian Student Christian Movement, A. Nikitin, who had been sent to Sofia in December 1932, these accusations were relayed by articles in the Bulgarian press and were swiftly directed against: "Archpriest S. Bulgakov, one of the directors of the Movement in Paris, who is unsteady dogmatically, . . . the books of the YMCA Press, which are openly atheistic, . . . the Institute of Theology, which receives money from the YMCA,"[33] and, in another article entitled "The Preachers of the YMCA: A New Sect," against the lecturers of the Academy, "Bulgakov, Berdyaev, Zenkovsky . . . who preach a new era," and so on. Like Zenkovsky and Chetverikov, Nikitin belonged to the neo-traditionalist fringe of the RSCM and was unable to give a convincing response. According to a report of the discussion that took place after the conference, Nikitin refused to defend the YMCA and gave the floor to a student, who stated that it had no importance for him whether the movement was for or against Metropolitan Anthony and reminded the audience that the RSCM was forming the Russian youth in exile against the Bolsheviks![34] As can be seen from a clarification by Chetverikov in the January 1933 issue of the *Messenger*, the conservative fringe of the RSCM, pushed up against a wall by Orthodox public opinion, felt increasingly ill at ease in its formal dependence on the YMCA rather than on Metropolitan Evlogy.

As the paranoid antagonism towards the Masonic octopus began to extend to the Russian immigrants in China, in March 1933, Anderson, the YMCA delegate to the RSCM, decided to put together, along with Lowrie, a detailed report that clearly confronted the ROCOR and responded to all the accusations. He also reacted by organizing another tour by Mott, in April and May, to Greece, Bulgaria, Romania, Yugoslavia, and, finally, France. The high point of Mott's visit to Europe was a conference held at Chantilly, May 28–30, 1933. This was the first formal meeting of the YMCA representatives and the ensemble of the different entities making up the School of Paris—the Academy, the St. Sergius Institute, and the Russian Student Christian Movement. The following participated in this conference: J. Mott, E. Colton, D. Davis, P. Anderson, D. Lowrie, B. Krutikov, and T. Baimakova for the YMCA; W. Visser't Hooft (World Student Christian Federation); Metropolitan Evlogy, S. Bulgakov, G. Florovsky, and G. Fedotov from St. Sergius; N. Berdyaev and B. Vysheslavtsev from the YMCA Press and the Academy; V. Zenkovsky from the Office of Religious Education; S. Chetverikov, L. Liperovsky, I. Lagovsky, Mother Maria Skobtsova, A. Nikitin, C. Peresneva, L. Zander, and N. Zernov for the RSCM; N. Federov, A. Morozov, F. Pianov, and S. Shidlovsky-Koulomzina from the RSCM in France; and S. Karashov, P. Kozlovsky, and Finisov from the Russian Higher Technical Institute and Courses by Correspondence. The participants listened to several talks describing the activities of each of the branches supported by the YMCA and, notably, that of Berdyaev on the Academy and "the journal, *The Way*, which the Academy edits." Then, after a roundtable discussion dedicated to "the dangers and problems of the youth of the Russian immigration," and a final declaration by Metropolitan Evlogy in which he personally thanked Mott for all his help, Mott himself summed up the results of the conference. He decided, first of all, to publish a brochure responding to all the accusations, second, to renew the financial aid to these organizations, and, finally, to modify the formal relationship with the RSCM. With respect to this last point, Mott gave three clarifications to questions posed by Zenkovsky. Zenkovsky had asked, first, if the YMCA would still be disposed to work with the RSCM when Russia was liberated; second, if the YMCA would not seek to work with organizations of the immigration other than the RSCM; and, third, what would be the best forms of coordination between the YMCA and the RSCM. Mott replied prudently regarding future prospects and tried not to commit himself too much with the RSCM regarding future work in Russia. He reaffirmed that the RSCM was their only partner for missionary work among the youth of the Russian immigration. At the end—and most importantly—he announced the creation of a coordinating committee between the YMCA, the RSCM, the Office of Religious Education, the Academy, and St. Sergius Institute.[35]

Thus, external tensions contributed to bringing the organizations together and transcending their internal bickering. In addition to the natural instinct to circle the wagons when confronted with the enemy, it is probable that the common vocation of these institutions—the transmission of a heritage in preparation for a return to a future Russia, which, as we have seen, was still a major preoccupation in 1933—made such unanimity possible. It is useful here to take a closer look at the evolution of the Academy, St. Sergius, and the RSCM and their mutual relations in order to understand better how the review was able to preserve its unity and homogeneity in the face of a new division in the Russian Church and the growing number of political differences among the right-wing and left-wing intellectuals.

The Academy of Religious Philosophy
Berdyaev was the director of both the YMCA Press publishing house and the Academy of Religious Philosophy. At Chantilly, he left the presentation on the publishing house to Vysheslavtsev and reserved the talk on the Academy for himself. The two presentations were quite similar. Vysheslavtsev stressed the committment of the Russian-American publishing house, "unique in all the world," to publish creative Russian thinking in the tradition of the pre-revolutionary publishing enterprise Put'. He emphasized the ecumenical openness of the YMCA. In his April 30, 1933, presentation at Chantilly on the Academy, Berdyaev reaffirmed that its first ambition was to impart to the young, as well as the not-so-young, a formation in "philosophical-religious, socio-religious, and cultural-religious problems"

and to thereby form a new apologetic discourse against atheism.[36] The second priority of the Academy was its participation in the ecumenical movement. The third and final aspect of its work was *The Way*, "the only organ of creative Orthodox thinking in the whole world."[37] Berdyaev reminded his listeners that there was no such thing as a Christian press in Russia and reasserted *The Way*'s aim of continuing the tradition of Russian religious thought while leaving room for different points of view. He insisted that *The Way* "consolidates all the Christian literary and scientific energies of the immigration, with the exception of the obscurantist wing of the extreme right which was hostile to any kind of thinking."[38] Berdyaev was glad to occasionally publish articles coming from the Soviet Union and also happy about the attention given to *The Way* by the Christian press of the West, even though the journal was published in Russian. He finished by affirming that the principal goal of *The Way* was "to reconcile tradition with the creative impulse, to preserve what is eternal in the past while looking ahead to the future."[39]

The classes and seminars at the Academy were held one evening a week, from 8:30 to 10:30 p.m., from November to May and cost sixty francs a year (two and a half francs a lecture). A student of Berdyaev, G. P. Kazatchkin, acted as the head. According to the journal of Lydia Berdyaeva, there were about a hundred regular students attending her husband's classes.[40] We know the names of some of them, who were also readers of the review. There was the intimate circle of those close to Berdyaev who regularly assisted at the Sunday afternoon teas at Clamart, such as Fritz Lieb, P. Ivanov, G. Fedotov, Rachel Ossorgina, Maria Kalash (Kurdiumov), F. Pianov, and Alexis Curilin-Kissiliov (whom the Berdyaevs looked upon as their adopted son). Some acquaintances passing through Paris also assisted at these courses, such as G. Sebrikov and V. Sezeman. There were the old-timers, such as B. Vysheslavtsev, Lev Gillet, and E. Rapp — whose sister-in-law had given a talk on creation and sin in 1930 — as well as younger participants such as G. and J. Kazatchkin, V. N. Pundik, and A. Karpov — who gave a conference on creation and liberty in 1930 — and Mother Maria Skobtsova, S. Zhaba, G. Fedotov, V. Ilyin, T. Baimakova, and D. Klepinin.

The couple Tamara Baimakova and Dimitrii Klepinin (they were married in 1937) were particularly representative of the connections between the YMCA, the RSCM, the Academy, and St. Sergius Institute. Born in 1897 in Pavlovsk, a suburb of St. Petersburg, Tamara was twenty years old when the revolution broke out. Her brother Boris was arrested and deported for being the son of a banker. After working in a meteorological station at Pavlovsk for years, she decided to join her family in Riga, where, thanks to her knowledge of English, French, and German, she put herself at the service of the YMCA. She collaborated with I. Lagovsky and F. Pianov, worked to extend the YMCA in the Baltic countries, and traveled as a delegate to the conference at Psherov in 1923, where she met Berdyaev for the first time. On returning to Riga, she had the responsibility of organizing Berdyaev's trip to Estonia in 1927. In 1930, after several stays in France, she profited from the Paris tour of a Russian opera company, which had engaged her as an interpreter, to settle in France. There she worked at the YMCA as an assistant to Anderson and MacNaughton. Having been very impressed by Berdyaev's book *La philosophie de l'esprit libre*, which appeared in 1927–28, she followed, after work, the weekly evening course and seminar of Berdyaev. As her biographer Harumi Matsuguchi writes, "she thus became, in our opinion, one of the best interpreters of Berdyaev."[41] Dimitrii Klepinin was the younger brother of Nikolai Klepinin, who in the 1920s had collaborated in Berdyaev's undertakings—the YMCA Press, the Academy, and *The Way*. Unlike his elder brother, Dimitrii chose to pursue his theological studies in Paris and was part of the first graduating class of the St. Sergius Institute in 1929. After a year in the United States, where he studied Pauline theology, he returned to France. Since he did not have a fixed job, he worked waxing floors during winter, and during the summer he served as a choir director in the vacation camps of the RSCM. He was very much shaped by the thought of Bulgakov and Berdyaev and followed their courses. Lowrie wrote that in 1932 Dimitrii and Tamara participated, along with Pianov, Mother Maria, Zhaba, and Fedotov, in a book club at Berdyaev's apartment, where they commented on *Le Christianisme et la lutte des classes*. Both were active participants in the projects of Berdyaev and Mother Maria during the 1930s.

The themes of the courses at the Academy varied each year, "depending on the preoccupations of the Russian public."[42] Several of these lectures appear as articles in the review. Those of Florovsky, for example, given in 1930, were published in the December 1930 issue under the title "The Dispute concerning German Idealism" (F47). Ilyin's 1932 presentations appeared in the July 1932 issue under the title "Goethe the Sage" (I27). Vysheslavtsev's lectures from 1933 were published in March 1934 as "The Problem of Power and Its Religious Significance" (V29), while those of

Fedotov in 1934 on the subject "The Religiosity of the Russian People as Seen in Their Poetry" appeared in March 1935 as "Mother-Earth: Towards a Religious Cosmology of the Russian People" (F15). Examples can also be given of public lectures at the Academy, many of which became the basis for articles in the review: March 9, 1930, Zenkovsky's lecture "The Problem of Beauty in the Worldview of Dostoevsky" (later Z37); Ilyin, "The Demonic in Art"; December 1931, Berdyaev, Bulgakov, Fedotov, and Ilyin, "Christianity Faced with Social Reality" (I26); November 27, 1932, Berdyaev, Vysheslavtsev, Fedotov, Shestov, "The Causes of Atheism in the World" (special issue); November 16, 1933, Shestov, "The Theological and Philosophical Ideas of Kierkegaard," in the presence of Berdyaev, Vysheslavtsev, Lazarev, Remizov, Florovsky, de Schloezer, and Mochulsky (Sh4R); October 28, 1934, Berdyaev, Vysheslavtsev, Zenkovsky, Fedotov, "The Christian Conscience and War"; May 5, 1935, Shestov, "Kierkegaard and Dostoevsky" (Sh5); May 28, 1935, Vysheslavtsev, "The Image of God in the Essence of Man" (V31).

In Berdyaev's case, his articles in *The Way* depended on his lectures at the Academy. The themes of his 1930–31 presentations on "Russian Spiritual Culture in the Nineteenth Century" appear in his articles on Jacob Boehme and the Russian sophiological currents and in "In Defense of Blok" (B52). His lectures of 1931–32, "The Finalities of Culture," can be found in the following articles published in 1931, 1932, and 1933: "Literary Currents and the Social Order" (B55), "The Spiritual State of the Contemporary World" (B60), and "Man and the Machine" (B65). The 1932 supplement to the journal entitled "Christianity and the Challenge of Contemporary Social Reality" echoed a public session of the Academy and was an extension of the 1932–33 seminar, which dealt with the social question. His courses of 1933–34 on nationalism can be found in his review of J. Schmidhauser (B68R), his review of G. Heering (B69R), and "Polytheism and Nationalism" (B70). Last, his article in the December 1935 issue entitled "The Russian Renaissance at the Beginning of the Twentieth Century and the Journal *The Way*" is the last chapter of his 1934–35 course, "The History of Russian Thought."

Parts of the archives of the Academy have been recovered, notably, the stenciled course materials for Vysheslavtsev's 1932 course "The Philosophy of Beauty" and Berdyaev's 1931–32 course "The Finalities of Culture." In his inaugural lecture, Berdyaev explained the theme chosen for that year:

In our times the problem of judging culture and its historical finalities is becoming very intense. My course will be devoted to the problem of relations between the Christian vision of world and culture. It will defend culture against the "obscurantist" attacks which are victimizing it and, at the same time, it will expose the contradictions of culture and pass judgment on it.[43]

It is impossible to comment here on these unpublished lectures and course materials, not all of which appeared in *The Way*. They reveal an unknown aspect of Berdyaev—that of a teacher—which would require special study. I simply note here that it was in the context of the Academy that Berdyaev, in commenting on Heidegger's *Being and Time*, in interpreting futurist and neoclassical currents, and in announcing the crisis of the intellectual elite, first developed the themes of "the myth of man" and "the myth of God" as the foundations of a cultural Renaissance. (See the courses of 1931–32.)

As has already been noted for the period from 1925 to 1929, Bulgakov's seminar was actually a workshop for his sophiology, where he could freely discuss his research on the Wisdom of God. It is very probable that his articles on "the dogma of the Eucharist" were fruits of his seminar, although this cannot be confirmed given the absence of archives. At least that is what can be supposed from the testimony of the wife of Nikolai Afanasiev, who participated in Bulgakov's seminar. Afanasiev arrived in Paris in 1929. He quickly became Zenkovsky's assistant at the Office of Religious Education and was named professor of canon law at St. Sergius. Marianne Afanasiev wrote that "he is more and more interested in dogmatic theology, an interest aroused ... by his participation in the 'seminar' of Father Sergius Bulgakov."[44] His interest in eucharistic theology had its origin in his attendance at this seminar and an article by Chetverikov published in *The Way* in 1929. Marianne Afanasiev's account also indicates the link between the Academy, St. Sergius, and *The Way*.

In the winter of 1932–33, Nikolai Afanasiev had, for the first time, the "vision" of his "eucharistic ecclesiology." I remember well those days when, in spite of the sorrows of that time (sickness, international crisis, first rumors of war), my husband went around as if inspired. He wrote a paper for the seminar of Father Sergius entitled "Two Concepts of the Universal Church." . . . Father Sergius was not enthusiastic about this paper, or at least did not sense a certain relationship of eucharistic ecclesiology with the doctrine of *Sobornost'* and with its lofty eucharistic aspiration; all the same he recommended the article to Berdyaev, who published it in *Put'*.[45]

This was the article "The Two Concepts of the Universal Church," which appeared in the November 1934 issue of *The Way*. Similarly, the two-part article of Bulgakov entitled "Judas Iscariot, Apostle-Betrayer" (B128 and B129), published in the February and April 1931 issues, was first presented in a public session of the Academy on November 23, 1930. This session was a good illustration of what united authors of *The Way* who participated in these meetings of the Academy: a taste for religious questions, an interest in an antinomic and sophiological approach to these questions, and, finally, the comparison—taken to extremes—of the problem being treated to the enigma of the destinies of Russia.[46]

The St. Sergius Institute

The St. Sergius Institute and the Academy had the same ambitions of forming leaders for the Russia of the future, of promoting intellectual research within the Orthodox tradition, and, finally, of constituting a missionary and ecumenical center. This is why the review opened its pages generously to articles submitted by professors at the Institute: Bulgakov, Vysheslavtsev, Florovsky, Zenkovsky, Ilyin, Bezobrazov, Kartashev, Afanasiev, and Veidlé. Certain articles are mentioned explicitly as being transcripts of talks given at the Institute on the occasion of the traditional ceremonies at the inauguration of the academic year (B131, F9, etc.). Other articles, like those of Ioann (Shakhovskoy), are mentioned explicitly as coming from the Institute (I5). In his history of the Institute, Alexis Kniazev relates that the theses of Vysheslavtsev which appear in his work *The Ethic of the Eros*, and which are summarized in his article in the August 1930 issue of *The Way*, were "the result of the courses in moral theology which he gave at the Institute."[47]

In a talk he gave on the Institute at Chantilly on April 30, 1933, Kartashev insisted on the fact that the St. Sergius professors looked upon their commitment as long-term. Kartashev, conscious that for Russian-speakers, St. Sergius was the only establishment of advanced theological teaching in the world, and fearing a conservative political and religious restoration in the Russia of the future, stated: "Our inspiration comes simply from the fact that we are not working among a self-enclosed nation of immigrants, but as one with Russia and the Russian Church. . . . We are the heirs of Russian theological science, and we are preparing enlightened pastors not just for the immigration community but for the Russia of the future."[48]

The St. Sergius Institute was above all a place where knowledge was transmitted. In 1932 the Institute had graduated its fifth class of students. Since its creation in 1924, fifty-three students had finished the complete cycle of four years of studies, and thirty more had followed a part of the cycle. Half of these students came from countries bordering Russia. Thirty of the fifty-three graduates had become priests and had returned to their respective countries, while the rest prepared themselves for a teaching career—such as B. Sové, who became a professor of Old Testament at the Institute in 1931. As Zander's "List of the Writings of Professors of the Russian Orthodox Theological Institute in Paris (1925–1933)" demonstrates, the Institute was a thriving center of intellectual creativity: no less than twenty-five books and four hundred articles are listed as having been written by professors of the Institute over a seven-year period. Most of the books, as well as the review of the Institute, *La Pensée Orthodoxe* (with a single issue in 1930), were published by the YMCA Press.[49] Finally, the Institute, through its teachers and students, accomplished important missionary work in the parishes of the immigration community and in the context of the Russian Student Christian Movement. The Confraternity of St. Sergius, which published *Sergievskie Listki*, also organized a system of courses by correspondence for children and a network of assistance for the needy. When faced with a 40 percent reduction of its budget due to the economic crisis in the United States and in England, which affected a great number of its benefactors, the Institute resolved to find new forms of financing. Zander, the Institute's financial secretary, had the idea of organizing fundraising tours by the choir of the students, which was directed by I. Denisov. These took place annually, beginning in 1933; the tours included Switzerland (1933), England (1933–34 and 1936–37), the Netherlands (1936–37), and Denmark, Norway, and Sweden (1938). The sustained participation of the professors in the ecumenical movement was one of the causes of the increasing influence of the Institute outside the borders of Orthodoxy. Bulgakov was a permanent member of the organizations

Faith and Order, and Life and Work. Kartashev gave lectures in Europe on a regular basis, notably in 1930–31, when he spoke in Protestant churches in Holland on the situation of the Russian Church. He also represented Metropolitan Evlogy at the 1932 conference in Velehrad on Eastern Rite Catholics. To take only one year, in 1933 Florovsky and Bulgakov participated in the meetings of the Anglo-Russian Fellowship of St. Alban and St. Sergius; Bezobrazov and Glubokovsky attended the conference of Protestant and Orthodox theologians at Novi Sad in Yugoslavia; and Bulgakov and Zenkovsky were invited to Germany for a conference of Life and Work on social Christianity. To cite one very significant incident, Bulgakov, in the talk he gave at Chantilly entitled "The Participation of Russians in the World-Wide Ecumenical Movement," pointed out that ecumenical work was incumbent upon the Institute and the RSCM through the very fact that, aside from Metropolitan Evlogy, no bishop, either in Russia—for Metropolitan Sergius had refused to participate in the 1930 Conference of Lambeth—or in the immigration, was attuned to this problem.[50] According to Bulgakov, "the majority of the members [of the Church of the immigration] are either indifferent or opposed to the ecumenical movement."[51]

Thus, the modernism that united the professors of the Institute was much more precious to them than the factors that divided them. Their common commitment to thinking through the problems of modernity, of preparing a Christian but nonreactionary future for Russia, and of meeting their Protestant, Catholic, and Anglican colleagues with complete liberty and without censorship was the inestimable achievement of the generation of the professors at the Institute.

The modernist character of the Institute found particular expression in the teaching of a new discipline, hagiology, a subject unheard of in the pre-revolution academies of theology—at least, not under the form it took with the enthusiastic George Fedotov. On November 9, 1930, Fedotov gave a lecture at the Institute entitled "The Tragedy of Medieval Russian Sanctity," which also appeared in the April 1931 issue of *The Way*. This lecture, whose audience was the professors and students of the Institute as well as an educated sector of the Russian Orthodox community of Paris, is still famous in the modernist milieus of the immigration. It is particularly interesting for our purposes because it shows how the Institute contributed, by its teaching, to the formation of a new consciousness of an intellectual generation.

In Fedotov's perspective, this history of sanctity in Russia was meant to manifest the spiritual sources of the Russian intelligentsia. Fedotov attempted to understand why the modern cultural elite of Russia, "the learned school of little-Russia," which emerged historically in the eighteenth century when culture was becoming secularized, had distanced itself from the state, which it saw as a heartless monster, from the church, seen as becoming increasingly submissive and servile, and from the people, whose deep religiosity was finding expression in all sorts of sects. By drawing on both a critical and a spiritual reading of the lives of the saints, legends, and popular spiritual poems, Fedotov argued that these facts of Russian history are the result of the tragic struggle, at the beginning of the sixteenth century during the reign of Basil III, between two spiritual currents represented by Joseph of Volokolamsk (1439–1515) and Nil of Sora (1433–1508). This battle between those who defended monastic property-holding and those who thought that the monasteries should not have possessions—but also between those who wanted to see heretics burnt at the stake and those who favored dialogue with Jewish sympathizers—ended "tragically," for it led to the persecution of the Jews, to the victory of the Josephites over the Trans-Volga monks, and, eventually, to the eviction of Avvakum and the disciples of Joseph at the end of the seventeenth century. According to Fedotov, the use of force and the interference of the tsar in the affairs of the church then became inevitable. As a historian who did not hesitate to travel freely between the past and the present, Fedotov argued that the consequences of this intervention "still do us great harm."[52] He enumerated the damages done: the paralysis of the principal spiritual currents in Russia, the fact that the church became a function of the state, the schism/*raskol* with the Old Believers, but also, as a reaction, the denationalization of the Russian Church, which opened itself to Catholic and Protestant tendencies, and, finally, the emergence of the modern intelligentsia.[53]

This critical work concerning the spiritual memory of the intelligentsia, which moved the myth of the origins of the intelligentsia from the Old Believers to Nil of Sora, was decisive, above all, for young intellectuals. For those who, like Berdyaev, had been marked by the "rebel" type of intellectual life characteristic of the nineteenth century, this new awareness came too late to immediately alter their spiritual profile. Berdyaev was criticized for this by Bitsilli in 1932 in *New City*; Bitsilli faulted Berdyaev for attributing the origins of the intelligentsia to the schism of the Old Believers in his 1931 book *La psychologie religieuse russe et l'athéisme communiste* (published in Paris by the YMCA Press).[54] Moreover, for the young intellectuals who were turning towards the Byzantine heritage of Russian history, the figure of Nil was venerated, essentially, for the hesychastic aspect. To be sure, there was no insurmountable chasm between fathers and sons, between "Muscovites" and "Byzantines." Earlier, in 1926, Bulgakov had presented Sergius of Radonezh as the father of Russian holiness who shaped the entire Russian theological tradition. All the same, Fedotov's intuition of a double foundation, both mystical and ascetical, and both communitarian and hierarchical, of the intelligentsia was critical, for it created a memory of balance for the younger generation, which, in the early 1930s, was still integrated with the older one. It was the common foundation of their engagements, the historical source of their cohesion.

The Russian Student Christian Movement
The 1933 conference at Chantilly took place at the height of the Russian Student Christian Movement's development. At that time, the movement had twenty-five centers in ten European countries and more than five hundred active members, half of whom were students; to that figure must be added another fifteen hundred who participated in dozens of biblical, charitable, and sport circles, plus twelve hundred children in the Sunday schools and the summer camps (eight per year). The deployment of activities among the young people of the Russian immigration community was such that, ten years after the foundation of the movement, few would have imagined that it would enter into a long period of a crisis beginning in the summer of 1933. The representatives of the intelligentsia who encouraged this youth movement, realizing that the return to Russia would not come about any time soon and, at the same time, seeing more than ever the necessity of forming citizens for the Russia of the future, engaged themselves in the RSCM with even more seriousness than they had done when the movement was founded. The younger generation, sensitive to the social-political context of the immigrant community, wanted to be realistic; they did not want to be lulled to sleep by formulas that might sound magnificent but that often lacked concrete form, such as "the churching of life" or "the presentation of the icon to the West," both of which were used at the conference of Psherov. Due to this dynamic realization and the energy it

evoked, the movement, during the period 1930–35, added to its existing youth programs (catechism, literary circles, summer camps) with new activities, which engaged it very concretely in its openness towards Russia by developing programs in the Russian-speaking countries bordering the USSR, notably, the Baltic States. It also multiplied its social, cultural, and ecumenical initiatives in Western Europe.

The Russian Student Christian Movement, thanks to the work of Tamara Baimakova, had already organized a conference by Zenkovsky in Latvia in 1928. This was held at the monastery of Pustin', with the participation of about sixty young people from all the neighboring countries.[55] The movement organized a first congress in January of 1929 at Riga, then a second one, with Zander, Liperovsky, and Lagovsky, at the monastery of Pechiora, near Pskov. This latter brought together some three hundred participants. Chetverikov spoke of the Eucharist as the center of Christian life (see C4). The following year, the annual congress took place on the border of the USSR, at the monastery of Pyuhtinsky in Estonia. Chetverikov, along with others, was present. Chetverikov, as noted in an article in the July 12, 1932, issue of *The Way* entitled "The Difficulties of Religious Life during Infancy and Adolescence," had a gift for speaking to young people, notably in describing his crisis of atheism when he was thirteen years old, and the way in which he overcame it (C5). These assemblies and the installation, at Riga, for a two-year period (1929–31), of Lev and Valentina Zander as delegates of the head office of the RCSM, contributed, according to B. Plyukhanov, to the founding of enthusiastic and very active local branches.

Each year brought an increase in the number of lectures by members of the movement. Among others were Ilyin (1930), Florovsky (1931), Zenkovsky (1932), Vysheslavtsev (1933), Berdyaev (1934), and Mother Maria Skobtsova (1935). Some of these lectures—such as that of Vysheslavtsev on "The Tragedy of Those Elevated and Speculation on Their Fall" (V25)— were published in *The Way*. This lecture and article by Vysheslavtsev provoked polemics in the May 1933 issue of *The Way*. Vysheslavtsev argued that materialism profaned the hierarchy of the degrees of being by rejecting the spirit. V. Rastorguev, a young Russian immigrant who was left-leaning but not a communist, wrote a critical response. The polemic between the two was a good illustration of the generational differences among the authors of the review. Rastorguev criticized Vysheslavtsev for his virulent and unsophisticated anti-Soviet stance. For Rastorguev, Marxism, rather than being a philosophy, is an "organization of action,"[56] and only the activity of Christians, not incendiary polemics, can confront it effectively. In his reply in the same issue, Vysheslavtsev rejected Rastorguev's arguments and affirmed again that Marxism was nothing more than economic materialism and that no moral values or judgments can be added to it without transforming it into idealism.[57] Fifty-six years old at the time, Vysheslavtsev lamented that "contemporary youth" were not aware of the tragic contradictions of Marxism. That was how things stood. It was as if the moment of division had not yet arrived, even though the Soviet frontier had become the focal point. This situation was further complicated by other difficulties originating in the Baltic countries. The Russian-speaking Christian youth were becoming increasingly nationalist and anti-communist, and this was frowned upon by the Baltic governments. Two months after Vysheslavtsev's lecture, the Soviet consul in Riga complained about "contra-revolutionary" agitation by the students.[58] Even though the executive committee of the RSCM had condemned all types of nationalism in October 1932, the Latvian government refused to let the movement organize its congress in July 1933. The installation of Lagovsky as general secretary of the Latvian branch of the movement permitted the continuity of certain activities (the development of the local network, lectures, the congress of the World Student Christian Federation in August 1934), but these were carried out with more discretion. *Vestnik RSKhD* (*Messenger*), the RSCM journal—under the direction of Fedotov until 1932, when he was replaced by Lagovsky—was considered at that time, according to Marc Raeff, as "the popular version of the review of religious philosophy *The Way*."[59] During 1932–33, it was published once every several months—a rhythm less consistent than in the 1920s. It published numerous articles on the situation in the Baltic countries and Russia.

In Western Europe, especially in France, the movement invested a good deal of energy in helping those in need. With the aid of ecumenical and charitable organizations such as the YMCA, the World Student Christian Federation, and the Appeal for the Russian Clergy and Church Aid Fund, and thanks to the personality of three women—A. Matteo, S. Zernova, and E. Skobtsova (Mother Maria)—the movement sponsored the creation, in January 1931, of a free cafeteria for those without work. Twenty thousand persons were fed over a period of fifteen months. In October 1932, a home for young women in difficulty (Avenue de Saxe) was opened, and in that same year a new hospice for the unemployed (forty-five beds, two hundred fifty meals a day, and medical care). In 1933, a medical clinic organized by the union of Christian physicians was begun, and in May 1935, the Center for the Assistance of Russians of the Emigration (CARE). Skobtsova was secretary of the Council of the RCSM for the dispersed Russian émigrés when she chose to enter religious life. Metropolitan Evlogy understood the unusual personality of this woman, who did not want to shut herself up in a convent, and had told her that her monastery would be "the desert of human hearts." She traveled the length and breadth of France in order to save young isolated Russian immigrants from despair, to free veterans of the White Army from the psychiatric hospitals where they had been erroneously confined due to their ignorance of French, and even to simply do housework for alcoholic Russian workers who were unable to fend for themselves. She succeeded in persuading the minister of public health at that time, whose wife was a Russian, to finance the treatment of Russians with tuberculosis while she found placement for them in sanatoriums. In the summer of 1932 she published a series of articles entitled "The Russian Geography of France" in the daily newspaper *Poslednie Novosti* (*Latest News*). These articles described the unbearable conditions in which numerous Russians were living in the provinces.[60] Although her philosophical writing had slowed, she continued to compose poems and publish articles in *The Way* and *New City*. Elisabeth Behr-Sigel, a French philosopher and theologian who had known her since 1928, wrote:

> One image remains engraved in my memory. Wearing heavy clumsy shoes, weighed down under a canvas bag full of food which she had bought cheaply or begged for as a gift from the merchants, she was returning from Les Halles markets with provisions for her household. There, at Avenue de Saxe, then at 77 rue de Lourmel in the 15th arrondissement, you would find, side by side, tramps, people without work, all sorts of miserable folk, but also the intellectuals: Berdyaev, Mochulsky, Zander, priests such as Lev Gillet and Cyprian Kern; a few nuns eventually joined Mother Maria.[61]

The principal cultural innovation came from Fedotov, the founder of the League of Orthodox Culture (LCO). Berdyaev presided over this association, which was founded on the margins of the RSCM, while Fedotov, aided by Skobtsova, was the secretary. The first congress took place on May 17–19, 1930, in Paris and the last in 1935 at rue de Lourmel, the headquarters of Orthodox Action. During these five years, about thirty conferences were organized around themes of general cultural or social and ecumenical questions. These conferences were also an occasion for intellectuals writing for *The Way* to meet one another outside of their respective institutions. Thus, for example, on September 24–26, 1932, the fourth conference of the LCO brought together approximately fifty people to discuss a variety of themes. In the presence of ecumenical figures who had become friends, such as F. Lieb and Rev. Widdrington, Bulgakov gave a talk entitled "The Dogmatics of the Common Task," Zenkovsky spoke on "The Difficulties in Building an Orthodox Culture," Fedotov talked about "The Relations between the Personal Principle and Culture," Veidlé presented "Christian Art," and Mother Maria spoke of her "Voyage in the Baltic Countries." Fedotov's lectures "Orthodoxy and Historical Criticism" and "The Holy Spirit in Nature and Culture" were published in the April and September 1932 issues of *The Way* (F12 and F13). At these conferences Berdyaev often opposed his prophetic concept of culture to Zenkovsky's more ascetic outlook. Yet both shared the eschatological idea that Fedotov developed in his second article, according to which the Person of the Holy Spirit, the foundation of all creation, who only appears in the Gospels under the symbolism "of wind, fire, and the dove," will reveal himself as a person on the last day when God judges the world.[62]

Alongside these conferences, the RSCM continued to organize its own congresses. In addition to the annual congresses organized in France, members of the movement gathered in Montfort l'Amaury on September 12–23, 1930, for the eighth general assembly of all its European sections. Berdyaev, who felt progressively more uncomfortable in the movement, stopped publishing reports of its congresses in *The Way*. The congress was notable, however, in that Skobtsova and Fedotov became part of the executive committee. Among the ecumenical activities of the movement—aside from its organic relationship with the YMCA—was the pan-Orthodox conference of Thessaloniki held on November 3–7, 1930, which was convoked on the initiative of the Youth Commission of the Ecumenical Council of Practical Christianity and the conference of Chamcoria in August 1935, organized by the World Student Christian Federation. In the course of this latter conference, the Russian Student Christian Movement became an associate member of the World Student Christian Federation. The Thessaloniki conference was attended by Zenkovsky, A. Chetverikova, Lagovsky, Sophie Shidlovsky [Koulomzin], and L. Zander, along with Orthodox representatives from Greece (N. A. Nissiotis), Yugoslavia, Romania, and Bulgaria, and four ecumenical delegates, one of whom was Visser't Hooft. Quite naturally, the separation between the jurisdiction of Metropolitan Evlogy and that of Metropolitan Sergius of Moscow was the subject of commentaries. As Lagovsky, whose report focused on the youth of the Russian immigration community, pointed out:

> The division of the Church (Karlovtsians, Evlogians, Patriarchals) has divided families; often the father and mother belong to a current different from that of their children. The upcoming generation is involuntarily caught up in bitter and passionate quarrels within the family and is poisoned by them. The abuse of excommunication, reciprocal false accusations of not being in the state of grace ... all this comes about as the result of the fact that the children of Karlovtsians avoid the followers of Metropolitan Evlogy because they think it is dangerous to have anything to do with those who are not in the state of grace.[63]

As will be seen, the 1931 separation between Metropolitan Evlogy and Metropolitan Sergius of Moscow disturbed people very deeply and was the occasion of numerous debates in the review, but it was not of the same nature as the schism with the Russian Orthodox Church Outside Russia. Lagovsky remained faithful to Metropolitan Sergius, while Zenkovsky followed Metropolitan Evlogy, but that did not prevent them from participating in the movement together.

Conclusion: Solidarity and Dissension

Given all these activities, it is understandable why Berdyaev, in spite of his misgivings about the neo-traditionalist tendency of the RSCM, chose to entitle his talk at the May 1933 Chantilly conference "The Importance of the Russian Student Christian Movement." But this defense of the movement should be seen as a case of reflexive solidarity. It did not prevent him, several months later, in July 1933, from entering into a violent polemic with Zenkovsky in the pages of the *Messenger*. The cohesion of the Russian modernist organizations supported by the YMCA in the face of the Russian Church Outside Russia did not mean that Berdyaev agreed with the evolution of the RSCM. This second anti-RSCM positioning of Berdyaev after that of 1929 suggests that the spiritual dissensions that appeared in 1926–29 had changed, between 1929 and 1934, into a genuine political confrontation within the movement between a nationalist, right-wing current and a socialist left-wing current. But it should be pointed out that this clear and profound opposition was still within a space common to both parties. The next step, in 1935, would be the withdrawal of the left-wing group from the RSCM.

In an article in the September–October issue of the *Messenger*, Berdyaev saw the RSCM going through a profound financial and ideological crisis and, without naming them, blamed three people. He criticized the movement for becoming too cozy with the church, since the original idea was to reach out from the church to the real problems of life. He accused it of being satisfied with giving the youth an education in sports and using militaristic and nationalistic methods to turn them into an image of "groups of Hitler Youth."[64] Berdyaev took aim at Fedorov in particular, since he was responsible for the youth programs in the movement. Berdyaev stated that while these programs pretended to be apolitical and apolitically nationalist, "there was a very clear political option of right-wing or fascist nationalism as if this were obviously linked to Orthodoxy. This is, in my opinion, intolerable."[65] Here Berdyaev was probably thinking of Nikitin, the movement's delegate to Bulgaria, a person close to nationalist right-wing milieus and a member of the National Union of Work of the New Generation (NTS), a nationalist and anti-democratic organization created at Belgrade in July 1930 by M. Georgievsky. The ideological directors of the movement—Zenkovsky, Vysheslavtsev, and Chetverikov—were all roundly criticized. The Russian philosopher ended his article by declaring himself a "friend of the movement" who was disappointed by the transformation of its leaders into "professional functionaries."[66]

As can be imagined, the ninth assembly of the RSCM, held on the estate of L'Oiseau Bleu near Boissy, on September 12–24, 1933, the last of its kind, was especially agitated. There were delegates from the Baltic countries, Germany, Czechoslovakia, Bulgaria, and France. The speakers—Bulgakov who spoke on "The Spiritual Life of the Movement," and Vysheslavtsev, who dealt with "Russian Culture and the Paths of the Movement"—attempted, in Berdyaev's absence, to refocus the concerns of the movement—above all in the Eastern countries—towards a greater engagement in social problems. But there had not been a general assembly for three years, and, during this time, the political and social context had changed considerably, and numerous mutual misunderstandings had accumulated. All the same, after several days and many debates, the RSCM decided to make a fresh start and reform its structures. The new council of the movement was made up of the following members: V. Zenkovsky (president), B. Vysheslavtsev (vice president), L. Liperovsky, G. Serikov, E. Mensikova, Mother Maria Skobtsova (social and missionary work), A. (Anna) Chetverikova, P. Anderson (struggle against atheism), Nicolas Zernov (ecumenism), L. Zander (finances), I. Lagovsky (Baltic countries), A. Nikitin (Bulgaria), V. Slepian (Berlin), F. Pianov (France), and A. Vissarionov (Brno). The new council was to replace the assembly due to the difficulty in convening the latter. Zenkovsky and also Fr. Chetverikov, the chaplain of the RSCM, headed this council. This structural reform, undertaken for financial reasons, was a failure—in spite of what Zernov would say later.[67] In fact, only two subsequent meetings of the RSCM could be organized—in 1935 and 1937—and tensions continued to increase. Moreover, the ideological malaise was accompanied by a financial crisis. On December 9, 1933, Paul Anderson sent a letter to the directors of the RSCM, the Office of Religious Education, the Academy, the YMCA Press, and the technical institute informing them that, due to the financial crisis in the United States, he had to reduce the subsidies for the year 1933–34 by 65 percent. For the RSCM, the Office, and the Institute, that meant that only the costs of the building at 10 Boulevard Montparnasse would be covered. The library, the publishing house, and the Academy would continue to receive subsidies, but these would be "severely reduced in comparison with the preceding years."[68]

While the RSCM was wallowing in this ideological and financial crisis, the backlash in France to the events of February 6, 1934, complicated things even more. On top of the institutional, economic, and social crisis in the country, there was an international crisis marked by the withdrawal of Japan and Hitler's Germany from the League of Nations. The Stavisky affair, involving a Ukrainian Jew who had received French citizenship, made manifest the venality of the press and the corruption of certain members of Parliament, and set off riots in Paris from January 27 to February 6, 1934, leaving fifteen dead and two thousand wounded. Édouard Daladier, the prime minister, resigned, and the right, with Doumergue and Tardieu, took over power on February 7. Thinking that this was not a simple uprising, the left panicked, for it saw the face of fascism in the riot led by Colonel de la Rocque. For the right, on the contrary, these events represented the hope that order would be reestablished. Ilyin notes in his memoirs that it was during this "tragic winter" that he broke off all contacts with Berdyaev, even though he admired him greatly. Believing that he had been rejected because of his nationalist views by Berdyaev, Mother Maria, and Pianov, he turned to the right. Politics took precedence over friendship. During the events of February, Ilyin was enthusiastic about "the successes of the fascist youth," for, as he wrote, the riots represent "the liberation of the workers," "the rejection of the chains of capitalism."[69]

The combination of the new political context in France with the ideological crisis denounced by Berdyaev, the failure of the reform statutes, and the financial crisis led to a dramatic split between the youth movement, headed by N. Fedorov, and the headquarters of the movement. After the events of February 6, Fedorov, in March, with Kartashev and Denisov as patrons, founded the Society of the Friends of the Heroes (*vitiazi*) and took with him the majority of the young men and a part of the young women. In his memoirs, Fedorov writes this concerning the directors of the RSCM: "they were ignorant of the nationalist character of education ... and of the traditions of the Russian Imperial Army."[70] The left-wing current of the movement tried to react by organizing a congress at Montfort l'Amaury on May 18–22, 1934, to condemn nationalism. But nothing came of it. The right-wing current, led by Nikitin, Ilyin, Zenkovsky, and Chetverikov, regretted the departure of the youth section, but that did not fundamentally change its pro-nationalist and virulently anti-Soviet attitude. Berdyaev, more and more worried about the "fascist" and "monarchist" evolution of the RSCM, wrote a new letter of warning to the movement's council on December 30, 1934, in which he criticized it for succumbing to the nationalist spirit of the times and to public opinion. According to Pianov, who assisted at the council, this letter was supported by "Bulgakov, Vysheslavtsev, and many others although there were some who did not agree with it."[71] But when the RSCM organized a congress at Boissy in July 1935, no one from the left wing of the movement attended—neither Fedotov, nor Mother Maria, nor Pianov.

Between Moscow and Constantinople

The Chain of Events

In his memoirs, Metropolitan Evlogy accused Berdyaev by name of having precipitated the crisis within the Russian Student Christian Movement. The image of Berdyaev held by the right-wing current of the movement is evident in the following lines.

> I blame Berdyaev. He is the one who began to stir up the political question by taking a very clear socialist line, by doing everything he could to push people to follow leftist political slogans. "Enough of bowing down to the great magnates. Let us prostrate ourselves at the feet of the proletariat," and other such irresponsible phrases have led those young people who have not forgotten the horrors of Bolshevism ... to protest energetically, and the result was that the peace and concord among the members of the movement disappeared.... The leftists (the disciples of Berdyaev, Mother Maria, Pianov) accused the right of not understanding the soviet reality, "the soviet new man," of not wanting to be reconciled with the soviet motherland and of digging a ditch between the past and the present. The right accused the left, saying: you do not teach nationalism, you betray Russia, you are ready to shake hands with the enemies of the Church ... the violent debates at Montparnasse were unending.[72]

In these words of Metropolitan Evlogy, accusing Berdyaev of, on the one hand, initiating the hostilities and, on the other, of offering his hand to the enemies of the church, we can see in outline that the principal criticism of the philosopher was that he chose to remain in the ecclesiastical jurisdiction of Metropolitan Sergius of Moscow in 1931. The monarchist bishop blamed "those of the right wing" without naming anyone and justifying their legitimate defense, and "those of the left wing" (Mother Maria and Pianov) by presenting them as disciples of Berdyaev. Unlike Berdyaev, these and others had chosen to remain faithful to Evlogy. Before returning to this settling of scores and the factors that enabled the intellectuals of the review to remain united until 1935, it is helpful to briefly sum up the chain of events and the different conflicting positions.

The Turning Point in the Summer of 1930
Unlike Metropolitan Anthony Khrapovitsky, in 1927 Metropolitan Evlogy had chosen to sign a declaration of spiritual loyalty to the Soviet state so that Metropolitan Sergius might canonically recognize his jurisdiction and so that peace might be restored to his parishes. But this declaration had the drawback of being very fluid and ambiguous. What did the term *loyalty* mean? Fedotov, alone at that time, had questioned this purely formal approach to canonical links. A tacit compromise was then found between Paris and Moscow when Metropolitan Sergius explained in a letter that "the term loyalty does not imply obedience to Soviet laws." But, at the same time, he asked Metropolitan Evlogy not to mix ecclesial affairs with political affairs. On January 29, 1928, in an interview that appeared in *Vozrozhdenie (Renaissance)*, Metropolitan Evlogy assured Metropolitan Sergius that he would not make any political declaration either in an ecclesial context or in public.[73]

But the modifications of religious legislation in the USSR that went into effect in April–May 1929, legalizing both religious communities and anti-religious propaganda, in fact opened the gates for the atheist agitation that reached its height between 1929 and 1930. The adoption in August 1929 of a continuous work week suppressed any possibility of celebrating Sunday. The collectivization of the countryside was nearly always accompanied by the closing of churches. To protest these persecutions, the Vatican, in 1929–30, organized a vast information campaign throughout Europe. Bishop Neveu, the apostolic administrator in Moscow, shocked by the declarations of loyalty by Metropolitan Sergius in 1927, wanted to help the suffering Russian Church by choosing the path of confrontation with the official church. He communicated his project for days of prayer to Bishop Chaptal, who transmitted it to the pope. On February 2, 1930, Pius XI addressed a letter to Cardinal Pompilj, which was published in the February 9 edition of the *Osservatore Romano* under the title "In Reparation for the Divine Rights Cruelly Violated in the Territory of the Russian State." The letter called upon Christians of every confession to unite themselves in prayer for those who were persecuted. Pius XI himself celebrated a mass on March 19, 1930, "for the end of persecutions" in Russia. According to the press of that time,[74] Catholic, Anglican, and Protestant parishes responded with fervor to the appeal of Pius XI. On February 16, Metropolitan Sergius denied that there was any persecution in Russia and accused the pope of aligning himself with "the English landowners and the Franco-Italian bourgeois" and "wanting to catholicize our Church." Stalin's reaction was different. He published an article in the March 2, 1930, issue of *Pravda* entitled "The Vertigo of Success," in which he attacked the "so-called revolutionaries who begin the creation of a collective by tearing down the bell towers."[75]

The situation of Evlogy became all the more critical in that the position of the Russian Orthodox Church Outside Russia in favor of these informational campaigns was much more credible among his parishioners than his own stance. When, in March 1930, the Archbishop of Canterbury invited Metropolitan Evlogy to London to participate in these days of prayer, the metropolitan accepted. He assisted at a prayer service presided over by the primate of the Church of England at Westminster Abbey and expressed all that was in his heart since 1928 about the persecutions in the USSR to a reporter from *The Morning Post*. Moscow wasted no time in reacting. On June 11, 1930, Metropolitan Sergius stripped Metropolitan Evlogy of his functions and asked that they be transmitted to Bishop Vladimir Tikhonitsky of Nice (1873–1953) or, if he refused, to another bishop of his diocese. Bishop Vladimir, already accused by some of being an agent of the GPU (it was rumored that he had been seen on a train to Berlin with a red fur cap), energetically refused this poisoned gift. Metropolitan Evlogy convoked his diocesan assembly from June 29 to July 4. All the bishops and members of the council approved his position. When the RSCM held its congress in July 1930, it also chose to support Metropolitan Evlogy—but not unanimously.

On December 26, Metropolitan Sergius confirmed his decision by placing the jurisdiction of western Europe under the authority of Metropolitan Eleutherius of Lithuania by a decree published in the immigration press a month later.

The Appeal to the Ecumenical Patriarch
Metropolitan Evlogy wrote in his memoirs that, "according to the canons of the Church, every bishop has the right to appeal to the Ecumenical Patriarch when there is an injustice in a Church."[76] In view of these canons, he decided to address himself to Ecumenical Patriarch Photius II, the patriarch of Constantinople. For the latter, this was a unique occasion to intervene in the affairs of the Third Rome. When the Russian bishop appealed to

him, he invited him and transmitted to him, on February 17, 1931, the *tomos* that changed his jurisdiction into an exarchate of the ecumenical patriarchate in western Europe. For Metropolitan Evlogy, this situation would last until "a central ecclesial authority is recognized by all and the normal conditions of existence for the Russian Orthodox Church are reestablished."[77] A diocesan assembly, composed of members of the clergy and lay representatives from the parishes, was convoked in June 1931, and it ratified, by a large majority, the decision taken by Metropolitan Evlogy. But if the great majority of the pastors and faithful of his diocese stood by him, this rupture of the canonical link between Metropolitan Evlogy and Metropolitan Sergius also brought about the emergence of a new jurisdiction that drew to itself the faithful from practically everywhere—in France (Paris and Nice), in Germany, and in Belgium. In Paris, the young French-speaking Orthodox community of Saint Genevieve and the Transfiguration, where Lev Gillet was the rector, was divided. Father Lev, who was teaching at the St. Sergius Institute, and a handful of the faithful, including Paul and Natasha Evdokimov, Elisabeth Behr-Sigel, Marguerite Zagorovsky, Leonid Chrol, G. Jouanny, Madame Abamelek—the director of the French-language bulletin *The Way*—and Nadezhda Gorodetsky (who brought along her friends Vsevolod de Voght and Marcel Péguy) remained faithful to Metropolitan Evlogy. But the Kovalevsky brothers, Vladimir Lossky, Leonid Uspensky, and Maria Kalash (Kurdiumov), objecting to the decisions of the diocesan assembly, put themselves under the authority of Metropolitan Eleutherius, bishop of Vilnius and all Lithuania. This group, sensitive to the interests of Western intellectuals in Orthodoxy, was close to the Catholic-Orthodox community of Bishop Winnaert. These hoped to obtain, through Moscow, recognition on the part of the Orthodox Church.[78]

Drawing Closer to the Synod
In 1933–34, Metropolitan Evlogy, without much regard for his flock's points of reference, sought to reconcile with his "old friend"[79] Metropolitan Anthony Khrapovitsky. Since he did not want to appear as a "Greek" in the middle of a diocese made up of Russians, Evlogy reasoned that the old feuds with the synod of Sremski Karlovtsy would be forgotten once his canonical status was consolidated, and that a common rejection of the Soviet government would unite them. In line with S. Troitsky, he thought

that even if he henceforth formally depended on the ecumenical patriarchate, the principle of Russian bishops in exile sharing territories was still a valid possibility. After several contacts, Metropolitan Evlogy decided to travel to Yugoslavia in May 1934 without telling anyone. Count Grabbe, the secretary of the synod and the principal adversary of the Parisian modernist current, took the bishop to the residence of Metropolitan Anthony. The two bishops became reconciled from this first meeting. But this encounter only revived passions. Count Grabbe declared publicly, in the month of August, that a council of the Russian Orthodox Church Outside Russia would meet to formalize this reconciliation but that first, the questions left suspended in 1929 had to be resolved, most notably, the doctrine of sophiology. During the summer of 1935, Metropolitan Evlogy, still eager to arrive at an agreement with the synod on the autonomy of the Russian dioceses of the immigration, agreed, with the blessing of the ecumenical patriarch, to return to Karlovtsy for a meeting of the principal hierarchs of the Russian immigration in order to define what their relationship would be.

The Debate in the Review

These events were the occasion for several series of articles in the immigration press, especially in *The Way*. Berdyaev had a threefold preoccupation. First, he wanted to show that, contrary to what the conservative press reported, religion was not dead in Soviet Russia. But he wanted to do this without minimizing the importance of the persecutions in the USSR, since this would involve Metropolitan Sergius. Berdyaev opened the pages of the journal to partisans of Metropolitan Sergius who emphasized the first aspect, while the partisans of Metropolitan Evlogy insisted on the second. Second, without taking sides, he was active in publishing articles coming from the USSR in order to maintain a dialogue with Russia. Third, he tried to provoke exchange between the two separated parties of the Russian Church while declaring that the journal was neutral. Until December 1931, the supporters of Metropolitan Evlogy engaged in dialogue with those of Metropolitan Sergius. After that date, the debate continued in the journal but without direct confrontation. The die had already been cast. For both sides, it was a question of reflecting on the reconstruction of a united Russian Orthodox Church on the ruins of the post-Constantinian church.

Echos of the Religious Situation in the USSR
In April 1930, an article by Julia Sazonova entitled "Religious Quests as Reflected in Soviet Literature" appeared in *The Way*. Sazonova claimed that the work of Yevgeny (Eugene) Zamiatin, the author of *We* [published in 1921 in the USSR, its fictional account of a thirteenth-century totalitarian state inspired George Orwell's *1984*], reveals "the despair of atheism which, in its essence, shows itself to be a religious quest."[80]

Because he often traveled to the borders of Russia, Lagovsky was considered one of the foremost authorities on the question. He also published an article on the religious situation in a special supplement of the September 1932 issue of the review. The author insisted, above all, on the reality of the persecutions. He provided a wealth of information on the liquidation of the *kulaks*, the deportation of entire families to "concentration camps,"[81] and the atheist education given in the collectives/*kolkhozes*. But— and this is characteristic of the Muscovite tendency of the journal—he also wrote of the vigor of religiosity, the eschatological atmosphere, the anticipation of the "new man," and the sect of "the red dragons" that expected the coming of the Archangel Michael.[82] Two other articles in the same tone by Kurdiumov appeared in the May 1933 and September 1934 issues of *The Way*. We will return later to these contributions of Sazonova, Lagovsky, and Kurdiumov, as well as Gofshtetter and Artemiev. The important thing to be noted here is that, throughout 1930 and up to 1934, the journal went overboard in depicting religious vigor within the USSR.

Berdyaev, for his part, distinguished his affiliation with the Moscow-based Russian Church from his civic convictions and did not hesitate to publish articles critical of the religious policy of the Soviet government. Unlike Lagovsky, the supporters of Metropolitan Evlogy were not particularly moved by accounts of religious fervor in Russia. Troitsky published two articles in the review, in August 1930 and April 1931, with the express purpose of rebutting the declarations of Metropolitan Sergius on the absence of persecutions in the Soviet Union (T7 and T8R). Based on Soviet legislation, the anti-religious press in Russia, and numerous publications in the West, he claimed that persecutions against Christians, Jews, and Muslims had been increasing since 1929. Klepinin's 1930 article in *The Slavonic Review* is cited, one in which the author noted that since 1921, 673 monastic churches had already been closed.[83] Troitsky described in detail the intolerable economic, juridical, and social status of priests who were overwhelmed with taxes, lacked any civic rights, and were obliged to live in shared apartments, and he rendered homage to the Russian martyrs. In his review of *Das Notbuch der Russischen Christenheit*, a collection published in Berlin with the collaboration of Protestant and Orthodox authors, including H. Koch, F. Lieb, K. Bem, N. Glubokovsky, and N. Arseniev, he described the de-Christianization that took place in the USSR during the collectivization process, from the promotion of free love to the legislation on bigamy and the transformation of Christian names into revolutionary names as part of the promotion of a cult of the personality.[84]

Beside these discussions, the journal entered into genuine dialogue with Soviet Russia through a few contributions. In the June 1930 issue, Berdyaev published the article of which he was probably the the most proud during the fifteen-year history of the review. It was, for the first time, a letter from a contemporary, coming from Russia and written expressly for *The Way*. Up to this time, Berdyaev had published articles written in Soviet Russia only by authors who had immigrated or by authors who had no particular intention of dialogue with *The Way* but, as it were, simply put letters in a bottle and threw them into the sea. The author was a twenty-nine-year-old philosopher, born in 1901, living in Vologda. He moved from atheism to Christianity thanks to the writings of Berdyaev, which he discovered in 1929, and the support of members of the "suffering Church." In his letter he told of his quest for God. He also wrote to the Russian philosopher to tell him that Berdyaev's position on the fanaticism of the Russian emigration, "whose echoes come to us from time to time as we live under the shadow of the 'seven seals,'"[85] brought him great joy. Thus Berdyaev discovered that, thirteen years after the revolution, he was still being read in Russia. Berdyaev finally had the impression that he was rediscovering a living dialogue with his homeland. An editor's note states that this "extremely interesting letter" testifies to "the depth of spiritual and intellectual life in Russia."

The following year, in February and then in June and August of 1931, Berdyaev continued this dialogue by publishing three articles from writers in the USSR. The first, on Blok, was written by "a priest from Petrograd," now deceased but whose archives had been sent from Russia. This article led to a debate with Berdyaev, of which I will treat later. The second and third articles were written by a young Russian monk-philosopher and concerned the economy. The sophianic overtones of these articles were a reminder that Florensky was still alive and attracting disciples. A fourth article, which also came from the Soviet Union and was published in *The Way*, summarized all that had been said about the position of the journal on the religious situation in the USSR. This article consisted of two sermons of one "Fr. Alexei B.," a parish priest in Moscow in 1925–30. The editors informed readers that the sermons, strongly marked by the influence of Fedorov, had been given in 1928, and added that the author had been arrested and was now in the Solovki concentration camp. This was in March 1934. For the authors of the review, Russia was very much alive, but was lying beneath the ruins, and there could be no direct contact with her outside of returning or through mystical union with her.

The Position of Neutrality
When, in July 1930, the RSCM chose to support Metropolitan Evlogy and his policy of firmness, this was not without some hesitation, notably on the part of Lagovsky. But between the summer of 1930 and February 1931, a number of painful questions concerning the future of the diocese remained unsolved. Fedotov, the editor of the *Messenger*, opened the debate in autumn 1930 with an article entitled "Concerning the Situation of the Russian Church." While explaining that his point of view was not shared by the whole of the editorial board of the RSCM's publication, Fedotov clearly took a position against Metropolitan Sergius. He considered that the persecutions in the USSR were worse than those of the Christians in the late Roman Empire insofar as they were half-concealed. He also questioned the argument invoked by Sergius for breaking off with Evlogy (not respecting neutrality) by pointing out that the declaration of loyalty was itself a political act. Above all, he denied that Sergius's actions could be justified by the principle of "economy," which, he wrote, in the Orthodox tradition did not signify lying or compromise but rather flexibility in the application of a judgment that is fundamentally just. Fedotov returned to his argument of 1927. He claimed that the diocese of Metropolitan Evlogy remained faithful to its source of legitimacy in the late Patriarach Tikhon (Belavin) and detached itself from Metropolitan Sergius but without returning to the jurisdiction of the Russian Orthodox Church Outside Russia.[86]

This article provoked a response in *The Way* several months later, written by Kurdiumov. But the new division within the immigration community threatened the very identity of the journal. The article was preceded

The Ecclesial Frontiers of a Generation 237

by a significant note from the editorial board that illustrated the nonconformist character of the journal and Berdyaev's desire to preserve unity among contributors: "The editorial board of the journal *The Way* should remain neutral in the recent ecclesial controversy and this is why it allows different points of view to be expressed." This kind of caution prefaced practically all the articles treating of this question up to 1935.[87] Although the journal had clearly taken a position against Metropolitan Anthony in the 1920s, in the August 1931 issue, at a moment when anything could happen, it published two divergent points of view, those of Kurdiumov and Fedotov.

The Breach between the Authors
In her polemical article, Kurdiumov compared the immigration community, riddled by divisions, with suffering Russia headed by Metropolitan Sergius. She raged against the maximalist immigrants with their Karamazovian temperament, who are ready to break all their bonds with what they loved most dearly, while she described all the riches of Christian maximalism to which the Russian martyrs bore witness. Convinced as she was that the revolution had been sent by God to punish the sinful Russian Church, the author summoned the immigrants to pray for their own sins rather than consider the Communist regime as a manifestation of the Antichrist. "There are two points of view," she wrote, "We curse. They pray."[88] Without naming him, the author accused Fedotov of not showing love when he accused the church of adapting to the conditions in which God had placed it. Kurdiumov even counterattacked by reminding Fedotov that Nil of Sora was essentially preoccupied with spiritual questions, and that if the immigrant community wanted to follow his path, it should not imagine that any kind of regime would be able to impede a society from growing spiritually.[89] The author concluded by recommending the "narrow road" of the apostolic way in Russia rather than the "indifferent boulevards of Western capitalist society." In her view, to abandon the church of Metropolitan Sergius would signify the loss of this Russian maximalism and be the equivalent of a definitive exile.

In his reply, published in the same issue, Fedotov had no difficulty in underlining the religious nationalism of his adversary. Trying to find a balance between the "lyricism" and the "pathetic" style of the article and its fundamental arguments, Fedotov attempted to reply to three questions raised by the author—concerning the immigration community, the Russian Church, and the social question. He thought that Kurdiumov was wrong when, without making clear distinctions, she divided the immigration from Russia to the point that, even if the "self-satisfied immigrant and the Russian martyr" were real, the internal differences between Metropolitans Evlogy and Anthony and between Metropolitan Sergius and the innovators were no longer apparent.[90] As for the necessary separation of the political from the ecclesiastical, Fedotov admitted "certain mistakes" committed by his jurisdiction but argued that these were minimal alongside the continual efforts of all the pastors of the church to avoid nourishing the nationalist and anti-Bolshevik passions of their flocks.[91] In Fedotov's opinion, it was not the followers of Metropolitan Evlogy who acted incorrectly but rather Metropolitan Sergius, who did all he could to get rid of Evlogy. What is more, by deviating from the morality of the Gospels by his falsehoods, the head of the Russian Church was pushing the young members of the Party (the "*komsomols*") even farther from the church. By describing the mechanisms of Stalinist terrorism—denunciations, mock trials, renouncements—Fedotov argued that the key to this strategy was the message, pounded into the heads of the people, that words have lost their meaning and weight in the course of events, and, consequently, anyone can say anything. The best contrary proof, he stated, was for Western public opinion to succeed in stemming the persecutions for a while by shouting out the truth. Moreover, the Russian historian claimed that he belonged to the tradition of Nil of Sora and that, during periods of tension, from the fourth-century Arian heresy to the synodal epoch of the Russian Church, it was not the hierarchy or the majority who preserved ecclesial truth but, more often, a few persecuted just people such as Nil. As for the social question, Fedotov claimed that Metropolitan Sergius was not a hierarch at the service of the proletariat, as Kurdiumov believed. He was, Fedotov wrote, the very prototype of the Russian bishop formed prior to the revolution, for whom the service of the monk was limited to asceticism, while that of the lay person began and ended with the liturgy. Such a spirituality left the social services, de facto, to Caesar, regardless of whether he is a revolutionary or a conservative.[92]

This article made clear the polemical battle—all the more so because the concrete aspect of the debate had been resolved since the ratification in June 1931 by the Parisian synod of their change to the jurisdiction of the Ecumenical Throne (the patriarch of Constantinople). All that was left to each side was to solidify their positions. By directly attacking the head of the Russian Church, in a tone unimaginable in the pre-revolutionary days, Fedotov had shocked that narrow but influential circle of Orthodox who were nationalists on the ecclesial level, adherents of a spirituality rooted in the *Philokalia*, and pre-revolutionary on a political level. The manager of the journal, Sergius Hautman de Villiers, a young Frenchman of Russian descent who had left the parish of Father Lev to join the eparchy of Metropolitan Eleutherius, threatened the editorial board with his resignation if *The Way* published any more harmful articles against Metropolitan Sergius, who had been "elected by the Holy Spirit."[93]

Kurdiumov replied in the December 1931 issue with a personal attack against Fedotov. In her article entitled "A Reply to G. Fedotov Concerning the *Raskol* in the Church," the author no longer used the term *quarrel* but the much stronger one—*raskol*. *Raskol*, which means separation, is not yet heretical schism, which is a separation on dogmatic points. *Raskol* is equivalent to a canonical separation. Kurdiumov accused Fedotov of being the "prosecutor" of Metropolitan Sergius, of having an "anti-hierarchical" obsession, and, worse still, of being a leftist intellectual who put more hope in the League of Nations than in God.[94] She also tried to damage Fedotov by observing that even if he pretended to be sacramentally united to the Russian Church, his real communion was with the jurisdiction of the patriarch of Constantinople, the head of the Russian Church of Metropolitan Evlogy. Concerning essentials, the author added to the debate an important argument borrowed from Troitsky. Formally speaking, Metropolitan Evlogy and the council of his diocese were responsible for the *raskol* and not Metropolitan Sergius because, canonically, there can only be an appeal to the authority of Constantinople if there is agreement between the two parties. The supporters of Metropolitan Evlogy, by creating the separation (*raskol*), have gone against "the total canonical submission" owed to the Mother Church of Russia.[95]

Berdyaev allowed the debate to play itself out. The editorial board replied to the young manager by telling him that "even if violent attacks against Metropolitan Sergius are intolerable, the editors reserved the right to publish articles that would shed light on the ecclesial question from different perspectives."[96] But there would be no more direct confrontation between the two sides until 1935. Fedotov, considering that everything had been said, refused to reply again. Moreover, the attacks of an "intellectual" on a hierarch of the church—even a separated hierarch—were not much appreciated by the diocesan officials of Metropolitan Evlogy's cathedral, the Cathedral of St. Alexander Nevsky on the rue Daru. The two sides, once intimately linked, abandoned all attempts at reconciliation. Yet each of the two parties, aware that the situation could only be temporary, sought to reflect on the future of the Russian Church. Three levels of analysis can be distinguished in the debate: the spiritual level, which concerned the limits of the church; the political level, which reflected on the ideal relations between the church and the state; and the ecclesial level, which considered the reconstruction of the visible church.

Three Aspects of the *Raskol*

The Spiritual Aspect
Although Kurdiumov appealed to Nil of Sora as an example, her own approach, like that of Artemiev, was more in continuity with the "Josephite" model of Russian holiness. Joseph of Volokalamsk was the principal representative of this form of spirituality, which was transmitted to the Old Believers, the elders of Optino, and certain of the intelligentsia, such as Konstantin Leontiev and Pavel Florensky.[97] Kurdiumov presented all the elements of this spiritual model in an article entitled "The Church and the New Russia," which appeared as a supplement to the May 1933 issue, and in another article, "On the Struggle against God and Gehenna," published in September 1934. The author had already demonstrated an interest in Russian maximalism and the religiosity of the Russian sects. In the 1933 article, she explained why she had not followed the path of the sects, in spite of the fact that power now lay in the hands of atheists.

> It is especially important to take note that, in a moment when a sector of the clergy, in a state of panic and expecting the end of the world, has summoned the laity to go underground and shut themselves in while they await the Second Coming of Christ, Metropolitan Sergius has called upon the hierarchs and clergy to accomplish the work of God in a fallen world.... Yet the opposition has reproached the Russian primate for not abandoning sinful Russia to Satan, for not having gone underground with the "elect"... for not having seen the end of the world but rather a phase of human history whose higher objectives have been authorized by "the action of God's Providence."[98]

She added: "It is not by chance, but by the providential action of the Divine Will that the Russian Church finds itself at the heart of the problem."[99] She rejoiced that the church has separated the Kingdom of God from that of Caesar and chosen the divine better part. "Outside of the Eucharist," the author claimed, the organization of the Church is "accessory."[100] While praising Metropolitan Sergius in Moscow for not having invoked the end of time, Kurdiumov was also drawn to the primitive church—this was contradictory but understandable—when bishops did not wear robes, and by the "proletarian" church, namely, the communion of Christians outside the walls of the institutional church.[101] Quoting the post-revolutionary review *Zavtra*, a left-wing nationalist publication of the group *Utverzhdentsy* ("The Affirmers"), she saw a sign of hope in the Christian profession of faith on the part of a member of the Communist Youth Movement.[102]

Although Berdyaev did not directly define his own position in the pages of the review, he chose to remain, in Paris, in the jurisdiction of Metropolitan Sergius. He also believed, as did others, such as Mother Maria Skobtsova, that the Russian Revolution was willed by Divine Providence. In the October 1931 issue of *The Way*, he wrote, "Christian truth had not been attained in all the fullness of life, so the forces of evil complete this truth through the power of the mysterious ways of the Providence of God."[103] Berdyaev, shaped by the Spirit-centered ecclesiology of Khomiakov, was not able to invest himself in the significance of competing and opposing juridical relationships within the church, such as those among the Russian Orthodox Church Outside Russia, Metropolitan Evlogy, and those loyal to Metropolitan Sergius of Moscow. Thus his recognition of Metropolitan Sergius should be considered, like that of Kurdiumov, as a formality. Even before the revolution, Berdyaev had appreciated contacts with the representatives of many denominations, churches, and traditions, and, like Bulgakov, had severely criticized the Russian Church in the debate concerning the monks who "adored the Name" [i.e., the "Imiaslavie" controversy of the early twentieth century, in which church authorities took a heavy-handed approach to Russian monks on Mt. Athos whose experience of the Jesus prayer led them to assert—heretically, according to authorities—that the name of God was God Himself]. All these elements explain why Berdyaev was sensitive to the arguments of Kurdiumov and wanted to remain faithful to the church of the martyrs. To be sure, this spiritual profile should be understood dynamically. Berdyaev had spiritual sources other than the eschatological tradition of the Old Believers. His lecture on Dostoevsky and his Christological evolution within the immigration community led him progressively closer to the "Nilian" current of Russian spirituality.

The spirituality bequeathed by Nil of Sora to Saint Philip, Metropolitan of Moscow, then to a certain fringe of the intelligentsia (Dostoevsky), and rediscovered within the émigré community,[104] was based on the idea that God had given total freedom to the world, even the power of rejecting Him.[105] This spirituality was shared by intellectuals such as Fedotov, Kartashev, Zernov, and Afanasiev. Their critical reflection led them to reject the non-canonical argument of the followers of metropolitans Anthony and Sergius. The canonists of the St. Sergius Institute easily parried this argument by citing canon 28 of the Council of Chalcedon, which stated that the authority of the Patriarch of Constantinople extends to communities implanted in "barbarian countries," that is, outside of the Roman Empire. Therefore it was natural for the émigré church to appeal to the Ecumenical Throne.[106] For them, however, the canons only served to facilitate the historical incarnation of the divine-human truth inscribed in dogma.

Nikolai Afanasiev, professor of canon law at the Institute, in an article in the July 1933 issue entitled "The Canons and Canonical Consciousness," gave the traditional explanation that the forms of ecclesial life can be modified in the measure in which "the canonical order is only the expression of the dogmatic doctrine on the Church."[107]

Here again, this distinction between the two spiritual currents that stemmed from Saint Sergius of Radonezh was a typology that permitted a wide range of views. Thus, in the camp of Metropolitan Evlogy, Kartashev recognized the grace of Metropolitan Sergius but believed that the Soviet state was not in a position to allow the church to lead an autonomous existence. Consequently, the two other sides of the *raskol* question should be examined—from a political viewpoint and an ecclesial viewpoint—in order to appreciate the full complexity of the breach established within the intellectual generation of the authors of *The Way*.

The Political Aspect
In opposition to the "Muscovite" position, which posited the submission of the church to the state, leaving the affairs of the world to Caesar and the nonworldly, liturgical part to God, Vadim Rudnev, the editor of the review

Contemporary Annals (*Sovremennye Zapiski*), published an article in the 37th edition entitled "Religion and Socialism." It proposed a lay version of the complete separation of church and state, inspired by the program of the Austrian Social Democrats, according to which the state should guarantee religious liberty as merely an aspect of the liberty of conscience.

Nikolai Sarafanov, a writer living in Constantinople, replied to this article in the April 1931 issue of *The Way*, stating that this approach posed two problems. First, a "society based only on physical relationships and material interests, outside of any spiritual bonds whatsoever, would not be a living social organism but a machine, a mechanical meeting of puppets without a soul."[108] The separation can only be made within the limits of the state itself, which should distinguish secular affairs from spiritual affairs.[109] In his conclusion, the author summed up his position. He believed that the church's spiritual authority is founded on freedom and that it should not seek anything else to legitimate it—neither the physical force of the power of the secular state nor the support of reasons that have no spiritual foundation.[110]

Faithful to the spirit of Nil of Sora, Kartashev, like Berdyaev and some other journal contributors, tried to synthesize, at the political level of the relationship between church and state, the mystical principle with the ascetic principle of organization, and the communitarian and creative principle with the hierarchical and organizational principle. In spite of the fact that politically he was a monarchist and a "theocrat," the former Ober-Procurator of the Holy Synod had invented, in 1923 at Pscherov, the formula that the Russian Church, after the council and the revolution, had "come out of the Constantinian phase of its history"—a view that could not be admitted either by the supporters of the ancient political order within the Russian Orthodox Church Outside Russia or by the partisans of the church's submission to the new religious legislation of the Soviet government. On February 19, 1931, two days after his diocese came under the jurisdiction of the Ecumenical Throne, Kartashev wrote an article entitled "Church and State, That Which Was and That Which Should Be in Russia," which had both a theological and a practical dimension. In this article, published in the April 1932 supplement of *The Way* (K15), the author, one of Metropolitan Evlogy's closest counselors, wrote: "We find ourselves faced with a problem which is absolutely practical and immediately vital: How can we begin to organize relations between the Russian Church, henceforth interiorly free, and the future national Russian State?"[111] For Kartashev, this question was all the more important because the local example of Russia could serve as a model for the universal church.

Kartashev argued that the church was bound to the state "without confusion or separation," "in the image of the two natures of Christ." This image implied the intangible principle of "rendering to Caesar what is Caesar's" but opposing Caesar when he claims "what belongs to God"—as did the martyrs, and not by political resistance.[112] As a historian, Kartashev enumerated the different forms of relationship between church and state. In the West, these range from the attempts of domination by Rome to the Protestant principle of the state's territorial primacy over the church. In the East, they range from the Byzantine principle of symphony, which proclaimed that the two entities are "two gifts of God" that should organize their respective spheres autonomously, to the reality in Russia of a state church and a theocratic state. Kartashev feared that, in the future Russia, because of this ponderous heritage, the state might try to impose a demagogic Orthodox propaganda. Therefore he recommended a complete separation between "free associations" and "the police"—but would leave the Orthodox Church with certain advantages as the dominant confession: through the official calendar, religious education in public establishments, and the primacy of the hierarchs in certain ceremonies, among other matters. In Kartashev's opinion, however, the hierarchical and theocratic principle should not disappear with the coming of a new democratic order. "It can be said that the paths of the theocratic service of the Church are democratized at present. The man of the Church, the theocrat, should now be a democrat, that is, a free social activist."[113] The church should put aside its old romantic dreams of unity in order to ensure, in collaboration with the creative forces in society, social services, education, and so forth. This solution would have the additional advantage of allowing the church to come out of its national framework and freely enter into relationships with the other autocephalous Orthodox churches, as well as with other confessions.[114] He concluded by echoing the slogan of the generation of the 1920s: "In this domain we should be realists, not dreamers—we should be modernists."[115]

The Ecclesial Aspect
As Kartashev pointed out at the end of his article, when he mentioned the problem of the relationship among churches, the political aspect of the *raskol* was inseparably linked to the problem of the church's internal

organization. The debate on nationalism that took place in the journal will be treated in full later. Yet, even at this point, it must be understood that the splintering of the Russian Church into three parties corresponded to three representations of the internal canonical organization of the church and, notably, of its rapport with the national body. Because the Russian Church had delegated all the powers to the state from the seventeenth century onward, it was difficult for it to define itself outside the national limits of the state and to establish nonpolitical relations with the other national churches—Bulgarian, Serbian, Greek, and so on. Once again— on this question of the establishment of a new ecclesial life—two points of view, *grosso modo*, can be found.

First, there was the traditional and hierarchical position defended by S. Troitsky, which counted among its adherents those bishops who were formed before the revolution, including metropolitans Anthony, Evlogy, and Sergius. According to this position, the limits of each church are territorial and political and the internal jurisdictional organization of these churches should follow the contours of these frontiers. This did not exclude horizontal contacts that remind believers of the universality of the Kingdom of God, such as common prayers and sacraments, meetings, and mutual programs. In practice, however, these remnants of the Byzantine Empire had very little influence on the internal national lives of these churches because of their dependence on the political vagaries and diplomatic preoccupations of the states to which they were subject. This explained why Evlogy, acting on the advice of Troitsky, attempted in 1935 to participate with Metropolitan Anthony in a council that would delimit a definitive sharing of zones.

The second point of view, shared by the modernist intellectuals of the review, was based on a more universal and horizontal vision of the church, both in theory and in practice. This vision did not question the historical and national inscription of the church. On the contrary, it gave the church its dynamic element. It was based on the idea that the church was the Body of Christ, where human nature, historically, responded unceasingly to the divine appeal and where "when one member suffers, the whole body suffers." Such a representation of the church necessarily called for a reform of the ecclesial body, both internally and externally.[116]

As for the international aspect and the necessary reform of the ecclesial organization, the points of view put forth by Kartashev in his 1932 book, published by the YMCA Press, and those expressed by Afanasiev in his review of it in *The Way*, were nearly identical. Kartashev developed a line of reasoning that included both communitarian and hierarchical elements of the church. Kartashev's book, one chapter of which was the transcription of a lecture delivered on November 15, 1931, was written in a very special context. At the moment when the internal divisions within the Russian Church came to light, the patriarch of Constantinople, who was experiencing increasing difficulties with the Turkish authorities, was trying to convoke a Great Council that would include all the Orthodox churches. A first pro-synod, with the participation of the patriarchs of Jerusalem, Antioch, Alexandria, and the autocephalous churches of Europe, except Russia, took place on Mount Athos in 1931, and a second was planned for 1932. Kartashev, who lamented that no one was informed about these meetings, proposed that the great pan-Orthodox council be prepared first on the level of the local churches and that it end with the formation of a permanent conciliar organ, which, like the Vatican, would be able to defend the national churches against infringements by the states. The author also dreamt of a new ecclesiology of sister-churches, which would one day render possible a great ecumenical council of the Eastern and Western churches, where there would no longer be any "memory of past anathemas nor the mutual sacrilegious negation of the dignity of ecclesial grace and of catholicity."[117] Kartashev pointed out that the principle of conciliarity, such as Khomiakov had envisaged it, is, "like holiness," a dynamic principle within history. In the name of this principle, he declared himself in favor of lay people participating in the council, even if it should be the patriarch, rather than the emperor, who convoked it. Finally, recalling the fifteen hundredth anniversary of the Third Ecumenical Council of Ephesus, which took place in 431, and the opposition between the theologians of Antioch (who insisted on the humanity of Christ and, therefore, on the non-confusion of his two natures) and those of Alexandria (who insisted on the unity of the Person in Christ and therefore on the non-separation of the two natures)—an opposition which played itself out in the council—he concluded his work with a new formula: "In our days, the times are Antiochizing!"[118]

In the context of the book, this formula signified that the separation of church and state, as the foundation of the internal and external conciliarity of the church, was on the agenda. N. Afanasiev, a colleague of Kartashev at the St. Sergius Intitute, in his review of the book in the February

1933 issue of *The Way*, praised the "talent" of the author in every respect.[119] But his commentary on the enthusiastic formula of Kartashev was more realistic: "It should be added that the times are also Alexandrizing!"[120] Afanasiev also recommended extreme prudence in preparing this council and urged that the conciliar work of the local churches be given special consideration. Finally, Afanasiev believed that, theoretically, the separation between clergy and laity that had appeared in the councils over the course of centuries was not healthy, for their divergent interests cannot be represented within the church. But he recognized that, on a practical level, a future council where only bishops would be represented could only aggravate the clergy-laity division.

The differences that began to appear in 1930 among the authors of the review regarding a question of an apparently purely jurisdictional order were serious. By revealing, within the modernist generation, two types of spirituality, that is, two types of relationships to evil, to grace, and to power, the debate introduced a split within the group, and this, in turn, led to different behavior and commitments. But until 1935, the division between the two jurisdictions—which was not as profound as the schism with the Russian Orthodox Church Outside Russia—had a connotation more political than spiritual or theological. Thus, thanks to an editorial consensus on the position of neutrality adopted by the review, the authors had the possibility of engaging in a dialogue in the pages of *The Way* and demonstrating a bit of creativity; and this, too, was evidence of the nonconformist unity of the generation of the early 1930s.

A Workshop in Search of a Third Way

The immigrant community—divided between the traditional left-wing and right-wing parties, between post- and pre-revolutionary movements, and between pro-Soviet and pro-Fascist currents—knew all the variants of political engagement that the Western democracies were experiencing. *The Way* did not support any party, maintaining its stance of giving ecclesial commitment priority over political commitment.[121] Ilyin wrote for the right-wing daily *Vozrozhdenie* (*Renaissance*), while Shestov wrote for the left-wing daily *Poslednie Novosti* (*The Latest News*). Kartashev and Zenkovsky frequented the monarchist milieus, Frank and Bulgakov felt more at ease with the right-wing liberal position of P. Struve, while Berdyaev and Fedotov, sensitive to the reproaches of passivity from the younger generation, were engaged in the movements known as post-revolutionary—according to the expression then in vogue.[122] *The Way*'s authors, united through the primacy of the spiritual principle, agreed on three points: criticism of the bourgeois spirit, rejection of both communism and capitalism, and rejection of nationalism. Very consciously, they rooted their positions in the myth of theanthropy (divine-humanity). Valentina Zander, who debuted in the pages of *The Way* in 1931 with an article entitled "The Symbolism of the Icon of the Holy Trinity by Andrei Rublev," clearly expressed—in the version translated into French in 1936—the common will of these intellectuals by insisting on the social implications of the Russian painter's task. In a style that recalled Solovyov at his purest, she wrote:

> It is, then, this cross inscribed in the Holy Trinity that becomes the principal law of human society. It is only though the cross that a society can become Christian, and the ideal Christian society is the Church. Thus the Church is the cross incarnate on earth in the lives of human beings. . . . People united among themselves and to their Creator by love and assembled around the Eucharistic table which is the witness and first fruits of the absolute reality of this love—this is the Christian social ideal—the Church as the eternal vision of all human society, the Church as the eternal source of the resolution of every social problem.[123]

But this primacy of the spiritual was also a source of discord. As soon as the myth of theanthropy was invoked in order to elaborate a positive and creative social or national doctrine, the authors found themselves occupying different positions as to the best means of actualizing the Kingdom of God. From this perspective, their various ideologies are simply dispersed and divergent attempts to actualize the myth of the Kingdom.

The Political Dimension

The spiritual foundation of the review's political position appears clearly in two articles by Berdyaev. The first, entitled "The Spiritual State of the Contemporary World," appeared in the September 1932 issue and was translated into French in 1949. The second bore the title "Man and the

Machine: The Question of the Sociology and Metaphysics of Technology" and was published in Russian in May 1933 and in French that same year in an edition of Je Sers. In addition to these two articles, a book entitled (in the title of its English translation) *The Fate of Man in the Modern World* was published by the YMCA Press in 1934 in Russian and by Stock in 1936 in French (*Le destin de l'homme dans le monde actuel*).

The first article by Berdyaev was a lecture given to a student congress organized by the World Student Christian Federation in May 1931 at Bad Bol in Austria. According to Berdyaev, the world was living through an era of "spiritual anarchy" characterized by the loss of faith in progress and democracy. Modern France, he wrote, was being corrupted by cultural skepticism. The philosophy of Heidegger regarded the world as irretrievably sinful and God as absent. Finally, the school of thought of Barth, "the most important among the theological currents" in Berdyaev's view, was marked by the exclusionary and bitter sentiment of sin. For the Russian philosopher, it was as if humanity were ready to swap a spiritual freedom that had exhausted itself for a force that would organize both its interior and exterior existence. Berdyaev analyzed three aspects of the process of this spiritual crisis: technology, democracy, and capitalism.

Technology
For Berdyaev, technology posed a spiritual problem involving the relationship between God and man. When man possesses such an important force, "the fate of all humankind depends on his spiritual state."[124] The significance of the intrusion of technology into the modern world was that all of human existence passed from the organic level to the organizational level. Berdyaev saw all the advantages in detaching one's self from a life overly centered on the cosmos. But, in his eyes, an excessive rationalization of social life would lead to unemployment in the West and to a "collective delirium" in the USSR. In his article "Man and the Machine," he added that for Taylorism, a view that transformed humanity into a machine, technology essentially dominated the spirit, with humanity thereby "changed into its image and likeness."[125] But the person is characterized by unity and integrity and cannot be transformed into a constitutive component, a means, a tool. In this article, Berdyaev sought to discover what meaning the coming of a new cosmos would have for human reality.

We should recognize the significance of the technological era, its religious significance above all, insofar as it means the end of the terrestrial epoch of history where mankind was defined by the soil—not just in the physical sense of the word, but in the metaphysical sense also.... This modification of our consciousness had already come about, theoretically speaking, at the beginning of modern times when the Copernican system replaced that of Ptolemy, when the earth ceased to be the center of the cosmos, when mankind discovered the infinity of worlds.... Mankind, feeling cheated by the loss of this cosmos where it held a hierarchical rank and felt itself surrounded by supreme powers, seeks to make up for it by finding a support in transferring the center of gravity into the self, into the subject. The idealist philosophy of this new history is an expression of this need for compensation.[126]

In Berdyaev's view, if the former culture endangered the human body by exhaustion from work, the mechanical-technological civilization, with its mastery of time by speed, was above all fatal for the soul. It demanded a greater spiritual intensity on the part of mankind in order to rediscover, through meditation, the depth and the eternity of the present moment.[127] Berdyaev concluded his reflection on the problem of technology by situating it within the tradition of the eschatological thought of Fedorov:

A remarkable attempt to resolve this problem was undertaken by the brilliant thinker Nikolai Fedorov, author of *The Philosophy of the Common Task*. For Fedorov, as for Marx and Engels, philosophy should not limit itself to a theoretical knowledge of the world but should actively transform it, it should be projective. Mankind is called to dominate the cosmic forces of nature which cause his death and to regulate and organize not only social life but also cosmic life.... If Christians do not unite in the common task destined to surmount the forces of the cosmos, to vanquish death and reestablish life everywhere, if they do not create a kingdom of work which is spiritualized in a Christian manner, if they do not overcome the dualism of theoretical reasoning and practical reasoning, of intellectual work and physical work, there will be no Christian truth. If the Christian does not practice fraternity and love in all the fullness of life, if he does not triumph over death by the combined forces of Christian love and science, then this will be the advent of the Antichrist, the end of the world, the last judgment and the accomplishment of all that is foretold in the Apocalypse. But, once again, all this can be averted if "the common task" is undertaken.[128]

Democracy
After World War II, V. Varshavsky, in his memoirs entitled *A Generation Which Nobody Noticed*, criticized Berdyaev for having had a negative influence on members of the post-revolutionary movements, by inciting them to be scornful of the state and democracy and thus encouraging some to return to the USSR.[129] Varshavsky did not cite any facts to support his thesis. This accusation was essentially based on a polemic that took place in the pages of *New City* between 1931 and 1933 and statements by Berdyaev during this time period. Stepun, in the third issue of the review in 1932, criticized Berdyaev for not distinguishing sufficiently between the bourgeois spirit and democracy.[130]

In order to evaluate Varshavsky's charge, one must examine Berdyaev's writings during this period. Clearly, certain proposals of Berdyaev in 1931–32 could be interpreted as anti-democratic by young Russian immigrants. The first issue of the journal *Affirmations* (*Utverzhdenia*) in 1931 began with the following words of Berdyaev:

> The spiritual struggle against Communism is the defense neither of private property nor of capitalism but of the spiritual principle of the person and the spiritual principle of liberty. The Italian Fascists and the National-Socialist Germans do not understand this because they are pagans; they are, on the whole, strangers to Christianity. The defense of the spirit and dignity of the person threatened by dangers should be absolutely free of any obligatory link with any sort of political regime such as, for example, liberal democracy.[131]

Moreover, in *The Fate of Man in the Modern World*, he wrote: "formal parliamentary democracy has compromised itself and is incapable of bringing about the social reformation of society. It has shown a terrible capacity for inertia."[132] But beginning with the first issue of *New City* in 1931, Berdyaev had asserted: "We shouldn't cry 'Long live Freedom' in front of a person who is deprived of bread.... In this sense truth is on the side of a social democracy rather than a liberal democracy."[133] Similarly, in the same book in which Berdyaev criticized the parliamentary system of the Third Republic, he stated:

> However, if there is an eternal principle in democracy, it is certainly not linked to the idea of the primacy of the nation, but rather to the concept of the subjective rights of the human person, to the freedom of the spiritual life, to the freedom of conscience, to the right to think, speak, and create. This concept of the inalienable rights of the human person does not come from Rousseau or from the Jacobins of the French Revolution, but from Christianity and the Reform movement. But the idea of the rights of the person and the citizen has been disfigured and hijacked in the capitalist and bourgeois societies of the nineteenth and twentieth centuries.... In general, it is not understood that the heart of the problem is not so much in the advent of this or that social organization and type of state in which society and the state would bestow freedom on the human person, but rather the affirmation of the freedom of the human person with respect to the unlimited power of the society and the state.[134]

It would seem, then, that Berdyaev maintained a twofold position on the question of democracy. In one sense, as he wrote in "The Spiritual Crisis," culture cannot attain perfection without the aristocratic principle, without choice. But in another sense, Berdyaev was pleased that progressively larger sectors of society shared the fruits of culture. The main problem was not with democracy in itself, but with the fact that the European cultural elite was detached from the masses, who aspired to take their rightful place in social life. According to Berdyaev, the masses were led by "myths, religious or social-revolutionary beliefs, and not by cultural and humanistic ideas."[135]

The debate on democracy between Berdyaev and the authors of *New City* ended with a showdown in the journal's seventh issue, where the two editors, Berdyaev and Fedotov, each contributed articles. Berdyaev, losing patience with the accusations against him and seeing that events were confirming his misgivings about parliamentary democracy, counterattacked in an article entitled "On Social Personalism." He criticized the young *New*

City writers for being democrats of the old school, incapable of imagining that institutions might have an interior life and paralyzed with fear by the developing conflicts in Europe. Moreover, he claimed that Fedotov and his friends erred in their excessive confidence in neo-capitalism, in making an overly radical distinction between politics and ethics, and in their lack of universalism.[136] Fedotov began his reply with these words: "Berdyaev, one of our closest and most appreciated collaborators on our review, wanted to turn his interesting article on social personalism into a criticism of *New City*. I must admit that we do not understand why Berdyaev has proceeded in this way."[137] Fedotov agreed with Berdyaev's ideas on the primacy of freedom over the collectivity and on the material aspects of capitalism. But he added a nuance, which was the real stumbling block between the two men, perhaps between the two generations, as far as the question of democracy was concerned. While Berdyaev, in his quest for the spirit, was turned towards the "not yet" of the Kingdom, Fedotov wanted to live in a society where the spirit was "already there." In his article, Fedotov, who thought that moral utopianism in politics was a crime, favored the autonomy of the political sphere with respect to the ethical sphere. This position differed from the thought of Berdyaev, for whom, according to Fedotov, the ideal of a completed culture was impossible. Because he considered economics to be the sphere where ethics should be applied, Berdyaev, in Fedotov's opinion, did not acknowledge what was specific to this sphere of knowledge, which consisted in satisfying humanity's natural needs. Fedotov wrote: "The apocalypse of culture does not mean a formless and disintegrated state but simply a preparation for its self-definition in the Kingdom of God."[138] In Fedotov's view, there was an iconoclastic element in Berdyaev's thought, for he sought to block any way for the spiritual to incarnate itself in culture, under the pretext that this could not be fully realized. But Fedotov, influenced by Bulgakov's sophiological understanding of the icon, asserted that "the autonomous spheres of culture are nothing more than the created icons of Divine-human religion. All culture should be understood as a veneration of icons."[139]

New City tried to be fair to Berdyaev. Alongside these articles were two others in the same 1933 issue — the first by the editors, "Germany has Awakened," and a second by Fedotov, entitled "Democracy Sleeps." The editorial recognized that "criticism of democracy was, from the beginning, considered as one of the principal tasks of *New City*, but the review never posed the question, 'democracy or fascism?'"[140] In his article, Fedotov, obviously stung by Berdyaev's criticism, underlined the weakness of democracy in the face of the violent acts of the fascist and nationalist states. Further, he opposed Berdyaev's idea of reforming the institutions of the Third Republic, in favor of a new "ideocracy, comparable to fascism or communism, but which would bring to the world not the tyranny of the idea but the liberation of the power of the idea."[141] However, we should not read too much into such words. Neither Berdyaev nor Fedotov questioned the foundations of democracy. Both were seeking, each in his own way and while there was still time, to lay down the basics of a "social personalism" or a "Christian democracy,"[142] the one on a philosophical level, the other on a political level, the one looking towards the kingdom which is to come, the other seeing this kingdom as already present.

Capitalism and Communism
In Berdyaev's perspective, the crisis of modern civilization, characterized by the submission of the person to technology and collectivization, meant that "the myth of man" as the image of God was threatened in the same way as "the myth of God," that is, the God-Man.[143] For Berdyaev, this process of dehumanization was historically rooted in the emergence, at the time of the Renaissance, of an industrial capitalism that transformed creative work into products for sale. Thus, for him, communism, with its need to reduce individuals to a collectivity, was the natural outcome of capitalism.[144] In his article entitled "The Truth and Lies of Communism," which appeared in the October 1931 issue of *The Way*, Berdyaev wrote that "there is nothing more opposed to the spirit of Christianity than the spirit of capitalism," that is, the spirit which made the life of society as a whole dependent upon the interplay of private interests.[145] Berdyaev also published a number of articles in *The Way* that were critical of capitalistic liberalism.

In November 1933, a young philosopher, Nikolai Reimers, published an article written in August 1932 and entitled "Freedom and Equality: Blueprint for a System of Philosophy of Law." The author, a taxi driver and professional philosopher, was known for his book *The Aesthetic Principle in History* and favored a personalist philosophy of law. For him, law should try, by the force of reason, to make the spirit the regulatory principle of personal relationships.[146] In the same issue, A. Polotebneva had an article entitled "An Essay on an Ethical and Religious Conception of Nature." The author deplored the lack of respect for nature on the part of industrial society, which destroyed forests, polluted the air, and caused tuberculosis and cancer. Polotebneva found it revolting that tons of coffee were thrown into the ocean to maintain its price on the market. For her, this was "offensive to nature's generosity."[147] She also protested that "millions of living beings are sacrificed daily for commercial profit."[148] The editorial board was unanimous in its criticism of capitalism. In the June 1931 issue, the following note can be found: "The editors believe that the problem of the relationship between Christianity and socialism can be discussed from various points of view in the pages of *The Way*. The only exception would be an attempt to defend a Christian conception of the capitalist reality of the nineteenth and twentieth centuries."[149]

Berdyaev was also criticized by Varshavsky for having provoked the return of young immigrants to the USSR because of the pro-Soviet positions expressed in the review. What Berdyaev himself wrote should be taken into consideration. He published several articles on the evolution of communism in the USSR between 1930 and 1935.[150] The criticism was on three levels—spiritual, philosophical, and apologetic.

Berdyaev kept hammering away at the fact that communism did not reject God in the name of humanity but rather in the name of the social collectivity. For Berdyaev, who wrote a review of Trotsky's autobiography for *New City*, the figure of the Bolshevik leader illustrated the tragic destiny of the egocentric person who believes that the end justifies the means. As he put it in "Truth and Lies of Communism," Communism replaced the Christian theanthropic myth by a "proletario-centrism."[151] Berdyaev had no qualms about comparing communism and fascism, "which are so much alike from a social morphological viewpoint."[152] The difference, for him, was that Marx worshipped society while Mussolini venerated the state.

Berdyaev closely followed the latest publications of Soviet philosophers.[153] He probably knew of the article written about him by I. K. Luppol in 1930 in *The Great Soviet Encyclopedia*.[154] Luppol was the director of the Institute of World History and specialized in the history of philosophy. He ruthlessly attacked Berdyaev's "reactionary social and mystical metaphysics."[155] In *The Way*, Berdyaev argued that for Marxism-Leninism, the primacy of being over consciousness was the cornerstone of materialism. But, he added, on this line of thought the material was a "myth disposing of divine attributes," such as that of auto-dynamism.[156] In his review of the book of V. F. Asmus, *An Essay on the History of Dialectic in New Philosophies* (published in Moscow, 1929), Berdyaev was pleased that, in spite of censorship, there existed a movement of philosophical thought in the USSR evolving from materialism and towards the dialectic of Hegel. Like Asmus, Berdyaev believed that being has primacy over consciousness, but he criticized Asmus for opposing spiritual metaphysics to dialectical materialism. For Berdyaev, there could only be a dialectic of the spirit and not a dialectic of atoms.[157]

The article entitled "The General Orientation of Soviet Philosophy and Militant Atheism," written a year later in July 1932, was more pessimistic. Berdyaev claimed that in the USSR, philosophy had been transformed into a theology, which assumed a revelation through scriptures, through the church fathers, and, above all, through its inquisition and heresies, from Plekhanov to Bogdanov and from Trotsky to Kautsky. The mechanical materialism of Bukharin and the dialectical idealism of Deborin and Karev were the two supreme heresies. Marxism-Leninism had become a type of scholasticism, which had to adapt itself unceasingly to the directives of Stalin, who, according to Berdyaev, "doesn't understand anything about philosophy."[158] In Berdyaev's view, speculation was totally paralyzed when it tried to lead the battle against religion since, "according to article 13 of the charter of the Communist Party, a communist must be an atheist and participate in anti-religious propaganda."[159] According to Berdyaev, what was most original in this line of thought was the permanent link between theory and practice—and in this respect it resembled the perspectives of Fedorov and Christianity. But in Marxism-Leninism, this link was conceptualized in a partisan and sectarian way, without any reflection on the hierarchy of values. In reality, the principal idea of the philosophy of class was that there only existed one logic, one ethic, one human nature. This is why it was impossible to engage in a discussion if one lacked the class consciousness of the proletariat. Not even facts can be used in an argument, for these depended on consciousness. Berdyaev stated, "For them, truth is only an instrument of combat, it is filled with hate. This truth is linked to the five-year plan and not to eternity."[160]

Berdyaev was not content with criticizing the foundations of Marxist-Leninism. Through the YMCA Press he launched a new series of brochures of twenty-four pages each entitled "Christianity on the Battle Line against Atheism," which aimed at being a popular, accessible response to Soviet propaganda. These were sold in the immigration community at three francs apiece and were distributed in regions adjoining the USSR. Berdyaev invited the authors of *The Way*, such as Frank ("Personal Life and Social Creation," no. 2 in the series) and Fedotov ("The Social Significance of Christianity," no. 3) to contribute. Berdyaev himself published an article ("Christianity and Human Creativity") in this series in 1933. It was principally in this brochure that he replied to the main argument of atheist propaganda: that the Christian religion denied the value of human activity and preached a passive submission to destiny, since only God was a true agent. In the countryside, Berdyaev wrote, the benefits of the tractor were set in opposition to vain prayers for a good harvest. He observed bitterly that such propaganda was successful because of the weakness of prerevolutionary theology, which used the doctrine of original sin to humiliate people and keep them in slavery without any other hope of salvation than a magical kind of grace. However, Berdyaev argued, Christianity was, above all, a revelation about humanity created in the image and likeness of God. "The essence of the Gospels is the quest for the Kingdom of God ... sin is vanquished by the active seeking of the Kingdom of God, of the best, most perfect, most complete, and most total life."[161] For Berdyaev, Christianity was the religion of the incarnate Spirit and of the transfiguration of the world. The very history of Christianity, he argued, was that the advances of science and of civilization issued from the message of the Gospels and in turn showed that this quest was a "fire." The inquisition and the torturers in the West or the lethargy of Oblomov in Russia should be understood as the revolt of the fallen element in humanity against the Christian message. Berdyaev reminded his readers that the words, "He who does not work, does not eat," are not from Marx but from Saint Paul.[162] Berdyaev concluded his counterattack by arguing that philosophical and historical materialism are less effectively active than Christianity because, in their perspective, humanity is simply the fruit of chance and social process.

It is true that Berdyaev treated roughly ideas that were widely accepted in the Russian émigré community. In his article "The Truth and Lies of Communism" of October 1931, he began as follows:

> Until now, the relationship with communism has been more emotional than intellectual. The psychological atmosphere was not at all propitious for an understanding of the ideal world of communism.

In the Russian immigration community, communism called forth an affective, emotional reaction against it on the part of people who had been hurt by it. Too many people replied to the question: "What is communism?" by "It's my broken existence," or by "It's my unfortunate destiny."[163]

Berdyaev felt that the time had come to change this way of thinking. What many would not forgive him was precisely this aim: to show the truth of communism, which believes in the possibility of a leap from eternity into time by passing from the domain of necessity to the society of the Soviets; and to describe communism as a "religious manifestation," a vision of the world as a whole, inspiring enthusiasm and sacrifices. For the generals of the Supreme Council of the Monarchy, it was scandalous to dare to compare the messianic project of Moscow–Third Rome of the monk Philotheus of Pskov to the Bolshevik project of the Third International. Berdyaev was opposed to their projects of restoring the prerevolutionary order or transforming Russia into a bourgeois society based on the nineteenth-century model, for "the future belongs to the working masses anyway. Integral communism can only be replaced by integral Christianity."[164] Elsewhere, in a public session of the Academy of Religious Philosophy in 1932, Berdyaev stated:

> We know that the symbol of the hammer and sickle has become a symbol hostile to the cross, but the reasons for this are complex. I think that this would not have come about were it not for the faults of Christians; fundamentally, the symbol of the hammer and sickle is more compatible with the symbolism of the cross than with that of Roman law and bank notes.[165]

Similarly, young intellectuals such as Varshavsky, who were psychologically walled in by their anti-communism, were scandalized by what Berdyaev had to say:

> Communism submits the life of a particular individual to objectives which are grandiose, worldwide, and supra-individualistic. In a new way the individual returns to understanding life as service— something that has completely disappeared from our dechristianized,

bourgeois, and liberal epoch. Every young person feels that he is constructing a new world. Even if it is a question of building the tower of Babel, communism gives to those who engage in its ways a meaning above and beyond their own lives. Economics is no longer a private affair; it is of worldwide importance. . . . What especially attracts the youth is that the world has become plastic, it can be transformed and reconstructed as much as one wants. The weight of the past, of history, of traditions, which count for so much in the West, is like ballast to be dumped. The creation of the world is to begin as if it were the original beginning. . . . Communism absolutely does not understand liberty as the possibility of choosing, the possibility of turning to the right or to the left, but exclusively as the possibility, once a direction has been taken, of realizing all of one's potential energies.[166]

To get an idea of the harshness of such proposals, one would have to read the hallucinatory notebooks of Poplavsky, the Russian Rimbaud, who died from a drug overdose in 1935, or the bitter account of the new Soviet reality by Ivan Boldyrev, *The Boys and the Girls*, published shortly before his suicide in 1933. Berdyaev, however, never called for a return to the USSR. Rather, he called for a creative spiritual effort. It is precisely because he understood the sufferings of these young writers, and was aware that his negative criticism of Marxism-Leninism would be insufficient to help them find a meaning for their existence, that he reached out to them. In a lecture given to *Kochevie*, the Union of Poets, which was published in the August 1931 issue of the review as "Literary Currents and the Social Order (On the Question of the Religious Meaning of Art)," he spoke of the solitude of the individual in the West, who had a social sense but no community, and of the difficulty confronting the immigrant writer in finding what Soviet jargon calls the "social order." He painted a picture of this uprooted writer, bowing under the weight of the great Russian literature of the nineteenth century, fascinated by the writings of Proust. But, Berdyaev affirmed, on the one hand, the future lay not in the psychological analysis in vogue in the West but in a mystical realism; and, on the other hand, the situation of the Russian writer had grown even worse because of "the horror of the government literary organizations in Soviet Russia, which forbade any creative liberty and restricted the awareness of this problem of the social order."[167] For Berdyaev, the individualistic humanism of the Renaissance was coming to an end and humanity was entering a new Middle Age, in which the artist would no longer be at the service of society or of a patron or of the state but rather at the service of "the conciliatory spirit."[168] Art does not constitute an autonomous sphere; it is at the service of the spirit, a transfiguration of life as witnessed (according to Berdyaev's pet genealogy) by "Dante, Michelangelo, Beethoven, Joseph de Maistre, Tolstoy, Dostoevsky, Kierkegaard, Nietzsche, and Léon Bloy."[169] He encouraged the young immigrant poets to make a spiritual effort to listen in their hearts to the voice of the spirit telling them to what service they are being called. And he indicated a path, the only path capable of transcending their desire to return to the homeland: "The dream of the advent of community, i.e., of communism in the religious sense of the word, is the loftiest dream of humanity." But to ensure that everything was clear, he added: "The greatest evil of communism is that it wants to bring about community, communion, mechanically, by the constraint of social organization.... But the social order of the community can only be realized through freedom."[170]

The Social Question

The primacy of the spiritual over the political provided cohesion to the generation of the authors of *The Way*, but it did not erase all their differences. On the contrary, precisely because their differences were spiritual, their debates were intense and often even violent. The nonconformist character of *The Way* preserved it from such violence in the first half of the 1930s, while encouraging reflection on the principal spiritual antinomies that came to the fore at the moment of the *raskol:* the division between contemplation and action, between subjectivity and objectivity, between freedom and responsibility, and between voluntary community and the organized state. From the beginning of the 1930s, a dividing line can be traced between two groups of authors concerning the two principal questions treated in the journal—the social question and the national question. On the one side were those who, with Berdyaev, believed that the solution to the problem of the social and national among individuals was the awareness that the person was more important than the collectivity. On the other side were those who, like Vysheslavtsev, believed the contrary— that the starting point was the natural and hierarchical bond that united individuals among themselves, and from this derived the solution to the problem of their own social and national identity.

N. Alekseev, whose article entitled "Christianity and Socialism" appeared in the June 1931 issue, belonged to the personalist faction of the journal. Alekseev used the example of the community life between Christ and his apostles and the writings of the Fathers of the Church to affirm that the social ideal of Christianity was founded on the primacy of the person. He thus rejected socialist doctrine. The socialist perspective did not situate the individual at the center of life in society, but rather replaced the person with society as a whole—whether in the name of the people, the church, the state, the proletariat, or all of humanity.[171] Such a social order, conceived as the reflection of the divine cosmos, forces mankind into submission. Alekseev thought that the purpose of dividing medieval society into three orders was to imitate a preestablished divine order. The reunification of the person—who has become aware of the fallen state of the world—with the social group can only take place in Christ, Alekseev argued, and not by seeing himself, according to a tradition running from Aristotle to Saint Thomas, as part of a political organism.[172] For Alekseev, society was not a collection of atoms. The person, by freely refusing to be master of his own existence, was capable, as was Christ with respect to his Father, of transforming the material into the spiritual. Alekseev recognized the dangers of individualism inherent in this doctrine. What was important was to keep the final objective in view. The apostles did not sell their possessions in order to create socialism; they did so in order to abandon themselves to God. Therefore, Alekseev concluded, the problem was not so much in the development of capitalism or socialism but in the formation of a state able to ensure, given the historical conditions, a harmony between the individual and the universal principles of social life in view of the development of the spiritual life of the person.[173]

In the same spirit, F. A. Stepun, one of the old pre-revolutionary acquaintances of Berdyaev ever since he was one of the first lecturers at the Free Academy of Spiritual Culture (VADK), the predecessor of the Academy of Religious Philosophy, published a letter from Germany (where he resided), which appeared in the August 1931 issue. This letter, which bore the title "Religious Socialism and Christianity," focused on the socialist-religious movement of Paul Tillich, one of the first contributors to *The Way* and a friend of Berdyaev. Berdyaev greatly appreciated in Tillich's theology of the *kairos*, of the prophetic moment, the link between the critical and the sacramental in mankind's relationship with history, which allowed for the foundation of a society that was both respectful of the sacred and open to creative liberty. But in 1929, Tillich's movement had entered politics by joining the Social Democratic Party. In his article, Stepun was quite critical of the German religious socialists, for whom the church, identified with the proletariat, was the foundation of social commitment. Stepun also denounced the position of the Protestant theologian and pastor as being "nationalist and bourgeois," as lacking any mystical vision of the church, and as preaching an "Aryan Christ."[174]

For reasons that will be examined later, Berdyaev's social personalism was not fully articulated until the next period of the journal, which I address in Part Three of this volume. His article of July 1935, "Personalism and Marxism," marked a turning point in a period dedicated to the criticism of Marxism as dialectical materialism. Berdyaev had been reading Tillich and Ragaz (see B67R and B79R). At the 1932 public session of the Academy of Religious Philosophy, which had as its theme "Christianity and Contemporary Social Reality," Berdyaev limited himself to preparatory work. He used as a starting point the fact that any Christian justification of the established order was impossible. Whether this justification based itself on suffering as a means of salvation or on the sanctification of all power insofar as it comes from God, it is always the social projection of human sin. Berdyaev was seeking a Christian vision of the worldwide regulation of economic activity and the organization of work. Such regulation was not based on individual talents, as it was during the centuries of a patriarchal society, but on social justice, as demanded by the new "workers' democracies."[175] At this same conference, Fedotov argued that even if social consciousness has been aroused, Christian reflection "still does not have an intellectual response to the question, 'what is to be done?'" (F11). He reviewed the different Christian attempts to remedy social problems, from Percy Widdrington's "The League of the Kingdom of God" in England to the first experiments with worker-priests in France in the context of the social teams of Robert Garric.[176]

Characteristically, Ilyin and Berdyaev, during this period of the journal, preferred to treat the social question according to its cosmic dimension, its "social-technical nature," and its ecclesial implications, "the divine energies in the Church."[177] In a series of articles that appeared in *New*

City in 1931–33, Bulgakov, looking for a solution to the social question, called for a Christian "dogma" of the economy able to reject the pagan dogmas of Epicureanism.[178]

For Vysheslavtsev, the social question was linked to the question of power. He wrote two articles for *The Way* in 1934 on the question of power, based on the debate in Germany among philosophers and theologians concerning the phenomenology of power. Vysheslavtsev warned his readers that the question of power, as Pushkin pointed out in *Boris Godunov*, was itself linked to the antinomy of good and evil. On the one hand there was the dominating figure of the Grand Inquisitor, and on the other, that of Christ, who proclaims "All power is given to me on heaven and on earth."[179] Vysheslavtsev tried to resolve this antinomy. He described power as consisting in the perfect execution of the relationship of order-execution between master and slave. This in turn was based, in Dostoevsky's words, "on the miracle, the mystery and authority," and the hierarchy, which presumed an organization without power.[180] "The Kingdom of God," Vysheslavtsev wrote, "is without power but not without principle, it is not anarchic; it is hierarchical because it supposes an order of sacred principles." For him, the question of the relationship between bosses and workers rested on this antinomy. The social question was the question of the power of one person over another. The two responses, the communist response and the capitalist response, were both unacceptable, for they were based on a decision system that was absolutely authoritarian. Vysheslavtsev imagined an eschatological relationship to power as the solution of this antinomy. He admitted that, in a fallen world, authoritarian power was superior to the chaos engendered by evil. But in the sphere of the Kingdom of God, already present on earth, power should constantly sublimate itself. According to Vysheslavtsev's definition, power was from God when it recognized something superior to itself, and the power of the Kingdom of God was above all other power.[181]

On this question, Vysheslavtsev also published a review of Georges Gurvitch's book *L'idée du droit social* (published in Paris in 1932). Vysheslavtsev, who had known Gurvitch for a long time, praised his friend's work, particularly the fact that he based himself on Khomiakov's ideal of conciliarity in introducing the notion of social law in France. It was understandable that the German lawyer Girke's idea of a new science adapted to every form of socialism, without state control, was appealing to Vysheslavtsev.

For him, Gurvitch was original in enlarging social law to include the entire process of the creation of community bonding, no matter what the activity—dancing, religious congregations, or factories. But Vysheslavtsev faulted Gurvitch for leaving social law on the periphery of private and public law and not making it the foundation of all laws. Indeed, for Vysheslavtsev, the basic juridical concept was the principle of organization, and this was what distinguished the hierarchical perspective from the communitarian perspective:

> What is the community, the ultimate juridical unity, the organism or the person? Fichte, Krause, and Girke speak of an "organic whole," of "the organism of freedom" . . . nowadays M. Scheler puts forth the concept of *Gesammperson*. There is, then, in every juridical unity, something which is linked to the organism and to the person. In spite of that, we should say that the fundamental category is neither the organism nor the person. We have another superior category at our disposition. By defining the ultimate spiritual unity as an organism or as a person, we stray from the definition of justice such as we had established previously. [I.e.: The person and the community have the same rights.] The organism and the person are more precious than their parts and their structural elements and submit these to themselves; this cannot be said of society as a whole. The theory of the organism or the person in its uniqueness leads to Leviathan and destroys the autonomous value of the individual person. . . . The ultimate juridical unity is the organization, the essence of law depends on its power of organization. . . . The organization supposes the person and is only possible among persons and yet it is not the person in its uniqueness, but the relationship among persons. The juridical person, from a philosophic point of view, is a fiction in the measure in which this person is without a personal identity. But the fictive concept is introduced here to designate the reality X which is the organization.[182]

Thus the principal opposition between Gurvitch and Vysheslavtsev was the following: for the former, there was a preexisting, non-organized communication, which the conscious activity of reason should organize through laws; for the latter, there is a subconscious and intuitive "organizing force" that underlies all conscious organization. Vysheslavtsev uses the example of rhythm, a subconscious norm, which organizes a dance. Even if a group is organized, it always seeks to find itself a *vozhd'*, a leader, or a *Führer*. This idea of an "auto-organizing" principle that is the basis of all laws allowed Vysheslavtsev to contradict Gurvitch, who can only conceive of social law in the context of a democracy. "Dictatorship and '*Vozhdism*' are also founded on social law, on a particular juridical awareness of the *demos*."[183]

Kartashev approached the social question in a manner that was more historical and political than philosophical and juridical, and more oriented to action than contemplation. In an article published in December 1932, the Russian Church historian took as a model of social engagement not the community of monks of the Trans-Volga, but the heritage left to tradition by the figure of St. Vladimir. According to the story told by his biographer, Metropolitan Hilarion, this engagement consisted in a charitable commitment, not merely personal but on the level of the state, with respect to the freedom of its populations.[184] Kartashev did not want the restoration of the patriarchal order, however—quite the contrary. In a June 14, 1934, article entitled "Personal and Communal Salvation in Christ," he advocated modifying the way the church is organized. In his eyes, the time had come to adapt the canonical system of church organization to modern society, because the parish system was no longer sufficient to ensure the "churching" of life. Like Vysheslavtsev, Kartashev began his reflection by recalling the kingship of Christ. He complained, further, that the Orthodox Church only taught individual asceticism and not social asceticism.[185] For him, this attitude had distorted the Orthodox religion into a kind of Buddhism and opened a space for "secularism," which, because of its rejection of Christ, was "the worst enemy of the Church." He urged the formation of "an army of the servants of the Church" made up of "fraternities" or "orders" of Christians engaged in social or cultural service.[186] Kartashev balanced his hierarchical and "Christocratic" exposition with a healthy dose of communal spirit and action and, most notably, a rejection of clericalism. Against a clerical approach he called for a bottom-up method (*molekularnym metodom*)—a typical nonconformist term—of these communities within institutions, academies, and universities.[187]

The National Question

From its beginnings in 1925, *The Way* took a very clear stance against nationalism, whether Fascist and National-Socialist or of Communist origin. Hitler's rise to power on January 30, 1933, and the favorable view of nationalism in Europe during the 1930s—the USSR included—provoked a multitude of articles on this question in *The Way*. It was becoming clear that simple moral condemnation was not enough to channel the passions of the intellectuals and the masses. Within democratic societies there was little recognition of the mask of chauvinism that was being donned and the increasing authority of heads of state. For the authors of *The Way*, the classical explanations of the military, political, economic, and social factors of the crisis were certainly decisive but nonetheless insufficient. In fact, these explanations did not take into consideration the general incapacity of the states, the churches, and social organizations, both in Germany and France, to curb the fears of the people. The only explanation had to be on the mytho-logical level.

A common approach, from Berdyaev to Zenkovsky, found the source of the collective European anguish in the crisis within Protestantism and, more fundamentally, in all the Christian churches. Indeed, the churches' traditional vision of the nation was eschatological. This was the case whether the nation was regarded as a Noah's ark, which would save its people from disaster, or whether the very identity of the nation was drowned in the ocean of the final project. What was deadly was the incapacity of Christians to collectively reevaluate the divine-human myth in contemporary language, that is, in the relationship between the national bond and the social bond, between hierarchy and fraternity, and between the memory of the past and the horizon of the future. The generation of Russian intellectuals who came together in *The Way* sought to renew these themes of reflection. But here as well, two streams could be distinguished among these authors. On the one side was Berdyaev, who considered the person as the foundation of the national bond and, on the other, Bulgakov, for whom the homeland constituted the historical foundation of the community.

The Diagnosis of the Crisis
The October 1933 issue contained two reviews by Berdyaev of works, published that same year in Germany and in France, dealing with the two aspects of nationalism—militarism and territorialism. The first book reviewed, *God and Caesar: The Deficiencies of the Churches Concerning the Problem of War*, was by G. I. Heering, a Dutch Protestant theologian. The preface was by André Philip, a Protestant of Barthian tendencies that Berdyaev approved, as well as a professor of political economy and a famous

figure in the Socialist Party. The thesis of these two Protestants was the condemnation of any Christian justification of war and the promotion of a radical Christian pacifism, a position also held by L. Ragaz, a Swiss Protestant who was a member of the movement of religious socialists. Berdyaev praised the condemnation of war "in the name of Christ" but categorically rejected an attitude that consisted in fleeing before the "terrible and satanic evil of war." Berdyaev asked: "Can France disarm while Hitler's Germany builds up its arms?"[188] Berdyaev, for whom a spiritual revival of societies was the only possible response, also rejected the description of Germany made by another Protestant, J. Schmidhauser, a Swiss Protestant historian who had published a history of the University of Hamburg. In his book, Schmidhauser showed sympathy for the popular and territorial aspects of Hitlerism and pointed out the appeal that Nietzsche and his passion for power had among young people. Berdyaev opposed this explanation. For him, National Socialism represented the social revolt of the petite bourgeoisie and the bourgeoisie against proletarian socialism and against the intellectual aristocracy symbolized by the figure of Nietzsche. On the political level, Berdyaev argued, this political party stood for the divinization of the state and of nationality. In Berdyaev's opinion, National Socialism was worse than communism because in the USSR, Christians are openly persecuted, whereas in Germany, the state seeks to transform the church into its docile instrument.[189]

Since some of the contributors to *The Way* lived in Germany, the review was able to follow the German intellectual and ecclesial debate rather closely. An anonymous author, S., probably Stepun,[190] sent two articles to *The Way* in 1933–34. One concerned a new book by Oswald Spengler, the other the presence of a Christian opposition in Germany. Spengler's book, *Jahre der Entscheidung: Deutschland und die weltgeschichtliche Entwicklung*, caused a sensation when it appeared in Germany in 1933. The anonymous author considered this book as typical of the ideas of a sector of the German intelligentsia, which criticized both the parliamentary system and Bolshevism, favored a hierarchically structured society, and longed for a return to Prussian order. Unlike Heidegger, whose voice belonged to the chorus of those who "glorify the reigning doctrine and seek to justify its vision of the world,"[191] Spengler, until recently considered one of the party ideologues, was really a dissident voice. He attacked the new masters, ridiculing their "zoological" vocabulary based on race. He would replace such racial talk by talk of the human species. Yet the Caesarism of Spengler leads him, in defiance of all logic, to hope for a dictator in Germany, like Lenin in Russia.[192] According to S., there is a gap between the chivalrous fervor of Spengler, which can only be nourished by the spirit in its activity in the world, and his rejection of Christianity, along with his conception of man as basically "a rapacious animal." S. concluded that Spengler was right in his criticism of rationalism and romanticism in the name of the spirit, but, since this criticism is not based on the spirit of authentic Christianity, it collapses into volitional rationalism and an escapist romanticism, which is even worse.[193]

Zenkovsky, in "The Crisis of German Protestantism," which appeared in the March 1934 issue, and again in his June 1934 review of an issue of the journal *Eine Heilige Kirche*, agreed with S. who published in the same June 1934 issue "The Voices of Christian Conscience in Germany." Both, in their analysis of events, situated the principal source of the crisis in the malaise of the Protestant Church. Zenkovsky put it this way: "It is clear that Hitler's rise to power is not just the consequence of the political and social effervescence created by the painful Versailles treaty, nor the fruit of a demagogic struggle with Judaism, etc.... but the sequence of complex processes in Germany's spiritual life which had been accumulating for a very long time but which had not found their expression until now."[194] One of these spiritual processes, "the most painful" according to Zenkovsky, is the division of the Protestant Church—which is all the more evident when compared to the force of the Catholic Church.[195]

For Zenkovsky, as for S., the emergence of the voices of German Christians was a testimony to the deep spiritual crisis of Protestantism, which was incapable of forming a coherent policy on nationalism. Zenkovsky thought that Protestantism suffered from a lack of a sense of history, of the separation that it brings about between the church and the world. Karl Barth's 1933 pamphlet "Theologische Existenz heute!," although courageous and powerful, cannot bring Protestantism "out of the impasse in which it finds itself."[196] For Barth, the people and the state do not, fundamentally, enter into the church, and thus the church cannot limit the state. In Barth's view, freedom of conscience is a freedom of the world and not for the world. That is why the faithful, even if they might be sensitive to Barth's protests, cannot be drawn to the church in order to find a response to their desires. S., in his "The Voices of Christian Conscience in Germany" (a discussion of Barth and Friedrich Heiler), published in June 1934, somewhat qualified Zenkovsky's vision. For S., the nationalism of the German Christians had little resonance among Germans in general. The crisis of Protestantism resided more in the liberal prewar theology that Barth had already condemned in 1919 in his *Commentary on the Epistle to the Romans*, than in the healthy distinction that the Calvinist theologian makes between God and the world. In the review *Hochkirche*, led by Friedrich Heiler, the head of the High Church movement, Heiler's quest for a genuine catholicity, according to S., reveals that nationality is a religious question.[197] But, S. added, it was clear that the position of Barth, because he chooses to speak in a radical manner and to turn exclusively towards eternity, inspired solely by "the fear of God," resembles that of a dove, who sits on the roof of a house while a tragic struggle is taking place within.[198]

The Personalist Approach
Berdyaev's article "Polytheism and Nationalism," which appeared in the June 1934 issue of *The Way*, was never translated from the Russian into any other language. Yet it is one of the rare attempts in the history of Russian thought—along with Bulgakov's article "The Nation and Humanity," which came out in *New City* around the same time—to understand the nationalist phenomenon from a mytho-logical point of view. The difference between the two authors is that Berdyaev was interested in purifying the personal principle of nationality from the "demons"—in the strict sense of the word—of nationalism, while Bulgakov wanted to see the love for the homeland as a manifestation of sophianic love.

Berdyaev was aware that it was useless to simply deny "the nationalist mood of today's youth,"[199] just as it was impossible to have a rational dialogue on kinds of behavior that have nothing rational about them. "Communist internationalism is easily transformed into Soviet nationalism and Stalinism is already hardly distinguishable from Fascism."[200] But Berdyaev was not going to refuse to discuss this. He began with a philosophical reflection, arguing that the present-day reappearance of the most ancient myths of Indo-European civilization was the fruit of a rationality detached from its spiritual foundation. In a second section of his article, he traced the history of the relationship between Christianity and nationality and pointed out that totalitarianism is the result of an imperfect incarnation of the Christian message. He ended with a consideration on the relationship between the nation and technology, which again brought into play the relationship between the particular and the universal.

The concepts of the individual and the universal were at the basis of Berdyaev's reflection. He distinguished the concept of the universal from the concept of the general:

> The general signifies the abstraction from everything concrete as in the case of a number. . . . The universal, on the other hand, is a total and indivisible quality as in the case of an individual. In this sense, the universal includes the individual in itself as a positive instance of being. The general, on the contrary, always abstracts from the individual, takes away the individual instances of being.[201]

This distinction explains why Berdyaev asserted that the universalism which affirmed the spiritual unity of humanity was a concrete, positive unity, which integrated within itself all the individual nationalities, while internationalism was an abstract idea that denied them. In the same way, nationalism, the other side of internationalism, was a revolt of naturalistic peculiarities against universalism, against humanity as a spiritual universal. Nationalism, Berdyaev argued, was the particularity of the individual who refused to see the meaning for human values of the spiritual quality of the universe and who merely perceived the general, the purely human, which for him was an abomination. Nationalism was polytheistic. It did not believe in the unity of humanity, whereas universalism was monotheistic and divine-human. Berdyaev noted that the conflict between the French and the Germans was a conflict between abstract humanism and naturalist particularity. Consequently, to struggle against paganism, one must not impose either the general or the abstract but rather the universal-spiritual. It was this distinction between nationality as individuality and nationality understood as generality that was, for the Russian philosopher, the key to the national problem. For Berdyaev, nationality, an individualizing step in the historico-natural process, was among the spiritual realities of the person and of humanity. When nationality is understood not as a natural individuality that is to be enlightened and spiritualized, thus enriching personal human existence, but as a superior and absolute value, as an idol, "it smothers, impoverishes, and even disfigures human personal existence."[202] It is at this moment that nonrational paths appear. For Berdyaev, just as for Dostoevsky, man must kneel before something that is superior to him. The irrational forces of nature invented ideals and idols if they were not channeled towards the spirit. "The creation of myths plays an enormous role in our era; they have more influence than the scientific theories, which are only interested in abstract truth, and the myth of race could be a real weapon for the self-affirmation of nationality."[203]

The victory of Christianity over polytheism, Berdyaev argued, took place during the Hellenistic era, when the national was separated from the religious. Christianity addressed itself not to a people but to all of humanity, and the relationship between the human being and God was not determined through the nation but through that spiritual society which is the church. In this sense, Berdyaev added, "Christ has been crucified in the name of nationalism—not just Jewish nationalism, as has been asserted so often, but of all nationalism, be it Russian, German, French, or English."[204] Christianity thus liberated humanity from the fear of fate, from the clannish mentality and the demons of nature. But in our modern age, nationalism has replaced medieval universalism. The de-Christianization of society resulted from the loss of faith in the universality of God. In France, at the moment of its revolution, "God was replaced by the nation."[205] Nationalism then found itself in need of the state in order to make effective its desire for power. "The contemporary idea of the total State," Berdyaev wrote, "which does not recognize any limits, which pretends to organize not just social life but also spiritual and intellectual life, is the fruit of nationalism."[206] Thus the ancient demons, formerly tamed and relegated to the unconsciousness "of race, blood, nationality, and sex," have risen up once again. New demons, fruits of the determinism and fatalism of capitalist civilization and technology, have also appeared—such as social class or the machine: "the myth of the chosen race and the myth of the elected class have been very active in our times."[207] Berdyaev completed his historical portrayal by opposing, to the National-Socialist and pagan synthesis of the principles of erotic nationality and of social ethic, a "personalist socialism, a trade union socialism," which unites the value of the person with that of the encounter.[208]

Berdyaev concluded by setting nationalism in opposition to technology. For him, technology, which was fundamentally international, was the principal force capable of standing up to a nationalism that was essentially particular. Berdyaev announced that "technology will show itself to be more powerful than nationalism because it affirms the universality of communication and does not authorize any kind of self-sufficient autarchy or any kind of world closed-in upon itself."[209]

The Patriotic Approach
Both Bulgakov and Kartashev, as they had already done in 1914, used the church as a starting point to give religious significance to the national question. Before Bulgakov gave his sophiological response to this question in *New City* near the end of 1934, Kartashev had already posed some points of reference in *The Way*. On July 1, 1932, he gave a lecture entitled "The Right of Nationalities and the Orthodox Church" during the League of Nations congress on minorities in Vienna (see K17). As the representative of the Orthodox Church, the Russian historian retraced the disastrous religious policy of the Russian Empire regarding nationalities. Against the advice of the Orthodox Church, which was not opposed to the development of national cultures, the imperial power imposed the Slavonic language nearly everywhere. Two years later, in September 1934, in an article entitled "The Church and Nationality" (K18), Kartashev moved from an historical approach to a dogmatic discussion, in which he sought to protect the nationality of the church itself, and then to a political perspective, where he defended the church from nationalism. He questioned the ascetic, ahistoric passivity of the Orthodox Church, which derived from its reading of the Apocalypse as a predetermination of history. Kartashev explained the origins of the historical cohabitation of the Orthodox Church and the Russian nation, which led the church, despite its universal vocation, to justify nationalism. This attitude, he wrote, came from a tragic presupposition—the rejection of any human effort to bring about the earthly city, since any such city would be corrupt, and therefore the choice to passively await the coming of the heavenly city. But for Kartashev, "the national principle, as well as the individual principle, is the holy principle of the diversity of countenances and of the beauty of God in this world, like the beauty of a field full of flowers."[210] Kartashev opposed the nation to the destructive principle of class, but he condemned any form of corrupted national egoism. He was in favor of "an ecclesiastical monarchy," similar to the Roman system, which would effectively sustain its churches against paganism—unlike Protestantism, which did not have

at its disposal this supranational hierarchic power.[211] Kartashev concluded by proposing that the patriarchates be reinforced by the addition of true conciliar assemblies of the autocephalous churches. This would give greater extraterritorial security to Orthodox churches that are overly nationalistic.

For Bulgakov, this diversity of flowers in a field corresponds to "the manifold wisdom of God," of which St. Paul speaks in his Epistle to the Ephesians (Eph. 3:10). In an article entitled "The Nation and Humanity," which appeared in *New City* in 1934, Bulgakov began by discussing the relationship between, on the one hand, the uncreated divine spirit in mankind and, on the other hand, the human soul and body, the wisdom created by God, which constitutes the person. The angel, a non-incarnate spirit, does not have a nature of its own; it knows no genre, but only hierarchy, or the choir. And yet, as a ray of the plenitude of the Divinity, each spirit has an individuality. Because of this, Bulgakov writes, the angels are the genii of places and eras, of peoples and churches. The angels of the peoples are the spiritual foundations of their being.[212] Mankind, unlike the angels, possessed an inherent generic foundation (*rodovoi*). The nation is part of corporal and psychic nature. For the Russian theologian, it was natural that the human being loved his psyche, that is, his genre (*rod*) and his Motherland (*rodina*), his people and his soil in all their complexity (language, characteristics, creation, history). Moreover, this love is a duty, for it is only through love that one arrives at knowledge. Here, it was not a question of the trihypostatic figure of supreme love that the three Persons of the Trinity manifested in their reciprocal relationship. "This is another type of love," Bulgakov continued, "it is, precisely, that of a person for his heritage [*k svoemu dostoianiyu*], which has its correspondence in the love of God for Sophia in His self-revelation. Such a self-revelation of the human being as creation of self in one's element is only realizable in the fullness of life in one's nature, in one's psyche."[213] This was why the nation should be subordinate to the spirit. It was not a fetish of the psyche but a creative task to be accomplished, a gift to offer to the spirit in order to be transfigured by it. And this contradicted any form of nationalism because, unlike wisdom which is plural, the spirit is universal: "Spiritual conciliarity unites all peoples and the universal Church is constituted by the different national Churches. . . . This is why spiritual asceticism should control the fire of national passions—without prejudice to the concreteness of the spiritual life which, in the nation, receives for itself matter and content, like a particular talent."[214] Bulgakov resolved the antinomy between universality and nationality, between the divine spirit and created wisdom, in a Christological manner. "For Christ," Bulgakov wrote, "was the Son of David, Son of Abraham." He wept over his city and his people, whom he wanted to gather together in himself. But he was also, Bulgakov concluded, the one who fulfilled his mission by sending the apostles to teach the Pentecost of the peoples in all languages.[215]

The Ecclesiastical Frontiers of a Generation

There is no doubt that there was a profound affinity among the intellectuals of *The Way*, which manifested itself in their social, jurisdictional, and political commitments within the Russian immigrant community. To borrow the image of Bulgakov, it can be said that there was a common spirit inherent in this generation, a spirit that manifested itself in a diversity of countenances. Whether it was their coexistence within the Russian village on boulevard Montparnasse and rue de Crimée, their common preoccupation with reconstructing the Temple of God—Jerusalem, Constantinople, Moscow—or, finally, their spiritual approach to politics, everywhere, the same generational spirit dominated the psyche of the Russian intellectuals. However, intellectual awareness of their unity could be obscured by the different commitments each had. In their common desire to transmit their heritage to future generations, one can note a split within the group between the anti-communist and the anti-nationalist authors. Similarly, once the link between ecclesial jurisdiction and intellectual milieu was broken, two types of spirituality corresponding to two different theodicies manifested themselves within the modernist generation. Finally, the nonconformist unanimity of the review in the political realm would be corrected by two different relationships to community bonds. One was based on the primacy of the divine-human Wisdom and on the hierarchical structure of the world of the spirit. The other was based on the primacy of the human person and postulated the superiority of the spirit over nature. This internal tension within Russian thought deserves close analysis. It is also the expression of two different spheres of commitment within the review—mytho-logical creation and participation in the ecumenical movement.

THE PARIS SCHOOL

A Nonconformist Memory

The Nonconformist Memory at Work

Between 1930 and 1935, the modernist tradition remained the main reference for the authors of the review. Articles on Dostoevsky, Fedorov, Bukharev, Solovyov, and, to a lesser degree, Khomiakov and Nesmelov were most prominent.[216] There was some variation from this pattern, with articles emphasizing Chaadaev, Kireevsky, and Leontiev making their appearance in the pantheon. In 1931, Frank wrote an article on the religious philosophy of N. I. Pirogov, a liberal and humanist physician (d. 1881). He placed Pirogov in "the classic line of Russian religious thought ... [of] Chaadaev, Khomiakov, Kireevsky, Dostoevsky, Leontiev, Fedorov," since Pirogov sought a synthesis between reason and faith "in the light of the ideal of the God-Man."[217] Berdyaev, in an article that summed up the work at the Academy of Religious Philosophy, entitled "On the Nature of Russian Religious Thought in the Twentieth Century," published in 1930 in *Contemporary Annals* (*Sovremennye Zapiski*), considered the modernist tradition, with its intuition of freedom and its demand for conciliarity, as the source of the three dynamic tendencies of Russian thought: "philokalic thought, anthropological thought, and cosmological thought."[218] This threefold division of the field of Russian religious thought, accurate for the 1920s, began to change substantially afterwards. The deliberate identification, during the 1930s, of the myth of the Kingdom with the source of this modernist tradition, namely, the myth of theanthropy—or, to use the expression of Pirogov, "the ideal of the God-Man"—would open up new horizons and greater freedom.[219]

This shift was first expressed in a return of generational memory towards the historic origins of modernism; first, towards new figures, writers, or searchers for God, and second, towards the Eastern nonrational aspect of Russian thought. In his biography of Ivan Kireevsky (1806–56), "for the 150th anniversary of his birth" (!), I. K. Smolitsch claimed that the thirst for "a vital knowledge" in the members of the society of The Friends of Wisdom was the result of a spontaneous and critical encounter between the philokalic spirituality of Elder Macarius of Optina and

Schelling's *The Philosophy of Revelation*.[220] In his portrait of Prince S. N. Trubetskoy (1862–1905), the disciple of Solovyov who became the liberal rector of Moscow State University, Florovsky shows that the thought of the author of *The Metaphysics of Ancient Greece* is ontological, for "he had a keen sense of the universal and conciliatory character of philosophical thought."[221] It is eschatological because "it is interested in the beginnings and the ends, the birth of thought from religiosity or myth, and the result of Hellenistic philosophy [in Patristic thought]." It is antinomic because Christ was able to bring about a synthesis between the wisdom of the Greek language and divine truth: "Wisdom could not help but reveal itself and the Word had to become flesh."[222] In June 1935, Princess O. N. Trubetskaya published, with an introduction, some material about S. N. Trubetskoy. She revealed that he wanted to write his thesis on the topic "The Doctrine of the Church and Holy Wisdom," but abandoned this project to write a treatise on astrology. In the extract that was published, Trubetskoy distances himself from the Slavophile movement, even though he praised the principle of freedom of conscience and the understanding of the universal church inherent in this movement.[223]

Among the new figures who were the objects of this work of memory were numerous writers, including Pushkin (F81, C11R), Gogol (B106ter), Chekhov (I35R), and Zhukovsky (M4R); and philosophers, including P. Bakunin (B106bis), L. Lopatin (F74), N. Pirogov (F77), B. Chicherin (A11), A. Ivanov (P11), and V. Pechorin (I39). For A. Ivanov, a radical of the 1860s, "the way towards the Kingdom of God"—wrote P. Prokofiev— "passes through beauty and art."[224] For P. Bakunin, the brother of the alleged anarchist, as described by P. Bitsilli, it was the "immortality of the person" that is primary.[225] From Pushkin and Gogol to Chekhov, the whole of Russian literature was revisited using the principle of the unity of creation and religiosity in the writer.[226] Along these lines, Frank retraced the religious evolution of Pushkin and countered Leontiev's representation of the writer as a "pagan rebel" with the image of "one of the most profound geniuses of the Russian Christian spirit"[227] who declared that he was born for "sweet tones and prayer."

Finally, the third sign of the evolution of generational memory— from the myth of the East to that of the God-Man—manifested itself, as soon as the ecclesial character of the reflection no longer needed to be proven, by a greater attention to the esoteric (B44, B130bis, S3, S4, S5, S6), to Buddhism (K29, X1), and to mythical thought (V2). This new awakening ranged from Far Eastern poetry to the legend of the Holy Grail and the alchemy of Angelus Silesius. A. Vanovsky, who published only one article in the review, lived in Japan, as indicated by a note on the bottom of the page. The note also explained that the author's lecture "The Mythology of Kojiki and the Bible" was given at a meeting of the Meiji association on April 26, 1932. Vanovsky noted all the similarities between Japanese mythology and the biblical account in Genesis, not only in the order but also in the principles of the creation of the world. But where the Japanese myth speaks of the birth of gods, the biblical myth speaks of the birth of mankind—something not without political implications. Vanovsky concluded by showing that the formation of the Japanese state imitated in its organization the foundational story of the Kojiki, of the creation of the world.[228] In his article "The Holy Grail," Bulgakov was not afraid of giving a sophiological reinterpretation of the legend of the Knights of the Round Table. He presented a sort of dogmatic exegesis of a Gospel passage (John 19:34) concerning the crucifixion of Christ: "but one of the soldiers pierced his side with a lance and, immediately, blood and water came forth." Bulgakov interpreted this verse as a sign and linked it to the legend of the Holy Grail. According to the legend, Joseph of Arimathea, at the foot of the cross, received the blood and water of Christ in a cup, which found its way to Glastonbury and was kept by the Knights of the Round Table of King Arthur. For Bulgakov, this legend testified to the intuition, in Western esotericism, of the continual presence of Christ on earth under the form of his living corporality.[229] The Holy Grail was a symbolic cup that represented the entire world. The Russian theologian used the anthroposophic expression "Christ-Impulse" to give a cosmic dimension to this presence, for "all of nature awaits the blood and body of Christ and communicates with them through the blood and water which flowed from the cross."[230] Bulgakov argued that the mystery of Golgotha "is invisibly prolonged in the world." This is why he ardently called for a liturgical life that was not simply based on the annual rhythm of feasts but would be able to surge beyond the walls of the church to become anthropo-cosmic. For Bulgakov, if, as the Evangelist proclaimed, people would do works even greater than those of Christ (John 14:12–13), then Fedorov's project of regulating nature in order to build the Kingdom of God on the earth should be taken into consideration. Scripture will only be fulfilled, according to Bulgakov, when there is no longer any separation between heaven and earth. Bulgakov concluded by citing the prophecy of Zechariah, which St. John evoked: "They will look upon him whom they have pierced" (John 19:37; cf. Zech. 12:10).[231]

Alexander Saltykov, who came from the esoteric circles of the immigration community, followed Bulgakov's lead to present his theses on the star of Bethlehem and the zodiacal rhythm of the Gospels (S5), on the mountain as a symbolic hieroglyph in the Bible (S4), and on the correspondence between alchemic constructions and the world of the stars (S6). In this last article, he claimed that the cosmogonic link between the sun and the earth in Genesis has led to a Christian esoteric tradition identifying the Son of God with "the golden color of life."[232]

The Ecclesial Frontiers of Memory

But these bold interpretations of sacred texts had their limits. The more traditional exegeses of Bezobrazov or Gillet did not disappear entirely (B100R, B101R, B102R, B103R, B105R, G2). Certain young authors who were deliberately anti-rationalist were published, although with great reservations on the part of the editorial board (see, for example, Menshikov, M2). Yet the principal consensus that the borders of ecclesial tradition marked the common ground of reflection was above all evident in the general turning of the memory towards the symbolist era, which was both near in time yet existentially relatively distant and thus open to a reevaluation. One of the eminent personalities of the Silver Age, Dimitrii Merezhkovsky, became more than ever *persona non grata* in the review. The gnosis he developed in *The Unknown Jesus* was vigorously attacked, first by Myrrha Lot-Borodin (L26R) and then by S. Bezobrazov (B104R). On the occasion of the 1929 republication of Pavel Florensky's major work, *The Pillar and Ground of the Truth*, Florensky, Bulgakov's friend, became the object of a virulent debate in the review between Ilyin, who defended his "dogmatic gnosis" against all the "obscurantists,"[233] and Florovsky, who criticized the absence of a "Christological chapter" in Florensky's theodicy.[234]

The most important figure of this era, the poet Alexander Blok, also became an identity marker for the authors of *The Way*, and this led some to a self-redefinition. On November 13, 1930, the literary circle *Kochevie* of Marc Slonim had organized an initial gathering dedicated to the lyric poet, with the participation of K. Mochulsky, M. Tsvetaeva, and B. Poplavsky. Three months later a polemic erupted when the journal published an article entitled "On Blok" by an anonymous author, "The Priest of Petrograd," who was strongly influenced by Florensky's ideas. Originally it had been a lecture given in January 1926 on the occasion of the fifth anniversary of the poet's death at a meeting of Leningrad writers. The author was critical of the "demonism" of Blok's poetry as manifested in his 1909 poems, "The Demon," "The Double," and "The Song of Hell," and, above all, in the 1918 poem, "The Twelve," which ends with the figure of the revolutionary anti-Christ being displaced by that of Christ, marching ahead of his apostles. Berdyaev, who, like Skobtsova and Bulgakov, knew the poet personally admitted in his response, "In Defense of Blok," that elements of "ontological corruption" affected the Russian religious renaissance at the beginning of the twentieth century.[235] But he also defended Blok's "quests for God and the Kingdom of God" and denied the right to make a religious judgment on the national poet of Russia. "The soul of Russia and of the Russian people," Berdyaev concluded, "was defenseless, just as the soul of Blok was; the Logos, in this soul, did not dominate the Cosmos."[236]

On the other hand, in December 1930, Rudolf Steiner, the head of the anthroposophic movement, was the target of Berdyaev's fury. Berdyaev, who had agreed to publish a letter written by the sister-in-law of Andre Biely, N. Turgeneva, who was one of the editors of the review *Anthroposophy* (a publication of the immigrant community), used the occasion to ruthlessly criticize the theosophic and anthroposophic movements that had emerged in Russia at the end of the nineteenth century and were prospering among the émigrés. Steiner, who knew Berdyaev personally, placed Christianity above Brahmanism—unlike H. Blavatskaya, who became a Buddhist in 1880. Berdyaev believed that in Steiner's case, due to the monism of theosophic thought, "the human spirit is not liberated from the cosmic forces."[237] For Steiner, Berdyaev wrote, "the Christ-Logos and the man Jesus are not united in the one person."[238] Berdyaev in particular attacked the esoteric argument *par excellence* invoked by Turgeneva, which claimed that anyone who has not experienced reincarnation cannot condemn it.

> With such a perspective, nothing whatsoever can be judged or criticized. A Catholic would say that papal infallibility cannot be condemned without having had the Catholic experience of papal infallibility; a Calvinist would say that the doctrine of predestination cannot be condemned without having had the Calvinist experience

of predestination; a Buddhist would say that Buddhism cannot be condemned without having had the Buddhist experience of liberation from the sufferings of existence in Nirvana; a Marxist-Communist would say that class warfare and the mission of the proletariat cannot be condemned without the experience of class warfare and of the proletariat, etc.[239]

Nonetheless, Berdyaev recognized the value of the questions posed by anthroposophy, such as the reconciliation between science and religion, the uncovering of ways for the spiritual life to grow, and the destiny of the human soul. Berdyaev thought that these questions were so important and widespread among the youth of the immigrant community that he brought together, in the venerable tradition of the symbolist generation, a group of authors to collaborate in a collection entitled *The Doctrine of the Transmigration of Souls: The Problem of Immortality in Occultism and Christianity*. This work was published by the YMCA Press[240] in 1935 and included contributions by Berdyaev, Bulgakov, Vysheslavtsev, Zenkovsky, Florovsky, and Frank. Alongside the traditional response of the church as formulated by Bulgakov—"One has to choose between Christianity and occultism"— more detailed responses appeared in the articles by Berdyaev and Vysheslavtsev. For Berdyaev, the classical doctrine of the church on the infusion of the soul at the moment of conception is not satisfactory. A "preexistence of souls in the spiritual world" should be admitted.[241] However, the salvation of the soul did not consist in the liberation of divinity in the human being, but rather in the deification of the whole person. Christianity did not deny that death was tragic, as did the doctrine of reincarnation, but rather it struggled with death. According to Vysheslavtsev, this was possible because, as Freud demonstrated, "the subconscious does not believe in death"; in the subconscious the eternal soul of the person lives.[242] The soul battles with death and finitude through the potentially infinite memory of the subconscious and through the conscious spirit, which has the capacity to draw near to eternity. For Vysheslavtsev, Steiner was right when he wrote that the soul possessed a super-individual and cosmic memory (*Akacha Khronika*), but Steiner interpreted this in a rationalistic sense. Vysheslavtsev considered for himself that the soul always retains its individuality.

> The super-individual and cosmic memory is not the memory of my incarnations but of those of others. In my memory and imagination,

in my conscious and subconscious, I find a plurality of souls and of "incarnations," for every imagination [*vo-obrazhenie*] is an incarnation [*vo-ploshchenie*] and every recollection [*vos-pominanie*] is a resurrection [*vo-kreshchenie*)] of my genus. A plurality of souls live within me, some anonymously and simply, others with a precise, individual imagination (heroes, prophets, the God-Man). Potentially, all these souls live and act in me. . . . It is in this general interpenetration of souls, in their conciliarity . . . that the eternal and super-temporal character of the soul resides. That is why the soul does not need to "transmigrate," or rather, one could say that the soul "transmigrates" and is "reincarnated" an incalculable number of times in the course of its brief existence, it transports and reincarnates itself through the memory and imagination.[243]

For Vysheslavtsev, "the myth of the transmigration of souls" should not be understood rationally. It was the symbol of the "evolution" of the soul, of its becoming and deployment through its potential and infinite memory.[244] In this sense, Vysheslavtsev restored the notion of *karma*, the ontological memory of evil acting within the limits of each individual soul, as the conscious or unconscious presence of "original sin." But he completed this with the Christian position, according to which karma or destiny is vanquished by redemption, the victory over both super-individual and individual sin.

Berdyaev's collection is a good example of the unanimity of the authors of the review, within the diversity of Russian mytho-logical thought, concerning questions outside the limits of dogma and its ecclesial understanding. And in general, the evolution of collective memory allowed these intellectuals to redefine the frontiers of their generational development and thus integrate some new members (Shestov, Karpov, Veidlé). *The Way's* authors collectively revived Solovyov's initial theanthropic intuition by liberating it from the past. However, a number of things need closer examination. Among them is the divergence in their modernist interpretations of the tradition of the church fathers, as well as certain new emphases in discussions and debates on the holy of holies, the divine-humanity.

The Tectonic Plates

The change in intellectual terrain within the review was situated at a deeper level of memory, where, so to speak, the tectonic plates of *mythos* and *logos* met. It was of a spiritual order. To render it intelligible, it is best to proceed analytically and to avoid trying to distinguish the spiritual experiences of the intellectuals holding different philosophical and theological systems. Such experiences were intimate, and they are hidden to the historian. Instead, I will try to show that the representations of these experiences can be differentiated. Among these intellectuals, there was no division between object and subject, as is the case with ontological monism, nor any separation between God and the world, as is the case with dualism. There was the image, the celestial Archetype, already present in the experience of the church and in personal experience, the primary source of reflection. The authors' viewpoints (on eschatology, ontology, antinomy) reveal notable nuances. Their intellectual representations of divine humanity (theanthropy) are divergent. To be sure, the group remained united in being centered on the divine-human relationship as the source of philosophical or theological discourse; by a common perception of antinomy as the unity of the divine and human in Christ "without confusion and without separation"; and, lastly, by a "kerygmatic" eschatology that interpreted the relationship between God and humans as a personal encounter leading to the transfiguration of time and space. But in the personal synthesis of faith and intelligence, each particular voice can be distinguished to such an extent that the reader of an article can recognize its author simply by its tone. This was especially the case with Berdyaev (in the anthropomorphic current) and Bulgakov (in the sophiocentric current), whose melodic accents stand out from the main choir of Russian religious thought (the theocentric current). In theocentric discourse, the question of hypostases, that is, God in his otherness, is first in ontology. In anthropocentric discourse, it is the image of God in himself, in his identity, which makes possible the revival of the myth of Mankind. And in sophiocentric discourse, speculation is entirely centered on the myth of Divine Wisdom, which reveals the divine-human relationship between God and the world.

The Theocentric Discourse

The common point in the theories of Shestov, Florovsky, Vysheslavtsev, or Frank is that they manifest an ontology that radically distinguishes hypostasis, the consciousness that God has of his own nature, from Being.

In philosophical terms, the discussion shifts from the relationship between beings and Being to the difference between them. God is not the divine Existent. He is a person who reveals himself to mankind as Father, Son, or Holy Spirit, and this makes it more difficult to grasp God in his unity, as Spirit, as Wisdom, and as a Person in his otherness.

By liberating metaphysics from the methodology of the physical, the opposition between, on the one hand, the person who bases his own essence in his hypostasis and, on the other, the Being of the world and mankind, becomes antinomic. The antinomy between God in his hypostatic identity and Being is aporetic (that is, contradictory, paradoxical). In its attempt to prevent any rationalization when speaking of the divine, this theory tried to avoid "any mixture and confusion" between divine nature and human nature, between divine Wisdom and fallen Wisdom. This relationship could not be of a substantial nature. From this perspective, the fundamental question was the nature of the relationship that God maintained with mankind and the world. Whether this relationship was realized by the Father, by the Son, or by the Holy Spirit, it was always the Wholly Other who made himself known to mankind. Even without forcing things, it was significant that each of these authors, in their discourse, insisted more particularly on one or another hypostasis.

Thus the eschatological mode of the relationship between human nature and divine nature, between wisdom and revelation, and between philosophy and theology, could only be accomplished through a dialogue of faith—understood as a leap outside of being—and of the revelation inspired by the uncreated energies.

The Figure of the Creator

Shestov's entry into the group of authors of the review was the sign of a notable change from the 1920s—a period when philosophy continued its work of undermining the pretensions of dialectic to produce "bread, water, or a symphony" from "the laws of oxygen and hydrogen." In the course he gave on Solovyov's thought at the Institute for Slavic Studies, Shestov situated Solovyov in a continuous line from Schelling, for whom "true freedom coincides with holy necessity," and Seneca, for whom "destiny leads those who consent and drags those who resist."[245] Berdyaev criticized Shestov's book *In Job's Balances* in the September 1929 issue, arguing that the Old Testament sources of the religious philosophy of his friend prevented him from hearing the Christian message concerning the law (B41R). Shestov nonetheless entered the journal through the publication of the lecture he gave on Rozanov at the French soirée of the review *Chisla*.[246]

By resurrecting the voice of the thinker "who adored Isiris," Shestov affirmed his difference from the outset. Rozanov had been shattered by his discovery of the powerlessness of God in the face of necessity and had been aided by some "educated Christians," such as Voltaire and Hegel. Like Rozanov, in the tradition of Dostoevsky, Shestov attacked the compromises made by Christian philosophers with the laws of reason or morality. In a review of two books on German philosophy by Richard Kroner, Shestov centered his criticism on Hegel. "Rationalism depends on this certitude that one has of his power, with the aid of his 'thought,' to discover the essence of the universe, to attain its depths and come away with its treasures, as Hegel puts it in his inaugural lecture at Berlin."[247] Shestov conceded that there was an "admirable" moment in the history of German idealism when the "I" of Kant attempted once again, with Schelling, to transport the center of gravity of reflection into the world. For Shestov, this showed that the "I" that rose up in its opposition to the world was no longer a human "I." "It is a divine 'I' living at the depths of our being."[248] It is also in the name of this divine "I" that Kierkegaard, whose philosophy would be presented by Shestov in two articles in 1934 and 1935, rose up against Hegel. Together with the Danish philosopher, Shestov declared himself in favor of an existential philosophy that was based on the absurd. He wanted to believe in repetition, in the possibility that the past did not remain what it was. To Spinoza's maxim, "Don't laugh, don't cry, don't hate but understand," he opposed the tears of Job on his dunghill, which moved God to restore all his blessings.[249] In another article on Martin Buber, he recounted the Hassidic legend of the eighteenth century according to which God worked a miracle just so that a poor bookbinder could honor the Sabbath, "that is, by buying candles, bread, and wine."[250] Along the same lines as Shestov, Adolf Lazarev published an article entitled "The Philosophical Destiny of William James" in 1932, in which he showed that the founder of pragmatism sought to believe in a personal God, as opposed to the Absolute of monist philosophy, by battling all forms of intellectualism.[251]

Shestov's and Lazarev's efforts can be considered mytho-logical in the sense that they sought to rediscover the myth of the living God while rejecting any rational representation of God. Shestov proposed a solution to the panic that Rozanov experienced before the powerlessness of the God of Hegel: faith in God, the Creator and the Almighty. For Shestov, absurdity and faith were synonymous. They opened up the possibility of representing God without the limitations of reason. Faith was "a new dimension of thought," which was neither theology nor speculative philosophy but rather existential philosophy. "Sin," Shestov wrote, "does not reside in being, it did not come from the hands of the Creator; sin, vice, insufficiency reside in our knowledge."[252]

The Figure of Emmanuel

Two types of the phenomenology of spiritual experience could be distinguished among the authors whose work centered on the figure of Jesus Christ. There was that which proceeded from the revelation of the divine Word to humanity, as expressed in the dogmas (Florovsky, Lot-Borodin, Chetverikov), and that which used the myth of creation as the foundation for the relationship of image and resemblance between humanity and the heavenly Lamb (Vysheslavtsev, N. Lossky). This distinction was accidental because, in both cases, the main fear of the authors was that of treating the second person of the Trinity as the man-Jesus of the Protestant tradition. In both cases, however, the presentation depended on a hermeneutic tradition handed down by the Fathers of the Byzantine Church to express the Mystery of God-with-us (Emmanuel).

Florovsky dedicated his 1930 article on German idealism to Shestov. In spite of all that separated the two, Florovsky, like his elder colleague, made a radical distinction between faith and knowledge. In this article he took historical knowledge in monist philosophy as an example. According to Florovsky, Christianity, unlike idealism, had a dynamic and nonmorphological concept of history. For idealism, the myth was a real symbol, but the myth was always above concrete time. "The revelation of God in the world is a series of events and not a chain of symbols. This is why knots which cannot be repeated form in the flesh of time; they appear as mysterious points of rupture. And the greatest of events is the incarnation of the Word. The Word is an event and not just a manifestation. . . . God must be seen *in history and not just through history.*"[253]

But Florovsky refused to follow Barth, who opposed to idealism an absolute dualism in the name of Christianity and who rejected any type of metaphysics in order to accede to the truth of the Reformation:

For history is witness to the fact that the Church has enlightened, not extinguished, metaphysical curiosity; from the outset, the Church sought to manifest and demonstrate that the truth of the apostolic teaching was a truth of the reason and for the reason. The Church has never affirmed that there is nothing in common between Jerusalem and Athens, between the "academy" and the Church. One must see a profound significance in the fact that it was precisely the Greek language which became the principal language of Christianity; it still is and always will be, for it is the language of the New Testament.[254]

This last affirmation—which was at the very least debatable, if the multiplicity of tongues at Pentecost were taken into consideration—was a sign of the importance that the phenomenology of revelation had for Florovsky and also of the secondary role he assigned to the hypostasis of the Holy Spirit. Thus, after logically rejecting both the "ascetic" path of the Reformation and the "Catholic compromise," which tends to baptize Aristotle without transforming him, Florovsky turned to the Greek tradition as alone capable of producing a "Christian metaphysics": "What is left is the creative path through the glorious past, through patristics, through these ancient experiences of the Christianization of Hellenism.... The future holds no other road than through the tradition of the Fathers of the Church."[255]

In this spirit he wrote two books in the space of three years, one consecrated to the Fathers of the fourth century, the other to the Fathers of the fifth to eighth centuries. Lot-Borodin wrote an unreservedly favorable review of the second book (L24). In the last articles that Florovsky wrote for *The Way*—with which he collaborated until 1934—he continued to apply his program by systematically criticizing the path of the Reformation (F54R) and Catholic modernism (F49R, F53R). He maintained an interest in certain figures of Russian modernist thought—Trubetskoy (F48), Solovyov (F55), Dostoevsky (F46R), Kireevsky (F50R), and the Ukrainian philosophers (F51R)—but they had less and less attraction for him. In fact, Florovsky, like Rozanov before him, discovered to his horror the full influence that German idealism had on Russian Christianity.

Florovsky developed his first elements of a Christian metaphysics in an article entitled "Theological Fragments" in the December 1931 issue of *The Way*. The foundations of Christian philosophy laid down by the Greek Fathers were, for him, a new concept of the person; a keen sense of history, understood as a dynamic process with a beginning and an end; a sanctification of the body with an affirmation of the resurrection of the dead; and the concept of created, manifested, and formed ideas. Unlike Shestov, for whom faith, that is, the experience of the revelation of God the Father, was identified with hope, Florovsky oriented faith not towards that which is yet to come but towards what is already accomplished, namely, the incarnation of the Word: "The object of faith is the eternal present or the divine plenitude revealed by and in Christ."[256] According to Florovsky the hermeneutic of this experience could only be ecclesial, that is, dogmatic.

> Dogma is a judgment of experience and not a speculative theorem. Its whole dynamic is to point out the divine reality. It is a *testimony of the concept*, concerning what is discovered, seen, and contemplated by the experience of faith. This testimony expresses itself in notions and definitions; dogma is a "noetic" vision, a contemplated truth. Let us say that it is an image, a logical "icon" of the divine reality. At the same time, dogma is a judgment. It is, therefore, essential that it have a logical form, that this "inner word" be fixed *ad extra* by a determined and literal expression.[257]

This radical distinction between experience and the dogmatic formulation *ad extra* in "words which are exact" led Florovsky to affirm the impossibility of a "development of dogma." The criterion of the truth of experience was not its spiritual intelligibility but tradition seen as the "memory of the Church,"[258] because this memory abolished the discontinuity of time. Tradition was "the principle of life, growth, and renewal." The memory of the church "integrates its experience of grace."[259] The consequences of this referral of the criterion of truth to "the inspiration of the Holy Spirit" which resided in the church were the following. On the one hand, there was the teaching authority of the bishop, "the voice of the church" and not superior to the church, who alone is authorized, in virtue of his priesthood given by the Holy Spirit, to proclaim the truth. On the other hand, there was the impossibility of expressing "private opinions" in the church and the negation of "unlimited freedom" in the absence of external authority in the church.[260]

In its pastoral translation, the approach of Chetverikov was similar to that of Florovsky. Chetverikov, however, added a spiritual touch. For him, it was not the Incarnation, the unity of God and Man, but the redemption, the sacrifice of the Son of God on Golgotha, which was actualized throughout the ages in the sacrament of the Eucharist.[261] Because of this representation of the "divine sacrifice," one should be "pure" at the moment of communion. Chetverikov therefore considered confession indispensable before receiving the Eucharist. He also urged the faithful to communicate "frequently," that is, "four times a year."[262]

Vysheslavtsev, N. Lossky, and Alekseev followed the same Christological reasoning as Florovsky and Chetverikov but began from the experience of the individual rather than that of the church. Vysheslavtsev produced a series of articles on "the ethic of sublimation" (V18R, V19R, V20R, V21R), as well as his book *The Ethic of the Transfigured Eros*, whose content was summarized in a 1930 article in *The Way* (V22). His sole concern was to show that, in order to move beyond Kant's moralism and the passivity inherent in the system of Jung, one had to recognize that the process of the sublimation of desire could only be brought about by the force of the imagination (*voobrazhenie*) acquired through asceticism, that is, by the identification of the human being, the image of God, with the supreme image of Christ, "the only Saviour."[263] Whether it was sexual libido (Freud), psychic energy (Jung), affective potential (Baudouin), the hunger for domination (Adler), or Eros (Plato), there was a thirst for incarnation in mankind, "thirst for the birth of the God-Man."[264]

This led to the question of how this divine-human thirst was satisfied. In the work of Vysheslavtsev, as in that of Florovsky, there was a radical separation between Christ and mankind, between the world of the spirit and the world of phenomena. This called for the postulation of an autonomous ethic, culminating in a system that was "hierarchical without power."[265] The patristic response of Dionysius the Areopagite and Maximus the Confessor, updated by Vysheslavtsev, was the deification of the Platonic Eros. Unlike the rationalist and normative morality of the "Pharisees," which could not encompass the subconscious, the church fathers suggested the process of identifying with Christ through the imagination. For Vysheslavtsev, the law seen as transcendent and exterior to the person could not enable a human being to rejoin the world of the spirit. Such a law could only end up in Puritanism. Only "auto-suggestion" could enable a person to live freely in the world of the spirit.[266]

This thesis was based on an anthropology of the Self (*samost*), "whose deepest level is the *Ungrund* or freedom." For Vysheslavtsev, Christ was the "incarnation of Wisdom."[267] Vysheslavtsev opposed the conscious and the subconscious, "the heart and the entrails." Only the '*Ia sam*', the Self distinct from the Absolute, the *Atman* of Hinduism, distinct from the *Brahman*, above and beyond any definition of the individual (negative anthropology), could overcome this antinomy. Vysheslavtsev pursued an exegesis of Genesis to demonstrate that from the beginning, mankind had a sphere of autonomy in relationship with God. He began his article humorously. "Celsus thought that myths were fables for children. From the point of view of contemporary psychology, you couldn't give a better compliment to myth."[268] Indeed, for Vysheslavtsev, "just as the geological structure was a summary of the history of the earth, myth was a summary of the history of the soul."[269] In Genesis, "God did not set down any law." He simply gave recommendations—to cultivate, to preserve, and to dominate—which, for Vysheslavtsev, meant to sublimate, to respect the hierarchy of values in order to actualize it, to arrive at "the fullness of freedom and creation."[270] He disagreed with Shestov because Shestov identified sin with the desire to know good and evil. For Vysheslavtsev, sin consisted in a rejection of the established hierarchy by the serpent who denied the ontological bond between evil and death. Thrown into "the fallen world," even though rejecting objective law, mankind could not avoid judgments of value that distinguished good from evil. This was why Vysheslavtsev maintained that value is the soul of Sophia.[271] But it was evident that the two writers used the same logic of opposition between God and Being, between grace (or faith) and the law.

Nikolai Lossky, in his review of Vysheslavtsev's *The Heart in Christian and Indian Mysticism*, noted the author's interest in the understanding of freedom as the source of the "I." This enabled him to resolve the antinomy between the heart as "judge without sin" and the heart as "source not only of good but also of evil."[272] Lossky did not entirely abandon substantialism, and he also evoked the ontological primacy of the Wisdom of God.[273] For him, the person was "an essence who employs volition."[274] This similarity of opinions—which confirmed the correspondence between the two thinkers—was not limited to ontology. In three articles between 1930 and 1935, Lossky developed a phenomenology of religious experience that completed Vysheslavtsev's psychological approach. Around 1930, Lossky came to a religious and philosophical turning point. In February 1931, on the occasion of his sixtieth birthday, the editorial board of

The Way honored him. A notice preceding his article "On the Resurrection of the Body" stated that Lossky, "after having created a general theory of intuition, ... has arrived at a Christian philosophy and has rejoined, in his own way, the principal tradition of Russian philosophical and religious thought."[275] Lossky sought to identify himself with the tradition of mytho-logical language. In "Magic and the Christian Cult," he confessed to having had a religious experience of the love between God and mankind and located his work in the tradition of Solovyov, Trubetskoy, Florensky, Bulgakov, Berdyaev, Frank, and Vysheslavtsev. In 1931, Lossky professed "a concrete organic ideal-realism (personalism)" and gave himself the task of "integrating the dogma [of the resurrection] into a philosophical vision of the world."[276] In continuity with the patristic tradition—but also invoking the thought of Leibniz—Lossky treated the myths of creation, of the Kingdom of God as opposed to the kingdom of being, and of the universal Body of Christ in which the synthesis of all the "substantial actors" is to be realized.[277] Recalling St. Gregory of Nyssa's doctrine of the *apokatastasis*, of the salvation of all at the end of time, he concluded the article by citing the well-known Easter sermon of St. John Chrysostom. Christ received the worker who arrived at the eleventh hour in the same way as he received the worker who began at the first hour. In his article entitled "The Visions of Saints and Mystics," Lossky used the major idea of Vysheslavtsev—that of "the incarnation of energy by the memories of the imagination"[278]—to explain the reality of the spiritual experiences of St. John of the Cross, Thérèse of Lisieux, and Solovyov. Like Vysheslavtsev, Lossky warned against the dangers of passivity in spiritual matters. He concluded that, as the experience of the Orthodox Church attested, one's spiritual vision was the result of a synergy because mankind is created in the image of God.[279]

The Figure of the Giver of Life

For Frank, Bubnov, Zenkovsky, and Fedotov, an understanding of the unity between God and the world does not come through the tradition of the Byzantine Church, as Florovsky believed, nor by the mediation of the fathomless Wisdom, as Vysheslavtsev and Lossky proclaimed, but rather through the energies and experience of life. In its theological formulation, this signifies that the union between the human spirit and the divine spirit is realized by the Holy Spirit, called "the Giver of life" in the church's tradition. A unity of the human nature and divine nature, "without separation or confusion," is realized by Christ, which renders meaningful the tendency of human life towards the spirit. On the level of religious experience, this translates into "the acquisition of the Holy Spirit," in the expression of Saint Seraphim of Sarov. For Frank or Zenkovsky, everything happens as if the Holy Spirit were identical to the Spirit of God, or as if the nature of God, his absolute unity, were realized by the third person of the Trinity. However, as was also the case for Shestov or Florovsky, the real issue on the level of logic was to distinguish the inaccessible from its representation in the consciousness. The spirit is not the Holy Spirit. Being, the absolute unity dear to Solovyov, is life, but life is not the Absolute. Frank wrote:

> Reality is life; it is based on the irrational mystery of being, on the inaccessible—it would be more accurate to say, in that final principle which can be philosophically attained, not according to the concepts of idea or spirit, but only according to the concept of inaccessibility, through which we realize what is, what we are ourselves, but which we cannot understand, that is, translate into concepts.[280]

What we have here is the patristic use of the apophatic method to avoid any rationalization of the mystery of being. At the International Congress of Philosophy at Prague in 1934, Frank gave a lecture on the theme "The Spiritual and Vivifying Significance of Negative Theology."[281] Frank's apophaticism explains why he could not find words sufficiently harsh against the "biological determinism" of the psychoanalysis of Freud.[282] In a 1930 book, Frank argued that the relationship between God and the world is neither causal-temporal nor logical-ahistoric but trans-rational. His ontological ethic, based on the divine-humanity, uses a "conciliar" phenomenology of the human spirit, similar to that of Wilhelm Dilthey, which gives access to the foundations of the understanding of society.[283] Vysheslavtsev reviewed this book in *The Way* and criticized, not the myth of divine-humanity, but the doctrine of the social ideal, which, in Frank's work, was based on the principles of service, duty, and obligation. "It's pure Kant," Vysheslavtsev complained; he set the ethic of grace in opposition to the ethic of law. For Frank, the law maintained a spiritual foundation in the category of obligation, whereas for Vysheslavtsev, there was a radical distinction between the law-as-power, which belonged to a fallen world, and the source of law, which was freedom.[284]

In *The Way*, Frank, unlike Shestov or Florovsky, tried to rehabilitate the history of thought as a temporal manifestation of the spirit using the examples, in the Russian tradition, of Lopatin ("his phenomenology of the life of the soul," F74), Dostoevsky ("his Christian humanism," F76), Pirogov ("his religious thought," F77), and Pushkin ("his religiosity," F81); in the German tradition, of Hegel ("his religious ontologism," F78) and Goethe ("his spiritual culture," F79), as well as Spinoza (F80) and Nicholas of Cusa. In the article on Spinoza, he argued that the idea of superrational knowledge, in the form of the unity of contrary concepts found in Nicholas of Cusa, comes, in fact, from negative theology.[285] To be sure, Frank affirmed that Spinoza's system suffered from rationalism and led to pantheism. But if Spinoza had developed the system of the *coincidentia oppositorum*, "his pantheism would have become a concrete panentheism."[286] Frank rejected the accusations of heresy directed against the philosopher and invoked the words of Christ, namely, that only the sin against the Holy Spirit was unpardonable. Frank ended his article on Spinoza's philosophy with these words: "The entire life and thought of Spinoza were an uninterrupted glorification of the Spirit and a dedication to it, even though in incomplete and erroneous forms."[287] N. Bubnov also followed Frank's approach in the reviews he wrote for the journal on contemporary German philosophers (H. Schwarz, H. Gross, H. Leisegang, K. Leese, R. Otto, and B. Christiansen). He defended the ontological tradition of Russian religious thought (B109R) and of German idealism, notably that of Lessing, a disciple of Spinoza (B111R), against the attempts of dialectical theology to reduce Christianity to the Bible and to the *Gesangbuch*, to Lutheran hymns (B110R).

Just as Frank distinguished life from the Absolute, V. Zenkovsky, in the pages of *The Way*, tried to show that created Wisdom, the spiritual nature of the world, a "living and concrete unity,"[288] cannot be identified with uncreated Wisdom, the absolute-unity. Hence Zenkovsky criticized Frank's 1916 book, *The Object of Knowledge*, in which the sophianic foundation of the created world was identified with the Absolute. The created world was wholly distinct from the uncreated Absolute. But, in reality, Zenkovsky followed the same path as Frank in the 1920s. The unity of God and the world realized in Christ can only be actualized in humanity. He wrote: "In humanity the sophianic foundation of the world attains a unity which reveals a certain 'unity of essence' [*edinosoushchie*] of humanity, of which Saint Paul speaks in Romans 5:12. The revelation of this moment, which is essential for sophiology, can only be given in anthropology."[289] In a second public lecture at the Academy of Religious Philosophy in February 1931, Zenkovsky took up this question, "The Problem of Beauty in the Worldview of Dostoevsky." Like Chetverikov, Zenkovsky used the redemptive character of the sacrifice of God to contradict Dostoevsky and to affirm that one cannot save one's self through nature alone—the temptation of naturalism. Indeed, for Zenkovsky, the sacrifice had priority over the accomplishment of the incarnation because, if there was only the incarnation, "the resurrection becomes useless."[290] The salvation of the world is accomplished by the restoration of the image of God in humanity, for that alone could restore the brightness "to the somber visage of created Wisdom."[291]

Other articles of Zenkovsky are essentially aimed against the Christocentric current of the journal, that is, against Florovsky (Z28R), Nikolai Lossky (Z30R, Z33R), and Vysheslavtsev (Z32R). In a review of Florovsky's 1931 book on the Eastern Fathers of the fourth century, he criticized the author's lack of a sense of history in his exposition of "the dialectical evolution of ideas." He preferred the work of Karsavin entitled "The Holy Fathers and Confessors of the Church," which was more in the spirit of Solovyov's divine-humanity.[292] Zenkovsky also reviewed N. Lossky's *Value and Existence* (1931) and *The Ways of Apprehending the World: An Introduction to Metaphysics* (1931). As for the theory of knowledge, Zenkovsky praised Lossky's attempt to link the sphere of ethics, of values, with the sphere of ontology. But with respect to ontology, he rejected Lossky's spiritualism, influenced by the philosophy of Leibniz, which did not give full weight to the reality of the material.[293] For Zenkovsky, this was due to an overly optimistic representation of freedom, which did not give sufficient consideration to the fact that this freedom is the origin of evil.[294] Lossky replied in 1932 by affirming that, in his opinion, "God does not participate in evil."[295] Finally, Zenkovsky, in his 1932 review of Vysheslavtsev's *The Ethics of Transfigured Eros*, detected "a mild naturalism" that did not distinguish the fallen eros from the divine eros, the result of a non-ecclesial and autonomous conception of sublimation.[296] For Vysheslavtsev, one loses one's self in God. God is the sole source of activity. This is why human freedom, outside of the immersion in one's innermost depths through the imagination, remained inactive. For Zenkovsky, true sublimation should go beyond the aesthetic imagination and should take place, along with the work of the spirit, in the "laborious harbor of the Cross," in voluntary and spiritual asceticism.[297]

> Without the illuminations of grace, the spiritual life cannot develop normally in us; it is on this point that we clearly distinguish ourselves from this doctrine of spiritual evolution found in Hinduism and neo-Hinduism, which relies entirely on the hidden forces of humanity. But these illuminations from on high do not act upon our heart magically. They suppose not only the free tending of the soul towards God (something Vysheslavtsev also recognizes) but also a certain *work*, an authentic interior activity.[298]

Vysheslavtsev replied indirectly in a review of Troitsky's book *The Christian Philosophy of Marriage*. Far from rejecting any action of the intellect in the subconscious life, he showed, on the contrary, all the weaknesses of Troitsky's neo-Kantian approach, which identified the intervention of practical reason in the sphere of desire as concupiscence. Such an approach, which forbade any intervention so as not to sink into evil, is based, whatever its intention, on a rational knowledge of good and evil. It thus unconsciously intervenes in the sphere of desire, and this leads, logically, to Shestov's rejection of the knowledge of good and evil. But for Vysheslavtsev, allowance for the work of the conscience on mankind's Dionysian desire does not mean returning to "the old traditional Pharisaic responses."[299]

Fedotov's articles in the review were also oriented towards the third hypostasis of the Trinity, but according to the particular problematic of its historical incarnation. Aside from the rediscovery of the spiritual tradition of Nil of Sora (F9), Fedotov was interested in the presence of the Holy Spirit in nature and culture, as the title of an article indicates (F13), as well as in historiography (in F12) and the cosmology of the Russian people (F15).

Unlike Florovsky, for whom truth is based on the tradition of the church, Fedotov made the case for personal knowledge of the past, aided by historical criticism. On an individual level, this corresponded to a religious value, to "repentance," which enables the soul to detach itself from a fault.[300] Criticism was what allowed the past to pass, that is, rejoin the present life. But the church, Fedotov wrote, had a tendency to regard the past as sacred, and thus it lost touch with its living, historic incarnation. The task of the theologian was to purify tradition, the church's memory of the church, from the accumulated material of history.[301] Fedotov proposed the elaboration of an Orthodox historiography that would avoid skepticism, naïveté, and rationalism but that was based on a "rigorous realism." It would witness not only to the presence of the Holy Spirit in history but also to the social reality of a fallen world.[302] The history of the world was a drama, the history of the divine-humanity, which extended beyond the borders of the visible church. In order to grasp this drama, Fedotov invoked the triune structure of a medieval theatre production, where the action takes place simultaneously in heaven, on earth, and in hell. In the same way, according to Fedotov, the historical recital should take into account these three corresponding levels: "holiness, daily life, and sin."[303] Fedotov took these historiographic principles from mythical Orthodox thought, as expressed in the Middle Ages in the lives of saints and in icons. Fedotov observed that the founder of modern Russian historical science, Vasilii Klyuchevsky, wrote his thesis on the topic "The Lives of Russian Saints as a Historical Source."[304] Fedotov also took up the difficult question of biblical exegesis, which, in his mind, will become one of the most acute problems "in the Russia of the future."[305] According to Fedotov, the fundamental principle in this case was that the approach should imitate the structure of the Bible itself, based on the Law and Grace, that is, it should put tradition ahead of the judgment of one's reason, so that the human reason might become "ecclesial reason."[306]

Fedotov, in his history of the religious cosmology of the Russian people, applied his principles in arguing that the "sophianic" cult of Mother Earth was essentially pneumatological. Using a study of *Spiritual Verses*, a collection of epic religious songs whose purpose was to recount the lives of the saints to the Russian people of the Middle Ages, but which remained popular until the nineteenth century, Fedotov demonstrated how mythical understanding tended to anthropomorphize the Earth. Out of all the cosmos, only mother-earth was endowed with a personal incarnation, and this, for Fedotov, revealed the feminine side of Russian spirituality. As the source of beauty and nourishment, she was the guarantor of moral life and interceded before God for the pardon of humanity's sins. Fedotov described this spirituality of *Spiritual Verses*, oriented towards the Holy Spirit, in the following terms:

> The world, divine as to its origins, sanctified by the blood of Christ and by the tears of the Mother of God, is penetrated through and through by the Holy Spirit or by the "holy spirits" sent by Christ. . . . The whole earth receives the Holy Spirit, who, according to the radical expression of a verse, becomes incarnate in her. . . . Living in nature, the Holy Spirit is perceived by the people in the breath of the air, of the wind, and in the perfumes of the earth.[307]

Fedotov expressed his pneumocentrism even more clearly in his article on the Holy Spirit that appeared in the journal in 1932. As in the case of Frank, Fedotov found the Holy Spirit in "living nature"—for example, in the mouth of the ass who spoke to Balaam the prophet.[308] Similarly, like Zenkovsky, he insisted on "the cross and ecclesial experience"[309] as necessary conditions for the incarnation of the Spirit in nature and in culture. For, Fedotov wrote, human nature was crucified in Christianity. Only the incarnation of Christ enables mankind to recover the "Breath," the "Giver of Life," and even the "Muses."[310]

As we have seen in the case of Chetverikov or Zenkovsky—and also Vysheslavtsev and Shestov—behind the question of the mode of relationship between God and humanity looms that of theodicy, of the origin of evil, and of the meaning of the incarnation. It will be helpful at this point to consider the theories of Berdyaev and Bulgakov, respectively. These two intellectuals, aware of the a priori importance of this question, sought to recapitulate the experience of the church and to give it a new expression.

Berdyaev: The Discourse Centered on Humanity

Berdyaev's thinking followed the same course as Shestov, Florovsky, or Frank, namely, a de-ontologizing of the Absolute. But he went further by denying the transcendent and static status of the Absolute, which negative theology retained after divesting it of the personal properties of being (love, proximity, joy, and so on). For Berdyaev, God was not the Absolute of ancient philosophy, the One of Plotinus, ever more inaccessible as one drew near. He was a living person, capable of going forth from himself in order to reveal himself to humanity. Apophatic theology was justified by its refusal to rationalize the mystery of creation, but it sank into irrationalism if it denied the personal character of the Absolute. This was because the process of negation, the refusal by the human spirit to objectify God, was itself based on the mystery of freedom, which was a personal reality. God reveals himself to us as "He who is" and not as He who is not. Because of these insights, Berdyaev, in 1929, formulated his representation of the abyss that separates God from the world in a new way, at the risk of differing from the traditional way in which the church represents creation.

Unlike Boehme, who placed the *Ungrund*, or nothingness, "in" God, Berdyaev made a decisive turnabout by clearly affirming that the "meonic" nothingness is situated "outside" of God. In an analysis awash in symbols, Berdyaev distinguished the divinity of apophatic theology, which "precedes" the emergence in eternity of the divine Trinity, from the nonbeing "outside" of God.[311] In his study of Boehme published in the February and April 1930 issues of *The Way*, Berdyaev sharpened the negative formulation of his representation of freedom. "I am inclined to interpret *Ungrund* as an absolutely original freedom, as a meonic freedom, not determined, not even by God."[312] And, he added, in a note: "Something in the sense of *me on* and not in the sense of *ouk on*." Following Schelling, Berdyaev distinguished two modes of representing negation in the language of Plato and Aristotle: *me on*, in the sense of "not yet," and *ouk on*, in the sense of "beyond which." This distinction was decisive. In the one case it posits *nothingness (le néant)* as the sphere of relative nonbeing, while in the other case nothingness is understood as *nonexistence (le rien)*, pure nonbeing.[313] This distinction was critical for understanding the mythology of Berdyaev. The world, or being, belonged to the sphere of being born from nothingness (*néant*), the not yet. Nothingness (*néant*) was nonexistent, but it had the possibility of an existence that was not hypostatic. Its foundationless origin (*Ungrund*) was freedom. In contrast, the divine and human Person belonged, according to Berdyaev's vision, to the sphere of nonexistence (*le rien*), of the "beyond-which" (*sur-quoi*), because this Person is not a "what" but a "who" and, consequently, defies objectification.[314] Given this initial logical distinction, we should study more closely the myths on which it was based in order to understand the personalist myth-ology that Berdyaev developed between 1930 and 1935 and the reactions it provoked.

Ontology

Berdyaev's ontology was mytho-logical. It was based on the following myths: boundless freedom as symbolized by darkness, Sophia as symbolized by light, and the Heavenly Man. "Only mythological consciousness has seen the irrational principle in being."[315] Freedom is understood as the desire or the "hunger" of nothing to become something.[316] This myth, whose importance for Berdyaev has already been pointed out in discussing his 1929 review of Koyré's book on Boehme's philosophy, was connected to his vision of the creation of the world. In his 1927 article "Some Reflections on Theodicy," Berdyaev linked his ontology to his rejection of the traditional explanation of the creation of the world, which was founded, in his opinion, on "the ontology of sin." In his article on Boehme, the Lutheran cobbler, he returned to this theme.

> I call the following conception of rational, cataphatic theology a comedy: God, so it seems, the perfect and immobile God, complete, satisfied, all-powerful, all-knowing and infinitely good, has created the world and mankind for his glory and for the good of creation.... God would have endowed his creature, the human being, with the fatal faculty of freedom.... But mankind would have used said freedom badly, rebelling against his Creator.... Having opposed the will of God, humanity would have been subjected to damnation.... Every creature moans and weeps. End of Act I. With Act II, redemption begins.... The person of the Creator is pushed into the background and the Redeemer takes center stage.... God, who created the world, has predestined it to be eternally lost for he knows the consequences of freedom.... He is playing a game with himself because he is the one who gives freedom and he knew its consequences since freedom is not unfathomable for him.[317]

Berdyaev's ontology of grace was an attempt at personalizing the Absolute of traditional theology, at revitalizing it. For Berdyaev, evil did not come from the freedom that originally was pure potentiality, but from using this freedom to make God an object. This is where Berdyaev's cataphatic and personalist about-face occurs. Freedom is not the static possibility of choosing between good and evil. It is the relationship of love between God and his creature. Berdyaev wanted to preserve this relationship and to absolve God from any participation in evil. He did so at the risk of scandalizing his readers, for he affirmed, on the one hand, that God is not all-powerful with respect to humanity, and, on the other hand, that God is not perfect and that the fullness of freedom is not entirely his. Following Boehme, Berdyaev speaks of a theogonic process. This did not mean, as it did for Hegel, that God was born in time. "The interior and eternal life of God reveals itself under the form of a dynamic process, of tragedy in eternity, of combat with the powers of non-being.... The creation of the world is part of the interior life of the divine Trinity, it cannot be something absolutely exterior to it."[318] The fact that Berdyaev conceived of a freedom outside of God did not mean that he considered it as something substantial. Even for Boehme, Berdyaev reminded the reader, "freedom as nothingness, as *me on*, does not have any substance in itself." Berdyaev continued: "Perhaps for the first time in the history of human thought, Boehme saw that at the foundation of being and before being, there is freedom without foundation ... he thus laid the bases for a particular metaphysical voluntarism [giving priority to the will over intellect and emotion] not known to ancient and medieval philosophers."[319] All the difficulty that reason experiences in grasping this non-hypostatic and non-substantial freedom or this emergence in eternity comes from the fact that thought transforms realities of the symbolic order into rational concepts. Such is the case for the symbols of anteriority and posteriority—and also for those of interiority and exteriority—of the images of nothingness "in" God and "outside of" God. These images should be understood as symbolic and not conceptual. These symbols do not belong to space or time and should not be understood according to these categories. They indicate a non-hypostatic mode of being. The final lines of Berdyaev's article are totally incomprehensible if the notions of abyss are understood in spatial and temporal terms. He writes:

> The doctrine of Boehme on the *Ungrund* should be developed along the lines of the distinction between, on the one hand, the divine abyss, the divine freedom, and, on the other hand, the meonic abyss and freedom. In the ultimate and inexpressible mystery, this distinction itself disappears, but, at the threshold of the mystery, the difference imposes itself.[320]

Berdyaev's ontology borrowed a second myth from Boehme—that of Sophia—which corresponds to the image and likeness of God in humanity, to the myth of the "androgyny of humanity," of its original integrity.[321] For Boehme, Christ was the model of the androgyne. But, Berdyaev assures us, Boehme "is not a monophysite." According to him, Christ realized the synthesis of celestial, androgynic humanity by incarnating himself in the masculine sex. In Berdyaev's thought, this myth was linked to that of the Heavenly Man, of the Adam-Kadmon of the Kabbalah.[322] He expressed this intuition in his *Spirit and Freedom*—published in 1927–28— when he wrote that "the whole generation of Adam is in the Son of God."[323] God became incarnate so that humanity might be divinized. In this perspective, the coming of the God-man should be seen dynamically, as the accomplishment of the project of creation, and only secondarily as the salvation of mankind. This was the source of Berdyaev's basic understanding of this myth: "In Christ, humanity is raised up to heaven, up to the Holy Trinity."[324]

The Mariology of Boehme is equally sophianic. The Virgin Mary brings about the synthesis between Sophia and its created nature though the Holy Spirit. Berdyaev wrote: "The cult of the Virgin is the cult of Sophia, of the Wisdom of God."[325] The myth of Sophia reaches into the depths of the Trinity. Berdyaev cites John Pordage (1607–81), the seventeenth-century English theosophist and disciple of Boehme: "Sophia says of herself: 'I am the virginal Wisdom of my Father, who cannot create anything without me, just as I can do nothing without the Father, Son, and Holy Spirit.'"[326] Sophia is by definition the possibility of the transfiguration of the created world.

The Personalist Turn

In returning to the very source of the Russian modernist tradition— in his studies on Boehme, he cites Fedorov, Dostoevsky, Bukharev, and Solovyov—Berdyaev found new energy. At the age of fifty-six, he entered another phase of his thinking, which he himself described as a personalist philosophy. He had always been sensitive to humanity's creative role in the divine-human relationship. This was at the heart of his outlook. But by specifying his discourse on being and freedom, and by separating, in a new and more antinomic way, the human spirit created in the image of God from human nature and issued from the meonic abyss, Berdyaev established the ontological foundations of his mytho-logy of the Person. The principal effect of situating nothingness outside of God was to mytho-logize, to give life to the notion of a person possessing a freedom that is absolutely original. This was not dualism. The human Person and the divine Person merge in eternity in the figure of the Heavenly Man and in time with Jesus Christ, true God and true Man, in whom is accomplished the synthesis between human freedom and divine freedom. The antinomy was no longer between the God-Absolute and Being but between the freedom of the God-Person and the freedom of Man.

This personalist evolution had impelled Berdyaev to immediately put into writing, in 1931, the foundations of a new anthropology, in his *The Destiny of Man*, and a new personalist sociology, in *The Self and the World of Objects* (published in English as *Solitude and Society*), which appeared in 1934. As of 1933, he wrote "from the point of view of existential philosophy" in the hope of being integrated into a group of philosophers of the spirit, but he immediately added that this had nothing to do with Heidegger and Jaspers. In fact, by making this turn Berdyaev experienced a profound solitude, which he described in *The Self and the World of Objects*. He probably should have written "from the point of view of mytho-logy," since for him, existence was based, above all, on the myth of the person. In his 1935 article entitled "Personalism and Marxism," Berdyaev continued with his mytho-logy of the person. He distinguished the individual, a biological and sociological category, from the person, a spiritual and religious category. The person is a whole and cannot be part of something more general. The person was not part of society—quite the opposite. Citing Nesmelov, he described the person as an "eruption" in the natural world. The person was unity in plurality, the structure in the movement. The person, Berdyaev stated, presumed a super-personal superior being, which it reflected, and super-personal values, which it realized and which constituted the riches of the content of its life. The person was not something already complete; rather, it created itself, it proceeded from itself towards others. This was not the rather passive idea of "life," which was the active principle of the person according to Scheler and Frank; it was the spirit. Berdyaev then called for a complete "revolution" of values: "Underlying personalism's conception of the social world one does not find the idea of equality or of justice but rather the idea of the dignity of every human person who should be given the possibility of realizing himself."[327]

For Berdyaev, just as for Shestov, Florovsky, and Frank, a central idea was that of no longer ontologizing God. What was unique in Berdyaev's thought was that, for him, in the sphere of the divine, there was no longer any object in general, for being had disappeared. As he wrote in his article "Two Ways of Understanding Christianity: The Debates about the Old and the New in Christianity": "In his deepest mystery, God is not an object and is not part of the objective world."[328] Being, understood as God, was dead. But God as object was also dead. God as person, in his otherness, is Spirit—and this is why a discussion on the myth of God is possible. For Man, created in the image of God, as a being-in-relation, also has a spiritual nature. This nature explains why the incarnation of God in man is possible. Man, integrated into the inner life of the Trinity, became the source of creation and activity. The objective world, which seemed to exist autonomously, was an illusion of our consciousness. In oppposition to those whom he called conservatives, those who believed that the subject, dominated by the object, is passive, Berdyaev did not hesitate to justify Spinoza, Voltaire, Kant, Hegel, Feuerbach, Marx, biblical criticism, the mythological theory, Nietzsche, and Rozanov.[329] The conservatives, according to Berdyaev, always believed that the world was a finished product, whereas Fedorov, on the other hand, launched an appeal to vanquish the established order in the name of the resurrection of all.

This ushered in a new ethic. In what could sound like a declaration of war on Florovsky, Berdyaev argued that, after the humanistic Renaissance, "it is impossible to return to a patristic or Thomistic anthropology."[330] He took aim in particular at the traditional doctrine of the church concerning hell and paradise. In his book *The Fate of Man in the Modern World*, he embraced a new eschatology directly based on his personalism. Human consciousness could no longer accept the fear of hell as a road towards the Kingdom of God. Berdyaev affirmed that from an "objective" point of view, on the level of divine omnipotence, hell had no ontological reality. "Moral consciousness began with the divine question: 'Cain, what have you done with your brother Abel?' It will find its consummation in this other question: 'Abel, what have you done with your brother Cain?'"[331] Like Origen, Berdyaev believed that Christ would remain on the Cross as long as there was a single person in hell. Berdyaev, however, rejected Origen's doctrine of the *apokatastasis*, according to which every creature will be "forced" to enter into the Kingdom of God. Berdyaev accepted hell from a "subjective" point of view, on the level of the individual person, in the realm of meonic freedom. Like paradise, hell became a symbol of spiritual experience. Hell was "an absorption in one's self such that eternity closes around itself. . . . The experience which gave birth to the idea of an eternal hell is that which a person lives in the subjective sphere, as endless. . . . But this infinity has nothing in common with eternity."[332] Hell corresponded to a meonic or nihilistic freedom that had degenerated into adversity. Only Christ, the redeemer and savior who descended into hell, enables the human being to abandon the creation of hell and consecrate himself to the creation of the Kingdom of God. Consequently, the ultimate maxim of ethics, in Berdyaev's system, was closer to that of Fedorov than to that of Kant. It can be summed up thus: Act by directing all the forces of your spirit towards Christ so as to deliver the dead from death and hell.[333]

Given the personal spirit of each human being, the realization of the Kingdom of truth depended, for Berdyaev, on the degree of communion among people. This is why he regarded apophatic knowledge as the purification of tradition of all its social mutations, and as the liberation of individuals from all the hellish fears that fill our collective subconscious.

> Christianity will bring about social justice, it will create a new life when it ceases to be, subconsciously, a social religion, a religion of a specific type, of the state, of the nation, of a certain class, of ratio, of law, and when Christians will hear the voice of God and not that of society, the voice of infinity rather than the voice of finitude.[334]

The Debate in *The Way*

These ideas were reflected in the pages of *The Way*. Berdyaev was obviously happy to cross swords with Ioann Shakhovskoy, Chetverikov, or Alekseev, since debate stimulated his personal reflection. To this end, he did not hesitate to use provocative expressions. Among the authors of the journal, the first to react to Berdyaev's turn was the poet-turned-monk Fr. Ioann Shakhovskoy (1902–89). In his 1931 review of Berdyaev's book *The Destiny of Man*, Shakhovskoy sharply criticized the philosopher for attacking the Fathers of the Church. He countered Berdyaev's glorification of human creativity by recalling that humanity cannot do anything without the glory of God, which is at work in the transfiguration of the world. Shakhovskoy also lamented the fact that Berdyaev was afraid of "being a fool in philosophy" and that he continued to use the logic of the theory of knowledge, instead of putting himself at the service of theology.[335] Thus the question of hell, for example, was not a philosophical "problem" for Shakhovskoy but rather a "given." Berdyaev should not try to "limit God by the ethical norm of a moral-meonic scope."[336] Shakhovskoy was least of all disposed to concede that human liberty "only half-comes" from God. He wrote: "Can it not be affirmed, on the contrary, that the meonic nothingness is the source of nonfreedom towards which the person who separates itself from God sometimes tends?"[337]

Everything indicates that Berdyaev was elated by the opportunity to reduce to ashes what he called "the pride of the humble." At home in his nontheological terrain, he was vehemently critical of the "Orthodox-ascetic" mentality, which, under the guise of humility, practiced unquestioning formal obedience. This "Orthodox mindset" was arrogantly proud of a tradition that despised humanity, philosophy, and culture. It "held court on Mount Athos in a fortress well defended against all the worries and events of this world."[338] Berdyaev prayed for the advent of a new monastic way of life in the world that would bring about a spiritual break between the tradition of the *Philokalia*—which he only knew in the abridged version of Theophan the Recluse—and the early church's tradition of the Gospels. Berdyaev acknowledged that Fr. Ioann belonged to a new type of monks, but only in the sense that these monks "pretend to show that they are troubled by what happens in this world."[339] In reality, their battle against reflection was a traditional one, motivated by the desire to preserve "the monopoly of the spirit."[340] In denouncing Russian obscurantism, which he described as an inheritance from monophysitism, Berdyaev recalled that the human being is called to "love God with his whole mind."[341]

> I affirm in good conscience that philosophy (and theosophy) are not servants of theology nor useful arms and techniques for the goals which religion sets for itself; rather they are the manifestation of the activity of humanity's creative knowledge precisely as human philosophy, as human love for wisdom, as the created gift bestowed on mankind which goes beyond itself and finds itself in the experience of the knowledge of the spiritual world.

Chetverikov, one of the representatives of the Christocentric current within the journal and, more importantly, the spiritual guide of the Russian Student Christian Movement, took on Berdyaev, but in a less polemical tone. Chetverikov first published an open letter to Berdyaev in March 1935, in which he asked him to define his position more precisely. With sensitivity and respect, he posed three questions concerning Berdyaev's pessimistic understanding of the role of God in the world, the place he allowed for the church in his ethics, and the possibility of a nondivine freedom. In his reply, in the same issue of *The Way*, Berdyaev limited his polemics to a simple dismissal of "the self-satisfaction of the Pharisees" and explained, more seriously, the tragic and antinomic characteristics of his thought. He rejected a Christianity that divided the saved, within the borders of the church, from the damned, who are outside these borders. Such a view was due to the fact that nature itself is antinomic. Moreover, he refused to have his ethics qualified as "pessimistic," because God, for him, was a God of love who recognized human freedom. If God, as he believed, was not at work in evil, this meant that evil had another source. Berdyaev concluded that there existed a "freedom of God and in relationship with God." It was because of these views that Berdyaev, although he understood "the limits of language," could dare to speak of "the powerlessness of God in the face of the freedom of evil" and of the possible solution to evil through God-the-Redeemer. Berdyaev was no more satisfied with the solution of agnosticism, of the impossibility of rationally solving the mystery of evil, than he was with the Augustinian theodicy of predestination. Indeed, "in theology as in metaphysics, this theory has never held up until the end, and there have always been theories which are humiliating for a sensitive conscience."[342]

In his conclusion, Berdyaev opposed his conception of the church as the Mystical Body of Christ to that of the church as a sinful social institution. Berdyaev complained that the necessity of repentance as a way of salvation, the necessity of taking upon one's self the sufferings of the world, was considered rhetoric by most Christians. "Job debated with God, those who consoled him were pious." But, he added, only Job was justified by God. Thus, for Berdyaev, optimism did not consist in believing that God was the savior of those who are within the church. Rather, one should struggle with God for the salvation of all.

Chetverikov was not satisfied with Berdyaev's replies. He took up the issue again in an article dated May 18, 1935. This final duel between

Berdyaev, who represented the neo-modernist current in the church, and Chetverikov, who defended the enlightened traditionalist current, was decisive, for it marked the end of the journal's nonconformist period. Both of them went as far as they could in their faith to try to find a common language. By the end of the summer of 1935, as we shall see, this possibility was out of the question.

Chetverikov rephrased his questions in a more direct manner: Does Christ's work continue on earth through the church? How is this noncreated freedom to be reconciled with the Christian affirmation that all things come from God? Chetverikov argued that Berdyaev's theodicy did not resolve the aporia or paradox of evil, for God, when he created mankind from meonic freedom, should have foreseen that humanity would use this freedom to its detriment. Why not accept the idea, Chetverikov continued, that God gave freedom to the human race not so that it might commit evil, but in order to choose between good and evil? Why not admit that God accepts evil by limiting his omnipotence in the name of that freedom which he gave to humanity? In his reply, Berdyaev reaffirmed the uninterrupted presence of Christ in the church but objected to a vision of a narrowly limited church. Above all, he returned to the question of theodicy. Berdyaev stated that, for him, the distinction between good and evil was already a consequence of the Fall, whereas freedom preceded it. Berdyaev's argument was as follows. If God grants freedom, he grants the freedom of good and of evil. This is why it is illogical to impute to God only the freedom to do good and to humanity only the freedom to do evil. Berdyaev reaffirms: "It is impossible to attribute the prevision of evil to God because evil has its source outside of being and outside of the world created by God."[343] Chetverikov, Berdyaev wrote, did not suppose that evil had not been vanquished by God, but he forgot that the traditional doctrine of the church admitted the eternity of hell, as if evil was indispensable for God.

Finally, Berdyaev put his finger on what was essentially at issue in the debate. The discourse on evil can only be mytho-logical, that is, founded on symbols, on antinomy, and on the goal of history. Freedom, as an irrational principle of the order of non-being, "cannot be grasped as a concept, it can only be spoken of in a mytho-logical way, with symbols."[344]

> The Fall cannot be understood rationally. It is a myth—which does not mean that it is opposed to reality. The creation of the world can

be interpreted as a struggle against non-being, against an adversity in the somber element of non-being. The freedom to sin and do evil that issued from non-being could not be overcome in the first act of the creation of the world by God the Father, but it is vanquished by God the Son, who descends into the somber depths of non-being; it is vanquished not by force but by the sacrifice of love. This is the whole mystery of Christianity.[345]

From the logic of this argument, freedom is shown to be twofold. But Berdyaev put truth above cataphatic thought. One could only speak of the "non-discursive mystery of God" in a negative way. "On this level there is no longer any dualism, any opposition between light and darkness; there is the pure divine light, which is darkness for reason, and there, hell is no longer possible nor can there be any trace of any sort of pessimism. This is the limit of thought, the sphere of mystical contemplation and of unity."[346]

If the criticisms of Shakhovskoy and Chetverikov came from traditional theology, those of Alekseev were based on phenomenological philosophy. Alekseev was the brother-in-law of Vysheslavtsev and shared his Boehmian vision of the undetermined in God. In his article "On the Idea of Philosophy and Its Social Mission," published in the September 1934 issue, he put Berdyaev's thought, as expressed in *The Self and the World of Objects*, into the philosophical context of the times. But he observed that the originality of Berdyaev with respect to Karl Jaspers consisted in the fact that Berdyaev, by rejecting the notion of object, arrived at "a philosophy of pure subjectivism."[347] This rejection of objectivity in the sphere of being, as well as in the sphere of divine-human relations, corresponded, in Alekseev's opinion, to a philosophy of uprooting (*déracinement*) that was characteristic of the social situation of the Russian émigré community. Thus, Alekseev wanted to distribute competencies between philosophy, the "gnosis" that is rooted in the subject-object dialectic, and "religion," which started from revealed truth and, to attain gnosis, made use of "prayer, spiritual effort [*podvig*], and asceticism."[348]

In his reply, Berdyaev stated that since the publication of his book *The Philosophy of Freedom* (translated into English as *Freedom and the Spirit*), he had always conceived his theory of knowledge not as a project of objectivization but as a coming together of the knower and being, made possible by the fact that the knower himself is a being, that is, an existent.[349] Berdyaev pointed out to Alekseev that he had not grasped the principal idea of his book—namely, the link between knowledge and the degrees of communication among people. In fact, in his book *The Self and the World of Objects*, he rejected the universality of reason in the objective sense given to it by rationalist philosophy. For him, "knowledge depends on the forms of communication [*soobshchenie*] and communion [*obshchenie*] among peoples."[350] Berdyaev did not deny the positive value of objective knowledge—in physics and mathematics, for example—but this type of knowledge was directed towards a world torn apart. Only the fallen world was subject to the law of "two plus two equals four," not persons. Berdyaev claimed that he had learned this lesson both from Marxism (according to which the proletarian knows things in a way that is different from that of the bourgeois) and from religion (which sees faith and love changing the results of knowledge).

Finally, Berdyaev justified his philosophical turn. He disassociated himself from subjective philosophy insofar as he believed that the "subject, the Self of German idealism, was not the human being."[351] But going beyond objectivization did not mean a withdrawal into the self, for even though philosophy might be anthropocentric, the human being is not. In the end, Berdyaev believed that personalism was the only philosophy capable of assuring the passage from communication to communion, from the sphere of the anonymous multitude to the coming together with the other and with God.

Bulgakov: The Discourse Centered on Sophia

In 1917, Bulgakov had insisted that there was an impassable line—impassable for humanity—between the Absolute and the revealed God of the Bible. He also denied that the Absolute could be qualified in any way, even as a Person.[352] Yet in spite of the unfathomable abyss between God and man, what linked the Absolute and the world was the revelation of Wisdom, present both in the world and in the depths of the Trinity, and forming, as he awkwardly expressed it, "a fourth hypostasis."[353] Faithful to his intuition of Wisdom, as he formulated it in his 1911 book *The Philosophy of Economy: The World as Household*, and hoping to situate himself in continuity with the work of St. Gregory Palamas, Bulgakov then directed his reflection towards an interpretation of the icon of the Wisdom of God, the source of the divine energies present in the cosmos. But after the Russian Revolution and his "linguistic turn," Bulgakov revisited the awkward formula he had used in 1917. In his 1925 article "Hypostasis and Hypostaticity" and his later essay "Chapters on the Trinity,"[354] he began a new stage in his thought, given over to clarifying this relationship of Wisdom to the Three Hypostases of the Trinity by examining in depth the question of "how."

In "Hypostasis and Hypostaticity," Bulgakov no longer saw Wisdom as a "person," for he realized that there is a non-hypostatic love, for example, the love of creation for its creator. The Psalms proclaim that creation "praises God." In "Chapters on the Trinity," he renounced the temptation to think of God as an "absolute object," but also the temptation, conversely, of thinking of Him as an "absolute subject": "It is necessary," he wrote, "to think of both at the same time, as an 'I' and as an 'Us.'"[355] Thus, between the approach of Shestov, Florovsky, and Frank, on the one hand, and that of Berdyaev, on the other, Bulgakov's project was to elaborate a sophio-logy that would permit one to logically represent the relationship between God in his identity ("I") and God in his otherness ("Us"). In his analysis of the icon of the Wisdom of God, published between 1925 and 1929 and dedicated, in its first part, to the angels, the Mother of God, and Saint John the Baptist—those who surround Wisdom seated on her throne—Bulgakov tried to resolve the same question: If one admitted that Wisdom was not a hypostasis, that its reality as a "lover" is distinct from the divine hypostases—notably the Holy Spirit—and that it is the "joy" of the Trinitarian love from all eternity (Prov. 8:30–31), how can Wisdom be both the loved one (object) and the lover (subject)?

Ontology

Bulgakov found an initial answer to this question at the beginning of the 1930s by turning towards the Trinity, that is, by replacing the question of "how" by that of "who." Indeed, as long as Wisdom was considered the divine foundation of creation, and as long as its consideration was relative to the doctrine concerning the world (the angels, the Virgin, Saint John the Baptist), Bulgakov could avoid facing up to the question of the nature of Sophia. By deciding to focus on the figure of Christ in glory, represented in the icon of Novgorod just above the figure of Wisdom seated on her throne, Bulgakov was led to postulate the following equation: The Sophia in the world presupposes the Sophia in God. From this seminal spiritual experience, expressed according to the mode of correspondence of the image to the archetype, Bulgakov arrived at three conclusions.

First, as he wrote in *The Way* in 1933, this equation signified that the Trinity possessed a nature in the sense that *ousia* had for the Fathers of the Church, which Bulgakov names *Sophia*.[356] Whereas in 1917 Bulgakov had asked, "Who is Sophia?" and replied negatively that "Sophia is not God,"[357] in 1933 he put the question differently. He asked, "Who is God?" The response concerning Sophia becomes positive: "The Holy Trinity possesses a nature or an *ousia* which is not only the unfathomable depth of the life of God but also *the self-revelation of God*, and, in this sense, the *ousia* is Sophia. . . . Sophia is the plenitude of divine life and, in this sense, is the divine world."[358] But if Sophia is God in his self-revelation, if God is Sophia, Bulgakov immediately adds that the contrary is not true: "Sophia is not God."

Second, Bulgakov introduced a duality into the concept of Sophia. There are two different modes of being in its relationship to God and to the world, which he defined as divine Sophia for the divine world and created Sophia for the created world. In *The Way*, he wrote: "They are identical in their foundation, distinct according to their mode of being. The first is the pre-eternal essence in God, the second, issued from 'nothing,' is a becoming, even though for this latter Sophia is both the foundation and the final term, the entelechy."[359] Humans consisted of an uncreated spirit and a nature, created Sophia, that constitutes their body and soul. The relationship between God and mankind was thus accomplished by Sophia, present both in the creator and the creature.

Finally, this redirection towards heaven meant that apophatic theology, the phenomenology of Sophia, could not avoid a "metaphysics" of Sophia, that is, a cataphatic discourse on Being. From 1921 on, Bulgakov had adopted a mytho-logical discourse, but, confronted with attacks from the Russian Orthodox Church Outside Russia, he had been trying to mask it in a classical theological discourse. He was convinced that the Orthodox Church could no longer ignore the mytho-logical problematic of Sophia, and in *The Way* he spoke openly of the need to provide a response to the antinomy between God and the world that is not only dogmatic but also theological.[360]

This discovery led to an intensification of his thinking and a rapid expansion in his output. Between 1930 and 1935, Bulgakov produced his second trilogy, *The Lamb of God* (started in September 1931, finished in September 1932, and published in 1933), *The Paraclete* [*The Comforter*], and *The Father* (started in August 1933, finished in July 1934, and published in 1936). In 1931, he returned to his sophiological methodology by publishing a "dogmatic essay," *The Veneration of Icons*. The following year, without any reference to the Wisdom of God, he published an apologetic book entitled *On the Gospel Miracles* and a book translated into French, later English, entitled *Orthodoxy* [*The Orthodox Church*]. In *The Way*, his studies on the dogma of the Eucharist and those concerning the question of predestination (with the example of Judas Iscariot) alone take up more than 170 pages.

The Sophiological Turn

The academic address given by Bulgakov in 1932 to the assembly of professors and students of the St. Sergius Institute was entitled "On the Paths of Dogma (After the Seven Ecumenical Councils)." It was published in the February 1933 issue of *The Way*. This address could be considered the symbolic climax of the cataphatic turn in Bulgakov's thought. Just as Berdyaev, after profound reflection, discovered the intuition of meonic freedom outside of God and was thus able to objectivize the entire modernist tradition starting from Boehme, similarly, Bulgakov, having had the logical inspiration that allowed him to fully accept the living face of Sophia, suddenly turned around and went back down the road to the very sources of dogmatic reflection and then heard the deafening dialogue of his thought with itself. "On the Paths of Dogma" was probably one of his three or four most important lectures.[361]

Bulgakov began his address with a bombshell. He announced to his listeners that the seven ecumenical councils had set a sacred frontier for ecclesial theology in Christological matters. But, he added, "They should not be taken as sacred oracles separated from one another, but as a unique whole,"[362] as expressing a common desire to understand how Christ can be both the Son of God and the Son of Man. He went so far as to affirm that dogmatic development, unlike dogmatic crystallization, was the result of dialogue between theologians, among whom figure the Fathers of the Church but also heretics. Heresy is a partial truth (*hairesis*) and only becomes an error when it is affirmed for its own sake.

In his address, Bulgakov launched into a vast, tragic, epic drama. In the first act, the curtain rose on Alexandria in the fourth century. The fiery Arius began to have doubts about the unity of nature between the Father and the Son and sought to understand the relationship between God and the created world.[363] A little later, in Laodicea in Asia Minor, Bishop Apollinarius the Younger questioned how (and no longer why) the Incarnation of God was possible. Both these men were condemned as heretics by the church. In the second act, Christological intrigue entered the scene with the combat between Cyril and the Alexandrian school, who affirmed the unity of the God-Man, and Diodorus of Tarsus and the Antiochian school, who put the emphasis on the duality of the two natures, human and divine, in Christ. This opposition was fatal, Bulgakov explained, because the two schools lacked an adequate terminology to express visions that were basically identical, yet with different emphases. The two schools used the distinction, taken from the *Metaphysics* of Aristotle, between primary essence and secondary essence. Cyril, however, thought that the unity of the divine and human natures (which do not have a concrete reality) of the God-Man was realized by the Incarnation (which corresponded, in his view, to the hypostasis, Aristotle's primary essence). Diodorus separated the two natures, divine and human, because, in his view, there could not be a nature that was not a hypostasis—and this prevented him from resolving the unity of the person.[364] The second act ended with Cyril pronouncing an anathema against Diodorus.

In the third act, the Antiochians took their revenge after the failure of the Robbers' Council, which the school of Alexandria had organized against them in 449 at Ephesus. In the fourth act, there was a general reconciliation of the warring factions, thanks to the intervention of the Pope of Rome, Leo the Great. The solution consisted in distinguishing the nature from the hypostasis and thus admitting that the human nature of Christ had a sole divine hypostasis. At the Fourth Council of Chalcedon, in 451, the "dogmatic miracle" occurred as the result of a compromise. Both schools affirmed the hypostatic unity of Christ but without abolishing his two natures—which represented a victory for the school of Antioch. These two natures were "without separation, without mixture, without confusion, and without change." So there was no dogmatic synthesis. For Bulgakov, this definition was a frontier for thought, "but not the thought itself, which can only be given by a positive definition."[365]

It is for this reason that, in the fifth act, hostilities resumed between the Monophysites and the Diophysites. The Sixth and Seventh Councils (680–681 and 787, respectively) succeeded in maintaining the consensus of the church by affirming, in the one case, the primacy of the divine will over the human will and, in the second case, the possibility of venerating icons. According to Bulgakov, this continual resurgence of disputes was explained by the fact that the dogma of the union of two natures in one hypostasis, formulated in a reified terminology by the Fathers, still left room for a mechanical interpretation of this unity. Thus, for example, it was a mistake, Bulgakov argued, to imagine that it was the human nature of Christ which wept on seeing the body of Lazarus, but his divine nature which expressed itself when he raised Lazarus from the dead. Such a division of natures is a camouflaged form of Nestorianism. The problem left unresolved by the Fathers was that, in the terminology of Aristotle, hypostasis is merely the sign of an essence, while the essence in general is an aggregate of characteristics constituting a whole.

Bulgakov then put the finishing touches on his long exposé. For him, only a personal approach, which perceived the spiritual character (rather than the reified aspect) of the divine and human natures, could resolve the enigma of the divine-human person.[366] He concluded his address by challenging the assembly not to fall asleep "on the dogmatic pillow of the seven ecumenical councils."

> Our era is called to elaborate a neo-Chalcedonian theology which would revive for us the problem of the *divine-humanity*, thereby prolonging the creative work of the seven ecumenical councils in all its plenitude and complexity.... The Son of God is the Son of Man in the *unity* of his divine-human life or of his theandric energy, in a true communion of characteristics, in the accord and reunion of wills—such is the dogmatic problem of Christology for our times. Along with the four negative declarations of Chalcedon a positive dogmatic assertion should be found and formulated, and this will not happen in the context of the Alexandrian-Antiochian dispute.[367]

Bulgakov believed that he had found the key to "the enigma of Chalcedon." For him, Christ is God in his divine-human self-revelation. The divine-humanity is Sophia, the pre-eternal, celestial humanity manifested by the Divinity in humanity. Before he formulated this conclusion, Bulgakov had laid the groundwork and, above all, influenced his contemporaries' perspectives through a series of three brilliant yet pedagogical studies, originally delivered as lectures, that appeared in the review: "The Holy Grail" (written in October 1930), which we have already discussed; "The Dogma of the Eucharist" (published in two parts, February and April 1930); and "Judas Iscariot" (published in two parts, February and April 1931). All of these studies dealt with the Christological problem. Because of their novelty and surprising durability, these studies would live on as stunning revelations in the memories of a great number among Bulgakov's audience, whether students or readers, including Paul Evdokimov, Alexander Schmemann, Constantine Andronikov, Elias Melia, Nadine Fuchs, Nicolai Afanasiev, and Alexis Kniazev.[368]

In his lengthy study of the Eucharistic dogma, Bulgakov used all the techniques of a police novel, setting up a dramatic intrigue. From the start, he warned his readers that his approach to the mystery of the transformation of the holy gifts would not be a traditional one, because it was metaphysical and not merely physical. He then introduced the reader to the very heart of the enigma by explaining that "for more than a thousand years in the history of the Church, there was no need to think about a dogma for the Eucharist,"[369] but now such a task had become indispensable. Having thus engaged his readers or listeners in this divine mission, and having put them in the position of the Fathers of the Church at the time of the ecumenical councils, Bulgakov began a dialogue with Luther and Thomas Aquinas, as if they were still alive. Standing on Bulgakov's shoulders, as it were, the horrified reader suddenly grasps that if the Western Church became divided at the moment of the Reformation because neither side knew how to extricate itself from Aristotelian terminology and its distinction between *ousia* and *accidentia*, then the Eastern Church,[370] in spite of its symbolism, was also marked by the Thomistic theology of transubstantiation, of the diophysitism that suppresses the process of transformation of the accidents and only allows for a miracle on the level of abstract substance. For Bulgakov, at the time of the Reformation and Counter-Reformation there no longer was an indissoluble connection between the representations of the substance of Christ and the accidents of bread and wine, between Christ and his appearance.[371] Added to this problem was the fact that, in the doctrine of transubstantiation, it was no longer just the body and blood of Christ that were present for communion, but it was the "whole Christ" (and this contradicted the doctrine of the Ascension) that was "present" (and this contradicted the notion that communion was based on the transformation of the holy gifts).[372]

Bulgakov, sure of the effect he had produced, gave a first clue to his solution. For him, the mystery of the transformation should be approached not by asking "what" (since this register is incapable of conceptualizing the Christian representation of the antinomic relationship of identity and otherness between the earthly and the heavenly) but by asking "who." If the reflection centered on communion, on the encounter between God and humanity, the problem shifted from the question of "how" to the question of the *meaning* of this mystery of God nourishing his creature. Following Gregory of Nyssa and John of Damascus and citing his *Philosophy of Economy*, Bulgakov reminded the reader that the act of eating, of transforming the world naturally, should be understood *analogously* in the act of communion as a meta-natural—but not counter-natural—transformation of the bread into His body and of the wine into His blood (that is, His soul).[373] There was, then, no passage from one substance to another, but rather the "meta-physical" realization, by the act of communion, of the unity of the spiritual body of Christ with the substance or the Eucharistic matter of this world. Therefore, of utmost importance was that, initially, the ascension should not be understood as an astronomical departure "*substantialiter et accidentaliter*" of Christ because, aside from his otherness, Christ had demonstrated, after his resurrection (notably by eating), the identity between his earthly body and his resurrected body. According to Bulgakov, Christ was able to manifest himself through the essence but not in the essence.[374]

> The heaven to which the Lord mounted in his ascension is not a place but a state of spiritual corporality, and the same can be said of his sitting at the right hand of the Father. This means that, after leaving the world, the Lord did not cease to be a man and dispose of a body—but this body has become so spiritual that it does not impede his presence in heaven, at the right hand of the Father as before the Incarnation.[375]

Consequently, the meaning of the Eucharistic dogma was that Christ, on leaving the world, maintained a spiritual and corporeal link with it, as his own words confirm: "All authority has been given to me in heaven and on earth" (Matt. 28:18).[376] After such a demonstration, when all might seem to be resolved, Bulgakov, keeping his reader in suspense, then concluded the first part of his study with these words: "We can now focus directly on the Eucharistic dogma, on the doctrine of the transformation of the holy gifts (to be continued in the next issue)."[377]

Two months later, in April 1930, Bulgakov continued the second part of his study in the same metaphysical-thriller style. He began with a summary of the preceding episodes. Then came the dramatic turn. Bulgakov proceeded to clarify all his conclusions by a "sophiological interpretation of the Eucharistic dogma."[378] He had already mentioned the myth of the Wisdom of God in *The Way*. But for the first time, even if he was careful to distinguish the form of his presentation—traditional in the first part, modernist in the second part—Bulgakov revealed his mytho-logy to the reader, the sophiocentric logic of his theological discourse. Those who were enthusiastic about the first part of his argument were obliged to recognize the validity of the sophiological discourse underlying it.

The exposé took on a new dimension. After treating the question of "who," Bulgakov returned, for the rest of his discourse, to the question of "how" and enlarged the discussion on the Eucharistic dogma to include the celebration by all creation of a divine-human liturgy of love. This time, Bulgakov introduced the reader into the heart of the Trinitarian mystery, for the image of God in humanity signified, inversely, the human nature of the Word from the very beginning.[379] Bulgakov then revealed his mythological discovery. Just as in humanity, the body and not the flesh is the "self-revelation of the spirit," the corporality of Christ is nothing other than the self-revelation of His Spirit, that is the Glory of God, one of the biblical figures of Sophia.[380]

> [The Glory of God] is the life of the tri-hypostatic divine subject, the unique essence [*edinosushchnoi*] of the Trinity, which possesses it not just in an ideal mode, *in potentia*, but as realized in reality, *in actu*, as the absolute content, the divine world. To reject this would mean limiting the life of God to subjectivism, to potentiality, to non-being. God, living a divine life, reveals His Divinity. This Divinity in God, the Glory of God, the Sophia, is precisely this divine corporality, which not only does not contradict the spirituality of God but realizes it

absolutely. This corporality is as spiritual as the essence of God, from which it cannot be distinguished, but it is, moreover, perfectly concrete, like the figure of all figures, the organism of ideas taken not just in their ideal content but also in their real existence through the power of the Word... and of the Holy Spirit, the Giver of life.... The corporality is the unity of the idea and the figure, of the content and existence, of thought and of life, of the Word and the Spirit who reveal the Father in His double-unity [*dvuedinstve*]. It is God who reveals Himself. This corporality is the divine Wisdom, present in the Holy Trinity, as the unity of life of the Three and as the life of each of the hypostases in their distinction but also in their bond and in their unity with one another. The trace of the Figure of God in Wisdom is given immediately by the Son as figure of the Father—but this is accomplished by the Holy Spirit as the "figure of the Son." This latter is, then, "the figure of the heavenly humanity," for the corporality of God, Sophia, is eternal humanity, the essence of the Divinity. This is precisely why it is the Son of God who became incarnate and walked the earth as a cosmo-urgic hypostasis *par excellence* but through the Holy Spirit, indivisibly with him (even if the hypostasis of the Holy Spirit did not become human).[381]

For the first time in his writings, Bulgakov distinguished, without separating them, created Sophia from divine Sophia.[382] Bulgakov returned to the creation of humanity to begin the narration of this myth. He affirmed that although the human body, at the moment of its creation, already possessed in itself, through created Wisdom, all the fullness of its predestination, it was still created from "the earth." Bulgakov identified the earth here with nothingness, meaning that humanity was still powerless with respect to the forces of life, that it had to nourish itself and could still fall, that is, die.[383] After the Fall, the sophianic character of humanity changed its condition, becoming flesh. This human sophianity revealed itself and realized itself by the reunion, in Christ, of its celestial corporality (divine Sophia) and its terrestrial corporality, that of Adam prior to the Fall (created Sophia). Bulgakov, quoting St. Paul (Phil. 3:21), explained that God was able to become incarnate in humanity because of the conformity of the image and the archetype but also thanks to the *kenosis* of uncreated Wisdom, the humiliation of the divine Glory which is unceasingly contained in human flesh.[384] In this perspective, the transfiguration on Mount Tabor of the God-Man in his glory, who had become the perfect master of the fullness of the spirit, was the supreme accomplishment of the creation of the world. The resurrection was definitively possible through this total victory of the spirit over the body. By his ascension, Christ did not leave the earth but rejoined the Father in order to finish his divine-human task. The union of the heavenly body of Christ with earthly substance during the liturgy is produced by the power of the Holy Spirit, but it is possible due to the fact that the bread and wine acquire a sophianic corporality. This divinization of the bread and wine is possible because of their ontological connection to the created nature of Christ, the original connection having been distorted by the Fall.[385] Thus it is that the Body and Blood of Christ, that is, the corporality of Christ, are nothing other than divine Sophia, the Glory of God, manifested not only in God but also in creation. So it can be said that Bulgakov's sophiological turn is both antinomic, with the distinction between uncreated Sophia and created Sophia, and eschatological, with this new theodicy founded on the Incarnation and integrating the Kingdom of God into history. This new intuition of Bulgakov, developed more fully in *The Lamb of God*, consisted in regarding the life of the church, the body of Christ, as the repetition of the historical life of Christ. He concluded on an eschatological note, which revealed the full social and economic dimension (i.e., the divine economy, or plan for the world) of his Eucharistic vision:

> This transfiguration of creation, which corresponds to the second coming of the Savior, is accomplished in a mysterious fashion, i.e., in a way that only the eyes of faith can see, upon the Eucharistic substance in the Divine Eucharist. What takes place in this mystery is realized at the end of time in the whole world, which is the body of humanity, itself the Body of Christ.[386]

Bulgakov used the same stylistic procedures and the same antinomic and eschatological reasoning in his article on Judas Iscariot. But because, unlike Berdyaev, Bulgakov refused to attribute all the potentiality outside of God to Sophia, he was less comfortable when he dealt with the question of human freedom. He started from the "enigma" presented by the fact that Christ, who, being God, could not make a mistake, chose as an apostle someone who would betray him. Bulgakov resolved this in an antinomic manner by arguing that, on the one hand, Judas became a traitor *progressively* because of his religious nationalism and, on the other hand, Christ chose him as an apostle because *in his eternity* God fashioned the soul of Judas to be an apostle. According to Bulgakov, the traditional doctrine of predestination could not resolve this paradox, because its transcendence prevented it from accepting that the world could have its own freedom and activity. The relationship between God and the world, Bulgakov wrote, is "interactive."[387] It was the fruit of the relationship between God and humanity according to the two modalities of Sophia, Wisdom in the eternity of God in Himself and Wisdom in the time of God as creator. This distinction between the two Wisdoms allowed Bulgakov to elaborate a new theodicy that made sense of the possibility that Judas failed in his divine mission. To do this, Bulgakov used three key concepts: creation out of nothing, self-determination, and self-positioning.

Bulgakov, following the principles outlined in his 1917 book *The Unfading Light*, believed that God has created the world out of nothingness in the sense of *ouk on*, "which, in itself, has no creative potentiality... and cannot summon itself into being by itself but needs, for this, the creative act of the Divinity."[388] This sterility of nothingness is, nonetheless, capable of being transformed into fruitfulness on entering into contact with "the sophianic seeds of being." Nothingness thus became the "principle of created freedom," which consisted in accomplishing or opposing itself to its fully realized sophianic essence, its entelechy. Having given this liberty to humanity, God could only intervene in the world through his creature's openness to the divine action.[389] But Bulgakov rejected any idea of indeterminism. The autonomy of the world was limited by the internal norm of being, which is created Sophia.[390]

In Bulgakov's view—and he stated it rather than demonstrated it—the person, the self as image of God, at the very moment of its creation, between eternity and time,[391] had, because of the principle of created freedom, the possibility of self-determination, that is, of participating in its own creation by saying "yes" to the divine summons.[392] Bulgakov's terminology was borrowed from Schopenhauer. His originality consisted in his adding that the individual, the consciousness of one's self, had the faculty of self-positioning itself, of actualizing or not, in time, its supra-temporal choice.[393] Bulgakov concluded by suggesting that God was not able to avoid the presence of Judas alongside Christ, to the same degree that the Incarnation has a prologue in heaven. As in the story of Job, God did not want the evil. He simply let Satan have his way in view of the final glorification of Job or, in the case of Judas, for the salvation of humanity.[394] For Bulgakov, Judas, far from being a puppet, was an authentically tragic figure, torn between the divine idea of his apostolic ministry and the final choice of betrayal.[395]

The Debate in *The Way*

Bulgakov recognized the distinction made by Shestov and Florovsky between God in his identity, and Being—which he named Wisdom—but rejected the unilateral character of Being. In effect, Being for him did not exist in itself, in a non-hypostatic way. In spite of this fundamental difference in viewpoint, however, the nonconformist period of *The Way* was the time when its authors—from N. Lossky and Vysheslavtsev to Ilyin and Zenkovsky—were most disposed to assimilating the sophianic problematic into their own thinking. On the other hand, Berdyaev and Bulgakov, without calling into question their mutual admiration and friendship, did not hide their distrust of each other's thought. Their relationship of "respectful distance" merits closer study, for it is indicative of the paradoxes of mytho-logical discourse.

As he had written in 1917, in *The Unfading Light* (see Part One of this volume), Bulgakov feared the possibility that Berdyaev's thought held a temptation from Lucifer—that of making created freedom an ontological reality. In 1935, Bulgakov, in a note to Metropolitan Evlogy, repeated what he had already declared in 1917: "There is another orientation of the sophianic doctrine, which Western mystics have followed (Boehme, Pordage, etc.) and which had a certain influence on Solovyov. For my part, I have nothing to do with this."[396] For his part, Berdyaev could not accept Bulgakov's idea of a one-sided freedom. In 1930, in his study on Jakob Boehme, Berdyaev had this to say of Bulgakov: "He wants to be a theologian and not a theosophist, and that is what makes his position so difficult."[397] What Berdyaev feared most in Bulgakov's "Platonism" (as well as in the thought of Blok and Florensky) was a Sophia separated from the Logos, a Wisdom without Christ.[398]

In this respect, the correspondence between the two thinkers is eloquent. In 1934, Bulgakov wrote a letter of congratulation to Berdyaev on the occasion of the publication of his book *The Self and the World of Objects*. "By its theme, the divine-humanity, and by its intensity, your book found echoes in my own thought—often to the point of a total convergence; in general, I do not find myself in contradiction with any of your essential ideas. The best and most interesting chapter is that concerning time."[399] But Bulgakov also pointed out to Berdyaev that what he calls "philosophy" goes beyond the borders of philosophy and that, as a consequence, his work had something "incomplete" about it, because metaphysics could not grasp the spiritual nature of the person. On the other hand, Berdyaev replied that same year that he had read Bulgakov's *The Lamb of God*, which he found "remarkable" and written with great freedom on the theological level. Yet he criticized elements of "naturalist metaphysics" in Bulgakov's philosophical discourse.

Fundamentally, both thinkers suffered from a lack of comprehension of the other's work, which stemmed from their different choices of approach. Their misunderstandings were linked both to the very recent character of the renewal of the mytho-logical approach in Orthodox thought and also to the many reciprocal wounds inflicted by the two different traditions. Bulgakov's persistent fear was that the God-Man was being transformed, in philosophical discourse, into a man-god. Berdyaev was fearful, when he read theological works, that humanity, "enveloped by a divine and cosmic energy," would become "imprisoned in a 'passive beatitude.'"[400] At this stage of the development of their thought, for Berdyaev as well as for Bulgakov, it was as if the concepts each employed, whether philosophical or theological, prevented them from recognizing what they shared in common. There was a common logic behind their individual formulations of the myth of divine-humanity, their common effort to go beyond the narrow limits of their respective disciplines so as to give a dimension to language that would be closer to their vision of the God-Man. From 1930 to 1935, both were devoted to the aims of not emptying God of his nature, of not digging a trench between God and Man, and of deepening the ideas of myth, antinomy, and finitude in their thinking. Bulgakov approached, if obliquely, Berdyaev's ideas when he wrote, in his sophiological interpretation of the Eucharistic dogma, that the earthly body was "the distinctive body of humanity and of creation."[401] The antinomic character of the earth, as both the work of God and what becomes the nothingness of humanity, could open a dialogue with Berdyaev's idea of an obscure *Ungrund* both within God and outside of God. In the end, Berdyaev and

Bulgakov arrived, each in his own way, at the same hypothesis of the presence of a non-hypostatic reality-outside-of-God, whose face was both obscure and luminous. It was only in 1937 that the two would realize the antinomic character of their approach.

Conclusions

The polemical relationship between the theocentric, anthropocentric, and sophiocentric approaches could be interpreted as a result of the impossibility of finding a language capable of expressing simultaneously the dynamic truth of these three "visions" of the myth of divine-humanity, which all three attempted to articulate. However, as the example of Berdyaev and Bulgakov has shown, these tendencies of Russian thought, in spite of their diversity, should be understood as a sole movement—a sole "judgment," as Bulgakov would have expressed it during the time of his "philosophy of Crimea." All three of these approaches were focused on the mystery of divine-humanity and its formulation in contemporary discourse. Alongside the approach of Shestov, Florovsky, and Frank, which focused on God-in-his-Hypostasis, God-in-his-identity, and alongside that of Berdyaev, which was oriented towards the Person of God, God-in-his-otherness, Bulgakov concentrated on Wisdom, that is, the nature of God, which manifests the Kingdom, the Power, and the Glory as the meeting place between God and humanity.

The attempts at a synthesis undertaken by members of the younger generation who wrote in *The Way* (I. Lagovsky, Mother Maria Skobtsova, N. Afanasiev, N. Zernov, L. Zander) are a witness to this common ground. In their articles, these authors, united by a common concern for Orthopraxy, for making discourse closer to life, dealt with the myth of God simultaneously as a tri-hypostatic Person, as a Trinitarian Hypostasis, and, finally, as the self-revelation of God to Himself.

Mother Maria, for instance, in her article entitled "Birth and Creation," published in October 1931, attempted a synthesis between wisdom and freedom by using, as a point of departure, a concrete interpretation of the hypostatic principles of generation (the cosmic principle of birth) and the procession (the anthropological principle of creation) within the Trinity. In the anthropological approach there were "two subjectively opposed ways of understanding the same ontological reality."[402] For Mother Maria, the birth of a free person into the world, of the same essence as its progenitor, did not imply an innate freedom. On the contrary, every human creation, which—by definition—was free, brought forth an essence that was not free. Humanity's solution to the antinomy of its condition as created and engendered, according to Mother Maria, was to be found in the hypostasis of Christ, which was both born and noncreated, that is, of the same essence as the Father *and* completely free in respect to the Father.

I. Lagovsky, in "Salvation and Culture," published in March 1932, tried to reconcile the three currents in the journal by a reflection on the practice of faith and of creation. He retained Bulgakov's idea that the body was a reality different from the spirit but not opposed to it. Lagovsky also based himself on Berdyaev's notion of the person as a miracle of individual union, without confusion, of two bodies. Finally, along with Vysheslavtsev, Lagovsky affirmed that every manifestation of the spiritual life of a person was linked to the function of incarnation, which always gave corporality to all the acts of the intelligence or emotions.[403] According to Lagovsky, the individual, in his religious practice, brought about a twofold objectivization of the spirit: in his personal body and in the social body, which culminates in the Incarnation of God and the creation of the church. Thus, the author sought to realize a synthesis between the corporal and liturgical incarnation of the spirit by "poetic" prayer and by "philokalic" repentance, and its cultural and social incarnation by "obedient" creation and by an intelligence "open to grace." Lagovsky understood prayer as the force that prevented the spirit from fixing itself in the material and that pushed the spirit to incarnate itself in the forms which belong to it—in the rites of the church, but also in the "liturgy of the world, which takes place outside of the church."[404] Repentance, humility but also audacity, and recognition of one's divine image, these three formed the road leading both to creation and to the love of beauty. In opposition to every spirituality cut off from the world, the "sophianic work" that Lagovsky defended tried to reconcile human creation and the created world in order to prepare a new heaven and a new earth, "the Glorious Kingdom of Christ" which was coming.[405]

AN ECCLESIAL COMMITMENT OFF THE BEATEN PATH

The renewal of the theanthropic or divine-human theological debate among the Russian intellectuals, provoked in part by their rediscovery of the Christian West—from Jakob Boehme to the legends of the Holy Grail—also led in the early 1930s to increased contact with Western intellectuals who were open to spiritual questions. However, the Russian intellectuals took little part in the usual institutional networks, such as through universities, major publications, or academic colloquia. Aside from perhaps Berdyaev and Shestov, they were not well known by the public, even though they benefited from the attribution of an ambiguous prophetic halo. And they were exasperated by how little Western intellectuals knew about Russia. Thus, they tended to create their own, primarily "nonconformist," networks.[406]

These nonconformist networks will receive special treatment here. They made a major contribution by bringing together Russians and Westerners, through groups interested in the USSR and in communism, those interested in the thought of Berdyaev and Shestov, and, finally, those interested in the ecumenical question. Moreover, since our study is focused on *The Way*, in this section the generational unity of these intellectuals will be observed through their encounters with Western philosophers, theologians, and even psychologists. In spite of the plurality of networks to which they belonged, throughout their debates with Bergson, Barth, or Jung, they all posed the question of theanthropy or divine humanity. Likewise—and this will be the third aspect of our account—the commitments of the intellectuals of *The Way* to ecumenical activity also varied, depending on the ways in which they interpreted the idea of divine-humanity.

The Nonconformist Networks

The Political Scene

In the early 1930s there was a surge of sympathy for the Soviet Union and of interest in Marxism on the part of the French intelligentsia. This was manifested by the influence of two rival publications, *L'Humanité* of Paul Vaillant-Couturier and *Monde* of Brice Parain—both communist; by a pro-revolutionary fad among surrealist writers; and by the founding, in March 1932, of the Association of Revolutionary Writers and Artists (AEAR) and the Group of French-Speaking Proletarian Authors.[407] French intellectuals were no longer quite so passionate about the pre-revolutionary Russia of Tolstoy and Dostoevsky. This shift in interest explains why J. Sazonova was invited to speak about new Soviet literature at the Franco-Russian Studio on November 4, 1930. But her approach, as manifested by the title of her talk—"Religious Quests as Reflected in Soviet Literature"—did not correspond to the expectations of her audience. The meetings at the Franco-Russian Studio arranged by V. de Vogt and N. Gorodetsky lost their significance, little by little, and ended in 1932.[408] André Gide, Malraux, and Vladimir Pozner were henceforth more interested in the successes of industrialization or in social realism in literature. Fondane related that a book by Shestov on Kierkegaard, which had been authorized by J. Paulhan of the *Nouvelle Revue Française* (Gallimard), was delayed by Malraux.

> When all was said and done, the publishing house depended solely on Malraux, who had often shown respect and admiration for Shestov. Three years earlier, he had criticized Shestov for paying attention to personalities like Bergson and Husserl. He told me [Fondane] that, when he wrote *The Royal Way*, he thought about Shestov and arrived at the same conclusions as the Russian. Yet when he returned from the Congress of Soviet Writers [September 11, 1934], Malraux vetoed the publication of Shestov's book, which Paulhan had promised to publish.[409]

On February 23, 1935, while assisting at a conference on Soviet writers organized by Jean-Richard Bloch at the Union for the Truth (Union pour la Verité), and with Ilya Ehrenburg present, Berdyaev felt himself humiliated when Malraux addressed the Soviet writer as if he were the sole representative of Russian literature. Berdyaev, both chagrined and amused by what he considered naïveté on the part of the French "intellectuels,"[410] published in *The Way* deadly reviews of Emmanuel Berl's *Mort de la morale bourgeoisie* (The Death of the Bourgeois Morality) (June, 1931) and Carlo Suarez's *La Comédie psychologique* (The Psychological Comedy) (September 1934). Both authors were eminent representatives of the new generation of French intelligentsia, succeeding that of Charles du Bos, Valery, and Bergson. Berdyaev sarcastically wrote that reading Berl "gives the impression of finding one's self again in the times of Chernyshevsky and Pissarev."[411] But Berl's justification of materialism, his defense of Soviet communism, and his criticism of Christianity revealed, more seriously, for Berdyaev, "the crisis of European culture and its decadence due to the separation between the cultivated classes and the social body."[412] Likewise, the elaboration of a metaphysics of communism by Carlo Suarez, who took upon himself the task of annihilating the human self in order to dispel the illusion of individual consciences, represented, in Berdyaev's view, nothing more than the prolongation of the comedy of egocentrism resulting from original sin. "The victory over original sin," he wrote, "is not the elimination of the self but its transfiguration, its union not with the 'something' but with God and, through God, with the world."[413]

Those who were interested in the spiritual position of *The Way* came from the nonconformist milieus that questioned the established disorder and suggested a third way apart from communism and capitalism. Berdyaev was one of the principal leaders of the journal *Esprit (Spirit)*. According to a note of its founder, Emmanuel Mounier, dated December 8, 1930, it would seem that the very idea of the journal *Esprit* and the related Personalist movement took shape that same day, during a meeting at Berdyaev's house at Clamart.[414] Berdyaev observed that he took part in the first meeting of the editorial committee at the home of G. Izary.[415] His name appeared alongside those of "Jacques Copeau, Daniel Halévy, René Schwob, Jules Supervielle," and others in the letter-questionnaire that Mounier sent out to several intellectuals on June 8, 1931. His name was the only one with any authority to appear in the table of contents of the first issue of the journal, published in October 1932. Berdyaev's article, "The Truth and Lies of Communism," contributed to the journal's nonconformist tone. After reading it, Georges Izard wrote Berdyaev in a letter dated September 18, 1931: "What I find wonderful in your article is the absence, on your part, of any prejudice in your outlook and in this examination, which is only undertaken in order to safeguard the spirit. God torn away from capitalistic hypocrisy and from Bolshevist negation—it is along these lines that we also see salvation."[416] On November 27, 1932, Mounier wrote to Berdyaev:

> I ought to tell you how much enthusiasm your article aroused on all sides. It was certainly one of the articles of our first issue which drew the most attention. You have, I am sure, seen the very favorable reports in the newspapers such as *Monde*. I am certain that it helped greatly, even prior to our special issue [The Rupture between Christianity and the Bourgeois World], to eliminate any misunderstanding between ourselves and some revolutionary milieus.[417]

The article published in *Esprit* also contributed to making Berdyaev's theological-political approach to the problem better known to his French friends. A letter of Charles du Bos, dated November 14, 1932, bears witness to this: "how agreeable and precious it is for me, every time I read a new text of yours, to sense an intensification of our spiritual bond."[418] During this period, Berdyaev, considered somewhat ambiguously as "the voice of the Orthodox world" by Mounier, published another article in *Esprit* in March 1933, entitled "Russian Christianity and the Modern World." Here he took up again some of his theses on the Russian eschatological tradition from Dostoevsky to Fedorov and the thirst for the kingdom on the part of the Communists in Russia.[419]

These articles gave Berdyaev the reputation of an expert on communism in the eyes of French intellectuals, both clerical and lay. In 1932–34, four anthologies of his articles were published: *L'homme et la machine* (Man and the Machine)—which contains the title article that was published in *The Way* in May 1933—by the Protestant publishing house Je Sers; *Christianisme et realité sociale* (Christianity and Social Reality), published by Demain; *Le Christianisme et la lutte des classes* (Christianity and Class Warfare), published by Desclée de Brouwer; and *Problème du communisme*, which included "Verité et mensonge" (Truth and Lies), as well as the article published in the July 1932 issue of *The Way*, "The General Orientation of Soviet Philosophy." Invitations to give lectures on these subjects began to multiply. Thus, for example, on May 24, 1933, Fr. Octave de Roux, S.J., asked Berdyaev to give a talk on the topic "Communism and Christianity" to the students at the Institute of Engineering, rue de Varenne. On September 7, 1934, it was the turn of Fr. Michel Riquet, S.J., who invited him to give a lecture on this theme to the French Federation of Catholic Students.

There can be no doubt, as Daniel-Rops, one of the witnesses of these times, wrote in *Le monde sans âme* (The World Without a Soul),[420] that Berdyaev contributed to the surge of enthusiasm among French intellectuals for "the great light glowing in the East." In the second chapter of Maritain's *Humanisme intégral* (Integral Humanism), which appeared in 1936—the same year Gide returned from the USSR—the author made a direct reference to Dostoevsky's "The Legend of the Grand Inquisitor" in the terms used by Berdyaev. Maritain also referred to the work of Helene Iswolsky (1896–1974), another author in *The Way*, to explain the roots of Soviet atheism.[421]

In the course of the Décades de Pontigny, organized by his friend Paul Desjardins around philosophical and literary themes as well as political ones, Berdyaev was able to converse with French intellectuals about communism. There he met the Protestant Socialist André Philip, along with C. du Bos, J. Schlumberger, R. Martin du Gard, A. Maurois, L. Brunschvicg, and J. Wahl. But he also entered into contact with others, such as B. Groethuysen (half Russian, half Dutch, a "refined skeptic," according to Berdyaev), Ramon Fernandez, R. de Becker, A. Koyré, D. Mirsky, and L. Shestov. In August 1935 he participated in a ten-day meeting devoted to asceticism (his presentation reappears in the fourth chapter of his book *Esprit et realité*), where he met Martin Buber and Ernesto Buanaotti, an Italian philosopher who had been excommunicated for his modernism. Finally, Berdyaev was a frequent visitor to another circle inspired by Desjardins, the Union pour la Verité. This was an association for mutual philosophical and civic education, with headquarters on the rue Visconti, where intellectual stars of the Latin Quarter gathered—personalities such as Jean-Richard Bloch, André Malraux, Julien Benda, Paul Nizan, and Max Hermant. On June 14, 1935, before a full house, Berdyaev debated the question of social humanism with Max Hermant, the author of *Idoles allemandes* (German Idols). Earlier, on March 16, 1935, he was invited to speak, on the same program as Paul Nizan, a friend of Jean-Paul Sartre, on the topic "The Person and Communism." In his reply to the French philosopher, in which he commented at length on the works of Lenin, Berdyaev criticized communism for rejecting the divine nature of the human being. Gide then spoke up and declared, "If I do not return to the Communist Party, it is for the reason of which Berdyaev speaks."[422] In his memoirs Berdyaev related his encounter with Gide as follows:

> I met André Gide after the publication of my article "Truth and Lies of Communism" in the first issue of *Esprit*. Gide, who, at that time, was beginning to take an interest in communism, liked the article very much as he himself writes in his journal. He insisted on our getting together. Our conversation was centered on Russian communism and the relationships between communism and Christianity. It seemed to me that Gide was absolutely sincere in his interest in communism.... Gide had not read very much about social issues, he did not have much experience and was still unfamiliar with communist literature.... For all these reasons I was the more active partner during our conversation.[423]

Through his articles in the July 1933 issue of *The Way* and in *New City* in 1934, Berdyaev contributed to making *Esprit* known to young Russian intellectuals. This is attested by the enthusiastic review of the first nine issues of *Esprit* by a collaborator of *New City*, identified as "A. M. I.," in 1933. Conversely, he introduced Fedotov and Iswolsky to Mounier. On December 30, 1931, Mounier wrote to Berdyaev: "Think about sending us your friends, whether they are in France or abroad. I have not received a reply from Fedotov. What is he up to?"[424] In *The Way*, Berdyaev described *Esprit* as having three strengths: first, it categorically affirmed the primacy of the spiritual principle over political or economic principles; second, its editorial policy defined itself as interconfessional; third, it defended personalist convictions on philosophical and religious levels that translated, on the social level, into a communitarian personalism in the tradition of Proudhon and Péguy. On December 20, 1934, Berdyaev was invited by the journal *Esprit* to give a lecture on the concept of the person before an audience that included Maritain, P. L. Landsberg, and Gabriel Marcel. Two months later, with Maritain, he replied to Landsberg concerning the person and death. That same year, in an article published in *New City* entitled "The Quests for Social Justice among the French Youth," he demonstrated his perfect familiarity with the nonconformist milieu and with the divisions that had taken place just after the events of February 6, 1934, by reviewing different political journals for younger readers: *Plans*, edited by J. Fabrègues, *Ordre Nouveau*, edited by Arnaud Dandieu, Alexandre Marc, and Daniel-Rops, and *Troisième Force*, founded by Georges Izard. Berdyaev knew of these groups all the more because Alexandre Marc—whose real name was Alexandre Lipiansky, and who was a Russian Jew of socialist-revolutionary tendencies who had converted to Catholicism—was one of his faithful readers.

The Networks of Berdyaev and Shestov

As D. Lindenberg wrote, one of the principal contributions of Russian religious philosophy in France was its interest in the "theological-political." Although it is difficult to sort out the reciprocal influences, Olivier Clément has shown the profound influence of Berdyaev's articles on Mounier—not only on a political level but also in matters philosophical, especially in Mounier's definition of the person as "a presence rather than a being,"[425] his reflections on the ages of the spiritual life, and his views on the ambivalence of technology, which could be both numbing and liberating. In a famous, program-proposing article, "Reflections on the Christian Idea of the Person," published in the December 1934 issue of *Esprit*, P. L. Landsberg—one of those who had introduced German phenomenology into France—underlined Berdyaev's importance in the articulation of the personalist philosophy, especially through his dialectic of the "making present."[426]

In reality, within the two principal networks of authors of *The Way*—that of Berdyaev and that of Shestov—the majority were oriented more towards philosophy than towards politics. One of the favored spots for philosophical discussions among French intellectuals—and for integration, as far as the Russian intellectuals were concerned—was the Catholic-Orthodox seminar that took place monthly at Berdyaev's home at Clamart, with the participation of many authors of the review, such as Fedotov, Vysheslavtsev, Shestov, and Veidlé. Florovsky told his biographer that these meetings were decisive for him, since they were his first experience of ecumenical dialogue. It is there that he became acquainted with Myrrha Lot-Borodin and, later, her husband Ferdinand Lot, a professor of medieval history at the Sorbonne. Florovsky's writings represented the first attempts at the elaboration of a neo-patristic synthesis. He stated, of the meetings: "There was the group of liberals, gathered around Berdyaev, and, in the other corner, there were the conservatives headed by Maritain and myself."[427]

Unlike preceding encounters during the 1920s, which, given the presence of Protestants, had a confessional character, the seminar organized by Maritain and Berdyaev was planned more as an open circle dedicated to philosophical and theological studies. Beginning in 1931, the two philosophers invited Étienne Gilson, Fr. Altermann (who had converted Mauriac, du Bos, and G. Marcel), Jean de Menasce, and Fr. Yves Congar to attend. The minutes of these meetings, taken by Count Jean de Pange, showed the impact of Berdyaev's ideas on the French intelligentsia. After Olivier Lacombe's December 16, 1930, lecture, "The Intellect and the Principle of Identity," Pange recorded that "Berdyaev pointed out that the happiest discovery of Hegel had been that one could only move as a result of contradiction. He thus introduces a dynamic into the dialectic. The principle of identity leads only to immobility. The mystery of non-being, which sets up the contradiction.... Take up again these doctrines in a study on corporation in scholasticism."[428] In discussing the lecture of Fr. Augustin Jakubiziak on May 5, 1931, entitled "Free Will and Predestination," Pange noted that "Berdyaev does not like the expression 'free will'... as it only leaves a freedom of choice and excludes creation.... Deep down, Christianity is not monotheistic but Trinitarian, and this notion must be reincorporated into Creation."[429] From Pange's notes, it can be seen that the principal bone of contention between Berdyaev and the French intellectuals is the question of uncreated freedom, which, as we have seen, he had reformulated during this period. On May 13, 1930, Berdyaev, in a presentation entitled "Negative Theology and German Mysticism," submitted his theses, published a few weeks earlier in his article on Boehme, to his Russian and French guests. Pange summarized:

> Boehme already had the idea of the necessity of the opposition of contraries, that nothing can develop without resistance. He postulates the *Ungrund* (which should not be translated, as Koyré did, by "Absolute" but rather by "Undetermined"). He also has the idea of the primacy of Liberty over Being, an idea especially dear to Berdyaev.... In order to disassociate God from any responsibility in human decadence, it must be supposed that the gift of liberty is not gratuitous but necessary, that prior to the world and to Being, there was not nothingness [*le néant*] but rather Freedom. Freedom is necessary to the order of the world. Like death, it is both the greatest evil and the greatest good. These ideas of Berdyaev provoked a great commotion in our little meeting place. Both the French and the Russians rose to their feet, all talking at the same time.[430]

Since Jacques Maritain was not able to present his own views at the meeting, due to all the controversy, he decided to write Berdyaev the very next day:

> The *Ungrund* is my main objection in this doctrine since it seeks in God something more profound than God Himself has revealed about Himself and His inner life.... Actually, Boehme postulates a human idea, myth, symbol, or concept—whatever you want to call it—the idea of *Ungrund* above and beyond all the dogmatically revealed truths and above and beyond the divine idea (the idea of the Holy Trinity). Thus it falls in the extremities of cataphatic theology.[431]

The debate continued throughout the 1930s. On March 24, 1931, Berdyaev presented his guests with his views on the topic "The Religious Anthropology of Max Scheler." He used the occasion to return to the theme of theodicy. Jean de Pange wrote in his notes:

> Is the history of the world only soteriology? After the Fall, however, there was the Incarnation, the new Adam. Since St. Augustine, we think of freedom only as the possibility to sin or not sin—but we do not think of it as creative of positive values.... Preexistence of freedom in relationship to humanity, this freedom being rooted in some way in the nothingness from which humanity was drawn forth.... Gabriel Marcel is afraid of the consequences of Berdyaev's hypothesis. Maritain: The problem of salvation is not so much escaping from sin as becoming God.[432]

Among the French intellectuals attracted by Berdyaev's ideas about Boehme was Jean Wahl (1888–1974), who first encountered Berdyaev in 1929 by reading his work *L'esprit de Dostoevski*. Berdyaev sent him his article on Boehme. In an undated letter, written in Lyon, Wahl described his reaction:

> You have brought out his antinomic thought and his "quite theological consciousness" in a very interesting way. From Boehme and even from Heraclitus up to Dostoevsky, you trace this itinerary which has always attracted me—thinkers who are not Apollonians nor even Dionysians, because their mysteries, where evil has its place, come from a world perhaps still more profound.[433]

The Sunday afternoon meetings at Berdyaev's home brought together primarily Russian, French, and German intellectuals, but there were also Venezuelans, Americans, and Indians who attended. On Sunday, November 11, 1934, Berdyaev introduced to Gabriel Marcel not only Raïssa Maritain, Vera Maritain, and Shestov, but also Marina Tsvetaeva, who read her poems, Helene Iswolsky, and André Karpov. On Sunday, December 23, 1934, Pierre Pascal, along with Mochulsky, Lazarev, Ilnitsky, and L. Krestovskaya, assisted at the habitual duel between Shestov and Berdyaev, or, as Lydia Judifevna put it, "between the Old and the New Testament." In 1934–35, Berdyaev also organized soirées at his house for young Russians and Frenchmen affiliated with *Esprit*, around themes such as morality. Moreover, Fritz Lieb and his friend Fritz Heinemann, a German philosopher expelled by Hitler's regime, regularly updated Berdyaev's Russian friends on the situation in Germany. On Sunday, February 3, 1935, the principal topic of discussion was, once again, the situation in Germany. The Landsbergs were present, along with Jules Cain, the director of the National Library, his wife, who was Berdyaev's translator, and Alekseev. Three weeks later, Paul Anderson and Donald Lowrie came to speak on the economic and spiritual situation in the United States. M. Lot-Borodin, M. Turgeneva, and H. Iswolsky were also present.

After the publication (in their French translations) in March 1933 of *Esprit et liberté* (*Spirit and Freedom*) and then of *De la destination de l'homme* (*The Destiny of Man*) in 1935 by the publishing house Je Sers, books in which Berdyaev formulated a number of his metaphysical theses, his audience continued to grow and, more importantly, allowed him to move outside exclusively Thomistic circles. On June 17, 1933, Léon Brunschvicg honored him with the prestigious Charles Lambert award of the Institut de France. After this date, the names of François Mauriac, Henri Corbin, Benjamin Crémieux, Henri Bergson, Emile Bréhier, Pierre Leyris, Eugène Porret, and Jean de Rougemont can be found in Berdyaev's correspondence. Maritain delayed his reply to Berdyaev's head-on criticism of Thomism in *Esprit et liberté*. When he finally responded on December 23, 1933, it was to express his regrets that Berdyaev, by affirming the primacy of freedom over Being, was putting his talent at the service of the "destruction of metaphysics."[434] From this time on, the two remained friends but avoided discussing metaphysical questions. On January 1, 1935, Berdyaev celebrated the new year at the home of the Maritains and met Marc Chagall. The following month, it was the turn of the Maritains to visit the Berdyaevs, along with F. Lieb, to debate the necessity of unity among Christians in the struggle against evil. In Berdyaev's archives there was nothing more from Maritain except a brief postcard from Argentina, dated October 23, 1936, in which he spoke of his "very great friendship" and signed it "Your Jacques Pavlovitch."[435]

On the other hand, René Le Senne, who was already familiar with the "beautiful article on Boehme," reacted with enthusiasm. Le Senne (1882–1954), a former professor at the Lycée Victor Duruy (where he awakened Simone Weil's interest in philosophy), then professor of preparatory courses (*khâgne*) at Marseille, had become a professor in the chair of ethics at the Sorbonne and a member of the Academy of Ethical and Political Sciences. In 1934, with Louis Lavelle, he founded the collection "Philosophie de l'Esprit" at the publishing house Aubier. Alongside his book *Obstacle et Valeur*, which appeared that same year, Aubier published the French translation of the principal works of Berdyaev, Solovyov, and Frank. Le Senne, a moralist, shared Berdyaev's battle against "ontism" [with its emphasis on mere factual or physical reality] and gave added value to the role that Berdyaev had attributed to creation—that is, the role of "keeping the spirit on fire." It is worthwhile to quote some passages from the letter he wrote to Berdyaev on April 19, 1933, for this letter is one of the best examples of Berdyaev's impact:

> I think that the truth is theandric—and this I believe as sincerely as you do. The reality is not God and I—it is God with me, that is, a relationship between two free persons that always animates our life as long as we do not passively hand ourselves over to nature. This spiritual ontologism excludes both a theological monophysitism, which would reduce us to the condition of a cadaver, and a naturalistic humanism, which would produce the same effect since the individual would be nothing more than an undisputable fragment of determinism.
> ... it is essential to show human freedom in the face of confessional servitude or materialism....
> ... I am still convinced that there is a true mythology. That is why I do not like Bergson's term 'fabulation' which seems to discredit what he recognizes.
> ... I am in complete agreement with the symbolic signification of nature and history.
> ... what you write concerning freedom and free will is very interesting.
> ... everything you have to say about the mediocrity of our modern art in which the spirit is absent, about not seeking an official union of the Churches but to wait upon the unorganized collaboration of free spirits, about the opposition of the bourgeois spirit in religion, the religion of custom, the social level and spiritual aristocratism on the personal level ... all these ideas and so many others seem to me to be profoundly true.[436]

Le Senne's single reservation with respect to Berdyaev's thought was, however, a weighty one, and it was typical of the view held by most French intellectuals towards Eastern philosophy. Once again, it was a question of Berdyaev's eschatology. "I'll admit that I find eschatology repugnant," Le Senne wrote. It is as if the French philosopher feared that by recognizing "a freedom ablaze" at the beginning of the cosmos, he would see all the fruits of culture and science, all forms of specifically human intelligence, disappear in the fire of the *Parousia*, the second coming of Christ. Maurice de Gandillac, in his review of *Esprit et liberté* in *Esprit*, concluded that, for Berdyaev, the created world was only an "ossification" of the spirit.[437] He preferred the scholastic approach of Thomism used by Maritain in his *Degrees of Knowledge*, where the proper value of science and created reality, with their distinctions and hierarchies, were more in evidence.

Mounier also preferred to rely on Thomistic cosmology, where materiality exists in an irreducible and autonomous manner, rather than venture into "the pallid universe of Boehme and Eckhart."[438] Mounier went so far as to postulate that "Shestov takes over from Dostoevsky and the iconoclasts of the East."[439]

Although Shestov sought to establish contacts mainly with philosophers and savants—Meyerson, Husserl, Buber, Einstein (whom he met in Berlin in 1927)—the French intellectuals who were interested in him were, above all, literary critics.

Among the friends of Shestov living in Germany were Edmund Husserl, Count Hermann von Keyserling, Martin Buber, and Richard Kroner. Keyserling met Berdyaev in 1923 and Shestov in 1926. In July 1932, he sent his book *South American Meditations* to his two Russian friends. Berdyaev reviewed it in *The Way*. He admitted that he felt more affinity with the emotional and passionate style of his German friend than with the intellectual and sensorial style of writers such as Proust or Gide. Berdyaev distanced himself from the earth-based cosmology of Keyserling, which he found infected by naturalism. But he was seduced by the "intuitive" thought of the German writer, who relied on symbols more than on concepts.

Shestov met Husserl on April 23, 1928, at the congress of the Philosophical Society of Amsterdam. Although they were very opposed on a philosophical level, they immediately became friends and saw one another again several times between 1928 and 1930. On November 9, 1928, Shestov gave a talk on Tolstoy in Freiburg, which both Husserl and Heidegger attended. Shestov was disappointed by his conversation with Heidegger. The two met again on June 22, 1930. On the other hand, Shestov became friends with Buber, whom he met in May 1928 in Frankfurt, through Max Scheler. Buber immediately published Shestov's article on Spinoza in his review *Kreatur*. Shestov and Buber also corresponded in 1933 concerning an article on the German theologian that Shestov was preparing. They saw one another again when Buber visited Paris in 1934. In France, unlike Germany, Shestov's studies of Dostoevsky, Tolstoy, and Pascal attracted attention, while his philosophical considerations (beginning with his study on Plotinus in 1924, he hardly wrote anything except philosophical essays) left most French intellectuals perplexed. Two exceptions were Gabriel Marcel[440] (for a while) and Lucien Lévy-Bruhl, whom Shestov met at the house of P. Boyer and who invited him to collaborate with *Revue philosophique de la France et de l'Etranger*. This perplexity was common in spite of two channels for Shestovian thought in France, namely, the writings of B. de Schloezer[441] and B. Fondane,[442] and in spite of the fact that Shestov was integrated into the most exclusive philosophical societies. In 1924 he became a member of several prestigious associations of Kantian and Nietzschian studies in Germany; he published his articles in German in *Logos*, the review of his friend Richard Kroner. On October 23–25, 1930, he participated in the congress of The International Society for Cultural Cooperation at Krakow, where he gave a talk, in French, entitled "The Sources of Metaphysical Truths."

The enthusiastic acclaim that Shestov received at the beginning of the 1920s for his literary criticism determined, in large measure, his reception in France. In 1920–21, Shestov was published in two prestigious literary reviews: *Le Mercure de France* and, later, *La Nouvelle Revue Française*. His works appeared in the collection Cahiers Verts of Daniel Halévy of Grasset Books, in the editions Plon of C. du Bos, in the "Editions of the Century" of Jules de Gaultier, and, finally, in the editions Pléiade of Jules Schiffrin. In 1923 and 1924 he was invited to the literary meetings of Pontigny. His network of acquaintances was framed by A. Gide and J. Rivière, and then, in the 1930s, by J. Paulhan of the *Nouvelle Revue Française*. In December 1932, Paulhan published an article of B. de Schloezer about Shestov and Wahl in *Cahiers du Sud*, which, between 1932 and 1935, also published three studies of Shestov by B. Fondane. Shestov knew how to employ this network, to which the group of Jewish intellectuals of the review *Palestine* could be added, as well as the young Russian nonconformists organized around the review *Les Cahiers de l'Etoile* of I. de Manziarli, particularly for the purpose of publishing in French the articles that Shestov wrote for *The Way*, but also to help many of Shestov's friends, from Ivan Bunin to Adolf Lazarev. In 1930 he supported the candidacy of Bunin for the Nobel Prize in literature and proposed him to Thomas Mann and the jury of Stockholm. (The Russian writer would receive this award in 1933.) In 1931 he introduced Lazarev, who lived in Strasbourg, to Berdyaev, with the hope of getting his work published in *The Way*. His first article in *The Way*, in fact, was published in 1932 (L4).

But when Fred Lefèvre, a reporter from the weekly *Nouvelles Littéraires*, with a circulation of 250,000, came to visit Shestov on October 24, 1931, for an article to be entitled "Une heure avec Léon Shestov," the only thing they discussed was literature.

The Ecclesial Networks

Pierre Andreu, a friend of Max Jacob and Marcel Péguy, whose name appears in nearly all of the nonconformist reviews of the 1930s, recounted in his memoirs that he was deeply moved by the "originality of Russian Christianity." He cited in particular Shestov's *The Night of Gethsemane* and Berdyaev's *The Spirit of Dostoevsky*.[443] This proximity of clergy and intellectuals in France during the early 1930s justifies the application of the notion of "nonconformist network" to the ecumenical networks of the Russian intellectuals of the Boulevard Montparnasse and rue de Crimée. Indeed, the feeling of urgency about ecumenical dialogue, which had prevailed within this active minority of the Russian Orthodox Church since the First World War and the Russian Revolution, the desire to find a solution to the "established disorder" represented by the division of the churches, and the attempts to build "molecular relationships"—according to the typically nonconformist expression used by Bulgakov at Chantilly in 1933[444]— shed new light on the extent of the nonconformist spirit in the 1930s.

The founding, in 1929, of the journal *Orient und Occident* by the Swiss Lutheran theologian Fritz Lieb, with the cooperation of Berdyaev, included German translations of some of the articles of *The Way*. It was among the initiatives hailed by both Florovsky and Vysheslavtsev. On receiving the fourth issue of the German review in February 1931, Vysheslavtsev wrote:

"The Russians are no longer astonished by the West's constant misunderstanding of the 'Russian question.' What astonishes us is when we find understanding or even a desire to understand."[445] Significantly, *Orient und Occident*, the younger sister review of *The Way*, appeared at a time between the two world wars when mutual interest among Russian and German intellectuals was at its highest point. This interest subsequently died out. In the 1929–34 period, *Orient und Occident* was published in seventeen issues, then another three in March and October 1936, before going out of business.[446]

One of the main networks for encounter and integration among the younger Orthodox writers was the Protestant Federation of France, whose headquarters was in Paris and whose review, *Le Semeur* (The Sower), published texts by Zander, Berdyaev, and Paul Evdokimov. On the Continental level, the main network was the World Student Christian Federation. Visser't Hooft, the very energetic general secretary of the World Student Christian Federation, multiplied initiatives. He invited Berdyaev to Bad Bol in Austria in May 1931, participated in the same year in the conference of the Fellowship of St. Alban and St. Sergius at High Leigh, and organized a seminar on ecumenical dialogue held on August 22–28 at Saldus in Latvia, in which Lagovsky and Zenkovsky participated. These contacts intensified when, in August 1935, during a meeting of the general committee at Chamcoria in Bulgaria, the Russian Student Christian Movement became a full member of the federation.

But the early 1930s was also a period of intense exchanges between Orthodox and Protestant theologians, thanks to the two commissions of the movements Faith and Order, and Life and Work (discussed in Part One). Beginning in 1934, these commissions worked closely together within an Ecumenical Council due to the effects of the economic crisis and the political and religious situation in Germany. During the period 1931–34, N. Arseniev and N. Zernov frequently traveled to northern European countries in their work for these two commissions. On the occasion of the ecumenical conference of the Life and Work group, which took place on April 8–14, 1934, in Paris (St. Germain) on the theme "Church and State: The Nature, Foundations, and Limitations of the Authority of the State," the authors of *The Way* who taught at St. Sergius (representing the Orthodox Church)—namely, Bulgakov, Florovsky, Vysheslavtsev, Fedotov, and Kartashev—had the opportunity to talk with a great number of theologians from all over the world: V. Demant, A. Lecerf, A. Garvie, E. Brunner, W. Menn, A. Runestam, and Max Huber. The Russian theologians demonstrated their common nonconformist position by unanimously condemning any type of nationalism (although not the idea of a nation), be it left-wing or right-wing. Their declaration stated:

> Political and even religious difficulties result from the complex relations between the Church and the Christian Nation. Doubtless nationalism, no less than communism, is one of the most terrible demonic forces of our times. And yet at the basis of our nationalism we find the nation, an organic and spiritual unity, forming a cultural entity of its own.[447]

This meeting was immediately followed by a Life and Work conference at Fanø, Denmark, on August 24–30, 1934, in which Pastor Boegner, Zernov, and Vysheslavtsev took part. During this conference, which took place three months after Karl Barth pushed for resistance to Nazism in his theological declaration of Barmen, a conflict broke out between Ludwig Müller, the new head of the Church of the Reich, and G. K. A. Bell, the bishop of Chichester and the president of the commission, who sided with the Evangelical Church of Germany on the question of racism.

Vysheslavtsev had the opportunity to meet Barth during the second international theological seminar, founded in 1934 by the secretariat of the Ecumenical Council. Eighty-five pastors and students, representing nineteen countries and nine churches, assembled in Geneva from July 22 to August 9, 1935. They heard talks by—among others—M. Dibelius (of Heidelberg), Karl Barth (Basel), A. Keller (Geneva), A. C. Bouquet (Cambridge), H. Lilje (Berlin), W. Visser't Hooft (Geneva, general secretary of the World Student Christian Federation), and F. Lieb (Basel—on the eschatology of Solovyov). According to *The Gazette of Lausanne*, in its issue of August 25, 1935,

> Professor Vysheslavtsev of the Orthodox Academy of Paris gave a brilliant presentation on Christian anthropology from an Orthodox point of view. He studies the different layers of the human personality, which reproduce those of the cosmic hierarchy. The microcosm is similar to the macrocrosm. But, unlike contemporary psychology, he explains

the inferior by the superior. This theme, by the way, is one which will be studied at the 1937 conference [at Edinburgh on the people, the state, and the church].[448]

For his part, Florovsky was invited in 1931 by Barth, whom he had met through Faith and Order, to his seminar at the University of Bonn, where he gave a lecture entitled "Revelation, Theology, and Philosophy," based on his article "Theological Fragments," which had been published in *The Way* and had provoked some lively discussions.

Berdyaev, although he did not officially represent the exarchate of the patriarchate of Moscow, was also an active participant in the ecumenical encounters with the Protestant and Anglican worlds—especially during the summer of 1935. In June he gave a talk at Geneva to the Ecumenical Council entitled "An Evaluation according to the Christian Conscience of the International Efforts of the Churches," and in July he joined his friends André Philip and Suzanne de Dietrich at a conference in Swanwick, England, centered on social and industrial problems. There he spoke on the topic "The Nature of Christian Social Action."

A twofold phenomenon could be discerned in the Roman Catholic Church. Whereas in France, the Catholic Church was experiencing a "golden age of intellectual activity" and an ecumenical renewal, in Rome, especially within the Pro Russia Commission but also in other institutions directly controlled by the Vatican, there was a more belligerent attitude towards the Russian immigrants as a result of the change of policy regarding Russia on the part of Pius XI in 1930. In 1930, Afanasiev reacted sharply and gave a masterful presentation on the conciliar nature of Orthodox ecclesiology to the Catholic theologians meeting in Velehrad (published in *The Way*, A1). Berdyaev felt himself obliged to give the right to reply to G. Bennigsen, a Catholic Russian immigrant living in England, who was offended by certain remarks of Polotebneva concerning the veneration of St. Francis of Assisi in Italy. For his part, Fedotov, in 1932, deplored the fact that the Belgian Benedictine review *Irénikon* had adopted a "pro-Uniate" position. In fact, in his reviews of articles in *The Way*, Clément Lialine, a Russian Benedictine, was becoming increasingly critical of them. Even when Bulgakov advocated the union of the Orthodox Church with the Catholic Church, the Benedictine monk adopted a triumphalist attitude and criticized the article that the Russian theologian wrote on the Eucharistic dogma. Lialine wrote: "In his [Bulgakov's] eyes, the efficacy of the sacraments *ex opere operato* has lost its irreligious magical character."[449] But this hardening of the Roman Church, always on the fringes of the ecumenical movement, did not alter the relationship of profound veneration on the part of Russian intellectuals towards the great tradition of Catholic spirituality, as evidenced by the articles of E. Belenson on feminine Catholic mysticism—from Melanie Calva of La Salette to Therese Neumann (B5); of Zenkovsky on the importance of a charitable sensitivity and the social implication of Catholic Christians, especially in the suburbs outside the big cities (Z29R); or of the young student A. Glazberg, who, full of wonder, described his stay at the Cistercian Abbey of Sept-Fons (G4). Conversely, the review *Irénikon* published a long study by K. Pfleger entitled "The Orthodox Gnosis of Berdyaev," which summed up the discreet attraction to Orthodoxy in certain Catholic circles.

> A defense of Berdyaev the schismatic? Of course not—but perhaps a discreet and—alas—insufficient defense of Berdyaev the Christian Gnostic. For although his gnosis cannot be accepted in all its details by the Catholic conscience, that does not stop us from doing justice to Berdyaev in his struggle for the justification of a Christian gnosis and, above all, a Christian Orient.[450]

The renewal of the Catholic Church in France was notably manifested by the openness to Orthodoxy among many Catholic intellectuals and clerics. In the circles associated with *Esprit*, Etienne Borne, who, at that time, lived at the Thiers Foundation, induced a group of students from l'École Normale to read Berdyaev. On April 24, 1932, he organized a lecture by Berdyaev on Orthodox spirituality. On October 17, 1933, the Dominican Yves Congar invited Berdyaev to speak on a subject of his choice at the Saulchoir near Tournai.[451] In his memoirs, Zernov thought that the principal contribution of the young Russians to the ecumenical movement was to enlist Abbé Paul Couturier (1881–1953) in the cause of ecumenism. In 1934, Couturier would launch the first Week of Prayer for Christian Unity.[452] *The Way* contributed to making known this renewal. When the book of the Belgian Jesuit Fr. Emile Mersch, *The Mystical Body of Christ*, appeared in 1933, with its ecclesiology centered, in the first volume, on Greek patristic texts, *The Way* published an enthusiastic review by Lot-Borodin.

Although she gently complained that Fr. Mersch seemed unacquainted with the work of Maximus the Confessor, she stated, "Every true Christian will joyfully endorse the remarkable words Fr. Mersch uses as a conclusion: 'Between the Incarnate word and any Christian in the Church which contains Christ ... there is a mystical, transcendent, supernatural union which God alone can make known, just as He alone can bring it about.'"[453]

Bulgakov's archives include two letters written in the spring of 1934, shortly after the appearance of the French translation of his book entitled *The Orthodox Church*. One is from Fr. Valentin Breton, a Franciscan priest and theologian living in Paris, the other from Fr. Martin Jugie, a priest of the Augustinians of the Assumption and professor of Oriental theology at the Atheneum of the Lateran at Rome and at the Catholic Institute of Lyon. Fr. Breton sensed a palpable "antipathy"[454] towards Catholicism on the part of Bulgakov and, provoked by his own reading of the Orthodox theologian's doctrinal presentation, set forth his "case of conscience":

> You categorically affirm that the Orthodox Church is the only true Church; you intend this word to have an exclusive meaning. May Christ be my witness that, in order to follow Him, I am ready to abandon everything in this world, and I think I am able to say that, through his holy grace—to Him benediction and thanksgiving!—I have left behind everything, not only by my monastic profession but also through the daily renouncements where I have given up even the meaning of my life.... As a Roman Catholic, am I not in Orthodoxy? Is not the Church the true Church of Christ? Does it not have the evangelical faith, the apostolic succession, the hierarchy, the sacraments, the witness of the Spirit and holiness? ... Can it not have its liturgy and its *theologoumena*, including, if the infallible conciliarity of its faithful approve them, its doctrine concerning the Pope and the Immaculate Conception of the All-Holy and Blessed *Theotokos*?[455]

Bulgakov replied to the Franciscan priest immediately, assuring him that he never questioned the fact that the Church of Rome was a true Church of Christ but held that it was not the only one, and invited Breton to visit him at the St. Sergius Institute. On March 21, 1934, Breton replied, declining the invitation but thanking Bulgakov for his letter:

My conscience can now be at peace; I can entrust myself to my Church and its interpretation of God's Word just as you confide in your Church. This is a practical solution we can both live with. As for knowing whether Christ has established a foundation on which you and I can come together in unity, that is a theoretical solution which I've forbidden myself to touch upon.[456]

Fr. Martin Jugie was known to the Russian philosophers, and Bulgakov considered him as one of the very best Western specialists on the Christian East. This is why he wasted no time in replying when, on May 2, 1934, Jugie, who had just finished a book to be published by Alcan, asked Bulgakov to send him his works so that he could study them systematically. On May 10, 1934, Fr. Jugie acknowledged the reception of the copies sent by Bulgakov and told him of his Roman Catholic vision of church unity. He brushed aside "childish quarrels" with a sweep of the hand: "It seems to me," he wrote, "that the old Byzantine schism, due, above all, to the scorn of the Byzantines for the Barbarians of the West, makes no sense in our day and age."[457] Next, Jugie lamented the fact that the Russians were attracted to Anglicanism, "whose *Prayer Book* contains notorious heresies." He concluded with an appeal to return to the house of the Father: "Doesn't the actual fragmentation of Orthodoxy suggest some useful reflections on the necessity of a common center of unity, that evoked by St. Irenaeus, the bishop of Lyon?"

The Jesuits Henri de Lubac and Hans Urs von Balthasar were also attentive readers of Bulgakov's theses on Catholic "Christomonism" and, especially near the end of the 1930s, both gave a more important role to the Holy Spirit in their sacramental theology.[458]

As can be seen by the abundant correspondence between Bulgakov and his Anglican friends—Bernard Pares, Geoffrey Curtes, and Charles Gillett—he felt a genuine attraction to the Anglican Church. The Russians were very moved by the support, both spiritual and financial, of Cosmo Lang, the archbishop of Canterbury, and a great number of the Anglican faithful for the persecuted Christians of Russia, as well as the Russian immigrants. This support was of great importance for the St. Sergius Institute. At the invitation of his American Anglican friends, who were disposed to find new financial sources for him, Bulgakov traveled twice to America (New York and Chicago) from September to November 1934 and from September to December 1936. He wrote of his journeys in his *Autobiographical Notes*, referring to his "revelation of Sophia in the ocean,"[459] but also to his many meetings with the board of the YMCA (P. Anderson, E. MacNaughten, Colton), with his Russian émigré friends (M. Rostovtsev at Yale, M. Karpovich at Harvard), and with Archbishop Athenagoras, the head of the Greek churches in America and future Patriarch of Constantinople. He also gave lectures on communism and Orthodoxy in Episcopalian seminaries, colleges, institutes, and churches. The Fellowship of St. Alban and St. Sergius was also at the origin of the postwar American career of Florovsky, who went on speaking tours in Anglican colleges nearly every year, beginning in 1933. He was also invited to Scotland several times, beginning in 1935.

The Anglican Church, which was in the midst of a religious renewal thanks to exceptional personalities such as bishops Frere and Gore, went so far as to consider, during the conference of Lambeth in June 1930, the question of sacramental union with the Orthodox Church. In the course of this meeting, to which the theologians depending on the Russian diocese under the protection of Constantinople were not invited, but in which N. Arseniev participated, alongside the Patriarch of Alexandria, a decisive step was taken in the ancient history of the relations between the two churches. Arseniev would write a report of the conference for *The Way*. The Orthodox delegation affirmed that it was satisfied that the apostolic succession had been maintained in the Anglican Church, since both churches had the same doctrine concerning the sacraments and the hierarchy (A39). But at a second conference at Lambeth, on October 14–21, 1931, the Orthodox theologians, for the most part Greek Orthodox, posed—in a "scholastic and non-Johannine" spirit, as Arseniev put it[460]—new conditions concerning the veneration of icons and of the Virgin Mary. With this, the hopes of rapidly arriving at full sacramental communion between the two churches fell through. All the same, these two conferences, held at the highest levels, constituted an additional stage in the process of the reconciliation of the Orthodox and Anglican Churches.

It is in this context that the meetings of the Fellowship of St. Alban and St. Sergius took place. Karpov gave reports of these sessions in *The Way* in 1930 and 1931. On April 25–30, 1930, a conference on holiness was held at High Leigh in England, with the participation of the Archbishop of Canterbury, Metropolitan Evlogy, S. Bezobrazov (with a talk entitled

"St. Paul and Holiness"), Bulgakov ("The Church—Holy and Conciliar"), Bishop Frere, Georges Florovsky ("The Appeal of the Sermon on the Mount"), G. Fedotov ("The Typology of Holiness"), and S. Chetverikov ("The Ways of Salvation"). On April 16–23, 1931, the fifth conference of the Fellowship had as its theme "the Church." Talks included Bulgakov's "Commentary on the Nicene Creed," Florovsky's "Freedom and Authority in the Church," Rev. Crum's "The Anglican Church as Historical Manifestation," Dr. Good's (a professor at Oxford) "Freedom and Authority in the Church," A. Kartashev and Prof. Kirk's "Church and State," and Canon Douglas's "The Lambeth Conference."

The sixth Anglo-Russian conference was held in London, as an exception, on March 30–April 4, 1932, on the theme "The Lord and Giver of Life." Participants included Anderson, MacNaughten, Visser't Hooft, Berdyaev (with the talk "Christianity and Communism"), Bulgakov, Fedotov, T. Baimakova, Xenia Braikevitch (secretary of the fellowship), Florovsky, Zernov, Zander, G. Henriod, and 127 guests, of whom ninety were Anglo-Irish and thirty were Russian.

Given the growing number of participants, the organizers decided to divide the conferences between those for students and those reserved for nonstudents. On June 23–27, 1933, the seventh (nonstudent) conference began at High Leigh with Bulgakov's presentation "The Eucharist and the Problems of Contemporary Society" as the principal lecture. This was followed, on June 27–29, by a congress with Bulgakov, whose lecture "By Jacob's Well" was later published in a collection by the YMCA Press.

On June 22–26, 1934, the eighth conference of the Fellowship returned to the theme of the Church. Several Greek, Romanian, and Old Catholic guests were present at this conference. Also among the 120 participants were O. Clarke, Nicholas Behr, Veidlé, and Lieb. The speakers were Florovsky, Bulgakov, H. Kelly (with a talk entitled "On the Universal Church"), the bishop of Gloucester ("The Structure and Nature of the Church"), and Kartashev ("The Church in Its Historical Realization," which was published in the June 1935 issue of *The Way*). On this occasion, Nicolas Zernov, who had been living in London for several years, became general secretary of the Fellowship and would remain in this position until 1947. He began by transforming its review, *The Journal of the Fellowship*, into a more important one, renamed *Sobornost'*. At the ninth conference on June 22–28, 1935, the theme was "God, Man, and Society," with the participation of two hundred guests. The principal speakers were Berdyaev, Florovsky, Relton (University of London), and Oldam. During this final conference, it was decided to organize, for the first time, a meeting of the Fellowship in France, at Bièvres, in December 1935 and, also for the first time, to plan for the concelebration of a liturgical service between Bishop Frere and Metropolitan Evlogy.

In view of the extent, formation, and hierarchical structure of the networks of the authors of the review, the following general hypothesis can be advanced concerning the processes of intellectual reception. These could well be the result of the appropriateness between the unconscious desire to accede to the savior prototype and the capacity of another to resemble the representation of this prototype. To put it more simply—if, among the political writers of the review, neither the monarchists, nor the radical anti-communist Vysheslavtsev, nor the liberal-democrat Frank were invited to participate in the arena of French intellectual debates, essentially this was because the only nonconformist discourse concerning Soviet reality was that of Berdyaev. Equally, if Berdyaev and Shestov were listened to with so much interest by the French intellectuals, it was not because of the originality of their thinking—both complained, throughout their lives, of having been misunderstood—but rather because they assumed a role of channeling German philosophy and the Byzantine patristic tradition within a tradition of Cartesian and Thomistic thought which was, at that time, in a situation of crisis and disintegration. In France, Shestov was the first to ask the Sorbonne to invite Husserl to Paris (February 1929) and the first to publish an article about him in February 1926. Encouraged by Husserl, Shestov, in the 1930s, was one of the principal disseminators of the thought of Kierkegaard in French existentialist circles. Berdyaev was the first to publish the *Mysterium Magnum* of Boehme in French, and he popularized the anthropology of Gregory of Nyssa among the younger generation, including such personalities as Jean Daniélou, Henri de Lubac, and Emile Mersch. The only book by Bulgakov to be translated into French during his lifetime was not one of his sophiological works but his *The Orthodox Church*—which was the first presentation in French of the theology of the Eastern Church. Frank only succeeded in being published in French in 1939 when he established himself as an expert in the philosophy of Nicholas of Cusa and apophatic theology. Here, we could also cite the examples of the place in French thought of Vysheslavtsev, Gurvitch, Lévinas, Koyré, and Kojève. This curiosity about communism, Germany, and Byzantium, this expectation—one might say, this unconscious desire for a controlled opening—regarding Eastern otherness on the part of the French intellectuals was the principal vector for the reception of Russian intellectuals in France. It was also the source of the distribution of honors that undoubtedly reinforced Berdyaev's prophetic figure and, within the young generation of the Russian intelligentsia, the positions of Florovsky, Vladimir Lossky, S. Bezobrazov, and M. Lot-Borodin—to the detriment of the more Russophile and modernist current as represented by N. Zernov, L. Zander, K. Mochulsky, G. Fedotov, and Mother Maria.

The Silent Confrontation

The confrontation between Western and Russian intellectuals during this period went unnoticed for the most part; it was, so to speak, subterranean. At least this was the feeling of the intellectuals of the review who suffered from not being sufficiently heard. How could it have been otherwise, given that their reception of the work of thinkers such as Bergson, Barth, or Jung came out essentially in Russian in *The Way*?

The reawakening of interest in Europe in the Orthodox Church in the early 1930s was echoed in *The Way*—at first by the publication of articles on different testimonies of Orthodoxy in the Western world, from the exposition of icons at Paris to diverse celebrations of Eastern liturgies throughout Europe (I22, I24, Z13). By introducing Fr. Lev Gillet, the first Orthodox priest to celebrate the Byzantine liturgy in French and the editor of the parish bulletin *La Voie*, Berdyaev also contributed to sustaining the growing current—notably among certain Catholics exasperated by Roman authoritarianism—in favor of a French Orthodox Church (G2). The Boulevard Montparnasse review also evidenced the European dimension of the ecumenical networks, especially through the contributions of V. Zenkovsky, "The Athens Conference" (Z24), and N. Arseniev, "The Religious Conferences in Newcastle and Cambridge"[461] and "The Movement for Christian Unity and the Problems of the Contemporary World";[462] or, in a more spontaneous style, through the report of G. Pronevitch, a student at St. Sergius, entitled "The Ecumenical Seminar in Geneva."[463] The fact that *The Way* published articles by non-Orthodox authors also testifies to the friendships that had grown up among Christian intellectuals. Whether these authors were K. Kirk, one of the principal supporters of

Orthodoxy at the University of Oxford, Frank Gavin, the American friend of Bulgakov, or Augustin Jakubiziak, Lydia Judifevna's confessor, who regularly attended Berdyaev's seminar at Clamart, the editorial board continued to publish firsthand information on non-Orthodox matters. But, along the same lines, many of the authors of *The Way*—especially Berdyaev, Zenkovsky, Florovsky, Vysheslavtsev, and Zernov—assumed the role of observing the Anglican, Protestant, and Catholic worlds. In general, the contributors to the journal regularly noted, with increasing worry, "the crisis of Protestantism in Germany" (as Zenkovsky put it), but they also made mention of all the interesting initiatives and personalities—especially John Mott—who gave them hope.

But the journal was also precious to Russian intellectuals thanks to its reviews of the principal books being published in Europe and the networks established by the authors living outside of France. In Germany, for example, the relationship that Bubnov and Stepun, the friend of Gadamer, had with the review *Logos* enabled the Russian intellectuals to orient themselves collectively in the maze of the intellectual networks of that epoch. If the field of intellectual interests of the authors of *The Way* or their travels throughout Europe or the composition of their libraries were to be depicted virtually, in the manner of archaeologists, it would probably be represented by a figure with six branches. These branches would depict, on the one hand, the centers of reflection consisting of the phenomenology of Heidegger, the dialectical theology of Barth, and the Thomism of Maritain; and, on the other hand, the poles of research represented, at that time, by myth, symbol, and dogma, and centered around Jung, Bergson, or Keyserling. In the background of this configuration, and given the opinions published in *The Way* that attest to a real confrontation between the Russian religious thinkers and the principal European intellectual currents—a silent confrontation since it was practically inaccessible to the non-Russian-speakers—one can find the common interest of the Russian intellectuals in theanthropy, the divine-human relationship.

With the Philosophers

The Eighth International Congress of Philosophy, held on September 2–7, 1934, at Prague and whose theme was "Philosophy and Life," was a good example of the intellectual solidarity of the Russian philosophers who had migrated to Europe. This meeting brought together intellectuals from

An Ecclesial Commitment off the Beaten Path   349

Germany, Belgium, Czechoslovakia, Poland, England, America, Italy, the Netherlands, and France. Among them were N. Hartmann, A. Lalande, L. Brunschvicg, E. Pshivara, and E. Radl. Husserl, who was unable to travel, sent a "letter," as did the sociologist Ferdinand Tönnies. Among the Russians who participated (N. Lossky, S. Frank, S. Guesen, G. Katkov, I. Lapshin, E. Spektorsky, B. Jakovenko), the themes of the Congress were represented in talks with the following titles: "The Christian Vision of the World as a Universal Synthesis" (Lossky), "The Spiritual and Living Significance of Negative Theology" (Frank), "Integrity as the Fundamental Principle of Pedagogy" (Guesen), and "Reflections on the Question of Theodicy" (Katkov). Frank, in his report on the congress that appeared in the December 1934 issue of *The Way*, emphasized that, unlike the general tone of the congress, which was characterized by a "rationalist optimism and a metaphysical pessimism," the Russians who participated had, without prior consultation among themselves, developed, from different angles, the same fundamental idea "of truth as universal plenitude and absolute unity."[464] He added that within "this parliament of philosophical thought," nationalist tendencies were clearly revealed:

> Thus the fidelity of French thinking to its immemorial rationalism; the Germans, by the solidity and depth of their reflections, have shown that they remain, above all, a people of philosophers. By its absence from the Congress, Soviet philosophy convincingly manifested its bankruptcy. On the other hand, independent Russian philosophy—numerically under-represented at the Congress—succeeded in reviving the original religious traditions of Russian culture.[465]

Berdyaev said much the same in his review of a book by his compatriot Gurvitch, entitled *The Current Trends in German Philosophy*,[466] which came out in 1930 with a preface by Léon Brunschvicg. This book was the first presentation in French of the different currents of German phenomenology. In this regard, it is significant to note that the three principal channels through which German phenomenology became known in France, namely, Gurvitch, Shestov, and Lévinas, were all immigrants from the former Russian empire.[467] Berdyaev gave a positive review of Gurvitch's work in *The Way*.[468] He used the occasion to take a few shots at the self-sufficiency of French thought—especially that of Brunschvicg. According to the latter, German philosophy was at a "pre-Cartesian" stage.

Not without humor, Berdyaev replied that it would be more accurate to say that French philosophy was at a "pre-Kantian" stage. For, he argued, with the exception of Bergson and Le Roy, the French philosophers are either Positivists, Cartesians, or Thomists, that is, at any rate naïve rationalists, who are unable to understand even the basic approach of the irrational that is typical of the German metaphysical genius.

The interest in Bergson mentioned by Berdyaev, as well as in the American philosopher William James, can be explained by a long-standing complicity on the part of the Russian intellectuals. At the beginning of the century, while still in Russia, N. Lossky, Shestov, and Frank had read and given passionate commentaries on Bergson's *L'Essai sur les données immédiates de la conscience* (1889) and, above all, his *L'Evolution créatrice* (*Creative Evolution*) (1906).[469] Moreover, as Lazarev indicated in his 1932 article in *The Way* entitled "The Philosophical Destiny of William James," the way in which the leader of American pragmatism questioned the absolute God of monist philosophy and the problem of evil aroused the interest of the heirs of Dostoevsky.[470] But, paradoxically, Berdyaev had reservations about the religious turn that Bergson took in 1932 with the publication of *Les deux sources de la morale et de la religion* (*The Two Sources of Morality and Religion*). Mochulsky, who reviewed the book in *The Way*, recognized the validity of the distinction Bergson made in his chapter on static religion between closed and open societies, and his interpretation of the "function of the fable," which neutralized the anarchic and destructive action of reason. But he was "disappointed" by the French philosopher's attempt to base morality and religion on the methods of scientific biology. Because of this attempt, the chapter that Bergson consecrated to "dynamic religion," to the nature of God, and to the problem of evil revealed, according to Mochulsky, a form of rationalism disguised under the veil of mysticism.[471]

Neither Shestov nor Berdyaev ever met Bergson. Their contact was limited to sending their books to one another, along with a friendly letter. Berdyaev, however, in his book entitled *Cinq méditations sur l'existence*, rendered homage to Bergson. He wrote: "The problem of time is the principal problem of human existence. It is not by chance that the two most remarkable philosophers of contemporary Europe, Bergson and Heidegger, put the problem of time at the center of their philosophy."[472]

The interest in German phenomenological philosophy dated from *The Way*'s very beginnings. Some of the authors, namely, Frank, Stepun, and Bubnov, were still living in Germany and ensured that the smallest ripples in speculation east of the Rhine found their echoes in the review. Like Hartmann, Heidegger, and Buber, Shestov, Vysheslavtsev, and Berdyaev had distanced themselves from the "rationalism" of Husserl[473] and shared an approach to the world that was both metaphysical and realist. In September 1934, Alekseev summed up the common opinion of the Russian philosophers when he affirmed that the phenomenological school was "the most remarkable phenomenon since the times of the great German systems of classical idealism."[474]

After the journal had twice drawn the attentions of its readers to the ethics of Hartmann (1882–1950), through articles by Frank and Berdyaev (F63R, B49R), Vysheslavtsev in the October 1933 issue wrote about Hartmann's ontological underpinnings. In his review of Hartmann's latest book,[475] Vysheslavtsev expressed his approval of the fact that the German thinker had retained only the "most congenial" elements of Kantianism, "that is, the thing in itself, the irrationality of being . . . and this signifies that being is more fundamental than knowledge."[476] But this irrational dimension of being, he argued, did not prevent Hartmann from trying to logically formulate the definition of the particular mode of spiritual existence in its relationship with natural existence and, notably, with personal existence, the summit of the hierarchical scale of being. Vysheslavtsev insisted on the religious foundations of Hartmann's thought; Hartmann, he wrote, "senses the cosmic depth of being, the presence within it of *Sophia*, of Wisdom" much more than Heidegger does.[477] With respect to freedom, however, Vysheslavtsev, differed from Hartmann, who denied any freedom to the disincarnate spirit and treated the relationship between spirit and nature as antinomic. According to Vysheslavtsev, freedom was of the very essence of the spirit.[478] In this sense, he concluded, the faculties of knowledge, imagination, and creation, which were inherent in the spirit, could not be limited by the laws of nature. Hartmann had been criticized for letting himself be impressed, while writing his book, by the prevalent ideological forces and, for a time, by Nazism.[479] In his article in *The Way*, Vysheslavtsev made no allusion to this criticism. On the other hand, however, when Heidegger joined the National Socialist Party in 1933, this did not go unnoticed in *The Way*. It was pointed out in December by an author who preferred to remain anonymous (S. for Stepun?).[480]

The anthropocentric representation of ontology, a vision dear to Russian personalist thought, was a favorite theme of Heidegger. In 1928, Sezeman had pointed out the importance of the philosophical revision made by Heidegger in 1927. In the October 1930 issue of *The Way*, Berdyaev joined his personal impressions of *Being and Time* to his review of Gurvitch's book. For Berdyaev, generally speaking, the main weakness of German phenomenologists was that they wanted to know being intuitively, while remaining free from any construction. He believed that such an attitude led them to turn aside from being or else to simply support its presence passively. "The object," Berdyaev argued, "enters into the subject in the act of knowledge. The subject then puts a phenomenological construction into play and opens itself passively to the object."[481] Hence, in the case of Scheler as well as in that of Heidegger, there is the presence of a metaphysical construction. Berdyaev wrote:

> Heidegger is profoundly right when he seeks the enigma of existence in humanity; but he neither founds nor justifies any such road of ontological elaboration. He absolutely does not consider his philosophy anthropological. He is convinced that the phenomenological method reveals essences to him. "Ontologie ist nur als Phänomenologie möglich." ... He studies being as *in-der-Welt-Sein*, as if it were thrown out and descended into the world and there the world reveals itself to it as a concern. "Dasein ist Seiendes, das Je ich selbst bin, das Sein ist ja meines."[482]

For Berdyaev, just as for N. Lossky—who, in 1931, also published a review of Gurvitch's book in *Contemporary Annals*—this metaphysical construction, although Heidegger failed to recognize it as such, is in reality a metaphysical construct with theological presuppositions. This point distinguished Gurvitch's approach from that of Berdyaev. While Gurvitch, who never published in *The Way*, carefully avoided linking the evolution of his thought with a spiritual evolution towards the atheism of Scheler, Hartmann, or Heidegger, Berdyaev showed that the logical reflection of these three personalities is inseparable from their representation of their gods. Thus for Berdyaev, the philosophy of Heidegger is a "Christian metaphysics without God," which associated elements of the Catholic doctrine on original sin with an ancient conception of death. That is why, Berdyaev held, Heidegger insisted on the fallen state of humanity without admitting that anxiety might have an origin distinct from the everyday world, subject to time.[483]

Frank's interpretation of Heidegger throughout the 1930s was clearly more sensitive to the German intellectual's ontology and was distinct from that of Berdyaev and N. Lossky. Much like Max Scheler—who criticized the pessimism of Heidegger, influenced, in his opinion, by the "neo-Calvinism" of Karl Barth—Frank gave a course on Heidegger at the University of Berlin in the early 1930s.[484] Although Frank preferred the intuitive approach to the hermeneutic approach of Heidegger in a theory of knowledge, the two agreed on the Greek understanding of *energeia* as the foundation of ontology.

With the Theologians

The attention to the religious foundations of German phenomenology in *The Way* corresponded to a collective frontal criticism of the absolute transcendentalism of the dialectical theology of Karl Barth and his followers F. K. Schumann, E. Brunner, and F. Gogarten. The Russian philosophers recognized that Barthianism was "the most remarkable religious current" in Europe during the period between the two wars,[485] because it represented a powerful reaction within Protestantism against the romanticism, pietism, and idealistic pantheism of the preceding centuries and because it revealed the "too human" character of the realities that people had made sacred, through their extreme desire to hear the voice of God behind those of men. In this sense, when Barth, in July 1933, criticized National Socialism, he was praised by Zenkovsky and by the author identified as "S.," even though they did not share certain of the anti-episcopal themes of the neo-Calvinist theologian.

But, as Berdyaev pointed out in his review of F. K. Schumann's 1929 book, this powerful movement of desacralization was accompanied by a rejection of naturalism and therefore wound up denying any form of mysticism, any form of sanctification and transfiguration of the earthly flesh. It was as if Barthianism, by rejecting magic, ended in rejecting any form of sacramentalism. Lev Gillet confirmed this analysis in 1932 in his criticism of the morphological exegesis of Bultmann, which took the Gospel tradition to be a sedimentation of fictions elaborated by the first Christian communities.[486] According to Berdyaev, however, "pantheistic mysticism is only the other face of the absolute negation of mysticism in Christianity."[487]

But, above all, this primacy of faith over human reason, the primacy of the freedom of God over human freedom, this theocentric conception of the church as opposed to any catholic imperialism seen as basely human—as Berdyaev indicated in his criticism of Emil Brunner's book *God and Man*—led to a monotheistic, Old Testament, non-Trinitarian understanding of God. According to Berdyaev,

> Here is what cannot be surpassed either by Brunner or anyone else. Revelation is a binomial and not a monomial; it supposes not just He who reveals but also the person to whom He reveals Himself, not only God but also humanity—and humanity cannot be just a passive receptor of revelation; it reacts actively to what has been revealed from on High in conformity with the structure of its conscience. And in the measure in which a person has an active and creative reaction to revelation through his thought, through the rational character of his essence, he necessarily has a philosophy in his reception of revelation. This is linked to the doctrine on humanity in the perspective of the concept of divine-humanity and is not sufficiently emphasized by Brunner and the neo-Barthian school.[488]

Florovsky was also attracted by the neo-apophatic tendency of dialectical theology. But, as he wrote in his review of a book by Paul Schütz, the Reformation, in its chronic desire to surpass human history—the source of its interest in and fear of revolutionary mystics—was a "hypereschatologism" incapable of understanding the meaning of the divine incarnation.[489]

This collective response explained why the authors of *The Way* felt more at ease with intellectuals such as Friedrich Heiler, "the best theologian in contemporary German Protestantism," according to S., or with Rudolf Otto, the great historian of religions, a professor at the faculty of theology of Marburg, and a friend of Vysheslavtsev. In 1934, Otto wrote a book treating the Gospel theme of the "Son of Man" as the key to a synthesis between the different representations of the "Kingdom of God" in the Aryan religions. Bubnov reviewed the book in the September 1934 issue of *The Way*. The book also aroused the interest of Shestov, who began to delve into the Hindu philosophy of the Upanishads (see B113R).

In a manner analogous to the philosophical currents of Protestantism, the Russian intellectuals were traditionally attracted to the ontological depths of the neo-Thomistic current, yet more at ease, on an ecclesial level, with the neo-modernist current and its emphasis on freedom.

In his 1932 book *Le songe de Descartes* (*The Dream of Descartes*), Maritain made a radical criticism of the rationalism characteristic of French thought and, at the end of the book, addressed himself to the Russian intellectuals, asking them to take into consideration the fact that there was more to French thought than Cartesianism. In so doing, Maritain echoed the debate that had occurred between himself and Vysheslavtsev at the meetings of the Franco-Russian Studio in 1931.

In the 1930s, however, the neo-Thomistic movement spearheaded by Maritain was heavily criticized by the Russian intellectuals. Zenkovsky, responding to the appeal of the French philosopher in a review in the July 1932 issue of *The Way*, admits that a rereading of Cartesianism could be a path towards the coming together of East and West. But, he continued, this should not obscure the real stumbling block between Russian and French intellectuals, and that stumbling block was Thomism.[490]

Shestov challenged Maritain's claim that metaphysics could be found in the Bible.[491] Rejecting all the pretensions of rationalism to ontologize revelation, he proposed the faith of Abraham as the foundation of all Christian philosophy.[492] Berdyaev confirmed this change of tone in the review regarding Thomistic ontologism. In his review of *La Providence et la confiance en Dieu*, a book by the Dominican Garrigou-Lagrange, who was considered the principal Thomistic theologian in virtue of his position as professor at the Pontifical University of St. Thomas Aquinas in Rome, Berdyaev did not hesitate to write that the book had such an influence on him that "while reading it, I became an atheist—and even a militant one!"[493] In his book, however, Garrigou-Lagrange did nothing more than repeat the theodicy of St. Augustine and Leibniz, for whom evil and suffering were as indispensable to the divine glory as shadow is to light. This "teleological" philosophy, which distinguished the natural and the supernatural and thus introduced a mechanical relationship between the Creator and the creature, was, according to Berdyaev, indicative of the "rationalist optimism" of Thomism.[494] For Berdyaev, "after Dostoevsky, Nietzsche, and Kierkegaard," Thomism could no longer base itself on a theodicy of this type. It should force itself to pass by the humble road of negative thought, "which gives priority to symbols rather than concepts."[495]

Even though Lucien Laberthonnière was, in his opinion, "more a religious moralist than a metaphysician," Berdyaev felt himself closer to the "personalism" of the head of the modernist movement than to the tradition of Aristotle and St. Thomas, which "ignores the problem of the person."[496] In Laberthonnière, Berdyaev recognized the great tradition of "the secret France," running from Pascal to Maine de Biran, with its emphasis on the freedom of conscience and its desire for realism.

The work of the Jewish philosopher Martin Buber (1878–1965) was contemporary with the return to Aristotle in the phenomenology of Heidegger and in the dialectical theology of Barth. But the fact that Buber's thought was rooted in the Bible—whose German translation he had revised in conjunction with Franz Rosenzweig—and in the Kabbalah[497] gave his work a realistic character, and this had a special appeal for the Russian intellectuals. In May and July 1933, Berdyaev and Shestov each published an article in *The Way* on the following books by Buber: *I and Thou* (Berlin: Inssel Verlag, 1923), *Hassidic Tales* (Berlin: Shoken Verlag, 1927), *The Dialogue of Life* (Berlin: Shoken Verlag, 1932), and *The Kingdom of God* (Berlin: Shoken Verlag, 1932). Arseniev, in August 1931, wrote a review of a book on Hassidism (A37R), *Priester der Liebe*, authored by Chaim Bloch, another Jewish philosopher contemporaneous with Buber. Although Berdyaev appreciated Buber's effort to put the Hassidic legends into contemporary language, he disagreed with his conception of freedom. For his part, Shestov lamented the fact that Buber, in his task of actualization, felt that he should relegate to the background, in his philosophical work, the fantastic nature of these legends. In Berdyaev's view, for there to be a true meeting between I and Thou, humanity should have the benefit of an uncreated, primordial freedom as the indispensable condition for the convergence, without fusion and without separation, of the I and the Thou in the God-Man. Shestov, unlike Berdyaev, but following a similar antinomic logic, reminded Buber of the biblical affirmation that there was a common nature between God and the world. Against the pretensions of human knowledge—which preferred to exile God from the earth rather than recognize its own incapacity to completely contain Him—Shestov opposed the biblical myth of *Sophia*, which is taken up again in the Kabbalah by the myth of the *Shekinah* of God through which "the design of God is accomplished in our world."[498] But both Russian philosophers agreed in thinking that Buber's attempt to "base his religious philosophy on Myth"[499] and to express the truth of the Bible in philosophical language was, regardless of its outcome, "worthy of the most profound sympathy."[500]

With the Psychologists

Vysheslavtsev was not satisfied merely with enthusiastic commentaries in the journal concerning the psychological studies of Paul-Emile Lévy (the school of Nancy), Charles Baudouin, and C. G. Jung. In the early 1930s he participated in the meetings of the "Gros caillou" of the Psychological Club of Paris. He also met Jung, the celebrated Swiss psychologist, on several occasions. Their first meeting was probably on August 4, 1933, in the course of a seminar at Jung's Psychology Club in Zurich—which was also attended by Hermann Hesse and Hermann Keyserling, among others. But Vysheslavtsev always felt out of step with Jung. He differed from Jung in that he believed in a form of "heteronomic suggestion," which corresponded to the "action of the Word, operating through the Spirit, at the deepest level of the Self,"[501] in the symbolic area of consciousness of the heart and the visceral-unconsciousness. In such a perspective, every form of symbolic representation—art (V21R), politics, religion—appeared as specific spheres where the action of suggestion and creation come into play. It is especially in the religious domain that their approaches differed. Vysheslavtsev, in his review of a book by K. Schjelderup on asceticism (V20R), and N. Lossky, in his article entitled "The Visions of Saints and Mystics," presented in *The Way* the imposing literature on the question of the traditional Western forms of the sublimation of the spiritual life. Both agreed, given the dangers of an imagination that is overly passive to any form of suggestion, to give more value to the active conception of the symbolic representation favored by the Fathers of the Eastern Church.[502]

Eschatological Awareness and Ecumenical Engagement

The Ecclesiological Debate

Although all the contributors to *The Way* sought to situate the discussion among Russian, German, and French intellectuals on the level of the church, their paths differed as to how to define the church and trace the ways of access leading to it. In 1933, rather symptomatically, the two principal approaches to this question—the traditional and the modernist— were expressed in separate publications. In February, Florovsky published a scathing article entitled "The Question of Christian Unity" (F54bis) in a supplement of *The Way* (but with reservations on the part of the editorial board, who thought it necessary to add a note at the bottom of the page stating that "there can be other points of view on the question"). That same year the YMCA Press (this time without Florovsky) published a collection of articles by Greek and Russian authors (among them, Bulgakov, Berdyaev, and Kartashev), which were very different from one another but whose tone was more conciliatory. It was entitled *Christian Reunion: The Ecumenical Problem in Orthodox Consciousness*.

Florovsky's article set off an explosion and provoked several reactions, which were published in the July 1933 issue: Zernov's article "Saint Cyprian of Carthage and the Unity of the Universal Church"[503] and Afanasiev's "The Canons and Canonical Consciousness."[504] Florovsky replied to this crossfire in July 1934 with his article "The Limits of the Church"[505] and was answered in October by Afanasiev, in his article "The Two Concepts of the Universal Church."[506] One must assume that the stakes were high because, after this polemic, Florovsky ended all collaboration with *The Way*, thus prefiguring the open and definitive break with his former colleagues that took place the following year.

Florovsky, the former bard of Eurasianism and, more recently, an apostle of neo-Byzantinism, had never been very flexible in his relation with Western Christianity. In the 1920s, however, even though contacts among Eastern and Western theologians had increased, the conception of Christian unity did not yet exist as such. The pacifist spirit of those times, the joy of mutual rediscovery during the meetings in Lausanne and Stockholm among Christians of the East and the West after centuries of separation, and, finally, the fact that the ecumenical movement did not have precise goals—all these facts enabled each person to participate freely. Florovsky—having become a priest, participating in the relatively restricted and organized meetings of Faith and Order, engaging in dialogue with theologians of Barthian tendencies on such subjects as grace and the hierarchy, and under pressure from Christians who wanted to see rapid and tangible results—found himself obliged, like most Russian intellectuals who participated in the ecumenical movement, to formulate his basic principles in order for the discussion to be honest, deep, and mutually enriching. In his January 1933 article for *The Way*, he situated himself in the tradition of Khomiakov and repeatedly asserted that "the church is one" and that the division is "dogmatic" in nature and not sentimental. But he made so many demands as conditions of reunion that he himself admitted that he had little faith in "theologians' conferences" and transferred his hope to an "eschatological twilight," that is, to the end of history, the moment of the authentic coming together. In fact, Florovsky dismissed both the hyper-eschatologism of Protestantism, which was the consequence of its expulsion of the sacred and of its religious individualism, and the hyper-historicity of Catholicism, which was the result of its lack of faith in the resurrection of Christ and in the fact that Christ continued to preside over historical destinies. So, for Florovsky, while the Reformation was "an empty house without a soul," "the Roman Church errs in matters of faith and is incapable of love."[507] Assertions such as these were not appreciated in ecumenical circles. In *Irénikon*, among the reviews of articles appearing in *The Way*, this can be found: "As for the categorical affirmations about the Roman Church, one is so used to finding them that they don't surprise anyone any more."[508] But the principal source of Florovsky's skepticism lay in the axiom attributed to St. Cyprian of Carthage, a third-century bishop: "the canonical limit of the Church is, at the same time, charismatic."[509] Florovsky could not accept the other principal definition of the limits of the church, namely, the branch theory [holding that Roman Catholics, Orthodox, and Anglicans are three branches, each legitimate, of one "tree"], which consisted in "Darwinizing" the Body of Christ.

The collection put together by the YMCA Press was the first attempt at a pluralistic formulation of the Orthodox position on ecumenism. Lay people were invited to contribute (N. Berdyaev, A. Kartashev, V. Zenkovsky, and the Athenian theologian Hamilcar Alivisatos), but so were clerics, bishops, and priests (Archbishop Gennady of Constantinople, Metropolitan Nectary of Bukovina, Protopresbyter Stefan Zankov of Sofia, and Fr. Sergius Bulgakov), Russians as well as Greeks and Romanians. The quality of the essays varied, but they had the merit of representing the diversity of views in the Orthodox world. This is the reason for focusing on the three essays of Bulgakov, Berdyaev, and Kartashev, which bring an entirely new dimension to the question of unity among the churches. In his contribution, entitled "By Jacob's Well," referring to the conversation between Christ and the Samaritan woman in the Gospel of John, Bulgakov turned the entire structure of traditional discourse upside down by insisting on the features that united Christians, namely, their prayer, their understanding of the Gospel as a verbal icon of Christ, and their common recognition of the sacrament of baptism, rather than the issues that separated them. Bulgakov was able to pull off this turnaround because he distinguished, in a more antinomic and thus more radical way than Florovsky, the church as Mystical Body—according the Gospel definition "When two or three are gathered in my name, I will be there in their midst"—from the historical local churches, which, because they belong, in part, to a fallen and divided world, suffer divisions and can actualize, individually, only a part of the life of the Mystical Body. In order to definitively leave behind any purely institutional and hierarchical definition of the church, Bulgakov pointed to the example of Christ, who declares to a non-Jew that he has not found a faith as great as his in all of Israel. Calling to mind the traditional faith of the church in the mystical communion of all the saints, Bulgakov dared to affirm—in the line of the Orthodox liturgical practice of admitting converts without rebaptizing them—that there is a sacramental life outside of the Orthodox Church, understood as an institutional church. This enabled Bulgakov to vigorously argue that he did not think it necessary to reestablish canonical and juridical links before permitting intercommunion among Christians. Bulgakov believed that putting dogmatic agreement before Eucharistic sharing was dubious, considering that something more precious was involved. "The mystical life of union in the table of the Lord" is sacrificed in the name of this or that disagreement rooted in the human conscience. With respect to such disagreement, Bulgakov repeated that the concept of heresy was historically meaningful only within the boundaries of the mystical church.

Bulgakov proposed, therefore, adopting a reasoning process that was both new and also traditional, in the sense that it was according to the mind of Christ. It consisted in "beginning to try to overcome the heresy we live before trying to overcome dogmatic heresies."[510] This "Eucharistic" process of Bulgakov was based on a mytho-logical vision that distinguished, antinomically, Christian unity as already given and therefore to be realized, and separation as a historical fact. To be sure, Bulgakov invited the Protestant world to reestablish an apostolic hierarchy, but he evoked the adage of Vincent of Lerins: *In necessariis unitas, in dubiis libertas, in omnibus caritas*—"In essential things unity, in uncertain things freedom, in all things love."

Berdyaev, in his essay "Universality and Confessionalism," argued that the principal preliminary condition for church unity is that every Christian should sense the lack of fullness of his own church, have the desire to repent for past errors, and endeavor to go beyond the provincialism of his own confession to rejoin the "divine-human process which is the Church."[511] In this relationship, the person is active, and thus there is a positive tendency to individualize the Word of God according to the different nations. But it could also be the case that a person is unready to receive this revelation in all its profundity. Hence there is a tendency to transpose certain tribal elements in the way the church is represented, and this explained, for Berdyaev, the primacy of sacramentalism over evangelization and the tendency of Orthodoxy to retreat within itself. It also explained Catholic imperialism and the inconstancy of the Protestant world. This was also the reason why Berdyaev rejected the expression "re-union of the churches" since, in his eyes, it was not the church that was divided but rather "Christian humanity."[512] Thus he put the emphasis on the unity between Christians of the East and the West and not on that of institutions. Berdyaev proposed focusing this human activity not on a theological level but on a social and, more importantly, on a spiritual level, for, according to the Gospels, Christ invited his disciples to seek first the Kingdom of God and the rest would be given.

> Universal Christianity can only be realized by means of a strong eschatological sense of life . . . . The idea of the Kingdom of God in Christianity goes deeper than the concept of Church insofar as the latter is the historical path towards the Kingdom of God. The idea of the Kingdom of God is eschatological and prophetic. Unity should be based on this concept. It is not a minimal unity but rather a maximal one, not an abstraction but a concrete reality. The perspective of acceding to absolute plenitude and unity is an eschatological perspective, it is the accomplishment of time. But the accomplishment of time is still realized within time.[513]

Kartashev's contribution to the collection, "The Reunion of the Churches in the Light of History," brought a historian's perspective and teachings drawn from the rich experience of the first centuries of the Christian church. For him, the Orthodox Church, wounded by a succession of mortal blows—from the crusades to the uniate council of Florence—had forgotten that re-union (*vozsoedinenie*), in the practice of the primitive church, meant a mutual recognition of faults followed by forgiveness. This practice was rooted in the primacy of the ontological unity of the church. "By the grace of the Holy Spirit" it acted on the divine-human dogmatic awareness, which, without being false, was necessarily insufficient due to its historical limitations. Following the logic of his openness, Kartashev, who noted both the separation of the Catholic Church "from the spirit of the councils" and the reality of "the miracles of Lourdes," proposed to the Orthodox that the Catholic concepts of the *Filioque* or the Immaculate Conception be recognized as "theologoumena," that is, as particular theological hypotheses.[514]

While he was in London, Zernov read Florovsky's article in *The Way* and decided to reply to it immediately. On January 16, 1933, he wrote an article entitled "Saint Cyprian of Carthage and the Unity of the Universal Church," in which he recommended "the highest degree of prudence" to those who seek to resolve contemporary problems by presuppositions that cannot be considered as expressing the authentic doctrine of the church. Zernov reminded his readers that Cyprian of Carthage, who was baptized into the church in 246 after studying Roman law, represented a turning point in its history. Cyprian contributed a thesis that ought to be highly debatable, namely, that it was the bishop—and no longer the community of the faithful—who was the source of charismatic grace within the church. Zernov recalled, moreover, that the tradition of the church never confirmed or denied Cyprian's doctrine that the bishop was the successor of Peter, "the unique founder of the universal Church." In referring to the evolution of the Docetist movement as well as the papist current in the West, both of which took their inspiration from Cyprian, Zernov noted that the African bishop's theses were in the long run more destructive than constructive. That is, Zernov believed that this doctrine, which, notably, did not solve the problem of collegiality among bishops, could be refuted.

> His [Cyprian's] error was precisely to attempt to establish the visible limits of the Church.... There are many reasons for considering that the pre-Cyprianic conception of the unity of the Church was more in harmony with the New Testament image and that the progressive return towards this conception constitutes the task of our times. This would facilitate, in many ways, the reunion of confessions currently separated within one Holy, Catholic, and Apostolic Church.[515]

Berdyaev published Zernov's article in July, in the same issue that included the supplement written by Afanasiev, "The Canons and Canonical Consciousness." A student of Bulgakov, Afanasiev also took a position opposed to certain allegations of Florovsky, notably, his frequent references to Byzantine canons that had fallen into disuse regarding the interdiction of having communion with those in divided churches. Afanasiev, a professor of canon law at St. Sergius Institute, noted that the basic rule of his discipline was that "canonical order is only the expression of the dogmatic doctrine concerning the Church."[516] Therefore one must guard against making the forms of ecclesial life absolute. He gave some striking examples, such as the prohibition of bishops changing their residence or the excommunication of those who "do not remain until the end of the Eucharistic liturgy."[517]

On July 18, 1934, on the feast of St. Sergius, Florovsky replied both to the essays in the collection of the YMCA Press and to the two articles described above by a contribution to *The Way* entitled "The Limits of the Church." This article was a rewrite of a piece published in the October 1933 issue of the *Church Quarterly Review*.[518] Since it was written for an Anglican and Orthodox readership, it was less polemic than the preceding one, although the approach was fundamentally the same. He accepted Bulgakov's argument (which he cited) according to which the sacramental practice of the church revealed an implicit recognition of the mysteries outside its visible canonical frontiers. But, he added, in a strange quote of "blessed Augustine," these sacraments are "real" but not "efficacious."

In his reply to Zernov, Florovsky was both conciliatory and intransigent. Agreeing with Zernov and differing from Cyprian's view that the sacraments were valid only within the church, he admitted that "where the sacraments are celebrated, there is the Church."[519] But Florovsky had not incorporated the antinomic approach of Bulgakov concerning the visible church and the mystical church, united without separation but also without confusion. He could not bring himself to distinguish these two because, for him, there was only one divine-human church, namely, the Orthodox Church. Thus he reaffirmed, in accordance with the "still actual" doctrine of the African bishop, that every schism was a departure from the authentic church.

Finally, Florovsky conceded to Afanasiev that the church was a mystical and not a canonical organism and recognized that the question of heretics in the church should be resolved in an "economic" manner, that is, in a philanthropic spirit rather than in a legal context. He considered, however, that this "economic" interpretation of the canons was the historical result of the decadent period of Greek theology. Thus, he implicitly indicated that he preferred rebaptizing heretics and neophytes, because, according to St. Augustine—with whom Florovsky sides—"grace might be active outside of catholicity but in this case it cannot save."[520] He concluded with a new diatribe against the "church branch theory," whose main error was precisely not knowing how to distinguish the limits of the sacramental life of the church.

Afanasiev's article "The Two Concepts of the Universal Church," although written before Florovsky's article appeared in number 44 of the review, was published in number 45, December 1934, as a sort of reply to Florovsky. According to the recollections of his wife, this article, the first attempt by Afanasiev to formulate his new eucharistic ecclesiology, was composed during the winter of 1932–33 when he was "preparing a paper for a seminar of Father Sergius."[521] Afanasiev's question concerning the nature of the church and the way to actualize this question found a much more satisfactory answer in Ignatius, a second-century bishop of Antioch, than in the theses of Cyprian. To Cyprian's vision of the church as a community of several communities united among themselves through the episcopal institution that ruled in the place of Christ—a vision that led Rome to Papocaesarism and Constantinople to Caesaropapism—Afanasiev contrasted the vision of Ignatius. For Ignatius, the ecclesial community—bishops and laity—formed a body through the Eucharist, thus rendering the Body of Christ into a multitude of decentralized local churches. That was why, Afanasiev wrote, if it was true that "the Church is there where the bishop is," since he alone can celebrate the Eucharist, it was necessary to add that "the bishop is there where the Church is," since the Eucharistic celebration was only possible because there was a gathering of Christians. This approach corresponded to a mystical, that is, sacramental—and not mechanical—definition of the church. As Afanasiev put it, "in each community there is the plenitude of the Catholic Church, just as the whole divine nature of the Holy Trinity is present in each hypostasis without separation or division."[522]

The Three Interpretations of the Church

The different positions can be summed up schematically in three logical principles that interpret the symbol of the church as the Body of Christ:

Bulgakov's definition of the church was cataphatic, sophiological, and eschatological. In practical terms, this meant that the unity given and "already present" of the Church (Divine Wisdom) was to be realized in history (created Wisdom) by the assembly of the faithful (*ekklesia*) participating in a common task (the liturgy).

Florovsky's definition was apophatic, Christological, and patristic. In this perspective, the broken unity of the mystical Body of Christ could only be restored by God himself at the moment of the Parousia. Since the sole criterion of ecclesiological truth is the Orthodox tradition of the ecumenical councils, which preserves all the dogmas concerning the divine humanity of Christ, it is the duty of Orthodox Christians to communicate this tradition through a theological dialogue with the other Christian traditions. In contrast, the definition proposed by Afanasisev was apophatic, pneumatological, and apostolic. In his perspective, the gifts of the Holy Spirit, communicated to all the faithful at Pentecost, make it possible to imagine the reunification of Christians through a progressive, conciliar approach involving the clergy, from the base (local councils) to the summit (ecumenical councils).

Finally, Berdyaev's definition of the church was cataphatic, personalist, and eschatological. This definition summoned persons who were created in God's image to freely come together, in small missionary and charitable communities, above and beyond any confessional allegiance, in the name of the Trinitarian Spirit, so that the Holy Spirit might communicate his gifts in this world and actualize the universal church.

These three logical principles of the symbol of the church resulted in a growing antagonism among the authors of the review as to the attitude that should be taken towards the Anglican Church, which, from every point of view, was the Christian tradition closest to the Russian Orthodox Church. The opposed viewpoints on the Anglican Church within the review will be studied next, as represented by Arseniev and Zernov. I will then treat of the activities of Bulgakov, Florovsky, and Berdyaev in England and in France.

The Anglo-Orthodox Laboratory

The Debate on the Anglican Church in The Way
With the passage of time, Arseniev, whose ideas were similar to those of Florovsky, became more radical in his approach to the Anglican Church,

and this revealed certain ambiguities in the grand declarations of friendship of the 1920s. At first he considered that "we do not have the right to turn away from a hand extended fraternally."[523] Then he held that the question of apostolic succession was the principal obstacle to the unification of the two churches. When this obstacle was surmounted in March 1931, he brought up new issues of disagreement to be reexamined in order to assure full theological unity, notably, the perennial stumbling block of the *Filioque*. "If these conditions are met ... full intercommunion is possible," Arseniev wrote in *The Way*.[524] At the same time, he tried to show that he was magnanimous by adopting certain of Florovsky's theses on the nonnecessity of reordination for the Anglican hierarchy. He justified this stance by explaining that it was a measure of "economy." Continuing in this tone, he argued that the Anglican Church, which at present found itself in a prejudicial situation by "being separated from the Church,"[525] would no longer be in a state of nonplenitude if it entered into communion with the Orthodox Church. In his last article published in *The Way*, in the September 1932 issue—after this date the modernism of the review caused Arseniev as well as Florovsky to discontinue their participation—he made a final effort to show his good will towards ecumenism by criticizing modernist Anglican theologians and citing the works of the most conservative theologians of Anglicanism (R. C. Moberly, Lionel Thornton), whose works on redemption he considered to be close to those of Metropolitan Anthony Khrapovitsky. This final article thus revealed Arseniev's conservative motivations. These motivations, in fact, had been present from the beginning. In 1931 he wrote that the "support" given to the Anglican Church was imperative in order to avoid "the danger of its passing" to the Catholic Church. But as long as the Russian Church was not concretely implicated in the process of reconciliation, this type of argument passed unnoticed. On the other hand, this final article by Arseniev provoked a reaction by Zernov on November 1, 1933, and again in 1934 at a moment when the Russians had to define themselves, this time directly, regarding the question of reconciliation.

In his article "Orthodoxy and Anglicanism," published in the April 1934 issue of *The Way*, Zernov referred to the "mistrust of certain Orthodox" concerning reconciliation with the Anglican Church and stated that "it is only the impossibility of assembling a pan-Orthodox Council that impedes the concrete realization of this reconciliation."[526] He attempted to convince the reticent Orthodox by explaining the meaning of such reconciliation. First of all, he wrote, this reconciliation process had a significant history, since the first attempts dated to the beginning of the eighteenth century, and later the 1830s, with the correspondence between Palmer and Khomiakov. Second, Zernov explained that theologians were committing an error by discussing matters on a "theoretical level," first by considering that outside the Orthodox Church there is nothing but paganism, and then by drawing improper conclusions from the true affirmation that "the Orthodox Church preserves the fullness of sacramental life." Zernov argued that this latter affirmation lacked dogmatic precision, for the whole church could not be identified with the Eastern Church. Above all, he added, it must be recognized that this church did not live according to its canons.[527] Finally, Zernov took direct aim at Florovsky by rejecting the proposition of "certain theologians" who proposed "following the ecumenical councils on the path of reconciliation." He argued that although the councils were "the living voice of the ecclesial conscience of their times," they could not be set up as "infallible oracles" for resolving new conflicts and problems.[528]

Zernov proposed a more pragmatic process for defining the boundaries of the church. Basing himself on the New Testament, where "the letter of the Law is no longer dominant but rather God's mercy towards sinful persons," he proposed three main signs that manifest the presence of the Holy Spirit in a gathering of the faithful: the continuity of ecclesial life, ecclesial creativity, and the evidence of the gifts of the Holy Spirit. For Zernov, these criteria were authentic guarantees, which "prevent the power of the Holy Spirit over the Church from being replaced by any exterior authority, be it that of the pope, Holy Scripture, or ecumenical councils."[529] Zernov finished his argument by claiming that the Anglican Church satisfied the three criteria he had put forth. Zernov based himself particularly on the fact that the Patriarch of Constantinople had recognized the apostolic primacy of the Anglican hierarchy in 1922. He also made reference to the support of the Anglican people for the Russian people—a clear testimony to the work of the Holy Spirit in the church. As a contrast, Zernov deplored Orthodox chauvinism and legalism, which turned *sobornost'* into bureaucracy. These defects, he wrote, are precisely the result of the separation among churches. He concluded with an appeal for Christian repentance for "the common sin of division" and for practical wisdom; "if one admits that it is not theories but the quality of ecclesial life which is the ultimate measure for judging the non-Orthodox and determining the boundaries of the Church, then one can again hope to rediscover a conciliatory wisdom for a correct response to the Anglican proposition to renew communion with their Church."[530]

In an essay dated May 12, 1934, Zernov replied to another important argument of Arseniev for putting off any reconciliation with the Anglican Church, namely, the diversity of theological currents within this church. After describing eight main currents of the Anglican Church in all their diversity—from the evangelical wing (Low Church) to the Anglo-Catholic one (High Church)—Zernov made an indirect reference to Arseniev's article by showing their historical unity; the importance of their theology of the Incarnation, as redemption but also as "sanctification of one's whole life";[531] and, above all, their common rejection of any exterior authority in the church, without, however, eliminating the institution of the episcopate, such as the Protestants had done. He concluded by inviting Orthodox theologians to avoid using the authoritarian Roman discourse and to return to the conciliar spirit of the early church, which authorized a plurality of opinions.

The Eucharistic Engagement
In this context, in June 1933, Bulgakov took a new and astonishing initiative. Drawing out the practical conclusions of the theses he laid out in the YMCA Press collection, he proposed, in a lecture on the Eucharist given to the Fellowship of St. Alban and St. Sergius, that a new step be taken in the work of reconciliation of the Anglo-Russian fraternity by inviting the participants of the two churches to commune from the same chalice. Indeed, for Bulgakov it was becoming "spiritually dangerous" to continue to unceasingly discuss differences when the goal of the Fellowship was to elaborate a more concrete approach to reconciliation. This proposal of Bulgakov sparked a passionate discussion. Zernov, Fedotov, and Kartashev in particular supported Bulgakov's proposition, while Arseniev and Florovsky opposed it. The Anglicans were also divided, and they decided to form an executive committee in the course of the year to resolve the question. Faced with the turmoil aroused by his proposition, Bulgakov added a number of qualifications. He suggested to this committee that "when a group of Anglicans and Orthodox (like those of the Fellowship) have found a certain basis of doctrinal agreement, especially through common prayer, intercommu-

nion can be authorized on certain occasions ... and it should be preceded by a sacramental blessing by religious authorities."[532] Bulgakov justified his position by arguing from the fact that intercommunion already existed in the spiritual and liturgical experience of the Fellowship.

This new proposal further amplified the discussions, for in the measure in which the perspective of unity became tangible, the Kingdom of God drew closer, and people became afraid. Bulgakov recognized these eschatological fears of the apocalypse and, in a conference given the following year, in June 1934, he tried to calm things down by distinguishing between the Kingdom of God, the human face of the church, which perpetually and prophetically actualizes the gifts of the Holy Spirit given at Pentecost, from the *Parousia*, the divine and eternal face of the church, which will be accomplished only at the end of time. To illustrate this distinction, he referred to the antinomic mystery of the church, which is static in its eternal aspect and dynamic in its historical realization. In a sort of resumé of the eschatological modernism of Russian religious philosophy, Bulgakov wrote:

> Many of us feel the fullness of the Church in its static sense, we consider that the only duty a Christian has is to preserve this fullness. This pious conservatism turns with suspicion to everything that is new. But according to the Gospel one can only preserve by creative expansion; Church statics are dynamic when immersed in history. The face of eternity is seen in time in which the eternal life of the Church is accomplished. The Church Universal combines within itself both this fullness of eternity and the integrity of time—the present which preserves the past and conceives the future, and the future itself which is the disclosing of the past and a fulfillment of the present. The Holy Spirit Himself grants to his Church this future and illuminates its paths.[533]

In spite of this clarification, Florovsky remained adamantly opposed to intercommunion and argued that first there had to be complete dogmatic agreement, that neither the Russians nor the Anglicans of the Fellowship were representative of the whole of their respective churches and could not make such a decision on their own, and, finally, that the idea of "partial intercommunion" is a contradiction in terms, for communion is a catholic, not a private, act. On the Anglican side, some, like Father O. Clarke, thought that it was false to think that the confraternity was wasting its time by too much discussion of differences because, as he wrote in the Fellowship journal (which he edited), "in the deepest sense of the word we benefit from our union in the Holy Spirit . . . but we cannot say that, because we are united in the Holy Spirit, our divisions in the human part of the Church are of little importance; the Church is a divine-human organism."[534] Clarke also pointed out that the émigré church did not have "canonical authority," and that this complicated official negotiations.

Unlike Florovsky, the other professors of the St. Sergius Institute, Kartashev and Zander, sided with their dean. They noted that the official negotiations among hierarchs needed the support and stimulus of the faithful. Moreover, the canons forbidding, in principle, common prayer among the Orthodox and non-Orthodox cannot be invoked. Kartashev, in an article published in the review *Sobornost'* in December 1935, entitled "Intercommunion and Dogmatic Agreement," took a public stance in favor of Bulgakov's proposal for Eucharistic sharing. "In the cup of the Eucharistic is to be found the whole mystery of the unity of the Church. Union through the cup solves the problem completely."[535]

After the June 1934 session of the Fellowship, Malcolm Spencer, a friend of both Bulgakov and Florovsky, tried to find an intermediate position—a characteristic example of the spiritual nonconformism of the early 1930s. He published an open letter to his friend Florovsky in the Fellowship journal. While declaring himself incompetent to judge Bulgakov's proposition, he put forward certain principles of action that would enable intercommunion without provoking a schism. Spencer rejected both the casualness of Protestantism and the rigidity of Catholicism concerning tradition. This is why, he writes, the Orthodox Church should be capable of proposing a third way to the West. It should be capable of showing that, while remaining firmly attached to church tradition, it was also receptive to historic creativity.

> The present proposal for a canonical advance, starting from the bottom up, experimentally and tentatively, and humbly ready to learn by catholic experience whether the action should be fully upheld by the voice of the Spirit in the Church—this proposal seemed to me to be of the kind which would tend to combine historic development with historical continuity; and demonstrate the reconciling mission of the Orthodox in the divided Church.[536]

Encouraged by declarations such as this, Bulgakov fought for a sacramental engagement of Christians in the ninth conference of June 1935. In his report of the conference, Zernov wrote that there was no unanimity when, once again, the members of the Fellowship posed the question of liturgical communion, "even though all were convinced of the necessity to work for its future realization."[537] Sensitive to the worsening of the political situation in Europe, he ended his article by insisting on the importance of the spiritual coming-together of Anglicans and Orthodox for the sake of "all the Christians of East and West, who, together, are faced with the terrible danger of a new paganism."[538] Equally aware of the imminence of the danger, Bulgakov, in an article "Ways to Church Reunion," which appeared in *Sobornost'* around the same date, repeated for one last time: "Why cannot separate parts of a group belonging to the different Church bodies, Orthodox, Roman Catholic, Anglican, unite in intercommunion, if that actually expresses their true dogmatic and Church relationship?"[539]

But as of the following autumn, the danger that Bulgakov sensed in 1933 came to pass. His sophiology became the target of the attacks of Florovsky and Vladimir Lossky, and the meetings of the Fellowship were poisoned by these inter-Orthodox divisions. Bulgakov then ceased to propose Eucharistic sharing among Christians, judging that the charismatic interval was closed.

Berdyaev's Communitarian Engagement
Berdyaev was quite interested in the Fellowship, and he traveled to England several times—notably on the occasion of the Fellowship conference of June 1932 and, above all, that of June 1935. Favorable towards Bulgakov's proposition, he published an article in the September 1934 issue of the Fellowship journal entitled "About the New Christian Spirituality." Here he stated that "in a divine-human perspective," the grace of the Holy Spirit is obtained not merely in contemplation but also by the creative actions of people. But he enlarged the ecclesial boundaries of this premise.

> The new Christian spirituality therefore will be characterized by recognition of the very positive value of the human element and by the creative vocation of man. Every single human action, the least as well as the greatest, represents a creative spiritual act, and every relationship of man to man, both in personal and social life, is of such a nature. The

problem of a new type of communion between men, of new relationships of man with man, which must find their own particular social projection, cannot fail to enter into Christian spirituality. Man is united with God, not emptied of his nature when this nature has been creatively illuminated and manifested in his relationships to other men and to the world.[540]

Berdyaev, inspired by this evangelical definition of the church, preferred to involve himself in interconfessional community initiatives. On two occasions, in 1932 and 1934, he participated in closed meetings that brought together not only Christian intellectuals of all denominations but also Hindus. These were organized by Suzanne de Dietrich at her family's chateau in Mutterhouse, near Bitche in Moselle. In May 1932, Berdyaev met there with Henri-Louis Henriod of the ecumenical commission of the World Student Christian Federation, W. Visser't Hooft, and pastors Maury and Boegner, as well as Father Brillet, the superior of the Oratorian Fathers in France, the Indian priest Rolla Ram, a Japanese priest, and an Austrian priest. Among the other Russians present were Vysheslavtsev, Bulgakov, and Zander. The Bulgarian priest Stefan Zankov also participated. Berdyaev was the president of Orthodox Action as of 1935 and played a decisive role in its attitude towards the Jewish world. It would be fitting to focus with more detail on his participation in "the community of the poor," founded by a young twenty-eight-year-old Belgian Catholic, Raymond de Becker. Such participation was characteristic of Berdyaev's nostalgia for the Pentecostal spirit of the Christian communities of the primitive church.

Becker, a partisan of an integral Christianity, had founded in 1931 a review called *Esprit nouveau*. The following year he had launched the Independent Catholic Youth of Belgium and, in 1932, organized the first political conference of the Belgian Catholic youth. He then became a monk at the Cistercian hermitage of the "Gate of Heaven," at the abbey of Tamié in Savoie, where two other monks lived—the poet Henry Bauchau, professor in the Faculty of Poetry at the University of Louvain, and Thierry d'Oultremont (to whom he dedicated the article he published in *The Way*).[541] The superior of the abbey, Fr. Alexis Presse, was held in high esteem by the nonconformist youth—he had been instrumental in the conversion of Daniel-Rops—because of his desire to celebrate the liturgy in French. Inspired by Berdyaev's ideas as he had expressed them in *Un nouveau Moyen-*

Age [published in English as *The End of Our Time*] and after having met the Russian philosopher through Mounier, Becker decided to open a correspondence with him following the publication, in their French translations, of *Freedom and the Spirit* in 1933 and then of *The Destiny of Man* in 1935. He fraternally criticized Berdyaev for identifying the Catholic Church with Latinism and cited in contrast John of the Cross and Catherine of Siena.[542] In his reply, Berdyaev, doubtlessly enthusiastic about the spirit of *sobornost'* that marked the young man's initiatives, encouraged him to invent "a new rhythm of religious life."[543] In 1934, Becker told Berdyaev of his project for a "Christian revolutionary movement," centered on a community based in Louvain and making use of an agricultural enterprise near Paris. He sent Berdyaev his pamphlet "The Community of the Poor," written in 1932, and the first issue of his journal *Communities*, dated November–December 1933, with the warning "strictly confidential." Finally, he invited Berdyaev to a meeting on April 14, 1935, whose purpose was to set up the community in Paris. Berdyaev attended this meeting, along with the Jesuit priest Paul Doncoeur, one of the main inspirers of Catholic boy scout groups, and Jean Revault d'Allonnes-Psichari.

In his pamphlet, Becker wrote that this community of "God's Poor" went beyond communism and fascism and was a lay religious order based on poverty, chastity, and humility, made up of "wandering brothers" and a "communion of saints" united in a spiritual revolt against the modern world, which they hope to undermine. The pamphlet further stated that this revolt should find its expression through an "exterior revolution, through the transformation of all institutions."[544] The young intellectual cited Berdyaev several times, but also St. Thomas, St. John Chrysostom, Guardini, Newman, Solovyov, Péguy, and Gandhi. In the chapter on liturgical prayer, Becker quoted "a remarkable Russian intellectual, Fedorov," who "speaks of a liturgy outside of the church as temple and which involves one's whole life." In the chapter "Techniques of Action," Becker urged all the brothers to "infiltrate" the non-Marxist revolutionary movements and "take them over."[545] In his journal *Communities*, Becker suggested that the brothers of the community follow an advanced program of intellectual formation but with the help of new university programs, which people such as "Fr. Doncoeur, Fr. Lavaud, Jacques Maritain, Nicholas Berdyaev" could invent and transmit.[546] Although he kept some distance, Berdyaev's participation extended at least until May 1936, when he accepted for publication in

The Way an article on mysticism submitted by Becker three years earlier (B1). In a note to this article, Berdyaev mentioned "the organization Community." But after this date, no trace can be found in the writings and archives of Berdyaev of his relationships with the community of the young Belgian. It is as if the abrupt changes of 1935–36 altered the focus—as it had also done in the case of the aborted charismatic initiative of Bulgakov. With the awareness of the imminence of a catastrophe, the time for dialogue, initiative, and encounter came to an end.

PART THREE

A Spiritual Journal

(1935–1940)

THE PARADIGM OF THE SPIRIT

Before World War I, Russian intellectuals, assembled in societies of religious philosophy, were inspired by a paradigm of "symbolic realism." After the revolution of 1917, the émigrés regrouped within the modernist quadrilateral that was the "School of Paris" (the Academy of Religious Philosophy, *The Way*, the St. Sergius Institute, and the Russian Student Christian Movement). Now, in 1935–40, when once again their world seemed on the brink of dissolution, a new self-definition became necessary. After a brief parenthetical moment of "nonconformism," during which those who contributed to *The Way* tried to synthesize tradition and modernity, community and hierarchy, and activism on the social level with activism on the national level, a new period, which could be described as "spiritual," emerged. Internally, this change was due to the growing awareness, among some of these Russian intellectuals, that only the Spirit could bring about the social, political, and intellectual syntheses to which they aspired; on an external level, it was due to the increasing polarization of political, social, and intellectual realms, which tended to accentuate the differences among the

Russian intellectuals themselves. This twofold evolution, which took place in three stages between 1935 and 1940, resulted in considerable changes in the composition of the editorial board as well as in the content and tone of the articles that appeared in *The Way*.

Internal Evolution

A renewed self-consciousness among the intellectuals who directed *The Way* began to manifest itself in 1934–35 through the writings of Berdyaev, Fedotov, and Bulgakov. It was first expressed by these three as a rediscovery of the spiritual nature of the group to which they belonged, namely, the intelligentsia, and of the prophetic mission of this group.[1] In the spring of 1934, Fedotov published "The Foundations of Christian Democracy" in the journal *New City*. Here he maintained that the antinomy between the power of the people and the liberty of the person was synthesized in the principle of conciliarity (*sobornost'*). He also argued that the source of the freedom of the person is found in prophecy, "the zone of maximum freedom in the Kingdom of God."[2] Berdyaev continued the debate on the role of intellectuals confronting this crisis in the tenth issue of *New City*, in an article entitled "The Prophetic Mission of the Word and of Ideas in the Understanding of Liberty." Berdyaev, having lost patience with the claims of French intellectuals regarding freedom of expression in the Soviet Union (which was vaunted during the international congress of authors held in Paris at the Maison de la Mutualité in August 1935), observed that "the cultural elite of Europe is in crisis because it no longer listens to the voice from on high."[3] He wrote that "only a spiritual understanding of freedom, which presupposes that human beings possess an innate element of independence regarding the state and society, can save freedom."[4] Berdyaev shared the theory of the two spheres—politics and intellectual critique—professed by Julien Benda, but reproached him for radically isolating the intellectual side. [Benda, in his 1927 book *La Trahison des clercs* (*The Treason of the Intellectuals*), had accused modern intellectuals of becoming political partisans of the Right or Left rather than keeping separate these two areas.] On the other hand, Berdyaev criticized the blind commitment of Gide in his attempt to lump together "Ivan the Terrible and Montaigne," and predicted that, "sooner or later," the incompatibility of this mixture of integral communism and individualism would become clear. In contrast, the prophet, according to Berdyaev, regards isolation and social service as antinomies, as a penetration into the mysteries of destiny, on the one hand, and as judgment on the powerful, on the other. Berdyaev portrayed the prophet, in his paradoxical role of loner and social critic, as one who "hears the voice of God, the voice of his conscience," who finds himself in permanent conflict with society, and who continues the genealogy of "the Old Testament prophets, Socrates, Michelangelo, Dante, Beethoven, Tolstoy, Dostoevsky, Ibsen, Kierkegaard, and Nietzsche."[5] He concluded with a vibrant appeal to "people of the word and people of the mind, who have safeguarded a spark of the prophetic spirit, to struggle against the dictatorship imposed on the human conscience by fascism as well as communism, to struggle for the liberty of the spirit."[6] In 1938, again in *New City*, in an article entitled "The Crisis of the Intellect and the Mission of Intellectuals," he returned to the same theme with his latest definition of intellectuals. According to Berdyaev, the intellect should not be understood theoretically or abstractly. It is one of the functions of the creative spirit. "The authentic *intellectuels*" (in French in his text) "are representatives of the spirit, that is, of freedom, of common sense, of value, of quality and not representatives of the state, or of a social class, or of particular interests. The representative of the spirit, the creator of a spiritual culture, has a prophetic mission."[7]

Evolution towards the Spirit

This new interpretation of the spiritual paradigm was not limited to the social awareness of the intellectuals. It also took place on theological, philosophical, and historical levels. In 1936, Bulgakov published *The Comforter*, in which he proposed a new interpretation of the Trinitarian dogma based on a crucial distinction between the Spirit of God and the Holy Spirit. He reviewed his own book in the April 1936 issue of *The Way*. Bulgakov began by showing that, up to the seventh century, the Fathers of the Church, both in the East and the West, could only formulate a binary, not a trinitarian, doctrine of the Trinity. For him, however, a correct understanding of the Trinity cannot be based solely on concepts of causality and origin. The life of the Trinity can only be founded on the premise that God is Spirit and Love and can only be described by using the concept of "mutual revelation." After these preliminaries, Bulgakov clearly distinguished the personality of the third divine hypostasis from its nature:

"If the Spirit of God is the tri-unity of the three hypostases in their differences, the Holy Spirit is their hypostatic unity in the third hypostasis."[8] In other words, the Spirit of God was always tri-hypostatic, while the Holy Spirit was the personal realization of the divine Spirit. The consequences of this distinction were twofold. It underscored the personal (and not abstract) dimension of the gifts of the Holy Spirit—communion, prophesy, asceticism, humility, love, and so forth—and, on the other hand, it brought closer together the figures of the Wisdom of God and the Spirit of God. Bulgakov wrote: "Certainly, taken in itself, the Divine Wisdom is also a spiritual principle; it is the spirituality of the tri-hypostatic spirit."[9] This pneumatological approach allowed him to finally explicate the object of his research and would lead him to undertake a third trilogy consecrated to the essence of sophiology, to the church that is "Sophia under its double aspect, divine and created, with their interaction expressed by their union."[10]

Around the same time, in 1935–36, Berdyaev was drawing out the philosophical consequences of his personalist turn during the preceding five years. This was evident in his book *Spirit and Reality* (*Esprit et réalité*), published in Russian by YMCA Press in 1937 and by Aubier in French in 1943. For Berdyaev, the spirit was a transcendent sphere, distinct from and opposed to "the state of the existent as it exists in the mind," for in this sphere the existent was neither an object nor a hypostasis but was incarnate in reality. "The philosophy of the spirit," he wrote, "is not a philosophy of being—an ontology—but rather a philosophy of existence."[11] This was the culmination of his reflection on divine-humanity and on the uncreated aspect of liberty. He went on to state that "the Spirit represents the divine element in man, but this is inseparable from the human element and thus it is that both operate conjointly. This is the mystery of divinized humanity."[12] Berdyaev would subsequently describe the characteristics of the spirit and of the new spirituality whose advent he ardently desired. Here, I merely point out one of the anthropological consequences drawn by the philosopher from his phenomenology of the spirit, that is, his criticism of intellectuals who have not become aware of their spiritual nature. "These intellectuals," he wrote, "and I mean the intellectual workers who do not focus on life in all its plenitude, are satisfied with an abstract conception of the spirit because they are obsessed with a false dichotomy between the spirit and the body, by a deluded opposition between spiritual and intellectual work on the one hand and manual and physical work on the other."[13]

Figure 1. Cover of the first number of *The Way* (*Put'*), 1925. *Photo courtesy of the author.*

Figure 2. Faculty and students of the St. Sergius Institute, Paris, Spring 1926. First row, seated from left to right: Fr. Gregory Shumkin, Lev Zander, Sergius (later Fr./Bishop Cassian) Bezobrazov, Anton Kartashev, Fr. Sergius Bulgakov, Metropolitan Evlogy, Bishop Benjamin, Nicholas Lossky, Vladimir Ilyin, Peter Kovalevsky. Second row, left to right: Michael Jashvill, Evgraph Kovalevsky, Rezhetsky, Alexis Stavrovsky, deacon George Fedorov, Vladimir Evdokimov, George Bobrovsky, Paul Evdokimov, Gregory Svetchin, Leonid Khrol, Konstantin Struve, Dmitrii Klepinin, Dmitrii (later Fr. Ioann) Shakhovskoy. Third row, left to right: Vsevelod Palashkovsky, Nicholas Ignatiev, Sergius Otman de Villiers, Revenko, Feodosy Spassky, Alexis Greve, Michael Sokolov, Alexis Tekutchev. *St. Sergius Archives (Lev Zander archives). Photo courtesy of the author.*

Figure 3. Meeting of the Russian Student Christian Movement, Chateau de Bierville, 1926. Seated at the table, left to right: Basil Zenkovsky, president; Alexander Nikitin, secretary; Fr. Sergius Chetverikov, chaplain. *Photo courtesy of the author.*

Figure 4. First Anglo-Russian conference, St. Albans, January 1927. This gathering led to the formation of the Fellowship of St. Alban and St. Sergius. First row: fourth from left, Fr. Sergius Bulgakov; ninth, Sergius (later Fr./Bishop Cassian) Bezobrazov; eleventh, Nicholas Zernov. *Archives of the Fellowship of St. Alban and St. Sergius. Photo courtesy of the author.*

Figure 5. Faculty and students of the St. Sergius Institute, Paris, 1930. First row, left to right: Lev Zander, L. Kisselevsky, Basil Zenkovsky, Metropolitan Evlogy, Fr. Sergius Bulgakov, Sergius (later Fr./Bishop Cassian) Bezobrazov, George Fedotov, Ivan Lagovsky. Second row: eighth from left, Fr. George Shumkin; ninth, Fr. Avraam Tereshkevich; tenth, Fr Issac Vinogradov; twelfth, Fr. Athanasius Netchaev; sixteenth, Michael Ossorguine. Photo courtesy of the author.

Figure 6. Meeting of the Russian Student Christian Movement, Paris, 1935. In the foreground, left to right: Basil Zenkovsky, Fr. Sergius Bulgakov, Fr. Sergius Chetverikov. Tamara Baimakova Klepinin is just behind Zenkovsky, and Mother Maria Skobtsova is standing behind her. Lev Zander is at the extreme right, third row up. Boris Vysheslavtsev stands to the right of Mother Maria, Fr. Victor Yureyv to her left. Ivan Lagovsky is seated at the table at the extreme right. Seated just behind Fr. Chetverikov is Fr. Alexander Tchekan. Fr. Lev Liperovsky stands just behind Fr. Tchekan. *Photo courtesy of the author.*

Figure 7. Members of the Fellowship of St. Alban and St. Sergius at a meeting in Paris, 1936. From left to right: Lev Zander, Anton Karpenko, Nicholas Afanasiev, two unknowns, Fr. Georges Florovsky, Elia Melia, two unknowns, Anglican Bishop Walter Frere, Vladislav Kulivov, Fr. Sergius Bulgakov, unknown, Paul Anderson, Fr. Cassian Bezobrazov, Evgeny Kisselevsky, Anton Kartashev, Boris Sové, Basil Zenkovsky. *University Archives, University of Illinois at Champaign-Urbana. Photo courtesy of Michael Plekon.*

Figure 8. Meeting of the Russian Student Christian Movement and YMCA, Paris, May 1937. Standing, from left to right: Paul Anderson, Donald Lowrie, Irina Okounev, Alexis Okounev, Alexandra Chetverikova, Feodor Pianov, Alexander Nikitin, George Fedotov, Lev Zander. Seated from left to right: Fr. Sergius Bulgakov, Fr. Widdrington, Duffus, Nikolai Berdyaev, Basil Zenkovsky, Mother Maria Skobtsova. *Photo courtesy of the author.*

Figure 9. Gathering of the Fraternity of the Holy Trinity in the apartment of Lev and Valentina Zander, Paris, 1937. First row, seated from left: Valentina Zander, Fr. Sergius Bulgakov, Mother Maria Skobtsova, Julia Reitlinger (facing right, later Sister Joanna), Basil Zenkovsky, Vladimir Ilyin, Boris Vysheslavtsev, Nicholas Afanasiev, Lev Zander. Below them are Mother Evdokia (Courtain), and Assia Obolenskaya. Standing from left, Vladimir Weidle (Veidlé), George Fedotov, Boris Sové. *Photo courtesy of the author.*

As we have already seen, the work of Fedotov between 1930 and 1935 was centered on the Holy Spirit. Between about 1934 and 1940, a similar paradigmatic evolution can be found in his anthropology of the Holy Spirit. He moved from a consideration of the Third Person of the Trinity, transcending history and culture, to that of the Spirit, human and divine, the image of God in man. Fedotov took the profound historical crisis of the intelligentsia as his starting point. In two articles published in *The Way* in July 1937 and September 1939, "Ecce Homo" and "In Defense of Ethics," Fedotov characterized the dominant spiritual current of his times as a mixture of voluntarism, racism, and irrationality, due to a rejection of ethics. Fedotov noted that in general, intellectuals in the broad sense of the term—from Virginia Woolf to Igor Stravinsky and Karl Barth—tended to reject certain qualities of the soul (sentiment, emotion, intelligence). He interpreted this as a reaction against the optimistic humanism of the early twentieth century. But in the tradition of the Fathers of the Church, nourished by the Neoplatonic philosophy of the *nous* and by the Christian revelation of the *ruakh-pneuma*, the spirit was not radically distinct from the soul. According to Fedotov, in the soul there was a superior reason, *um* in Russian, the intellect in conjunction with the heart, which was in contact with the world of the spirit. For Fedotov, the majority of the intellectuals had adopted a dualistic vision of humanity, which opposed spirit and body. Because of this tension they tended towards either an angelic immateriality or a form of bestiality. The intellectuals of the West, tempted by intellectualism, and the intellectuals of the East, tempted by asceticism, did not realize that by stifling the soul, they were involving the spirit and, consequently, such qualities as contemplation, tenderness, or authentic rationality. Fedotov advanced his own tripartite definition of the person as spirit, soul, and body.

The decisive development of Fedotov with respect to the preceding period consisted in his recognition that the spirit had a twofold source, divine and human. He affirmed that the will has a double origin. "On the one hand, the will is spiritual, on the other it is a corporeal tension."[14] The consequence of this evolution, which was linked, as we shall see, to the conflict between Fedotov and the St. Sergius Institute, was that Fedotov would reconsider his concept of "the foundations of the moral act."[15] It was no longer a question of the intellectuals being on one side and the people on the other. "At this moment, when millions of persons are held in death camps,"[16] Fedotov realized that the divisions between social castes had been eliminated. The spirit was no longer the property of clerics alone. The spirit belonged to every Christian who received the royal, priestly, and prophetic anointing at the moment of his baptism.

Evolution of Generational Memory

This redefinition of the intellectual as spiritual and the paradigmatic shift from the theme of divine-humanity to that of the spirit led Bulgakov, Berdyaev, and Fedotov to reinterpret their earlier thought and opened up new perspectives for the future. This meant the turning of a page in the history of the intellectuals who collaborated in *The Way*. It was only very gradually, through dialogue, that their individual awareness of this shift was communicated to the other members of the journal. During the period 1935–36, in a political and social context that had become explosive, this caused an intensification of the divergences not only between the School of Paris and the conservative elements of the immigration, but even within *The Way* itself, between the adherents of the theocentric, anthropocentric, and sophiocentric tendencies. This tension would last until 1937–38, when members of the review came to share an unspoken but collective realization of their spiritual unity, linking social commitment, intellectual reflection, and ecumenical engagement.

In a highly characteristic manner, at the convocation commemorating the tenth anniversary of the St. Sergius Institute, Bulgakov gave a lecture entitled "On the Banks of the Chebar River," which was also published in the June 1935 issue of *The Way*. Here he defined the "modernism" of the School of Paris as prophetic, free, and ecclesial. He compared the intellectuals who had come out of the School of Paris to the prophets Ezekiel and Daniel. When the people of Israel were captives in Babylon, these prophets dreamed of returning to Jerusalem and contributed to the spiritual renewal of their people. "In like manner, our work at Paris is not just local and provincial. It is also on a global scale." According to Bulgakov, the task was universal insofar as it was part of a general search among Christians for unity through ecumenism.[17] To be sure, he continued, implicitly referring to the debates raging in the Institute, "the gift of spiritual freedom" was a precious gift, which could be dangerous. However, the spiritual quest required audacity. Bulgakov concluded by characterizing the work of the

School of Paris as an ecclesial service insofar as it springs from "prayer and the Eucharistic inspiration of the altar."[18]

In the same commemorative style, as a sign of the consummation of a historical rupture, and with the same goal of deepening the modernist aspect of the religious mentality of the immigration, Berdyaev published an article in the October–December 1935 issue of *The Way* entitled "The Russian Religious Renaissance . . . and the Journal *The Way*," in honor of the journal's tenth anniversary. From the outset, the author explained that the principal lacuna of the symbolist generation of the Golden Age was to have been "more cultural than spiritual," the work "of an elite detached from the people."[19] *The Way*, anchored in the tradition of Russian spirituality, wanted to be "modernist." But Berdyaev judged the term ambiguous and specified that this modernism was characterized by "pneumocentrism."[20] "The defense of modernism," he wrote, "is the defense of life, of movement, of creation, of freedom, of ideas."[21] This was why *The Way* was not a partisan magazine, nor was it properly a theological journal. Rather, it was a journal of "spiritual culture." The new tasks of regular contributors to *The Way* consisted of Christian responses to the efforts towards the reunification of the churches, to contemporary social challenges, and to the crisis of culture. In 1935, Fedotov gave the same orientation to his journal *New City*. The tenth issue, published in December 1935 after an interruption of a year, began with an editorial that emphasized the primacy of the spiritual in the life process and identified, in the phenomena of the mechanization of life and of individualism and collectivism, signs of the final stage of the "disintegration of the spirit."

This spiritual awareness manifested itself among the authors of *The Way* in three ways, described here as follows: by one's self (the *raskol* of a generation), in one's self (the conflict between two spiritualities), and for the other (the common horizon of war and the New Jerusalem).

THE *RASKOL* OF A GENERATION OF INTELLECTUALS

The new awareness of the self as spiritual, together with the different theocentric, sophiological, and personalist tendencies of authors of the journal, revealed a new line of demarcation among them. On the one hand, there was a pneumocentric, socialist, and ecumenical line of thought; on the other, an ontological, nationalist, and pan-Orthodox one. Although these problems were real, they were not insurmountable. In fact, those who were the most ardent opponents of Bulgakov, Berdyaev, and Fedotov, that is, Lossky, Chetverikov, and Florovsky, did not necessarily seek a rupture, but they feared that too much freedom would threaten the very foundations of the church. They now preferred to use the language of authority rather than to discuss matters. In his correspondence with Bulgakov in 1938–39, Florovsky reiterated his sentiments of respect and admiration several times. On April 11, 1943, he wrote from Sofia: "I very strongly believe that, in spite of our differences, we are working towards a common goal."[22] On November 16, Vladimir Lossky wrote a very typical letter to Bulgakov, stating: "We have always criticized your doctrine, but neither I nor the other members of the Fraternity—among whom are many of your former students at the Institute—have ever ceased to have a great personal respect and love for you and consider you as our master, our spiritual father, and, in brief, as one of the most remarkable exponents of contemporary theological investigation."[23] With hindsight, one can identify to what degree the radical and disintegrating spirit of the times contributed to a spiral of violence and to the interruption of the dialogue between the modernist and traditionalist currents, which had marked the nonconformist years.

Unlike the years 1930–34, the public ecclesial, political, and social context of Europe during the period under consideration had become polarized and radicalized. This was not, however, a continuous or fatal evolution. Upon close examination of the milieu of the Russian immigration, it appears that the periods of identity loss (Spring 1935–Spring 1936; Spring 1938–Summer 1939) alternated with periods of collective re-identification (Summer 1936–Winter 1937; Fall 1939–Summer 1941). The enthusiasm for the mythical among the thinkers of the Russian immigration in 1935–36 was the result of a triple phenomenon. On the political level, the catalyst for the majority of the Russian intellectuals, who defined themselves as anticommunist, was the Franco-Soviet pact of alliance promulgated on May 2, 1935. Stalin's new strategy, initiated in 1934, of aligning with democratic countries to form a block against Hitler, shook up the image that the Russian immigrants had of themselves. This strategy included the entry of the Soviet Union into the League of Nations in 1934 and, in July–August 1935, the adoption by the seventh congress of the Cominterm of a new policy of unity with "the forces of democracy against Fascism." For French intellectuals, the political crisis reached its height when Mussolini's Italy invaded Ethiopia on October 2, 1935.

Moreover, on the ecclesial level, the Russian Church did not present a clear and consistent position to the faithful in the face of communism and nationalism, as did the Roman Church under Pius XII. In addition, metropolitans Anthony and Evlogy made efforts to bridge the gaps between them as the diocese of rue Daru began to free itself from Moscow's sphere of influence, while, on the other hand, Metropolitan Sergius of Moscow tried to control the émigré church. During the summer and fall of 1935, this provoked another explosive situation. For the young émigrés, this twofold development, together with the difficulties of social and professional assimilation, resulted in a sense of powerlessness, mingled with a desire for order and authority. Nina Berberova, in her novella *Astachev in Paris*, has described this confusion. "He dreamed of an order—of an individual who would be able to hold in his hands all of Europe and the whole universe. And he too, Astachev, would get himself a pair of those nice, shiny boots of the kind worn by those who had acquired a true discipline. And he felt that he was indispensable in this world."[24]

Several factors, however, contributed to calming the spirits of the intellectuals of *The Way* during the summer of 1936 and the spring of 1938: the victory in France of the Popular Front in June 1936 (which put an end to the institutional crisis brewing since February 1934 and permitted a new government to undertake a series of important social reforms); the tacit but effective distancing of those opposed to the School of Paris—the metropolitans Sergius and Anthony, as well as certain members of the review who found themselves in the minority; and, finally, the friendly pressure of the ecumenical movement on the intellectuals of *The Way* for greater internal cohesion. All this helped to unite the members of the journal for a period of time and fostered the development of a number of creative initiatives. The principal sources of conflict, however, continued to evolve. On the one hand, the democratic countries were unable to curb Hitler's desire for revenge, which became evident in March 1938 after the annexation of Austria and culminated in August 23, 1939, with the signing of the pact of alliance between Russia and Germany. On the other hand, the European governments in general, and the Third Republic in particular, were hard-pressed to respond to the popular aspirations for a synthesis between fraternity and liberty, authority and the constitutional state, and socialism and nationalism. Analogously, the inability of the Russian émigré church to unanimously recognize a legitimate authority and to organize itself around a common goal, plus the internal tension between the two ideological tendencies—socialist and nationalist—of the intellectuals of the review would soon revive the conflicts in the Russian immigration, beginning in February–March 1938.

These would continue until September 1939, when Berdyaev once again succeeded in overcoming fears of the Russian intellectuals by publishing the sixtieth issue of *The Way* with a new editorial board, a reaffirmed ethical commitment, and, as we shall see, a new, winnowed community of writers and readers ready for spiritual struggles. In order to appreciate the evolution of the tensions in this intellectual generation of the authors who contributed to *The Way*, it is necessary to distinguish and compare the three sources of conflict: the interecclesial dispute centered on the sophiology of Bulgakov, the debates concerning socialism and nationalism, and, finally, the opposition within the youth movement between those who treated it as a Scout organization and and those who treated it as a vehicle for social commitment.

The Interecclesial Dispute about Sophia

Attacks on the School of Paris, 1935–1937

According to Vladimir Lossky's letter to Bulgakov, it would seem that the initiative for the condemnation of sophiology by Metropolitan Sergius in September 1935 came from Moscow. Lossky wrote that during the summer of 1935—"following up on a request from Metropolitan Sergius [for a report] on *The Lamb of God* to his bishop in Western Europe, Metropolitan Eleutherius"—he sent a preliminary report, criticizing the positions of the Russian theologian. Lossky stressed, however, that in this report, the question was that of "a dynamic attempt to interpret the Church's dogmas in the context of the ecclesiological moment we are now living." At the same time, Alexis Stavrovsky (born 1905), a former student of the St. Sergius Institute who did not complete his studies and who was president of the Brotherhood of St. Photius, put together, "according to the instructions of Metropolitan Eleutherius" (for whom he was secretary), a report based on quotations from *The Lamb of God*. Both agreed in their conclusions that Bulgakov's sophiology was pantheistic and that it removed the limits between God and his creatures.

Before gathering the Holy Synod, according to traditional Orthodox practice, and without waiting for the more detailed memorandum that Lossky had promised in his letter, Metropolitan Sergius hastily signed decree number 1651 on September 7, condemning the sophiological doctrine of Bulgakov. The main criticisms of Metropolitan Sergius were on three levels—dogmatic, soteriological, and ecclesiological. For Metropolitan Sergius, who objected to Bulgakov's uses of pagan philosophical sources, there can be no such thing as an an-hypostatic love. Moreover, there was a danger of divinizing sexual relations (as did Rozanov) by distinguishing Logos and Sophia. The Creator is not the cause of man's fallen nature. It is sin that determines the Incarnation of the Son of God, not some reason within the Divinity. And, finally, it is not the *apokatastasis* that is the goal of history but rather the deification of the person in Christ. The decree declared that this teaching is "foreign to the Holy Orthodox Tradition" and called for "all the Orthodox faithful to return to the holy doctrine." Metropolitan Sergius also criticized Bulgakov personally, accusing him of being a "pure intellectual."[25] He concluded with the following warning: "Even though Fr. Sergius Bulgakov is not at present in communion with the Orthodox Church of the Patriarchate of Moscow," should it ever occur that his reintegration be considered, he "must present a written renunciation of his sophiological interpretation."[26]

Four months later, on December 27, Metropolitan Sergius signed a new decree condemning Bulgakov's interpretation of "the dogma of the two natures and unique hypostasis of Our Lord Jesus Christ." It is probable that this additional pressure from Metropolitan Sergius was part of a new strategy to recover the émigré Russian parishes under Metropolitan Evlogy. In fact, six months later, on June 16, 1936, at the request of the Brotherhood of St. Photius, Metropolitan Sergius consented to receive into his jurisdiction a community led by Fr. Winnaert, which had broken off from Catholicism. This policy of Metropolitan Sergius was also probably linked with the promotion of his own status within the Patriarchate of Moscow. Indeed, on the same day of his promotion, December 27, 1936, the Russian Church published a decree ordering all the churches under the patriarchate to commemorate, in every liturgy, "the blessed Metropolitan Sergius" as "*locum tenens* (*mestobliustitelia*) of our patriarch." Even though this decree said nothing about the death of Metropolitan Peter Krutitsky, *locum tenens* of Patriarch Tikhon during the 1920s and for whom Metropolitan Sergius was the deputy, it presupposed his death. Since Metropolitan Sergius had dissolved his synod by decree on May 18, 1935, B. Sové, who knew the patriarch personally, concluded that the Russian Church was governed in "a monarchical manner."[27]

Metropolitan Evlogy was aware of the danger this presented to the stability of his diocese, but he also feared the attacks of the Synod of the ROCOR, which was trying to gain control of parishes, especially in Germany and Belgium, under the pretext that they had become "Greek" and thus hostile to the Russian Church.[28] This, as we have seen, led him to travel to Karlovtsy in October 1935, with the approbation of Ecumenical Patriarch Photius, to try to consolidate his jurisdictional rights. Isolated and on the verge of a nervous breakdown, Metropolitan Evlogy, while reserving his right to remain under the Patriarch of Constantinople, signed a protocol of agreement for the administration of the Russian Church that was intended to put an end to the public campaigns of attack, but at the price of reinforcing the authority of the ROCOR Synod over the dioceses of the Russian immigration, including those of Western Europe. Moreover, at the end of the synod, the bishops themselves decided to condemn Bulgakov's doctrine as heretical, this time relying on the 525-page report by Archbishop Seraphim Sobolev. This condemnation was redacted in a polemical tone and published in *Karlovatskikh Tserkovnykh Vedomostiakh* on October 30, 1935. The bishops justified their action by simply affirming that "sophiology does not have enough basis in the Word of God and the writings of the Holy Fathers of the Church" and "that there is not, nor has there ever been, any theological problem in the relationship between God and the world in both the Old and New Testaments."[29] Upon his return, Metropolitan Evlogy had no choice but to name a diocesan commission to study the accusations of heresy leveled against Bulgakov. Fr. I. Smirnov, the rector of St. Alexander Nevsky cathedral, presided over the commission, composed of Frs. I. Ktitarev, C. Bezobrazov, and G. Florovsky and the lay faculty members A. Kartashev, V. Zenkovsky, and B. Sové.

These events seriously destabilized the cohesion of the diocese of the rue Daru. The entire immigrant community, from Harbin to Berlin, from Riga to Warsaw, was caught up in a violent polemic.[30] Certain intellectuals affiliated with the Institute, such as S. Chetverikov and Florovsky, both priests working with the Russian Student Christian Movement in 1936, took a public stance against the sophiology of Bulgakov.[31] The spiritual core of the review began to fall apart. At a public session of the Academy, B. Vysheslavtsev and Maxim Kovalevsky came to blows after a debate on Sophia.

The level of discussion degenerated. In the postwar years, Fr. Eikalovich, a former student at the Institute, wrote a history of the debate on Sophia. Although he was against the "private opinion" of Bulgakov, he tried to maintain a neutral attitude. He stressed, however, the "absence of fair play" on the part of V. Lossky, from the moment he was revealed to be the author of the secret report.[32] The eighty-seven page booklet by Lossky, *Spor o Sofii* (*The Dispute about Sophia*), published in January 1936, confirmed this opinion. There Lossky systematically condemned the theses of Bulgakov and concluded with a list of twenty points of accusation—an approach that had little in common with the fraternal correction recommended by the Gospel. Moreover, this report, both in substance and in form, did not measure up to the academic requirements necessary for treating such matters. Lossky, who affirmed without demonstrating anything, rarely cited the passages of Bulgakov that he was criticizing. Without proof, he accused Bulgakov of professing all sorts of heresies, from neo-Apollinarianism[33] to pantheism.[34] In an intimidating tone, he demanded that "anathemas" be published against Bulgakov as soon as possible. Finally, he hinted at the psychological instability of the Institute professor, a former student of Marx, and accused him of "having already betrayed his ideals once by entering into the Church."[35]

In this vein, Lossky launched a harsh criticism of the "sophianic mythology" of Bulgakov. He reproached him for not wanting to "understand that apophatic theology ... is the only true theology."[36] Without referring to the chapters where Bulgakov treated the subject, the young theologian judged that the principal flaw in sophiology was that "it confuses nature and person."[37]

As will be seen in the reply made to Lossky by I. Lagovsky, Lossky's attack was linked to Bulgakov's criticism of tri-theism. This doctrine, which was condemned in the early years of the church, consisted in interpreting the Trinitarian unity as substantial and recognizing the divinity as personal only insofar as it was realized in three hypostases. But for Bulgakov, there could be no nature without hypostasis. Bulgakov ascribed the quality of person to the Father, the only God, and the quality of hypostasis to the Father, to the Son, and to the Holy Spirit in their self-revelation. In *The Lamb of God*, Bulgakov recalled that the Spirit of God was above all personal insofar as it is personal consciousness. Thus God, while having one nature, that is, a unique life, has a personality consisting of three relationships to himself. He arranges his life by the Father, by the Son, and by the Holy Spirit. While God is triune, he reunites in his unique personal consciousness all the modes of the personal principle—I, You, He, Us, They. Man possesses all the modes except the ecstatic I (the I outside oneself). The personal principle in its fulfillment is a person of three individual consciousnesses. "Neither three nor one," affirmed Bulgakov, "but, uniquely, three in one."[38] In his presentation on the Father at the end of *The Comforter*, Bulgakov returned to this theme. He defined the "personalism of Christian philosophy": "The superior and primordial form of the Absolute is to be personal existence which is, in an absolute manner, in the aggregate personality of the triple divine unity, of the tri-hypostatic hypostasis."[39] Bulgakov's reasoning added a new dimension to the perspectives of the Fathers of the Christian Church. If, in the doctrine of the uncreated energies of St. Gregory Palamas, the "how" of the relation between the divine essence and the energies was explained, the "who" of the relation between the Person and the divine essence still had to be answered. In *The Bride of the Lamb*, written between 1936 and 1938, Bulgakov stated:

> The core idea of St. Gregory Palamas is that there exists, outside of God's transcendent "essence," a multiform manifestation of God in the world, his shining forth in his energies. Yet his theory of the essence and the energies remains disjoined from Trinitarian dogma, especially with regard to the doctrine of three distinct Hypostases and the unique Holy Trinity. The idea of the divine multiplicity and equality of the energies in God corresponds to the Wisdom of God, *polypoikilos Sophia tou theou* ("the manifold Wisdom of God," Eph. 3:10).[40]

Bulgakov, however, sought to explore this link between essence, the energies, and hypostasis in continuity with the doctrine of Gregory Palamas, which he considered an "incomplete sophiology" insofar as the Byzantine theologian himself contemplated the energies under the aspect of "the light of Tabor," that is, the Wisdom of God.

Byzantine reflection, shattered by fourteen centuries of Christological controversy and by foreign invasions, feared any rationalization of the divine mystery. Six centuries after Gregory Palamas, Bulgakov lifted the prohibition on logical discourse and probed the relationship of the essence and energies with the Trinitarian hypostases, thus giving a creative impetus to his intellectual generation and even to those who considered it their duty to protect ecclesial traditions. Indeed, this cataphatic vision of the divine unity was at odds with the apophatic perspective of Vladimir Lossky, who had been L. Karsavin's disciple. Lossky claimed that he based himself exclusively on revelation, and he denied any possibility of a philosophical understanding of mystical realities.[41] All the same, Lossky was obliged to recognize certain errors of Metropolitan Sergius.[42] It was impossible to avoid the sophianic problem.

Reactions in *The Way*, 1935–1936

Counting on the support of *The Way* and the YMCA publishing house, Bulgakov wasted no time in responding. He wrote two successive reports to Metropolitan Evlogy, one a reply to Metropolitan Sergius in October 1935 (published by the YMCA Press), the other a reply to the Russian Church Outside Russia, published in a supplement of *The Way*. In contrast, probably because he was saddened by Vladimir Lossky's report, he made no effort to reply to it. Bulgakov had already clearly expressed his opinions on the question of the relationship between nature and person in the first two chapters of his book concerning the Incarnate Word.

In his reply to Metropolitan Sergius, Bulgakov began by criticizing the form of the Russian hierarch's report and claiming that it failed to show "the precise points which are opposed to the doctrine of the Church."[43] Further, he argued that it failed to take into account the fact that the value of Sophia as a *theologoumenon* to describe the divine nature was recognized by the Russian Church at the Council of 1917. Bulgakov rejected the accusation of Gnosticism and declared that, in continuity with the patristic tradition, he was trying to understand the relationship between God and the world by using biblical sources, yet without rejecting the insights of ancient philosophy. He then counterattacked by affirming that, on the one hand, Metropolitan Sergius had obviously not read all his works "due to the fact that the Soviet authorities prohibit these types of books,"[44] and, on the other hand, that the metropolitan had acted without ecclesial validity by signing a decree with no pretense of *sobornost'*. Moreover, according to Bulgakov, the opinions of Metropolitan Sergius on the doctrines of incarnation and salvation "tend towards an a-dogmatic Protestantism."[45]

Focusing on the basics, Bulgakov reasserted that he never identified Sophia as a fourth hypostasis of the Trinity. Rather, he had continued the reflections of the Cappadocian Fathers on the heavenly archetypes and those of Gregory Palamas (who was himself accused of polytheism by his contemporaries) on the divine energies. He added "that persons are not the only ones capable of loving,"[46] and he cited biblical passages showing that "creation and the Church" are capable of loving in a non-hypostatic manner ("All the earth praises the Lord"). Furthermore, Bulgakov regretted that Metropolitan Sergius had "not understood at all" his distinction between the second and third hypostases in the divine Sophia[47] and, consequently, could not grasp his doctrine on the masculinity and femininity of the Trinitarian God. Concerning Metropolitan Sergius's belief "that God foresaw but did not will" the fall of mankind, Bulgakov ironically observed that this meant that the Incarnation of God "was the result of an accident."[48] Quoting St. Irenaeus of Lyon, Bulgakov emphasized that for the church, "the *Logos* was meant to become flesh from the beginning." His harshest words were directed at the "occasionalist soteriology" of the Moscow hierarch, which was inspired by Anselm's theory of redemption. To this, Bulgakov opposed his doctrine of salvation through deification. According to Bulgakov, Metropolitan Sergius professed a "Nestorianism" and an "extreme kenotism" that led to the negation of the divinity of Christ. Bulgakov concluded with an appeal *pro domo*: "As an Orthodox priest, I confess all the authentic dogmas of Orthodoxy. My sophiology does not touch the content of these dogmas but only their theological interpretation."[49]

In his reply to the synod of the Russian Church Outside Russia, Bulgakov refused to engage with their discourse—which was more polemic than academic—and instead presented a minicourse on the dogmatics of sophiology. This did not prevent him from characterizing the synod's position as subordinationist and Nestorian. He began this reply by quoting numerous passages from the Bible and the Fathers of the Church (particularly the doctrine of the two Wisdoms of Athanasius the Great)[50] that legitimated a sophiological interpretation of the Trinitarian mystery. He then explained that the Wisdom of God "reunites the world and God since it is the principle God had at the beginning when he created the world."[51]

Without this understanding of creation as a self-revelation of God in Wisdom, and, consequently, of the world as the creation of the Father by the Word and the Holy Spirit, one inevitably would fall, according to Bulgakov, into a subordinationist and Arian perspective, namely, that God created the world "by means of the Son."[52] The union of the two natures, divine and human, in one Person should not be understood as a *deus ex machina*, "but supposes a primordial correspondence or an ontological correlation of the two natures, the divine *Sophia* and the created one."[53] Worse still, Bulgakov was appalled by the expression "extreme subjectivism" that the synod used to characterize his doctrine of the sinlessness of the Virgin Mary. Bulgakov pointed out that, according to the doctrine of the church as expressed in its hymnography and iconography, Mary, the Mother of God, was perfectly pure of all sin even though her human nature bore the consequences of original sin. In Bulgakov's opinion, the fundamental problem was that the bishops, due to their Nestorianism, did not believe that Christ descended from on high "in His Divinity." This would explain why not only their Mariology but also their understanding of the doctrine of the Incarnation and Ascension were in error.

> Once again it is hard to believe one's eyes when we read that, according to the document of condemnation (of the bishops), an eschatology of this sort is reserved for the future, that the Kingdom of Christ will not be realized in this world created on earth, but in the Heavenly Kingdom of the Holy Trinity, that is, when glorified humanity will be taken up to heaven and into the heart of the Holy Trinity. Where did they get this strange and unorthodox doctrine of a universal ascension, which, we must obviously conclude, will take place after the Second Coming and supposes, evidently, a second ascension of Christ on high, this time with all of humanity? Such a doctrine has no basis in the teachings of the Church. . . . The most astonishing aspect is that this strange doctrine is justified by a text of the Apocalypse (21:3) that refers precisely to the Heavenly Jerusalem descending upon earth and the Kingdom of Christ on earth.[54]

Berdyaev, who formally belonged to the Patriarchate of Moscow, chose to support his former classmate and thus exposed himself to the danger of excommunication. In December 1935, he published an article in *The Way*, "The Spirit of the Grand Inquisitor: Concerning the Decree of Metropolitan

Sergius Condemning the Theological Opinions of Fr. Sergius Bulgakov." This article attacked both the "denunciation" of the Brotherhood as an exercise in "ecclesial fascism"[55] and the "placing on the Index" of Bulgakov's works by Metropolitan Sergius, who is identified with the Grand Inquisitor of *The Brothers Karamazov* "but without his poetry." Berdyaev believed that this *ukaz* against "the intellectual Bulgakov" was directed against Russian religious thought as a whole. He defended the Russian intelligentsia, "which has always suffered from censorship," as "Khomiakov, Bukharev, Dostoevsky, Nesmelov, Solovyov, and Fedorov" all bear witness.[56] Berdyaev was also shocked by the Metropolitan's scorn for the philosophy of Plato and Plotinus, since such a negation of philosophy led him to negate theology as well. Berdyaev felt that the idea that God became incarnate to make reparation for the sins of mankind was a "utilitarian comprehension of the Incarnation." Since it was founded on "the fear of eternal damnation," it gave clergy enormous influence over peoples' souls.[57] Berdyaev defended "the principal idea put forth by all of Russian religious thought"— that of "divine humanity," namely, that the Incarnation is not just the work of salvation: it is, above all, "the continuation of the creation of the world."[58]

To be sure, Berdyaev acknowledged that "for complex philosophical reasons," he had some reservations about sophiology. Above all, he feared that "conservative conclusions may be drawn from this doctrine" and that it could lead to a "sacralization of history." However, Berdyaev was of the opinion that the problem implied by this doctrine was of great importance. He offered philosophical criticism of certain concepts in Orthodoxy— "domination over the collective religious conscience of its adherents" and a concept of heresy "based on an instinct of power and sadism." On a sociological level, Berdyaev wrote: "Marxist orthodoxy isn't any different from religious orthodoxy," and for this reason he preferred to use the categories of "truth and of error."[59] Finally, it was his judgment that the ukase of Metropolitan Sergius—which should be evaluated on the existential level rather than the scientific level—was a "real heresy against Christian life," because it only demonstrated his disbelief "in the Spirit."[60]

This article created quite a stir, and responses were swift. In the April issue, Berdyaev published two letters—one from Vladimir Lossky dated November 23, 1935, and the other, dated March 2, 1936, from S. Chetverikov. Lossky's article, a reply to an unpublished letter of Berdyaev, was characteristic in revealing the malaise of a segment of the young generation, which complained about not being taken seriously or being published.

Lossky wrote: "The press is closed to us."⁶¹ By the same token, despite his refusal to recognize Berdyaev as an Orthodox philosopher, Lossky stressed that he nevertheless felt very close to certain themes of the Russian philosopher "concerning the ecclesial bourgeoisie, the power of nationalism in the Church, the importance of the aristocratic principle, the way Leontiev is to be understood."⁶²

Lossky denied the accusation that he had denounced Bulgakov and affirmed that he had merely responded to a request from the hierarchs. He justified his defense of the principle of power in the church by appeal to a text of St. Paul, which affirms the presence of a "gift of government" in the church (1 Cor. 12:28).⁶³ Lossky's main argument was that the conscience of the church, of which the bishops are the guardians, should have precedence over the individual consciences of its members.

> The dogmas of the Church are basically apophatic insofar as they teach the intellect to reject its habitual ways of reasoning and testify to the limits and partial nature of its knowledge. This does not mean that the dogmas become manifest by something exterior to them, like a *Deus ex machina*; this means that the Holy Spirit not only transmits the Truth to the Church but also reveals the ways to arrive at this Truth in a perfect, conscious, and creative manner. Yet the dialectic of this acquisition is different from that of any other art. At the outset there is the principle of obedience, i.e., the recognition that the Truth does not depend on my creative efforts, that I cannot add anything to it. . . . [Since you reject this way of free obedience to the Truth], you remain a subject in face of an exterior object (the Truth) or you make the object itself a means to create a subject.⁶⁴

Chetverikov, in an open letter to Berdyaev, declared that he was shocked by the latter's arrogant judgments of the Russian Church. He defended the most authentic representatives of Russian spirituality—from the monks of the monastery of Kiev to the *startchestvo* of the nineteenth century. Although he believed that the decree of Metropolitan Sergius was "too hasty," Chetverikov, unlike Berdyaev, held that "Truth is a value greater than freedom, for it is truth alone that guarantees full freedom" (John 8:32).⁶⁵ Chetverikov sided with Metropolitan Sergius's soteriology and cited Matthew 25:46 on "eternal punishment" to justify the doctrine of hell.

Berdyaev replied to both in an article entitled "On Authority, Freedom, and Humanity." He stated that he did not reject the principle of power. Rather, he believed that in certain cases—for example, to prevent the victory of Fascism—force should be used to defend freedom. All the same, he observed, a report turns into a denunciation when it is addressed to hierarchs who consider themselves "the kings of peoples."[66] Berdyaev pointed out that Lossky, the troubadour of apophaticism, used a cataphatic ecclesiology based on a monarchical principle whenever it suited him. He ironically thanked Lossky for authorizing him, "as a nonspiritual person," to pronounce the most heretical teachings ever devised. But he renounced this permission and preferred his own freedom to search for and defend the truth, "however imperfectly."[67] Berdyaev also replied to the argument on the humility of knowledge:

> Every thinking person defends his conception of truth—not because it is a personal conception but because he is convinced of the truth of his conception. Show him the error of his conception and he will detach himself from it. For me, obedience to the Truth is rooted in the need for an absolute knowledge—but it is a question of obedience to a truth and not to a power, and certainly not to ukases and decrees, of obedience to God and not to man or any human power.[68]

Berdyaev replied to Chetverikov, again ironically, that he could not be accused of being "against the Russian Church" for the simple reason that he was officially a member of the Moscow patriarchal diocese, while Chetverikov belonged to the jurisdiction of the patriarch of Constantinople. But for all this, Berdyaev did not exonerate the Russian Church. He called to mind that many conservative Orthodox—Berdyaev was thinking, for example, of Theophan the Recluse, one of the principal authorities in the nineteenth-century Russian Church—"defended serfdom, capital punishment, autocracy, anti-Semitism, and nationalism." Berdyaev argued in his own commentary on the Gospel passage cited by Chetverikov that the Greek term *eon*, used in Scripture to indicate the length of time of the decadent fall of the world and of individuals, should be interpreted as "a long time" rather than "eternity."[69] "There is no dogma having to do with the eternal pains of Hell." Finally, he agreed with Chetverikov in placing truth above freedom, but, he added, "there is also a Christian truth concerning freedom. It is the knowledge of the truth that sets us free . . . but the knowledge of the Truth must be uncoerced. . . . Truth and freedom cannot be separated, and freedom cannot be denied in the name of truth."[70]

Consensus Restored and a New Crisis, 1936–1940

The replies of Berdyaev and Bulgakov in *The Way* were followed by articles by other writers favorable to sophiology, notably in the right-wing press, such as those by Ilyin in October 1935 and Timashev in March 1936. Moreover, in June 1936 the diocesan council rejected the new proposal for the reorganization of the Russian Church, which Metropolitan Evlogy had unfortunately signed and which threatened the diocese and the Institute. The bishops of the Russian Church Outside Russia, who were furious, immediately attempted to take over the German parishes of Metropolitan Evlogy, but they were unsuccessful. More importantly, the theological commission of the diocese charged with verifying the accusations against Bulgakov arrived at a verdict on July 6, 1937. Under the leadership of Bishop Ioann Leontshukov, it fully rehabilitated the Russian theologian. The commission unanimously rejected any accusation of heresy on the grounds that the "theological opinions" of Bulgakov were licit in the church and did not contradict any dogma. However, in an attached document, two members of the commission who found themselves in the minority, Chetverikov and Florovsky, noted three points in Bulgakov's doctrine that were "weak and unacceptable."

In the first place, according to these two, church tradition had always associated the Wisdom of God with the Second Person of the Trinity. They conceded, however, that before the fourth century, certain Fathers associated the Wisdom of God with the Person of the Holy Spirit. Second, both recognized that Bulgakov did not make Wisdom a fourth Person of the Trinity, but they criticized him for "giving such an impression." Finally, while the two agreed in judging the condemnation overly hasty, they were, in general, in favor of an authoritarian solution of this question "by the power of the Church." Chetverikov and Florovsky backtracked during the diocesan assembly of November 26–29, 1937. But the commission of the diocese, on the basis of the verdict of the theological commission, likewise absolved Bulgakov of any heresy, while taking into consideration the three points put forth by the two priests.[71]

Despite these minor reservations, Bulgakov emerged victorious. Florovsky, humiliated, left for Greece to teach at the French School of Athens for eight months and from there went to Mount Athos, where he remained until September 1938. Chetverikov, who lost his good standing with the youth movement and was without support in the diocese, also left France in the summer of 1938 to enter the monastery of New Valaam in Finland. Moreover, a new commission was set up in the St. Sergius Institute, including all the professors with the exception of Florovsky, namely, Fr. Cassian Bezobrazov, A. Kartashev, G. Fedotov, B. Vysheslavtsev, V. Zenkovsky, V. Ilyin, V. Veidlé, B. Sové, N. Afanasiev, L. Zander, Fr. Lev Gillet, and P. Kovalevsky. This commission fully endorsed Bulgakov and went on the offensive to attack Metropolitan Sergius, stressing that the act of accusation was not canonical because it was not signed by the synod of bishops of the Russian Orthodox Church. More importantly, in the summer of 1937 a number of the Institute's faculty, namely, A. Kartashev, I. Lagovsky, V. Zenkovsky, N. Afanasiev, V. Ilyin, G. Fedotov, L. Zander, C. Kern, C. Bezobrazov, and B. Sové, circled the wagons around Bulgakov by publishing a collection entitled *Living Tradition* (*Zhivoe Predanie*), a good example of the "spirit"—both traditional and creative—of the Paris School. The collection began with a statement from St. Paul that the Christian should serve not the letter but the Spirit, for "the letter kills, but the Spirit gives life" (2 Cor. 3:6).[72] According to the professors of St. Sergius who signed the general introduction, tradition was as much an act as it is a fact, and as much an interpretation as a given doctrine. This is why, they wrote, Christ himself "makes the Scriptures intelligible" for those "who have ears to hear."[73]

The spirit-centered (pneumo-centric) tone of the articles making up this collection was evident. Bulgakov presented an exposition of dogmatic methodology, which he defined as "a philosophy of revelation" and as "religious philosophy."[74] He argued that the field of dogma was "wider than the patristic tradition."

> It is thus an error and somewhat historically naïve to demand that, for all problems, we should reason "as did the Fathers," and to reject or put into doubt any problem for the sole reason that we do not find it in their writings. If we examine the history of dogma in its creative cycles, we can see that each age has its own problems, which are new with respect to those of the past, and is not afraid to innovate while

taking care not to break with tradition. It is clear that an attitude of mistrust or rejection of a new problem and, consequently, of a new doctrine is to fall into an anti-historic Talmudism and, at the same time, into a specific patrological heresy.[75]

Bulgakov claimed that most of the confessional wars were rooted in the absence of a distinction between a dogma and a dogmatic opinion. He concluded with the audacious idea "of a dogmatic development within Orthodoxy." This idea was based on the antinomy between the mystical nature of the church, which received the fullness of the Spirit at Pentecost, and its historical nature, which assimilated the gospel truths collectively and progressively. Zander continued along these lines in his essay "The Essence of the Ecumenical Movement," in which he justified the commitment of Christians who share a kinship in the same Spirit. Kartashev, in "The Freedom of Scientific and Theological Research and the Authority of the Church," interpreted this development as a "new awareness" on the part of the church.[76] To support his thesis, he pointed out the way in which the church, in the early centuries of its existence, needed time to assimilate new ideas—for example, in the domain of Trinitarian teaching. Afanasiev also called for a creative attitude with regard to the canons of the church, which are often marked by monophysitism.[77] Fedotov gave an exposition of ecclesial eschatology based on the principle of a development and of an incarnation of the Spirit in cultures. He contrasted this to the eschatology of the end of history and to the aestheticism of "certain Eastern Christians" who approach the church "in the hope of seeing Byzantium and not Christ."[78] Bezobrazov, a New Testament professor at the Institute, explained that all dogmatic development was founded on the belief that the scriptures are inspired by the Spirit and on the principle of consensus in Tradition—a consensus itself based on a multidisciplinary commentary on the same scriptures. Bezobrazov suggested that in extreme cases, the dogmatic interpretation, faithful to Tradition, had priority over the historical interpretation.[79] Sové, professor of liturgy at the Institute, also showed that the tradition of liturgical practices (infrequency or frequency of communion, the anaphora and other prayers of the liturgy recited in near silence rather than aloud, and the very recent requirement of confession and absolution before communion) was not written in stone but had been the result of a process of historical adaptation in function of the needs of the church at given moments. Kern's article was typical of this new awareness of "clericalism," to which reference has already been made. A professor of pastoral theology at St. Sergius, Kern contrasted the figure of the Levite to that of the prophet to demonstrate the evolution of the priestly function in the course of history. Kern juxtaposed the creative, dynamic, and visionary spirit of the priest-prophet with the static and Talmudic spirit of caste characteristic of the Old Testament priesthood.

Several essays in the collection incorporated the idea of the Wisdom of God, such as those by Zenkovsky, Ilyin, and Lagovsky. Zenkovsky, who taught philosophy at St. Sergius, was not afraid to affirm (even though he was close to Florovsky and Chetverikov) that "we should recognize that what is ideal in the cosmos bears the image of the divine Sophia and can rightly be called the created Sophia."[80] It must be noted that, at the same time, Zenkovsky's stance was ambiguous, since he also declared in private to his students at the Institute that he agreed with the sophiology of Bulgakov as long as it was not a question of the divine Sophia, the "uncreated Sophia."[81]

The article by Lagovsky, "The Return to the House of the Father," merits extensive discussion since it directly concerns the polemic surrounding Sophia.[82] Lagovsky's position was all the more intriguing in that he belonged to the Moscow patriarchate and, because of this allegiance, had left his teaching post at St. Sergius.

Lagovsky explained the debate between Bulgakov and his opponents as a confrontation between two philosophical attitudes, realism and nominalism. Lagovsky identified nominalism with rationalism and characterized it as the reduction of being to the level of a concept, one applicable only to individuals. Realism, on the other hand, was defined by "a sense of hierarchical primacy of being over consciousness," a symbolic—and nonmaterialistic—understanding that knowledge was a self-revelation of the Divinity.[83] Whereas realism, according to Lagovsky, was able to integrate the gospel revelation of the Kingdom as "growth" of being, nominalism, which had lost contact with the depths of the Divinity, had a static approach to the spiritual world.[84] It was this divergence between realism and nominalism, according to Lagovsky, that led to the opposition between Bulgakov and his accusers. In his opinion, their nominalism led them to formulate theses in matters of anthropology, soteriology, and triadology that did not conform to the dogmatic experience of the church.

Let us examine these theses, which represent an authentic "pneumatological boundary," distinguishing the School of Paris from its detractors in the Orthodox Church. Lagovsky wrote that the anthropology of the Orthodox Church was founded on the concept of *perichoresis*, elaborated by St. John of Damascus in the eighth century, according to which "each nature in Christ acts with the participation of the other." Thus the hypostatic union of two natures in Christ was not the "co-presence of two natures in a single receptacle" but the reunion, by the agency of the Divine Spirit, of the divine and human natures.[85] The synod of Karlovtsy, however, had formulated the following definition: "The Church expresses its faith that an integral human nature composed of spirit, soul, and body was united to the Word of God in such a manner that, as a result of this union, a Divine person appeared."[86] Lagovsky demonstrated that this was an Apollinarian and Nestorian interpretation of the doctrine of Chalcedon. On the one hand, it presented the hypostatic union as a result, as if it were the consequence of a synthesis, a third nature in addition to the divine and human natures. Moreover, it affirmed that the spirit was a part of human nature, and this contradicted patristic anthropology. For a realistic theology, Lagovsky continued, it was not the Lord Jesus Christ who "puts on a human nature composed of the *spirit*, of the soul and of the body," but the human nature "composed of a soul (intelligent) and body" that receives the divine Spirit, which is, in the case of Christ, the Logos. Thus, Lagovsky asserted, there were not two personal actions of Christ which could be opposed to one another, but the realization of the human nature in the divine nature "by the force of the divine Hypostasis."[87]

Concerning soteriology, Lagovsky again quoted Metropolitan Sergius:

We believe that if man . . . had progressed in his likeness to God, the incarnation of the Son in man would not have taken place. . . . At the beginning, man was not destined to occupy such an exceptional place in creation and in Divine Providence as was the case after the incarnation of the Son of God, who came to save one of the hundred expressions of his creative power.[88]

Lagovsky noted that this was an "occasionalist soteriology," a rationalization of the significance of salvation by making it an accidental event in the eternal plan of creation. Lagovsky explained that, according to the scriptures, even though the incarnation brought about the salvation of humanity, it was, from the beginning, seen as the fulfillment of creation so that, as John the Evangelist says, "whoever believes in him shall not perish but have eternal life" (John 3:16).[89]

Lagovsky concluded with the weakest point in the accusation—the triadology. He quoted the words of Metropolitan Sergius in his document of accusation: "The unique and inseparable Spirit can have three faces, that is, three consciousnesses or three 'I's,' which are not interchangeable."[90] Lagovsky maintained that this was a heresy, known in church history as tritheism, which deviated from the faith of the church in its proclamation of a unique "Trinitarian I." According to Lagovsky, Metropolitan Sergius, because of his nominalism, considered the mystery of the divine Being as if it were "a common abstract essence which only really existed in the Hypostases . . . the 'common nature' can and should be an abstract being, a 'representation'"—and from this came his temptation to interpret Sophia as an abstract intermediary between God and the world.[91] Lagovsky showed that this nonrecognition of "God outside of revelation" explained why those opposed to apophatic theology believed that it was based on "a presumption that the 'thing-to-be-known' was inaccessible to the intellect." For Lagovsky, on the contrary, the inaccessibility was an aspect of the Divine Absolute in the measure in which it signified "an inexhaustibility in spite of its accessibility."[92]

The publication in 1939 of an article by Elisabeth Behr-Sigel, who was close to both Vladimir Lossky and Bulgakov, put the finishing touches on the intellectual "victory" of Bulgakov's sophiology among the "modernists" of the Russian immigration on the eve of the war. Behr-Sigel gave a balanced and scholarly presentation of Bulgakov's thought. She wrote: "By constantly referring to the patristic tradition, Fr. Bulgakov seems to have, in great measure, avoided the danger which Solovyov could not escape, that is, to introduce into the Divinity a dualism which would be logically and ontologically prior to its Trinitarian structure."[93] Although she endorsed an article by Fr. Lev Gillet published in *Oecumenica* in 1936, in which the author lamented that Bulgakov had displaced the center of gravity from Christ to Sophia, Behr-Sigel emphasized that Sophia, for Bulgakov, was not a hypostasis but rather a "hypostasibility."[94] This essential point meant that the attacks of the neo-patristic movement were neutralized within that very segment of Francophone Orthodoxy allied with Vladimir Lossky. Expressing gratitude to Bulgakov for awakening the theologians from their "intellectual torpor," Behr-Sigel wrote: "His living ontology leads us out of the woods of Aristotelian scholasticism in which our Trinitarian theology was often mired."[95] Behr-Sigel, however, concluded her article by posing the following question, which shows how deeply she had penetrated the dynamics of Bulgakov's thought: "How can the concept of the progressive deification of the world be reconciled with the catastrophic eschatology of the New Testament?"[96] Unknown to Behr-Sigel, Bulgakov was working on a reply to this precise question in his final book, *The Bride of the Lamb* (which was not published until after the war).

This period of consensus with respect to Bulgakov and Metropolitan Evlogy helped to calm the tensions in the diocese between 1935 and the beginning of 1938. Aside from these internal reasons, there was also the fact that from 1936 to 1937, the Russian Church endured a new wave of violent persecution. In an article in the July 1937 issue of *The Way*, "The Present Situation of the Russian Church," Sové wrote: "As of May 1936, there were 9,126 members of the clergy in concentration camps."[97] In addition, the Russian constitution of 1936 contained new discriminatory measures against religious confessions. The fact that Metropolitan Sergius was preoccupied with these events explains, perhaps, why he exerted little pressure on the diocese of Metropolitan Evlogy.

On February 25, 1938, however, Hitler signed a decree that placed the possessions of the Russian Church under the authority of the Ministry of Cults and handed over their administration to representatives of the Synod. These representatives, with the support of the German police, obliged the clergy faithful to Metropolitan Evlogy to become members of the Synod. In August 1938 the Synod, for the first time since 1921, summoned a council of the whole church of the immigration but excluded the jurisdiction of Metropolitan Evlogy. The successor of Metropolitan Antony, the self-proclaimed Metropolitan Anastassy Gribanovsky, speaking in the name of the Synod, condemned Metropolitan Evlogy, imposed the use of Slavonic as the liturgical language throughout the world, confirmed the existence of a sole legal Russian Church in Germany, and accused "international Judaism" of acting in collaboration with the Catholic Church to undermine Christianity.[98] Unlike the council of 1921, this one did not call for a return of the monarchy but instead expressed hope for "a healthy, strong, and unique Russian State." During the war, Metropolitan Seraphim was sent to Paris by the Synod in conformity with a policy of close collaboration with the German government. This led to several interrogations of Metropolitan Evlogy by the Gestapo. On another front, the patriotic attitude of Metropolitan Sergius in 1941 and Stalin's recognition of a new status for the church in 1943 did much to unite the anti-German and anticommunist immigrants under the Muscovite jurisdiction. After the war, Metropolitan Evlogy—like Metropolitan Seraphim, now exarch of the patriarchate of Moscow—once again turned towards the Moscow patriarchate. He concelebrated a liturgy with Metropolitan Nicholas Krutitsky in the cathedral of rue Daru in August 1945. The reservations of Zenkovsky and Kartashev made him hesitate, however, and he died in August 1946 without being able to complete this final reversal of history.

Different Representations of the Kingdom

The Way's Position in the Conflict between Right and Left, 1935–1936

The Franco-Soviet rapprochement, which began with the first meeting of the two countries' ministers of Foreign Affairs, Pierre Laval and Maxim Litvinov, on December 5, 1934, and culminated May 2, 1935, with a treaty of alliance and the subsequent visit of Laval to Moscow on May 13, caused a crisis among the émigrés. It was no longer possible to sit on the fence; each one had to choose a side. Between 1935 and 1937, the Mladoross Party leaders, A. Kazem-Bek and N. Fedorov, the head of the Association of the *Vitiazi*, became the standard-bearers of right-wing nationalism, while the Eurasians, S. Efron and N. Klepinin, opted to return to the USSR on October 22, 1937. In 1936, the publisher Desclée de Brouwer brought out a book by Nadezhda Gorodetsky.[99] It described the uprooted young generation of the Russian emigration, torn between their desire to return to the USSR—as does Nina, the young heroine—and their incredible passivity, their feelings of resentment towards the preceding generation.[100] This evolution had its effects on the review as well.

On February 1, 1935, one "P. Sazonovich" published an article entitled "Berdyaev's Ideology of the Return" in *Renaissance*, the most popular daily newspaper of the émigré community. The article accused the editor of *The Way* of having facilitated the return of S. Efron through his contacts with the Soviet Union and the NKVD and of nurturing an admiration for the accomplishments of the Russian Communist Party. As soon as the article appeared, Tamara Baimakova, who was close to Berdyaev, immediately recognized the style of Ilyin under the pseudonym of Sazonovich, thanks to certain expressions favored by the philosopher in referring to Berdyaev, such as "red general" or "defender of the KGB"—terms that the professor at St. Sergius was spreading throughout Paris at that time. Once unmasked, Ilyin sent a letter to Berdyaev, dated February 10, in which he acknowledged his authorship and made his apologies. Berdyaev did not enter into the polemic. He simply commented to his wife, "But what right has he to judge me?"[101] Meanwhile the discussions continued in the émigré salons.

No one defended Berdyaev against these accusations until a month after Ilyin's article appeared. Shestov reacted on March 2 with a "letter to the editor" in the review *Poslednie Novosti* (*Latest News*).[102] He took apart Sazonovich's arguments, affirmed that Berdyaev had never advocated a return, and expressed his indignation that a prestigious daily could publish such nonsense. This letter was co-signed by Fondaminsky, Vysheslavtsev, Kurdiumov, Iswolsky, Mochulsky, and Fedotov. Two days later, in the same publication, sixteen others announced their support of this letter and condemned Sazonovich's "assault on Russian culture." The right-wing press, however, seized upon this unhoped-for support of a writer of *The Way* to back up their theory that Berdyaev's review was a tool of the Soviet Secret Services. They harped on this all year long.

All this only encouraged Berdyaev to open the pages of the review to nonconformist left-wing authors. Particularly notable was an article by Gofshtetter in the May–October 1936 issue, following the victory of the Popular Front and during the first trial against Zinovev and Kamenev in Moscow. The article, "The Philosophical Foundations of Socialism," was preceded by a notice that the editors "leave to the author the responsibility for his defense of state capitalism." In his article, Gofshtetter affirmed that "the political genius of Lenin was to install state capitalism as a necessary transition step towards the socialism of the future."[103] He also ended by praising Stalin for having brought back salary scales [as part of 1931 wage reforms]: "As a good disciple [of Lenin,] Stalin continued his work."[104] As soon as this issue of *The Way* was published, Ilyin again took up his pen to write—this time without a pseudonym—a vitriolic article for *Renaissance*, in which he declared himself scandalized that "a review of religious philosophy" would publish "bad articles of Soviet propaganda."[105] These attacks against the review as a whole by Ilyin coincided, ironically, with a period in which Berdyaev was being harshly criticized from within the Soviet Union. In December 1935, *Izvestiia* published two violent diatribes by Bukharin against Berdyaev's book *Le destin de l'homme dans le monde actuel* (*The Fate of Man in the Modern World*), which the Soviet philosopher had read in German. He treated Berdyaev as one of the "white guard" and a propagator of "cultural phyletism."[106]

This criticism by Bukharin, who had been following closely Berdyaev's articles in the émigré press,[107] did not occur randomly. It corresponded to a transition in Berdyaev's political philosophy from criticism of Marxism to his development of a "personalist socialism" or a "religious socialism," which he considered a valid ideological alternative to the Stalinist regime. The evolution from a metaphysical personalism to the elaboration of a political doctrine centered on the person took place between July 1935, the date of the publication of "Personalism and Marxism," and October of that same year, when he wrote reviews in *The Way* of two books, one by E. Mounier, *Révolution personnaliste et communautaire*, the other by L. Ragaz, *Du Christ à Marx et de Marx au Christ*. While Berdyaev left off his studies of Soviet communism once he had completed, before the summer of 1935, *Les sources et le sens du communisme russe* (*The Origin of Russian Communism*), in March 1936 he composed *De l'esclavage et de la liberté de l'homme* (*Slavery and Freedom*), his personalist synthesis. In his essay "Personalism and Marxism" in *The Way*, he made his own the Marxist doctrine of mercantile fetishism, according to which the German philosopher defined capital not as something real but as "the social relationship among people in the course of the production process" and sought to displace the center of gravity of economics from the product to human activity. But Berdyaev contrasted his new existential sociology, which viewed the person as an eruption in the world of nature, to Marxist sociology, which affirmed that the person is the result of a social process. Citing Nesmelov, Berdyaev asserted that it was not the person who was part of society; rather, society was a part of the person. Differing from Max Scheler, who based the person on the life principle, Berdyaev affirmed that it was the spirit, an active—not passive—principle, which defined the person. In Berdyaev's perspective, this reversing of values should inspire a genuine social revolution. "The foundation of the social conception of the world of personalism is neither the idea of equality nor that of justice but the idea of the dignity of every human person, which gives him the right to the possibility of self-realization."[108] Finally, Berdyaev, for the first time in the review, abandoned his neutral stance of "neither capitalism nor communism" and expressed his convictions and political commitment.

> Socialism must be defined as the construction of the new classless society in which a greater degree of social justice will prevail and where the exploitation of man by man will not be authorized. The realization of the new man and the fraternity of peoples is a spiritual and religious task and implies an inner rebirth. This is what communism, itself a religion, does not want to accept. This is why a Christian can be a socialist and even, in my opinion, should be a socialist. But it is difficult for him to be a communist, for he cannot accept the totalitarian vision of communism. . . . Christian personalism should not only not be opposed to the creation of a classless society; it should contribute to its realization. . . . In a period of acute social struggle, the social system which best corresponds to Christian personalism is the system of personalist socialism.[109]

From this point on, Berdyaev progressively developed his political doctrine, building on the insights of other theorists of religious socialism, such as Leonard Ragaz, a Swiss Protestant theologian, Paul Tillich, Henri de Man, André Philip, and Emmanuel Mounier, among others. Later on I address the question of what Berdyaev held in common with these authors and where he differed from them. For now, it is worth noting that Berdyaev's ideas, especially the personalist justification for the refusal of private property, attracted a certain number of young Russian émigrés. Berdyaev published an important article by D. Semenov Tian-Shansky in March 1937, entitled "Work, Creativity, and Freedom," in which the author dealt with some controversial contemporary issues such as the necessity of reducing the numbers of hours worked and the transition from a society based on machines to a community founded on the development of creative trades in view of the public good.[110]

Fedotov followed a similar path. As a left-wing Christian, in 1935–36 he felt that the time had come to become more involved in the political arena. He began to write articles on contemporary political issues both at home and abroad, which were published regularly in the new weekly founded by Kerensky in 1936, *Novaia Rossiia* (*New Russia*). Fedotov, who was formerly a Eurasian, was once appreciated by certain right-wing elements of the immigration for the patriotic overtones of his reflections. The rapid evolution of the political context by 1935, the very evident prodemocratic involvement of the editor of *New City*, and, above all, the large-scale collapse of the simplistic ideological conceptions that divided the world into socialism and nationalism, all combined to make Fedotov the scapegoat of the conservative press. The first article of his that provoked the thunderbolts of this press was entitled "Stalinocracy." It was published in 1936 in *Contemporary Annals* (no. 60) and subsequently reproduced in French in 1937 in *Esprit* (no. 56). It claimed to be a "photograph of Russia on January 1, 1936." In it, Fedotov rebutted the idea, traditional in monarchist and conservative circles, that Stalin was the living incarnation of Marxist-Leninism. On the contrary, Fedotov compared Stalin, "the red tsar," to Bonaparte. He warned those "young elements of the emigration who wanted to return to Russia" that this pseudo-transformation of Bolshevism to Fascism and then to a pure and simple dictatorship depended on a system of "concentration camps, deportations to Siberia, inhuman labor, and death."[111] A little later, Fedotov published an article entitled "Passionaria" in *New Russia*, in which he defended Spanish democracy against the Falangists of Franco, who hid their nationalism under the Christian cross. That was too much. Metropolitan Evlogy, who was his confessor and spiritual father, demanded that Fedotov cease publishing political articles. The conservative elements completely flew off the handle when, in 1937, Fedotov published a new essay entitled "How Stalin Sees Russian History," in which he demonstrated the pseudomorphosis of the Bolshevik ideology from internationalism to nationalism. The nationalist circles close to the Russian General Military Union (ROVS), irritated by this article that questioned their very identity, put pressure on Metropolitan Evlogy, the rector of the St. Sergius Institute, who demanded that Fedotov choose between his teaching position and his journalistic activity.

The Desire for Unity, 1937–1938

The position taken by Berdyaev in favor of socialism and the glowing tribute he paid to Léon Blum, the head of the French government in 1936–1937, and then again in 1938, in the pages of *The Way*—"one of the most honest, idealistic, and cultivated politicians in this country" (Berdyaev and Blum met personally in 1938 at the request of the prime minister)[112]—did not mean that everyone associated with the journal had become a socialist. Within *The Way*, however, no one dared to argue politics with Berdyaev. Thus, Berdyaev's commitment caused *The Way* to be considered a socialist publication by force of public opinion. One of the consequences was that this clarified the situation and calmed down disputes. Once again, Berdyaev was reconciled with Ilyin through the mediation of Bulgakov, and in October 1938 he published an article by Ilyin. This article was without political undertones; rather, it was a sophiological meditation on death and resurrection.

Moreover, the separation of the nationalist and democratic currents within the Russian Student Christian Movement contributed to the reinforcement of the anti-nationalist position of the review. This position had been laid down by Berdyaev against the Eurasians as early as 1925 and reaffirmed when Hitler came to power in 1933. Berdyaev and Mochulsky continued to maintain this intransigent line. In December 1937, Berdyaev published yet another violent criticism of totalitarianism in Germany. This article was directed at the German Protestant theologians who were unable to participate in the ecumenical conference at Oxford in June 1937, but who published a collection of essays entitled "The Church, the People, and the State." Berdyaev voiced his dismay at their lack of freedom and the fact that he was scandalized by their religious justification of eugenics in the name of racial purity, their anti-Semitism, and their anti-personalism.[113] He compared the conformism of the German theologians with that of the Soviet philosophers and paid tribute to the Orthodox and Protestant dissidents who struggle against the totalitarian state.

In 1937 an extraordinary event shook up the émigré community and dampened the zeal of the conservatives in their efforts to unmask the Bolshevik enemy in the free socialist press. On a September morning, both the Russian and French press shocked the immigrants by revealing that the Russian General Military Union, the spearhead of the anti-communist campaign, was itself infiltrated by the KGB. General Nicolas Skoblin was the aide of General Miller, the head of the ROVS, the principal military organization of the emigration, and since 1930 he had been working for both the Soviet and German secret services.[114] In 1936 he met two KGB agents, who asked him to participate in fabricating evidence that would implicate Marshal Tukhachevsky in a Hitler-inspired plot against Stalin. In exchange, they promised that General Miller, who mistrusted Skoblin, would be taken care of. On September 22, 1937, seven years after the kidnapping of General Kutepov, General Miller was kidnapped in the center of Paris and left France, the next day, on the ship *Maria Oulianova* with the complicity of the Russian embassy in France. Skoblin, unmasked, succeeded in escaping but left his wife, Nadezhda Plevitskaya, in the hands of the French police. After a widely publicized trial she was condemned, in December 1938, to twenty years in prison.[115] This shocked the immigrant community. Also disturbing were the return of Eurasians to the Soviet Union in October 1937, the warming of Franco-Soviet relations that began in 1935, and the troubling rumors of a reign of terror in Russia. All these events led a large sector of the Russian emigration to regroup and to rediscover a common identity between 1937 and 1938. In 1937, Berdyaev, Mother Maria, and Fedotov had the idea of founding a "Christian league for the defense of human rights," with the participation of many associations and reviews representing both the left-wing and right-wing tendencies of the immigration. This search for unity was apparent above all in 1937, the jubilee year of Pushkin, and again in 1938, the jubilee year of the baptism of St. Vladimir (988), when the emigration commemorated its past and sought to rise above its internal quarrels in honoring these two historic and nonconflictive personalities. On February 28, 1937, Bulgakov, Kartashev, and Fedotov celebrated the memory of Pushkin side by side at St. Sergius.[116] On June 3, 1938, in the presence of representatives of the organizations of the immigration assembled for the occasion, Kartashev concluded his talk on the celebration of the 950th anniversary of the baptism of St. Vladimir with the following words: "We Orthodox have no doubts that, in this situation of freedom, under the standard of St. Vladimir, our heavenly protector who has transmitted to us the creative heritage of the Orthodox culture, of Christian governance, and of a just social order, we will triumph."[117]

The Rekindling of Tensions, 1938–1940

After the Munich pact, which completely discredited the democratic powers, Fedotov chose to leave the St. Sergius Institute. He arranged a six-month leave of absence to write a new book on Russian spirituality and moved to

England. But when General Denikin launched an appeal to all the organizations of the immigration to reunite in the face of the dangers of war, Fedotov took up his pen and published an article in *New Russia* entitled "Make Haste!" Statements such as these provoked a lively reaction:

> It is thought that the tyrant is smothering Russia only because of the priorities of the International. People think like that only because they cannot represent the radical evil elsewhere than in the figure of the International and cannot imagine that the service of the International also demands an effort on one's part, a sacrifice for the good of the other—something Stalin is incapable of doing. To be absolute Master of a country and to decide to link one's name forever with the history of this country, as well as to sacrifice the country to the interests of humanity and to the fraternity of workers, really demands an ultra-Christian spirit of sacrifice. Every bandit who becomes master of a country ceases to distinguish between the interests of the state and his own interests. Stalin, like the German emperors at Petersburg in the eighteenth century, is the master of Russia. But he is a barbaric master, cynical and stupid, who, in the name of his caprices and idiocy, smothers the land and lays waste to its resources. To his natural barbarism, fear must be added. The struggle for his personal safety and the conservation of power dictate everything the tyrant does. On the eve of war, he destroys his army to frustrate any plots against him—that sums up Stalin.[118]

Renaissance immediately launched a press campaign against Fedotov. Semionov, the editor-in-chief of the journal, and the journalist Goriansky accused Fedotov of pro-Soviet agitation by his declarations "in favor of the International." Metropolitan Evlogy, fearful for the reputation of the St. Sergius Institute, decided to call a meeting of its board of directors. On February 8, 1939, the board—which included most of the professors of the Institute—officially demanded that Fedotov sign a written promise not to publish any more political articles. Without trying to hide his political motives, Metropolitan Evlogy sent a letter to Fedotov dated February 10 ordering him to cease "all socialist declarations."[119] He criticized him above all for having affirmed in "sacrilegious" fashion that the cause of the International "demanded an ultra-Christian sacrifice." The salary he received from the Institute was the main source of revenue for Fedotov, his wife, Elena, and his daughter, Nina. Nevertheless, Fedotov, with his wife's agreement, preferred to risk expulsion from the Institute and unemployment rather than submit to the demands of the Metropolitan. He was supported in his battle for "the freedom of expression for all Orthodox writers" by his wife, who was in Paris at that time, by students at the Institute (E. Lampert, K. Kostandi, V. Dubrovsky, I. Morozov, A. Kniazev, E. Melia, and others), and by the Orthodox Action group.

On February 13, Fedotov replied to the board of directors, asking its members to reconsider their decision. He justified his request by claiming that it was not the role of the St. Sergius Institute to judge his journalistic activities. What is more, he wrote, his opinions did not in any way threaten the Institute, given that the smear campaign against his articles came from a journal and a circle that offered "neither material nor moral" support to the Institute.[120] On the contrary, Fedotov believed, if the decision of the Institute became public, it would reflect negatively on the dignity of the church of the Russian emigration and especially on the Institute. This sharp reply of Fedotov put the St. Sergius professors in an awkward position— it revealed their ideological motivations and genuinely threatened the Institute, since its main benefactors were Anglicans and Protestants on the side of democracy. Two professors, Zenkovsky and Florovsky, were especially sensitive about their reputation in ecumenical circles and made another effort to convince Fedotov to stop writing about politics. Zenkovsky wrote to him on February 20: "My God, how little value freedom has compared to the possibility of working for the spiritual and intellectual renaissance of the Church and, through it, of Russia."[121] On March 7, Florovsky and Zenkovsky wrote to him, "in the name of all your colleagues at the Institute," that "political activities are incompatible with a commitment to the service of the Church through the Institute of theology."[122] One month later and without explanation, Elena Fedotov ceased to receive her husband's salary from the Institute. Fedotov, however, would not yield.

At this point, Berdyaev came to Fedotov's assistance by making the affair public. In April 1939, he published a famous article entitled "Does Freedom of Thought and Conscience Really Exist in Orthodoxy?" (B91). This article was subsequently considered a manifesto on the same level as Tolstoy's pamphlet "I Cannot Keep Silent."[123] Berdyaev began with a citation from Nietzsche's *Zarathustra*: "You have become small and are going to become still smaller. That is what you get from your doctrine on humility and obedience."[124] After summing up the affair of the "ultimatum" issued to Fedotov by the St. Sergius Institute, Berdyaev posed the following question: "Can an Orthodox be a democrat and a socialist while teaching at an institute of theology?" The professors of the Institute, he stated, were not intellectual Philistines, but they were smothered by the traditionalist and nationalist circles surrounding them. But, Berdyaev argued, "our world is in the process of dying because of nationalism; it is going towards a blood bath because of those who 'think of the nation.' The Church should condemn nationalism as a heresy against life."[125] Berdyaev noted that what the nationalist circles attacked in Fedotov was his lack of attachment to the nation and, more profoundly, his belonging to the intelligentsia. For Berdyaev, this latter allegiance was characterized by an evangelical attachment to truth and justice, whereas nationalism, whose only characteristic was the sacralization of traditions, was religious tribalism. This led to the core of Berdyaev's attack.

> Slavery, servitude—presented in the catechism of Philaret—the despotic state, the retardation of scientific knowledge, all that was a sacred tradition. . . . There are no conclusions more frightening than those that Orthodoxy, in the course of its history, has drawn from the concepts of humility and obedience. In the name of humility people were forced to subscribe to evil and lies. Humility became a school of servility. Thus were formed souls of slaves, bereft of any virility and trembling before the forces and powers of this world. Civic manliness and the sentiment of honor were incompatible with such an understanding of humility and obedience. That is where the subservience in Soviet Russia comes from. The Russian clergy, the hierarchs of the Church have always wagged their little tails when faced with the power of the State, adapting themselves to it to the point of submitting the Church to it. And this continues even in our times when, thank God, this lie of a "State orthodoxy" no longer exists. Today the people of the Church wag their little tails when faced with the right-wingers of the immigration.[126]

Berdyaev called for a "reform" of Orthodoxy in the line of a tradition that extended from "Nil of Sora to Solovyov." Such a reform should include a new way of understanding the myth of original sin that would enable us to finally liberate ourselves from our servility before Caesar and to respond to all the new questions being posed to society. He stated that he had had enough of hearing the church talk all the time about divine-humanity without responding to the problems presented by the conflicts between workers and capitalists. He reminded readers that John Chrysostom was a communist and that he saw "more Christian humanitarianism in the politics of Blum than in those of the right-wingers with their constant appeals to murder and violence."[127] To conclude, Berdyaev contrasted the example of Jacques Maritain, who, thanks to the perspicacity of Pius XII, could write against Franco and teach at a Catholic university, with the attitude of the nationalist circles "who think that the Gospel is a Baptist book!"[128]

Even though Berdyaev prefaced his article with a note from the editors of *The Way* stating that "the author assumes exclusive responsibility for this article,"[129] this scathing attack by the editor of the review—which was also published in Kerensky's *New Russia*—let loose a new polemic among the writers and readers of *The Way*. Lydia Judifevna Berdyaev took note of it in her diary:

> May 26 [1939] A bomb has exploded! Publication in *The Way* of an article by Ni [Nikolai Berdyaev], "Does Freedom of Thought and Conscience Really Exist in Orthodoxy?" The first reaction to this article was a letter from Professor Zenkovsky of the Institute of theology. He feels offended and has decided to resign from the editorial staff of *The Way*. . . . Ni is worked up and getting ready for the battle. He is waiting to see how things evolve. Personally, I'm quite happy. I think this Fedotov affair has been providential. The severance of links with those who use the authority of the Church to cover goals which have nothing to do with Christianity has been long overdue.[130]

With the exceptions of Vysheslavtsev, Mochulsky, Lev Gillet, and Bulgakov, all of the other professors of St. Sergius withdrew from the review, namely, Florovsky, Zander, Bezobrazov, Kern, Ilyin, Kartashev, Afanasiev, and Sové. In his correspondence with Fedotov, Berdyaev referred to a conflict with Paul Anderson, who considered this article "a heavy blow to the Institute and to *The Way*—and a still more serious conflict with Vysheslavtsev with whom I can no longer work."¹³¹ The Institute found itself obligated to issue a convoluted press release, published, notably, in the *Messenger* of the Russian Student Christian Movement, which promised, as a sign of its "good faith," to publish all the documents relative to this affair (something that was never done). It read thus:

> The directors of the theological institute feel obliged to indicate that the whole article of N. A. Berdyaev is based on a totally false presentation of the facts. . . . It is especially false to say that an ultimatum has been given to Professor Fedotov. It is also false to say that he was summoned to cease his journalistic activities and to renounce his political commitment. . . . The directors simply passed a judgment on the political writings of Professor Fedotov, concluded that they would lead a great number of the faithful into error, and requested that, in the future, Professor Fedotov refrain from declarations that could be harmful to the institute of theology.¹³²

The departure of the pro-nationalist writers of the review encouraged Berdyaev to break off definitively with the Christian right wing and with Frank in particular. In September 1939, Berdyaev published an article by Frank entitled "The Problem of Christian Socialism," in which the author affirmed that if the social question was not just a matter of individual almsgiving, the Christian could not rely on a social utopia, "because he knows that human tragedies have a deeper root . . . to which political measures cannot have access." Consequently, according to Frank, "Christian love cannot be legislated, for the law is an obligation, whereas the Spirit breathes where He wills." Thus the Christian, although not remaining inactive, believes that any reform should be accompanied by spiritual growth. Frank went on to affirm that this was why the spiritual quest for the Heavenly Kingdom should have precedence over the struggle for social reforms in this world. Frank concluded his article by defending the democratic and capitalist regimes that have been capable of welcoming Christian socialists and by criticizing the German and Soviet dictatorships, where "Christian socialism is an almost inconceivable phenomenon."¹³³

Berdyaev chose to reply to this article with moderation but also firmness. He criticized Frank's conclusion that the system most compatible with Christianity was based on "property without limits, on economic 'freedom,' on the individual's 'freedom' to dispose of his riches." He pointed out that this was precisely "the capitalist system, which claimed to be founded on freedom but which was motivated by egoism, individual interests, competition, the quest for profits, the bestial indifference to needs, to exploitation, and to human poverty, a system where man is crushed by man and made a thing."[134] For Berdyaev, the law of elementary justice for all must be realized before we can speak of "spiritual deepening":

> To eliminate slavery, it was not necessary to wait for an increase of Christian charity; there was a social act which brought it about, which changed the structures of society. It's the same thing today.... The socialist system might be as sinful as all the other regimes in the world. But man's elementary dignity... will be upheld. Only then can we ask ourselves more in depth whether men treat one another as brothers— and that is a question that goes beyond the social order.[135]

Berdyaev concluded by defending a personalist socialism against national socialism and state socialism or fascism; a personalist socialism "refuses to submit man to the power of the State, to national glory, or to economic development."[136]

The decision to make the debate public and the ensuing separation among the authors of the journal according to their convictions served to calm things down. To be sure, Berdyaev did not set foot in the St. Sergius Institute again, except once, in July 1944, on the occasion of the death of Bulgakov. Fedotov's case was different. In May 1939, Berdyaev published an article by Fedotov entitled "In Defense of Ethics," which he considered "a reply to Fr. Sergius [Bulgakov] and those who follow him." In the Kantian tradition, Fedotov defended the autonomy and primacy of the ethical sphere alongside the domains of epistemology and aesthetics. Fedotov— who observed that the Christ of the Gospels taught how to love one's neighbor and not "how to write poems or do mathematics"[137]—compared the moral act to prophesy in the sense that both demand listening to the will of God and a commitment *hic et nunc*.[138] For Fedotov, the "renaissance of the Russian Church" had the great merit of restoring prayer to the very heart of ethics. But this renewal shut itself up in a liturgical and ascetic universe "that doesn't resolve all of life's problems"[139] and that can impede Christian action insofar as it habituates a person to passivity and the interior life.

During the following month, Fedotov, in a letter to Berdyaev thanking him for his article, confided that he no longer felt he had enough strength left to return to teaching at the Institute, even if he were invited to do so.[140] Bulgakov, however, who had just undergone a serious throat operation that left him unable to speak, sent Fedotov a letter dated July 19 in which he requested a "reciprocal amnesty."[141] When war was declared in September 1939, Zenkovsky and Zander were arrested by the French police on suspicion of collaboration with the German-Soviet enemy. At that time, Florovsky, whom Fedotov considered "the center of resistance" to his return to the Institute in virtue of his lobbying Metropolitan Evlogy to this end, was in Switzerland. Florovsky decided to take refuge in Belgrade with P. Struve and the Russian Orthodox Church Outside Russia. From this moment, the professors at the St. Sergius Institute forgot their quarrels and welcomed Fedotov back to the faculty. In September 1939, Fedotov published an article in *The Way* entitled "Pages of St. Sergius" ("Serguievskie listki," a review of the latest issues of the journal of St. Sergius), signed only with his initials and edited by two students at the Institute, V. Dubrovsky and E. Lampert. The article was a homage to those who stood by him during his painful skirmish with the directors of the Institute.[142]

Dissolution and Restructuring within the Review

The Crisis of 1935–1936

The spiritual evolution of the writers contributing to *The Way* had points of convergence but also of divergence, and this, in turn, affected the journal's makeup. After the events of February 6, 1934, and the departure of Fedorov, the leaders of the Russian Student Christian Movement maintained an apolitical attitude. This stance contributed to splitting the Orthodox youth movement into three factions: the pro-nationalist tendency of *Vitiazi*, the anti-nationalist current of Orthodox Action, and the pro-nationalist youth orientation of those who remained members of the Russian Student Christian Movement. The principle of apoliticism proved fatal to the RSCM since, on the one hand, the nationalist ideologues who were responsible for elaborating the relationship that its members should have with the world were not in a position to condemn or oppose political and social realities that contradicted or opposed Christian ethics—and, on the other hand, this ideology contradicted itself and lost its appeal when it abandoned apolitical prudence to condemn communism. Whereas Fedorov had left the movement in 1934 because of its links with the YMCA, Berdyaev and Mother Maria left it in September 1935 because of the dominant nationalistic ideology.

This schism became inevitable after the Congress of Boissy l'Aillery, held June 1–4, 1935—just before the tempest regarding Sophia—with the participation of about a hundred delegates from all of the countries of Europe. In his inaugural address on June 2, Zenkovsky, who had been reelected president, reaffirmed the general principles of "unshakeable anti-bolshevism" and of collaboration only with apolitical youth organizations.[143] A. Nikitin, the head of the pro-national tendency, replaced F. Pianov, a friend of Berdyaev, in the movement's council, and Chetverikov was confirmed in his functions as chaplain of the movement. Recognizing the split with the followers of *Vitiazi*, the Congress decided to change the structure of the RSCM to a "union of local autonomous movements," which would enable it to reintegrate the movement of Fedorov. However, the Congress postponed the election of a secretary in charge of coordination until the following year.

By autumn, Nikitin's election as general secretary of the RSCM in France had brought about a hardening of the right-wing tendencies in the movement and provoked the creation of Orthodox Action by Mother Maria and Berdyaev, who hoped to thus regroup the anti-nationalist currents. In an attempt to appease Fedorov, Nikitin arranged for separation of the RSCM from the YMCA. In fact, the RSCM received only minimal financial support from the American organization (2,500 French francs out of a budget of 83,350 French francs). This led to the decision by the RSCM to move its offices to a new site—91 rue d'Olivier de Serres, near the Versailles gate in Paris. Thanks to financial aid from the World Student Christian Federation, the move took place on December 1, 1935. The last days of cohabitation between the YMCA (on which the Academy of Religious Philosophy and *The Way* depended) and the RSCM at Boulevard Montparnasse were very tense. When Berdyaev gave his lecture on the Grand Inquisitor in defense of Bulgakov on November 24, on the occasion of a public session of the Academy, Chetverikov sought to have Berdyaev expelled from the RSCM for insubordination to ecclesiastical authorities. But Berdyaev retaliated with a speech on the freedom of conscience in

Orthodoxy so passionate that no one dared to initiate the process of expulsion.[144] On the other hand, S. Hautman, the manager of the journal, resigned. Berdyaev asked Fr. Lev Gillet, who was then living at Orthodox Action, to replace him. The departure of the RSCM caused the YMCA—which was the seat of the review—to move to 29 rue Saint Didier in the 16th arrondissement of Paris in May. Paul Anderson joined with other editors of the Russian immigration to open a bookstore there under the name of Les Éditeurs Réunis, which carried, among other literature, issues of *The Way*.

If the administrative address of the journal was now on the Right Bank in the 16th arrondissment, the real intellectual and spiritual center of *The Way* had been transferred to the seat of Orthodox Action, at 77 rue de Lourmel, on the Left Bank in the 15th arrondissement. During the first semester of 1936, there were still classes at Boulevard Montparnasse. It was significant that Berdyaev focused his courses on the topic of "different types of spiritual life." In the next semester, however, in October 1936, the Academy of Religious Philosophy, which edited the journal, decided to transfer its activities to the rue de Lourmel. This was done at the request of Mother Maria, who wanted to reinforce her "missionary center" of Orthodox Action. As will be seen, this geographic change corresponded to the spirit-centered evolution of the most influential members of the review—Berdyaev and Mother Maria, but also Fedotov, Bulgakov, and Mochulsky, who were leaders of the social consciousness of the intellectuals who made up *The Way*.

After the congress of 1935, Mother Maria, with the blessing of Metropolitan Evlogy, had decided to create her own organization. Even though she herself had no money, she had been able to acquire a run-down building in the rue de Lourmel in 1934, thanks to the gifts of some Anglican friends of Paul Anderson. This building was in a neighborhood where Russian émigrés were particularly numerous.[145] She decided to create Orthodox Action after discussing the matter with Berdyaev, who came up with the name for the new venture. This association, financed in part by the YMCA, had a threefold objective: to provide material, pedagogical, and liturgical assistance to the neediest of the Russian émigré community. Mother Maria was the president, K. Mochulsky the vice president, F. Pianov the secretary, and Fr. Chertkov the treasurer. Berdyaev, Bulgakov, and Fedotov were the first members. As for the younger generation, Mother

Maria invited certain former members of the RSCM, such as Tamara Baimakova, of the Academy, G. Kazatchkin, and certain members of The Circle (*Krug*)—founded about the same time by I. Fondaminsky and revolving around the review *New City*—such as S. Zhaba.

In October 1935, with the help of Mother Eudoxia, another nun who came from Russia, Mother Maria moved the home for single women and its chapel from the Villa de Saxe to her building at rue de Lourmel. The first priest who served at the modest chapel set up in the courtyard of the building was Fr. Lev Gillet. Thirty-two women could be housed there. The kitchen served 120 meals daily. Mother Maria also set up a home for men a short distance away, at rue Felix Fauré. These men were very often chauffeurs without families, but they also included the unemployed, delinquent expatriates threatened with expulsion, and former soldiers considered mentally ill and vegetating in psychiatric hospitals. According to Elisabeth Behr-Sigel, Fr. Lev Gillet often accompanied Mother Maria as she made the nightly rounds of the bars near des Halles seeking out Russian vagabonds in order to bring them help and comfort. This "monastery" of Mother Maria, the temporary home for unemployed Russian émigrés, scandalized many who were accustomed to the ascetical and liturgical ambience of classical Russian monasteries. In a letter dated November 9, 1935, to Elisabeth Behr-Sigel, Fr. Lev Gillet gave this tongue-in-cheek description of the "monastery": "It is a strange pandemonium: we have some young girls, basket cases, people who have been expelled, people who are unemployed, and, at this moment, the choir of the Russian Opera and the Gregorian choir of Dom Malherbe, a missionary center, and, now, services in the chapel every morning and evening."[146]

In autumn of 1935, Berdyaev had decided to relaunch *New City*, which published one issue a year until 1939. The review echoed the commitment of Mother Maria by publishing an article of hers entitled "Orthodox Action," in which she justified her activities by stating how tired she was of listening to lofty theoretical speeches on ways to reconstruct Russia after the collapse of communism. Rather, she pleaded for modesty, realism, and respect for the "little things" of the daily life of the émigrés. This article could be considered the manifesto of Orthodox Action and a new concept of commitment on behalf of the nation: namely, service to one's neighbor here and now. It signified a radical shift from the projects of the 1920s of the Russian Student Christian Movement, the Academy of Religious Philosophy, and the St. Sergius Institute, which had viewed the formation of the younger generation in terms of a return to Russia in the near future. Mother Maria wrote:

> It would be much more difficult for me to launch such an appeal if I didn't feel surrounded by a significant group of persons who had already agreed among themselves to enter into this common project which we call "Orthodox Action." We don't just theorize but, in the measure of our poor and insufficient possibilities, we try to put our theories into practice. We have a hospice, for women and for men . . . we distribute books. We dream of building a little Orthodox city within this gigantic and foreign Paris! . . . It is not our fault if this cannot be an enormous State or even all of humanity. We have been placed in a very reduced space and we want to be faithful to it.[147]

The journal *New City* also attempted to stimulate the ideas of Christian democracy and religious creativity that had been discussed in its pages by opening a new feature significantly entitled "The Spiritual Front." In this feature the review echoed the discussions of a group dedicated to political and literary reflection, The Circle *(Krug)*, founded October 21, 1935, by Fondaminsky with the participation of Mother Maria and Fedotov. It was oriented especially towards the young intellectuals, writers, and artists of the emigration. This circle, which met on the second Sunday of each month in Fondaminsky's home, became one of the principal centers of diffusion for the reviews of the YMCA, *The Way*, and *New City*. Among the members of the circle—who opted to meet in less prominent or more informal ways by 1938—were G. Adamovich, G. Terapiano, K. Mochulsky, V. Varshavsky, V. Veidlé, G. Raevsky, N. Felzen, Z. Oldenbourg, and V. Yanovsky. The appearance of Berdyaev at meetings of this sort impressed a great number of the young immigrants. Yanovsky recalled one of these meetings in his memoirs: "It was from him that I first heard that you shouldn't talk about the Holy Spirit to someone who is hungry. That would be a sin against the Holy Spirit."[148]

The Armistice (1936–1939)

The attacks of the Russian Orthodox Church Outside Russia and the Patriarchate of Moscow on the diocese of Metropolitan Evlogy and on Bulgakov reinforced the unity of the RSCM. On April 6, 1936, in a special issue commemorating its tenth anniversary, the *Messenger* of the Russian Student Christian Movement published an article by Bulgakov on the Holy Spirit and another by Lagovsky defending his sophiology. Moreover, Florovsky resigned as vice-chaplain of the movement, thus weakening the position of Chetverikov. What was more, the RSCM, in its editorial, no longer presented itself as an anti-Bolshevik movement. Instead, it portrayed itself as a movement of unity among young people faithful to the service of the Orthodox Church and capable of leading a struggle against "contemporary materialism and atheism."[149]

Finally, the election of Lev Zander as general secretary of the movement during the last meeting of the international committee on October 1, 1936, brought peace to what had been a most contentious period. Zander was to be responsible for coordinating the activities of the different "autonomous movements." A professor of logic at the St. Sergius Institute and close to Bulgakov, Zander was enthusiastically engaged in ecumenism, and he was approved by all the various groups in the RSCM. He sought to transform its structure into a genuine federation of the different "circles in Russian Orthodox society." He obtained sufficient financial support from Orthodox Action and the St. Sergius Fraternity, as well as from the Anglo-Russian Fellowship, to resume the publication of the *Messenger* from December 1936 until 1939, with Zenkovsky as editor-in-chief. In a sign of openness, reference to the RSCM no longer appeared on the cover. The only goals of the review were the development of the idea of "an active Christianity" and extended information on "the work of Christian forces in the world." Eventually, on June 16–19, Zander succeeded in bringing together, in the presence of Metropolitan Evlogy, representatives of the RSCM, the St. Sergius Fraternity, and Orthodox Action. In addition to articles in the *Messenger* by Fedotov, Florovsky, Mother Maria, and Zenkovsky, room was made for ecumenical contributions. Among these were articles by Fr. Widdrington of the Fellowship of St. Alban and St. Sergius ("The Anglican Social Movement"), Emmanuel Mounier of the review *Esprit* ("Social Movements among French Catholics"), Suzanne de Dietrich of the World Student Christian Federation ("The Ecumenical Theme in Religious Work in India and South America"), and J. Bosco, the general secretary of the Protestant Federation of France ("Work among the Students").

Zander continued to organize meetings in France as well as in the rest of Europe. The final one was in Slovakia, August 22–29, 1939. He received support in his work of reconciliation from Zernov, Lagovsky, and the couple Tamara Baimakova and Dimitrii Klepinin. The latter was a former student at St. Sergius who, after his marriage to Baimakova, was ordained a priest by Metropolitan Evlogy. In 1938 Klepinin replaced Chetverikov at the church of the Presentation of the Virgin in the Temple, which was the church of the Russian Student Christian Movement. Then, in 1939, he became rector of the church of the Protection of the Mother of God, which was attached to Mother Maria's hostel and Orthodox Action on 77 rue de Lourmel.

Thanks to the organizational talents of Zander's collaborators, the division between the left and right wings of the movement gave way to a desire for dialogue. In April 1937, Zenkovsky published a polemic between Chetverikov and Mother Maria in the *Messenger* and added his own conclusions in favor of Mother Maria—which demonstrated how greatly the context had changed. In his article, Chetverikov criticized a number of statements by Mother Maria that had appeared in the previous issue of the journal concerning the subordination of the Russian Church to the state during the synodal period. He also called the attention of the editorial staff to the reactions of a reader defending the Holy Russia of Seraphim of Sarov and John of Kronstadt. Mother Maria replied that she did not question the reality and depth of the spirituality of the Russian people. She insisted, however, on all the damage done to the church by its subjection to the state and by those who "consider Orthodoxy as only a detail of their national identity."[150]

This polemic showed that the split of the RSCM in 1934–35 was not due exclusively to external factors. It coincided with a fresh awareness ("fresh" as compared with the years 1920–30) on the part of some of the authors of *The Way* of the profound crisis that the revolution had provoked not only in the structures of the church but also in its traditional spirituality. Unlike the preceding period, when Berdyaev's fulmination against the paralysis of the pre-revolution church was more or less accepted as characteristic of his mentality as an intellectual, the group united around Orthodox Action, from now on, would attempt to create a new mode of evangelical and Spirit-centered Christian life corresponding to the newfound conditions of freedom they enjoyed. An essay entitled "The Types of Religious Life," recently found in the archives of Mother Maria and written in 1937, contrasted precisely this more Gospel-oriented understanding of

Christian life to different types of Russian Orthodox piety—the "synodal," canonical, ascetic, and aesthetic. She reflected on the Beatitudes, in which Christ promised the Kingdom of Heaven to "the poor in spirit." Mother Maria argued that these words should be interpreted not as an injunction to embrace material poverty or to reject intellectual activity, but as an invitation to place the salvation of the other above one's own personal salvation. "He who is poor in spirit," she stated, "is he who ... offers this spirit in love, who does not economize his spiritual riches."[151]

In *The Way*, Mother Maria continued with her phenomenology of evangelical spirituality by contrasting the figure of the martyr to that of the Pharisee. She was attempting a synthesis between the conservative spirituality of Chetverikov and her own revolutionary ardor. In "A Defense of Phariseeism," published in June 1938, she argued that the figure of the Pharisee should be rehabilitated. When the prophetic spirit wanes, as in Russia after Peter the Great, the function of preserving the law is carried out by the "Pharisees," the clerical guardians of the church, and their messianic waiting for the Savior becomes immensely important. But when the church in Russia is persecuted and "all of humanity is on fire," the wisdom and sobriety of the Pharisees are no longer enough. For, alongside their other qualities, the Pharisees "try to protect the Church from the authentic Christian fire and from all fire in general; they only protect their riches and do not allow anyone to have access to them."[152] In an article published in *The Way* in April 1939, entitled "On the Imitation of the Mother of God," Mother Maria argued that to become a true prophet, one should not turn only to the figure of Christ. The figure of the Virgin must also be discovered, she who is the Spirit-Bearer (*Pneumatophore*) par excellence. One should not only freely choose to carry one's cross. A person must know "the mystery of the cross changed into a sword."[153] In the same article, which was her last contribution to the review, written just after she had learned of the death of her daughter Gaiana, who had recently returned to the USSR, Mother Maria wrote:

> If man is not only the image of God but also the image of the Mother of God, he should see in every other person the image of God and the image of the Mother of God. In the divine-maternal human soul, ... there is not only Christ who is born; there is also a clairvoyance of the image of Christ in other souls which manifests itself. In this sense the

divine-maternal part of the human soul begins to see others as its own children, to adopt them.... The human heart should be pierced by two-edged swords... the crosses of others... [and the soul] should participate in the destiny of its neighbor. And it does not choose these swords—they are chosen by those who have taken them up like a cross on their shoulders. The human soul, like its archetype, the Mother of God, tends toward Golgotha, in the footsteps of her son, and is unable not to walk in that direction and is unable not to shed blood. I believe that the true mystical foundations for relationships among people are rooted in this.[154]

Inspired by this fresh interpretation of the Gospels, Mother Maria intensified her efforts within Orthodox Action. In 1936–37 she founded a nursing home in Noisy-le-Grand for about fifty victims of tuberculosis, as well as a parish and a Russian school at Montrouge. Fr. Valentin Bakst was the first parish chaplain. Along with Sophia Mikhailovna Zernov, she opened several old-age homes for immigrants and participated in the creation of a center for abandoned children at Montgeron. In October 1936, with the help of F. Pianov, she opened a home for about fifty people at 42 rue Francois Gérard in the 16th arrondissment. This home also included the center of assistance for the unemployed under the direction of Sophia Zernov, who was in charge of the Russian branch in Paris of the Fellowship of St. Alban and St. Sergius (Confrérie de Saint Alban et Saint Serge), and the office of the Union of Christian Doctors. In January 1937, the Committee for Unemployment Assistance became the Committee for Social Assistance of Russian immigrants, in affiliation with the Russian Student Christian Movement. Mother Maria was tireless in visiting the Russian communities at Le Creusot, Lyon, and Grenoble. In the midst of all this she took up poetry again. In the April–June 1937 issue of *The Way*, Mochulsky reviewed her collection that was published by Petropolis under the simple title *Poems*. He noted that the religious poetry of Mother Maria was a justification of martyrdom based on the maternal sentiment of compassion for all of humanity. He quoted the verses of intercession that the poet made to God for "her brothers, the bandits, the drunks": "And the brothers: Is it their fault / if they have become like a battlefield?"[155]

Certain conferences of the Academy of Religious Philosophy were open to the general public for the purpose of outreach. In April 1937, a public conference was held at Orthodox Action, with Archimandrite Kyprian Kern, Mother Maria, V. Bakst, and Bulgakov speaking on the theme "The Cross, the Beauty of the Church." On December 18, 1938, after the death of Shestov, Berdyaev organized a memorial session and invited Zenkovsky. Classes were held on Thursday evenings. In 1937–38 the class presentations were as follows: Berdyaev, "Man Confronted with His Internal Contradictions" (begun 11/26) and "Man Confronted with History"; Vysheslavtsev, "The Tragedy of Life and Ways of Salvation"; Fedotov, "Christianity and the Nation"; and Mochulsky, "Russian Religious Thought in the Nineteenth Century." In 1938–39 the presentations were: Berdyaev, "The Fundamental Themes of Russian Religious Thought" and "Man, the World, and God"; Vysheslavtsev, "The Problems of Contemporary Philosophy"; Frank, "The Person and the World"; and Mochulsky, "Russian Poets."

In 1937–38, *The Way* reflected both unshakeable support for Bulgakov and a search for a consensus by both sides. Berdyaev allowed all of the differing members of the St. Sergius Institute to express themselves (for instance, Bulgakov, Zander, Zenkovsky, Bezobrazov, Kern, Fedotov, Sové, Vysheslavtsev, Ilyin). While still preferring the standbys (Shestov, N. Lossky), he also allowed younger writers to make themselves heard (Alexandrov, Lebedev, Tian-Shansky, Shvarts, Volkonsky, Ilnitsky). He also permitted older thinkers to become better known (Mother Maria Skobtsova, Smolitch, Mochulsky, Lot-Borodin, Zernov, Pletnev, Ivanov, Kurdiumov, Belenson, Lazarev, Polotebneva). The most noteworthy names absent from the review in this period were Bubnov, Stepun, and Frank, who were preoccupied with trying to get out of Germany; A. Kartashev, whose patriotic articles were lambasted in 1937 in a stinging response by Lot-Borodin; and, finally, G. Florovsky and S. Chetverikov, who were shunned after their failed coup.

The New Editorial Team (1939–1940)

The Fedotov affair encouraged Orthodox Action to consolidate its forces and create its own journal, named after the organization. The first issue, which had a marked "Christian socialist" overtone,[156] included contributions from Lev Gillet, Berdyaev, Mother Maria, Mochulsky, and Fedotov. In an article entitled "Love and Sociology," Fedotov explained—with a veiled reference to his ostracicism from the St. Sergius Institute—that friendship was not only inseparable from piety but was one of its preconditions. For

Fedotov, the essence of Christianity was in the link between the double commandment of love of God and love of neighbor. He noted that in the early church, diaconal service was social service. For him, the crisis of secularized societies arose from the fact that they have forgotten that the church is the metaphysical foundation of all social relationships. Thus, according to Fedotov—building on the intuitions of Fedorov—liturgical life should be understood not merely in the narrow sense of Eucharistic service but also in a sociological sense as the mystery or sacrament of encounter.

In the next issue of *Orthodox Action*, an editorial by Mother Maria summed up the work of Orthodox Action from its prehistory in 1932 and its creation in 1935. She contrasted the exterior success of the association, namely, the "collaboration with the Academy of Religious Philosophy, which considerably strengthens our cultural presence,"[157] with her interior dissatisfaction, resulting from her inability to transform the different activities of Orthodox Action—providing food and refuge, a parish, medical services—into a coherent whole that would be experienced as such by each person participating in or benefiting from this work. This contrast was all the more painful for Mother Maria in that she now realized, based on experience, that her decision to commit herself to the poor of the emigration to the detriment of the original project of training youth to return to Russia could, paradoxically, serve as a model for the future renewal of the Russian Church. She now imagined seeing, "maybe in a hundred years," an Orthodox fraternity bringing together people moved by the same ideal of realizing a liturgy "outside the walls" and the generalization of a personalist education in all institutions in which this fraternity was present. "What we are doing here is a sort of laboratory for Russia; this is why the value of our work resides in its ideological and methodological purity and not in the search for rapid and grandiose results. We should try to find a method of Orthodox inspiration, both conciliatory and personal."[158]

The declaration of war and the leftist stance taken by the editorial committee of *The Way* in September 1939 explained why the journal *Orthodox Action* ceased publication. After the departure of certain professors from the St. Sergius Institute (Zenkovsky, the president of the RSCM, took along with him L. Zander, his general secretary), Berdyaev took advantage of the situation to bring together a restricted number of contributors to the journal—twenty-five in all—as a collective body. Berdyaev became the sole editor-in-chief. Vysheslavtsev, who represented the right wing on the editorial staff, was now just one among others in the assembly of authors.

Among those members of the St. Sergius Institute who remained faithful were Bulgakov, Vysheslavtsev, and Veidlé. Among those of Orthodox Action were Mother Maria, Mochulsky, Fedotov, and Lev Gillet (who was in England at that time). Thirteen authors formed the real core of the journal. They were faithful to it from its beginning until its end: N. Alekseev, N. Berdyaev, S. Bulgakov, B. Vysheslavtsev, P. Ivanov, M. Kurdiumov, N. Lossky, Mother Maria, I. Smolitsch, G. Fedotov, J. Sazonova, D. Chizhevsky, and S. Frank. Ten authors who appeared between 1930 and 1935 were also in this group: P. Bitsilli, V. Veidlé, H. Gofshtetter, N. Zernov, L. Gillet, A. Lazarev, M. Lot-Borodin, K. Mochulsky, "the Russian monk," and F. Stepun. Finally, there were two new arrivals: Nadezhda Gorodetsky (who was, at that time, professor of Russian literature at Oxford and who did not have the time to contribute articles to the review—aside from a translation of Lev Gillet in 1931) and Helene Iswolsky. The latter, the daughter of the last Russian ambassador to Paris and who became a Catholic in 1921, was particularly close to Berdyaev, two of whose books she translated, to Mounier, who invited her several times to contribute to his journal *Esprit*, and to G. Fedotov, who welcomed her as an associate in *New City*.

The Academy functioned up to the arrival of the Germans in Paris in June 1940. The cessation of its activities also put an end to the publication of *The Way*. The last issue appeared in March 1940. It concluded with a violent criticism of National Socialism by N. Alekseev, who compared Hitler to Stavrogin, one of the heroes of Dostoevsky's *The Possessed*.[159] The spiritual, antinomic, and eschatological tone of the review was characterized, on the one hand, by a pro-democratic and anti-nationalistic commitment with room for debate between liberalism and socialism and, on the other hand, by a personalist and ecumenical reflection that did not preclude articles of theocentric tendencies (Vysheslavtsev, Lossky). The editorial of the next-to-last issue of September 1939—the first editorial since 1925—described this spiritual vision of the group brought together by Berdyaev. The editorial, quoted below almost in its entirety, was, like the review's first editorial, written by Berdyaev:

> Our journal ... does not have to judge events from a political point of view. The catastrophe of war which has engulfed all of Europe has a spiritual aspect and a spiritual meaning. It is not just a battle for material interests; more profoundly, it is a battle for spiritual values. It is a battle not just of states and peoples but of ideas and principles. Will

Europe preserve the liberty of the spirit, the freedom to think and to breathe, in short, everything which founds human dignity—or will it succumb to the slavery of totalitarian regimes founded on a morality of gangsters? Germany, famous in times past for its giants of thought and creation, has allowed itself to fall into an unimaginable servitude and wants to submit other peoples, even the whole world, to this slavery. The imperialistic desire for power leads to folly. Germany has refused to submit either to God or to human freedom and has fallen into the grip of destiny, of somber, irrational forces. The diabolical desire for power in this world should be crushed. It has definitively separated itself from the morality of the Gospels and returned to paganism. This has been an apostasy with respect to the hierarchy of the supreme principle of life and of values. The same can be said for any type of fascism and racism, including communist fascism.... This war, which should end with the victory of freedom over slavery, poses the problem of reconstruction—not only on a national and social level but also regarding spiritual changes in human societies. We must hope for a reawakening of the nostalgia for freedom, for humanity, and for spirituality.[160]

On the first Sunday of November 1939, Berdyaev, now installed at Clamart, 83 rue du Moulin de Pierre,[161] began the courses of the Academy for the school year 1939–40, centered on the theme "Idols and Ideas," with a public lecture entitled "War and Eschatology." In her journal, Lydia Berdyaeva noted the event:

Sunday, November 5 [1939]: Ni [Nikolai Berdyaev] gave a lecture at our house today on "War and Eschatology." The central idea of the lecture is that the end of the world takes place every time man accomplishes what is good and thus triumphs over evil. Evil is finite, good is infinite. N. Alekseev, G. Fedotov, Mother Maria participated in the discussions. As always, the ideas of Ni are very complicated and often paradoxical and I don't think that many people understand them. You have to know his whole philosophical system; otherwise they cause misunderstandings and the discussions are often sterile.[162]

This lecture appeared in *The Way* and was the last article by Berdyaev published in the journal. It inaugurated a new line of reflection on the philosophy of history that would lead to Berdyaev's final philosophical book, first published in French in 1946: *Essai de métaphysique eschatologique* (*The Beginning and the End: Essay on Eschatological Metaphysics*). This revival of the eschatological problematic, which also appeared in another lecture he gave at his home in 1940, was his response to the question posed in his editorial on the spiritual sense of contemporary events. In contrast, Alekseev's final book on metaphysics, *The Last Things*, was never published.[163] However, this convergence of investigations, which will be treated later, helps to explain why the generational spirit—one of self-revelation by the personal conscience that hence was communitarian as regards the question confronted—as expressed in *The Way* over a period of fifteen years (1925–40), continued after the journal had ceased its activity.

TWO CONFLICTING SPIRITUALITIES

After National Socialism had triumphed in Germany in January 1933, after Stalin came out with his *Remarks on the Project for a Manual of the History of the USSR* in July 1934, in which he resolutely adopted a national ideology close to that of Eurasianism,[164] and after the improvement of Franco-Soviet relations in May 1935, which abruptly brought Soviet reality to the very doors of the Russian émigré community, the writers of *The Way* felt impelled to reflect on the foundations of Russian identity. Although most of their research on this topic was published between 1935 and 1936, the debates continued until the war broke out.

Between March 1935 and December 1936, Fedotov, Zernov, Lot-Borodin, and Kartashev all published their reflections on the philosophy of Russian history. During this time Berdyaev wrote his book *The Sources and Meaning of Russian Communism* and Florovsky came out with *The Ways of Russian Theology*. It was also during this period that the journal published two important commemorative speeches; that of Berdyaev for the tenth anniversary of *The Way* and that of Bulgakov for the tenth anniversary of the St. Sergius Institute. Both presented a revitalized philosophy of history and offered a new horizon of a spirit-centered future to the immigrant community.

All agreed on one point: the history of the Russian Church was central to the definition of Russian national identity. Like all historians, they conceived of this history by means of powerful myths—the state, society, the nation—which shaped their narratives. These myths were interpreted as divergent conceptions of the relationship between time and eternity, movement and structure, space and identity. For some, the historical driving force of the Russian Church was the Russian people, who were predestined for a particular mission (Bulgakov, Kartashev). For others, the creative structure was the evolution of various intellectual presentations: for Shestov, the history of universal philosophy; for Florovsky and Lot-Borodin, the history of Orthodox theology; for N. Lossky and Zenkovsky,[165] the history of Russian philosophy; for Fedotov and Zernov, the history of religious mentalities. And finally, for Berdyaev and Mother Maria, it was human freedom, working beneath the surface, that determined the course of events much in the manner of volcanic eruptions.

But these mythologies depended on a still more powerful religious myth. These three conceptions of Russian history revealed three different representations of the church: as the Wisdom of God, as the Body of Christ, and as the place where the Spirit disclosed itself. For these intellectuals, the church was not merely a concept. As the assembly of the faithful (*ecclesia*), it had a mythical, divine-human nature, which was forever in movement. For this reason the historical destiny of the church was the result of a process both esoteric (the relationship between its divine and human natures) and exoteric (the relationship between the historical consciousness and the unconscious memory). The synthesis of this twofold process was the creation of secularized forms of the myth of the church—the God-bearing people on the sophiological line of thought, the theocratic state on the theocentric one, and the legendary City of Kitezh, protected by the *raskolniki* or schismatics, on the personalist one.

These secularized forms of the myth, however, were seriously challenged by political realities. In 1935–40 the violent opposition between partisans of the God-bearing Russian people, of the Byzantine golden age, and of salvation through the intelligentsia revealed the limits of a nationalistic definition of Orthodoxy, be it Greek or Russian.

This provoked a certain number of contributors to the review who represented the different tendencies (Bulgakov, Berdyaev, Mother Maria) to revise their own conceptions and propose a new interpretation of Russian identity as it appeared rooted in the history of the Russian Church, yet with universal significance. Their new interpretation rejected an ontological understanding of the church. It attempted to purify the church's memory of all nationalistic pretensions without, however, denying the historical forms of its incarnation. In their view, an overly static understanding of the church, which gave rise to the separation between the people, the state, and the intelligentsia, was the cause of the secularization of the church, its submission to the state, and its transformation into a bureaucratic organization that distrusted the intelligentsia. The synthesis of the three tendencies—sophiological, theocentric, and personalist—led to the revival of the messianic myth of Moscow, the Third Rome, but in a spirit that was radically anti-nationalist. This was in opposition to the myths of Holy Russia and the golden age of Byzantium.

As we shall see later, this intellectual trend did not alter the fundamentals of the mytho-logical systems of the contributors to the review. As we know, among the contributors there were three different modes of interpreting the divine-human myth of the church, represented by Bulgakov, by Shestov/N. Lossky–Vysheslavtsev/Zenkovsky–Frank, and by Berdyaev. These interpretations varied principally according to their ontology, eschatology, and the focal point of antinomic reflection: whether the question was of the relationship between God and the world (the sophiological approach), of the internal relationships in the Godhead (the theocentric approach), or of the relationship between God and mankind (the anthropocentric approach). It is clear that between 1935 and 1940, in spite of the attempts at a synthesis, each side did nothing more than delve more deeply into its own interpretation of the world. This intellectual division, the repeated attacks on sophiology, and the disdain for the personalist works of Berdyaev by large sectors of the émigré community—a disdain evidenced by the nearly complete absence of public reaction to Berdayev's publications in that community[166]—practically wiped out the climate of dialogue and synthesis that had been established during the nonconformist era.

And yet, at the end of the day, the debate begun in the journal and continued in other venues by Shestov, Bulgakov, and Berdyaev left the hope that a spiritual synthesis of the three principal tendencies of Russian mytho-logical thought was in the process of maturing.

Eschatology of the Spirit and Messianisms

The Memory of Holy Russia

In October 1936, Kartashev published an essay entitled "Russian Christianity" in *The Way*. From the very first lines, he went straight to the core of his thesis by justifying a "Russian Christianity" as a divine-human phenomenon, understood according to an "absolute-relative" mode. "For the Christian," he wrote, "this is not a paradox but rather the holy antinomy of the dogma of Chalcedon, which saves us from the contrary heresies of Nestorianism (a folklore without faith) and Monophysism (a pseudo-Christian spirituality).[167] After this brief introduction, and without addressing the ideological connotations of his terminology, Kartashev launched into a historical analysis of "the racial and national Russian temperament."[168] Kartashev was especially interested in the Russian people, who, he argued, were "liturgized rather than catechized."[169] Of the attacks made on Russia, the one that especially offended the president of the High Monarchical Council was that made by I. Hecker in the review *Christendom* in 1934, where Hecker affirmed that the Russian people had not been seriously Christianized by the Orthodox Church. The Russian historian, furious with Hecker, whom he accused of being a "Bolshevik agent," revealed the essence of his thought in his reply to the Protestant theologian: "[If it was not the Orthodox Church], who, then, formed this 'most Christian of peoples,' those called 'Godbearers' by Dostoevsky?"[170] This affinity with the populist strains in Dostoevsky appeared again later in the article. For Kartashev, the Old Believers were "the best, the most ardent in their faith. If they left the "official Church" in the seventeenth century, it was in the name of a profound mysticism that was inherent in them and was expressed in their rituals.[171] Alongside this mysticism, the Greeks, according to Kartashev, are mere altar boys and "liberals."

For Kartashev, the characteristics of popular Russian piety are a mixture of asceticism, humility, patience in suffering, a mythic and plastic mode of thinking, a faith in the uncreated energies and the transfiguration of the material, an opposition to the official church even concerning the divinity of the very name of God [a reference to the "Imiaslavie" controversy], and, finally, a sophianic cult of the forgiving and compassionate Mother of God. The Russians, Kartashev claimed, are the "sons of Paul"— probably referring to a 1931 article of Bulgakov on Judas. This relationship, this spiritual and eschatological kinship, was archaic in its roots. According to Kartashev, certain traits inherited from antiquity—such as nomadism—"preserved in the Russian blood-line and transforming the Russian soul," explained the eschatological quest of the Russian people for the "new City."[172]

Thus, for Kartashev, "the Church ... for a thousand years was the life-giving sun that illuminated ... the Russian countryside.... For a thousand years the Church was the unique light, joy, and authentic culture of the Russian people. It almost spoke their native tongue."[173] Kartashev's conclusion reemphasized what was at stake in this debate. He cited Gogol, who dreamt of one day seeing Christ returning to Russia in glory, and added: "That could happen soon when the seal of Pilate, affixed to the three-day tomb of Holy Russia by the Third International, falls to the ground without resistance."[174]

This article irritated both the neo-Byzantine and the left-wing intellectuals. In the name of the first group, Lot-Borodin lashed out vigorously at Kartashev's "intolerable religious nationalism,"[175] while Fedotov, in the name of the second group, tried to reply on the question of liturgical language. Berdyaev expressed his disagreement by inserting the following note with the article: "The editors believe that this interesting article of A. Kartashev idealizes one aspect of Russian Christianity—but this also has other aspects."[176]

Lot-Borodin had converted to Orthodoxy in 1934 under the influence of Florovsky and the patristic renewal in Russian theology. For her, the idealization of Russian religiosity by Kartashev was the sign of a lack of spiritual vigor, characterized by a chimerical quest for a lost paradise and by the invention of a scapegoat, the Third International, the heir, in fact, of the pagan myth of Moscow as the Third Rome. She added, however, that in this domain she appreciated the thesis of Zernov—to be discussed later—concerning the universal and ecumenical interpretation of the myth of the monk Philotheus of Pskov.[177] According to Lot-Borodin, the idea that the essence of Russia was found in its God-bearing people is a "vainglorious" form of messianism.[178] Even though she admitted that the Russian identity was eschatological, especially as compared with Western rationalism, she refused to sanction the historical errors of the Russian Church. In particular she regretted that the submission of the church to the state had impeded the "development of personal and intimate prayer" and, consequently, the "emancipation of the person."[179]

Lot-Borodin preferred to return to the patristic sources of Orthodoxy and in particular to the theology of Nicholas Cabasilas, as opposed to the "Old Testament spirituality, the only spirituality authorized by synodal Russia." The latter is marked by a separation that contradicts the principle of conciliarity between clergy and laity and that is symbolized by the iconostasis. She set herself up against "an exaggerated ritualism," which is the opium of Russians who "do not understand the Eucharist well," and against the primacy given to humility over love and charity, which has prevented Russian spirituality from integrating the mystical marriage of God with the church and the soul of which *The Canticle of Canticles* sings. In opposition to the pagan Slavic concept of Mother Earth and the anti-dogmatic attitude of the people, which has led to a passive sentimentality and an understanding of the divine bordering on magic, Lot-Borodin cited Maximus the Confessor on the cooperation of creation with the divine energies.[180] Finally, against the chauvinism of Kartashev, she defended Western spirituality, which also preserves the cult of the Wisdom of God as a prefiguration of the Mother of God.[181]

In brief, Lot-Borodin considered it impossible to identify Holy Russia with the Body of Christ. Nonetheless, she wished for the rebirth of the Russian Church, but one purified and washed clean of all nationalism. Although she rejected the "thesis of the Polish Jesuits"[182] according to which the submission of the church to the state is the result of its separation from the Roman Church, Lot-Borodin assigned an ecumenical mission to the future Russian nation. She concluded by praying with her whole heart that "new revelations of the unique theophany of the Invisible Church might become incarnate on Russian soil, of that Church over which the gates of Hell have not—and will never have—any power."[183]

Without referring directly to Kartashev, Fedotov preferred to reply to his colleague at the Institute by focusing solely on the thesis according to which "the Russian Church almost spoke the native tongue of the people." Fedotov admitted that the question of liturgical language was difficult because, on the one hand, the political context was not propitious for reforms and, on the other hand, "the liturgy is not just a prayer; it is also a mystery."[184] The Slavonic of the Russian liturgy was, in his view, "obscure without being incomprehensible" and facilitated "the passage to another level of reality." However, Fedotov thought that this aesthetic trait was a form of magic. Moreover, he emphasized that the church had a missionary role in the world and that the Slavonic language had become an obstacle to the evangelization of Russia. This result was contrary to the "living tradition" and specifically to the intentions of the inventors of Slavonic, Cyril and Methodius, who wanted Slavonic to be a vehicle of intelligibility.

So he was aware that this question "will be a preoccupation for the Russian Church in the future" and will be an element in the redefinition of a national identity. He then opened the debate on the possible translations of certain texts, notably the Psalms, from Slavonic to Russian. Fedotov argued that the real advantages of Slavonic, that is, its proximity to Greek, its musical rhythm, and the aristocratic veneer that time has given to certain terms, "are not linked to the Slavonic language as such" but are the fruit of a heritage, due to the passage of time or the personal gifts of hymnologists.[185]

On the other hand, Fedotov argued, Slavonic had a number of drawbacks. Above all, insofar as it never was the language of a great civilization, it had failed to become a language of thought or of poetry. In contrast with Latin, of which even Kant had made use, Slavonic had remained liturgical and didactic; even in the twelfth century, the famous *Tale of Igor's Campaign* had been translated into Russian. Fedotov used the example of the translation of the Bible into Slavonic—a literal translation from Greek—to prove that even in the Middle Ages, Russians were incapable of writing in Slavonic without making mistakes. Greek in its syntax, half-Greek in its semantics, and Bulgarian-Macedonian in its etymology, Slavonic, according to Fedotov, suffered from being an artificial language and had never been really understood by the people.[186] The second problem in the use of Slavonic was the difference in spirituality between the Greeks and the Russians, between the "pompous" style of Byzantine Greek and the more simple style of Russian spirituality dominated by the concept of the *kenosis* [self-emptying] of Christ. This gap, which was the source of a great number of Hellenisms and errors of translation in the Gospels, the letters of St. Paul, and the Psalms, had always been anecdotal material for seminarians. Fedotov attacked an intelligentsia that had little experience of the culture of the people and was, at present, seduced by "the luxury of the Byzantine-Slavonic muse" and thus incapable of grasping the ironies perceived even by seminarians.

Consequently, for Fedotov, "it is indisputable that our Slavonic translation is in need of a reform." In order to continue "the work begun by Nikon in the seventeenth century," Fedotov proposed two possibilities: either a correction of the Slavonic text while retaining its syntax but giving more meaning to the words, or a new translation into the language of Karamzin and Lomonosov. For aesthetic reasons, Fedotov preferred the second solution, provided that the poet also be familiar with scholarship.

He himself recognized that this radical solution was "dangerous" and that the Russian language, which had borrowed heavily from Slavonic, had "more riches than one might think."[187] But Fedotov added that his choice was also made for a profound reason, one that concerned the debate over the future of the Russian Church and its national identity. There can be no doubt that this conclusion by Fedotov was addressed as much to Bulgakov as to Florovsky:

> Today two profound currents of Orthodox spirituality are struggling among themselves in the Russian Church: the kenotic Russian with the transcendent Byzantine. This is not, of course, a struggle to eliminate one or the other, but to decide which will dominate and give direction. Which will win? Sergius of Radonezh or Dionysius the Areopagite? The result of this face-to-face confrontation will decide the destiny of the Slavonic or Russian liturgy.[188]

Fedotov's historical criticism, which demystified the Slavonic language considered sacred by the majority, provoked a violent reaction in the circles close to Metropolitan Evlogy. His "anti-national" treatment of the liturgical language in the context of an increasing national hysteria was probably the main reason for his exclusion from the St. Sergius Institute three months after the publication of this article. The fact of the matter is that Fedotov, throughout the years 1937–39, published political articles (as discussed above), violating the 1936 interdiction by Metropolitan Evlogy. Finally, the theme of religiosity in the Third International, which served as a pretext for the release of anger against Fedotov, was an old story to the professors of the Institute and Kartashev in particular. But no one, on the other hand, from the beginning of the exile up until now, had dared to question an element so inherent to Russian identity as the "native tongue."

This is the only way to explain why Bulgakov, certainly influenced by Kartashev, participated in the expulsion of Fedotov from the St. Sergius Institute. It is well known, moreover, that Fedotov, from England, asked his wife to resign herself to Bulgakov's state of mind. Bulgakov in fact shared the Dostoevskian myth of the God-bearing Russian people and accepted the sophianic dimension of the liturgical language. He had explained his views on the Russian people, who, he stated, bear "the seal of the apostolate of St. John," in his 1931 article on Judas. Notably, using the biblical symbolism of the twelve apostles, who represented the spiritual plenitude of the twelve tribes of Israel, Bulgakov had justified the idea that peoples have particular spiritual missions, which they are called upon to carry out.[189] Moreover, in his book *The Philosophy of the Name*, which he was constantly revising, Bulgakov wrote: "The word is cosmic by nature, for it belongs not only to the consciousness which is its source, but, more fundamentally, to being."[190] The conclusion is that to play with language, especially liturgical language, is a profanation of the manifestation of created Wisdom.

After his throat operation, which brought him close to death and was the occasion of a profound spiritual experience, Bulgakov asked Fedotov to forgive him. Perhaps Bulgakov remembered that he himself, in 1918, had roundly criticized "Greco-Russian" Orthodoxy in Crimea, next to the walls of the Cathedral of Chersonese, where St. Vladimir was baptized. Later, during the emigration, Bulgakov had sided with the conservative circles mainly out of anti-communist sympathy. However, in 1939–41, Bulgakov made his examination of conscience. Shocked by the violence of nationalism and anti-Semitism, Bulgakov decided to revise his philosophy of history—or rather, to readjust his antiquated conception of people and race as part of the evolution of his sophiological doctrine. After the German army entered Russian territory, Bulgakov felt the need to draw out the political consequences of the spirit-centered development of his sophiology by dedicating the final years of his life to more existential notions of people and race. In an essay written during the winter of 1941–42, entitled "Racism and Christianity," Bulgakov criticized the "naturalism and paganism" of racism as expressed by its principal ideologue, Alfred Rosenberg, in his book *The Myth of the Twentieth Century*.[191] In his essay "The Doctrine of the People and Racism in the Light of Sophiology," Bulgakov launched into a thorough criticism of "nationalism" and of the Old Testament "biology" that affirmed that "the souls of animals are in their blood."

Bulgakov explained that from a sophiological point of view, the unity of the human race was "spiritual." This primacy of the spirit led him to personalism:

> Neither the race nor the nation nor any biological collectivity constitutes an original reality ... as is the case of the person. This truth, insupportable for racism, is affirmed in both the Old and the New Tes-

tament as the foundation of the human being. Humanity is composed not of races but of persons who find their common source, as individuals, in the unique total person, in the new Adam, in Christ.[192]

Yet this spirit-centered view did not debilitate Bulgakov's messianism, which involved a reconciliation with Judaism. He wrote: "A new force appears in historical Christianity which will become, as in its first days, its spiritual heart—Judeo-Christianity."[193]

The Memory of Byzantium

Despite differences, there were many similarities in the ecclesiologies of Shestov, Florovsky, and Fedotov. In fact, even though Shestov never pretended to be orthodox and was drawn to Hinduism near the end of his life, and even though Florovsky and Fedotov were radically opposed in the realm of spirituality, all three intellectuals failed to clarify the relationship between the heavenly city and the earthly city, the mystical church and the visible church. The result of this intellectual apophaticism was a tendency to identify the church with the visible church. Theocentric in its source (Father, Son, and Holy Spirit), this kind of ecclesiology defined the church by the borders or limits of the outpouring of grace. Historically and geographically, these limits were revealed by the Law and the Prophets, dogmas and hierarchy, and religious culture and holiness. The history of the church, therefore, is a history of philosophical, theological, or spiritual representations. It should be focused on the figures of prophets (from Abraham to Kierkegaard), theologians/mystics, and saints. This identification of the church with the visible church explained how each crisis in the church led to a rejection. For Shestov, this was the case for the church as a whole when it was unable to integrate Judaism and surrendered to Hellenic influences. For Florovsky, this was the case for the Russian Church when it did not remain faithful to its Byzantine heritage. For Fedotov, this was the case for the synodal period of the Russian Church (from 1721, following the church reforms of Peter the Great), when it was unable to assimilate the evangelical tradition of the Trans-Volga monks.

Although Shestov wrote little on the national question between 1935 and 1940, he had always been sensitive to the Zionist question. It was not by chance that he traveled to Palestine in 1936, when the identity crisis in the Russian immigration was at its peak. Lovtzki, who had organized the trip, wrote, "The oldest dream of L. I. [Lev Isaakovitch Shestov] was realized. We visited the land of our ancestors where my grandfather and his are buried on the Mount of Olives."[194] In his correspondence, Shestov wrote mainly about the conflict between Jews and Arabs, showing his interest in a future Jewish state in Palestine.

Fedotov and Florovsky were both Eurasians. Both roundly criticized the *raskolnik*/schismatic Avvakum—who rejected the reforms of Nikon, which favored a return to Byzantine sources—as well as the Russian intelligentsia, who had led Russia to catastrophe through their anti-state attitude and their alienation from the general population. Even in the 1930s, both took positions in favor of a renaissance of Imperial Russia—but for different reasons. Florovsky, imbued with the Byzantine model of Christ *Pantocrator*, could only imagine a strong state authority and a powerful hierarchy in the church. On the other hand, Fedotov, who inclined towards the figures of the Holy Spirit and the Virgin of Tenderness, could not imagine the church as a political force that possessed and administered lands. Florovsky finished his book on the history of the Russian Church, *Ways of Russian Theology*, in 1936. Here he claimed that the initial drama of Rus' was to have been cut off from Byzantium in the eleventh century, just when it had become aware of itself as a national entity. "The essence of the Muscovite crisis is found in the rejection of the Greeks."[195] From this premise, Florovsky proceeded to show that the Russian Church had never been able to develop a theology of its own and, consequently, a Christian identity of its own. Thus, according to him, after the crisis of the Council of a Hundred Chapters in the sixteenth century, under Ivan the Terrible—a sort of counter-reformation that broke with the Byzantine patristic heritage—Russian theology came under the influence of Latin theology in the seventeenth century, during the time of Peter Mohila. Then, after the schism with the Old Believers and the implementation of Mohila's reforms, it was poisoned by Protestant ecclesiology. Florovsky argued that the heresy of "the apocalyptic utopia" of the Old Believers, once grace had disappeared, shifted from the Tsar towards man: "Since visible grace had abandoned the apostate State, which henceforth had to be opposed, everything now depended on man, his continence, and his ascetic efforts." Florovsky located the irresponsible anarchy of the Russian intellectuals of the eighteenth and nineteenth centuries, namely, the Freemasons, Occidentalists, and Slavophiles, in the continuation of this heresy. With the exception of an eminent theologian and bishop, Philaret, Metropolitan of Moscow (1820–67) [canonized by the Russian Orthodox Church in 1997], Orthodox theology did not succeed, in Florovsky's opinion, in liberating itself from Western influences. In the final chapter Florovsky did not mince words against Berdyaev and Bulgakov. On the eve of the revolution the intelligentsia, alienated from their roots and influenced by German Idealism and certain troubling Gnostic currents, tried to rejoin the church, but they did not possess the spiritual forces to oppose the revolution. In conclusion, Florovsky assigned Russian theology the task of liberating itself from captivity "by a return to the patristic tradition, not as an interpretation of the past but as a creative realization of the future."[196]

Berdyaev published Florovsky's book though the YMCA Press and reviewed it in July 1937. Simply put, Berdyaev made target practice of it. This book, he wrote, was a sign of the "pathological anxiety of Orthodoxy," "of a need for an inner order," of an anti-humanism typical of the times that followed the Great War and the revolution. But just like the anti-romanticism of Maurras, the anti-romanticism of Florovsky hides a romanticism. The proof is the quest by the Russian theologian for Byzantinism, "this nostalgia for a vanished world."[197] Berdyaev was also disturbed by the author's tendency "to give out certificates of orthodoxy or heresy" to everybody. Berdyaev was equally critical of many other elements—Florovsky's historical observations were in error, as was his schematic opposition of Russia and the West, which led to a caricature of the West. Berdyaev attacked his naïveté concerning the so-called independence of Byzantine Orthodoxy regarding Neoplatonic philosophy, and his false identification of Russian religious thought with German thought. In the end, Berdyaev concluded, Florovsky "protects and defends traditional Orthodoxy but, fundamentally, he does not recognize any authority."[198]

Zernov's article "Moscow, the Third Rome," although written in April 1935, well before this polemic, and appearing in the October 1936 issue of *The Way,* could be considered a synthesis between Florovsky's quest for universality and Berdyaev's defense of Russian spirituality. The fact that Mother Maria, who was close to Berdyaev, used this theme of "the third Rome" and the favorable reaction to the article by Lot-Borodin illustrated the real possibility of a synthesis of the two tendencies on the basis of Zernov's interpretation—if political considerations and personal interests were put to the side. Zernov situated himself within Fedotov's theocentric position, and in his introduction he praised the historian of Russian sanctity. But he departed from this perspective by arguing for a new messianism based on three principles: the "churching" of life (and of the state in particular), the rejection of violence by taking upon one's self the sufferings associated with waiting for the fullness of Christian life,[199] and, finally, an extension of the limits or borders of the church by rooting the Russian Church in the universal church.[200] This last characteristic witnessed to a very distinct development that had taken place within the theocentric wing of the intelligentsia. Even if this tendency did not dogmatically identify the universal church with the Russian Church, its historical preoccupations were centered exclusively on the destinies of the latter. But after the debates from 1930 to 1935 on the antinomic nature of the dogma of Chalcedon, the possibility had emerged of a cataphatic approach that interpreted the relationship between the mystical church and the visible church dynamically rather than statically.

Zernov was strongly influenced by the way in which Bulgakov's sophiology responded to the question of the relationship between the two Wisdoms, between time and eternity. Like Florovsky, but in a different spirit, he took the mystical and universal church as a given fact, as an eternal reality, already present, which the visible church should actualize. It was up to humankind to creatively invent new ways to permit the reciprocal and concrete recognition of both churches and an awareness of the common task to be accomplished. Zernov became personally involved in this path, both intellectually and practically. He published an article in the October 1938 issue of *The Way,* written from this perspective: "An English Theologian in Russia at the Time of Emperor Nicholas I: William Palmer and Alexei Khomiakov." In the introduction to his article, Zernov explained that the extensive debate among the Russian émigrés on the justification of ecumenical relations was nothing new. According to him, this was why the disputes should not be considered as the consequences of a difficult historical situation, that is, the emigration, but rather as the result of "the absence in Orthodox theology of a universally recognized definition of the Church and its visible borders."[201] Anticipating a new objection on the part of Orthodox traditionalists, Zernov explained that the need for a definition of the church was due not so much to the contact with the West as to the danger that Orthodoxy faced of splitting apart in an infinite number of schisms. How Zernov responded to this challenge is considered below. Here, we should note the mission he assigned to the Russian intelligentsia:

> It can be said that contemporary Orthodoxy has no task more essential than that of defining the principal objectives that determine whether a given religious community belongs to this Church which is one, holy, catholic, and apostolic and in which we confess our faith in each liturgy. Important and indispensable materials for solving this problem are presently accumulating in our Church of the immigration. But those who participate in the gathering of these materials can hardly be expected to sort them out and study them. This will certainly be the work of future generations.[202]

The Memory of the City of Kitezh

In his book *Les sources et le sens du communisme russe* (*The Origin of Russian Communism*), written in 1935, Berdyaev developed his thesis on the religious roots of communism. With Kartashev, Berdyaev shared the myth of the God-bearing Russian people. On the other hand, he agreed with Florovsky and Fedotov in considering the intellectuals as the heirs of the *raskolniki* [the Old Believer schismatics]. But he differed with their assertion that the *raskolniki*, like the intellectuals, were Utopians who wanted to realize the Kingdom of God in the state and not in the church. Berdyaev defended the *raskol* [those of the Old Believer schism], who, in his opinion, knew how to preserve, although with distortions, the Christian messianic truth of the Kingdom of God on earth. That was why, according to Berdyaev, the true church was invisible. It was swallowed up in the lake of Kitezh. [According to legend, in the thirteenth century the city of Kitezh was under threat from the Mongol invasion but was miraculously saved when the entire city disappeared beneath the surrounding waves of Lake Kitezh. It was said that only the pure in heart could henceforth see the invisible city.] Berdyaev differed here from Kartashev, for whom the truth preserved by the *raskolniki* was that of the Muscovite Kingdom, of the mode of Christian life illustrated by the *Domostroi* [the sixteenth-century Russian handbook for the detailed pious ordering of domestic life], and of the cosmological sentiment of the uncreated energies present in creation. Berdyaev aligned himself with the *raskolniki* in their rejection of a state that had become anti-Christian and in their combat for liberty of conscience against the dictates of the Orthodox hierarchs.

Thus Berdyaev's philosophy of Russian history was neither a history of piety, as it was for Kartashev, nor a radical criticism of the history of the Russian Church, as it was for Florovsky. Instead it was the history of the formation of an intellectual conscience, of an intelligentsia, issued from the people of the *raskolniki*, whose messianic faith rejected the apostate state and sought justice and truth. Although no one dared to directly oppose this vision of history, which was close to anarchy and Protestantism, several factors led Berdyaev to revise his philosophy of Russian history between 1935 and 1941. These included Fedotov's work, Zernov's article, and his contacts with Mother Maria, who wrote an unpublished article, probably near the end of the 1930s, entitled "Our Era." Whether Berdyaev read it is unknown. But there can be no doubt that this article, which tried to synthesize the positions of Berdyaev, Bulgakov, and Zernov, was discussed at Clamart or rue de Lourmel during the frequent meetings between Mother Maria and Berdyaev in this period. For Mother Maria, as for Berdyaev, the Russian intellectuals were the "mouthpieces" of Russian history.[203] Like Zernov, she believed that if the thick coat of "chauvinism"[204] was stripped away, the myth of Moscow as the Third Rome could be justified as the desire of the Russians to "religiously establish a created form of life—the State." And yet Mother Maria, like Bulgakov, found the origin of this eschatological thirst in an original sophiological intuition. The Russians, she wrote, have tried to solve the problem of the relationship between God and creation. But, she continued, "in the beginning the world was created in such a way that it might discover the Wisdom of God within itself, placed there as the divine image and likeness."[205] Thus, for Mother Maria, who had studied the evolution of the interpretation of the Russian Church from Khomiakov to Bulgakov (and in nihilism as well), "Russian thought was sophiological from its beginning."[206] She proposed a personalist history that studied the incarnation of universal characters in individuals and not as part of a collectivity. But such a history authorized the possibility of an autonomous and super-personal reality, namely, "the people," who were entrusted with the accomplishment and historical realization of an eternal divine energy.

These approaches found an indirect echo in *The Way*. In 1936, Mochulsky, who was close to Mother Maria, Berdyaev, and Bulgakov, published a book on Solovyov in which he demonstrated that the foundation stone of the work of the Russian philosopher was his mystical intuition of Wisdom. This book was reviewed in the March 1937 issue of *The Way* by Zenkovsky. Characteristically, the reviewer, while describing the book favorably as "the best introduction to the study of the work of Solovyov,"[207] criticized its interpretation of Solovyov's work and preferred to give precedence to the idea of pan-unity (*vseedinstvo*) as the Russian philosopher's foundational concept, rather than his sophiology.

In *The Russian Idea*, which Berdyaev began to write in June 1943, several months after the battle of Stalingrad, the Russian philosopher took under consideration Mother Maria's historical synthesis between personalism and sophiology, Fedotov's observations on the role of Nil of Sora and the ecclesiastical roots of the intelligentsia, and, lastly, Zernov's justification of a new messianism. Thus his history was no longer simply the history of the intelligentsia. Rather, it became the history of an archetype, of a national "idea." In writing, in the introduction, that the book was meant to be more a work of love than a history, his personalist philosophy and his sophiology were united.

> The mystery of each individual is only found through love, and in this mystery there is always something which doesn't let itself be discovered completely, in its ultimate depth. I'm not so much interested in what Russia was empirically as in knowing what the Creator of Russia intended, what the intelligible figure of the Russian people was according to God's idea.[208]

In Berdyaev's opinion, this idea/myth, which created a vast spiritual synthesis, was found in the history of Russia's holiness, of its revolutionary movements, and of its religious philosophy. This is why Berdyaev harked back to the holy princes Boris and Gleb in the eleventh century and emphasized the role of Nil of Sora as "the precursor of the libertarian tendency of the Russian intelligentsia"—more by his rejection of power in itself than by the rejection of the state in the proper sense of the term.[209] Berdyaev concluded that this idea consisted in a certain form of religiosity, a manner of thinking that was essentially eschatological, and a straining towards the salvation of all.[210] He ended with his desire for "fraternal" relations with Germany in the future and stressed the spiritual dimension of the national idea:

The Russian people, through their eternal idea, are not disposed to settle in an earthly city, and tend towards the city which is to come, the new Jerusalem. The new Jerusalem is not conceived as separated from the great Mother Russia but is linked to it and will integrate it. Community and fraternity among all peoples are indispensable for the new Jerusalem, and for that it is indispensable to continue to live in the epoch of the Holy Spirit, during which there will be a new revelation on the nature of society. This was prepared in Russia.[211]

Three Logical Antinomies

As we have seen, the theme of theodicy, of the origin of evil, is central to Russian religious thought. This theme constitutes the antinomian axis of the mytho-logical systems of the contributors to *The Way*, whatever might be their metaphysics. For some, it was the question of the relationship between God and the Absolute, for others, the relationship between God and humanity, and, for a third group, the relationship between God and the world. Between 1935 and 1940, a sizable number of articles in *The Way* dealt with the question of the origin of evil—a tragic one for the younger contributors during the months preceding the outbreak of hostilities (Gofshtetter, Alexandrov, Lebedev), a more reasoned one for the older writers (Zenkovsky, Vysheslavtsev, Bulgakov). If the myth of theanthropy, the humanity of God, was still and always the only response to the problem of evil, the eschatological modalities of this myth and its antinomian foundations were sources of different logical interpretations.

The Theocentric Current: God and the Absolute

For the theocentic group, freedom came from God the Absolute and from him alone. This premise was fatal in rational terms. It could lead to making God responsible for evil. It wound up introducing an impermeable separation between the God of the philosophers—that is, the image of the Absolute that we create for ourselves—and the personal Absolute of the Old Testament revelation, who is invisible, unknowable, and ineffable. In this perspective, God's freedom is more important than human freedom. For Shestov, Vysheslavtsev, and Zenkovsky, what was important was to stress the biblical revelation of God as all-powerful.

The Position of Shestov and Lazarev
According to Shestov and Lazarev, all of theodicy was contained in Genesis. The Fall was provoked by the serpent who suggested to man that he become "like God" by knowing good and evil. For these two philosophers—as for Kierkegaard—"what does not come from faith is sin." This was why, as discussed later, Shestov and Lazarev, in their articles on Lévy-Bruhl, Jaspers, and Jules Lequier, argued that the pretensions of reason in the preceding era had attempted to enchain the God of the Bible and transform him into an abstract and inhuman absolute. According to Shestov, these pretensions of reason were rooted in the fact that human nature is afraid of change, to the point of deifying death, which has neither beginning nor end. "But," he wrote, "perhaps all our terrors are in vain, perhaps our reason is mistaken.... Perhaps the link between change and the end, death, which we observe according to the conditions of our existence and our terror-ridden thoughts, has been raised up to the level of an a priori and immutable truth, whereas this link by no means has the force of law or of a general rule that has a power over mankind."[212]

This combat against reason led to an eschatology of rupture. At a meeting of the Academy of Religious Philosophy on December 15, 1935, to mark the twenty-fifth anniversary of the death of Tolstoy, Shestov gave a lecture entitled "Yasnaya Polyana and Astapovo." This gathering was one of the most successful of those sponsored by the Academy. Lydia Berdyaeva, who participated, wrote in her journal:

> There were so many people that most had to remain standing throughout the session. Ni [Berdyaev] and Shestov were particularly inspired. Adamovich was more lyrical. Fedotov was not in form; his presentation lacked enthusiasm. All in all, the affair was wonderful. The shadow of Tolstoy succeeded in accomplishing what the members of the Academy had failed to do during twelve years of exile: reunite, through their love for Tolstoy, representatives of all the different sectors of the Russian colony: those on the right, those on the left, Christians and non-Christians.[213]

During this conference, Shestov, who had met Tolstoy a year before his death, related how the famous writer, who was installed in his house at Yasnaya Polyana, struggled unsuccessfully against his reasoning, which affirmed that the principle of nonresistance to evil was "absurd." But near the end of his life, Tolstoy, like Abraham, preferred the absurd faith in "the unproved truth" of the Gospel commandment to the "repugnant enemy" of the proven truth.[214] He went out, not knowing where he was going, and wound up dying in the little train station of Astapovo. For Shestov, this episode of the absurd yet salutary departure of the great writer demonstrated that the meaning of life, whether personal or universal, was not in our hands but in the hands of God. The one who understands has no choice but to abandon his security and venture out. This opposition between faith and fallen reason, between the personal and unknowable God and the God of the philosophers, between the divine nature and human nature, leads to an eschatology that does not depend on the clock of human time. Shestov stressed that Christ promised to return "as a thief in the night" and not in the context of some earthly scenario.

For Shestov, as for Lazarev, faith was not merely a defense mechanism against the constant assaults of reason. The passage from apophatic thought to cataphatic thought occurred when faith became the principle of creation, when the principle of contradiction came from God and not from an a priori judgment. As Yves Bonnefoy put it, Shestov replied to the biblical serpent that God did not know good and evil: "God doesn't 'know' anything, God 'creates' everything."[215]

In October 1938, Berdyaev published an article by Lazarev in *The Way* entitled "The Philosophical Project of Jules Lequier." Lequier was a French philosopher of the nineteenth century, a contemporary of Charles Renouvier, whose memory had been revived by Jean Grenier in 1936 by an article and the republication of fragments of his writings entitled *La liberté*.[216] Lazarev's article was the subject of a lecture at the Academy and was published simultaneously in French by L. Lévy-Bruhl in *La Revue philosophique*. Shestov thought that it was excellent. Here is what he said about Lazarev's essay to Fondane. "He wanted to write about me, but I discouraged him as much as I could.... It's fine to compare Lequier to Kierkegaard, who is very famous even in France ... those who know me will have understood."[217]

Lazarev agreed with Lequier, the philosopher of freedom, when the latter placed creation (the "making")—which was based on the freedom to act according to one's will—above knowledge, which depended on causality and change. In opposition to Descartes or Kant, who sought scientific criteria for truth, evidence, or morality, Lazarev cited this profession of faith in creation by the French philosopher: "Make, do not become, and in making, be made."[218]

Starting from this positive approach of faith as a new dimension of thought, Shestov progressively, during the 1930s, recognized the possibility of a religious philosophy—on the condition that this philosophy freed itself from all restraints, ceased to propose as its objective the task of consoling and ordering human existence, and accepted the integration of mysticism, especially Hindu mysticism, with faith and reason. Shestov's new philosophy, as expressed in his 1937 book, *Athènes et Jérusalem*, had pure creation as its sole principle and was based not on concepts but on myths, the receptacles of revelation. This philosophy proclaimed: "Since we do not know anything, we are bound by nothing."[219]

From this starting point, Shestov proposed beginning the journey as did Abraham and Tolstoy, by abandoning all the spiritual riches that reason had accumulated and dreaming of a new order where even the past might not have happened. On this road, the principle of contradiction was no longer the organizing principle of all things but rather a tool at the service of the divine-humanity. Shestov wrote:

> Are we not free to admit that certain things among all the things which have been will never be effaced, while others will disappear and become nonexisting, and that, consequently, the principle of contradiction, submitted to a superior principle, will protect certain pages of the past until the end of time and will destroy others in such a way that the past itself will be modified? We are, of course, free to admit this possibility; but we will not admit it for the sole reason that we "are afraid" . . . that we will have to transform all our logic or (and this is what seems to be the most terrible consequence) renounce the services of previously prepared criteria and "lose footing." Instead of asking, we will have to respond; instead of obeying, we will have to command, choose our own Eurydice, and descend into hell in order to oblige it to recognize our rights. Is this too much to ask of man, of man mortal and weak?[220]

The Position of Vysheslavtsev, Lossky, and Alekseev
Although Florovsky had ceased publishing in *The Way* between 1935 and 1940, N. Lossky, Vysheslavtsev, and Alekseev continued to try to overcome the absolute dualism between the figure of the Creator-God and that of

fallen man in the pages of the journal. For Lossky, salvation came from the freedom of the creature entirely separated from his Creator, while for Vysheslavtsev it came from man's spiritual resemblance with God, which was rooted in the *Ungrund*, in Divinity. Lossky and Vysheslavtsev gave the myth primacy over logic and the supra-rational self primacy over intellectual awareness, and they deliberately situated themselves in a "metalogical sphere, that is, a sphere not subject to the law of identity, of contradiction and of *tiers exclu* [excluded third possibility].[221] Alekseev, on the contrary, sought to maintain a logical discourse. In the primacy of meaning over being, he saw a sign that the individual consciousness, apart from all revelation, could nonetheless dynamically be connected to meaning.

During this period Vysheslavtsev tried to reconcile his own theocentric approach—according to which human freedom came exclusively from Divinity—with the personalism of Berdyaev and the sophiology of Bulgakov. In the domain of theodicy he used a theology of negation, and in the domain of the theory of knowledge he employed a negative anthropology. The central question for Vysheslavtsev throughout the three studies published between December 1935 and March 1940 was, as he himself put it, the tragic antinomy between the two natures of the God-Man: "Christ is the Divinity infinitely elevated and infinitely precious, but he is absolutely defenseless when confronted with violence."[222] Thus, for Vysheslavtsev, the antinomy is between the figure of the Father, all-powerful but not necessarily good, and that of the Son, full of love but powerless before Pilate. According to Vysheslavtsev, Marcion interpreted this antinomy as an opposition between two gods. Vysheslavtsev, for his part, believed that the *Ungrund*, the uncreated freedom, the source of this antinomy between humanity and divinity, was to be found in God himself. He proposed a synthesis of the antinomy by suggesting the image of a "blind energy of being" opening the creative possibilities to infinity so as to give birth to "the best of possibilities."[223] Man had no reason to complain about the "indifference of nature," of nature's capacity to do evil as well as to do good, for, Vysheslavtsev argued, it is this neutrality "that makes possible man's creative freedom."[224] This justification of creation and of all-powerfulness, however, was still insufficient to explain why Christ found himself "abandoned by God" at the crucifixion. Vysheslavtsev did not give an answer to this question. He believed that it lay in the realm of mystery. However, he stated that this abandonment "only lasts a minute." In the end, God restored

Job's riches to him and raised his Son. For Vysheslavtsev, the eschatological meaning of Christianity consisted in this final revelation of a just God, in the expectation of the Kingdom of God at the end of time.

Before this presentation of a theology of negation, Vysheslavtsev had laid out his negative anthropology in a series of conferences at the Academy in 1935. These were published in the first two articles, "The Image of God in the Essence of Man" (December 1935) and "The Image of God in the Fall" (April 1938). As will be discussed later, Vysheslavtsev, in these essays, tried to counter the dialectic theology of the school of Barth, which deduced an opposition between the free and all-powerful Absolute and man, who was weak and powerless from this separation between the power of the Father and the powerlessness of the Son.[225] For his part, Vysheslavtsev saw in the theocentric antinomy of Father and Son an anthropocentric antinomy between the created and uncreated natures of man.

Unlike Feuerbach, Freud, and Jung, for whom God was only the ideal of the self, Vysheslavtsev took seriously man's desire to embody the archetypes of the subconscious in symbols, gestures, and words. Man did not create God in his image, he affirmed; rather, God created man in his image and likeness. Even if, Vysheslavtsev argued, symbols could be suspected of being the product of subjectivity, the fact of the transcendent movement that sought to represent an objective reality was nevertheless indisputable. Differing from Berdyaev, Vysheslavtsev distinguished the "Self" of the "spiritual conscience" or "spiritual person." Above and beyond intellectual consciousness, the *nous*, there was, he wrote, man in himself, the self, the authentic definition of the absolute person whose symbolic place was the heart and not the intellect. The person, he added, was inaccessible to "rational thought" and to psychology, "as Jung himself had clearly stated."[226]

> The authentic reality of the Absolute is not eliminated by the sole fact that the archetype of the person, the archetype of the Father, is transposed on it. We affirm that this transfer is perfectly valid, for the archetype of the Father reveals the adequate symbol of the Absolute.... In the person itself there is something which resembles the absolute: the person exists in itself, by itself, and for itself. The same can be said of the Absolute.... In a word, the person is auto-creation, the self, and the Absolute is auto-creation, the self. It is in *aseitas* [existence in itself] that they are comparable, existing in themselves and for themselves.[227]

Unlike Shestov, Vysheslavtsev justified knowledge by this likeness to Divinity. But the foundation of knowledge was turned upside down. A human being no longer identified God with his concepts, and his imagination concerning God and the world was no longer a representation of the human consciousness as in Jung. The foundation of knowledge, according to Vysheslavtsev, was that man, the "icon of Divinity," transcended himself in his searching and in all his creation in order to rejoin his Archetype.

Thus, "just as God creates, man creates," Vysheslavtsev stated, citing Berdyaev.[228] Negative anthropology could then be the source of positive knowledge. Vysheslavtsev, in a manner typical of the Russian intellectual consciousness of those times, thought that the self, as center of conscience, as *ego cogitans*, was not the most profound dimension of the person. He cited Baratynsky's "Amo ergo sum." The self, the incarnate spirit that dominated cosmic being, the "super-consciousness" that united the me, the you, and the him without confusing them, was the worthy image and resemblance of God. It is for this reason, he added, that "the person cannot be defined through a system of concepts."[229]

Vysheslavtsev did not explain how man, God's creature, could be able to fall. But he took up perspectives offered by Mother Maria in her article "Birth and Creation" to recall that man was not only a creature of God. He was also "born of the Father." If his nature was created, his spirit was infused by God. As St. Gregory the Theologian wrote, man was a creature whose mission was to become God. This is why even if man, as a creature, could fail in his mission, then as spirit, as son-of-the-Father, he could attain deification—"the main idea of Christianity," according to Vysheslavtsev.[230]

Differing from Vysheslavtsev, N. Lossky, in his article "Of the Creation of the World by God," published in December 1937, did not hesitate to attribute man's freedom exclusively to God. He understood creation in two steps. He first postulated—to avoid any accusation of pantheism—an act of free creation of the world by God out of divine nothingness as the foundation of the "radical ontological separation between God and the world."[231] But God only created the ideal being and left the task of creating the concrete being to man. In the line of the substantialist thought of Leibniz and Spinoza, which he embraced, Lossky made essence precede existence in order to distance God from man's sinful action. In this perspective, evil was not a fatality: "The freedom of created essences is necessarily linked to the possibility of choosing the way of evil—a possibility which, it is true, might never become a reality."[232] The source of evil, Lossky claimed, was not in the essence but in the "pride" of "created actors who have overestimated the value of their personality."[233] According to the logic of his "theism," Lossky, in his interpretation of the incarnation of the Logos, stressed that the two natures of Christ, though not separated, are "without confusion."[234] Lossky concluded with a criticism of the "pantheism" of Bulgakov and, in general, of the idea of pan-unity (*vseedinstvo*) deriving from Solovyov.[235]

Alekseev, who had more affinity with Kant than with Spinoza, thought that the source of freedom was found in the depths of the subjective consciousness. This consciousness, he believed, was itself in relationship with the Absolute, which Alekseev called the "living meaning." The mystery of this relationship led Alekseev to develop an apophatic philosophy that dethroned the all-powerfulness of being and drew a radical distinction between philosophy and theology. In dealing with the problem of evil, Alekseev did not allow himself any recourse to revelation. The separation of God and the world was surpassed, he argued, by the fact that "being is not the highest category of philosophy."[236] Indeed, Alekseev claimed that being necessarily found itself in a dialectic with nothingness. Consequently, for him, only meaning can coordinate the relationship between being and nothingness, above and beyond all conceptualization and in an antinomian manner. But, Alekseev argued, meaning was not something purely logical. Referring to Dilthey, Heidegger, and Berdyaev, Alekseev held that meaning was interpreted increasingly as "one of the aspects of the living meaning."[237] For Alekseev, this philosophy of life and living meaning should be in relationship with the consciousness of the individual, which was the receptacle of freedom and which came from nothing.

The Positions of Zenkovsky and Frank

Like Shestov and Vysheslavtsev, Zenkovsky and Frank believed that man's freedom came exclusively from God. However, unlike them, they believed that the freedom thus offered did not imply a radical separation between God and the world. Evil, the fruit of freedom, had no ontological reality and could not affect God's omnipotence. This was why, for them as for Shestov—to use a religious mode of expression—the world was in the hands of God; it does not have the autonomy that would give freedom, as Vysheslavtsev and Lossky thought. While Shestov opposed the tree of life to the tree of the knowledge of good and evil, and Lossky, Alekseev, and Vysheslavtsev opposed the Divinity, the God-Creator, the Living Meaning, to abandoned, sinful, and relative Being, Frank, Troitsky, and Zenkovsky regarded Being as fractured by sin but not destroyed by it.

Unlike Alekseev, Zenkovsky thought that the problem of evil should be treated by religious philosophy. In his article published in June 1938, "Evil in Man," Zenkovsky agreed with Vysheslavtsev that "Orthodox anthropology" was based on the fact that man was created in the image of God.[238] Zenkovsky differed from Vysheslavtsev in rejecting any recourse to Boehme and postulating that, even before the Fall, human activity in Paradise—hence in the Divinity—had a double source: a divine source and an autonomous source (*samobytnost*). Zenkovsky stated, "The catastrophe is that this autonomy was transformed into an illusion of man's total independence."[239] For him, this was why, after the Fall, "alongside the principle of light and truth, an active center of darkness and sin appeared in the depths of man."[240] However, Zenkovsky, who wanted to absolve the Creator, insisted that this was not a question of metaphysical dualism but only of a "meta-empiric" dualism, which did not touch man's deepest essence.

In February 1939, Frank published *The Inaccessible*, in which he distinguished apophatically the inaccessible God of the Absolute. As N. S. Plotnikov has pointed out, Frank, in this book, continued the interrogation of Heidegger on the meaning of the being of the existent.[241] In order to avoid Heidegger's shift from an analysis of the meaning of being to an analysis of the history of being, however, Frank sought to root all the forms and regions of being in a sole inaccessible being. This monistic philosophy thus succeeded in restoring the pan-unity in the world of objects, in human existence, and in the divine realm. In his effort to understand the relative independence of these spheres, Frank considered the question of evil at the end of his book. But he held that it was impossible to answer this question, even though he shared the perspective of Zenkovsky that "evil as such is not an essence."[242] He concluded that the only way to approach this mystery was to postulate the personal responsibility of the individual regarding evil.

Personalism: God and Man

Berdyaev wrote a review of Frank's book in *The Way* in the September 1939 issue. His principal objection to the ontological approach of Frank was that it was based on an objectification of the products of the mind, on a "logical universalism,"[243] and on an impersonal representation of the Absolute.[244] Moreover, regarding the question of evil, he thought that Frank's agnosticism was incompatible with a rigorous philosophy of unity since it ended up introducing evil into the inner essence of the divinity.[245] This criticism of Frank revealed something of the intellectual evolution of Berdyaev during the years 1935–40. During the preceding period, by situating the source of liberty both "in" God and "outside of" God, Berdyaev had shifted the antinomian axis of the "all-powerful Absolute/God made manifest" towards the axis of the "divine Person/human person." This evolution was part of an effort to de-ontologize the Absolute and introduce movement within the Divinity. Berdyaev, who situated himself in the existentialist movement, put the finishing touches on this process in 1935 with his *Spirit and Reality*. Defining the *Ungrund* as the primal, pre-ontological liberty,[246] he ceased granting any reality to abstract being and inaugurated a metaphysic of the spirit that was markedly eschatological.

> The spirit is not an objective reality. Moreover it cannot be categorized as "being" insofar as this is a rational category. The spirit is never, under any aspect, a real object. The philosophy of the spirit is not a philosophy of being—an ontology—but rather a philosophy of existence. The spirit is a reality but a reality very different from that of the world of nature, of the world of objects.[247]

In this book Berdyaev returned to the problem of evil and insisted that "evil cannot be conceptualized; it can only be thought of mythically."[248] From this perspective, he used the symbol of maternity to describe the mystery of freedom. Irrational freedom gives "birth" to evil and to good: "freedom does not choose," he wrote, "but engenders." Because of this, he continued, "the goal of the spiritual life is not to explain or justify life's sufferings, but to illuminate them and to live them spiritually."[249] In his *The Beginning and the End: Essay on Eschatological Metaphysics* written in 1940–41, Berdyaev held that eschatology consisted in realizing that the fallen state was a state of objectification, which could only be vanquished by a reaching towards the final state.[250]

As Berdyaev wrote in an article published in *The Way* in April 1936, entitled "The Problem of Mankind: Towards a Christian Anthropology," this primacy of the spirit should lead us to consider the divine image in man as a capacity to go beyond one's own self and to create.[251] But this also led him to reformulate his philosophy of history. Renouncing his positions on the meaning of history as expressed in 1923, he wrote that history was anything but an "uninterrupted divine-human process."[252] On the contrary, Berdyaev observed, history was indifferent to man and suffocated the person. "History," he stated, "is the failure of the Kingdom of God; it only continues because the Kingdom of God is not being realized." For him, history had a religious meaning—that of the Kingdom of God—only in the degree to which the meta-historic penetrated it here and there and saved actual persons. In a talk given at Clamart on November 5, 1939, and published in March 1940, entitled "War and Eschatology," Berdyaev stated that in times of war or revolution, people understood better than at other times that the Apocalypse was not a fate decreed but the revelation of a judgment within history and an appeal to human creativity. Berdyaev believed that there would be an end to history, but he refused to interpret this end solely in fatalistic terms. He offered an original exegesis of the phrase of the Apocalypse, "Behold, I make all things new" (Rev. 21:5), in that for him it was addressed to mankind's eschatological creativity as well as to God's.

> Every act authentically moral, spiritual, and creative is an eschatological act in that it finishes one world and makes of it another, a new one. Every moral act is a victory of liberty over necessity, of the divine humanity over the natural inhumanity. If you give something to eat to someone who is hungry or if you free the Blacks from slavery—I am taking the most elementary examples—you are accomplishing an eschatological act, for this world is hunger and slavery.... The Kingdom of God comes without fanfare, without theatrics. It comes in each triumph of humanity; the end of this world, this world of cruelty, of slavery, of inertia, draws near in a true liberation, in an authentic creation.[253]

According to Berdyaev, the end of the world did not take place in time. Rather, it was the end of time itself. In 1940, when the German army had occupied Paris, he was living in Pila-sur-Mer, in the Arcachon Bay area. Driven by his personalist vision of eschatology, he completed the essential parts of his book *Conscience de soi, essai d'autobiographie philosophique* (*Dream and Reality: An Essay in Autobiography*). He refined this theme in his *The Beginning and the End: Essay on Eschatological Metaphysics*. People tended, he wrote, to objectify the end, using the concepts of this world. The ideas of Hell and Paradise were characteristic of this kind of exteriorization. But, he explained, the end of the world cannot be disassociated from the end of each individual. It was for this reason that he accepted the principle of metempsychosis, or the transmigration of souls, not merely on one level—that would contradict the corporal and spiritual integrity of the person—but on several levels, before birth and after death, a process that leads up to the resurrection of souls and bodies.[254]

Sophiology: God and the World

During the summer of 1935, before the great polemic on Sophia, Bulgakov wrote an article for *The Way* entitled "The Problem of Conditional Immortality: An Introduction to Eschatology." He criticized the doctrine of conditional immortality that had originated in Protestant circles during the second half of the nineteenth century and that claimed that eternity was promised only to those who followed the evangelical counsels while on earth. Bulgakov saw in this doctrine a form of eschatological thought that considered man only from an exterior point of view and failed to take into consideration the divine-human process of deification, which takes place in each and every person.[255] This article was written—as we shall see—from a perspective of ecumenical dialogue and was intended as the point of departure for a new treatise on the church, in which Bulgakov hoped to formulate an Orthodox approach to eschatology. For him, this approach had to free itself both from a penal vision—inherited from the Middle Ages—of the sufferings meted out to people after death, and from a humanitarian vision—inherited from modern times—that denied the reality of suffering in hell.

This research was delayed for a year and a half. Bulgakov made another trip to the United States in 1936, from September 29 to November 6. He gave a series of lectures to raise funds for the St. Sergius Institute, but, unlike the previous visit, he found himself in a country undergoing an economic and political renewal. He also participated in the first International Congress of Orthodox theologians held in Athens between November 29 and December 3, 1936. Bulgakov decided to give his lecture there on the theme of the church. After all the polemics, it was becoming urgent to renew Orthodox ecclesiology. It was no longer possible to disguise the sophiological problematic, as had been the case in the studies on the doctrine of the church published in *The Way* in 1925–26. At a few meters from the Agora and before a public of young theologians in quest of a neopatristic synthesis, Bulgakov added three new aspects (cosmic, historical, and eschatological) to the traditional definitions of the church (treasury of the gifts of grace and source of eternal life). Three weeks later, on Christmas night, 1936, Bulgakov began a third trilogy consecrated not to Wisdom in the world—as in 1925–29—nor to Wisdom in God—as in 1930–35— but to the relationship between uncreated Wisdom and created Wisdom, that is, the church. The trilogy [which appeared as a single book with three parts: "The Creator and Creation, "The Church, History, and the Afterlife," and "Eschatology"] was finished on October 27, 1938, but published only in 1945 after his death (*The Bride of the Lamb*). However, his contemporaries were able to consult a summary of his theses on the church in a book published in English in 1937 entitled *The Wisdom of God*. This book was the result of lectures given by Bulgakov in 1936 at Mirfield, England, where he shared his sophiology with members of the Fellowship of St. Alban and St. Sergius. After two throat operations in March and April 1939, Bulgakov lost his voice. However, he partially recovered in 1941 and gave a course at the St. Sergius Institute on the theology of St. John. This led to his final book, completed during the summer of 1943, *The Apocalypse of St. John*—which he considered the conclusion of all his work.

The ecumenical implications of the ecclesiology of Bulgakov will be examined later. What is important to emphasize here is that in presenting the cosmic dimension of the church, Bulgakov once again tried to resolve the problem of evil. According to Bulgakov, the fundamental antinomy was not between the Absolute and God, nor between God and man, but between God and the world, that is, between God and Wisdom. He was critical of those who, like Berdyaev, postulated a meonic freedom outside of God. Bulgakov insisted that the world was created by God from "nothing."[256] In the logic of Bulgakov, even nothing (*me on*) had been created by God. But Bulgakov could not accept the point of view of those who would not allow the world its own autonomy, or who would have it receiving only a partial freedom from its Creator. For Bulgakov, the world has genuine autonomy, which is based in the freedom created by God alone and which could lead it even to reject God. Bulgakov's interpretation was close to that of Shestov but differed in that it situated sin not only in knowledge but even in the angelic world. which revolted against its ontological dependence. Bulgakov thus assumed the biblical account in its entirety and believed that evil did not have a rational cause; it was the mark of a universe unfulfilled.

A good understanding of eschatology and of the meaning of creation was essential to this perspective. Bulgakov did not interpret the biblical "In the beginning," the *Bereshit*, according to the Kabbalah tradition as the affirmation of the Law from the very origin of the world. Nor did he interpret it according to modern tradition, as chronological time. Instead, it was the secret presence of the divine and eternal Wisdom manifested in God as the created and spatial-temporal Sophia. Thus Bulgakov included the creation of the world in the very life of the Divinity. For Bulgakov, God created the world from nothing, that is, of himself, of his eternity. By an act of love, of tri-hypostatic self-determination, God let this eternal world, which he possessed in himself and for himself, take on an independent, temporal mode of being.[257] Referring to Plato as much as to the Bible, Bulgakov formulated his central antinomy in the following terms:

> The divine Sophia and the created Sophia are not two. They are one Sophia but distinguished according to their mode of being; as an ideal reality with an eternal mode, and as an entelechy of the created, in the mode of the autonomous being proper to the world of creatures. It is precisely because of the unity of Sophia under its two forms that the world is created and is not, that it belongs to the temporal order by its being [autonomous existence] and to eternity in virtue of its principle.[258]

For Bulgakov, the historical expression of this relationship between the divine Sophia and the created Sophia was tragic and, according to the testimony of the Apocalypse, would end in a catastrophe. But in an eschatological perspective, this catastrophe would not be the final word. Similarly, the division between paradise and hell, which are merely ontological states, could not be eternal.[259] The history of the church found its fulfillment in the epiphany of divine Wisdom in created Wisdom, in the return of Christ, by the revelation of the hypostasis of the Holy Spirit. In the apocalyptic theme of the Bride of the Lamb, Bulgakov saw the prefiguration of the face of the Third Hypostasis of the Trinity: the Mother of God.

> She, the Spirit-bearer, is the "Spirit and the Bride" who reveals, by her very being, the image of the hypostatic Spirit of God. The final words of the New Testament proclaim her [Rev. 22:17, 20]. "And the Spirit and the Bride say: Come! And let him who understands say: Come! Amen, come Lord Jesus."[260]

The Logic of the Spirit

Although the contributors to *The Way* read one another's works and sometimes sought to overcome their differences concerning the problem of evil, it was evident—and this was one of the causes of the demise of the journal—that on the eve of the Second World War, they were unable to find a synthesis that incorporated their distinct points of view. Moreover, in the period 1936–38 the three most significant representatives of the theocentric, anthropocentric, and sophiocentric positions, namely, Shestov, Berdyaev, and Bulgakov, published three articles, one after the other, that were unusually polemical—thus effectively ending the quest for a synthesis that had marked the nonconformist period. Things arrived at such a point that, after the conflict was over and the protagonists were deceased, Zenkovsky and Nikolai Lossky believed that the time had come for each of them to write a history of Russian philosophy, which would put to rest the most audacious attempts to elaborate a mytho-logical discourse. These histories contained a radical criticism of the "irrationalism" of Shestov, of the "neo-romanticism" of Berdyaev, and of the "monism" of Bulgakov's sophiology.

Some Violent Farewells

The three articles in which Berdyaev, Shestov, and Bulgakov violently took on one another were all published—and this is of importance—not in the generational sanctuary of *The Way* but in *Contemporary Annals* (*Sovremennye Zapiski*). Berdyaev started things off in 1936 by publishing a review of a book by Shestov on Kierkegaard. From the very first lines he denounced the "despotic thinking" of Shestov, who "divides the world into two irreconcilable spheres"—on the one hand, the sphere of Socrates and Hegel, for whom reason and morals are necessities, and on the other hand, the sphere of the Bible—"and still only a few words of the Bible"—and of Kierkegaard, for whom life and freedom are above the knowledge of good and evil.[261] Berdyaev showed the dilemma caused by this "Manicheism." Shestov believed that faith alone—for example, the faith of Kierkegaard that he will find his beloved again in spite of all the evidence to the contrary—was a source of salvation. But at the same time Shestov recognized that, aside from the example of Abraham, such a saving faith was impossible. Berdyaev had no qualms about qualifying Shestov's religiosity as "quietist." For the source of this religious dead end, according to Berdyaev, came from the fact that Shestov had a passive understanding of the Kingdom—for him, "faith marks the end of the tragedy"[262]—and he gave no attention to the central figure of Moses, to the divine revelation of the Law. Concerning the central definition in Shestov's thought of God as "unlimited possibility," Berdyaev asked: "But why is Shestov so convinced that God, who is absolutely free (God's freedom almost becomes arbitrariness), wants to give Regine Olsen to Kierkegaard? . . . Perhaps God does not want that at all and prefers that Kiekegaard not recover his fiancée. . . . [I]n this case the hopes of Kierkegaard and Shestov are in vain."[263] Moreover, Berdyaev stigmatized Shestov's "Jewish heritage," made manifest by the ease with which his reason arrived at believing in an all-powerful God while it was a paradox for reason to imagine an incarnate God. At the conclusion of his article, Berdyaev charged that Shestov was as rationalistic as his opponents, since, like them, he believed in the universality and oneness of reason, whereas reason varied according to the quality of the relationships among people.[264]

Shestov responded to Berdyaev near the end of fall 1937, after the publication of the Russian version of *Spirit and Reality*. His reply bore the title "Nicolas Berdyaev, Gnosis and Existential Philosophy." Although written in a friendly tone, it attempted to tear apart Berdyaev's personalist philosophy. A few days after writing it, Shestov suffered an intestinal hemorrhage that confined him to his bed for a month. Aside from a piece dedicated to the memory of Husserl, this was the last article of Shestov published while he was still alive. He died on November 20, 1938. The reply to Berdyaev was published one month earlier in *Contemporary Annals* and had the tone of a philosophical testament. Shestov began by pointing out that Berdyaev's latest book, *Spirit and Reality*, marked a "spirit-centered" evolution in the philosopher's thinking. But Shestov held that this development was the logical consequence of Berdyaev's theandrism, which tended to "transform itself into anthropotheism."[265] This pseudo-existentialist evolution, Shestov argued, was not based on Kierkegaard and less still on Scripture, "which never says that freedom is uncreated, that freedom is the faculty of choosing between good and evil."[266] According to Shestov, Berdyaev's evolution was the result of his dabbling in Gnosticism, mysticism, and German idealism. For Shestov, it was characteristic of this tradition to consider, on the one hand, that God cannot vanquish an obscure freedom and, on the other hand, that all suffering was justifiable because man had been given the freedom to do good or to do evil. But this tradition, Shestov maintained, was based on an individual spiritual experience that did not intend to be restrictive but only reproduced, hidden behind its desire to offer "flights towards other worlds," the strict morality of ancient philosophy. Further, Shestov claimed,

> Berdyaev is almost horrified by the idea that man could have been imagined in a world without liberty, without this liberty which enables him to do evil: he would have been an automaton of good.... Even in the face of what Berdyaev calls, in philosophical terms, "the dialectic of Ivan Karamazov" (the martyred children evoked by Dostoevsky), even then the gnosis does not hesitate; of course, it is undoubtedly evil, but God is powerless. We are obliged to abandon the children to their torments lest we take away from adults the possibility to choose between good and evil and deprive them of their original freedom. Berdyaev harkens to the voice of Schelling: "true freedom harmonizes itself with holy necessity—for the only thing which links the spirit and the heart is their own law, which voluntarily affirms what is necessary." But he doesn't understand the question of Dostoevsky: What is the sense in having this diabolical good and evil if the price to pay is too great? It is in no way because of indifference or hardness of heart that he does not understand. On the contrary: Berdyaev's writings show that he is extremely sensitive and compassionate: but the little boy torn to pieces by the general's dogs and before his mother's eyes is a fact; the small girl who cries out

through her tears, "My little beloved God!" is likewise a fact. It is a holy necessity.[267]

Whereas Berdyaev, like the Stoics, asked that suffering be accepted by "penetrating it with light," Shestov sided with Job, who, through the force of revolt, obtained "the repetition" from God, the restoration of all his goods, and with Kierkegaard, who, "in virtue of the Absurd," recovered his fiancée.[268] Shestov also reclaimed the reference to Moses, no matter what Berdyaev might think. He held that when Moses was on the mountain, face to face with God, there was no law. Shestov quoted the phrase of the Apostle Paul: "the law came later, to increase the trespass" [Rom. 5:20].[269] In the face of the fear of the void and the ethic of the law, which Berdyaev defended, Shestov proclaimed the ethic of the Good News. He pointed out that, in reply to the question about which of the commandments is first, Christ did not answer with a "You should" but with "Hear, O Israel! The Lord your God is the One God" [Mark 12:29; cf. Deut. 6:4]. Shestov also answered Berdyaev's accusation by affirming that his faith was in no way quietism but, on the contrary, "a desperate struggle to obtain the impossible."[270] It was in the name of this struggle that Shestov understood the Incarnation and not in the name of the Christian version "of the religion of a suffering god." He considered once again Luther's extraordinary hope of a new creation of the world by God:

> Luther says: "God called his Son and said to him: it is not Peter who denied you, David was not an adulterer, the thief on the cross never killed anyone, Adam never ate the forbidden fruit, it is you who did all that." And that is the true meaning of the Savior's work, that is what inspired the prophecies of Isaiah and Daniel and determines the orientation of existentialist philosophy. If Peter did not deny, if David did not commit adultery, if Adam never tasted the fruit of the tree of knowledge, then everything that Kierkegaard has said about Job, about the poor young man, about his rights over Regine Olsen—all that passes from the domain of the forever-impossible to that of reality *par excellence*.[271]

Berdyaev's criticism of Bulgakov's sophiology has already been mentioned. The reciprocity of their intellectual antipathy can be measured by the swiftness of Bulgakov's reaction after he read Shestov's article. The very same day, Bulgakov sent an enthusiastic letter to Shestov:

> Dear L. I.,
> ... I feel like greeting you, like shaking your hand.... In my opinion this article (even though these last few years I've fallen behind in reading your writings just as you have doubtlessly done with mine) is one of your most interesting and brilliant works. And, surprisingly enough, some convergences came to light—at least on certain points ... as to the understanding of "the liberty of the creature," and no other understanding is possible, I find an ally in you.[272]

Shestov replied with a letter brimming with respect and sympathy. He invited the theologian to visit him in Boulogne and included a copy of his latest book, *Athènes et Jérusalem*. He died several weeks later, without having seen Bulgakov again.

Contemporary Annals asked Bulgakov, as a spiritual authority, to write an article in memory of Shestov. In spite of their final exchange of letters, Bulgakov did not hide his disappointment on reading Shestov's last book. In his article, "Some Aspects of L. Shestov's Religious Vision of the World," which appeared in 1939, Bulgakov stated that Shestov was more of an "essayist," who was "constantly repeating himself," than a true philosopher.[273] Bulgakov was still more disappointed by the "blind faith" of Shestov. The danger in this sort of thinking, Bulgakov pointed out, was a sort of "negative theology" which, in trying to oppose the "first truths" of Greek philosophy and "panlogism," winds up rejecting thought itself, "the Logos and the logical link."[274] Shestov's "fideism" turned into a "militant agnosticism."[275] According to Bulgakov, Shestov's error consisted in confusing the content of faith (revelation) with the act of faith (which Shestov pretended to consider as lacking any rational element). Convinced that the power of the absurd was a "utopian abstraction,"[276] Bulgakov did not spare his criticism of a philosophy that was not rooted in a dogmatic doctrine. For him, the omnipotence of God should be thought of ontologically and not abstractly. God, he explained, "cannot commit sin or interrupt his existence."[277] Similarly, God could not capriciously destroy his creation and wipe out the past. On the contrary, he "prolongs existence and transfigures it."[278] In concluding, Bulgakov also noted Shestov's Judaism: "the unity of God has not been revealed to him as a trinity, which is unique in essence."[279] Carried away by his criticism, he argued that Christ's saying that "everything is possible to him who believes" (Mark 9:23) should not be understood "literally" but "in a divine context." Bulgakov even went so far as to compare Shestov's irrational waiting for a miracle to the temptation of Satan addressed to Christ and urging him to descend from the cross![280]

The Underground Dialogue

The violence of these words is astonishing, considering that it was customary to speak only well of the dead. It was all the more shocking in that, as Bulgakov himself pointed out, his friendship with Shestov stretched back thirty-five years. Of Shestov, Bulgakov wrote: "You could not help loving him."[281] Bulgakov recalled that when he was still living in Kiev, he, Shestov, and Berdyaev had formed a "group" in solidarity. He remembered that many years later, in the immigration, his rare walks with Shestov in the Bois de Boulogne were "always friendly and joyful occasions."[282] Going even further, Bulgakov wrote in his last letter to Shestov: "I always knew and clearly sensed that your apotheosis of the uprooting [the Russian émigré exile] had hidden roots in the revelation of the Old Testament which, in your conscience, has evidently become that of the New Testament."[283]

Berdyaev, for his part, wrote very simply in his autobiography that Shestov—"one of the best persons I ever had the good fortune to meet"—was his "only friend."[284] Berdyaev dedicated two articles honoring Shestov in *The Way*: in the April 1936 issue on the occasion of his seventieth birthday and after his death in the January 1939 issue.[285] He began the first article by stating, "We have been old friends with L. Shestov and for thirty-five years we have been carrying on discussions about God, good, and evil, the nature of knowledge."[286] Without denying his disagreements with Shestov, Berdyaev explained that, nonetheless, their principal differences on the theme of the utility of knowledge were not very deep: "Sometimes it seems to me that questions of terminology play an exaggerated role in the dispute with Shestov."[287] He concluded with a vibrant homage to Shestov, "one of the most original thinkers of the Russian spiritual renaissance."[288]

After the death of his friend, Berdyaev became president of the committee responsible for the publication of Shestov's works—a committee that included P. Milyukov, V. Rudnev, J. de Gaultier, and L. Lévy-Bruhl.

Berdyaev organized a session at the Academy of Religious Philosophy in memory of Shestov on December 18, 1938. There was a full house. Along with Zenkovsky, Lazarev, and M. Zitrone, Berdyaev spoke on the topic "The Fundamental Idea of L. Shestov." He explained that the primary existential experience was difficult to communicate. In view of this difficulty, he proposed to formulate the principal idea of his friend and defend it against "all easy criticism." He wrote in the version published in *The Way*: "L. Shestov is not at all fundamentally opposed to scientific knowledge, or against the use of reason in everyday life. That was not his problem. He is against the pretensions of science and reason to resolve the problem of God . . . when reason and reasonable knowledge seek to limit such possibilities."[289]

Shestov, in spite of a violent dispute with Berdyaev on December 23, 1934, at Clamart[290]—which Pierre Pascal remembered for a long time[291]— had been the first to defend his friend in an article in *Latest News* on March 2, 1935, in response to the attack of Ilyin in *Renaissance*. In his last letter of reply to Bulgakov, Shestov had written concerning Berdyaev: "I cherish and appreciate N. A. very much—I think this is clear in my article."[292] He also made plain his friendship with Bulgakov: "I thank you whole-heartedly for your letter. It gave me great pleasure to find sympathy for my ideas in a person who, like you, has dedicated his whole life to the service of religion."[293] Shestov and Berdyaev had both been present when Bulgakov was ordained on June 11, 1918. Berdyaev remembered this event, when he wrote to Bulgakov in 1933, "as a symbolic moment in the history of the self-awareness of the Russian intelligentsia." And Berdyaev added that he often thought of the intellectual pilgrimage that they have made side by side. He reaffirmed his solidarity with Bulgakov during the Sophia affair in a letter of support dated October 8, 1935.[294] Later, during the Fedotov affair, Berdyaev was careful to spare Bulgakov from his anger against the St. Sergius Institute. He wrote: "Some remarkable people, such as Fr. Sergius Bulgakov, are victims of this domineering atmosphere of the servility of Church people to the right-wing elements of the immigration."[295] Bulgakov followed the work of Berdyaev very closely. In 1933 Bulgakov wrote to Berdyaev that their spiritual paths were like two parallel lines, which could not meet in Euclidean space but which joined above and beyond this space.[296] In 1937, after having read *Spirit and Reality*, he wrote to Berdyaev: "[Between] proximity and remoteness, there is this *and* which somehow exists between the two of us. The *and* brings together and opposes. For my part, I like the antinomy. . . . I believe that it exists in our *and.*"[297] Bulgakov went so far as to confide his discovery of Berdyaev to Shestov: "It is evident that there is no great contradiction between the philosophy of positive nothingness . . . of the 'freedom of the anti-God' in Berdyaev's works—and both my sophiology and my philosophy of existence."[298]

A Three-Part Discourse

The contrast between their declarations of friendship in their correspondence and in *The Way* and the violence of their exchanges in *Contemporary Annals* shows the gap between the solidarities of two of these thinkers arrayed against the other and their common awareness of being part of a same generation. The desire to crush an intellectual opponent was mixed with the sentiment of wanting to say the same thing as the opponent, without being able to do so. All this leads us to look for a three-part discourse beneath the fiery polemics. It was as if the rational logic of "subject-verb-object," once considered the source of the history of Western philosophy, was being transformed, on the basis of a certain level of spiritual density, into a new discourse of "Person-Wisdom-Hypostasis," the reflection of a divine logic in the human intellect. On this "non-Euclidean" level, the historical personalities became the subjects of one and the same voice, which whispered to them an ineffable music. Three essential questions occupied the representatives of the anthropocentric, sophiocentric, and theocentric currents—the origin of evil, the foundations of knowledge, and the meaning of history. Without denying all that separated Berdyaev, Bulgakov, and Shestov, a contemporary observer can find a certain number of bridges uniting these three authors on these three themes.

Let us first consider the question of the origin of evil. As we have seen, Bulgakov, from 1934 onward, no longer hesitated to identify Wisdom with the Spirit. Conversely, Berdyaev was no longer afraid to use the term "divine energies" to express the work of the spirit in the world. Both thinkers considered that freedom and wisdom were *both* in God and outside of God. But with Bulgakov insisting on the non-hypostatic nature of Wisdom, and Berdyaev insisting on the uncreated dimension of freedom, each feared that the other's position ran the danger either of being swallowed up by the cosmic forces or being confronted with Satanism. All the same, both wound up admitting—whether consciously or unconsciously has little importance here—the twofold origin of mankind and the world through the mediation of the biblical figure of Wisdom with God at the moment of creation and the figure of the Word in God and with God at the beginning of the world (John 1:1). This is why Bulgakov could write to Shestov that he no longer thought that the positive nothingness of Berdyaev was Luciferian in meaning. Berdyaev himself insisted on this point in replying to Shestov's article:

> I do, in fact, appreciate J. Boehme very much and he has meant a lot to me. But I understand freedom differently. For Boehme the *Ungrund*, which I interpret as freedom, is found in God as an obscure nature— while I see freedom as something exterior to God. Along these lines I am more of a dualist than a monist, but both these terms are inaccurate. Dostoevsky and Nietzsche have played a much more important role in my life than Schelling and German idealism.[299]

For his part, Shestov never denied that in the Garden of Eden there were two sources of existence for mankind, that is, the tree of life and the tree of knowledge. His main problem was, as Berdyaev put it, not to mix these two sources; on the other hand, Bulgakov, as we have seen, sought to avoid separating Athens from Jerusalem.

The spatial antinomy in this manner of understanding God and divinity had a temporal corollary. As an analysis of their texts shows, these three thinkers were speaking from different points of view. From the point of view of God, that is, the point of view of eternity, it is difficult to question Shestov's conception of the all-powerfulness of the Father without questioning the very concept of a Creator-God. But from the point of view of the person, Berdyaev could not admit that God be objectified as all-powerful. This is why he affirmed that in the world of objects, "God has less power than a policeman." Finally, from the point of view of Wisdom, both eternal and temporal, Bulgakov needed only to take the book of Job to affirm the rights of Wisdom or of being, in the face of "the creature's total liberty" and the "all-powerfulness" of God: "Where were you when I formed the earth? Speak up if you know.... Have you ever once in your life commanded the morning?"[300]

The mystery of evil can be formulated only in antinomian and symbolic terms and not in terms of causality—they all agreed on this. The relationship between God and Wisdom, between the person and liberty, and between the Creator and life becomes, as Mother Maria put it, a love story, the call and the response between the one who gives and the one who receives, the "free creation of what is not free" and "the birth of what is not free from what is free," so that in the nonfreedom of human nature the "Free One, Born and not created" might be revealed."[301]

When we see the profound unity of these three men on the question of theodicy, we understand better, first of all, that the opposition between the sophiology of Bulgakov, the existentialism of Shestov, and the eschatology of Berdyaev is purely formal. Second, we see that the opposition between the gnosis of Berdyaev and the existentialism of Shestov is one of terminology. Third, we recognize that the differences between Berdyaev and Bulgakov, on the one hand, and Shestov, on the other, concerning the utility of the intellect are groundless. Indeed, if Berdyaev and Shestov rejected traditional ontological metaphysics, their purpose was, as they themselves wrote, to communicate better with the world of the possible or with the reality of the spirit without objectivizing the latter. Through his readings of Shestov, Bulgakov realized that his own philosophy was profoundly existentialist in the sense that he could not conceive of being independently of the divine and personal existence. In his letter to Shestov, Bulgakov referred to his sophiology, "which would also be an 'existentialist philosophy'"; and, "at that point, like the bourgeois of Molière, I learned that I was writing prose and not poetry."[302] The philosophy of Berdyaev, which was increasingly opposed to the hypostasizing of ideas, was similarly not in contradiction with the existential philosophy of Shestov. Berdyaev may have used the works of the mystics more than Shestov did, but he did not reject Kierkegaard's battle with Hegel. In reality, both of them were afraid, above all, that their thought would be assimilated to that of Heidegger and Jaspers. Berdyaev criticized Heidegger and Jaspers in a conference at the Sorbonne on the occasion of the Ninth International Congress of Philosophy in August 1937, as follows:

> They pretend to resolve new problems as, for example, those caused by anxiety ... in an academic format, scientifically, with the aid of rational concepts.... Nonetheless, it seems to us that to envisage philosophical knowledge from this angle is to keep it under the domination of objectivization. In brief, in the philosophy of Heidegger and Jaspers, there is not a sense of the existentiality of the subject.[303]

Conversely, Shestov, whose writing against Jaspers in the December 1937 issue of *The Way* will be studied further, implicitly recognized that reason was more than a mere stone wall since he was intellectually engaged with the thought of Kierkegaard. Moreover, in spite of the critique of irrationalism by Berdyaev and Bulgakov, Shestov did not deny that the tree of the knowledge of good and evil had been created by God. He simply added that true knowledge, faith, is in God—a claim that Berdyaev and Bulgakov would certainly not question. As Bulgakov wrote, the philosophy of Shestov "has nothing of the absurd" in the light of common sense. It is rather a question of a negative philosophy.

Similarly, Bulgakov, although more sensitive than the others to the unity and ontological value of thought from Plato to the Fathers of the Church, did not conceive original freedom as the possibility of doing good or evil. In *The Bride of the Lamb* he described the primitive angelic state following creation: "The fact that they [the angels] are immersed in the divine life is the source of their own life, which is an unlimited deification by grace."[304] Evil, he wrote, is not a substance, "it is a state of created being."[305]

> Good and evil, with their contradiction, are not present at the beginning; they belong to the created (and fallen) earth; "The light shines in the darkness." The darkness is, as it were, the base of the light, invisible and, in this sense, nonexistent; they correspond to the nothing of pre-creation (from an ontological—not chronological—point of view, of course): "God is Light and there is no darkness in Him" (1 John 1:5). As darkness, nothingness acquires a certain actuality in the creature in the course of its evolution, which is essentially a *chiaroscuro*. The darkness becomes a reality when the clear-obscure balance is broken, when the shadows cease to be simply a means of light and open passage to darkness.[306]

In this passage, nothing distinguishes Berdyaev's mystery of uncreated freedom, Shestov's affirmation of the omnipotence of God over nothingness, and Bulgakov's vision of the Burning Bush at the heart of creation.

Since knowledge is possible and since it is mytho-logical, it necessarily looks towards the finality of history. However, as we have seen, Berdyaev and Bulgakov disputed Shestov's postulate that it was possible to believe that "what once was, has never been." It was clear that the formulation used by Shestov was ambiguous and did not correspond to what he wanted to say, that is, not "Job did not lose his wealth"—which would contradict his faith in the omnipotence of God—but "God restored all his wealth to Job." These two statements are not the same thing. Shestov himself had lost his only son and could not but know the reality of suffering. Shestov was not denying the existential depth of suffering. He was denying its ontological reality, its capacity for lasting.

For their part, Berdyaev and Bulgakov, throughout their lives, never ceased to repeat that Fedorov's eschatological project of the resurrection of the dead was something extraordinarily new and congenial. The originality of Fedorov did not lie in defending the fact of the resurrection of the dead, which has always been one of the foundation stones of Christianity. It consisted in the fact that—for the first time, according to them—someone took seriously the words of Christ which promise that it will be given to human beings, in the name of the dogma of the divine Trinity that affirms the unity of all in everything, to resurrect the dead. Above all, in Fedorov's vision, the Apocalypse no longer appeared as a *fatum*. Instead, it was a theanthropic deed that brought about the Kingdom of God on earth. Actually, Bulgakov and Berdyaev, even though they criticized the positivist formulation of some of Fedorov's theses, prolonged this tradition. To be sure, Berdyaev often quoted the phrase of Léon Bloy: "Suffering passes; to have suffered will never pass." But although he was aware of the existential depth of suffering, he could never bring himself to accept the injustice underlying it. When he wrote his autobiography, he tried to transfigure the past. "My memory will be knowingly active as regards my life and my pilgrimage; in other words—it will be a creative effort of thought, of my awareness such as it is today."[307] If Berdyaev viewed eschatology more from a personal point of view, he did not hesitate to prophesy the coming of a new age of the Spirit, which would affect all humankind. Conversely, if Bulgakov saw eschatology principally as the achievement of all history, as the descent upon earth of the Heavenly Jerusalem at the end of time, his spiritual experience during his serious illness in 1926 and then in 1939 made him aware—as he wrote in his final book on the Apocalypse of John—of the paradoxical truth of the words of Christ found at the end of the Bible: "My return is near at hand" (Rev. 22:20).

Moreover, Bulgakov and Berdyaev, even though they could not find words sufficiently harsh to condemn the utopia of Shestov, admitted that in their own eschatology there was no place in the Kingdom of God for paradise or hell. If we can imagine—wrote Berdyaev—that in paradise, Abel could not accept the idea that Cain was being consumed in the flames of hell, that is, in a different *place* where there was no grace, why can we not imagine, here from a temporal perspective, that at the end of time, the poor young man would continue to hope to marry, *one day,* the king's daughter? Bulgakov, for whom the divine and eternal Wisdom established and transfigured created and temporal Wisdom while leaving it all its consistency, would hardly be able to admit that Judas, one of the Twelve, be *forever* branded by Scripture as a traitor—something Judas had freely chosen to *become.* We cannot know the answer. Let it be simply noted in conclusion that, even though these three men had different interpretations, their eschatology was essentially based on the same passage of the Apocalypse:

> I heard a voice crying from the throne: "Behold the dwelling place of God among people. He will dwell with them: they will be his people and He will be their God. He will wipe all tears from their eyes: death will be no more: there will be no more tears, nor cries, nor pains, for the old world has passed away." Then He who sits on the throne will declare: "Behold I make all things new." Then he added: "Write: these words are certain and true" (Rev. 21:3–5).

THE COMMON HORIZON OF THE WAR AND THE NEW JERUSALEM

Around 1934–35, as we have seen, certain intellectuals of the journal became more aware of their spiritual identity. This was the result of a development in their representation of the divinity and caused an internal schism within the Paris School, not only on the social level but also in the realm of the ecumenical engagement that had been the foundation stone of the integration of these intellectuals with Western reality. At the end of the 1920s, the originality of Florovsky and Bulgakov consisted in their willingness to break off from the spiritualist traditions of the Russian intelligentsia. This tradition, inherited from Khomiakov and represented by Berdyaev in particular, was motivated by an opposition to the Caesaropapism of the church's synodal period, but, at the same time, it refused to accept that Christianity needed to incarnate itself in visible forms in order to develop. This provoked, as we have seen, an in-depth discussion during the early 1930s among the sophiological, Christological, and personalist approaches to the theanthropic/divine-human dimension of the structures and limits of the church. The three approaches were able to coexist as long as they searched for a common synthesis in their dialogue. Three factors, however, contributed, on the one hand, to bringing about a schism between those intellectuals who sympathized with Berdyaev and Bulgakov and those who preferred the neo-patristic synthesis favored by Florovsky. And, on the other hand, they contributed to the emergence of a pneumocentric or spirit-centered hermeneutic of church unity, which was simultaneously sophianic, personalist, and tri-hypostatic.

The highly charged political atmosphere near the end of the 1930s deeply affected European intellectuals. Most were persuaded that war was inevitable and that one had to choose one's side, and this conviction no doubt also formed the background of the disputes that divided the Russian intellectuals. The political bipartition of French intellectuals, which became evident at the outbreak of the Italo-Ethiopian War, became only more confirmed with time and extended to the literary sphere. In the ecumenical domain, the opposition between the official German theologians and the partisans of a theology free of all traces of nationalism reflected this permeation of the spiritual dimension by the political. The young right-wing generation in the Russian immigration sought to break their ties to the older, ex-Marxist generation, and they expressed this desire by openly accusing the latter of having precipitated the Communist Revolution by their abstract and irresponsible spiritualism. Conversely, following the "denunciation" by Vladimir Lossky and the attacks by Florovsky on Bulgakov, Berdyaev's and Fedotov's opposition to the neo-Byzantine current became radicalized. They ceased to see it as a way to purify classical theology through a return to the church fathers, insofar as it placed its hopes in the hierarchy of the "Red Church" or the "White Church." On January 19, 1936, while the authors of the review were gathered at Berdyaev's home, an incident typical of this about-face occurred. Berdyaev, as his wife noted, thought that the position of Myrrha Lot-Borodin was "too orthodox and very right wing." She attempted to reply. Furious, he snapped at her, "to prove to her that, in the Church, there is no authority nor should there be."[308]

The political divergences brought out the doctrinal oppositions. Take the ecclesiological views of Florovsky. For him, the assembly of the ecclesial community around the bishop, viewed as a charismatic leader, was paramount. His position, therefore, was that any doctrine not in conformity with the tradition of the ecumenical councils was heretical, and he insisted on the necessity of the conversion of the Western churches to Orthodoxy. These views were similar to those of Metropolitan Anthony Khrapovitsky. Florovsky cited the works of the head of the Russian Orthodox Church Outside Russia with increasing frequency, and the latter—according to a former student of the theologian at the St. Sergius Institute, Alexander Schmemann—sent a letter to Florovsky shortly before his death, in which he congratulated him for protecting the Orthodox tradition from "outside deformations" in his writings.[309] While Berdyaev celebrated the "secret" France of the French novelist Joris-Karl Huysmans and of the "little Flower," St. Thérèse of Lisieux, and while Bulgakov prayed every day before the icon of the Wisdom of God of Novgorod, Florovsky and Vladimir Lossky by the end of the 1930s vigorously rejected the history of Russian and French spirituality as non-Christian and advocated a return to Merovingian France or Byzantine civilization. The young Orthodox theologians considered any idea not drawn from the Fathers of the Church as gnostic. As Olivier Clément wrote, Vladimir Lossky "had no great liking for Berdyaev, whom he took literally, in order to demonstrate the absurdity, the 'mythified' conception of freedom (mythified but not mystifying if rightly understood)."[310]

Along the same lines, Florovsky, after his burial of Russian theology in his 1936 book and in spite of the sophiological crisis, was still participating in ecumenical gatherings in 1937 with Berdyaev and Bulgakov. He continued, however, to criticize their "gnosticism." As his biographer, Andrew Blane recounts, Florovsky was above all motivated by the desire to correct the errors of those whom he otherwise respected.[311] It might be added that the ecumenical world, as a network of contact and integration, had considerable social importance for the young immigrant theologian. Although he hesitated at the beginning of the 1930s, Florovsky realized that he had a larger audience in the newly forming ecumenical world—because he was seen as representative of the Eastern Church—as an intransigent defender of Orthodoxy rather than as an heir of Khomiakov.[312] Moreover, if Florovsky was considered a traditionalist by the theologians of the Paris School, he appeared as a modernist to the Greek theologians. According to John Zizioulas, when Florovsky, after his debates with Bulgakov and Zernov, accepted and subsequently promulgated the idea that the charismatic frontiers of the church went beyond its canonical boundaries, he shocked a great number of theologians with his "very advanced" views.[313] Be that as it may, the rupture between the two lines of thought, prepared by the Sophia dispute, took place in an ecumenical context. As his biographer tells it, certain émigrés attacked Florovsky during the Congress of Edinburgh in August 1937, charging him with maintaining a systematic campaign of disparagement of sophiological and personalist "gnosis" in both Orthodox and Protestant circles and of usurping Bulgakov's place in ecumenical events.[314]

A number of factors helped Florovsky at the expense of Bulgakov. One was the very superficial knowledge of Eastern Orthodoxy on the part of the great majority of Western Christians. This knowledge was based on the intellectual proximity of the neo-Byzantine current with neo-Thomism and, even more so, with Barthianism. Another was the reluctance to deal on an official level with lay theologians whose hierarchical support came exclusively from the liberal diocese of Metropolitan Evlogy. A third was the preference for the neo-patristic line of thought on the part of the hierarchs of not only the Greek Church but also of the Eastern European churches. The result of all this was that the ecumenical participants in the Congress of Edinburgh, which took place from August 3 to August 18, 1937, preferred the candidacy of Florovsky to that of Bulgakov. Florovsky thus became one of the two official representatives of the Orthodox Church on the fourteen-member executive commission of the World Council of Churches. This election undeniably sealed—for at least half a century—the victory of the neo-Byzantines in ecumenical relations.

In pre-war France, it was the prophetic vision, open to the world, of the Orthodoxy of Berdyaev that was better known than the more traditional approach of Vladimir Lossky. This was due, in part, to the positive reception of Berdyaev's personalist theses by the group of the journal *Esprit*. However, even before the war, Lossky had a genuine influence on a number of intellectuals in the newly evolving Catholic-Orthodox Church in France—among them Maurice de Gandillac[315]—who were attracted by his apophatic and cosmic theology of the uncreated energies. This tension between Lossky and Berdyaev resurfaced after the war when a group of intellectuals who had disassociated themselves from *Esprit* and reorganized around Marcel Moré refused to invite Berdyaev to participate in their journal *Dieu vivant* (*The Living God*).[316]

Another determining reason for the tension between Berdyaev and Lossky was the split among the contributors to *The Way* between the intransigent neo-Palamist group and the Russophile group, who truly believed in the possibility of ecumenical reunion. There was a progressive awareness, beginning in 1937–38, by Bulgakov and Berdyaev, as well as by the younger generation of Lagovsky, Zander, and Zernov, that a synthesis might be possible between an ecclesiology turned towards the world and an ecclesiology turned towards the church. The result was a lack of interest in further dialogue with Florovsky and Lossky, whose theocentric ecclesiology seemed to them clearly unilateral and insufficiently attentive to the internal life of the Triune God, the resting of the Holy Spirit upon Christ. Freed from the fear of being unfaithful to tradition, yet realistic concerning the difficulties to be overcome on the path to unity, these intellectuals were nonetheless guided by the eschatological vision of the New Jerusalem, which, at the end of time—that is, from now on, according to their expectations—would descend from heaven to take the place not only of Rome, Geneva, and London, but also of Byzantium and Moscow. From this point on, Bulgakov, Berdyaev, and the younger generation of spiritual intellectuals came together in a common understanding of the church as the "House of the Father," composed of "several dwellings," and they mutually recognized the possibility of engaging themselves in the church defined as the Temple of the Holy Spirit or Body of Christ. These three aspects will be explored below.

The House of the Father

Let us begin by examining the converging movements of the ecclesiologies of Berdyaev, Bulgakov, and Fedotov. Whereas Florovsky stopped publishing in *The Way* in 1935 and Vladimir Lossky only contributed a protest letter, Bulgakov and Berdyaev simultaneously published two a priori and diametrically opposed visions of the church in the review. Called upon to address the question of the organization and limits of the church, Berdyaev chose a layman's definition, using what he called a "personalist socialism." In contrast, Bulgakov, speaking as a theologian, favored the idea of "hierarchical conciliarity." However, as we shall see, their ecclesiological approach—whether personalist or sophiological—was based on the same revelation of the unique tri-hypostatic Spirit, and this led to a common vision of the church as the "House of the Father." Unlike the apophatic vision, this concept left space for the confident integration of the "several dwellings" mentioned in the Gospel.

Personalist Socialism

As we already know, Berdyaev believed that "the social system most compatible with Christian personalism is the system of personalist socialism."[317] From 1935, he completely identified his ecclesiology with his vision of the Kingdom. In his book *De l'esclavage et de la liberté de l'homme* (*Slavery and Freedom*), Berdyaev claimed that the church was not an objective social reality that crushed the individual. It was, above all, his body. Every human being is called by the *epiklesis*, by the invocation of the Holy Spirit, to spiritualize not only his or her own body but also the social body and, in this sense, build up the Body of Christ on earth. For Berdyaev, the fundamental definitions of the church are to be found in the injunction of the Apostle Paul to Christians to consider their bodies as the temple of the Holy Spirit and the promise of Christ to be present when two or three are gathered in his name. After a period of intense reflection on Marxism and the sources of Russian Communism—which culminated in his 1935 book *Les sources et le sens du communisme russe* (*The Origin of Russian Communism*)—Berdyaev opposed personalism to Marxist logic and communist practice. From this point on, he no longer hesitated in comparing the socialist vision of the Kingdom to the primitive Christian vision of "the classless society where the exploitation of man by man will no longer be authorized."[318] In such a perspective, the principal characteristic of this ecclesiology was to be oriented, above all, towards individuals and the world. In a break with ontologism, Berdyaev questioned his own philosophy of history—too teleological for his taste—as expressed in his *Sens de l'histoire* (*The Meaning of History*). This eschatology, now become personalist, was regarded by Berdyaev as the possibility of personal participation in the Kingdom here and now. This probably prevented him from seeing the work of the Holy Spirit over time, in Tradition, and in the gradual awareness by Christians of the universality of the church. However, the mytho-logical transition from being to spirit, formalized by Berdyaev in 1935, was itself based on an evolution of his vision of the figure of the Holy Spirit, previously conceived as the invisible source of human liberty and now seen as the Third Hypostasis of the Triune God. This evolution somewhat modified his ecclesiology. The personalist eschatology of Berdyaev included the idea that the visible forms of the church could be not only the mark of the manifestation of the Holy Spirit but also the sign of its secret presence in history.

Thus Berdyaev, who already counted Paul Tillich and Emmanuel Mounier as old friends, resolved to give a more active orientation to the political and social program of the religious socialist movement. He became interested in the work of the founders of religious socialism in Germany in the nineteenth century—Johann Blumhardt (1805–80) and his son, Christoph Blumhardt (1842–1919). The fundamental idea of the Blumhardts, similar to that of Khomiakov, consisted in locating the center of gravity of Christianity not in a pietistic cult but in the transfiguration of the world into the Kingdom of God through the workings of the Holy Spirit. At a meeting of the Décades de Pontigny, Berdyaev met André Philip (1902–70), a young Protestant who belonged to Christianisme Social, a movement started by the pastors Elie Gounelle and Wilfrid Monod, which stressed political action. In 1936 Philip became the first militant Christian to be elected deputy of the Socialist Party (Section Française de l'Internationale Ouvrière) in the Rhône region. Berdyaev also discovered the work of Reinhold Niebuhr (1892–1971), the American Protestant theologian who had been a pastor in Detroit. Through his friend Fritz Lieb, he came into contact with the work of Leonhard Ragaz, a Swiss Protestant theologian who became famous in 1914 after his appeal against the War, alongside Romain Rolland, Lenin, and Trotsky. As the principal voice of religious socialism, Ragaz was closer to the humanism of Henri de Man than to the dualism of Karl Barth. In 1935 he published a book in German entitled *Von Christus zu Marx—Von Marx zu Christus*. Berdyaev reviewed it in the December 1935 issue of *The Way*. Berdyaev and Barth shared the idea that the church appeared because "the Kingdom of God has not arrived." For this reason, Berdyaev appreciated the socialist messianism in Ragaz's book, which he found closer to that of St. Francis of Assisi than to that of Marx.[319] But Berdyaev also found Ragaz overly optimistic and unable to comprehend that, "as a religion, Marxism is a lie."

Berdyaev accompanied his review of Ragaz's book with a review of Mounier's book *Révolution personnaliste et communautaire*, published by

Montaigne Press that same year. In his discussion of Mounier's work, Berdyaev reaffirmed his conviction that "personalist socialism is the system most compatible with Christian personalism."[320] Berdyaev was especially appreciative of Mounier's ethical commitment, his desire — in the name of the group of young intellectuals who surrounded him — to testify to the truth and not seek success, and his rejection of capitalism, which transforms people into utilitarian means or simply things. Berdyaev saw in Mounier the symbol of a new generation trying to take shape around certain Christian principles, such as asceticism, humility, and the revolutionary refusal of the bourgeois world. Berdyaev wrote: "This is a collective and conciliatory task of the conscience." With amiable humor, the philosopher remarked that "Mounier links the person with the community to such a point that he doesn't want to say 'I' — he wants to say 'us.' This is very close to what Orthodoxy calls *sobornost*."[321] Finally, Berdyaev considered "very healthy" Mounier's rejection of the deification of the state and of the "secret Nietzscheism" of the New Order group. Mounier, he claimed, was not a "doctrinal democrat" holding on to the ideology of 1789 seen as "bourgeois radicalism," but a democrat "in the Christian understanding of the word."[322] The entire development of Berdyaev's thought from spiritualism to spiritual realism, which he formalized in 1935, was evident in his positive evaluation of Mounier's political commitment — not in the traditionalist sense of a political career, but in the elaboration of new forms of social engagement. Even though Berdyaev would have liked Mounier to be constantly aware that "spiritual reevaluation" was the basis of all action, he was enthusiastic about the way in which the personalist movement was concerned with its "social projection" in the community. Berdyaev wrote: "He [Mounier] approaches the revolution not just interiorly, in a spiritual sense — but also in an exterior, social sense."[323]

But Berdyaev was not content merely to encourage the movement voiced in the journal *Esprit* — he wanted to correct and reorient it. Thus he criticized the position of Mounier and the Catholic Church regarding private property. Mounier recognized property based on work and accepted the Catholic Church's justification of property as a guarantee of family stability. Berdyaev, in this case closer to Proudhon, attacked the principle of inheritance rights as the source of "innumerable nightmarish family dramas." For him, "family egotism and family property are the foundation of the bourgeois world, and it is this foundation that the personalist revolution should destroy."[324] Berdyaev concluded by directing a philosophical critique at Mounier. He questioned the validity of the idea of "the community as a person."

> This business of applying the category of person not to a man but to communitarian and social entities is a very complex problem. Can the Church be thought of as a person, for example? That hasn't been worked out by Mounier. Along the same lines, his fear of understanding the person as a creative act provokes certain reservations. In this domain one senses the influence of Thomism, which does not see man as a creator.[325]

Hierarchical Conciliarity

When Bulgakov was designated by Metropolitan Evlogy as the representative of the Orthodox Church of the diocese of rue Daru to the Faith and Order Commission, he insisted that the question of the hierarchy and the sacraments of the church be included in the agenda. For Bulgakov, this question was fundamental in the dialogue with the Protestant world. It was also of prime importance for resolving the internal debate between the partisans of the view that the hierarchy was the sole source of grace (e.g., Florovsky) and the vision of the visible church as a Eucharistic community (a position outlined in *The Way* by N. Afanasiev). In the first instance, the church was based on the figure of Christ, "the pillar and foundation of truth," whereas in the second case, the Holy Spirit was the source of the love among the faithful, who form, at the moment of the liturgy which brings them together in a common project, a *koinonia*, an authentic community. As for the church's social organization, the first definition of the church tended — as we have seen in the case of Cyprian of Carthage — to consider the bishop as the exclusive successor of the Apostle Peter, himself the successor of Christ, in order to accentuate the divine character of the hierarchy. Inversely, the *koinonia* vision of the church reminds us that in the early days, ordinary laity were empowered, that is, elected to celebrate the Eucharist and were, therefore, dispensers of grace. There was no clerical caste. As noted above, this opposition between the two ecclesiologies had a political projection in the opposition between hierarchic nationalism and universal socialism.

More profoundly, in the one case, the good governance of the church was of a republican mode. It was centered on what is public, on the "what" rather than the "who," on the dogmatic truth preserved by an oligarchical elite rather than on the faithful themselves. This was why Florovsky had difficulty in accepting the presence of Christians outside of the dogmatic boundaries of the Orthodox Church. In the other case, the "who" prevailed over the "what," and the mode of good governance was of the democratic variety, based on those of the faithful who were worthy to participate in the mystery/sacrament of the sharing of the Eucharistic bread and wine. In this perspective, all of the believers are kings, priests, and prophets and are only distinguished among themselves according to the mode of their functions and the principle of representation. This was why Afanasiev was fiercely opposed to lay people taking the place of bishops at councils, because the grace of the bishops resided more especially in their mode of existence, that is, their quality as "chosen"—and not in their ontological capacity to preserve the dogmatic truth of the church, since this function belonged to the whole body of the faithful at the moment of the "reception" of the decisions made by the councils. In the mid-1930s Bulgakov proposed a synthesis of the two approaches, between the "what" and the "who," by shifting the center of gravity in ecclesiology towards the figure of the Spirit of God, and by reuniting the mystical church and the historical church on an antinomian and eschatological level. His article, "Hierarchy and Sacraments," appeared in the December 1935 issue of *The Way* and was translated into English in the collection *The Ministry and Sacraments* for the meeting of the Faith and Order Commission held in Edinburgh in July 1937. It was, however, addressed especially to Protestant theologians and ecclesiastics. Only in 1938, after his rupture with Florovsky, did Bulgakov explain his dogmatic synthesis of the church and the good use of ecumenical practice in an article in *The Way* addressed primarily to Orthodox readers.

In "Hierarchy and Sacraments," Bulgakov called on Christians to avoid both the temptation of papalism—here the theologian addressed himself especially to the Orthodox—and the danger of turning liturgical ministers into functionaries—here he pointed to the Protestant Church in Germany.[326] To avoid this double danger, Bulgakov proposed above all considering the church as having a divine-human nature, eternal and temporal at the same time, thus justifying the possibility of historical development. For Bulgakov, this double nature of the church was the basis of the "hierarchical conciliarity" that historically has been the way the church conducted its internal affairs. Bulgakov began with an historical survey, from which he drew his dogmatic conclusions. He gave only relative importance to certain "myths," such as that of an unbroken apostolic succession, the foundation stone of the hierarchical principle, which, he stated, can only be "postulated" but is not apparent in its triadic people-priests-bishops form until the second century. To support his thesis on "the emergence of the hierarchy in history," Bulgakov pointed out that the apostles, and later the hierarchs, are not the only recipients of the grace of the Holy Spirit. At the moment of the birth of the visible church, that is, at the moment of Pentecost, when the flames of the Holy Spirit descended upon the followers of Jesus, these flames came down not merely on the apostles but also on the Virgin Mary and many others. That meant, Bulgakov explained, that the hierarchs are not the only ones able to lead the church. The twelve apostles represent the whole body of the church, hierarchy and laity, men and women. Hence, Bulgakov concluded, "we cannot speak of apostolic grace limited to the hierarchy alone."[327]

For Bulgakov, however, the historical appearance of the hierarchy—and the ontological primacy of the church over the hierarchy—did not call into question its divine origin through apostolic succession but rather designated its functional usage through its indefectible connection with the local church (the parish) at the moment of the Eucharistic celebration. Although apostolic succession is indispensable for the bishop's office, the bishop, in the early church, was in fact designated by the local church through common prayer and only later by election. Bulgakov underlined the universal dimension of episcopal ordination by evoking Cyprian's principle of *in solidum*, whereby the new bishop is always ordained in the presence of two or three bishops from neighboring dioceses. This, he argued, bears testimony to the conciliar bonds among Christians not only on the historical and apostolic level but also on a geographical, interjurisdictional plane. Bulgakov believed that such an approach to the question of hierarchy could reconcile not only Catholics and Protestants but also, within Orthodoxy, the perspectives of Florovsky and Afanasiev. Bulgakov admitted that the *post factum* canonical formalization of the emergence of the hierarchical principle could have suffered "legalistic" deformations in the Roman Church, against which the Reformation reacted. But Bulgakov affirmed, nonetheless, that the conciliar practice of the historical church did not place the bishop above the laity since the laity were, by baptism, priests, prophets, and kings. This historical practice of close association between the bishop and the laity confirmed, in Bulgakov's mind, the dogmatic principle that "the whole Church is hierarchical, as the Body of Christ and as the temple of the Holy Spirit, and the hierarchical service is not the foundation but rather the function of this hierarchy."[328] Bulgakov pointed out that the principle of the royal priesthood of all believers was proclaimed in Protestantism but was not realized except in the pastors because the principle of differentiated orders, or ministries, was not recognized. So he directed an appeal to "our Protestant brothers" to show some "practical wisdom" by recognizing the usefulness of a hierarchy in the church, in order to activate the principle of the royal priesthood of all the faithful.[329]

Bulgakov distinguished what he called "hierachical conciliarity" from papalism and Quakerism. In secular terms—and here one comes back to the consequences for the laity of the different ways of defining the church—he understood "hierarchical conciliarity" to be distinct both from monarchy, which is founded on succession without a consensus process, and from democracy, which is founded on election but without tradition:

> Ordination is not a magic act, a *deus ex machina*, the power of a single bishop over the Church; in it is realized the ecclesial ministry itself. By the principle of succession (that is, the *in solidum* of Cyprian), it is the structured life of the ministry. This structured life corresponds in a much more consequential way to the idea of universal ministry than an elective ministry without sacramental signification.... In reaction against this legalism (of the Western Church), the Reformation went further than its adversary. The bureaucratic delegation of the *ministerium*, anti-hierarchical ecclesial democracy, signifies that secularization has been authorized to penetrate the Church.[330]

In support of his thesis, Bulgakov argued that if the power of teaching and of jurisdiction had been historically confided to the bishops, they only retained this power jointly with the people to the extent that the people have the capacity of ratifying or rejecting the decisions taken by the councils—the principle of reception. However, Bulgakov immediately added that bishops were not the only ones at the councils. Lay members (such as monks and the emperor himself) also participated. Bulgakov summed up his position: "teaching is not a sacramental privilege of the hierarchy ... lay people can also teach."[331] For Bulgakov, bishops are "the mouthpiece of the Church," and it is their role, with the consent of the people, to take initiatives—notably, he clarifies, in the area of "sacramental intercommunion."[332] Yet Bulgakov, instructed by his experience in the Fellowship of St. Alban and St. Sergius, took a step backwards with respect to the desire that he had expressed for intercommunion among Christians of different confessions. It should be prepared by the people and not decreed by the hierarchy. This prudence of his was also motivated by the fact that "in the Church there is an immediate and direct reception of the gifts of the Holy Spirit through the force of prophecy."[333] Finally, by the same title that Rome disposes of the primacy over the other dioceses in a functional—but not ontological—manner, Bulgakov judged that the principle *primus inter pares* (first among equals) should take precedence in relations between all the dioceses and within each diocese, and that this would justify the existence of metropolitans and patriarchs or, in other words, the existence of a multipolar world.

The Myth-ology of the Church

The approaches of Berdyaev and Bulgakov, although different, would converge in a rhythm similar with the merging of the ecumenical commissions Life and Work and Faith and Order in the World Council of Churches (WCC). Indeed, after the congresses of Oxford and Edinburgh agreed, in the summer of 1937, to unite in a single ecumenical organization (although because of the war this did not take place until 1948, with the founding of the WCC), the Russian intellectuals close to Berdyaev and Bulgakov became aware of the spiritual unity between the two approaches. In opposition to the "neo-Byzantine" vision of Florovsky, who conceived of ecumenical dialogue as an unrealizable project to convert the "other" to the truth of Orthodoxy, the contributors to *The Way* were unanimous in believing that the unity of the church was already realized in its spiritual depths and that it was the task of the visible church to manifest this unity *hic et nunc*, here and now. To the sophiological, antinomic, and eschatological visions of the Kingdom of God, the authors of *The Way* added a properly Trinitarian, personalist, and tri-hypostatic dimension to the nature of the church. I. Lagovsky's article in the 1937 collection *Living Tradition* (*Zhivoe Predanie*), emblematically entitled "The Return to the House of the Father," made it clear that his defense of sophiology indicated a spiritual movement of dogmatic awareness. Similarly, the intellectuals writing for the journal drew ecclesiological conclusions from their newfound awareness of the integrally personal reality of the divine Spirit. The church appeared to them not as either an impersonal hierarchical structure or an amorphous spiritualism, but as the most profound reality of the unique life of the tri-hypostatic Spirit, a reality to which the dogmatic definitions pointed symbolically. In this mytho-logical perspective, the church was the "House of the Father" but also the "Body of Christ" and the "Temple of the Holy Spirit."

For both Berdyaev and Bulgakov, this new formulation of the dogma of the church did not imply any compromise. On the contrary, it was a liberation. Their Spirit-centered vision of the church was proclaimed more vigorously than ever. In January 1939, Berdyaev published an article by Cyprian Kern on pastoral theology—thus giving proof of his openness to the neo-patristic current at the St. Sergius Institute. But when Kern recommended that Orthodox pastors be on their guard against "innovators" and "people who have just recently entered the Church without being liberated from nonecclesial and purely secular influences but who think they are already mentors," Berdyaev flew off the handle. In a note he pointed out that "the editorial staff did not want to infringe on freedom of conscience but thought it necessary to indicate that this passage contradicted the overall tone of the article. This passage could be interpreted in such a way as to restrict the right of religious creativity to the spiritual hierarchy while denying it to the laity."[334] His criticism of the hierarchy, however, was not unilateral. In April 1939 he accompanied his article defending freedom of conscience in Orthodoxy with a letter by Pastor Christoph Blumhardt and a text praising Pope Pius XI. This juxtaposition was meant to signify that Berdyaev's ethical and personalist vision of the church was rooted in the eschatological spirituality of the Protestant pastor, that it situated the quest for the Kingdom above confessional allegiances, and that it found expression in the person of the primate of the Catholic Church.

Pastor Blumhardt, who had been elected deputy for Wurtemberg, had written a letter to the Royal Consistory explaining his commitment to serve the most helpless. He was subsequently stripped of his functions as pastor by the national church. Blumhardt decided to make his letter public so that his friends might understand the reasons behind his stance. His letter was a vibrant plea for opening the doors of the church as wide as possible.

> How many times do we sense a stronger presence of God in the souls of those whose reason rejects Him than in the souls of those who give Him merely formal recognition! Who is not aware of the number of

superstitions and contradictions in official Christianity? Can we blame someone who uses his intelligence if he chooses the road of negation?[335]

Berdyaev's admiration for Blumhardt's deep solidarity with the proletariat did not prevent him from also rendering homage to Pius XI. Berdyaev presented the pope as a defender of "the freedom of the spirit," who denounced "the lived heresies and not the doctrinal ones."[336] By this Berdyaev was referring to the fact that Pius XI, in spite of "the horrible Roman bureaucracy" and the "fascist cardinals" who surrounded him, condemned both capitalism and communism and thus oriented the church towards a healing role in the face of modernity. Even though he glided over the attitude of Pius XI concerning General Franco and failed to mention his condemnation of the ecumenical movement, Berdyaev wanted to state publicly his recognition of the value of the principle of authority in the church when it was associated with ethical principle and not restricted to hierarchal principle.

In the same issue of the review, an article by Maria Kurdiumov appeared entitled "The Church and the World." Kurdiumov, who lacked Berdyaev's ecumenical experience, had less faith than he did in the possibility that the visible church could open itself to the modern world, but she was sympathetic to Berdyaev's arguments on the functional role of the hierarchy. Her article illustrates a similar evolution of the eschatological current towards an engagement of the church—and not just of individual Christians—in the world. Rejecting both spiritualism, as an obstacle to "posing the social problem correctly," and Caesaropapism, which considered social injustices as "God's will," she favored a return to the conciliar life of the early church, thus eliminating the phenomenon of clerical domination of the laity—something which was an historical fact rather than a dogmatic necessity.[337]

Fedotov's evolution was much more typical of the change taking place within the left-wing faction of the intelligentsia. In the January 1939 issue of *The Way*, Fedotov published a review of the French translation of Johann Adam Moehler's ground-breaking book on the unity of the church,[338] on the occasion of the hundredth anniversary of the death of this German Catholic theologian. Fedotov presented Moehler as a "precursor of Khomiakov" and located him in the classical spiritual tradition of the Russian intelligentsia, for which *sobornost'* meant unity in truth. But Fedotov added something new in his article.

Unity in truth does not exclude differences. The different rites and forms of life are necessary for an organic, non-authoritarian unity. However, unity in love seeks and finds social expression in the hierarchy, in the context of a vertical perspective ... of the centers of ecclesial life: bishop, metropolitan, pope. What is characteristic of Moehler's hierarchy is that the idea of authority or personal power is practically excluded. Power becomes a crystallization of love. The distinction between clergy and laity is a distinction of charismas where the ministry of each is recognized. But hierarchy is not constructed on the basis of democratic principles, from below, for its source is not an election but rather a communication of the gifts of the Holy Spirit. It is remarkable that Moehler bases papal primacy on the same principle.[339]

In April 1938 an article, this time from the ranks of the theologians, had appeared in *The Way* entitled "The New Testament in Our Times," This was the text of a lecture that Bezobrazov had delivered in Athens at the International Congress of Theology in December 1936 in the presence of Florovsky and Bulgakov and that he gave again at St. Sergius Institute on December 21, 1936. His ecclesiology took its point of departure from a perspective different from that of Berdyaev or Fedotov, in that it was deeply rooted in Scripture. All the same, it led to an eschatological vision of the church, which, on the one hand, rested on the mutual action of the three persons of the Trinity, and, on the other hand, emphasized the presence of the divine energies in the world. Although he drew inspiration from Bulgakov, Bezobrazov questioned the latter's distinction between the Person of Spirit and the hypostasis of the Holy Spirit as it appeared in Bulgakov's 1936 book *The Comforter*. As Bezobrazov wrote later, in 1939: "The distinction made between the gift of the Spirit and the hypostasis of the Spirit and which would permit the affirmation of a quantitative difference between two revelations, John 20 and Acts 2, is ... a misunderstanding, which cannot be defended without imprudence."[340] Yet Bezobrazov endorsed the principle "clearly" formulated by Bulgakov concerning "the dyadic relationship between the Word and the Holy Spirit." In the 1938 article, his final contribution to *The Way*, he made love the essence of the church—both the internal love of the three hypostases and the love between human beings and God.[341] The salvation of the world is only possible "through the action of the Holy Spirit in the Church," and this action itself depends on our fidelity to the sacrificial testimony of Christ. This personalist, antinomic, and cataphatic vision of the church was based on an eschatological intuition. He asked: "How can we explain this undeniable truth—that the presence in the Church of the Son of God, ascended into heaven and sitting at the right hand of the Father, becomes accessible through the action of the Spirit?"[342] Bezobrazov replied to this question by affirming two scriptural facts: the departure of Jesus from this world, and the distinction between the figures of Christ and the Holy Spirit. In his view, the only response was to accept that there are two types of eschatologies—not only the ontological one (the *Parousia*) but also the existential one (the Eucharist). He proposed an exegetical study of the apparently contradictory words of Christ concerning his presence in the world until the end of time and his return in glory at the *Parousia*. He found an answer to this antinomy through his interpretation of the last words of Christ to his disciples: "In the house of my Father there are many dwellings" (John 14:2), and "Yet a little while and you will no longer see me and yet another while and you will see me again" (John 16:16). Bezobrazov concluded: "The presence of Christ in the Church is revealed in the action of the Spirit because Christ has returned in the Spirit."[343] This Christocentric approach to the divine life also opened up perspectives for a new interpretation of the scriptures regarding the antinomy between the fallen world and the salvation of all in God.[344]

In the January 1939 issue of *The Way*, an article by Bulgakov illustrated the converging evolution of his ecclesiology. Entitled "*Una Sancta*: The Foundations of Ecumenism," it was a lecture that Bulgakov had given in 1938 at the meeting of the Fellowship of St. Alban and St. Sergius at High Leigh from June 30 to July 6. While Berdyaev used his personal talents as a publicist to passionately defend his ecumenical vision of the church, Bulgakov used theological discourse to calmly demonstrate to an audience of church people that the church is the *Una Sancta*, according to the expression of Pope Boniface VIII in his bull of 1302. Bulgakov argued that, on the one hand, the unified church was a reality which already existed and that this fact presupposed the "reunion of the Churches" and, on the other hand, that the profound movement of an ecclesial awareness of the universality of the church would continue to gain momentum. Thus it could be said that the question, for Bulgakov, was not "what" or "who," since the history of the church revealed the phenomenon of the self-revelation of the "what" in the "who." The remaining question was "how."

Bulgakov began by rejecting the strategy of integration. According to him, such a strategy was based on the identification of the church with the visible church. But, aside from being an empirical organization, the church was also, in Bulgakov's mind, both "the Mystery ... hidden in God for ages, the infinitely resourceful Wisdom deployed by God" (Eph. 3:9–10), "the body of Christ" (Rom. 12:5), "the Temple of the Holy Spirit" (1 Cor. 3:16), "the Plenitude" (Eph. 1:22), "the Bride of Christ," "the Glory of God," "the divine City," "the kingdom of God," and so on.[345] But Bulgakov also rejected the strategy of pluralism. He recognized the complexity of the human reality of the empirical church—all the more so in that this was confirmed by the messages in the Apocalypse to the seven churches of Asia from the One who sat on the throne (Rev. 2–3). For his part, Bulgakov believed that Christians could not accept the justification of the separation between the visible church and the invisible church as long as they prayed in the name of the Trinitarian God and recognized the divine humanity of Christ.[346]

Bulgakov proposed a third way of orthopraxis, of unity based on a sophiological vision of Trinitarian life. Similar to the way he had shown, in his 1933 book *The Lamb of God*, that Christ became aware of his Divine-humanity only progressively, Bulgakov characterized the history of the church as a phenomenon of "growth in plenitude."

> Prophecy is the dynamic factor in the life of the Church, while hierarchism is what makes it static. It is only the coming together of both which forms the *Una Sancta*, the Divine-humanity *in actu*. This life is not limited to the visible ecclesial organization; it overflows its boundaries. . . . There, at this depth, we meet and mutually recognize our unity in Christ and in the Holy Spirit, as children of the one Heavenly Father. . . . For "there are many dwellings in the house of my Father" (John 14:2), but they all belong to the same house. "There is, to be sure, a diversity of spiritual gifts, but it is the same Spirit" (1 Cor. 12:4), as Christ is "the same yesterday, today, and forever" (Heb. 13:8). . . . ["I have given them the glory which you have given me] so that they might be one as we are one, as You, Father, are in Me and I in You, so that they might be perfect in unity" (John 17:21).[347]

It is from this sophiological, personalist, and tri-hypostatic perspective that Bulgakov encouraged the Orthodox Church to prioritize the historical obligation of unity by affirming the truth of its faith, by manifesting a "special confessional asceticism," and, last, by firmly believing that with a "spirit of love and tolerance" the theological task of dogmatic creativity will be able to overcome disagreements.[348]

Lev Zander dedicated to Bulgakov an article he wrote on "the essence of the ecumenical movement" for the 1937 collection *Living Tradition*, in which he justified the necessity of ecumenical work. In spite of his difficulties with a "liberal Protestantism that denied the divinity of Christ," Zander, who had participated even before the Russian Revolution in ecumenical meetings with the YMCA and World Student Christian Federation, was certain that all dogmatic awareness was contained "in the profession of faith in the Name of Christ."[349] Like Bulgakov, Zander rejected both proselytism and indifference and affirmed that ecumenical dialogue had meaning only when one looked on the other Christian as one's brother. Refusing to "place a gag on the Holy Spirit," Zander assured the reader that, if there was a fraternal relationship, then Christians, as Christ-bearers, would manifest the Lord.[350] Zander used the image of a wounded face, already divine and soon restored, to underline the antinomic dimension of ecumenical eschatology. Nonetheless, Zander thought that ecumenical dialogue should be based on a certain number of practical rules, which included the condemnation of proselytism, strict confessionalism, recognition of the presence of the Holy Spirit in the sacraments of others—but without participation—and revision of the canons of the ancient church that forbade "praying with heretics."[351] Zander concluded his essay by stressing the prophetic dimension of the ecumenical movement and recalling that, according to the author of *The Brothers Karamazov,* "we have to believe in life more than logic."[352]

In an article entitled "At the Crossroads of the Church," written after the congresses of Oxford and Edinburgh, N. Zernov announced that he agreed with Zander's approach.[353] But Zernov wanted to go further than his older colleague. In his article on the English theologian William Palmer and Alexei Khomiakov, dated December 29, 1937, Zernov argued that although the visible union of the Orthodox and Anglican Churches had not been possible in the nineteenth century because of the *Filioque* question, "contemporary Orthodox theology," following the contributions of V. Bolotov and Bulgakov, "no longer judged this addition a heresy."[354] From this, Zernov deduced that the use made by Orthodox theologians of the segment of the symbol of faith concerning the procession of the Holy Spirit from the Father "and from the Son" as a stumbling block to any attempt at interecclesial reunion was only a pretext—less and less successful—to cover the absence of a precise definition of the church. Drawn in opposite directions by its struggles with the Greek Catholic Church and with the *raskol* of the Old Believers, the Orthodox Church, according to Zernov, hesitated between a broad definition (the Nicean symbol of faith) and a very narrow definition (the Russian Church) of the visible church. In Zernov's mind, the dogmatic vacuum was the cause of both the submission of the Orthodox Church to the state and its basically negative attitude towards other religions. He thus proposed a return to the situation that had marked the primitive church until the fourth century: local and autonomous churches, which mutually recognized one another by the profession of the same *credo* (which could have several textual variations) and through the institution of bishops with apostolic succession (which did not exclude a difference in the rites and rules of these churches). In an article dated December 24, 1939, entitled "Anglican Ordination and the Orthodox Church," Zernov argued that there was nothing to prevent an effective union of the Orthodox Church with the Anglican Church. He rejected Bulgakov's idea of a spiritual communion, of a grace given by God to the non-Orthodox "outside of the sacraments" and solely on the basis of their faith.[355] Zernov believed that this type of reasoning led to the abandoning of sacramental life. Once again, he rejected the approach of the bishops Ignatius Brianchaninov and Anthony Khrapovitsky, who refused to recognize the existence of any authentic ecclesial life in the West, and he challenged Orthodox theologians to rediscover "the objective efficacy of the holy sacraments." To this end he posed the following condition:

> The first condition for this is the recognition that the sacramental life of the Church is a gift God makes to that part of humanity which believes that Jesus Christ is the Saviour of the world and is baptized in the name of the Holy Trinity. All those who confess the Incarnation and who present themselves to receive the sacraments are, by that fact in itself, members of the one, holy, catholic and apostolic Church. The Orthodox practice which forbids the rebaptism of non-Orthodox Christians who are reunited to our Church bears silent witness to this truth.[356]

The close proximity of the ecclesiologies of the authors of the review, who represented different spiritual positions, political opinions, and age generations, is striking. As we know, the way in which the intellectuals of *The Way* represented the church and understood the paths that led to unity determined—in great part—their integration into Western society and their involvement in setting up networks of intellectual friendships. Actually, a double phenomenon can be observed at the end of the 1930s. A sense of the urgency of Christian unity on the eve of a great conflict, together with a clearer vision of the church, encouraged the intellectuals to become more involved in the ecumenical movement. However, depending on the configuration of the theological discourse of each thinker, some of them started from the level of the invisible church, while others started from its concrete, visible boundaries in order to promote unity. And yet the ecclesiological convergence among the writers of the review appeared principally in their practical contacts with the Western world. They shared the same concern for placing ethical principles at the heart of their involvement. Similarly, they represented a collective expression of an intuition of the mystical and dogmatic reality of the church. Finally, they shared a sense of hastening the coming of the New Jerusalem.

The Temple of the Holy Spirit

If the church, for Berdyaev, Fedotov, or M. Kurdiumov, was, above all, the House of the Father, it was present in history as "the temple of the Holy Spirit." This meant that their relationship with the Kingdom of God was focused on the world. In their contacts with Western intellectuals, as expressed in *The Way*, they passionately and meticulously debated three topics—social and national politics, the status of the intellect, and, finally, the evolution of capitalist society. In all three cases, the modalities of the realization of the Kingdom of God upon earth were at stake. Although their left-wing engagement dated back some time, it had been catalyzed by political events and the aftereffects for French intellectuals. Their mobilization appeared on the occasion of the first international congress of writers for the defense of culture, held at the Mutualité on June 21–25, 1935. This congress gave birth to an association of the same name, including members such as R. Rolland, H. Mann, A. Huxley, A. Gide, I. Ehrenburg, A. Tolstoy, and M. Gorky. In November 1935, on the eve of the Popular Front, the weekly *Vendredi* (*Friday*) was founded, directed by Jean Guéhenno, who left the Communist-controlled review *Europe*. The creation of this publication shows the breadth of the French intellectuals who were rallying against fascism—among them, Gide, Giono, Alain, Malraux, Maritain, and Nizan. That same year Gide and Malraux published two strong texts—*Les Nourritures terrestres* and *Le Temps du Mépris*—each with a preface in defense of communism. Conversely, after the victory of the Popular Front, the new generation of Maurrasian intellectuals, Robert Brasillach, Lucien Rebatet, and Dominique Sordet, united on May 4, 1936, in founding the right-wing weekly *Je suis partout* (with a circulation of 100,000 copies), which went from admiration for Italy to enthusiasm for Germany as well as for the conservative political and literary weekly *Gringoire* (350,000 copies). But the evolution of Pierre Drieu la Rochelle between 1936 and 1938, for example, reveals that, over and above the rational intellectual exchanges over socialism and nationalism, the divisions among the intellectuals were mainly a question of choice between the restrictive duty to serve a sad truth and the desire for a supra-rational commitment to an authentic community. As M. Winock wrote, what Drieu asked of fascism, others found in communism: "the condemnation of a decadent bourgeois world . . . at the opposite pole is the heroic life . . . , the fraternity of young warriors."[357]

In the face of the increasing power of the right/left opposition, the nonconformist groups such as *Esprit*, where Mounier followed the Victor Serge affair very closely, or the Collège de Sociologie under Roger Caillois, were forced either to take a stand or to disappear. [Victor Serge was a Russian revolutionary, journalist, and writer in France; born Victor Lvovich Kibalchich (1890–1947), he became well known for his pro-socialist but anti-Stalinist views, especially during the Spanish Civil War.] The "spiritual means," articulated politically as pacifism, were incapable of opposing the invasion of Ethiopia. Thus the Christian Democrat weekly *Sept*, founded by the Dominicans, was obliged to close down in August 1937, after publishing an interview with Léon Blum, which some regarded as too favorable and also criticized because they were not extremely opposed to the Spanish Republicans.[358] After the Spanish Civil War broke out in July 1936, the left's united front progressively disintegrated. The division between interventionists and pacifists in the weekly review *Friday* illustrated the malaise that finally led to the downfall of the second government of Blum in March 1938. While Hitler was annexing Austria, the right regained power with P. Daladier and P. Reynaud on April 12, 1938. On September 30, however, with the Munich Pact between Hitler, Mussolini, Daladier, and Chamberlain, the democracies capitulated to the German chancellor and recognized the annexation of the Sudetenland. In the view of Winock, the two figures representing one faction of the intelligentsia on the eve of the war were both "men of faith"—André Gide, the left-wing Protestant, and Georges Bernanos, the right-wing Catholic.[359] Each in his own manner, over and above the right/left split, embodied an ethical attitude towards the world and towards truth, which contrasts with the dogmatic attitude of another faction of the intelligentsia, those devoted to serving an absolute cause.

The Russian intellectuals were divided in their attitude towards the unfolding political events. While Berdyaev condemned the Munich accords, Fedotov approved of them. Similarly, as we have seen, Berdyaev distanced himself from Vysheslavtsev, who was drifting towards National Socialism for both political and philosophical motives. Yet they all shared a desire for dialogue with French intellectuals, over and above dogmatic differences, in the hope of ecumenical reconciliation. Whether this be on the level of individuals such as Maritain, Mounier, or Suzanne de Dietrich, or on an institutional level with the circle of the Union pour le Verité, or the congress of Life and Work, those intellectuals involved in the spirit of *The Way* were marked by certain traits of a part of the French intelligentsia: its ethical engagement, the desire to embody new political forms in social involvement, its respect for ecclesial hierarchy, and the freedom it drew from that.

The Debate on Communism, Anti-Semitism, and the War

In 1935 the position of the socialist-religious Russian intellectuals of the review *The Way* became more troubling for French intellectuals. Those on the left wing suspected that the anti-communism of the Russian religious thinkers was anti-Soviet, while those on the right thought that their social involvement was incompatible with anti-communism. Only *Esprit* would publish Fedotov's vigorous criticism of Stalin in 1936.

Similarly, it was thanks to his friendship for Berdyaev that P. Van der Meer, the director of the publishing house Desclée de Brouwer, agreed to publish Helene Iswolsky's 1936 book, *L'Homme 1936 en Russie soviétique—*

a severe portrait of the *homo sovieticus*.[360] In the context of the alliance of the French left wing with international communism, the anti-Soviet patriotism of Berdyaev was replaced by Gide. For his part, Berdyaev was quite ill at ease with the reception given by the members of the Vigilance Committee of Anti-Fascist Intellectuals to Ehrenburg, whom they considered the true representative of living Russian thought.[361] In *The Way*, Berdyaev sketched "the drama of French intellectuals" who are tempted by Marxism but refuse "the tyranny of orthodoxy."[362] In his view, Gide, after his book *Retour de l'URSS*, released on November 13, 1936 (with 150,000 copies printed all told) and his *Retouches à mon retour d'URSS*, released in June 1937, was able to find a way out of this dilemma "honorably."[363] The question posed by Gide's attitude was at the very heart of a philosophy of engagement. J. Grenier, Albert Camus's professor of philosophy in Algiers, in his book *Essai sur l'esprit d'orthodoxie*, published by Gallimard in 1938, criticized the approval by French intellectuals of totalitarian systems, whether of the left or of the right. Grenier's book concluded with an open letter to Malraux, summoning him to abandon his Marxist dogmatism. Earlier, in 1936, in an article for the *Nouvelle Revue Française*, Grenier wrote: "Being a Marxist in 1935 is like being a republican in 1880."[364] Berdyaev was sufficiently interested in Grenier's book to review it in *The Way*. It reminded him, Berdyaev stated, of his younger years when he was a philosophical Kantian and a political Marxist and his comrades reproached him for deviating from the party line. For Berdyaev, Grenier was correct in defending the right of conscience, yet his opposition to Russian Marxism was overly intellectual and insufficiently voluntaristic. Berdyaev argued that communist hostility to philosophical ideas was not an intellectual phenomenon. There was something religious about it. "Dogmatism," he wrote, "is the result of the socialization of religion."[365] Demonstrating a perfect familiarity with the Parisian intellectual world, Berdyaev added that Grenier had missed the mark when he took aim at Malraux, who "is more Nietzschean than Marxist."

> Intellectuals should realize that they are representatives of the spirit, not of a society, a state, a people, or a class.... Marx and Nietzsche, the two most influential thinkers in our world today, modified, each in his own way, the understanding of truth as a function of different objectives. The truth has become the fruit of social struggle or the

will to power. . . . Communism and fascism deny the existence of truth as it has been traditionally understood in the name of the principle of totality. It is necessary to understand what is signified by the pretension of totality, because this is the case of a truth which has been deformed. Christianity is also totalitarian; it is a total truth engaging the totality of life, but such a totalitarianism has nothing in common with orthodox Marxism and totalitarian states. The truth of totalitarianism is spiritual and is relative to the human person, not to society, the state, the nation. . . . Society cannot pretend to embrace totality and plenitude; only the person can do this, and not as a given but as a task to accomplish.[366]

Although he was angry with French intellectuals for a period of time (and ceased identifying them with "the intelligentsia"),[367] Berdyaev continued to attend their intellectual and philosophical gatherings. He became friends with R. Rolland, whose spouse was Russian and related to him,[368] but he did not share Rolland's pacifism. A common love of Péguy, Bloy, and Tolstoy, as well as a mistrust of the established church, united them. In his book on Péguy, written during the war, Rolland described Berdyaev as "a great religious philosopher, whom Péguy was unable to know . . . yet who was one with him in his ideas concerning God, the spirit, grace, and liberty."[369] The influence of Berdyaev on personalist circles was particularly evident in the work of Maritain. Maritain's *Humanisme intégral*, which appeared in 1936, echoed aspects of Berdyaev's thought.

> This new humanism, which has nothing in common with bourgeois humanism, and which is all the more human in that it does not worship mankind, truly and effectively respects human dignity and recognizes the integral needs of the person. We conceive this humanism as oriented towards a social-temporal realization of this evangelical attentiveness to what is human—an attitude that should not exist on a purely spiritual level for it demands to become incarnate—and towards the ideal of a fraternal community. It does not ask men to sacrifice themselves for the dynamism or imperialism of a given race or class or nation; it demands this sacrifice for a better life for their brothers and for the concrete good of the community of human persons; . . . from this point of view it cannot be anything other than a heroic humanism.[370]

On May 23, 1936, Paul Desjardins organized a session at the Union pour la Verité in honor of Berdyaev on the occasion of the publication of the Russian philosopher's book *Le destin de l'homme dans le monde actuel* (*The Fate of Man in the Modern World*). Jean Hyppolite,[371] who was enthusiastic about Berdyaev's presentation, sent the philosopher a letter a few days later expressing his admiration for him.[372] On August 1, 1936, it was the turn of Roger Martin du Gard to write a very friendly letter to Berdyaev. The author of *Les Thibault* and future recipient of the Nobel Prize (1937) had this to say to Berdyaev about his book:

> My wife and I have passed whole evenings discussing this work, which is so dense, so measured also, so enriching for those who, like myself, have trouble accepting your point of departure if not your point of arrival. . . . For me, the important thing is that you not have any doubts of the lively and enduring interest which I have taken in these new clarifications of your thought nor of my gratitude to you for having sent me this book nor of the great esteem and liking I have for you personally.[373]

Berdyaev also had found increasing acceptance among those Christian intellectuals who favored social reforms. François Mauriac, in the May 29, 1936, issue of *Sept*, expressed his interest in the Russian philosopher's way of criticizing the institutional church: "During these times, we are profoundly sensitive to what Berdyaev wants to say when he writes that, on a temporal level and in the measure in which the Church is a human society, Christianity has been contaminated by history."[374] Similarly, in the July 14, 1936, issue of *Le Figaro*, Guermantès congratulated Berdyaev for the success of his book. In the following year, Daniel-Rops persuaded Berdyaev to give him his article "Personalism and Marxism," which had appeared in *The Way*, for inclusion in a collection entitled *Le communisme et les chrétiens*, which also featured contributions by Father Ducatillon, François Mauriac, Alexandre Marc, and Denis de Rougemont. De Rougemont expressed a very Berdyaevan idea in his essay: "Christians are much more responsible for the success of Marxism among the people than Marxism is responsible for the decline of the churches in the modern world."[375] In 1938, Berdyaev's book *Les sources et le sens du communisme russe* (*The Origin of Russian Communism*), translated into French from the Russian original, appeared in the series *Les essais* published by

Gallimard. Léon Blum, the head of the French government, wanted to meet Berdyaev after having read and appreciated the book. In his memoirs, Berdyaev recalled this meeting. "He impressed me as being a very cultivated person, intelligent, very human, very pleasant conversationalist. I believe that with his personal qualities, he is one of the better French politicians. I agreed with his social reforms. But he didn't impress me as being a revolutionary or a statesman with a strong will."[376]

In fall 1939, after the German-Soviet pact and the entry of France into the war, and again in January 1940, Emmanuel Mounier—even though he had been mobilized—proposed to Berdyaev that the journal *Esprit* run a special issue on Russia.[377] Berdyaev asked his friends in the Academy of Religious Philosophy and in Orthodox Action to collaborate in this project. Mounier thought that Bulgakov's article was too long, liked the articles by Fedotov, Alekseev, and Iswolsky, but rejected those submitted by Mochulsky and Mother Maria, which he wanted to replace by contributions from B. Parain and B. de Schloezer. All copies of this issue were lost during the German offensive in May 1940.[378]

One of the contributors to the review, Elisabeth Belenson, a Russian-Jewish intellectual who had converted to Catholicism, used to frequent the Judeo-Catholic circle of Oscar de Ferenzy, which included S. Fumet, A. Pallière, Bishop Beaussart, and the Jesuit theologian Henri de Lubac. Belenson's article in *The Way* in March 1937, entitled "The Mission of Israel," began with an editorial note condemning the persecution of the Jews. (The main thrust of the article, however, was the hope of converting the Jewish people to Christianity.)[379] In June 1938, Berdyaev joined his voice to that of French intellectuals in the condemnation of racism and anti-Semitism. After the condemnation of Nazism on March 14, 1937, by Pius XI, many left-wing Catholics, including Jacques Maritain, E. Mounier, and Maurice Blondel, vigorously condemned racism. Berdyaev's article "Christianity and Anti-Semitism: The Religious Destiny of Judaism" appeared in the June 1938 issue of *The Way*. He had it translated into French by one of his readers, Princess Theodore, and published as a brochure—the first time a text in French had been published by the Academy of Religious Philosophy.[380] Berdyaev began by demonstrating the mytho-logical process of the diffusion of "the myth of the Aryan race elaborated by Gobineau." One by one, he rejected the intellectual atheists such as Céline, whose book *Mort à crédit* was a "real call for a pogrom," and the anti-Semitic intellectuals who pretend to be Christian but who "ought to repent."[381]

Not only racial anti-Semitism but any sort of racism cannot stand up to criticism from three points of view: religious, moral, and scientific.... Contemporary anthropology thinks that the very concept of race is dubious. In fact, racism belongs more to the realm of the mytho-logical than to the realm of science. The notion of a select race is a myth of the same order as that of a select class. Yet a myth can be very dynamic; it can contain an explosive power within itself and provoke mass movements among those who have no interest in scientific truth—or in any kind of truth for that matter. We live in times in which myths are particularly abundant, but their quality is—alas— very inferior.[382]

Quoting Franz Rosenzweig, "that remarkable Jewish religious philosopher," Berdyaev argued that the principal source of anti-Semitism was the belief on the part of most Christians that the Kingdom of God would only be realized in heaven, and that this explained their passivity regarding earthly matters. "But," Berdyaev pointed out, "the ancient Hebrew prophets" were the first to stand up for truth and justice in social relationships. Konstantin Mochulsky, Berdyaev's colleague in Orthodox Action, also recognized the ethical authority of Pius XI in his November 1938 article, "Racism and Western Christianity." He cited the example of the Catholic Church, which, acting through its primate, condemned the "religion" of National Socialism in the encyclical *Mit Brennender Sorge (With Burning Anxiety)*. Mochulsky used the example of Goering's phrase, "Our Gospel is *Mein Kampf*."[383] He cited Karl Barth of the "Free or Confessing Church" (*Freie oder Bekenntnis Kirche*), who had immigrated to Switzerland, in his protests against Ludwig Müller, the Reich-bishop, against the new Trinitarian dogma of "blood, race, and the sun," and against the concentration camps.[384]

When the war broke out, the Academy of Religious Philosophy was obliged to suspend its activities, including the review. Fondaminsky, who was a Jew, a socialist, and close to Christianity thanks to the circle he had created with Mother Maria, had the idea of continuing the group's meetings under a different rubric. With Berdyaev's agreement and the support of Orthodox Action, he organized meetings in Berdyaev's house to study "the spiritual significance of events" and invited not only Russian but French, German, and Spanish intellectuals. The first of these gatherings took place on February 5, 1940, at rue Moulin de Pierre. Berdyaev gave a talk with Jean Wahl, H. Iswolsky, G. Fedotov, Mother Maria, Paul-Louis Landsberg, and I. Fondaminsky in attendance. This was a success. At the second gathering on March 3 in Fondaminsky's home, there were about thirty in attendance—among them, V. Yanovsky, Gabriel Marcel, and Jean Schlumberger, as well as Hindu, Chinese, and Spanish participants. The text that Berdyaev presented, in French, at the first of these meetings has been found in his archives. In it, he articulates his eschatology:

> When we go out into the darkness, when we have to make our way in obscurity in the streets of Paris, we need a flashlight, a light which we have with us and not a light from outside—for outside everything is extinguished. The same thing happens to us on the spiritual level.... This is because the world has collapsed into an intrinsic anarchy, where there is no longer unity either in the realm of religious belief or in the exterior forms, and this leads the world to have recourse to a dictatorial regime.... There is not only a light which comes from the past but also a light which comes from the future. This is a paradoxical formula but one admitted by all the authors of a philosophy of history, for it is only by this light that the meaning of History can be known.... Last year, when the representatives of France and England met with Hitler at Munich, I had the very clear impression that we were witnessing a conflict between destiny [*fatalité*] and reason. The representatives of France and England took a reasonable point of departure, whereas Hitler had on his side the dark powers of destiny.... Of all the politicians in the universe, Hitler alone takes counsel of God—a terrible God but one who is consulted.... What is this voice he hears? It is not the voice of God but the voice of destiny. It is a principle totally different from any divine or human principle.... Christianity finds itself in a moment when the light coming from the past has been diminished and the light which should come from the future is not strong enough. Yet the Christianity which will enter into a new era, when the light of the future will be more powerful, will be an eschatological Christianity.[385]

The Debate on Myth, Reason, and Gnosis

Daniel Lindenberg remarked that at the beginning of the "underground years" (1937–47), a "conservative revolution" could be observed among

French intellectuals.[386] The themes of myth, of Eastern civilizations, and of community were dominant on the eve of the war in the works of intellectuals such as Georges Dumezil, Roger Caillois, and Jean Guitton. Behind the interest in myth lay a desire to go beyond rationalism; it was a need for renewal through a return to the origin of things and a religious quest. This was fertile ground for meetings between French and Russian intellectuals. Lev Shestov, who, near the end of his life, had a growing interest in Hinduism, met young specialists such as Olivier Lacombe at the Maritains' home. Conversely, Henri Corbin, a specialist in Islamic mysticism and a professor at the l'École Pratique des Hautes Études, learned to appreciate the Fedorovian eschatology of Berdyaev. On March 7, 1939, he wrote to Berdyaev: "It seems to me that, in these times, it is so very important and urgent that the voice of Greco-Russian Orthodoxy be heard."[387] Together with Alexandre Kojève, who was related to A. Kozhevnikov, an eminent specialist in the thought of Fedorov, Corbin translated *The Socialist Idea* of Henri de Man in 1935. Kojève had written a thesis on Solovyov before dedicating himself to the study of Hegel. Raymond Aron, Jean-Paul Sartre, and Jacques Lacan all attended Kojève's seminar on German philosophy at L'École Pratique des Hautes Études, where, in 1934, he had replaced Alexandre Koyré. Kojève analyzed the work of Hegel from the point of view of Heidegger.

Also noteworthy, under the rubric of the religious restlessness common to both Russian and French intellectuals, was the emergence of a new literary genre. In 1939, Nathalie Sarraute, who was of Russian descent, published her first novel, *Tropismes*, inaugurating what would later be called the *nouveau roman*, with its mixture of anguishing day-to-day banality and implicit theology.

Another example of the proximity between Russian and French intellectuals is the "groupe du Troca[déro]." Shortly before the war, Paul Rivet, the director of the Musée de l'Homme, one of the Meccas of anthropology and ethnology, hired Vildé and Levitsky, two young immigrants who were members of the circle of Fondaminsky. Boris Vildé had married Berdyaev's translator, Irene Lot, daughter of Myrrha Lot-Borodin, and met regularly with Georges Bataille at Place du Trocadéro. As Denis Hollier points out, Bataille's lecture on the myth of the sorcerer's apprentice was the best example of the philosopher's contributions to the new College of Sociology. In this lecture, Bataille, who greatly appreciated the works of Shestov, delared that "the myth is perhaps a fable, but this fable is the complete opposite of fiction if one considers the people who make it dance and act and for whom it is living reality."[388]

The convergence with the religious thinkers who contributed to *The Way* is evident. However, as we know, Russian mytho-logical thought was rooted in the Judeo-Christian tradition and, above all, in an intellectual history which had already passed through the moment when thought explodes, with all the risks and extremities that this implies, from esotericism to the anticipation of a dictatorship. The Russian religious philosophers did not want to escape from the strict categories of conceptual rationality only to rediscover the boundaries—carefully protected by "living tradition"—of a revealed truth ruled by logical rationality. They could not but be opposed to the neo-pagan mythology of René Guénon, Henri de Montherlant, or Louis Rougier. The ecumenical work carried out in common by Mochulsky, Shestov, and Berdyaev, over and above their differences, with French intellectuals who were tempted either by rational abstraction—such as J. Danzas or E. Gilson—or by metalogical realism—such as Benjamin Fondane and Henri Corbin—insisted on the necessity of preserving the reality of history from the seduction of myths that explained everything. They sought to propose an alternative to a purely ethical existentialism and, finally, to affirm that the union of Athens and Jerusalem is not necessarily synonymous with a betrayal of reason.

Shestov's work in this domain was significant. His seventieth birthday on February 13, 1936, was the occasion for displays of friendship and recognition on the part of Russian and French intellectuals. The influence of Shestov extended from Nadezhda Teffi, a humorist writer who was well known in the immigration community, to Paul Desjardins and Jean Paulhan. In May 1936, Fondane published a book entitled *La conscience malheureuse* in which he expressed his admiration for Shestov. Shestov had helped him to put the finishing touches on his studies of Heidegger and Husserl.[389] B. de Schloezer in *Vendredi*, Marc Hérubel, a young Protestant who contributed to *Le Semeur*, E. Bréhier in *La Revue philosophique*, Fondane in *Cahiers du Sud*, Grenier in *La Nouvelle Revue Française*, and Emmanuel Lévinas in *Revue des études juives* all popularized the theses of Shestov presented in his *Kierkegaard and Existential Philosophy*, a work published in July 1936.[390] In 1937, Shestov gave several series of lectures on Radio-Paris concerning Dostoevsky and Kierkegaard. The publication of *Athènes et Jérusalem* in June 1937, first in German and then in French, and the death of Shestov on November 20, 1938, gave rise to a series of eulogistic reviews and testimonies of homage, such as that of Jules de Gaultier in *La Revue philosophique*, of Vladimir Veidlé in *Les nouvelles littéraires*, and of André Miroglio in *Le Semeur*.

Shestov's dialogue with Gilson and Lévy-Bruhl, on the one hand, and with Husserl and Jaspers on the other, is particularly indicative of the religious and ecclesial dimension of the debate between French, German, and Russian intellectuals. *Revue philosophique* asked Shestov for an article on Gilson's *L'esprit de la philosophie médiévale*, published in January 1935. The article, translated into French by de Schloezer, came out in two installments, in December 1935 and February 1936. Shestov took an interest in Gilson's thesis that the Judeo-Christian revelation was a religious source of philosophical development. Shestov agreed with Gilson when the latter affirmed that St. Paul wanted to "eliminate the apparent wisdom of the Greeks, which is, in reality, a folly, in the name of the apparent folly of the Christians, which is, in reality, wisdom."[391] And yet, Shestov stated, the history of philosophy showed that reason sought to invent laws so as to safeguard human liberty from the arbitrariness of God. Thus the source of Russian philosophy was to maintain, in the spirit of Tertullian and Luther, the opposition between reason and faith in order to avoid repeating the suffocation of truth such as that of the medieval Scholastics. According to Shestov, the opposition between Athens and Jerusalem was the necessary basis for the emergence of a new philosophy founded on the notion of "created truth" and placing the divine-human will above all laws.

> The "will to power" of Nietzsche, his "beyond good and evil," his "morality of the masters"—which he contrasts to the "morality of slaves"—and through which appears the concept of the "truth of the masters" (of the truth of which one disposes as the Son of Man disposes of the Sabbath)—all these are desperate attempts to leave the tree of knowledge and return to the tree of Life.[392]

On March 11, 1936, after having read his article, Gilson replied to Shestov. His letter showed that the ecumenical problematic is at the heart of the debate between the French and Russian intellectuals:

> What seems remarkable to me is that, in a communication in 1924 . . . I also cited Tertullian's phrase but adding this response: what is there

in common between Athens and Jerusalem? The response: Rome. That is evidently the crux of the debate—You keep coming back to Luther, or to what there is of Luther in your dear Dostoevsky. I believe, on the contrary, that God speaks through the Church of Rome, that revelation continues through its mediation, and that it has, moreover, the mission to keep the totality of revelation before our eyes.[393]

In April 1936, an article by Shestov appeared in *The Way* entitled "Myth and Truth: Toward a Metaphysics of Knowledge." This was a review of Lucien Lévy-Bruhl's *Primitive Mythology*, published by Alcan in 1935. Shestov had written his very favorable review of it in August 1935, which Lévy-Bruhl had asked Koyré to publish in *Recherche philosophique*, but Koyré never followed through. The article also appeared in translation in the Netherlands and in Yugoslavia. Lévy-Bruhl's book questioned the rationalism of Western civilization, which, in his view, based being and truth exclusively on what was verifiable by experience. For Shestov, citing Lévy-Bruhl, knowledge based on myth did not impose itself on the intellect; it opened the intellect to the noblest of experiences, the mystical experience. But Shestov encouraged the neo-Kantian philosopher to go still deeper in his discoveries: being depended on knowledge, to be sure, but that meant that one could not be satisfied with a theory of knowledge. Shestov concluded that a true metaphysics of knowledge should be elaborated that would draw out all the consequences of this "fluidity" of reality such as it appears to the aborigines of Australia.[394]

A criticism of Husserl's phenomenology by N. Lossky appeared in *The Way* in 1939, which did not add anything to a critique written by Shestov back in 1917. However, for Shestov, who wrote a new article, this time more positive towards Husserl, dated April 26, 1938, what was of interest in Husserl's phenomenology was not its methodology but its existential dimension, its faith in the possibility of a science of absolute truths. Shestov did not hide his admiration for Husserl's religious dedication to reason, even though he had fought with him all his life. But Shestov held that philosophy was struggle and not reflection. He stated: "Husserl, by absolutizing the truth, finds himself forced to relativize being or—more exactly—human life."[395]

On the other hand, Shestov was far more critical of the work of Jaspers, whose book *Reason and Existence* had appeared in 1935. In Shestov's eyes, Jaspers had betrayed the heritage of Kierkegaard by defending reason and imperceptibly reintroducing a constraining ethic into existentialism, which thus suffocated revealed truth "without the shedding of blood." Shestov's article "*Sine effusione sanguinis*" was written in October 1936 and appeared in *The Way* in December 1937 and, in a French translation, in the review *Hermès* in January 1938. Shestov reproached Jaspers for accepting the rational principle of God's immutability in the name of the ethic of a distant God, even though that meant that God had abandoned his Son on the cross through impotency, because God cannot intervene in history. Shestov did not reject rationality, but he questioned its pretense of immutability—even though it rested on moral presuppositions—which led to paralyzing people, by presenting being as unchangeable.

> It would be easy to cite many more judgments of the reason . . . which clearly demonstrate that reason does not stop at enlightening being and rendering it transparent. The light it proposes is not light at all; reason does not enlighten, it judges. These "inexorabilities" and "impossibilities" of which Jaspers speaks do not come from fact but from reason. And Kant never denied it: according to Kant, reason is the source, the only source, of synthetic *a priori* judgments. But all the judgments of which we have just treated are synthetic—not analytic—judgments, and insofar as they are synthetic, they neither admit nor recognize any other instance than reason: *Roma locuta, causa finita*. The idea of the infallibility of the Church, the idea of the power of the keys, is far from being an idea peculiar to Catholicism. The medieval conviction that philosophy was *ancilla theologiae* is rooted in a misunderstanding; on the contrary, it is theology which was and still is the servant of philosophy. The revealed truth, as such, satisfies people but rarely and very little; thus they have always tried to package it in reason, to justify it before reason, to make it reasonable, to make it "that which was always believed everywhere, always, and by all" [quoting St Vincent of Lérins, the "Vincentian Canon"]—or, better, "what should be believed."[396]

Mochulsky used the pages of *The Way* to present Protestant thinking. But in his review of Denis de Rougemont's book *Love in the Western World*, published by Plon in 1939, Mochulsky's criticism was the very opposite of that made by Shestov with respect to Jaspers. Mochulsky faulted the young Swiss essayist, a collaborator of the journal *Esprit*, for not sufficiently respecting historical rationality. De Rougemont used as a starting point the fact that *The Romance of Tristan and Isolde* was a myth about adultery, which had its origin in the Bogomil and Manichean religion of the eleventh- and twelfth-century troubadours of Provence. In support of his thesis, de Rougemont claimed: "Myth appears when it would be dangerous or impossible to speak clearly of a certain number of social or religious facts, or of emotional relationships, which one wants, however, to protect or which cannot be destroyed."[397] Using the literature of courtly love as a starting point, he followed the evolution of the myth up to its renaissance in the works of Wagner and from there extended his study to the entire history of European culture, from Orthodox mysticism to military science. The author concluded his panoramic view with an appeal to religious and ecumenical authorities to rehabilitate the idea of Christian marriage, understood not as love from afar—which is really the devouring passion of death that is found in us all—but as love for one's neighbor. Although Mochulsky appreciated the originality of de Rougemont's thesis of love-passion as a quest for death and the link between Eros and Mars in the art of war, he found it regrettable that the author wanted to explain everything—from the dissolution of the family to the springing up of totalitarian ideologies—by means of the myth of love-passion. The theses of de Rougemont lacked historical foundations: "An elementary familiarity with Provençal lyricism is enough to make one realize that the theses of de Rougemont are doomed to failure."[398]

The urgency with which the Russian philosophers discussed the problem of evil and the myth of original sin aroused the curiosity of French intellectuals. Berdyaev was invited on October 10, 1935, by the Union pour la Verité, who met at rue Visconti, to present his book *De la destination de l'homme* (*The Destiny of Man*), centered on ethics and the origin of good and evil. The following year, a ten-day meeting, from August 21 to September 4, 1936, was held at Pontigny to discuss the problem of evil. Berdyaev participated, along with M. de Gandillac, J. Wahl, V. Jankelevitch, M. Buber, J. Madaule, and A. Koyré. Berdyaev gained increasing respect within academic and university circles. In 1937 he presented papers at the Eleventh International Congress of Aesthetics and at the Ninth International Congress of Philosophy. He was also invited to speak by the University of Lille. Berdyaev participated often and gladly in the circle of phenomenological philosophy which met at the home of Gabriel Marcel. On December 11, 1936, during one of these meetings, he discussed his objections to the existentialism of Jaspers with Jeanne Hersch, who had just published *L' illusion philosophique*. Later, and until 1939, Berdyaev participated in meetings with Eugène Minkowski on the topics "Time as Lived" and "The Structure of Psychic Reality," with Louis Lavelle on "Evil and Suffering," and with Gaston Fessard on "The Principles of Political Decision." Berdyaev, however, kept his distance from the existentialist phenomenology that was practiced in the circle of Marcel because he thought that it was too superficial. He preferred the thought of Paul-Louis Landsberg, Marcel Moré, and Jean Wahl, young philosophers eager to pose the question of the meaning of being. Jean Wahl's existentialist interpretation of Hegel was much closer to Berdyaev's position than to the reading of Kojève. In January 1936, Wahl, who had read all of Berdyaev's books, sent him a letter expressing his "keen interest" in his book *Cinq méditations sur l'existence*, which had just been translated into French by Irène Vildé-Lot and published by René Le Senne in the series La philosophie de l'esprit of Aubier Press.

> I greatly appreciated the ideas you put forth: the objective value of emotion, the rooting of the subject in being on the one hand, and, on the other hand, the ultimately non-objective conception of being. This in such a way that the ontologism which appeared initially is quite different from an objectivist ontology. Concerning time—this time which here does not point towards despair but ... is, above all, pointed towards hope— ... you put forth ideas which are meaningful and important. I particularly liked what you say about the face.[399]

Berdyaev also took time to respond to the accusation of Catholicism against Gnosticism. As can be seen from the articles of N. Lossky and Volkonsky in *The Way*, there had been a raging debate between Orthodox and Catholic intellectuals ever since the pontifical commission "Pro Russia" in Rome, which had been reorganized on December 21, 1934, had adopted a more belligerent attitude towards the Soviet Union.[400] In October 1936, Berdyaev published a review by N. Lossky of a book by the Polish Jesuit B. Yasinowsky—*Le christianisme oriental et la Russie*. Yasinowsky argued that sophiology was "a gnostic sexualization of the Divinity," that Russian religious philosophy denied all knowledge of God by its apophatic approach, and, finally, that Russian literature, from Dostoevsky to Merezhkovsky, was infected with Manicheism. Lossky complained that Yasinowsky's book was "driven by hatred" and replied to it point by point, in particular by explaining that the impossibility of expressing God through concepts should not be confused with a knowledge of God, which gives full recognition to the apophatic approach. He concluded by paying homage to Russian religious thought that had elaborated concepts such as *sobornost'* (Khomiakov). According to Lossky, this tradition had also transposed the principle of the uni-substantiality of the Trinitarian nature to the metaphysical realm (Florensky). Finally, in the tradition of intuitivism so dear to the author, Russian religious thought had brought about a synthesis between empiricism and rationalism (Kireevsky).[401]

In the same issue, Berdyaev replied to Julie Danzas. Danzas was a Russian Catholic who, after the revolution, had been sent to a gulag in Solovki because of her religious beliefs. After she succeeded in immigrating to France, she collaborated with the bimonthly review *Russie et Chrétienté*, founded in 1934 by Istina, the Dominican Center for Russian Studies, with a view to helping toward "the triumph of the faith over Marxist materialism and the restoration of Christian unity between Russian Orthodoxy and the Catholic Church." Of the authors who contributed to *The Way*, Veidlé also collaborated with the Dominican review, notably with his 1936 article "The Marxist Theory of Art in Soviet Russia."[402] In the summer of 1936, Danzas published an article in *Russie et Chrétienté*, entitled "The Path of Russian Religious Philosophy," which was centered on Berdyaev's journal and the Academy of Religious Philosophy. That same year she amplified her study with her book entitled *L'itinéraire religieux de la conscience russe*.[403] In "The Path of Russian Religious Philosophy" she stated:

> This Academy is closely related to the Russian Institute of Theology of Paris [St. Sergius], and together they represent the avant-garde of the religious movement which is trying to infuse new life into the Russian Church by bringing modern or renewed philosophical concepts to its doctrines and traditions. The official organ of this movement is the quarterly review *The Way*, which will soon celebrate its tenth anniversary.... For whoever wants to know modern Russian religious thought and follow its present evolution, the study of this review is indispensable.[404]

In spite of these favorable references to *The Way*, the purpose of Danzas's article was to demonstrate that the line of thought presented in *The Way* was the "old gnosis," which went so far as to deny "the transcendence of God" and which was full of prejudice against Western spirituality. Danzas cited, in particular, the articles of Zenkovsky, Ilyin, and Kartashev and lamented that there was "a lack of good will to seek the bonds that unite."[405] In Berdyaev and Bulgakov, the author found "traces of a Marxism which has been vanquished but not wiped from their mentality,"[406] as witnessed by the excessive importance they attribute to the material side of human nature. She was especially critical of the review's ecumenical stance.

> It will suffice for us to state that *The Way* takes a clearly anti-Roman position in these problems [ecumenical]: if it does not entirely accept the Protestant thesis of a federation of all the branches of Christianity opposed to the Catholic Church on the basis of a spiritualism free of dogmatic formulas, it comes close to doing so by a conception of Orthodoxy where the principle of authority in the Church is completely sacrificed to a very vague universalism, dressed in the exterior forms of Orthodox worship and saturated in religious aestheticism.[407]

In her book, Danzas added to this critique the claim that Russian spirituality is Manichean and that the church is divided between a structure which is submissive to the state and a body at the mercy of all sorts of sects.

Berdyaev reviewed Danzas's book in the October 1936 issue of *The Way*. He bewailed the fact that Catholicism was not well known by Orthodox authors, yet he set himself up as a defender of Orthodoxy. He took exception to the "tendentious allegations" of the author and her attitude, which he described as "missionary" and "provincial."[408] He added, however, that "in our times" this type of literary propaganda corresponded so little to the modern mentality that it was "without danger."[409] Despite this dismissal, Berdyaev replied to Danzas that if the Orthodox Church were really responsible for the Russian Revolution, then Catholicism was also at fault because it did not warn the West of "religious indifference and atheism."[410] He also defended the cosmic spirituality of the Russian people and regretted that Danzas did not mention Russian holiness. Finally, the philosopher responded to the accusation of gnosticism:

Fundamentally, all religious philosophy could be called gnostic. It is only scholastic theologies that are not gnostic, but there is no element of creative thought in them. Having said this, Russian philosophical and religious thought has nothing in common with the gnostics of the first centuries of Christianity, and there is no proof of an influence of any sort here. . . . The one who came closest to gnosticism was Vladimir Solovyov, whom Catholics consider one of their own.[411]

Berdyaev continued to publish the works of Catholic authors in *The Way*, in spite of this criticism. Fedotov wrote a review of the book by Pierre Pascal on Avvakum, and in 1936 he published an article by Raymond de Becker, "In the Darkness," in which one finds the mixture of religious quest and a thirsting for community that was typical of that era. This type of inquiry was behind the creation during the war, by Roger Schutz, an ecumenical Protestant, of the community at Taizé, near Cluny, which brought together believers from different horizons.

The Social Debate

In the second half of the 1930s, the neo-Slavophile and nonconformist criticism of capitalist society on the part of contributors to the review changed to a commitment to the ecumenical movement on the social level as well. Berdyaev, as noted in Part Two, dramatically increased his efforts in 1935. In June 1935 he was in Geneva for a conference at the office of Life and Work on the attitude of the ecumenical movement towards war. After his return to Paris he departed almost immediately for a conference of the Fellowship of St. Alban and St. Sergius at High Leigh on June 22–28. There he gave a talk entitled "God, Man, and Society," with Anglican intellectuals and Florovsky in attendance. On July 15–21, Berdyaev, at the invitation of Suzanne de Dietrich, participated in the conference of the World Student Christian Federation at Swanwick, England, on social and industrial problems. There he spoke on the topic "The Nature of Christian Social Action," with André Philip, Sir Arthur Salter, and R. H. Tawney present. From December 30, 1935, to January 3, 1936, he participated in the congress of the Fellowship of St. Alban and St. Sergius near Paris, on the theme "The Church and the World." This congress was exemplary in that Russian thinkers representing the two ecumenical currents in *The Way* participated. More than a hundred people attended lectures given by Berdyaev, Bulgakov, Florovsky, Kartashev, Fedotov, Bishop Frere, and M. Morton. There, for the first time, an Anglican priest celebrated a service in the Orthodox church on rue Daru. A few weeks later, on January 28–30, and once again at the invitation of Suzanne de Dietrich, Berdyaev participated in a weeklong series of ecumenical talks in the Latin Quarter in the company of André Philip, Marc Boegner, W. Visser't Hooft, P. Archambault, and G. Izard. The following year he accepted the invitation of Wilfrid Monod to participate in the congress for social Christianity at Toulouse. In 1936 and 1938 he participated in ecumenical meetings organized by Suzanne de Dietrich at Mutterhouse chateau along with Catholics and Protestants, but also including some Hindus and others.

This ecumenical engagement brought out new admirers of Berdyaev. Eugène Porret, a young Swiss Protestant, president of the Federation of Christian Socialists, began to meet with Berdyaev on a regular basis in order to write a book about him. Even before the publication of his book in 1944, he popularized Berdyaev's thought in the reviews *Foi et vie*, *Le Christianisme social*, and *Les Cahiers protestants*.[412] On the Catholic side, P. Archambault, in 1937, published a study entitled "The Drama of Freedom in the Philosophy of Berdyaev" in the review *Politique*.[413]

The contributors to *The Way* were also attentively following the evolution of Catholic social thought. Iswolsky's article entitled "The New Doctrines of Catholic Social Thought in France" appeared in the September 1939 issue. It stressed, along with the importance of Jacques Maritain's *Humanisme intégral* and *Questions de conscience* (1938), the determining role of the Catholic Semaines Sociales ["Social Weeks," courses of lectures by Catholics on social and economic issues] and the important research of the young nonconformist generation including Etienne Borne and Jean Lacroix, who participated in a collection called *Options pour demain* published by *Cahiers de la Nouvelle Journée* in 1939. Iswolsky insisted on the importance of efforts to "Christianize" the conscience of the working class, especially by working actively in trade unions.

The ecumenical commitment of the pneumocentric group within *The Way* was apparent at the ecumenical congress of Life and Work held at Oxford, July 12–26, 1937, on the theme "The Church, the Nation, and the State."[414] The Oxford conference brought together 425 official members of most of the Christian churches (among them forty Orthodox) from fifty countries, with a clear Anglo-Saxon Protestant dominance. Absent were delegates representing the Roman Catholic Church, the German

Churches—Hitler blocked the participation of the German delegation—and the Church of the Soviet Union.[415] The project of the joint committee was to continue the Lausanne movement. The participants were divided into six sections: "Church and Society," "Church and the Economic Order," "Church and State," "Church and Education," "Church and Nation," and "Universal Church and International Order." Although the congress did not want to encroach on purely political terrain, it published a declaration of solidarity with "our Christian brothers of Russia" and with "our brothers of the German Evangelical Church." The representatives of dialectical theology, headed by E. Brunner, P. Maury, and W. Vissert'Hooft, put through a number of resolutions, notably within the section Church and Nation, including one concerning civil disobedience when a certain threshold of oppression is breached.

In addition to Metropolitan Evlogy, other members of the review present at the congresses in Oxford and Edinburgh were Berdyaev, Zernov, Zander, Bulgakov, Kartashev, Zenkovsky, Gorodetsky, Vysheslavtsev, Alekseev, Florovsky, and Fedotov, who published an enthusiastic report in *The Way*. Fedotov was particularly pleased that the economic section stated in its resolution that, for a Christian, the most desirable social order would be a "social-personalist" order.[416] He agreed with the absolute condemnation of war and with the declaration stating that "the unconditional sovereignty of the nation is an evil."[417] As reported by Alekseev in *New City*, there were major tensions among the Russian delegates on the question of whether or not Christians had the obligation to participate in warfare. Alekseev defended a certain participation if the state demanded it from its citizens, while Fedotov accepted participation only if the war were defensive and liberating.[418] On the other hand, Alekseev and Fedotov agreed in lamenting the indifference reigning "in our parishes," which are so worried about individual salvation and the disunity of the Orthodox churches that they are incapable of putting the social question on the agenda.[419]

The Body of Christ

Until the end of the 1930s, the authors of *The Way*, in spite of their differences, were conscious of a profound unity among themselves in their relationships with the ecumenical world. Their confessional adherence and their common intellectual history gave them a shared understanding of the most pressing problem for the theology of that era, namely, cosmology, or the relationship of God to the world. As Bezobrazov put it in his lecture in December 1936, "unlike Barthianism, contemporary Orthodoxy has a vision of a rehabilitated world."[420] But this transfiguring vision of the world gave rise to two different types of commitment. Whereas for Fedotov and Berdyaev, human dignity was the foundation upon which the Kingdom of God should be constructed, for Bulgakov and Florovsky, Christian baptism was the cornerstone of the visible church.

Bulgakov and Florovsky had a Christocentric vision of the church, understood as the visible, historical, and sacramental incarnation of the mystical Body of Christ on earth. But as can be seen from the theological works of these two men during the period in question, Bulgakov developed a pneumatological ecclesiology that was, simultaneously, personalist, sophiological, and eschatological, whereas Florovsky developed a Christological ecclesiology that was, simultaneously, apophatic, patristic, and historiographical.

Bulgakov was convinced that the Orthodox Church contained all the fullness of the life of the church. Yet the unity of the mystical church with the visible church, that is, the Orthodox Church, did not in itself mean that other Christian confessions were outside of the church. And, above all, for Bulgakov, the rediscovery by the visible churches of their profound unity corresponded to the first phase of a new evangelization of the universe.

Florovsky, as we have seen, refused to separate the mystical church from the visible church and believed that this spiritualism was the principal cause of the troubles of the Russian Church. In an article published in *The Way* in 1933, "The Question of Christian Unity," he had affirmed the depths of the divisions between East and West and the impossibility for "theological conferences and congresses of hierarchs" to arrive at a theological agreement. Such an accord, in his view, could only take place at the end of time, at the *Parousia*.[421] In 1939, at the Amsterdam conference, Florovsky declared to the magazine *Reform*: "The differences between Orthodoxy and Protestantism are dogmatic; it is a question of faith. In this perspective (in particular on the question of apostolic succession) an agreement among them *will never be reached* [emphasis in the text]."[422] This type of declaration is in sharp contrast with what was being proposed in the ecumenical press by the disciples of Bulgakov and of Zander in particular, whose article "The Essence of the Ecumenical Movement" appeared in the journal *Social Christianity* and in the 1937 collection *The Living Tradition*. Florovsky, although he made some contradictory statements on this question, remained faithful until the end of his life to his unilateral identification of the mystical church with the Orthodox Church. As he wrote in 1978, theology should be historical, understood "not as a dialectic of concepts but as a profession of faith," Christocentric and Hellenocentric.[423] Also, for Florovsky, the sacramental border separating the Orthodox Church from the other churches could only be breached, according to George Williams, by the return of Protestantism to the church of the ecumenical councils.[424] This is why the intransigence of Florovsky was, at the same time, the source of his desire for dialogue with the ecumenical world. As he reaffirmed in 1949, Florovsky saw his participation in the ecumenical movement as a "conversation" in view of a "missionary activity."[425] The rediscovery of the riches of Greek patristics should permit other confessions to follow the same route that led Russian theology to the primitive church.

The ecclesiology of Florovsky was all the more successful in that it corresponded to the dominant philosophy in the Christian world at that time—Barthianism in Protestantism and Neo-Thomism in Catholicism. These doctrines had a point in common with the neo-patristic synthesis insofar as they rejected the liberal Protestant ecclesiology of the nineteenth century and underlined the distinction between God and human representations of the Divinity. This led to the victory of the neo-patristic line of thought even prior to the Second World War, both in the Anglican and in the Protestant worlds. Nevertheless, the polemic between these two Orthodox visions of the church continued to divide Orthodoxy after the war.[426]

Dialogue with the Catholics

If relations between the journals *The Way* and *Russie et Chrétienté* were strained, those with *Irénikon*, the review of the Benedictines of Chevetogne, were more cordial. In his account of the issues of *Irénikon* between 1935 and 1937, Zenkovsky gratefully pointed out the review's attitude of openness towards Orthodoxy, thanks to its editor Dom Clément Lialine. But Zenkovsky believed that the "incomprehension of Protestantism" manifested in the journal constituted a stumbling block with respect to Orthodoxy. Zenkovsky was bitterly critical of the "insensitivity" of Rome and its lack of repentance—aside from some rare exceptions—for the role it played in the division of Christians.[427] This point of view should be counterbalanced by that of Lot-Borodin, who in April 1939 wrote a very favorable review of a book by Yves Congar, *Chrétiens désunis, principes d'un oecumenisme catholique*, which was published in 1937 by Éditions Cerf. This work of Congar, a young Dominican and editor of the *Revue des sciences philosophiques et religieuses*, abundantly cited Berdyaev, Bulgakov, and Florovsky, and was hailed by Lot-Borodin as "the first clear voice from a non-official representative of the Catholic Church."[428] Florovsky's friend stressed "the call to reform," the desire to "return to the Fathers of the Church," the criticism of "the left wing of the ecumenical movement," that is, of Life and Work, and the "opening up to Orthodoxy." Above all, Lot-Borodin appreciated Congar's vision of the church as founded on the *Corpus Mysticum* of Christ. Lot-Borodin, however, in the name of "Oriental Christo-pneumatology," was harshly critical of Western Christianity in its cataphatic and rational approach, which identified the church with the institutional church and which limited the "regime of pedagogy, of the exercise of authority" exclusively to the hierarchy.[429] In spite of this criticism, the book review led to an understanding of the reasons why Catholic theologians of the younger generation were so favorable to Florovsky's neo-patristic synthesis. During the Athens Congress in 1936, when Florovsky gave two lectures, "The Western Influence on Russian Theology" and "Patristics and Contemporary Theology," the two Dominicans who were present, Christopher Dumont and Charles Moeller, stated that they were most impressed by the renewal of Orthodox theology as exemplified by the St. Sergius Institute professor.[430]

Dialogue with the Protestants

The second congress of Faith and Order took place on August 3–18, 1937, in Edinburgh, presided over by Dr. William Temple, the Anglican archbishop of York [later Archbishop of Canterbury], and in the presence of John Mott and 414 delegates representing 122 confessions from 43 different countries. Among the delegates from the Russian exarchate of Western Europe were Metropolitan Evlogy, Bulgakov, Zernov, Zander, Bezobrazov, Zenkovsky, and Kartashev. The delegates were divided into five commissions or sections, on "The Grace of our Lord Jesus Christ," "The Church and the Word of God," "Ministry and Sacraments," "The Communion of the Saints," and "The Unity of the Church in Life and Liturgical Service."

Zander and Zernov reported on the congress in *The Way*. Zander endorsed the declaration of the ensemble of Orthodox delegates protesting the parliamentary procedure adopted by the Protestant majority. He reported, however, that in certain points of doctrine, such as the question of the antithesis between works and faith as sources of salvation, there was a convergence of approaches even if there was no agreement. Zander stressed, above all, the decisive role played by Bulgakov, the fruit of ten years of work, in the adoption of a resolution on the Mother of God, the angels, and the saints, which was included in the fifth section. This resolution emphasized "the great respect which should be given to Mary in Christian consciousness."[431] But given the difficult discussions in the other sections and considering the interconfessional character of the liturgical celebrations, Zander noted, the congress shattered many illusions, and he concluded that unity was not feasible at present.[432]

Nonetheless, Zander observed that the congress was a "spiritual event" and revealed the growing awareness, on the part of many, of the unity of the Christian world and the responsibility of each in the face of disunity.[433] In his report, Zernov called attention to the fact that the Orthodox delegation was equally divided between those who held to an "absolutist" approach, for whom unity was a return to the sheepfold, and the representatives of an "organic" approach, for whom the church is "founded by God but cannot be identified with its structures of direction."[434] The internal division among the Orthodox became apparent to the participants on the final day when the group led by Florovsky refused to participate in the voting on the resolutions, while the group that followed Bulgakov chose to take part. According to Zernov, the absolutist members were principally opposed to a third approach, which represented the majority—the liberal approach. According to the liberal approach, since each confession only represented a part of the truth, there should be a federation of Christian churches based on a minimal dogmatic accord. He wrote: "The principal difference between the absolutist, liberal, and organic approaches concerning the divisions in the Church is that the liberal current and the absolutist currents try to show that, in reality, there is no division, while the organic current has the courage to recognize that the unique body of the Church is historically divided because of the sin of its members."[435] From this perspective, Zernov thought that the future of the ecumenical movement depended on the capacity "of the Orthodox Church to rediscover a conciliar life and to establish relations with the West." The Orthodox

Church, he regretfully stated, did not draw out all the consequences of its ancestral recognition—through its own liturgical practice—of the presence of a sacramental reality outside of Orthodoxy. Zernov saw in the Eucharistic renewal an authentic source that would allow the Orthodox Church to overcome its internal divisions (ecclesiological, but also national) and to transform the ecumenical movement from a parliamentary institution into an authentic fraternity.

As we have seen, the Edinburgh Conference and the Life and Work Movement approved the creation of a single institution and named an executive commission of fourteen members, including J. Mott, W. Visser't Hooft, Metropolitan Germanos of Thyateira, G. Florovsky, and M. Boegner. A crowning honor for Florovsky in September 1937 was his reception of a doctorate *honoris causa*, bestowed on him by the University of St. Andrews together with Martin Dibellius and Karl Barth. Even though Florovsky's selection to the commission represented an undeniable victory for those advocating a neo-patristic synthesis, it did not prevent the disciples of Bulgakov from continuing their ecumenical involvement. After the Utrecht Conference in May 1938, during which the commission adopted a projected constitution for the World Council of Churches, Zander and Zernov were active participants—from Stockholm to Madras, India—in the preparatory meetings for the new assembly. On August 29, 1938, Bulgakov participated in a meeting of Faith and Order at Clarens. He fell ill at the beginning of 1939, however, and was unable to continue his ecumenical activities.

Aware of the imminence of war, the commission made it a priority to communicate the accomplishments of the ecumenical movement to the younger generation of Christians. From July 24 to August 4, 1939, another Ecumenical Congress of Christian Youth took place in Amsterdam. This congress was organized by the Preparatory Committee of the World Council of Churches in conjunction with the World Student Christian Federation (of which the Russian Student Christian Movement had been a full member since 1935), the YMCA, and the YWCA. It brought together two thousand delegates from seventy-five countries (including one hundred Orthodox delegates), 80 percent of whom were under the age of twenty-five. To avoid repeating the mistakes of past conferences, Zernov and Zander took it upon themselves to organize a Eucharistic liturgy in three languages for all of the participants so that the delegates of non-Orthodox confessions might be able to understand and participate in the

Orthodox ritual—without, however, receiving communion. This was a "first" for the ecumenical movement. In the report he wrote for *The Way* from London on December 28, 1939, Zernov stated that this congress constituted a "turning point" in the history of the ecumenical movement. It marked the end of a first period which "consisted in getting to know one another" and the beginning of a new era shaped by the start of the war but also by the tragic consciousness of the universality of the church.[436]

Dialogue with the Anglicans

The high point of the coming together of Orthodox and Anglicans had taken place near Paris on the occasion of the Conference of the Fellowship of St. Alban and St. Sergius from December 30, 1935, to January 3, 1936. This conference, as discussed earlier, was centered on the theme "The Church and the World," and it reunited all the groups of the Paris School, from Berdyaev and Bulgakov to Florovsky. It culminated in a liturgical service—not Eucharistic, of course—concelebrated for the first time in common between the Anglican and Orthodox hierarchs, Metropolitan Evlogy and Bishop Walter Frere, in the cathedral on rue Daru. But the tensions generated by the debate on intercommunion and the polemic concerning Sophia changed the atmosphere of the meetings. From April 16, 1936, during the tenth conference of the Fellowship at Digswell, the debate shifted and focused on the divisions that were tearing apart the Orthodox Church. Bulgakov gave a talk on sophiology. Ten days later, Bishop Frere organized a conference at Mirfield, in the monastic Community of the Resurrection, to give the Russian theologian the chance to present his doctrine again, this time in a more relaxed setting. His lectures led to the publication in 1937 of a book in English entitled *The Wisdom of God*. Zander followed up the action of his spiritual father by publishing sophiological essays in different ecumenical reviews.[437] He developed the activities of the Fellowship by popularizing the idea of fraternity in the different Orthodox parishes of France.

Bulgakov continued to defend the cause of sophiology when he visited the United States from September 29 to November 6, 1936 (where he met Archbishop Athenagoras, the future ecumenical patriarch), and subsequently in Greece. He made the same presentation everywhere. The following is an excerpt:

There are two polarizing attitudes in the Christian conception of the world, both erroneous because of their unilateral character: Manicheism, which negates the world, which separates God from the world by an abyss that cannot be crossed and that divides and, consequently, abolishes theanthropy [divine humanity]; and secularism, which consists in receiving the world such as it is and bowing down before its system of values. . . . Is there a ladder which goes from earth to heaven along which the angels descend and mount? . . . The created world is united to the divine world by the divine Sophia. . . . And God does not live only in heaven but also on earth, in the world, with man. . . . Theanthropy is a dogmatic appeal to spiritual asceticism as well as to creative activity in order to save ourselves from the world, as well as to save the world itself. . . . What is more, there is an essential difficulty . . . and that is the absence of a dogma of the Church. . . . And what is the meaning of the union of the Churches in one Church? Does that correspond to a "pact" or to an act, as the manifestation of a unique Church, as the revelation of the Theanthropy, of the Wisdom of God? . . . History reveals itself to us as apocalypse; the apocalypse as eschatology; the end as the accomplishment; the coming of Christ as *Parousia*, as his welcome by the Church.[438]

Bulgakov's final act of participation in the Fellowship of St. Alban and St. Sergius was at the conference from June 30 to July 6, 1938, where he presented a paper entitled "*Una Sancta*," which, in the absence of Florovsky, sealed his "victory" within the fraternity over his younger colleague in the intellectual joust they were waging.[439] But this victory did not last long. Florovsky, having become the editor of the Fellowship's review, which had been renamed *Sobornost'*, also became the vice president of the Fellowship in 1937. Moreover, one of Bulgakov's principal supporters, Bishop Frere, the president of the Fellowship, died in the spring of 1938. In the May issue of *The Way*, Bulgakov paid him final homage, hailing him as the pioneer of church unity.[440] In the spring of 1939, while Bulgakov was absent due to illness, Florovsky was back at High Leigh again. In July 1939, the last meeting of the Anglo-Russian fellowship prior to the outbreak of the war took place, with the theme "The God Who Speaks," in an atmosphere of tension between Fedotov and Florovsky following the threats to expel the Russian historian from the St. Sergius Institute.[441]

Conclusion:

The Two "Bodies" of the Review

The Way was not merely a publication, a body of work that for more than fifteen years brought together the most eminent representatives of Russian religious thought. As we have been able to see throughout this account, it was also a "spiritual body," a community of Russian intellectuals who were in the process of discovering their roles as spiritual figures. Although its publication may be ended, a journal lives on for some time via other modes of communication. This was the case for *The Way* until after the Second World War, when a number of deaths, the rise of other intellectual figures throughout the world, and, especially, the emerging spirit of a new generation ultimately brought its history to a close.

THE END OF THE REVIEW'S HISTORY (1940–1948)

The Review's Ethical Commitment

Between June 1940—when he left Paris to spend three months at Pyla-sur-Mer, near Arcachon—and January 1945, after the last German soldier had left France, Berdyaev did not publish a single article, either in *The Way*, whose publication came to an end in March 1940, or in any other review. As early as September 1940, Berdyaev, as an opponent of the Hitler movement, felt threatened. Intent on remaining thoroughly independent of the occupying forces, he decided, together with Paul Anderson, to end the activities of the Academy of Religious Philosophy as well as the publication of *The Way*. Thus, the review remained faithful to the ethical tradition of the Russian intelligentsia to the last. Beginning in 1940 and throughout the war, the Sunday afternoon gatherings at Berdyaev's residence in Clamart became the émigrés' "center of Russian patriotism," according to one American observer.[1] Among the most assiduous members of the inner circle of the journal we find Mother Maria, Pianov, Mochulsky, Zhaba, Adamovich, the poet Piotrovsky, the writer Stavrov and his wife, Ms. Kliiachkin, and Maria Kurdiumov. In 1943, Berdyaev began writing *The Russian Idea*. In November 1944 he gave a lecture on the theme "The Russian Ideal and the German Ideal" and then, through Jean Schlumberger, sent the "Manifesto of Russian Authors" to the review *Combat*.[2] In response to criticism for compromising with the communist government, Berdyaev reiterated his position after the war in his *Spiritual Autobiography*, a position considered intolerable by the right-wing emigration ever since his arrival from Berlin: "Nothing has changed, essentially, in my attitude toward Soviet Russia. I consider the Soviet government to be the sole national Russian government. . . . This does not mean that I approve of it entirely."[3] Nevertheless, among the French intellectuals most devoted to the group in Clamart during the war, we find R. Le Senne and P. Leyris. In his memoirs, Maurice de Gandillac recalls the "prophet of *A New Middle Ages* [published in English as *The End of Our Time*]—fully heir to knowledge and wisdom, unsatisfied with Pontigny, both disturbing and stimulating for Maritain, Mounier, and Moré—at the time of the siege of Stalingrad, assessing in his Clamart villa his contrasting relationships with Marx and Schelling."[4]

This intellectual, patriotic, and ethical resistance to the invading forces ended tragically for some of the authors of the review. In Germany, I. Stratonov's allegiance to the patriarchate of Moscow cost him his life. Arrested by the Gestapo in 1941, he died in a concentration camp in 1942. Lagovsky came to the same tragic end, although at the hands of the Soviet invaders. He was arrested by the Red Army in Tallinn in 1940 and, on April 25, 1941, was condemned to death as an anti-Soviet agent by the Leningrad tribunal (article 58-4). He was killed by a firing squad on July 3, 1941.[5]

The End of the Review's History (1940–1948) 521

In France, because they were in charge of the Russian Student Christian Movement, Zenkovsky and Zander were the first authors of *The Way* to be arrested, in September 1939, by the French police, who were wary of members of the Russian immigration following the German-Soviet alliance. They were released in November 1940 and supported Paul Anderson and the YMCA in their efforts on behalf of prisoners of war. In 1942, Zenkovsky was ordained a priest by Metropolitan Evlogy. Zander was sent once again to Compiègne in June 1941. The group known as Résistance—also the title of the journal whose name bore the legacy we all know—which was founded by Boris Vildé (1908–42) and his friend Anatole Levitsky (1901–42) in the basement of the Musée de l'Homme in Paris, was the first to be decimated in 1941, despite the appeals of F. Mauriac, P. Valéry, and G. Duhamel. Although Vildé and Levitsky were not contributors to *The Way*, we know to what extent Vildé, the husband of Berdyaev's translator Irene Lot and thus the son-in-law of Myrrha Lot-Borodin, was influenced by the Academy of Religious Philosophy and by those gathered around Fedotov and Fondaminsky, where there was an ongoing exchange of Russian religious thought. General de Gaulle posthumously conferred upon Vildé and Levitsky the medal of the Resistance. Fondaminsky refused to leave Paris and faithfully attended the gatherings of Berdyaev. He was arrested on June 22, 1941, and sent to a holding camp in Compiègne. He was baptized there. Rejecting any plan of escape out of solidarity with the Jewish prisoners, he died at Auschwitz in 1943.

In February 1943, the very core of the review was hit when the central figures of Orthodox Action were arrested. Fr. Dimitrii Klepinin was the first to be arrested, for providing forged baptismal certificates to a number of Jews; the arrests of Mother Maria and her son, Yuri, of Fyodor Pianov, Anatole Viskovsky, and George Kazachkin—all members of Orthodox Action—soon followed. On February 27, the men were transferred from the prison in Romainville to the camp in Compiègne.[6] A clandestine correspondence began between Fr. Dimitrii and his wife via the American sector of the camp in Royaullieu. The main concern of the group Orthodox Action at the time was the possibility that Metropolitan Evlogy would give in to the conservative and collaborative elements of the emigration, represented especially by Bishop Anastassy Gribanovsky, successor to Metropolitan Anthony Khrapovitsky as head of the Russian Orthodox Church Outside Russia. On September 8, 1943, when Metropolitan Sergius Stragorodsky, the patriarch-elect of all Russia, sent a pastoral letter encouraging

Christians the world over to unite against Nazism, the members of Orthodox Action took comfort in the hope of reuniting with the mother church. On December 13, 1943, Fr. Dimitrii was transferred to Germany, to the forced-labor camp of Buchenwald, then sent on to the Dora labor camp, where he died on February 9, 1944, at the age of thirty-nine. On March 30, 1945, Mother Maria died in the gas chambers at Ravensbrück. Out of the group of Orthodox Action, the sole survivors were Fyodor Pianov, who spent the last years of his life putting together an index for *The Way*, and George Kazachkin, the former secretary of the Academy of Religious Philosophy.

Not all of the authors of the review achieved such acts of heroism. Some merely sought refuge in places where they felt safe. When war broke out in 1939, Florovsky was in Switzerland, at a gathering of the Faith and Order Commission. He decided to join the Russian Orthodox Church Outside Russia in Yugoslavia. He taught history to the Corps of Cadets, first in Bela Tserkva and then in Belgrade in 1942. Alekseev also moved to Belgrade, but he was removed from the university in 1942 for his pro-Soviet stance. P. Bitsilli, the liberal historian, remained in Sofia, where he openly declared himself to be anti-fascist and pro-Russian. In 1942, Nikolai Lossky moved from Prague to Bratislava, where he was elected to teach at the school of philosophy. F. Stepun, like I. Smolich, lived in Germany throughout the conflict, during which he clearly sided with the Soviet Union. As early as 1938, Fr. Lev Gillet left France for London, where he joined N. Zernov and N. Gorodetsky. Fedotov, like Iswolsky, left for the United States. He arrived in New York on September 14, 1941, and taught at Yale University. In 1943 he began teaching history at St. Vladimir's Theological Seminary in New York. He was joined there, after the war, by Nikolai Lossky, G. Florovsky, and N. Arseniev.

S. Frank, a Jew with a Jewish family, was under threat from the invading German forces—like Vladimir Lossky, whose wife was Jewish—and hid in France throughout the war. After the French liberation, he left for England. Among the authors of the last editorial committee who remained in France were Veidlé, Ivanov, Kurdiumov, Lazarev, Lot-Borodin, Mochulsky—who narrowly escaped being deported in 1943—and Bulgakov, who continued to teach almost up to his death on July 12, 1944. Alexis Kniazev has compiled the epic account of the life of the St. Sergius Institute during the war. As a former German Lutheran institution that had been confiscated by the French authorities in 1918, the Institute received several visits from the Gestapo. But a German officer in Paris, the son of Bodelschwing, the pastor who had been the founder of the old Lutheran church and diaconal center, protected the Institute. In the spring of 1943, through an invitation made by the rector, Metropolitan Evlogy, and the dean, Bulgakov, the St. Sergius Institute ceremoniously received his Excellency Beaussart, the auxiliary bishop of Paris, who came as a representative of the cardinal archbishop. It was the first time a Catholic bishop had visited the Institute.[7]

Although the review as a whole expressed its opposition to the invading German forces, two authors of *The Way*, B. Vysheslavtsev and V. Ilyin, chose to collaborate with the Nazi government as a way of supporting its fight against the Soviet Union. Ilyin had left the authors of *The Way* as early as 1934, while Vysheslavtsev had lost his position as assistant editor-in-chief when the time came to renew the review's editorial committee in 1939. Although he was married to a Jewish woman, Vera Pundik, Ilyin left for Berlin in 1941 and spent one year serving as a translator for the Reich. He returned to Paris in 1942 and was soon ostracized by the Russian intelligentsia. He then wrote, in the same year, a set of rather bitter memoirs against the milieu of the emigration.

Like D. Merezhkovsky, Vysheslavtsev was delighted by the entry into Soviet territory of German troops, on June 21, 1941. There are no sources indicating precisely what Vysheslavtsev did during the conflict. V. Yanovsky wrote only that Vysheslavtsev traveled back and forth between France and Germany, where he collaborated with the Reich's department of propaganda. In 1943 he left France for Switzerland, thanks to his membership in the International Society for Psychology. After the war, he remained in Switzerland so as not to have to face the French courts.[8]

Pneumatology and Eschatology

Because *The Way*'s publication was interrupted by the war, it is difficult to outline the continuing intellectual evolution among its authors. Nevertheless, one may consider the convergence of Berdyaev's, Bulgakov's, and Mother Maria's research on the subject of eschatology as representing a kind of epilogue to the intellectual adventure of their generation, that of *Vekhi/Landmarks*.

After having drafted his *Autobiographie spirituelle* (*Dream and Reality: An Essay in Autobiography*) in 1940 (completed in 1947), Berdyaev wrote his last great philosophical work, *Essai de métaphysique eschatologique*

(*The Beginning and the End: Essay on Eschatological Metaphysics*), in 1941 (it was published by Aubier in 1946). He then devoted himself, in 1944–45, to a new philosophical/religious meditation, *Dialectique existentielle du divin et de l'humain* (*The Divine and the Human*), in which he took up a number of his favorite themes but from a more eschatological perspective. Berdyaev's last book, *Royaume de l'Esprit et royaume de César* (*The Realm of the Spirit and the Realm of Caesar*), which he completed in 1948, retained the same eschatological bent. During the war he took part in meetings at Marie-Madeleine Davy's center for philosophical and spiritual research, which were also attended by J. Hyppolite, M. Butor, G. Deleuze, and M. Tournier, among others. In 1943 a colloquium of la Fortelle took place near Paris—prompted by Davy—on his recently published book, *Esprit et réalité* (*Spirit and Reality*), with M. Moré, abbé G. Fessard, V. Lossky, N. Poltoratsky, and others in attendance. Berdyaev also visited Marcel Moré, where he met Teilhard de Chardin, G. Bataille, P. Klossowski, M. Blanchot, Jean Daniélou, and Jean-Paul Sartre. Berdyaev gave two lectures there to a crowd of 150 to 200 people on the subjects of religious messianism and the drama of Nietzsche's religious thought. As he told his wife on June 26, 1943, upon returning from a meeting at Marcel Moré's: "Eschatology is now at the center ... the Spirit cannot be objectified as I once thought it could."[9]

In the first part of his *The Beginning and the End: Essay on Eschatological Metaphysics*, Berdyaev undertook a critique of the relationship between a thing in itself and the phenomena suggested by Kant, Hegel, and Husserl. In the second part he suggested replacing ontology with a form of pneumatology, since in his view "the spirit is a reality of another order than that of objective nature or of objectivity as produced by reason."[10] From then on, Berdyaev declared himself a proponent of a new metaphysics, based no longer on conceptual causality but on creative imagination. In the fourth and final part of the work, Berdyaev made corrections along more pneumatological lines to the reflections on time and history which he had begun to lay out in his works *Le sens de l'histoire* (*The Meaning of History*) and *Le moi et le monde des objets* (*Solitude and Society*). "Within objectified time," he wrote, "there is neither beginning nor end, but only an infinite middle. The beginning and the end are part of the existential realm."[11] From this perspective, only the resurrection can give meaning to the destiny of the human person. Berdyaev stated: "Man is a temporal being who contains eternity within himself and who demands eternity. Metaphysics inevitably becomes eschatological."[12] After having read his *The Beginning and the End*, Frank expressed his agreement with Berdyaev but nevertheless brought some nuances to bear. In 1946 he wrote:

> I am not as strongly opposed to you as you think. That creation and freedom have greater depth than a completed being, I fully recognize. Likewise, I recognize the primal, ontological significance of the personal spirit. I disagree with you only insofar as I do not share your negations, the *bezpochvennost'* [groundlessness, formlessness] and defiance. I am afraid that your attack on objectivization amounts to a negation of the idea of the incarnation, to an abstract spiritualism.[13]

The Apocalypse of John, drafted by Bulgakov between 1940 and 1944, was the dogmatic centerpiece of his rethinking during that period of the entire question of history and Judaism. Like Berdyaev, Bulgakov made a clearer distinction between the synergistic sense of history, on the one hand, and its personal and eschatological meaning, on the other. The strange vision of John the Evangelist, to whom Christ refers as a "Son of Thunder," led Bulgakov to "rethink Revelation as the final word in dogmatic theology, and particularly in ecclesiology and eschatology."[14] Overwhelmed by the vision of Christ's return in glory described in the Book of Revelation, Bulgakov did not hesitate to evoke a "new sense of life" conveyed by the ultimate revelation, the coming of the Kingdom, and eternity entering time. He produced a line-by-line commentary on the last book of the Bible, which led in particular, in his treatment of chapters 2 and 3, to an ecclesiology divided into seven charismatic types. Most important, Bulgakov offered a sophiological interpretation of the events described in Revelation: the seven seals, the seven trumpets, the seven cups, the nuptial feast of the Lamb and his Bride, meaning Christ and the divine-human Church, followed by a first battle against the Beast, the millennial reign, a definitive victory over evil, and, finally, in chapters 21 and 22, the reunion of divine Wisdom with created Wisdom, of the Spirit and the Bride, and the eschatological recreation of the world. From this Bulgakov produced a new philosophy of history in which he distinguished between two forms of metahistory. On the one hand, the world's history must be understood from a synergistic perspective as tending towards the millennial reign, as a preparation for the nuptial banquet and an authentic manifestation of the Kingdom of God on earth. On the other hand, it must be seen as an eschatological process evolving on a spiritual level where evil is definitively eradicated.

Mother Maria Skobtsova also experienced the war as an invitation to deepen her eschatological understanding of history. In an article entitled "The War as Revelation," she wrote:

> War is a call. War is what opens our eyes. This call, this trumpet sound of the Archangel, is one to which we can respond in various ways. We can be like the dignified attendants at a funeral service and respond with polite and indifferent sadness . . . but if we open our hearts to God, suddenly our temporal, fallen life will plummet into the depths of eternity, our human cross will become like the cross of God become man.[15]

In 1942–43, Mother Maria wrote a mystery play (in the medieval sense of the term) entitled *The Seven Cups*,[16] where she set up a dialogue between two monks, Procor and Ioann. The scene takes place on a desert island with a number of jobless people crushed by their humiliation, a crowd ready to fight, three women downtrodden by war and misery, soldiers, prisoners, and some Jews all taking the full brunt of the six cups. Mother Maria ends her story with Procor experiencing a (Bulgakovian) vision of the seventh cup, namely, the encounter of the earthly and angelic realms. "Baptized in the fire of the Spirit / We take part in the Burning Bush."[17]

After the War: A New World

In 1946, despite the dissolution of the group of Russian intellectuals, Berdyaev decided to establish the Society for Spiritual Culture, at 77 rue de Lourmel, as a replacement for the Academy of Religious Philosophy. He took advantage of the presence in Paris of Nikolai Lossky and N. Arseniev by giving them each a course to teach: on the history of Russian thought (which Lossky later published as a *History of Russian Philosophy*) and on mysticism (Arseniev). Mochulsky, who had taken over as president of Orthodox Action after Mother Maria was deported, held a class on Dostoevsky.

As for Berdyaev, who was now lecturing in French to an audience of nonspecialists, he chose to devote his last courses to two themes: "Man and the Modern World" and "The Currents of Modern Thought." Thanks to one of his students, A. Lequeux, a portion of the notes from these classes has survived.[18] Drawing lessons from World War II and from the advent of the atomic bomb, Berdyaev sought to understand the mystery of the relationship between darkness and light. He continued his rigorous critique of Marxism and communism, but also of Nietzsche, Heidegger, Jaspers, and Sartre. Although Berdyaev considered Marxism to be "of little interest" on an intellectual level, he urged Christians to ponder the extraordinary vitality of communism and inveighed against the anticommunist movement for its part in pushing the Soviet Union into a defensive posture. He also studied the vital elements of Christianity within Catholicism (for instance, Daniélou, Balthasar, Fessard), Protestantism (Barth, Tillich, Ragaz), and Russian Orthodoxy ("from a distance one might think it unified, but this is false, for there are many currents"). His last class was devoted to the crisis within Christianity. "We are witnessing a passage from historic Christianity, shining with a light from the past, to an eschatological Christianity, where the light comes from the future. . . . This presupposes a greater prophetic revelation. The Church is the means and the Kingdom of God is the goal."[19]

Berdyaev saved his own ideas for a group of specialists gathered within the framework of the Collège Philosophique, at 44 rue de Rennes, which was organized after the war by M. M. Davy and J. Wahl. In the company of E. Lévinas (*Parole et silence*) and B. de Schloezer, Berdyaev led a course on the topic "The Philosophical Contradictions of Freedom." He also lectured at 15 rue Cujas and at 184 Boulevard St. Germain on "The Philosophical Contradictions of Marxism" and "Forms of Atheism in the Contemporary World." Among the other lecturers were E. Weil, G. Bataille, V. Jankelevitch, P. Emmanuel, R. Aron, J. Lacan, M. Merleau-Ponty, A. Koyré, J. Paulhan, M. Leiris, G. Bachelard, J. Desanti, G. Canguilhem, and G. Gurvitch. Berdyaev also frequented the residence of Gabriel Marcel, where he was invited to share in private gatherings with Lévinas, Minkowski, Wahl, and Landsberg, and to listen to Vladimir Jankelevitch interpret Fauré's *Nocturnes* on the piano.[20]

This mingling of Russian and French intellectuals was also apparent in the new review launched by Berdyaev in late 1945: *Les Cahiers de la*

Nouvelle Époque. He had decided not to start up *The Way* again. At more than seventy years of age, after having undergone a major operation in 1942, and after having lost his wife, Lydia Judifevna, in September 1945, he did not feel he had the stamina for such an undertaking. Furthermore, most of the authors on the last committee of the journal were either deceased (Bulgakov, Mother Maria) or out of the country (Alekseev, Fedotov, Gillet, Gorodetsky, Iswolsky, Zernov, Lossky, Frank, Stepun). Ultimately, Berdyaev probably thought that the time had come to establish a French-language, fully ecumenical and social review that would also provide precise information regarding the situation in the Soviet Union. He teamed up with M. Vilshkovsky (editor-in-chief) and Admiral D. Verderevsky, a former secretary of the navy in the provisional government of 1917 who had turned pro-Soviet after the victory of the Red Army. He also invited Paul Anderson to join, from among the former members of *The Way*. From among the Russian immigration, he called on N. Poltoratsky and G. Annenkov. On the French side, he joined with M. M. Davy, A. Philip, and J. Madaule, and he extended invitations as well to M. de Gandillac, Constantin de Grunwald, P. Burgelin, and Audiberti, among others. In their first editorial, the authors called on their readers to discover a new era, dominated by "spiritualist, universalist, and social" tendencies, and to bear in mind especially the Russian contributions to this new civilization. Only two issues came out containing articles by Berdyaev: "Personality and Community in Russian Thought" and "Social Revolution and Spiritual Awakening." In February 1947, Berdyaev also included these two articles in a collection of his essays entitled *Au Seuil de la Nouvelle Époque* (*Towards a New Epoch*). Disenchanted by the authoritarian development of the Stalinist regime (see "Freedom to Create and the Fabrication of Souls" in this collection) and by the nihilist bent of the intellectual debate in France (see "Sartre and the Future of Existentialism"), Berdyaev brought his editorial activities to a close, affirming the advent of a new Christian conscience.

Conclusion

Although Berdyaev was able to revive *The Way* indirectly for a time, between 1945 and 1948, through the review *Les Cahiers de la Nouvelle Époque*, this effort did not survive the death of its main proponent. On March 14,

1948, at the residence of Emmanuel Mounier, Berdyaev took part in a debate revolving around Gandhi. The following Sunday he presided at his usual meeting in Clamart. He died suddenly, at his desk, on March 23, 1948. A half-smoked cigar and an open Bible were found by his side. He had been writing a book on creation, for which the outline found in his archives reads as follows: "Nothingness, Being and Creation, God, and Freedom; The Creative Incarnation, Inspiration, The Advent of What Had Not Existed; The *Mytho-creative* Process; The Artistic Creative Act; Creative Knowledge; Sin, Grace, and Creation: The Religious Significance of Creation: Responding to God; Creation and Work; Creation and Freedom; Creation, Objectivization, and the Incarnation; Creation, Love, and Compassion."[21]

After his death, numerous people expressed their friendship to his sister-in-law, Evgenia Rapp: Pierre Leyris, J. Mott, S. Frank, G. Fedotov, P. Anderson, G. Florovsky, M. Lot-Borodin, N. Arseniev, F. Lieb, Abbott Hardy, Pastor Porret, V. Zenkovsky, V. Ilyin, G. Kuhlmann, P. Suvchinsky, N. Lossky, Rev. Clark, and E. Mounier.[22] Mounier wrote:

> Not fifteen days ago, we had the pleasure of welcoming Nicolas Berdyaev to Chatenay. He was visibly tired, but how intellectually lucid and spiritually alert. It was he who led the gathering, and I am moved at the thought that we received his last public address. We all owe him everything! Our friend who loved Christ with all his faith has the mysterious honor of imitating him in his final hour. Have no doubt that he will soon be in His light, and we pray that he will continue to light our way.

The new political, social, and theological climate was characterized by the beginning of the Cold War, the accession of Barthian, neo-Thomist, and neo-patristic elements to seats of power in ecumenical circles, the rise of neo-Hegelian currents and Sartrian existentialism in philosophy, the disintegration of the Russian immigration as a homogeneous social milieu, the advent of new ecumenical institutions, and, finally, the rise of a new, younger generation of Orthodox intellectuals with almost no experience of Russia (such as A. Schmemann, B. Bobrinskoy, J. Meyendorff, C. Elchaninov, C. Andronikov, and A. Kniazev). All these elements contributed to the ultimate breakdown of the homogeneity of the old intellectual conscience that had asserted itself in Moscow, in 1909, through an anthology of the writings of its major figures (*Vekhi/Landmarks*). New connections began forming among the Orthodox émigrés at the St. Sergius Institute in Paris and St. Vladimir's Seminary near New York, but also within the reemerging Russian Student Christian Movement, and then within Syndesmos, the international Orthodox youth movement founded at Montgeron in 1953. While their elders set about burying the past (Zenkovsky, N. Lossky), a new generation of theologians and philosophers emerged, characterized by a shared desire to root the Orthodox Church within the Byzantine patristic tradition, united by a common rejection of philosophical/religious gnosis, and unanimous in its radical criticism of the atheistic Soviet government. This group was led by G. Florovsky, Vladimir Lossky, and Paul Evdokimov, and, between 1948 and 1989 it also experienced a number of trials, divisions, and renewals.

THE RECOLLECTIONS OF A GENERATION IN RUSSIA

Although the history of *The Way* came to a full close at Berdyaev's death in 1948, the story of the many recollections of *The Way* was far from complete. And although this story is fascinating in many ways, the history behind it must be distinguished from the various recollections, since these are addressed to the present age, directly confront the great figures who shaped the spirit of a given age, and are particularly susceptible to the distortions of specific perspectives. The phenomenon of recorded memorials sheds light on the close connection between recollection and the social and political life of a country. Thus, if in 1989 Merezhkovsky was posthumously held in high regard in Russia—while in the West he had been all but forgotten—it was because his name had been linked with the remembrance of a long suppressed and only recently rediscovered golden age. But when nostalgia for the "Belle Époque" began to give way, in 1995, to the great commemoration of the fiftieth anniversary of the victory over Germany, the discovery by the general public of this Russian author's pro-Nazi leanings relegated him to another period of purgatory.

Nevertheless, the recollections of the generation of Russian intellectuals from *The Way* must be understood first and foremost as a symbolic phenomenon. It is impossible to write a strictly social or political history of the extraordinary phenomenon of recovering the cultural heritage of the emigration that took place in Russia between 1988 and 1998. By taking into account only *perestroika* and *glasnost'*—or conversely, the autonomy of their agents with respect to political life—as the causes of change, one simply misses the more complex phenomena that provide a better sense of the evolution of this recovery.

Clearly, the recovery of the heritage of Russian religious thought initially followed a symbolic motif that was at once political (the anticommunist symbol), national (the symbol of the pure and authentic Russia of the emigration, as opposed to the USSR), and religious (the symbol of religious renewal). This period witnessed the publication in Russia of certain books by Bulgakov, Berdyaev, and Fedotov in enormous print runs (up to 200,000 copies), most often undertaken by government reviews or publishing houses. It was only later, and at greater length, that a stage of conceptualization and objectification led to categorizing the heirs of the emigration's religious thought as social democrats (Yavlinsky) and liberals (Gaidar), but also as "Europeanists" (Kostikov) and Eurasians (Routskoy), and finally as neo-Byzantines (Horuzhy) and ecumenists (Krekshin). This period also corresponded with a growing awareness of the intellectual heritage in the provinces and in universities and seminaries, with the systematic publication of authors' complete works, but there was a dramatic drop in print runs. Finally, it was only after a long silence—humility of a sort, in the face of the mountain of material to be discovered—that the younger generation of politicians, clergy, and scholars began taking seriously the works of writers whom their elders had labeled nihilists, in an effort to create their own syntheses. While the religious thought of the emigration seemed to have gone out of style in the media, more and more theses on Florovsky, Berdyaev, or Fedotov were being defended in the universities. After a period of recovery and of living memory, then of instrumentality and objectification of recollections, there had to be a period of creation, of rediscovered memory.

Symbolic history relies first and foremost on the temporality of communal conscience, rather than on chronological time; thus there is no precise boundary between these metamorphoses of memory. This is why, rather than writing a linear history of this recovery, I have favored a rather meandering account, made up of constant exchanges between history and memory, between time parsed out and time lived out. Likewise, I favor a traditional universalistic account over one fragmented into various "space-time" elements, as astrophysicists might put it, or various *chronotopes*, in Bakhtin's terminology, and made up of three mnemonic components (nation, church, intellectuals). For this purpose I rely primarily on the bibliography—nonexhaustive but sufficiently rich to be of significance—of publications of the authors of *The Way* within the USSR/Russia between 1988 and 1998.

The National Community: Memory in Search of Identity

Russia's national community was restored just as it began discovering, between 1988 and 1991, the political writings of the anticommunist authors who had been run out by the Soviet government. We need not revisit the critique of "bourgeois philosophy" initiated by Lenin in 1909, furthered by Bukharin in the 1930s, and taken up again by the Soviet philosophers through the 1980s.[23] The wholesale critique of the works of Merezhkovsky, Berdyaev, Frank, Bulgakov, and Struve helped forge the myth of the emigration's ideological unity of thought. Furthermore, after 1988, when the high-volume reviews—*Novy Mir, Moskva, Iunost'*—regained their freedom, they started publishing essays of the "post-October Russian philosophers of the emigration."[24] Berdyaev's *The Russian Idea* was published by *Voprosy Filosofii* in 1990, at 85,000 copies. Another of his books, bearing the catchy title *The Destiny of Russia*, sold over 200,000 copies in 1990–91. Fedotov's work entitled *The Saints of Ancient Russia* was printed in 1990 at 150,000 copies by the publisher Rabochi. It included a preface by Dimitri Likhachev and Fr. Alexander Men, both of whom emphasized the spiritual dimension of Russian identity. Despite the efforts of Gorbachev's government, this particular dimension, which had already been emphasized in 1988 during the millennial celebration of the baptism of Russia, remained among the assets of the opponents to the communist regime. The collections *Vekhi/Landmarks* and *De profundis*, against the "Marxist pseudo-intelligentsia," underwent several reprints of 30,000 copies in 1990–91.

In his book on the emigration, Yeltsin's future spokesman, Vyacheslav Kostikov, after some research among the oldest surviving representatives of the emigration, recounted especially the recollections of struggles between the democratic and patriotic Paris School and the conservative, monarchist currents of the Synod. With no knowledge of the works of

Paul Evdokimov or Lev Zander, Kostikov explained to his compatriots that "the activities of the Academy of Religious Philosophy and of the Russian Student Christian Movement bore no fruits after the death of those who had inspired them." Nevertheless, Kostikov showed a certain measure of sentimentality by assimilating the emigration to a sense of patriotism. "The creative and spiritual legacy of the Russian Student Christian Movement," he wrote, "lies not in the works that were left behind, but in the fact that this student movement initiated thousands of children of the emigration into Russian culture."[25]

A deep movement of national unity, in which the couple Alexander Sakharov and Elena Bonner participated and which was skillfully appropriated by Yeltsin, led to the proclamation of the Russian Federation in 1991. One of Yeltsin's first measures, therefore, was to offer citizenship to the Russian "compatriots" of the emigration. With the ideological contributions of the third emigration, reinforced by the writings of such dissidents as Alexander Solzhenitsyn and Mikhail Heller, a national, democratic rift began making its mark in the Russian political sphere.

The unanimity that had reigned among the prodemocratic leadership regarding the anti-Soviet authors of the emigration soon gave way to a serious confrontation between "Eurasian" democrats, supporting H. Hasbulatov, the president of the Federation Council, the heirs of the works of Savitsky and Ilyin, and the "European" democrats, supporting the president of the republic and his team. The Russian Church herself was divided into a national, anti-Yeltsin group (the priest-monk Nikon Belovenets left to join the delegates at the White House in October 1993) and a democratic group demanding an account from the hierarchs (one delegate, Fr. Gleb Yakunin, was prevented from serving as a priest in 1993). This dividing line between "Eurasians" and "Europeans" was significant, despite being somewhat overshadowed by the dissolution of the Federation Council in 1993 and the adoption of a new constitution, which essentially vindicated the second of the two groups. It followed the lines of confrontations in the early 1920s—sometimes explicitly, in the context of debates—between the national, liberal current of P. Struve and I. Ilyin and the spiritual and social current of Berdyaev and Kerensky. During the same period, a strong demand arose on the part of Russian society as a whole for historical works. Karamzin and Klyuchevsky were republished, at over 75,000 copies. In 1993, with the blessing of the patriarch, *Saint Alexander*

Nevsky,[26] written by the Eurasian historian of *The Way*, Nikolai Klepinin, was also published at 50,000 copies. The following year, the Iskusstvo publishing house produced a two-volume collection of articles from Berdyaev, Veidlé, Fedotov, Florovsky, Frank, Bulgakov, and Stepun, on "the Russian idea."[27] And Solzhenitsyn, in his work *The Russian Question at the End of the Twentieth Century*,[28] completed in March 1994 and immediately distributed throughout the media and translated, cites three philosophers in support of his patriotic stance: Struve, Berdyaev, and Bulgakov.

The cinematographic evolution of the producer and delegate Nikita Mikhalkov, who had read Ivan Ilyin and was a typical representative of Soviet-turned-Eurasian *nomenklatura*, is especially telling in this regard. After hailing Yeltsin's accession to power and Russia's recovery of its national symbolism, Mikhalkov was deeply shocked—as was evident in his film *Anna 6–18*—by the tremendous Westernization of Russia from 1991 to 1993. After revealing the charm of Russo-Mongolian Eurasia, in *Urga* (*Close to Eden*), in 1991, he brought back, in 1995, the image of the émigré-traitor in his film *Burnt by the Sun*. In 1996, he accepted second place in the pro-governmental listing of the political party of Boris Yeltsin, Our Home Is Russia (*Nash Dom Rossia*). But in 1998, Mikhalkov and Yeltsin parted ways. As the very popular president of the cinematographer's union, in 1999, in the midst of the war in Kosovo, he introduced his *The Barber of Siberia*, a veritable ode to the great Imperial Russia over against a decadent America.

In contrast to Mikhalkov 's evolution, we may consider that of Yavlinsky, the leader of the social democratic party Yabloko. After a brief role in Gorbachev's government in 1990, Yavlinsky created his own party, which, between 1993 and 1999, accumulated approximately 10 percent of the vote in the legislative elections. Remaining quite hostile to the government, as he was to the Communist Party, in 1994 Yavlinsky took a stance against the war in Chechnya, thereby gaining the support of figures such as E. Bonner and S. Kovalyov. Yavlinsky was close to Likhachev and openly claimed to be a part of the spiritual current of the Russian intelligentsia, initiated by the monks of the Trans-Volga and brought to light by Fedotov, Berdyaev, and Bulgakov. Some of the principal writings of this intellectual generation, such as that of Bulgakov on the intelligentsia that appeared in *Vekhi/Landmarks* in 1909, can be downloaded from the Yabloko Party website.

Close to Yavlinsky was Boris Nemtsov, the former governor of Nizhni-Novgorod turned first vice prime minister in 1997, who surrounded himself with intellectuals influenced by the religious thought of the emigration, such as Victor Aksyuchits. The latter had just produced a book, *In the Shadow of the Cross*, which was introduced on television in March 1998 in the context of a primetime political program, *Geroi Dnia* (Hero of the Day). In his book, Aksyuchits, the former leader of the Christian Democratic Movement—very much a product of Russian religious thought—espoused an "enlightened patriotism" and a "constitutional monarchy." He also favored a creative attitude with regard to tradition and, in a rather eclectic manner, developed an "ontology of the person" inspired by both Florovsky and Lossky, but also by Bulgakov and Berdyaev.

Nemtsov entrusted Victor Aksyuchits with organizing the celebration for the interment of the bodies of the imperial family, discovered in a forest not far from Ekaterinburg. Although the ceremonies were not attended by Patriarch Alexy II of Moscow, for fear he would be criticized by ROCOR, on the one hand, for venerating possible false relics, and by a large segment of the Russian political body, on the other, the event did finally take place on July 18, 1998, in St. Petersburg, in the presence of Boris Yeltsin, as well as that of Nikita Mikhalkov and Dimitrii Likhachev.[29] Bowing before the tomb of Nicholas II, the Russian president officially expressed repentance on behalf of the Russian state for the persecution carried out by the Communist government against the imperial family and all the victims of the revolution.

Thus, despite a period of enthusiastic and somewhat naïve rediscovery of the message of the Russian emigration, the fact that it was rather tarnished by its complexity and its inability to address immediate issues—what kind of regime? which national anthem? which economic model? which borders?—and a decline in public interest, it was nevertheless able to outline responses to a certain number of existential questions for the young Russian nation: What is the nature of Russian identity? How does one explain the tragedy of the communist persecutions in the twentieth century and what was the responsibility of the Christian community in this process? The fact that the interment of the imperial family took place in the presence of the two most significant representatives of the heritage of the emigration within current Russian political circles demonstrated, once and for all, as Ricoeur himself wrote, that only forgiveness makes it possible to move from repetitive to creative remembrance.

In 1990 a collection was published under the title *Pushkin in Russian Philosophical Criticism*, which included articles about the Russian poet from authors of *The Way*, in continuity with their predecessors Solovyov and Rozanov. Apart from a short preface, not a single Soviet author was to be found in this anthology of "Russian Philosophical Criticism" (despite the fact that the author of *Eugene Onegin* was the USSR's favorite poet). The lavish celebration in June 1999, from Moscow to Vladivostok, of the bicentennial of Pushkin's birth, *the* heroic figure of both the emigration and the Soviet Union, revealed that the Russian-Soviet Empire was in the process of becoming a nation state. It also indicated that the two once-rival perspectives were converging in a common understanding of their progressive estrangement from a bygone era, which nevertheless oddly repeats itself in images such as Christ the Savior Cathedral or the never-ending war in Chechnya.[30]

The Ecclesial Community: Memory, a Pathway to Tradition

While the emigration helped redefine Russian identity within the national community, the collective memory of the intellectual generation of Berdyaev, Bulgakov, and Florovsky also played a decisive role for many believers who were searching for existential answers to their religious questions. Just as they had done for the national community, Orthodox intellectuals first turned to the authors of the "Paris School" as representatives of a church free from any compromise with the Soviet state and as faithful to church tradition. With little concern as to whether these authors were part of a traditional or a reforming current within Orthodoxy, Russian editors published the principal works of Fedotov, Florovsky, and Zenkovsky, as well as those of Berdyaev, Metropolitan Evlogy, and Fr. Alexander Elchaninov.

The Period of Reconstruction

Fr. Alexander Men, known for being persecuted by the KGB and for his great learning, which was much appreciated by intellectuals, dissidents, and Western diplomats, became, along with Metropolitan Anthony Bloom— the only Russian bishop to have participated in the "Paris School" venture— the main voice of Orthodoxy during *perestroika*. He contributed significantly to the popularization and realization of the democratic, ecological, and existential ideals of the émigré intellectuals. In 1995 a collection of his talks from 1989–90, on Russian religious philosophers, was published

The Recollections of a Generation in Russia 537

in Moscow with a print run of 10,000 copies. Men presented Merezhkovsky, Berdyaev, Bulgakov, Frank, Fedotov, and Mother Maria as belonging to a single intellectual generation descended from the tradition of Solovyov, Tolstoy, and Sergei Trubetskoy, and, deeper still, from Metropolitan Philip, Maximus the Greek, Lomonosov, and Khomiakov, among others. Although he was somewhat reluctant to adopt the notion of uncreated freedom in Berdyaev and was not especially sensitive to sophiological doctrine, Men nevertheless respected the opinions of all. He regarded the resurgence of Berdyaev's works in Russia as a "feast," and he decried the accusation of heresy against Bulgakov as unjust. Concerning the review *The Way*, he wrote: "It is not a journal, it is a treasury of thought! Its sixty issues are truly a treasure, a legacy which we are now receiving. May God preserve them for our descendants."[31]

After Men's assassination in September 1990, a current of democratization and reform flowed through the Russian Church until 1994. Men's disciples published dozens of their teacher's books in substantial print runs. *The Son of Man*, for example, was published in 1991 at 100,000 copies (and reprinted at up to 4 million copies). While millions were asking to be baptized and churches were being rebuilt throughout the country, many intellectuals pursued Men's popularization of the religious thought of the emigration. Several teaching and publishing centers emerged in the former Soviet Union with a mission to popularize Russian religious thought. Remarkably, the majority of the schools devoted to scientific atheism in the Soviet universities turned into schools for religious studies.

The Russian Christian Institute for the Humanities was created in St. Petersburg. A research facility was put in place at the State University of Omsk to study the Russian emigration; in Riga, N. Bolshakova founded the review *Khristianos*. A European research center was dedicated to the comparative study of Russian-Ukrainian philosophy and contemporary philosophy in the Moghila Academy itself, in Kiev. But the majority of initiatives were concentrated in the Russian capital.

In 1990, Fr. George Kotchetkov, with the support of Sergei Averintsev, founded the St. Philaret Institute. He also created the review *The Orthodox Community* (*Pravoslavnaia Obshchina*), which, with the patriarch's blessing, published texts by Alexander Schmemann on the early church and parish life, but also articles by Afanasiev, Bulgakov, and Fedotov, among others, from *The Way*.[32] Some of the intellectuals from the period of the

1960s were converted. Under the influence of Fr. Shargunov, I. Vinogradov, the editor in chief of *Kontinent*, asked to be baptized. The review regularly published articles by Kotchetkov, Metropolitan Anthony Bloom, and Alexander Kyrlezhev.

Fr. Ioann Ekonomtsev, the director of education for the Moscow patriarchate, became the rector of an important Orthodox university situated within the Vyssoko Petrovsky monastery in Moscow and, with the help of Valentin Nikitin, published a review under the suggestive title *The Way of Orthodoxy*, where one could find articles by Vysheslavtsev, Bulgakov, and Vladimir Lossky. Ekonomtsev had Lossky's *Dogmatic Theology* and his *Mystical Theology of the Eastern Church* published at 100,000 copies.[33] He encouraged Alexis Bodrov, a young physicist who was taken by the teachings of Alexander Men, to create an independent university supported by Archimandrite M. Mudyugin, Metropolitan Anthony of Sourozh, Dimitrii Pospielovsky, and Fr. I. Pavlov. It developed a significant publishing program (*The World of the Bible*, and so on). Soon afterward, the St. Andrew Institute of Biblical and Theological Studies, known by the name of Fr. Alexander Men, wanting to offer its students a recognized diploma, separated itself from the Orthodox University of Alexander Men, where Fr. George Chistiakov continued to teach.

Also close to the patriarch were Frs. Vladimir Vorobyov and Valentin Asmus and Deacon Andrei Kuraev, who in 1992 founded the St. Tikhon Institute within the State University of Moscow. Kuraev, having once held the position of secretary to the patriarch, also participated in the creation in 1994 of the biblical journal *Alpha and Omega*, together with Fr. Ignaty Krekshin and Sergei Averintsev. The first issues of the journal contained numerous articles by Florovsky, Meyendorff, and Schmemann, as well as works by Mother Maria, Rilke, and Origen.

The Period of Division

The climate within the Russian Church began to change dramatically after a number of events: the bombing of the parliament building (the "White House," as it is known) in October 1993, which divided the Russian Church; the invasion of Chechnya in 1994, which the patriarch supported, to the dismay of a large number of the faithful; the discovery of all the complexities of the émigré heritage, divided between the "aggressive" attitude of the synod of the Russian Orthodox Church Outside Russia and the "dangerous" modernity of the Constantinopolitan diocese of rue Daru; and, finally, the recognition by the priests and the faithful of the lack of renewal within the hierarchy and the lack of repentance on the part of the church in Russia. If one adds to this the sense that the consolidation of a democratic regime was underway in Russia after the adoption of a new constitution and that some priests and hierarchs feared they might be accused of having collaborated one way or another with the Soviet system, it becomes clear why a time of settling scores would follow a period of openness for the Russian Church. The old anti-Semitic tendencies in particular, represented by the Radonezh Society, with a radio station founded in 1991 and a journal entitled *Rus' Derzhavniy* (*Sovereign Rus'*), and which had remained inconspicuous in the preceding period, began putting increasing pressure on church hierarchs to halt the overwhelming development of Christian communities considered to be Protestant sects. History began to repeat itself following the Eurasian scenario. The factions that had arisen within the church of the emigration in 1921, then again in 1931, were once again dividing the church of post-Soviet Russia.

A conference organized by the patriarchate on the theme of church unity, which took place in Moscow on November 15 and 16, 1994, was the last time that Frs. G. Kotchetkov, A. Borisov, A. Shargunov, D. Smirnov, V. Asmus, and V. Vorobyov all came together. Fr. Arkady Shatov (now Bishop Panteleimon) was the first to condemn the "modernism" of Kotchetkov on the basis of an old article the latter had published in 1979 under a pseudonym in the review of the Russian Student Christian Movement, *Vestnik RKhD* (the *Messenger*, formerly *Vestnik RSKhD*).[34] Arguing that the appearance of a "Protestant" Eucharistic renewal movement was "extremely dangerous for the Church," Shatov warned Kotchetkov of the risks of heresy.[35] An interesting detail is that Shatov used the writings of Fr. John Meyendorff to accuse and condemn Kotchetkov.

In reality, during this period, a group at the St. Tikhon Institute was leaning in the same direction as the St. Sergius Institute of Paris—with which it signed a publication agreement—and St. Vladimir's Seminary in New York. Nikita Struve and Nicholas Lossky met regularly with Patriarch Alexy II, who, being from the Baltic countries, had participated in the Russian Student Christian Movement prior to the war and had studied religion under Ivan Lagovsky. Profiting from the isolation of the modernists, the Brotherhood of St. Mark of Ephesus published several collections against the "renewal" movement. The reform group of Kotchetkov, Borisov, Krekshin, Chistiakov, and Sviridov was compared to the movement of "The Living Church," which had collaborated with the Bolshevik government against the Russian Church in the 1920s. Significantly, in a 1996 editorial on a collection of essays entitled *The Contemporary Reform: An Eastern Rite Protestantism*, concerning Archbishop Serafim Sobolev of the Russian Church Outside Russia—the one who accused Bulgakov in 1935—Shatov, Asmus, and Deacon Kuraev all agreed in judging that Bulgakov's sophiology was heretical, in criticizing the ecumenism of the Soviet hierarchs, and in rejecting the modernism of Schmemann, Afanasiev, and Berdyaev. Vladimir Lossky's *The Debate on Sophia* was republished in Moscow in 1996, sixty years after its condemnation by Metropolitan Sergius.

Although they were very different in their spiritual orientations, Kotchetkov, Borisov, Krekshin, Chistiakov, and Sviridov found themselves together within a reform movement made up of several parishes, institutes of formation, and diverse channels of communication such as Radio Sofia, the reviews *Kontinent* and *Vestnik RKhD*, and the religious supplement of the weekly émigré journal *Russian Thought*. They all had in common the fact that they posed the sacrilegious question of translating the Slavonic liturgical offices into modern Russian. A new publishing house, The Way (Put'), published not only the works of these authors but also those of theologians who were not Russian Orthodox, such as Olivier Clément.[36] In 1997, Fr. Chistiakov's *Reflections with the Gospel in One's Hands* appeared through this publisher, in which the author strongly condemned war in general and, more particularly, the bombing of Grozny in Chechnya. In this book and also in his numerous public lectures on television and radio, Chistiakov referred increasingly to the spiritual and social heritage of Mother Maria Skobtsova. In 1995, most of the members of this group assisted at a conference of the RSCM in Moscow organized by its foundation, "Aid for the Christians of Russia." The theme was social service and formation in the church.

A counter-conference on the same theme was organized the following year by the patriarchate of Moscow and the Radonezh Society. After several complaints from the conservative groups, the accusation of "modernism" finally led, in 1997, to the prohibition of Kotchetkov from celebrating the liturgy and to the excommunication of several members of his parish. Kotchetkov was convinced that he was a victim of the same phenomena that made a scapegoat out of Bulgakov in 1935, and he was not mistaken. On October 15, 1997, he inaugurated a conference entitled "The Living Tradition" in reference to the collection published in Paris fifty years earlier. But unlike the reaction of the diocese of Metropolitan Evlogy, and in spite of the attacks of I. Vinogradov in *Kontinent* against Orthodox fundamentalism, there was no holy rallying around the victim this time. From this point on, the ecclesial world was divided into two camps. In an apologetic book published in January 1998, of which 15,000 copies were printed, Deacon Kuraev wrote that "1997 was the year I destroyed my own manuscripts."[37] That same year, the publication in *Vestnik RKhD* of Mother Maria's essay "Types of Religious Life," written in 1937 and discovered in the cellar of Berdyaev's house, threw a match, as it were, on the gasoline.[38] The founder of Orthodox Action, by comparing the different types of spirituality—synodal, ascetic, formalist, and aesthetic—to evangelical spirituality, involuntarily provoked the anger of the conservative groups of St. Tikhon Institute and the Radonezh Soceity. In July 1998, in the theological seminary of Ekaterinburg and with the blessing of the local bishop, there was a burning of "modernist" books by Men, Schmemann, and others. As Olivier Clément wrote in *Le Monde*, after a trip to Russia at the invitation of the French University College of Moscow, an atmosphere of inquisition hung over the Russian Church. Several priests—such as the famous iconographer, the priest-monk Fr. Zenon—were suspended for having communed with Catholic priests. Others were simply stripped of their functions because of simple questions of rivalries—such as Fr. Martiri Bagin of Moscow in October 1998. Others, finally fed up with the unceasing attacks of the conservatives and by the nationalist positioning of their bishops, decided to leave the country—as did Fr. Ignaty Krekshin.

The Period of Dissemination

These violent struggles were nothing other than the actualization in the memory of the Russian Church of the profound lines of fracture that had appeared within the intellectual generation of the journal *The Way*. The first consequence of this fratricidal combat was that the heritage of Russian religious philosophy was now transmitted primarily within lay institutions rather than within the official church. The appearance in January

1997 of a monthly religious supplement, *NG-Religiya*, to the daily paper *Nezavisimaya Gazeta* (circulation 60,000) has made a considerable contribution to the diffusion of the political and social ideas of Russian religious thought and has opened up a spectrum of information to the various religions existing in Russia—including the phenomenon of popular superstition. The publication in March 1998 of an article on the work of Berdyaev by Ilya Solovyov, on the front page of *NG-Religiya*, was a sign of this turnaround in the evolution of the memory of the Russian religious conscience.[39] Similarly, the role played by the Library of Foreign Literature, directed by Ekaterina Genieva, a former disciple of Men and president of the Soros Foundation in Russia, has been decisive. In addition to the hall of religious philosophy, which is open to the general public, the library provides a program for disseminating religious thought on the Internet. Moreover, several libraries of religious philosophy have been opened by Nikita Struve, with the support of the French embassy, in over a hundred Russian cities. The principal one was in Moscow in the House of Russian Immigration, which Solzhenitsyn inaugurated in 1996.

An important phenomenon of the 1990s has been the emergence of a new generation of Russian students who believe that the debates between modernists and conservatives are relics of a bygone era and who seek a free path towards the transcendent, calling upon all sorts of tendencies for possible direction. At the MGUIMO, the famous institute for international relations at Moscow State University, Professor K. M. Dolgov, a specialist in the thought of Bulgakov, along with A. Sarov, organized a conference on May 21, 1997, on the topic "The Church and International Relations." On this occasion several Christian student reviews, such as *Foma* and *Tatianin Den'*, the journal of the University of Moscow, joined forces to reflect on the link between Russia's spiritual heritage and the "geostrategy" of the Russian government. At RGGU, the state university for human sciences founded by the historian Yuri Afanasiev, the faculty of religious studies, in association with the École Practique des Hautes Études of Paris, regularly organized colloquiums and publications on the theme "Religion and Society."[40]

Moreover, in spite of the restrictions of the new law of 1997 on religious organizations, the rapid development of Catholic and Methodist communities in Russia has contributed to reinforcing the tendency to look back on the ecumenical experience acquired by the immigration community. The ecumenical weekly *Russian Thought*, with a circulation of more than 50,000, has discontinued its religious supplement but still publishes articles by Chistiakov and reviews of books on Russian religious thought. Several "bridge personalities," enthusiasts of things Russian, such as Georges Nivat and Fr. de Laubier, regularly invite Russian intellectuals to the University of Geneva in Switzerland or to the Vatican. Certain Orthodox intellectuals who are open to ecumenism, such as Yakov Krotov, are eminent specialists in Russian religious thought, from Solovyov to Berdyaev, and take public positions in the press on religious and social questions. The St. Andrew Theological Institute, in its review *Stranitsy* (*Pages*), founded in 1996, regularly publishes articles by non-Orthodox authors such as Enzo Bianchi, the prior of the ecumenical monastic community of Bose in Italy, and Karl Christian Felmy, a member of the German Evangelical Church (who became Christian Orthodox afterwards), as well as the works of figures of the immigration such as Mother Maria Skobtsova.[41] Publishing houses and ecumenical magazines such as *Istina i Zhizn'* (*Truth and Life*) publish the works of Frank and Mother Maria, among others.

Finally, on the sidelines of the confrontation between the heirs of the pneumocentric current and the new generation of intellectuals formed in religious institutions inherited from the Soviet period, a neo-Byzantine current that follows the tradition of Florovsky, Lot-Borodin, and Vladimir Lossky has become progressively apparent within the Moscow Patriarchate. Metropolitan Hilarion Alfeyev, with doctorates from both St. Sergius and Oxford, is now head of the Moscow Patriarchate's external affairs division. He is a protégé of Patriarch Kyrill and the author of numerous volumes, including a treatise on dogmatic theology entitled *The Mystery of Faith*. Earlier he might have been described as representative of this new generation, although more recent writings and statements are suggesting otherwise. At St. Tikhon Institute or the institute of Father Ekonomtsev, young intellectuals are rediscovering the path of the Orthodox tradition, over and above the polemics.

The review *Alpha and Omega*, following the departure of Kuraev and then of Krekshin, continued to publish texts by Metropolitan Anthony Bloom of Sourozh as well as articles from *The Way* by Frank, Vysheslavtsev, Smolitsch, Lev Gillet, and Alexis Kniazev.[42] Behind the façade of a new official jargon, with its obligatory citations of Florovsky and the Fathers of the Church, a new nonconformist research was emerging.

The most evident sign of the profound effect of the memory of Russian religious thought in the immigration community was the publication, on April 18, 1998, of an essay by Fr. Boris Danilenko on *The Way* and the republication of the complete journal on CD-ROM. The principal themes of Danilenko's essay are worth pointing out since they reveal the contemporary impact of this memory in the ecclesial milieu. As the title of the essay—"Grains of a Unique Bread"—indicates, the author's main concern was to preserve the myth of the great and indivisible tradition of Russian religious thought. "Even though the authors of *The Way* did not always agree among themselves," he wrote, they were nonetheless "all united by the same ardent and sincere faith in the Risen Christ."[43] Danilenko quoted a highly relevant poem of Lot-Borodin, published in 1939, in which she wrote, "Only the Spirit, . . . only the radiance of the Eternal Glory prevents them from falling into the abyss." Significantly, the only bone of contention that Danilenko points out is the debate between Lossky and Bulgakov concerning Sophia, which, according to the Russian priest, ended in favor of Frank, who "couldn't see the utility of sophiology."[44]

The second important point for Danilenko was that the unity of the intellectual generation of the authors of *The Way* defined itself, on a political level, by a common rejection of fascism and communism. There is no use in recalling the narrowness of such a claim, which does not take into account the evolution of Karsavin or Vysheslavtsev.

Finally, Danilenko tried to legitimate the authors of *The* Way to his readers by insisting on the fact that they opposed Catholic expansion in Russia, the Russian Orthodox Church Outside Russia, and the movement of the "renovationists" (*obnovlentsy*). He could not avoid mentioning Berdyaev's "original philosophical judgments" and a certain instability in the lay intellectuals who moved from Marxism to Christianity, but he insisted on their sensitivity and understanding with respect to "the different aspects of the life of Orthodoxy."[45] After having drawn up a martyrology of the journal—Lagovsky, Stratonov, Mother Maria—he also stressed that the journal was in contact with the authors of the Soviet Union who were persecuted for their faith.[46] He added—thinking of Patriarch Alexy II, who was from Estonia—that the review was known in the Baltic countries prior to the war, when the Russian minority was likewise persecuted. Aware that he had forgiven much and worked for reconciliation, the author concluded by citing the Gospel passage, "unless a grain of wheat falls into the earth and dies, it remains alone; but if it dies, it bears much fruit (John 12:24)." For Danilenko, what was most painful was a past which does not go away.

The Community of Philosophers: Memory in Search of a Synthesis

The Myth of the Uninterrupted Tradition

After Alexander Yakovlev, the head of ideology on the Politburo of the Russian Communist Party, gave the order in 1988 that authorized the publication of Russian religious philosophers, a tidal wave of articles in the major journals and reviews followed, articles both by and about Berdyaev, Karsavin, Frank, and Vysheslavtsev. Paradoxally, however, freedom of the press did not coincide with the liberation of minds. The main "bridge personalities" who were charged with commissioning, prefacing, and commenting on these publications belonged to the generation of the 1960s. They were either professional philosophers convinced of the "nihilism" of these authors (P. Gaidenko and R. A. Galtseva on Berdyaev and Shestov), literary critics who had no specific theological training (I. Rodnyanskaya on Bulgakov), or scientists hostile to any mixture of reflection and revelation (S. Horuzhy on Bulgakov and Karsavin).

In continuity with the works of the Soviet authors Saveliev[47] and V. Kuvakin,[48] Galtseva, in an essay on Berdyaev, Shestov, and Florensky, criticized "Russian utopian thought."[49] In 1997, P. Gaidenko, of the Institute of Philosophy, published a compendium entitled *The Breakthrough towards the Transcendent*. After having criticized the mystical revolutionism of Berdyaev, which she did not hesitate to compare to the nihilism of Sartre, she expressed her preference for a new "Christian ontologism."[50] On a more serious level, in 1991, Horuzhy published an important book entitled *After the Pause: The Paths of Russian Philosophy*. Situating himself as the heir to the great tradition of pan-unity (*vseedinstvo*) "from Heraclitus to Bakhtin," he revived V. Lossky's criticism of Bulgakov. After plunging into the mysticism of Palamite hesychasm, he announced the advent of a new philosophy of "Orthodox energeticism" as a means of proving that the communist parenthesis of philosophy was definitively closed. In 1995, in collaboration with V. Bibihin, he published a collection in the same vein entitled *Synergy: Problems of Orthodox Asceticism and Mysticism*.[51] The first part was fittingly dedicated to John Meyendorff (1926–92). Without question, this group of authors had the merit of presenting the works of forgotten authors to the general public.

The roadblocks set up by certain philosophers against the religious thought of the Russian immigrant community, which they qualified as utopian or gnostic, did not prevent intellectuals from wanting to judge for themselves. The subterranean memory was nourished by the *samizdat* during the Soviet period. It was represented either by immigrants returning to their country, such as Mother Elena at Saint Petersburg or Fr. Boris Stark at Yaroslav, or by a certain number of intellectuals who had discovered the émigré philosophy during the 1970s (Y. Krotov, V. Poresh, A. Ogorodnikov). Above all, many were curious about this topic, which was sometimes forbidden, at other times denounced. All these factors led to an impressive editorial phenomenon throughout Russia: more than thirty authors of *The Way* were published (their most important books but also several sets of complete works) in Russia in the space of ten years, often for the first time, and—until the inflation of 1993—with an astronomical number of copies. Reviews such as *Voprossy Filosofii* published numerous texts of Frank, Bulgakov, and Vysheslavtsev. Particular note should be taken of the publication, in 1994, of a very detailed study by Evgeny Gollerbah on the generation of the authors who were united around the publishing house The Way during the period 1910–19.[52] The publishing house Respublika published an entire series of authors of *The Way* (Zenkovsky, Berdyaev, Bulgakov, N. Lossky). A significant number of copies were printed, especially when the subject matter was of general interest—eroticism, history, and the like—or when it was question of handbooks. Sixty thousand copies of *The Ethic of the Transfigured Eros* were printed in 1994. In 1990, a collection of articles entitled *The Russian Eros or the Philosophy of Love in Russia*, with contributions from Bulgakov, Karsavin, and Vysheslavtsev, along with pieces by Solovyov, Rozanov, and Merezhkovsky, sold 100,000 copies. *The History of Russian Philosophy* by N. Lossky sold 50,000 copies when it was first published in 1991, and it went through several subsequent editions. *An Essay on the History of Russian Philosophy* by Levitsky was also published. Like the works of Lossky and Zenkovsky, this book was written to criticize Soviet philosophy.[53] In 1994, the Russian Christian Institute of Human Sciences of St. Petersburg began publishing a very well received series entitled *Pro and Contra*. By publishing reviews both favorable and unfavorable of writers as admired as Rozanov, Florensky, and Berdyaev, these collections gave readers the opportunity to measure their distance from these authors. Several reviews sprang up that disseminated the thought of the authors of *The Way*, such as *Stupeni* and *Nachala*. But—like the rebuilding of the Cathedral of Christ the Savior in Moscow as a nearly identical replica of the original—a constructive critical distance towards Russian religious thought was lacking, and this impeded any attempt to allow a creative synthesis to see the light of day.

The most characteristic example of repetitious memory—as a mixture of fascination for the past of the immigration community and the incapacity to actualize this heritage—was the 1992 publication of the first six issues of *The Way* and the founding, by Yakovlev, of a journal with the same name as Berdyaev's in the hope of reviving the great tradition of Russian religious thought. The hopes of Yakovlev were never realized. The review did not sell and ceased to exist in 1997. In July 1996, Alexander Dobrokhotov, a professor of philosophy at the University of Moscow, published an article in *Esprit* in which he took stock, rather bitterly, of Russian philosophy in the past decade. He noted that the religious thought of the Silver Age, far from being surpassed, had simply not inserted itself into post-Soviet intellectual life. He wrote:

> The second illusion was to believe that the Russian philosophy of the Silver Age was going to be revived. This is a period which contained—and, indeed, still contains—an enormous potential which could serve as a platform for the future. It faced up to problems similar to the ones we are facing and discovered some excellent antidotes against the "demons" of its epoch, and this is why we spontaneously turned towards it. This impulse was shared by all the movements.... But, as in the legend, the weapon awaits the one who will show himself worthy of it.[54]

The Deployment of Post-Soviet Philosophy

With the ban on the Communist Party in 1991, and alongside the faddish popularity, mixed with reservations, for émigré religious philosophy, a threefold phenomenon in philosophical circles could be observed: an attraction to authors on the margins of official philosophy, an interest in cultural studies, and the discovery of the Western philosophy of the last fifty years. A great enthusiasm for the thought of Alexei Losev (1893–1988) and Merab Mamardashvili (1930–90) marked the period of 1990–94. Losev's *The Dialectic of Myth* was published in 1991 with a printing of 100,000 copies.[55] These two phenomenologists, who were known to have been persecuted during their careers, enjoyed quick success, but it was in circles that progressively distanced themselves during the 1990s.

Among the disciples of Losev can be found V. V. Bibihin, the translator of *Being and Time*, V. Molchanov, and S. Averintsev.[56] A. Ahutin, a student of Bakhtin who became the promoter of Bakhtin's philosophy of dialogue, deserves special mention. Ahutin, who was highly critical of the way the Russian immigration philosophers treated the philosophy of Kant, distinguished himself particularly in his edition of the works of Shestov. Moreover, the prestigious school of Tartu, directed by Yuri Lotman during the 1970s, was forming specialists in semiotics and culture, such as V. Toporov. Many literary critics banded together in the review *Arbor Mundi* and the weekly *NLO*. Mamardashvili, one of the members of a group of four that was active at the University of Moscow in the 1950s (the other three were A. Zinoviev, E. Ilyenkov, and G. Shedrovitsky), had a profound influence on intellectuals such as Yuri Senokosov. M. Ryklin and V. Podoroga, who were also influenced by the Georgian philosopher and were anxious to extract themselves from the provincialism into which Soviet philosophy had fallen, introduced the postmodernist perspective in Russia. Thanks especially to the publishing houses Ad Marginem and Gnosis, the Russian public became acquainted with the works of Derrida, Lacan, Deleuze, Baudrillard, and Foucault.

The review *Logos*, the organ of the Russian Phenomenological Society at the State University for Human Sciences, strove to reflect these three tendencies. It was founded in 1992 by a group of young philosophers who distanced themselves from religious philosophy and who were attracted by the thought of Husserl and Heidegger, as well as by that of Deleuze and Derrida (V. Anashvili, I. Chubarov, and others). It became progressively torn, however, by a conflict between the Germanophile current of pure phenomenology—represented by Molchanov—and a Francophile current, critical of reflexive thought, led by Ryklin and N. Avtonomova. In 1996 the review *Logos* published an article by Vladimir Malakhov that was very critical of the school of phenomenology and accused it of hiding, behind the controversial personality of Alexei Losev, the profound discontinuity between the Silver Age and the present.[57] As a sign of the times, in

1998, Chubarov published, through the publishing house Gnosis, a history of phenomenology in Russia (Gustav Shpet—but also Shestov and Lossky).

Attempts at a Synthesis

Based on a lengthy consideration of Russian religious thought and Western philosophy, several modern attempts at a synthesis of the two traditions can be discerned. One must keep in mind, first of all, that the criticism of Losev's work by the authors of *Logos* was, in certain respects, similar to the break between the authors of *The Way* and Platonic philosophy. On the other hand, an uncrossable line based on the experience of totalitarianism should not be drawn between Mamardashvili and Berdyaev, insofar as both of them evolved from Marxism towards Kant and Husserl.

One must also take into consideration the fact that certain works of the Russian religious thinkers became known only in recent decades. Be it the 1994 publication of Berdyaev's *The Beginning and the End: Essay on Eschatological Metaphysics* or Bulgakov's *The Philosophy of the Name*, republished in 1997, the publication of the most mature works of the émigré intellectuals took place slowly—probably because they were the least known.

More generally, the movement of dis-ontologization undertaken, in particular, by the students of Podoroga has something in common with the criticism of ontological metaphysics as expressed by Florovsky or Berdyaev. Imperceptibly, the postmodern Russian philosophers, like the young Derrida when he read *Athens and Jerusalem*, discovered the depth of Shestov's criticism.

Following a visit by Derrida to Moscow philosophers in 1993, the repeated visits of Paul Ricoeur—who had been a friend of Paul Evdokimov—to Moscow in 1995 and 1996, by invitation of the French University College of Moscow, and to Kiev in 1997, represented a growing awareness of the modernity of Russian philosophy's personalism. Certain young philosophers close to Sergei Averintsev, such as Konstantin Sigov at Kiev, tried to update the ethical teachings of Frank or Berdyaev by using Ricoeur's philosophy of testimony in *Oneself as Another* (1992). The contemporary mythological reflection of Stanislas Breton, a friend of Althusser, Derrida, and Badiou, on the philosophy of the Cross is not unfamiliar to Russian or Ukrainian religious philosophy.

Moreover, a certain number of contemporary issues in Russia, such as the question of the relationship between secular governance and religion [*laïcité*] and the foundations and practice of law by the state, led researchers in human sciences to consult their existing heritage. In 1993, *Russian Philosophy of Property (XVIII–XXth Century)* was published containing essays by Bulgakov, Berdyaev, Frank, and Stepun.[58] In 1995, Jurist Editions of Moscow published *History of Political and Legal Doctrines in Russia (XI–XXth Century)*, which situated the thought of Berdyaev, Fedotov, Kistyakovsky, and Novgorodtsev in the continuity of Russian history, from the eleventh-century "Sermon on Law and Grace" by Metropolitan Hilarion of Kiev to Trotsky's history of the Russian revolution.[59] On the literary terrain, there was the example of the works of Mochulsky, which were only discovered in 1995 but which brought about an important renewal in the traditional criticism of the writings of Gogol, Dostoevsky, and Solovyov. The poet Natalia Strizhevskaya, citing the literary critics of the immigration, tries to bring together the formalist criticism of the word (*slovo*) of Yuri Tynianov and Bakhtin and the Christian revelation of glory (*slava*).[60] Olga Sedakova, one of the most brilliant contemporary poets, also tries to find a synthesis between her Christian faith and her openness to Western culture.

Last, the introduction of the history of Russian thought into school and university programs, alongside the general history of world philosophy, brought about the questioning of the myth that national thought was hermetically sealed off from the rest of the world. Beginning in 1996, several courses of lectures on the history of Russian philosophy appeared in university curricula, as well as encyclopedias, which, by force of these new circumstances, placed the two intellectual traditions side by side. In 1996–98, the Soros Foundation financed authors from the Institute of Philosophy to edit a new manual for students on the history of philosophy. The last volume, written by N. Motroshilova, N. Gromov, and J. Melih, sought to place the work of Berdyaev, Shestov, Novgorodtsev, N. Lossky, Frank, and Karsavin within the great movements of twentieth-century thought (phenomenology, philosophy of life [Dilthey, Bergson], psychoanalysis, and others).[61] Certain young philosophers, such as A. Kozyrev, a veteran of the review *Logos*, who specialized in Solovyov, began to publish comparative studies of European and Russian philosophy. This integration of Russian religious thought into academic programs boosted research. At Kiev a society of Russian philosophy, which originated in the Institute of Philosophy of the Academy of Sciences, organized a colloquium on Berdyaev in March 1999. More than one hundred researchers from various Ukrainian universities attended this event.

THE DEVELOPMENT OF MEMORY IN FRANCE

In the West, the evolution of the memory of the authors of *The Way* followed a logic that was simultaneously historical and political, social, institutional and generational, and, finally, personal and spiritual. The emigration milieu, because it had to preserve its very existence, was central to the conservation and transmission of Russian religious thought. But it was not the only such milieu. Certain intellectuals who were heirs of the interwar culture and certain universities and institutions, as well as ecumenical structures, cultivated the memory of the Russian intellectuals. We will concentrate, however, on the milieu of the Russian emigration in France because, first, it was the origin of *The Way*; second, because the mythical aspect of memory-keeping is particularly visible within a mnemonic community relatively united through institutions; and finally, because the émigré community was, in one way or another, in contact with other memorial networks. But the work of certain researchers, such as T. Schipflinger[62] and F. Polyakov in Germany,[63] T. Spidlik in Italy,[64] H. Matsuguchi in Japan,[65] Georges Nivat in Switzerland,[66] and Marc Raeff in the United States,[67] shows that the study of the thought of the authors of *The Way* is a worldwide phenomenon. According to events, cultural circumstances, and personalities, the memory of the work of Berdyaev, Shestov, and Frank has been refreshed at the end of the twentieth century. Questions must now be asked concerning the meaning and consequences of this revival of remembrance.

Remembrance of Russian Religious Thought
Prior to Russian Independence

The emigration, as a homogeneous cultural milieu, disappeared little by little, and, as it did, the memory of Russian religious thought, which was still active in the 1960s, progressively shrank during the 1980s. Certain institutions that played a role in the beginning, such as the Russian Student Christian Movement, the YMCA Press—whose facilities were transferred to the RSCM after the war by Paul Anderson—and the St. Sergius Institute, managed to maintain themselves until the breakup of the Soviet Union. In collaboration with other vectors of Russian immigrant culture, such as the weekly *Russian Thought*, the different youth movements, and certain Orthodox dioceses, they contributed to orienting the memory of religious thought in three directions: the deepening of the spiritual heritage of Orthodoxy, ecumenical and social engagement, and contacts with the USSR.

Immediately after the war, these institutions sought to ensure their own survival by regularly reviving the memory of their origins and freeing themselves from the past through a long grieving process. At the St. Sergius Institute, after the death of Zenkovsky, the course on the history of Russian philosophy was assumed by Constantin Elchaninov and then by Dimitri Shakhovskoy. Several colloquiums on Bulgakov, Mother Maria, and Shestov were organized at Bièvres and later at Montgeron. Progressively, during these conferences, the RSCM gave a greater importance to the spiritual dimension of its philosophical heritage than to its national dimension and thereby prepared its members to focus on the reality of the Orthodox Church in France.

On this score, the Moscow diocese, which integrated the Fraternity of St. Irenaeus and the heritage of the movement begun by Fr. Lev Gillet and Vladimir Lossky in favor of a French-speaking Orthodox Church, was well in advance. Immediately after the liberation, Vladimir Lossky (d. 1958) and Evgraph Kovalevsky began to teach dogmatic theology and church history in French at the Institut Saint-Denis, which, until 1953, belonged to the patriarchate of Moscow. Vladimir Lossky brought G. Marcel, M.-M. Davy, and Dom Lambert Beauduin to Saint Denis.[68] In 1949, Jean Balzon, a layman and lawyer who was interested in theology, founded—after the end of the adventure with the journal *Dieu vivant*—the review *Contacts*. This review, after it was "refounded" in 1959 by Elisabeth Behr-Sigel, Boris Bobrinskoy, Lev Gillet, and Olivier Clément, would assume the heritage of *The Way* as regards religious philosophy.

In 1953, former students of St. Sergius Institute, who had been influenced by Zander and Zenkovsky as well as by Alexander Schmemann and John Meyendorff, founded Syndesmos, the World Fellowship of Orthodox Youth. This organization promulgated the ideas of the interwar period in many countries—in particular, Lebanon, Finland, and the United

States. In 1955, Paul Evdokimov (1900–1970), a former student of Bulgakov and Berdyaev and later a professor at St. Sergius, founded, in conjunction with Zander and Clément, a center for Orthodox studies in French. In the 1960s, the jurisdictional wounds of the past became less important. In 1963, on the initiative of Cyrille Elchaninov and with the active support of Clément, Fr. Cyrille Argenti, Nicholas V. Lossky (the son of Vladimir Lossky), and Fr. Pierre Struve, the Coordinating Committee of Orthodox Youth was founded. The Orthodox Fraternity of Western Europe grew out of this initiative. From Annecy in 1971 to Dijon in 1974, Amiens in 1977, and Paray-le-Monial in 1999, the reality of a local Orthodox Church in France is emerging.

The heritage of religious thought was diffused in ecumenical circles thanks to the presence of personalities such as Florovsky and Zander within the authority structure of the World Council of Churches, which, since 1948, had its headquarters in Geneva. After the war, these two former writers for *The Way* were at odds with one another over the road to follow in ecumenical dialogue. Florovsky, even though he held an important position in the World Council, could only see a return of wayward sons and daughters to the Orthodox Church. Zander, for his part, published a short work entitled *Western Orthodoxy*[69] in which he favored a spiritual coming together, outside of all institutional links. He referred to an Orthodoxy "outside of church walls." The year 1963 marked the beginning of a period full of spectacular gestures—notably, the proclamation of the lifting of the anathemas between the Catholic Church and the Orthodox Church and the exchange of the kiss of peace between Pope Paul VI and Ecumenical Patriarch Athenagoras I. It is well known that the Greek Patriarch, who knew Bulgakov personally, was very appreciative of Russian religious thought. In regard to Catholics, significant roles were played by Afanasiev and Evdokimov, who were summoned as official observers to the third session of Vatican II, and by Olivier Clément, who communicated Orthodox spirituality and religious philosophy in the French media. Boris Bobrinskoy—relying, in large part, on the theses of Bulgakov concerning the Holy Spirit resting on the Son—contributed to ending the very ancient polemic over the *Filioque.*

To be sure, Russian religious thought was subject to theological criticism, as witnessed, for example, by Jean-Louis Segundo's demolition of the "apophatic ontology" of Berdyaev in 1963.[70] All the same, in reviews like *Irénikon* or *Istina*, or at the Institut Supérieur d'Études Oecuméniques (ISEO) at the Institut Catholique de Paris, Russian religious thought was the subject of numerous commentaries. Thanks to the translations of Constantin Andronikov, certain authors such as Louis Bouyer, Hans Urs von Balthasar, and Cardinal Daniélou popularized the ideas of Bulgakov among Catholics and drew parallels with the sophiology of Teilhard de Chardin.

With respect to Protestants, Zander and Evdokimov were intermediaries in passing on the ideas of Russian religious thought, the former through organizations such as the World Student Christian Federation, the latter through the Institute of Ecumenical Studies at Bossey and through CIMADE, an ecumenical commission dedicated to the reception of refugees, on whose behalf he directed a student hostel at Sèvres. In 1970, Éditions du Cerf published Paul Evdokimov's book *Le Christ dans la pensée russe* (*Christ in Russian Thought*). The volume carefully examined Russian Christology, both as it derived from the Eastern patristic tradition and in its continuity with the thought of St. Sergius of Radonezh and Solovyov. Evdokimov distinguished three well-defined strands: religious philosophy, neo-patristic theology, and Eucharistic ecclesiology.[71]

The attraction of certain Protestant movements to Marxism in the 1970s led the Russian Student Christian Movement to break off its ties to the World Student Christian Federation. In the 1980s, the ecumenical movement became more theologically oriented. N. Lossky, Clément, Fr. Bobrinskoy, and Fr. Michel Evdokimov participated in mixed committees organized between the Orthodox Church, on the one hand, and Catholics and Protestants, on the other. These meetings were at the origin of a certain number of texts, such as BEM (Baptism, Eucharist, and Ministry), the World Council of Church's Faith and Order document that was signed at Lima in 1982. The dialogue between the Orthodox Churches and the pre-Chalcedonian Churches, which began in 1964 and became official in 1985, took place in this context and drew inspiration from the theological revival inspired by the Paris School.

In addition, the institutions of the émigré community, with a great deal of resolve, turned their attention towards Russia. In 1961, after spending some time in Russia, Cyrille Elchaninov, the general secretary of the Russian Student Christian Movement, set up a foundation called Aid for the Faithful of the USSR. He put into place an underground network to distribute within Russia books of religious thought (e.g., works of Berdyaev, Florovsky, Schmemann) and writings by dissidents (e.g., I. Ogurtsov, A. Ogorodnikov, V. Popkov). These new opportunities for contact with Russian citizens, made possible by the "Thaw," encouraged the younger members of the RSCM to promote culture.[72] In 1966, Nikita Struve, the editor of the RSCM *Vestnik*, joined forces with E. Barabanov and transformed his slim publication into a thick review, which published all the contemporary religious thinking of the immigration community as well as that of Soviet dissidents. In 1969 he began publishing Solzhenitsyn, and the following year he received Solzhenitsyn's novel *August 1914*. On December 28, 1973, the YMCA Press published *The Gulag Archipelago*, with a first edition of 50,000 copies—an astronomical number, far surpassing anything else published by the émigré community. The shock caused by this publication is well known—notably, for certain new philosophers such as A. Glucksmann and B.-H. Lévy.

The YMCA Press received a fresh infusion of life from the Soviet Union by publishing not only other works of Solzhenitsyn but also those of V. Shalamov, N. Mandelshtam, and J. Dombrovsky. *Russian Thought*, which regularly published authors of *The Way* such as N. Lossky, Veidlé, and Ilyin, also received a new breath of life when, in the 1960s, it added dissidents such as A. Ginzburg and M. Heller to its editorial board. In the 1980s, the weekly, under the direction of I. Illovayskaya-Alberti, along with other organs of the press such as The Orthodox Press Service, founded by Jean Tchekan, and the publications of the RSCM, contributed to informing the West about the dissidents and the religious persecutions in the USSR. Most important, Soviet citizens were able to have access to religious thought thanks to certain radio broadcasts such as *The Voice of Orthodoxy*, founded by B. Bobrinskoy, and *Radio Liberty*, in which Veidlé and Schmemann participated. In 1990, for the seventieth anniversary of the publishing house of the Rue de la Montagne Sainte Geneviève, the *Vestnik RKhD*, the oldest review of the immigration community, was published in Russia. At the same time, about 30,000 copies of *Russian Thought* were distributed in Russia.

In France, Russian religious thought had trouble integrating itself into the intellectual forum after the war, due to the deep tradition of secularity (*laïcité*) that distinguishes the public sphere from the religious sphere. All the same, in the topography of the intellectual landscape, the shadow of the authors of *The Way* is always present. The memory of Russian religious thought has, first of all, marked French territory—be it by the cemetery of Sainte Geneviève-des-Bois, the Berdyaev museum at Clamart, or the different onion-domed churches in Paris or in the provinces. The Orthodox Church also makes use of radio and television programs carried by national channels. These broadcasts have played a major role in the diffusion of the heritage of Russian religious thinking. Finally, from P. Kovalevsky to C. Goussev and M. Gorbov, the émigrés and their descendents carefully preserved the memory of a country "which does not appear on any map."[73]

Certain secular institutions of education and research, such as the Institut d'Études Slaves, the Institut des Langues Orientales, the Institut d'Études Politiques de Paris (IEP), and the École des Hautes Études en Sciences Sociales, with their reviews—notably, *Notes on the Russian and Soviet World*—also played an important role in transmitting information and ideas. The first major colloquium dedicated to Russian thought took place at Aix-en-Provence in 1968. The conference enjoyed a number of distinguished guests, such as O. Clément, P. Pascal, J. Scherrer, and N. Struve. The authors of *The Way* were commonly characterized as intellectuals who had passed from Marxism to idealism, as clearly found in the works of Pierre Pascal,[74] of Guy Planty-Bonjour,[75] and of A. Besançon.[76]

The Institut d'Études Slaves published bibliographies of the works of Lossky, Frank, Berdyaev, and Bulgakov as well as a certain number of bibliographies of the reviews of the émigré community and studies on Berdyaev and Shestov. Jean-Claude Marcadé, the secretary of the Association of the Friends of Berdyaev, organized a colloquium on Berdyaev in 1975. At the École des Hautes Études en Sciences Sociales, Jutta Scherrer, a former student of Florovsky, dedicated a large number of her seminars to the study of Russian thought. At the Institut des Langues Orientales, Cyrille Elchaninov gave a course on the history of Russian civilization, which led many students to discover the thought of Berdyaev and Bulgakov. Both at the Institut d'Études Politiques as well as in her own writings, Hélène Carrère d'Encausse was especially attentive to the liberal current in the history of Russian political theory.

A number of publishers contributed to the dissemination of Russian religious thought. After the war, Gallimard published translations of Veidlé (*La Russie absente et présente*) in 1949, of Berdyaev (*Les sources et le sens du communisme russe*) in 1951, and of Zenkovsky (*Histoire de la philoso-

phie russe) in 1953. In the 1970s and 1980s, the publishing house L'Age d'Homme continued this trend by publishing Andronikov's translation of the works of Bulgakov. Desclée de Brouwer and Éditions du Cerf also published authors such as Berdyaev, Florovsky, and Vladimir Lossky. These publications were often prepared and commented upon by a certain number of *passeurs*, cross-cultural "translators." Among those who commented on Shestov were Gabriel Matzneff, Boris de Schloezer, Vladimir Jankelevitch, and Yves Bonnefoy. Those who continued the heritage of the review *Esprit* and of Berdyaev's personalism counted among their number the personalist philosopher Jean Lacroix,[77] Marie-Madeleine Davy,[78] Olivier Clément—who edited whole series of studies for the review *Contacts*— and Henri Corbin, the president of the Association of the Friends of Berdyaev ("what we owe to him ... was, above all, the discovery of sophiology").[79] André Fontaine, the editor of the well-known daily *Le Monde*, was particularly sensitive to the thesis of the author of *The Origin of Russian Communism*. For his part, Maurice de Gandillac, a friend of Frank, Vladimir Lossky, Koyré, and Berdyaev, popularized the neo-Platonic current of Russian religious philosophy through the colloquiums of Cerisy and Chantilly.[80]

The Remembrance of Religious Thought from 1991 Onwards

Russia's accession to independence and the collapse of the Communist Party were considered a victory by the immigration community. YMCA Press quickly created a Franco-Russian publishing house, Russkii Put', directed by V. Moskvin, which published, directly within Russia, a certain number of works by Bulgakov, Berdyaev, and others. In nearly a hundred Russian cities and towns, the YMCA Press, in collaboration with the French embassy, opened libraries of religious philosophy. Thus, for example, the mayor of Livny, Bulgakov's hometown, announced in June 1996 that the Square of the Proletariat would henceforth be named after Bulgakov.[81] Through A. Bogoslovsky, the correspondent of *Vestnik RKhD* in Russia, the YMCA renewed contact with B. Pliuhanov and V. Miliutina, the wife of I. Lagovsky, and, through them, with the heritage of the Russian Student Christian Movement in the Baltic countries.

The Aid for the Faithful of the USSR, now known as Aid for the Christians of Russia, reorganized its activities by developing aid programs focusing on plans both for training and for social and humanitarian help.

Moreover, it continued to inform Western public opinion about the religious and social evolution of Russia. There were several organizations, such as the AREP, an émigré association of businessmen with Russian backgrounds, which had a subsidiary of expatriates in the Commonwealth of Independent States (former Soviet republics). The weekly newspaper *Russian Thought* opened offices in Moscow, and its editorial board underwent an important renewal by adding authors who were living in Russia. It reported regularly on new publications in the domain of religious philosophy.

The crisis of 1994–96 between the patriarchate of Constantinople and the patriarchate of Moscow concerning the jurisdiction of Estonian parishes disgusted the immigration community. It quickly quieted down, however. Mindful of the fruitless postwar initiatives by Metropolitan Evlogy to reconcile with the patriarchate of Moscow, Metropolitan Sergius, the archbishop of the Russian diocese under the Ecumenical Patriarchate of Constantinople, tried to approach Alexis II. In 1996, the two religious leaders concelebrated in Moscow. At the same time, a "Metropolitan Evlogy Association," composed of laity and priests, was created in France to support a return to the jurisdiction of the Moscow patriarchate. Simultaneously, in other segments of the immigration community, the rediscovery of the figure of Mother Maria Skobtsova encouraged some émigrés, along with some Catholics and Protestants, to ask that she be canonized by the Orthodox Church. But in Russia, although certain individuals such as Father Ekonomtsev favored this action, the majority of the episcopate was thinking more about canonizing the imperial family. [Editor's note: In May 2004, Mother Maria and her companions, Fr. Dimitrii Klepinin, her son Yuri, and Ilya Fondaminsky, were proclaimed martyr saints by the Ecumenical Patriarchate of Constantinople in the same cathedral of St. Alexander Nevsky on rue Daru where they had prayed.]

After a period of tension in the early 1990s in Catholic-Orthodox relations, some ecumenical initiatives were taken. Following a voyage to Russia in 1993 by Bishop Gerard Daucourt, the head of ecumenical relations for the French bishops' conference, the Benedictine monastery of Sainte Esperance at Mesnil-Saint-Loup, near Troyes, edited a series of texts on ecumenical agreements in conjunction with the Orthodox monastery of the Nativity of the Mother of God at Bobrenevo, near Kolomna. Several monasteries, such as Chevetogne and, above all, Taizé, received a great number of visitors from Russia. The review *Simvol*, run by the Jesuits of

Meudon, put out previously unpublished texts of religious philosophy such as "Beneath the Walls of Chersonese" by Bulgakov.[82] Four books by Olivier Clément were rapidly translated into Russian (*Conversations with Patriarch Athenagoras, The Roots of Christian Mysticism, The Way of the Cross to Rome,* and *You Are Peter: An Orthodox Reflection on the Exercise of Papal Primacy*). In the spring of 1995, John Paul II asked the Pontifical Council for Christian Unity to "clarify" the traditional doctrine of the *Filioque* in such a way that it would be in "complete harmony with what the Ecumenical Council of Constantinople, in 381, confesses in its symbol: the Father as the source of the whole Trinity, the sole origin of the Son and the Holy Spirit."[83] Then, on May 25, 1995, the pope signed an encyclical, *Ut Unum Sint,* dedicated to ecumenism and calling for a fraternal dialogue with the Orthodox Sister-Church on the exercise of his ministry. But this warming of relations stumbled upon the question of the Greek-Catholic Church in the Ukraine.

At the World Council of Churches, Ion Bria, George Lemopoulos, and Todor Sabev published, during the 1990s, several works in which the writings of Russian thinkers such as Florovsky, Evdokimov, Lossky, and Mother Maria were given prominence.[84] In 1995, the World Student Christian Federation celebrated its centenary and rendered homage to Evdokimov, Zander, and Bulgakov, among others. The World Council of Churches also organized missions in Russia, notably from the perspective of preparing for the WCC general assembly in Harare, Zimbabwe, in 1998. Konrad Raiser, the general secretary of the World Council, accompanied by N. V. Lossky (as noted above, son of Vladimir Lossky, and a scholar on the ecumenical movement), was received rather coldly at the Moscow Theological Academy in Sergiev Posad when he visited in 1997. He was thus able to see for himself that ecumenical progress, realized in the West thanks to the intellectuals of the Paris School, was far from being fully received by the Russian bishops.

These contacts with Russia gave a new vitality to the study of religious thought in France. In 1990–91 alone, two books on Berdyaev appeared.[85] In 1993, Pastor Laurent Gagnebin again published a work on the editor of *The Way*. The originality of Olivier Clément's *Berdiaev: Un philosophe russe en France* consisted, notably, in the attention he gave, based on certain articles of Berdyaev in "that great journal of the Russian emigration, *Put,*"[86] to the encounter and collaboration between French and Russian émigré thought during the 1925–50 period.

Today, when not only economic relations but also cultural and spiritual relations have resumed between France and Russia, where Europe, whose roots are above all Christian—although not exclusively so—ought to integrate both its east and its west, it seems to me that Berdyaev has much to say to us. Along with others, but playing a principal role, his thought, which had become secret even in Russia itself, has contributed to the fall of the colossus with feet of clay.... The thought of Nicolas Berdyaev is a creative spirituality, it is a vision of the divine-humanity which opens us, with the correct criteria ("without separation, without confusion"), to all experiences of the divine and to all human experience, in the light of faces that are already iconic. The perspective then grows wider; it is no longer European but planetary. It does not separate the "hand of God" from that of humanity, the "light" of critical reason from the light of the Transfiguration. It is an "all-embracing torrent, a dynamic creativity in liberty."[87]

In 1991 the French translation of the *Life of Lev Shestov* was published by La Différence, as well as the first volume of Florovsky's *The Ways of Russian Theology*, which was put out by Desclée de Brouwer. The following year, Gallimard republished Zenkovsky's *The History of Russian Philosophy*. Other publications concerning the Russian émigré community and the authors of *The Way* appeared, such as the biography of Lev Gillet by Elisabeth Behr-Sigel, a collection of Mother Maria's texts, *Le sacrement du frère* (published by Le Sel de la Terre in 1995), and Vladimir Lossky's memoir, *Sept jours sur les routes de France* (published by Éditions du Cerf in 1998). Finally, C. Andronikov succeeded in publishing his translations (some of which had been completed since the end of the war) of the principal works of Bulgakov. As a preface to the translation of *The Comforter*, which appeared for the first time in French in 1996, Andronikov invited the writer Vladimir Volkov to give his opinion. Volkov wrote that Bulgakov "is the modern theologian *par excellence* because—and he was criticized enough for it—he does not limit theology to patristics.... Bulgakov's theory of Sophia ... is a hardy and promising hypothesis."[88]

In the domain of inter-university exchanges and research, a certain number of initiatives in the 1990s revived the study of Russian religious thought. In 1992 a Research Group on the Russian Immigration (GRER), headed by Nikita Struve, was founded in Paris at the Institute of Research and Studies on the New Eastern Institutions and Societies. In 1993, in conjunction with the MSH (Maison des Sciences de l'Homme) and the Academy of Sciences in Russia, the GRER organized a vast congress in Moscow on the cultural heritage of the Russian immigration. It also organized a colloquium on Shestov in 1993, on Berdyaev in 1998, and on the historians of the Russian immigration in 1999. With the help of a branch in Russia directed by L. Mnuhin, it launched a project to publish an extended chronology of the Russian immigration. The final volume appeared in 1997. Among Slavists, Michel Evdokimov and Georges Nivat referred to the authors of *The Way* on several occasions.[89] Mention should also be made of the initiative of P. de Laubier and B. Dupire, who, in 1991, founded a Vladimir Solovyov Society, which organized several conferences in France, Switzerland, and Russia on Russian religious thought. Among the French who participated could be found Father F. Rouleau, B. Marchadier, J. de Proyart, and M. Dennes,[90] while Russians were represented by E. Genieva, I. Vinogradov, and N. Kotreliov. Four years later, Frances Nethercott published her thesis on early twentieth-century Russian reception of Bergson's thought.[91] The Solovyov Society published several works that included French and Russian intellectuals.[92] Beginning in 1994, the Solovyov Society organized an annual seminar at the MSH on Russian religious philosophy with the participation of young French intellectuals. In their manifesto of 1994, the founders of the Solovyov Society wrote:

> During the last seventy-five years, the Christians of Russia have, in their flesh, paid the price of that liberty which is not a return to economic liberalism nor even that of the exigencies of democracy; it is above all the price of a liberty which they have professed and reclaimed in the *samizdat* by invoking and citing the names of Solovyov, Bulgakov, and Berdyaev. Such is the price of a liberty which they intend to share today with other Christians, an "ecumenical" liberty in the strongest sense of the word.[93]

The Waning of the Emigration and the Implications of a School of Thought

The emigration community progressively realized that the demise of the USSR meant, at the same time, the end of the emigration—or at least, the end of the spiritual and political significance of the post-revolutionary emigration. This historic questioning of the identity of the émigré community paralyzed some people.[94] One after the other, various émigré institutions commemorated the anniversaries of their foundation or the anniversaries of the deaths of authors of *The Way*[95] by organizing jubilees and publishing commemorative brochures.[96] Nikita Struve published his *70 ans de l'émigration russe* with Fayard in 1996. In all such cases, the past was scrutinized for signs of what the future would bring, or there was a collective questioning of the ways to realize, in the present situation, a spiritual and incarnate heritage, a social heritage that did not reject the church hierarchy, that was ecumenical yet faithful to tradition.

The waning of the emigration is linked to the horizon of the future of the Orthodox Church in France. The Orthodox Church in France since 1996 is organized theoretically as an assembly of autonomous bishops, and each of the representatives of the different jurisdictions (Greek, Russian, Romanian, Serbian) continues to depend on his church of origin. The consequence of this situation is that, in practice, the Orthodox Church in France has only a sacramental unity. Because of internal rivalries, often nationalistic, the Orthodox Church has been incapable of uniting its forces in ecclesial practice (social, missionary, ecumenical, and so forth) and is, at present, incapable of offering possibilities for development to its younger members. Moreover, the conservative hardening of the Russian Church constitutes a genuine obstacle to the vague desire to leave the "Greek Church." Therefore the waning of the ecclesial organization, as it was elaborated provisionally between the two wars, is accompanied by renewed reflection on the nature and boundaries of the church, and this is happening on the basis of discussions that took place between Bulgakov, Florovsky, and Afanasiev in the 1930s.

To be sure, this new incarnation, which the Orthodox Church must bring about, is not unrelated to its rapport with the Catholic Church, whose primacy has always been recognized in principle, and whose jurisdiction over French territory has been respected to the point that the Orthodox Church has not erected an episcopate in Paris. Here, too, the most advanced ecclesiological reflection on the ecumenical movement is still probably that found in the dialogue between Berdyaev, Bulgakov, and Florovsky. Olivier Clément, in his *You Are Peter: An Orthodox Reflection on the Exercise of Papal Primacy*, explicitly discusses concrete steps towards a reunion of the Catholic Church and the Orthodox Church, with respect for the spiritualities and practices of each confession. Clément, moreover, realizes a personal synthesis of the work of the Russian religious philosophers representing the neo-patristic line of thought. Neo-patristic reflection, exemplified by Lossky, Florovsky, and Meyendorff, has an apophatic vision of the Trinity, which does not allow for imagining the church otherwise than according to the mode of division among Christian confessions and which makes a distinction between Eucharistic communities and episcopal institutions; in contrast, the cataphatic and eschatological vision of the Kingdom as already present, of God as Tri-Hypostatic Person, revealing himself as Father, Son, and Holy Spirit, allows for imagining together the three traditional definitions of the Church (Body of Christ, Temple of the Holy Spirit, and House of the Father). For Clément, the divine unity refers not to a neutral essence but to the Person of the Father. At a time when the World Council of Churches is trying to reform itself, when the Roman pontiff is questioning the way his authority is exercised in the Catholic Church, and when the Orthodox Churches, confronted with modernity and secularization, are passing through a profound identity crisis, the vision of the church reformulated by Clément as a "Unique Humanity in a multitude of persons" opens new perspectives.

The second aspect of the waning of the emigration concerns the Russian Church. The Paris School played a considerable role in the evolution of the dogmatics and practice of the émigré Orthodox Church. The anti-Semitic tradition of the Fathers of the Church was denounced and criticized. The practice of the sacraments, from confession to baptism, was renewed. The Eucharistic movement brought clergy and laity closer together and invited the latter, men and women, to a more active participation in liturgical life. The belief that Slavonic is a sacred language was refuted in theory and in practice. Today, however, in the Russian Church, these acquisitions of religious reflection are being threatened, perhaps more seriously than in the era of stagnation. Or, to put it differently, the Russian Church continues to live according to the rhythm of the Julian calendar without knowing how to integrate the movement of history with the preservation of the riches of its tradition.[97] There is not yet sufficient perspective to write an objective history of the resistance, when "people of good will, not heroes in the style of James Bond, but modest people"[98] participated in the liberation of minds in the USSR. In Russia, the *passeurs*, the transmitters of this history of resistance (G. Kotchetkov, A. Kyrlezhev, and others) are targets of attack by religious authorities. In France, the heirs of the defunct Russian immigration continue to mobilize, but with a view to avoiding auto-da-fés and excommunications. In 1997 certain intellectuals, such as N. Struve, J. Tchekan, and N.V. Lossky, asked Patriarch Alexy to lift the interdict on Kotchetkov, but nothing came of this. Shortly afterwards, the patriarch himself was challenged by Clément and the Canadian historian Dimitry Pospelovsky. In this context, the discreet and indispensable labor of numerous groups of Christians, without any other means, as realized in such works as the foundation Aid for the Christians of Russia, is particularly important. As an observer of religious life in Russia, the foundation is able to detect the dynamic and tolerant sectors and point out the activities of conservative groups to Western public opinion. But this is becoming less the responsibility of the immigration community as such and more the responsibility of all those who cherish liberty of conscience and the integration of the countries of the former Soviet Union into the concert of the secular and democratic European nations.

The final implication of the current commemorations of the immigration is of an intellectual, philosophical, and theological order. A certain number of works published in Russia, either unknown in France—such as Bulgakov's *The Tragedy of Philosophy*—or by contemporary philosophers—such as Losev's *The Dialectic of Myth*—are new evidence of the modernity of a profoundly mytho-logical reflection. The rediscovery of the diversity in the heritage of émigré religious thought by a young generation of Orthodox intellectuals makes possible the realization that, behind the façade of the unanimous celebration of the Paris School, lies a hidden skepticism as to the very possibility of religious reflection. Moreover, this rediscovery of Russian religious thought reveals a certain number of "white spots" (to use Soviet terminology) in the history of the neo-Palamite development of Orthodox theology. Whether it was the question of the polemic concerning Sophia or the rejection of Berdyaev's personalist ecclesiology, today it is clear that it cost dearly to arrive at the myth of the indivisible unity of the tradition of Orthodox thought. But as Clément wrote, the distance between Vladimir Lossky and Bulgakov, amplified by the polemic spirit of the 1930s, is not insurmountable. Moreover, a certain number of lively debates during the last ten years over such issues

The Development of Memory in France 565

as the reorganization of ecumenical institutions, the place of women in the church, Christian responsibility for the environment, or the question of the rapport between ethics and religion show that the theology of the uncreated energies does not have the answer to everything. And, above all, just as neo-Thomism and Barthianism have long since become outmoded in Christian intellectual milieus, similarly, fears of Gnosticism and the apophatic wall found among Orthodox theologians also now appear outdated.

Silently, in fact, certain movements of contemporary thought are converging towards Russian mytho-logical reflection, to the point that D. Janicaud could denounce "the theological tendency of French phenomenology,"[99] which began with the publication of Emmanuel Lévinas's *Totalité et infini* in 1961. At the end of the 1980s, the hidden affinities between the works of Shestov and Lévinas were discovered. Marie-Anne Lescourret recalled in particular that as soon as he read Shestov's *Kierkegaard et la philosophie existentielle* in 1936, Lévinas had grasped the full implications of a reflection that "blew up the synthesis of the Greek spirit and the Judeo-Christian spirit which the Middle Ages thought it had realized."[100] In his intellectual autobiography published in 1995, the philosopher Paul Ricoeur wrote: "If the time is given to me, I have the imperative to confront head on the question ... of the conflictive-consensual relationship between my philosophy, without an absolute, and my biblical faith, which has been nourished more by exegesis than theology."[101] At the height of his fame and without abandoning the purely philosophical perspective, Ricoeur proceeded to explore new possibilities. The editor of the *Revue de métaphysique et de morale* confirmed this new orientation of his research in 1998 with the publication of *Thinking Biblically*, coauthored with André Lacocque, in which both authors interpret key passages of the Hebrew Bible.[102]

On the theological level, the 1998 encyclical of John Paul II, *Fides et Ratio*, gave an unexpected legitimacy to Russian sophiology. Having taken up again the question of the relations between faith and reason, a topic not treated at this level since the 1879 encyclical of Leo XIII, *Aeterni Patris*, the pope-philosopher invoked, for the first time, the "great philosophical and theological tradition" incarnated in particular, "in an Eastern context," by names such as "Vladimir S. Soloviev, Pavel A. Florensky, Petr Chaadaev and Vladimir N. Lossky."[103] "To be consonant with the word of God, philosophy needs first of all to recover its *sapiential dimension* as a search for the ultimate and overarching meaning of life. This first requirement is in fact most helpful in stimulating philosophy to conform to its proper nature."[104] The pope concluded by identifying the relationships of the Virgin, the throne or seat of Wisdom, and of Christ with those of philosophy and theology: "Just as the Virgin was called to offer herself entirely as human being and as woman that God's Word might take flesh and come among us, so too philosophy is called to offer its rational and critical resources that theology, as the understanding of faith, may be fruitful and creative. . . . May Mary, Seat of Wisdom, be a sure haven for all who devote their lives to the search for wisdom."[105]

It can also be briefly pointed out that the "present humanization of the social sciences" in France, noticed by François Dosse and based on interdisciplinarity, intersubjectivity, and ethical concern, corresponds to the anthropocentric movement of the philosophies of Frank and Berdyaev. The work of two contemporary sociologists, Luc Boltanski and Laurent Thévenot, transmitters in France of the American debate over John Rawls and his theory of the foundations of justice, is a perfect illustration of this movement. L. Boltanski and L. Thévenot, in their book *De la justification: Les économies de la grandeur*, published in 1991, present the break with the critical sociology of Durkheim and Weber in the 1970s as a given.[106] The object of sociology is no longer the presupposed background world to the acts of "agents in the social field" but is rather the world itself. As Éric Vigne writes in *L'Essai*, "what becomes constitutive of the person is no longer just his ability to live in several worlds, but also of being able to live there in conflicts, in the name of the desire for justice, and to elaborate compromises within it."[107] This echoes Berdyaev's preoccupation with placing the "dignity of the person" at the heart of sociological reflection and practical wisdom, orthopraxis, as the foundation stone of modern justice. To be sure, there is no explicit reference to divine-humanity, as Solovyov understood it, in the works of Thévenot and Boltanski. Similarly, when Jean-Pierre Vernant, in his 1996 autobiography, described how much his research on Greek antiquity and his political engagement (which led him to Russia, where he met Mamardashvili) was influenced by the place of myth in history, he excluded any religious interpretation of his writings. All the same, as he himself wrote, "the feeling of being indebted remains."[108] As Olivier Mongin states, the dividing line is less about what distinguishes believers from others and more about what separates those who recognize "that there is a preliminary gift, a donation, an originating creation" from those who, among the heirs of Nietzsche, reject this perspective as alienating and "prefer the idea of a primordial chaos."[109] Through their evolution and their recognition of this gift to religious philosophy, Shestov and N. O. Lossky have much to say to the former. And by their criticism of the "last judgment" and of the patristic vision of hell—which Deleuze stigmatized as the "doctrine of judgment" and of the "infinite debt"—Berdyaev and Bulgakov have much to interest the latter.

Taking things from this point, certain Orthodox philosophers and theologians, recognizing that the "theological-political" is pervasive in French thought and aware of the dialogical dimension inherent in Russian religious reflection, are progressively leaving behind the hieratic and unshakeable image of the School of Paris and rediscovering the inspiration of the living tradition. Annick de Souzenelle, influenced by the thought of Berdyaev and Evgraph Kovalevsky, but also by the Kabbalah, rereads the Bible and Greek myths in order to offer, as much to exegetes as to psychologists, a new understanding of the human body and the masculine-feminine relationship.[110] Bertrand Vergely, professor of philosophy at the Institute for Political Studies, is another example of the vitality of contemporary Orthodox philosophical speculation. In 1997 he published a book on philosophical ethics with Gallimard Press entitled *La souffrance*. In recovering certain accents in the work of Michel Henry, he realizes a synthesis of Berdyaev's personalist anthropology, Bulgakov's sophiology, and Frank's philosophy of life to arrive at a reinvigorating hymn of creation. By working in centers of palliative medicine, Vergely also fulfills the wish of the younger generation of Zander, Lagovsky, and Mother Maria, who wanted to reconcile Orthodoxy and orthopraxis. He also echoes the interrogation of Russian mytho-logical thought on the origin of evil and suffering. He writes: "Between the forgetfulness of suffering due to our rationalizations of life and the forgetfulness of life because of our desperation when faced with suffering, there is the meaning of life in the face of suffering."[111] André Borrely, for his part, offers new ecclesiological perspectives.[112] Although he remains within the neo-patristic tradition, this French Orthodox theologian is shocked by the separation, in certain Orthodox milieus, between the proclamation of a doctrine which affirms that God acts (*energei*) outside of his own essence and the reality of a practice which forbids a cardinal to go beyond the narthex of an Eastern church! Echoing the sophiology of Bulgakov, the personalism of Berdyaev, and the ethics of Frank, he invites Christians to rediscover the purity of their tradition.

> This implies ... approaching this mystery of the Church more dynamically, without, however, conceding anything to minimalism or doctrinal relativism, closing the gap of imposture which too often separates "ortho-doxy" from "hetero-praxis"; it implies baptizing the world of the third millennium by living within it the silent but radiant testimony of the Christian faith in the divine Trinity and in humanity as image of the Trinity invited to the divine nuptial feast[,] ... revealing the possibility of uniting wisdom and science, reflection and life, knowledge and love: this would be, it seems to us, what is at stake in the effort of Christians towards unity in reconciled diversity.[113]

Having arrived at the end of this study, we can offer a tentative reply to the question of historical significance as formulated in the introduction to this volume.

The intellectual generation of the authors who contributed to *The Way* is a place of memory, a symbolic reality. The close study of the intellectuals of the review reveals a certain number of oppositions and conflicts within a generational conscience that was in perpetual redefinition. Moreover, while based on facts, the memory of the contribution of the Russian intelligentsia in exile has been deformed over the years by the historical factors that overtook it. All the same, there is a profound historical reality in the symbol of an "intellectual generation," first expressed in *The Way* by a modernist configuration, then a nonconformist one, and, finally, a spiritual one. Taken together, it represented the advent within the religious and cultural Orthodox tradition of a modern conscience that is ethical, mytho-logical, and ecumenical, an advent which, at the same time, is in continuity with patristic thought.

As Pierre Nora puts it, writing the history of memory is not the same as writing a history of the Fourth Republic. While distinguishing the past which no longer exists from the future which is yet to come, it is also enlightening to be aware of the permeability between the space of experience and the horizon of anticipation—to use Reinhart Koselleck's expression.[114] The history of *The Way*, the chronological and synthetic narrative of a generation, is, in itself, by itself, and for others, a testimony to the interpenetration between the two planes of being and existence. Whether it is a question about the period between the two wars—when Berdyaev, Florovsky, and Bulgakov were constantly reinventing the future of Russia, according to their generational experience—or about the present moment, when Russian and Western intellectuals search in the thesaurus of *The Way* for answers to the questions that preoccupy them now, the history which is being made is never very far from the history which is being written.

In *Russia Absent and Present*, Vladimir Veidlé writes:

> (Ancient) Russia was only separated from the West because of the difference between Byzantine Christianity and Western Christianity, between the spirit of classical antiquity as transmitted by Byzantium and this same spirit as inherited from Rome. This means that there is no reason why this separation should become total and definitive. In the historical perspective of Europe, Rome is no longer separable from Athens, nor Athens from Rome, and both are inseparable from Jerusalem to which they are linked once and for all by the mission of Peter and that of Paul. But Constantinople, which had become the second Rome, also received the heritage of the Acropolis and that of Golgotha; what it transmitted to its own heirs cannot be considered alien to the most precious patrimony of Europe.[115]

The story of the life of a few Russian intellectuals in France seems a good example of this consideration, so full of future promises, by one of the authors of *The Way*.

Afterword to
the English Translation

During the summer of 1998, I finished writing this book as a doctoral thesis on *The Way*—a journal that many specialists consider the most brilliant of those produced by the Russian intelligentsia in the course of the twentieth century. Back then, my plan was to offer a synthesis between the different memories of the generation of intellectuals that participated in this earlier intellectual adventure and the political, ecclesial, and intellectual developments of the final years of the twentieth century. In spite of the positive reviews that this research received, both in academia and in the press,[1] it remained confined to a narrow circle of specialists. There was the impression, among some, that the ideas and figures that I tried to make known had very little influence on contemporary political, ecclesial, and intellectual developments in Russia, Ukraine, France, and beyond.

For the most part, this impression was probably my fault. All too often, I have neglected to actively promote the results of my research. Developments in world affairs seemed to leave us very distant from the ideas being debated in the 1930s. This I now regret, having learned a greater appreciation of the connections and relevance of the early to the late twentieth century. Above all, when I observe the intellectual, ecclesial, and political developments of recent years, it only confirms for me the urgency of rediscovering the religious thought of the émigré Russian community based in Paris.

On an intellectual level, my research on the authors of *The Way* demonstrated that the thinking of these Russian émigrés should be understood as mytho-logical, that is, as neither purely symbolic nor purely Cartesian but rather a synthesis of both. This synthesis was made possible by their acceptance, in principle, of the hypothesis of the incarnation of the Trinitarian God. If for no other reason, the esteem enjoyed by these Russian intellectuals throughout the twentieth century among such moral and intellectual authorities as John Mott, Patriarch Athenagoras, Thomas Merton, Dorothy Day, Pope John Paul II, Enzo Bianchi, Alexander Solzhenitsyn, Paul Ricoeur, John Milbank, Peter Berger, Andrea Riccardi, and Rowan Williams, among others, made it clear to me that this renewal of mytho-logical thinking within the Russian immigration community was not in the least provincial and, indeed, was extremely important. If this line of thinking has been underrated, this was, in my opinion, due to the evolutions suffered by modern secular reflection—a fact admirably demonstrated by Charles Taylor in his masterful studies.[2]

Several intellectual developments have confirmed my intuition that this "religious thought"—a rather pejorative designation in Parisian intellectual circles—was not only profound but very real. To measure the degree to which secular thinking has opened itself to mytho-logical thought—limiting myself to the French scene—it suffices to read the works of François Dosse on the crisis of structuralist thought and the renewal of hermeneutic phenomenology in modern human sciences,[3] to realize the growing demand in French society for what religion has to offer,[4] to note the rediscovery of Catholic religious thinkers such as Maurice Zundel,[5] Pierre Teilhard de Chardin, Jean Guitton,[6] or Michel de Certeau (all of whom had been relegated to Purgatory), to see eminent intellectuals such as Luc Boltanski convert to Christianity, or to immerse one's self in the works of philosophers such as Jean-Louis Chrétien, Jean-Luc Marion, and Jean-Yves Lacoste.[7]

These last three writers, specialists in the work of Nietzsche, Heidegger, and Derrida, abandoned theoretical constructions organized around the concept of religious sentiment (à la Schleiermacher) or around the idea that the sole element of knowledge is through concepts (à la Hegel). The "pleasure of the concept" was, for Hegel, the source of blessedness. But it was not really necessary that people—notably, children and the spiritually simple—lead the life most worthy of the God who has made Himself their ally (Lacoste). This is why Chrétien, Marion, and Lacoste are turning today, in the line of the liturgical and iconic phenomenology of Bulgakov, towards a doxological way of thinking, where "liturgy" designates "the logic which presides over the meeting between humanity and God."[8] As for Paul Ricoeur, he has delivered contemporary philosophy from a vision focused exclusively on a preoccupation with temporality by pursuing the intuitions of the eschatological metaphysics of Berdyaev. In his central work, *La Mémoire, l'histoire et l'oubli*, published in 2000, this friend of Paul Evdokimov invoked the act of remembering and the joy that makes us live in a present untroubled by the future, in a rediscovered abandonment to the Providence of God.

But we must look beyond the intellectual garden that is France to be convinced of the profundity of the rehabilitation of Christian mytho-logy. In 1998, John Paul II published his encyclical *Fides et Ratio*, in which he quoted Russian thinkers such as Vladimir Lossky and Pavel Florensky. The pope proposed an *aggiornamento* of traditional neo-Thomist thought and made an appeal, along the lines of the religious thought characteristic of the Russian immigrant community, for a new synthesis, one that is both rooted in the wisdom of God and also personalist, between faith and reason. For his part, Pope Benedict XVI, in his 2006 discourse at Regensburg, insisted, in terms that echo Florovsky, on the necessity of rediscovering Christian Hellenism in order to arrive at this goal. In a totally different milieu, one of the most popular writers in France today, Maurice G. Dantec, a former punk guitarist, a disciple of Gilles Deleuze, a reader of Berdyaev, and a recent convert to Christianity, has contributed to such a synthesis of faith and reason by rehabilitating the work of the medieval philosopher John Duns Scotus. According to the author of *Grande Jonction*, it would also be profitable to rehabilitate the theories of Georg Cantor, the German mathematician of Russian descent and one of Florensky's teachers:

> Cantor and Scotus practice the same fundamental operation six centuries apart: a radical break with Aristotle's order of indefinite succession by substituting the actual simultaneity of all the successive units,

and it is through this fundamental ontological rupture with the numerical "collection" of finite numbers that, suddenly, the domain characteristic of the infinite opens up. Here this rupture shows the absolute power of naming and of naming the totality of the infinite. This rupture demonstrates, on the deepest level imaginable, the absolute liberty on which is based the creation of humanity, the Image of a Being infinitely and sovereignly free.[9]

Several years after the encyclical of John Paul II, the movement known as "Radical Orthodoxy" appeared with considerable controversy, first in England, then in the United States. This lay intellectual movement, which was originally composed of postmodern philosophers, is characterized by the rediscovery of the trans-modernity of Christian *kerygma*. Here is what Catherine Pickstock, one of the spiritual heirs of Bishop Charles Gore, the Anglo-Catholic friend of Fr. Sergius Bulgakov, had to say:

> Radical Orthodoxy is both the ally and enemy of post-modern thought: enemy because we believe that differences, if they are to be real, should coexist and collaborate with one another—otherwise they would disappear due to their antagonism and the war they would wage on one another; ally because, like the post-modern thinkers, we believe that we live on the surface of a world of changing and mysterious symbols which we are constantly called upon to decipher. This world is that which has been created *ex nihilo*, as St. Augustine puts it—things do not exist by themselves, they are only the faint reflection of God, their Creator. For his part, the post-modern thinker adopts a position which is almost nihilist; for him there is nothing under this inrush of signs. Radical Orthodoxy seeks to resituate this nihilism: the flow of signs escapes from nothingness in the measure in which it is the reflection of God who is everything.[10]

Whatever one might think of John Milbank, of Catherine Pickstock, or of William Cavanaugh, it is indisputable that their participatory vision of reality furnishes a new understanding of the evolution of quantum physics at the same time as it gives new insights concerning the most complex subjects, from the theology of Fr. Henri de Lubac to climatic disturbances. John Milbank considers Bulgakov as nothing less than the greatest thinker of the twentieth century.[11] The Anglican philosopher holds that Hans Urs von Balthasar neglected the personal character of the Divine Essence as such by reducing the Trinitarian Persons to "autonomous centers of being," and he credits the Russian Orthodox thinker with seeking to conceptualize this personal reality in Sophia.[12] Although not himself part of the Radical Orthodoxy movement, the archbishop of Canterbury, Rowan Williams, is a specialist in twentieth-century Russian theology and has not only published on Bulgakov, Evdokimov, and Vladimir Lossky but also brought out a profound examination of theological themes in Dostoevsky.[13]

I conclude this brief overview of the contemporary intellectual pertinence of the philosophy of the Russian immigrant community by mentioning the work of the Greek Orthodox philosopher Christos Yannaras. In his book *Postmodern Metaphysics*,[14] a vast fresco that evolves into a postmodern metaphysical ontology, Yannaras tries to realize a creative synthesis between personalism, sophiology, and theocentrism. In my opinion, this triangle represents an essential key. On the one hand, it enables an understanding of the work of Berdyaev, Bulgakov, Shestov, Florovsky, and Fedotov. Moreover, insofar as Yannaras has grasped, through their dialogue, the principal elements of theological, philosophical, and contemporary scientific knowledge that are at stake, his work is not an isolated case. Russian religious thought is also hailed by such famous astrophysicists as Basarab Nicolescu, a member of the French National Center of Scientific Research (CNRS) and of the Romanian Academy. In his book *Nous, la particule et le monde*, the transdisciplinary theorist centers his analysis of quantitative fields on the bootstrap theory. This theory is based on the "principle of informational organization of matter, that of autoconsistency, which has the advantage of also being the principle that structures the different levels of Reality."[15] Here, too, can be heard the echo of the theory of matter as it was formulated by the Russian religious philosophers. François Euvé, a physics professor and a Catholic theologian, has written of a synthesis between anthropology and cosmology, basing himself on the idea of "playfulness," an attribute of the Wisdom of God. For the Jesuit theologian, "playfulness is neither pure accident nor unfailing determinism. It implies an element of uncertainty which is tempered by rules. . . . The biologist Manfred Eigen applies the image of playfulness to the process of evolution, where it has a regulatory role."[16]

On the ecclesial side, certain hypotheses of my research have also been gradually confirmed in recent years, even though they have not yet been very widely received. When I studied the ecumenical engagements of Russian immigrants such as Florovsky, Zernov, or Zander, I insisted upon their prophetic realization that they were living in a post-confessional and post-Constantinian world. They all agreed on the fact that the Church of Christ extends beyond the sacramental limits of the different Christian confessions. This realization was so revolutionary that, even today, the churches are unable to thwart the neo-traditionalist currents that are reemerging within them. One need only mention the declaration of July 2007 by the Vatican's Congregation for the Doctrine of the Faith ("Responses to Some Questions Regarding Certain Aspects of the Doctrine of the Church"), which refuses the right of churches other than the Roman Catholic Church to affirm that the Church of Christ subsists in them. It is a well-known fact that most of the Orthodox churches, even though they participate in the World Council of Churches, have the same reservations regarding non-Orthodox churches—as the Anglican theologian Mary Tanner points out.[17] It is also evident how much the new Evangelical churches in the world are ill at ease with the ecumenical movement.

But if these churches wanted to reread attentively books such as *The Bride of the Lamb* by Fr. Sergius Bulgakov, they would realize that one does not betray the Orthodox faith by recognizing that the sacramental boundaries of the churches do not necessarily coincide with their canonical boundaries. In so doing, they would open themselves to the most contemporary research of the ecumenical world.[18] The common point among American theologians as diverse as Geoffrey Wainwright, Brian Daley, and John Erickson is that the church should no longer be understood either in a spiritualist or rationalist sense. If the church is no longer considered as a *what* but rather as a *who*, as a divine-human body pulsing with the relationships among people, the cosmos, and their Creator, if modern thought would associate history with eschatology, then new perspectives would open up for our contemporary societies corroded by despair and the amnesia of being: neither sacralization nor secularization but baptismal, eucharistic, and pastoral eschatology. In this time-space continuum, it is not concurrence that defines inter-ecclesial or inter-religious relations but rather the awareness of the fact that human communities all live according to different levels of consciousness, all of them loved by God and developing in the measure in which the divine image finds expression in them. In this Eucharistic space-time perspective, the life of human beings is not determined by the dialectic of fear and of the social contract, as Hobbes, Locke, and Rousseau proclaimed; it is the gratuitous and disinterested gift which becomes the driving force for a durable and just economic growth. In the perspective of a society with an inter-generational and inter-communitarian sharing, each is concerned that the maximum number of his neighbors benefit from the same gifts which he himself benefited from.[19]

Having arrived at this point, those theologians throughout the world who are still working in the many mixed ecumenical commissions to reach consensus on the fundamental questions regarding full communion would not have much ground to cover. Bulgakov, Berdyaev, Zernov, and their friends had opened the way in the 1930s on several points of dissension. They emphasized the importance of mutual recognition of baptism in the early church, the possibility of inter-communion among Christians given certain conditions, the orthodoxy of the non-Chalcedonian churches, and the necessity for the Protestant world to rediscover the veneration of the Virgin, as well as the necessity of recognizing the apostolicity of the Anglican ministries. They urged this recognition not in a mechanical sense but rather in an eschatological context, the personal and not biological or mechanical nature of the relationship between the Son and the Spirit, the indispensable synthesis—for good governance in the church and, consequently, in the state. They recognized the interdependence that holds between the authority of responsibility or of regulation of Peter, the utopian authority of love of the beloved disciple John, and the authority of freedom or resistance of Paul.

And during recent years a number of documents and publications bear witness that the ecumenical movement is rediscovering and deepening these prophetic intuitions. Apart from official agreements (such as the Declaration on Justification in 1999 between Catholics and Protestants, the Declarations of Reuilly in 2000 on the mutual recognition of ministries between Protestants and Anglicans, the mutual recognition of baptism among the Christian churches of Germany in 2007, the Declaration of Velehrad, Czech Republic, in July 2000 between Greek Catholics and

Orthodox, and more),[20] I briefly mention publications such as the document of the Dombes Group (Groupe des Dombes) concerning Mary,[21] the 2003 document of the ecumenical centers of Strasbourg, Tübingen, and Bensheim in favor of inter-communion among Christians,[22] the work of Fr. Bernard Sesboüé on the ministry of Peter,[23] and that of the late Ukrainian Orthodox Archbishop of Chicago, Vsevolod (Maidanski) of Scopelos.[24]

I might add that, as I had expected, the Russian Church experienced several new developments linked to the non-reconciliation of different memories of the ecclesial separations in the years 1920–30. In June 2007, the patriarchate of Moscow reunited with many of the parishes of the Russian Orthodox Church Outside Russia. But even more parishes under Russian archbishops passed over to the jurisdiction of the patriarchate of Constantinople during the interwar period, along with some from the diocese of Sourozh in England. It seems to me that this makes evident the fact that reconciliation among the Orthodox will not be possible until the whole of Orthodoxy accepts the new definition of Orthodoxy set forth in Paris in 1931, that is, that Orthodoxy is not an institution but rather a style of life, "the life in Jesus Christ in the Holy Spirit."[25] What Sergius Bulgakov, Anton Kartashev, Lev Gillet, and Paul Evdokimov once used to say is being taken up again throughout the world by a growing number of eminent figures of the Orthodox Church, such as Olivier Clément,[26] the recently deceased French lay theologian, and Archbishop Anastasios (Yannoulatos) of Tirana, the primate of the Orthodox Church in Albania.

But I had not expected that one of the principal contributors to the journal *The Way*, Mother Maria Skobtsova, would be canonized so early (January 2004) by the Orthodox Church, along with three other friends of the journal (her son Yuri, Fr. Dmitrii Klepinin, and Ilya Fondaminsky). I rejoice that this took place in Paris, in the presence of the late Cardinal Lustiger, who requested that all the Catholic faithful of his diocese commemorate these saints of the universal church every year on July 20. I also rejoice in all the publications and iconographic creations that anticipated or accompanied this profound movement of collective memory.[27] My dream today would be that this same memory might turn itself towards other actors of this extraordinary renewal of Christian consciousness which took place in the darkest hours of totalitarian persecutions of Christians. I am thinking in particular of the starets Sophrony (Sakharov), of Ivan Lagovsky,[28] of Fr. Sergius Bulgakov,[29] and of Paul Anderson.

Without Anderson,[30] a Presbyterian from Iowa who, in the 1920s, became director of the YMCA mission to Russian immigrants in Europe, a great number of the Orthodox projects—such as the St. Sergius Institute, the Russian Student Christian Movement, and Orthodox Action—would never have had the impact that they did. I was able to work in Anderson's personal archives in Chicago. There is no doubt in my mind that this associate of John Mott and Mother Maria Skobtsova, the friend of the patriarchs Alexii I and Athenagoras, and the editor of Berdyaev and Solzhenitsyn, deserves to be canonized today by the universal church. This would also be a way of doing homage to the extraordinary generosity of innumerable American patrons such as John Rockefeller and to recall to the YMCA that it played a decisive role in the renewal of Christian thought.

I will conclude with the political consequences of this revival of the memory of Russian religious thought. When I was writing the final chapter of my book during the summer of 1998, the Yeltsin regime was living its final hours. By kneeling with representatives of the Russian cultural elite before the remains of the imperial family when they were reburied in the Cathedral of Saints Peter and Paul in Saint Petersburg, Boris Yeltsin witnessed by this very gesture that communist ideology had failed. But, at the same time, democracy and liberal capitalism were failing just as badly in convincing the new generation of Russians. Indeed, during the month of August, the devastating stock market crisis occurred, which ruined the emerging middle class and, above all, given the specter of the dissolution of the Russian Federation, terrorized it for a long time.

Several months later, Vladimir Putin, a former KGB officer, came to power. The new president, seeking a new ideology for the Russian state, did not receive any support from the moral authorities of the country when he wanted to revive links with the ideas of the Russian immigration— neither from the Russian Orthodox Church nor from Nikita Mikhalkov, president of the Union of Film Makers. At the beginning of his mandate, Vladimir Putin often referred in his speeches to Ivan Ilyin and extended his hand to Solzhenitsyn, one of Ilyin's contemporary intellectual heirs. That could have been the occasion of a fruitful debate with the Orthodox thought that had emerged from the immigration. In this book I have made special reference to the importance of the debate in the 1920s between Berdyaev and Ilyin—a debate that echoed that of the neo-democrats with the neo-monarchists of the immigration community—on Hegel's philosophy and the moral foundations of violence.[31] If this debate had taken place on the highest levels, with the participation of intellectuals and large sectors of the population, if, in particular, Ivan Ilyin's evolution towards Nazism had been kept in mind, I am convinced that, in large measure, the current authoritarian evolution of the Russian government, with its imprisonment and banishment of former oligarchs and the disappearance of an independent media, could have been averted. According to most independent observers, the Russian state is, in fact, now trying to rehabilitate the dignity of the Soviet era and restore a neo-national corporate regime.

I cannot help thinking that if the Russian elites had attentively read the book of the Russian immigrant historian George Fedotov, *The Saints of Ancient Russia*—published in 1990 with a preface by Fr. Alexander Men and Dimitrii Likhachev—they would have avoided supporting the neo-imperialist politics of Russia towards its close neighbors. The tensions between Russia and the Baltic nations are innumerable. The catastrophic intervention of Russia in Ukrainian affairs during the Orange Revolution of November 2004,[32] the increasing tensions between secular and Muslim fundamentalists in the Caucasus, and the repeated launching of missiles on Georgian territory and military conflict in several provinces in Georgia are all testimonies to the fragilities of the Russian state. The European Union and the United States are now distancing themselves because of Russia's use of its natural gas as political blackmail.

George Fedotov was the first Russian historian to find a solution for the atavist imperialism of the Russian state. He did so by clearly distinguishing between the history of the Rus' of Kiev and that of the Russia of Peter the Great and the tsars who succeeded him. His thesis was that Muscovy became an imperial and authoritarian state when it cut itself off from its spiritual roots. If, for Fedotov, the golden age of Russian spirituality is the fifteenth century, the tragedy of Russian identity began in the sixteenth century when Moscow, cut off from its Byzantine roots for a long time because of the Tartar yoke, developed, in pride and solitude, the thesis that it would be the "Third Rome," the only place called upon to realize the city of God here on earth. Unable to find a synthesis in the conflict between the monks who were hostile to property and the monasteries that were favorable to an accommodation with the state, the Russian Church progressively abandoned the Christian "ecumenism" that was still alive in the Rus' of Kiev in the fifteenth century.

There is an immense historical and theological effort to be undertaken in our times in order to reconcile memories concerning the advent of Russia, a state without a nation, and Ukraine, a nation without a state. Such an effort, if it is done seriously, would not necessarily, as many Russians fear, lead to a questioning of Russian identity.[33] On the contrary, it might, as Zernov already suggested in a 1936 article in *The Way*, enable a rediscovery of the spiritual and fully universal meaning of the myth of Moscow as the Third Rome.[34] In particular, it would be the occasion to rediscover all the contemporary potentialities of the motto of the Rus' of Kiev, *Za Rus', Za veru*: "For Rus' and for the Faith"—a motto taken up by the boy scout organizations of the Russian immigration. Thus it is not "For Russia and for Orthodoxy," as proclaimed by the new ideology of Putin, which wants to be the uncritical heir of Tsar Nicholas I and of his motto, "Autocracy, Nationality, Orthodoxy." To be sure, one must first rid oneself of the scheme of an exclusivist, genealogical history in order to arrive at the multi-vectored historiography of the founding symbol of the state of the Eastern Slavs—the baptism of Vladimir in 988.[35] In the new historiographical perspective, this motto now signifies especially the promotion of a common symbolic space, within which each state-principality makes use of its political independence, while sharing its resources in the mutual interest of each of the others. It also signifies a postmodern reconciliation of states and churches, which is centered not on an authoritarian social contract based on the fear of an illusory primitive violence but—along the lines of a deeper understanding of the model of the medieval city of Novgorod— on the primacy of an openness to faith in a Trinitarian God and authentic respect for the liberty of conscience of each person.

The political ideas presented in the articles of *The Way* do not merely concern the future of the contemporary territories of *Rus'*. They concern, more generally, the future of parliamentary democracies and of consumer societies eroded by populism and threatened by debauchery. The authors of the review wanted to rehabilitate theological-political thinking. They criticized the concept of sovereignty as it had been developed in modern times, from Bodin to Bismarck, and they preferred ethical principles such as the priority given to respect for human dignity. On this point also, I regret that, for the most part, contemporary Orthodox thought still rejects the heritage of the Russian émigré community. How many Orthodox theological schools now teach the religious thought of this community? Most of the time, the Paris School is placed on a pedestal, but in practice, Bulgakov's work is still considered heretical, the thinking of Berdyaev is seen as not ecclesial, and Shestov remains ignored.

The recent publication of the journals of the late Father Alexander Schmemann, the dean of St. Vladimir's Seminary, is a case in point. Schmemann expressed his reservations about Bulgakov's sophiology, which, he admits, he does not understand.[36] But that does not mean that Schmemann himself, as I mentioned in my study, did not find inspiration in the work and liturgical practice of his teacher for the development of his own liturgical theology. This is something which is forgotten too often—to the point that the Paris School is considered merely as the place where the absolute superiority of the Fathers of the Church was rediscovered. Such a view permits these same readers to quickly pass over other passages of Fr. Schmemann such as this: "Orthodoxy refuses to recognize the fact of the collapse and breakup of the Orthodox world."

But contemporary authors around the world who are influential in the media, charitable organizations, or international institutions such as the World Trade Organization—authors such as Jim Wallis in the United States, Robert Van Drimmelen in Holland,[37] or Pascal Lamy in France— are rediscovering, without necessarily being familiar with Russian philosophy, the validity of the nonconformist political position of *The Way* and its spiritual vision of the cosmos as creation, of technology as a divine and human tool, and of an economy founded on sharing rather than competition. Whether it be a question of sustainable agriculture, of micro-credit, of bioclimatic architecture, of the protection of biodiversity, or ecotourism, there are enormous fields for the promotion of the orthopraxis of Orthodox thought. Several Orthodox theologians are convinced that with the liturgical practice of gift and counter-gift, Christianity holds the key to the new economy: to give without seeking to receive in return does not deprive the giver—on the contrary, it increases his well-being. [38]

In France, Jean-Baptiste de Foucauld has initiated the putting into practice of a spiritual democracy along the lines traced by Berdyaev, Mother Maria, and Fedotov in the 1930s. Foucauld, a high-ranking public servant in the Ministry of Finances (1970–2011) and a disciple of Raymond Abellio and Michael Walzer,[39] believes that only a development project that is sustainable, equitable, and in solidarity, centered on the material, social, and spiritual development of each person, can unite social liberals, Christian democrats, social democrats, and ecologists. In Foucauld's view, this demands working simultaneously on the three principal structures or political cultures of our modern world—regulation, resistance, and utopia. This immediately calls to mind the theses of Solovyov on Christ's three apostles, Peter, Paul, and John, symbols of the three poles of trinitarian life in human cultures. For Foucauld, "things become much more luminous if there is recourse to this triune culture so profoundly present in the Gospel: the Gospel denounces the injustice, egoism, corruption, and hypocrisy of the powerful; it is an appeal to an extreme radicalism, that of the Kingdom to come whose gate is narrow; and, in the meantime, human nature being what it is, progressing slowly by fits and starts, it allows for more moderate social rules so that people might live together such as they are rather than as they should be. The good grain and the weeds are mixed together."[40]

It may be said that this is not a very scholarly afterword. I take responsibility for my choice. Even though I chose to leave the professional framework of the Ministry of Foreign Affairs and enter that of the Catholic University of Ukraine, I have learned my lesson concerning the risks of conceptual hyper-specialization in an academic setting. Russian religious thought should really be studied in a critical context—that of microhistory and the places of memories. But it should not be enclosed in this context. Otherwise it would be a posthumous stratagem of reason.

All that is left is to profoundly thank Fr. Michael Plekon, whom I am honored to have as a friend. My infinite thanks for all the confidence he had in me, for the titanic efforts of Jerry Ryan in his translating in order to make this publication possible, and to Natalia Ermolaev and Fr. John Jillions, who also assisted in editing. I am very grateful to Rebecca DeBoer, from Notre Dame University Press, whose precise work allows this American edition of my book to become the reference one. Above all, I am grateful for their love for the Orthodox, Catholic, and Protestant Churches and for the Russian religious thinkers in this study.

Antoine Arjakovsky

NOTES

Notes to Introduction

1. The full title of the journal in Russian is: *Put'. Organ russkoi religioznoi mysli*. In French: *La voie, organe de la pensée religieuse russe*, Paris, Académie de philosophie religieuse, nos. 1–61, 1925–1940.
2. Pierre Pascal, "Les grands courants de la pensée russe contemporaine," *CMRS (Cahiers du Monde russe et soviétique)*, Paris/The Hague, January–March 1962, 5–89.
3. Marc Raeff, *Russia Abroad: A Cultural History of the Russian Emigration (1919–1939)* (New York: Oxford University Press, 1990).
4. Olivier Clément, *Berdiaev: Un philosophe russe en France* (Paris: Desclée de Brouwer, 1991), 4th page of cover.
5. The translated articles are: Nikolai Berdyaev, "'L'Orient et l'Occident' dans 'L'Orient et l'Occident,'" *Cahiers de la Quinzaine*, ser. 20, no. 9, June 5, 1930, 5–60; Berdyaev, "Verité et mensonge du communisme," *Esprit*, October 1932, no. 1, 104–128; Berdyaev, "La ligne générale de la philosophie soviétique," in *Problème du communisme* (Paris/Bruges: Desclée de Brouwer, 1933); Berdyaev, "La technique et l'âme," French trans. of his Russian essay "Man and the Machine" (B65), in *L'Homme et la machine* (Paris: Je Sers, 1933); Berdyaev, "Deux concepts du christianisme," French trans. of "Two Ways of Understanding Christianity" (B62), *Zofingue* (Switzerland), no. 3, 1936; Lev Shestov, "Kierkegaard et Dostoïevski," French trans. of "Hegel or Job, Concerning the Existentialist Philosophy of Kierkegaard" (Sh4R), in *Kierkegaard et la philosophie existentielle* (Paris: LALC-Vrin, 1936).
6. Nikolai Berdyaev, "De l'esprit bourgeois" and "La situation spirituelle du monde contemporain," in *De l'Esprit bourgeois, essais* (Neuchâtel: Delachaux et Niestlé, 1949): Berdyaev, "L'Ungrund et la liberté" and "La doctrine de la Sophia et l'androgyne, Jaköb Boehme et les courants sophiologiques russes," in *Jacob Boehme: Mysterium magnum* (Paris: Aubier, 1946); Berdyaev, "L'idée fondamentale de Léon Chestov," *Le Messager orthodoxe*, 1966, nos. 1/2 (33/34), 16–21; Berdyaev, "La guerre et l'eschatologie," *Vie, art, cité*, no. 3, 1948; Berdyaev, "La liberté n'est pas un droit mais une obligation," French trans. by P. Pascal of "On Authority, Freedom and Humanity" (B81), *Le Monde*, March 23/24, 1952; Sergius Bulgakov, "Le dogme du

Vatican," trans. of "Notes on the Doctrine of the Church IV" (B123, B124), *Le Messager orthodoxe*, 1959, no. 6: 19–33, no. 7, 30–41, no. 8: 11–22, no. 10: 18–26; Bulgakov, "Le saint Graal," *Contacts*, no. 28, 1975, 281–318; Lev Shestov, "V. V. Rozanov," "Deux livres de R. Kroner," "Martin Buber, un mystique juif de langue allemande," "Job ou Hegel?" "Le mythe et la verité. A propos de la métaphysique de la conaissance. La mythologie primitive de L. Lévy-Bruhl," and "*Sine effusione sanguinis*. De la probité philosophique. Vernunft und Existenz de K. Jaspers," in *Spéculation et révélation* (Lausanne: L'Age d'Homme, 1982); George Fedotov, "Le saint Esprit dans la culture et dans la nature," *Contacts*; Georges Florovsky, "Révélation, expérience, tradition," trans. of "Theological Fragments"(F52), in "La Tradition, recueil," *La pensée orthodoxe*, no. 17/5 (Paris: L'Age d'Homme, 1992), 54–72; Mother Maria Skobtsova, "A Justification of Pharisaism," in *Mother Maria Skobtsova: Essential Writings* (Maryknoll, NY: Orbis, 2003), 116–125; Skobtsova, "Les sources de l'acte créateur," in *Le sacrement du frère* (Paris: Le sel de la terre, 1995), 173–186.

7. See *L'Emigration russe en Europe. Catalogue collectif des périodiques en langue russe*, by T. Ossorgin and A. M. Volkov, vol. 1, 1855–1940 (Paris: Institut d'Études Slaves, 1976), 360 pages. Also see T. Gladkova and T. Ossorgin-Bakunin, *L'Emigration russe, revues et recueils; index général des articles*, vol. 1, 1920–1980 (Paris: Institut d'Études Slaves, 1988), 664 pages.

8. A. P. Obolensky, *Index of the Authors, Themes and Reviews of the Journal, The Way, Paris (1925–1940)* (New York: Zapiski russkoi akademicheskoi gruppy v SShA, 1968). Even though there are numerous errors and omissions in the index, it classifies articles to facilitate comparative research. It is to be hoped that these errors and omissions can be corrected in the index of articles to *The Way*.

9. Raeff was not able to contain in the limited number of pages he devoted to *The Way* the theological, philosophical, and cultural debates in the review. He also is mistaken in claiming that the review did not have a literary dimension.

10. Raeff, *Russia Abroad*, 144–145.

11. In the 1960s, Fr. Alexander Men, a priest in the village of Novaia Derevnia near Moscow, received a number of copies of the journal.

12. CD-ROM, Business Forms Company, 1998. It is accompanied by a pamphlet containing the above-mentioned introduction by Fr. Danilenko with the index of articles, all in Russian. The scanned issues of *The Way* are now also available in Russian at http://www.odinblago.ru/path.

13. Also see E. Gollerbakh's study of the publishing house *The Way: K nezrimomu gradu. Religiozno-filosofskaia gruppa Put' (1910–1919) v poisakh novoi russkoi identichnosti* (St. Petersburg: Aletheia, 2000). Certain authors in this publishing house created the review of the same name, *The Way*, after the revolution.

14. P. Nora, "Comment écrire l'histoire de France," in *Les lieux de mémoire*, t. III, *Les France*, vol. 1, *Conflits et partages* (Paris: Gallimard, 1992), 20.

15. One cannot find in any study a unique and definitive version of the accomplishments of the intelligentsia of the Russian emigration, although such versions are implicitly present throughout. Each historian focuses on particular details,

but the framework is always the same in that it is necessary to distinguish the émigré memoir from the Soviet memoir. For the memoir of emigration, Nikita Struve defines what is at stake: "Russia abroad has been the legitimate inheritor and the continuation of Russia always more so than within the historical borders of the land, where one finds a regime alien by its ideology and nature seeking to annihilate the historic Russia and the soul of her people." N. Struve, *70 ans d'émigration russe, 1919–1989* (Paris: Fayard, 1996). One can also consult the principal historical reference for this intellectual generation: Nicolas Zernov, *The Russian Religious Renaissance of the Twentieth Century* (New York: Macmillan, 1963; in Russian, Paris: YMCA Press, 1974). In Soviet historiography one essentially stops with the departure of the renegade intellectuals. V. Kostikov's book *Ne budem proklinat' izgnanie* (*Let Us Not Curse the Exiles*) has come to fill the gap.

16. A. Brossat, *A l'est la mémoire retrouvée* (Paris: La Découverte, 1990), 15.

17. From V. Bolshakov, *The Russian Shores near Paris* (Moscow, 1990) (in Russian).

18. G. Nivat, *Russie, Europe, la fin du schisme: Études littéraires et politiques* (Paris: L'Age d'Homme, 1993), 651.

19. P. Nora, *Les lieux de mémoire*, t. I, *La République*, xx.

20. V. Kostikov, *Ne budem proklinat' izgnanie* [*Let Us Not Curse the Exiles*] (Moscow: "Mezhdunarodnye otnosheniia," 1990), 21.

21. A. Abramov, "Preface," in *Put'*, reprint (Moscow: Inform Progress, 1992), 6.

22. A. A. Yakovlev, "Putting the Tradition into Practice," editorial, *The Way, an International Philosophical Review*, Moscow, Inform Progress, 1992, no. 1, 8 (Russian).

23. Ibid., 3–5.

24. Raeff, *Russia Abroad*, 10.

25. N. Struve, *70 ans d'émigration russe*, 94.

26. Ibid., 25.

27. In both Yannaras and Lossev one finds a synthetic presentation of the distinction between mythical and conceptual thought: Christos Yannaras, *Philosophie sans rupture*, 2nd ed. (Paris: Labor et Fides, 1980); V. Lossev, *Philosophy, Mythology, Culture*, Moscow (in Russian) (IPL, 1991), especially from paragraph 3 of the introduction, "The Genealogy of Mythological Thought."

28. O. Clément, *Rome autrement* (Paris: Desclée de Brouwer, 1997), 123–124.

29. H. Carrière d'Encausse, *La gloire des nations ou la fin de l'empire soviétique* (Paris: Fayard, 1990), 313.

30. M. Evdokimov, *Une voix chex les orthodoxes* (Paris: Cerf, 1998), 90–91.

31. See Philippe Arjakovsky, "L'inscription de la philosophie dans la langue et la culture russe" (unpublished). The blindness of Russian culture, for him, lies in the absence of any horizon of interpretation in Russian culture in relation to its Greek sources and because of the grafting on of the Slavonic language. He cites Yuri Lotman and Boris Ouspensky, *Sémiotique de la culture russe* (Lausanne, 1990), for whom Russian culture transformed the absence of this intercultural dialogue according to the principle of temporal polarity, between the new and the ancient (Hilarion), the

Slavonic language being interpreted as the very language of revelation, even more sacred than Greek, which was polluted by paganism. The *iazychnik*, the "pagan," is the one who could not speak a higher language. Russian philosophy began to properly speak only in the eighteenth century, in the dialogue between the Slavophiles and the Westernizers—and was completely shaped by the philosophy of history of German idealism (A. Koyré, *La philosophie et le problème national en Russie au début du XIXe siècle* [Paris, 1973; original ed. 1929], 155). The dialogue was a painful interrogation about the justification of culture as a human and national creation. There then begins a deliberate and discursive questioning of the relationships between word and thought. P. Arjakovsky says: "Russian thinkers totally distanced themselves, one could say, from the Hegelian opposition between the Romantic approach and that of the dialectic of knowing the absolute, in order to find a third way between the dialectic of the pure concept and the abstraction of immediate sensation, the way which they loved to call 'myth'" (ibid., 13).

32. C. Andronikov, preface to *Bibliographie des oeuvres de S. Boulgakov* (Paris: Institut d'Études Slaves, 1984), 6–41.

33. The label "Paris School" meant at first the St. Sergius Theological Institute in Paris and later came to describe a reforming school of Orthodox thought that had regrouped in Paris. Used first by the opponents of St. Sergius, this label has progressively passed into the vernacular as a synonym for "modernism," both in the positive and very negative connotations of this term. On March 18, 1927, the synod of the Russian Orthodox Church Outside Russia condemned the "doctrinal modernism" of the "intimate collaborators" of Metropolitan Evlogy or the "reformers" of the "Paris School" (Epistle no. 341). In 1935, on the other hand, Bulgakov used the label in the first or positive meaning: "A distinctive school has been created, Paris theology, which despite its complex harmony and dissonance, possesses its own personality and is quite singular in its perspective." B134, 67. [Editor's note: On May 17, 2007, the feast of the Ascension, an event took place in the newly rebuilt cathedral of Christ the Savior in Moscow which defied the decades of animosity with the Russian Orthodox Church Outside Russia, the descendant of the Karlovtsy Synod, which condemned not only the Moscow patriarchate but also Bulgakov. Its first hierarch, Metropolitan Laurus, concelebrated the liturgy along with Patriarch Alexii II of Moscow and numerous other bishops and clergy of both churches, thereby ending their schism by the reestablishment of eucharistic communion. What was unthinkable for decades became possible in just a few years, less than five, and for the express purpose of uniting Orthodox Christians of the Russian tradition worldwide. The factors that enabled this reunion and the long-term impact are most complex and are far from clear. Nevertheless, this improbable reunion is intimately linked to the issue of collective memory pursued in this study.]

34. Paul Ricoeur, "La marque du passé," *Mémoire, histoire, revue de métaphysique et de morale*, January–March 1998, no. 1, 17.

35. Antoine Prost, *Douze leçons sur l'histoire* (Paris: Seuil, 1996), 290.

36. Raymond Aron, *Introduction à la philosophie de l'histoire* (Paris, 1937), 234.

37. Jacques Revel, *Jeux d'échelles, La micro-analyse à l'expérience* (Paris: Gallimard, Le Seuil, Hautes Études, 1996), 11.
38. Christophe Charle, *Les intellectuels en Europe au XIXe siècle, essai d'histoire comparée* (Paris: Seuil, 1996), 20.
39. Ibid., 30–31.
40. Antoine Prost, "Histoire, vérité, méthodes, des structures argumentatives de l'histoire," *Le Débat*, Paris, no. 92, November–December 1996, 127–140.
41. Bernard Lepetit, "De l'échelle en histoire," in Revel, *Jeux d'échelles*, 71–94.
42. Jeffrey Andrew Barash, "Les sources de la mémoire," in *Mémoire, histoire* (cited n. 34 above), 137–148.
43. Ricoeur, " La marque du passé," 18.
44. In Nora, ed., *Les lieux de mémoire*, t. III, *Les France*.
45. Ricoeur, "La marque du passé," 28.
46. J. Le Goff, *Les intellectuels au Moyen-Age* (Paris, 1957).
47. P. Bénichou, "Parcours de l'écrivain, entretien avec Paul Bénichou," *Le Débat*, Paris, no. 54, April 1989, 24–32.
48. C. Charle, *Les intellectuels en Europe au XIXe siècle*, notes that this term "intelligentsia," coming from the German *Intelligenz* (in the sense of an ensemble of learned people), is even more ancient. See O. W. Müller, *Intelligensia: Untersuchungen zur Geschichte eines politischen Schlagwortes* (Frankfurt: Athenäum, 1971), chap. 6.
49. D. Likhachev, "The Russian Intelligentsia," *Novyi mir*, Moscow, 1993, no. 2, 5.
50. Ibid., 8.
51. Nora, "La génération," in *Les lieux de mémoire*, t. III, *Les France*, vol. 1, *Conflits et partages*, 936.
52. Ibid., 959.
53. Ibid.
54. Jean-Francois Sirinelli, *Génération intellectuelle, khâgneux et normaliens dans l'entre-deux guerres* (Paris: Fayard, 1988). See also his article "La khâgne," in *Les lieux de mémoire*, t. II, *La nation*, vol. 3, 589–624.
55. Jutta Scherrer, "Les sociétes de philosophie religieuse," in Acts du colloque "La philosophie idéaliste en Russie," Aix-en-Provence, March 25–29, 1968, no. 7, 1–24. Also see her essay "Intelligentsia, religion, révolution, premières manifestation d'un socialisme chrétien en Russie (1905–1907)," *CMRS*, 1969, XVII, 4, pp. 427–466; XVII, pp. 5–32.
56. Known by the acronyms RSCM in English, RSKhD in Russian, and ACER in French (Action Chrétienne des Etudiants Russes).
57. N. Berdyaev: "The authentic intellectuals are representatives of the spirit," in "On the Prophetic Mission of the Word and Spirit," *Novyi grad*, no. 13, 1935, 9. The spiritualizing of the term "intellectual" should not be confused with its clericalization. The qualification of "intellectual" also means a certain desire for independence within the church. From 1935, Patriarch Sergius of Moscow, wishing to discredit Father Bulgakov, called him an "intellectual." Berdyaev did not deny his

friend's identity: "The name Bulgakov is inscribed in the history of Russian intelligentsia, those who could not forgive him were the old bourgeois class of Orthodox seminarians." B78, 73.

58. I use the expression "nonconformist" here in the sense that Jean Touchard, Jean-Louis Loubet del Bayle, Jean-François Sirinelli, and Pascal Ory used it for the 1930s, that is to say, it refers to a stream of intellectuals born in the years 1900–1910, gathered together in certain reviews such as *Esprit, Ordre Nouveau,* or *Combat,* and united, despite their divergences from each other, by an attitude of reaction to the intellectual order established by a rejection both of communism and of capitalism. See Pascal Ory and Jean-François Sirinelli, *Les intellectuels en France, de l'affaire Dreyfus à nos jours* (Paris: Armand Colin, 1986), 89–92.

59. Michel Trébitsch, "Les réseaux intellectuels européens de Colpach à Pontigny," in Actes du colloques "Les revues européennes de l'entre-deux guerres," April 22–23, 1994, Berlin, Centre de Recherches en Sciences Sociales, Institut d'Histoire du Temps Présent (IHTP), 1994. See also Michel Trébitsch, "Les revues européennes de l'entre-deux-guerres," *Vingtième siècle: Revue d'histoire,* no. 44, October–December 1994, 135–138.

60. Jacques Julliard, "Le monde des revues au début du siècle," *Cahiers Georges Sorel* (Paris, 1987), 6–8.

61. Since Berdyaev, the rich period of Russian literary creativity in the first two decades of the twentieth century is known as "The Silver Age." It included the poetry of Alexander Blok, Anna Akhmatova, Ivan Bunin, Marina Tsvetaeva, Osip Mandelstam, and others.

62. The best study on the publishing house Put' is E. Gollerbakh, "Religiozno-filosofskoe izdatel'stvo 'Put'," *Voprosy filosofii,* 1994, nos. 2 and 4, 129–163.

63. Publication was set at four issues a year in 1925, at a yearly subscription of $2.25, or seventy cents per issue (twenty cents less than *Sovremennye zapiski*). This was increased to six issues per year, still at an annual subscription of $2.25 or sixty cents an issue. In September 1933 the price was stated in francs: 15 francs for each issue and an annual subscription of 56.25 francs for six issues. But during the winter of 1933–34 the financial crisis took its toll on the review, and it returned to four issues a year, at 10 francs per issue, or 35 francs for the yearly subscription of four issues. There was no further fluctuation in the price or the number of issues until the sixty-first and last issue in March 1940.

64. Archives of Paul Anderson from YMCA Press, VII-I (General Russian periodical), "Minutes of the meeting," December 4, 1924, 2. YMCA Archives.

65. A list of the names of 128 people who received a free copy of the first issue of the review exists (prepared by Paul Anderson for N. Berdyaev, dated November 6, 1925, YMCA Archives). This list accounts for 10 percent of the journal's readers and thus can serve as a good basis for judging the readership among older readers. It is necessary to add to this list the names of authors in the review who are not already mentioned. (See the articles in the list of References at the back of this volume.) One can reasonably estimate that these readers formed the nucleus of subscribers. And

the readers of the review were also clients of the publishing house, the YMCA Press. In a memo addressed by Paul Anderson to Gustave Kuhlman on September 29, 1924, one discovers the network of the YMCA Press distribution. This included circles of students, other periodicals, intellectuals, parishes, and YMCA booksellers. On the other hand, a May 2, 1925, meeting report entitled "Notes on a conference held at Annemasse, near Geneva" states that the editors of the review intended to distribute it "among groups of students, in homes, factories, in associations and clubs, among lawyers, engineers, physicians, Russian correspondence school students, and those who were YMCA clients." A bit further on, one reads that the following periodicals were contacted as well: the *Yale Review*, *University of Chicago Review*, and *The Christian Century*. As for the younger readers of the review, one can turn to the libraries of the Russian Student Christian Movement, St. Sergius Institute, and Berdyaev at Clamart. The collection of issues at St. Sergius is particularly rich in annotations to the pages. Finally, a third source of readers of the review came from the correspondence and lectures of authors who published in it, particularly its editors Berdyaev and Vysheslavtsev.

66. Personal archives of Berdyaev, excerpt of a letter of Ivan Shmelev, 1925. Beyond these archives, one can consult those of the review itself kept in the Berdyaev museum in Clamart and at CGAALI (the Russian Central State Archive of Literature and Art in Moscow: Tsentralni Gossudarstvenij Arkhiv po Literaturi I Iskusstv). Likewise consulted are the YMCA archives and those of St. Sergius Institute in Paris. Lastly there are the personal archives of a great many of the review's authors, such as Vysheslavtsev, Ilyin, Kartashev, Anderson, Bulgakov, Mother Maria, Zander, Bezobrazov, and Shestov.

67. *(Re)lire Suvtchinski: Textes choisis par Eric Humbert Claude, La Bresse*, ed. E. Humbert Claude (Paris: Efflorescence, 1990), 248–249.

68. Actes du colloque "La philosophie idéaliste en Russie," Aix-en-Provence, March 25–29, 1968.

69. M. Grabar, "La renaissance de la philosophie religieuse en Russie au tournant du siécle: De la crise d'idéalisme au réalisme symboliste," doctoral thesis manuscript, EHESS (L'École des Hautes Études en Sciences Sociales), Paris, 1996, 326–327.

70. Mircea Eliade, *Aspects du mythe* (Paris, Gallimard, 1963). For Jean-Pierre Vernant, mythology is "a unified narrative ensemble which represents, by an extension of its field and its internal coherence, a system of original thought, which is as complex and rigorous as, in a different context, the construction of a philosopher." Vernant, *Mythe et société en Grèce ancienne* (Paris: La Découverte, 1974; Seuil, 1992), 207.

71. F. W. Schelling, *Philosophie de la mythologie*, préface by M. Richir (Paris: J. Million, 1994).

72. C. Yannaras, *Philosophie sans rupture* (Paris: Labor et fides, 1986).

73. S. N. Trubetskoy, *Works* (Moscow, 1900; repr., Mysl, 1994).

74. Yannaras, *Philosophie sans rupture*, 28.

75. Trubetskoy, *Works*, 233.

76. John. D. Zizioulas, *Being as Communion* (Crestwood, NY: St. Vladimir's Seminary Press, 1985), 88.

77. Yannaras, *Philosophie sans rupture*, 85.
78. P. Ricoeur, *Soi-même comme un autre* (Paris: Seuil, 1990), 21.
79. Ibid., 21.
80. Ibid., 27.
81. F. W. Schelling, *Introduction à la philosophie de la mythologie*, 8th lesson, vol. 1 (Paris: Aubier, 1945), 238.
82. J. Grondin, *E. Kant* (Paris: Citérion, 1991), 163.
83. V. Solovyev, *La crise de la philosophie occidentale* (Moscow, 1874; Paris: Aubier, 1947), 194.
84. A. Koyré, "Hegel en Russie," *Le Monde slave*, n.s. 13, May–June 1936; *Études sur l'histoire de la pensée philosophique en Russie* (Paris: Vrin, 1950).
85. B21, 64.
86. M. Richir, Préface, in Schelling, *Philosophie de la mythologie*, 7–8.
87. F78, 48.
88. B76, 72.
89. In his last book, *Royaume de l'Esprit et royaume de César* (Paris: Delachaux et Niestlé, 1951), 20, Berdyaev writes the following, a confirmation of the mythologic of his thought: "The new existentialists can say that my philosophical point of view presupposes the myth of God and the myth of the Spirit. They can call this myth if they like. This does not trouble me greatly. These are the most universal and integral of myths. But here is what is most important: this myth is equally the myth of the existence of the Truth, without which it is difficult to speak of the truth of what ever may be, not only of the Truth, but of truths. It is not possible and is otherwise useless to demonstrate the reality of the myth of God, of the Spirit, of the Truth. It is a question of choice finally linked to freedom. I have the right to consider myself an existentialist even though I can in large measure appeal to my philosophy: the philosophy of the Spirit and even better, an eschatological philosophy."
90. B21, 64–65.
91. N. Berdyaev, *Esprit et liberté* (Paris: Desclée de Brouwer, 1984), 83–84.
92. Ibid., 87.
93. Ibid., 92.
94. The work under review is L. Lévy-Bruhl, *La mythologie primitive* (Paris: Alcan, 1935).
95. Sh6R, 65.
96. S. Bulgakov, *La tragedie de la philosphie*, in *Oeuvres*, vol. 1 (Moscow: Nauka, 1993), 425.
97. F47, 80.

Notes to Part One

1. On the concept of the generation between the wars, see J. F. Sirinelli, "Générations intellectuelles," *Les Cahiers de l'IHTP*, no. 6, Nov. 1987; J. P. Azéma and M. Winock, "Les générations intellectuelles," *Vingtième siècle: Revue d'histoire*, no. 22, April–June 1989, 17–38.

2. R. Girardet, *Mythes et mythologies politiques* (Paris: Seuil, 1986).

3. Girardet cites the following definition of myth from Mircea Eliade: "The myth recounts a sacred story; it relates an event which took place in time immemorial, the fabled time of origins. Put differently, myth tells how a reality came into existence, whether the totality of reality, the cosmos, or only a part of this: an island, a natural location, a human behavior, an institution" (ibid., 13, referring to M. Eliade, *Aspects du mythe* [Paris: Gallimard, 1963; 2nd ed., 1988]).

4. Walter F. Otto, *Essais sur le mythe*, trans. Pascal David (Mauvezin, France: Trans-Europ-Repress, 1987), 52. Also see Ernst Cassirer, *Le mythe de l'Etat* (Paris: Gallimard, 1993; original ed., 1946).

5. S. Bernstein, "L'esprit des années vingt," in J. J. Becker and S. Bernstein, *Victoire et frustrations (1914–1929)* (Paris: Seuil, 1990), 391.

6. See J. Luchaire, *Une génération réaliste* (Paris: Librairie Valois, 1929).

7. The naturalized French coming from Russia grew from 5,800 in 1926 to 11,000 in 1931. See Catherine Gousseff and Nicolas Saddier, *L'émigration russe en France, 1920–1930*, Master's thesis of history, Paris I, October 1983, 209–223.

8. See M. Eliade, *La nostalgie des origines* (Paris: Gallimard, 1971; 2nd ed., 1991); M. Eliade, "La nostalgie du paradis dans les traditions primitives," in *Mythes, rêves et mystères* (Paris: Gallimard, 1957; new ed., 1989), 78–94. In general, page numbers are cited from the newer editions.

9. B43R, 114.

10. B120, 28.

11. B120, 14.

12. R. Girardet, *Mythes et mythologies politiques*, 105.

13. M. d'Herbigny and A. Deubner, *Evêques russes en exil*, Orientalia Christiana, vol. 21, no. 1 (Rome: I. P. O., 1931), 118.

14. R3, 7.

15. R3, 7.

16. [Editor's note: Biographical sketches for many individuals are included in the French and Russian versions of this book, as well as in Nikita Struve's previously cited *70 ans de l'émigration russe* and Nicolas Zernov's *Russian Religious Renaissance*.]

17. B77, 16.

18. R3, 7.

19. YMCA Archives, Anderson Foundation, N. Berdyaev, untitled, March 6, 1925, 4. A part of the YMCA Archives consulted for this volume consists of family archives. Another part is at the library of the University of Illinois. See Paul B. Anderson Papers, 1909–1988, University of Illinois Archives. For a description of the YMCA Archives, see also http://archives.library.illinois.edu/uasfa/1535054.pdf. The YMCA Press Archives are found in the Paul Anderson Archives at the University of Illinois and at the YMCA Press office in Paris.

20. Following is a list of the seventy-four contributors to the journal between 1925 and 1929: N. N. Alekseev, P. F. Anderson, Cardinal Andrieu, P. Archambault, N. S. Arseniev, E. Belenson, N. A. Berdyaev, S. S. Bezobrazov, N. Bubnov, S. N. Bul-

gakov, "A Catholic," S. Chetverikov, D. Chizhevsky, V. Ekkersdorf, A. Elchaninov, E. El'son, H. Erenburg, G. Fedotov, N. Fedorov, G. Florovsky, S. L. Frank, S. Fumet, M. A. Georgievsky, N. Glubokovsky, V. Grinevich, priest-monk Ioann, V. Ilyin, P. Ivanov, I. Ivask, "K. A.," "K. N.," A. Karpov, L. P. Karsavin, A. Kartashev, S. Kavert, N. Klepinin, L. Kozlovsky, T. S. Ku, G. Kuhlmann, M. Kurdiumov, I. Lagovsky, F. Lieb, P. Lopukhin, N. Lossky, J. Maritain, "A Russian monk," O. Nalimov, P. Novgorodtsev, S. Ollard, A. Petrov, Pius XI, A. Pogodin, "A priest of Petrograd," D. Remenko, A. Remizov, P. Savitsky, J. Sazonova, V. Sezemen, E. Skobtsova, I. Smolitsch, V. Solovyov, V. Speransky, I. Stratonov, P. Suvchinsky, P. Tillich, N. Timashev, S. Troitsky, G. N. Trubetskoy, S. N. Trubetskoy, G. V. Tsebrikov, R. Valter, B. Vysheslavtsev, L. Zander, V. Zenkovsky.

21. Each time the editors of *The Way* were in serious disagreement with the author of an article they published, they indicated this by means of a note on the bottom of the first page (see for example C1, 85). Otherwise, when the editors were themselves divided on the publication of an article of Berdyaev himself, they signaled this likewise by a note (see for example B22, 110).

22. Elizabeth Skobtsova, in her memoirs of the poet Alexander Blok, records that the intellectual elite to which she belonged was comparable to that of the last Romans, for both were aware of their isolation and lack of relationship to the rest of society and of the imminent catastrophe. She writes: "Russia was uneducated, but in our circle the entirety of universal culture was concentrated. One could quote the ancient Greeks by heart, there was great enthusiasm for French symbolism, one claimed as one's own Scandinavian poetry, one knew the philosophy, theology, history, and poetry of the world . . . it was just like Rome in the final, decadent days." E. Skobtsova, "Encounters with Blok," *Uchenye zapiski Tartuskogo universiteta*, no. 209, 1968, 168.

23. For general bibliographical information, see the editor's note 16 above.

24. N. Berdyaev, *The Philosophy of Freedom* (Moscow: Put', 1911; new ed., Pravda, 1989), 28.

25. S. Bulgakov, "Economic Materialism as Philosophy and as Science," in *The Philosophy of Economy*, part 1 (Moscow: Put', 1912; new ed., Moscow: Nauka, 1993), 276–297.

26. On the idea of economics, again, not conceptualized by reason but, following the iconoclastic crisis, as the foundation of a new sense of symbol, see the approach of Marie-José Mondzain, *Image, Icône, économie, les sources byzantines de l'imaginaire contemporain* (Paris: Seuil, 1996).

27. S. L. Frank, *Knowledge and Being* (Petrograd: R. G. Sreder, 1915); French trans. (Paris: F. Aubier, 1937), 315.

28. N. Berdyaev, *Essai d'autobiographie spirituelle* (Paris: Buchet-Chastel, 1958), 257.

29. P. Struve, "Preface," in *De profundis, a Collection of Articles on the Russian Revolution* (Moscow: Iz Glubin, 1918; new ed., 1989), 5.

30. V. Zenkovsky, "On My Life," in *An Anthology in Memory of Father Vasilii Zenkovsky* (Paris: R. S. H. D., 1984), 84 (Russian).

31. Sergius Bulgakov, "My Atheism," in *Autobiographical Notes* (Paris: YMCA Press, 1946; new ed., 1991), 25–33 (Russian).

32. D. Beaune, G.P. Fedotov, *What Remains (Reflections on the Russian Revolution)*, doctoral thesis, University of Provence-Aix-Marseilles publications, Aix, 1990, p. 18.

33. *Free Voices*, notice of the editors, Petrograd, 1918, n. 1, p. 1 (Russian).

34. Berdyaev, *Essai d'autobiographie spirituelle*, 218.

35. For the question of the monks, worshippers of the Name, defended by Bulgakov and Berdyaev against the Synod's accusation of magism, see the thesis of Antoine Nivière and the works of D. Pospielovsky, *The Orthodox Church in the History of Rus', of Russia and of the Soviet Union* (Moscow: BBI, 1996).

36. See the section in the introduction, "The Epistemological Stance of Russian Religious Thought."

37. S. Bulgakov, *The Tragedy of Philosophy (The Philosopher and Dogma)*, Prague, March 1925, in S. Bulgakov, *Works* (Moscow: Nauka, 1993), 311–518; N. Berdyaev, *The Philosophy of Freedom* (Moscow: Put', 1911). See also N. Berdyaev, "Symbol, Myth and Dogma," in *Freedom and the Spirit* (Paris: YMCA Press, 1927) (Russian); French trans., *Esprit de Liberté* (Paris: Je Sers, 1933; repr., Paris: Desclée de Brouwer, 1984), 67–96. Berdyaev, rejecting both agnosticism and "the rationalist hypothesis which supposes that the mystery of the divine being is accessible to concepts," defines symbolism as that "which admits the transfusion of divine energy into this world, which separates and joins two worlds, and recognizes that the divine being only symbolizes itself while remaining unfathomable and mysterious" (75). He defines theology "as the symbolic expression of the spiritual path" (80). After all, "the foundation of mystical and symbolic knowledge is not a philosophical proposition, but rather a mytho-logical representation. A concept gives birth to philosophical proposition, while a symbol produces a mytho-logical representation.... Religious philosophy is, by itself, a creation of myths, an imagination" (81).

38. S. Bulgakov, *The Unfading Light* (Moscow: Put', 1917) (Russian); French trans., *La Lumière sans déclin*, trans. Constantin Andronikov (Paris: L'Age d'Homme, 1990), 72. I quote from the French translation.

39. Ibid., 80 (French trans.).

40. Ibid., 82.

41. See the thesis of M. Grabar, "The Renaissance of Religious Philosophy in Russia at the Turn of the Twentieth Century," Paris, January 1996, manuscript.

42. S. Bulgakov, *The Tragedy of Philosophy*, op. cit., 317–318.

43. A third-century heresy that tried to synthesize Christian revelation with Greek substantialism by portraying God as a sole hypostasis transforming itself into tri-unity.

44. Bulgakov, *The Tragedy of Philosophy*, 319.

45. Ibid., 389.

46. *Vekhi: Sbornik statei o russkoi intelligentsii* (Moscow: V. M. Sablin, 1909; new ed., Frankfort: Posev Verlag, 1967) (Russian). In English, under the title *Sign-*

posts, trans. Marshall S. Shatz and Judith E. Zimmerman (Irvine, CA: C. Schlacks, Jr., 1986).

47. A. Arjakovsky, "Landmarks (1909), Criticisms of the Russian Intelligentsia," Master's dissertation under the tutelage of F.-X. Coquin, Paris-Sorbonne, June 1989; and *Les Jalons: Cent Ans Apres,* ed. Antoine Arjakovsky, with Georges Nivat, Paul Valliere, Olga Sedakova, Enzo Bianchi, Walter Kasper, and John Milbank (Lviv: Éditions de L'Institut d'Études Écumeniques, Université Catholique d' Ukraine, 2010).

48. I. Gardenin, "Landmarks as a Sign of the Times," in *Landmarks as a Sign of the Times (A Collection of Articles)* (Moscow: Zveno, 1910), 8.

49. V. Lenin, "Concerning *Landmarks,*" in *Complete Works,* vol. 16, 1909–1910, 127, cited by N. Poltoratsky, *Russia and the Revolution* (Tenafly, NJ: Hermitage Press, 1988), 53–47 (Russian).

50. Metr. A. Khrapovitsky, *Slovo,* May 10, 1909. See N. Berdyaev, "An Open Letter to Archbishop A.," in *The Spiritual Crisis of the Intelligentsia* (St. Petersburg: Obshchestvennaia pol'za, 1910), 289.

51. The most documented study is that done by N. Poltoratsky, "The Points of Reference and the Russian Intelligentsia," *Mosty,* no. 10, Munich, 1963, 292–304 (Russian), translated into English as "The Dispute over the Signification of 'Points of Reference,'" *Canadian Slavonic Papers,* vol. 9, no. 1, 1967, 86–106; this article reappears with notes in N. Poltoratsky's *Russia and the Revolution* (n. 49 above), 53–74 (Russian). See also *Vekhi, Pro and Contra,* edited by V. Sapov (Moscow: SPb, Ruskij Put', 1998), 256.

52. A. Kartashev, "The Revolution and the Council of 1917–1918," *Russia and Christianity,* nos. 1–2, 7–12, 1950. Also see Hyacinthe Destivelle, *Le concile de Moscou 1917–1918* (Paris: Cerf, 2006).

53. Michel Heller, "First Warning: The Lash of the Whip. The History of the Expulsion of Cultural Personalities from the Soviet Union in 1922," *Notebooks of the Russian and Soviet World,* no. 2, 1979, 131–172; L. A. Kogan, "Expel Abroad without Pity (Once More on the Emigration of the Spiritual Elite)," *Voprosy filosofii,* no. 9, 1993, 61–84 .

54. V. Kostikov, *Ne budem proklinat' izgnanie* [*Let Us Not Curse the Exiles*], 176–177.

55. B77, 16.

56. R3, 4.

57. V8, 110–119.

58. V9, 136.

59. R3, 8.

60. N. Berdyaev, Iakov Bukshpan, F. Stepun, and S. Frank, *Oswald Spengler and the Decline of Europe* (Moscow: Bereg, 1922).

61. See especially N. Berdyaev, *The Meaning of History* (Berlin: Obelisk, 1923); V. Zenkovsky, *Russian Intellectuals and Europe: The Criticism of European Culture by Russian Intellectuals* (Belgrade: Nova Europa, 1929; new ed., Paris: YMCA Press, 1955).

62. B12, 12.
63. B12, 10.
64. Z18, 54. Quote from Kant, *The Critique of Practical Reason* (in French trans.), 8th ed. (Paris: Presses Universitaires de France, 1983), 173.
65. Z18, 55.
66. F26, 32.
67. F58, 10.
68. B22, 113.
69. N3, 69.
70. B16, 180.
71. O. Böss, *Die Lehre der Eurasier: Ein Beitrag zur russischen Ideengeschichte des 20. Jahrhunderts* (Wiesbaden, 1961); N.V. Riasanovsky, "The Emergence of Eurasianism," *California Slavic Studies*, vol. 4, 1967, 39–72; M. Bassin, "Russia Between Europe and Asia: The Ideological Construction of Geographical Space," *Slavic Review*, Spring 1991; [special edition] *The Foundation Stones (Nachala)*, no. 4, Moscow, 1992, 112 (Russian).
72. A. A. Troyanov and R. I. Vildanova, "Bibliography of Eurasianism," in *Foundation Stones*, 103–112.
73. The Editors, "Preface," in *The Going-Forth Towards the East: Affirmations of the Eurasians* (Sofia, 1921); new ed., *The Paths of Eurasianism: The Russian Intelligentsia and the Destinies of Russia* (Moscow: Russkaia Kniga, 1992), 313.
74. P. Suvchinsky, "The Eternal Foundation," in *On the Roads: Affirmations of the Eurasians*, no. 2 (Berlin: Guelikon, 1922), 109 (Russian).
75. N. Trubetskoy, "The Tower of Babel and the Confusion of Tongues," *Evraziiskii vremennik*, no. 3, Berlin, 1923, 107–124. See also Patrick Sériot, *N. S. Troubetzkoy, l'Europe et l'humanité: Essais linguistiques et paralinguistiques*, Philosophy and Language (Sprimont, Belgium: P. Mardaga, 1996), 126.
76. G. Florovsky, "Just Patriotism and Sinful Patriotism," in *On the Roads*, 230.
77. B9R, 134.
78. B9R, 135.
79. V. Solovyov, *The Russian Idea* (Paris: Librairie Académique Didier, 1888); republished as V. Solovyov, *Sophia and the Other French Writings* (Paris: La Cité–L'Age d'Homme, 1978), 102.
80. R3, 5.
81. B16, 182; F26, 27. See also N. Berdyaev, "Democracy, Socialism and Theocracy," in *The New Middle Age* (Berlin: Obelisk, 1924); French trans. (Paris: Plon, 1927; repr., Paris: L'Age d'Homme, 1985), 113–133. Berdyaev writes: "Without the realization of the supreme spiritual life, i.e. without a rebirth, without a new spiritual birth, it is not possible to accede to a perfect society or a perfect culture. It is not possible to be content with symbolizing the supreme spiritual life and finally simulating it; it must be attained in truth.... It is not possible to return to the ancient theocracies, be they those of the East or those of the West, for there can be no possible return to the exterior celebration of the Kingdom of God if one has not truly attained it" (129).

82. R3, 7.
83. L15, 34.
84. F62R, 191.
85. L15, 47. See V. Ilyin, *The Six Days of Creation* (Paris: YMCA Press, 1930; repr., Paris: YMCA Press, 1992), 51.
86. L15.
87. L15, 41.
88. R. Kroner, *Vom Kant bis Hegel*, 1929.
89. Jean Wahl, *Le malheur de la conscience dans la philosophie de Hegel* (Paris: Rieder, 1929).
90. B39R, 104.
91. B39R, 106.
92. F65R, 90.
93. N. Hartmann, *Ethik* (Berlin: Walter de Gruyter, 1926).
94. F70, 83.
95. F63R, 136.
96. S13R, 117.
97. Olivier Clément, *Hesychasm*, Collectanea Cisterciensia, 53, fasc. 1, 3–19.
98. V7, 80.
99. John Meyendorff, *Initiation à la théologie byzantine* (Paris: Cerf, 1975), 103. This method, in principle, goes back to the beginnings of monasticism, but it was not until 1368, when St. Gregory Palamas was canonized, that it became explicit on a theological level. In Russia, the fourteenth-century renewal of monastic holiness corresponded exactly with the penetration of hesychasm—notably through St. Sergius of Radonezh (1314–92). The dominating figure of St. Nil of Sora (1433–1508) is a fruit of this renewal. In his monastery, St. Nil stressed an interior asceticism, which gave preference to liberty and submission to Christ over obedience to one's confessor; he also inaugurated a critical exegesis of hagiographies. In the council of 1503, he opposed those who favored the death penalty for heretics and those who defended the church's possession of lands and serfs (S20, 60). In the eighteenth century, the Eastern hesychastic tradition was consigned to writing by Nicodemus the Hagiorite, a monk of Mount Athos and a promoter of frequent communion, in an anthology of texts entitled *Philokalia*—a word which means love of beauty—which was published in Venice in 1782. It was translated into Slavonic by a Ukrainian living in Moldavia, Paisius Velichkovsky (1722–94), and became the preferred spiritual nourishment of the Russian monks, of Seraphim of Sarov and the elders of Optino. Ilyin, in the book reviewed by Lossky for *The Way*, insists on the joyful nature of this spirituality. He quotes St. Seraphim: "Joy is not a sin, little mother [*matushka*]. It takes away our fatigue. Fatigue engenders sadness and that is the worst of things. When I entered the monastery, little mother, I went to sing in the choir. My joy, I was so happy!" (L11R, 153).
100. S. Bulgakov, *La Lumière sans déclin*, 101–168.
101. C3, 44–45.

102. Moreover, the rediscovery in Russia, at the beginning of the twentieth century, of the more Christocentric vision of the Fathers of the Church led to an awareness by certain intellectuals of the risks of falling into a Buddhist-like spirituality that was exclusively dedicated to "the acquisition of the Holy Spirit" (according to the formula used by St. Seraphim in his dialogue with Motovilov). That is why the collection of texts presented in the article "Intellectual and Interior Prayer: Extracts from the Fathers . . . ," published in the July 1926 issue of *The Way*, were all dated earlier than the fourteenth century (A22).

103. *Brhad-aran*, Upanishad IV, 3; V7, 83.
104. V7, 89.
105. V16, 91.
106. Vysheslavtsev corresponded with Rudolph Otto. See B. Vysheslavtsev file at the YMCA Press Archives, Paris.
107. V15R, 109.
108. L10, 24.
109. A18, 103.
110. K13.
111. V14R, 125.
112. A18, 103.
113. A18, 101.
114. F29R, 84.
115. B77, 16.
116. Aristotle, *Metaphysics* IV.3, 1005b19. Translation W. D. Ross.
117. Pavel Florensky, *The Pillar and Ground of the Truth* (Moscow: Put', 1914; Paris: L'Age d'Homme, 1975), 101. English trans. Boris Jakim (Princeton: Princeton University Press, 2004).
118. Ibid. (French ed., 1975), 105. See also P. Florensky, *The Cosmological Antinomies of Kant* (Sergiev Posad: Editions of the Academy of Theology Saint Sergius, 1909).
119. Florovsky took particular interest, in the pages of *The Way*, in the thought of the French neo-Kantian philosopher Charles Renouvier precisely because, for the latter, God is above all the Creator (F36R, 115).
120. Florensky, *The Pillar*, 98.
121. Immanuel Kant, *The Critique of Pure Reason* (French trans.), under the direction of Ferdinand Alquié (Paris: Gallimard, 1980), 408–415.
122. S. Bulgakov, *La Lumière sans déclin*, 171.
123. B41R, 91.
124. V. Ilyin writes: "For the Christian believer, the a priori fundamental truth is that the world was created by one and the same Logos, by one and the same Wisdom, and that this is manifested in the holy book (sophianic), the Bible. . . . The Logos incarnate himself said, 'I am the Way, the Truth and the Life' (John 14:16)." V. Ilyin, *The Six Days of Creation, the Bible and Science Concerning the Creation and the Origin of the World* (Paris: YMCA Press, 1991; original pub., 1930), 9 (French).

125. Ibid., 15.
126. Ibid., 16.
127. T4, T5, T6.
128. B41R, 100.
129. B41R, 103.
130. These differences reappear in their different interpretations of the revolution. For Berdyaev, Shestov "reasons as positively and rationally as P. N. Miliukov" (B41R, 104).
131. F71, 126.
132. B41R, 88–90.
133. N. Berdyaev, *The Spirit of Dostoevsky* (Prague: YMCA Press, 1923) (Russian); French trans., *L'esprit de Dostoevski*, trans. L. Julien Cain (Paris: Éditions Saint-Michel, 1929).
134. B24. See also Z10. The idea of making reparation to God is the Anselmian theory of atonement, commonly known as the satisfaction theory.
135. B24, 57–58.
136. B23R, 131.
137. V13, 15.
138. P. de Laubier, *L'Eschatologie* (Paris: Presses Universitaires de France, 1998).
139. E. Dacque, *Urwelt, Sage und Menschheit* (Munich: Oldenbourg, 1924).
140. F66R, 92.
141. E. Dacque, *Leben als Symbol: Metaphysik einer Entwicklungslehre* (Munich and Berlin: R. Oldenbourg, 1928); L. Bolk, *Das Problem der Menschwerdung* (Jena, 1926); M. Scheler, *Die Stellung des Menschen im Kosmos* (Darmstadt, 1928).
142. F72R, 129.
143. In *The Pillar and Ground of the Truth*, Florensky writes: "The theory of knowledge, by means of the notion of transcendental intuition, with all the acts of apprehension, of reproduction and recognition which accompany it, make memory the fundamental cognitive principle of reason. Plato expresses the same conviction, clothing it with images of the myth.... We would like, however, to know more about the ontological aspect of memory.... It is the activity of intellectual assimilation, i.e., its work consists in reestablishing, creatively, basing itself on representations, what is revealed in Eternity to the mystical experience; put otherwise—memory creates, in Time, the symbols of Eternity.... The past, as well as the present and the future, in order to make a place *now* for the mystical symbolism, must themselves be experienced *together*—still as elements belonging to different times but suddenly seized *sub specie aeternitatis*: according to the threefold role of the memory, the activity of thinking expresses Eternity in the language of Time; the act of this expression is precisely *memory*.... Thus memory is the creative principle of thought; it is the thought within the thought, it is, strictly speaking, *thought* ... recalling, God thinks; by thinking he creates" (French ed., 135–136).
144. For the contribution to history of this Freudian approach of the manifestations of collective memory, cf. Henry Rousso, *The Vichy Syndrome* (Paris: Seuil, 1987).

145. N. Berdyaev, *A. Khomiakov* (Moscow: La Voie, 1912).
146. S27.
147. I1.
148. F2.
149. In "Carmen Saeculare," the Russian historian brings into play his idea that the spirit is linked to the soul but also to the body by pointing out that the new cult of the body and the practice of sports in the West could represent a new form of chivalry, provided that these spiritual forces be submitted to the Holy Spirit and not to the Beast (F7).
150. Fedorov's editor was N. A. Setnitsky (1888–1937), a Russian economist who was a disciple of V. A. Kozhevnikov and a friend of the Moscow intellectuals V. N. Muravev (1885–1932) and A. K. Gorsky (1886–1943) (pseudo. Gornostaev). In his capacity as engineer, Setnitsky was sent to Harbin by the Soviet government to work on the project of a trans-Manchurian railway. Thanks to this, he was able to serve as a link between the intellectual milieus of Harbin, Moscow, and Paris. As of 1927, he entered into correspondence with the Russian emigrants in Paris. In 1928, P. Suvchinsky published "Extract From the Correspondence of N. Fedorov with V. Kozhevnikov Concerning Turkestan" in the third issue of *Versts* (*Versty*, no. 3, 277–288; see also N. Setnitsky's article "The Communist Order in the Representations of N. Fedorov," 259–277) and, in the editorial, called the reader's attention to the "actuality" of the common project, understood as the indivisibility of the individual and the collectivity (*Versty*, no. 3, 6). In the April 1927 issue of *The Way*, Berdyaev reviewed an anonymous work marked by the ideas of Fedorov. It was in fact a book by N. Setnitsky and A. Gorsky. Berdyaev writes: "We can only have an extreme interest in religious thought within Russia" (B25R, 122). Thanks to this connection, Ilyin received a book by V. Muravev, one of the authors of the collection *De Profundis* who had remained in Russia. A professor at the State Academy of Sciences and Art, Muravev, prior to his arrest in 1929, had succeeded in founding a circle of religious philosophy at Moscow and made known the ideas of Fedorov to V. Mayakovsky, Platonov, and Pasternak. (The ideas of N. Fedorov were taken up by Boris Pasternak in *Doctor Zhivago*. His father, Leonid Pasternak, was a friend of Fedorov and had painted a portrait of him.) Muravev's book, also marked by the ideas of Fedorov, was entitled *The Conquest of Time* and had been edited at the author's expense in Moscow in 1924. The book was reviewed by Ilyin in the January 1928 issue of *The Way* (I16R). (It was also reviewed by another Eurasian, V. Sezeman, in *Versty*, no. 3, 172–175.) Three months later, Berdyaev published a new unedited extract from the work of N. Fedorov (F22). In 1928–29, Setnitsky published the books of A. Gorsky, *Before the Visage of Death, L. Tolstoy and N. Fedorov,* and *Paradise on Earth. The Ideology of F. Dostoevsky: F. Dostoevsky and N. Fedorov*. During the summer of 1928, he visited Paris, where he met Suvchinsky and Berdyaev. After this meeting Berdyaev reviewed the works of Gorsky in the June 1928 and November 1929 issues (B32, B43R) and published, in September 1929, new, unedited manuscripts of Fedorov (F23).

151. B25R.
152. B32.
153. B8, 52.
154. F58, 30.
155. B8, chapter 3.
156. B43R, 116.
157. L13, 13.
158. N. Berdyaev, *The Meaning of the Creative Act* (Moscow: Put', 1914), 291 (Russian).
159. B11, 41.
160. V18R.
161. F67, F69.
162. B30R.
163. F7.
164. Berdyaev, "The Charm of Men of Culture," in N. Berdyaev, *Types of Russian Religious Thought* (Paris: YMCA Press, 1989), 524 (Russian).
165. R7, R8, E1, T17; Zaitsev was part of the first editorial board but never published an article.
166. I19R, 111.
167. S15, 67–68.
168. B42R, 117–118.
169. A. Koyré, *La philosophie de J. Boehme* (Paris: Vrin, 1929).
170. B19R, 119.
171. The different Russian editions of translations of Boehme, dating back to the end of the seventeenth century, cite the term *Ungrund* textually. See the introduction to the Russian translation of J. Boehme, *Christosophia* (St. Petersburg: A-CAD, 1994). Cf. also "The Russian Translations of Jakob Boehme," *Bibliograficheskie zapiski* (Moscow, 1858), note 5.
172. K9, 125.
173. K12, 47.
174. F29R, F39R.
175. I20R.
176. Proverbs 8:22–23.
177. F23.
178. S. Bulgakov, *La Lumière sans déclin*, 145.
179. Ibid., 161.
180. B118, 15.
181. S. Bulgakov, *Kupina neopalimaia* (*The Burning Bush*) (Paris: YMCA Press, 1928); French trans., *Le buisson ardent* (Paris: L'Age d'Homme, 1987), 122.
182. B35, 19.
183. V. Solovyov, *Sophia and Other French Writings* (Paris: La Cité–L'Age de l'Homme, 1978) (French).
184. B42R, 120.

185. B38R, 99.
186. A. Khomiakov, *Oeuvres*, 3rd ed. (Moscow, 1900), vol. 1, 283.
187. Z19, 3–22.
188. Z19, 14.
189. Z19, 17.
190. A. Khomiakov, *Oeuvres*, vol. 2, 230.
191. N. Berdyaev, *A. Khomiakov*, 36.
192. I9, 92.
193. I9, 94.
194. I9, 94.
195. K13, 44.
196. F28R, 130.
197. F27, 69; F40, 5.
198. John 16:14.
199. F27, 77.
200. F27, 78.
201. F40, 7.
202. F40, 14.
203. B18, 52.
204. B118, 18.
205. Eph. 1:23; Col. 3:11.
206. Luke 4:16.
207. B115, 62.
208. B116, 47–58.
209. R. Girardet, *Mythes et mythologies politiques*, 12.
210. Ibid., 105.
211. Ibid., 136.
212. R3, 5.
213. Bernard Marchadier, "The Exhumation of the Relics in the First Years of the Soviet Government," *Notebooks of the Russian and Soviet World*, no. 1, 1981, 67–88.
214. Metropolitan Anthony Khrapovitsky was born in Novgorod in a family of the aristocracy. He finished his studies at the Academy of Theology of Moscow in 1885 and began to teach at the St. Petersburg Academy. At the age of twenty-eight he became rector of the Academy of Theology at Moscow, but his modernist teachings, influenced by the school of moralist theology of the end of the century, led to his transfer to the Academy of Theology of Kazan in 1895. In 1900 he became bishop of Ufa, then of Volynia, and finally of Kharkov. At the council of 1917–18, he was one of the three candidates for the patriarchal throne. After the revolution he became metropolitan of Kiev and of Galicia but had to leave Russia along with the White Army in 1920. His theological modernism found its most notable expression in his book, edited by the YMCA Press in 1925, where, in treating of the dogma of redemption, he links salvation not only to the death of Christ on the cross but also to the night of Gethsemane.

215. Metropolitan Evlogy Georgievsky was also a monarchist. In fact, he had been a monarchist deputy in the Duma.

216. *Acts of the Council of the Church in Exile* (Sremski Karlovtsy, 1992), 50.

217. See *Histoire du Christianisme*, under the direction of J. M. Mayeur (Paris: Desclée de Brouwer, 2000), vol. 12, *Guerres mondiales et totalitarisme (1914–1958)*, 760.

218. This was the argument of Stratonov in *The Way* in 1929 (S37, S38).

219. Berdyaev was still in Russia at the time and thus witnessed firsthand the hardening of the Soviet government vis-à-vis the church in the wake of the council of the émigré church. In 1926 he condemned, in the pages of *The Way* and in the name of the tradition of "Khomiakov, Dostoevsky, and Solovyov," the violence employed by the monarchists at the council of Karlovtsy (B16, 178).

220. I33, 147.

221. *The Messenger of the Synod (Vestnik sinoda V.C.U)*, no. 7, Moscow, 1928, 76 (Russian).

222. T11, 120.

223. M. Heller and A. M. Nekrich, *L'Utopie au pouvoir: Histoire de l'U.R.S.S. de 1917 a nos jours* (Paris: Calmann-Levy, 1982), 137. In English, *Utopia in Power: The History of the Soviet Union from 1917 to the Present*, by Aleksandr Nekrich and Mikhail Heller (New York: Summit Books, 1986).

224. N1, 3.

225. N1, 3.

226. See N. Struve, *Les chrétiens en URSS*, 2nd ed. (Paris: Seuil, 1964).

227. N1, 4.

228. N1, 9–11.

229. S32, 114.

230. In French, the Russian Student Christian Movement was known as the Christian Action of Russian Students, after its model, the Catholic Action movement. The important idea of "movement"—implied in the term *dvizhenie*—was lost in translation.

231. Manuel Quintero, "Notes on WSCF Ostpolitik," *WSCF Journal*, August 1990, 20–24.

232. The YMCA also created Russian centers in Riga and at Harbin.

233. Z23R, 120.

234. P. Anderson, *No East or West* (Paris: YMCA Press, 1985), 30; see also A. Kartashev and N. Struve, *70 ans des éditions YMCA-Press* (Paris: YMCA Press, 1990).

235. YMCA Press Archives, Vysheslavtsev file, letter of 4/14/1922 to E. MacNaughten.

236. YMCA Press Archives, Vysheslavtsev file, letter of 8/17/1922 from Pianov to Kuhlmann.

237. The creation of this institute was also aided by the intervention of the philosopher I. Yashchenko, who, in a letter to Berdyaev dated 10/21/1922, wrote that he has heard of considerable praise for the Free Academy of Spiritual Culture and

proposed a new academy of this type in Berlin, which would be financed by an American.

238. The seminars organized by the Academy gave hundreds of students the opportunity to attend lectures by Stepun on Spengler, P. Florensky on magic, and Berdyaev on theosophy.

239. M. d'Herbigny relates that this took place at the local of a Masonic lodge, in *Orientalia Christiana*, vol. 3, 1, no. 11, 1924, 201; mention should also be made here of the periodical of the Union of Churches, in which reference is made to the modernism of the Academy of Religious Philosophy: *Union of Churches*, nos. 19–20, July–August 1926, 120–123, and to M. d'Herbigny and A. Deubner, "Russian Bishops in Exile," *Orientalia Christiana*, vol. 21, 1, no. 67, 1931.

240. P. Anderson, *No East or West*, ch. 3, "1922–1939," 27–79.

241. *Problems of the Russian Religious Conscience* (a collection) (Berlin: YMCA Press, 1924) (Russian).

242. F70, 86.

243. YMCA Press Archives, Vysheslavtsev file, "Report on the Winter Semester of the Russian Student Work in Germany from October 15, 1924, to April 4, 1925," 5.

244. Among these thirty-seven students were fifteen men and twenty-two women; twenty-three were under twenty-five years old. There were twenty-four Orthodox, six Protestants, and five Jews. Thirty-two of them had financial problems.

245. P. E. Kovalevsky, *The Russia of the Emigration* (Paris: Library des cinq continents, 1971, 1973), 2 vols. (Russian).

246. After I. Eihenvald, a philosopher who specialized in Schopenhauer, was tragically crushed under a streetcar on December 17, 1928, Frank, his fellow student and friend at the Society of Russian Philosophy (SPR) of Berlin, published a memorial article in *The Way*, describing him as "one of the best contemporary literary critics" (F71).

247. In 1925 the Academy of Religious Philosophy moved to 9 rue Dupuytren.

248. For several years Frank continued to give talks in Germany under the auspices of the already famous Academy of Religious Philosophy.

249. In his memoirs, Berdyaev writes that the initiative for the project came from G. G. Kuhlmann. See Berdyaev, *Essai d'autobiographie spirituelle*, 294–297.

250. G. G. Kuhlmann, "Minutes of a Conference between P. B. Anderson, G. G. Kuhlmann, Professors Berdyaev, and Vysheslavtsev Regarding the Project of Publishing a Russian Religious Periodical," Paris, October 20, 1924, YMCA Press Archives, 4.

251. Ibid., 2.

252. G. G. Kuhlmann, "Project of a Russian Religious Periodical. Minutes," YMCA Press Archives, 2.

253. Ibid., 2.

254. "Minutes of the Meeting on the New Russian Religious Journal. Held at Paris on December 4, 1924," YMCA Press Archives.

255. Ibid., 1. It is noteworthy that the authors hesitated over the subtitle of the review; it was not until June 1925 that they finally chose the subtitle "a journal of Russian religious thought" rather than "a journal of Russian Christian thought," as initially planned.

256. *Put'* can be translated as "the road" as well as "the way"; both terms evoke the ideas of evolution, of contemplation, and of a beginning and an end. The latter is signified by the emblem of the review—the sign XP intertwined (*Khristos*), an ancient Christian Christological symbol which appears on the cover of each issue, bordered by the two letters that begin and end the Greek alphabet, the alpha and omega. Hence it is possible to think that the term *Put'* evokes the response of Christ to Thomas as recorded in the Gospel of John (John 14:6), translated into Russian as "Ia put', i istina i zhizn" and into English as "I am the way, and the truth, and the life." I have retained the French translation as indicated on the review itself: "Voie (Way), A Russian Revue Appearing four times a year." We know from the Acts of the Apostles that the first Christians described themselves as adherents of "the way."

257. "Notes on the Conference held at Annemasse near Geneva, May 2, 1925," YMCA Press Archives, 4.

258. Ibid., 1.

259. During this conference the stipends for the contributors was also agreed upon. For an article of 36,000 characters, the review would pay $20, or about $1.60 a page. This stipend may have varied, since the archives of B. Vysheslavtsev indicate, for example, that for shorter articles—such as that of L. Zander on the 1926 RSCM congress—the author received the sum of $13.30, or $2.50 a page. On the other hand, a letter of December 9, 1924, from P. Anderson to E. Colton indicates that the overall budget for the production and distribution planned for a year (or four issues) was $2,500. YMCA Press Archives.

260. YMCA Press Archives.

261. D. Lowrie, *Saint Sergius in Paris, the Orthodox Theological Institute* (London, 1954), 119; Alexis Kniazeff, *L'institut Saint-Serge* (Paris: Beauchesne, 1974), 152.

262. B96, 130.

263. The titles of the papers were as follows: Bulgakov, "The Ways and Forms of Christian Activism," Berdyaev, "The Specificity of Russian Religiosity," Kartashev, "The Russian Religious Movement of the Nineteenth and Twentieth Centuries," Zenkovsky, "The Psychology of Religious Crises," and A. Nikitin, "The Missionary Duties of the Christian." See "The Pan-Russian Conference of Christian Students at Prague," in *The Spiritual World of Students: Messenger of the Russian Student Christian Movement in Europe*, no. 2, October 1923, Prague, Leguiografia, 19.

264. S. Frank, *The Fall of the Idols* (Berlin: YMCA Press, 1924) (Russian).

265. Z14, 123.

266. Z14, 125.

267. Z14, 121–127.

268. Z23R, 120.

269. *Acts of the Congress of the Russian Church Outside Russia* (Sremski Karlovtsy, 1921), 77.

270. YMCA Press Archives, Vysheslavtsev file, Bishop Benjamin, "Literature to Help Acquire the Spirit of Christian Orthodoxy," October 24, 1923, 2.

271. S. Bulgakov, *Svet nevechernii* (Moscow: Put', 1917), 212.

272. Metropolitan Anthony, *Novoe vremia*, no. 1005, Sept. 4, 1924 (Russian).

273. The preceding conferences were held in Moravia in July 1924, centered on the theme of church-state relations; at Argeron in July 1924; at Sternberg in July 1925, concerning the church, the confraternities, and the different forms of Christian life. See *The Spiritual World of Students*, July 1924, Argeron.

274. Z1, 113–114.

275. *Novoe vremia*, April 3, 1925, YMCA Press Archives, Anderson file, VII-1.

276. S. Bulgakov, *Vechernee vremia*, October 13, 1924, no. 170.

277. B118, 19.

278. Z1, 119.

279. Z3, 105.

280. Metropolitan Anthony, *The Dogma of the Redemption* (Paris: YMCA Press, 1925).

281. B17R, 183.

282. M. Zyzykin, *The Power of the Tsar and the Law of Succession in Russia* (Belgrade, 1924).

283. B8, 42.

284. I. Brianchaninov, *The Mystery of the Church, One, Holy, Catholic, and Apostolic* (St. Petersburg, 1863).

285. P1, 139.

286. In 1924 the YMCA Press published Ilyin's book *The Religious Signification of Philosophy: Three Conferences, 1914–1923*.

287. P. Struve, "Political Journal," *Vozrozhdenie (Renaissance)*, Paris, no. 7, June 25, 1925 (Russian); see N. Poltoratsky, *I.A. Ilyin and the Polemic Concerning His Ideas on Resistance to the Forces of Evil* (London and Canada: Zaria, 1975).

288. I. Demidov, "The Created Legend," *The Latest News*, Paris, June 25, 1925 (Russian).

289. M. Kolkov, "The Rejuvenation of the Gospel," *Pravda*, Moscow, no. 137, June 19, 1925 (Russian).

290. Bulgakov Archives, at the St. Sergius Institute, Paris, letter from N. Berdyaev on September 23, 1925, box XI, 23-1.

291. See Berdyaev Archives at Clamart.

292. In his reply, Berdyaev states that he is only writing in his own name (B13, 140).

293. B13, 143.

294. T15, 172–175.

295. B16, 177.

296. B16, 110–111.

297. B16, 108.
298. B16, 115.
299. B16, 104.
300. N. Struve, *Les chrétiens en URSS* (Paris: Seuil, 1961), 39. In the January 1928 issue of *The Way*, I. Stratonov published a detailed analysis of this declaration of Metropolitan Sergius. The author viewed this recognition of the state by the church favorably in the sense that "the Church's fundamental vocation is the salvation of people; this is why the hopes—as elevated as they might be—that repose on the Church should be abandoned if they trouble or impede the accomplishment of this essential task" (S34, 62). Stratonov also pointed out that the temporary synod organized by Metropolitan Sergius only has a consultative role, and this allows the maintaining of the principle of personal authority in the Russian Church. Finally—in the same way that Metropolitan Evlogy, on November 15, signed a declaration of "spiritual loyalty" to the Soviet State—Stratonov believed that the term "loyalty" should not be construed as implying submission to the laws of the state (72).
301. This was only published in *The Way* in April 1928.
302. Z9, 75.
303. Z9, 76.
304. In 1926, this school had three hundred ninety-two students in twenty-three countries throughout the world. See the YMCA Archives, Anderson file, P. Anderson, "Russian Service in Europe, Annual Report for the Year 1926," 4.
305. V12.
306. YMCA Archives, Anderson file, P. Anderson, "The YMCA and the Russian Orthodox Church," 3.
307. Ibid., 10.
308. YMCA Archives, Anderson file, "Russian Area Conference," Chantilly, May 28–30, 1933; E. T. Colton, "1927 Agreement," November 7, 1927, 6–7.
309. A. Kartashev, "The Schism of the Russian Church," *Vozrozhdenie*, no. 41, May 1925 (Russian).
310. *Tserkovnye vedomosti*, nos. 13–24, 10 (Russian).
311. *Messenger (Vestnik RSKhD)*, 1926, no. 10, 25 (Russian).
312. Z4, 117.
313. L9, 113.
314. L9, 114.
315. Z5, 123.
316. L9, 118.
317. B18, 42.
318. B18, 49.
319. B18, 54.
320. B18, 46.
321. *Tserkovnye vedomosti*, nos. 5–6, 1927, 8–9 (Russian).
322. *Tserkovnye vedomosti*, nos. 3–4, 1927, 1–2.

323. A. Kartashev, "The Reform, the Reformation, and the Accomplishment of the Church," *Na Putiakh*, Berlin, Éditions Eurasienne, no. 2, 1922, 30–98 (Russian).
324. ROCOR, Pastoral Letter no. 341, March 18, 1927, cited by M. Herbigny, *Éveques russes en exil*, op. cit., 147.
325. Ibid., 148.
326. Ibid., 149.
327. F4, 120.
328. F4, 120.
329. Thirty-seven of the fifteen-hundred parishioners in Paris, half of a parish in Berlin, and a quarter of the parish in London left Metropolitan Evlogy. See YMCA Archives, Anderson file, P. Anderson, "Russian Service in Europe," 3.
330. *Manuscript Note Presented by Professor and Protopresbyter Sergius to Metropolitan Eulogius*, Spring 1927, 58. St. Sergius Institute, Paris.
331. I12R, 157.
332. I34, 128.
333. V. Zenkovsky, "Concerning the Book of I. A. Ilyin 'Resistance to the Forces of Evil'," *Sovremmennye Zapiski*, no. 29, 1926, 284–307.
334. N. P. Poltoratsky, *I. A. Ilyin and the Polemic Concerning His Ideas on Resistance to the Forces of Evil*, 31.
335. K4.
336. A32.
337. K4, 106.
338. B22, 114.
339. B22, 114.
340. A32, 103.
341. B22, 111.
342. In October 1926, *Trest* mounted a false Eurasian congress in Moscow, to which it invited P. Savitsky. See R. Gul', *Ia unes Rossiiu s soboi*, vol. 1 (New York, 1984), 173; A. B. "Les Eurasiens et Trest," *La Renaissance*, no. 30, 1953, 117–127; S. L. Voichekhovsky, *Trest: Souvenirs et documents* (London, Ont., 1974), 28.
343. I16R, 94. L. Karsavin, *The Church, the Person, and the State* (Paris: Éditions Eurasienne, 1927) (Russian).
344. I16R, 94.
345. K28, 73.
346. K12, 37.
347. F58, 30.
348. B8, 46.
349. A7, 30.
350. A7, 32.
351. A7, 41; A8, 30–31.
352. A9, 34.
353. A9, 40.
354. A9, 57.

355. B9R, 134.
356. F64, 19.
357. *Eurasianism: An Attempt at a Systematic Exposition* (Paris: Éditions Eurasienne, 1926) (Russian).
358. B27R, 141.
359. B27R, 144.
360. I.V. Stalin, *Collected Works (Sochineniia)* (Moscow, 1947), vol. 11, 63.
361. M. Heller and A. M. Neckrich, *L'Utopie au pouvoir*, 183–184.
362. R. Brasillach, *Notre avant-guerre* (Paris, 1992), 14.
363. See especially the study on naturalizations in the Russian emigration, Gousseff and N. Saddier, *Le émigration russe en France, 1920–1930*, 209–223.
364. Robert Williams, *Culture in Exile: Russians in Germany* (Ithaca, NY: Cornell University Press, 1972).
365. P6.
366. Z10.
367. K34.
368. B. Varshavsky, *Nezamechennoe pokolenie (A Generation Nobody Noticed)* (New York: Chekhov Publishing House, 1956).
369. *RSKhD za granitsei (The Russian Student Christian Movement Abroad)* (Paris: MCER, 1928), 10–11.
370. I2, I3.
371. G5.
372. B40R.
373. T4, T5, T6.
374. J. Scherrer, "Les sociétés de philosophie religieuse," *Actes du colloque: La philosphie idéaliste en Russie*, VII, 7. See also J. Scherrer, "Intelligentia, religion, révolution: premiéres manifestations d'un socialisme chrétien en Russie, 1905–1907," *CMRS*, 1976, XVII-4, 427–466; ibid., 1977, XVIII-1/2, 5–32.
375. According to Metropolitan Anthony, it is moral experience that justifies the dogmas. See Paul Evdokimov, *Le Christ dans le pensée russe* (Paris: Cerf, 1970), 124.
376. T4, 31.
377. T6, 7.
378. T2, 58.
379. T3, 60.
380. S35, S36, S37, S38.
381. B35, 19.
382. B35, 19.
383. B40R.
384. I18, 60.
385. I18, 67.
386. I18, 74.
387. B3, 89.

388. "Berdiaev i berdiaevshchina," *Rossyia i slavianstvo*, Belgrade, February 2, 1929, 1.

389. B37, 94.

390. B37, 87.

391. B37, 88.

392. B37, 91–92.

393. B37, 86.

394. B37, 89.

395. YMCA Archives, Anderson file, P. Anderson, "Russian Service in Europe," 9.

396. 131 Av. Jean Jaures, in the offices of the Cabinet de Pédagogie Religieuse.

397. S. Bulgakov, *Lestvitsa iakovlia* (Paris: YMCA Press, 1929); *Jacob's Ladder*, trans. Thomas Allan Smith (Grand Rapids, MI: Eerdmans, 2010).

398. I20R, 139.

399. G. Struve, *Russkaia literatura v izgnanii* (*Russian Literature in Exile*) (New York: Chekhov Publishing House, 1956; repr., YMCA Press, 1984), 194.

400. B36, 5.

401. B36, 14.

402. B36, 20.

403. Z20, 77.

404. B36, 29–30.

405. Berdyaev, "Po voprosu ob ideologii RSKhD" (On the Question of the Ideology of RSCM), *Messenger*, no. 6, 1928.

406. Kartashev, "Eshche raz k voprosu ob ideologii" (Again on the Question of Ideology), *Messenger*, no. 11, 1929.

407. Zenkovsky, "Ocherk ideologii RSKhD" (Outline of the Ideology of RSCM), *Messenger*, nos. 5, 6, 8, 9, 1929.

408. Berdyaev wrote: "In our times the separation of fathers and sons is deeper than it was in the past for there is, between them, the catastrophes of the Great War and the revolution.... These last few years, new tendencies are appearing in the emigration which are not linked to the events taking place in Russia in the same way, as was the case with the first émigrés. These tendencies are characterized by a return to the Russia of the past" (B36, 3, 6–7).

409. F39R.

410. F4, 119.

411. F4, 119.

412. T11, 120.

413. N. Klepinin, *Sviatoi, blagovernyi velikii kniaz' Aleksandr Nevskii* (*The Holy, Just and Great Prince Alexander Nevsky*) (Paris: YMCA Press, 1926; Moscow: Strizen, 1993), 81.

414. I13R, 158. The unanimity concerning this book encouraged the RSCM to choose St. Prince Alexander Nevsky as its holy protector.

415. G. Fedotov, *Sv. Filipp, mitropolit Moskovskii* (*Saint Philip, Metropolitan of Moscow*) (Paris: YMCA Press, 1928), 4.

416. Prince Kurbsky, *Skazaniia*, ed. Istrialova, 2nd ed., 1842.
417. G. Fedotov, *Sv. Filipp*, 5 and 95.
418. G. Florovsky, "Evraziiskoe iskushenie" (The Eurasiianist Temptation), *Contemporary Annals*, no. 34, 1928, 312–346 (Russian).
419. Archives V. Kozovoi, published by A. Sobelev, "Evraziistvo, L. Karsavin i drugie" (Eurasianism, L. Karsavin, and the Others), *The Foundations* (*Nachala*), no. 4, 1992, 57.
420. I17R, 133.
421. K33, 98.
422. K33, 102.
423. K33, 111.
424. B32, 90.
425. F33, 9.
426. K13, 44.
427. F7, 111.
428. F7, 112.
429. B27R, 141.
430. D. Sviatopolk-Mirsky, "O Tolstom [On Tolstoy], 1828–1928," *Evraziia* (*Eurasia*), no. 1, November 24, 1928, 6.
431. This is the opinion of A. K. Chkhidze, *Chkhidze archives at Prague*, F. A. P., no. 1, 237.
432. *Evraziia*, December 8, 1928, 8.
433. The editorial staff, "Put' evraziistva" (The Road of Eurasianism), *Evraziia*, no. 8, January 12, 1929.
434. N. Alexiev, V. Ilyin, and P. Savitsky, *O gazete "Evraziia" (Gazeta "Evraziia"—ne evraziiskii organ)* [*Concerning the Journal Eurasia (The Journal Eurasia—Not a Eurasian Organ)*], Paris, 1929.
435. B37, 88–90.
436. Gerard Noiriel, "Français et étrangers," in *Les lieux de mémoire*, t. III, vol. 1, 281.
437. Gousseff and Saddier, "La situation juridique des réfugies russes," in *L'émigration russe en France, 1920–1930*, 163–223.
438. Isabelle Repiton, *L'opinion française et les émigrés russes, 1920–1939, à travers la littérature française de l'entre-deux-guerres*, mémoire de DEA (Paris: Institut d'Études Politiques, 1986). See also Florence Silve, *Des émigrés parmi d'autres: Recherches sur la colonie russe de l'agglomération lyonnaise durant la période 1920–1939*, Master's thesis, University of Lyon III, 1980.
439. Ralph Schor, *L'opinion française et les étrangers, 1919–1939* (Paris: Presses de la Sorbonne, 1985), 20.
440. Zoé Oldenbourg, *Visages d'un auto-portrait* (Paris: Gallimard, 1977).
441. Berdyaev, *The Spirit of Dostoevsky*, op. cit.
442. N. Zernov, *The Russian Religious Renaissance of the Twentieth Century*, chap. 10, "The Meeting with the Christian West" (New York: Harper & Row, 1963), 250–282.

443. R3, 7.
444. Etienne Fouilloux, "Traditions et expériences françaises," in *Histoire du christianisme*, gen. ed. Mayeur, vol. 12, 779.
445. Ibid., 780.
446. *Acta Apostolicae Sedis*, vol. 12, 1920, 595.
447. Etienne Fouilloux, "Vatican et Russie soviétique (1917–1939)," *Relations internationales*, no. 3, 1981, 303–318; Antoine Wenger, *Rome et Moscou 1900–1950* (Paris: Desclée de Brouwer, 1987), 648.
448. *Russia and Latinism* (Berlin: Éditions Eurasienne, 1923), 11–12 (Russian).
449. Ibid., 9.
450. T12R, 175.
451. T12R, 175.
452. S40, 134.
453. T13, 135.
454. G. Trubetskoy was particularly close to the archbishop of Malines, who shared his monarchic opinions and anti-communist commitment. He also considered Mercier's action on behalf of church unity as a model to follow. When Cardinal Mercier died, the Russian diplomat wrote an article for *The Way* in which he rendered homage to the Belgian bishop, whom he considered a saint (T14, 125).
455. O. Clément, *Berdiaev: Un philosphe russe en France* (Paris: Desclée de Brouwer, 1991), 79–140.
456. B14R, 146.
457. Berdyaev, in 1914, was the first Russian intellectual to make Bloy known in Russia through an article entitled "The Knight of Poverty," *Sofia*, no. 6, 1914, 49–78 (Russian).
458. F84, 154–160.
459. Z15R.
460. Z16R.
461. A28, 166.
462. A28, 164; see also Zenkovsky's article, Z17R.
463. A28, 165.
464. M. d'Herbigny, "L'aspect religieux de Moscou en Octobre 1925," *Orientalia Christiana*, vol. 5, t. 3, no. 20, January 1926.
465. B14R, 145.
466. A30, A31.
467. B20R, 132.
468. Ivan Kologrivov, S.J., "Royaume de Dieu et Royaume de César d'aprés la pensée d'un philosophe russe," *Orientalia Christiana*, no. 24, May 1926, 139–160.
469. The priory was transferred to Chevetogne in 1939.
470. There are two main studies on this subject: O. Clément, *Berdiaev: Un philosophe russe en France*, 81–105; F. Damour, *Berdyaev*, Master's thesis, Paris, Sorbonne, 1993.
471. N. Berdyaev, "Le destin de la culture," *Chroniques*, Le Roseau d'Or, Works and Chronicles, no. 2 (Paris: Plon, 1926), 73–100.

472. Berdyaev Archives, file no. 1496-1, doc. 605.
473. N. Berdyaev, *Un nouveau Moyen-Age*, Le Roseau d'Or, Works and Chronicles, no. 13 (Paris: Plon, 1927).
474. Berdyaev Archives, file no. 1496-1, doc. 568.
475. Ibid., doc. 459.
476. Ibid., doc. 453.
477. Ibid., doc. 453.
478. J. Maritain, *Refléxions sur l'intelligence* (Paris: Nouvelle Librarie Nationale, 1925).
479. R. Garrigou-Lagrange, *Le sens commun: La philosophie de l'être et les formules dogmatiques* (Paris: Nouvelle Librairie Nationale, 1925).
480. B10R, 169.
481. B10R, 171.
482. M1, 100.
483. B14R, 147.
484. M. Blondel, *L'Action* (Paris: Alcan, 1893).
485. R. P. Moncheuil, "Introduction," in *M. Blondel, Pages Religieuses* (Paris: Aubier, 1942), 9–57.
486. Concerning Suzanne de Dietrich, see Berdyaev Archives, file no. 1496-1, doc. 464.
487. These meetings were cloaked in mystery and have yet to be studied in detail. Some information about them can be found in: N. Zernov, *Abroad: Belgrade, Paris, Oxford—The Chronicle of the Zernov Family (1921–1972)* (Paris: YMCA Press, 1973) (Russian); Berdyaev Archives, file no. 1496-1, doc. 605; N. Berdyaev, "The Truth of Orthodoxy," *The Student World*, 21, July 1928, 249–263; J. Maritain, *Carnet de Notes* (Paris: Desclée de Brouwer, 1965); Marc Boegner, *L'exigence œcuménique, Souvenirs et perspectives* (Paris: Albin Michel, 1968).
488. From the book by V. Bourne, *La divine contradiction*, cited in F. Damour, *Berdyaev* (Master's thesis), 36 (n. 470 above).
489. A19, A23.
490. N. Berdyaev, *Essai d'autobiographie spirituelle*, 326.
491. I9, 89.
492. K12, 32.
493. F3R, 128.
494. F3R, 129.
495. N. Zernov, *Chronicle* (n. 487 above).
496. F6, 60.
497. F6, 70.
498. F6, 72.
499. In its account of the articles appearing in *The Way*, the review *Irénikon* hails the August 1927 issue as "the most remarkable." "Chronique des revues," *Irénikon*, t. III, no. 6, October 1927, 358.
500. V1.
501. S9, 121.

502. R. Rémond, *Les catholiques dans la France des années 1930s* (Paris: Éditions Cana, 1979).
503. Ca1, 85.
504. H. Massis, *Défense de l'Occident*, Le Roseau d'Or (Paris: Plon, 1927).
505. A. Malraux, *La tentation de l'Occident*, 1926; René Guénon, *Appels de l'Orient*; Grousset, *Réveil de l'Asie*; Muret, *Crépuscle des races blanches*.
506. R. Brasillach, *Notre avant-guerre*, 47.
507. J. Maritain, *Primauté du spirituel*, Le Roseau d'Or (Paris: Plon, 1927).
508. H. Massis, *Défense de l'Occident*, 56.
509. B28R, 145.
510. B28R, 146.
511. B28R, 147.
512. "Chronique des revues," *Irénikon*, t. III, no. 6, October 1927, 360.
513. F. Damour, *Berdyaev*, 50.
514. J. Maritain, *Pourquoi Rome a parlé* (Paris: Spes, 1927).
515. J. Maritain, *Primauté*, 268.
516. Ibid., 267.
517. B30R, 120.
518. B30R, 115.
519. In January 1928, the review published an account of the religious situation in China by the Russian émigré sinologist living in Harbin, T. S. Ku. Going against all the ideas he received from the Eurasians, the author mentions the presence in China of a westernizing current, which is "young, energetic and scientifically cultivated" as opposed to the ancient tradition of Chinese thought, which is turned towards aesthetics (K31, 54).
520. The circulation of the daily, *Action Française*, dropped rapidly—from 90,000 in 1926 to 40,000 in 1929; G. Cholvy and Y.-M. Hilaire, *Histoire religieuse de la France contemporaine*, 3 vols. (Toulouse: Privat, 1985–1988), vol. 2, 307. Berdyaev, in August 1927, recognized a great force in Catholicism and in the institution of the papacy due to its capacity to preserve its memory of the past, and he pays tribute to it (B26, 133).
521. B26, 131–132.
522. In January 1928, the review *Irénikon* could still write: "*Ex Oriente Lux* is not only true for the past, for the unique event: the birth of our Savior in Palestine; even today it would be to our great advantage if we could receive from our dear Orthodox brothers—who, to be sure, are wrong in being separated from Rome—the good lesson of this virtue of religion which too often is lacking in us." "Chronique," *Irénikon*, t. V, January 1928, 62.
523. In October 1928, Ilyin limited himself to expressing his solidarity with the German Benedictine C. Panfoeder (I19R).
524. F34R, 123.
525. F34R, 123.
526. Simeon the New Theologian, *Hymnes* I, ed. J. Koder, trans. J. Paramelle, *Sources Chretiennes* 156 (Paris, 1969).

527. F34R, 123.
528. F37R, 103.
529. B31R, 132.
530. B34R, 120.
531. F7, 114.
532. F7, 114.
533. B121, 74.
534. B121, 80.
535. B121, 77.
536. B121, 72.
537. B121, 78.
538. B121, 74.
539. B121, 81; Bulgakov already foresaw the determining role that *The Criticism of Abstract Principles* of Solovyov could play in the traditional controversies between Catholics and Protestants.
540. E. Behr-Sigel, *Un moine de l'Eglise d'Orient, Lev Gillet* [*A Monk of the Eastern Church, Lev Gillet*] (Paris: Cerf, 1993).
541. Metropolitan Evlogy, *Put' moiei zizni* [*The Way of My Life*], ed. T. Manoukhina (Paris: YMCA Press, 1947), 445. I quote from the Russian. In French, *Le chemin de ma vie*, trans. Pierre Tschesnakoff (Paris: Presses Saint Serge, 2005).
542. To distinguish it from Berdyaev's journal, the letter (F) was later added to the title of Fr. Lev's journal.
543. *The Way, Monthly Bulletin of the French Orthodox Community (F)*, managed by Fr. Lev Gillet, February 1929, 3.
544. Berdyaev Archives, March 5, 1928, doc. 605.
545. J. de Pange, *Journal*, vol. 1 (1927–1930) (Paris: Grasset, 1964), 155–156.
546. Z22R, 123.
547. J. Sazonova, "The Influence of French Literature on Russian Writers," in "Rencontres," ed. R. Sébastien et W. de Vogt, *Cahiers de la Quinzaine*, Paris, special issue, 1930.
548. In this sense, the 1929 publication of the French translation of Berdyaev's book only confirmed the observations of Maxence. N. Berdyaev, *L'esprit de Dostoevski*, trans. L. Julien Cain (Paris: Éditions Saint-Michel,1929).
549. S. Bulgakov, *U Sten Hersonisa, Dialogui*, in *Trudy po Sociologui i Teologui* (Moscow: Nauka, 1997), 351–500; S. Bulgakov, *Sous les remparts de Chersonése*, trans. B. Marchadier (Paris: Ad Solem, 2000).
550. B118.
551. B124, 47.
552. S. Bulgakov, *Kupina neopalimaia*, 120.
553. B123, 39.
554. B123, 50.
555. J. Meyendorff, *Initiation à théologie byzantine* (Paris: Cerf, 1975).
556. B124, 35.
557. B124, 47.

558. YMCA Press Archives.

559. Jean Baubérot, "L'organisation internationale du protestantisme: Le COE," in *Histoire du christianisme*, gen. ed. Mayeur, vol. 12, 44.

560. Suzanne de Dietrich, *50 Years of History, 1895–1945* (Geneva: WSCF, 1993), 13.

561. *The Orthodox Church and the Ecumenical Movement, Documents and Statement, 1902–1975*, ed. G. Patelos (Geneva: World Council of Churches, 1978), 27–33.

562. Ibid., 40–43.

563. Metropolitan Evlogy, *The Way of My Life*, 480 (Russian).

564. Raymond Winling, *La théologie contemporaine* (Paris: Le Centurion, 1983), 39–52.

565. A28, T1.

566. A33, 100.

567. A28, 162.

568. T1, 154.

569. K22, 123.

570. N. Zernov, *Chronicle*.

571. Z5, 125.

572. Z2, 120–121.

573. K32, 93.

574. K32, 96; Z2, 120–121.

575. E4, 89.

576. 1 Cor. 13:6–7.

577. B119, 91.

578. B119, 91.

579. B119, 92.

580. Z20.

581. K23.

582. A34, 111.

583. B121, 82.

584. A34, 106; S. Bulgakov, *The Orthodox Church*, rev. trans. Lydia Kesich (Crestwood, NY: St. Vladimir's Seminary Press, 1988), 116–128. Zernov also treats of this incident in *The Russian Religious Renaissance*, 262–263.

585. S. Zankov, *Das Orthodoxe Christentum des Ostens: Sein Wesen und seine Gegenwarige Gestalt* (Berlin: Furche Verlag, 1928).

586. A34, 108.

587. B121, 73.

588. B121, 79.

589. F30R, 129.

590. F38R, 107.

591. F35R, 113.

592. F41R, 118.

593. Z21R, 136.

594. W. Monod, *Du Protestantisme* (Paris: F. Alcan, 1928).
595. Z21R, 136.
596. Z23R, 121.
597. F26.
598. Z19.
599. *Orient und Occident: Staat, Gesellschaft, Kirche*, Blätter fur Theologie, Ethik und Soziologie, 1929–1934, nos. 1–17; March–October 1936, nos. 1–3 (Leipzig: I. C. Hinrichs).
600. L7, 71.
601. L7, 80.
602. L7, 74.
603. N. Berdyaev, *Essai d'autobiographie spirituelle*, 349.
604. L7, 80.
605. L7, 81.
606. John 11.
607. B98, 8.
608. B98, 17.
609. B98, 18.
610. John 11:8–10.
611. B98, 14.
612. B99, 94.
613. B99, 103.
614. Philippians 3:10.
615. Philippians 2:5–11.
616. B99, 98.
617. B99, 102.
618. O1, 124.
619. K1, 100.
620. Khomiakov, *Oeuvres*, vol. 8, 130.
621. N. Berdyaev, *A. Khomiakov*, 43 (French).
622. Metropolitan Evlogy, *The Way of My Life*, 481–484 (Russian).
623. H. Nickerson, *The Christian East*, no. 6, 2, June 1925, 90.
624. G5, 141.
625. Metropolitan Evlogy, *The Way of My Life*, 483 (Russian).
626. L. Zander, "Chronicle of the Institute of Theology," *Orthodox Thought*, Works of the St. Sergius Institute, Paris, no. 2, 1930, 206 (Russian).
627. B117, 5.
628. B117, 13.
629. B117, 24.
630. K3, 109.
631. B97, 3.
632. K3, 111.
633. K3, 110.

634. K3, 112.
635. Bezobrazov, in his report, erroneously gives the dates as November 30–December 17, 1927.
636. B97, 15.
637. A16, 114.
638. G12, 92.
639. F8, 104.
640. F8, 104.
641. F8, 106.
642. F8, 107.
643. Berdyaev, "'L'Orient et l'Occident' dans 'L'Orient et l'Occident,'" *Cahiers de la Quinzaine*, ser. 20, no. 9, June 5, 1930, 5.
644. Ibid., 11.
645. Ibid., 12.
646. Ibid., 29.
647. Ibid., 54.
648. Ibid., 56.
649. Ibid., 60.

Notes to Part Two

1. Emmanuel Mounier would frequently use the expression "nonconformist youth," as in I28, 65; *Esprit*, no. 2, November 1933, 281; and see M. Winock, *Esprit: Des intellectuels dans la cité (1930–1950)* (Paris: Seuil, 1975, 1996).
2. Jean Touchard, *Histoire des idées politiques* (Paris: Presses Universitaries de France, 1959, 1981), 2:815–839.
3. M. Winock, *Esprit: Des intellectuels dans la cité (1930–1950)*, 71.
4. E. Mounier, "Plaidoyer pour l'enfance d'un siècle," *Esprit*, no. 150, November 1948, 681.
5. Daniel Lindenberg, *Les années souterraines* (Paris: La Découverte, 1990), 33–35.
6. Vladimir Veidlé was a cousin of the filmaker Sergei Eisenstein. He was trained in both the history of art and literature. Throughout his life he maintained connections with writers, poets, and artists both of Europe and of the Russian emigration, with links to Akhmatova, Merezhkovsky, and Chukovsky. He wrote on Chagall, Malraux, and T. S. Eliot and brought his commitment to the arts and humanities to St. Sergius Institute, where he taught in these disciplines for over thirty years.
7. V3, 35.
8. V4, 56.
9. V4, 58.
10. N. Berdyaev, *O Naznachenia Cheloveka* (Paris: Sovremennye Zapiski, 1931). Translated in French as *De la destination de l'homme* (Paris: Je Sers, 1935) and in English as *The Destiny of Man* (London: G. Bles, 1937).

11. Lev Shestov, *Athènes et Jérusalem, un essai de philosophie religieuse* (Paris: Flammarion, 1967), 285.
12. Full names and dates include Nikolai Nikolaevich Afanasiev (1893–1966), Lev/Louis Gillet (1893–1980), Nicholas Alexandrovich Reimers (1894–1964), Lev Alexandrovich Zander (1893–1964), Nikolai Mikhailovich Zernov (1898–1980), Adolf Markovich Lazarev (1873–1944), Myrrha Lot-Borodin (1882–1957), Yakov Mikhailovich Menshikov (1888–1953), Lev Isaakovich Shestov (1866–1938), Evgeny Vassilevich Spektorsky (1875–1951), and Feodor Augustovich Stepun (1884–1965).
13. P8.
14. "Editorial," *New City*, no. 1, Paris, 1931, 5 (Russian).
15. Ibid., 7.
16. N. Afanasiev, *L'Église du Saint Esprit* (Paris: Cerf, 1975), preface by Marianne Afanasiev, 15.
17. R3, 7.
18. The archives of the review *The Way* are scattered about in several locations: at Clamart in the office of Berdyaev, at CGAALI (Tsentralni Gossudarstvenij Arkhiv po Literaturi I Iskusstv) in Moscow, at the Paul Anderson Archives at the University Library of Urbana-Champaign, Illinois (many thanks to William Maher and to the Ukrainian Catholic Education Foundation), and at Paris in the archives of the YMCA Press (many thanks to Alik Khananie for having given access to them).
19. Andrew Blane, *Georges Florovsky: Russian Intellectual and Orthodox Churchman* (Crestwood, NY: St. Vladimir's Seminary Press, 1993), 47.
20. YMCA Press Archives: Vysheslavtsev, correspondence with N. Lossky.
21. M2, 104.
22. I28, 60.
23. I28, 58.
24. I28, 62.
25. I28, 64.
26. Berdyaev Archives, Clamart, letter of V. Ilyin, 1.
27. Ibid., 2.
28. Ibid., 7.
29. Z24, 118.
30. *Tserkovny Vestnik* (*Church Messenger*), November 1932, 1.
31. But in reality, this article was written by Metropolitan Seraphim, as later became clear following a denial by the Russian Orthodox Church Outside Russia. Metropolitan Seraphim lived in Paris and closely surveyed the activities of the modernist groups.
32. *Tsarsky Vestnik*, no. 310, 3–4.
33. YMCA Archives, report by D. G., 1.
34. YMCA Archives, report by D. G., 2.
35. YMCA Archives, Anderson file, "Russian Area Conference," op. cit., 5.
36. Berdyaev, in "Russian Area Conference," 38.
37. Ibid., 39.
38. Ibid.

39. Ibid., 40.

40. "Journaux Intimes de L. I. Berdyaeva," Moscow, *Zvezda*, no. 10, 1995, 140–166.

41. Harumi Matsuguchi, "Tamara Klepinine (1897–1987): Ein Leben im Umkreis von N. Berdjajew (1874–1948)," *Japanese Slavic and East European Studies* 11, 1990, 45–58. See also Harumi Matsuguchi, "Berujiyaefu to 'Atarashi shukyo ishiki' Berujiyaefu no kuredo," *Hannan ronschu*, Osaka, no. 3, 1982, 65–74; Harumi Matsuguchi, "Geschichte der Einführung der Philosophie N. Berdjajews in Japan," *Kyoto Sangyo daigaku ronschu*, Kyoto, no. 4, 1985, 246–283 (with a bibliography of 117 studies on Berdyaev in Japanese, pp. 276–283).

42. The program of courses and seminars of this period was as follows: 1930–31: Berdyaev, "Russian Spiritual Culture in the Nineteenth Century" (second semester); Ilyin, "The Creation and Destruction of the World"; Vysheslavtsev, "The Subconscious and Its Mysteries"; Florovsky, "The Religious Meaning of History"; seminar by Berdyaev, "Concerning the Book, *The Destiny of Man*"; seminar by Bulgakov, "Asceticism and Christian Culture."

1931–32: Berdyaev, "The Destinies of Culture" (5 cycles of 4 conferences): culture, nature, and religion, the contradictions and destinies of culture, the culture of the social process, the spiritual crisis of contemporary European culture, the types of culture and the judgment of culture; Vysheslavtsev, "The Philosophy of Beauty" (1 cycle); Ilyin, "The Philosophical and Religious Meaning of Goethe's Faust" (1 cycle); seminar of Berdyaev, "Christianity and Creation (the Principal Tendencies of Contemporary European Culture)"; seminar of Bulgakov, "Orthodoxy and Modernity."

1932–33: seminar by Berdyaev, "The Social Question as Seen in the Light of Christianity" (biweekly every other Friday from 8:30 to 11:00 p.m.).

1933–34: Berdyaev, "The Destinies of the Russian National Idea" (universality and nationalism, nationalism and imperialism, messianic hope and racial theory, Christianity and Judaism, Christianity and war, Fascism and National Socialism, contemporary nationalism); Vysheslavtsev, "The Problem of Power and Christianity"; Mochulsky, "The Religious Life of France (Péguy, Bloy, A. Gide, St. Thérèse of the Child Jesus)"; Ilyin (?); seminar by Berdyaev, "The Person and Society; the Meaning and Finality of Theatre and Cinema"; seminar by Bulgakov (at St. Sergius), "Orthodoxy and Modernity."

1934–35: Berdyaev, "The History of Russian Thought"; Vysheslavtsev, "Man, Problems of Anthropology" (second semester); Mochulsky, "The Catholic Renaissance of France (Claudel, Teresa of Avila, St. John of the Cross)"; Fedotov, "The Religiosity of the Russian People as Seen in Their Spiritual Poetry"; seminar by Bulgakov, "Orthodoxy and Modernity."

43. YMCA Archives, cycle 1, conference 1, 1.

44. Afanasiev, *L'Église du Saint Esprit*, 17.

45. Ibid., 17–18.

46. Bulgakov had, in fact, developed a thesis according to which the figure of Judas Iscariot had not yet been fully revealed to the mind of the church. The church,

influenced by the Gospel of St. John, had the tendency to summarily condemn a man, greedy from the outset, without fully realizing that Christ, who could not be suspected of having deceived himself, had chosen the one who would betray him. To support his thesis, Bulgakov made an inventory of the Synoptic Gospels, enumerating all the spiritual actions that Judas accomplished along with the other apostles—the healings, the confession with Peter that Christ is the Son of God, the Last Supper. Bulgakov came to the conclusion that Judas, far from being a wolf among sheep, "*became a traitor*" (B128, 19) when he realized that Christ no longer incarnated his ideal—much more glorious for the Son of Man—of national Messianism. But that only shifted the problem. Bulgakov dedicated the second part of his lecture to a sophiological explanation of the antinomy between the Synoptic Gospels and the Gospel of St. John. Why did Christ, knowing from all eternity that Judas was going to betray him, historically choose him as an apostle? Can it be thought that Judas was a puppet in the hands of God? This posed the problem of predestination, debated by Augustine and Calvin and on which, to Bulgakov's dismay, the Eastern churches had never spoken. Differing from Western transcendentalism, which posed the relationship between God and the world in the same dimension, Bulgakov believed that in order to reply to this question, it was better to consider this relationship in an antinomic way. The world, he said, depended on God, but it was autonomous in its relationship with God. The relationship of God and the world in the Providence of God was interactive: "The unique Sophia and the unique divine world exist both in God and in creation, but according to two different modes: in eternity and in time, in an absolute way and in a relative, created way" (B129, 11). Passing from the cosmological antinomies of Kant to the theses of Origen concerning the preexistence of souls and to the doctrine of reincarnation of the Theosophists, Bulgakov returned to Judas and concluded that, in the image of the sophianic relationship between God and the world, God created the soul of Judas in his eternity so that he might become an apostle (which is why Christ chose him), but with his personal freedom, Judas transformed his ministry into treason (and the God-Man, the Lamb of God immolated from the beginning, experienced this liberty of the world unto the crucifixion) (B129, 23–27). It is well known that *publicistika* is a genre characteristic of Russian religious thought, where the most abstract considerations are mixed with political positions. The presentation by Bulgakov furnished a good example. Indeed, for Bulgakov, Judas, by his greed, that is, by his materialistic economy, and by his religious messianism, that is, his national socialism, was the archetypical figure of the "Bolshevik" (B128, 10). More generally, the tragedy of Judas had become the tragedy of an entire people, of Holy Russia, which, by betraying its apostolic mission for "thirty denarii" of economic progress, had transformed its religious energy into the persecution of the Church of Christ. The devil entered into the soul of the Communist oligarchy, as he had of old entered into the soul of Judas (B129, 34). Bulgakov concluded his thesis by asking if Lenin and Stalin would not wind up being hung, as was Judas. He prayed that the Russian people, like St. Paul, would rediscover the path to the Kingdom of God. With accents reminiscent of Dostoevsky, he concluded: "The murder of Christ in the hearts and in the souls in Russia dissimulates the resurrection of Christ. It is beginning from this day on: Christ is rising in Russia" (B129, 42).

47. Alexis Kniazev (Knieazeff), *L'Institut Saint-Serge* (Paris: Beauchesne, 1974), 81.

48. A. Kartashev, in "Russian Area Conference," 45.

49. The library of the St. Sergius Institute, which had just received an important gift of books through the intermediary of Florovsky—books left behind by the Methodist mission in Prague—had about six thousand volumes.

50. S. Bulgakov, in "Russian Area Conference," 47.

51. Ibid., 48.

52. F9, 44.

53. In order to put this struggle within the church in perspective, Fedotov began his talk by going back to the emergence of sanctity in Kiev with the two figures of Anthony and Theodosius, the founders of the Monastery of the Caves in the eleventh century. He stated that between Anthony, who brought the severe and hermit-centered spirituality of Mount Athos to Russia, and Theodosius, who mediated the simple, gentle, and cenobite Palestinian spirituality, the Russian people felt closer to the latter, given that he was canonized less than thirty-five years after his death. This spirituality flourished, Fedotov argued, in the fourteenth century with the figure of Sergius of Radonezh. Continuing in the tradition of Theodosius, Sergius wore old liturgical vestments, used wooden liturgical vessels, did not hesitate to give advice to great princes, and never punished his disciples. Influenced by the spirituality of hesychasm, of the prayer of the heart, the life of Sergius was a model of equilibrium between the mystical life in the desert and the ascetical life in the world. The fifteenth century, the golden age of Russian holiness, was also the period when two different currents began to appear among the disciples of Sergius. On the one hand was the mild and contemplative current, favorable to intellectual work and to the interpretation of Scripture, and living in total poverty. This was centered around the figure of Cyril, then Nil in northern Russia. On the other hand was the current that was turned towards the world, founded on a sense of asceticism, and recommending the discipline of a spiritual father on the journey towards the Kingdom. This was centered around Paphnutius of Borovsk, then Joseph of Volokalamsk in the southern Muscovite district. Fedotov set up a parallel between those who "were the issue of love (for God)" and those "born from the fear of God" (F9, 66), between those whose spiritual nourishment came from the Byzantine Fathers, while maintaining their "Russian-ness," and those who elaborated a religious nationalism, making the tsar the head of a Third Rome; between those who cherished their independence from temporal power, and those who put themselves at the service of the tsar in order to accomplish their social work. The real shame, Fedotov stated, was the liquidation of the Trans-Volga monks by the Josephites, who accused them of being Jewish sympathizers, and next the persecution of Maximus the Greek, who, by this fact alone, could hardly be considered the incarnation of

the lay model of Russian holiness. Fedotov did not hide his own preferences. He concluded by emphasizing that sanctity was able to enter Russia and maintain itself in the eighteenth and nineteenth centuries thanks to Paisius Velichkovsky, Tikhon of Zadonsk, and Seraphim of Sarov. "With them, the time has come to rehabilitate Nil, whom Moscow forgot to canonize, but who was ecclesiastically venerated in the nineteenth century. Nil represents the deepest and most beautiful expression of Russian medieval holiness" (F9, 70).

54. Bitsilli, "Russian Religious Psychology and Communist Atheism," *New City*, no. 3, 1932, 87–89. Likewise, if Shestov, whose thinking in many respects constituted the Old Testament pole of Russian spirituality, could be sensitive to the spiritual profile of Nil as the partisan of dialogue with the Judaizers, Nil could not compete with the figure of Abraham.

55. Priest-monk Ignatius (Ozerov), "A la conférence du RSHD en Lettonie en août 1928," Warsaw, ST [publisher], 1929 (Russian).

56. R1, 81.

57. V26, 83.

58. J. G. Lockhart, "The Russian Student Christian Movement in the Baltic States," London, ARCCF [Anglo-Russian Fellowship publishing house], n.d., 2.

59. Raeff, *Russia Abroad*, 137.

60. E. Skobtsova, "Marseille," *Poslednie Novosti*, III, 6/25/1932, no. 4112; IV, 7/2/1932, no. 4119 (Russian).

61. Quoted by H. Arjakovsky, "Mother Marie Skobtzoff, 1891–1945," *Service Orthodoxe Presse*, no. 171, September–October 1992, 30.

62. F13, 19.

63. I. Lagovsky, in *Jeunesses Orthodoxes* (Geneva: CJCOCP [World Student Christian Federation publishing house], n.d.), 68.

64. Berdyaev, "The Ideological Crisis of the Movement," *Messenger*, no. 9–10, 1933, 31.

65. Ibid., 30.

66. Ibid., 33.

67. N. Zernov, "The Life of the Russian Student Christian Movement Outside Russia 1933–1953," Geneva, no. 0133, World Student Christian Federation, 1954, 1.

68. YMCA Archives, Letter of P. Anderson, 12/9/33, p. 1. As another effect of this financial crisis, *The Way*—as we have seen—was forced to return to its pattern of four issues per year.

69. Ilyin Archives, *Memoires*, 63.

70. N. Fedorov, "The Birth of the Nationalist Organization at Vitiazi," *Politika*, Moscow, 1991, no. 6, 16.

71. L. Berdyaeva, *Professia: žena filosofa [Job Description: Philosopher's Wife (The Journals of Lydia Berdyaeva)]*, ed. Elena Vladimirovna Bronnikova (Moscow: Molodaja Gvardia, 2002), 160 (Russian). Cited as *Journals of Lydia Berdyaeva*, ed. Bronnikova.

72. Evlogy, *The Way of My Life*, 492 (Russian).

73. *Vozrozhdenie*, 1/29/1928, *poslanie* of Metropolitan Evlogy, 1.
74. A. Wenger, *Rome et Moscou*, 390.
75. Ibid., 396.
76. Evlogy, *The Way of My Life*, 571 (Russian).
77. Ibid., 574.
78. E. Behr-Sigel, *Un moine de l'Eglise d'Orient, Lev Gillet*, 210.
79. Evlogy, *The Way of My Life*, 576.
80. S10, 83. Two months later, H. Gofshtetter, a member of the post-revolution left, went further than Sazonova in that he implicitly justified atheism. Without referring to the situation in the Soviet Union, he noted that man's struggle against God had its origin in the Judeo-Christian tradition, namely, with the struggle between Jacob and the angel and Job's dispute with God himself (G7). In this same vein, Kurdiumov, one of the principal adversaries of Metropolitan Anthony in the pages of the review, in an article entitled "Orthodoxy and Bolshevism," affirmed that thirteen years after the revolution, there was a "volcanic effervescence of religious forces" in the USSR (K36, 67). In this historiosophical essay, the author established a parallel between the pre-revolution sects and the battalions of atheists, between the cult of Mother Earth and that of electricity, between the popular songs of the "twelve bandits" and the groups of *komsomols*. She argued that the Russian sects had always sought either to approach God through mystical ecstasies or to realize the Kingdom of God on earth (K36, 75), but they did so in a primitive way, without distinguishing the kingdom of Caesar from that of God. In this respect, the church bore an enormous responsibility, in that the sects of the *Khlystys* or of "Common Hope" were marked by formalism, a representation of an avenging God, the importance of obedience, providentialism, and fatalism. Testimony concerning religiosity in the Soviet Union underscored these observations. Artemiev, a young author and recent émigré, contributed an article in the December 1930 issue of the journal with the dramatic title "Is Russia Alive?" (A41). For him, socialist materialism was a new religion with its holy scriptures (Marx and Engels for the Old Testament, Lenin for the New Testament), its scholastic theology (dialectical materialism), and its inquisition (the KGB) (A41, 20). Artemiev also gave the journal an article coming from Russia by an anonymous author. Artemiev presented the author as a professor, a Bakunin specialist, who had given classes in 1927 on mystical anarchism in the basement of the Kropotkin Museum (X1). The article was a stenographic copy of this class, in which Buddha, Sophia, and Villiers de L'Isle Adam all entered into play.
81. L3, 4.
82. L3, 11.
83. T7, 74.
84. T8R, 104–105.
85. A26, 93.
86. G. Fedotov, "Concerning the Situation of the Russian Church," *Messenger*, no. 10, 1930, 13–17; no. 11, 10–14.
87. K37, 49.

88. K37, 63.
89. K37, 62.
90. F10, 68.
91. F10, 70.
92. F10, 76–77.
93. H1, 103.
94. K38, 97.
95. K38, 90.
96. H1, 102.
97. This spirituality is founded on the idea that "everything (even the sufferings of innocents) is according to the holy will of God." God can authorize that man be tempted by evil. God governs the world in its most minute details through the Holy Spirit sent by Christ to mankind at the moment of his ascension. In such a view, Caesar, the secular arm of Providence, received his authority from God himself, and that is why the tsar should be anointed by the Spirit. Whether it is the tsar or a mere bishop, the hierarchical and organizational principle is the surest vector of grace. Therefore discipline, respect for the rule, and submission to the hierarchical leader are the guarantees of the ecclesial life in Christ. When the leader acts badly, that means that the last times have come and the Anti-Christ announced in the Gospels is now in control. Salvation can only be obtained by fleeing from the visible church. In both cases, the privileged means of contact with God are, on the one hand, liturgical service, mysticism, and hymns, and, on the other hand, a social organization, developed through asceticism and discipline, for charitable purposes.
98. K39, 15–16.
99. K39, 8.
100. K39, 4.
101. K39, 18.
102. K39, 18. Artemiev argued that Bolshevism was a providential disease sent as a punishment from heaven (A41,7). Unlike Kurdiumov, he believed that the last days had arrived. The Russia of the Bolsheviks was governed by "the prince of darkness," the "anti-Christ" (A41, 8). The article ended on a tone of poetic frenzy with a vision: "I see the Archangel Michael.... He hastens to the aid of Russia and to strike the dragon with a fatal wound.... I see a contemporary Church where the last Russians are gathered together," and so forth (A41, 20–21). Stratonov pleaded the same case as Artemiev but for canonical rather than apocalyptical reasons. In an article entitled "The Origins of the Present Organization of the Patriarchal Russian Church," published as a supplement to issue no. 40 in October 1933, he limited himself to showing the exemplary role played by Metropolitan Sergius in the face of the different schisms in the church up to the year 1928. In a book that appeared a year earlier, *The Crisis of the Russian Church, 1921–1931*, Stratonov stated that the only just ecclesial position was to recognize the authority of Metropolitan Sergius (Z49R). Ishevsky, in the January 1935 issue of *The Way*, told of his meeting with Metropolitan Eleutherius, who was in charge of the Moscow jurisdiction in Western Europe.

As with other authors, he repeated that "Atheistic Bolshevism must be considered as coming from Christ" (I32, 40) to punish the church for having submitted itself to temporal power. The argument of Avvakum reappears here. At the same time, Ishevsky painted a flattering portrait of Metropolitan Sergius. Paradoxically, in the division of labor between the temporal and the spiritual—the latter being called upon to rediscover its autonomy through mysticism—Ishevsky proposed the completion of the task undertaken by Patriarch Tikhon, that is, of submitting the church to the state, because the atheistic powers would accomplish the work of salvation without knowing it (I32, 45). Indeed, for the author, "persecutions confirm the faith" (I32, 45).

103. B55bis, 4.

104. In the same vein, N. Zernov wrote in "The Jurisdictional Disputes in the Russian Immigration Church," *Messenger*, no. 114, 1974, 120–125, that the distinction between the Josephites and Nilians distinguished the representatives of the Russian Orthodox Church Outside Russia and the School of Paris, which was ecclesiastically under Constantinople.

105. This doctrine gave birth to two lines of thought within the intelligentsia—that of Berdyaev and Dostoevsky, which rejected this tragic divine scenario and gave back to God their "ticket to Paradise," for this freedom was too burdensome to be assumed; and that of Bulgakov, for whom the freedom that was offered was not removed, and who could not imagine Christ playing with Judas as if he were a puppet. In this second view, it was man who was mysteriously responsible for evil and who should assume responsibility for his own actions. To do so, he should develop his own critical reflection, which enabled him, thanks to a personal and immediate contact with Christ, to orient himself without stumbling. Dogma took precedence over canons, for the first was divine-human and reconciling—not a fixed law imposed from without. Eschatology does not take place at the end of history, as in its spirit-centered version, but rather at each instant, for Christ did leave the world when he returned to his Father. Like the monks of the Trans-Volga, man should flee from power in order to create a community of free persons, where authority was based on mystical experience. Man should not hesitate to oppose Caesar, just as Philip of Moscow confronted Ivan the Terrible, or as Athanasius stood up to the Arian bishops in the fourth century. The hierarchical principle is not thereby rejected, for Christ, the true King, directs the world through the intermediary of His Church. Thus, man should dedicate himself to building up His Church in the image of His divine-human Body. This meant a separation of the Kingdom of God from the kingdom of Caesar (but in order to transfigure it from within) and the participation of all the baptized, and kings, priests, and prophets in the work of the church, and a social commitment that is personal and total (the selling of one's possessions, the rejection of property).

106. E. Behr-Sigel, *Un moine de l'Eglise d'Orient, Lev Gillet*, 209.

107. A3, 3.

108. S7, 81.

109. S7, 91. The real problem for Sarafanov was not the separation of church and state but rather the separation of the church from any state power in a democratic context. The state should commit itself not to intervene in spiritual affairs unless this is done through the churches. Second, Sarafanov rejected the implicit philosophy in the program of the Social Democrats. for whom an areligious science, such as they wanted to be taught in secular schools, was more open than religious science, which was subordinated to dogmas. According to Sarafanov, Christian philosophy was more open than areligious science because, unlike the constraining truths of science to which one can only submit, it did not impose anything more than the free choice to believe in God, outside of all logic. For Sarafanov, this choice did not call into question the validity of reflection. On the contrary, this freedom permitted science to progress by continually questioning its foundational axioms. Therefore, he argued, the only truly egalitarian community is that founded on a faith that is free, for this faith would be accessible to all and require no knowledge.

110. S7, 93.
111. K15, 1.
112. K15, 3.
113. K15, 18.
114. K15, 20.
115. K15, 19.

116. Two historical articles in the journal concerned attempts to introduce reforms in the Russian Church at the beginning of the twentieth century. These attempts sought to return to an organization more in conformity with the spirit of Orthodoxy, without neglecting the national aspect. The first article was written by Smolitsch, who was also the author of an article on Nil of Sora that appeared in *The Way* in 1929. In December 1931, Smolitsch, who lived in Berlin, wrote a new article, published in the May 1933 issue, entitled "The Pre-Council Assembly of 1906." He stressed the relevance of this reforming assembly for the present time, "On the 25th Anniversary of the Attempt at Ecclesial Reform in Russia." The author related the way in which the church tried to reconsider the synod-type organization, which had been inspired by Protestantism and imposed by Peter the Great in 1721. The pre-council assembly of 1906 led to the reestablishment of freedom of conscience for other confessions and, thanks to the role of certain intellectuals such as E. Trubetskoy and Aksakov, called for the convocation of a Great Council with the participation of lay people—as was the case in the second and third centuries—in view of restoring the patriarchate. The author noted that the work preparatory to the council of 1917 was interrupted in 1907. He pointed out that it was significant that Moscow was given preference over the capital, St. Petersburg, in order to symbolize the return to a hierarchical and national concept of the church (S22).

Zernov was in the tradition, simultaneously hierarchical and communitarian, of the disciples of Nil of Sora. He recognized the importance of the patriarchate in the church, but in his article he also insisted on the necessity of reviving the principle of conciliarity for the reform of the Russian Church. In "Russian Church Reform and the Pre-Revolution Episcopate," which appeared in December 1934, he wrote: "The Russians are so accustomed to the absolute immobility of Orthodoxy that they can only imagine two types of responses to the religious question: either leave the Church once and for all, or recognize indefectibly the unchangeable and indestructible character of all its actual rules and customs.... For the majority of Russians, the doctrine of the Church as a living organism, continuously growing, extending its influence to all aspects of life, appears, at present, as a dangerous novelty which goes against the tradition of the homeland.... The conviction, very deeply rooted in the consciences of the people, that Russian Orthodoxy should not and cannot change, is founded, in general, on the argument of the silence observed by our clergy" (Z53, 4–5). In his article, Zernov went on to show that, according to a poll taken by the holy synod in 1905, the bishops, on the eve of the synod council, were suffering from the immobility of their church on questions concerning the general organization of the parish (election of the priest by the parish, liberation of the priests from functioning as policemen, the restoration of the diaconate, and so on), the liturgy (incomprehension of Slavonic, which favored the development of sects, the length of the services, the reading aloud of the Eucharistic prayers), and the composition of the council. He concluded: "We [the members of the Church] are not able to resolve all these questions which concern the whole Russian Church, but we can, given the conditions of liberty and security which we enjoy, think and act on ways to reanimate the conciliar principle in Russian Orthodoxy" (Z53, 15).

117. Kartashev, *The Roads towards the Ecumenical Council* (Paris: YMCA Press, 1932), 27 (Russian).

118. Ibid., 137.

119. A2R, 97.

120. Perhaps in implicit reference to the recent union of church and state in the USSR; A2R, 94.

121. At the beginning of the 1930s, two types of political formation could be distinguished in the immigrant community—those originating in the pre-revolutionary tradition and those arising from the acceptance of the fact of the revolution. The first spanned the entire political spectrum, from the right wing to the left wing. The organ of press of the monarchist right was the review *Dvuglaviy Oryol* (The Double-Headed Eagle). The Supreme Council of the Monarchy (VMS), headed by N. E. Markov, had pronounced itself, in November 1922, in favor of the Grand Duke Nicholas. But Nicholas, as well as General Wrangel, died in 1929. Nicholas was replaced by the Grand Duke Kirill, who became the new pretender to the throne. Before his death, the Grand Duke Nicholas had confided the direction of the very important Russian General Military Union (ROVS) to General Kutepov. The kidnapping of Kutepov on January 26, 1930, by V. Volovich, the chief of Stalin's bodyguards, echoed like a clap of thunder in the immigration community, three quarters of whom were monarchists. General Miller, who was known for his firm-handedness and integrity, took charge of the ROVS. His deputy, General Skoblin, had become well known because of his marriage to the famous singer Nadezhda Plevitakaya. On

the center-right were the liberal conservatives. These were at a disadvantage because of the departure, in 1928, of P. Struve, the editor of the daily newspaper *Vozrozhdenie* (*Renaissance*) (circulation 23,000), who left for Serbia, where he was editing the review *Rossia i Slavianstvo* (1928–34) together with K. Zaitsev. The heirs of the Cadet Party had the daily newpaper *Rul'*, edited by I.V. Guesen in Berlin, but this paper ceased publication in 1931. On the center-left were the heirs of the left wing of the Cadet Party, with the Republican Democratic Union, founded in 1924 by P. Milyukov, the editor of the daily *Poslednie Novosti* (circulation 40,000). To the left of Milyukov, the Republican Socialist Party of A. Kerensky was represented by the daily newspaper *Dni* up until 1933 and then, until 1936, by the weekly *Svoboda*. Finally, on the extreme left were a series of groups, from the Socialist-Revolutionaries (*Contemporary Annals*) and the Mensheviks organized around F. Dan, the publisher of *Socialisticheski Vestnik*, to the anarchist trade unionists. The new organizations that sprang up in the immigration community shared the idea of a "common destiny" with Russia and sought a concrete link with the Motherland (see M. Nazarov, *The Mission of the Russian Immigration* [Moscow: Rodnik, 1994], chap. 9). The left wing of the Eurasian movement, with S. Efron, became an openly pro-Soviet organization, called The Union for the Return, with its headquarters at rue de Buci in Paris; it maintained contacts with the Soviet Embassy in France. The right wing still published a collection of writings entitled *The 1930s—Affirmation of the Eurasians*, with articles by Savitsky and Ilyin. After the movement of the "changes in points of reference" and Eurasianism fell apart, four new developments appeared on the political scene at the beginning of the 1930s: the fascist groups, the *mladoross* groups, the solidarity groups, and the post-revolutionaries (divided into four groups—the national-maximalists, the Affirmers, *Novogradsy*, and *Tret'aia Rossia*).

The Pan-Russian Fascist Organization (VFO), characterized by its opposition to Freemasonry and its anti-Semitism, was founded by Anastasy Vonsiatsky in Paris in 1927. It became associated with the Pan-Russian Fascist Party (RFP), of pro-Christian, then pro-Stalin tendency, which had been founded in Manchuria by Constantin Rodzaevsky in 1931. From their merger, in April 1934, was born the Pan-Russian Fascist Organization of the Third Russia (VFP). The two groups separated in 1935. The party of Vonsiatsky took the name of the Pan-Russian National Revolutionary Party (VNRP).

The Union of Russian Youth was founded in Munich, in January 1923, by Alexander Kazem-Bek and had as its motto "God, the Czar, and the Motherland." In 1925 it became the Union of *Mladoross* (Young Russians). Originally in favor of a social monarchy, the movement first veered to the right, then gradually evolved towards a pro-Soviet nationalism. In December 1933, the Union arrived at a pact with the Pan-Russian Fascist Organization (VFO), but in September 1934 it was replaced by the Mladoross Party, and in 1935 A. Kazem-Bek proclaimed that his party had become a second Soviet opposition party. In January 1935, the party organized a congress, with a Hitler-style production (party members wearing blue uniforms, slogans for a cooperative state, the idea of awaiting the arrival of the leader). The party had about twenty publications—among them, *Mladorosskaya Iskra* (1931–40) and the review *Bodrost'* (1934–39).

The National Union of Russian Youth, created in 1930 by M. Georgievsky, became the National Union of the New Generation in 1931 and then, in 1936, the National Workers Union of the New Generation (NTSNP). Georgievsky was very hostile to the *mladoross* because of their wait-and-see position. Moreover, he favored a dictatorial regime. But, like the *mladoross*, the solidarity groups were anti-democratic and anti-liberal and militated in favor of nationalism and social justice. For the NTSNP and its review *Za Rosiyu*, edited in Sofia, the national revolution could take place only within Russia. Thus the task of the immigration community was to form revolutionary groups within the country. As partisans of "idealism, nationalism, and activism" (Nazarov, *Mission of the Russian Immigration*, 245), the young members of this group recognized Ivan Ilyin and E. Spektorsky, among others, as ideological guides. With the help of the ROVS, the NTSNP organized several expeditions into the USSR, with tragic consequences—notably, the death of M. Florovsky, the brother of G. Florovsky, at the Romanian border in 1933.

122. In 1931–32, *The Way* had no qualms about publicizing two reviews belonging to the "post-revolutionary" current, namely, *Affirmations* (*Utverzhdenia*) and *New City* (see the cover page of *The Way*, no. 32, as an example). Alhough the post-revolutionary movement was divided into three wings, all regarded Berdyaev as their principal mentor. They also shared a Christian worldview. Prince Yuri Shirinsky-Shakhmatov, the ideologue and founder of the National-Maximists in the late 1920s, published *Affirmations* between 1931–32, putting out three issues. The journal achieved great popularity, and the prince named its members *Utverzhdentsy* ("The Affirmers"). Sirinsky-Shakhmatov himself was descended from a prominent Russian aristocratic family. He participated in the founding of the Mladoross movement in Germany and later settled in Paris. He was married to Evgenia Ivanova, Boris Savinkov's widow. The prince, who earned his living as a taxi driver, brought together former Eurasians and even captured the interest of Berdyaev, who contributed two articles to his journal. Other authors of *The Way* joined Berdyaev in doing so, including E. Skobtsova (Mother Maria), F. Stepun, M. Artemiev, N. Timashev, N. A. Reimers, H. Iswolsky, and N. Turgeneva.

Affirmations called for a new social order, both anti-capitalist and anti-communist, based on Christian values. The younger members of the movement, N. Klepinin and A. Jarmidze, also founded the review *Tomorrow* (*Zavtra*). These neo-democrats favored a democracy with "less plutocracy and more Christianity" (Varshavsky, *A Generation Which Nobody Noticed*, 47 [Russian]). In July 1933, the movement organized a congress and established a union of post-revolutionaries, which included the National-Maximists, neo-democrats, and national Christians, among others. Among points of ideological agreement, the Union's charter affirmed: (a) Christian truth as social truth; (b) the primacy of the spiritual principle as the means to overcome all forms of contemporary worship of the material (capitalism and communism); (c) understanding authentic nationalism as the collective service

of God and for peace, according to its own historic itinerary; and so forth (Varshavsky, *A Generation Which Nobody Noticed*, 49).
The journal *New City*, founded by G. Fedotov, F. Stepun, and I. Bunakov-Fondaminsky with the support of Berdyaev and the publishing house YMCA Press, published nine issues between 1931 and 1934 (and five others from 1935 to 1939). From the moment of its foundation in 1931, the review distanced itself from Shirinsky-Shakhmatov's movement and the new parties within the immigration community—including the Mladoross Party. In the first issue of *New City*, P. Bitsilli, one of the contributors to *The Way*, criticized the Affirmers for their ambiguous attitude towards the Soviet regime (P. Bitsilli, "What Aspects of the Affirmations Must Be Denied," *New City*, no. 1, 1931, 83). *New City* also criticized members of a group of young intellectuals, among them P. Boranecky, who had gathered around the review *The Third Russia, Organ of Post-Revolutionary Synthesis* (*Tret'aia Rossiia, Organ Porevolutsionnaia Sinteza*), for basing themselves more on Nietzsche than on Christianity (Stepun, "Tret'aia Rossia," *New City*, no. 3, 1932, 48). On the other hand, the review regarded itself as somewhat in continuity with *The Way*. Like the authors of *The Way*, those of *New City* were influenced by the thought of Fedorov and his project of a common task. Bunakov-Fondaminsky announced the journal's aim in his first article—to contribute to the renaissance of the intelligentsia. Fondaminsky was a former Socialist-Revolutionary who, as commissioner of the Black Sea Fleet, had participated in the revolt of the battleship Potemkin. A non-practicing Jew, he had his first experience of God while in prison after his conviction. In the immigration community, he was one of the founders and leaders of the journal *Contemporary Annals*. Since he was relatively well-off compared to others, he was able to take the initiative for a great number of projects, notably, the literary soirées with Vladimir Nabokov. Drawn towards Christianity, he sought contact with the modernist authors of *The Way*. In the first issue of *New City* can be found the following contributors to *The Way*: Stepun, "The Path of Creative Revolution"; Fedotov, "The Twilight of the Motherland," "Quadragesimo Anno," and "A. Bremond, P. Lhande, R. Garric"; Maxence and Gorodetzky, "Charles Péguy"; P. Valery, "Thoughts on the World of Today"; Bulgakov, "The Soul of Socialism"; Berdyaev, "The Paradoxes of Liberty in Social Life" and "*My Life* by Lev Trotsky"; Guesen, "The Five Year Plan and the Educational Policy of Soviet Power"; Bitsilli and N. Lossky, "N. Berdyaev, *Concerning Man's Destiny.*" Later, Mother Maria, Mochulsky, and Vysheslavtsev were regular contributors to *New City*. In the same first issue, there is also a review of issues 28 and 29 of *The Way* by Fedotov, who singled out the articles of Alekseev, Stepun, and the Russian monk. In the third issue of *New City*, Stepun praised Berdyaev and *The Way* as "the torch-bearers of the post-revolutionary conscience" (F. Stepun, "The Tasks of the Immigration," *New City*, no. 3, 1932, 80–83). The older generation of the Russian intellectuals of the immigration reproached the *New City* writers, above all, for their eschatology. In 1933, G. Adamovich wrote about *New City* in *Chisla*: "They want to construct, concretely, in time and in history, without a sense of an 'either-or' and, in so doing, divide Christianity and the future" (*Chisla*, no. 7–8, quoted by

Varshavsky, *A Generation Which Nobody Noticed*, 296). *New City* did not aim to construct a political platform, yet it defended certain principles: the relationship between the spiritual and the political realms, the rejection of communism and capitalism, the defense of neo-democracy and of formal liberties, that is, human and civic rights, the formation of a Europe composed of nations, and the rejection of any return to Russia in the short term.

123. Z13. See also V. Zander, *The Social Implications of the Doctrine of the Trinity*, Editions of the Orthodox Fraternity of the Holy Trinity (Paris, 1936), 17–19.

124. B60, 59.

125. B65, 11.

126. B65, 17–18.

127. B65, 23.

128. B65, 33.

129. Varshavsky, *A Generation Which Nobody Noticed*, 48.

130. Stepun, *New City*, no. 3, 1932, 17.

131. Berdyaev, "Open Letter to the Post-Revolutionary Youth," *Affirmations* (*Utverzhdenia*), no. 1, 1931, 15.

132. Berdyaev, *Le destin de l'homme dans le monde actuel* (Paris: Stock, 1936), 23–24. I quote from the French edition. Published first in Russian: *Sudba tcheloveka v sovremmennom mire* (Paris: YMCA Press, 1934), and in English as *The Fate of Man in the Modern World*, trans. Donald A. Lowrie (London: SCM Press, 1935, 1938).

133. Berdyaev, "The Paradoxes of Liberty in Social Life," *New City*, no. 1, 1931, 4.

134. Berdyaev, *Le destin de l'homme*, 24–25.

135. B60, 63.

136. Berdyaev, "On Social Personalism," *New City*, no. 7, 1933, 44–60.

137. Fedotov, "Answer to N. A. Berdyaev," *New City*, no. 7, 1933, 81.

138. Ibid., 83.

139. Ibid.

140. "Editorial," *New City*, no. 7, 1933, 3. That said, Bitsilli had published an article in 1932 on the thought of B. de Jouvenel, in which he stated that he preferred "a state led by the trade unions rather than a democracy" (*New City*, no. 5, 1932, 102).

141. G. Fedotov, "Democracy Is Sleeping," *New City*, no. 7, 1933, 34.

142. Fedotov, "The Pillars of Christian Democracy," *New City*, no. 8, 1934, 3–14.

143. B60, 67.

144. B60, 66.

145. B55bis, 5.

146. The author went on to develop a theory in vogue at that time, according to which the history of the juridical development of societies is characterized by a struggle among three types of understanding. The military intelligence, founded on the power of the sword, is typical of the feudal period, while the perspective of the merchant and industrial baron, founded on the power of money (plutocracy), is typical of the societies of the nineteenth and twentieth centuries. Reimers foresaw the neces-

sary passage from the power of money to the power of the spirit (pneumocracy). Philosophical understanding, he wrote, would enable the relationship of teacher/student to replace that of employer/employee, for power has always sought to be adequate to the spiritual values of a people.

147. P8, 72.
148. P8, 61.
149. A12, 32. Accepting "spiritual" articles in *The Way* was a deviation from its policy of "neither right nor left." Among the young authors included by Berdyaev was a philosopher residing in Greece, Hyppolite Gofshtetter, who was hostile to the parliamentary system and who made no secret of his hope of seeing the Stalinist regime become progressively democratic. In an article entitled "Social Christianity" in the December 1933 issue, Gofshtetter argued that "an authentic servant of Christ cannot justify the exploitation of one human being by another" (G9, 79). He criticized Marxism as Lenin's personality cult, but he praised the Russian spirituality that he saw partially present in Bolshevism insofar as the latter seeks (in the author's opinion) a synthesis of the religious and the social. He also attributed the "success" of collectivization to this Russian spirituality and believed that Stalin treated official atheism with irony and distanced himself from it (G9, 96). A note from the editorial board warned about the tendentious character of this article because of certain anti-ecumenical propositions of Gofshtetter. This note was inserted at the bottom of the first page of the text: "The article of Gofshtetter is interesting and valuable as a manifestation of the awakening of the Christian conscience to social problems, but it contains false judgments regarding Western Christianity, Catholicism, and Protestantism. The editorial board lets the author assume the sole responsibility for these judgments" (G9, 73).

150. For the sake of completeness, other articles by Berdyaev must also be mentioned. These articles will be examined in more detail in the third part of this book. First of all, in *The Way*: a review of V. F. Asmus's *Essay on the History of Dialectic in New Philosophies*, in April 1931; "The Truth and Lies of Communism (For an Understanding of the Religion of Communism)" in October 1931 (French trans. in *Esprit*, no. 1, 104–128; see also the anthology *Problèmes du communisme* [Paris-Bruges: Desclée de Brouwer, 1933] and "The General Orientation of Soviet Philosophy and Militant Atheism" in the July 1932 supplement); and "Personalism and Marxism" in July 1935. In addition, in other journals: "*My Life* by Lev Trotsky" (*New City*); "The Metamorphosis of Marxism" (*Blackfriars*, February 1934, no. 167; *American Review*, September 1934, no. 4); "Marxism and the Conception of the Personality" (*Christendom*, December 1935, no. 2); "The Christian and Marxist Conceptions of History" (Geneva: COECP, November 1935, in German; French trans., Paris: Le Centurion, 1975). See also *Russian Religious Psychology and Communist Atheism* (Paris: YMCA Press, 1931); *Christianity and Class Warfare* (Paris: YMCA Press, 1931; French trans., ed. Demain, 1932); *Christianity and Human Activity* (Paris: YMCA Press, 1933, French trans.); cf. the anthology *Christianity and Social Reality* (Paris: Je Sers, 1934); *The Fate of Man in the Modern World* (Russian ed., 1934; French trans., *Le destin de l'homme dans le monde actuel*, 1936) (see n. 132 above).

151. B55bis, 25.
152. Berdyaev, *Le destin de l'homme*, 37.
153. B59, 1.
154. I. K. Luppol, "Berdyaev," *BSE*, vol. 5, Moscow, 1930, 586–587.
155. Ibid., 587.
156. B59, 16.
157. B53R, 109.
158. B59, 4.
159. B59, 20.
160. B59, 28.
161. Berdyaev, *Christianity and Human Activity*, 4–6.
162. Ibid., 6.
163. B55bis, 3.
164. B55bis, 34.
165. B58, 9.
166. B55bis, 22–23.
167. B55, 81.
168. B55, 84.
169. B55, 89.
170. B55, 84.
171. A12, 41.
172. A12, 50.
173. A12, 66.
174. S33, 43.
175. B58, 7.
176. See, concerning R. Garric, G. Chovly, and Y.-M. Hilaire, *Histoire religieuse de la France contemporaine*, vol. 2, 337.
177. B58, 12 and 30.
178. Bulgakov, "The Soul of Socialism," *New City*, no. 1, 1931, 54.
179. V29, 17.
180. V29, 15–16.
181. V29, 21.
182. V30R, 80–81.
183. V30R, 81.
184. K16, 76.
185. K19, 32–33.
186. K19, 34.
187. K19, 35.
188. B69R, 71.
189. B68R.
190. Stepun began to collaborate with the review in 1931, with a political-religious account of events in Germany. He lived in Munich, where Spengler's book was published, and he held a post at the university, which was why he felt threat-

ened. He had collaborated with Berdyaev in publishing a series of articles on Spengler in 1922.
191. S1R, 105.
192. S1R, 109.
193. S1R, 110.
194. Z38, 56.
195. The context in which these two articles of Zenkovsky and "S." were written must be kept in mind. In Thuringia in 1929, an ecclesiastical movement of German Christians was founded, whose goal was to unite the Teutonic cross and the Christian cross within "working communities of National-Socialist pastors" (*Histoire du Christianisme*, gen. ed. Mayeur, vol. 12, 587). Three years later, the head of the Nazi Party at Landtag, Prussia, entrusted Pastor Hossenfelder with the task of reuniting the diverse groups of German Christians in a movement called the "Faith Movement of German Christians" (*Glaubensbewegung Deutscher Christen*). This movement had a notable success in the elections of the Prussian synod in November 1932, garnering a third of the votes. After becoming Chancellor, Hitler named Pastor Ludwig Müller, a "German Christian," to be head of Protestant affairs, a post he held until the spring of 1935. When the United Church, *Reichskirche*, appeared in 1933, the German Christian party suffered a setback: Pastor F. von Bodelschwingh, who was elected first bishop of the Reich, refused to exclude non-Aryans. But under pressure from Hitler and abandoned by the Lutheran bishops, he had to cede his post to Müller in July 1933, in spite of appeals for resistance on the part of pastors Martin Dibelius, Martin Niemoller, and Dietrich Bonhoeffer. The German Christian party finally divided between a left wing, which confessed a German faith hostile to Christianity, and a right wing, which affirmed the unshakeable authority of the Bible. In July 1933, Karl Barth wrote a brochure entitled "Theologische Existenz heute!" which was printed in 30,000 copies. He then participated in the writing of two declarations, one dated January 4, the other May 31, 1934, on the occasion of two Free Reformed synods that were held at Barmen in the Rhur. These declarations condemned the movement of German Christians and strongly affirmed the Reformed faith and the independence of the church vis-à-vis the state. Barth also rejected any idea of a super-bishop in the church, for, in the church as in the state, the head should be a reality given by God. Barth recognized the authority of a charismatic leader in the church but rejected the episcopal institution as a source of power, for the one head of the church is Christ (S2, 65). These two synods of the "confessing church" made Hitler retreat, abandon his idea of dividing the Protestant Church from within, and led him to adopt a politics of de-Christianization by creating, in July 1935, a Ministry of Ecclesiastical Affairs to assure that the Protestant Church be under state supervision.
196. Z38, 65.
197. S2, 67.
198. S2, 66.
199. B70, 15.
200. B70, 15.

201. B70, 4.
202. B70, 5–6.
203. B70, 6.
204. B70, 7.
205. B70, 9.
206. B70, 10.
207. B70, 11.
208. B70, 13.
209. B70, 14.
210. K18, 11.
211. K18, 13.
212. S. Bukgakov, "The Nation and Humanity," *New City*, no. 8, 1934, 29.
213. Ibid., 31–32.
214. Ibid., 34.
215. Ibid., 37.
216. F24, F46R, F55, F76, G13, K5, K6, P3, P4, Z11R, Z37, and so on.
217. F77, 81.
218. Berdyaev, "Of the Nature of Russian Religious Thought in the Twentieth Century," *Contemporary Annals*, no. 42, 1930, 309–343, in N. Berdiaev, *Les Types de la pensée religieuse russe* (Paris: YMCA Press, 1989) (Russian).
219. The quest for the Kingdom in the pages of the review attracted an increasing number of new authors from different horizons, from Evgeny Spektorsky, who reviewed a Slavic book entitled *A Book About God*, to Fr. Lev Gillet, whose article on the original evangelical tradition (G2) was translated into Russian by Nadezhda Gorodetsky. The younger generation, such as V. Zander in her article "The Symbolism of the Icon of the Holy Trinity by Andrei Rubliev" (Z13) and B. Vrevsky in his article "From Faith to the Recognition of God," is especially in quest of "a faith founded on the awareness of the living God" (V6, 26).
220. S21, 54–59.
221. F48, 118.
222. F48, 120–121.
223. T10, 13.
224. P11, 47.
225. B106bis, 26.
226. C11R, 105.
227. F81, 39.
228. V2, 49.
229. B130bis, 7.
230. B130bis, 14–15.
231. B130bis, 42.
232. S6, 63.
233. I21R, 117.
234. F43R, 104.

235. B52, 109.
236. B52, 112.
237. B51, 106.
238. B51, 114.
239. B51, 112.
240. In a letter dated April 24, 1935, from Paul Anderson to Vysheslavtsev, it is stated that YMCA Press paid 300 francs for a manuscript of 40,000 words and wanted it submitted before September 15, 1934. See Vysheslavtsev Archives, typewritten.
241. Berdyaev, *The Doctrine of the Transmigration of Souls: The Problem of Immortality in Occultism and Christianity* (Paris: YMCA Press, 1935), 76 (Russian).
242. Ibid., 115.
243. Ibid., 119–120.
244. Ibid., 128.
245. L. Shestov, "Speculation and Apocalypse: The Religious Philosophy of V. Solov'ev," in *Spéculation et révélation* (Lausanne: L'Age d'Homme, 1982), 37.
246. This article provoked a rather confused response, in 1931, in the review of young Hyppolite Gofshtetter (G8).
247. Sh2R; French trans. in *Spéculation et révélation*, 84.
248. Sh2R; French trans. in *Spéculation et révélation*, 82.
249. Sh4R, 141.
250. Shestov, "Speculation and Apocalypse," in *Spéculation et révélation*, 89.
251. L4, 47.
252. Sh5, 37.
253. F47, 71.
254. F47, 77.
255. F47, 80.
256. F52; French trans. in "La Tradition, recueil," *La pensée orthodoxe*, no. 17/5 (Paris: L'Age d'Homme, 1992), 59.
257. Florovsky, "La Tradition, recueil," *La pensée orthodoxe*, 60.
258. Ibid., 67.
259. Ibid., 68.
260. Ibid., 69–70.
261. C4, 13.
262. C4, 22.
263. V22, 3.
264. V22, 17.
265. V29, 17.
266. V19R, 72.
267. V22, 23.
268. V24, 3.
269. V24, 4.
270. V24, 9.
271. V24, 17.

272. L17R, 107.
273. L16, 71.
274. L18, 4.
275. L16, 61.
276. L16, 62.
277. L16, 70.
278. L19, 26.
279. L19, 34.
280. F78, 48.
281. F82, 74.
282. F75, 48.
283. S. Frank, *The Spiritual Foundations of Society: An Introduction to Social Philosophy* (Paris: YMCA Press, 1930; repr., Moscow: *Respublika*, 1992) (Russian).
284. V17R, 108–109.
285. F80, 65.
286. F80, 66.
287. F80, 67.
288. Z26, 12.
289. Z26, 12.
290. Z37, 46.
291. Z37, 48.
292. Z28R, 102.
293. Z33R, 107.
294. Z30R, 91.
295. L18, 16.
296. Z32R, 91.
297. Z32R, 96.
298. Z32R, 97.
299. V27R, 85. Troitsky continued his polemic with Vysheslavtsev in the pages of the review in the October 1936 issue (T9R), but without adding new elements to the debate.
300. F12, 17.
301. F12, 5.
302. F12, 9.
303. F12, 11.
304. F12, 12.
305. This is confirmed by the article of K. Serezhnikov that was published in the May 1933 issue (S12) and dedicated to this question. Serezhnikov questions the principles expressed by S. Bezobrazov in 1928.
306. F12, 17.
307. F12, 8.
308. F13, 3–4.
309. F13, 19.

310. F13, 9.
311. B44, 76.
312. B44, 57; this also appeared in Berdyaev's preface to the 1946 French translation of *Mysterium Magnum* (*Jacob Boehme: Mysterium magnum* [Paris: Aubier, 1946]), 12, but the French translation is defective.
313. Schelling, *Darstellung*..., as cited by Bulgakov in *The Unfading Light*: French trans., *La lumière sans déclin* (Paris: L'Age d'Homme, 1990), 402, n. 169.
314. Berdyaev, *Esprit et liberté*, 79.
315. B44, 76.
316. B44, 61.
317. Berdyaev, preface, *Jacob Boehme: Mysterium magnum*, 14.
318. B44, 60.
319. B44, 62.
320. B44, 79.
321. B46, 34.
322. B46, 40.
323. Berdyaev, *Esprit et liberté*, 140.
324. B46; Berdyaev, preface, *Jacob Boehme: Mysterium magnum*, 32.
325. B46, 45.
326. B46, 50.
327. B75, 7.
328. B62, 17.
329. B62, 36.
330. B62, 28.
331. Berdyaev, *Le destin de l'homme*, 356.
332. Ibid., 346.
333. Ibid., 361.
334. B62, 43.
335. I4R, 60.
336. I4R, 67.
337. I4R, 62.
338. B56, 70.
339. B56, 72.
340. B56, 75.
341. B56, 73.
342. B73, 32–33.
343. B76, 71.
344. B76, 72.
345. B76, 72.
346. B76, 72.
347. A13, 32.
348. A13, 35.
349. B71, 44.

350. B71, 45.
351. B71, 47.
352. "Thus it is not even possible to say of the Divinity, under its transcendent aspect, that it is. Indeed by doing so, we make it a Who...." Bulgakov, *La lumière sans déclin*, 104–105.
353. "This 'fourth hypostasis', which receives the revelation of the mysteries of God, introduces, *by and in itself*, a distinction, an order in the life of the divine Tri-Unity," ibid., 200.
354. S. Bulgakov, "Ipostas i ipostasnost" [Hypostasis and Hypostaticity], in *Sbornik statiei posviachennykh Petru Berngardovitch Struve* [Collection of Essays in Honor of P. B. Struve] (Pragua: Plamia, 1925), 353–371; "Glavy o troitchnosty" [Chapters on the Trinity], in *Pravoslavnaja Mysl'* (*Orthodox Thought*), no. 1, 1928, 31–88; no. 2, 1930, 25–85 (Russian).
355. L. Zander, *Bog I Mir, Mirosozercanie otca Sergija Bulgakova* [God and the World, The Vision of the World of Father Sergius Bulgakov], 2 vols. (Paris: YMCA Press, 1948), vol. 1, 104.
356. B132R, 102.
357. Zander, *Bog I Mir*, vol. 1, 71.
358. B132R, 102.
359. B132R, 102.
360. B132R, 101.
361. In my discussion I also make use of the article entitled "The Dialectic of the Idea of Divine-Humanity during the Patristic Era," which Bulgakov himself cited in his introduction as a reference for the reader to a more detailed study.
362. B131, 3.
363. B131, 7.
364. B131, 26.
365. B131, 19.
366. B131, 26.
367. B131, 33.
368. See, for example, the testimony of the late Alexis Kniazev, former dean of the St. Sergius Institute: "I owe all my theological formation to him." *The Orthodox Messenger*, Paris, no. 98, 1985.
369. B126, 8.
370. B126, 21.
371. B126, 13.
372. B126, 20.
373. B126, 25.
374. B126, 34.
375. B126, 41.
376. B126, 44.
377. B126, 46.
378. B127, 21–33.

379. B127, 21-22.
380. B127, 24.
381. B127, 23-24.
382. B127, 24.
383. B127, 25-26.
384. B127, 29.
385. B127, 32.
386. B127, 33.
387. B128, 11.
388. B129, 16-17.
389. B129, 14.
390. B129, 15.
391. B129, 21.
392. B129, 19.
393. B129, 22.
394. B129, 24.
395. Fr. Sergius finished with a lyrical flourish, in which he identified the tandem "John the Beloved/Judas the Traitor" with that of "Holy Russia/Soviet Russia."
396. Bulgakov, "Dokladnaja zapiska predstavlennaja Mitropolitu Evloguiou v okt. 1935," in S. Bulgakov, *O Sofii, Premudrosti Bojiei* (Paris: YMCA Press, 1935). See also C. Andronikov, "The Sophianic Problematic," *The Orthodox Messenger*, no. 98, 1985, 49.
397. Berdyaev, preface, *Jacob Boehme: Mysterium magnum*, 41.
398. B47; in Berdyaev, preface, *Jacob Boehme: Mysterium magnum*, 40.
399. Berdyaev Archives, Clamart.
400. Berdyaev, preface, *Jacob Boehme: Mysterium magnum*, 41.
401. B127, 26.
402. S16, 35.
403. L2, 22.
404. L2, 33.
405. L2, 33.
406. Jean-Louis Loubet de Bayle, *Les non-conformistes des années trente* (Paris: Seuil, 1969).
407. Jean-Pierre Morel, *Le Roman insupportable: Internationale littéraire et la France (1920-1932)* (Paris: Gallimard, Bibliothèque des Idées, 1985), 426.
408. Before Sazonova's talk, two earlier meetings had focused on the two literary idols of the younger Russian writers, Marcel Proust (February 25, 1930) and André Gide (March 25, 1930). These meetings brought together the elite of the literary intelligentsia, from Nina Berberova to Marina Tsvetaeva, and included several authors of the review, such as Mochulsky, Veidlé, Berdyaev, and Fedotov. Among the French intellectuals who assisted at these meetings were J. Maxence, G. Marcel, R. Lalou, A. Maurois, A. Malraux, A. Arnoux, and S. Fumet. The four speakers were R. Honnert and Vysheslavtsev (on Proust) and Louis-Martin Chauffier and G. Adamovitch (on

Gide). Vysheslavtsev's talk was published in the fifth issue of *Cahiers de la Quinzaine* in 1930.

409. 11/21/1931, B. Fondane, *Rencontres avec Shestov*, 70–71, quoted by Nathalie Baranoff Chestov (N. Baranova) in her *Vie de Léon Chestov* (Paris: Éditions de la Différence, 1991), vol. 2, 152–153. In 1930, Malraux had written in the copy of *La Voie Royale* which he offered to Shestov the following dedication: "I'd imagine, my friend, that you hardly have time to read novels even though this one is one of the rare French novels which absolutely dominated the tragedy from which you have drawn philosophy. This is why I allow myself to offer you it as a gift." See N. Baranoff (N. Baranova), *Vie de Léon Chestov*, vol. 2, 286.

410. Here, Berdyaev used the term "intellectuals," which he preferred to "intelligentsia" and which he wrote in French in the text when he wanted to set himself apart from his French colleagues.

411. B54R, 104.

412. B54R, 106.

413. B72R, 72.

414. *Bulletin des amis d'E. Mounier*, no. 33, February 1969, 5, cited in O. Clément, *Berdiaev: Un philosophe russe en France*, 91.

415. Berdyaev, *Essay d'autobiographie spirituelle*, 314; this was probably the meeting of June 24, 1931, with J. Maritain, G. Marcel, A. Deleage, G. Izard, O. Lacombe, and P. van der Meer; van der Meer, the director of publications at Desclée de Brouwer, a novelist, and godson of Léon Bloy, entered the Benedictine order in 1933.

416. Berdyaev Archives, CGAALI, no. 497.

417. Letter of E. Mounier to Berdyaev, 11/27/32; Berdyaev Archives, Clamart.

418. CGAALI Archives, no. 367.

419. *Esprit*, no. 6, 1933, 933–941.

420. Daniel-Rops, *Le monde sans âme*, as cited by F. Damour, *Berdyaev*, Master's thesis, Paris, Sorbonne, 1993, 100.

421. H. Iswolsky, *L'Homme 1936 en Russie soviétique* (Paris: Desclée de Brouwer, Courrier des Iles, 1936; repr., Montaigne, 1968), 44–103.

422. *Journals of Lydia Berdyaeva*, ed. Bronnikova, 147 (Russian).

423. Berdyaev, *L'essai autobiographie spirituelle*, 407.

424. Letter of 12/30/31 to Berdyaev, Berdyaev Archives, Clamart.

425. E. Mounier, *Personalisme* (Paris, 1949), 53.

426. P.-L. Landsberg, "Quelques réflexions sur l'idée chrétienne de la personne," *Esprit*, no. 27, 1934, 393, cited by O. Clément, *Berdiaev: Un philosphe russe en France*, 90.

427. A. Blane, *Georges Florovsky*, 48.

428. J. de Pange, *Journal*, vol. 1 (1927–1930) (Paris: Grasset, 1964), 256–357.

429. J. de Pange, *Journal*, vol. 2 (1931–1933) (Paris: Grasset, 1967), 29–30.

430. Ibid., vol. 1, 297–298.

431. Berdyaev Archives, CGAALI, letter of J. Maritain, in Russian, 3/14/30, no. 605.

432. J. de Pange, *Journal*, vol. 2, 20–21.

433. Berdyaev Archives, CGAALI, no. 378, Letter of J. Wahl to Berdyaev, undated, Lyon.
434. CGAALI Archives, J. Maritain, 12/23/33, no. 605.
435. CGAALI Archives, J. Maritain, 10/23/36.
436. CGAALI Archives, Le Senne, 4/19/33.
437. Cited by O. Clément, *Berdiaev: Un philosphe russe en France*, 109.
438. E. Mounier, *Les certitudes difficiles*, in *Oeuvres* (Paris, 1950), IV, 75; cited by O. Clément, *Berdiaev: Un philosphe russe en France*, 109.
439. E. Mounier, *L'espoir des désespérés*, 1953, in *Oeuvres*, IV, 327, cited by O. Clément, *Berdiaev: Un philosphe russe en France*, 110.
440. G. Marcel told B. Fondane that his *Le monde cassé* (Paris: Desclée de Brouwer, 1933) was written in the 1920s under the influence of Shestov.
441. B. de Schloezer (1881–1969) was of Russian descent on his father's side, Belgian on his mother's side. He did some of his studies in Russia, then left for Paris and Brussels. He met Shestov at the house of the Balashkovskys at Kiev in 1918. After the revolution of 1921, he immigrated and rejoined his friend in Paris. He became a literary critic and secretary of a musical review. It was he who presented Shestov to J. Rivière, who was preparing an issue on Dostoevsky. He then became Shestov's principal translator.
442. B. Fondane (1898–1944) was a French writer, born in Romania, who settled in Paris in 1923. His meeting with Shestov in 1924 was decisive and inspired him to write several pieces—*Rimbaud le voyou* (1933), *La consciene malheureuse* (1936), and *Faux traité d'esthétique* (1938). He was arrested in May 1944 and died at Auschwitz on October 3, 1944. Shestov considered him as one of his disciples. In 1982, the publishing house Plasma put out his *Rencontres avec Léon Shestov*.
443. Pierre Andreu, *Le rouge et le blanc* (Paris: La Table Ronde, 1977).
444. S. Bulgakov, "Participation of Russians in the World Ecumenical Movement," in YMCA Archives, Anderson file, "Russian Area Conference," 48.
445. V23R, 125.
446. See also S. Troitsky, *Das Notbuch*, 4/27/31, 101–108, ecumenical compilation on the persecutions in the USSR.
447. Memorandum submitted by a study group of Russian Orthodox theologians, Paris, in "Universal Christian Council for Life and Work, Ecumenical Study Conference, April 8–14, 1934," typescript, Vysheslavtsev Archives.
448. Pastor Arnold Mobbs, "La vie religieuse," *La Gazette de Lausanne*, August 25, 1935, 2.
449. Dom C. Lialine, "Orthodoxie à propos d'oecumenisme," *Irénikon*, vol. 10, no. 4, 1933, 311.
450. K. Pflegler, "La gnose orthodoxe de Berdiaev," *Irénikon*, vol. 9, July–August 1932, 355.
451. Berdyaev Archives, CGAALI, no. 886.
452. P. Pierre Michalon, *L'Abbe Paul Couturier* (Mesnil Saint Loup: Le Livre ouvert/Ouverture, 1998). Father Couturier discovered the Orthodox Church while serving Russian refugees at Lyon in 1923. He became a Benedictine oblate at

Amay-sur-Meuse in 1933. In 1936, in the liturgical setting of the feast of Pentecost, he decided the foundation of what has come to be known as the Dombes Group (le Groupe des Dombes) which, in its beginnings, brought together about thirty Catholic priests, pastors of the Reformed faiths, and Lutherans at the Trappist monastery of Dombes, near Bourg in Bresse. He was in contact particularly with Visser't Hooft and Roger Schutz, the founder of the community of Taizé.

453. L25R, 95.
454. Bulgakov Archives, St. Sergius Institute, box XI, 15.1, (first) letter of F. Valentin Breton.
455. Ibid.
456. Bulgakov Archives, St. Sergius Institute, box XI, 15.1, (second) letter of F. Valentin Breton, March 21, 1934.
457. Bulgakov Archives, St. Sergius Institute, box XI, 15.5.
458. R. Winling, *La théologie contemporaine*, 56.
459. S. Bulgakov, *Autobiographical Notes* (Paris: YMCA Press, 1991), 116 (Russian).
460. A38, 86.
461. A35.
462. A38.
463. P12.
464. F82, 74.
465. F82, 75.
466. G. Gurvitch, *Les tendances actuelles de la philosophie allemande: E. Husserl, M. Scheler, E. Lask, N. Hartmann, M. Heidegger* (Paris: Vrin, 1930).
467. The first article of Lévinas on Husserl appeared three years after Shestov's article. Cf. "Sur les 'Ideen' of M. E. Husserl," *Revue philosophique de France et de l'Etranger*, March–April 1929, 230–265.
468. Gurvitch was behind the creation of The International Institute of Philosophy, of Law, and of Legal Sociology, whose president was Louis Le Fur, and which contributed to making known eminent German intellectuals such as Hans Kelsen and H. U. Kantorovicz (of Kiel). This institute, which had branches in Germany, Italy, England, and the United States, held its first session on the theme "The Sources of Positive Law" on October 7, 1933, in which two friends of Gurvitch participated— Vysheslavtsev and Alekseev. (See Vysheslavtsev Archives.)
469. N. Baranoff (N. Baranova), *Vie de Léon Chestov*, vol. 2, 119.
470. L4, 38.
471. Shestov had the same reaction as Mochulsky. In his conversations with Benjamin Fondane, Shestov summed up, in an ironical tone, Bergson's evolutionism as it was formulated in his latest work: "Human intelligence had been made, by nature, only for action. But, suddenly, this intelligence discovers that it is superior to the task it has been assigned; it starts to think for itself; that is how it came to create gods. The gods then, according to Bergson, have been made by the Collège de France, and these sorts of gods are what the Bible calls idols." See B. Fondane, *Rencontres avec Léon Chestov* (Paris: Plasma, 1982), 107.

472. Berdyaev, *Cinq méditations sur l'existence* (Paris: Fernand Aubier, 1936), 117. English translation, *Solitude and Society* (London: G. Bles, 1938).
473. Shestov, "Momento Mori, à propos de la théorie de la conaissance de Edmond Husserl," *Revue philosophique*, January–February 1926, no. 1–2, 5–62.
474. A13, 27.
475. N. Hartmann, *Das Problem des Geistigen Seins: Untersuchungen zur Grundlegung der Geschichtsphilosphie und der Geisteswissenschaften* (Berlin and Leipzig: Walter de Gruyter, 1933).
476. V28R, 72.
477. V28R, 75.
478. V28R, 76.
479. J. L. Dumas, *Histoire de la pensée*, vol. 3 (Paris: Tallandier, 1990), 268.
480. S1R, 105.
481. B49R, 117.
482. B49R, 119.
483. B49R, 119.
484. Bakhmetev Archives at Columbia University, course presented by F. Boubaier, cited in N. S. Plotnikov, "S. Frank and Heidegger," *Voprosy Filosofii*, no. 9, 1955, 169–185.
485. B45R, 116. See also Z27R.
486. G2, 85; see also B100R–B103R.
487. B45R, 116.
488. B50R, 124.
489. F54R, 96.
490. Z35R, 72.
491. Shestov, "A propos du livre d'Etienne Gilson, *L'Esprit de la philosophie médiévale*," *Revue philosophique*, November–December 1935, no. 11/12, 305–349; January–February 1936, no. 1/2, 32–79.
492. Shestov, *Athènes et Jérusalem*, 285.
493. B61R, 97.
494. B61R, 98.
495. B61R, 99.
496. B57R, 104.
497. See G. Scholem, *Les grands courants de la mystique juive* (Paris: Payot, 1960).
498. Sh3, 68.
499. B66R, 87.
500. Sh3, 76.
501. V19R, 71–72.
502. L19, 33.
503. Z51.
504. A3.
505. F56.
506. A4.
507. F54bis, 8–9.

508. *Irénikon*, vol. 11, no. 6, November–December 1934, 602.
509. F54bis, 13.
510. Bulgakov, "By Jacob's Well," in *Christian Unity: The Ecumenical Problem in the Orthodox Conscience* (Paris: YMCA Press, 1933), 31 (Russian). See also *Tradition Alive*, ed. Michael Plekon (Lanham, MD: Rowman & Littlefield/Sheed & Ward, 2003), 55–65.
511. Berdyaev, "Universality and Confessionalism," in *Christian Unity: The Ecumenical Problem in the Orthodox Conscience*, 65.
512. Ibid., 75.
513. Ibid., 79.
514. Kartashev, "The Reunion of the Churches in the Light of History," in *Christian Unity: The Ecumenical Problem in the Orthodox Conscience*, 120.
515. Z51, 38.
516. A3, 3.
517. A3, 11.
518. Florovsky, "The Limits of the Church," *Church Quarterly Review*, vol. 117, no. 233, October 1933, 117–131.
519. F56, 16.
520. F56, 25.
521. Afanasiev, *L'Église du Saint Esprit*, 17.
522. A4, 26.
523. A38, 85.
524. A39, 48.
525. A39, 51.
526. Z52, 49.
527. Z52, 55–56.
528. Z52, 57.
529. Z52, 59.
530. Z52, 60.
531. Z54, 60.
532. As quoted in Rev. O. Clarke, "The Healing of Schism," *Journal of the Fellowship of St. Alban and St. Sergius*, no. 25, September 1934.
533. In Bulgakov, "The Church Universal," *Journal of the Fellowship of St. Alban and St. Sergius*, no. 25, September 1934, 10–14.
534. Clarke, "Healing of the Schism," 5.
535. A. Kartashev, "Intercommunion and Dogmatic Agreement," *Sobornost'*, no. 4, December 1935, 42. Also in *Tradition Alive*, ed. Plekon, 213–220; see also 205–212.
536. "Letter by Malcom Spencer to Fr. Florovsky," *Journal of the Fellowship of St. Alban and St. Sergius*, no. 25, September 1934, 34.
537. Z55, 84.
538. Z55, 85.
539. Bulgakov, "Ways to Church Reunion," *Sobornost'*, no. 2, June 1935, 7–14.

540. Berdyaev, "About the New Christian Spirituality," *Journal of the Fellowship of St. Alban and St. Sergius*, no. 25, September 1934.
541. Others among the "brothers" included Théo Léger, Jean Grenier, and Jo Artru.
542. CGAALI Archives, no. 330.
543. "Communities," typescript of Becker's journal, Berdyaev Archives, Clamart, 2.
544. R. de Becker, "The Community of the Poor," typescript, Berdyaev Archives, Clamart, 1.
545. Ibid., 10.
546. R. de Becker, in "Communities," typescript of Becker's journal, Berdyaev Archives, Clamart, 14.

Notes to Part Three

1. Marc Raeff has pointed out that this growing spiritual awareness of the Russian intellectuals coincides with the evolution of certain intellectual currents in France. M. Raeff, "Le Front populaire et la presse émigré russe," in *Russes, slaves et soviétiques* (Paris: Institut d'Études Slaves, Publications de la Sorbonne, 1992), 427.
2. Fedotov, *New City*, no. 8, 1934, 14.
3. Berdyaev, *New City*, no. 10, 1935, 63.
4. Ibid., 60.
5. Ibid., 61.
6. Ibid., 63–64.
7. Berdyaev, *New City*, no. 13, 1938, 9.
8. B136R, 67.
9. Bulgakov, *The Comforter*, trans. Boris Jakim (Grand Rapids, MI: Eerdmans, 2004), 154–155.
10. Bulgakov, *L'Epouse de l'Agneau* (Paris: L'Age d'Homme, 1984), 197; *The Bride of the Lamb*, trans. Boris Jakim (Grand Rapids, MI: Eerdmans, 2002), 253.
11. Berdyaev, *Esprit et realité* (Paris: Aubier, 1943), 10. I quote from the French edition.
12. Ibid., 53.
13. Ibid., 54.
14. F16, 35.
15. F20, 7.
16. F20, 8.
17. B134, 68.
18. B134, 69.
19. B77, 3.
20. B77, 16.
21. B77, 21.

22. S. Bulgakov Archives, letter no. 2316 from Florovsky, April 11, 1943, 1.
23. S. Bulgakov Archives, letter no. 2314 from V. Lossky, November 16, 1935, 1–2.
24. Nina Berberova, *Astachev à Paris* (Paris: J'ai Lu, 1991), 105.
25. Metropolitan Sergius, decree no. 1651, quoted by Eikalovich: Igumen Gennadii (Eikalovich), *Delo prot. Sergiia Bulgakova: Istoricheskaia kanva spora o Sofii* (San Francisco: Globus, 1980), 6.
26. Ibid., 18.
27. S29, 67.
28. Evlogy, *The Way of My Life*, 579 (Russian).
29. Bulgakov, *Dokladnaia Zapiska* (Paris: YMCA Press, 1936), 3; Igumen Gennadii (Eikalovich), *Delo prot. Sergiia Bulgakova*, 14.
30. Cf. letters of Lagovsky to Bulgakov in the Bulgakov Archives; N. Arseniev, *Wisdom in Theology* (Warsaw, 1936); *A Discussion of Seven Orthodox on Sophia* (Berlin: Za Tserkov, 1936) (author or editor unknown).
31. As we shall see, the motivations of these two personalities were not purely theological. According to A. Blane, *Georges Florovsky*, 72–73, certain rumors circulated that Florovsky had profited from the crisis to replace Bulgakov in his role in the WCC just prior to the Edinburgh Congress in August 1937. As for Chetverikov, his role as spiritual guide of the youth movement was compromised by the theses of Bulgakov; he had to react.
32. Igumen Gennadii (Eikalovich), *Delo prot. Sergiia Bulgakova*, 18.
33. V. Lossky, *Spor o Sofii* [*The Dispute about Sophia*] (Paris: St. Photius Brotherhood, 1936), 63.
34. Ibid., 66.
35. Ibid., 85.
36. Ibid., 21.
37. Ibid., 68.
38. Bulgakov, *The Lamb of God*, trans. Jakim, 94.
39. Bulgakov, *The Comforter*, trans. Jakim, 369.
40. Bulgakov, *The Bride of the Lamb*, trans. Jakim, 15–16.
41. Vladimir Lossky, who, without admitting it, used Neoplatonic concepts, saw the divine Person in an abstract perspective, without any link to its own nature. By insisting on the separation between the divine spirit and human nature, he quite naturally arrived at supporting ideas close to Nestorianism. In fact, taking the very doubtful postulate of "the confusion of hypostasis and nature" in Bulgakov's writings and using it as a leitmotiv, he affirmed that sexuality belongs only "to human nature and not to the person" (V. Lossky, *Spor o Sofii*, 32). Likewise he postulated a radical separation in Christ between his human traits, notably his being a Jew, and his personality.
42. Lossky felt obliged to justify these errors. He ended up defending the "occasionalist sophiology" of Metropolitan Sergius and declaring that "it's better to think that Satan . . . was the cause of good than to make God the cause of evil"!

(*Spor o Sofii*, 59). In opposing the argument of Bulgakov that there existed an anhypostatic reality capable of loving God, i.e., the church, Lossky had a very strange explanation for a Christian theologian: this argument is not convincing because "the Church belongs to the created world" and has nothing to do with "the divine essence of the Holy Trinity" (ibid., 27).

43. Bulgakov, *Note to Metropolitan Evlogy* (Paris: YMCA Press, 1935), 24.
44. Ibid., 21.
45. Ibid., 32.
46. Ibid., 35.
47. Ibid.
48. Ibid., 39.
49. Ibid., 51.
50. B137, 4.
51. B137, 5.
52. B137, 8.
53. B137, 13.
54. B137, 21.
55. B78, 73.
56. B78, 74.
57. B78, 77.
58. B78, 78.
59. B78, 78.
60. B78, 79.
61. L23, 31.
62. L23, 31.
63. L23, 27.
64. L23, 28–29.
65. C8, 33.
66. B81, 37.
67. B81, 42.
68. B81, 39.
69. B81, 48.
70. B81, 48.
71. Nikolai O. Lossky dedicated a long article in *The Way* to the defense of the theses of his son and to demonstrating that the sophiology of Bulgakov was a disguised form of pantheism, but he severely condemned the accusations of the synod and of Metropolitan Sergius.
72. *Zhivoe Predanie* [*The Living Tradition*] (Paris: YMCA Press, 1937; repr., Moscow: Institute St. Philaret, 1997), 6. The essays of Berdyaev, Afanasiev, Bulgakov, Kern, Kartashev, and Zander from *Zhivoe Predanie* appear in English translation in *Tradition Alive*, ed. Michael Plekon (Lanham, MD: Rowman & Littlefield, 2003). That of Sové can be found at http://www.holy-trinity.org/liturgics/sove-eucharist.html.
73. *The Living Tradition*, 7 (Russian).

74. Ibid., 24.
75. Bulgakov, "Dogma and Dogmatics," in *The Tradition in Orthodox Thought* [in French], trans. C. Andronikov (Paris: L'Age d'Homme, 1992), 28. Originally published in *Living Tradition*.
76. *The Living Tradition*, 33 (Russian).
77. Ibid., 106.
78. Ibid., 135.
79. Bezobrazov took as an extreme example of interpretation the Gospel passage where Christ, at the Last Supper, gave a piece of bread to Judas. At this moment, according to the Evangelist, "Satan entered Judas" (John 13:27). Even though the personal consciousness of the God-Man is a mystery, Bezobrazov believed that this act must be understood as a last effort to convert Judas rather than as a reply to the disciple's request that the traitor be named. Ibid., 193.
80. Ibid., 10.
81. See the testimony of Fr. Elie Melia, a student who entered the Institute in 1934, in "Father Sergius Bulgakov Such As We Knew Him," *Le Messager orthodoxe*, Colloquium S. Bulgakov, no. 98, I-II, 1985, 138.
82. This article can be set side by side with one he published in the *Messenger*: "The Dogmatic Experience and the Dogmatic Schemes," Paris, no. 12, 1936, 25–36. In the latter, Lagovsky pointed out the impossibility of a condemnation *ex sese* ("from outside"—for example, by a decree of Metropolitan Sergius without the support of his synod) in the Orthodox Church, the error of setting up in the church a single system of interpretation of dogma, and, lastly, the reduction to which the judges of Bulgakov submitted the dogmatic experience of the church.
83. *The Living Tradition*, 47 (Russian).
84. Ibid., 51.
85. Ibid., 54.
86. Ibid.
87. Ibid., 57.
88. Ibid., 59.
89. Ibid., 60.
90. Ibid., 67.
91. Ibid., 68.
92. Ibid., 60.
93. E. Behr-Sigel, "La sophiologie du père Serge Bulgakov," *Revue d'histoire et de philosophie religieuse*, no. 2, 1939, 130–158, reprinted in *Le Messager orthodoxe*, Centenary of Fr. Sergius Bulgakov, no. 57, I, 1972, 21–48.
94. Ibid. (1972 reprint), 43.
95. Ibid., 48.
96. Ibid.
97. S29, 68.
98. Dimitry Pospielovsky, *The Russian Orthodox Church under the Soviet Regime, 1917–1982*, 2 vols. (Crestwood, NY: St. Vladimir's Seminary Press, 1984), 266.

99. N. Gorodetsky, *L'exil des enfants* (Paris: Desclée de Brouwer, 1936).
100. P. Sazonovich, "Ideologicheskoe Vozvrashchenstvo," *Vozrozhdenie*, February 1, 1935, no. 3530, 2.
101. "Journal of Lydia Berdyaeva," *Zvezda*, no. 11, notebook no. 2, 141. In *Journals of Lydia Berdyaeva*, ed. Bronnikova (Moscow: Molodaja Gvardia, 2002) (Russian).
102. "Pismo v redaktsiu," *Poslednie Novosti*, no. 5091, March 2, 1935, 4.
103. G10, 57.
104. G10, 57.
105. Ilyin, "*The Way*, no. 51," *Vozrozhdenie (Renaissance)*, October 1936, 2.
106. Bukharin, "The Philosophy of Cultural Phyletism," *Izvestiia*, December 8, 1935, 4; December 10, 1935, 6.
107. M. Heller and A. M. Nekrich, *L'Utopie au pouvoir*, 242.
108. B75, 7.
109. B75, 18–19.
110. S11, 30.
111. G. Fedotov, "Stalinocracy," in *The Destiny and Sins of Russia* (St. Petersburg: Sofia, 1992), vol. 2, 84.
112. B88, in French translation: N. Berdiaeff, *Christianisme et antisémitisme*, trans. la princesse Théodore (Paris: Éditions de l'Académie de Philosophie religieuse, n.d.), 4.
113. B87R, 75.
114. Marina Gorboff, *La Russie Fantôme, L'émigration russe de 1920 à 1950* (Lausanne: L'Age d'Homme, 1995), 150–153.
115. Fr. Lev Gillet, in his role as Orthodox chaplain, visited her in prison.
116. *The Face of Pushkin: Address Given at the Special Ceremony of the Institute of Theology* (Petseri, Estonia: Put Zizni, 1938) (Russian).
117. Kartashev, *The Holy Prince Vladimir, Father of the Russian Culture* (Paris: Éditions de la rue Daru, 1938), 24 (Russian).
118. G. Fedotov, "Make Haste!," *New Russia*, no. 59, 1939.
119. "On the 110th anniversary of G. Fedotov," *Zvezda*, no. 10, 1996, 120. This article contains excerpts on the Fedotov affair, from the Fedotov Archives, Columbia University, New York, published in *Zvezda* by Daniele Beaune.
120. Ibid., 125.
121. Ibid., 127.
122. Ibid., 135.
123. See the letter of Sablin to Fedotov, *Zvezda*, no. 10, 1996, 149; Fedotov Archives, Columbia University.
124. B91, 46.
125. B91, 48.
126. B91, 50.
127. B91, 53.
128. B91, 49.

129. B91, 46.
130. "Journal of Lydia Berdyaeva," May 26, 1939. In *Journals of Lydia Berdyaeva*, ed. Bronnikova (Russian).
131. Berdyaev Archives, Clamart, correspondence with Fedotov, letter of 1939.
132. *Zvezda*, no. 10, 1996, 149; Fedotov Archives, Columbia University. The text of the St. Sergius Institute was also published in the RSCM *Messenger* in 1939.
133. F83, 31.
134. B93, 33.
135. B93, 34.
136. B93, 36.
137. F20, 11.
138. F20, 13.
139. F20, 14.
140. *Zvezda*, no. 10, 1996, 145; Fedotov Archives, Columbia University.
141. Ibid., 151.
142. F21bisR.
143. N. Zernov, "The Congress of Boissy," *Messenger*, 1935, 22–36.
144. Donald A. Lowrie, *Rebellious Prophet: A Life of Nicolai Berdyaev* (New York: Harper, 1960), 196.
145. See E. Behr-Sigel, *Un moine de l'Eglise d'Orient, Lev Gillet*, 281.
146. Cited by E. Behr-Sigel, ibid., 282.
147. Mother Maria, "Orthodox Action," *New City*, no. 10, 1935, 115.
148. V. Yanovsky, *Les Champs Elysées* (New York: Serebrianii vek, 1938), 161.
149. *Messenger*, December 1935–February 1936, 3.
150. Mother Maria, "Letter to the Editor," *Messenger*, no. 3–4, 1937, 26.
151. Mother Maria, "The Types of Religious Life," first published in *Vestnik RKhD* (the *Messenger*), no. 176 (1997), 5–50, quotation p. 45. Also see *Mother Maria Skobtsova: Essential Writings*, 140–186. As indicated in the Conclusion, the RSCM *Messenger* was renamed in 1974 (no. 111) from *Vestnik RSKhD* to *Vestnik RKhD*.
152. S18, 43. For the entire essay see *Mother Maria: Essential Writings*, 116–125.
153. S19, 27. For the essay see *Mother Maria: Essential Writings*, 61–74.
154. S19, 27–28.
155. M5R, 87.
156. *Pravoslavnoie Delo* (Paris: Les Éditeurs Réunis, 1939), collection no. 1, 78.
157. Mother Maria, *Sotchinenia* (St. Petersburg: Iskusstvo, 2004).
158. Ibid., 262.
159. A15, 26.
160. R4, 3.
161. The move of the Berdyaevs from 14 rue de St. Cloud to 83 rue du Moulin de Pierre at Clamart took place in 1938, thanks to a gift of money from Mrs. Florence West.

162. "Journal of Lydia Berdyaeva," *Vstrechi s proshlym*, no. 8 (Moscow: Russkaia Kniga, 1996), 330.

163. V. Zenkovsky, *Histoire de la philosophie russe* (Paris: Gallimard, (1953), vol. 2, 386. I consult the French edition. In English, V.V. Zenkovsky, *History of Russian Philosophy* (London: Routledge, 1953).

164. Heller, *Utopia*, 243.

165. In April 1936, Zenkovsky published an obituary in commemoration of Professor G. Chelphanov, who had died in the Soviet Union. They had known each other well. The daughter of Chelpanov was married to Brice Parain, who worked at Gallimard Press and who entrusted the responsibility of writing a history of Russian philosophy to Zenkovsky.

166. T. Klepinine and W. Wallace Cayard, *Bibliography of Studies on N. Berdyaev* (Paris: Institut d'Études Slaves, 1992). See also T. Klépinine, *Bibliography of N. Berdyaev* (Paris: YMCA, 1978).

167. K21, 19.
168. K21, 20.
169. K21, 25.
170. K21, 25.
171. K21, 26.
172. K21, 23.
173. K21, 24.
174. K21, 31.
175. L27, 45.
176. K21, 19.
177. L27, 46.
178. L27, 46.
179. L27, 47.
180. L27, 50.
181. L27, 53.
182. L27, 47.
183. L27, 55.
184. F18, 4.
185. F18, 11.
186. F18, 7.
187. F18, 27.
188. F18, 28.
189. B129, 29.

190. S. Bulgakov, *La philosophie du Verbe et du Nom* [*The Philosophy of the Verb and of the Name*] (Paris: L'Age d'Homme, 1991), 27.

191. Bulgakov, in *Christianity and the Jewish Question* (Paris: YMCA Press, 1991), 27 (Russian).

192. Ibid., 140.

193. Ibid.

194. N. Baranoff, *Vie de Léon Chestov*, vol. 2, 172.
195. Florovsky, *Ways of Russian Theology*, trans. Robert L. Nichols (Belmont, MA: Nordland, 1979), vol. 1, 12.
196. Ibid., vol. 2, 301.
197. B84R, 54.
198. B84R, 65.
199. Z56, 17.
200. Z56, 12.
201. Z58, 59.
202. Z58, 59.
203. Mother Maria, *Memories, Articles, Essays*, vol. 2 (Paris: YMCA Press, 1992), 11.
204. Ibid., 13.
205. Ibid., 14.
206. Ibid., 15.
207. Z43R, 79.
208. Berdyaev, *L'idée russe*, translation in French by H. Arjakovsky (Paris: Mame, 1969), 5.
209. Ibid., 15.
210. Ibid., 253.
211. Ibid., 255.
212. L. Shestov, *Athènes et Jérusalem*, 316.
213. "Journals of L. J. Berdyaeva," *Zvezda*, no. 10, 154 (Russian).
214. Shestov, *Spéculation et révélation*, 113.
215. Y. Bonnefoy, in Shestov, *Athènes et Jérusalem*, 11.
216. Jean Grenier, *Le philosophie de Jules Lequier* (Paris: Les Belles Lettres, 1936); Jules Lequier, *La liberté* (Paris: Vrin, 1936).
217. B. Fondane, *Rencontres avec Shestov*, 166, quoted by N. Baranoff (N. Baranova) in *Vie de Léon Chestov* (Paris: Éditions de la Différence, 1991), vol. 2, 208.
218. L5, 39.
219. Shestov, *Athènes et Jérusalem*, 320.
220. Ibid., 326.
221. L21, 3; V31–V33.
222. V33, 15.
223. V33, 19.
224. V33, 20.
225. V31, 66.
226. V31, 54.
227. V31, 50.
228. V31, 59.
229. V31, 60.
230. V31, 68.
231. L21, 3.

232. L21, 10.
233. L21, 9.
234. L21, 14.
235. L21, 18–19.
236. A14, 39.
237. A14, 42.
238. Z47, 22.
239. Z47, 30.
240. Z47, 23.
241. N. S. Plotnikov, "S. L. Frank on Heidegger: Towards a History of the Reception of Heidegger by Russian Thought," *Voprosy Filosofi*, no. 9, 1995, 169–185; article sent by Maryse Dennes.
242. Frank, *The Inaccessible* (Paris: Sov. Zap., 1939); reprinted in *Works* (Moscow: Pravda, 1990), 544 (Russian).
243. B94R, 65.
244. B94R, 66.
245. B94R, 67.
246. Berdyaev, *Esprit et réalité*, 182.
247. Ibid., 9.
248. Ibid., 145.
249. Ibid., 146–147.
250. Berdyaev, *Essai de métaphysique eschatologique* (Paris, Aubier, 1946), 63. I cite from the French edition. It was published in Russian a year later: *Opyt eshatologuiceski metafiziki* (Paris: YMCA Press, 1947).
251. B80, 9.
252. B80, 23.
253. B95, 11.
254. Berdyaev, *Essai de métaphysique eschatologique*, 271.
255. B138, 18.
256. Bulgakov, *The Bride*, trans. Jakim, 6.
257. Ibid., 47–49.
258. Ibid., 60–61.
259. Ibid., 500–501.
260. Ibid., 526.
261. Berdyaev, "L. Shestov and Kierkegaard," in *Types of Russian Religious Thought* (Paris: YMCA Press, 1989), 400.
262. Ibid., 401.
263. Ibid., 404.
264. Ibid., 406.
265. Shestov, "Nicolas Berdyaev, Gnosis, and Existentialist Philosophy," in *Spéculation et révelation*, 181 (French).
266. Ibid., 181.
267. Ibid., 187–188.

268. Ibid., 191.
269. Ibid., 201.
270. Ibid., 190.
271. Ibid., 195.
272. Baranoff, *Vie de Léon Chestov*, vol. 2, 219.
273. Bulgakov, "Some Aspects of the Religious Vision of L. I. Shestov," *Contemporary Annals*, no. 68, 1939, 305–323, reprinted in Bulgakov, *Works* (Moscow: Nauka, 1993), 519–537.
274. Ibid., in *Works*, 525.
275. Ibid., 531.
276. Ibid., 536.
277. Ibid., 536.
278. Ibid.
279. Ibid., 533.
280. Ibid., 537.
281. Ibid., 519.
282. Ibid., 520.
283. Baranoff, *Vie de Léon Chestov*, vol. 2, 220.
284. Berdyaev, *Essai d'autobiographie spirituelle*, 157.
285. B81bis; B90.
286. B81bis, 50.
287. B81bis, 52.
288. B81bis, 52.
289. B90, 45.
290. See "Journal of Lydia Berdyaeva," *Zvezda*, no. 11, notebook no. 2. In *Journals of Lydia Berdyaeva*, ed. Bronnikova (Russian).
291. See *Colloquium N. Berdyaev* (Paris: Institut d'Études Slaves, 1975).
292. Baranoff, *Vie de Léon Chestov*, vol. 2, 221.
293. Ibid., 220.
294. See Bulgakov, Archives of the St. Sergius Institute, no. 23.1.
295. B91, 50.
296. Berdyaev Archives, Clamart.
297. Berdyaev Archives, Clamart.
298. Baranoff, *Vie de Léon Chestov*, vol. 2, 219–220.
299. Ibid., 223.
300. Job 38:4, 12.
301. S16, 47; S19.
302. Baranoff, *Vie de Léon Chestov*, vol. 2, 220.
303. Berdyaev, "The Philosopher and Existence," *Bulletin of the N. Berdyaev Association*, no. 2–3, 1954–57, 6.
304. Bulgakov, *The Bride*, trans. Jakim, 126.
305. Ibid., 118.
306. Ibid., 121.

307. N. Berdyaev, *Essai d'autobiographie spirituelle*, 8.
308. "Journal of Lydia Berdyaeva," *Zvezda*, no. 11, notebook no. 2, 156. In *Journals of Lydia Berdyaeva*, ed. Bronnikova (Russian).
309. A. Schmemann, "Roll of Honor: A Sixtieth Anniversary Salutation to Georges Florovsky," *St. Vladimir Seminary Quarterly* 2, no. 1 (1952/53), 7.
310. O. Clément, *Berdiaev: Un philosphe russe en France*, 116.
311. Blane, *Georges Florovsky*, 73.
312. Emilianos Timiadis, "Georges Florovsky," in *Ecumenical Pilgrims: Profiles of Pioneers in Christian Reconciliation* (Geneva: World Council of Churches, 1995).
313. Metropolitan John of Pergamon, "The Self-Understanding of the Orthodox and Their Participation in the Ecumenical Movement," in *The Ecumenical Movement, the Churches, the WCC* (Geneva: WCC-Syndesmos, 1995), 39.
314. Blane, *Georges Florovsky*, 73. Also see O. Clément, *Berdyaev: Un philosphe russe en France*, 106.
315. Personal interview with M. de Gandillac in 1993.
316. O. Clément, *Berdyaev: Un philosphe russe en France*, 116.
317. B75, 19.
318. B75, 19.
319. B79R, 87.
320. B79R, 91.
321. B79R, 90.
322. B79R, 90.
323. B79R, 90.
324. B79R, 89.
325. B79R, 90.
326. B135, 47.
327. B135, 26.
328. B135, 33.
329. B135, 37.
330. B135, 37.
331. B135, 43.
332. B135, 43.
333. B135, 44.
334. K26, 24.
335. B107, 40.
336. B92, 56.
337. K41, 18.
338. J. A. Moehler, *L'unité dans l'Eglise ou le principe du catholicisme d'aprés l'esprit des Pères des trois premiers siécles de l'Eglise* (Paris: Cerf, 1938).
339. F19R, 65.
340. Archimandrite Cassian (Bezobrazov), *La Pentecôte Johannique* (Valence sur Rhone: Imprimeries Réunies, 1939), 17.
341. B106, 21–22.

342. B106, 17.
343. B106, 18.
344. B106, 19.
345. B142, 5.
346. B142, 8; Bulgakov added that intercommunion can frustrate the very goal it seeks when it tries to go beyond the sacramental frontiers "prematurely or superficially." He noted that the sacramental efficiency *ex opere operato* also depends on the sacramental reception *ex opera operantis*. "St. Theophan the Recluse once said of the Protestant sacraments 'that these will be given to them through faith.'" Finally, Bulgakov reminded his readers, the gifts of the Holy Spirit mentioned by Paul are not linked to the hierarchy. B142, 11–12.
347. B142, 12–13.
348. B142, 13.
349. L. Zander, "On the Essence of Ecumenical Participation," in *Tradition Alive*, ed. Plekon, 227.
350. Ibid., 228.
351. Even before the war Zander was in conflict with Florovsky—not only because of the dispute revolving around Sophia but also because Zander suspected that Florovsky, in spite of his participation in the ecumenical movement, did not genuinely desire reconciliation among churches. Thus he proposed a revision of the concept of heretic, a term used constantly by Florovsky. Zander argued that the heretic is not the one who thinks he has preserved dogmatic truth but "the one who does not want the reconciliation of the churches." Ibid., 235.
352. Ibid., 238.
353. Z57, 70.
354. Z58, 66.
355. Z59, 68.
356. Z58, 68.
357. Michel Winock, *Le siècle des intellectuels* (Paris: Seuil, 1997), 243.
358. P. Ory and J. F. Sirinelli, *Les intellectuels en France, de l'affaire Dreyfus à nos jours* (Paris: Armand Colin, 1986), 107.
359. Bernanos wrote *Le Journal d'un curé de campagne* in March 1936 and his most important work, *Les grands cimetières sous la lune*, in April 1938.
360. H. Iswolsky, *L'Homme 1936 en Russie soviétique* (Paris: Desclée de Brouwer, Courrier des Iles, 1936).
361. Cf. "Journal of Lydia Berdyaeva," *Zvezda*, no. 11, notebook no. 2. In *Journals of Lydia Berdyaeva*, ed. Bronnikova (Russian).
362. B89R, 84.
363. On December 1, 1936, Berdyaev published an article in Russian entitled "The Illusions and Disillusions of Andre Gide" in the socialist weekly of Kerensky, in which he stigmatized the contradictions of those French intellectuals seduced by communism (N. Berdyaev, *New Russia*, no. 17, December 1, 1936, 6–7). Berdyaev's collaboration with the Russian socialist weekly of the immigration, *Novaia Rossiia/*

New Russia, edited by A. Kerensky, had begun in the first issue of March 8, 1936, with an article entitled "Religious Socialism and the Religion of Socialism."
364. J. Grenier, "L'âge des orthodoxies," *Nouvelle Revue Française*, April 1936, cited by M. Winock, *Le siècle des intellectuels*, 294.
365. B89R, 85.
366. B89R, 85.
367. From 1935–36 on, Berdyaev ceased to identify the term "intelligentsia"— which had a very specific spiritual and therefore ethical connotation for him— with the term "intellectuals," which he used more to designate a cultivated man of letters. See chapter 1 of his *The Origin of Russian Communism*.
368. Mrs. Rolland was the widow of Berdyaev's nephew, Prince Sergius Kudachev.
369. R. Rolland, *Péguy* (Paris: Albin Michel, 1944), vol. 2, 224.
370. J. Maritain, *Humanisme intégral* (Paris: Aubier, 1936; repr., 1968), 15.
371. This famous professor of the École Normale Supérieure became the philosophy teacher of Michel Foucault.
372. Berdyaev Archives, CGAALI, no. 497.
373. Berdyaev Archives, CGAALI, no. 412.
374. Berdyaev Archives, CGAALI, no. 927.
375. D. de Rougemont, "Changer la vie ou changer l'homme," in *Le communisme et les chrétiens* (Paris: Plon, 1937), 218.
376. Berdyaev, "Cinq passages inédits de l'autobiograhie," *Bulletin de l' Association Berdyaev*, Paris, no. 4, March 1975, 21.
377. Berdyaev Archives, Clamart.
378. This issue was also mentioned by O. Clément, *Berdyaev: Un philosophe russe en France*, 93.
379. B6, 56.
380. The text was reprinted in *Le Christianisme social* in 1939.
381. Berdyaev, *Le christianisme et l'antisémitisme* (Paris: Édition de l'APR, 1938), 6.
382. Ibid., 12.
383. M6, 28.
384. M6, 32.
385. Berdyaev Archives, Clamart.
386. D. Lindenberg, *Les années souterraines*, 101.
387. Berdyaev Archives, CGAALI, no. 531.
388. Georges Bataille, "L'apprenti sorcier," in D. Hollier, *Le Collège de sociologie* (Paris: Gallimard, 1979; repr., 1995), 323.
389. N. Baranoff, *Vie de Léon Chestov*, vol. 2, 177.
390. *Bibliographie des oeuvres sur L. Chestov* (Paris: Institut d'Études Slaves, 1978); cf. especially E. Lévinas, "L. Shestov, Kierkegaard et la philosophie existentielle," *Revue des études juives*, Paris, July/December 1937, II, no. 1/2, 139–141.
391. L. Shestov, "De la philosophie médiévale," in *Athènes et Jérusalem*, 215.

392. Ibid., 284.
393. N. Baranoff, *Vie de Léon Chestov*, vol. 2, 157.
394. Sh6R, 65.
395. L. Shestov, "A la mémoire d'un grand philosophe, E. Husserl," in *Spéculation et révelation*, 214.
396. Sh7; French translation in *Spéculation et révelation*, 159–160.
397. D. de Rougemont, *L'amour et L'Occident* (Paris: Plon, 1939; repr., 1972), bk. 1.
398. M7R, 77.
399. Berdyaev Archives, CGAALI, no. 378.
400. Wenger, *Rome et Moscou 1900–1950*, 458–459.
401. L20R, 74.
402. W. Veidlé, "The Marxist Theory of Art in Soviet Russia," *Russie et Chrétienté*, no. 3, May–June 1936, 96–102.
403. J. Danzas, *L'itinéraire religieux de la conscience russe* (Juvisy: Cerf, Istina, 1936).
404. J. Danzas, "La voie de la philosophie religieuse russe," *Russie et Chrétienté*, no. 3, May–June 1936, 214–215.
405. Ibid., 235.
406. Ibid., 238.
407. Ibid., 222.
408. B83R, 74.
409. B83R, 76.
410. B83R, 75.
411. B83R, 76.
412. E. Porret, "La philosophie chrétienne en Russie, Nicolas Berdiaeff," in *Etre et penser*, no. 8, Édition La Baconnière, Neûchatel, October 1944, 172.
413. P. Archambault, "Le drame de la liberté dans la philosophie de Berdiaeff," *Politique*, Paris, February 1937, 123–143.
414. *Histoire du Christianisme*, no. 12, 68–71.
415. The discovery of the importance of the Protestant community in Italy (100,000 people) at the Oxford congress encouraged Berdyaev to ask his Italian correspondent, Polotebneva, to write an article on the subject—which she did in June 1938.
416. F17, 59.
417. F17, 60.
418. N. Alekseev, "The World Congress of Practical Christianity at Oxford," *New City*, no. 13, 1938, 152–162.
419. F17, 61; Alekseev, "The World Congress of Practical Christianity at Oxford," 158.
420. B106, 22. See also Z46R.
421. F54bis, 4–15.
422. "Professor L. A. Zander's Reply to G. Florovsky," quoted in *The Christian East*, vol. 2, no. 5/6, Summer 1953, 2.

423. Blane, *Georges Florovsky*, 156.
424. G. Williams, "The Neo-Patristic Synthesis of G. Florovsky," chap. 5, in Blane, *Georges Florovsky*, 327–338. See also Yves-Noel Lelouvier, *Perspectives russes sur l'Eglise, un théologien contemporain, G. Florovsky* (Paris, 1968).
425. G. Florovsky, "Orthodox Participation in the Ecumenical Movement," *Journal of the Exarchate of the Russian Orthodox Church of Western Europe*, Paris, May 1949, 2.
426. "Professor L. A. Zander's Reply to Fr. G. Florovsky," cited in *The Christian East*, vol. 2, no. 5/6, Summer 1953.
427. Z44R, 86.
428. L28R, 74.
429. L28R, 75–76.
430. Blane, *Georges Florovsky*, 67. See also the collection *Christian Sources* by Etienne Fouilloux (Paris: Cerf, 1995).
431. Z12, 67.
432. Z12, 63.
433. Z12, 70.
434. Z57, 70.
435. Z57, 75.
436. Z60, 25.
437. Bulgakov, "The Central Problem of Sophiology" [German translation by L. Zander], *Kyrios*, no. 2, 1936, a theme taken up again in the RSCM *Messenger*, no. 101–102, 1971, 104–108.
438. Bulgakov, *The Wisdom of God* (Hudson, NY: Lindisfarne Press, 1993), 14–15.
439. See B141, 67.
440. B141, 66–68.
441. See *Zvezda*, no. 10, 1996, 142; Fedotov Archives, Columbia University.

Notes to Conclusion

1. D. Lowrie, *Rebellious Prophet*, 269.
2. See the Berdyaev Archives, CGAALI, no. 799.
3. Berdyaev, *Essai d'autobiographie spirituelle*, 418.
4. M. de Gandillac, *Le siècle traversé* (Paris: Albin Michel, 1998), 441.
5. After the war, another former author of the review, Lev Karsavin, who had fled to the Baltic States, was arrested and died in a concentration camp at Abez in 1952.
6. "Extraits du journal de Dimitri Klepinin," *Khristianos*, no. 8, Riga, A. Men Fund, 1999, 33–41. [Editor's note: The entire exchange between Fr. Dimitrii and his wife Tamara, along with biographical material, has been translated and published by their daughter, Hélène Arjakovsky-Klépinine, *Et la vie sera amour* (Paris/Pully: Cerf/Le Sel de la Terre, 2005). In May 2004, as noted later in this conclusion, Mother

Maria Skobtsova, Fr. Dmitrii Klepinin, Yuri Skobtsov (Mother Maria's son), and Ilya Fondaminsky were canonized as martyr saints in the cathedral at rue Daru, Paris, by the archdiocese of the Orthodox Church of the Russian tradition in Europe, under the Ecumenical Patriarchate. Materials on the canonization: http://www.pages orthodoxes.net/saints/mere-marie/mmarie-intro.htm and http://incommunion.org/contents/mother-maria (accessed January 2008).

7. Bulgakov Archives, St Sergius Institute.

8. V. S. Yanovsky, *Elysian Fields*, trans. Isabella Yanovsky and V. S. Yanovsky (DeKalb: Northern Illinois University Press, 1987), 149.

9. Journal of L. Berdyaeva, *Vstrechi s proshlim*, no. 8, 360 (Russian).

10. Berdyaev, *Essai de métaphysique eschatologique* (Paris: Aubier, 1946), 112.

11. Ibid., 234.

12. Ibid., 259.

13. Berdyaev's personal archives, excerpt of a handwritten letter from Frank, 1946.

14. S. Bulgakov, *The Apocalypse of John* (Paris: YMCA Press; repr., Moscow, MBTOY, 1991), 7 (Russian).

15. *Mother Maria Skobtsova: Essential Writings*, 138–139.

16. M. Maria Skobtsova, *Poèmes* (Paris, 1949).

17. Ibid., 99.

18. N. Berdiaev's personal archives; notebook from 1946.

19. Ibid.

20. Marie-Anne Lescourret, *Emmanuel Lévinas* (Paris: Flammarion, 1994), 194.

21. Berdiaev Archives, Clamart.

22. Ibid.

23. See, for example, V. A. Kuvakin, *Critique de l'existentialisme de Berdiaev* (Moscow: MGOU, 1976) (Russian).

24. See *Sur la Russie et la culture philosophique russe, les philosophes de l'émigration russe d'après octobre, Berdiaev, Vycheslavtsev, Zenkovsky, Sorokin, Fedotov, Florovsky* (Moscow: Nauka, 1990), 50,000 copies.

25. V. Kostikov, *Ne budem proklinat' izgnanie* [*Let Us Not Curse the Exiles*], 56.

26. N. Klepinin, *Saint Alexandre Nevsky* (Moscow: Stryzev, 1993).

27. *L'idée russe* (Moscow: Iskusstvo, 1994).

28. A. Solzhenitsyn, *Le problème russe à la fin du XXe siècle* (Paris: Fayard, 1994).

29. Likhachev died a year later, in St. Petersburg, in October 1999.

30. *Pushkin dans la critique philosophique russe* (Moscow: Knigua, 1990), 30,000 copies (Russian).

31. A. Men, *La culture spirituelle mondiale* (Moscow: A. M., 1995), 514 (Russian).

32. See esp. no. 34 of *Pravoslavnaia Obshchina*, 1996, 50–62, where Bulgakov's "*Una Sancta*" appeared.

33. V. Lossky, *La théologie dogmatique* and *L'Essai sur la théologie mystique de l'Église d'Orient* (Moscow: SEI-Tribuna, 1991).

34. The name of the RSCM *Messenger, Vestnik RSKhD*, was changed under Nikita Struve in 1974 (no. 111) to *Vestnik RKhD*. Issues of *Vestnik* are available at http://www.rp-net.ru/book/vestnik.

35. A. Shatov, "The Evolution of the Concept of Community in Contemporary Modernism," *Edinstvo Tserkvi*, Moscow, 1996, 212–221.

36. O. Clément, *Sources* (Moscow: Put', 1994).

37. A. Kuraev, *The Heritage of Christ* (Moscow: Blagovest, 1998), 3.

38. *Mother Maria Skobtsova: Essential Writings*, "Types of Religious Life," 140–186.

39. I. Solovyov, "50 Years Have Passed since the Death of N. Berdyaev," *NG-Religiya*, no. 3 (14), March 1998, 9.

40. See *Dia-logos* (Moscow: Istina I zhizn', 1997).

41. *Stranitsy*, no. 2 (4), 1997. See also the collection *Reconciliation* published in Moscow by the BBI in 1997. It is dedicated to a colloquium on ecumenism organized at Chevetogne; likewise the collection *Sobornost'*, which reprints articles of Fedotov, Zernov, and Nicholas Lossky, with a preface by Anthony Bloom, etc., of the Fellowship of Saint Alban and Saint Sergius, published in Moscow in 1998.

42. *Alpha and Omega*, no. 1 (15) and no. 2 (16), Moscow, 1998.

43. Boris Danilenko, "Grains of a Unique Bread," Moscow, Synodal Library of the Patriarchate of Moscow, 1998, 14.

44. The author adds in a footnote that "the least passionate presentation" of the meaning and evolution of the polemic is that of Zenkovsky, as published in *Vestnik RKhD* in 1987, no. 149, 61–65. Even though the position of Zenkovsky was very critical of sophiology, he accepted to defend Bulgakov at the St. Sergius Institute after the theologian was rehabilitated by the diocesan commission. It was, then, a veiled rehabilitation by a representative of the patriarchate of Moscow. See Danilenko, "Grains of a Unique Bread," 7.

45. Ibid., 3.

46. He suspected that the Russian monk was the future Archbishop Vsevolod Krivoshein (1900–1985).

47. S. N. Saveliev, *The Ideological Bankruptcy of the Quest for God in Russia* (Leningrad: University of Leningrad, 1987).

48. Valerii Kuvakin, *Religious Philosophy in Russia* (Moscow: Mysl', 1980).

49. R. Galtseva, *Essay on Utopian Russian Thought in the Twentieth Century* (Moscow: Nauka, 1992).

50. P. Gaidenko, *The Breakthrough Towards the Transcendent* (Moscow: Respublika, 1997).

51. *Synergy: Problems of Orthodox Asceticism and Mysticism*, under the direction of S. Horuzhy (Moscow: Di-dik, 1995).

52. E. Gollerbakh, "The Publishing House The Way," *Voprosy Filosofii*, no. 4, 1994, 129–164.

53. S. Levitsky, *An Essay on the History of Russian Philosophy* (Moscow: Kanon, 1996).

54. A. Dobrokhotov, "Philosophy, While Waiting for Godot," *Esprit*, no. 223, July 1996, 137.

55. A. Losev, *Philosophy, Myth, Culture* (Moscow: Politizdat, 1991); M. Mamardashvili, *Philosophy as I Understand It* (Moscow: Progress, 1992), 25,000 copies.

56. In the face of accusations against Losev of collaboration with the Communist regime, Aza Taho-Godi, the philosopher's wife, published, in 1997, a biography of Losev through the publishing house Molodaya Gvardia in 1997 in an effort to rehabilitate him. Similarly, the discovery in 1996 of pro-Stalinist projects for reform of the state written by Florensky in 1933 while he was in prison had a singular chilling effect on the popularity of the Russian philosopher—even though these documents could have been written under pressure from the NKVD (Florensky, *Works*, vol. 1 [Moscow: Mysl', 1996], 647–681).

57. V. Malakhov, "Is Russian Philosophy Possible?" *Logos*, no. 8, 1996, 117–131.

58. *Russian Philosophy of Property (XVIII–XXth Century)*, a collection of texts of Bulgakov, Berdyaev, Frank, and Stepun (St. Petersburg: Ganza, 1993).

59. I. Isaev and N. Zolotuhina, *History of Political and Legal Doctrines in Russia (XI–XXth Century)* (Moscow: Jurist, 1995).

60. N. Strizhevskaya, *On the Poetry of Joseph Brodsky* (Moscow: Graal, 1997).

61. *History of Philosophy*, vol. 3 (Moscow: Cabinet Greco Latin, 1998).

62. Thomas Schipflinger, *Sophia-Maria, Eine Ganzheitliche Vision der Schöpfung* (Munich-Zurich: Verlag Neue Stadt, 1997; Moscow: Gnosis-Skarabel, 1998).

63. F. Polyakov, "Myrrha Lot-Borodine: Wegzeichen und Dimensionen des west-östlichen Dialoges in der russischen Diaspora," in *Festschrift fur Hans-Bernd Harder zum 60. Geburstag* (Munich: Otto Sagner, 1995).

64. Tomas Spidlik, *The Russian Idea* (Paris: Fates, 1994).

65. H. Matsuguchi, "Geschichte der Einfuhrung der Philosophie N. Berdjajews in Japan," *Kyoto Sangyo daigaku ronschu*, Kyoto, no. 4, March 1985, 246–283.

66. Georges Nivat, *Russie-Europe, la fin du schisme: Études litteraires et politiques* (Paris: L'Age d'Homme, 1993).

67. Raeff, *Russia Abroad*.

68. Alexis Van Bunnen, "An Orthodox Church of the Western Rite, the Orthodox Catholic Church of France," Louvain la Neuve, 1981, mimeographed thesis.

69. L. Zander, *Western Orthodoxy* (Paris: CEO, 1958).

70. J.-L. Segundo, *Berdyaev, une réflexion chrétienne sur la personne* (Paris: Montaigne, 1963).

71. P. Evdokimov, *Le Christ dans la pensée russe* (Paris: Cerf, 1970; repr., 1986).

72. For instance, with several newpapers, such as *Kliutch* (1954–61); the Dostoevsky Circle, founded in 1964 and led by Fr. P. Struve; theatrical productions, and so forth.

73. M. Gorboff, *La Russie fantôme* (Paris: L'Age d'Homme, 1995).

74. Pierre Pascal, *Les grands courants de la pensée russe contemporaine en 1971* (Paris: L'Age d'Homme, 1971).

75. Guy Planty-Bonjour, *Hegel et la pensée philosophique en Russie (1830–1917)* (The Hague: Martinus Nijhoff, 1974).

76. Alain Besançon, *Les origines intellectuelles du léninisme* (Paris: Calmann-Lévy, 1977).
77. Jaen Lacroix, *Panorama de la philosophie française contemporaine* (Paris: Presses Universitaires de France, 1966).
78. Marie-Madeleine Davy, *Berdjaev, l'homme du huitième jour* (Paris: Flammarion, 1964).
79. See Colloquium Berdiaeff, Paris, Institut d'Études Slaves, 1975, 50.
80. M. de Gandillac, *Le siècle traversé*, 440.
81. See N. Struve, *70 ans d'émigration russe*, 163.
82. S. Bulgakov, "Beneath the Walls of Chersonese," *Simvol*, no. 35, 1991, 167–342.
83. *Greek and Latin Traditions Concerning the Procession of the Holy Spirit* (Vatican: Pontifical Council for Christian Unity, 1996), 4.
84. *Ecumenical Pilgrims* (Geneva: World Council of Churches, 1995).
85. R. Clavet, *N. Berdiaeff, l'équilibre du divin et de l'humain* (Montreal: Paulines, 1990); O. Clément, *Berdiaev: Un philosophe russe en France*.
86. O. Clément, *Berdiaev: Un philosophe russe en France*, 9.
87. Ibid., 8–10.
88. V. Volkoff, Preface, in S. Bulgakov, *Le Paraclet* (Paris: L'Age d'Homme, 1996), 2.
89. See especially M. Evdokimov, *Le Christ dans la tradition et la littérature russes* (Paris: Desclée de Brouwer, 1996).
90. Maryse Dennes, *Russie-Occident, philosophie d'une différence* (Paris: Éditions Mentha, 1991).
91. Frances Nethercott, *Une rencontre philosophique: Bergson en Russie (1907–1917)* (Paris: L'Harmattan, 1995).
92. *Oecumenisme et eschatologie selon Soloviev*, collection (Paris: FxG., 1994); *L'Unité*, collection (Paris: Solov'ev Society, 1996).
93. *Oecumenisme et eschatologie selon Soloviev*, 3.
94. This was the case for members of the Russian Student Christian Movement, only a handful of whom spoke correct Russian. The RSCM did not dare to change its name in 1994 but merely added the initials MJO, for Movement of Christian Youth (Mouvement de Jeunesse Orthodoxe), to its acronym.
95. See no. 170 of *Vestnik RKhD* on the fiftieth anniversary of the death of Bulgakov as an example.
96. See A. Kartashev and N. Struve, *70 ans des éditions YMCA-Press* (Paris: YMCA Press, 1990); *L'Institut de Théologie Orthodoxe Saint-Serge, 70 ans de théologie orthodoxe à Paris* (Paris: Hervas, 1997); and *1923–1998, Regard sur 75 ans d'activités Catalogue de l'exposition photographique réalisée à l'occasion du 75ᵉ anniversaire de l'ACER-MJO*, Paris, ACER, November 1998.
97. The example of the practice of confession is an illustration. Whereas in the Russian émigré community, following the theses presented in *The Way* in 1929 by Professor Nalimov (N2), the sacrament of confession has been distinguished from the sacrament of communion, in Russia the two remain mechanically linked.

98. C. Elchaninov, "Il y a 25 ans," *Bulletin de l'Aide aux croyants de l'URSS*, no. 50, Spring 1986.

99. D. Janicaud, *Le tournant théologique de la phénoménologie française* (Paris: L'Éclat, 1991).

100. Emmanuel Lévinas, "Leon Chestov, Kierkegaard et la philosophie existentielle," *Études juives*, July–December 1937, II, no. 1–2, 141; cited by Marie-Anne Lescourret, *Emmanuel Lévinas* (Paris: Flammarion, 1994), 180.

101. P. Ricouer, *Réflexion faite, autobiographie intellectuelle* (Paris: Esprit, 1995), 82.

102. André Lacocque and Paul Ricoeur, *Thinking Biblically: Exegetical and Hermeneutical Studies*, trans. David Pellauer (Chicago: University of Chicago Press, 1998).

103. John Paul II, *Fides et Ratio* (September 14, 1998), no. 74. Available at www.vatican.va.

104. Ibid., no. 81.

105. Ibid., no. 108.

106. L. Boltanski and L. Thévenot, in their book *De la justification: Les économies de la grandeur* (Paris: Gallimard, 1991)

107. Eric Vigne et al., *L'Essai* (Paris: ADPF/Ministère des Affaires Etrangères, 1997).

108. J. P. Vernant, *Entre mythe et politique* (Paris: Seuil, 1996), 628.

109. O. Mongin, *Face au scepticisme* (Paris: La Découverte, 1994).

110. A. de Souzenelle, *Le Féminin de l'Etre, pour en finir avec la côte d'Adam* (Paris: Albin Michel, 1997).

111. B. Vergely, *Le souffrance* (Paris: Gallimard, 1997), 47.

112. A. Borrely and Max Eutizi, *L'oecuménisme spirituel* (Geneva: Labor et Fides, 1988).

113. Ibid., 247–248.

114. R. Koselleck, *Vergangene Zukunft, Zur Semantik geschichtlicher Zeiten* (Frankfurt am Main: Suhrkamp, 1979), quoted by P. Ricoeur, *Temps et récit*, vol. 3, *Le temps raconté* (Paris: Seuil, 1985), 375.

115. V. Weidlé, *La Russie absente et présent* (Paris: Gallimard, 1949), 17.

Notes to Afterword

1. The thesis was defended in April 2000 at the Institute for Higher Education in Social Sciences (L'École des Hautes Études en Sciences Sociales) and accepted as "Très Honorable avec les félicitations du jury." It was published in Russian as *Zhurnal Put'* (Kiev: Phenix, 2000) and in French as *La Géneration des penseurs religieux de l'émigration Russe* (Kiev and Paris: L'Esprit et la Lettre, 2002). At Moscow, Lviv, and Kiev, the book was presented and discussed on several occasions. During these sessions, numerous intellectuals, such as the theologians Olivier Clément, Mi-

haylo Dymyd, and the late George Chistiakov, as well as philosophers such as Konstantin Sigov and Sergei Krymski and the poet Olga Sedakova, took up and improved the general theses which I defended in the book. Among the reviews were: Olivier Clément, "The Generation of the Religious Thinkers of the Russian Immigration," *Contacts*, no. 204, October–December 2003, 463–466 (in French); Michel Winock, "Paris, The Capital of Russia," *L'Histoire*, no. 274, March 2003, 26–27 (in French); "The Russian Intellectuals in France," *Revue des études Slaves*, Paris, vol. 73/2–3, 2001, 461–464; "A Doctoral Thesis on Religious Thought in the Russian Immigration Community," *SOP*, no. 248, May 2000, 6 (in French); T. Andrussevitch, "A. Arjakovsky: The Review *The Way* (1925–1940)," *Dukh i Litera*, nos. 7–8, 2001, 488–491 (in Ukrainian); T. Andrussevitch, "The Review *The Way* and the Return of Theological Memory to the Motherland," *Vera I Kultura*, Spring 2001, 4–5 (in Ukrainian); S. Makhun, "A New Departure for *The Way* in Kiev," *Collegium*, no. 11, 2001, 214–219 (Ukrainian); Yuri Pavlenko, "The Spiritual Dialogue between Kiev and Paris," Kiev, *Dialogues*, September 2002, 158–159; Yuri Pavlenko, "The Return," *Zerkalo nedeli*, no. 4, January 27, 2001, 14 (in both the Ukrainian and Russian issues); Klara Gudzik, "The Orthodox Renaissance at Paris," *Den'*, no. 16, January 26, 2001, 18 (in both the Ukrainian and Russian issues); Youri Vestel, "The Roads of Russian Orthodox Thinking during the Exile," *Khristianskaia mysl*, Kiev, June 2002, 12–32 (in Russian).

2. Charles Taylor, *The Malaise of Modernity*, Massey Lectures (Canadian Broadcasting Corporation, 1991), *Sources of the Self: The Making of the Modern Identity* (Cambridge, MA: Harvard University Press, 1989), and *A Secular Age* (Cambridge, MA: Harvard University Press, 2007).

3. François Dosse, *L'Empire du sens* (Paris: La Decouverte, 1997). François Dosse later wrote works on Michel de Certeau and Paul Ricoeur.

4. Frédéric Lenoir, *Les Métamorphoses de Dieu* (Paris: Plon, 2001). Cf. also: "The new scientific paradigm, through the diversity of its logics, pretends to assume not only the mythos but also the logos.... It is precisely by this movement of thought that it is possible to bring about the junction of different registers of intelligibility, to integrate the imaginary in the sphere of the rational and to recognize the structures of the imaginary itself." Lenoir, *Sciences et archetypes: Fragments philosophiques pour un réenchantement du monde* (Paris: Dervy, 2002), 37–38.

5. Cf. Bernard de Boissière and France-Marie Chauvelot, *Maurice Zundel* (Paris: Petite Renaissance, 2007).

6. Jean Guitton, *Mon testament philosophique* (Paris: La Renaissance, 2007): "the foundation of reason is prayer" (259).

7. On the issue of Russian religious thought and contemporary French philosophy, see my "Notre génération," in *Les Jalons Cent Ans Après*, ed. Antoine Arjakovsky (Lviv and Paris: Institut d'Études Œcuméniques, François Xavier de Guibert, 2009).

8. Jean-Yves Lacoste, *Expérience et Absolu* (Paris: Presses Universitaires de France, 1994), 2.

9. Maurice G. Dantec, *Grande jonction* (Paris: Albin Michel, 2007), 548.

10. Catherine Pickstock, "L'Orthodoxie est-elle Radicale," in *Radical Orthodoxy, Pour une Révolution Théologique* (Geneva: Ad Solem, 2004).

11. Cf. the presentation by Milbank on Bulgakov at Cambridge in 2006: "Sophiology and Theurgy," available online: http://theologyphilosophycentre.co.uk/papers/Milbank_SophiologyTheurgy.doc (last accessed Fall 2007).

12. John Milbank, *The Suspended Middle: Henri de Lubac and the Debate Concerning the Supernatural* (Grand Rapids, MI: Eerdmans, 2005).

13. Rowan Williams, *Sergii Bulgakov: Towards a Russian Political Theology* (Edinburgh: T&T Clark, 1999), and *Dostoevsky: Language, Faith and Fiction* (Waco, TX: Baylor University Press, 2008).

14. Christos Yannaras, *Postmodern Metaphysics* (Brookline, MA: Holy Cross Orthodox Press, 2004).

15. Basarab Nicolescu, *Nous, la particule et le monde* (Paris: Rocher, 2002), 52.

16. François Euvé, *Science, foi, sagesse* (Paris: Éditions de l'Atelier, 2004), 180.

17. Mary Tanner, "The Significance of the Special Commission," in *Grace in Abundance* (Geneva: World Council of Churches, 2006), 117.

18. *The Ecumenical Future*, ed. Carl E. Bratten and Robert W. Jensen, background papers for *In One Body Through the Cross: The Princeton Proposal for Christian Unity* (Grand Rapids, MI: Eerdmans, 2004). See also Peter Neuner, *Théologie oecuménique: La Quête de l'unité des Eglises Chrétiennes* (Paris: Cerf, 2005).

19. I developed this idea in my book *Church, Culture and Identity: Reflections on Orthodoxy in the Modern World* (Lviv: Ukrainian Catholic University Press, 2007).

20. The texts concerning the dialogue between Catholics and Orthodox in the United States can be found in John Borelli and John H. Erickson, eds., *The Quest for Unity* (Crestwood, NY: St. Vladimir's Seminary Press, 1996).

21. *Mary in the Plan of God and the Communion of the Saints*, Groupe des Dombes (Paris: Bayard, Centurion, 1999).

22. *Abendmahlsgemeinschaft ist möglich: Thesen zur eucharistichen Gastfreundschaft* (Frankfurt am Main: Lembeck, 2003).

23. Bernard Sesboüé, *Le Magistère à l'épreuve* (Paris: Desclée de Brouwer, 2001).

24. Archbishop Vsevolod of Scopelos, *We Are All Brothers* (Fairfax, VA: Eastern Christian Publications, 2006).

25. I develop this theme in two books: *Le Père Serge Boulgakov, philosophe et théologien chrétien* (Paris: Parole et Silence, 2006), and *Church, Culture and Identity* (n. 19 above).

26. Olivier Clément, *Mémoires d'espérance* (Paris: Desclée de Brouwer, 2003).

27. I am thinking especially of two books by Father Michael Plekon, *Living Icons* (Notre Dame, IN: University of Notre Dame Press, 2002), and *Hidden Holiness* (University of Notre Dame Press, 2009).

28. Ivan Lagovsky was canonized by the Russian Orthodox Church in 2012.

29. Bishop Gabriel of Comanes started a process of glorification of Fr. Sergius Bulgakov after the Russian Student Christian Conference in 2011 at Loisy.

30. See Paul Anderson, *No East or West* (Paris: YMCA Press, 1985).
31. See the section "Debate on the Use of Force," pp. 105–108 in this translation.
32. Cf. Andreas Kappeler, *Histoire de l'Ukraine* (Paris: IES, 2004).
33. Anna Politkovskaya and Georges Litvinenko, recent victims of the hardening of President Putin's regime, both had Ukrainian roots.
34. See "The Catholicity of Russian Orthodoxy," in my *Church, Culture and Identity*, 13–19.
35. Kappeler, *Histoire de l'Ukraine*.
36. *The Journals of Father Alexander Schmemann* (Crestwood, NY: St. Vladimir's Seminary Press, 2000), 169. This English translation consists of a selection of journal passages. The full journals, kept in the last ten years of Schmemann's life, have now been published in both the original Russian as well as a French edition: *Dnevniki (1973–1983)* (Moscow: Russkii Put', 2005), and *Journal (1973–1983)* (Paris: Éditions des Syrtes, 2009). In a lecture which I gave at Saint Vladimir's Seminary in 2004, I also recalled that the reservations of Fr. John Meyendorff about the sophiology of Fr. Bulgakov did not invalidate sophiology itself (which John Meyendorff was unable to understand because Fr. Sergius did not lecture on it at the St. Sergius Institute). Nor does it reflect on Meyendorff (who had all the reason in the world to reject the gnostic and Solovyovian vision of Sophia, which he mistakenly attributed to Bulgakov). [Editor's note: Paul Valliere's correspondence with Fr. Meyendorff just before the latter's death suggests that he was reassessing his earlier critical stance toward Bulgakov and sophiology. See Paul Valliere, *Modern Russian Theology: Bukharev, Soloviev, Bulgakov* (Grand Rapids, MI: Eerdmans, 2000), 396.] On the other hand, Meyendorff's rejection of confessionalism is very much in the line of the theological renewal carried out by the School of Paris. See Meyendorff's *Catholicity and the Church* (Crestwood, NY: St. Vladimir's Seminary Press, 1983).
37. Robert Van Drimmelen, *Faith in a Global Economy* (Geneva: World Council of Churches, 1998).
38. See Petros Vassiliadis, *Eucharist and Witness: Orthodox Perspectives on the Unity and Mission of the Church* (Geneva: World Council of Churches, 1998).
39. Michael Walzer, *The Revolution of the Saints: A Study in the Origins of Radical Politics* (Cambridge, MA: Harvard University Press, 1965).
40. Jean-Baptiste de Foucauld, *Les trois cultures du développement humain* (Paris: Odile Jacob, 2002), 166.

REFERENCES

Articles Published in *The Way*

The scanned issues of *The Way* are available at http://www.odinblago.ru/path.

Articles are coded by the first letter of the author's last name and ascending numbers. Articles with codes ending in "R" are reviews of the publication(s) listed immediately after the article code. A few author names are not in alphabetical order, matching the French edition or as a result of English transliteration of proper names. Cross-references have been added for these authors. The pattern followed below is:

Author Name

Article Code
Title of *The Way* article (translated into English from Russian); or, the author(s) and title(s) of the work(s) under review by *The Way* article (Russian and French titles translated)
(*The Way* issue number: month/year, page numbers), or,
(*The Way* issue number: month/year, page numbers—"Title of review article")

AFANASIEV, N. N. (Father)

A1 "The Ecumenical Councils. Concerning the 'Address to Orthodox Theologians'"
(25: 12/30, pp. 81–92)
A2R A. V. Kartashev: *The Paths to the Ecumenical Council*. Paris: YMCA Press, 1932, 140 pp.
(37: 2/33, pp. 91–92)
A3 "The Canons and Canonical Consciousness"
(Supplement to issue no. 39, 16 pp.)
A4 "The Two Concepts of the Universal Church"
(45: 10–12/34, pp. 16–29)

ALEXANDROV, A. A.

A5 "The Book of Job"
(58: 11–12/38–1/39, pp. 57–63)

ALEKSII, B. (Father)

A6 "Two Sermons Delivered in Soviet Russia"
(42: 1–3/34, pp. 68–79)

ALEKSEEV, N. N.

A7 "The Concept of the 'Earthly City' in Christian Doctrine"
(5: 10–11/26, pp. 20–41)

A8 "Christianity and the Concept of Monarchy"
(6: 1/27, pp. 15–31)

A9 "The Russian People and the State"
(8: 8/27, pp. 21–57)

A10 "Russian Westernizing"
(15: 2/29, pp. 81–111)

A11 "B. N. Chicherin and His Religious-Philosophical Ideas in Light of His Memoirs"
(24: 10/30, pp. 98–110)

A12 "Christianity and Socialism"
(28: 6/31, pp. 32–68)

A13 "On the Idea of Philosophy and Its Social Mission"
(44: 7–9/34, pp. 27–43)

A14 "On the Highest Comprehension of Philosophy"
(53: 4–7/37, pp. 37–52)

A15 "Demonocracy. On the Books of Rauschning"
(61: 10/39–3/40, pp. 26–32)

Alexandrov, A. A. See A5

ANDERSON, P. F.

A16 "The Anglo-Russian Fellowship of the Martyr Saint Alban and Saint Sergius of Radonezh"
(10: 4/28, pp. 112–114)

ANDRIEU, Cardinal (Archbishop of Bordeaux)

A17 "A Letter on Action Francaise" / Translation of an article that appeared in the *Religious Weekly of Bordeaux* 27: 8/26
(6: 1/27, pp. 81–83)

ANONYMOUS

A18 "Public Session of the Religious-Philosophical Academy Dedicated to the Memory of Vladimir Solovyov" / With the participation of Fr. S. Bulgakov, N. Berdyaev, and B. Vysheslavtsev
(2: 1/26, pp. 101–104)

A19 "A Meeting of Orthodox, Catholics and Protestants in Paris" / Report
(3: 3–4/26, p. 150)

A20 "Russian Religious Thought in German"
(3: 3–4/26, pp. 151–152)

A21R V. Solovyov: *The Spiritual Foundations of Life*. 2 vols. Paris: YMCA Press, 1926
(3: 3–4/26, p. 153—Notice of a New Edition)

A22 "Intellectual and Interior Prayer. Extracts from the Fathers of the Church, Saint Basil the Great, Gregory the Theologian, John Chrysostom, Macarius the Great, Simeon the New Theologian, Mark of Ephesus, Gregory Palamas"
(4: 5–7/26, pp. 117–120)

A23 "Chronicle of the Spiritual Life"
(1) An Interconfessional Meeting / Report, December 1926
(2) Session of the Religious-Philosophical Academy on the Topic of the Church and State / Report, January 1927
(7: 4/27, p. 121)

A24 "The Philosophy Society of Prague" / A brief history of its foundation, list of participants, and conferences from 1924 to 1927
(8: 8/27, pp. 139–140)

A25R Father Pavel Florensky: *The Pillar and Ground of the Truth: An Essay in Orthodox Theodicy in Twelve Letters*. Berlin: Rossica, 1929
(18: 9/29, p. 124—Notice of a New Edition)

A26 "Letter to N. A. Berdyaev from Russia"
(22: 6/30, pp. 93–96)

ARCHAMBAULT, P.

A27 "The Philosophy of Action. Maurice Blondel and Abbe Laberthonnière"
(4: 7/26, pp. 121–126)

ARSENIEV, N. S.

A28 "Contemporary Currents in Catholicism and Protestantism in Germany"
(1: 9/25, pp. 161–168)

A29 "Life in Abundance. Mysticism and the Church"
(3: 3–4/26, pp. 148–149)

A30 "Pessimism and Mysticism in Ancient Greece"
(4: 6–7/26, pp. 88–102)
A31 "Pessimism and Mysticism in Ancient Greece" (continuation and conclusion)
(5: 10–11/26, pp. 67–86)
A32 "The Spirit of the Times and Its Understanding. Concerning the recent articles of N. A. Berdyaev" / Summary title: "The Spirit of Our Times"
(6: 1/27, pp. 102–104)
A33 "The Present Situation of Christianity"
(7: 4/27, pp. 99–106)
A34 "The Lausanne Conference"
(10: 4/28, pp. 102–111)
A35 "The Religious Conferences in Newcastle and Cambridge"
(20: 2/30, pp. 88–92)
A36 "The Religious Significance of the Contemporary Youth Movement in Germany (*Jungendbewegung*)" / Summary title: "The Religious Youth Movements in Germany"
(23: 8/30, pp. 110–119)
A37R Chaim Bloch: *Priester Der Liebe. Die Welt Der Chassidim.* Almathea Verlag, 1930, 266 pp.
(29: 8/31, pp. 93–94)
A38 "The Movement for Christian Unity and the Problems of the Contemporary World"
(31: 12/31, pp. 75–88)
A39 "Meetings with the Anglican Church"
(33: 4/32, pp. 44–51)
A40 "Contemporary Anglican Theology"
(35: 9/32, pp. 68–82)

ARTEMIEV, M. M.

A41 "Is Russia Alive? (The Story of a Russian Exile)"
(25: 12/30, pp. 3–21)
A42 "Freedom of the Will"
(32: 2/32, pp. 43–72)
A43 "The Path of Transfiguration" (A Preface) / cf. X1 in this list
(39: 7/33, pp. 41–43)

BECKER (de), R.

B1 "In Darkness (Dedicated to Theodore d'Ultremont)"
(51: 5–10/36, pp. 32–45)

BELENSON, E.

B2 "The *Podvig* of Holy Foolishness"
    (8: 8/27, pp. 89–98)
B3 "The Hidden Christ of the Jews"
    (13: 10/28, pp. 87–92)
B4 "The Secret Path (Marie de Vallais, 1590–1656)"
    (17: 7/29, pp. 96–103)
B5 "Catholic Women Mystics of the Nineteenth and Twentieth Centuries"
    (28: 6/31, pp. 89–98)
B6 "The Mission of Israel"
    (52: 11/36–3/37, pp. 56–66)

BENNIGSEN, G. M. (Father)

B7 "Letter to the Editor"
    (44: 7–9/34, pp. 63–67)

BERDYAEV, N. A.

B8   "The Kingdom of God and the Kingdom of Caesar"
     (1: 9/25, pp. 31–52)
B9R "The Eurasianists" (*The Eurasianist Messenger*, bk. 4, Berlin, 1925)
     (1: 9/25, pp. 134–139—"The Eurasianists")
B10R Jacques Maritain: *Reflections on the Intellect and Its Specific Activity*. Paris: Nouvelle Librairie Nationale, 1925, 388 pp.
     (1: 9/25, pp. 169–171—"Neo-Thomism")
B11 "Salvation and Creation: Two Ways of Understanding Christianity (In Memory of V. Solovyov)"
     (2: 1/26, pp. 26–46)
B12 "The Bourgeois Spirit"
     (3: 3–4/26, pp. 3–13)
B13 "Reply to the 'Letter from a Monarchist'"
     (3: 3–4/26, pp. 140–144)
B14R Michel d'Herbigny, S.J.: "The Religious Aspect of Moscow in October, 1925." *Orientalia Christiana*, vol. 5, no. 20 (January 1926)
     (3: 3–4/26, pp. 145–147—"Father d'Herbigny and the Religious Rites in Moscow in October 1925")
B15R I. Ilyin: "Resisting the Forces of Evil"
     (4: 6–7/26, pp. 103–116—"The Nightmare of the Evil Good")
B16 "The Philosopher's Journal. The Debate about Monarchy, the Bourgeois Spirit, and Freedom of Thought" / under the rubric "The Philosopher's Journal"
     (4: 6–7/26, pp. 176–182)

B17R   Emile Dermenghen: "Joseph de Maistre, the Mystic," 1923
       Georges Goyau: "The Religious Thought of Joseph de Maistre," 1921
       Count Joseph de Maistre: "Free Masonry. Memoir for the Duke of Brunswick" (Introduction by E. Dermenghen)
       (4: 6–7/26, pp. 183–187—"Joseph de Maistre and Freemasonry")
B18   "The Discords in the Church and the Freedom of Conscience"
       (5: 10–11/26, pp. 42–54)
B19R   Heinrich Barnkamm: "Luther Und Bohme," 1925
       Jacob Boehme: "Gedankabe Der Syadt Gorlitz Zu Seinem. 300 Jahringen Todestage." Herausgegeben Von Richard Hecht, 1924
       Paul Hankamer: "Jacob Bohme." Gestalt und Gestaltung, 1924
       (5: 10–11/26, pp. 119–122—"Recent Books on J. Bohme")
B20R   Louis Rougier: *Celsus or the Conflict Between Ancient Civilization and Primitive Christianity* (The Masters of Anti-Christian Thought). Paris: Éd. du Siècle, 1926, 440 pp.
       (5: 10–11/26, pp. 131–132—"Anti-Christian Thought")
B21   "The Study of Religion and Christian Apologetics"
       (6: 1/27, pp. 50–68)
B22   "On the Spirit of the Times and on the Monarchy" / under the rubric "The Philosopher's Journal"
       (6: 1/27, pp. 110–114)
B23R   N. Lossky: *The Freedom of the Will.* Paris: YMCA Press, 1926, 180 pp.
       (6: 1/27, pp. 130–131)
B24   "Some Reflections on Theodicy"
       (7: 4/27, pp. 50–62)
B25R   Anonymous: "The Deification of Death: The Source of Heresies, of Divisions and of Deviations from the Correct Doctrine of the Church. Dogmatic Studies (1926)" [On the thought of N. F. Fedorov—manuscript received from the USSR]
       (7: 4/27, pp. 122–124)
B26   "A Conference in Austria: April 30–May 6, 1927
       (8: 8/27, pp. 131–133)
B27R   *Eurasianism: An Attempt at a Systematic Exposition.* Éd. Eurasienne, 1926
       (8: 8/27, pp. 141–144—"The Utopian Statism of the Eurasianists")
B28R   Henri Massis: *In Defense of the West.* Le Rouseau d'or, 1927
       (8: 8/27, pp. 145–148—"An Accusation of the West")
B29   "The Metaphysical Problem of Freedom"
       (9: 1/28, pp. 41–53)
B30R   Action Française: *Why Rome Spoke. The Great Debate in French Catholicism.* Éd. Spes. Cahiers de la Nouvelle Journée
       Jacques Maritain: *The Primacy of the Spiritual.* Le Roseau d'or.
       (10: 4/28, pp. 115–123—"Action Française and Catholicism")

B31R Jean Izoulet: *Paris, Capital of Religions or the Mission of Israel.* Paris: Albin Michel, 1925
(10: 4/28, pp. 130–133)

B32 "Three Anniversaries (N. Tolstoy, G. Ibsen, N. Fedorov)"
(11: 6/28, pp. 76–99)

B33R A. Jakubisiak: "An Essay on the Limits of Space and Time"
(11: 6/28, pp. 127–129)

B34R Henri Delafosse: *The Fourth Gospel: The Writings of Saint Paul, The Epistle to the Romans, The First Epistle to the Corinthians.* Éd. F. Rieder et Cie
L. Gabrilovitch: *Christianity, Marcionism, Antitheism.* Éd. Rieder et Cie., in the collection The Chronicle of Ideas
(12: 8/28, pp. 116–121—"Marcionism")

B35 "Obscurantism"
(13: 10/28, pp. 19–36)

B36 "Illusions and Reality in the Psychology of Emigré Youth"
(14: 12/28, pp. 3–30)

B37 "The Philosopher's Journal (On the Means and the Ends, On Politics and Morality, On Christian Politics and Humanist Politics, On the Two Ways of Understanding the Task of the Emigration)"
(16: 5/29, pp. 82–94)

B38R Fr. S. Bulgakov: *Jacob's Ladder. On the Angels.* Paris, 1929, 229 pp.
(16: 5/29, pp. 95–99—"On Sophiology")

B39R Jean Wahl: *The Ordeal of the Conscience in the Philosophy of Hegel.* Éd. Rieder.
(17: 7/29, pp. 104–107)

B40R Baron G. Grabbe: *Alexis Stepanovich Khomiakov.* Warsaw: Typography of the Synod, 1929
(17: 7/29, pp. 108–111)

B41R Lev Shestov: *In Job's Balances.* Paris: Éd. des Annales Contemporaines, 1929, 371 pp.
(18: 9/29, pp. 88–106—"The Tree of Life and the Tree of Knowledge")

B42R A. Koyré: *The Philosophy of Jakob Boehme.* Paris: Vrin, 1929
(18: 9/29, pp. 116–122)

B43R A. Gornostaev: *Paradise on Earth. The Ideology of F. Dostoevsky: F. Dostoevsky and N. Fedorov.* 1929
(19: 11/29, pp. 114–116)

B44 "Studies on J. Boehme (1) The Doctrine of the *Ungrund* and Freedom"
(20: 2/30, pp. 47–79)

B45R Friedrich Karl Schumann: *Der Gottesgedanke und Das Zerfallen der Moderne.* Tübingen: Verlag von Mohr (Paul Siebeck), 1929
(20: 2/30, pp. 113–116)

B46 "Studies on J. Boehme (2) The Doctrine of *Sophia* and the Androgyny. J. Boehme and the Currents of Russian Sophiology"
(21: 4/30, pp. 34–62)

B47 "Prince G. P. Trubetskoy *(in memoriam)*"
(21: 4/30, pp. 94–96)

B48	"The East and the West"
	(23: 8/30, pp. 97–109)
B49R	Georges Gurvitch: *Current Trends in German Philosophy: E. Husserl, M. Scheler, E. Lask, N. Hartmann, M. Heidegger.* Paris: Vrin, 1930
	Martin Heidegger: *Sein und Zeit.* Herste Hälfte, 1929
	(24: 10/30, pp. 115–121—"The New Trends in German Philosophy")
B50R	E. Brunner: *Gott und Mensch. Vier Untersuchungen über das Personhafte Sein.* Tübingen: Verlag von I. C. B. Mohr, Paul Siebeck, 1930
	(24: 10/30, pp. 122–124)
B51	"The Debate over Anthroposophy (Reply to N. Turgeneva)"
	(25: 12/30, pp. 105–114)
B52	"In Defense of Blok"
	(26: 2/31, pp. 109–113)
B53R	V. F. Asmus: *An Essay on the History of Dialectic in the New Philosophies.* USSR, Gosizdat
	(27: 4/31, pp. 108–112)
B54R	Emmanuel Berl: *The Death of the Bourgeois Morality.* Éd. Nouvelle Revue Française.
	(28: 6/31, pp. 70–75)
B55	"Literary Currents and the Social Order (On the Question of the Religious Meaning of Art)"
	(29: 8/31, pp. 80–92)
B55bis	"The Truth and Lies of Communism (For an Understanding of the Religion of Communism)"
	(30: 10/31, pp. 3–34)
B56	"The Pride of the Humble. A Response to Hieromonk Ioann"
	(31: 12/31, pp. 70–75)
B57R	P. Laberthonnière: *Selected Writings* (Introduction and notes by Thérèse Friedel). Paris: Vrin, 1931
	(32: 2/32, pp. 103–105)
B58	"Christianity and the Challenge of Contemporary Social Reality" (Conference)
	(Supplement to issue no. 32, pp. 1–10)
B59	"The General Orientation of Soviet Philosophy and Militant Atheism"
	(Supplement to issue no. 34, 28 pp.)
B60	"The Spiritual State of the Contemporary World" / Lecture given at the WSCF Conference at Bad-Bol, May 1931
	(35: 9/32, pp. 56–68)
B61R	H. Garrigou-LaGrange, O.P.: *Providence and Confidence in God.* Desclée de Brouwer
	(35: 9/32, pp. 97–99)
B62	"Two Ways of Understanding Christianity. The Debates about the Old and the New in Christianity"
	(36: 12/32, pp. 17–43)

B63R Count Herman de Keyserling: *South American Meditations*. Librairie Stock, 1932
(36: 12/32, pp. 89–93)
B64R N. A. Setnitsky: *The Extinguished Idea*. Harbin, 1932
(36: 12/32, pp. 93–95)
B65 "Man and the Machine: The Question of the Sociology and Metaphysics of Technology"
(38: 5/33, pp. 3–37)
B66R Martin Buber: *Die Chassidischen Bucher*. Hellereau: J. Hegnev, 1928
Martin Buber: *Ich und Du*. Leipzig: Insel Verlag, 1923
Martin Buber: *Zwiesprache*. Berlin: Schoken Verlag, 1934
Martin Buber: *Koenigtum Gottes*
(38: 5/33, pp. 87–91)
B67R *Esprit*, no. 6, "The Spiritual and Social Quests of the French Youth"
(39: 7/33, pp. 78–82)
B68R Julius Schmidhauser: *Der Kampf um das Geistige Reich*. Hamburg: Hanseatische Verlag Sans Talt, 1933
(40: 9–10/33, pp. 66–70)
B69R G. I. Heering: *God and Caesar. The Deficiencies of the Churches Concerning the Problem of War*.
(40: 9–10/33, pp. 70–72)
B70 "Polytheism and Nationalism"
(43: 4–6/34, pp. 3–16)
B71 "Knowledge and Communication" (A Reply to N. N. Alexeev)
(44: 7–9/34, pp. 44–49)
B72R Carlo Suarez: *The Psychological Comedy*
(44: 7–9/34, pp. 68–72—"The Comedy of Original Sin")
B73 "Concerning Christian Optimism and Pessimism" (Concerning Fr. Sergii Chetverikov's Letter)
(46: 1–3/35, pp. 31–36)
B74R Theodore Haeker: *Was ist des Mensch?* Leipzig: Jacob Hegner
(47: 4–6/35, pp. 86–89—"What Is Man?")
B75 "Personalism and Marxism"
(48: 7–9/35, pp. 3–19)
B76 "A Return to the Subject of Christian Pessimism and Optimism" (A Reply to Fr. Sergii Chetverikov)
(48: 7–9/35, pp. 69–72)
B77 "The Russian Renaissance at the Beginning of the Twentieth Century and the Journal *The Way*: On the Occasion of the Tenth Anniversary of Its Founding"
(49: 10–12/35, pp. 3–22)
B78 "The Spirit of the Grand Inquisitor: Concerning the Decree of Metropolitan Sergius Condemning the Theological Opinions of Fr. Sergius Bulgakov"
(49: 10–12/35, pp. 72–81)

B79R   E. Mounier: *The Personalist and Communitarian Revolution*. Ed. Montaigne
       Leonhard Ragaz: *Von Christus Zu Marx—Von Marx Zu Christus*
       (49: 10–12/35, pp. 88–91—"Religious Socialism")
B80   "The Problem of Mankind: Towards a Christian Anthropology"
       (50: 1–4/36, pp. 3–26)
B81   "On Authority, Freedom, and Humanity (Reply to V. Lossky and Fr. Chetverikov)"
       (50: 1–4/36, pp. 37–42, 42–49)
B81bis "Lev Shestov"
       (50: 1–4/36, pp. 50–53)
B82   "G. I. Chelpanov (*in memoriam*)"
       (50: 1–4/36, pp. 56–57)
B83R   I. N. Danzas: *The Religious Itinerary of the Russian Conscience*. In the collection "Istina." Juvisy, Cerf
       (51: 5–10/36, pp. 74–76)
B84R   G. V. Florovsky: *The Ways of Russian Theology*. Paris: YMCA Press, 1937, 574 pp.
       (53: 4–7/37, pp. 53–65—"Orthodoxy and Humanity")
B85   "A. F. Karpov (*in memoriam*)"
       (54: 8–12/37, pp. 72–73)

no B86

B87R   Kirche, Volk un Saat: *Stimmen aus der Deutschen Evangelischen Kirche zur Oxforder Weltkirchenkonferenz*. Berlin: Furche-Verlag, 1937
       (54: 8–12/37, pp. 74–76)
B88   "Christianity and Anti-Semitism: The Religious Destiny of Judaism"
       (56: 5–6/38, pp. 84–86)
B89R   J. Grenier: *Essay on the Spirit of Orthodoxy*. Paris: Gallimard
       (57: 8–10/38, pp. 84–86)
B90   "The Fundamental Idea in the Philosophy of L. Shestov"
       (58: 11–12/38–1/39, pp. 44–48)
B91   "Does Freedom of Thought and Conscience Really Exist in Orthodoxy?" / In defense of G. P. Fedotov
       (59: 2–4/39, pp. 46–54)
B92   "Pope Pius XI (*in memoriam*)"
       (59: 2–4/39, pp. 55–56)
B93   "Christianity and the Social Order (Reply to S. Frank concerning his article 'The Problem of Christian Socialism')"
       (60: 5–9/39, pp. 33–36)
B94R   S. Frank: *The Intangible. An Ontological Introduction to the Philosophy of Religion*. Paris: La Maison du Livre, Les Annales Contemporaines, 1939, 323 pp.
       (60: 5–9/39, pp. 65–67)
B95   "War and Eschatology"
       (61: 10/39–3/40, pp. 3–14)

BEZOBRAZOV, S. S. (Bishop Cassian)

B96 "The Russian Orthodox Institute of Theology in Paris"
(1: 9/25, pp. 128–133)

B97 "The Principles of an Orthodox Exegesis of the Word of God" / provisional title: "The Principles of Orthodox Teaching on the Holy Scriptures"
(13: 10/28, pp. 3–18)

B98 "The Raising of Lazarus and the Resurrection of Christ"
(16: 5/29, pp. 3–18)

B99 "The East-West Scholarly-Theological Conference in Novi Sad (Yugoslavia), August 9–10, 1929"
(19: 11/29, pp. 93–103)

B100R E. B. Allo: *Saint John. The Apocalypse: Biblical Studies.* Paris: Gabalda, 1921, 976 pp.
(21: 4/30, pp. 97–106)

B101R R. H. Charles: *A Critical and Exegetical Commentary on the Revelation of Saint John. With Introduction and Notes, also the Greek Commentary,* 1920. Vol. 1, 373 pp.; vol. 2, 498 pp.
(21: 4/30, pp. 106–112)

B102R Theodor Zahn: *Die Offenbarung des Johannes. Kommentar zum Neuen Testament.* Herausgegeben von Th. Zahn. Vol. 18, Parts 1 and 2. Leipzig: Erlangen, 1926, 633 pp.
(21: 4/30, pp. 112–117)

B103R Ernest Lohmeyer: *Die Offenbarung des Johannes. Handbuch zum Neuen Testament.* Herausgegeben von Hans Lietxman. Tübingen: Mohr, 1926, 203 pp.
(21: 4/30, pp. 117–128)

B104R D. S. Merezhkovsky: *The Unknown Jesus.* Vol. 1, Belgrade, 1932; vol. 2, part 1, Belgrade, 1933
(42: 1–3/34, pp. 80–87)

B105R Hieromonk Lev Gillet: *Jesus of Nazareth, The Historical Facts.* Paris: YMCA Press, 1934, 165 pp.
(48: 7–9/35, pp. 73–77)

B106 "The New Testament in Our Times: History and Theology" / Lecture given at the Orthodox Institute of Theology of Paris on December 21, 1936
(55: 1–4/38, pp. 3–23)

BITSILLI, P.

B106bis "P. A. Bakunin"
(34: 7/32, pp. 19–38)

B106ter K. Mochulsky: *The Spiritual Evolution of Gogol.* Paris: YMCA Press, 1934
(45: 10–12/34, pp. 77–79)

BLUMHARDT, C. (Pastor)

B107　"Open Letter from Pastor Blumhardt" / On Religious Socialism
(59: 2–4/39, pp. 38–45)

BUBNOV, N.

B108R　David Baumgardt: *Franz von Baader und die Philosophische Romantik.* 1927
(11: 6/28, pp. 124–127—"A Recent Book on Franz Baader")
B109R　Hermann Schwarz: *Gott Jenseits von Theismus und Pantheismus.* Berlin, 1928
(20: 2/30, pp. 94–101—"Understanding God and the Theory of Values")
B110R　Helmut Gross: *Der Deutsche Idealismus und das Christtentum.* 1927
(31: 12/31, pp. 104–109—"German Idealism and Christianity")
B111R　Hans Johannes Leisegang: *Lessings Weltanshauung.* Leipzig: F. Meiner, 1931
(33: 4/32, pp. 67–72—"A Recent Book on Lessing's Vision of the World")
B112R　Kurt Leese: *Die Krisis und Wende des Christlichen Geistes*
(35: 9/32, pp. 91–94)
B113R　Rudolph Otto: *Reich Gottes und Menschenson.* 1934
(44: 7–9/34, pp. 73–75)
B114R　Broder Christiansen: *Der Neue Gott.* 1934
(44: 7–9/34, pp. 77–80)

BULGAKOV, S. (Father)

B115　"Notes on the Doctrine of the Church"
(1: 9/25, pp. 53–78)
B116　"Notes on the Doctrine of the Church II: Does Orthodoxy Have the External Authority of Dogmatic Infallibility?"
(2: 1/26, pp. 47–58)
B117　"Notes on the Doctrine of the Church III: The Church and 'Heterodoxy'"
(4: 6–7/26, pp. 3–26)
B118　"Saint Sergius' Blessed Precepts for the Russian Theological Tradition" / Lecture at the Convocation of the Orthodox Theological Institute of Paris on July 7, 1926
(5: 10–11/26, pp. 3–19)
B119　"Reply to a Letter from Professor H. Erenberg"
(5: 10–11/26, pp. 90–92)
B120　"Concerning the Kingdom of God" / Address in English at the Second Anglo-Russian Conference of the Students of Saint Alban on December 30, 1927
(11: 6/28, pp. 3–30)

B121 "The Lausanne Conference and the Papal Encyclical" (of Pope Pius XI, *Mortalium Animos*)
(13: 10/28, pp. 90–92)

B122 "G. V. Williams, deceased November 18, 1928" (Obituary)
(14: 12/28, pp. 108–110)

B123 "Notes on the Doctrine of the Church IV: The Vatican Dogma"
(15: 2/29, pp. 39–80)

B124 "Notes on the Doctrine of the Church IV: The Vatican Dogma (Conclusion)"
(16: 5/29, pp. 19–48)

B125 "On the Issue of the Discipline of Confession and Communion" (Response to the theses of Professor T. Nalimov) (See Nalimov, 18: 9/29, pp. 79–87)
(19: 11/29, pp. 70–78)

B126 "The Dogma of the Eucharist"
(20: 2/30, pp. 3–46)

B126bis "Orthodoxy and Socialism" (Letter to the Editor)
(20: 2/30, pp. 88–95)

B127 "The Dogma of the Eucharist" (continued)
(21: 4/30, pp. 3–33)

B128 "Judas Iscariot, Apostle-Betrayer. Part One (History)"
(26: 2/31, pp. 3–60)

B129 "Judas Iscariot, Apostle-Betrayer. Part Two (Dogmatics)"
(27: 4/31, pp. 3–42)

B130 "Christianity and Contemporary Social Reality" (Conference)
(**Supplement to issue no. 32, pp. 27–31**)

B130bis "The Holy Grail (an Exegesis of John 19:34)"
(32: 2/32, pp. 3–42)

B131 "On the Paths of Dogma (After the Seven Ecumenical Councils)" (Lecture at the Orthodox Institute of Theology of Paris in 1932)
(37: 2/33, pp. 3–35)

B132R Fr. Sergius Bulgakov: *The Lamb of God. On Divine-Humanity*, vol. 1 / Christology. Paris: YMCA Press, 1933, 468 pp.
(**Review by Author.** 41: 11–12/33, pp. 101–105)

B133 "Fr. Alexander Elchaninov"
(45: 10–12/34, pp. 56–59)

B134 "On the Banks of the Chebar River" / Lecture at the Convocation of the Orthodox Institute of Theology of Paris on the Occasion of Its Tenth Anniversary
(47: 4–6/35, pp. 66–70)

B135 "Hierarchy and Sacraments"
(49: 10–12/35, pp. 23–47)

B136R Fr. Sergius Bulgakov: *The Comforter. On Divine-Humanity*, vol. 2 / Doctrine of the Holy Spirit, Pneumatology. Paris: YMCA Press, 1936, 449 pp.
(**Review by Author.** 50: 1–4/36, pp. 68–69)

B137 "More on the Question of Sophia, the Wisdom of God. Concerning the decisions of the Karlovtsy Synod" (Memorandum sent to Metropolitan Evlogy) / Title: "On Sophia, the Wisdom of God. Reply to the Bishops of Karlovtsy"
(Supplement to issue no. 50: 1–4/36, p. 24)

B138 "The Problem of Conditional Immortality: An Introduction to Eschatology"
(52: 11/36–3/37, pp. 3–23)

B139 "The Problem of Conditional Immortality: An Introduction to Eschatology" (continued)
(53: 4–7/37, pp. 3–19)

B140 "Frank Gavin"
(56: 5–6/38, pp. 63–65)

B141 "Bishop Walter Frere, 1863–1938 (*in memoriam*)"
(56: 5–6/38, pp. 66–68)

B142 "*Una Sancta*: The Foundations of Ecumenism." Address Given at the Anglo-Russian Conference of Students at High Leigh in 1938
(58: 11–12/38–1/39, pp. 3–14)

"A CATHOLIC"

Ca1 "Peter's Ladder" (Some Observations on the Ideas of D. Merezhkovsky)
(6: 1/27, pp. 85–88)

CHETVERIKOV, S. (FATHER)

C1 "From the of Historical Tradition of the Russian Elders, I–II. In Search of the Paths to Christ (from the History of the Childhood and Youth of the Moldavian Elder Archimandrite Paisius Velichkovsky)"
(1: 9/25, pp. 99–115)

C2 "The Practice of Mental Spiritual Activity and Spiritual Sobriety"
(3: 3–4/26, pp. 65–83)

C3 "From the of Historical Tradition of the Russian Elders, III. The Writings of Elder Paisius Velichkovsky on Mental Prayer"
(7: 4/27, pp. 23–49)

C4 "The Eucharist as the Central Focus of Christian Life"
(22: 6/30, pp. 3–23)

C5 "The Difficulties of Religious Life during Infancy and Adolescence"
(34: 7/32, pp. 52–63)

C6 "Open Letter to N. A. Berdyaev concerning His Book *The Fate of Man in the Modern World*"
(46: 1–3/35, pp. 28–30)

C7 "On World Evil and the Saving Power of the Church" (Concerning an Article by N. A. Berdyaev, "On Christian Pessimism and Optimism") (See Berdyaev, 46: 1–3/35)
(48: 7–8/35, pp. 60–68)

C8   "Open Letter to N. A. Berdyaev Concerning His Article 'The Spirit of the Grand Inquisitor'" (See Berdyaev, 49: 10–12/35, pp. 72–81)
(50: 1–4/36, pp. 32–36)

CHIZHEVSKY, D.

C9   "The Philosophy of G. S. Skovoroda (1722–1794)"
(19: 11/29, pp. 23–56)

C10R "J. Boehme in Russia." R. M. Bluth: *A Christian Prometheus. The Influence of Boehme on the Third Part of Mickiewicz's "Dziady"* (from Works of the Commission for the Study of Literature and Civilization), vol. 3. Warsaw, 1929, pp. 178–212
(21: 4/30, pp. 129–130)

C11R Sergei von Shtein: *Pushkin the Mystic: An Historical-Literary Essay*. Riga, 1931, 117 pp.
(32: 2/32, pp. 105–107)

EKKERSDORF, V.

E1   "Little Nicholas" (Dedicated to N. A. E.) / short story
(3: 3–4/26, pp. 84–109)

ELCHANINOV, A. (Father)

E2   "The Bishop-Elder. Memories of Bishop Antonii Florensov"
(4: 6–7/26, pp. 157–165)

EL'SON, E.

E3   "Madness and Faith"
(2: 1/26, pp. 137–138)

ERENBERG, H.

E4   "Letter From Professor Hans Erenberg to Father Sergius Bulgakov concerning Orthodoxy and Protestantism"
(5: 10–11/26, pp. 87–89)

"F."

F1   "The Russian Religious Library of the Methodist Mission in Prague"
(4: 6–7/26, pp. 194–195)

Fedorov, N. F. See F22–F24

FEDOTOV, G. P.

F2 "On the Goodness of the Antichrist"
 (5: 10–11/26, pp. 55–66)
F3R Jerome and Jean Tharaud: *Our Dear Péguy*. 2 vols. Paris: Plon, 1926
 (6: 1/27, pp. 126–129—"Péguy's Religious Journey")
F4 "Discords in the Émigré Church"
 (7: 4/27, pp. 119–120)
F5R *Irénikon* (Monthly Bulletin of the Monks of the Union of Churches, Priory of Amay-sur-Meuse), vol. 1, nos. 8–9 (November–December 1926) Hieromonk Lev Gillet: "Orientations of Contemporary Russian Thought," no. 1, 1927
 (7: 4/27, pp. 124–126)
F6 "Saint Genevieve and Saint Simeon the Stylite"
 (8: 8/27, pp. 58–72)
F7 "Carmen Saeculare. Concerning Contemporary Culture"
 (12: 8/28, pp. 101–115)
F8 "High-Leigh (The Conference of Anglo-Russian Youth)"
 (19: 11/29, pp. 104–108)
F9 "The Tragedy of Medieval Russian Holiness" (Lecture given at the Orthodox Institute of Theology of Paris on September 11, 1930)
 (27: 4/31, pp. 43–70)
F10 "An Unfortunate Defense" (Reply to M. Kurdiumov concerning the article on 'Christian Maximalism')
 (29: 8/31, pp. 68–79)
F11 "Christianity and Contemporary Social Reality" (Conference)
 (Supplement to issue no. 32, pp. 17–26)
F12 "Orthodoxy and Historical Criticism"
 (33: 4/32, pp. 3–17)
F13 "The Holy Spirit in Nature and Culture"
 (35: 9/32, pp. 3–19)
F14R *Irénikon*, vols. 7–9 (1930–1932)
 (36: 12/32, pp. 96–97)
F15 "Mother-Earth: Towards a Religious Cosmology of the Russian People"
 (46: 1–3/35, pp. 3–18)
F16 "Ecce Homo (Concerning Several Persecuted 'Isms')"
 (53: 4–7/37, pp. 20–36)
F17 "Oxford" / Ecumenical Conference
 (54: 8–12/37, pp. 57–62)
F18 "The Slavonic or the Russian Language for Religious Services"
 (57: 8–10/38, pp. 3–28)

F19R   Johann Adam Moehler: *The Unity of the Church or the Principle of Catholicism According to the Fathers of the First Three Centuries of the Church* (trans. Lilienfeld). Paris: Cerf, 1938
(58: 11–12/38–1/39, pp. 64–66)

F20   "In Defense of Ethics"
(60: 5–9/39, pp. 4–17)

F21R   Pierre Pascal: *Avvakum and the Beginnings of the Schism*. Paris, 1938, 618 pp.
(60: 5–9/39, pp. 68–69)

F21bisR   "Pages of St. Sergius: New Series, nos. 1–2 (1938–1939)" / A review of the latest issues of the St. Sergius journal
(60: 5–9/39, pp. 69–70)

FEDOROV, N. F.

F22   "Excerpts from the Third Volume of 'The Philosophy of the Common Task'"
(10: 4/28, pp. 3–42)

F23   "Excerpts from Posthumously Edited Manuscripts. Augustus and Augustine: The Former Built the Earthly City, the Latter Built the City of God"
(18: 9/29, pp. 3–24)

F24   "What is the Good? (Concerning Opinions on Tolstoy)"
(40: 9–10/33, pp. 3–15)

FLOROVSKY, G. (FATHER)

F25   "A Heart of Stone (Concerning the Polemic Against the Eurasianists)"
(2: 1/26, pp. 128–133)

F25bis   "A Letter to the Editor of *The Way*" (Collective Letter of the Eurasianists)
(2: 1/26, pp. 128–133)

F26   "The Metaphysical Assumptions of Utopianism (Dedicated to the Much Mourned P. I. Novgorodtsev of Glorious Memory)"
(4: 4–7/26, pp. 27–53)

F27   "The House of the Father" / A definition of the Essence of the Church
(7: 4/27, pp. 63–86)

F28R   Johann Adam Moehler: *Die Einheit in der Kirche oder das Prinzip des Katholizismus Dargestellt im Geiste der Kirchenvater der Drei Ersten Jahrhunderte*. Mathias Grunwald Verlag, 1925.
(7: 4/27, pp. 128–130—"Moehler's Book on the Church")

F29R   S. M. Lukianov: *The Youth of V. Solovyov. Biographical Material*. Vol. 1, Pgr. 1916, 439 pp.; vol. 2, Pgr. 1918, 190 pp.; vol. 3, Pgr. 1921, 365 pp.
(9: 1/28, pp. 83–88)

F30R   Stephan Zankow: *Das Orthodoxe Christendum des Ostens. Sein Wesen, und seine Gegenwartige Gestalt*. Berlin: Furche-Verlag, 1928, 142 pp.
(10: 4/28, pp. 127–129)

F31R   *The Review of Ecclesiastical History*. Vol. 24, no. 1, Louvain, January 1928
(10: 4/28, pp. 129–130—"Concerning Russian Books")

F32R   P. Moghila: *The Orthodox Confession of Peter Moghila, Metropolitan of Kiev (1633–1646),* Approved by the Greek Patriarchs of the Seventeenth Century. Unedited Latin Text published with an Introduction and Critical Notes by A. Malvy and M. Viller, S.J. Rome, Paris, *Orientalia Christiana,* vol. 10, no. 39, 1927, 223 pp.
       (11: 6/28, pp. 120–124—"**An Orthodox Confession**")
F33   "Philaret, Metropolitan of Moscow"
       (12: 8/28, pp. 3–31)
F34R   *Theologia Dogmatica Christianorum Oreintalium ab Ecclesia Catholica Dissedentium.* Auctore Martius Jugie, ex August. Ab Assumptione. Vol. 1, *Theologiae Dogmaticae Graeco-Russorum Origo. Historia, Fontes.* Paris, 1926
       (12: 8/28, pp. 121–123—"**A Latin Book on the Orthodox Church**")
F35R   E. Brunner: *Der Mittler zur Besinnung über den Christus Glauben.* Tübingen: Mohr, 1927, 565 pp.
       (13: 10/28, pp. 112–115)
F36R   Abbe L. Foucher: *Renouvier as a Young Man and His First Philosophy (1815–1854).* Paris: Vrin, 1927, 231 pp.
       O. Hamelin: "Renouvier's System (Course Given at the Sorbonne, 1906–1907)." Paris: Vrin, 1927, 464 pp.
       G. Milhaud: "The Philosophy of Renouvier (Course given at Montpellier in 1905)." Paris: Vrin, 1927, 160 pp.
       P. Mony: *The Concept of Progress in Renouvier's Philosophy.* Paris: Vrin, 1927, 205 pp.
       (14: 12/28, pp. 111–116)
F37R   Nicetas Stetathos: *A Great Byzantine Mystic: The Life of Simeon the New Theologian (949–1022).* Unedited Greek Text Published with an Introduction and Critical Notes by Father Ireneus Hauscher, S.J., and a French Translation in Collaboration with Father Gabriel Horn, S.J. Rome, *Orientalia Christiana,* vol. 12, no. 45, 1928, 225 pp.
       (16: 5/29, pp. 99–103—"**The Life of Saint Simeon the New Theologian**")
F38R   Karl Holl: *Gesammelte Aufsätze zur Kirchengeschichte.* Vol. 2, *Der Osten.* Tübingen: Mohr, 1928, 464 pp.
       (17: 7/29, pp. 107–108)
F39R   E. de Faye: *Origen, His Life, His Work, and His Thought.* 3 vols. Paris: Leroux, 1923, 1928
       (18: 9/29, pp. 107–115—"**The Contradictions in Origenism**")
F40   "The Eucharist and *Sobornost*'" (Extracts from a Book on the Church)
       (19: 11/29, pp. 3–22)
F41R   Hans Koch: *Die Russiche Orthodoxie im Petrinischen Zeitalter. Ein Beitrag zur Geschichte Westlicher Einflusse auf das Ostslavische Denken.* Osteuropa Institute in Breslau, Quellen und Studien. Breslauund Oppeln: Priebatsch's Buschhandlung, 1929, 191 pp.
       (19: 11/29, pp. 116–118)

F42R D. Chizhevsky: *Philosophy in Ukraine. An Historiographical Essay*. Prague, 1926, 200 pp.; 2nd ed., vol. 1, Prague, 1928, 142 pp.
(19: 11/29, pp. 118–119)

F43R Father Pavel Florensky: *The Pillar and Ground of the Truth: An Essay in Orthodox Theodicy in Twelve Letters*. Berlin: Rossica, 1929
(20: 2/30, pp. 102–107—"The Stifling of the Spirit")

F44R *Orient und Occident*: "Blatter fur Theologie, Ethik und Soziologie." In Verbindung mit Nikolai Berdjajew. Herausgegeben von Fritz Lieb und Paul Schutz. Leipzig: Verlag der J. C. Hinrichsschen Buchhandlung
(22: 7/30, pp. 129–130)

F45R Charles Gore: *Jesus of Nazareth*. New York, London, Home University, Library of Modern Knowledge, no. 130, 1929, 619 pp.
(23: 8/30, pp. 130–135)

F46R W. Komarowitsch: *Die Urgestalt der Bruder Karamasow Dostojevskis Quellen*. Entwurfe und Fragmente erlautert von W. Komarowitsch. Munich: R. Pipper and Cie, 1929, 619 pp.
(23: 8/30, pp. 121–125)

F47 "The Dispute concerning German Idealism (Dedicated to Shestov)"
(25: 12/30, pp. 51–80)

F48 "Prince S. N. Trubetskoy, 1862–1905 (*in memoriam*)"
(26: 2/31, pp. 119–122)

F49R Jean Rivière: *Modernism in the Church. A Study of Contemporary Religious History*. Paris: Letouzey and Ane, 1929, 589 pp.
(26: 2/31, pp. 123–125)

F50R A. Koyré: *Philosophy and the Problem of the Russian Nation in the Early Nineteenth Century*. Paris, 1929, 213 pp.
(30: 10/31, pp. 91–93)

F51R D. Chizhevsky: *Outlines for a History of Philosophy in Ukraine*. Prague, 1931, 175 pp.
(30: 10/31, pp. 93–94)

F52 "Theological Fragments"
(31: 12/31, pp. 3–29)

F53R A. d'Alès: *The Dogma of Ephesus*. Paris, 1931
(33: 4/32, pp. 72–76—"On the History of the Council of Ephesus")

F54R Paul Schütz: *Zwischen nil und Kaukasus. Ein Reisebericht zur Religions Politischen Lage im Osten*. Munich: Chr. Kaiser, 1930, 246 pp.
Paul Schütz: *Sakulare Religion. Eine Studie über Ihre Erscheinung in der Gegenwart und Ihre Idee bei Schleiermacher und Blumhardt*. Beiträge zur Systematischen Theologie, 2. Tübingen: J. Mohr, 1932, 224 pp.
(35: 9/32, pp. 94–97)

F54bis "The Question of Christian Unity"
(Supplement to issue no. 37)

F55 "Tiutchev and V. Solovyov" (Chapter of the book dedicated to P. B. Struve)
(41: 11–12/33, pp. 3–24)

References   689

F56 "The Limits of the Church" / On the Separation and the Schism
     (44: 7–9/34, pp. 15–26)

no F57

FRANK, S. L.

F58 "The Religious Foundations of Society"
     (1: 9/25, pp. 9–30)
F59R Franz Rosenzweig: *Der Stern der Erloesung*. Frankfurt am Main: Kaufman, 1921, 532 pp.
     (2: 1/26, pp. 139–148—"The Mystical Philosophy of Rosenzweig")
F60 "Religion and Science in the Contemporary Mentality"
     (4: 6–7/26, pp. 145–156)
F61R Franz von Baader: *Die Herdflamme, Schriften zur Gesellschafts Philosophie*, Herausgegeben von Johaness Sauter. Jena: Gustav Fitscher, 1925
     (4: 6–7/26, pp. 188–189)
F62R Ernst Cassirer: *Philosophie der Symbolischen Formen*. Vol. 2, *Das Mythische Denken*. Berlin, 1925
     (4: 6–7/26, pp. 190–191—"The Neo-Kantian Philosophy of Mythology")
F63R Nicolai von Hartmann: *Ethics*. Berlin: Verlag Walter de Gruyter, 1926
     (5: 10–11/26, pp. 133–137—"The New Ethics of German Idealism")
F64 "The Church and the World, Grace and the Law"
     (8: 8/27, pp. 3–20)
F65R A. F. Losev: *The Cosmos of the Ancients and Modern Science*. USSR, edition of the author, 1927
     A. F. Losev: *The Dialectic of Artistic Forms*. USSR, edition of the author, 1927
     A. F. Losev: *The Philosophy of the Name*. USSR, edition of the author, 1927
     (9: 1/28, pp. 89–90—"A New Russian Philosophical System")
F66R Edgar Dacque: *Urwelt, Sage und Menschheit*. Munich: R. Oldenbourg, 1924
     (9: 1/28, pp. 91–93)
F67 "The Mysticism of Rainer Maria Rilke"
     (12: 8/28, pp. 37–52)
F68R Fritz Lieb: *Franz Baaders Jugendgeschichte*
     (12: 8/28, pp. 124–126—"A Recent Book on Franz Baader")
F69 "The Mysticism of Rainer Maria Rilke"
     (13: 10/28, pp. 37–52)
F70 "Max Scheler" (Obituary)
     (13: 10/28, pp. 83–86)
F71 "I. Eihenvald (*in memoriam*)"
     (15: 2/29, pp. 125–26)

F72R   L. Bolk: *Das Problem des Menschwerdung.* Jena, 1926
Edgar Dacque: *Leben als Symbol. Metaphysik einer Entwick-Lungslehre.* Munich, Berlin, R. Oldenbourg, 1928
Max Scheler: *Die Stellung des Menschen im Kosmos.* Darmstadt, 1928
(15: 2/29, pp. 132–135—"New German Literature on the Philosophy of Anthropology")

F73R   Oskar Goldberg: *Die Wirklichkeit der Hebraer Einleintung in das System des Pentateuch.* Vol. 1. Berlin, 1925
(19: 11/29, pp. 109–113—"The Philosophy of the Old Testament World")

F74   "L. M. Lopatin (*in memoriam*)"
(24: 10/30, pp. 125–126)

F75   "Psychoanalysis as a Worldview"
(25: 12/30, pp. 22–50)

F76   "Dostoevsky and the Crisis of Humanism (On the 50th Anniversary of Dostoevsky's Death)"
(27: 4/31, pp. 71–78)

F77   "Pirogov, a Religious Thinker (On the 50th Anniversary of His Death, November 23, 1881)"
(32: 2/32, pp. 73–84)

F78   "The Philosophy of Hegel (On the 100th Anniversary of His Death)"
(34: 7/32, pp. 39–51)

F79   "Goethe and the Problem of Spiritual Culture"
(35: 9/32, pp. 83–90)

F80   "The Fundamental Idea of Spinoza's Philosophy (On the 300th Anniversary of His Birth, November 24, 1632)"
(37: 2/33, pp. 61–67)

F81   "Pushkin's Religiosity"
(40: 9–10/33, pp. 16–39)

F82   "Philosophy and Life" (International Philosophical Conference in Prague, September 2–7, 1934)
(45: 10–12/34, pp. 69–76)

F83   "The Problem of Christian Socialism"
(60: 5–9/39, pp. 18–32)

FUMET, S.

F84   "The Pilgrim of the Holy Sepulcher. Léon Bloy" (Translated from French. An article especially written for *The Way*)
(1: 9/25, pp. 154–160)

GAVIN, F.

G1   "Christianity in America"
(20: 2/30, pp. 80–87)

Gessen, S.G. See G13

GILLET, L. (HIERMONK)

G2   "In Quest of the Original Evangelical Tradition" (Article translated by N. Gorodetsky)
(36: 12/32, pp. 81–88)

GIORGIEVSKY, M. A.

G3   "Ancient Christian Communism"
(18: 9/29, pp. 25–53)

GLAZBERG, A.

G4   "At the Monastery of Sept-Fons"
(43: 4–6/34, pp. 72–77)

GLUBOKOVSKY, N. N.

G5   "Christian Unity and Theological Instruction According to an Orthodox Perspective" (Conference Given at King's College of London, July 8, 1925)
(4: 6–7/26, pp. 39–144)
G6   "The Old Testament Law: Its Origin, Meaning and Value According to Galatians 3:19–20"
(10: 4/28, pp. 43–52)

GOFSHTETTER, H.

G7   "The Struggle with God. The Meaning of Jacob's Courage and Job's Equity"
(22: 6/30, pp. 52–66)
G8   "Captives of Philosophical-Theological Confusion (On Rozanov, Hegel, and Shestov)"
(28: 6/31, pp. 52–66)
G9   "Social Christianity"
(41: 11–12/33, pp. 73–100)
G10 "The Philosophical Foundations of Socialism"
(51: 5–10/36, pp. 46–57)
G11 "The Mystery of the Night at Gethsemani"
(58: 11–12/38–1/39, pp. 36–43)

GRINEVICH, V.

G12 "Religious and Philosophical Thought in England (Contemporary Tendencies)"
(19: 11/29, pp. 79–92)

GESSEN, S. G.

G13 "The Tragedy of Evil (The Philosophical Signification of the Character of Stavrogin)"
(31: 12/31, pp. 44–74)

HAUTMAN DE VILLIERS, S.

H1 "Open Letter to the Editor of *The Way*" (Concerning G. Fedotov's article "An Unfortunate Defense") (See Fedotov, 29: 8/31, pp. 68–79)
(31: 12/31, pp. 102–103)

Iakubiziak, A. (Abbot). See J1

Ilnitsky, S. See I30–I31

Ilyin, V. N. See I6–I29

IOANN (HIEROMONK, later Bishop) (Prince D. A. SHAKHOVSKOY)

I1 "On the Rights of Discussion" (The Apocalypse and Contemporary Reality)
(5: 10–11/26, pp. 115–118)
I2 "Lent"
(13: 10/28, pp. 66–70)
I3 "Freedom from the World"
(17: 7/29, pp. 25–29)
I4R N. A. Berdyaev: *The Destiny of Man. An Essay on Paradoxical Ethics*. Paris: Sovremennye Zapiski and YMCA Press, 1931, 318 pp.
(31: 12/31, pp. 53–69—"On the Destiny of Humanity and the Paths of the Philosopher")
I5 "The Baptism of Knowledge"
(39: 7/33, p. 317)

ILYIN, V. N.

I6 "Letter to the Editor of *The Way*" (Collective Letter of the Eurasianists)
(2: 1/26, p. 134)
I7 "Monasticism and the *Podvig*"
(4: 6–7/26, pp. 72–87)
I8R L. P. Karsavin: *De Principiis. An Essay on Christian Metaphysics*. Vol. 1, *God and Creation*. Obelisque, 1925
(4: 6–7/26, pp. 192–193)
I9 "On Heavenly and Earthly *Sobornost*'" (Concerning Deviations from Conciliarity, Papal-Caesarism, and Caesaro-Papism)
(6: 1/27, pp. 89–94)

I10R L. P. Karsavin: *The Holy Fathers and Doctors of the Church. The Revelation of Orthodoxy through Their Work*
(7: 4/27, pp. 126–128)

I11R Fr. Sergius Bulgakov: *The Friend of the Bridegroom. On the Orthodox Veneration of the Forerunner.* Paris: YMCA Press, 1927, 227 pp.
(8: 8/27, pp. 154–155)

I12R Metropolitan Antonii Khrapovitsky: *The Dogma of Redemption.* Sremski Karlovtsy, 1926
(8: 8/27, pp. 156–157)

I13R N. A. Klepinin: *The Holy, Just and Great Prince Alexander Nevsky.* Paris: YMCA Press, 1926, 202 pp.
(8: 8/27, p. 158)

I14R Fr. K. Smirnov: *The Liturgy: A Reconstruction with an Introduction and Historical Commentary. Material for the Up-Coming Council.* Le Bedin, 1924, 71 pp.
(8: 8/27, p. 158)

I15 "A Project for an Encyclopedia of Orthodoxy"
(9: 1/28, pp. 81–82)

I16R Valerian Muravyov: *The Conquest of Time.* Moscow, published by the author, 1924, 127 pp.
L. P. Karsavin: *The Church, the Person, and the State.* Paris: Éditions Eurasienne, 1927, 30 pp.
(9: 1/28, p. 94)

I17R G. P. Fedotov: *Saint Philip, Metropolitan of Moscow.* Paris: YMCA Press, 1928, 224 pp.
(10: 4/28, pp. 133–134)

I18 "Christ and Israel"
(11: 6/28, pp. 59–75)

I19R Chrisostomus Panfoeder: *Christus unser Liturge.* Mainz: Mathias Grunewald Verlag, 1924, 104 pp.
Chrisostomus Panfoeder: *Das Opfer.* Mainz: Mathias Grunewald Verlag, 1926, 184 pp.
Chrisostomus Panfoeder: *Das Personöliche in der Liturgie.* Mainz: Mathias Grunewald Verlag, 1925, 171 pp.
Christosomus Panfoeder: *Die Kirche als Liturgische Gemeinschaft.* Mainz: Mathias Grunewald Verlag, 1924, 116 pp.
(13: 10/28, pp. 110–111)

I20R Fr. Sergius Bulgakov: *Jacob's Ladder: On the Angels.* Paris: YMCA Press, 1929, 229 pp.
(15: 2/29, pp. 137–139—"The Angels and the Doctrine of Holy Sophia, the Wisdom of God")

I21R Fr. Pavel Florensky: *The Pillar and Ground of the Truth: An Essay in Orthodox Theodicy in Twelve Letters.* Berlin: Rossica, 1929
(20: 2/30, pp. 116–119)

I22 "Concerning the Second Exposition of Icons (December 27, 1929–January 5, 1930)"
(22: 6/30, pp. 126–128)

I23R Hanns Lilje: *Das Technische Zeitalter*. Second printing. Berlin: Furche Verlag, 1928, 175 pp.
(25: 12/30, pp. 131–132)

I24 "The Aesthetic, Theological, and Liturgical Significance of Bell Ringing"
(26: 2/31, pp. 114–118)

I25R "Orthodox Thought: Works of the Orthodox Institute of Theology at Paris." Vol. 2. Paris, 1930
(30: 10/31, pp. 86–89)

I26 "Christianity and Contemporary Social Reality" (Conference)
(Supplement to issue no. 32, pp. 11–16)

I27 "Goethe the Sage" (Dedicated to L. I. Kuris)
(34: 7/32, pp. 64–70)

I28 "The Profanation of Tragedy: The Confrontation of Utopia, Love, and Death"
(40: 9–10/33, pp. 54–65)

I29 "Holy Saturday. On the Mystery of Death and Immortality (Dedicated to the Memory of Fr. Alexander Elchaninov)"
(57: 8–10/38, pp. 48–57)

ILNITSKY, S.

I30 "At the Sources of the Faith. Impressions of Dahomey"
(46: 1–3/35, pp. 60–65)

I31 "Pray for the Peace of Jerusalem" (Travel Journal)
(52: 11/36–3/37, pp. 70–73)

ISHEVSKY, D.

I32 "'God's' and 'Caesar's.'" (An Interview with His Holiness Metropolitan Eleutherius, Metropolitan of Lithuania and Vilensk)
(46: 1–3/35, pp. 37–50)

Iswolsky, H. See I40

IVANOV, P. K.

I33 "The Episcopal Meeting in Moscow Held to Choose the Members of the Council of 1932"
(1: 9/25, pp. 139–147)

I34 "The True Meaning of the Occurrences within the Russian Orthodox Church (Mysticism and Psychology)"
(8: 8/27, pp. 122–130)

I35R M. Kurdiumov: *An Unquiet Heart. On the Works of Chekhov*. Paris: YMCA Press, 1934
(46: 1–3/35—"The Beauty of Chekhov")

I36 "The Testament of the Apostle Paul" (On the Crucified Christ, on Love, and on the Spirit of the Antichrist)"
(55: 1–4/38, pp. 41–52)

I37R D. S. Merezhkovsky: *Francis of Assisi*. Ed. Petropolis
(58: 11–12/38–1/39, pp. 66–71)

IVASK, Iu.

I38 "The Proletarian and the Machine"
(17: 7/29, pp. 81–95)

IZIUMOV, A.

I39 "V. S. Pechorin's Spiritual Return to the Motherland (according to unpublished letters to A. I. Hertzen and N. P. Ogarev)"
(47: 4–6/35, pp. 28–50)

ISWOLSKY, H.

I40 "The New Doctrines of Catholic Social Thought in France"
(60: 5–9/39, pp. 57–64)

JAKUBIZIAK, Augustin (Abbot)

J1 "The Calling of Saint Joan of Arc"
(30: 10/31, pp. 48–58)

"K. A."

K1 "Relations between the Anglican Church and the Orthodox Church" (How the Orthodox Church is perceived by the Anglican Church)
(5: 10–11/26, pp. 100–103)

"K. N."

K2 "In Glorious Memory of the Igumena Ekaterina (Countess Evgenia Borisovna Efimovskaya)"
(4: 6–7/26, pp. 166–171)

K3 "The Conference of Saint Alban, January 11–15, 1927"
(7: 4/27, pp. 107–112)

KARPOV, A.

K4   "On the Monarchy"
(6: 1/27, pp. 105–109)

K5   "A. M. Bukharev (Archimandrite Fedor)"
(22: 6/30, pp. 24–51)

K6   "A. M. Bukharev (Archimandrite Fedor), Conclusion"
(23: 8/30, pp. 25–47)

K7   "The Anglo-Russian Conference of High Leigh (April 25–30, 1930)" (On Holiness)
(24: 10/30, pp. 87–97)

K8   "The Fifth Anglo-Russian Conference of High Leigh (April 16–23, 1931)" (The Doctrine of the Church)
(30: 10/31, pp. 59–70)

KARSAVIN, L. P.

K9   "Reply to N. Berdyaev's Article Concerning the Eurasianists"
(2: 1/26, pp. 124–127)

K10   "Letter to the Editorial Board of *The Way*" (Collective Letter of the Eurasianists)
(2: 1/26, p. 134)

K11   "An Essay in Apologetics"
(3: 3–4/26, pp. 29–45)

K12   "The Dangers of an Abstract Christianity and How They Can Be Overcome"
(6: 1/27, pp. 32–49)

K13   "Prolegomena for a Study of Personhood"
(12: 8/28, pp. 32–46)

KARTASHEV, A.

K14   "The Influence of the Church on Russian Culture"
(9: 1/28, pp. 33–40)

K15   "Church and State, That Which Was and That Which Should Be in Russia"
(**Supplement to issue no. 33, 20 pp.**)

K16   "The Testament of the Holy Prince Vladimir"
(36: 12/32, pp. 75–80)

K17   "The Ecclesial Question at the Conference of Minorities in Vienna (June 26–July 1)"
(40: 9–10/33, pp. 40–53)

K18   "The Church and Nationality"
(44: 7–9/34, pp. 3–14)

K19 "Personal and Communal Salvation in Christ"
(45: 10–12/34, pp. 30–36)
K20 "The Church in Its Historical Incarnation"
(47: 4–6/35, pp. 15–27)
K21 "Russian Christianity"
(51: 5–10/36, pp. 19–31)

KASSIAN (Bishop). See BEZOBRAZOV, S.

KAVERT, S.

K22 "The Road Towards a True and International Church" (Concerning the World Conference at Stockholm on Questions of Practical Christianity, August 10–30, 1925)
(2: 1/26, pp. 122–123)
K23 "The Different Currents of Religious Life in America"
(7: 4/27, pp. 94–98)

KIRK, K.

K24 "The Ideals of the Anglican Church"
(32: 2/32, pp. 85–89)

KERN (Cyprian, Archimandrite)

K25R R. P. F. Mercenier: *The Prayer of the Church in the Byzantine Rite*. Priory of Amay-sur-Meuse, Belgium, vol. 1, 450 pp.
(55: 1–4/38, pp. 82–84)
K26 "The Problem of Pastoral Formation" (On the Question of the Teaching of Pastoral Theology)
(58: 11–12/38–1/39, pp. 1–39)

Kirk, K. See K24

KLEPININ, N. A.

K27 "The Fraternity and the Paths of the Orthodox Student Movement"
(3: 3–4/26, pp. 127–133)
K28 "Thoughts on the Religious Significance of Nationalism"
(6: 1/27, pp. 69–80)

KOLPAKCHI, G.

K29 "A Comparative Study of Buddhism and Christianity"
(39: 7/33, pp. 60–66)

KOZLOVSKY, L.

K30 "The Evening Hymn of the Soul" (Jan Kasprovich, 1866–1926)
(11: 6/28, pp. 113–119)

KU, T. S.

K31 "The Collision of Religious and Cultural Currents in China"
(9: 1/28, pp. 54–60)

KUHLMAN, G. G.

K32 "Protestantism and Orthodoxy" (Lecture at the Conference of Christian Students in May 1926 at Ban' Kostenec, Belgium)
(5: 10–11/26, pp. 93–96)

KURDIUMOV, M.

K33 "The Holiness of St. Sergius of Radonezh and the Affair of Metropolitan Sergius"
(11: 6/28, pp. 95–112)
K34 "In the Power of Temptation" (On the Quarrels within the Church)
(13: 10/28, pp. 93–105)
K35 "In the Light of Tabor" (On Pre-Revolution Russian Orthodoxy)
(17: 7/29, pp. 30–53)
K36 "Orthodoxy and Bolshevism"
(22: 6/30, pp. 67–92)
K37 "On Christian Maximalism (The Ways of the Russian Church)"
(29: 8/31, pp. 49–67)
K38 "A Reply to G. Fedotov Concerning the *Raskol* in the Church"
(31: 12/31, pp. 89–101)
K39 "The Church and the New Russia"
(Supplement to issue no. 38, 12 pp.)
K40 "On the Struggle against God and Gehenna"
(44: 7–9/34, pp. 50–62)
K41 "The Church and the World"
(59: 2–4/39, pp. 3–18)

LAGOVSKY, I. A.

L1 "There Where They Fight with God (Outside of the Frontiers of the Church)" (The Anti-Religious Propaganda in the USSR)
(10: 4/28, pp. 86–101)

L2 "Salvation and Culture" (On Prayer and Repentance)
    (33: 4/32, pp. 18–43)
L3 "Collectivization and Religion"
    (Supplement to issue no. 35, 20 pp.)

LAZAREV, A.

L4 "The Philosophical Destiny of William James"
    (35: 9/32, pp. 20–55)
L5 "The Philosophical Project of Jules Lequier"
    (57: 8–10/38, pp. 27–47)

LEBEDEV, V.

L6 "The Religious Crisis of Contemporary Society"
    (59: 2–4/39, pp. 31–38)

LIEB, F.

L7 "Orthodoxy and Protestantism" (trans. V. Unru)
    (16: 5/29, pp. 69–81)

LITVYAK, M.

L8 "Extracts from a Diary. On Sinners and the Just. On Faith and Skepticism"
    (39: 7/33, pp. 53–59)

LOPUKHIN, P. S.

L9 "Concerning the Articles of L. A. Zander on the Bierville Conference"
    (7: 4/27, pp. 113–118)

LOSSKY, N. O.

L10 "Vladimir Solovyov and His Successors in Russian Religious Philosophy"
     (2: 1/26, pp. 13–25)
L11R V. Ilyin: *Saint Seraphim of Sarov*. Paris: YMCA Press, 1925, 215 pp.
     Boris Zaitsev: *Saint Sergius of Radonezh*. Paris: YMCA Press, 1925, 101 pp.
     (2: 1/26, pp. 153–156)
L12 "Vladimir Solovyov and His Successors in Russian Religious Philosophy"
     (continuation)
     (3: 3–4/26, pp. 14–28)

L13 "The Culture of Technology and the Christian Ideal"
(9: 1/28, pp. 3–13)
L14R Fr. W. Foerster: *Religion and Character Building*. Zurich and Leipzig: Rotapfel Verlag, 1925, 464 pp.
(9: 1/28, pp. 95–96)
L15 "Mythical Thought and Contemporary Scientific Thought"
(14: 12/28, pp. 31–55)
L16 "On the Resurrection of the Body"
(26: 2/31, pp. 61–85)
L17R B. Vysheslavtsev: *The Heart in Christian and Indian Mysticism*. Paris: YMCA Press, 1929, 77 pp.
(28: 6/31, pp. 106–107)
L18 "Magic and the Christian Cult"
(36: 12/32, pp. 3–16)
L19 "The Visions of Saints and Mystics"
(43: 4–6/34, pp. 17–34)
L20R B. Yasinowski: *Wschodnie Chrzestijanstwo a Rosja*. Vilnius, 1933, 173 pp.
(51: 5–10/36, pp. 68–74)
L21 "Of the Creation of the World by God"
(54: 8–12/37, pp. 3–22)
L22 "Husserl's Transcendental-Phenomenological Idealism"
(60: 5–9/39, pp. 37–56)

LOSSKY, V. N.

L23 "Letter of November 23, 1935, to N. A. Berdyaev"
(50: 1–4/36, pp. 27–32)

LOT-BORODIN, M.

L24R G. V. Florovsky: *The Byzantine Fathers of the 5th–8th Centuries* (from a course given at the Orthodox Institute of Theology of Paris). Paris: YMCA Press, 1933, 259 pp.
(38: 5/33, pp. 91–93)
L25R Emile Mersch, S.J.: *The Mystical Body of Christ. A Study in Historical Theology*. 2 vols. Louvain, 1933
(42: 1–3/34, pp. 93–95)
L26R D. S. Merezhkovsky: *The Unknown Jesus*. Vol. 1, Belgrade, 1932; vol. 2, part 1, Belgrade, 1933
(47: 4–6/35, pp. 71–86 — "The Forgotten Church; Concerning the Unknown Jesus")
L27 "A Critique of 'Russian Christianity'"
(52: 11/36–3/37, pp. 45–55)

L28R   M. J. Congar, O.P.: *Divided Christians: Principles of a Catholic Ecumenism.* Paris: Cerf
(59: 2–4/39, pp. 74–76)

MARIA (Mother). See SKOBTSOVA, E. Iu.

MARITAIN, J.

M1   "Metaphysics and Mysticism" (translated from French, article written especially for *The Way*)
(2: 1/26, pp. 88–100)

MENSHIKOV, Y.

M2   "The Soul of Things"
(22: 6/30, pp. 104–115)

MOCHULSKY, K. V.

M3R   Henri Bergson: *The Two Sources of Morality and Religion.* Paris: Alcan, 1932
(37: 2/33, pp. 88–93)

M4R   Dr. Z. Kobilinski-Ellis: *Das Goldene Zeitalter der Russischen Poesie. W. A. Joukovski, Seine Personlichkeit, Sein Leben und Sein Werk.* Paderborn: Verlag F. Schoningh, 1937
(45: 10–12/34 pp. 79–80)

M5R   Mother Maria Skobtsova: *Poems.* Ed. Petropolis, 1937
(53: 4–6/37, pp. 86–87)

M6   "Racism and Western Christianity"
(58: 11–12/38–1/39, pp. 26–35)

M7R   Denis de Rougemont: *Love and the Western World.* Paris: Plon, 1939
(59: 2–4/39, pp. 76–77)

MONK, the Russian

M8   "The Spiritual Life and Economy"
(28: 6/31, pp. 3–31)

M9   "The Economy of Nature"
(29: 8/31, pp. 3–19)

"N."

N1   "Concerning the Russian Church (A Letter from Russia)"
(2: 1/26, pp. 3–12)

NALIMOV, O. (Father)

N2 "Theses of Professor O. Nalimov of the Academy of Petrograd Concerning the Contemporary Discipline of Repentance"
(18: 9/29, pp. 79–87)

NOVGORODTSEV, P.

N3 "The Restoration of the Sacred (Dedicated to the Memory of V. D. Nabokov)"
(4: 6–7/26, pp. 54–71)

OLLARD, S. L.

O1 "Anglicanism"
(3: 3–4/26, pp. 120–124)

PETROV, A.

P1 "A Monarchist's Letter to the Editorial Board of *The Way* (Concerning N. Berdyaev's article 'The Kingdom of God and the Kingdom of Caesar')"
(3: 3–4/26, pp. 134–139)

PIUS XI (POPE)

P2 "Letter of His Holiness Pope Pius XI to Cardinal Andrieu"
(6: 1/27, p. 84)

PLETNEV, R.

P3 "Dostoevsky and the Gospels"
(23: 8/30, pp. 48–68)
P4 "Dostoevsky and the Gospels (Conclusion)"
(24: 10/30, pp. 58–86)
P5 "Dostoevsky and the Bible: The Old Testament (A Small Chapter from the Book *Dostoevsky and Spiritual Literature*)"
(58: 11–12/38–1/39, pp. 49–56)

POGODIN, A.

P6 "Progress and Christianity"
(13: 10/28, pp. 53–65)

POLOTEBNEVA, A.

P7 "From Italian Religious Life: Assisi"
 (37: 2/33, pp. 68–73)
P8 "An Essay on an Ethical and Religious Conception of Nature"
 (41: 11–12/33, pp. 61–72)
P9 "From Italian Religious Life: Italian Protestants"
 (56: 5–6/38, pp. 47–62)

PRIEST OF PETROGRAD

P10 "On Blok"
 (26: 2/31, pp. 86–108)

PROKOFIEV, P. (pseud. Chizhevsky)

P11 "The Religious Utopia of A. A. Ivanov"
 (24: 10/30, pp. 41–57)

PRONEVICH, G.

P12 "The Ecumenical Seminar in Geneva (July 29–August 18, 1934)"
 (46: 1–3/35, pp. 51–59)

Rashheev, D. See R2

RASTORGUEV, V.

R1 "A Tragic Lack of Sensitivity (Concerning the Article by B. Vysheslavtsev 'The Tragedy of Those Elevated and Speculation on Their Fall')"
 (38: 5/33, pp. 76–81)

RASHHEEV, D.

R2 "Letter to the Editor from Romania"
 (38: 5/33, pp. 84–86)

REDACTION (EDITORS)

R3 "The Spiritual Tasks of the Russian Immigration"
 (1: 9/25, pp. 3–8)
R4 "A Decisive Hour of Historical Destiny"
 (60: 5–9/39, p. 3)

REIMERS, N. A.

R5   "Freedom and Equality: Blueprint for a System of Philosophy of Law"
     (41: 11–12/33, pp. 25–60)

REMENKO, D.

R6   "The Religious Foundation of the Miracle"
     (18: 9/28, pp. 54–78)

REMIZOV, A. M.

R7   "A Moscow Bee. Extract from the Book *Pleteshok*"
     (2: 1/26, pp. 59–87)
R8   "The Nativity"
     (6: 1/27, pp. 3–14)

"S." See also Stepun, F. A.

S1R Oswald Spengler: *Jahre der Entscheidung. Erste Teil: Deutschland und die Weltgeschichtliche Entwicklung.* Munich: Becksche Verlags Buchhandlung, 1933
     (41: 11–12/33, pp. 105–109)
S2   "The Voices of Christian Conscience in Germany (K. Barth, F. Heiler)"
     (43: 4–6/34, pp. 62–71)

SALTYKOV, A. A.

S3   "A Latest Movement for the Knowledge of Christianity"
     (25: 12/30, pp. 115–126)
S4   "The Mountain in the Bible"
     (30: 10/31, pp. 71–85)
S5   "On the Cosmic Rhythm of the Gospels"
     (37: 2/33, pp. 74–87)
S6   "The Elements of Alchemy in the Religious Tradition"
     (45: 10–12/34, pp. 60–68)

SARAFANOV, N.

S7   "An Open Letter to V. V. Rudnev Concerning the Separation of Church and State"
     (27: 4/31, pp. 79–94)

SAVITSKY, P. N.

S8   "Letter to the Editors of *The Way*" (Collective Letter of the Eurasianists)
     (2: 1/26, p. 134)

SAZONOVA, Iu. L.

S9   "Three Catholic Figures: Marie-Angelique, Saint Theresa, Saint Theophan"
     (8: 8/27, pp. 108–121)
S10 "Religious Quests as Reflected in Soviet Literature"
     (21: 4/30, pp. 76–93)

SEMENOV TIAN-SHANSKY, D.

S11 "Work, Creativity, and Freedom"
     (52: 11/36–3/37, pp. 22–44)

SEREZHNIKOV, K. G.

S12 "Toward a Problematics of the Historical-Religious Conflict"
     (38: 5/33, pp. 38–64)

SEZEMAN, V.

S13R Martin Heidegger: *Sein und Zeit*. Vol. 1, 1927
      (14: 12/28, pp. 117–123)

SHAKHOVSKOY, D. A. (Prince). See IOANN (HIEROMONK)

Shcherbatov, S. See Sh9

Shestov, L. I. See Sh1–Sh7 *(following S40)*

Shvarts, M. N. See Sh8

SKOBTSOVA, E. Iu. (Mother Maria)

S14 "The Holy Land"
     (6: 1/27, pp. 95–101)
S15 "The Search for Synthesis"
     (16: 5/29, pp. 49–68)
S16 "Birth and Creation"
     (30: 10/31, pp. 35–47)

S17 "The Sources of Creativity"
(43: 4–6/34, pp. 35–48)
S18 "A Defense of Phariseeism"
(56: 4–6/38, pp. 37–46)
S19 "On the Imitation of the Mother of God"
(59: 2–4/39, pp. 19–30)

SMOLITSCH, I. K.

S20 "The Great Elder Nil of Sora (Toward a History of the Russian Elder)"
(19: 11/29, pp. 57–69)
S21 "I. V. Kireevsky (On the 125th Anniversary of his Birth)"
(33: 4/32, pp. 52–66)
S22 "The Pre-Council Assembly of 1906 (On the 25th Anniversary of the Attempt at Ecclesial Reform in Russia)"
(38: 5/33, pp. 65–75)
S23R Die Ostkirche Betet: *Hymnen aus den Tagzeiten der Byzantinischen Kirche. Die Vorfastenzeit*. Übertragung aus dem Griechischen und Vorrede von P. Kilian Kirchof, O. F. M. Einfuhrung über den "Aufbau des Byzantinischen Breviers" von Prof. Anton Baumstark. Leipzig: Verlag Jacob Hegner, 1934, 2038 pp.
(49: 10–12/35, pp. 91–93)
S24R Archimandrite Cyprian Kern: *Father Anthony Kapustin, Archimandrite and Superior of the Russian Mission in Jerusalem (1867–1894)*. Belgrade, 1934, 209 pp.
(52: 11/36–3/37, pp. 74–78)
S25R Die Ostkirche Betet: *Liturgische Vorbemerkung*, von Prof. Dr. Baumstark. Band II: Erste bis Dritte Fastenwache. Band III: Vierte bis Sechste Fastenwache. Leipzig: Verlag Jacob Hegner, 1935, 288 pp. and 318 pp.
(52: 11/36–3/37, pp. 78–79)
S26R A. Ehrard: *Veberlieferung und Bestand der Hagiographischen und Homiletischen Literatur der Griechischen Kirche von den Anfängen bis zum Ende des 16 Jns: Die Verberlie Ferung*. Leipzig: Hinrichs Verlag, 1937, 717 pp.
Karl Heussi: *Der Ursprung des Mönchtums*. Tübingen: Verlag von J. C. B. Mohr (Paul Siebeck), 1938, 308 pp.
Julius Tyciak: *Die Liturgie als Quelle Oestlicher Frömmigkeit*. Freiburg: Herder and Co., 1937, 148 pp.
Julius Tyciak: *Die Ostkirche Betet. Hymnen aus den Tagseiten der Byzantinischen Kirche. The Heilige Woche*. Aus dem Griechischen Übertragen von P. Kilian Kirchoff, O. F. M., Liturgische Vorbemerkung von Prof. Anton Baumstark. Leipzig: Verlag Jacob Hegner, 1937, 208 pp.
Georg Wunderle: *Aus der Heiligen Welt des Athos, Studien und Erinnerungen*, Würzburg, 1937, 61 pp.
(56: 5–6/38, pp. 69–74—"The New German Literature on Orthodoxy")

SOLOVYOV, V. S.

S27 "Letter to L. Tolstoy Concerning the Resurrection of Christ"
(5: 10–11/26, pp. 97–99)

SOVÉ, B. I.

S28 "Theses on the Holy Scriptures of the Old Testament (For the First Conference of Orthodox Theologians at Athens in November 1936)"
(52: 11/36–3/37, pp. 67–69)
S29 "The Present Situation of the Russian Church"
(53: 4–7/37, pp. 66–84)

SPEKTORSKY, E. V.

S30R Franz Veber: *A Book About God.* Celje, 1934, 454 pp.
(46: 1–3/35, pp. 70–73—"A Slovakian Book About God")

SPERANSKY, V. N.

S31 "A Quarter Century Ago" (*in memoriam*, V. Solovyov)
(2: 1/26, pp. 105–108)
S32 "Religious-Psychological Sketches of Contemporary Russia"
(5: 10–11/26, pp. 109–114)

STEPUN, F. A.

S33 "Religious Socialism and Christianity"
(29: 8/31, pp. 20–41)

STRATONOV, I. A.

S34 "Recent Documents of the Patriarchal Church of All Russia"
(9: 1/28, pp. 61–74)
S35 "The Moment the Present Crisis in the Russian Church Began"
(12: 8/28, pp. 76–100)
S36 "The Growth of Ecclesial Confusion Following the First Council of Karlovtsy (1922)"
(14: 12/28, pp. 80–90)
S37 "The Growth of Ecclesial Confusion Following the First Council of Karlovtsy (Conclusion)"
(15: 2/29, pp. 112–124)
S38 "The Crisis of the Russian Church and Its Consequences Abroad" (1923)
(17: 7/29, pp. 62–80)

S39 "The Origins of the Present Organization of the Patriarchal Russian Church"
(Supplement to issue no. 40, 16 pp.)

SUVCHINSKY, P. P.

S40 "Letter to the Editors of *The Way*" (Collective Letter of the Eurasianists)
(2: 1/26, p. 134)

SHESTOV, L. I.

Sh1 "V. V. Rozanov"
(22: 6/30, pp. 93–103)
Sh2R Richard Kroner: *Die Selbstver Wirklichung des Geites. Prolegomena zur Kulturphilosophie.* Tübingen: Verlag von J. C. B. Mohr, Paul Siebeck, 225 pp.
Richard Kroner: *Von Kant bis Hegel.* Vol. 1, 612 pp.; vol. 2, 526 pp. Tübingen: Verlag von J. C. B. Mohr, Paul Siebeck
(27: 4/31, pp. 95–100)
Sh3 "Martin Buber"
(39: 7/33, pp. 67–77)
Sh4R Søren Kierkegaard: *Repetition.* Alcan
(42: 1–3/34, pp. 88–93—"Hegel or Job, Concerning the Existentialist Philosophy of Kierkegaard")
Sh5 "Kierkegaard and Dostoevsky, Voices Crying in the Desert"
(48: 7–9/35, pp. 20–37)
Sh6R Lucien Lévy-Bruhl: *Primitive Mythology.* Alcan, 1935, 335 pp.
(50: 1–4/36, pp. 58–65—"Myth and Truth: Toward a Metaphysics of Knowledge")
Sh7 "*Sine Effusione Sanguinis.* On Philosophical Honesty"
(54: 8–12/37, pp. 23–51)

SHVARTS, M. N.

Sh8 "Georg Zimmel as a Philosopher of Life and of Culture"
(55: 1–4/38, pp. 53–67)

SHCHERBATOV, S.

Sh9 "The Crisis of Art"
(45: 10–12/34, pp. 37–55)

TILLICH, P.

T1 "Dialectical Theology. Spiritual Life in the West" (Translated from German by Sophie Lorie, article written for *The Way*)
(1: 9/25, pp. 148–154)

TIMASHEV, N. S.

T2 "The Church and the Soviet State"
(10: 4/28, pp. 53–85)
T3 "The Codification of Soviet Ecclesiastical Law"
(17: 7/29, pp. 54–61)

TROITSKY, S.

T4 "Marriage and the Church"
(11: 6/28, pp. 31–58)
T5 "Marriage and Sin. Marriage before the Fall"
(15: 2/29, pp. 3–38)
T6 "Marriage and Sin. Marriage after the Fall"
(17: 7/29, pp. 3–24)
T7 "Why Churches Are Being Closed in Russia"
(23: 8/30, pp. 69–96)
T8R *Russian Christianity: The Book of Martyrs* (collection of articles)
(27: 4/31, pp. 101–108)
T9R "In Defense of a 'Christian Philosophy of Marriage'" (response to criticisms of S. Troitsky, *Hrisjanka Filozofja Braka*. Belgrade, 1934 [Serbian])
(51: 5–10/36, pp. 58–67)

TRUBETSKOY, O. N. ("T.")

T10 "Prince Sergei N. Trubetskoy on Holy Wisdom, the Russian Church, and the Orthodox Faith: His Relationship with the Slavophiles"
(47: 4–6/35, pp. 3–14)

TRUBETSKOY, G. N.

T11 "In Memory of the Most Holy Patriarch Tikhon"
(1: 9/25, pp. 116–120)
T12R Michel d'Herbigny, S.J.: "The Russian Religious Soul According to Their Most Recent Publications," *Orientalia Christiana*, no. 11, September–November 1924

Michel d'Herbigny, S.J.: "Information on Russian Orthodoxy Outside of Russia," *Orientalia Christiana*, no. 12 (December 1924–February 1925), no. 14 (April–May, 1925)
(1: 9/25, pp. 171–176—"A Catholic Theologian Writes About Russian Religious Psychology")

T13 "A Reply to the Letter of the Eurasianists"
(2: 1/26, pp. 135–136)

T14 "In Memory of Cardinal Mercier"
(3: 3–4/26, pp. 125–126)

T15 "The Dispute over the Monarchy"
(4: 6–7/26, pp. 172–175)

TRUBETSKOY, N. S.

T16 "Letter to the Editors of *The Way*" (Collective Letter of the Eurasianists)
(2: 1/26, p. 134)

Trubetskoy, O. N. See T10

TSEBRIKOV, G. V.

T17 "Antimins" (Dedicated to Prince D. A. Shakhovskoy) / Nouvelle
(7: 4/27, pp. 87–93)

TURGENEVA, N. A.

T18 "Reply to N. A. Berdyaev Regarding Anthroposophy"
(25: 12/30, pp. 93–104)

VALTER, R.

V1 "Angelus Silesius"
(8: 8/27, pp. 99–107)

VANOVSKY, A. A.

V2 "The Mythology of Kojiki and the Bible" (Lecture given in Tokyo to the association "Meiji" on April 26, 1932; original title "Japanese Mythology and the Bible")
(42: 1–3/34, pp. 38–55)

VEIDLÉ (WEIDLE), V. V.

V3 "The Degeneration of Art"
(42: 1–3/34, pp. 22–37)

V4 "The Renaissance of the Marvelous"
(48: 7–9/35, pp. 38–59)

VOLKONSKY, M.

V5 "The Secret Causes of the Russian Aristocracy's Attraction to Catholicism"
(54: 8–12/38, pp. 52–56)

VREVSKY, B.

V6 "From Faith to the Recognition of God"
(46: 1–3/35, pp. 19–27)

VYSHESLAVTSEV, B. P.

V7 "The Meaning of the Heart in Religion"
(1: 9/25, pp. 79–98)
V8 "The Paradoxes of Communism"
(3: 3–4/26, pp. 110–119)
V9 "The Two Paths of Social Development"
(4: 6–7/26, pp. 127–138)
V10R Prof. Charles Richer: *Treatise on Metaphysics*. 2nd ed. Paris: Alcan
(5: 10–11/26, pp. 123–127—"The Science of Miracles")
V11R Dr. Alexandre Lescinskij: *Nervous States and Their Treatment. Psychological Theories and Practical Indications for the Sick and Their Families*. Geneva: Atar
(5: 10–11/26, pp. 128–130—"The Religious-Ascetical Signification of Neurosis")
V12 "Balkan Impressions: Serbia, Bulgaria, and Greece"
(8: 8/27, pp. 134–138)
V13 "A Tragic Theodicy"
(9: 1/28, pp. 14–32)
V14R Plotinus: *The Enneads*. Vols. 1, 2, 3. Text established and translated by E. Bréhier. Paris: Belles Lettres, 1924
Plotinus: *The Enneads*. Philosophical translation from the Greek text by Abbé Alta, vols. 1, 2, 3. Paris: Bib. Charconac, 1926
(10: 4/28, pp. 124–127—"New Translations of Plotinus")
V15R Rudolf Otto: *West-Ostliche Mystik. Vergleich und Unterscheidung zur Wesensdeutung, Bucherei der Christlichen Welt*. Gotha: Leopold Klotz Verlag, 1926, 397 pp.
(13: 10/28, pp. 106–109)
V16 "Krishnamurti: The Completion of Theosophy"
(14: 12/28, pp. 91–107)

V17R S. Frank: *The Spiritual Foundations of Society. An Introduction to Social Philosophy.* Paris: YMCA Press, 1930, 317 pp.
(20: 2/30, pp. 107–111)

V18R C. G. Jung: *Psychological Types. A Selection of Studies in Analytical Psychology* (edition authorized under the general direction of E. Metner, translation by S. Lorie). Mussaget, 1929, 475 pp.
(20: 2/30, pp. 111–113)

V19R C. G. Jung: *Psychological Types* (above)
C. Baudouin: *Psychology of Suggestion and Auto-Suggestion.* Paris: Delachaux and Niestle
Dr. A. Leseinsky and S. Lorie: *A Medical-Psychological Essay on Auto-Suggestion—Methods of the New School of Nancy*
(21: 4/30, pp. 63–75)

V20R K. Schjelderup: *Die Askese. Ein Religion-Psychologische Untersuchung.* Berlin and Leipzig, 1929
(22: 6/30, pp. 133–135)

V21R C. Baudouin: *The Psychoanalysis of Art.* Paris: Alcan, 1929
(22: 6/30, pp. 135–139)

V22 "The Ethic of Sublimation as the Negation of Moralism"
(23: 8/30, pp. 3–24)

V23R *Orient und Occident, Blatter für Theologie und Soziologie.* 4 Heft. "Der Russische Geist im Kampf um seine Existenz und der Protestantismus" (G. G. Kul'man, N. Berdjaev, G. Florovskij, F. Lieb, Reisner). Leipzig: Hinrichs Verlag, 1930.
(26: 2/31, pp. 125–127)

V24 "The Myth of the Fall"
(34: 7/32, pp. 3–18)

V25 "The Tragedy of Those Elevated and Speculation on Their Fall"
(Supplement to issue no. 36, 16 pp.)

V26 "On the Inability to Feel and Understand Tragedy. A Reply to V. Rastorguev"
(38: 5/33, pp. 82–83)

V27R S. Troitsky: *The Christian Philosophy of Marriage.* Paris: YMCA Press, 1933, 227 pp.
(39: 7/33, pp. 82–85)

V28R Nicolai Von Hartmann: *Das Problem des Geistigen Seins. Untersuchungen zur Grundlegung der Geschichtsphilosophie und der Gestesweissenschaften.* Berlin und Leipzig: Verlag Walter de Gruter, 1933, 482 pp.
(40: 9–10/33, pp. 72–77)

V29 "The Problem of Power and Its Religious Significance"
(42: 1–3/34, pp. 3–21)

V30R Georges Gurvitch: *The Idea of Social Law.* Paris: Sirey, 1932, 710 pp.
(43: 4–6/34, pp. 78–82)

V31 "The Image of God in the Essence of Man"
(49: 10–12/35, pp. 48–71)

V32 "The Image of God in the Fall"
(55: 1–4/38, pp. 24–40)
V33 "God's Abandonment"
(61: 10/39–3/40, pp. 15–21)

WEIDLE, V. See VEIDLÉ, V. V.

"X."

X1 "The Path of Transfiguration" (an article from Russia; mimeographed notes of a course by Professor X. given at Moscow in 1927, secretly disseminated. Introduction by M. Artemiev)
(39: 7/33, pp. 41–52)

ZANDER, L. A.

Z1 "The Conference of Argeron (Normandy)"
(2: 1/26, pp. 109–116)
Z2 "The Conference of Hopovo"
(2: 1/26, pp. 116–121)
Z3 "Three Student Conferences" (Bulgaria, Yugoslavia, Germany)
(5: 10–11/26, pp. 104–107)
Z4 "The Conference of Clermont" (1926)
(6: 1/27, pp. 115–119)
Z5 "The Conference of Bierville" (1926)
(6: 1/27, pp. 120–125)
Z6R Miguel de Unamuno: *The Agony of Christianity*. Paris, 1925, 162 pp.
(6: 1/27, pp. 131–133)
Z7R *The Archives of Dostoevsky*. Munich: R. Piper
(6: 1/27, pp. 133–134)
Z8R J. Popovich: *The Philosophy and Religion of Dostoevsky* (in Serbian). Sremski Karlovtsy: IHG, 1924
(8: 8/27, pp. 149–153—"A New Book on Dostoevsky: An Introduction to a Vision of the Orthodox World")
Z9 "A Conference Concerning Russia" (Clermont II, 1927)
(9: 1/28, pp. 78–80)
Z10 "A Sad Paradise" (On the work of Dostoevsky)
(14: 12/28, pp. 56–79)
Z11R A. L. Bem: *On Dostoevsky* (a collection of essays edited by A. L. Bem). Prague, 1929, 164 pp.
(25: 10/30, pp. 127–131)
Z12 "The Conference of Christian Churches at Edinburgh"
(54: 8–12/37, pp. 63–71)

ZANDER, V. A.

Z13 "The Symbolism of the Icon of the Holy Trinity by Andrei Rublev"
     (31: 12/31, pp. 30–52)

ZENKOVSKY, V. V.

Z14   "The Religious Youth Movements in the Russian Emigration"
      (1: 9/25, pp. 121–127)
Z15R H. Delacroix: *Religion and Faith*
      (2: 1/26, pp. 149–151)
Z16R Saint Thérèse of the Child Jesus: *The Story of a Soul*
      (2: 1/26, p. 151)
Z17R Dr. M. Pfliggler: *Die Deutsche Jugendbewegung und Jungkatholischer Geist*
      (2: 1/26, p. 152)
Z18   "Autonomy and Theonomy"
      (3: 3–4/26, pp. 46–64)
Z19   "Freedom and *Sobornost*'"
      (7: 4/27, pp. 3–22)
Z20   "Facts and Reflections" (On the psychology of contemporary youth)
      (8: 8/27, pp. 73–88)
Z21R W. Monod: *On Protestantism*. Alcan, 1928
      (15: 2/29, pp. 135–137)
Z22R K. Müth: *Wiederbegegnung von Kirch und Kultur in Deutschland. Eine Festgabe fur Karl Müth*. Munich
      (18: 9/29, pp. 122–125)
Z23R V. F. Marcinkovsky: *Notes of a Believer. From the History of the Religious Movement in Soviet Russia*. Prague, 1929
      (19: 11/29, pp. 120–121)
Z24   "The Athens Conference"
      (22: 6/30, pp. 116–125)
Z25R Max Pribilla, S.J.: *Um Kirchliche Einheit*. Stockholm, Lausanne, Rome: Freiburg, 1929
      (23: 8/30, pp. 120–121)
Z26   "Overcoming Platonism and the Problem of the Sophianicity of the World"
      (24: 10/30, pp. 3–40)
Z27R R. B. Hoyle: *The Teachings of Karl Barth, An Exposition*. London: BSCM Press, 1930
      (26: 2/31, pp. 127–129)
Z28R G. Florovsky: *The Eastern Fathers of the 4th Century*. Paris: ISNEFS, 1931, 239 pp.
      (28: 6/31, pp. 101–102)

Z29R	Pierre Lhande: *Christ of the Suburbs* and *The God Who Moves* (28: 6/31, pp. 102–104)
Z30R	N. Lossky: *Value and Existence*. Paris: YMCA Press, 1931 (30: 10/31, pp. 89–91)
Z31R	F. Heiler: *Im Ringen um die Kirche, Gesammelte Aufsätze und Vorträge*. Vol. 2. Munich, 1931 (31: 12/31, pp. 110–111)
Z32R	B. Vysheslavtsev: *The Ethics of Transfigured Eros*. Paris: YMCA Press, 1931 (32: 2/32, pp. 90–102— "The Place of Imagination in the Spiritual Life")
Z33R	N. Lossky: *The Ways of Apprehending the World. An Introduction to Metaphysics*. Paris: Sovremennye Zapiski, 1931, 183 pp. (32: 2/32, pp. 107–109)
Z34R	L. A. Matveev: *Do Miracles Exist? A Scientific Analysis of the Miracles of Jesus Christ and the Apostles*. Belgrade, 1931 (33: 4/32, pp. 76–77)
Z35R	J. Maritain: *Descartes' Dream and Other Essays*. Paris: R. A. Correa, 1932, 344 pp. (34: 7/32, pp. 71–72)
Z36R	World Committee of the YMCA: "Report: Facing a World Crisis." Geneva, 1932 (34: 7/32, pp. 72–73)
Z37	"The Problem of Beauty in the Worldview of Dostoevsky" (37: 2/33, pp. 36–60)
Z38	"The Crisis of German Protestantism" (42: 1–3/34, pp. 56–67)
Z39R	B. Mathews: *J. R. Mott, World Citizen*. New York, London, 1934, 454 pp. (43: 4–6/34, pp. 82–83)
Z40R	*Eine Heilige Kirche*, no. 4, 1934 (January–March), herausgeber Fr. Heiler (43: 4–6/34, p. 83)
Z41R	*Oekumenika. A Journal of Theological Synthesis*, no. 1, 1934, published under the auspices of the Council for Religions Outside of the Anglican Communion (44: 7–9/34, p. 75)
Z42	"Professor G. I. Chelpanov (*in memoriam*)" (50: 1–4/36, pp. 53–56)
Z43R	K. V. Mochulsky: *The Life and Teachings of V. Solovyov*. Paris: YMCA Press, 1936, 79 pp. (52: 11/36–3/37, p. 79)
Z44R	*Irénikon*: The Monthly Bulletin of the Monks of Church Unity, Priory of Amay-sur-Meuse, 1935–1937 (53: 4–7/37, pp. 85–86)
Z45R	Igor Smolitsch: *Leben und Lehren den Startzen*. Vienna: Thomas Verlag, 1936 (54: 8–12/37, pp. 76–77)

Z46R   E. Brunner: *Der Mensch im Widerspruch: Die Christliche Lehre von Wahren und Wirlichen Menschen*. Berlin: Furche Verlag, 1937
(55: 1–4/38, pp. 81–82)

Z47   "Evil in Man"
(56: 5–6/38, pp. 19–36)

ZERNOV, N. M.

Z48R   Prof. A. Kartashev: *The Paths to the Ecumenical Council*. Paris: YMCA Press, 1932
(34: 7/32, pp. 73–75—"The Russian Church and Universal Orthodoxy")

Z49R   Prof. I Stratonov: *The Crisis of the Russian Church, 1921–1931*. Berlin, 1932, 204 pp.
(34: 7/32, pp. 73–74)

Z50R   S. Troitsky: *Separation or Schism*. Paris: YMCA Press, 1931, 148 pp.
(34: 7/32, p. 74)

Z51   "Saint Cyprian of Carthage and the Unity of the Universal Church"
(39: 7/33, pp. 18–40)

Z52   "Orthodoxy and Anglicanism"
(43: 4–6/34, pp. 49–61)

Z53   "Russian Church Reform and the Pre-Revolutionary Episcopate"
(45: 10–12/34, pp. 3–15)

Z54   "The Unity of the Anglican Church"
(47: 4–6/35, pp. 51–65)

Z55   "The Ninth Anglo-Orthodox Congress (1935)"
(49: 10–12/35, pp. 51–65)

Z56   "Moscow, the Third Rome"
(51: 5–10/36, pp. 3–18)

Z57   "At the Crossroads of the Church"
(55: 1–4/38, pp. 68–80)

Z58   "An English Theologian in Russia at the Time of Emperor Nicholas I: William Palmer and Alexei Khomiakov"
(57: 8–10/38, pp. 58–83)

Z59   "Anglican Ordination and the Orthodox Church"
(59: 2–4/39, pp. 57–73)

Z60   "The World Christian Youth Conference (Amsterdam, July 24–August 2, 1939)"
(61: 10/39, pp. 3–40)

INDEX

Abamelek, Madame, 232
Abellio, Raymond, 582
About V. Solovyov, 41
Abramov, Aleksander, 7
Absolute, the, 28, 289, 291, 292; Berdyaev on, 296–97, 298, 453; Bulgakov on, 308, 388; Hegel on, 29, 70; relationship to God, 444–52, 453
Academy of Religious Philosophy, 16, 21, 64, 92, 95–96, 100, 116, 122, 125, 207, 209, 210, 211–16, 375, 387, 418, 423–24, 426, 445, 520, 521; and Berdyaev, 52, 93, 94, 95, 129–31, 210, 211–12, 213, 214–15, 258, 262, 275, 496, 497–98, 520; and ecumenism, 150; and *The Way*, 1–2, 94, 95–97, 203, 417, 506–7; YMCA funding of, 227, 416
Action Française, 149, 153–58, 186
Adamovich, G., 419, 445, 520
Afanasiev, Marianne, 215–16
Afanasiev, Nikolai, 93, 194, 314, 396, 397, 540; articles in *The Way*, 197, 215–16, 242, 245–47, 322, 340, 358, 363, 364, 478, 537; "The Canons and Canonical Consciousness," 242, 358, 363; ecclesiology of, 245–47, 340, 363, 364, 365, 478, 479, 480; ecumenical activities, 553; on the Eucharist, 364, 478; on Orthodox Church, 562; political views, 412; "The Two Concepts of the Universal Church," 215–16, 358, 364
Afanasiev, Yuri, 542
Affirmations, 241, 251
Ahutin, A., 548
Aid for the Christians of Russia, 557–58, 564
Aid for the Faithful of the USSR, 554–55, 557
Aksyuchits, Victor: *In the Shadow of the Cross*, 535
Alekseev, Nikolai, 19, 40, 41, 43, 51, 57, 94, 133, 137, 203, 288, 333, 427, 496, 528; articles in *The Way*, 118–19, 201, 202, 261, 303, 307–8, 426, 447–48; on Being, 448, 451, 452; on Berdyaev, 307–8; ecumenical activities, 510; eschatology of, 428; on freedom, 451; on German phenomenology, 351; on God, 307, 447–48; on Hitler, 426; *The Last Things*, 428; on meaning and Being, 448, 451; political views, 53, 118–19, 426; on the state, 118–19, 132; during World War II, 522
Alexander III, 39

Alexandrov, 424, 444
Alexei II, Patriarch, 3, 535, 539, 544, 558, 564, 579
Alexei, St., 91
Alivisatos, Hamilcar, 359
Alpha and Omega, 538, 543
Altermann, Fr., 330
Althusser, Louis, 549
Anashvili, V., 548
Anastasios (Yannoulatos) of Tirana, Archbishop, 578
Anastassy (Gribanovsky), Metropolitan, 401
Anderson, Paul, 19, 92, 94, 95, 96, 168, 208, 213, 227, 333, 344, 345, 412, 417, 520, 521, 528, 529, 578–79; as director of YMCA Press, 93, 96, 171, 184, 552; ecumenical activities, 93, 101, 169, 210; "The YMCA and the Russian Orthodox Church," 110
Andreu, Pierre, 337
Andrieu, Pierre-Paulin Cardinal, 19, 153
Andronikov, Constantine, 11, 314, 529, 554, 557, 560
Angelus Silesius, 153, 277
Anglicanism, 12, 19, 20, 21, 38, 98, 123, 230, 231, 512; and ecumenism, 141, 144, 165, 168–69, 179–86, 218, 340, 343–45, 365–71, 420, 488–89, 508–9, 516–17, 577; *Prayer Book*, 343. *See also* Fellowship of St. Alban and St. Sergius
Annales de Philosophie Chrétienne, 149
Annenkov, G., 528
Anselm, St., 390
Anthony (Khrapovitsky), Metropolitan, 49, 101, 104, 122, 123, 209–10, 237, 242, 366, 472, 489, 521; *The Dogma of Redemption*, 116; and ecumenism, 171, 180, 181; and loyalty to Soviet state, 230; on morality, 124, 125; *The Moral Significance of the Dogma of the Holy Trinity*, 125; relationship with Metropolitan Evlogy, 115, 124, 138, 232–33, 238, 245, 383; relationship with Florovsky, 472; role in ROCOR schism of 1927, 114–15; on sophiology, 102, 103; and Synod of Karlovtsy, 89, 90, 110, 111
Anthony Bloom of Sourouzh, Metropolitan, 536, 538, 543
anthroposophy, 279–80
Antichrist, 72, 88
anti-Semitism, 88, 102–3, 496, 539, 563
Apocalypse: 2–3, 487; 21:3, 391, 454; 21:3–5, 470; 22:17, 20, 458; 22:20, 469; myth of Kingdom of God in, 38, 72, 391
apokatastasis, 177, 290, 302, 385
Apollinarianism, 312, 387, 399
apophatic theology, 27, 62, 170, 296–97, 303, 307, 387, 393, 400, 473, 505, 506, 511, 565; vs. cataphatic theology, 310, 365, 389, 394, 446, 475, 563; of Frank, 291, 292, 346, 452
Appeal for the Russian Clergy and Church Aid Fund, 182, 222
Aquinas, Thomas, 70, 80, 147, 314, 350; neo-Thomism, 147, 355–56, 473, 478, 512, 529, 564, 573
Arbor Mundi, 548
Archambault, Paul, 19, 149, 156, 509
archetypes, celestial, 282, 390
archteypes of holiness, 132–34, 138
AREP, 558
Argenti, Fr. Cyrille, 553
Aristotle, 65, 147, 286, 297, 313, 314, 356, 573; on primary vs. secondary essence, 27, 312

Arius, 312, 391
Aron, Raymond, 13, 15
Aron, Robert, 190, 206, 499, 527
Arseniev, Nikolai, 19, 40, 41, 44, 51, 57, 93, 95, 96, 145, 169, 201, 235, 522, 526, 529; on Anglicanism, 365–66, 367; articles in *The Way*, 170, 201, 344, 347, 356, 366; ecumenical activities, 173, 174, 176, 338, 344, 365–66, 368; political views, 53, 117
Artemiev, M. M., 198, 234, 240
asceticism, 81, 152, 273–74, 288, 294, 304, 477
Asmus, Fr. Valentin, 256, 538, 539, 540
Association of Revolutionary Writers and Artists (AEAR), 324
Association of the *Vitiazi*, 402, 415, 416
Association of Writers for the Defense of Culture, 490–91
Athanasius, St., 42, 75, 390
atheism, 44, 45, 49, 108–9, 221, 230, 234, 240, 327, 530; Berdyaev on, 46, 104, 109, 157, 161, 212, 256–57, 352, 496, 507; Fedotov on, 161–62
Athenagoras I, Patriarch, 344, 516, 533, 572, 579
Attempt at a Systematic Exposition, An, 120
Audiberti, Jacques, 528
Augustine, St., 54, 119, 305, 332, 355, 364, 574
Averintsev, Sergei, 537, 538, 548, 549
Avtonomova, N., 548
Avvakum, 438, 508

Bachelard, G., 527
Badiou, Alain, 549
Bagin, Fr. Martiri, 541
Baimakova, Tamara, 21, 210, 212–13, 221, 345, 403, 418, 421

Bainville, Jacques, 157
Bakhtin, Mikhail, 548, 550
Bakst, Fr. Valentin, 423, 424
Bakunin, P., 276
Balthasar, Hans Urs von, 343, 527, 554, 575
Balzon, Jean, 552
baptism, 360, 480, 511, 577
Barabanov, E., 555
Barash, Jeffrey Andrew, 14
Baratynsky, Yevgeny, 450
Barbey d'Aurevilly, Jules, 144
Barth, Karl, 172, 324, 347, 356, 379, 497, 515, 527; Berdyaev on, 249, 353; on church and state, 268–69; dialectical theology of, 169–70, 348, 353, 356; ecclesiology of, 476; ecumenical activities, 339, 340; eschatology of, 176; on freedom of conscience, 268; influence of, 169–70, 171, 175, 267, 353, 358, 473, 512, 529, 565; on metaphysics, 285; on Nazism, 339, 353; *Der Römerbrief*, 169–70, 269
Basil III, Patriarch, 115, 219
Basil the Great, St., 61
Bataille, Georges, 190, 499–500, 524, 527
Bauchau, Henry, 372
Baudelaire, Charles, 144
Baudouin, Charles, 357
Baudrillard, Jean, 548
Beaudouin, Dom Lambert, 146, 552
Beaussart, Bishop Roger-Henri-Marie, 496, 523
Becker, Jean-Jacques, 191
Becker, O., 61
Becker, Raymond de, 19, 328, 372–74, 508
Behr, Nicholas, 345
Behr-Sigel, Elisabeth, 223, 232, 400–401, 418, 552, 560

Being, 25–28, 42, 60, 64, 289, 320; abyss as foundation of, 77–78; Alekseev on, 448, 451, 452; as antinomian, 77; being as energy (*energoumenon*), 27–28; being in relation (*prosopon*), 27; being oneself (*hypostasis*), 27, 28, 48, 49, 66, 83, 102, 103, 114, 116, 282–83, 312, 313, 322, 387–88, 399; Berdyaev on, 31, 302, 505; Cappadocian Fathers on, 27–28, 63; ontic conception of, 26, 27; personal conception of, 25, 27–28; rationalist conception of, 26; Solovyov on, 291
Belenson-Elson, Elisabeth, 19, 41, 51, 127, 201, 341, 424, 496
Belgrade Academy of Theology, 93–94
Belinsky, Vissarion, 15, 29; "Letter to Gogol," 18
Bell, G. K. A., 339
Belovenets, Nikon, 533
Bely, Andrei, 29, 50, 93
BEM (Baptism, Eucharist, and Ministry), 554
Bem, K., 235
Benda, Julien, 328, 376
Benedictines, 21, 75–76, 145, 146, 151, 159, 340, 512, 558
Benedict XV, 142
Benedict XVI, 573
Bénichou, Paul, 15
Benjamin (Kazansky), Metropolitan, 90, 98
Benjamin, Bishop, 101–2, 116, 180–81
Bennigsen, Fr. G., 19, 198, 340
Berberova, Nina, 186, 383
Berdyaeva, Lydia (Lydia Judifevna), 46, 153, 212, 332, 348, 427, 445, 528
Berdyaev, Nikolai, 10, 12, 15, 16, 19, 22, 34, 44, 50, 60, 61, 64, 86, 93, 170, 177, 191, 196, 209, 210, 216, 223, 243, 282, 290, 324, 337, 338, 347, 358, 382, 408, 424, 451, 500, 575, 579; on the Absolute, 296–97, 298, 453; and Academy of Religious Philosophy, 52, 93, 94, 95, 129–31, 210, 211–12, 213, 214–15, 258, 262, 275, 496, 497–98, 520; on anthroposophy, 279–80; on antinomianism, 65, 69, 77, 305; on anti-Semitism, 496–97; on art, 259–60; on atheism, 46, 104, 109, 157, 161, 212, 256–57, 352, 496, 507; on Barth, 249, 353; on Being, 31, 302, 505; on Bergson, 350; on Berl, 325–26; on Boehme, 77–78, 80, 193, 214, 297, 298, 299, 300, 311, 331–32, 333–34, 466; on Brunner, 354; on Buber, 356; on Bulgakov, 464; on capitalism, 54, 253, 254, 490; on Catholicism, 144, 145, 147–48, 155–57, 361, 483, 484, 505–6, 507–8; on Christification, 58; on communism, 251, 255, 256–59, 260, 269, 280, 326–28, 346, 402–3, 405, 441, 475, 493–94, 495–96, 520, 527; on creation, 298, 306–7, 334; on creativity, 74, 75, 84, 300, 303, 450, 454; on culture, 74–75, 224; on Danzas, 507–8; death, 528–29, 530; on democracy, 251–54; on dialectic, 256; on dogma, 31, 47, 84; on Dostoevsky, 140, 146, 242, 332, 337, 416; on East and West, 186–88; ecclesiology of, 84–85, 140, 153, 241, 327, 354, 365, 371–72, 429–30, 441, 474–78, 483, 490; ecumenical activities, 95, 129, 140, 141, 144–45, 146–49, 150, 151, 158, 159, 161, 162–64, 177, 183, 186–88, 198, 334, 340, 341, 345, 346, 348, 359, 360–61, 371–74, 472, 484, 508–9, 510, 516,

562, 577; as editor-in-chief of *The Way*, 1–2, 18, 20, 36–39, 52, 95–97, 197–98, 199–200, 201, 202–6, 213, 224, 233, 234, 235–36, 237, 239–40, 255, 337, 373–74, 384, 403, 424, 425, 426–27, 432, 483, 508; as editor-in-chief of YMCA Press, 93, 94, 200, 211–12, 213, 439; education of, 39, 40, 41, 46; and epistemology, 22, 42, 307–8; eschatology of, 73, 104, 117, 128, 159, 224, 335, 361, 365, 427–28, 453, 454–55, 467, 468–70, 474, 475–76, 499, 523–26, 527, 573; on Eurasian movement, 57, 119–20, 130, 137, 153, 199, 407; on evil, 68–70, 127–28, 138, 161, 296, 298–99, 305, 306–7, 332, 355, 444, 453, 466–67, 504; family of, 40; on Fedorov, 73, 135, 136, 250–51, 256, 469; on Fedotov, 410–11; on Florovsky, 439; on freedom, 30, 46, 62, 69, 77–78, 80–81, 113, 157–58, 242, 251–52, 260, 275, 297, 298–99, 300–301, 303, 304, 305, 306–7, 320, 331, 333, 334, 354, 356, 376–77, 394–95, 413–14, 416–17, 429, 453, 456, 460–61, 465, 466, 468, 472, 476, 483, 537; on Freemasonry, 104–5; on French intellectuals, 493–94; on German nationalists, 55; on gnosticism, 507–8; on God as Creator, 67, 69, 148, 298, 299, 306–7, 355, 392, 443, 450, 529; on God as person, 296–97, 302; on God's energies, 465; on God's love, 298–99, 305; on Grenier, 493–94; on Hegel, 59–60, 580; on Heidegger, 352, 353, 467–68, 527; on hell, 302–3, 304, 306, 307, 394, 470, 567; on

Holy Spirit, 148, 158, 205–6, 371, 444, 475–76, 524; on humility and obedience, 411; on individualism, 260; influence of, 38, 213, 235, 328, 329–35, 346, 347, 372–73, 405, 513, 531, 534, 535, 536, 542, 545, 550, 553, 560; on intellectuals, 376–77, 378; on Jaspers, 467–68, 504–5, 527; on Jesus Christ, 30, 68–69, 84–85, 104, 107–8, 128, 148, 271, 298, 300, 301, 302, 303, 305, 306, 321, 361, 392, 469; on Kartashev, 432; on Kingdom of God on earth, 34, 36, 74, 85, 102, 117, 130, 257, 303, 441, 454, 475, 490, 511; on knowledge of God, 66–67; on Maritain, 147–49; on Marxism, 135, 136, 256–57, 259, 262, 308, 475, 476, 493–94, 495, 527; on Massis, 154, 155, 165; on materialism, 257; on metempsychosis, 194; on modernism, 36–38, 52, 381; on Mounier, 476–78; on myth of Heavenly Man, 298, 301; on myth of Sophia, 298, 300; on mythologic thought, 24, 29–31, 59–60, 66–67, 77, 298, 301, 306–7, 475–76, 496; on nationalism, 266–67, 269–72, 407, 411–12; native town, 40; on negation, 297, 299; on Neoplatonism, 65; on Nietzsche, 267, 527; on Old Believers, 441–42; ontology of, 298–300, 302, 467, 505, 549, 553; on original sin, 67–68, 128, 257, 306–7, 326, 412; on origins of the Russian intelligentsia, 219–20; and Orthodox Action, 416, 417, 424, 497; on Orthodox Church, 37–38, 46, 62, 80, 97, 112, 113, 131, 155–57, 241–42, 302, 304,

Berdyaev, Nikolai (*cont.*)
306, 361, 392, 411–12, 421, 429, 471, 495; personalism of, 23, 24, 31, 86, 191–92, 262, 266, 296–97, 300–303, 308, 323, 329, 330, 355–56, 361, 365, 404–5, 414, 430, 443, 448, 452–55, 466, 471, 473, 474–78, 494, 557, 564, 566, 567, 568; political views, 43, 52, 53, 55, 57, 57–58, 104–8, 117, 118, 119, 120, 126, 127–28, 226, 228, 229, 247–48, 251–54, 404, 405, 406–7, 412, 471, 490, 492, 493, 534, 580; on power, 394; on property, 477; on the prophet, 376–77; on Protestantism, 107, 361, 483; on Providence of God, 241; and Put' publishing house, 18; on racism, 496–97; on Ragaz, 476; on reason, 31, 65, 308, 354; on reincarnation, 279–80; relationship with Bulgakov, 320–22, 407, 414, 461–62, 463, 464–66; relationship with Chelpanov, 40; relationship with Ilyin, 228; relationship with Maritain, 146–49, 156–57, 163–64, 330, 331, 333, 494, 520; relationship with Tillich, 261–62; relations with French intellectuals, 326–35; remembrance of, 461, 531, 532, 533, 534, 535, 536, 537, 540, 542, 544, 545, 549, 550, 551, 553, 555, 556, 557, 559, 560, 561, 562, 566, 567, 569, 573, 582; on resurrection of Christ, 74; on return to Russia, 109; on revelation, 354; on Rougier, 145–46; and RSCM, 99, 100, 109, 112, 126, 130–31, 202, 221, 224, 225–26, 229, 416–17; on Russian intellectuals, 442; on Russian national identity, 429–30, 441, 443–44; on Russian religious thought, 275; on Russian Revolution, 241; on Sartre, 527; on Shestov, 283–84, 458–59, 463–64, 466, 468–70; on sin, 257, 262; on socialism, 271, 404, 405, 406–7, 413–14, 474–78; on social justice, 303; and Society for Spiritual Culture, 526; on Solovyov, 65, 73, 80; on sophiology, 77, 80–81, 129, 300, 318, 320, 391–93, 443, 461–62, 557; on the souls, 280; on spirituality, 157, 241–42, 250, 251, 329, 371–72, 376–77, 378, 380, 381, 404, 453, 470; on the state, 271, 407, 411–12; on Steiner, 279; and St. Sergius Institute, 129, 424, 464; on Suarez, 325, 326; symbolism of, 47, 69–70, 146, 186, 187, 188, 224, 306, 334, 355; on technology, 249–51, 271–72, 330; and The Circle, 419; on theosophy, 279–80; on theurgy, 75; on Thomism, 355–56, 478; on time, 350, 505; on the Trinity, 106, 300, 302, 331, 476; on truth, 256, 307, 394–95, 411, 493–94; on the *Ungrund*, 193, 196, 297, 299, 321, 453; on the universal vs. the general, 270; during World War II, 519–20, 524; on younger generation, 129–30
Berdyaev, Nikolai, works of: "About the New Christian Spirituality," 371; "The Accusation of the West," 155; articles in *Esprit*, 326–27, 328–29; articles in *New City*, 376–77; articles in *The Way*, 2, 18, 34, 54, 65, 68–69, 73–75, 77, 80–81, 104, 113, 127–28, 129–31, 144–45, 154, 158, 161, 186, 193, 194, 201, 202–3, 214–15, 248–60, 254,

255–56, 257–58, 259, 262, 269, 279, 283–84, 297, 298–99, 301–8, 325–26, 327, 329, 349–50, 351, 352, 355, 356, 381, 391–92, 394–95, 404–5, 410–14, 426–28, 439, 452–54, 458, 463, 474–75, 476–77, 483–84, 490, 493, 496–99, 506, 507–8, 546, 559; *Au Seuil de la Nouvelle Époque*, 528; "The Bourgeois Spirit," 54; *Le Christianisme et la lutte des classes*, 213, 327; *Christianisme et realité sociale*, 327; "Christianity and Anti-Semitism," 496–97; "Christianity and Human Creativity," 257; "Christianity and the Challenge of Contemporary Social Reality," 214; *Cinq méditations sur l'existence*, 350, 505; *Conscience de soi/Dream and Reality*, 455; "The Crisis of the Intellect and the Mission of Intellectuals," 377; *De l'esclavage et de la liberté de l'homme*, 404, 475; "The Destiny of Culture," 147; *The Destiny of Man*, 196, 301, 303–4, 333, 373, 504; *The Destiny of Russia*, 532; *Dialectique existentielle du divin et de l'human*, 524; "Does Freedom of Thought and Conscience Really Exist in Orthodoxy?," 410–14; *Esprit et realité*, 328; *Essai de métaphysique eschatologique/The Beginning and the End*, 428, 453, 455, 523–25, 549; *The Fate of Man in the Modern World/Le destin de l'homme dans le monde actuel*, 249, 251–52, 302, 404, 495; "The Finalities of Culture," 214–15; "The Fundamental Ideal of L. Shestov," 464; "The General Orientation of Soviet Philosophy and Militant Atheism," 194, 256, 327; "The History of Russian Thought," 214; *L'homme et la machine*, 327; "Illusions and Realities in the Psychology of the Youth of the Emigration," 129–31; "In Defense of Blok," 214, 279; "Joseph de Maistre and Freemasonry," 104; "The Kingdom of God and the Kingdom of Caesar," 73–74, 104–5, 146; "Literary Currents and the Social Order," 214, 259; "Man and the Machine," 214, 248–50; "Manifesto of Russian Authors," 520; *The Meaning of History*, 158, 475, 524; *The Meaning of the Creative Act*, 74–75; *Le moi et le monde des objets (Solitude and Society)*, 524–25; *Un nouveau Moyen-Age/The End of Our Time*, 147, 372–73, 520; "Obscurantism," 80, 127; "On Authority, Freedom and Humanity," 394; "On Social Personalism," 252–53; "On the Nature of Russian Religious Thought in the Twentieth Century," 275; "Personalism and Marxism," 262, 301, 404–5; "Personality and Community in Russian Thought," 528; "A Philosopher's Journal," 127–28, 137; *Philosophy of Freedom*, 42, 213, 307–8; "Polytheism and Nationalism," 214, 269–71; *Problème du communisme*, 327; "The Problem of Mankind," 453–54; *La Psychologie religieuse russe et l'athéisme communiste*, 220; "The Quests for Social Justice among the French Youth," 329; *Royaume de l'Esprit et royaume de*

Berdyaev, Nikolai, works of (*cont.*)
César, 524; "Russian Christianity and the Modern World," 327; *The Russian Idea*, 443, 520, 532; "The Russian Religious Renaissance . . . and the Journal *The Way*," 214, 381; *The Self and the World of Objects*, 301, 307, 321; "Social Revolution and Spiritual Awakening," 528; "Some Reflections on Theodicy," 68–69, 298–99; *Les sources and le sens du communisme russe*, 404, 428, 441, 475, 495–96, 556, 557; *Spirit and Freedom*, 158, 300, 333, 335, 373; *Spirit and Reality*, 378, 453, 459, 460, 464–65, 524; *The Spirit of Dostoevsky*, 68, 332, 337; "The Spirit of the Grand Inquisitor," 391–92; *Spiritual Autobiography*, 520, 523; "The Spiritual Crisis," 252; "The Spiritual State of the Contemporary World," 214, 248, 249; "The Truth and Lies of Communism"/ "Verité et mensonge," 2, 254, 255, 257–58, 326–27, 328; "Two Ways of Understanding Christianity," 302; "Universality and Confessionalism," 360–61; *War and Eschatology*, 454
Berger, Peter, 572
Bergson, Henri, 22, 24, 35, 149, 324, 325, 333, 334, 347, 348; influence, 191, 350, 550, 561; on vital impulse/*élan vitale*, 71, 191
Berl, Emmanuel, 325–26
Bernanos, Georges, 492
Berstein, Serge, 33, 191
Besançon, A., 556
Besant, Annie, 63
Bezobrazov, Fr. C., 386, 396

Bezobrazov, Sergei, 40, 44, 51, 199, 344–45, 347; articles in *The Way*, 19, 97, 99, 178, 201, 216, 424, 485; on divine revelation, 36; on dogma, 397; ecclesiology of, 485–86; ecumenical activities, 176, 178–79, 182, 184, 218, 513; education of, 41; eschatology of, 485–86; on exegetical symbolism, 184; on Holy Scripture, 36, 278; on Holy Spirit, 397, 485–86; on love, 485; on metahistory, 184; political views, 53, 412; on raising of Lazarus, 178; on resurrection of Jesus, 178; and St. Sergius Institute, 98, 99
B., Fr. Alexei, 19, 236
Bianchi, Enzo, 543, 572
Bibihin, V., 548; *Synergy*, 545–46
Bibliothèque Nationale, 2
Bidault, G., 156
Bilimovich, A., 105
Bitsilli, Piotr, 19, 133, 198, 219–20, 276, 426, 522
Blanchot, M., 524
Blane, Andrew, 203–4, 472
Blavatskaya, H., 279
Bloch, Chaim, 356
Bloch, Jean-Richard, 325, 328
Blok, Alexander, 235, 278–79, 320; "The Demon," 279; "The Double," 279; "The Song of Hell," 279; "The Twelve," 279
Blondel, Maurice, 147, 149, 496
Bloy, Léon, 22, 35, 144–45, 147, 469, 494
Blumhardt, Christoph, 19, 177, 476, 483–84
Blumhardt, Johann, 476
Blum, Léon, 406–7, 412, 491, 496
Boborykin, Pyotr, 15
Bobrinskoy, Fr. Boris, 529, 552, 553, 554, 555

Bobrovsky, G., 123
Bodrov, Alexis, 538
Boegner, Pastor Marc, 150, 339, 372, 509, 515
Boegner, Philippe, 150
Boehme, Jakob, 59, 131, 324, 335, 452; on Being, 77–78; Berdyaev on, 77–78, 80, 193, 214, 297, 298, 299, 300, 311, 331–32, 333–34, 466; on freedom, 77–78, 299; on God, 307; influence of, 24, 77–78; on Jesus Christ, 300; on Lucifer and evil, 78; Mariology of, 300; *Mysterium Magnum*, 346; on opposition of contraries, 331; on Sophia, 300; on the *Ungrund*, 193, 297, 299, 331, 466; on Wisdom of God, 77–78, 79, 80, 320
Bogoslovsky, A., 557
Boldyrev, Ivan, 259
Bolk, L., 71
Bolotov, V. V., 166, 488
Bolshakova, N., 537
Bolshakov, V., 6
Boltanski, Luc, 566, 572
Boniface VIII, 486
Bonnefoy, Yves, 446, 557
Bonner, Elena, 533, 534
Borisov, Fr. A., 539, 540
Borne, Etienne, 341, 509
Borrely, André, 567–68
Bosco, J., 420
Bouquet, A. C., 339
Bourdieu, Pierre, 13
Bouyer, Louis, 554
Boyer, Paul, 21, 336
Braikevich, Xenia, 184, 345
Brasillach, Robert, 154, 491
Bréhier, Emile, 65, 333, 500
Brent, Charles, 168, 173
Breton, Fr. Valentin, 342–43
Breton, Stanislas, 11, 549
Bria, Ion, 559

Brianchaninov, Ignatius, 101, 104, 123, 489
Briand, Aristide, 110, 121
Brillet, Fr., 372
British Student Christian Movement (BSCM), 182, 183–84
Brossat, Alain, 6
Brotherhood of St. Mark of Ephesus, 540
Brotherhood of St. Photius, 384, 385
Brotherhood of St. Sophia, 105–6, 115
Brunner, Emil, 170, 175, 339, 353, 354, 510
Brunschvicg, Léon, 328, 333, 349–50
Buanaotti, Ernesto, 328
Buber, Martin, 127, 284, 328, 335, 336, 351, 504; *The Dialogue of Life*, 356; "Hassidic Tales," 356; "I and Thou," 356; *The Kingdom of God*, 356
Bubnov, Nikolai, 19, 201, 290, 292, 348, 350–51, 354, 424
Buddhism, 20, 63, 129, 277, 279, 280
Bukharev, Alexandr: influence of, 36, 37, 52, 74, 84, 128, 203, 275, 300, 392
Bukharin, Nikolai, 120, 256, 404, 532
Bulgakov, Sergius, 10, 12, 15, 16, 19, 25, 44–45, 50, 52, 64, 94, 95, 96–97, 98, 106, 150, 155, 156, 158, 177, 200, 202, 203, 209, 210, 224, 279, 280, 282, 290, 358, 382, 389, 408, 415, 417, 442, 451, 472, 488, 496, 507, 511, 522, 528, 574; on the Absolute, 308, 388; on Anglicanism, 368–69; on *apokatastasis*, 131; on apophaticism, 62; on baptism, 511; on Being, 320; on Berdyaev, 464–65; on body and spirit, 323; on Catholicism, 162, 166–67, 342–43, 480, 481; on Christ as God-Man, 35; Clément on, 9, 564;

Bulgakov, Sergius (*cont.*)
on creativity, 75; on dogma, 24, 31–32, 47, 49, 116, 166–68, 193, 215, 263, 311–16, 321, 341, 360, 377–78, 385, 388, 390, 396–97, 462, 479–80, 483, 525; ecclesiology of, 85–86, 172, 173, 360, 363, 365, 429–30, 456, 473, 474–75, 478–82, 483, 486–87, 511, 525; ecumenical activities, 159, 161, 162–63, 164, 166–67, 172, 173–75, 176, 177, 182–83, 184, 217–18, 218, 337, 338–39, 340–41, 342–44, 345, 359–60, 368–69, 370, 371, 372, 374, 455, 472, 473, 486, 489, 508–9, 510, 514, 515, 516, 577; education of, 41; and epistemology, 22; eschatology of, 159, 176, 318, 365, 369, 401, 455, 457–58, 468–70, 474, 511, 517, 523, 525–26; on the Eucharist, 173, 193, 215–16, 311, 314–16, 318, 321, 340–41, 360, 368–69, 370, 371, 480, 482; on evil, 456–57, 466–67, 468; on faith, 462; on Fedorov, 469; on freedom, 456–57, 468; on God as Creator, 309, 319, 390–91, 456–57, 468; on God as omnipotent, 462; on God's freedom, 66; on hell, 455, 470, 567; on Holy Spirit, 85, 86, 116, 309, 318, 369, 377–78, 388, 391, 397, 420, 458, 465, 478, 480, 481, 482, 485, 553; on human freedom, 318–19; influence of, 38, 129, 213, 253, 382, 513, 531, 534, 535, 536, 545, 550, 553, 554; on Jesus Christ, 35, 85–86, 196, 274, 277, 309–10, 311–19, 321, 359–60, 385, 390, 391, 437, 463, 469, 487, 525, 553; on Judaism, 437; on Judas, 318–20; on Kant, 66; on Kingdom of God on earth, 34–35, 76–77, 277–78, 369, 391, 526; on Knights of the Round Table, 277; on language, 48–49; on love, 273; on materialism, 42; on modernism, 380; on monistic thought, 48–49; on Mother of God, 79–80, 173–74, 458; on mytho-logic thought, 24, 42, 47–48, 310, 316; on nationalism, 266, 269, 272, 273–74, 436; native town of, 40; on Neoplatonism, 65; on original sin, 318; on Orthodox Church, 166–67, 173–75, 182–83, 310, 342, 429, 470–71, 487–88, 511, 562, 578; on the Parousia, 35; on personalism, 388, 436–37, 511; political views, 43, 45, 53, 228, 247, 412, 534; on predestination, 311, 319; on Protestantism, 455, 480, 481; on reason, 48–49; relationship with Nikolai Afanasiev, 215–16; relationship with Berdyaev, 320–22, 407, 414, 461–62, 463, 464–66; relationship with Novgorodtsev, 40; remembrance of, 531, 532, 534, 535, 536, 537, 541, 545, 546, 547, 549, 550, 552, 553, 554, 556, 557, 559, 560, 561, 562, 564, 567, 568, 569, 573, 574–75, 578, 582; and ROCOR, 310, 386, 389, 395, 419–20, 540; and RSCM, 99, 100, 112, 202, 218, 226–27, 540; on Russian national identity, 429–30, 435–37; on salvation, 390; on the Self, 48–49; on St. Sergius, 79–80; on Sergius of Radonezh, 220; on Shestov, 462–63, 468–70; on sin, 457; on Slavonic language, 435–36; on social problems, 263; on Solovyov, 65, 79; sophiology of, 23, 42, 62, 76–77, 78–81, 85,

86, 102, 103, 111, 114, 115, 193, 196, 215, 253, 269, 272, 282, 308–20, 321, 322, 365, 371, 378, 384–95, 398–401, 419–20, 435, 436–37, 440, 442, 448, 455–58, 461–62, 464, 465, 466, 467, 470, 471, 473, 474–75, 487–88, 511, 516–17, 525, 540, 544, 560, 567, 568, 575, 581; on spirituality, 376, 380–81, 436–37, 470; and St. Sergius Institute, 99, 129, 396, 428, 435, 483; on substance, 48–49; symbolism of, 47, 85, 277; on the Trinity, 32, 48, 49, 85–86, 309–10, 316–17, 377–78, 387–88, 390–91, 487; during World War II, 522, 523

Bulgakov, Sergius, works of: *The Apocalypse of St. John*, 456–58, 469, 525–26; articles in *The Way*, 2, 79, 85–86, 103, 162, 166–67, 182, 193, 201, 214, 216, 277, 309, 310, 311–13, 314, 377–78, 380–81, 424, 426, 444, 455, 458, 474–75, 479–80, 486–88, 517, 537, 538, 546; *Autobiographical Notes*, 344; "Beneath the Walls of Chersonese," 559; *The Bride of the Lamb*, 388, 401, 456, 468, 576; *The Burning Bush*, 79, 166–67; "By Jacob's Well," 345, 359–60; "Chapters on Trinitarity," 79, 309; *The Comforter*, 377, 388, 485, 560; "The Doctrine of the People and Racism in the Light of Sophiology," 436–37; *The Dogma of Redemption*, 104; "The Dogma of the Eucharist," 314; *The Father*, 311; *Friend of the Bridegroom*, 79; "Hierarchy and Sacraments," 479–80; "The Holy Grail," 277, 314; "Hypostasis and Hypostaticity," 103, 309; *Jacob's Ladder*, 79; "Judas Iscariot," 216, 314, 318–20, 431, 436; *The Lamb of God*, 196, 311, 318, 321, 384, 388, 487; "The Lausanne Conference and the Papal Encyclical," 162; "The Nation and Humanity," 269, 272; "Notes on the Doctrine of the Church," 85; "On the Banks of the Chebar River," 380–81; *On the Gospel Miracles*, 311; "On the Paths of Dogma (After the Seven Ecumenical Councils)," 311–13; *Orthodoxy*, 311, 342, 346; *The Paraclete*, 311; *Philosophy of Economy*, 42, 308, 315; *The Philosophy of the Name*, 436, 549; *The Philosophy of the Word*, 47–48; "The Problem of Conditional Immortality," 455; "Racism and Christianity," 436; *The Saints Peter and John*, 79; *Tragedy of Philosophy*, 47–48, 79, 564; "*Una Sancta*," 486–88; *The Unfading Light*, 62, 65, 78–79, 102, 319, 320; *The Veneration of Icons*, 311; "Ways to Church Reunion," 371; *The Wisdom of God*, 456, 516

Bulgarian Orthodox Church, 207, 225, 245
Bultmann, Rudolf, 170, 353
Bunin, Ivan, 196, 337
Burgelin, P., 528
Butor, M., 524

Cabasilas, Nicholas, 27, 432
Cahiers de la Nouvelle Époque, 527–28
Cahiers de la Nouvelle Journée, 149, 157, 509
Cahiers de la Quinzaine, 165, 186
Cahiers de l'Etoile, 337
Cahiers du Sud, 336

Caillois, Roger, 491, 499
Cain, Jules, 333
Calvat, Mélanie, 144, 341
Calvinism, 279–80
Camus, Albert, 22, 493
Canguilham, G., 527
Canticle of Canticles, 433
Cantor, Georg, 573–74
capitalism, 254–55, 263, 326, 413–14, 477, 579; Berdyaev on, 54, 253, 254, 490
Cappadocian Fathers: on Being, 27–28, 63; on heavenly archetypes, 390
Carrère d'Encausse, Hélène, 556
Carroll, Lewis, 195
Cassirer's *Philosophy of Symbolic Forms*, 58–59
cataphatic theology, 311, 331, 440, 513; vs. apophatic theology, 310, 365, 389, 394, 446, 475, 563
Catherine of Siena, 373
Catholic Action movement, 164
Catholicism, 46, 84, 94, 174, 180, 230, 268, 286, 370, 502, 503, 527, 542, 572; Berdyaev on, 144, 145, 147–48, 155–57, 361, 483, 484, 505–6, 507–8; Bulgakov on, 162, 166–67, 342–43, 480, 481; and ecumenism, 140, 141, 142–67, 169, 176, 182, 183, 218, 330–32, 340–43, 372–74, 484, 507, 509, 512–13, 544, 553–54, 554, 558–59, 562, 576, 577; Florovsky on, 159–61, 359; Immaculate Conception, 166, 362; papal infallibility, 83, 157, 162, 166, 167, 279; and private property, 477; Thomism/neo-Thomism, 70, 80, 147, 314, 350, 355–56, 473, 478, 512, 529, 564, 573; Vatican I, 167; Vatican II, 553; Zenkovsky on, 164, 341, 512–13

Cavanaugh, William, 574
Céline, Louis-Ferdinand, 496
Celsus, 146, 289
Center for Religious Literature of the Russian Emigration, 3
Center for the Assistance of Russians of the Emigration (CARE), 223
Certeau, Michel de, 572
Chaadaev, Pyotr: influence of, 22, 275, 565
Chagall, Marc, 333
Chamberlain, Neville, 492
Chaptal, Bishop Rafael, 163, 230
Charle, Christophe, 13
Chechnya, 536, 538, 540
Chekhov, Anton, 165–66, 276
Chelpanov, G., 40
Chertkov, Stefan, 21, 417
Chesterton, G. K., 195
Chetverikova, Anna, 225, 227
Chetverikov, Sergius, 19, 41, 51, 61, 62, 86, 97, 201, 209, 210, 215, 226, 285, 296, 303, 345, 387, 424; on Berdyaev, 305–7, 392, 393, 394–95; on Christ and the church, 306; on the Eucharist, 221, 287–88; on freedom, 382; political views, 228; on redemption, 287–88, 293; and RSCM, 122–23, 202, 305, 416, 420, 421–22; on sophiology, 395, 396, 398; on spirituality, 422
Chicherin, B., 276
Chistiakov, Fr. George, 538, 540, 543
Chizhevsky, Dmitrii, 19, 41, 77, 94, 201, 426
Chrétien, Jean-Louis, 572–73
Christ and Freedom, 45–46
Christianisme Social, 476
Christian mysticism, 63, 155, 164, 175, 353, 460
Christian Reunion, 358, 359–62, 363, 368

Christiansen, B., 292
Christian universalism, 139–40, 144, 159, 170, 206, 245, 271, 361, 380, 486, 507
Chrol, Leonid, 232
Chrysostom, St. John, 61, 290, 373, 412
Chubarov, I., 548
Chukov, Nicolas, 98
churching of life, 55, 85, 99, 100, 220, 265, 440
CIMADE, 554
Circle, The (*Krug*), 418, 419
City of Kitezh, 159, 429, 441–44
Clarke, O., 182, 183, 345, 369–70
Clark, Rev., 529
Claudel, Paul, 35
Clément, Olivier, 329, 540, 541, 552, 553, 554, 556, 557, 564, 578; *Berdiaev*, 559–60; on Bulgakov, 9, 564; ecclesiology of, 563; on mytho-logic thought, 9; *Rome autrement*, 9; on *The Way*, 1–2, 9; *You Are Peter*, 562–63
Cohen, Hermann, 58
Collège de Sociologie, 491
Colton, Ethan, 93, 97, 210, 344
Combat, 520
communism, 16, 54, 100–101, 263, 324, 326, 339, 491, 544; Berdyaev on, 251, 255, 256–59, 260, 269, 280, 326–28, 346, 402–3, 405, 441, 475, 493–94, 495–96, 520, 527; Russian Communist Party, 3, 51, 105, 108, 256, 403, 545, 547, 557; Russian Revolution, 2, 3, 5, 19, 37, 43, 45, 52–53, 56, 57, 87, 89, 96, 99, 180, 237, 241, 309, 439, 471, 507; Third International, 121, 258, 382–83, 409, 432, 435
Communisme et les chrétiens, Le, 495
Communities, 373
Comte, Auguste, 70

conciliarity (*sobornost'*), 50, 90, 216, 246–47, 275, 365, 368, 390, 433, 477, 484; Bulgakov on, 162; as hierarchical, 474–75, 478–82; Khomiakov on, 81–83, 263, 506
concupiscence, 124, 125
Confraternity of St. Sergius, 217
Congar, Fr. Yves, 330, 341
Congregation Pro Ecclesia Orientali, 142–43
Constitutional Democrat Party, 43, 49, 51
Contacts, 552, 557
Contemporary Annals, 9, 243, 275, 352, 406, 458–63, 465
Contemporary Reform, The, 540
contributors to *The Way*, 18–20, 24, 247–48, 384; common experience of exile, 39, 51–58; on editorial committee, 38, 95–96, 97, 203–4, 412, 425–26, 522, 528; generational differences, 197–98, 200–203, 221–22; intellectual trajectories, 41–43; modernist identity, 16–17, 34, 35–39, 47, 51, 87–88, 114–15, 137, 140, 141, 200–201, 218, 245, 248–49, 275, 281, 300, 311, 347, 366, 380; monarchists as, 53, 104–8, 117, 126, 201, 532–33; republicans as, 53, 104–8, 532–33; residences of, 19–20; social backgrounds, 40
Coordinating Committee of Orthodox Youth, 553
Copeau, Jacques, 326
Corbin, Henri, 333, 499, 500, 557
1 Corinthians, 172; 3:16, 487; 12:4, 487; 12:28, 393
2 Corinthians 3:6, 396
Council of Chalcedon, 83–84, 242, 312, 313, 399, 431, 440
Council of Ephesus, 246
Council of Florence, 167

Council of Nicea, 489
Couturier, Abbé Paul, 341
creativity, 74–76, 77–78; Berdyaev on, 74, 75, 84, 300, 303, 450, 454; cultural creativity, 73, 74–75; Mother Maria on, 75, 76, 322–23
Crémieux, Benjamin, 333
Croce, Benedetto, 127
Crum, Rev., 345
cultural creativity, 73, 74–75
Curilin-Kissiliov, Alexis, 212
Curtes, Geoffrey, 343
Cyprian of Carthage, St., 358, 359, 362–63, 364, 478, 480, 481
Cyril, St., 312, 433

Dacque, Edgar, 71
Daladier, Édouard, 228, 492
Daley, Brian, 576
Damien of Jerusalem, Patriarch, 180
Dandieu, Arnaud, 190, 206, 329
Daniélou, Jean Cardinal, 346, 524, 527, 554
Daniel-Rops, Henri, 189, 327, 329, 372, 495
Danilenko, Fr. Boris: "Grains of a Unique Bread," 3, 8, 544–45; on *The Way*, 8, 544–45
Dantec, Maurice G., 573–74
Danzas, Julie, 500; on Academy of Religious Philosophy/*The Way*, 506–7
Darwin, Charles, 71, 185
Daucourt, Bishop Gerard, 558
Davis, Donald E., 92, 173, 208, 210
Davy, Marie-Madeleine, 524, 527, 528, 552, 557
Day, Dorothy, 572
Deborin, 256
Debussy, Claude, 22
Décades de Pontigny, 24, 147, 164, 328, 336, 476, 520
Delacroix, H., 145

Delafosse, H., 161
Déléage, André, 190
Deleuze, Gilles, 524, 548, 566, 573
Demant, V., 339
Demidov, I., 105
democracy, 55, 244, 251–54, 265, 266, 481, 532–33, 539, 579, 581
Democratic Union, 94
Deniken, Anton, 409
Denisov, I., 217, 228
Dennes, M., 561
De Profundis, 16, 41, 43, 53, 96, 532
Dermenghem, Emile, 147, 164
Derrida, Jacques, 22, 548, 549, 572
Desanti, J., 527
Descartes, René, 446; on the *Cogito*, 28; influence of, 350, 355
Desjardins, Paul, 24, 35, 147, 164, 328, 495, 500
Deuteronomy 6:4, 461
D'Herbigny, Monsignor Michel, 21, 35–36
Diaghilev, Serge de, 18
dialectical theology, 169–70, 292, 348, 353, 356, 510
Dibelius, Martin, 173, 179, 339, 515
Dietrich, Suzanne de, 150, 340, 372, 420, 492, 508, 509
Dieu vivant, 474, 552
Dilthey, Wilhelm, 291, 451, 550
Dimitrii of Serbia, Patriarch, 181
Diodorus of Tarsus, 312
Dionysius the Areopagite, 64, 288, 435
diophysitism, 313, 314
Dobrokhotov, Alexander, 547
Docetist movement, 362
Doctrine of the Transmigration of Souls, 280
dogma, 39, 66, 188, 242, 285, 290, 348, 384, 393, 440, 543, 552; Berdyaev on, 31, 47, 84, 483; Bulgakov on, 24, 31–32, 47, 49, 116, 166–68, 193, 215, 263, 311–16, 321, 341, 360, 377–78, 385, 388, 390,

396–97, 462, 479–80, 483, 525; dogmatic interpretation of sophiology, 78–80; dogmatic symbolism, 37, 47, 200, 483; Florovsky on, 24, 31, 32, 83–84, 286, 287, 365, 369, 511; Vladimir Ilyin on, 82–83
Dolgov, K. M., 542
Dombes Group, 578
Dombrovsky, J., 555
Domostroi, 441
Doncoeur, Paul, 373
Donskoy, Dmitri, 134
Doriot, J., 121
Dorotheos, Patriarch, 169
Dosse, François, 566, 572
Dostoevsky, Fyodor, 29, 62, 146, 166, 177, 271, 292, 336, 431, 502, 550, 575; *The Brothers Karamazov*, 140, 392, 460, 488; death sentence, 52; eschatology of, 71–72, 327; on the Grand Inquisitor, 68–69, 72, 140, 155, 263, 327, 391, 416; influence of, 5, 22, 24, 36, 37, 38, 39, 51, 52, 54, 55, 57, 64, 68–69, 70, 71–72, 74, 76, 97, 128, 137, 203, 242, 275, 284, 286, 300, 335, 350, 435, 466, 488; *The Possessed*, 426; on problem of evil, 68–69; on Pushkin, 155
Douglas, Canon J. A., 21, 173, 345
Doumergue, Gaston, 228
Dreyfus affair, 165
Drieu la Rochelle, Pierre, 491
du Bos, Charles, 164, 195, 325, 327, 328, 330, 336
Dubrovsky, V., 410, 415
Ducatillon, Fr., 495
Duhamel, G., 521
Dumezil, Georges, 499
Dumont, Christopher, 513
Duns Scotus, John, 573–74
Dupire, B., 561
Durkheim, Émile, 566

Eastern Pontifical Institute, 142
ecclesiology: of Afanasiev, 245–47, 340, 363, 364, 365, 478, 479, 480; of Berdyaev, 84–85, 140, 153, 241, 354, 365, 371–72, 429–30, 441, 474–78, 483, 490; of Bulgakov, 85–86, 172, 173, 360, 363, 365, 429–30, 456, 473, 474–75, 478–82, 483, 486–87, 511, 525; Caesaropapism, 37, 83, 111, 142, 151, 364, 470–71, 484; as Christocentric, 83–85; Church as Body of Christ, 82, 83–84, 86, 172, 245, 305, 318, 359, 360, 364–65, 429, 474, 483, 510–17, 563; Church as House of the Father, 474–90, 483, 563; Church as Temple of the Holy Spirit, 474, 483, 490–510, 563; ecumenical councils, 83–84, 86, 162, 174, 242, 246, 247, 311, 312, 313, 314, 362, 365, 367, 399, 431, 440, 472, 481, 489, 512, 559; of Fedotov, 437, 474, 484–85, 490; of Florovsky, 83–84, 140, 357–59, 363–64, 365, 366, 437, 440, 472–73, 474, 478, 479, 480, 482, 511–12, 513, 563; of Karsavin, 83, 265; of Kartashev, 244–47, 272–73; of Khomiakov, 81–83, 84, 112, 241, 246, 506; as spirit-centered, 81–83, 482–83; as wisdom-centered, 85–87; of Zander, 474, 488; of Zernov, 366–68, 440–41, 473, 474, 488–89, 514–15
Eckhart, Meister, 59, 63, 335
École des Hautes Études en Sciences Sociales, 556
École Normale Supérieure, L', 156
Ecumenical Council of Constantinople (381), 559
ecumenism, 129, 138–81, 274, 324, 381–82, 383, 433, 470–71, 490, 508–10, 529, 543, 568, 576–77;

ecumenism (cont.)
and Anglicanism, 141, 144, 165, 168–69, 179–86, 218, 340, 343–45, 365–71, 420, 488–89, 508–9, 516–17, 577; and Metropolitan Anthony, 171, 180, 181; and Catholicism, 140, 141, 142–67, 169, 176, 182, 183, 218, 330, 340–43, 372–74, 484, 507, 509, 512–13, 544, 553–54, 554, 558–59, 562, 576, 577; Christ and Freedom, 45–46; Declaration of Velehrad, 577–78; Declaration on Justification, 577; Declarations of Reuilly, 577; Ecumenical Congress of Christian Youth (Amsterdam, 1939), 511, 515–16; and Metropolitan Evlogy, 169, 173, 180, 218, 225, 344, 346, 510, 513, 516; and intercommunion, 181, 182, 185, 360, 366, 369, 370–71, 482, 516, 577, 578; and Protestantism, 140, 141, 149–50, 153, 158, 162, 168–81, 182, 218, 330, 337–40, 407, 488, 508, 509–10, 513–16, 554, 576, 577; and RSCM, 101, 171, 182, 184, 208, 218, 224–25, 515; and St. Sergius Institute, 164–65, 176, 184, 217–18, 370; World Council of Churches, 11, 169, 473, 482, 515, 553, 554, 559, 563, 576; and YMCA, 168, 173, 224, 344, 488, 515, 579
editorial policy of *The Way*, 96, 197, 198, 202–6, 237, 239–40, 247, 255, 278
Efron, S., 133, 136, 402
Ehrenburg, Ilya, 325, 490, 493
Eigen, Manfred, 575
Eihenvald, I., 68, 105
Eikalovich, Fr., 387
Eine Heilige Kirche, 268
Einstein, Albert, 191, 335
Ekkersdorf, Victor, 19–20, 75
Ekonomtsev, Fr. Ioann, 538, 543, 558

Elchaninov, Alexander, 19, 40, 41, 43, 51, 536
Elchaninov, Constantin, 529, 552
Elchaninov, Cyrille, 553, 554–55, 556
Eleutherius of Lithuania, Metropolitan, 231, 232, 239, 384–85
Eliade, Mircea, 24
Eltchaninov, Fr. Alexander, 197
Emmanuel, P., 527
Encausse, Hélène d', 10
"Encyclopedia of Orthodox Theology" (1901–1911), 4
Endokimov, Paul, 100
Engels, Friedrich, 250
Ephesians, 272; 1:22, 487; 3:9–10, 487; 3:10, 388
Epicurus, 70, 263
epistemology, 11, 21–32, 42, 307–8, 465, 468
Erenburg, Hans, 19, 172
Erickson, John, 576
eschatology, 70–73, 75, 85, 87, 146, 163, 266, 276, 282, 283, 482, 576; of Berdyaev, 73, 104, 117, 128, 159, 224, 318, 327, 335, 361, 365, 427–28, 453, 454–55, 467, 468–70, 474, 475–76, 499, 523–26, 527, 573; of Bulgakov, 159, 176, 318, 365, 369, 401, 455, 457–58, 468–70, 474, 511, 517, 523, 525–26; of Dostoevsky, 71–72, 327; of Fedorov, 134–35, 250–51, 327, 499; of Fedotov, 159, 224, 397; of Florovsky, 159, 359, 511; of Khomiakov, 71–72, 81; Last Judgment, 72; of Mother Maria, 523, 526; of Solovyov, 72, 73, 339
Esprit, 190, 330, 333, 341, 406, 473, 474, 547, 557; articles by Berdyaev in, 326–27, 328–29; and Mounier, 2, 190, 326–37, 329, 420, 426, 477–78, 491, 492, 496
Eucharist, the, 241, 248, 288, 363, 364, 433, 478, 479, 486, 515–16, 554,

563; Afanasiev on, 364, 478;
Bulgakov on, 173, 193, 215–16,
311, 314–16, 318, 321, 340–41,
360, 368–69, 370, 371, 480, 482;
Chetverikov on, 221, 287–88;
Florovsky on, 84; intercommunion,
181, 182, 185, 360, 366, 369,
370–71, 482, 516, 577, 578
Eurasian movement, 56–58, 82,
117–20, 129, 133–37, 138, 140,
143–44, 155, 428, 533–34, 539;
Berdyaev on, 57, 119–20, 130,
137, 153, 199, 407; division in,
133–34, 192–93; and Fedotov,
132, 133, 135, 137, 151–52, 438;
and Florovsky, 56, 57, 133, 135,
358, 438; and Karsavin, 118, 151;
and Sergei Trubetskoy, 56, 57
Euvé, François, 575
Evdokimov, Michel, 10, 554, 561
Evdokimov, Natasha, 232
Evdokimov, Paul, 10, 21, 100, 150, 232,
314, 338, 530, 533, 549, 553, 573;
Le Christ dans le pensée russe, 554;
ecumenical activities, 554; on
Orthodox Church, 578;
remembrance of, 559, 575
evil: Berdyaev on, 68–70, 127–28, 138,
161, 296, 298–99, 305, 306–7, 332,
355, 444, 453, 466–67, 504;
Bulgakov on, 456–57, 466–67,
468; Frank on, 452; Nikolai Lossky
on, 450–51; origin of, 68–70, 80,
185, 296, 298–99, 305, 306–7, 332,
350, 355, 444, 445–47, 450–51,
460, 465–67, 504, 567; Shestov on,
444, 445–47, 460–61, 466–67
Evlogy, Metropolitan, 21, 89, 90, 93, 98,
104, 108, 111, 112, 122, 123–24,
125, 126–27, 131, 132, 163, 201,
209, 210, 234, 241, 242, 320, 344,
385, 386, 395, 419, 420, 521, 536,
541; and ecumenism, 169, 173,
180, 218, 225, 344, 346, 510, 513,

516; and loyalty to Soviet state,
230, 231–33, 236, 243–44;
political views, 138, 229, 230, 435;
relationship with Metropolitan
Anthony, 115, 124, 138, 232–33,
238, 245, 383; relationship with
Berdyaev, 229; relationship with
Bulgakov, 389, 478; relationship
with Fedotov, 406, 409–10, 415,
435; relationship with Mother
Maria, 223; relationship with
Metropolitan Sergius, 207, 208,
225, 230, 231, 232, 236, 238,
239–40, 401, 558; role in ROCOR
schism of 1927, 113–14, 115, 116;
during World War II, 402, 521, 523
evolution, 71, 185

Fabrègues, Jean de, 190, 329
Fairfield, Zoe, 182
faith: Florovsky on, 285, 287; Lazarev
on, 24, 445, 446–47; and reason,
188, 275, 282, 284–85, 354,
445–47, 501, 565–66, 573;
Shestov on, 24, 196, 284–85, 287,
445, 446, 447, 459, 462, 467
Faith and Order, 168, 169, 173–75,
218, 338, 340, 358, 471, 482,
513–15, 522
Fall, the, 35, 67–68, 80, 445, 452
fascism, 55, 57, 121, 127, 382–83, 494,
544; in Italy, 251, 255; Nazism,
107, 251, 265–69, 339, 351, 382,
401–2, 407, 426–27, 428, 491–92,
492, 496, 497, 520, 580
Fatherland Notes, 17–18
Fathers of the Church, 38, 45, 69, 78,
140, 313, 314, 377, 379, 388–89,
471, 472, 513, 543, 563, 582;
Cappadocian Fathers, 27–28, 63,
390; Fathers of the Eastern
Church, 39, 285, 286–87, 290,
293, 310, 311, 357. *See also* neo-
Byzantinism

Faye, E. de, 78
Fedorov, Nikolai, 201, 256, 303, 392; eschatology of, 134–35, 250–51, 327, 499; influence of, 35, 36, 37, 72–73, 128, 134–37, 203, 236, 275, 300, 425, 469, 499; on Kingdom of God on earth, 277, 469; on overcoming of death, 136; *The Philosophy of the Common Task*, 73, 100, 250–51; political views, 302, 402; on resurrection of the dead, 469; and RSCM, 210, 226, 228, 415, 416; on salvation, 74; on sophiology, 77, 78; and St. Sergius Institute, 99
Fedotov, George, 12, 16, 25, 44, 51, 57, 125–26, 134, 137, 155, 158, 185, 200, 201, 203, 210, 212, 213, 222, 223–24, 242, 252, 253, 290, 329, 330, 347, 381, 382, 396, 403, 408–12, 417, 419, 420, 427, 428, 429, 441, 442, 445, 471, 496, 498, 521, 528, 529, 534, 537, 575; on authority, 131–32; on biblical exegesis, 295; on capitalism, 253, 490; on cult of Mother Earth, 295–96; on democracy, 253, 254; ecclesiology of, 437, 474, 484–85, 490; ecumenical activities, 151–53, 159, 161, 162–63, 164–65, 185–86, 338–39, 340, 345, 368, 509, 510; education of, 41; eschatology of, 159, 224, 397; and Eurasian movement, 132, 133, 135, 151–52, 438; family of, 40; on freedom, 115, 376; and hagiology, 218; on historiography, 294–95; on holiness, 133; on Holy Spirit, 224, 294–95, 296, 379, 397; influence of, 531, 534, 536; on intellectuals, 379–80; on Kartashev, 432; on Kingdom of God on earth, 490, 511; on love of God and love of neighbor, 425; native town, 40; and *New City*, 192, 200, 252–53, 376, 381, 406; and Orthodox Action, 424–25, 426; on Orthodox Church, 132, 230, 294–95, 433–34; on Péguy, 151; political views, 43, 45, 53, 228, 248, 253, 405–6, 409–13, 435, 464, 490, 492; on prayer, 414; on reason, 295, 379; relationship with Grevs, 40; on religious persecution in Soviet Union, 236–39; remembrance of, 582; on repentence, 295; on Russian history, 202; on Russian intelligentsia, 219–20, 443; on Russian state, 580–81; on separation of generations, 129; on Slavonic language, 433–35; on social problems, 262; on the soul, 379; on Spanish Civil War, 406; on spirituality, 376, 379–80; on *Spiritual Verses*, 295–96; on Stalin, 406, 492; on the state, 133, 135, 219; and St. Sergius Institute, 379–80, 406, 409–11, 412–13, 415, 424–25, 435, 464, 517; on truth, 294–95; on the will, 379; during World War II, 522

Fedotov, George, works of: articles in *The Way*, 18, 72, 115, 129, 135, 151–52, 161–62, 214, 218–19, 224, 236–39, 257, 294–95, 379, 414, 415, 424, 426, 484–85, 508, 510, 537; "Carmen Seculare," 129, 135, 161–62; "Christ and Freedom" founded by, 45–46; "Concerning the Situation of the Russian Church," 236–37; "Democracy Sleeps," 253; "Ecce Homo," 379; "The Foundations of Christian Democracy," 376; "The Holy Spirit in Nature and Culture," 224, 294; "How Stalin Sees Russian History," 406; "In

Defense of Ethics," 379, 414; "Make Haste!," 409; "Mother-Earth," 214; "On the Goodness of the Antichrist," 72; "Orthodoxy and Historical Criticism," 224; "Pages of St. Sergius," 415; "Passionaria," 406; "The Prophetic Mission of the Word and of Ideas in the Understanding of Liberty," 376; "Saint Genevieve and Saint Simeon the Stylite," 152–53; *Saint Philip, Metropolitan of Moscow*, 133; *The Saints of Ancient Russia*, 532, 580; "The Social Signification of Christianity," 257; "Stalinocracy," 406; "The Tragedy of Medieval Russian Sanctity," 218–19
Fellowship of St. Alban and St. Sergius, 184, 185, 218, 338, 344–46, 368–74, 420, 423, 456, 482, 486, 508–9, 516, 517
Felmy, Karl Christian, 543
Felzen, N., 419
Ferenzy, Oscar de, 496
Fernandez, Ramon, 328
Fessard, Gaston, 505, 524, 527
Feuerbach, Ludwig, 302, 449
Fichte, Johann, 28, 29, 49, 107, 264
Filioque, 82–83, 166, 180, 362, 366, 488–89, 553, 559
First Ecumenical Council, 162
Florensky, Fr. Pavel, 12, 51, 96, 177, 240, 290, 545, 546; articles in *The Way*, 133; on Eurasian movement, 133; on incarnation of the Word, 286; influence of, 45, 59, 177, 236, 279, 565, 573; *The Pillar and Ground of the Truth*, 45, 66, 78, 278; on reason, 66; remembrance of, 559, 573–74; on sophiology, 77, 78, 320, 356; and St. Sergius Institute, 99; on the Trinity, 506; on truth, 66

Florovsky, Georges, 12, 19, 25, 44, 62, 64, 66, 94, 97, 131, 143, 150, 199, 201, 202, 203, 204, 210, 214, 221, 278, 280, 291, 293, 302, 309, 322, 337, 347, 386, 387, 420, 424, 429, 432, 435, 441, 447, 529, 573, 575; on authority of the church, 287; on baptism, 511; on Catholicism, 159–61, 359; on Christian dogma, 24; on Christian metaphysics, 285–87; on Christification, 57–58; Christocentrism of, 176; on dogma, 24, 31, 32, 83–84, 286, 287, 365, 369, 511; ecclesiology of, 83–84, 140, 357–59, 363–64, 365, 366, 437, 440, 472–73, 474, 478, 479, 480, 482, 511–12, 513, 563; ecumenical activities, 140, 141, 149, 162–63, 164, 175, 176, 177, 183, 218, 330, 338–39, 340, 344, 345, 346, 348, 358–59, 367, 368, 369, 410, 472, 473, 482, 508, 509, 510, 511–12, 514, 515, 516, 517, 553, 576; education of, 41; eschatology of, 159, 359, 511; on the Eucharist, 84; and Eurasian movement, 56, 57, 133, 135, 137, 358, 438; on faith, 285, 287; and Fellowship of St. Alban and St. Sergius, 517; on freedom, 382; on German idealism, 285–86; on God and Being, 320; on heresy, 472; on immanentism, 55; influence of, 513, 535, 536, 543; intellectual predecessors of, 24–25; on Jesus Christ, 285; native town, 40; neo-Byzantinism of, 32, 86, 160–61, 330, 471, 472, 473, 513, 515, 530, 543, 563; ontology of, 282–83, 296, 302; on Orthodox Church, 159–61, 363, 437, 438–39, 442, 511–12, 562; political views, 43, 57, 57–58, 412; on Protestantism, 359, 511;

Florovsky, Georges (*cont.*) on reason, 285–86; on the Reformation, 354; relationship with Metropolitan Anthony, 472; relationship with Novgorodtsev, 40; remembrance of, 534, 535, 536, 543, 549, 555, 557, 559, 560, 562, 569; on revelation of God, 285; on Russian history, 202; on Russian Orthodoxy, 160; on St. Simeon, 159, 160–61; on Solovyov, 65; on sophiology, 371, 395, 396, 398, 473; on spirituality, 470, 472, 511; on S. N. Trubetskoy, 276; on truth, 287, 294; during World War II, 415, 522

Florovsky, Georges, works of: articles in *The Way*, 2, 18, 84, 131, 159–61, 175, 194, 201, 213, 216, 286–87, 340, 357–59, 362, 363–64, 474, 511, 538; "The Dispute concerning German Idealism," 32, 213; "The Eucharist and *Sobernost*'," 84; "The Limits of the Church," 358, 363–64; "The Question of Christian Unity," 194, 357–58, 511; "Theological Fragments," 286–87, 340; *The Ways of Russian Theology*, 428, 438–39, 560

Fondaminsky, Ilya, 20, 200, 403, 419, 497, 498, 499, 521, 558, 578

Fondane, Benjamin, 325, 336, 500

Fontaine, André, 557

force, use of, 105–8, 267, 445–46, 491, 494

Foucauld, Jean-Baptiste de, 582–83

Foucault, Michel, 14, 548

Fouilloux, Etienne, 142

Fournier, Alain, 195

France: French intellectuals, 11, 12, 15, 87, 194, 196–97, 324–37, 346–47, 355, 376, 471, 490–91, 492–93, 495, 496, 499–505, 520, 527–28; interest in *The Way* in, 1, 2, 6–7, 9–10, 11; *laïcité* in, 555; memory of *The Way* in, 551–57, 558–59; myth of golden age in, 33–34; Popular Front government, 383–84, 403, 406–7, 412, 490–91; preparatory courses for superior schools (CPGE), 16; relations with Russia, 39; relations with Soviet Union, 382, 402, 428; Revolution of 1789, 271; after World War I, 33–34, 139

Francis of Assisi, St., 44, 340, 476

Franco, Francisco, 406, 412, 484

Franco-Russian Studio, 325, 355

Frank, Simeon, 10, 19, 47, 57, 63, 77, 86, 93, 94, 95, 96, 280, 290, 309, 322, 334, 350–51, 424, 430, 528, 529; apophaticism of, 291, 292, 346, 452; on Being, 452; on Berdyaev, 525; education of, 40, 41; on epistemology, 42–43; on evil, 68, 452; on evolution, 71; on freedom, 60–61, 413–14, 451–52; on God and world, 291–92, 451; on God as all-powerful, 451; on Hartmann, 60–61; on Heidegger, 353; on Holy Spirit, 291, 296; influence of, 38, 545, 550; as Jew, 47, 522; on living knowledge, 42–43; on Losev, 60; on mythologic thought, 30, 71; on number, 59; ontology of, 282–83, 296, 302; on the person, 24, 301; on Pirogov, 275; political views, 43, 53, 55, 118, 247, 346, 413–14; on property, 413–14; on Pushkin, 276; on reality as life, 291; relationship with Novgorodtsev, 40; remembrance of, 532, 534, 537, 543, 544, 545, 549, 550, 551, 556, 557, 566, 567, 568; on Scheler,

60–61; on scientific thought, 59, 71; on sin, 452; on Spinoza, 292
Frank, Simeon, works of: articles in *The Way*, 18, 55, 58, 59, 60–61, 71, 74, 119–20, 194, 201, 257, 275, 292–93, 349, 351, 426, 543, 546; "The Church and the World, Grace and the Law," 119–20; *The Fall of the Idols*, 99–100; *The Inaccessible*, 452–53; *Knowledge and Being*, 42–43; "The Neo-Kantian Philosophy of Mythology," 58, 59; "The New German Literature on the Philosophy of Anthropology," 71; *The Object of Knowledge*, 292–93; "Personal Life and Social Creation," 257; "The Problem of Christian Socialism," 413; "Psychoanalysis as a Worldview," 194; "The Religious Foundations of Society," 55, 74
Fraternity of the Presentation of the Virgin in the Temple, 202
Free Academy of Spiritual Culture (VADK), 60, 93, 261
freedom: Berdyaev on, 30, 46, 62, 69, 77–78, 80–81, 113, 157–58, 242, 251–52, 260, 275, 297, 298–99, 300–301, 303, 304, 305, 306–7, 320, 331, 333, 334, 354, 356, 376–77, 394–95, 413–14, 416–17, 429, 453, 456, 460–61, 465, 466, 468, 472, 476, 483, 537; Boehme on, 77–78, 299; Bulgakov on, 456–57, 468; Fedotov on, 115, 376; Frank on, 60–61, 413–14, 451–52; of God, 301, 306, 354, 444, 459; Kant on, 66; Nikolai Lossky on, 293, 448, 450–51; Mother Maria on, 76, 322–23, 429, 467; Shestov on, 451–52, 501; Vysheslavtsev on, 288–89, 292, 294, 351, 448, 451; Zenkovsky, 82, 410, 451–52
Freemasonry: accusations of, 88, 103, 104, 110, 111, 113, 123–24, 127, 129, 207, 208–11, 438
Free Voices, 45–46
Frere, Bishop Walter, 21, 181, 184, 185, 344, 345, 346, 509, 516, 517
Freudian psychology, 23, 191, 280, 291, 449
Fuchs, Nadine, 314
Fumet, Stanislas, 19, 144–45, 147, 150, 186, 187–88, 496

Gabrilovitch, L., 161
Gadamer, Hans-Georg, 22
Gagarin, Prince Ivan, 140
Gagnebin, Pastor Laurent, 559
Gaidar, Yegor, 531
Gaidenko, P., 545
Galtseva, R. A., 545
Gandhi, Mahatma, 155, 373, 529
Gandillac, Maurice de, 335, 473, 504, 520, 528, 557
Garric, Robert, 156, 262
Garrigou-Lagrange, Reginald, 147, 355
Garvie, A. E., 173–74, 339
Gasparri, Pietro Cardinal, 169
Gaultier, Jules de, 336, 463, 501
Gavin, Frank, 19, 20, 198, 348
Gazette of Lausanne, The, 339–40
Genesis, Book of, 183, 184, 277, 278, 289, 445
Genevieve of Paris, St., 152
Genieva, Ekaterina, 3, 542, 561
Gennady of Constantinople, Archibishop, 359
Georgia, 580
Georgievsky, M., 226
German idealism, 11, 28–29, 32, 284, 285–86, 292, 308, 439, 460, 466
Germanos (Stronopoulos), Metropolitan, 169, 180

Germanos of Thyateira, Metropolitan, 515
Germany: alliance with Soviet Union, 383, 496, 521; National Socialism in, 107, 251, 265–69, 339, 351, 382, 401–2, 407, 426–27, 428, 491–92, 492, 496, 497, 520, 580; Protestantism in, 268–69, 348, 353; Social Democratic Party, 262; withdrawal from League of Nations, 227
Gessen, Sergei, 20, 94
Ghéon, Henri, 149, 186
Gide, André, 24, 325, 327, 328, 335, 336, 376, 490, 491, 492, 493
Gillet, Fr. Lev, 21, 150, 151, 186, 188, 197, 212, 223, 232, 347, 396, 412, 417, 418, 522, 543, 552, 560; biblical exegesis of, 278, 353; conversion, 163; and orthodox action, 424, 426; on Orthodox Church, 578; on sophiology, 400
Gillett, Charles, 343
Gilson, Étienne, 146, 164, 330, 500, 501; *The Spirit of Medieval Philosophy*, 196, 501–2
Ginzburg, A., 555
Ginzburg, M. A., 98
Giono, Jean, 195
Gippius, Zinaida, 105, 129
Girardet, Raoul: on myth and historical upheaval, 33; on mythical constellations, 87; on nostalgia and hope, 88
Glazberg, A., 197, 341
Glory of God, 316–18
Glubokovsky, Nikolai, 19, 20, 41, 44, 123, 169, 173, 181, 218, 235
Glucksman, A., 555
Gnosticism, 65, 78, 131, 341, 460, 505, 506, 507–8, 530, 546, 565
Gobineau, Joseph Arthur de, 496

God: as Creator, 9, 27, 66, 67–70, 148, 248, 283–85, 289, 298, 299, 306–7, 309, 319, 355, 385, 390–91, 392, 400, 443, 446, 447–48, 450–51, 452, 456–57, 466, 467, 468, 529, 574; energies of, 62, 78, 433, 465, 473, 564; Essence of, 78; existence of, 28; as Father, 27, 56, 63, 286, 312, 315, 317, 318, 323, 388, 391, 448, 449, 466, 474–90, 559, 563; freedom of, 301, 306, 354, 444, 459; grace of, 73, 78, 110, 289, 294, 437, 478, 480, 489; knowledge of, 65, 66–67; love for, 309; love of, 298–99, 305; mankind as image of, 254, 290, 293, 300, 302, 316, 319, 379, 422–23, 449–50, 452; as omnipotent, 444, 459, 462, 466, 469; Providence of, 145, 241, 573; relationship to the Absolute, 444–52, 453; revelation of, 36, 283, 285, 286, 317, 354; as Trinity, 27, 32, 56, 57, 63, 70, 76, 79, 82–83, 85–86, 102, 103, 106, 114, 115–16, 135, 139, 206, 248, 282–83, 291, 297, 299, 300, 302, 309, 316–17, 322–23, 331, 364, 377–78, 387–89, 390–91, 395, 400, 437, 463, 469, 471, 474, 475, 482, 485, 487–88, 489, 506, 559, 563, 568, 572, 575, 583; and truth, 66, 110; will of, 313; Wisdom of, 9, 42, 77–81, 85, 103, 114, 115–16, 272, 273, 282, 283, 289, 290, 292, 300, 308–10, 313–14, 316–18, 319, 322, 356, 378, 384–95, 398, 400, 429, 433, 442, 456, 465–66, 467, 470, 516–17, 544, 566, 575
Goering, Herman, 497
Gofshtetter, Hyppolite, 198, 234, 403, 426, 444
Gogarten, Friedrich, 170, 173, 353

Gogol, Nikolai, 276, 432, 550
Gollerbah, Evgeny, 546
Good, Prof., 345
Gorbachev, Mikhail, 532
Gorbov, M., 556
Gore, Bishop Charles, 173, 174, 180, 182, 183, 184, 344, 574
Goriansky, 409
Gorky, Maxim, 105, 490
Gornostaev, A., 34, 136
Gorodetsky, Nadezhda, 186, 232, 325, 402, 426, 510, 522, 528
Gounelle, Elie, 476
Goussev, C., 556
Grabar, Michel, 22–23
Grabbe, Count George, 89, 127, 233
Great Depression, 189
"Greek and Slavic Archives of the Library of the Holy Synod, The," 4
Greek Catholic Church, 489, 559, 577–78
Greek Orthodox Church, 169, 225, 245, 473, 577–78
Green Lamp society, 129
Gregory of Nyssa, St., 27, 42, 290, 315, 346
Gregory Palamas, St., 11, 24–25, 62, 63, 78, 308, 388–89, 390, 474, 545
Gregory the Theologian, St., 61, 450
Grenier, Jean, 446, 493, 500
Grevs, I., 40
Gribanovsky, Bishop Anastassy, 521
Grigorii, Metropolitan, 91
Grinevich, V., 185
Gringoire, 491
Groethyusen, B., 328
Gromov, N., 550
Gross, H., 292
Group of French-Speaking Proletarian Authors, 324
Grunwald, Constantin de, 528
Guardini, Romano, 145, 373
Guéhenno, Jean, 491

Guénon, René, 500
Guermantès, 495
Guesen, G., 198, 349
Guettée, Vladimir, 140, 163
Guitton, Jean, 499, 572
Gukasov, A., 117
Gurvitch, Georges, 23, 61, 94, 346, 352; *The Current Trends in German Philosophy*, 349–50; *L'idée du droit social*, 263–65
Gutvitch, G., 527

hagiology, 218
Halévy, Daniel, 186, 326, 336
Halifax, Lord, 144
Hardy, Abbott, 529
Harnack, Adolf von, 35, 161
Hartmann, Nicolai, 40, 60–61, 349, 351, 352
Hasbulatov, H., 533
Hausherr, Irenée, 159
Hautman de Villiers, Sergius, 163, 239, 417
Hebrews 13:8, 487
Hecker, I., 431
Hecker, Julius F., 93
Heering, G. I., 214, 266–67
Hegel, G. W. F., 49, 292, 302, 467, 499, 505, 524, 529; on the Absolute, 29, 70; Berdyaev on, 59–60, 580; on concepts, 573; dialectic of, 256, 330; on God, 299; influence of, 29, 58, 59–60; on myth, 32; neo-Hegelianism, 58, 59–60; on philosophy and religion, 59–60; rationality of, 284; Shestov on, 284, 285; on the state, 107; on universal memory, 14
Heidegger, Martin, 249, 267, 301, 335–36, 348, 350, 356, 451, 499, 548, 572; anthropocentric ontology of, 351–53; on Being, 452; *Being and Time*, 61, 215, 352;

Heidegger, Martin (*cont.*)
  Berdyaev on, 352, 353, 467–68, 527; on *Dasein*, 61; Nazi Party joined by, 351; Sezeman on, 61, 351–52
Heiler, Friedrich, 173, 269, 354
Heinemann, Fritz, 333
Heller, Michel, 91
Heller, Mikhail, 533, 555
Hello, Ernest, 144
Henriod, G., 345
Henriod, Henri-Louis, 372
Henry, Michel, 567
Heraclitus, 66
Herbigny, Michel d', 142–43, 145
heresy, 6, 49, 311–12, 360, 363–64, 392, 438–39, 472, 488, 540, 581
Hermant, Max, 328
hermeneutics, 48
Hersch, Jeanne, 505
Hérubel, Marc, 500
Hesse, Harmann, 357
hesychastic spirituality, 61–63, 220, 545
Hilarion (Alfeyev), Metropolitan, 265, 543
Hilarion of Kiev, Metropolitan, 550
Hinduism, 63, 289, 294, 354, 372, 437, 447, 499, 509
History of Political and Legal Doctrines in Russia, 550
Hitler, Adolf, 265, 268, 383, 401, 407, 408, 426, 492, 498, 510
Hobbes, Thomas, 577
Hochkirchlich-Oekumenischer Bund, 170
Hollier, Denis, 499
Holl, Karl, 175
Holy Alliance movement, 140, 168
Holy Spirit, 56, 63, 84, 287, 300, 343, 375, 393, 429, 471, 485–86, 577; Berdyaev on, 148, 158, 205–6, 371, 444, 475–76, 524; Bezobrazov on, 397, 485–86; Bulgakov on, 85, 86, 116, 309, 318, 369, 377–78, 388, 391, 397, 420, 458, 465, 478, 480, 481, 482, 485, 553; Church as Temple of the, 474, 480, 483, 487, 490–510, 563; Fedotov on, 224, 294–95, 296, 379, 397; *Filioque*, 82–83, 166, 180, 362, 366, 488–89, 553, 559; Frank on, 291, 296; gifts of the, 365, 367, 369, 378, 482, 485, 487; as Giver of Life, 290–96, 317; Zenkovsky on, 291, 296
Honnert, Robert, 186
Horuzhy, S., 531; *After the Pause*, 545; *Synergy*, 545–46
Hotovitsky, D., 168
Huber, Max, 339
Hugo's *Les Misérables*, 44
human dignity, 301, 405, 414, 427, 494, 511
Humanité, L', 324
Humanity of God, 23
humility, 323, 373, 394, 411, 431, 433, 477
Husserl, Edmund, 22, 28, 60, 61, 335–36, 346, 349, 351, 459, 501, 502, 524, 548, 549
Huxley, A., 490
Huysmans, Joris-Karl, 22, 472
Hyppolite, Jean, 495, 524

Iakubiziak, A., 198
icons: icon of Novgorod, 310; veneration of, 180, 253, 344, 472
Ignatius, bishop of Antioch, 364
Illovayaskaya-Alberti, I., 555
Ilnitsky, S., 194, 198, 332, 424
Ilyenkov, E., 548
Ilyin, Ivan, 94, 120; on Metropolitan Anthony, 116; political views, 107, 117, 118, 202, 580; remembrance of, 579–80; *The Resistance to the Forces of Evil*, 105, 106–8

Ilyin, Vladimir, 19, 42, 51, 61, 77, 94, 97, 125–26, 199, 201, 203, 212, 221, 262, 278, 396, 529, 533, 555; on anti-Semitism, 127; articles in *The Way*, 18, 66, 75–76, 82–83, 118, 127, 129, 132, 134, 204–6, 213, 214, 216, 407, 424, 507; on Berdyaev, 402–3, 464; as collaborator, 523; on creation, 67; on creativity, 75; on dogma, 82–83; ecclesiology of, 82–83; education of, 41; eschatology of, 159; on *Eurasia*, 137; and Eurasian movement, 57, 132, 143, 151; on the *Filioque*, 82–83; on knowledge, 67; on the liturgy, 75–76; on myth, 67; native town of, 40; on original sin, 205; political views, 107, 228, 247, 403–4, 412; "The Profanation of Tragedy," 204–6; relationship with Berdyaev, 228; relationship with Chelpanov, 40; on sophiology, 77, 78, 320, 395, 398, 407; on Soviet Union, 205–6; and St. Sergius Institute, 99
Imiaslavie controversy, 241, 431
immanentism, 55
individualism, 135, 145, 170, 191, 260, 261
Innokenty of Beijing, Archbishop, 113
Institut des Langues Orientales, 556
Institut d'Études Politiques, 556
Institut d'Études Slaves, 556
Institute of Ecumenical Studies, 554
Institut Supérieur d'Études Oecuméniques (ISEO), 554
interconfessionalism, 101, 171, 208
International Congress of Philosophy, Eighth, 348–49
Ioann (D. A. Shakhovskoy), Fr., 40, 307, 552; articles in *The Way*, 72, 123, 201, 216, 303–4

Iosif, Metropolitan, 91
Irenaeus, St., 343, 390
Irene, Grand Duchess, 186
Irénikon, 146, 151, 163, 340, 341, 359, 512, 554
Ishevsky, D., 198
Istina, 506, 554
Iswolsky, Fr., 21
Iswolsky, Helene, 327, 329, 332, 333, 403, 426, 496, 498, 522, 528; *L'Homme 1936 en Russie soviétique*, 492–93; "New Doctrines of Catholic Social Thought," 509
Italo-Ethiopian War, 383, 471, 491
Iunost', 532
Ivanov, A., 276
Ivanov, Piotr, 20, 75, 90, 201, 212, 522
Ivanov, Vyacheslav, 29, 41, 44, 47, 205, 206, 522
Ivan the Terrible, 133, 134, 376, 438
Izard, Georges, 190, 326, 329, 509
Izary, G., 326
Izoulet, Jean, 161

Jacob, Max, 337
Jakovenko, B., 349
Jakubiziak, Augustin, 19, 150, 330–31, 348
James, William, 284, 350, 426
Janet, P., 117
Janicaud, D., 565
Jankelevitch, Vladimir, 504, 527, 557
Japan, 277
Jaspers, Karl, 301, 307, 445, 467, 501, 502–3, 527
Je suis partout, 491
Jesus Christ: Ascension, 315–16, 318, 391, 486; Beatitudes, 422; Church as Body of, 82, 83–84, 86, 172, 245, 305, 318, 359, 360, 364–65, 429, 474, 481, 483, 487, 510–17, 563; cleansing of the Temple,

Jesus Christ (*cont.*)
107–8; Crucifixion, 277, 288, 293, 302, 448–49, 503; as God-Man/Incarnation, 30, 35, 63–64, 66, 69, 79, 83–84, 85, 106–7, 110, 196, 246, 254, 275, 282, 285, 287–88, 288, 291, 296, 300, 301, 302, 311–18, 320, 321, 323, 332, 342, 356, 385, 390, 391, 392, 399, 448, 451, 461, 487, 489, 572; and Judas, 318–20; *kenosis* of, 434; on Kingdom of God, 361; last words to disciples, 486; as *Pantocrator*, 438; promise to be present at gatherings, 475; raising of Lazarus, 178, 313; as Redeemer/Savior, 298, 303, 305, 392, 462, 485, 489; on rendering to Caesar what is Caesar's, 128; Resurrection, 73, 74, 177, 178, 290, 293, 315–16, 318; Second Coming/*Parousia*, 35, 72, 74, 76, 318, 335, 365, 369, 446, 457, 485, 511, 517, 525; on sin, 292; as Son, 56, 63, 278, 307, 311–12, 313, 317, 385, 388, 448, 449, 485, 489, 503, 553, 559, 563, 577; as Word become flesh, 276, 285, 287, 288–89, 316, 342, 399, 451, 566

Jesus Prayer: Mt. Athos tradition of, 44
Joachim III, Patriarch of Constantinople, 168
Joan of Arc, St., 144, 157
Job, 24, 284, 305, 320, 449, 461, 466
John, Gospel of: 1:1, 466; 3:16, 400; 8:32, 393; 12:24, 545; 14:2, 486, 487; 14:12–13, 277; 16:16, 486; 17:21, 487; 19:17, 278; 19:34, 277
1 John 1:5, 468
John of Damascus, St., 26, 315, 399
John of Kronstadt, St., 421
John of the Cross, St., 290, 373

John Paul II, 572; *Fides et Ratio*, 565–66, 573; *Ut Unum Sint*, 559
John the Baptist, St., 309
John, the beloved disciple, 577, 583
Joseph of Arimathea, 277
Joseph of Volokalamsk, 119, 219, 240
Jouanny, G., 232
Jouhandeau, Marcel, 195
"Journals of Theological Academies in Russia," 4
Journet, Fr. Charles, 164
Jouvenel, Bertrand de, 191
Judaism, 20, 25, 47, 102–3, 127, 459, 462–63
Judas Iscariot, 318–20, 470
Judifevna, Lydia. *See* Berdyaeva, Lydia
Jugie, Fr. Martin, 159, 342, 343
Julliard, Jacques, 17
Jung, Carl, 22, 288, 347, 348, 357, 449

"K. A.," 19
Kabbalah, 127, 300, 356, 457, 567
Kalashnikov, Fr., 21, 182
Kamenev, Lev, 93
Kant, Immanuel, 107, 288, 291, 302, 303, 434, 446, 493, 503, 548, 549; on autonomous ethics, 54; *Critique of Pure Reason*, 40, 66; on freedom, 66; and idealism, 28; influence of, 5, 24, 40, 41, 44, 66, 284, 414, 451; neo-Kantianism, 40, 41, 42, 58–59; on thing-in-itself, 23, 66, 67, 524
Karamzin, Nikolai, 533
Karashov, S., 210
Karev, 256
Karpov, Andrei, 53, 117, 201, 212, 281, 332, 344
Karpovich, Mikhail, 20, 344
Karsavin, Lev, 12, 32, 34, 38–39, 42, 57, 63, 77, 93, 96, 120, 150, 155, 389, 550; articles in *The Way*, 40, 64, 83, 118, 135, 293, 545, 546; *The*

Church, the Person, and the State, 118; ecclesiology of, 83, 265; ecumenical activities, 162–63, 218, 370; education of, 39, 40, 41; eschatology of, 159; and Eurasian movement, 118, 143, 151; on individualism, 135; native town, 40; on Orthodox Church, 265; political views, 43, 133, 136, 243, 544; "Prolegomena for a Study of Personhood," 64, 83, 135; "The Reform, the Reformation, and the Accomplishment of the Church," 114; relationship with Grevs, 40; on Solovyov, 64–65; on sophiology, 78, 80; and St. Sergius Institute, 98

Kartashev, Anton, 40, 41, 43, 44, 50, 51, 57, 95, 96, 111, 124, 131, 150, 242, 358, 386, 396, 408, 428; articles in *The Way,* 165, 194, 201, 216, 243–45, 265, 272, 345, 397, 424, 430–32, 507; on Catholicism, 362; on church and state, 243–45; on dogma, 47; ecclesiology of, 244–47, 272–73; ecumenical activities, 165, 338–39, 345, 359, 361–62, 368, 509, 510, 513; "Intercommunion and Dogmatic Agreement," 370; on modernism, 244; on nationalism, 272–73; on Orthodox Church, 272, 361–62, 402, 430–42, 578; political views, 53, 94, 201, 228, 247, 412; "The Reunion of the Churches in the Light of History," 361–62; and RSCM, 99, 100; on Russian national identity, 429, 430–32, 441, 442; on St. Sergius, 216–17; on social question, 265; and St. Sergius Institute, 97, 98, 114, 435

Katkov, G., 349
Kavert, Fritz, 19

Kavert, Samuel, 20, 170–71, 173
Kazachkin, Georgii, 21, 212, 418, 521, 522
Kazatchkin, J., 212
Kazem-Bek, Alexandr, 121, 402
Keller, A., 339
Kelly, H., 345
kenosis, 161, 434, 435
Kerensky, Alexander, 406, 412, 533
Kern, Fr. Cyprian, 40, 223, 396, 398, 412, 424, 483
kerygma, 574
Keyserling, Hermann von, 21, 94, 335, 348, 357
Khomiakov, Alexei, 29, 50, 62, 75, 392, 440, 484, 488; on conciliarity, 81–83, 263, 506; ecclesiology of, 81–83, 84, 112, 241, 246, 263, 506; ecumenical activities, 180, 367; epistemology of, 81; eschatology of, 71–72, 81; influence of, 16, 36, 37, 38, 42, 45, 51, 52, 54, 71–72, 74, 76, 81–82, 84, 97, 99, 112, 124, 128, 137, 153, 172, 176, 177, 203, 241, 246, 263, 275, 358, 470, 506, 537; on Kingdom of God on earth, 81, 139, 476; on love, 81–82; *On the Church,* 82–83; on the Trinity, 139; on truth, 81–82
Khristianos, 537
Kierkegaard, Søren, 24, 170, 284, 325, 445, 459, 461, 467, 468, 503
Kingdom of God on earth, 16, 50, 55, 57, 71, 75, 87, 120, 170, 199, 248, 254, 263, 277, 323, 469, 475, 482, 563; Berdyaev on, 34, 36, 74, 85, 102, 117, 130, 257, 303, 441, 454, 475, 490, 511; Bulgakov on, 34–35, 76–77, 277–78, 369, 391, 526; Fedorov on, 277, 469; Fedotov on, 490, 511; Khomiakov on, 81, 139, 476; Solovyov on, 139–40

Kireevsky, Ivan, 29, 42, 177, 275, 286, 506
Kirk, Kenneth, 19, 198, 345, 347–48
Kistyakovsky, Bogdan, 550
Klepinin, Dimitrii, 21, 40, 42, 51, 57, 129, 212, 213, 421, 521, 522, 558, 578
Klepinin, Nikolai, 93, 103, 109, 111, 112, 118, 133, 182, 213, 234, 402; *The Holy, Just, and Great Prince Alexander of the Neva*, 132, 533
Kliiachkin, 520
Klossowski, P., 524
Klyuchevsky, Vasilii, 295, 533
Kniazev, Alexis, 216, 314, 410, 522, 529, 543
Kochevie, 278–79
Koch, Hans, 175, 235
Kodzik, 194
Kojève, Alexandre, 346, 499, 505
Kologrivov, Fr. Ivan, 146
Kontinent, 540, 541
Koselleck, Reinhart, 569
Kostandi, K., 410
Kostikov, Vyacheslav, 7, 531, 532–33
Kothetkov, Fr. George, 537, 538, 539, 540–41, 564
Kotreliov, N., 561
Kovalevsky, Evgraph, 150, 163, 232, 552, 567
Kovalevsky, Maxim, 387
Kovalevsky, Piotr, 100, 232, 396, 556
Kovalyov, S., 534
Koyré, Alexandre, 23, 29, 77, 131, 298, 328, 331, 346, 499, 502, 504, 527, 557
Kozhevnikov, A., 499
Kozlovsky, Lev, 19
Kozlovsky, P., 210
Kozyrev, A., 550
Krasnitsky, V., 89, 90
Krause, 264

Krekshin, Fr. Ignaty, 531, 538, 540, 541, 543
Krestovskaya, L., 332
Krishnamurti, Jiddu, 63
Kroner, Richard, 59, 60, 284, 335, 336
Krotov, Yakov, 4, 543, 546
Krutikov, B., 210
Ktitarev, Fr. I., 386
Kuhlmann, Gustav, 19, 92, 95, 97, 101, 198, 203, 529; articles in *The Way*, 171–72; conversion of, 176; ecumenical activities, 171–72
Kuraev, Deacon Andrei, 538, 540, 541, 543
Kurbsky, Prince, 119, 133
Kurdiumov-Kalash, M., 40, 122, 134, 212, 232, 234, 236–38, 403, 520, 522; articles in *The Way*, 194, 236–37, 239, 240–41, 424, 426, 484; on capitalism, 490; ecclesiology, 484, 490; on the Eucharist, 241; on Kingdom of God on earth, 490; political views, 490
Ku, T. S., 20
Kutepov, Alexander, 408
Kuvakin, V., 545
Kyrill, Patriarch, 543
Kyrlezhev, Alexander, 538, 564

Laberthonnière, Fr. Lucien, 35, 149, 150, 157, 163, 355–56
Lacan, Jacques, 499, 527, 548
Lacocque, André, 565
Lacombe, Olivier, 164, 186, 188, 330, 499
Lacoste, Jean-Yves, 572–73
Lacroix, Jean, 509, 557
Lagovsky, I., 40, 100, 123, 194, 199, 201, 203, 210, 213, 221, 222, 225, 227, 236, 338, 396, 539; articles in *The Way*, 234, 322, 323; on Bulgakov, 398–99; death of, 520, 544;

ecclesiology of, 474; on Kingdom of God on earth, 323; on prayer, 323; on religion in Soviet Russia, 108–9, 234; remembrance of, 557, 567, 578; "The Return to the House of the Father," 398–99, 482; on salvation, 399–400; on sophiology, 398–99, 420, 482; on tritheism, 400
Lalande, A., 349
Lalou, R., 187
Lamour, Philippe, 190
Lampert, E., 410, 415
Lamy, Pascal, 582
Landmarks (*Vekhi*), 5, 12, 16, 41, 49–50, 96, 523, 530, 532
Landsberg, Paul-Louis, 329–30, 333, 498, 505, 527
Lang, Cosmo Gordon, 180, 343
Lapshin, I., 94, 349
Latest News, 94, 105, 223, 247, 403, 464
Laubier, Fr. P. de, 543, 561
Lausanne conference (1927), 162, 173–76, 183, 510
Laval, Pierre, 402
Lavelle, Louis, 334, 505
Lavrov, P., 41
Lazarev, Adolf, 198, 214, 332, 337, 424, 464, 522; articles in *The Way*, 284, 350, 426, 446–47; on faith, 24, 445, 446–47; on freedom, 446–47; on Genesis, 445; on sin, 445
League of Nations, 227, 382
League of Orthodox Culture (LCO), 223–24
Lebedev, Vyacheslav, 19, 21, 424, 444
Lebreton, Jules, 164
Lecerf, A., 147, 150, 151, 339
Leese, K., 292
Lefebvre, 147
Lefèvre, Fred, 337
Legaut, Marcel, 156

Le Goff, Jacques: *History and Memory*, 14; on intellectuals, 15
Leibniz, Gottfried Wilhelm von, 49, 290, 450; influence of, 69, 293; theodicy of, 70, 355
Leiris, M., 527
Leisegang, H., 292
Lemopoulos, George, 559
Lenin, Vladimir, 5, 15, 72, 98, 328, 403, 476, 532; on *Landmarks*, 49; New Economic Policy (NEP), 51, 120
Lenin Library Literary Archives, 3
Leonchukov, Ioann, 98, 395
Leonid (Verninsky), Bishop, 89
Leontiev, Konstantin, 36, 157, 158, 240, 275, 276, 393
Leo the Great, 312
Leo XIII, 142; *Aeterni Patris*, 565
Lepetit, Bernard, 14
Lequeux, A., 527
Lequier, Jules, 445, 446–47
Lermontov, Mikhail, 39
Le Roy, E., 147, 350
Lescourret, Marie-Anne, 565
Le Senne, René, 333–35, 520
Lessing, Gotthold Ephraim, 292
Lévinas, Emmanuel, 23, 346, 349, 500, 527, 565
Levitsky, Anatole, 499, 521, 546
Lévy, B.-H., 555
Lévy-Bruhl, Lucien, 31, 147, 336, 445, 446, 463, 501, 502
Lévy, Paul-Emile, 357
Leyris, Pierre, 333, 520, 529
Lialine, Clément, 340–41, 512
Library of Foreign Literature, 542
Lieb, Fritz, 19, 176–77, 178, 212, 224, 235, 333, 337–38, 339, 345, 476, 529
Life and Work, 169, 178, 218, 338, 482, 492, 508, 509–10, 513, 515
Lighthouse (*Maiak*), 92, 93, 101, 112

Likhachev, Dimitrii, 10, 532, 534, 535, 580; on Maxim the Greek, 15; on Russian intellectuals, 15
Lilje, H., 339
Lindenberg, Daniel, 498–99; *Les années souterraines*, 190; on Russian religious philosophy in France, 329
Liperovsky, Lev, 21, 44, 93, 100, 123, 210, 221, 227
liturgy, 11, 75–76, 84, 89
Litviak, 198
Litvinov, Maxim, 92, 402
Living Tradition, 396–98, 482–83, 488, 511, 541
Locke, John, 577
Lodyzhensky, P., 93
Lo Gatto, Ettore, 21
logic, 25–26, 29–30, 65–66; principle of contradiction, 65–66, 446, 447, 448; principle of identity, 448; principle of *tiers exclu*, 448
Logos, 336, 348, 548, 549
Loisy, Alfred, 35, 37, 149
Lomonosov, Mikhail, 537
Lopatin, Lev Mikhailovich, 69, 276, 292
Lopukhin, Piotr, 19, 51, 111, 112–13
Losev, Alexei, 12, 547–48, 549; *The Cosmos of the Ancients and Modern Science*, 60; *The Dialectic of Artistic Forms*, 60; *The Dialectic of Myth*, 564; *The Philosophy of the Name*, 60
Lossky, Nicholas, 539, 553, 554, 559, 564
Lossky, Nikolai, 12, 42, 45, 61, 63, 93, 94, 96, 204, 288, 349, 350, 400, 429, 430, 458, 528, 529, 530, 549, 550, 555; on Being, 452; on causality, 59; education of, 40, 41; and epistemology, 22; on evil, 450–51; family of, 40; on freedom, 293, 448, 450–51; on God as Creator, 447–48, 450–51; on Heidegger, 352, 353; on Husserl, 502; on Jesus Christ, 451; on myth, 290, 448; on myth of creation, 285; native town of, 40; on number, 59; ontology of, 289, 293; on the person, 24; political views, 43, 45, 53, 117; remembrance of, 556, 559, 567, 575; on resurrection, 290; on salvation, 448; on scientific thought, 59; on sophiology, 320, 371; and St. Sergius Institute, 98; on technology, 74; during World War II, 522
Lossky, Nikolai, works of: articles in *The Way*, 19, 64, 74, 201, 289–90, 357, 424, 426, 447–48, 450–51, 502, 505–6, 546; "The Culture of Technology and the Christian Ideal," 74; *The Freedom of the Will*, 69; *History of Russian Philosophy*, 526, 546; "Magic and the Christian Cult," 290; "Mythical Thought and Contemporary Scientific Thought," 58–59; "Of the Creation of the World by God," 450–51; "On the Resurrection of the Body," 290; *Value and Existence*, 293; "The Visions of Saints and Mystics," 290, 357; "Vladimir Solovyov and His Successors in Russian Religious Philosophy," 64; *The Ways of Apprehending the World*, 293
Lossky, Vladimir, 232, 347, 385, 389, 392–93, 394, 400, 522, 524, 575; on Bulgakov, 371, 382, 387, 393, 471, 544, 545, 564; *Dogmatic Theology*, 538; influence of, 473–74, 535, 545; *Mystical Experience of the Eastern Church*,

538; neo-Byzantinism of, 32, 163, 472, 530, 543, 563; remembrance of, 530, 535, 538, 543, 544, 552, 553, 557, 559, 563, 565, 573; *Sept jour sur les routes de France*, 560; on sophiology, 131, 371, 382, 384, 387, 544; *Spor o Sofii (The Dispute about Sophia)*, 387, 540
Lot-Borodin, Myrrha, 150, 330, 333, 347, 428, 439, 521, 522, 529; articles in *The Way*, 198, 278, 286, 341, 424, 426, 432–33, 439; on Congar, 513; on Kartashev, 429, 432–33; on Orthodox Church, 432–33, 471; remembrance of, 543, 544; on spirituality, 285, 432–33
Lot, Ferdinand, 21, 330
Lotman, Yuri, 548
Loubet del Bayle, Jean-Louis, 190
Louis, St., 157
Louis XIV, 157
love, 63, 69, 70, 85, 116, 124–25, 467; of God, 298–99, 305; for God, 309; Khomiakov on, 81–82; myth of love-passion, 503–4; of neighbor, 425
Lovtzki, 438
Lowrie, Donald, 21, 92, 99, 210, 213, 333
Lubac, Henri de, 343, 346, 496, 574
Lukianov, Sergei, 78
Luppol, I. K., 255
Lustiger, Jean-Marie Cardinal, 578
Luther, Martin, 59, 78, 80, 119, 314, 461, 501, 502

Macarius of Optina, Elder, 275–76
Macarius the Great, St., 61–62, 74
MacNaughten, Edgar, 92, 97, 208, 213, 344, 345
Madaule, Jacques, 190, 504, 528
Maistre, Joseph de, 144

Makarii (Bulgakov), Metropolitan: *Dogmatic Theology*, 51
Malakhov, Vladimir, 548
Malebranche, Nicolas, 28
Malraux, André, 187, 325, 328, 491, 493
Mamardashvili, Merab, 548, 549, 566
Manciarli, Irina de, 165
Mandelshtam, N., 555
Man, Henri de, 405, 476, 499
Manicheism, 78, 459, 504, 506, 507, 517
Mann, H., 490
Mann, Thomas, 337
Manziarli, I. de, 337
Marcadé, Jean-Claude, 556
Marc, Alexandre, 329, 495
Marcel, Gabriel, 164, 329, 330, 332, 336, 498, 504, 505, 527, 552
Marchadier, B., 561
Marcinkovsky, V. F., 92, 101, 175
Marcion, 448
Marie-Angelique, St., 153
Marion, Jean-Luc, 572–73
Maritain, Jacques, 19, 24, 140, 150, 155, 187, 191, 329, 348, 412, 492; on Boehme, 331; *Degrees of Knowledge*, 335; on faith, 148; *Humanisme intégral*, 327, 494, 509; "Metaphysics and Mysticism," 148; on Orthodoxy and Catholicism, 156–57; *Primauté du spiritual*, 156–57; *Questions de conscience*, 509; on racism, 496; relationship with Berdyaev, 146–49, 156–57, 163–64, 330, 331, 333, 494, 520; on salvation, 332; *Le Songe de Descartes*, 355; on the *Ungrund*, 331
Maritain, Raïssa, 332
Maritain, Vera, 332
Mark: 9:23, 463; 12:29, 461

Mark of Ephesus, St., 62
Markov II, 115
Markov, N., 104, 132
marriage, 124–25
Marrou, H. I., 35
Martin du Gard, Roger, 328, 495
Martin, V., 170, 173
Marxism, 5, 12, 23, 41, 53, 221–22, 255, 324, 392, 549, 554; Berdyaev on, 135, 136, 256–57, 259, 262, 308, 475, 476, 493–94, 495, 527
Marx, Karl, 70, 250, 302, 520; vs. Fedorov, 135, 136–37; influence of, 12, 41, 493–94; *Das Kapital*, 12, 41; on mercantile fetishism, 404; on society, 255; on the state, 53
Mary, Mother of God/Blessed Virgin, 152, 166–67, 180, 183, 300, 309, 344, 391, 422–23, 431, 433, 480, 514, 566, 578; Bulgakov on, 79–80, 173–74, 458
Massignon, Louis, 164
Massis, Henri, 146, 147, 149, 154–55, 165, 186, 187
materialism, 42, 255, 256, 257
Matsuguchi, Harumi, 213, 551
Matteo, A., 222
Matthew: 25:46, 393; 28:18, 316
Matzneff, Gabriel, 557
Maupassant, Guy de, 165–66
Mauriac, François, 195, 330, 333, 495, 521
Maurois, A., 328
Maurras, Charles, 146, 155, 157, 439, 491
Maury, Pastor Pierre, 150, 372, 510
Maxence, Jean-Pierre, 165, 166, 186, 187, 190
Maxim the Greek, 15, 537
Maximus the Confessor, 27, 288, 342, 433
Mechev, Fr. Alexei, 43

Melia, Elias, 314, 410
Melih, J., 550
memory: of Byzantium, 437–41; of City of Kitezh, 429, 441–44; development in France, 551–69; and historical truth, 1, 14; of Holy Russia, 57, 430–37; the intellectual as locus of, 15–16; and nonconformism, 201, 275–82; Nora on, 4, 6, 14, 15; as repetitious, 547; Ricoeur on, 14, 17, 535; *The Way* as locus of, 4–11, 12, 18, 530–69
Menasce, Jean de, 330
Men, Fr. Alexander, 532, 536–37, 538, 541, 580
Menn, W., 339
Menshikov, Yakov, 198, 204, 278
Mensikova, E., 227
Mercier, Désiré Cardinal, 144, 162, 181
Mercule de France, Le, 336
Merezhkovsky, Dmitrii, 47, 50, 96, 129, 154, 278, 523, 530, 532, 546
Merleau-Ponty, M., 527
Mersch, Fr. Emile, 341–42, 346
Merton, Thomas, 572
metempsychosis, 194, 455
Methodius, St., 433
methodology, 1, 11–17
Meyendorff, Fr. John, 529, 538, 539, 545, 552, 563
Meyer, A., 45
Meyerson, Isaac, 335
MGUIMO (Moscow State University), 542
Michels, Fr. Thomas, 145
Micou, Paul, 97
Mikhalkov, Nikita, 535, 579; *Anna 6–18*, 534; *The Barber of Siberia*, 534; *Burnt by the Sun*, 534; *Our Home Is Russia*, 534; *Urga (Close to Eden)*, 534
Mikhailovsky, N., 41

Milbank, John, 572, 574–75
Miliukov, Pavel, 80, 94, 463
Miliutina, V., 557
Miller, Yevgeny (E.), 126, 407, 408
Ministry and Sacraments, The, 479
Minkowski, Eugène, 505, 527
Miroglio, Abel, 140, 150, 156
Miroglio, André, 501
Mirsky, D., 118, 133, 328
Mladoross Party, 402
Mnuhin, L., 561
Moberly, R. C., 366
Mochulsky, K., 186, 198, 199, 214, 223, 278, 332, 347, 403, 407, 412, 417, 419, 424, 426, 496, 500, 520, 522, 526, 550; articles in *The Way*, 350, 423, 497, 503–4; on Bergson, 350; ecumenical activities, 500; on Rougement, 503–4; on Solovyov, 442–43
modernism, 10, 147, 157–58, 163, 184, 185, 207, 244, 281, 328, 539–41, 568; anthropocentric reflection in, 73–76, 81, 86; cosmologic reflection in, 73, 76–81, 86; ecclesiological reflection in, 73, 81–87; hesychastic spirituality in, 61–63; as independence from forms of power, 37, 51; and marriage, 124–25; modernist identity of contributors to *The Way*, 16–17, 34, 35–39, 47, 51, 87–88, 114–15, 137, 140, 141, 200–201, 218, 245, 248–49, 275, 281, 300, 311, 347, 366, 380; and social justice, 37; and universality, 37
Moehler, Johann, 83, 484–85
Moeller, Charles, 513
Moghila, Petro, 438; *The Orthodox Confession*, 159, 160
Molchanov, V., 548
monarchianism, 49

monarchists, 87, 118, 119, 123, 125, 127–28, 132, 138, 144, 153–58, 199, 201, 203, 247; as contributors to *The Way*, 53, 104–8, 117, 126, 201, 532–33; High Monarchist Council, 104, 115; National Committee of Monarchists, 94; and *New Time*, 102; in RSCM, 100, 126
Monde, 324, 326
Mongin, Olivier, 566–67
Monnier, Prof., 150
Monod, Wilfred, 150, 151, 173, 175, 476, 509
monophysitism, 106–7, 304, 312–13, 397, 431
Montaigne, Michel de, 376
Montherlant, Henri de, 500
Morand, Paul, 154
Moré, Marcel, 505, 520, 524
Morozov, A., 210
Morozova, Margarita, 18, 96
Morozov, I., 410
Morton, M., 509
Moscow Library of Foreign Literature, 3
Moscow Observer, 17–18
Moscow Weekly, 41
Moses, 459, 461
Moskva, 3, 532
Mother Earth, 295–96, 433
Mother Maria. *See* Skobtsova, Mother Maria
Motroshilova, N., 550
Mott, John, 21, 92, 93, 95, 97, 98, 169, 207, 208, 210–11, 348, 513, 515, 529, 572, 579
Motu proprio Orientalis catholici, 142
Mounier, Emmanuel, 22, 164, 191, 206, 335, 405, 520, 529; Berdyaev, 529; and *Esprit*, 2, 190, 326–37, 329, 420, 426, 477–78, 491, 492, 496; on racism, 496; *Révolution personnaliste et communautaire*, 404, 476–77

Mt. Athos, 44, 241, 246, 304, 396
Mudyugin, Archimandrite M., 538
Müller, Ludwig, 339
Munich Pact, 492, 498
Museum of the Russian Emigration, 3
Musset, Alfred, 197
Mussolini, Benito, 255, 383, 492
Mystery of God-with-us (Emmanuel), 285–96
mytho-logic thought, 23, 39, 58–73, 136–37, 138, 205, 266, 274, 290, 320, 500, 564, 565, 568, 572–74; anthropocentric/personalist current in, 86, 282, 296–308, 380, 381, 429, 430, 452–55, 458, 465, 566; antinomy, 32, 34, 65–67, 70, 71, 77, 188, 206, 216, 263, 276, 282, 283, 300–301, 305, 306, 315, 318–19, 321–22, 332, 351, 356, 360, 363, 369, 376, 377, 397, 426, 430, 431, 444–58; Berdyaev on, 24, 29–31, 59–60, 66–67, 77, 298, 301, 306–7, 475–76, 496; Bulgakov on, 24, 42, 47–48, 310, 316; Clément on, 9; creation and evil in, 67–70; defined, 572; and ecclesiology, 482–90; eschatology in, 70–73; Frank on, 30, 71; genealogy of, 24–32; idealist mytho-logy, 25, 28–29; vs. logical thought, 25–26, 29–30, 65–66; and nationalism, 269; Neoplatonic current in, 86; patristic mytho-logy, 25–28; and racism, 496–97; sophiocentric current in, 86, 282, 308–22, 380, 381, 429, 430, 455–58, 465; symbolist mytho-logy, 25, 29–32, 47; theocentric current in, 282, 380, 381, 426, 429, 430, 437, 440, 444–52, 458, 465, 575
myths, 188, 194, 195–96, 447, 502; chosen race, 271; creation, 285, 289; the émigré religious intelligentsia, 5–6, 14; the Fall, 35, 67–68, 80, 445, 452; Gaia and the Great Mother, 42; golden age in France, 33–34; Heavenly Man, 298, 301; Holy Grail, 277, 324; Japanese creation mythology, 277; Kingdom of God, 38, 72, 391; Knights of the Round Table, 277; Nikolai Lossky on, 290, 448; love-passion, 503–4; man as image of God, 254, 290; Moscow as Third Rome, 183, 430, 432, 442, 580; mythology defined, 24, 25; the *Parousia*, 35, 72, 76; Schelling on, 24, 28–29, 59; Sophia, 298, 300; sorcerer's apprentice, 499–500; the uninterrupted tradition, 545–47; the West, 87, 138, 141, 143–49

Nachala, 547
Nalimov, Fr. O., 19, 42
National-Bolsheviks, 121
nationalism, 228, 229, 245, 260–61, 265–74, 339, 382, 383, 384, 406, 415–16, 429, 433, 471, 478, 491; Berdyaev on, 266–67, 269–72, 407, 411–12; Bulgakov on, 266, 269, 272, 273–74, 436; Kartashev on, 272–73
National Union of Work of the New Generation (NTS), 226
Natorp, Paul, 40
Nectary of Bukovina, Metropolitan, 359
Nemtsov, Boris, 534–35
neo-Byzantinism, 11, 25, 47, 159–61, 358, 400, 432, 435, 437–41, 471–73, 482, 483, 512, 529, 554, 567; of Florovsky, 32, 86, 160–61, 330, 471, 472, 473, 513, 515, 530, 543, 563; of Lossky, 32, 163, 472, 530, 543, 563
Neoplatonism, 64–65, 85, 86, 379, 439

Nesmelov, V., 36, 37, 203, 275, 301, 392, 404
Nestorianism, 313, 390, 391, 399, 431
Nethercott, Frances, 561
Neumann, Therese, 341
Neveu, Bishop, 230
New City (Novy Grad), 199–200, 223, 251–54, 255, 262–63, 269, 272, 273, 329, 376–78, 418–19, 426, 510; and Fedotov, 192, 200, 252–53, 376, 381, 406
New Economic Policy (NEP), 51, 120
New Jerusalem, 474, 490
Newman, John Henry, 180, 373
New Order, 477
New Time, 102
New Way, 41, 96
New World, 18
NG-Religiya, 542
Nicholas (Krutitsky), Metropolitan, 402
Nicholas I, 581
Nicholas II, 39, 535, 579
Nicolas of Cusa, 31, 64, 69, 292, 346
Nicolescu, Basarab: *Nous, la particule et le monde*, 575
Niebuhr, Reinhold, 476
Nietzsche, Friedrich, 191, 267, 302, 524, 527, 572; on doubt, 28; influence of, 5, 22, 23, 41, 466, 493–94, 567; on master vs. slave morality, 501; *Zarathustra*, 410–11
Nikitin, A., 44, 93, 99, 209, 210, 226, 227, 228, 416
Nikitin, Valentin, 538
Nikolai, Baron Paul, 92
Nil of Sora, St., 62, 119, 133, 219, 220, 237, 238, 240, 242, 243, 294, 411, 443
Nissiotis, N. A., 225
Nivat, Georges, 543, 551, 561; on Russian emigration, 6; on the Russian myth, 139

Nizan, Paul, 328
NLO, 548
non-Chalcedonian churches, 554, 577
nonconformism, 189–200, 265, 337, 339, 346, 370, 491, 543; and memory, 201, 275–82; *The Way* as nonconformist, 17, 206, 247, 260, 274, 275–82, 306, 320, 375, 430, 508, 582
Nonjurors, 179–80
Nora, Pierre: on intellectuals, 15; on memory, 4, 6, 14, 15, 568
Notbuch der Russischen Christenheit, Der, 235
Notes on the Russian and Soviet World, 556
Nouvelle Revue Française, La, 190, 325, 336
Novaia Rossiia (New Russia), 406, 409, 412
Novgorodtsev, Pavel, 19, 40, 41, 42, 51, 93, 97, 550; political views, 43, 53, 55
Novikov, Nikolai, 77
Novy Mir, 532

Oblomov, Ilya, 257
Obolensky, A. P., 2
Occidentalists, 438
Oecumenica, 400
Ogorodnikov, A., 546, 555
Ogurtsov, I., 555
Oldam, 346
Old Believers, 219–20, 240, 242, 431, 438, 441, 489
Oldenbourg, Zoé, 139, 419
Ollard, S. L., 19, 179
onomatodox monks, 46
On the Roads, 56
Options pour demain, 509
Ordre nouveau, L', 190, 329
Orientalia Christiana, 143, 146
Orient und Occident, 177, 337–38

Origen, 302, 538
original sin, 67–68, 125, 281, 306–7, 318, 332, 352, 391, 504
Orthodox Action, 410, 415, 420, 421, 521–22, 579; and Berdyaev, 416, 417, 424, 497; and Fedotov, 424–25, 426; and Mother Maria, 416, 417–19, 423–24, 425, 426, 526, 541
Orthodox Church in France, 473, 552, 553, 562, 567–68
Orthodox Community, The, 537
Orthodox Thought, 123
Orwell's *1984*, 234
O. Spengler and the Decline of Europe, 41
Ossorgina, Rachel, 212
Ossorgin, Mikhail, 98, 99
Otsup N., 165
Otto, Rudolph, 21, 63, 292, 354
Otto, W., 33
Oultremont, Thierry d', 372
Oxford Movement, 180

Pages from the St. Sergius Institute, 124
Paisius Velichkovsky, St., 61
Palestine, 337
Pallière, A., 496
Palmer, William, 180, 367, 440, 488
Panfoeder, Chrysostom, 75–76
Pange, Count Jean de, 164, 186, 187–88, 330–31, 332
Parain, Brice, 324, 496
Pares, Bernard, 343
Pascal, Blaise, 24, 336
Pascal, Pierre, 332, 464, 508, 556; on *The Way*, 1, 203–4
Patriarchate of Constantinople, 119, 168, 242, 246, 367, 394, 558, 578; Athenagoras I, 344, 516, 533, 572, 579; Basil III, 115, 219; Photius II, 231–32, 386
Paulhan, Jean, 325, 336, 500, 527

Paul, St., 132, 577, 583; on body as temple of the Holy Spirit, 475; on folly and wisdom, 501; on gift of government, 393; on the law, 461; on letter vs. Spirit, 396; on manifold wisdom of God, 272; on unity, 64; on Wisdom of God, 388; on working and eating, 257
Paul VI, 553
Pavlov, Fr. I., 538
Pechorin, V., 276
Péguy, Charles, 37, 151, 165, 186, 187–88, 191, 329, 373, 494
Péguy, Marcel, 232, 337
Pentecost, 274, 286, 365, 368, 369, 397, 480
Peresneva, C., 210
perichoresis, 399
personalism, 11, 69, 429, 482–83, 487–88, 549, 575; of Berdyaev, 23, 24, 31, 86, 191–92, 262, 266, 296–97, 300–303, 308, 323, 329, 330, 355–56, 361, 365, 404–5, 414, 430, 443, 448, 452–55, 466, 471, 473, 474–78, 494, 557, 564, 566, 567, 568; Bulgakov on, 388, 436–37, 511
Peter (Krutitsky), Metropolitan, 116, 386
Peter, St., 577, 583
Peter the Great, 437, 580
Petit, Edouard, 21
Petrashevsky Circle, 52
Petrov, A., 104–5, 106
Pflegler, K., 341
phenomenology, 58, 60–61, 63, 307–8, 348, 349–52, 356, 502, 504, 548–49, 550. *See also* Heidegger, Martin; Husserl, Edmund
Philaret (Drozdov), St., 24, 411
Philaret of Moscow, Metropolitan, 135, 139, 438

Philip, André, 191, 266–67, 328, 340, 405, 476, 508, 509, 528
Philip le Bel, 157
Philippians, 179; 3:21, 317
Philip, St., Metropolitan of Moscow, 242, 537
Philokalia, 62, 123, 160, 239, 275–76, 304
philosophers' boats, 5, 12, 51
Philotheus of Pskov, 258, 432
Photius II, Patriarch of Constantinople, 231–32, 386
Photius of Alexandria, Patriarch, 180, 181
Pianov, Fedor, 2, 93–94, 210, 212, 213, 228, 416, 417, 423, 520, 522; arrest of, 521; political views, 229
Pickstock, Catherine, 574
Piotrovsky, 520
Pirogov, N. I., 275, 276, 292
Pisarev, Dmitri, 44
Pius X, 149
Pius XI, 19, 142, 156, 164, 230–31, 340, 483, 484; Action Française condemned by, 153, 154; and ecumenism, 144, 158–59, 162, 163; *Mortalium animos*, 158–59, 162, 163; on racism, 496, 497
Pius XII, 383, 412
Plans, 190, 329
Planty-Bonjour, Guy, 556
Plato, 65, 69, 147–48, 297, 392, 457; on Eros, 288
Plekhanov, Georgii, 15
Pletnev, Rostislav, 19, 198, 204, 424
Plevitskaya, Nadezhda, 408
Pliuhanov, B., 557
Plon publishing house, 151
Plotinus, 64, 65, 296, 392
Plotnikov, N. S., 452
Plyukhanov, B., 221
Pobedonostsev, Konstantin, 80
Podoroga, V., 548, 549
Pogodin, A., 102–3, 122
Poincaré, Raymond, 34, 121
Poliakov, F., 3
political philosophy, 73, 199–200
Polotebneva, Anastasia, 19, 198, 340, 424; "An Essay on an Ethical and Religious Conception of Nature," 254–55
Poltoratsky, N., 524, 528
Polyakov, F., 551
Pompilj, Basilio Cardinal, 230
Popkov, V., 555
Poplavsky, Boris, 165, 186, 197, 259, 278–79
Pordage, John, 300, 320
Poresh, V., 546
Porret, Eugène, 333, 509, 529
Portal, Fernand, 144
Portal, M., 156
positivism, 41, 49, 145, 350
Pospelovsky, Dimitrii, 538, 564
postmodernism, 574
Pouget, M., 156
Pozner, Vladimir, 325
prayer of the heart, 44, 61–63
predestination, 279–80, 305, 311, 319
presenting the icon to the West, 99, 220
Presse, Fr. Alexis, 372
"Priest of Petrograd, The," 279
principle of symphony, 244
Problems of Idealism, 41, 96
Problems of Life, 41
Problems of Philosophy, 7–8
Problems of the Russian Religious Conscience, 93, 96–97
Prokofiev, P., 276
Pronevitch, G., 347
Pro Russia Commission, 340, 505
Prost, Antoine: on factual proof vs. systematic proof, 13; on historical methods, 13; on methodology of history, 13

Protestant Federation of France, 338, 420
Protestantism, 12, 19, 20, 82, 101, 123, 183, 230, 244, 266–67, 272–73, 368, 370, 479, 512, 527; Berdyaev on, 107, 361, 483; Bulgakov on, 455, 480, 481; and ecumenism, 140, 141, 149–50, 153, 158, 162, 168–81, 182, 218, 330, 337–40, 407, 488, 508, 509–10, 513–16, 554, 576, 577; Florovsky on, 359, 511; in Germany, 268–69, 348, 353; Reformation, 32, 119, 168, 285, 286, 314, 354, 359, 481
Protocols of the Elders of Zion, 102–3
Proudhon, Pierre-Joseph, 191, 329, 477
Proust, Marcel, 22, 335
Prov. 8:30–31, 309
Proyart, J. de, 561
Psherov conference, 213, 220
Pshivara, E., 349
publicistics (*publitsistika*), 18, 75, 76
Pundik, Vera, 199, 212
Pushkin, Alexander, 39, 166, 276, 292, 408; *Boris Godunov*, 263
Pushkin in Russian Philosophical Criticism, 535–36
Putin, Vladimir, 579–80, 581

Quakerism, 481
Questions of Philosophy and Psychology, 41

Racine, Nicole, 17
Radical Orthodoxy, 574
Radio Liberty, 555
Radl, E., 349
Radonezh Society, 539, 540, 541
Raeff, Marc, 551; *Russia Abroad*, 2–3; on Russian emigration, 2–3, 8–9; on *The Way*, 1, 2–3, 8–9; on *Vestnik RSKhD*, 222

Raevsky, G., 419
Ragaz, L., 262, 267, 404, 405, 476, 527
Raiser, Konrad, 559
Ram, Rolla, 372
Rapp, Evgenia, 212, 529
Rasheev, D., 198
Rastorguev, V., 123, 198, 221–22
Rawls, John, 566
Réaction, 190
reason, 154, 155, 175, 191, 299, 308, 500; Berdyaev on, 31, 65, 308, 354; and faith, 188, 275, 282, 284–85, 354, 445–47, 501, 565–66, 573; Fedotov on, 295, 379; Shestov on, 445–46, 459, 464, 468, 501, 502, 503
Rebatet, Lucien, 491
Reimers, Nikolai A., 20, 197, 254–55; *The Aesthetic Principle in History*, 254; "Freedom and Equality," 254
Religious-Philosophical Society, 41
Relton, Herbert Maurice, 346
Remizov, Aleksey, 40, 42, 43, 51, 57, 75, 214
Rémond, René, 153
Renaissance (*Vozrozhdenie*), 94, 104, 105, 106, 111, 117, 230, 247, 402–4, 409, 464
Renouvier, Charles, 446
repentance, 295, 305, 323
Research Group on the Russian Immigration (GRER), 560–61
Revault d'Allonnes-Psichari, Jean, 373
Revel, Jacques, 13
Revue de philosophie et des religions, 24
Revue des Jeunes, 156
Revue Française, 190
Revue philosophique de la France et de l'Etranger, 336, 501
Reynaud, Paul, 492
Riccardi, Andrea, 572
Richir, M.: on mythological thought, 30

Ricoeur, Paul, 11, 572; on Cartesian *Cogito*, 28; on historical truth, 13, 14; "The Mark of the Past," 13; *La Mémoire*, 573; on memory, 14, 17, 535, 573; *Oneself as Another*, 549; *Thinking Biblically*, 565
Rilke, Rainer Maria, 538
Rimbaud, Arthur, 5
Riquet, Fr. Michel, 327
Rivet, Paul, 499
Rivière, J., 336
Robbers' Council, 312
Robertson, Rev., 182
Rockefeller, John, 579
ROCOR. *See* Russian Orthodox Church Outside Russia
Rocque, Colonel de la, 228
Roditi, Georges, 191
Rodnyanskaya, I., 545
Rolland, Romain, 155, 476, 490, 494
Romance of Tristan and Isolde, The, 504
Romanian Orthodox Church, 225
Romans, 127; 5:12, 293; 5:20, 461; 12:5, 487; Barth's *Römerbrief*, 169–70, 269
Rosenberg, Alfred: *The Myth of the Twentieth Century*, 436
Rosenzweig, Franz, 356, 497
Rostovtsev, M., 344
Rouault, Georges, 195
Rougemont, Denis de, 190, 191, 495; *Love in the Western World*, 503–4
Rougemont, Jean de, 333
Rougier, Louis, 146, 500
Rouleau, Fr. F., 561
Rouse, Ruth, 92, 99
Rousseau, Jean-Jacques, 577
Rousselot, Fr. Pierre, 149
Routskoy, Alexander, 531
Roux, Fr. Octave de, 327
Rozanov, Vasily, 36, 66, 124, 125, 196, 284, 286, 302, 385, 536, 546

RSCM. *See* Russian Student Christian Movement
Rudnev, Vadim, 242–43, 463; "Religion and Socialism," 243
Rueff, Jacques, 191
Runestam, A., 339
Rus' Derchavniy, 539
Rus' of Kiev, 580–81
Russia: famine of 1922, 143; interest in *The Way* in, 1, 2, 3–5, 6, 7–9, 10–11, 199
Russia and Slavism, 127
Russian Academic Group, 2
Russian Christian Institute for the Humanities, 537, 546
Russian civil war, 19, 51, 53
Russian Eros or the Philosophy of Love in Russia, The, 546
Russian General Military Union (ROVS), 406, 407–8
Russian national identity, 37–38, 428–37, 532; as Holy Russia, 57–58, 430–37
Russian Orthodox Church, 16, 20, 43–50, 61, 154, 244–47, 272, 579, 580–81; Council of the Russian Church (1917–18), 50, 83, 89, 90, 92, 98, 140, 389; and ecumenism, 168–69, 175, 177–81; as Living Church, 37–38, 89–91, 106, 127, 142, 540; relations with Soviet government, 88–91, 108–9, 110, 116, 117, 120–21, 126, 134, 230, 231–33, 236, 243–44; and waning of Russian emigration, 563–64, 581–82. *See also* Sergius (Stragorodsky), Metropolitan
Russian Orthodox Church Outside Russia (ROCOR), 80, 127, 203, 208, 226, 233, 236, 241, 243, 415, 521, 535, 544, 578; Bulgakov attacked by, 310, 386, 389, 395, 419–20, 540; relations with

Russian Orthodox Church Outside Russia (ROCOR) (*cont.*) RSCM, 102, 111–13, 209; relations with YMCA, 100, 101–4, 110, 111, 209; schism of 1927, 87, 88, 110–25, 132, 137–38, 140, 141, 173, 183, 207, 225, 247; Synod of Karlovtsy, 89, 90, 91, 101, 113–14, 116, 140, 154, 207, 225, 386, 390, 399, 539. *See also* Anthony (Khrapovitsky), Metropolitan; Evlogy, Metropolitan

Russian Philosophy of Property, 550

Russian religious thought: definitions of, 1, 22–24, 275

Russian Student Christian Movement (RSCM), 16, 21, 35–36, 44, 95, 115, 116, 125–26, 199, 207, 217, 220–26, 231, 338, 375, 387, 407, 415, 419–22, 423, 521; and Berdyaev, 99, 100, 109, 112, 126, 130–31, 202, 221, 224, 225–26, 229, 416–17; Boissy conference, 228; and Bulgakov, 99, 100, 112, 202, 218, 226–27, 540; Chantilly conference, 210–12, 216–17, 218, 220, 225–26; and Chetverikov, 122–23, 202, 305, 416, 420, 421–22; and ecumenism, 101, 171, 182, 184, 208, 218, 224–25, 515; and Metropolitan Evlogy, 236; and Fedorov, 226, 228, 415, 416; founding of, 99–101; and Kartashev, 99, 100; *Messenger*, 100, 131, 184, 209, 210, 222, 225–26, 236, 413, 420, 421, 539, 540, 541, 555, 557; Montfort l'Amaury conference, 224; and Mother Maria, 222, 223, 224, 227, 416, 420, 421–22; neo-traditionalists in, 122, 209–10, 225; and persecution of Christians in Russia, 108–9; relations with ROCOR, 102–4, 111–13; relations with YMCA, 92, 99, 100, 109, 110, 208, 209–11, 416, 417, 579; right-wing and left-wing factions in, 226, 227–28, 229; after World War II, 530, 533, 540, 551–52, 554–55, 557; and Zander, 420–21, 521; and Zenkovsky, 99, 100–101, 112, 126, 221, 225–26, 227, 416, 420, 521

"Russian Theologians and Church Historians of the Emigration," 4

Russian Thought, 41, 43, 540, 543, 552, 555, 558

Russie et Chrétienté, 506, 512

Russie et le latinisme, 143

Ryklin, M., 548

"S." (Stepun?), 267, 351, 353, 354

Sabev, Todor, 559

Saint-Simon, Henri de, 53

Sakharov, Alexander, 533

Salter, Sir Arthur, 508

Saltykov, Alexander, 194, 278

salvation, 74, 102, 280, 281, 287–88, 290, 320, 332, 422, 429, 448, 459, 510, 514; Jesus as Savior, 298, 303, 305, 392, 462, 485, 489; Metropolitan Sergius on, 390, 393, 399–400

Sangnier, Marc, 37, 157

Sankara, 63

Sarafanov, Nikolai, 198, 243

Sarov, A., 542

Sarraute, Nathalie: *Tropismes*, 499

Sartre, Jean-Paul, 15, 499, 524, 527, 529

Satan, 320

Saveliev, S. N., 545

Savitzky, Piotr, 19, 41, 51, 56, 57, 94, 133, 134, 137, 143, 533

Sazonova, Julia, 19, 153, 165–66, 185, 201, 426; on Soviet literature, 234, 324–25

"Sazonovich, P.," 402–3
Scheler, Max, 60, 71, 94, 264, 301, 336, 352, 353, 404
Schelling, Friedrich Wilhelm Joseph, 49, 283, 284, 460, 520; influence of, 24, 28–29, 297, 466; on myth, 24, 28–29, 59; *The Philosophy of Revelation*, 276
Scherrer, Jutta, 15, 556
Schiffrin, Jules, 336
Schjelderup, K., 357
Schleiermacher, Friedrich, 573
Schloezer, Boris de, 214, 336, 496, 500, 527, 557
Schipflinger, T., 551
Schlumberger, Jean, 328, 498, 520
Schmemann, Alexander, 21, 314, 472, 529, 537, 538, 540, 541, 552, 554, 555, 582
Schmidhauser, J., 214, 267
Scholasticism, 501
Schopenhauer, Arthur, 319
Schor, Ralph, 139
Schumann, F. K., 353
Schütz, Paul, 176, 354
Schutz, Roger, 508
Schwartz, H., 292
Schwob, René, 326
Sebastien, Robert, 165, 186
Sebrikov, G., 212
Sedakova, Olga, 550
Segundo, Jean-Louis, 553
self, the, 16, 48, 63
Semionov (*Renaissance*), 409
Semeur, Le, 24, 94, 338
Seneca, 283
Senokosov, Yuri, 548
separation of church and state, 243–44, 246–47
Sept, 491, 495
Seraphim, Metropolitan, 401–2
Seraphim of Finland, Archbishop, 116

Seraphim of Lubny, Bishop, 113–14
Seraphim of Sarov, St., 61, 63, 291, 421
Serbian Brotherhood, 12
Serbian Orthodox Church, 245
Serezhnikov, K., 197
Serge, Victor, 491
Sergius (Stragorodsky), Metropolitan, 90–91, 113, 115, 124, 137, 138, 218, 229, 233, 237, 245, 383; on absence of religious persecution in USSR, 234, 236; on incarnation, 390; on loyalty to the Soviet state, 108, 110, 116, 117, 132, 133, 134, 230–32, 236, 240, 242; on Nazism, 521–22; relationship with Metropolitan Evlogy, 207, 208, 225, 230, 231, 232, 236, 238, 239–40, 401, 558; on salvation, 390, 393, 399–400; on sophiology, 384, 385–86, 389–90, 391–92, 396, 400, 540; *The Orthodox Doctrine of Salvation*, 102; on the Trinity, 400
Sergius of Prague, Bishop, 108
Sergius of Radonezh, St., 61, 79, 124, 134, 184, 220, 242, 435, 554
Serikov, G., 227
Serkievskie Listki, 217
Sertillanges, Fr., 156
Sesboüé, Fr. Bernard, 578
Setnitsky, N., 72–73, 135, 136
Sezeman, Vasilii, 19, 40, 41, 42, 51, 57, 212; on Heidegger, 61, 351–52
Shakhovskoy, D. A. *See* Ioann (D. A. Shakhovskoy)
Shalamov, V., 555
Shargunov, Fr. A., 538, 539
Sharshun, S., 186
Shatov, Fr. Arkady, 539, 540
Shedrovitsky, G., 548
Sheptytsky, Andrei, 21

Shestov, Lev, 12, 47, 94, 202, 203, 281, 291, 292, 294, 309, 322, 324, 328, 330, 332, 349, 350, 351, 354, 403, 429, 430, 450, 499, 500, 575; on Being and consciousness, 31; on Berdyaev, 459–62, 464; on Buber, 356; on Bulgakov, 464; death of, 424; and epistemology, 22; on evil, 444, 445–47, 460–61, 466–67; existentialism of, 23, 284, 467, 502–3; on faith, 24, 196, 284–85, 287, 445, 446, 447, 459, 462, 467; on the Fall, 67–68; on freedom, 451–52, 501; on Genesis, 445; on Gilson, 501–2; on God and Being, 320; on God as all-powerful, 444, 459, 466, 468, 469; on God as Creator, 446, 468; on Hegel, 284, 285; on Husserl, 502; influence of, 346, 500–501, 545; intellectual predecessors of, 24; on Jaspers, 468, 502–3; on Jesus Christ, 446, 461; as Jew, 24, 154, 198, 437–38, 459; on Kierkegaard, 284, 325, 346, 458–59, 461, 468, 503; vs. Lévinas, 565; on Lévy-Bruhl, 31; on Maritain, 355; on Moses and the law, 461; on mytho-logy, 24; on Nietzsche, 501; ontology of, 282–83, 296, 302, 467; on original sin, 67–68; on the past, 284, 468–69; political views, 247; on principle of contradiction, 446, 447; on problem of evil, 68, 296; on reason, 445–46, 459, 464, 468, 501, 502, 503; relations with French intellectuals, 335–37; remembrance of, 545, 548, 549, 550, 551, 552, 556, 557, 560, 561, 565, 567, 582; on Rozanov, 284–85; on salvation, 459; on sin, 285, 289, 445, 457; on Tolstoy, 445–46; on truth, 501, 502

Shestov, Lev, works of: articles in *The Way*, 2, 24, 196, 198, 201, 214, 284, 337, 356, 424, 458, 468, 502–3; *Athènes et Jérusalem*, 447, 462, 500–501, 549; "Athens and Jerusalem," 196; *In Job's Balances*, 67, 283–84; "Kierkegaard and Dostoevsky," 214; *Kierkegaard and Existential Philosophy*, 500, 565; "Myth and Truth," 502; "Nicolas Berdyaev, Gnosis and Existential Philosophy," 459–62; *The Night of Gethsemane*, 337; "Parmenides Enchained," 196; "The Second Dimension of Thought," 196; "*Sine effusione sanguinis*," 503; "The Theological and Philosopical Ideas of Kierkegaard," 214; "Yasnaya Polyana and Astapovo," 445–46
Shidlovsky-Koulomzina, Sophie, 210, 225
Shirinsky-Shikhmatov, Prince Yuri, 121, 137
Shmelev, Ivan: "The Sun of the Dead," 20; on *The Way*, 20
Shpet, Gustav, 549
Shvarts, M. N., 424
Sigov, Konstantin, 549
Sillon, Le, 37
Silver Age, 18, 25, 39–50, 99, 140, 169, 193, 205, 278–79, 547, 548
Simeon the New Theologian, St., 24, 62, 159, 160–61
Simeon the Stylite, St., 152
Simmel, Georg, 40
Simvol, 558–59
Sirenelli, Jean-François, 15–16
Skoblin, Nicolas, 407–8
Skobtsova, Elizabeth, 76
Skobtsova, Mother Maria, 16, 42, 44, 199, 200, 203, 210, 212, 213, 221, 228, 279, 347, 408, 427, 439, 496,

497, 498, 579; arrest of, 521, 526; on Berdyaev and Bulgakov, 81; on creativity, 75, 76, 322–23; death of, 12, 522, 528, 544; education of, 41; eschatology of, 523, 526; family of, 40; on freedom, 76, 322–23, 429, 467; influence of, 540; on Jesus Christ, 323, 422; on love, 467; native town, 40; and Orthodox Action, 416, 417–19, 423–24, 425, 426, 526, 541; on Orthodox Church, 442; political views, 43, 53, 202, 228, 229; remembrance of, 537, 538, 540, 543, 552, 558, 559, 560, 567, 578, 582; on return to Russia, 109; and RSCM, 125–26, 222, 223, 224, 227, 416, 420, 421–22; on Russian intellectuals, 442; on Russian national identity, 429–30; on Russian Revolution, 241; on sophiology, 442–43; on spirituality, 421–22, 541; on the Trinity, 322–23; during World War II, 520, 526

Skobtsova, Mother Maria, works of: articles in *The Way*, 2, 76, 201, 223, 322, 422, 424, 426; "Birth and Creation," 322–23, 450; "A Defense of Phariseeism," 422; "On the Imitation of the Mother of God," 422–43; "Our Era," 442; *Poems*, 423; "The Russian Geography of France," 223; *Ruth*, 45; *Le sacrement du frère*, 560; *The Scythian Shards*, 45; *The Seven Cups*, 526; "The Types of Religious Life," 421–22, 541; "The War as Revelation," 526

Skobtsov, Yuri, 558, 578
Skovoroda, Hryhorii, 77
Slavonic language, 11, 45, 89, 163, 272, 401, 433–36, 540, 563

Slavophile movement, 438, 508; neo-Slavophile movement, 43, 54, 56
Slepian, V., 123, 227
Slonim, Marc, 278–79
Smirnov, Fr. D., 539
Smirnov, Fr. I., 386
Smolitsch, Igor, 19, 51, 62, 132–33, 201, 275–76, 424, 426, 522, 543
Sobolev, Archbishop Seraphim, 386, 540
sobornost'. *See* conciliarity (*sobornost'*)
Social Democrat Party, 45, 49
socialism, 45, 46, 53, 267, 271, 384, 404, 405, 406–7, 413–14, 491
Socialist Revolutionary Party, 43, 49, 51
social question, 37, 45, 260–65
Society for Spiritual Culture, 526
Society of Russian Philosophy (SPR), 93, 94
Society of the Friends of the Heroes, 228
Söderblom, Nathan, 169, 173
Sofia manifesto, 56
Solovyov, Ilya, 542
Solovyov, Vladimir, 29, 140, 167, 177, 283, 286, 290, 334, 392, 508, 536, 546, 550, 566; on Being, 291; on the death penalty, 51–52; on divine Sophia, 42; ecumenical activities, 140; eschatology of, 72, 73, 339; influence of, 5, 16, 22, 36, 37, 38, 41, 42, 44, 45, 47, 51–52, 54, 57, 63–65, 66, 71, 72, 73, 74, 76, 97, 118, 125, 128, 141, 174, 178, 203, 248, 275, 281, 293, 300, 373, 411, 451, 537, 554, 561, 565; on Kingdom of God on earth, 139–40; *The Meaning of Love*, 125; on pan-unity, 64; and sophiology, 77, 78, 79, 80, 115–16, 320, 443; on the state, 74, 118; *A Tale of the Antichrist*, 72, 139–40, 177; on three apostles, 583; on the Trinity, 400

Solzhenitsyn, Alexander, 3, 533, 542, 572, 579; *August 1914*, 555; *The Gulag Archipelago*, 555; *The Russian Question at the End of the Twentieth Century*, 534
sophiology, 6, 9, 11, 216, 429, 471, 482, 537, 564; Berdyaev on, 77, 80–81, 129, 300, 318, 320, 391–93, 443, 461–62, 557; Bulgakov on, 23, 42, 62, 76–77, 78–81, 85, 86, 102, 103, 111, 114, 115, 193, 196, 215, 253, 269, 272, 282, 308–20, 321, 322, 365, 371, 378, 384–95, 398–401, 419–20, 435, 436–37, 440, 442, 448, 455–58, 461–62, 464, 465, 466, 467, 470, 471, 473, 474–75, 487–88, 511, 516–17, 525, 540, 544, 560, 567, 568, 575, 581; Chetverikov on, 395, 396, 398; created vs. divine Sophia, 173, 274, 292–93, 300, 310, 317, 318, 319, 365, 398, 440, 456, 457–58, 466, 470, 525; dogmatic interpretation of, 78–80; and *Fides et Ratio*, 565–66; Florensky on, 77, 78, 320, 356; Florovsky on, 371, 395, 396, 398, 473; Vladimir Ilyin on, 77, 78, 320, 395, 398, 407; Karsavin on, 78, 80; Lagovsky on, 398–99, 420, 482; metaphysical interpretation of, 78, 80–81; patristic interpretation of, 78; Metropolitan Sergius on, 384, 385–86, 389–90, 391–92, 396, 400, 540; and Solovyov, 77, 78, 79, 80, 115–16, 320, 443; Zenkovsky on, 77, 292–93, 320, 398
Sophrony (Sakharov), Archimandrite, 578
Sordet, Dominique, 491
Sorel, Georges, 191
Souzenelle, Annick de, 567
Sové, B., 217, 386, 396, 397–98, 401, 412, 424

Spanish Civil War, 406, 412, 491
Spektorsky, Evgenii, 19, 40, 51, 94, 198, 349
Spencer, Malcolm, 370
Spengler, Oswald, 157, 160, 191, 267–68
Speransky, V., 41, 42, 91
Spidlik, T., 551
Spinoza, Baruch, 28, 49, 284, 292, 302, 450, 451
spirituality, 274, 282, 290, 357, 507, 519; Berdyaev on, 157, 241–42, 250, 251, 329, 371–72, 376–77, 378, 380, 381, 404, 453, 470; Bulgakov on, 376, 380–81, 436–37, 470; Byzantine spirituality, 79–80, 86–87; criticism of Western spirituality, 53–55; Fedotov on, 376, 379–80; Florovsky on, 470, 472, 511; hesychastic spirituality, 61–63, 220, 545; Josephite, 219, 240; Lot-Borodin on, 432–33; Mother Maria on, 421–22, 541; Nilian spirituality, 62, 119, 133, 219, 220, 237, 238, 240, 242, 243, 294, 411, 443; primacy of the spiritual, 190, 198, 199, 248; spiritual identity, 17; spiritual independence, 200; spiritual reality, 190–91, 199
Spiritual Verses, 295–96
Spolaikovitch, M., 186
Stalin, Joseph, 80, 134, 197, 256, 403, 404, 406, 409, 528; collectivization under, 120, 234, 235; consolidation of power, 34, 108, 110, 121, 126; policies regarding religion, 108, 402; popular front strategy, 382; *Remarks on the Project for a Manual of the History of the USSR*, 428; "The Vertigo of Success," 231
St. Andrew Institute of Biblical and Theological Studies, 538, 543
Stanitsy (Pages), 543

Stark, Fr. Boris, 546
Stavisky affair, 227–28
Stavrosky, Alexis, 384–85
Stavrov, 520
Steiner, Rudolf, 20, 279–80
Stepun, Feodor, 19, 51, 105, 198, 200, 251, 348, 350–51, 424, 426, 522, 528, 534, 550; "Religious Socialism and Christianity," 261–62; on Russian emigration, 7; as "S."?, 267, 351, 353, 354
Stetathos, Nicetas, 159
Stock Exchange News, The, 41
Stockholm conference (1925), 169–72
Stoicism, 70, 461
St. Philaret Institute, 537
St. Photius Brotherhood, 163
Stratonov, I., 127, 194, 520, 544
Stravinsky, Igor, 22, 379
Strizhevskaya, Natalia, 550
Strossmayer, Bishop J.-G., 167
Struve, Fr. Pierre, 553
Struve, Nikita, 3, 108, 539, 542, 555, 556, 560, 564; *Seventy Years of the Russian Emigration (1919–1989)*, 9, 562; on *The Way*, 9
Struve, Piotr, 53, 97, 103, 105–6, 117, 127–28, 138, 247, 415, 532, 534
St. Sergius Fraternity, 420
St. Sergius Orthodox Theological Institute, 16, 21, 122, 126, 155, 207, 209, 216–20, 242, 375, 418–19, 426, 506, 522–23, 530, 539, 552, 579; and Berdyaev, 129, 424, 464; and Bezobrazov, 98, 99; and Bulgakov, 99, 129, 396, 428, 435, 483; criticism of, 114, 115, 116, 123; and ecumenism, 164–65, 176, 184, 217–18, 370; and Fedotov, 379–80, 406, 409–11, 412–13, 415, 424–25, 435, 464, 517; founding of, 92, 97–99, 111; funding of, 123–24, 182, 217, 243–44, 455; hagiology at, 218; and Kartashev, 97, 98, 114, 435; library, 2; Office of Religious Education, 109, 130, 210, 211, 215, 227; *La Pensée Orthodoxe*, 217; and Vysheslavtsev, 99, 216; and Zenkovsky, 99, 109, 425
St. Sophia Brotherhood, 95
St. Tikhon Institute, 538, 539, 541, 543
Studio Franco-Russe (SFR), 165
Stundists, 172
Stupeni, 547
St. Vladimir's Seminary, 530, 539
Suarez, Carlo, 325
Supervielle, Jules, 326
Supreme Council of the Monarchy, 258
Suvarin, Boris, 105
Suvchinsky, Pierre, 22, 38, 51, 56, 57, 118, 133, 134, 136, 143, 529
Sviatopolk-Mirsky, D., 136
Sviridov, 540
symbolism, 15, 71, 152, 154, 171, 183, 184, 194, 200, 258, 278–79, 280, 314, 348, 357, 449, 466, 489, 568, 572, 583; of Berdyaev, 47, 69–70, 146, 186, 187, 188, 224, 306, 334, 355; in biblical exegesis, 178, 184, 436; of Bulgakov, 47, 85, 277; dogmatic symbolism, 37, 200, 483; and freedom, 30; French Symbolism, 39; and marriage, 124–25; and myth, 24, 25, 28–29, 30–31; realistic symbolism, 22–23, 47, 48, 375; symbolic history, 530–32; symbolist mytho-logy, 25, 29–32, 47; of *The Way*, 8–9, 16, 568
Syndesmos (World Fellowship of Orthodox Youth), 530, 552–53
Synod of Karlovtsy, 89, 90, 91, 101, 113–14, 116, 140, 154, 225, 386, 390, 399, 539
synthetic a priori judgments, 45, 73, 503

Tagore, Rabindranath, 154
Talberg, N., 104, 132
Tale of Igor's Campaign, 434
Tanner, Mary, 576
Taoism, 20
Tardieu, André, 228
Tartu, school of, 548
Tatlow, Tissington, 182
Tawney, R. H., 508
Taylor, Charles, 572
Tchekan, Jean, 555, 564
Teffi, Nadezhda, 186, 500
Teihard de Chardin, Pierre, 524, 554, 572
Temple of God, 274
Temple, William, 513
Terapiano, G., 419
Tertullian, 501–2
theodicy. *See* evil
Theodore, Princess, 496
Theophane Venard, St., 153
Theophan of Poltava, Archbishop, 111, 115
Theophan the Recluse, 62, 101, 123, 201, 304, 394
Theophilus (Pashkovsky), Bishop, 21
Theosophy, 63, 77, 129, 279
Thérèse of Lisieux, St., 145, 153, 290, 472
Thessaloniki conference, 224–25
"The Thaw," 3, 18, 555
Thévenot, Laurent, 566
Third Rome, 430, 432, 439–40, 442, 580
Thornton, Lionel, 366
Thurneysen, Eduard, 170
Tian-Shansky, D. Semenov, 405, 424
Tikhon (Belavin), Patriarch, 45, 88–89, 90, 91, 98, 110, 114, 168, 180, 236, 386
Tikhon (Liashenko), Bishop, 111
Tikhonitsky, Vladimir, Bishop of Nice, 231

Tillich, Paul, 19, 21, 24, 170, 261–62, 405, 476, 527
Timashev, N. S., 41, 126, 395
Titlinov, B. V., 89
Todorov, Tzvetan, 138–39
Tolstoy, A., 490
Tolstoy, Leo, 36, 39, 106, 107, 129, 166, 335, 336, 445–46; "I Cannot Keep Silent," 410, 537; influence of, 105, 494
Tönnies, Ferdinand, 349
Toporov, V., 548
Touchard, Jean, 190
Tournier, M., 524
"Tower," 41
Trans-Volga monks, 133, 437, 534
Trébitsch, Michel, 17
Trest, 117
Troisième Force, 329
Troitsky, Sergei, 19, 21, 41, 42, 43, 44, 50, 123, 194, 232, 239, 245; articles in *The Way*, 67, 124, 125, 201, 234–35; on Being, 452; *The Christian Philosophy of Marriage*, 294; on marriage, 124, 125; political views, 89; on religious persecution in Soviet Union, 234–35; on sin, 452
Trotsky, Leon, 51, 108, 255, 476, 550
Trubetskoy, E. N., 41
Trubetskoy, Grigorii, 40, 41, 42, 43, 50, 94, 96, 98, 112, 150, 192–93, 197, 290; articles in *The Way*, 91, 105, 106; ecclesiology of, 140; ecumenical activities, 140, 141, 143–44, 149; on Living Church, 90, 91; political views, 53, 106, 126, 132; on Uniatism, 143–44
Trubetskoy, Nikolai, 19, 38, 40, 41, 51, 57, 133–34, 143; on Fedorov and Marx, 136–37; "The Tower of Babel and the Confusion of Tongues," 56

Trubetskoy, O. N., 276
Trubetskoy, Sergei, 29, 276, 286, 537; "The Doctrine of Logos," 25; and Eurasian movement, 56, 57; on personal conception of Being, 25; on realization of divine Trinity on earth, 57
truth: vs. authenticity, 5; and God, 66, 110; as historical, 1, 14; speculative vs. practical, 5
Tsarsky Vestnik, 209
Tsebrikov, Georgii, 19, 75
Tsvetaeva, Marina, 278, 332
Tukhachevsky, Mikhail, 408
Turgeneva, N., 186, 194, 279–80, 333
Tvardovsky, Aleksandr, 18
Two-Headed Eagle, The, 115, 127
Tynianov, Yuri, 550
Tzvetaeva, Marina, 332

Ukrainian Orange Revolution, 580
Una Sancta, 170, 173
Uniatism, 143–44, 151, 340
Union pour la Verité, 328, 492, 504
Universal Evangelical Church, 168
Uspensky, Leonid, 232

Vaillant-Couturier, Paul, 121, 324
Valéry, Paul, 34, 146, 191, 325, 521
Van der Meer, P., 492–93
Van Drimmelen, Robert, 582
Vanovsky, Alexander, 20, 277
Varshavsky, V., 165, 255, 419; *A Generation Which Nobody Noticed*, 197, 251; political views, 258
Vedensky, A., 89
Veidlé, Vladimir, 198, 199, 201, 224, 281, 330, 345, 396, 419, 501, 522, 555; articles in *The Way*, 193, 194–95, 216, 426, 506; "The Degeneration of Art," 194–95; on faith, 195; "The Marxist Theory of Art in Soviet Russia," 506; "The Renaissance of the Marvelous," 193, 194, 195; *Russia Absent and Present*, 556, 569
Vekhi. See *Landmarks*
Vendredi, 491, 500
Venturi, Franco, 17–18
Verderevsky, D., 528
Vergely, Bertrand, 567
Vernant, Jean-Pierre, 566
Verne, Jules, 195
Versts, 56, 118
Vialatoux, J., 156
Vigilance Committee of Anti-Fascist Intellectuals, 493
Vigne, Éric, 566
Vildé, Boris, 499, 521
Vilshkovsky, M., 528
Vincent of Lérins, St., 181, 360, 503
Vinogradov, I., 538, 541, 561
Vishniak, M., 186
Viskovsky, Anatole, 521
Vissarionov, A., 227
Visser't Hooft, W., 210, 225, 338, 339, 345, 372, 509, 510, 515
Vladimir Solovyev Society, 561
Vladimir the Great, St., 56, 265, 408, 436, 581
Vogt, Vsevolod de, 165, 186, 187, 232, 325
Vogüe, Melchior de, 35
Voice of Orthodoxy, The, 555
"Voices of Christian Conscience in Germany, The," 268–69
Voie, La, 163, 347
Voisin, André, 191
Volkonsky, Mikhail, 19, 424, 505
Volkov, Vladimir, 560
Voltaire, 284, 302
Vorobyov, Fr. Vladimir, 538, 539
Vrevsky, B., 197
Vsevolod (Maidanski) of Scopelos, Archbishop, 578

764   Index

Vysheslavtsev, Boris, 19, 22, 40, 42, 57, 93, 94, 97, 109, 137, 150, 188, 200, 203, 204, 210, 211, 212, 214, 221, 290, 320, 330, 337–38, 387, 396, 403, 430, 545; and Academy of Religious Philosophy, 129; as assistant editor of *The Way*, 95; on Being, 452; on Christian anthropology, 339–40; as collaborator, 523; ecumenical activities, 177, 186, 338, 339–40, 348, 372, 510; as editor of YMCA Press, 93; education of, 40, 41; eschatology of, 449; on the eternal in Russian philosophy, 22; on ethic of sublimation, 288; on Frank, 291–92; on freedom, 288–89, 292, 294, 351, 448, 451; on God, 294, 307, 444, 447–48; on Gurvitch, 263–65; on Hartmann, 351; on hesychastic spirituality, 62–63; on Jesus Christ, 288–89, 448; on Jung, 357; on Kingdom of God on earth, 263; on Marxism, 53, 221–22; on morality, 288; on myth, 448; on myth of creation, 285, 289; on mytho-logical thought, 86; on national identity, 260–61; ontology of, 282–83; on organization, 264–65; political views, 43, 107, 226, 228, 346, 412–13, 425, 492, 544; on power, 263; on problem of evil, 70, 296; and RSCM, 226–27; on salvation, 448; on sin, 289; on social question, 263; on Solovyov, 64; on the soul, 280–81; on spirituality, 323, 449; and St. Sergius Institute, 99, 216; on Troitsky, 294; on the *Ungrund*, 448
Vysheslavtsev, Boris, works of: articles in *The Way*, 18, 53, 61, 62–63, 70, 125, 194, 201, 213, 214, 216, 221–22, 263–64, 288–89, 351, 357, 424, 426, 444, 447–48, 538, 543, 546; "The Ethics of Fichte," 40; *The Ethics of Transfigured Eros*, 216, 288, 293–94, 546; "The Heart in Christian and Indian Mysticism," 289; "The Image of God in the Essence of Man," 214, 449; "The Image of God in the Fall," 449; "The Meaning of the Heart in Religion," 61; "The Paradoxes of Communism," 53; "The Problem of Power and Its Religious Significance," 213; "The Tragedy of Those Elevated and Speculation on Their Fall," 194, 221–22; "A Tragic Theodicy," 70; "The Two Paths of Social Development," 53

Wahl, Jean, 59–60, 164, 328, 332, 336, 498, 504, 505, 527
Wainwright, Geoffrey, 576
Wakefield, Russell, 180
Wallis, Jim, 582
Walter, Reinhold von, 77, 153
Walzer, Michael, 582
Way of Orthodoxy, The, 538
Way of the Pilgrim, The, 62
Way, The (Put') (publishing house), 18, 54, 74, 96, 211
Weber, Max, 566
Week of Prayer for Christian Unity, 341
Weil, E., 527
Weil, Simone, 333
Widdrington, Percy, 224, 262, 420
Williams, George, 512
Williams, Rowan, 572, 575
Windelband, Wilhelm, 40
Winnaert, Bishop Louis Charles, 232, 385
Winock, Michel, 190, 491, 492
Woolf, Virginia, 379
World Alliance for International Friendship, 169
World Congress of Missions, 168

World Council of Churches, 11, 169, 473, 482, 515, 553, 554, 559, 563, 576
World of Art, The, 18
World Student Christian Federation, 12, 21, 44, 92, 93, 95, 98, 99, 101, 111, 158, 179, 182, 208, 210, 338, 420, 559; ecumenical activities, 168, 171, 222, 224–25, 416, 488, 508, 515, 554; founded, 168; Orthodox criticisms of, 110
World Trade Organization, 582
World War I, 19, 33–34, 142, 143, 168
World War II, 6, 12, 425, 426–27, 496, 497–98, 519–22
Wrangel, Pyotr, 89
Wundt, M., 40
Wurmser, André, 190

Yabloko Party, 534
Yakovenko, B.V., 94
Yakovlev, Aleksander, 7, 545, 547
Yakovlev, Anatolii, 7–8
Yakunin, Fr. Gleb, 533
Yannaras, Christos, 11; on myth, 25; *Postmodern Metaphysics*, 575
Yanovsky, V., 165, 419, 498, 523
Yasinowsky, B.: *Le christianisme oriental et la Russie*, 505–6
Yavlinsky, Grigory, 531, 534
Yeltsin, Boris, 7, 533, 534, 535, 579
YMCA (Young Men's Christian Association), 12, 21, 88, 97, 98, 171, 176, 193, 208–13, 222, 521; and ecumenical movement, 168, 173, 224, 344, 488, 515, 579; Orthodox criticisms of, 88, 110, 111, 119, 142, 207, 208–11, 226; relations with Academy of Religious Philosophy, 227, 416; relations with ROCOR, 100, 101–4, 110, 111, 209; relations with RSCM, 92, 99, 100, 109, 110, 208, 209–11, 416, 417, 579

YMCA Press, 92–93, 104, 166, 204, 210, 217, 220, 227, 245, 249, 256, 280, 344, 345, 378, 389, 551–52, 555, 557; Berdyaev as director, 93, 94, 200, 211–12, 213, 439; *Christian Reunion*, 358, 359–62, 363, 368; index of publications, 2; and *New City*, 200; *The Way* published by, 2, 9, 16, 21, 95–96, 109–10, 140, 168
Young-Russians, 121
Youth Movement (*Jugendbewegung*), 145
Yugoslav Orthodox Church, 225
Yundt, A., 150, 151

Zagorovsky, Marguerite, 232
Zaitsev, Boris, 61, 97
Zaitsev, K., 126
Zamiatin, Yevgeny, 234
Zander, Lev, 12, 21, 40, 41, 43, 44, 51, 93, 99, 102, 150, 197, 199, 203, 210, 217, 221, 223, 225, 227, 338, 345, 347, 396; articles in *The Way*, 201, 322, 424, 514; ecclesiology of, 474, 488; ecumenical activities, 370, 372, 420–21, 488, 510, 513, 514, 515–16, 553, 554, 576; "The Essence of the Ecumenical Movement," 397, 511; on Holy Spirit, 488; influence of, 552; political views, 412; remembrance of, 533, 552, 553, 559, 567; and RSCM, 420–21, 425, 521; "A Sad Paradise," 122; *Western Orthodoxy*, 553; during World War II, 415
Zander, Valentina, 19, 20, 40, 221, 248
Zankov, Protopresbyter Stefan, 173, 174, 175, 177, 359, 372
Zavtra, 241
Zdziechowsky, 156
Zechariah 12:10, 278
Zenkovsky, Marianne, 202

Zenkovsky, Vasilii, 12, 19, 42, 44, 93, 94, 95, 96, 98, 123, 130, 131, 150, 202, 203, 209, 210, 211, 215, 225, 269, 280, 290, 386, 396, 402, 429, 430, 458, 464, 521, 529, 530; on Barth, 353; on Being, 63, 452; on bourgeois ethic, 54–55; on Catholicism, 164, 341, 512–13; on culture, 224; death of, 552; on Dostoevsky, 293; ecumenical activities, 162–63, 171, 172–73, 175, 176, 177, 208, 218, 338, 347, 348, 359, 410, 510, 513; education of, 41; eschatology of, 224; on evil, 452; on the Fall, 452; on Frank, 292–93; on freedom, 82, 410, 451–52; on God as all-powerful, 444, 451; on God as Creator, 452; on Hitler, 268; on Holy Spirit, 291, 296; on immanentism, 55; influence of, 536, 552; on Lossky, 293; on nationalism, 266; native town of, 40; pneumocentrism of, 176; political views, 43, 53, 117, 126, 201, 226, 228, 247, 412; relationship with Chelpanov, 40; on resurrection, 293; and RSCM, 99, 100–101, 112, 126, 221, 225–26, 227, 416, 420, 521; *Russian Thinkers and Europe*, 22; on sin, 452; on sophiology, 77, 292–93, 320, 398; and St. Sergius Institute, 99, 109, 425; on Thomism, 355; on the Trinity, 82; on Vysheslavtsev, 293–94; on Wisdom, 292; during World War II, 415

Zenkovsky, Vasilii, works of: articles in *The Way*, 12, 18, 82, 100–101, 108, 125, 145, 164, 175, 201, 214, 216, 268, 292–94, 347, 355, 424, 443, 444, 452, 507, 546; "The Athens Conference," 347; "The Crisis of German Protestantism," 268; "Evil in Man," 452; "Freedom and *Sobornost*'," 82; *Histoire de la philosophie russe*, 556–57, 560; "The Problem of Beauty in the Worldview of Dostoevsky," 214; "The Religious Youth Movements in the Russian Emigration," 100–101; *Russian Thinkers and Europe*, 22

Zenon, Fr., 541
Zernova, S., 222
Zernov, Maria, 109, 176
Zernov, Militsa, 3
Zernov, Nicolas, 3, 12, 93, 100, 123, 150, 151, 171, 176, 182, 184, 197, 210, 227, 242, 347, 428, 429, 442, 522, 528; on Anglicanism, 365, 366–67; articles in *The Way*, 19, 201–2, 322, 358, 362–63, 366–67, 424, 426, 439–41, 514, 516, 581; on St. Cyprian, 358, 362–63; ecclesiology of, 366–68, 440–41, 473, 474, 488–89, 514–15; ecumenical activities, 199, 338, 339, 341, 345, 348, 366–68, 371, 440, 510, 513, 514, 515–16, 576, 577; on Holy Spirit, 367; messianism of, 443; on Moscow as Third Rome, 439–40; on Orthodox Church, 440–41, 488–89, 514–15; on Philotheus of Pskov, 432; on Russian intelligentsia, 441

Zernov, Sophia Mikhailovna, 423
Zhaba, S., 212, 213, 418, 520
Zhukovsky, Vasily A., 276
Zinoviev, A., 548
Zinoviev, G., 108
Zionism, 437–38
Zitrone, M., 464
Zizioulas, John, 473
Zoroastrianism, 56
Zundel, Maurice, 572
Zwischen den Zeiten, 170
Zyzykin, M., 104

ANTOINE ARJAKOVSKY

is research director at the Collège des Bernardins in Paris and founding director of the Institute of Ecumenical Studies and professor of ecumenical theology at the Ukrainian Catholic University in Lviv, Ukraine. He is the author of a number of books, including *Qu'est-ce que l'orthodoxie?*